NASA/TP-1999-206568

Fifty Years of Flight Research: An Annotated Bibliography of Technical Publications of NASA Dryden Flight Research Center, 1946–1996

David F. Fisher
NASA Dryden Flight Research Center
Edwards, California

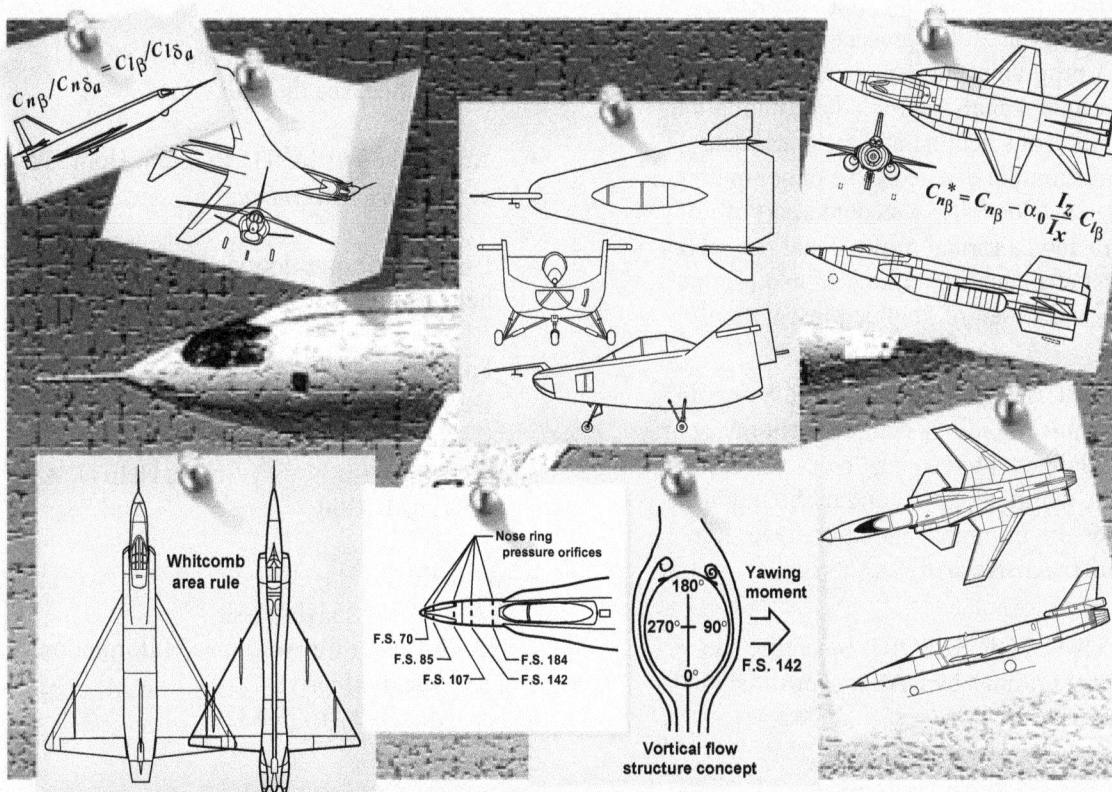

May 1999

The NASA STI Program Office... in Profile

Since its founding, NASA has been dedicated to the advancement of aeronautics and space science. The NASA Scientific and Technical Information (STI) Program Office plays a key part in helping NASA maintain this important role.

The NASA STI Program Office is operated by Langley Research Center, the lead center for NASA's scientific and technical information. The NASA STI Program Office provides access to the NASA STI Database, the largest collection of aeronautical and space science STI in the world. The Program Office is also NASA's institutional mechanism for disseminating the results of its research and development activities. These results are published by NASA in the NASA STI Report Series, which includes the following report types:

- TECHNICAL PUBLICATION. Reports of completed research or a major significant phase of research that present the results of NASA programs and include extensive data or theoretical analysis. Includes compilations of significant scientific and technical data and information deemed to be of continuing reference value. NASA's counterpart of peer-reviewed formal professional papers but has less stringent limitations on manuscript length and extent of graphic presentations.

- TECHNICAL MEMORANDUM. Scientific and technical findings that are preliminary or of specialized interest, e.g., quick release reports, working papers, and bibliographies that contain minimal annotation. Does not contain extensive analysis.

- CONTRACTOR REPORT. Scientific and technical findings by NASA-sponsored contractors and grantees.

- CONFERENCE PUBLICATION. Collected papers from scientific and technical conferences, symposia, seminars, or other meetings sponsored or cosponsored by NASA.

- SPECIAL PUBLICATION. Scientific, technical, or historical information from NASA programs, projects, and mission, often concerned with subjects having substantial public interest.

- TECHNICAL TRANSLATION. English-language translations of foreign scientific and technical material pertinent to NASA's mission.

Specialized services that complement the STI Program Office's diverse offerings include creating custom thesauri, building customized databases, organizing and publishing research results...even providing videos.

For more information about the NASA STI Program Office, see the following:

- Access the NASA STI Program Home Page at *http://www.sti.nasa.gov*

- E-mail your question via the Internet to help@sti.nasa.gov

- Fax your question to the NASA Access Help Desk at (301) 621-0134

- Telephone the NASA Access Help Desk at (301) 621-0390

- Write to:
  NASA Access Help Desk
  NASA Center for AeroSpace Information
  7121 Standard Drive
  Hanover, MD 21076-1320

NASA/TP-1999-206568

Fifty Years of Flight Research: An Annotated Bibliography of Technical Publications of NASA Dryden Flight Research Center, 1946–1996

David F. Fisher
NASA Dryden Flight Research Center
Edwards, California

National Aeronautics and
Space Administration

Dryden Flight Research Center
Edwards, California 93523-0273

May 1999

ACKNOWLEDGMENTS

The author acknowledges Dryden Librarian Dennis Ragsdale for his help in finding many of the entries in this bibliography and Library Technicians Charito Lopez and Lisa Carbaugh for their help scanning and typing many of the missing abstracts. Also, the author thanks the Dryden Graphics Office; Steve Lighthill, chief, Justine Mack, James Zeitz and Dennis Calaba for the many airplane three-view drawings and cover. The author is especially grateful to the Dryden Technical Publications Office; Camilla McArthur, chief, editorial assistants Lois Williams, Mary Whelan, and Karen Wick, editors Sue Luke and Muriel Khachooni for their patience and persistence in seeing this bibliography through to publication.

Available from the following:

NASA Center for AeroSpace Information (CASI)
7121 Standard Drive
Hanover, MD 21076-1320
(301) 621-0390

National Technical Information Service (NTIS)
5285 Port Royal Road
Springfield, VA 22161-2171
(703) 487-4650

CONTENTS

FOREWORD

The legacy of a research organization is the written history of its findings, whether the results were expected or unexpected, whether the predictions were valid or not.

The search for understanding and the advancement of ideas to technology is often a non-linear path. Ideas beget ideas, and data changes the reference point. Without written evidence of this progress, the map ends. Future explorers may have to retrace and relearn at great time and cost.

I am pleased to have the bibliography of technical publications of the NASA Dryden Flight Research Center published for future researchers to have. The first entries in this document deal with transonic and supersonic flight research at the dawn of the high speed aircraft era at Muroc. The latter entries deal with tailless flight, hypersonic flight, and civil transport safety.

The technical publications of the Dryden Flight Research Center are a reflection of the progress made in NASA's aeronautics research and technology program. They show what teams of people believed could fly or be flown. They document the claims, hopes, and aspirations of designers from across the country. These reports document the real and the imagined, the overlooked, and the unexpected, as Dr. Hugh L. Dryden would say.

I hereby dedicate this annotated bibliography of technical publications of the Dryden Flight Research Center to the memory of Dr. Hugh L. Dryden, scientist, engineer, manager, father, and technical author. His own research provided some of the foundation of the transonic flight exploration which spawned what is now the Dryden Flight Research Center.

I acknowledge the outstanding work of Mr. David Fisher, a research engineer at Dryden, to produce this bibliography.

Kenneth J. Szalai
NASA Dryden Flight Research Center Director 1994–1998

Fifty Years of Flight Research:

An Annotated Bibliography of Technical Publications of NASA Dryden Flight Research Center, 1946–1996

David F. Fisher
NASA Dryden Flight Research Center
Edwards, California 93523-0273

ABSTRACT

Titles, authors, report numbers, and abstracts are given for more than 2200 unclassified and unrestricted technical reports and papers published from September 1946 to December 1996 by NASA Dryden Flight Research Center and its predecessor organizations. These technical reports and papers describe and give the results of 50 years of flight research performed by the NACA and NASA, from the X-1 and other early X-airplanes, to the X-15, Space Shuttle, X-29 Forward Swept Wing, and X-31 aircraft. Some of the other research airplanes tested were the D-558, phase 1 and 2; M-2, HL-10 and X-24 lifting bodies; Digital Fly-By-Wire and Supercritical Wing F-8; XB-70; YF-12; AFTI F-111 TACT and MAW; F-15 HiDEC; F-18 High Alpha Research Vehicle, and F-18 Systems Research Aircraft. The citations of reports and papers are listed in chronological order, with author and aircraft indices. In addition, in the appendices, citations of 233 contractor reports, more than 200 UCLA Flight System Research Center reports and 25 video tapes are included.

INTRODUCTION

In September of 1946, a small band of engineers and technicians came to Muroc Army Air Field in southern California from the National Advisory Committee for Aeronautics (NACA) Langley Memorial Aeronautical Laboratory at Hampton, Virginia. These people were to assist in a supersonic flight research program involving the Bell XS-1 aircraft. The following year, the small group, which became known as the NACA Muroc Flight Test Unit, were key participants in the first known supersonic flight of an airplane on October 14, 1947. In 1949, they became the NACA High-Speed Flight Research Station (HSFRS), a division of the Langley laboratory and during 1950, they published 19 technical reports on various aspects of pioneering flight research. In 1954, the HSFRS became the NACA High-Speed Flight Station and moved from the south base location shared with the Air Force to the present location north of the base flight line. In 1959, after the creation of the National Aeronautic and Space Administration (NASA), the center was designated NASA Flight Research Center (FRC). On March 26, 1976, the center was redesignated Hugh L. Dryden Flight Research Center, in honor of the American aerospace pioneer, former Director of NACA and the first Deputy Director of NASA. In 1981, the center became a facility as part of Ames Research Center. In 1994, the facility became an independent NASA Center again as the Hugh L. Dryden Flight Research Center.

This document attempts to capture all the unrestricted reports, papers, and journal articles published by authors while they were employed by the NASA Dryden Flight Research Center and its predecessor organizations from September 1946 to December 1996. Also included are NASA Contractor Reports that were sponsored by DFRC. Reports from the UCLA Flight Systems Research Center under NASA Dryden Grant NCC2-374 are included in Appendix B. Many of the citations are from NASA CASI

RECON and RECONplus databases, the NASA Dryden card catalog, as well as information from the authors that was not included in the databases. The author regrets any documents that may have been inadvertently left out.

Some of the highlights of the first 50 years of what is now known as the Hugh L. Dryden Flight Research Center are as follows:

Sept. 30, 1946	Five NACA engineers, headed by Walter Williams, arrive at Muroc Army Air Base, California (now Edwards AFB) by this date from Langley Memorial Aeronautical Laboratory (now NASA Langley Research Center, Virginia), to prepare for X-1 supersonic research flights in a joint NACA-Army Air Forces program. First NACA-NASA presence is established at the Mojave Desert site. (Note: Some sources report the arrival of 13 individuals, but an early chronology shows that 13 were not present at Muroc until December.)
Dec. 9, 1946	Bell pilot Chalmers Goodlin flies the first successful rocket-powered flight of the X-1 (then designated XS-1).
Aug. 20, 1947	D-558-1 sets a world speed record of 640.7 mph.
Sept. 7, 1947	The NACA Muroc Flight Test Unit receives permanent status from Hugh L. Dryden, the NACA Director of Research. The staff now includes 27 people with Walt Williams as Head.
Oct. 14, 1947	X-1 exceeds the speed of sound in history's first supersonic flight flown by then - Maj. Charles E. Yeager, attaining maximum Mach number of 1.057.
Nov. 25, 1947	Howard C. Lilly is first NACA pilot to fly the jet-powered D-558-1 Skystreak.
Mar. 10, 1948	Herb Hoover becomes first NACA pilot and first civilian to fly supersonic in the X-1.
Nov. 14, 1949	The NACA Muroc unit, with about 100 people, is designated NACA High-Speed Flight Research Station (HSFRS), with Walt Williams remaining as director.
Sept. 25, 1950	John Griffith is first NACA pilot to fly the X-4 aircraft, studying flying qualities of tailless vehicles.
Mar. 4, 1952	Joe Walker is first to fly the variable-swept-wing X-5 to a full 60-degree angle. This concept is used today on F-14, F-111, and B-1 aircraft.
Apr. 9, 1953	The NACA first flight of XF-92A, a delta-wing aircraft used to study the problem of pitching up during maneuvering caused by the delta configuration.
Oct. 14, 1953	Last flight of XF-92A by the NACA. The flight research with this aircraft, the D-588-2 and the X-15, showed the desirability of low horizontal tail surface. That low horizontal tail configuration was later used on such supersonic swept-wing fighters as the F-100 Super Saber and F8U Crusader.
Nov. 20, 1953	The NACA pilot Scott Crossfield, in a rocket-powered D-558-2 Skyrocket, is the first to fly at twice the speed of sound, Mach 2.005.
Jun. 26, 1954	The NACA personnel move from the old south base site to new facilities that make up the original core of today's Dryden complex. The cost to build the new facilities was $3.8 million. Personnel on this date number more than 200.

Jul. 1, 1954	The NACA HSFRS is redesignated the NACA High-Speed Flight Station.
Aug. 23, 1954	Joe Walker makes the first of 20 NACA research flights in the X-3 "Flying Stiletto" supersonic program.
Aug. 27, 1956	The NACA research pilot Joe Walker makes the first flight by NACA of an F-104A aircraft (the seventh F-104 aircraft off the assembly line).
Sept. 27, 1956	Air Force Capt. Milburn G. Apt flies the X-2 to Mach 3.2 in the first flight of an aircraft beyond 3 times the speed of sound. Unfortunately, he subsequently loses control of the airplane due to inertial coupling, and it crashes, killing him and destroying the vehicle. The NACA never flew the X-2 but did assist the program with advice and data analysis.
Oct. 1, 1958	National Advisory Committee for Aeronautics (NACA) becomes National Aeronautics and Space Administration (NASA).
Oct. 15, 1958	First of three X-15 rocket research aircraft arrive at NASA High-Speed Flight Station as preparations move ahead for the highly successful NASA-Air Force-Navy program that lasts 10 years to investigate hypersonic flight.
Nov. 7, 1958	John McKay makes last flight in the X-1E, final model flown of the X-1 series. This aircraft is now displayed in front of Dryden headquarters building.
Jun. 8, 1959	First unpowered glide flight of the X-15 is flown, with Scott Crossfield at the controls, is made from NASA's "003," B-52 launch aircraft.
Sept. 15, 1959	Paul F. Bikle succeeds Walt Williams as director of NASA High-Speed Flight Station.
Sept. 27, 1959	NASA High-Speed Flight Station at Edwards is redesignated NASA Flight Research Center. NASA personnel number about 340.
Mar. 25, 1960	First NASA X-15 aircraft flight is made, piloted by Joe Walker.
Mar. 7, 1961	First piloted flight above Mach 4 is made; Mach 4.43 is achieved by X-15 flown by USAF Capt. Robert M. White.
Jun. 23, 1961	First piloted flight above Mach 5 is made; Mach 5.27 is achieved by X-15 flown by USAF Capt. Robert M. White.
Nov. 9, 1961	First piloted flight above Mach 6 is made; Mach 6.04 is achieved by X-15 flown by USAF Capt. Robert M. White.
Early 1962	Flight tests begin with the Paraglider Research Vehicle (Parasev). Developed to study ways of returning Gemini and Apollo spacecraft to Earth using a hang-glider-type wing. Pilot is Milt Thompson.
Apr. 5, 1963	M2-F1 lightweight lifting body is towed into the air over Rogers Dry Lake for the first time by a Pontiac convertible tow vehicle with Milt Thompson as pilot. Sets the stage for research with several lifting body designs to study atmospheric reentry of a vehicle like a Space Shuttle.
Aug. 22, 1963	Joe Walker flies X-15 to unofficial world altitude record of 354,200 ft.

Oct. 30, 1964	Joe Walker pilots the first flight of the Lunar Landing Research Vehicle (LLRV), "Flying Bedstead." LLRV used to develop techniques of landing a spacecraft on the moon's surface.
Mar. 11, 1966	High Temperature Loads Laboratory is formally accepted. With this facility, a complete YF-12 would be heated and loaded to simulate a high-speed flight.
Jul. 12, 1966	First flight of a heavyweight lifting body, the M2-F2, piloted by Milton O. Thompson.
Apr. 25, 1967	First NASA flight of the XB-70A with Air Force Col. Joe Cotton and NASA research pilot Fitz Fulton at the controls. The XB-70 flights investigated the stability and handling qualities of large, delta-wing aircraft flying at high rates of speed.
Oct. 3, 1967	X-15 sets world's absolute speed record for winged aircraft—4520 mph or Mach 6.72—with Air Force Maj. William Knight as the pilot.
Oct. 24, 1968	Last X-15 flight, 199th mission, is piloted by NASA pilot Bill Dana. World's first hypersonic aircraft is most successful research aircraft to date.
Dec. 17, 1968	Last research flight of XB-70 is flown by Fitz Fulton and Air Force Lt. Col. Ted Sturmthal, reaching Mach 2.53. Program produced data on sonic booms, flight dynamics, and handling qualities associated with large supersonic aircraft. Flight is on 65th anniversary of Wright Brothers flight at Kitty Hawk, North Carolina.
May 9, 1969	HL-10 becomes first lifting body to fly supersonic. John Manke, later to become Dryden site manager, is pilot.
Mar. 5, 1970	First NASA checkout flight of YF-12A, with Fitz Fulton as pilot.
Jun. 2, 1970	First flight of the M2-F3 lifting body is made by Bill Dana.
Oct. 14, 1970	NASA research pilots Tom McMurtry and Hugh Jackson reach a Dryden single-day record of six missions flown, in an F-104B while deployed to obtain data for the "Big Boom" experiments that sought to focus the energy from a sonic boom over a limited area.
Mar. 9, 1971	First flight of supercritical wing flown by NASA pilot Tom McMurtry. Unusual wing profile, tested on a modified F-8, increases flight efficiency and lowers fuel usage. This concept is now used widely on commercial and military aircraft.
Oct. 14, 1971	A Piper PA-30 Twin Commanche becomes testbed to develop remotely piloted aircraft techniques from a ground-based cockpit. This concept leads to successful projects such as three-eighths-scale F-15 spin research vehicle, HiMAT, and Boeing 720 jetliner purposely flown to a controlled crash landing in FAA test of anti-mist fuel additive.
May 25, 1972	First flight of aircraft with all-electric fly-by-wire flight control system, the NASA F-8 Digital Fly-By-Wire research aircraft, with Gary Krier as pilot. This concept is now used in many aircraft, including Space Shuttles.
Aug. 1974	The Boeing 747 shuttle carrier aircraft is used in wake vortex research program to study ways of reducing clear air turbulence trailing behind large aircraft.

Aug. 5, 1975	NASA pilot John Manke lands X-24B lifting body on Edwards runway, showing that a space shuttle-like vehicle can be landed safely on a designated runway after returning from orbit.
Mar. 26, 1976	NASA Flight Research Center is dedicated in honor of the late Hugh L. Dryden. NASA personnel number more than 560.
Aug. 12, 1977	First free-flight of the space shuttle Enterprise from the top of the Boeing 747 shuttle carrier aircraft. Enterprise piloted by Fred Haise and Gordon Fullerton. The 747 SCA was piloted by Fitz Fulton and Tom McMurtry, Vic Horton and Lewis (Skip) Guidry were the flight engineers.
Oct. 26, 1977	Last of 13 captive and free-flight tests with space shuttle prototype Enterprise, proving the shuttle glide and landing characteristics.
Oct. 31, 1979	Last research flight of the NASA YF-12 research program, with Fitz Fulton as pilot and Victor Horton flight test engineer on a YF-12A, one of three YF-12s flown during the program. Nearly 300 research flights explored high-speed, high-altitude flight, and yielded information on thermal stress, aerodynamics, high-altitude environment, and propulsion and flight control systems.
Dec. 21, 1979	AD-1 first flight is flown by NASA research pilot Thomas C. McMurtry.
Apr. 14, 1981	Three hundred and twenty thousand people at Edwards watch Columbia, the first orbital space shuttle, land. Dryden VIPs number 20,000, and 300,000 are at the East Shore public viewing site.
Oct. 1, 1981	Dryden is consolidated with Ames Research Center, Moffett Field, California, to become the Ames-Dryden Flight Research Facility. Position of Dryden director is renamed site manager and John Manke is selected for the post. NASA personnel number 491.
Jul. 4, 1982	President Ronald Reagan heads list of 45,000 guests at Dryden watching the fourth space shuttle landing. Crowd of 500,000 watches from East Shore public viewing site.
Sept. 22, 1983	A modified Schweizer SGS1-36 sailplane is flown in controlled, stabilized flight at 72 degrees angle of attack by research pilot Einar Enevoldson.
Oct. 30, 1984	NASA Dryden retires its oldest aircraft, the C-47 that towed the M2-F1 lifting body aloft during that program's early days and was used to support many other projects.
Dec. 1, 1984	A remotely-piloted Boeing 720 test aircraft used in the joint FAA/NASA Controlled Impact Demonstration erupts in flames as it slides through the impact site on the dry lakebed, demonstrating that, contrary to expectations, an anti-misting fuel additive did not substantially inhibit fuel fires.
Apr. 2, 1985	Steve Ishmael is first NASA pilot to fly the X-29 research aircraft investigating forward-swept wings, composite construction concepts, and integrated flight controls.
Sept. 9, 1985	Data Analysis Facility opens as new home for general computer and associated engineering support and flight data operations.

Jul. 10, 1986	F-111 Mission Adaptive Wing research aircraft flies Mach 1 for the first time, with Rogers Smith part of two-person crew. This program tested the wing with no ailerons, flaps, or slats. Camber changed mechanically in flight based on performance and mission.
Dec. 1, 1987	Groundbreaking held for $16.1 million Integrated Test Facility featuring interdependent systems testing, systems troubleshooting, and rapid pre-and post-flight systems checkout on several aircraft simultaneously.
Sept. 18, 1989	Ed Schneider flies the 100th mission in the F-18 High Angle of Attack Research aircraft in Phase 1 of the three-phase program investigating the high angle-of-attack, "alpha," regime.
Dec. 18, 1989	First self-repairing flight control system demonstrated on the F-15 HiDEC (Highly Integrated Digital Electronic Control) aircraft, with Jim Smolka as pilot. System identifies control surface failures or damage then automatically repositions other control surfaces to allow the pilot to continue the mission or land safely.
Feb. 15, 1990	First of three SR-71s arrive at Dryden for a program to investigate a host of disciplines to help development of future high-speed civil and military aircraft. (Three YF-12s, prototypes for a fighter-interceptor version of the SR-71, were flown at Dryden from 1969 to 1979 in an earlier high-speed program.)
Apr. 5, 1990	Pegasus® space booster is successfully air-launched from the NASA B-52 in one of the first successful flights of a commercially developed space launch vehicle placing a payload into earth orbit. The launch was off the California coast, with a NASA-Navy payload placed in a polar orbit 320 miles high.
May 3, 1990	First flight in NASA's first program to investigate laminar flow control at supersonic speeds. Program uses the only two F-16XL prototypes to investigate passive and active methods of reducing turbulence on wing surfaces at high speeds.
Oct. 25, 1990	Final test in a series of eight using B-52 No. 008 to validate drag chute deployment system for use on space shuttle to improve their landing efficiency. The tests with 008 were on the lakebed and main runway.
Dec. 3, 1990	Position of Dryden site manager redesignated as director in reorganization that strengthens Dryden's role as a national flight research installation, with Ken Szalai, chief of Dryden's Research Engineering Division, named to new position. Dryden personnel number 430.
May 15, 1991	Full-scale X-30 structural test component, representing a wing control surface, arrives at Dryden's Thermostructural Research Laboratory for loads and temperature testing.
Jul. 12, 1991	First flight of F-18 High Alpha (Angle-of-Attack) Research Vehicle (HARV) with thrust vectoring system engaged to enhance control and maneuvering at high angles of attack; 104th flight of the HARV, which arrived at Dryden Oct. 22, 1984, and initially flew a series of missions without thrust vectoring to obtain experience with aerodynamic measurements at high angles of attack and to develop the flight research techniques needed for this measurement.

®Pegasus is a registered trademark of Orbital Sciences Corporation, Fairfield, Virginia.

Aug. 14, 1991	First all-NASA SR-71 flight with research pilots Steve Ishmael and Rogers Smith in the cockpit. It was the first Mach 3 mission flown at Dryden since the final YF-12 flight Oct. 31, 1979.
Sept. 30, 1991	Seven-year X-29 Advanced Technology Demonstrator program ends after 362 research missions with the two forward-swept wing aircraft. No. 1 aircraft was flown 242 times to validate design concepts. X-29 No. 2 was flown 120 times in high-angle-of-attack studies. Joint USAF/NASA program later flies No. 2 in vortex control study.
Oct. 3, 1991	Dryden aeronautical engineer Marta Bohn-Meyer becomes first female crewmember to fly in an SR-71.
Nov. 1, 1991	Tests of pressure-sensitive luminescent paint end, opening door for a new method of measuring surface pressures on aircraft.
Dec. 12, 1991	F-18 high-angle-of-attack research aircraft, with pilot Ed Schneider, achieves design point of roughly 70 degrees angle of attack.
Apr. 23, 1992	First flight of an X-31 aircraft from Dryden following relocation of X-31 International Test Organization from Air Force Plant 42 in Palmdale, in a DOD study of thrust vectoring for air combat at high angles of attack.
May 16, 1992	Maiden landing of the space shuttle Endeavour, built to replace Challenger. Landing is viewed by an estimated 125,000 people, including 2,500 school students.
Jul. 1, 1992	Single-day Dryden record of six missions tied by X-29 No. 2 after the aircraft returns to flight for a 60-flight USAF/NASA study using vortex flow controls on nose to study improved control at high angles of attack.
Oct. 24, 1992	Integrated Test Facility (ITF) officially opens, giving Dryden a unique capability to carry out interdependent systems testing, systems troubleshooting, and rapid pre-and post-flight systems checks on several aircraft simultaneously.
Dec. 22, 1992	Flights begin with Dryden's CV-990 Landing Systems Research Aircraft, equipped with a space shuttle landing gear fixture that later led to increased orbiter cross wind landing limits at the Kennedy Space Center, and aided in the decision to resurface the Kennedy runway.
Jan. 4, 1993	Judy Janisse Child Development Center is dedicated. The $700,000 facility is named after a former NASA employee, killed in a commercial airline accident, who was instrumental in the development of the center.
Mar. 9, 1993	NASA SR-71 flies on first science mission, taking a JPL ultraviolet camera to 85,000 feet for night photo studies. Flight was also first SR-71 night mission.
Apr. 21, 1993	The F-15 Highly Integrated Digital Electronic Control (HiDEC) is landed using only engine power to turn, climb, and descend. Gordon Fullerton is pilot on milestone event.
Apr. 29, 1993	The thrust-vectored X-31 executes a minimum radius 180-degree turn—the "Herbst Maneuver"—while flying at more than 70-degrees angle of attack, well beyond the aerodynamic limits of any other aircraft.

May 21, 1993	First research flight with Dryden's F-18 Systems Research Aircraft checks out an electric actuator that monitors and controls one of the aircraft's ailerons, and becomes a testbed for advanced electric and fiber optics components.
Jun. 15, 1993	Modified F-15 called ACTIVE—Advanced Control Technology for Integrated Vehicles—replaces the HiDEC as Dryden's integrated systems aircraft. The ACTIVE F-15 features forward canards and will be fitted with thrust-vectoring nozzles to study their use for pitch and yaw control.
Jun. 24, 1993	Replica of X-15 rocket research aircraft, displayed at the corner of Lilly and Lakeshore Drives, is dedicated.
Nov. 1, 1993	The space shuttle Columbia, on mission STS-58, lands at 7:06 a.m. (PST), the last planned landing of a shuttle at Edwards. Nearly 35,000 people, including about 5000 Dryden guests, view the event.
Dec. 21, 1993	The Perseus remotely piloted aircraft flies for the first time in a project to develop technologies to be used to construct and fly unpiloted vehicles on high-altitude science missions.
Feb. 3, 1994	Final flight of an F-104 at Dryden, a symbolic farewell with NASA 826, is piloted by Tom McMurtry, Chief, Flight Operations Division. First acquired in 1956, 11 F-104s flew at Dryden over a 38-year period as chase and research aircraft. Last research mission with NASA 826 was Jan. 31, 1994. The other remaining F-104, NASA 825, was flown on its last research mission Jan. 24, 1994.
Mar. 1, 1994	Dryden named a NASA Center again. Transition period to institute independent administrative functions ends Sept. 30, 1994.
Mar. 18, 1994	Ten thousandth research mission is logged by Dryden's Western Aeronautical Test Range, a flight with the F-18 HARV. Facility was developed in the 1950s to support the X-15 program.
Jul. 20, 1994	Twenty-fifth anniversary of Apollo 11 features salute to Dryden's Lunar Landing Research Vehicle (LLRV), used to develop moon-landing training techniques.
Aug. 3, 1994	Sixth and last Pegasus® mission using NASA B-52 No. 008 as the launch vehicle is successful. Future airborne launches to be with an L-1011 owned and operated by Pegasus developer, Orbital Sciences Corp.
Aug. 4, 1994	X-31 logs 438th flight, new record for experimental aircraft. Record holder had been X-29, set on its last flight in 1992.
Oct. 1, 1994	Dryden assumes full Center status, as NASA's Center of Excellence in Flight Research. NASA personnel number 465.
May 13, 1995	X-31 completes final research flights, making a total of 555 for the program.
Jun. 11, 1995	The NASA B-52, No. 008, turns 40 years old. Based at Dryden since mid-1959, it is the oldest B-52 still flying.

Aug. 11, 1995	CV-990 Landing Systems Research Aircraft completes study of space shuttle landing gear, with a total of 155 research flights. Final tests subjected orbiter wheels to total failure modes on lakebed surface and concrete runway.
Aug. 29, 1995	Aided by NASA-developed propulsion controlled aircraft (PCA) system, an MD-11 makes first-ever, safe landings of an actual transport aircraft using only engine power for control.
Sept. 11, 1995	Pathfinder sets new altitude record for solar-powered aircraft. The remotely controlled, unpiloted prototype attained an altitude 50,500 ft during a nearly 12-hour flight. Solar cells on the top surface of the all-wing aircraft power six electric, propeller-turning motors for propulsion. Pathfinder is part of the NASA Environmental Research Aircraft and Sensor Technology (ERAST) Program.
Oct. 13, 1995	First flight of the F-16XL with the active glove installed. The two-seat F-16 XL was piloted by Dana Purifoy, and begins a program researching laminar flow at supersonic speeds using a suction panel that covers 60 percent of the wing chord. Previous studies with the single-seat F-16XL used a glove that covered only 20 percent of the chord.
Nov. 17, 1995	Center Director Ken Szalai renames the Integrated Test Facility as the Walter C. Williams Research Aircraft Integration Facility.
Nov. 30, 1995	Improved software enables an MD-11 to make a final landing at Edwards without the need for the pilot to manipulate the flight controls while using only engine power for control.
Jul. 2, 1996	NASA announces award of X-33 contract to Lockheed Martin Corp. to design, build, and fly a vehicle that will demonstrate advanced technologies to dramatically increase reliability and lower the cost of putting a pound of payload in space. The test vehicle was projected to fly from DFRC in the year 2000.
Sept. 6, 1996	F-18 High Alpha Research Vehicle (HARV) makes final flight in 385-flight research program that investigated improved maneuverability of tactical aircraft at high angles of attack.
Nov. 1, 1996	F-15 ACTIVE research aircraft conducts first thrust vectoring of engine exhaust at speeds approaching Mach 2.
Nov. 24, 1996	First flight of Tu-144LL flying laboratory inaugurates year-long flight test program in support of NASA's High-Speed Research program.
Nov. 26, 1996	Year-long Supersonic Laminar-Flow Control program concludes with 45th flight on highly modified F-16XL research aircraft. Program proved that laminar–or smooth–airflow could be obtained over a significant portion of an aircraft wing's chord at speeds of Mach 2 by use of a suction system pulling turbulent boundary-layer air through tiny holes in the wing skin.

More information on the history of Dryden Flight Research Center can be found in the references 1 through 9 on the following page.

REFERENCES

1. Hallion, R. P.: <u>On the Frontier: Flight Research at Dryden 1946–1981</u>, NASA SP-4303, 1984.

2. Wallace, Lane E.: <u>Flights of Discovery 50 Years at the NASA Dryden Flight Research Center</u>, NASA SP-4309, 1997.

3. Stillwell, Wendell H.: <u>X-15: Research Results with a Selected Bibliography</u>, NASA SP-60, 1965.

4. Thompson, Milton O.: <u>At the Edge of Space</u>, Smithsonian Institution Press, 1992, TL789.8.U6X578.

5. Powers, Sheryll Goecke: <u>Women in Flight Research at NASA Dryden Flight Research Center From 1946 to 1995</u>, Monograph in Aerospace History No. 6, 1997.

6. Day, Richard E.: <u>Coupling Dynamics in Aircraft: A Historical Perspective</u>, NASA SP-532, 1997.

7. Saltzman, Edwin J.; and Ayers, Theodore G.: <u>Selected Examples of NACA/NASA Supersonic Flight Research</u>, NASA SP-513, May 1995.

8. Reed, R. Dale (with Darlene Lister; foreward by Chuck Yeager): <u>Wingless Flight: The Lifting Body Story</u>, NASA SP-4220, 1997.

9. Kempel, Robert W.; Painter, Weneth D.; and Thompson, Milton O.: <u>Developing and Flight Testing the HL-10 Lifting Body: A Precursor to the Space Shuttle</u>, NASA RP-1332, April 1994.

ACRONYMS AND ABBREVIATIONS

AAS   American Astronautical Society, Washington, D. C.

AASE   Department of Aerophysics and Aerospace Engineering, Mississippi State University, Starkville, Mississippi

ACTIVE   Advanced Control Technology for Integrated Vehicles–a NASA Dryden test program

AEDC   Arnold Engineering Development Center, Arnold Air Force Base, Tennessee

AFB   Air Force Base

AFFTC   Air Force Flight Test Center, Edwards, California

AFWAL   Air Force Wright Aeronautical Laboratory, Dayton, Ohio

AGARD   Advisory Group for Aeronautical Research & Development, Paris, France

AHS   American Helicopter Society, Alexandria, Virginia

AIAA   American Institute of Aeronautics and Astronautics, Washington, D. C.

AICHE   American Institute of Chemical Engineers, New York, New York

AIR   Aerospace Information Report–a military report

AIST   Agency of Industrial Science and Technology, Japan

ARC   Ames Research Center, Moffett Field, California

ARS   American Rocket Society–became AIAA in 1963 with IAS

ASCE   American Society of Civil Engineers, Washington, D. C.

ASEE   American Society for Engineering Education, Washington, D. C.

ASME   American Society of Mechanical Engineers, New York, New York

BuAero   Bureau of Aeronautics, Department of the Navy, 1921–1959

CAI   Canadian Aeronautical Institute, Ottawa, Ontario

CASI   NASA Center for Aerospace and Scientific Information, Hanover, Maryland

CP   Conference Proceedings, NASA report

CR   Contractor Report, NASA report

DGLR   Deutsche Gesellschaft fuer Luft-und Raumfahrt, Germany

DOD	Department of Defense, Washington, D. C.
DTIC	Defense Technical Information Center, Ft. Belvoir, Virginia
ERAST	Environmental Research Aircraft and Sensor Technology program—a NASA Dryden test program
FAA	Federal Aviation Agency / Administration, Washington, D. C.
FED	Fluids Engineering Division (ASME), New York, New York
FRC	Flight Research Center, NASA facility at Edwards AFB 1959–1976
HARV	F-18 high alpha research vehicle
HiDEC	F-15 highly integrated digital electronic control
HSCT	High speed civil transport
HSFRS	High-Speed Flight Research Station
IAA	International Aerospace Abstracts–a monthly publication of recent international and AIAA Conference information in abstract form, AIAA, New York, New York
IAS	Institute of Aeronautical Sciences, Inc.—became AIAA in 1963 with ARS
ICAS	International Council of Aeronautical Sciences, Les Mureaux Cedex, France
ICASE	Institute for Computer Applications in Science and Engineering, Hampton, Virginia
ICASSP	International Conference on Acoustics, Speech, and Signal Processing
IEEE	Institute of Electrical and Electronics Engineers, New York, New York
IES	Institute of Environmental Sciences, Mount Prospect, Illinois
IFAC	International Federation of Automatic Control, Uppsala, Sweden
ISA	Instrument Society of America, Triangle Park, North Carolina
ITC	International Telemetering Conference
ITEA	International Test and Evaluation Association, Fairfax, Virginia
ITF	Integrated Test Facility, at Dryden since 1987
IUTAM	International Union of Theoretical and Applied Mechanics, Stuttgart, Germany
JPL	Jet Propulsion Laboratory, Pasadena, California
JSASS	Japan Society for Aeronautical and Space Sciences, Japan

LLRV	lunar landing research vehicle
MIT	Massachusetts Institute of Technology, Cambridge, Massachusetts
NACA	National Advisory Committee for Aeronautics–a NASA Precursor
NASA	National Aeronautics and Space Administration, Washington, D. C.
NIWC	National Institute of Materials and Chemical Research, Japan
NTIS	National Technical Information Service, Springfield, Virginia
PCA	propulsion controlled aircraft
RAE	Royal Aircraft Establishment, England
RECON	A CASI database to archive scientific and technical reports
RECONplus	A CASI database to archive scientific and technical reports
RM	Research Memo, a NACA report
RP	Reference Publication, NASA Report
SAE	Society of Automotive Engineers, Warrendale, Pennsylvania
SCA	shuttle carrier aircraft
SETP	Society of Experimental Test Pilots, Lancaster, California
SFTE	Society of Flight Test Engineers, Lancaster, California
SIAM	Society for Industrial and Applied Mathematics, Philadelphia, Pennsylvania
SP	Special Publication, a NASA report
SPIE	The International Society for Optical Engineering, Bellingham, Washington
TM	Technical Memorandum, a NASA report
TN	Technical Note, a NACA or NASA report
TP	Technical Paper, a NACA or NASA report
USAF	United States Air Force
USN	United States Navy
USN/NAWC	United States Navy/Naval Air Warfare Center

ORDERING INFORMATION

Ordering sources for the different types of materials given below:

Sources	Types of material	Accession number examples:
Document Delivery/AIAA Dispatch 800-662-1545 816-926-8794 FAX dispatch@lhl.lib.mo.us http://www.lhl.lib.mo.us/pubserv/ AIAA/dispatch.htm	AIAA papers and worldwide literature from conferences and periodicals available through AIAA.	A90-12345 90A12345 AIAA paper no. 97-1234
National Technical Information Service (NTIS) 703-487-4650 703-321-8547 FAX orders@ntis.fedworld.gov http://ntis.gov	Report literature having no distribution limitations.	N95-12345 95N12345 19970012345 AD-A123456
NASA Center for Aerospace Information (CASI) 301-621-0390 301-621-0134 FAX help@sti.nasa.gov http://www.sti.nasa.gov	Report literature having no distribution limitations. Report literature with some type of distribution limitation.	N95-12345 95N12345 19970012345 X97-12345 97X12345
Defense Technical Information Center (DTIC) 800-225-3842 703-767-8228 FAX help@dtic.mil http://dticam.dtic.mil/	Report literature from U. S. Government Agency or AGARD.	AD-A123456
NASA libraries or NASA CASI	Pre-1962 reports and papers.	87H12345 93R12345
Libraries	Books	TL123.C66.D7

KEY TO CITATIONS

Typical Citation and Abstract

(1)**1993.**(2)Burcham, Frank W., Jr.; Maine, Trindel; and Wolf, Thomas.(3)**Flight Testing and Simulation of an F-15 Airplane Using Throttles for Flight Control.** (4)NASA TM-104255,(5)H-1826,(6)NAS 1.15:104255,(7)AIAA Paper 92-4109.(8)Presented at the AIAA Flight Test Conference, Hilton Head, SC, 24 Aug. 1992.(9)August 1992,(10)92N32864,(11)#(12)(see also 2004).

Flight tests and simulation studies using the throttles of an F-15 airplane for emergency flight control have been conducted at the NASA Dryden Flight Research Center. The airplane and the simulation are capable of extended up-and-away flight, using only throttles for flight path control. Initial simulation results showed that runway landings using manual throttles-only control were difficult, but possible with practice. Manual approaches flown in the airplane were much more difficult, indicating a significant discrepancy between flight and simulation. Analysis of flight data and development of improved simulation models that resolve the discrepancy are discussed. An augmented throttle-only control system that controls bank angle and flight path with appropriate feedback parameters has also been developed, evaluated in simulations, and is planned for flight in the F-15.

1 Chronological number of citation

2 Author(s)

3 Title

4 NASA publication number

5 NASA Dryden production number

6 GPO number

7 Assigned conference publication number

8 Conference name, place, and date

9 Date of publication (underlined)

10 Accession number

11 Available on microfiche (#)

12 Chronological number of cross-reference citation

BIBLIOGRAPHY

1947 Technical Publications

1. Beeler, De E.; and Gerard, George: **Wake Measurements Behind a Wing Section of a Fighter Airplane in Fast Dives.** NACA TN 1190, March 1, 1947, 93R11438.

Wake measurements made in a vertical plane behind a wing-section of a fighter airplane are presented for a range of Mach number up to 0.78. Since evidences of reverse flow were found in a large part of the surveys—possibly because of interference of the rake support—the computed profile-drag coefficients are considered to be only qualitative. The results showed that the large increase in drag coefficient beyond critical Mach number indicated by wind-tunnel tests was also obtained under flight conditions and that the wake width was extended sharply when shock was encountered. The wake extension occurred first at the upper surface since the highest local velocity was obtained on that surface. The large increase in drag coefficient for the wing section tested did not occur until after the critical Mach-number had been exceeded by approximately 0.05. Comparison of the profile-drag measurements with total airplane drag measurements showed that the large increases in drag in both cases started to occur at the same value of Mach number. The results further indicated that wake measurements made in three dimensional-flow after shock had occurred cannot, in general, be interpreted in terms of section profile-drag coefficient because of the existence of the strong lateral flow indicated by tuft behavior in the dead-air region behind the shock.

2. Beeler, De E.: **Air-Flow Behavior Over the Wing of an XP-51 Airplane as Indicated by Wing-Surface Tufts at Subcritical and Supercritical Speeds.** NACA RM L6L03, April 24, 1947, 86H23988.

Results are presented in this report of the air-flow behavior over the wing of an XP-51 airplane including photographs of tuft attached to the wing surface and chordwise pressure distributions. A comparison of tuft studied is made of the flight results with those obtained from wind-tunnel tests. The results indicate that steady flow is obtained over the wing until the critical speed has been exceeded by about 0.04 to 0.05 in Mach numbers. At higher Mach numbers the flow is unsteady and becomes very rough and turbulent over the rear 50 percent of the chord after the limit maximum pressure coefficient has been reached. Observation of surface tufts alone without benefit of prevailing pressure distributions may indicate separated flow before separation actually occurs. Comparisons made of the flight and wind-tunnel data show a similar tuft behavior throughout the Mach number range.

1948 Technical Publications

3. Beeler, De E.; and Mayer, John P.: **Measurements of the Wing and Tail Loads During the Acceptance Tests of the Bell XS-1 Research Airplane.** NACA RM L7L12, April 1948, 87H24183.

During the acceptance tests of the XS-1 airplane, strain-gage measurements were made of wing and tail loads up to a Mach number of 0.80. The maximum lift and buffet boundaries were also determined. The loads encountered were well within the design loads and showed fairly good agreement with wind-tunnel and calculated data.

EC72-3431

XS-1 (X-1) Airplane

4. Williams, Walter C.; and Beeler, De Elroy: **Results of Preliminary Flight Tests of the XS-1 Airplane (8-Percent Wing) to a Mach Number of 1.25.** NACA RM L8A23A, April 6, 1948, 86H18960.

The data obtained in flight with the XS-1 airplane with 8-percent-thick wing up to and beyond the speed of sound at an altitude of 37,000 feet and above show that most of the trim and force changes expected in the transonic range have been experienced. Although conditions are not normal, the airplane can be flown under control through a Mach number of 1 at altitudes of 37,000 feet and above. In detail, the following has been noted: (1) Buffeting has been experienced in level flight but has been mild. The horizontal-tail loads associated with the buffeting have been small. (2) The airplane has experienced longitudinal trim changes in the speed range from 0.8 up to 1.25. The largest control force associated with these trim changes was 25 pounds. The pilot has been able to control the airplane. The relatively small magnitude of the control force may be attributed to the small size of the elevator and the high altitude of the flight. (3) The elevator effectiveness has decreased more than 50 percent in going from a Mach number of 0.7 to 0.87. There is evidence of further reduction in elevator effectiveness above a Mach number of 0.87. This loss in elevator effectiveness has affected the magnitude of the trim changes as noted by the pilot but the actual trim changes for the most part have been caused by changes in the wing-fuselage moment. (4) No aileron buzz or associated phenomena have been experienced. The airplane becomes right wing heavy with increasing Mach number up to a Mach number of 1.10, but can be trimmed with the ailerons.

5. McLaughlin, Milton D.; and Clift, Dorothy C.: **Results Obtained During a Dive Recovery of the Bell XS-1 Airplane to High Lift Coefficients at a Mach Number Greater Than 1.0.** NACA RM L8C23A, April 6, 1948, 86H31136.

Measured quantities are presented which were obtained on the Bell XS-1 airplane with an 8-percent-thick wing and a 6-percent-thick horizontal tail during a dive recovery at a Mach number greater than 1.0. The data obtained show that it is possible to obtain fairly high load factors with the airplane at Mach numbers greater than 1.0 if the stabilizer is used for longitudinal control. Lift coefficients approaching low-speed maximum-lift values have been obtained at a Mach number of 1.1 with no indication that these values are the maximum obtainable for the airplane. At the Mach number and lift coefficient reported, there was little or no buffeting.

6. Drake, Hubert M.; McLaughlin, Milton D.; and Goodman, Harold R.: **Results Obtained During Accelerated Transonic Tests of the Bell XS-1 Airplane in Flights to a Mach Number of 0.92.** NACA RM L8AO5A, April 19, 1948, 86H18537.

An accelerated flight program using the Bell XS-1 airplane has been undertaken to explore the transonic-speed range. The flying was done by an Air Force pilot, and the data reduction and analysis were made from NACA instrumentation by NACA personnel. This paper presents the results of tests obtained up to a Mach number of 0.92 at altitudes around 30,000 feet. The data obtained show that the airplane has experienced most of the difficulties expected in the transonic range, but that it can be flown satisfactorily to a Mach number of at least 0.92 at altitude above 30,000 feet. Longitudinal trim changes have been experienced but the forces involved have been small. The elevator effectiveness decreased about one-half with increase of Mach number from 0.70 to 0.87. Buffeting has been experienced in level flight but it has been mild and the associated tail loads have been small. No aileron buzz or other flutter phenomena have been noted.

7. Williams, Walter C.; Forsyth, Charles M.; and Brown, Beverly P.: **General Handling-Qualities Results Obtained During Acceptance Flight Tests of the Bell XS-1 Airplane.** NACA RM L8A09, April 19, 1948, 86H18538.

During the acceptance tests conducted by the Bell Aircraft Corporation on the Bell XS-1 transonic research airplane, NACA instruments were installed to measure the stability and control characteristics and the aerodynamic loads. Tests were made in gliding flight and in powered flight. Two Bell XS-1 airplanes were used during the program: one airplane had wing and tail thicknesses of 10 percent and 8 percent of the chord, respectively, and the other airplane had wing and tail thicknesses of 8 percent and 6 percent of the chord, respectively. The results for the stability and control measurements are presented in this paper.

8. Williams, Walter C.: **Limited Measurements of Static Longitudinal Stability in Flight of Douglas D-558-1 Airplane (BuAero No. 37971).** NACA RM L8E14, June 24, 1948, 86H17021.

During airspeed calibration flights of the D-558-1 airplane being used by NACA for high-speed-flight research, some measurements were obtained of the static longitudinal stability up to a Mach number of 0.85. These data showed that the airplane possessed positive static longitudinal stability up to a Mach number of 0.80. A trim change in the nose-down direction occurred for Mach numbers above 0.82.

E49-090

D-558-1 Airplane

9. Beeler, De E.; McLaughlin, Milton D.; and Clift, Dorothy C.: **Measurements of the Chordwise Pressure Distributions Over the Wing of the XS-1 Research Airplane in Flight.** NACA RM L8G21, August 4, 1948, 86H25805.

Measurements of the chordwise pressure distribution over the 8-percent-thick wing of the XS-1 research airplane have been made at a section near the midspan of the left wing. Data presented are for a Mach number range of 0.75 to 1.25 at a normal-force coefficient of about 0.33 and for normal-force coefficients up to 0.93 at a Mach number of approximately 1.16. The results show that there is a rearward shift of section center of load with an increase in Mach number due to the rearward movement of shock with a corresponding extension of the region of supersonic flow. The load center moves from about 25 to 51 percent of the chord as the Mach number is increased for 0.75 to 1.25. During the rearward movement of load from the forward to rearward limit position, there is a rapid and large shift of the center of load within these limits for a Mach number range of 0.82 to 0.88. It is expected that large changes in trim, with corresponding large changes in load factor at low altitude, may occur within this Mach number range.

10. Drake, Hubert M.; Goodman, Harold R.; and Hoover, Herbert H.: **Preliminary Results of NACA Transonic Flights of the XS-1 Airplane With 10-Percent-Thick Wing and 8-Percent-Thick Horizontal Tail.** NACA RM L8I29, October 13, 1948, 87H24234.

Contains results of exploratory flights at altitudes of about 40,000 feet to a maximum Mach number of 1.06. Data are presented showing the longitudinal trim changes, elevator effectiveness in producing acceleration, and rudder effectiveness as a function of Mach number. Data on lateral oscillations are also presented.

11. Goodman, Harold R.; and Drake, Hubert M.: **Results Obtained During Extension of U.S. Air Force Transonic-Flight Tests of XS-1 Airplane.** NACA RM L8I28, November 16, 1948, 86H18957.

Limited data covering extension of the U.S. Air Force transonic-flight tests of the XS-1 airplane are presented. These data show that successful flight to a Mach number of 1.35 has been achieved at altitudes above 40,000 feet. Longitudinal trim changes were experienced to the highest Mach numbers attained, with the wheel forces remaining small and the pilot able to control the airplane with ease. The airplane becomes right-wing heavy above a Mach number of 0.8 but can be trimmed with the aileron. No aileron buzz or flutter phenomena have been encountered. Buffeting has been light, when encountered in the range of Mach number and lift coefficient covered by these data.

12. Matthews, James T., Jr.: **Effect of Downwash on the Estimated Elevator Deflection Required for Trim of the XS-1 Airplane at Supersonic Speeds.** NACA RM L8H06A, November 1948.

This report contains the results of an investigation to determine from linearized theory, which has recently become available, the downwash at supersonic speeds at the tail of the XS-1 airplane and the effect of the downwash on the elevator deflection required for trim. The results are presented in the form of curves showing the variation of downwash angle with angle of attack and elevator deflection required for trim plotted against Mach number. The calculations indicate that increasing up-elevator deflection is required with increasing Mach number (unstable variation) in level flight between Mach numbers of 1.1 and 1.6. A slight reduction in up-elevator deflection occurs between Mach numbers of 1.6 and 2.0. The stabilizer angle has a similar variation, that is, unstable up to a Mach number of about 1.6 and then becoming slightly stable up to a Mach number of 2.0. The reduction of downwash with increasing Mach number is not the main cause of the increase in up-elevator deflection. The main reasons for this trend are that the pitching-moment coefficients due to the wing camber, the wing lift, and the lift of the stabilizer are all in a nose-down direction, and as the Mach number increases, these pitching-moment coefficients apparently decrease less rapidly than the elevator effectiveness.

1949 Technical Publications

13. Drake, Hubert M.: **Stability and Control Data Obtained From First Flight of X-4 Airplane.** NACA RM L9A31, February 7, 1949, 86H17466.

NACA instrumentation has been installed in the X-4 airplanes to obtain stability and control data during the Northrop conducted acceptance tests. The results of the first flight of the X-4 number 1 airplane are presented in this report. These data were obtained for a center-of-gravity position of about 22 percent of the mean aerodynamic chord. A maximum indicated airspeed and pressure altitude of 290 miles per hour and 11,000 feet, respectively, were obtained during the flight. Results of the flight indicated that the airplane is slightly unstable, stick fixed, in gear-up, flaps-up configuration for a center-of-gravity position at 21.4 percent of the mean aerodynamic chord. The pilot reported that it was difficult to maintain steady flight in this configuration. There was no indication of a snaking or lateral oscillation for the speed range covered. For gear-down configuration at low lift coefficients with the center of gravity at 22.4 and 21.6 percent of the mean aerodynamic chord the airplane was longitudinally stable; however, at high lift coefficients, it was indicated that the airplane was longitudinally unstable. The rudder effectiveness appeared to be low in the gear-down, low-speed condition. The maximum rate of rudder motion of 25 degrees per second available with the present control system was considered by the pilot to be too slow.

E-359

X-4 Airplane

14. Williams, Walter C.: **Flight Measurement of the Stability Characteristics of the Douglas D-558-1 Airplane (BuAero No. 37971) in Sideslips.** NACA RM L8E14A, April 18, 1949, 86H17022.

Measurements have been made of the stability characteristics of the D-558-1 airplane in steadily increasing sideslips at various Mach numbers from 0.50 to 0.80 at 10,000 feet altitude and at Mach numbers from 0.50 to 0.84 at 30,000 feet altitude. The results of these tests show that the apparent directional stability of the airplane is high and increases with increasing Mach number and dynamic pressure. The dihedral effect is positive at all speeds, there is little or no change in pitching moment with sideslip, and the cross-wind force is positive.

15. Barlow, William H.; and Lilly, Howard C.: **Stability Results Obtained With Douglas D-558-1 Airplane (BuAero No. 37971) in Flight Up to a Mach Number of 0.89.** NACA RM L8K03, April 22, 1949, 86H17024.

Measurements have been made of some of the high-speed characteristics of the D-558-1 airplane up to a Mach number of 0.89. The results of these tests showed that the stabilizer incidence drastically affected the longitudinal trim characteristics above a Mach number of 0.80. With a stabilizer incidence of 2.3 degrees, the airplane became nose heavy above a Mach number of 0.8. With a stabilizer incidence of 1.4 degrees, the airplane became tail heavy above a Mach number of 0.83. The airplane also became right-wing heavy above a Mach number of 0.84 and the airplane felt uncertain laterally to the pilot. The longitudinal stability in accelerated flight was positive throughout the speed range from a Mach number of 0.50 to 0.80 and increased above a Mach number of 0.675. The buffet boundary was defined up to a Mach number of 0.84 and was similar to that for the Bell XS-1 airplane with the same wing section, 65-110.

16. Drake, Hubert M.: **Measurement of the Dynamic Lateral Stability of the Douglas D-558-1 Airplane (BuAero No. 37971) in Rudder Kicks at a Mach Number of 0.72.** NACA RM L9D06A, May 31, 1949, 86H17025.

Contains results of flight measurements of the dynamic lateral stability of the Douglas D-558-1 airplane at a Mach number of 0.72 and a pressure altitude of 8500 feet.

E49-059

D-558-1 Airplane

17. Drake, Hubert M.: **Measured Characteristics of the Douglas D-558-1 Airplane (BuAero No. 37971) in Two Landings.** NACA RM L9D20A, June 3, 1949, 86H18900.

Records were obtained of two landings of the Douglas D-558-1 airplane made during the stability and control investigation. These two records show that the maximum normal-force coefficient used during the landings, 0.95, was considerably below the maximum, 1.2, estimated to be available. The approaches were made at 150 percent of the possible minimum speed, and the actual contacts were at about 115 percent of minimum speed. The rate of descent in the approach was 1200 to 1800 feet per minute at the start of the landing flare.

18. Drake, Hubert M.: **Measurements of Aileron Effectiveness of Bell X-1 Airplane Up to a Mach Number of 0.82.** NACA RM L9D13, June 20, 1949, 86H27619.

Abrupt, rudder-fixed aileron rolls have been made with the Bell X-1 airplane having a 10-percent-thick wing in glides to a Mach number of 0.82 at about 30,000 feet pressure altitude. Aileron movements were between one-fourth and one-half of full deflection. These aileron rolls indicate that Mach number has little effect on the aileron effectiveness up to a Mach number of 0.82.

19. Williams, Walter C.: **Results Obtained From Second Flight of X-4 Airplane (USAF No. 46-676).** NACA RM L9F21, July 18, 1949, 86H17468.

NACA instrumentation has been installed in the X-4 airplanes to obtain stability and control data during the Northrop-conducted acceptance tests. The results of the second flight of the X-4 number 1 airplane are presented in this report. This flight was made with the center of gravity at 19.7 percent of the mean aerodynamic chord and with the rudder-boost system removed. The results of the flight showed that the longitudinal stability was positive in the clean condition and in the gear-down, flaps-up condition. Records taken during landing approach and in a steady run at 170 miles per hour showed that the lateral oscillation is poorly damped. The pilot reported that the rudder control was adequate.

20. Drake, Hubert M.; and Wall, Helen L.: **Preliminary Theoretical and Flight Investigation of the Lateral Oscillation of the X-1 Airplane.** NACA RM L9F07, July 19, 1949, 86H17642, 87H24281.

A small-amplitude, undamped, lateral oscillation has been encountered in flight tests of the X-1 airplane. The oscillation occurs in subsonic and supersonic flight, in maneuvers, and power on and off. The calculations indicate that a change, in the positive direction, of the inclination of the principal axis with respect to the flight path should have a considerable stabilizing effect.

21. Goodman, Harold R.; and Yancey, Roxanah B.: **The Static-Pressure Error of Wing and Fuselage Airspeed Installations of the X-1 Airplanes in Transonic Flight.** NACA RM L9G22, July 22, 1949, 86H63671.

Measurements were made in the transonic speed ranges of the static-pressure position error at a distance of 0.96 chord ahead of the wing tip of both the 8-percent-thick-wing and the 10-percent-thick-wing X-1 airplanes, and at a point 0.6 maximum fuselage diameter ahead of the fuselage nose of the X-1 airplanes.

22. Drake, Hubert M.: **Measurements of Aileron Effectiveness of the Bell X-1 Airplane at Mach Numbers Between 0.9 and 1.06.** NACA RM L9G19A, August 4, 1949, 87H24295.

Presents results of flight measurements of aileron effectiveness of the X-1 airplane up to a Mach number of 0.94. The data indicate a 75 percent loss of aileron effectiveness between M = 0.82 and M = 0.94.

23. Valentine, George M.: **Stability and Control Data Obtained From Fourth and Fifth Flights of the Northrop X-4 Airplane (USAF No. 46-676).** NACA RM L9G25A, August 4, 1949, 86H17473.

NACA instrumentation has been installed in the Northrop X-4 airplane to obtain stability and control data during the Northrop-conducted acceptance tests. The results of the fourth and fifth flights of the Northrop X-4 number 1 airplane are presented in this paper. These data were obtained for a center-of-gravity position of approximately 19.5 percent of the mean aerodynamic chord. The results of this flight showed that the directional stability as measured in steadily increasing sideslips was positive and high and that the effective dihedral was positive. The results also show the airplane to be longitudinally stable, stick fixed, with the center of gravity at 19.5 percent of the mean aerodynamic chord.

24. Sjoberg, Sigurd A.: **Preliminary Measurements of the Dynamic Lateral Stability Characteristics of the Douglas D-558-II (BuAero No. 37974) Airplane.** NACA RM L9G18, August 18, 1949, 86H17031.

This paper presents some data on the dynamic lateral stability characteristics of the Douglas D-558-II (BuAero No. 37974) airplane. For the airplane in the clean condition, the lateral oscillations are lightly damped. In the landing condition, the airplane performs a constant-amplitude lateral oscillation.

E-1441

D-558-II Airplane

25. Williams, Walter C.: **Results Obtained from Third Flight of Northrop X-4 Airplane (USAF No. 46-676).** NACA RM L9G20A, September 9, 1949, 86H17471.

NACA instrumentation has been installed in the Northrop X-4 airplane to obtain stability and control data during the Northrop-conducted acceptance tests. The results of the third flight of the X-4 number 1 airplane are presented in this paper. The results of this flight showed that the directional stability as measured in steadily increasing sideslips was positive and high and that the lateral stability was positive.

26. Goodman, Harold R.: **The Static-Pressure Error of a Wing Airspeed Installation of the McDonnell XF-88 Airplane in Dives to Transonic Speeds.** NACA RM SL9I12, September 23, 1949.

Measurements were made, in dives to transonic speeds, of the static-pressure position error at a distance of one chord ahead of the wing tip of the McDonnell XF-88 airplane. The airplane incorporates a wing which is swept back 35° along the 0.25-chord line and utilizes a 65-series airfoil with a 9-percent-thick section perpendicular to the 0.25-chord line. The section in the stream direction is approximately 8 percent thick. Data up to a Mach number of about 0.97 were obtained within an airplane normal-force-coefficient range from about 0.05 to about 0.68. Data at Mach numbers above about 0.97 were obtained within an airplane normal-force-coefficient range from about 0.05 to about 0.38.

27. Sjoberg, S. A.; and Champine, R. A.: **Preliminary Flight Measurements of the Static Longitudinal Stability and Stalling Characteristics of the Douglas D-558-II Research Airplane (BuAero No. 37974).** NACA RM L9H31A, October 18, 1949, 86H17086.

Contains results of brief flight measurements of the static longitudinal stability and stalling characteristics of the Douglas D-558-II (BuAero No. 37974) research airplane.

1950 Technical Publications

28. Matthews, James T.: **Results Obtained During Flights 1 to 6 of the Northrop X-4 Airplane (USAF No. 46-677).** NACA RM L9K22, January 12, 1950, 86H17475.

NACA instruments were installed in the Northrop X-4 number 2 airplane (A.F. No. 46-677) to obtain stability and control data during the acceptance tests conducted by the Northrop Company. The results of flights 1 to 6 are presented in this report. These data were obtained for a center-of-gravity position of about 19.5 to 20.0 percent of the mean aerodynamic chord. The data presented include a time history of a complete pull-up, time histories of several level and accelerated flight runs, and the effect of dive-brake extension on the longitudinal and lateral trim. The pilot reports the mechanical trim device to be unsatisfactory for any stick-free or dynamic stability and control analysis because the stick force cannot be trimmed to zero sufficiently well to permit the stick to be released during a maneuver without the airplane performing a divergence. In addition, the trim device is inoperative when more than 8.0 degrees up elevon angle is required for trim. A short-period longitudinal oscillation with relatively poor damping was present, but this oscillation was not objectionable to the pilot. The airplane has a stable variation of longitudinal-control angle with normal-force coefficient for the indicated airspeed ranges of 180 to 300 miles per hour at about 30,000-foot pressure altitude. Extension of the dive brakes up to ±30 degrees has no appreciable effect on the longitudinal trim at indicated airspeeds of 160 miles per hour with landing gear down, and at airspeeds of 300 miles per hour with the landing gear up, at altitudes of 8,500 and 10,000 feet, respectively. A slight tendency to roll to the left was indicated in the landing-gear-down case.

29. Sadoff, Melvin; and Sisk, Thomas R.: **Stall Characteristics Obtained From Flight 10 of Northrop X-4 No. 2 Airplane (USAF No. 46-677).** NACA RM A50A04, February 27, 1950, 86H30240.

NACA instrumentation has been installed in the X-4 airplanes to obtain stability and control data during the acceptance tests conducted by the Northrop Aircraft Corporation. This report presents data obtained on the stalling characteristics of the airplane in the clean and gear-down configurations. The center of gravity was located at approximately 18 percent of the mean aerodynamic chord during the tests. The results indicated that the airplane was not completely stalled when stall was gradually approached during nominally unaccelerated flight but that it was completely stalled during a more abruptly approached stall in accelerated flight. The stall in accelerated flight was relatively mild, and this was attributed to the nature of the variation of lift with angle of attack for the 0010-64 airfoil section, the plan form of the wing, and to the fact that the initial sideslip at the stall produced (as shown by wind-tunnel tests of a model of the airplane) a more symmetrical stall pattern.

30. Sjoberg, S. A.: **Flight Measurements With the Douglas D-558-II (BuAero No. 37974) Research Airplane. Static Lateral and Directional Stability Characteristics as Measured in Sideslips at Mach Numbers Up to 0.87.** NACA RM L50C14, May 19, 1950, 86H17088.

Flight measurements were made in sideslips of the static lateral and directional stability characteristics of the Douglas D-558-II (BuAero No. 37974) research airplane. The directional stability of the airplane was positive in both the clean and landing conditions at all test speeds. About 2 degrees of rudder deflection were required to produce 1 degree of sideslip in both the clean and landing conditions. There was no decrease in the effectiveness of the rudder in producing sideslip up to the highest Mach number reached (0.87).

31. Thompson, Jim Rogers; Roden, William S.; and Eggleston, John M.: **Flight Investigation of the Aileron Characteristics of the Douglas D-558-I Airplane (BuAero No. 37972) at Mach Numbers Between 0.6 and 0.89.** NACA RM L50D20, May 26, 1950, 86H27648.

Abrupt, rudder-fixed aileron rolls have been made with the Douglas D-558-I airplane (BuAero No. 37972) at Mach numbers between 0.6 and 0.89. Rolls were made at aileron deflections between one-eighth and one-half the maximum available deflection. The results obtained indicate that the aileron effectiveness is independent of Mach number and deflection within the range investigated. Limited information on the lateral trim and handling qualities of the airplane at high Mach numbers is presented.

32. Sadoff, Melvin; and Sisk, Thomas R.: **Longitudinal-Stability Characteristics of the Northrop X-4 Airplane (U.S.A.F. No. 46-677).** NACA RM A50D27, June 29, 1950, 86H48899, 86H17213.

The results obtained from several recent flights on the Northrop X-4 No. 2 airplane are presented. Information is included on the longitudinal-stability characteristics in straight flight over a Mach number range of 0.38 to about 0.63, the longitudinal-stability characteristics in accelerated flight over a Mach number range of 0.43 to about 0.79, and the short-period longitudinal-oscillation characteristics at Mach numbers of 0.49 and 0.78. It was shown that the stick-fixed and stick-free static longitudinal stability, as measured in straight flight, were positive over the test speed range with the center of gravity located at about 18.0 percent of the mean aerodynamic chord. During the longitudinal-stability tests in accelerated flight an inadvertent pitch-up of the airplane occurred at a Mach number of about 0.79 and a normal-force coefficient of about 0.45 (normal acceleration factor, the ratio of the net aerodynamic force along the airplane Z axis to the weight of the airplane = 5), in which the acceleration built up rapidly to the ratio of the net aerodynamic force along the airplane Z axis to the weight of the airplane = 6.2 (which was in excess of the load factor, 5.2, required for demonstration of the airplane) before recovery could be initiated. A comparison of the experimentally determined elevon angles required for balance and the elevon-angle gradients with values estimated from limited wind-tunnel data showed fairly good agreement. Wind-tunnel data, however, were not available in the region where the pitch-up occurred so that an evaluation in this regard was not possible. The short-period oscillation was lightly damped and did not meet the Air Force requirements for satisfactory handling qualities. The pilot, however, did not object to the low damping characteristics of this airplane for small-amplitude oscillations. Theory predicted the period of the short-period longitudinal oscillation fairly well; however, the damping evaluated from the theory indicated considerably greater damping than was actually measured in flight, especially at the higher Mach numbers.

33. Mayer, John P.; Valentine, George M.; and Mayer, Geraldine C.: **Flight Measurements with the Douglas D-558-II (BuAero No. 37974) Research Airplane. Determination of the Aerodynamic Center and Zero-Lift Pitching-Moment Coefficient of the Wing-Fuselage Combination by Means of Tail-Load Measurements in the Mach Number Range From 0.37 to 0.87.** NACA RM L50D10, July 11, 1950, 86H18984.

Determination of the aerodynamic center and zero-lift pitching-moment coefficient of the wing-fuselage combination by means of tail-load measurements in the Mach number range from 0.37 to 0.87.

34. Wilmerding, J. V.; Stillwell, W. H.; and Sjoberg, S. A. **Flight Measurements with the Douglas D-558-II (BuAero No. 37974) Research Airplane: Lateral Control Characteristics as Measured in Abrupt Aileron Rolls at Mach Numbers Up to 0.86.** NACA RM L50E17, July 20, 1950, 93R15435.

Flight measurements were made of the lateral control characteristics of the Douglas D-558-II airplane in abrupt rudder-fixed aileron rolls. In the Mach number range from 0.50 to 0.86 the aileron rolling effectiveness is substantially constant and the rate of change of the maximum wing-tip helix angle with total aileron deflection (rate of change of maximum wing-tip helix angle with total aileron deflection, radians per degree) has a value of 0.0027 radian per degree. Extrapolated data indicate that in this Mach number range full aileron deflection of 30 degrees will produce a maximum wing-tip helix angle $pb/2V$ of about 0.08 radian. As the speed is reduced below a mach number of 0.50 a marked decrease occurs in the maximum value of $pb/2V$ obtainable with a given aileron deflection. This decrease $pb/2V$ occurs because the dihedral effect increases with decrease in speed and the adverse sideslip angles reached in the rolls at low speed are larger. At an indicated airspeed of 150 miles per hour in the landing condition, full aileron deflection will produce a maximum $pb/2V$ of 0.04 radian, which for standard sea-level conditions corresponds to a rolling velocity of 40 degrees per second. In the opinion of the pilots this rolling velocity is sufficiently high for the landing condition with this airplane.

It is the opinion of several NACA pilots that the maximum usable rolling velocity is on the order of 2.5 radians per second. In the Mach number range from 0.42 to 0.86 at an altitude of 15,000 feet rolling velocities greater than 2.5 radians per second can be obtained with less than full aileron deflection. The data indicate that in going from high to low lift coefficient the yawing moment due to rolling changes direction. At high lift coefficients the sideslip due to roll is in the same direction as the roll (right roll produces right sideslip), but at low lift coefficients the opposite tendency is present.

35. Gates, Ordway B.; and Sternfield, Leonard: **Effect of an Autopilot Sensitive to Yawing Velocity on the Lateral Stability of the Douglas D-558-II Airplane.** NACA RM L50F22, August 17, 1950.

A theoretical investigation has been made to determine the effect on the lateral stability of the Douglas D-558-II airplane of an autopilot sensitive to yawing velocity. The effects of inclination of the gyro spin axis to the flight path and of time lag in the autopilot were also determined. The flight conditions investigated included landing at sea level, approach condition at 12,000 feet, and cruising at 12,000 feet at Mach numbers of 0.80 and 1.2. The results of the investigation indicated that the lateral stability characteristics of the D-558-II airplane for the flight condition discussed should satisfy the Air Force - Navy period-damping criterion when the proposed autopilot is installed. Airplane motions in sideslip subsequent to a disturbance in sideslip are presented for several representative flight conditions in which a time lag in the autopilot of 0.10 second was assumed.

36. Mayer, John P.; and Valentine, George M.: **Flight Measurements With the Douglas D-558-II BuAero No. 37974 Research Airplane. Measurements of the Buffet Boundary and Peak Airplane Normal Force Coefficients at Mach Numbers Up to 0.90.** NACA RM L50E31, August 28, 1950, 86H91836.

Measurements of the buffet boundary and peak airplane normal force coefficients at Mach numbers up to 0.90.

37. Stillwell, W. H.; Wilmerding, J. V.; and Champine, R. A.: **Flight Measurements With the Douglas D-558-II BuAero No. 37974 Research Airplane. Low-Speed Stalling and Lift Characteristics.** NACA RM L50G10, September 5, 1950, 86H92789.

The low-speed stalling and lift characteristics of the D-558-II airplane were measured in a series of 1-g stalls in four different airplane configurations. With the slats locked closed and the flaps up or down, the airplane was unstable at angles of attack greater than about 9 degrees. With the flaps up this corresponds to a normal-force coefficient of about 0.8 and with the flaps down, about 1.07. Because of this instability, the airplane tended to pitch to high angles of attack; at these high angles of attack, violent rolling and yawing motions sometimes occurred. In one case with the flaps down and the slats locked the airplane went into a spin after pitching up to high angles of attack. The pilots considered the stalling characteristics of the airplane with the slats locked to be very objectionable. No data are presented in this paper on the stalling characteristics in maneuvering flight, but the pilots considered the longitudinal instability particularly objectionable in maneuvering flight. With the slats unlocked and the flaps up or down the airplane was unstable at angles of attack greater than about 23 degrees. Uncontrolled-for rolling and yawing motions due to stalling were present when the airplane was unstable in the high angle-of-attack range. With the slats unlocked and the flaps and landing gear up or down, there was adequate stall warning in the form of buffeting and lateral oscillations of the airplane. With the slats locked, slight buffeting of the airplane occurred at a normal-force coefficient slightly less than the normal-force coefficient at which the airplane became longitudinally unstable. With the flaps up and the slats locked, the highest normal-force coefficient obtained was 1.13 at an angle of attack of about 17.5 degrees. The highest normal-force coefficient obtained with the flaps up and the slats unlocked was 1.46 at an angle of attack of 36 degrees, and in the angle-of-attack range from 23 degrees to 30 degrees the normal-force coefficient had a substantially constant value of 1.32. At the lower angles of attack with the slats locked or unlocked deflecting the flaps produced an increment in normal-force coefficient at a given angle of attack of about 0.26. The highest normal-force coefficient obtained with the flaps down and the slats locked or unlocked was about 1.65. This value was attained at an angle of attack of about 35.5 degrees with the slats locked and at an angle of attack of about 38 degrees with the slats unlocked. However, in the angle-of-attack range from 12 degrees to 32 degrees considerably greater normal-force coefficients were obtained with the slats unlocked than with the slats locked.

38. Carner, H. Arthur; and Knapp, Ronald J.: **Flight Measurements of the Pressure Distribution on the Wing of the X-1 Airplane (10-Percent-Thick Wing) Over a Chordwise Station Near the Midspan, in Level Flight at Mach Numbers from 0.79 to 1.00 and in a Pull-Up at a Mach Number of 0.96.** NACA RM L50H04, September 12, 1950, 86H89804.

Measurements of the chordwise pressure distribution over the 10-percent-thick wing of the X-1 research airplane have been made at a section near the midspan of the left wing. Data presented are for a Mach number range from 0.79 to 1.00 at a section normal-force coefficient of about 0.32 and for section normal-force coefficients up to 1.00 at a Mach number of approximately 0.96. The results show that the section center of load moves aft from about 32 percent chord at Mach number 0.79 to 40 percent chord at Mach number 0.84, and then forward to 18 percent chord at Mach number 0.89. The section center of load moves aft to 45 percent chord at Mach number 0.95 and then remains approximately constant at Mach numbers up to 1.00. At a section normal-force coefficient of 0.32 a shock exists on the upper surface at the lowest test Mach number of 0.79 and supersonic flow exists over approximately 50 percent of the chord on the upper

surface. The first indication of a shock on the lower surface occurs at a Mach number of about 0.84. At Mach numbers above 0.95 the shocks on both surfaces occur near the trailing edge and the pressure distribution over both surfaces is quite similar. An increase in the normal-force coefficient at a Mach number of approximately 0.96 causes a slight increase in the section stability at the higher normal-force coefficients.

39. Carner, H. Arthur; and Payne, Mary M.: **Tabulated Pressure Coefficients and Aerodynamic Characteristics Measured on the Wing of the Bell X-1 Airplane in Level Flight at Mach Numbers from 0.79 to 1.00 and in a Pull-Up at Mach Number of 0.96.** NACA RM L50H25, September 18, 1950, 86H91513.

Tabulated pressure coefficients and aerodynamic characteristics are presented for six spanwise stations on the left wing of the Bell X-1 research airplane. The data were obtained in level flight at Mach numbers from 0.79 to 1.00 and in a pull-up to an airplane normal-force coefficient of 0.91 at a Mach number of approximately 0.96.

40. Drake, Hubert M.; and Carden, John R.: **Elevator-Stabilizer Effectiveness and Trim of the X-1 Airplane to a Mach Number of 1.06.** NACA RM L50G20, November 1, 1950, 87H24582.

The relative elevator-stabilizer effectiveness of the X-1 has been determined to decrease from a value of 0.25 at a Mach number of 0.78 to a value of 0.05 at a Mach number of 1.0. At supersonic speeds the effectiveness increases. The various stabilizer settings are caused by the variation in effectiveness and the fact that the effectiveness is nonlinear at Mach numbers between 0.94 and 0.97. It was found that, with the elevator fixed at zero, only about 0.5 degrees of stabilizer movement would be required to trim through the Mach number range from 0.78 to 1.02.

41. Knapp, Ronald J.; and Wilken, Gertrude V.: **Tabulated Pressure Coefficients and Aerodynamic Characteristics Measured on the Wing of the Bell X-1 Airplane in Pull-Ups at Mach Numbers From 0.53 to 0.99.** NACA RM L50H28, November 1, 1950, 86H93182.

Tabulated pressure coefficients and aerodynamic characteristics are presented for six spanwise stations on the left wing of the Bell X-1 research airplane. The data were obtained in 10 pull-ups at Mach numbers from 0.53 to 0.99.

42. Angle, Ellwyn; and Holleman, Euclid C.: **Determination of Longitudinal Stability of the Bell X-1 Airplane From Transient Responses at Mach Numbers Up to 1.12 at Lift Coefficients of 0.3 and 0.6.** NACA RM L50I06A, November 7, 1950, 86H91094.

A number of free-flight transient responses resulting from small stabilizer movements were obtained during flight tests of the Bell X-1 airplane (8-percent-thick wing and 6-percent-thick tail). Responses were analyzed to obtain a measure of the longitudinal stability characteristics of the airplane over the Mach number range from 0.72 to 1.12 at lift coefficients of 0.3 and 0.6. The data presented indicate three significant features: (1) The damping varies greatly with Mach number, maximum damping occurring at Mach numbers of 0.82 and 1.08 and a minimum damping at about 0.93; (2) some uncertainty of damping between Mach numbers of 0.91 to 0.95 appears although good agreement with model tests exists throughout the Mach number range covered; and (3) the static stability of the airplane increases with Mach number to a Mach number of about 0.93 and decreases with further increasing Mach number. Data above a Mach number of 0.90 indicate some lift-coefficient effects. Agreement of the full-scale flight data and model data over the Mach number range is good.

43. Drake, Hubert M.: **Effects on the Lateral Oscillation of Fixing the Rudder and Reflexing the Flaps on the Bell X-1 Airplane.** NACA RM L50I05, December 11, 1950, 86H93173.

Flight tests have been made on the Bell X-1 airplane having the 10-percent-thick wing and the 8-percent-thick tail to evaluate the effects of fixing the rudder and changing the inclination of the principal axes of inertia by reflexing the landing flaps on the snaking which has been encountered over practically the entire range of Mach number and normal-force coefficient. The data were obtained during power-off glides at altitudes between 32,000 and 16,000 feet. The results showed that fixing the rudder reduced the amplitude of snaking, but did not eliminate it at a Mach number of 0.84. It was also found that reflexing the flaps to change the inclination of the principal axis of inertia 1 and 3/4 nose up increased the dynamic lateral stability, but had only a small effect on the snaking oscillation at a Mach number of 0.85.

44. Sadoff, Melvin; and Sisk, Thomas R.: **Summary Report of Results Obtained During Demonstration Tests of the Northrop X-4 Airplanes.** NACA RM A50I01, December 13, 1950, 86H93149.

Results obtained during the demonstration flight tests of the Northrop X-4 No. 1 and No. 2 airplanes are presented. Information is included on the static and dynamic longitudinal- and lateral-stability characteristics, the stalling characteristics, and the buffet boundary. The data indicated that the airplane was almost neutrally stable in straight flight at low Mach numbers with the center of gravity located at about 21.4 percent of the mean aerodynamic chord for the clean configuration. In accelerated flight over a Mach number range of about 0.44 to 0.84 the airplane was longitudinally stable up to a normal-force coefficient of about 0.4. At higher values of normal-force coefficient and at the higher (approximately Mach 0.8) Mach numbers a longitudinal instability was experienced. The X-4 airplane does not satisfy the Air Force specifications for damping of the short-period longitudinal oscillation. The pilot, however, did not consider the low damping characteristics of the airplane objectionable

for small disturbances. An objectionable undamped oscillation about all three axes was experienced, however, at the highest test Mach number of 0.88. Theory predicted the period of the short-period longitudinal oscillation fairly well, while, in general, the theoretical damping indicated a higher degree of stability than was actually experienced. This discrepancy was traced to a considerable error in the estimation of the rotational damping factor. The directional stability of the X-4 airplane as measured in steady sideslips was high and essentially constant over the speed range covered, while the dihedral effect decreased considerably with an increase in airspeed. The damping of the lateral oscillation does not meet the Air Force requirements for satisfactory handling qualities over the Mach number range covered. The data indicated decreased damping as the flight Mach number was increased above about 0.5, and at high Mach numbers (M>0.8) and at high altitudes the X-4, in common with other transonic research airplanes, experienced a small amplitude undamped lateral oscillation. The dynamic lateral-stability characteristics were estimated fairly well by theory at low Mach numbers and at a pressure altitude of 10,000 feet. At 30,000 feet, however, at Mach numbers above about 0.6, the theory again indicated a higher degree of stability than was actually obtained. For the conditions covered in these tests the stalling characteristics of the X-4 airplane, as measured in stall approaches in straight flight and in an accelerated stall to about 1.6g, were, in general, satisfactory. Both the stall approaches and the stall were characterized by a roll-off to the right. The X-4 buffet boundary showed a sharp drop-off in the normal-force coefficient for the onset of buffeting as the flight Mach number exceeded 0.8. The boundary was almost identical to that obtained for the D-558-II research airplane at comparable Mach numbers.

45. Keener, Earl R.; and Pierce, Mary: **Tabulated Pressure Coefficients and Aerodynamic Characteristics Measured in Flight on the Wing of the Douglas D-558-I Airplane for a 1-G Stall, a Speed Run to a Mach Number of 0.90, and a Wind-Up Turn at a Mach Number of 0.86.** NACA RM L50J10, December 15, 1950, 86H91866.

Tabulated pressure coefficients and aerodynamic characteristics are presented unanalyzed for six spanwise stations on the right wing of the Douglas D-558-I research airplane (BuAero No. 37972). The data were obtained in a 1 g stall at subcritical Mach numbers, in a speed run to a Mach number of 0.90 and in a wind-up turn at a Mach number of 0.86.

46. Mayer, John P.; Valentine, George M.; and Swanson, Beverly J.: **Flight Measurements With the Douglas D-558-II (BuAero No. 37974) Research Airplane: Measurements of Wing Loads at Mach Numbers Up to 0.87.** NACA RM L50H16, December 26, 1950, 86H91869.

Measurements of wing loads at Mach numbers up to 0.87.

1951 Technical Publications

47. Drake, Hubert M.; and Clagett, Harry P.: **Effects on the Snaking Oscillation of the Bell X-1 Airplane of a Trailing-Edge Bulb on the Rudder.** NACA RM L50K01A, January 16, 1951, 86H94153.

A rudder bulb was installed on the trailing edge of the rudder of the Bell X-1 airplane having the 8-percent-thick wing and 6-percent-thick tail. Several flights were made to investigate the effects of the bulb on the snaking oscillation at Mach numbers between 0.75 and 1.0. It was found that the rudder bulb had no noticeable effect on the snaking oscillation over the Mach number range tested.

48. Sjoberg, S. A.; Peele, James R.; and Griffith, John H.: **Flight Measurements With the Douglas D-558-II (BuAero No. 37974) Research Airplane: Static Longitudinal Stability and Control Characteristics at Mach Numbers Up to 0.87.** NACA RM L50K13, January 17, 1951, 86H94865.

The paper presents the results of flight measurements of the longitudinal stability and control characteristics of the Douglas D-558-II research airplane. Data are presented in the speed range from the stalling speed of the airplane up to a maximum Mach number of 0.87.

49. Mayer, John P.; and Valentine, George M.: **Flight Measurements With the Douglas D-558-II (BuAero No. 37974) Research Airplane: Measurements of the Distribution of the Aerodynamic Load Among the Wing, Fuselage, and Horizontal Tail at Mach Numbers Up to 0.87.** NACA RM L50J13, January 19, 1951, 86H91625, 93R15887.

Flight measurements of the aerodynamic wing and tail loads have been made on the Douglas D-558-II airplane from which the distribution of the aerodynamic load among the wing, fuselage, and horizontal tail has been determined at Mach numbers up to 0.87. These measurements indicate that, for normal-force coefficients less than 0.7, the distribution of air load among the airplane components does not change appreciably with Mach number at Mach numbers up to 0.87. The measurements also indicate that, for all flight configurations, the increase in airplane normal-force coefficient above the angle of attack at which the wing reaches its maximum normal-force coefficient is due principally to the contribution of the fuselage to the airplane normal-force coefficient.

50. Keener, Earl R.; Peele, James R.; and Woodbridge, Julia B.: **Tabulated Pressure Coefficients and Aerodynamic Characteristics Measured in Flight on the Wing of the Douglas D-558-I Airplane Throughout the Normal-Force-Coefficient Range at Mach Numbers of 0.67, 0.74, 0.78, and 0.82.** NACA RM L50L12A, January 29, 1951, 86H92973.

Tabulated pressure coefficients and aerodynamic characteristics measured in flight are presented for six spanwise stations on the right wing of the D-558-I research airplane (BuAero No. 37972). The data were obtained throughout the normal-force-coefficient range at Mach numbers of 0.67, 0.74, 0.78, and 0.82. This paper supplements similar tabulated data which have been presented in NACA RM L50J10. (See also 45.)

51. Carman, L. Robert; and Carden, John R.: **Lift and Drag Coefficients for the Bell X-1 Airplane (8-Percent-Thick Wing) in Power-Off Transonic Flight.** NACA RM L51E08, June 1951, 87H24264, 86H96412.

Drag coefficients have been determined by the accelerometer method for the Bell X-1 airplane with 8-percent-thick wing and 6-percent-thick tail in power-off flight over a Mach number range of 0.64 to 1.14 and at lift coefficients from 0.1 to 1.2.

52. Stillwell, W. H.; and Wilmerding, J. V.: **Flight Measurements With the Douglas D-558-II (BuAero No. 37974) Research Airplane: Dynamic Lateral Stability.** NACA RM L51C23, June 18, 1951, 87H24199, 86H96642.

The paper presents flight measurements of the dynamic lateral stability of the D-558-II (BuAero No. 37974) research airplane. Data are presented for a range of calibrated airspeed from 167 miles per hour to 474 miles per hour.

53. Smith, Lawrence A.: **Tabulated Pressure Coefficients and Aerodynamic Characteristics Measured on the Wing of the Bell X-1 Airplane in an Unaccelerated Stall and in Pull-Ups at Mach Numbers of 0.74, 0.75, 0.94, and 0.97.** NACA RM L51B23, June 19, 1951, 87H24185.

Presents tabulated pressure coefficients and aerodynamic characteristics measured on the wing of the Bell X-1 research airplane in an unaccelerated stall and in pull-ups at Mach numbers of approximately 0.74, 0.75, 0.94, and 0.97.

54. Sadoff, Melvin; Roden, William S.; and Eggleston, John M.: **Flight Investigation of the Longitudinal Stability and Control Characteristics of the Douglas D-558-I Airplane (BuAero No. 37972) at Mach Numbers Up to 0.89.** NACA RM L51D18, June 1951, 87H24220, 86H97408.

Results and analysis pertaining to the longitudinal stability and control characteristics of the Douglas D-558-I airplane (BuAero No. 37972) are presented. The results indicated that large and rapid changes in elevator deflection and force were required for balance above a Mach number of 0.84. Analysis indicated that a major part of these changes were due to a loss in elevator effectiveness. A large increase in the apparent stick-fixed stability parameter $d\delta_e/dC_N$ was also noted due to a loss in elevator effectiveness combined with an increase in airplane stability.

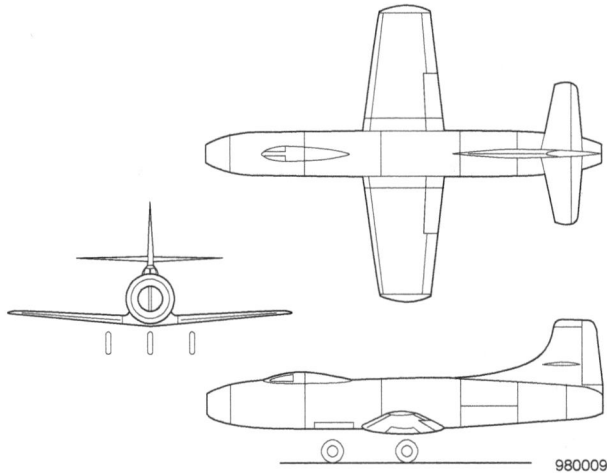

D-558-I Airplane, Three-View Drawing

55. Keener, Earl R.; and Bandish, Rozalia M.: **Tabulated Pressure Coefficients and Aerodynamic Characteristics Measured in Flight on the Wing of the D-558-I Research Airplane Through a Mach Number Range of 0.80 to 0.89 and Throughout the Normal-Force-Coefficient Range at Mach Numbers of 0.61, 0.70, 0.855, and 0.88.** NACA RM L51F12, August 1951, 87H24327, 86H98165.

Presents tabulated pressure coefficients and aerodynamic characteristics obtained in flight from pressure distributions over six chordwise rows of orifices on a wing of the Douglas D-558-I research airplane (BuAero No. 37972). It includes data obtained throughout a Mach number range of 0.80 to 0.89 and throughout the normal-force-coefficient range at M = 0.61, 0.70, 0.855, and 0.88.

56. Beeler, De E.; Bellman, Donald R.; and Griffith, John H.: **Flight Determination of the Effects of Wing Vortex Generators on the Aerodynamic Characteristics of the Douglas D-558-I Airplane.** NACA RM L51A23, August 1951, 87H24172, 86H93919.

Tests were made to determine the effects of wing vortex generators on the handling and buffeting characteristics of the Douglas D-558-I airplane. Measurements of the chordwise pressure distribution over one section of the wing, the total-head losses in a portion of the wing wake, the total airplane drag, and the buffeting and handling characteristics were made with the basic configuration and with vortex generators of an arbitrary size, shape, and location installed on the wing.

57. Knapp, Ronald J.: **Tabulated Pressure Coefficients and Aerodynamic Characteristics Measured on the Wing of the Bell X-1 Airplane in an Unaccelerated Low-Speed Stall, in Push-Overs at Mach Numbers of 0.83 and 0.99, and in a Pull-Up at a Mach Number of 1.16.** NACA RM L51F25, September 1951, 87H24339.

Presents tabulated pressure coefficients and aerodynamic characteristics measured on the wing of the Bell X-1 research airplane in an unaccelerated low-speed stall, in push-overs at Mach numbers of 0.83 and 0.99, and in a pull-up at a Mach number of 1.16.

58. Drake, Hubert M.; Carden, John R.; and Clagett, Harry P.: **Analysis of Longitudinal Stability and Trim of the Bell X-1 Airplane at a Lift Coefficient of 0.3 to Mach Numbers Near 1.05.** NACA RM L51H01, October 1951, 87H24599.

An analysis has been made of the flight test data obtained with two X-1 airplane shaving 10-percent-thick wings and an 8-percent-thick tail and 8-percent-thick wings and a 6-percent-thick tail. The variation with Mach number of the rate of change of downwash angle of attack, the static stability, and the airplane trim were obtained at a lift coefficient of 0.3.

59. Sadoff, Melvin; Ankenbruck, Herman O.; and O'Hare, William: **Stability and Control Measurements Obtained During USAF-NACA Cooperative Flight-Test Program on the X-4 Airplane (USAF No. 46-677).** NACA RM A51H09, October 26, 1951, 93R16101.

Results obtained during the Air Force testing of the Northrop X-4 airplane are presented. Information is included on the stalling characteristics, the static and dynamic longitudinal- and lateral-stability characteristics, and the lateral-control characteristics. The data indicated that the stalling characteristics of the X-4 airplane in straight flight and in accelerated flight at low Mach numbers were satisfactory, but that at Mach numbers above 0.68, the airplane became longitudinally unstable at moderate lift coefficients.

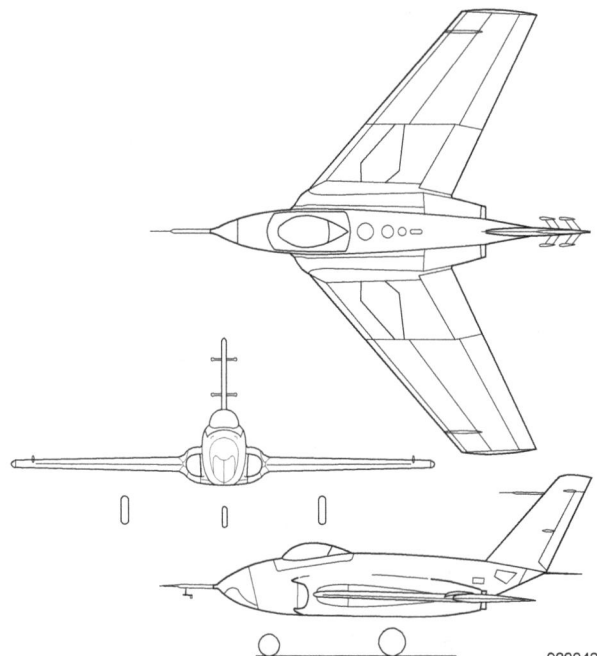

X-4 Airplane, Three-View Drawing

60. Williams, W. C.; and Crossfield, A. S.: **Handling Qualities of High-Speed Airplanes.** NACA Conference on High-Speed Airplane Aerodynamics, Langley Field, Virginia, <u>December 4–5, 1951</u>, pp. 171–188.

This paper discusses the handling qualities and stability of the X-1, D-558-I, D-558-II, X-4, F-86A, and XF-92 airplanes.

61. Drake, H. M.; and Stillwell, W. H.: **Landing Experience With Transonic Research Airplanes.** NACA Conference on High-Speed Airplane Aerodynamics, Langley Field, Virginia, <u>December 4–5, 1951</u>, pp. 269–280.

This paper discusses landing experiences with the D-558-I and the X-4 airplanes.

62. *Soule, Hartley A.; and Beeler, De. E.: **Review of High-Speed Buffeting Problems.** NACA Conference on

High-Speed Airplane Aerodynamics, Langley Field, Virginia., <u>December 4–5, 1951</u>, pp. 327–340.

*NACA - Langley Aeronautical Laboratory.

This paper discusses buffeting results from the X-1, D-558-II, X-4, and XF-92A airplanes.

1952 Technical Publications

63. Williams, W. C.; and Crossfield, A. S.: **Handling Qualities of High-Speed Airplanes.** NACA RM L52A08, <u>January 1952</u>, 87H24815.

Because there have been such drastic changes in the speed range and the configuration of airplanes in the past decade it becomes necessary to re-examine the requirements for satisfactory handling qualities as proposed by Gilruth in

E-842

NACA High Speed Flight Station Research Aircraft, circa 1952 (clockwise from front center), Northrop X-4, Douglas D-558-I, Douglas D-558-II, Convair XF-92A, Bell X-5, and Bell X-1-2

1940. This paper does not attempt to describe completely the handling qualities of all the research airplanes but does attempt to describe the objectionable characteristics and those which indicate review of the requirements. The research airplanes discussed are the X-1, D-558-1, D-558-2, X-4, F-86A, and the XF-92A.

E-1326

F-86 Sabre Airplane

64. Angle, Ellwyn E.; and Holleman, Euclid C.: **Longitudinal Frequency-Response Characteristics of the Douglas D-558-I Airplane as Determined From Experimental Transient-Response Histories to a Mach Number of 0.90.** NACA RM L51K28, February 1952, 87H24557.

Transient responses from elevator pulses of the Douglas D-558-I research airplane are analyzed by the Fourier transform to give the longitudinal frequency response of the airplane to a Mach number of 0.90 at altitudes between 30,000 and 37,000 feet.

65. Huss, Carl R.; Andrews, William H.; and Hamer, Harold A.: **Time-History Data of Maneuvers Performed by a McDonnell F2H-2 Airplane During Squadron Operational Training.** NACA RM L52B29, May 1952, 87H24976.

Preliminary results of 276 maneuvers of all types performed by an F2H-2 jet fighter airplane during normal operational training are presented in time history form and are summarized as plots of load factors and angular accelerations against indicated airspeed.

66. Rogers, John T.; and Dunn, Angel H.: **Preliminary Results of Horizontal-Tail Load Measurements of the Bell X-5 Research Airplane.** NACA RM L52G14, August 15, 1952, 87H24757.

Horizontal-tail load measurements were made during the Bell acceptance tests of a transonic speed research airplane having wings variable in flight between 20 degrees and 60 degrees sweepback. Load measurements were made during sweep changes in level flight from Mach numbers of 0.5 to 0.85, and during pull-ups at a Mach number of 0.83 at sweep angles of 20 degrees, 45 degrees, and 59 degrees.

E-810

X-5 Airplane

67. Holleman, Euclid C.: **Longitudinal Frequency-Response and Stability Characteristics of the Douglas D-558-II Airplane as Determined From Transient Response to a Mach Number of 0.96.** NACA RM L52E02, September 1952, 87H25163.

By an application of the Fourier transformation to transient-flight data the longitudinal frequency response of the Douglas D-558-II airplane has been determined over a Mach number range of 0.62 to 0.96 at altitudes between 21,000 and 43,000 feet; however, the results have been reduced to airplane stability derivatives which are presented as functions of Mach number.

68. Sisk, Thomas R.: **Flight Investigation of the Aileron Effectiveness of the Republic XF-91 Airplane Over a Mach Number Range From 0.40.** NACA RM L52E07A, September 1952, 87H25188.

A flight investigation has been conducted to determine the aileron effectiveness of the Republic XF-91 airplane. The tests were conducted over a Mach number range from 0.40 to

28

0.91 at approximate altitudes of 13,000, 24,000, and 32,000 feet.

E-475

XF-91 Airplane

69. Day, Richard E.; and Stillwell, Wendell H.: **First Landing of Bell X-2 Research Airplane.** NACA RM L52I11, October 1, 1952, 93R16608.

The Bell X-2 supersonic research airplane is equipped with a skid main landing gear and a nose wheel. Pending completion of the rocket engine, glide flights are being performed to determine low-speed handling qualities of the airplane and the landing characteristics with the ski type landing gear. The present paper presents data obtained during the approach and landing of X-2 airplane on its first flight.

E-2822

X-2 Airplane

70. Jones, Ira P. Jr.: **Measurements of Aerodynamic Heating Obtained During Demonstration Flight Tests of the Douglas D-558-II Airplane.** NACA RM L52I26A, November 1952, 87H24932.

Measurements of transient skin and canopy-glass temperature and stagnation temperature were made on the Douglas D-558-II research airplane up to a Mach number of 1.89 and to an altitude of about 77,000 feet. The maximum

temperatures that were obtained for the positions measured were not great enough to cause loss in structural strength.

1953 Technical Publications

71. Knapp, Ronald J.; and Johnson, Wallace E.: **Flight Measurements of Pressures on Base and Rear Part of Fuselage of the Bell X-1 Research Airplane at Transonic Speeds, Including Power Effects.** NACA RM L52L01, January 1953, 87H24836.

Flight measurements of the pressure distribution over the base and rear portion of fuselage of the Bell X-1 rocket-propelled airplane at transonic speeds, including power effects, are presented.

72. Childs, Joan M.: **Flight Measurements of the Stability Characteristics of the Bell X-5 Research Airplane in Sideslips at 59-Degree Sweepback.** NACA RM L52K13B, February 1953, 87H24781.

Flight measurements of the stability characteristics of the Bell X-5 research airplane were made in steady sideslips at 59 degree sweepback at Mach numbers from 0.62 to 0.97 at altitudes varying from 35,000 to 40,000 feet.

73. Finch, Thomas W.; and Briggs, Donald W.: **Preliminary Results of Stability and Control Investigation of the Bell X-5 Research Airplane.** NACA RM L52K18B, February 1953, 87H24804.

Results obtained during the acceptance tests of the X-5 airplane are presented. Information on the stalling characteristics, static longitudinal stability characteristics, and lateral control characteristics at various sweep angles is included.

74. Finch, Thomas W.; and Walker, Joseph A.: **Flight Determination of the Static Longitudinal Stability Boundaries of the Bell X-5 Research Airplane With 59-Degree Sweepback.** NACA RM L53A09B, February 1953, 87H24925.

Results obtained during flights of the Bell X-5 airplane with 59 degree sweepback are presented showing the variation with Mach number of the normal-force coefficient at the longitudinal reduction in stability. Results are given for a Mach number range of 0.67 to 0.98.

75. Bellman, Donald R.: **Lift and Drag Characteristics of the Bell X-5 Research Airplane at 59-Degree Sweepback for Mach Numbers From 0.60 to 1.03.** NACA RM L53A09C, February 1953, 87H24926.

Lift and drag coefficients for the 59-degree sweptback configuration of the Bell X-5 airplane were determined from flight tests covering the Mach number range 0.60 to 1.03. A brief comparison is made between the 20-degree and 59-degree sweptback configuration.

76. Ankenbruck, Herman O.; and Dahlen, Theodore E.: **Some Measurements of Flying Qualities of a Douglas D-558-II Research Airplane During Flights to Supersonic Speeds.** NACA RM L53A06, March 1953, 87H24908.

Results of measurements of lateral and longitudinal flying qualities of the Douglas D-558-II research airplane in flight to a Mach number of 1.87 and an altitude of 67,000 feet are presented.

77. Sisk, Thomas R.; and Mooney, John M.: **Preliminary Measurements of Static Longitudinal Stability and Trim for the XF-92A Delta-Wing Research Airplane in Subsonic and Transonic Flight.** NACA RM L53B06, March 1953, 87H24972.

Preliminary longitudinal-trim and static longitudinal stability measurements were made on the XF-92A delta-wing research airplane from Mach number of 0.18 to 0.97 at altitudes from 11,000 to 40,000 feet.

E-953

XF-92A Airplane

78. Fischel, Jack; and Nugent, Jack: **Flight Determination of the Longitudinal Stability in Accelerated Maneuvers at Transonic Speeds for the Douglas D-558-II Research Airplane Including the Effects of an Outboard Wing Fence.** NACA RM L53A16, March 1953, 87H24937.

The results of transonic flight measurements of the longitudinal stability characteristics of the Douglas D-558-II research the wings are presented. The levels of normal-force coefficient at which the stability decreases and pitch-up starts have been determined for both airplane configurations at Mach numbers up to about 0.94.

79. Dahlen, Theodore E.: **Maximum Altitude and Maximum Mach Number Obtained With the Modified Douglas D-558-II Research Airplane During Demonstration Flights.** NACA RM L53B24, April 1953, 87H24989.

The maximum values of Mach number and altitude obtained with the Douglas D-558-II all-rocket research airplane and determined by the radar-phototheodolite method are presented in this paper.

80. Baker, Thomas F.: **Some Measurements of the Buffet Region of a Swept-Wing Research Airplane During Flights to Supersonic Mach Numbers.** NACA RM L53D06, May 1953, 87H25036.

Limited measurements have been made of the region in which buffeting has been experienced by the swept-wing Douglas D-558-II research airplane during flights to supersonic Mach numbers. Buffet intensities and frequencies are given.

81. Johnson, H. I.: **The Background of Flying or Handling Qualities.** Presented to the Flight Test Panel of AGARD, May 1953, 65N88424.

82. Holleman, Euclid C.; Evans, John H.; and Triplett, William C.: **Preliminary Flight Measurements of the Dynamic Longitudinal Stability Characteristics of the Convair XF-92A Delta-Wing Airplane.** NACA RM L53E14, June 1953, 87H26860.

Longitudinal airplane oscillations obtained during U.S. Air Force performance tests of the Convair XF-92A airplane have been analyzed to give limited static stability and damping measurements for a Mach number range of 0.59 to 0.94.

83. Knapp, Ronald J.; and Jordan, Gareth H.: **Flight-Determined Pressure Distributions Over the Wing of the Bell X-1 Research Airplane (10-Percent-Thick Wing) at Subsonic and Transonic Speeds.** NACA RM L53D20, June 1953, 87H25070.

Aerodynamic section characteristics for various span locations, as determined by pressure distribution measurements in flight to high lift at Mach numbers between 0.30 and 1.19, are presented for the 10-percent-thick wing of the Bell X-1 research airplane.

84. Drake, Hubert M.; and McKay, John B.: **Aileron and Elevator Hinge Moments of the Bell X-1 Airplane Measured in Transonic Flight.** NACA RM L53E04, June 1953, 87H26857.

Hinge moments have been measured on the aileron and elevator of the Bell X-1 airplane having the 10-percent-thick wing and 8-percent-thick tail. The aileron measurements were made by means of strain gages and pressure distributions while the elevator measurements were made by means of the wheel-force strain gases. The elevator hinge-moment characteristics were determined to a Mach number of 1.18 and the aileron hinge moments to a Mach number of 1.13.

85.   Drake, Hubert M.; Robinson, Glenn H.; and Kuhl, Albert E.: **Loads Experienced in Flights of Two Swept-Wing Research Airplanes in the Angle-of-Attack Range or Reduced Stability.** NACA RM L53D16, June 1953, 87H25066.

Loads imposed upon the Bell X-5 and Douglas D-558-II swept-wing research airplanes during flights in which reductions of longitudinal stability followed attempted moderate-lift maneuvers are discussed. Information regarding horizontal- and vertical-tail loads, wing loads, and normal-force coefficients obtained during the high-angle-of-attack, unstable portions of the flights are presented.

86.   Day, Richard E.: **Measurements Obtained During the Glide-Flight Program of the Bell X-2 Research Airplane.** NACA RM L53G03a, July 30, 1953, 93R17091.

Results obtained during the glide-flight program of the Bell X-2 research airplane are presented. Landing characteristics and limited data evaluating static longitudinal stability at low speeds are included.

87.   Martin, James A.: **Longitudinal Flight Characteristics of the Bell X-5 Research Airplane at 59-Degree Sweepback With Modified Wing Roots.** NACA RM L53E28, August 10, 1953, 87H26865, 93R16939.

In an attempt to improve the longitudinal stability characteristics of the Bell X-5 research airplane at 59-degrees sweepback the wing-root leading edge was modified, the original 52.5-degrees sweptback leading-edge fillets being replaced by rounded leading-edge fillets. The two fillet configurations are compared in this paper on the basis of results obtained from maneuvers into the region of reduced stability at pressure altitudes from 28,000 to 40,000 feet and in the Mach number range from that for stall approach in the clean condition to a Mach number of 0.97.

88.   Baker, Thomas F.: **Results of Measurements of Maximum Lift and Buffeting Intensities Obtained During Flight Investigation of the Northrop X-4 Research Airplane.** NACA RM L53G06, August 1953, 87H26873.

The variation of the intensity of buffeting experienced throughout the operational region of the semitailless Northrop X-4 airplane and the values of maximum and peak normal-force coefficients in the Mach number range from 0.42 to 0.92 have been determined. The results are compared

with data obtained with the swept-wing Douglas D-558-II airplane.

89.   Peele, James R.: **Transonic Flight Measurements of the Aerodynamic Load on the Extended Slat of the Douglas D-558-II Research Airplane.** NACA RM L53F29, August 1953, 87H24933.

The results of transonic flight measurements of the aerodynamic load encountered over a partial-span leading-edge slat on the 35-degrees sweptback wing of the Douglas D-558-II research airplane are presented for the lift range at Mach numbers from 0.45 to 0.98.

90.   Saltzman, Edwin J.: **Flight Measurements of Lift and Drag for the Bell X-1 Research Airplane Having a 10-Percent-Thick Wing.** NACA RM L53F08, September 1953, 87H24842.

Lift and drag results have been obtained from power-off flight tests of the Bell X-1 (10-percent-thick wing) airplane for Mach numbers 0.68 to 1.01. Comparisons of drag are made with 8-percent-thick-wing flight tests and 10-percent-thick-wing wind tunnel results.

91.   Rogers, John T.: **Horizontal-Tail Load Measurements at Transonic Speeds of the Bell X-1 Research Airplane.** NACA RM L53F30, September 1953, 87H26871.

Flight measurements of aerodynamic tail loads have been made on the Bell X-1 research airplane from which the balancing tail loads, the static-longitudinal stability parameter $(dC_M/dC_L)_{WF}$, wing-fuselage aerodynamic center, and zero-lift wing-fuselage combination pitching moment coefficient have been determined from a Mach number of 0.7 to a Mach number greater than 1.0. A comparison was made of measured tail loads and loads calculated using available wing-tunnel data.

92.   Baker, Thomas F.: **Some Measurements of Buffeting Encountered by a Douglas D-558-II Research Airplane in the Mach Number Range From 0.5 to 0.95.** NACA RM L53I17, November 1953, 87H24978.

Measurements of the intensity of buffeting were made with a swept-wing Douglas D-558-II research airplane at subsonic speeds. The variation of buffet intensity with lift, angle of attack, and Mach number is presented. The results are compared with similar measurements made with another Douglas D-558-II airplane at high subsonic and supersonic speeds.

93.   Knapp, Ronald J.; and Jordan, Gareth H.: **Wing Loads on the Bell X-1 Research Airplane (10-Percent-Thick Wing) as Determined by Pressure-Distribution Measurements in Flight at Subsonic and Transonic Speeds.** NACA RM L53G14, November 1953, 87H26874.

The wing loads (including some wing-to-fuselage load carry over) and some aerodynamic characteristics as determined by pressure-distribution measurements in flight to high lift at Mach numbers from 0.50 to 1.19 for the 10-percent-thick wing of the Bell X-1 research airplane are presented.

94. Knapp, Ronald J.; Jordan, Gareth H.; and Johnson, Wallace E.: **Fuselage Pressures Measured on the Bell X-1 Research Airplane in Transonic Flight.** NACA RM L53I15, November 1953, 87H24970.

Fuselage pressure distributions and integrated normal load on the fuselage of the Bell X-1 research airplane (10-percent-thick wing) in flight during pull-ups to near maximum lift at Mach numbers of about 0.78, 0.85, 0.88, and 1.02 are presented.

1954 Technical Publications

95. Bellman, Donald R.; and Sisk, Thomas R.: **Preliminary Drag Measurements of the Consolidated Vultee XF-92A Delta-Wing Airplane in Flight Tests to a Mach Number of 1.01.** NACA RM L53J23, January 1954, 87H25168.

Lift and drag data for the Consolidated Vultee XF-92A delta-wing airplane were obtained for Mach numbers from 0.63 to 0.90. The drag coefficients for a lift coefficient of 0.08 are extended to a Mach number of 1.01.

96. Baker, Thomas F.: **Measured Data Pertaining to Buffeting at Supersonic Speeds of the Douglas D-558-II Research Airplane.** NACA RM L53L10, February 1954, 87H25252.

Data pertaining to buffeting have been measured at supersonic speed and high lift with the Douglas D-558-II airplane. Buffeting was encountered at normal-force coefficients greater than about 0.7 in the Mach number range from 0.96 to 1.27 but at a Mach number of 1.57, a peak normal-force coefficient of 0.80 was attained with no indication of buffeting. Buffet intensities at normal-force coefficients up to 1.5 are given for low supersonic Mach numbers. Sample records of flight in rough air at supersonic speed are included.

97. Ankenbruck, Herman O.: **Determination of Longitudinal Stability in Supersonic Accelerated Maneuvers for the Douglas D-558-II Research Airplane.** NACA RM L53J20, February 1954, 87H25139.

Flight tests were performed with the Douglas D-558-II research airplane to investigate the longitudinal stability of the airplane in accelerated flight at supersonic speeds to a Mach number of 1.67. This paper shows the conditions where instability occurs at supersonic speeds.

98. Fischel, Jack: **Effect of Wing Slats and Inboard Wing Fences on the Longitudinal Stability Characteristics of the Douglas D-558-II Research Airplane in Accelerated Maneuvers at Subsonic and Transonic Speeds.** NACA RM L53L16, February 1954, 87H25262.

The results of subsonic and transonic flight measurements of the longitudinal stability characteristics of the Douglas D-558-II research airplane for several wing-slat and inboard wing-fence configurations are presented at Mach numbers up to 1.0. The improvement provided by fully extended slats, compared to the stability characteristics of the slats-retracted configuration, is shown; and the effects of inboard wing fences on the stability characteristics with slats fully extended are also discussed. Limited data obtained with slats half extended indicated the similarity of this configuration to the slats-retracted configuration. The effects of a bungee (which improved the stick-free stability characteristics) in alleviating the stability changes apparent to the pilot are also discussed.

99. Peele, James R.: **Flight-Determined Pressure Measurements Over the Wing of the Douglas D-558-II Research Airplane at Mach Numbers Up to 1.14.** NACA RM L54A07, March 12, 1954, 93R17395.

A flight investigation of the section and panel characteristics and loads obtained from pressure measurements over a 35-degrees sweptback wing at level-flight lifts has been made through the Mach number range of 0.65 to 1.14. The section pressure distributions at the root, midspan, and tip stations varied from a subsonic type of distribution at a Mach number of 0.65 to a supersonic type of distribution at Mach numbers above 1.0.

100. Crossfield, A. Scott: **Subjective Experiences and Reactions During Flight Testing in the Transonic Region.** 4th General Assembly of AGARD, Schevenigen, The Netherlands, May 3–7, 1954. (See excerpts in *Aerospace Engineering Review*, Vol. 13, No. 9, Sept. 1954, pp. 49 and 87.)

101. Briggs, Donald W.: **Flight Determination of the Buffeting Characteristics of the Bell X-5 Research Airplane at 58.7-Degrees Sweepback.** NACA RM L54C17, May 24, 1954, 93R17481.

Flight measurements were made of the buffeting characteristics of the Bell X-5 research airplane at 58.7-degrees sweepback in the Mach number range from 0.65 to approximately 1.03 at altitudes from 37,000 to 43,000 feet. Maximum airplane normal-force coefficients were attained for Mach numbers up to 0.96.

102. Finch, Thomas W.: **A Flight Investigation of the Effects of Inclination of the Principal Axis of Inertia on the Dynamic Lateral Stability of the Republic XF-91 Airplane.** NACA RM L53I28, July 1954, 87H25044.

A flight investigation has been conducted to determine the effect of variable wing incidence angle on the dynamic lateral stability of the Republic XF-91 airplane. The tests were conducted over a Mach number range of 0.3 to 0.9 at altitudes of 10,000, 20,000, 30,000 and 37,500 feet at wing incidence angles of –2 degrees, 2 degrees, 4 degrees, and 5.65 degrees.

103. Sadoff, Melvin; and Crossfield, A. Scott: **A Flight Evaluation of the Stability and Control of the X-4 Swept-Wing Semitailless Airplane.** NACA RM H54G16, August 1954, 87H24527.

A flight evaluation of the handling qualities of the swept-wing semitailless X-4 airplane was made. Static and dynamic stability and control investigation covered a speed range from stall to Mach numbers of 0.92. Typical swept-wing instability at moderate lifts was encountered. Unsatisfactory and dangerous self-excited dynamic motions occurred at the high-speed end of the range investigated.

104. Nugent, Jack: **Lift and Drag Characteristics of the Douglas D-558-II Research Airplane Obtained in Exploratory Flights to a Mach Number of 2.0.** NACA RM L54F03, August 4, 1954, 93R17490.

A flight investigation was made of the Douglas D-558-II swept-wing airplane in the slats-retracted configuration. Lift and drag were determined for Mach numbers up to 2.0. The lift-coefficient range extended from below 0.1 to about 0.7.

105. Keener, Earl R.: **Wing Pressure Distribution at Low Lift for the XF-92A Delta-Wing Airplane at Transonic Speeds.** NACA RM H54H06, October 1954, 87H24530.

Wing pressure distribution from dives at transonic speeds for the Convair XF-92A delta-wing airplane are presented. The data were obtained from five chordwise rows of orifices on the left wing throughout the Mach number range of 0.74 to 1.01 at an airplane normal-force coefficient of about 0.09, for which the left deflection was about 2 degrees up.

106. Fischel, Jack; and Brunn, Cyril D.: **Longitudinal Stability Characteristics in Accelerated Maneuvers at Subsonic and Transonic Speeds of the Douglas D-558-II Research Airplane Equipped With a Leading-Edge Wing Chord-Extension.** NACA RM H54H16, October 1954, 87H24531.

On the basis of improved longitudinal stability characteristics exhibited in wind-tunnel model tests, the Douglas D-558-II research airplane was modified to include wing at Mach numbers up to about 1.0. The results of subsonic and transonic flight measurements of the longitudinal stability characteristics of the airplane are presented. The levels of normal-force coefficient at which the stick-fixed stability decays and pitch-up starts have been determined through speed range tested as have the variation of the stability

parameters d delta (sub) e/dC (sub) N (sub) A, dF (sub) e/dn, and dC (sub) N (sub) A/d sigma with Mach number. Comparisons of these data with comparable data for the unmodified airplane are also presented.

107. Crossfield, A. Scott: **Flying Techniques With the Research Airplanes.** Preprint 497, Inst. Aero. Sci., 1954, CAI-IAS International Meeting, Montreal, Canada, October 14–15, 1954 (see also in *Aerospace Engineering Review*, Vol. 14, No. 1, Jan. 1955, pp. 56–59).

108. Ankenbruck, Herman O.: **Determination of Longitudinal Handling Qualities of the D-558-II Research Airplane at Transonic and Supersonic Speeds to a Mach Number of About 2.0.** NACA RM H54G29A, November 1954, 87H24529.

Flight tests were performed with the Douglas D-558-II research airplane to investigate the longitudinal handling qualities and trim characteristics at transonic and supersonic speeds. This paper describes the changes with Mach number of the lift, maneuvering, and trim characteristics with elevator and stabilizer to a Mach number of about 2.0.

109. Bellman, Donald R.; and Murphy, Edward D.: **Lift and Drag Characteristics of the Douglas X-3 Research Airplane Obtained During Demonstration Flight to a Mach Number of 1.20.** NACA RM H54I17, December 1954, 87H24532.

Lift and drag data for the Douglas X-3 airplane were obtained during some of the demonstration flights. The data extend over the Mach number range from 0.82 to 1.20 and for certain constant Mach numbers the lift coefficient range from 0 to 1.0 is covered. A comparison of the flight data with wind-tunnel and rocket-model tests shows that the model tests satisfactorily predict the performance of the airplane.

E55-01994

X-3 Airplane

110. Ankenbruck, Herman O.; and Wolowicz, Chester H.: **Lateral Motions Encountered With the Douglas**

D-558-II All-Rocket Research Airplane During Exploratory Flights to a Mach Number of 2.0. NACA RM H54I27, <u>December 1954</u>, 87H24533.

Flight tests were performed with the Douglas D-558-II research airplane to investigate the lateral motions obtained during exploratory flights at supersonic speeds. This paper describes the effects of Mach number and angle of attack on the lateral handling qualities during oscillations at supersonic speeds. Some calculations of period and damping are included. Also shown are the results of some measurements of the variation of rudder hinge moments with sideslip and the effects of power on the variation.

1955 Technical Publications

111. McKay, John B.: **Rolling Performance of the Republic YF-84F Airplane as Measured in Flight.** NACA RM H54G20A, <u>January 1955</u>, 87H24528.

Flight measurements of the rolling performance of the Republic YF-84F airplane were made at altitudes of 10,000, 25,000, and 40,000 feet. The tests were conducted over a Mach number range from 0.35 to 0.95.

(Photo courtesy of Langley Research Center) L-84926

YF-84F Airplane

112. Johnson, Clinton T.; and Kuhl, Albert E.: **Flight Measurements of Elevon Hinge Moments on the XF-92A Delta-Wing Airplane.** NACA RM H54J25A, <u>January 1955</u>, 87H24534.

Elevon hinge-moment measurements were made during flight tests of the Convair XF-92A delta-wing airplane over the Mach number range from 0.70 to 0.95. Hinge moments were measured during longitudinal elevon pulses, aileron rolls, and wind-up turns. Data are presented giving the variation of $C_{h\delta}$ and $C_{h\alpha}$ as determined from these tests.

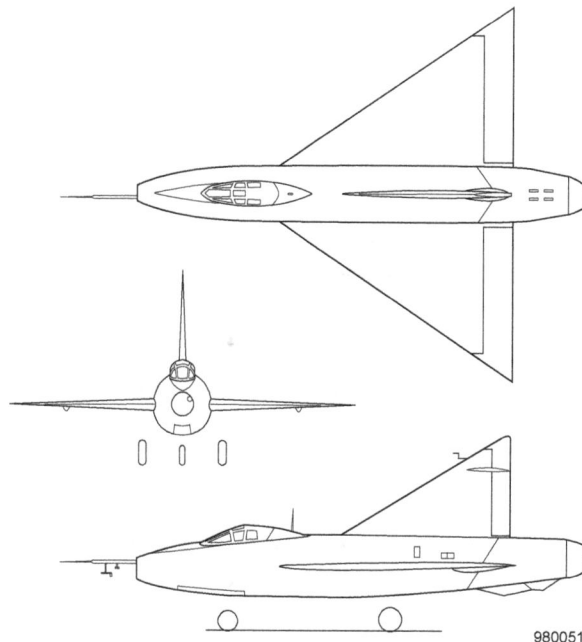

XF-92A Airplane, Three-View Drawing

113. Holleman, Euclid C.; and Triplett, William C.: **Flight Measurements of the Dynamic Longitudinal Stability and Frequency-Response Characteristics of the XF-92A Delta-Wing Airplane.** NACA RM H54J26A, <u>January 1955</u>, 87H24535.

Results of dynamic longitudinal flight test conducted with the XF-92A delta-wing airplane over a Mach number range of 0.42 to 0.94 at an altitude of about 30,000 feet are presented. The data were analyzed by measuring the airplane oscillatory characteristics, by matching the airplane system with an analog computer, and by determining the frequency-response characteristics of the airplane. Wherever possible, stability derivatives were computed and are presented as a function of Mach number.

114. Saltzman, Edwin J.: **The Effect of the Blunt-Trailing-Edge Elevons on the Longitudinal and Lateral Handling Qualities of the X-4 Semitailless Airplane.** NACA RM H54K03, <u>January 1955</u>, 87H24537.

The effects of thickening the trailing edges of the elevons on the static longitudinal stability and control, lateral control for the X-4, a swept-wing semitailless airplane, are presented. The results of this study are compared with similar tests for the X-4 with conventional elevon trailing edges.

115. Sisk, Thomas R.; and Muhleman, Duane O.: **Longitudinal Stability Characteristics in Maneuvering Flight of the Convair XF-92A Delta-Wing Airplane Including the Effects of Wing Fences.** NACA RM H54J27, <u>January 1955</u>, 87H24536.

The longitudinal maneuvering stability characteristics are evaluated on the Convair F-92A delta-wing airplane in wind-up turns over the Mach number range from 0.70 to 0.95 at altitudes between 22,000 and 39,000 feet. A longitudinal stability reduction evidenced as a pitch-up encountered over the Mach number range tested is evaluated along with the airplane behavior in the region of reduced stability. Two wing fence configurations are evaluated and compared with the basic airplane configuration characteristics.

116. Stillwell, Wendell H.: **Results of Measurements Made During the Approach and Landing of Seven High-Speed Research Airplanes.** NACA RM H54K24, February 1955, 87H24267.

Measurements made during the approach and landing of the X-1, X-3, X-4, X-5, D-558-I, D-558-II, and XF-92A research airplanes are presented. Data are also presented for the effect of lift drag ratio on the landing characteristics of the X-4 airplane.

117. Anon.: **Flight Experience With Two High-Speed Airplanes Having Violent Lateral-Longitudinal Coupling in Aileron Rolls.** NACA RM H55A13, February 4, 1955, 93R17938.

During flight tests of two high-speed airplane configurations, violent cross-coupled lateral and longitudinal motions were encountered following abrupt rudder-fixed aileron rolls. The speeds involved ranged from a Mach number of 0.7 to 1.05. The motions were characterized by extreme variations in angles of attack and sideslip which resulted in load factors as large as 6.7g (negative) and 7g (positive) normal acceleration and 2g transverse acceleration.

118. Robinson, Glenn H.; Cothren, George E.; and Pembo, Chris: **Wing-Load Measurements at Supersonic Speeds of the Douglas D-558-II Research Airplane.** NACA RM H54L27, March 1955, 87H24539.

Flight measurement of the aerodynamic wing loads on the D-558-II airplane have been made in the Mach number range from 1.0 to 2.0. Results of measurements of the wing-panel normal-force, bending moment, and pitching-moment coefficients, normal-force-curve slope, lateral center of pressure, and chordwise center of pressure are presented.

E-3995

D-558-II Airplane, Top View

119. Jordan, Gareth H.; and Keener, Earl R.: **Flight-Determined Pressure Distributions Over a Section of the 35-Degree Swept Wing of the Douglas D-558-II Research Airplane at Mach Numbers Up to 2.0.** NACA RM H55A03, March 1955, 87H24287.

Presented are pressure distributions and section characteristics for a wing-midsemispan station perpendicular to the 30-degree common-chord line of the 35-degree sweptback wing of the Douglas D-558-II research airplane at Mach numbers from 1.17 to 2.00.

120. *Gates, O. B., Jr.; Weil, J.; and *Woodling, C. H.: **Effect of Automatic Stabilization on the Sideslip and Angle of Attack Disturbances in Rolling Maneuvers.** In *NACA Conf. on Autom. Stability and Control of Aircraft,* March 30, 1955, pp. 25–41, (see N72-73193 12-99), 72N73195.

Time histories are presented that illustrate the large motions which have been encountered in flight tests of some of the present-day fighter airplanes. Results of some analog studies are discussed which indicate that variations in certain of the airplane stability derivatives could have an appreciable effect on these undesirable motions.

*Langley Aeronautical Laboratory, Hampton, Virginia.

121. Cole, H. A., Jr.; Brown, S. C.; and Holleman, E. C.: **Effects of Flexibility on the Longitudinal and Lateral Dynamic Response of a Large Airplane.** NACA RM A55D14, *NACA Conf. on Autom. Stability and Control of Aircraft,* March 1955, pp. 57–70, (see N72-73193 12-99), 72N73197.

In recent years the desire to increase the range and speed of large airplanes has led to sweptback wings of high aspect ratio, thin airfoils, and fuselages of high fineness ratio. The dynamic effects are especially important in the design of automatic control systems because structural modes may introduce instabilities which would not arise with a rigid airplane. It is important for the automatic-control designer to consider the effects of flexibility on control systems.

122. Jordan, Gareth H.; and Hutchins, C. Kenneth: **Preliminary Flight-Determined Pressure Distribution Over the Wing of the Douglas X-3 Research Airplane at Subsonic and Transonic Mach Numbers.** NACA RM H55A10, April 1955, 87H24540.

Preliminary flight-measured chordwise pressure distributions have been obtained at a wing midsemispan station of the Douglas X-3 research airplane through an angle-of-attack range at Mach numbers of 0.61, 0.78, 0.94, and 1.10. The results of the investigation indicate that the maximum section normal-force coefficient increased from about 0.7 at the lower Mach numbers to about 1.2 at a Mach number of 1.10. The pressure distributions at Mach numbers of about 0.61, 0.78, and 0.94 showed good agreement with wind-tunnel results.

At Mach numbers of 0.94 and 1.10 leading-edge flap normal-force and hinge-mount coefficients increased with increase in angle of attack throughout the angle-of-attack range tested and resulted in high normal-force and hinge-moment coefficients at the higher angles of attack.

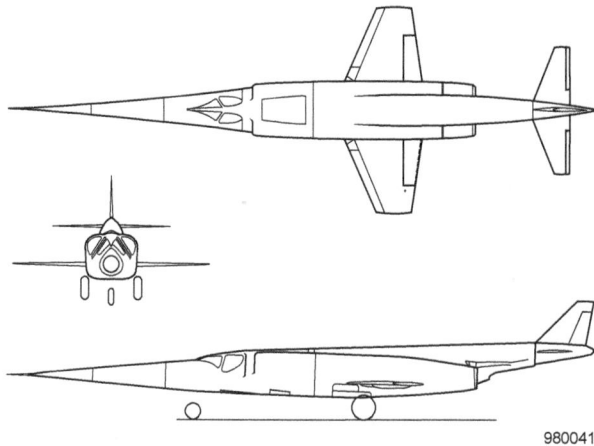

X- 3 Airplane, Three-View Drawing

123. Banner, Richard D.; Reed, Robert D.; and Marcy, William L.: **Wing-Load Measurements of the Bell X-5 Research Airplane at a Sweep Angle of 58.7 Degrees.** NACA RM H55A11, April 1955, 87H24541.

A flight investigation has been made over an altitude and lift range to determine the wing loads of the Bell X-5 research airplane at a sweep angle of 58.7 degrees at subsonic and transonic Mach numbers. The wing loads were nonlinear over the angle-of-attack range from zero to maximum wing lift. The nonlinear trends were more pronounced at angles of attack above the "pitch-up" where there is a reduction in the wing lift and an inboard and forward movement in the center of load. No apparent effects of altitude on the wing loads were evident from the data obtained in these tests.

124. Baker, Thomas F.; and Johnson, Wallace E.: **Flight Measurements at Transonic Speeds of the Buffeting Characteristics of the XF-92A Delta-Wing Research Airplane.** NACA RM H54L03, April 1955, 87H24538.

Measurements were made on the XF-92A delta-wing airplane of buffet-induced fluctuations in normal acceleration at the airplane center of gravity and of fluctuations in wing structural shear load in the Mach number range from 0.6 to 0.96 at altitudes from 25,000 to 38,000 feet. Airplane normal force coefficients in the order of 0.7 were attained at Mach numbers less than 0.9. Buffet frequencies and the variations with Mach number, lift, and angle of attack of buffet intensity are given.

125. Sisk, Thomas R.; and Muhleman, Duane O.: **Lateral Stability and Control Characteristics of the Convair XF-92A Delta-Wing Airplane as Measured in Flight.** NACA RM H55A17, May 1955, 87H24299.

The lateral stability and control characteristics of the Convair XF-92A delta-wing airplane are determined for sideslips, aileron rolls, and rudder pulses. A limited amount of data with wing fences installed at 60 percent of the wing semispan is presented for comparison with the basic airplane configuration.

126. Finch, Thomas W.: **Flight Determination of the Longitudinal Stability and Control Characteristics of the Bell X-5 Research Airplane at 58.7 Degrees Sweepback.** NACA RM H55C07, May 1955, 87H24301.

Flight tests were performed with the Bell X-5 research airplane at 58.7 degrees sweepback to measure the longitudinal stability control characteristics from elevator and stabilizer maneuvers at 40,000 feet and elevator maneuvers at 25,000 feet and 15,000 feet. Results are presented for Mach numbers up to 1.0 and include trim characteristics, apparent stability parameters, relative control effectiveness, stick-force gradient, normal-force-curve slope, and effect of dynamic pressure and engine power. Comparison is made with wind-tunnel data.

127. Kuhl, Albert E.; and Johnson, Clinton T.: **Flight Measurements of Wing Loads on the Convair XF-92A Delta-Wing Airplane.** NACA RM H55D12, May 1955, 87H24304.

Aerodynamic loads were obtained from strain-gage measurements during the NACA flight test program of the XF-92A research airplane. Wing-panel loads were measured during longitudinal pulses and wind-up turns over the mach number rang from 0.43 to 0.95. The wing-panel loads due to elevon deflection and angle of attack were determined for the Mach number range of these tests.

128. Cooney, T. V.; Andrews, William H.; and McGowan, William A.: **Preliminary Results From Flight Measurements in Gradual-Turn Maneuvers of the Wing Loads and the Distribution of Load Among the Components of a Boeing B-47A Airplane.** NACA RM L55B02, June 27, 1955, 93R17884.

129. Day, Richard E.; and Fischel, Jack: **Stability and Control Characteristics Obtained During Demonstration of the Douglas X-3 Research Airplane.** NACA RM H55E16, July 1955, 87H24543.

Results obtained from flights of the manufacturer's demonstration program and from U.S. Air Force evaluation flights of the Douglas X-3 research airplane are presented. Data evaluation includes static longitudinal directional, and lateral stability and control for Mach numbers up to 1.21 at pressure altitudes from 12,800 feet to 34,000 feet. Comparisons are made with wind-tunnel and rocket-model tests.

130. Weil, Joseph; Gates, Ordway B.; Banner, Richard D.; and Kuhl, Albert E.: **Flight Experience of Inertia**

Coupling in Rolling Maneuvers. NACA RM H55E17B, July 1955, 87H24318.

A brief discussion is presented of the flight tests of two airplanes which have exhibited strong coupling between their lateral and longitudinal motions. Results are presented which indicate the effect of directional stability and vertical tail size on the tail shear loads encountered in rolling maneuvers.

131. Reed, Robert D.: **Flight Measurements of Horizontal-Tail Loads on the Bell X-5 Research Airplane at a Sweep Angle of 58.7 Degrees.** NACA RM H55E20A, July 1955, 87H24544.

Flight measurements of the horizontal tail loads on the Bell X-5 research airplane have been made in accelerated maneuvers at Mach numbers from 0.61 to 1.00 at an altitude of 40,000 feet. At this altitude the aerodynamic and balancing tail loads were determined at all normal-force coefficients up to near maximum lift. Comparisons were made with flight and wind-tunnel data obtained at 25,000 feet and 15,000 feet over a limited lift range.

132. Fischel, Jack; and Reisert, Donald: **Effect of Several Wing Modifications on the Low Speed Stalling Characteristics of the Douglas D-558-II Research Airplane.** NACA RM H55E31A, July 1955, 87H24545.

The low-speed stalling and lift characteristics of the Douglas-D-558-II research airplane were measured in a series of 1g stalls performed with several wing modifications designed to alleviate swept-wing instability and pitch-up. The various configurations investigated include the basic wing configurations and two wing-fence configurations in combination with retracted free-floating, or extended slats, and a wing leading-edge chord extension configuration. All configurations were investigated with flaps and landing gear retracted and extended.

133. Holleman, Euclid C.: **Flight Measurements of the Lateral Response Characteristics of the Convair XF-92A Delta-Wing Airplane.** NACA RM H55E26, August 1955, 87H24323.

Rudder pulse maneuvers were performed with the XF-92A 60 degrees delta-wing airplane at 30,000 feet over a Mach number range of 0.52 to 0.92. Tests were conducted with and without a wing fence. Representative data were analyzed to give airplane stability derivatives and frequency responses.

134. Drake, Hubert M.; and Stillwell, Wendell H.: **Behavior of the Bell X-1A Research Airplane During Exploratory Flights at Mach Numbers Near 2.0 and at Extreme Altitudes.** NACA RM H55G25, September 1955, 93R18135.

A flight program has been conducted by the U. S. Air Force consisting of exploratory flights to determine the Mach

number and altitude capabilities of the Bell X-1A research airplane. On two flights of the X-1A airplane, one reaching a Mach number of about 2.44, the other a geometric altitude of about 90,000 feet, lateral stability difficulties were encountered which resulted in uncontrolled rolling motions of the airplane at Mach numbers near 2.0. Analysis indicates that this behavior apparently results from a combination of low directional stability and damping in roll and may be aggravated by high control friction and rocket motor misalignment. The deterioration of directional stability with increasing Mach number can lead to severe longitudinal-lateral coupling at low roll rates. The misalignment of the rocket motor could induce sufficiently high roll velocities to excite these coupled motions. Adequate control of these motions was virtually impossible because of the high control friction. In the absence of rolling, poor lateral behavior might be expected at somewhat higher Mach numbers because wind-tunnel data indicate neutral directional stability at about $M = 2.35$.

E55-01799

X-1A Airplane

135. Drake, Hubert M.; Finch, Thomas W.; and Peele, James R.: **Flight Measurements of Directional Stability to a Mach Number of 1.48 for an Airplane Tested With Three Different Vertical Tail Configurations.** NACA RM H55G26, October 1955, 87H24547.

Directional stability characteristics have been determined from the measured period and damping of a fighter-type airplane over the Mach number range from 0.72 to 1.48 at altitudes of 40,000 feet and 30.000 feet. Three different vertical tails of varying aspect ratio or area, or both, were employed.

136. Sisk, Thomas R.; and Andrews, William H.: **Flight Experience With a Delta-Wing Airplane Having Violent Lateral-Longitudinal Coupling in Aileron Rolls.** NACA RM H55H03, October 1955, 87H24548.

A time-history presentation is made of aileron rolls performed by a high-speed delta-wing airplane between Mach numbers of 0.7 and 0.8 including a one-half deflection aileron roll at a Mach number of 0.75 where violent cross-coupled lateral and longitudinal motions were experienced.

137. Videan, Edward N.: **Flight Measurements of the Dynamic Lateral and Longitudinal Stability of the Bell X-5 Research Airplane at 58.7 Degrees Sweepback.** NACA RM H55H10, October 1955, 87H24549.

Longitudinal and lateral dynamic-response characteristics to elevator and rudder pulse deflections have been measured on the Bell X-5 research airplane at 58.7 degrees sweepback. Flight records were obtained at altitudes of 40,000 feet and 25,000 feet. Period and damping, including nonlinear damping effects, are presented, and comparison is made with U.S. military lateral dynamic stability criteria. Engine gyroscopic coupling effects are discussed, and frequency response calculations are presented.

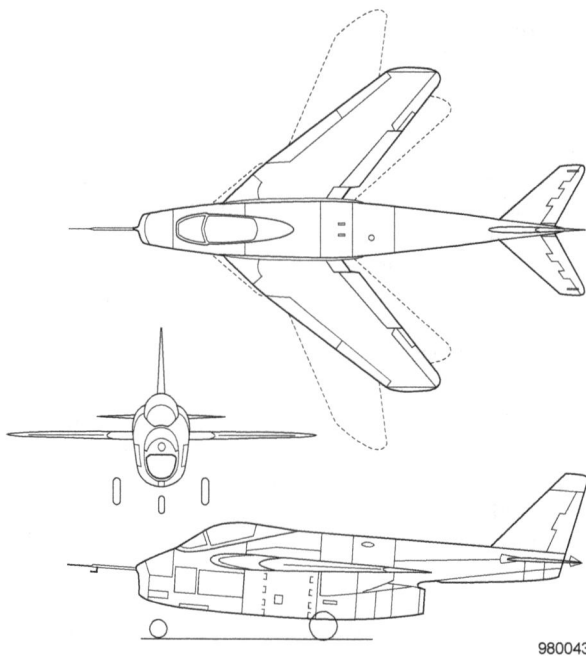

980043

X-5 Airplane, Three-View Drawing

138. Johnson, Clinton T.: **Flight Measurements of the Vertical-Tail Loads on the Convair XF-92A Delta-Wing Airplane.** NACA RM H55H25, October 1955, 87H24551.

Vertical-tail loads as obtained from strain-gage measurements during the NACA flight test program of the Convair XF-92A research airplane were measured during rudder pulses rudder-fixed oscillations, and gradually increasing sideslips over the Mach number range from 0.50 to 0.87. The vertical-tail loads resulting from rudder deflection and sideslip angle were determined for the Mach number range of the these tests.

139. Williams, Walter C.: **Flight Research at High Altitudes and High Speeds With Rocket-Propelled Research Airplanes.** SAE Paper 601, October 1955, 87H28633.

140. Thompson, Jim Rogers; Bray, Richard S.; and Cooper, George E.: **Flight Calibration of Four Airspeed Systems on a Swept-Wing Airplane at Mach Numbers Up to 1.04 by the NACA Radar-Photoheodolite Method.** NACA TN 3526, November 1955, 93R13513.

The calibrations of four airspeed systems installed in a North American F-86A airplane have been determined in flight at Mach numbers up to 1.04 by the NACA radar-photoheodolite method. The variation of the static-pressure error per unit indicated impact pressure is presented for three systems typical of those currently in use in flight research, a nose boom and two different wing-tip booms, and for the standard service system installed in the airplane. A limited amount of information on the effect of airplane normal-force coefficient on the static-pressure error is included. The results are compared with available theory and with results from wind-tunnel tests of the airspeed heads alone. Of the systems investigated, a nose-boom installation was found to be most suitable for research use at transonic and low supersonic speeds because it provided the greatest sensitivity of the indicated Mach number to a unit change in true Mach number at very high subsonic speeds, and because it was least sensitive to changes in airplane normal-force coefficient. The static-pressure error of the nose-boom system was small and constant above a Mach number of 1.03 after passage of the fuselage bow shock wave over the airspeed head.

141. Keener, Earl R.; and Jordan, Gareth H.: **Wing Pressure Distributions Over the Lift Range of the Convair XF-92A Delta-Wing Airplane at Subsonic and Transonic Speeds.** NACA RM H55G07, November 1955, 87H24546.

Chordwise and spanwise pressure distributions are presented for the left wing of the Convair XF-92A delta-wing airplane at Mach numbers from 0.30 to 0.93. Reynolds number based on the mean aerodynamic chord of the wing varied between 22 x 10 to the 6 power and 49 x 10 to the 6 power. The data cover the lift range from level flight to near-maximum lift. Effects of wing section stall upon the elevon-section loads are included.

1956 Technical Publications

142. Williams, Walter C.; and Phillips, William H.: **Some Recent Research on the Handling Qualities of Airplanes.** NACA RM H55L29A, February 1956, 87H24556.

Results of recent research on the handling qualities of airplanes are reviewed. Among the subjects considered are dynamic longitudinal stability, transonic trim changes, pitch-up due to decreasing airspeed, dynamic lateral stability, aileron control, and mechanical characteristics of power control systems.

143. Brunn, Cyril D.; and Stillwell, Wendell H.: **Mach Number Measurements and Calibrations During Flight at High Speeds and at High Altitudes Including Data for the D-558-II Research Airplane.** NACA RM H55J18, March 1956, 87H24552.

This paper contains data concerning research equipment and techniques pertaining to measurements of airspeed and altitude, with particular reference to high Mach number and altitude. Computations are presented for errors in determining Mach number for altitudes of 40,000 feet to 140,000 feet. Illustrative examples are included for maximum Mach number and altitude flights of the Douglas D-558-II research airplane.

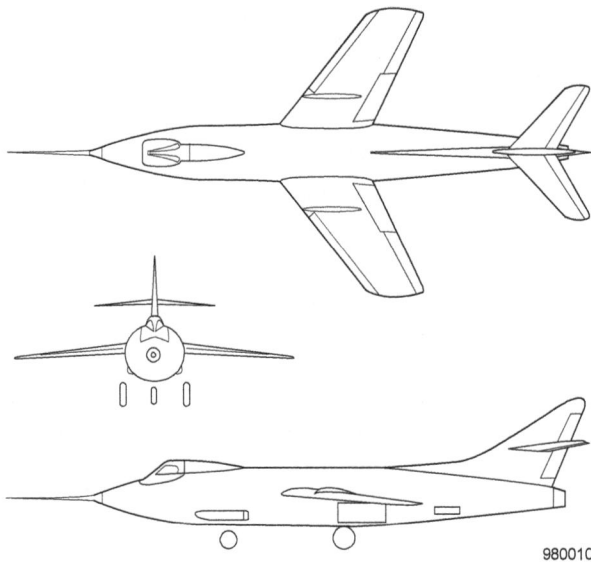

D-558-II Airplane, Three-View Drawing

144. Weil, Joseph: **A Brief Review of NACA Flight Research Relating to Roll Coupling.** Symposium on Roll Coupling, Dayton, Ohio, March 1, 1956.

145. Bellman, Donald R.; and Kleinknecht, Kenneth S.: **Operational Experience With Rocket Propelled Airplanes.** IAS-F75-038, 11th Annual Flight Propulsion Meeting of IAS, Cleveland, Ohio, March 9, 1956, 87H28957.

146. Finch, Thomas W.; Peele, James R.; and Day, Richard E.: **Flight Investigation of the Effect of Vertical Tail Size on the Rolling Behavior of a Swept-Wing Airplane Having Lateral-Longitudinal Coupling.** NACA RM H55L28A, April 1956, 87H24554.

The rolling behavior of a swept-wing airplane having lateral longitudinal coupling has been determined over a Mach number range of 0.73 to 1.39 at altitudes of 40,000 feet and 30,000 feet with three different vertical tails of varying aspect ratio or area, or both. Increasing the tail area 27 percent and the tail aspect ratio 32 percent greatly improved the rolling behavior. The adverse sideslip during the rolls decreased with increasing speeds to negligible values near Mach numbers of 1.00 to 1.05, then increased in the favorable direction at higher speeds. Stabilizer motion during the rolls greatly affected the rolling behavior.

147. Stephenson, Harriet J.: **Flight Measurements of Horizontal-Tail Loads on the Douglas X-3 Research Airplane.** NACA RM H56A23, April 1956, 87H24562.

Horizontal-tail loads were obtained from strain-gage measurements during flight tests of the Douglas X-3 research airplane over a Mach number range of 0.65 to 1.16. The horizontal-tail-panel lift-curve slope was obtained from stabilizer pulses. Balancing-tail loads, downwash, and total airplane pitching moment were obtained from wind-up turns and pull-ups.

148. Weil, Joseph; and Day, Richard E.: **An Analog Study of the Relative Importance of Various Factors Affecting Roll Coupling.** NACA RM H56A06, April 1956, 87H24558.

An analog study of the roll coupling problem has been made for a representative swept-wing and a tailless delta-wing configuration. The investigation, conducted primarily for subsonic flight conditions, included determination of the effects of wide variations in many of the pertinent aerodynamic derivatives on the motions developed in rolling maneuvers. The influence of large changes in principal axis inclination and mass distribution was also considered.

149. Weil, Joseph; Campbell, George S.; and Diederich, Margaret S.: **An Analysis of Estimated and Experimental Transonic Downwash Characteristics as Affected by Plan Form and Thickness for Wing and Wing-Fuselage Configurations.** NACA TN 3628, April 1956, 87H24920.

This paper presents a summary of the effects of changes in wing plan form and thickness ratio on the downwash characteristics of wing and wing-fuselage configurations in the Mach number range between 0.6 and 1.1. Data obtained by the transonic-bump technique at two tail heights have been compared with theoretical estimations made in the subsonic and supersonic Mach number range.

150. Finch, Thomas W.; and Walker, Joseph A.: **Flight Determination of the Lateral Handling Qualities of the Bell X-5 Research Airplane at 58.7 Degrees Sweepback.** NACA RM H56C29, May 1956, 87H24570, 93R19517.

Flight tests were performed with the Bell X-5 research airplane at 58.7 degrees sweepback to measure the lateral handling qualities over a Mach number range up to 0.97 at altitudes of 40,000, 25,000, and 15,000 feet. The dynamic characteristics were influenced by aerodynamic and engine gyroscopic coupling, and the damping was nonlinear at the higher Mach numbers. The positive apparent directional stability and the high apparent effective dihedral increased rapidly at higher Mach numbers. The low aileron effectiveness was adversely affected by the high effective dihedral. Directional divergence and aileron overbalance occurred at high lifts. An abrupt wing-dropping tendency existed and single-degree-of-freedom flutter occurred on the rudder at low supersonic Mach numbers.

151. Wolowicz, Chester H.: **Time-Vector-Determined Lateral Derivatives of a Swept-Wing Fighter Type Airplane With Three Different Vertical Tails at Mach Numbers Between 0.70 and 1.48.** NACA RM H56C20, June 1956, 87H24567.

The time-vector method was used to obtain the lateral stability derivatives C_{Y_β}, C_{n_β}, C_{ι_β}, C_{ι_p}, ($C_{n_r} - C_{n_\beta}$) of a swept-wing fighter-type airplane. The airplane was tested over a Mach number range of 0.71 to 1.48 at altitudes extending from 30,000 to 43,000 feet to obtain static and dynamic lateral stability characteristics. Four configurations were employed: three different vertical tails and an extended wing. Available wind-tunnel data and theoretical calculations were used for comparison purposes.

152. Fischel, Jack; and Reisert, Donald: **Effect of Several Wing Modifications on the Subsonic and Transonic Longitudinal Handling Qualities of the Douglas D-558-II Research Airplane.** NACA RM H56C30, June 1956, 87H24575, 93R19515.

The subsonic and transonic longitudinal handling qualities of the Douglas D-558-II research airplane were measured with several wing modifications designed to alleviate swept-wing instability and pitch-up. Airplane configurations investigated include the basic wing configuration and two wing-fence configurations in configurations in combination with retracted, free-floating, or extended slats, and a wing leading-edge chord-extension configuration. Results indicated that the comparative effects of these wing modifications on airplane pitch-up and trim-stability and on the stability parameters $d\delta_e/dC_N$, dF_e/da_n, and C_{N_σ} were essentially negligible. The various modifications had some measurable effect on airplane buffeting characteristics.

153. Nugent, Jack: **Lift and Drag of the Bell X-5 Research Airplane in the 45-Degrees Sweptback Configuration at Transonic Speeds.** NACA RM H56E02, July 1956, 87H24585.

Lift and drag coefficients for the 45-degrees sweptback configuration of the Bell X-5 research airplane were determined from flight tests covering the Mach number range from 0.61 to 1.01 and were compared to data obtained with the 59-degree sweptback configuration. Below the drag rise the 45-degree configuration had a zero lift drag coefficient of

0.020 as compared with 0.0175 for the 59-degree sweptback configuration. The lift-drag ratio for the 45-degree configuration exceeded that for the 59-degree configuration for a Mach number range from 0.61 to 0.88 with a maximum difference of about 0.7 at a Mach number of 0.82.

154. Saltzman, Edwin J.; Bellman, Donald R.; and Musialowski, Norman T.: **Flight-Determined Transonic Lift and Drag Characteristics of the YF-102 Airplane with Two Wing Configurations.** NACA RM H56E08, July 1956, 87H24588.

The flight lift and drag characteristics of the YF-102 airplane, a 60-degree delta-wing interceptor, were determined for a symmetrical wing configuration and for a configuration with cambered wing and reflexed tips. The Mach number range extended from 0.6 to 1.17 and altitude varied from 25,000 feet to 50,000 feet. The cambered wing configuration experienced a considerable reduction of drag-due-to-lift, resulting in about 0.01 lower drag coefficient at about 0.3 lift coefficient and an increase of about 20 percent in lift-drag ratio. Comparable wing-tunnel data are included.

E-2550

YF-102 Airplane

155. Beeler, De E.; Bellman, Donald R.; and Saltzman, Edwin J.: **Flight Techniques for Determining Airplane Drag at High Mach Numbers.** NACA TN 3821, AGARD Report #84, presented to the Flight Test Panel of Advisory Group for Aeronautical Research and Development, Brussels, Belgium, August 27–31, 1956, August 1956, 93R13811.

The accelerometer method has proven to be the most satisfactory method for the flight measurement of total airplane drag during research investigations of high-speed airplanes by the NACA High-Speed Flight Station. The method requires special instrumentation and measuring techniques which are described in detail. Method for separating the flight measured overall drag into drag components and for comparing the flight data with wind-tunnel-model data are presented.

156. Williams, Walter C.; Drake, Hubert M.; and Fischel, Jack: **Comparison of Flight and Wind-Tunnel Measurements of High-Speed-Airplane Stability and Control Characteristics.** NACA TN 3859, <u>August 1956</u>, 93R13946.

Comparisons of wind-tunnel and flight-measured values of stability and control characteristics are of considerable interest to the designer, since the wind-tunnel method of testing is one of the prime sources upon which estimates of the characteristics of a new configuration are based. In this paper comparisons are made of some of the more important stability and control characteristics of three swept-wing airplanes as measured in flight and in wind tunnels. Wind-tunnel data from high-speed closed-throat tunnels, a slotted-throat transonic tunnel, and a supersonic tunnel are used. The comparisons show that, generally speaking, the wind tunnels predict all trends of characteristics reasonably well. There are, however, differences in exact values of parameters, which could be attributed somewhat to differences in the model caused by the method of support. The small size of the models may have some effect on measurements of flap effectiveness. When nonlinearities in derivatives occur during wind-tunnel tests, additional data should be obtained in the region of the nonlinearities in order to predict more accurately the flight characteristics. Also, nonlinearities in static derivatives must be analyzed on the basis of dynamic motions of the airplane. Aeroelastic corrections must be made to wind-tunnel data for models of airplanes which have thin surfaces and are to be flown at high dynamic pressures. Inlet effects can exert an influence on the characteristics, depending upon air requirements of the engine and location of the inlets.

157. Williams, Walter C.; Drake, Hubert M.; and Fischel, Jack: **Some Correlations of Flight-Measured and Wind-Tunnel Measured Stability and Control Characteristics of High-Speed Airplanes.** NACA RM H56AG62, <u>August 1956</u>, 87H29107, (also AGARD Report 62).

Comparisons of wind-tunnel and flight-measured values of stability and control characteristics are of considerable interest to the designer, since the wind-tunnel method of testing is one of the prime sources upon which estimates of the characteristics of a new configuration are based. In this paper comparisons are made of some of the more important stability and control characteristics of three swept-wing airplanes as measured in flight and in wind tunnels. Wind-tunnel data are used from high-speed closed-throat tunnels, a slotted-throat transonic tunnel, and a supersonic tunnel. The comparison shows that, generally speaking, the wind tunnels predict all trends of characteristics reasonably well. There

are, however, differences in exact values of parameters, which could be attributed somewhat to differences in the model caused by the method of support. The small size of the models may have some effect on measurements of flap effectiveness. When non-linearities in derivatives occur during wind-tunnel tests, additional data should be obtained in the region of the non-linearities. Also, non-linearities in static derivatives must be analyzed on the basis of dynamic motions of the airplane. Aeroelastic corrections must be made to the wind-tunnel data for models of airplanes which have thin surfaces and are to be flown at high dynamic pressures. Inlet effects can exert an influence on the characteristics, depending upon air requirements of the engine and location of the inlets.

158. Weil, Joseph; and Day, Richard E.: **Correlation of Flight and Analog Investigations of Roll Coupling.** NACA RM H56F08, <u>September 1956</u>, 87H24591, 93R19575.

A brief review of NACA flight experience relating to the roll-coupling problem is presented. Conditions rated by pilots and intolerable, marginal, and good are discussed and correlated with calculated results. A suggested flight test procedure for roll-coupling investigations and a discussion of several other items of general interest are also presented.

159. Drake, Hubert M.: **Flight Experience With Present Research Airplanes.** Research-Airplane-Committee Report on Conference on the Progress of the X-15 Project, Langley Aeronautical Laboratory, Langley Field, Virginia, <u>October 26, 1956</u>, 93R21716. Declassified per NASA ccn 14, dated 25 April 1967.

The North American X-15 airplane is being designed for speeds and altitudes considerably greater than those presently being encountered by airplanes. This paper explores the status of flight research with the current research airplanes to see what experience and planned research are pertinent to the X-15 project.

E-5251

X-15 Airplane

160. Banner, Richard D.; and Malvestuto, Frank S., Jr.: **Skin and Structural Temperature Measurements on Research Airplanes at Supersonic Speeds**. Research-Airplane-Committee Report on Conference on the Progress of the X-15 Project, Langley Aeronautical Laboratory, Langley Field, Virginia, <u>October 26, 1956</u>, 93R21723. Declassified per NASA ccn 14, dated 25 April 1967.

Skin and structural temperatures of airplanes in flight at supersonic speeds have been determined by use of thermocouples and temperature resistance gages installed on various research airplanes. Such data have recently been obtained on two research airplanes, the Bell X-2 and the Bell X-1B. The object of this paper is to show some of the actual magnitudes and trends in the structural temperatures that exist in an airplane experiencing the effects of aerodynamic heating.

E-2539

X-1B Airplane

161. Stillwell, Wendell H.: **Control Studies. Part B: Studies of Reaction Controls**. Research-Airplane-Committee Report on Conference on the Progress of the X-15 Project, Langley Aeronautical Laboratory, Langley Field, Virginia, <u>October 26, 1956</u>, 93R21728. Declassified per NASA ccn 14, dated 25 April 1967.

The attitude-control method selected for the North American X-15 for flight at extremely low and zero dynamic pressures utilizes the reaction forces developed by small-rocket units located on the airplane to produce rolling, pitching, and yawing moments. An investigation of reaction control similar to those selected for the X-15 has shown that unique control problems exist for flight at the low dynamic pressures where this type of control is used. Although the Bell X-1B configuration was utilized for this investigation, a range of variables was covered to determine the significant effects of various factors on flight with reaction controls. It was also of interest to determine fuel requirements for the rocket units. The investigation consisted of analog-computer studies and ground-simulator tests. The significant results of this investigation is discussed in this paper.

162. Taback, I.; and Truszynski, G. M.: **Instrumentation for the X-15**. Research-Airplane-Committee Report on Conference on the Progress of the X-15 Project, Langley Aeronautical Laboratory, Langley Field, Virginia, <u>October 26, 1956</u>, 93R21729. Declassified per NASA ccn 14, dated 25 April 1967.

The development of a research airplane which extends manned flight into regions where extremes of temperature and pressure are reached requires the simultaneous development of new instrumentation technique not only to ensure safe operation of the aircraft but also to derive a maximum of research data throughout the operational range of the aircraft. The instrumentation required for the North American X-15 airplane project consists of ground range and for research measurements. This paper outlines a plan for a ground range, which is based upon developed equipment already in use, and also discusses the airborne instrumentation and some of the special airborne devices which are made necessary by the extended performance capabilities of this airplane.

163. Marcy, William L.; Stephenson, Harriet J.; and Cooney, Thomas V.: **Analysis of the Vertical-Tail Loads Measured During a Flight Investigation at Transonic Speeds of the Douglas X-3 Research Airplane**. NACA RM H56H08, <u>November 1956</u>, 87H24605.

An analysis of the vertical-tail loads obtained from strain-gage measurements during a flight investigation of the Douglas X-3 research airplane in the transonic speed range is presented. Data from rudder pulses, gradually increasing sideslips, and rudder-fixed aileron rolls were used to obtain rudder effectiveness and the effective lift-curve slope of the vertical tail. The variation of airplane yawing-moment coefficient with sideslip as determined from the measured vertical-tail loads is also presented.

164. Weil, Joseph: **Review of Recent Rate of Roll Investigations at the NACA High-Speed Flight Station**. Symposium on Roll Requirements, <u>November 14, 1956</u>, 87H29700.

165. Keener, Earl R.; and Jordan, Gareth H.: **Wing Loads and Load Distributions Throughout the Lift Range of the Douglas X-3 Research Airplane at Transonic Speeds**. NACA RM H56G13, <u>December 1956</u>, 87H24598.

Wing loads and load distributions were obtained in flight by differential-pressure measurements between the upper and lower surfaces of the left wing of the Douglas X-3 research airplane. The effects of angle of attack and Mach number on the wing characteristics at transonic Mach numbers are shown. The wing has an aspect ratio of 3.09 and a modified 4.5 percent-thick hexagonal section. Data cover the range from near-zero lift to maximum lift, over a Mach number range of 0.71 to 1.15. Reynolds number based on the mean aerodynamic chord of the wing varied between 16 x 10 to the 6 power and 26 x 10 to the 6 power.

166. Andrews, William H.; Sisk, Thomas R.; and Darville, Robert W.: **Longitudinal Stability Characteristics of the Convair YF-102 Airplane Determined From Flight Tests.** NACA RM H56I17, December 1956, 87H26846.

The longitudinal stability and trim characteristics for the cambered-wing configuration of the Convair YF-102 airplane are determined up to M = 1.18 at altitudes of 25,000, 40,000, and 50,000 feet from level-flight speed runs, stall approaches, wind-up turns, and elevator pulses. Trim data are also included for the symmetrical-wing version. The trim characteristics are conventional. The static stability more than double between M = 0.60 and 1.16 and there is a loss of 50 percent in control effectiveness between M = 0.90 and 1.0. No severe pitch-up was exhibited except in cases resulting from speed change in the trim region. A preliminary analysis of the artificial-feel system was made as a result of the poor stick-force characteristics exhibited around 1.5g and 2.0g.

1957 Technical Publications

167. Sisk, Thomas R.; Andrews, William H.; and Darville, Robert W.: **Flight Evaluation of the Lateral Stability and Control Characteristics of the Convair YF-102 Airplane.** NACA RM H56G11, January 1957, 87H24594.

The lateral stability and control characteristics of the Convair YF-102 delta-wing airplane with cambered-reflexed wings are determined from side-slips, aileron rolls, rudder pulses, trim runs, and wind-up turns. Violent inertial coupling has been encountered on this airplane and a summary of the rolling and sideslip characteristics is presented. The relation of the reciprocal of the cycles to damp to one-half amplitude with phi/Ve (Military Specification) varies from unsatisfactory to marginally satisfactory. Comparison is shown between the pilot's rating of the rudder pulse

E-2889

NACA High Speed Flight Station Research Aircraft, circa 1957 (clockwise from lower left), Bell X-1A, Douglas D-558-I, Convair XF-92A, Bell X-5, Douglas D-558-II, Northrop X-4, and Douglas X-3 (center)

43

maneuvers and the military requirement. A directional divergence that was encountered at high lift coefficient (alpha = 20 degrees) is presented.

168. Larson, Terry J.; Stillwell, Wendell H.; and Armistead, Katharine H.: **Static Pressure Error Calibrations for Nose-Boom Airspeed Installation of 17 Airplanes.** NACA RM H57A02, March 1957, 87H26847.

Static-pressure error calibrations made for nose-boom airspeed installations of 17 airplanes are presented. The calibrations are given in the form of true Mach number against indicated Mach number, Mach number error, and static-pressure error per recorded impact pressure. Static-pressure errors are compared and are shown to be dependent on nose-boom length, fuselage diameter, and nose fineness ratio. Information is presented to provide a useful means for predicting the static-pressure errors for similar airspeed installation. Designation Airplane A, D-558-I; B, F-86A; C, F-86F; D, X-5; E, F-100A; F, XF-92A; G, YF-102; H, X-4; I, F-89; J, F-89; K, X-1; L, X-1; M, X-1A; N, D-558-II; O, D-558-II; P, X-3; and Q, B-47A.

E55-02094

F-100A Super Sabre Airplane

169. Matranga, Gene J.; and Peele, James R.: **Flight-Determined Static Lateral Stability and Control Characteristics of a Swept-Wing Fighter Airplane to a Mach Number of 1.39.** NACA RM H57A16, March 1957, 87H26848.

Flight tests were performed with a swept-wing fighter-type airplane at an altitude of 40,000 feet over a Mach number range from 0.72 to 1.39 to determine the lateral stability and control characteristics. Results are presented for three different vertical tails and two different wing areas, and include plots of lateral stability derivatives against Mach number.

170. Wolowicz, Chester H.: **Dynamic Longitudinal Stability Characteristics of a Swept-Wing Fighter Type Airplane at Mach Numbers Between 0.36 and 1.45.** NACA RM H56H03, April 1957, 87H24602.

Longitudinal pulse maneuvers were conducted on a swept-wing fighter-type airplane for an original-wing and an extended wing-tip configuration at altitudes from 10,000 to 40,000 feet over a Mach number range from 0.36 to 1.45. Variations of the period, damping and the derivatives C_{L_σ}, C_{m_σ}, and ($C_{m_q} + C_{m_\sigma}$) are presented as functions of Mach number. Comparisons are made with wind-tunnel data. Some consideration is given to pilot opinion in regard to the dynamic longitudinal behavior of the airplane during simulated combat maneuvers.

171. McGowan, William A.; and Cooney, T. V.: **An Analysis of Vertical-Tail Loads Measured in Flight on a Swept-Wing Bomber Airplane.** NACA RM L57B19, May 7, 1957, 93R18908.

An analysis is presented of vertical-tail loads measured on a swept-wing bomber airplane at altitudes to 35,000 feet and Mach numbers to 0.82. Flight data obtained from rudder-step, rudder-pulse, aileronroll, and steady-sideslip maneuvers were used in the analysis to determine lift-curve slopes, centers of pressure, and wing-fuselage, tail, and airplane static-directional-stability parameters. Results are compared, where possible, with values used in design and with theoretical values. Theoretical values of the lift-curve slopes were in agreement with flight values when fuselage flexibility was considered.

172. Saltzman, Edwin J.: **Flight-Determined Induction-System and Surge Characteristics of the YF-102 Airplane With a Two-Spool Turbojet Engine.** NACA RM H57C22, June 1957, 87H29841.

Total-pressure recovery and distortion at the compressor face have been recorded for a twin-side inlet, two-spool turbojet engine combination during turns, sideslips, and speed runs at altitudes between 33,000 and 50,000 feet. In addition, conditions prior to several compressor surges have been recorded. The Mach number range covered extends from about 0.6 to 1.1. The investigation showed that engine surge as experienced is not related to distortion at the compressor face. Mismatching existed for most flight conditions.

173. Jordan, Gareth H.; Keener, Earl R.; and Butchart, Stanley P.: **Airplane Motions and Loads Induced by Flying Through the Flow Field Generated by an Airplane at Low Supersonic Speeds.** NACA RM H57D17A, June 1957, 87H24646.

Data are presented for the maximum sideslip angles and vertical-tail loads induced on a swept wing fighter-type airplane as a result of flying through the flow field generated by a similar airplane at low supersonic Mach numbers. These data were obtained during side-by-side passes at various passing rates (5 fps to 50 fps) and interval separation distances. Significant airplane sideslip angles and vertical-tail loads were obtained during close-proximity passes at a passing rate near the natural period of the airplane in yaw.

174. Banner, Richard D.: **Flight Measurements of Airplane Structural Temperatures at Supersonic Speeds.** NACA RM H57D18B, <u>June 1957</u>, 93R19049.

Skin and structural temperature distributions were obtained during transient supersonic flights of the X-1B and X-1E airplanes at Mach numbers up to approximately 2.0. Extensive temperature measurements were obtained on the X-1B. No critical temperatures were experienced over the range of the test. The measured temperatures were compared with simplified calculations.

E-1927

X-1E Airplane

175. Malvestuto, Frank S.; Cooney, Thomas V.; and Keener, Earl R.: **Flight Measurements and Calculations of Wing Loads and Load Distributions at Subsonic, Transonic, and Supersonic Speeds.** NACA RM H57E01, <u>July 1957</u>, 87H24650.

Presented in this report is a summary of local and net angle-of-attack wing-panel loads measured in flight on six airplanes. In addition, a comparison of these loads measured in flight with calculations based on simple theory is presented.

176. Nugent, Jack: **Effect of Wing-Mounted External Stores on the Lift and Drag of the Douglas D-558-II Research Airplane at Transonic Speeds.** NACA RM H57E15A, <u>July 1957</u>, 87H24654, 93R19584.

Lift and drag measurements were made during a flight investigation with the Douglas D-558-II(145) airplane in the basic and 150-gallon DAC store configurations over a

Mach number range from 0.48 to 1.03. The addition of stores increased the drag at all Mach numbers tested. Below the drag rise the increase was of about the same magnitude as the increase in wetted area caused by the addition of the stores. The peak lift-drag ratio was reduced by about 14 percent, and for lift coefficients of 0.2 and 0.4 a reduction in drag-rise Mach number was noted. Little change in lift-curve slope was observed for Mach numbers less than about 0.8.

177. Saltzman, Edwin J.; and Asher, William P.: **Transonic Flight Evaluation of the Effects of Fuselage Extension and Indentation on the Drag of a 60 Degrees Delta-Wing Interceptor Airplane.** NACA RM H57E29, <u>September 1957</u>, 87H26849, 71N72659.

The flight lift and drag characteristics of a 60 degrees delta wing interceptor airplane incorporating fuselage extension and indentation were determined over the Mach number range from 0.7 to 1.15 and the altitude range from 25,000 to 50,000 feet. Comparison is made with a similar airplane which did not utilize fuselage extension or indentation. The results indicate that the modifications (extension and indentation) reduced the transonic drag coefficient about 50 drag counts (0.0050) at a Mach number of about 1.1. Three sets of comparable low Reynolds number data are included which indicate reductions in transonic drag coefficient ranging from about 0.0025 to 0.0045 at a Mach number of about 1.1.

178. Fischel, Jack; Darville, Robert W.; and Reisert, Donald: **Effects of Wing-Mounted External Stores on the Longitudinal and Lateral Handling Qualities of the Douglas D-558-II Research Airplane.** NACA RM H57H12, <u>October 1957</u>, 87H24664.

The subsonic and transonic handling qualities of the Douglas D-558-II research airplane were investigated with several configuration of midsemispan external stores in the altitude region between 20,000 and 40,000 feet. The configurations tested consisted of an underslung pylon on each wing, pylons plus simulated DAC (Douglas Aircraft Co.) 1,000-pound bombs, and pylons plus DAC 150-gallon-fuel tanks. Comparisons of the results obtained were made with comparable data from the clean airplane. The trends exhibited in the characteristics measured with each configuration were generally the same as for the clean airplane; however, significant changes in the magnitude of the parameters measured with the pylon-tank configuration were sometimes apparent, particularly at the higher speeds tested.

179. Baker, Thomas F.; Martin, James A.; and Scott, Betty J.: **Flight Data Pertinent to Buffeting and Maximum Normal-Force Coefficient of the Douglas X-3 Research Airplane.** NACA RM H57H09, <u>November 1957</u>, 87H26850.

The X-3 airplane, which has a straight, 4.5-percent-thick wing, was flown to maximum wing lift at Mach numbers from 0.7 to 1.1 at an average altitude of 30,000 feet. Airplane

E57-2952

NACA High Speed Flight Station Century Series Fighter Aircraft, circa 1957 (clockwise from left), Lockheed F-104, McDonnell F-101, Convair F-102, and North American F-100

and wing maximum normal-force coefficients and buffeting characteristics were determined. Wing maximum normal-force coefficients at low supersonic speeds were almost twice the values at subsonic speed (M nearly equal to 0.8). At transonic speeds the buffet boundary abruptly increased, rather than decreased, with Mach number. The buffeting encountered did not constitute either an operational or a structural problem. The effective longitudinal maneuverability limit was defined by maximum wing lift. Limited data at subsonic speeds on the effects on lift and buffeting of deflecting the wing leading edge flaps 7 degrees are included.

180. Drake, Hubert M.; and Kincheloe, Iven C.: **Flight Research at High Altitude.** SLN: 63423, November 8, 1957, 87H29332.

In the past ten years the Air Force, Navy, and the NACA, in the research airplane program have obtained considerable experience in flight research at high altitude. The present paper details some of this experience, discusses some of the problems encountered and being investigated, and a quick look into future is taken.

181. Fischel, Jack; Holleman, Euclid C.; and Tremant, Robert A.: **Flight Investigation of the Transonic Longitudinal and Lateral Handling Qualities of the Douglas X-3 Research Airplane.** NACA RM H57I05, December 1957, 87H26851.

A flight investigation was performed to determine the longitudinal and lateral handling qualities of the Douglas X-3 research airplane in the clean configuration and with wing leading-edge flaps deflected. Static and dynamic stability and control characteristics were determined during trimmed and maneuvering flight at an average altitude of 30,000 feet over a Mach number range from 0.7 to 1.16. Statically and dynamically determined stability and control derivatives are presented, as well as pilot evaluation of the airplane.

182. Saltzman, Edwin J.: **In-Flight Gains Realized by Modifying a Twin Side-Inlet Induction System.** NACA RM H57J09, December 1957, 87H24669.

The effects of modifying a twin side-inlet duct system have been recorded and analyzed over an altitude range from about 25,000 to 51,000 feet and throughout the transonic region to a Mach number of about 1.2. The modification consisted primarily of redesigning the inlet lip, increasing the cross-sectional area of the inlet and diffuser, and adding a region of duct contraction ahead of the engine. These changes greatly improved the pressure-recovery characteristics and provided a 50-percent reduction in compressor-face distortion (pressure-profile variation).

183. Drake, H. M.: **Flight Research at High Altitude, Part 1.** AGARD *Proceedings of the Seventh AGARD General Assembly,* 1957, pp. 74–75, (see N82-73409 12-01), 82N73414, #.

46

Aerodynamic problems associated with flight at high Mach numbers and/or low dynamic pressures include reduction or directional stability, poor dynamic stability, low control effectiveness, and aerodynamic heating, and instrumentation problems. These are briefly indicated. Some of the high-altitude investigations on the X-1B aircraft are discussed. Including preliminary studies on an analogue computer used as a simulation.

184. Williams, Walter C.; and Drake, Hubert M.: **The Research Airplane—Past, Present, and Future.** IAS Summer Meeting, June 18, 1957, Preprint 750, 1957, 87H29153.

This paper discusses briefly the problems that have been studied by the NACA during the past ten years using research airplanes.

185. Beeler, De Elroy: **Flight Loads Measurements on NACA Research Airplanes.** AGARD Report 109, Structures and Materials Panel, 1957, 87H29112.

Summarizes results from flight loads investigations conducted primarily for the purpose of confirming wind-tunnel results by comparing full-scale results with comparable wind-tunnel results. Data have been selected from three research aircraft having a wide range of configuration. (X-1, X-5, & XF-92A). Flight loads were determined by use of calibrated strain gauges. Pressure distribution measurements were also made of fuselage & wing of the X-1.

186. Cole, Henry Ambrose; Brown, Stuart C.; and Holleman, Euclid C.: **The Effects of Flexibility on the Longitudinal Dynamic Response of the B-47 Airplane.** Preprint IAS 678, 1957, 87H29016. (See also 121.)

The frequency response of the B-47 to elevator control is presented for ranges of frequencies including the airplane oscillatory short period mode, the wing first-bending mode. Comparisons are made between response measured in flight and those predicted by pseudostatic analysis and by dynamical analysis. In the application of pseudostatic analysis, the importance of mass distribution is emphasized. Selection of dynamic degrees of freedom and the apparent disappearance of modes under forced oscillation is discussed. The frequency response at various points on the airplane is measured and calculated to find optimum locations for automatic control pickups. The points of low response to structural vibrations determined in flight are compared with those predicted by dynamical analysis and those measured in ground vibration tests.

E-1044

B-47 Airplane

187. Banner, R. D.: **Flight Measurements of Airplane Structural Temperatures at Supersonic Speeds.** In NACA Conference on Aircraft Loads, Structures, and Flutter, 1957, (see N71-75382), 71N75404.

188. Jordan, Gareth H.; Keener, Earl R.; and Butchart, Stanley P.: **Airplane Motions and Loads Induced by Flying Through the Flow Field Generated by an Airplane at Low Supersonic Speeds.** NACA Conference on Aircraft Loads, Structures, and Flutter, 1957, (see N71-75382), 71N75394.

An exploratory flight investigation was conducted to determine the disturbances to an airplane while flying in formation with another airplane at low supersonic speeds. The most significant motions were encountered as a result of flying through the flow field of the lead airplane. Several of these supersonic passes were made using two sweptwing fighter-type airplanes in order to evaluate the gross effects of time to pass through the flow field, lateral distance, and altitude within a Mach number range from 1.2 to 1.3.

189. Malvestuto, Frank S.; Cooney, Thomas V.; and Keener, Earl R.: **Flight Measurements and Calculations of Wing Loads and Load Distribution at Subsonic, Transonic, and Supersonic Speeds.** NACA Conference on Aircraft Loads, Structures, and Flutter, 1957, (see N71-75382), 71N75385.

1958 Technical Publications

190. Holleman, Euclid C.; and Boslaugh, David L.: **A Simulator Investigation of Factors Affecting the Design and Utilization of a Stick Pusher for the Prevention of Airplane Pitch-Up.** NACA RM H57J30, January 1958, 87H26852.

Presented are the results of a simulator study of the factors affecting the design of a device, a stick pusher, for preventing a representative supersonic airplane from entering the pitch-up region. The effects of varying the stick-pusher-activation boundaries, sensing parameters, and magnitude of stick-pusher force on the controllability of the airplane pitch-up were investigated. The possible tactical importance of the loss in available supersonic maneuverability caused by angle-of-attack limiting in turns and zoom maneuvers is also discussed.

191.   Williams, Walter C.; and Drake, Hubert M.: **The Research Airplane—Past, Present, and Future.** *Aeronautical Engineering Review*, Vol. 36, January 1958.

192.   Marcy, William L.: **High-Speed Landing Loads Measured on the Douglas X-3 Research Airplane.** NACA RM H57L06, February 1958, 87H24675.

Measured loads are shown for several landings of the Douglas X-3 at speeds from about 310 to 420 feet per second. Sinking speeds were between 2 and 5 feet per second. Some loads during taxiing and turning are also shown.

193.   Matranga, Gene J.; and Armistead, Katharine H.: **Flight Evaluation of the Effects of Leading-Edge-Slat Span on the Stability and Control Characteristics of a Sweptwing Fighter-Type Airplane During Accelerated Longitudinal Maneuvers at Transonic Speeds.** NACA RM H58A03A, March 1958, 87H26853.

Accelerated longitudinal maneuvers were performed at transonic speeds with a swept-wing fighter-type airplane having several slat-span configurations. The effects of these slat-span configurations on the stability and control characteristics of the airplane are discussed and compared with existing wind-tunnel data.

194.   Drake, Hubert M.; Bellman, Donald R.; and Walker, Joseph A.: **Operational Problems of Manned Orbital Vehicles.** NACA Conference on High Speed Aerodynamics, March 18–20, 1958, pp. 89–102, (see N71-75285), 71N75292.

195.   Banner, R. D.; McTigue, J. G.; and Petty, G., Jr.: **Boundary-Layer Transition in Full-Scale Flight.** NACA Conference on High-Speed Aerodynamics, March 18–20, 1958, pp. 467–475, (see N71-75285), 71N75319.

Because of greatly increased need for knowledge of full-scale boundary-layer transition and the difficulty of simulating actual flight conditions, a program has been initiated to provide a better understanding of the boundary-layer flow as it exists in supersonic flight. This paper shows the results obtained in the early flight tests which determined the content of laminar flow that could be obtained with practical wing-surface conditions.

196.   Taillon, Norman V.: **An Analysis of Surface Pressures and Aerodynamic Load Distribution Over the Swept Wing of the Douglas D-558-II Research Airplane at Mach Numbers From 0.73 to 1.73.** NACA RM H58A30, April 1958, 87H26196, 87H24678.

The variation of the measured pressures and loads with lift is presented, covering the speed range at airplane normal-force coefficients from about 0 to 0.8. Spanwise load distributions are compared with theory at subsonic and supersonic Mach numbers. The wing is swept back 35 degrees, has a streamwise thickness ratio varying from 8.7 percent at the root to 10.4 percent at the tip, an aspect ratio of 3.57, and 3 degrees incidence.

197.   Kuhl, A. E.; Little, M. V.; and Rogers, J. T.: **Analysis of Flight-Determined and Predicted Effects of Flexibility on the Steady-State Wing Loads of the B-52 Airplane.** NACA RM H57C25, April 23, 1958, 87H26193, 87H24615, 66N39617, #.

An analysis is made of the steady-state wing loads measured during a flight investigation conducted on the Boeing B-52 airplane. The investigation covers the speed range of the airplane up to a Mach number of 0.90. The measured loads are analyzed in terms of the effects of Mach number, lift, and dynamic pressure. In addition, the measured loads are compared with predicted loads and the effects of varying some of the structural and aerodynamic properties in the predictions are presented.

198.   McLeod, Norman J.; and Jordan, Gareth H.: **Preliminary Flight Survey of Fuselage and Boundary-Layer Sound-Pressure Levels.** NACA RM H58B11, May 1958, 87H26854, 87H26199.

Presented are the results of a preliminary flight investigation of noise inside fuselages and in the fuselage boundary layer. The overall noise and frequency spectrum are presented for the B-47A at subsonic speeds. Measurements were made internally at three longitudinal locations and in the fuselage boundary layer at one location. The overall noise level is presented for one internal location of the D-558-II at subsonic and low supersonic speeds. The relative importance of engine noise and aerodynamic noise due to the boundary layer at various airspeeds and engine operating conditions is discussed for the locations at which measurements were made.

199.   Johnson, Clinton T.: **Flight Investigation of the Aerodynamic Forces on a Wing-Mounted External-Store Installation on the Douglas D-558-II Research Airplane.** NACA RM H58B24, May 1958, 87H26203, 87H24680.

Aerodynamic forces have been measured on an external-store arrangement on the Douglas D-558-II research airplane. Aerodynamic loads on the store-pylon combination and the pylon alone were determined from angle-of-attack and angle-of-sideslip maneuvers over the Mach number range from 0.50 to 1.03. Wing-panel aerodynamic loads have also been determined for the store configuration and the clean-wing configuration. A brief discussion is presented for the measured loads on the fins of the external store.

200. Larson, Terry J.; Thomas, George M.; and Bellman, Donald R.: **Induction System Characteristics and Engine Surge Occurrence for Two Fighter-Type Airplanes.** NACA RM H58C14, <u>May 1958</u>, 87H26206, 87H24681, 71N70251.

Total-pressure recovery and distortion at the compressor face are presented as variations of angle of attack and mass-flow ratio for two fighter-type airplanes with similar two-spool turbojet engines, but with dissimilar inlets. One airplane has a normal-shock nose inlet, and the other has two engines and triangular-shaped inlets located in the wing roots. In addition, data are presented for engine surge occurrences of these two airplanes and also for a third single-engine airplane having two semicircular-shaped side inlets.

201. Pembo, Chris; and Matranga, Gene J.: **Control Deflections, Airplane Response, and Tail Loads Measured on an F-100A Airplane in Service Operational Flying.** NACA RM H58C26, <u>June 1958</u>, 87H26211, 87H24682.

Results are presented from 20 hours of service operational flying of an instrumented North American F-100A fighter airplane. Air Force pilots at Nellis Air Force Base, Nev., performed air-to-air gunnery, simulated air-to-ground attacks, air-combat maneuvering, acrobatics, and transition-type flights to altitudes slightly in excess of 50,000 feet and at Mach numbers up to 1.22. Measurements of pilot control deflections, throttle movement, airplane motions, and tail loads are presented primarily as envelope curves of maximum recorded values. An overall comparison of these results with results from earlier investigations with other airplanes is made. A limited analysis of the factors affecting horizontal- and vertical-tail loads is included.

202. Drake, Hubert M.; Bellman, Donald R.; and Walker, Joseph A.: **Operational Problems of Manned Orbital Vehicles.** NACA RM H58D21, <u>July 1958</u>, 87H26216, 87H24686.

Some of the operational problems of escape, piloting, orbit selection, flight termination, and range requirements are considered, including the effects of configuration. It is indicated that configuration materially affects operations, that survival considerations may preclude optimum procedures, and that use of the pilot can considerably simplify design and increase reliability.

203. Holleman, Euclid C.; and Stillwell, Wendell H.: **Simulator Investigation of Command Reaction Controls.** NACA RM H58D22, <u>July 1958</u>, 87H26855, 87H26220.

Reaction controls that command velocity and attitude have been investigated and are compared to controls that command acceleration. Velocity and attitude command systems facilitated the task of orientation and stabilization and minimized the effects of dynamic pressure. The simulation of an entry maneuver by dynamic-pressure buildup showed that successful entry could be made with any of the three systems, but the task was easier with the velocity or the attitude system.

204. Holleman, E. C.; and Stillwell, W. H.: **Simulator Investigation of Command Reaction Controls.** In NACA Conference on High-Speed Aerodynamics, <u>1958</u>, pp. 157–165, (see N71-75285), 71N75297. (See also 203.)

205. Keener, Earl R.; McLeod, Norman J.; and Taillon, Norman V.: **Effect of Leading-Edge-Flap Deflection on the Wing Loads, Load Distributions, and Flap Hinge Moments of the Douglas X-3 Research Airplane at Transonic Speeds.** NACA RM H58D29, <u>July 1958</u>, 87H26221, 87H24690.

Data were obtained in flight by differential-pressure measurements between the upper and lower surfaces of the wing, covering the range from near-zero lift to maximum lift over the Mach number range of 0.5 to 1.15 with flap undeflected and 0.5 to 0.9 with flap deflected. The unswept wing has an aspect ratio of 3.09, a taper ratio of 0.39, and a modified 4.5-percent-thick hexagonal section. The plain, constant-chord leading-edge flap extends from the wing root to the wing tip. Reynolds number based on the mean aerodynamic chord of the wing varied between 16×10^6 and 26×10^6. A brief comparison with wind-tunnel results is included.

206. Banner, Richard D.; McTigue, John G.; and Petty, Gilbert: **Boundary-Layer-Transition Measurements in Full-Scale Flight.** NACA RM H58E28, <u>July 1958</u>, 78N78570, 87H26856, 87H26226. (See NASA TM-79863).

Chemical sublimation employed for boundary-layer flow visualization on the wings of a supersonic fighter airplane in level flight near a Mach number of 2.0 has shown that laminar flow can be obtained over extensive areas with practical wing surface conditions. Heated temperature resistance gages installed in a Fiberglas "glove" installation on one wing continuously monitored the conditions of the boundary layer. Tests were conducted at speeds from a Mach number of 1.2 to a Mach number of 2.0, at altitudes from 35,000 feet to 56,000 feet. Data obtained at all angles of attack, from near 0 degrees to near 10 degrees have shown that the maximum transition Reynolds number on the upper surface of the wing varies from about 2.5×10^6 at a Mach number of 1.2 to about 4×10^6 at a Mach number of 2.0. On the lower surface, the maximum transition Reynolds number varies from about 2×10^6 at a Mach number of 1.2 to about 8×10^6 at a Mach number of 2.0.

207. Fischel, Jack; Cooney, Thomas V.; and Bellman, Donald R.: **Flight-Testing Techniques of Manned Hypersonic and Satellite Vehicles.** IAS, Los Angeles, California, July 10–11, 1958, 87H29821.

The desire of man to fly at ever increasing speeds and altitudes has resulted in a constantly accelerating performance growth. The technology has advanced at such a rate that future flight vehicles are planned not for small incremental performance increases as in the past, but rather, in multiples of present performance. With these increases in performance it is the problem of the flight test engineer to assure that his methodology is compatible with the vehicle. It is well, then, to take the case of a boost-glide vehicle capable of speed up to that required for orbital flight, examine its characteristics and problems, and outline the approach to the flight test of such a vehicle.

208. *Finch, Thomas W.; *Matranga, Gene J.; *Walker, Joseph A.; and *Armstrong, Neil A.: **Flight and Analog Studies of Landing Techniques.** This paper is from the Research-Airplane-Committee Report on Conference on the Progress of the X-15 Project held at the IAS Building, Los Angeles, California on July 28–30, 1958, NACA-CONF-30-Jul-58, July 30, 1958, pp. 83–93, 93R21698. Declassified per NASA ccn 14, 29 Nov. 1966.

The approach and landing operation of unpowered rocket airplanes has always required considerable pilot concentration but has been completed without undue demands on piloting technique. The X-15 airplane will land in a range of lift-drag ratio l/d markedly lower than previous rocket airplanes have used. This paper presents the results of a flight and analog study of landing to assess the potential difficulty of landing the X-15 at low l/d and to determine whether different techniques would be required in the landing maneuver.

*NACA High Speed Flight Station, Edwards, California.

209. *Rowen, Burt.: **Aeromedical Support of the X-15 Program.** Research-Airplane-Committee Report from Conference on the Progress of the X-15 project held at the IAS building, Los Angeles, California on July 28–30, 1958, NACA-CONF-30-Jul-58, July 30, 1958, pp. 129–146, 93R21680. Declassified per NASA ccn 14, 29 Nov. 1966.

Report describes the human factors or aeromedical support program for the X-15. The overall objective is to obtain quantitative physiological data and to make the pilot's actual flight task a realistic continuation of previous experience and training. During the flight phase of the X-15 aircraft, physiological data will be telemetered so that a flight surgeon observing the ground read-out can tell when the pilot is approaching the limit of his physiological tolerance.

*Air Force Flight Test Center, Edwards AFB, California.

210. Truszynski, G. M.; and Mace, W. D.: **Status of High-Range and Flow-Direction Sensor.** Research-Airplane-Committee Report from Conference on the Progress of the X-15 project held at the IAS building, Los Angeles, California on July 28–30, 1958, NACA-CONF-30-Jul-58, July 30, 1958, pp. 151–158, 93R21682. Declassified per NASA ccn 14, 29 Nov. 1966.

This paper describes the two systems used to provide certain research measurements for the X-15 aircraft. These systems are: (1) a probe and associated system that will be capable of operating throughout the extreme temperature environment encountered on reentry to provide a measure of the angle of attack and sideslip to the pilot, and (2) an instrumented ground range capable of monitoring the flight of the airplane throughout its entire trajectory.

211. *Beeler, De E.: **X-15 Research Objectives.** Research-Airplane-Committee Report from Conference on the Progress of the X-15 project held at the IAS building, Los Angeles, California on July 28–30, 1958, NACA-CONF-30-Jul-58, July 30, 1958, pp. 327–338, 93R21697. Declassified per NASA ccn 14, 29 Nov. 1966.

Paper presents the areas of research interest for the most important and urgent problems at the present time. Indications are given of other types of data that will be obtained, as well as possible additional research uses of the X-15. In the course of conducting the flight research for the X-15, the emphasis will change from one area to another and problems of new and different significance will result. Those problems that are found to be real will be better understood as a result of the flight investigations and those problems that have been imagined will be replaced with unexpected or overlooked problems.

*NACA High Speed Flight Station, Edwards, California.

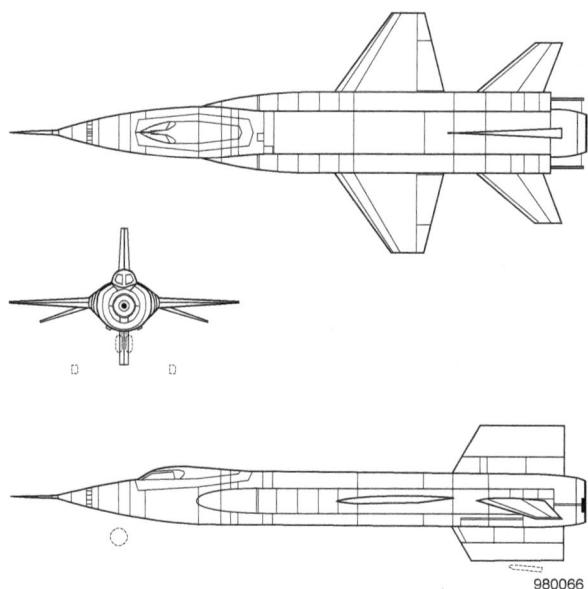

980066

X-15 Airplane, Three-View Drawing

212. Wolowicz, Chester H.; and Rediess, Herman A.: **Effects of Jet Exhaust on Flight-Determined Longitudinal and Lateral Dynamic Stability Characteristics of the Douglas D-558-II Research Airplane.** NACA RM H57G09, <u>August 1958</u>, 87H24659.

A flight investigation over a Mach number range from 0.67 to 1.61 was made to determine the longitudinal and lateral stability characteristics of the D-558-II airplane with particular reference to the jet exhaust effects of the rocket engine. Longitudinal stability was not affected because of the high horizontal tail. The rudder-fixed lateral stability was adversely affected in the supersonic region. Rudder-free lateral stability during power-on supersonic yawed flight was better than for rudder-fixed conditions.

213. Cooney, Thomas V.: **The Service Pilot as a Test Pilot.** *SETP Quarterly Review,* <u>Summer 1958</u>.

214. Stillwell, Wendell H.; and Drake, Hubert M.: **Simulator Studies of Jet Reaction Controls for Use at High Altitude.** NACA RM H58G18A, <u>September 1958</u>, 87H26229, 87H24697, 93R19525.

An investigation has been made of the use of pilot-controlled jet reaction forces for vehicle attitude control in regions of extremely low dynamic pressure. The effects of various control configurations, control magnitudes, control techniques, dynamic pressure, and aerodynamic stability were investigated. The results of analog computer studies and mechanical simulator tests indicate that control techniques are somewhat different from those used with aerodynamic controls at normal flight speeds and that constant attention to the control task is required. Because of the ease of overcontrolling with large control powers, much lower control power than that required for aerodynamic controls was preferred. Moderate values of effective dihedral produced a noticeable increase in the amount of roll control required to maintain trim at dynamic pressures up to 20 pounds per square foot.

E-2578

Iron Cross Reaction Controls Simulator

215. Wolowicz, Chester H.; and Holleman, Euclid C.: **Stability-Derivative Determination From Flight Data.** Presented to AGARD Flight Test Panel, Copenhagen, Denmark, <u>October 20–25, 1958</u>, Report 224 OTP-1958, October 1958, 87H29966, 87H29964.

A comprehensive discussion of the various factors affecting the determination of stability and control derivatives from flight data is presented based on the experience of the NASA High-Speed Flight Station. Factors relating to test techniques, determination of mass characteristics, instrumentation, and methods of analysis are discussed.

216. Fischel, Jack; Butchart, Stanley P.; Robinson, Glenn H.; and Tremant, Robert A.: **Flight Studies of Problems Pertinent to Low-Speed Operation of Jet Transports.** NASA Conference on Some Problems Related to Aircraft Operations, <u>November 5–6, 1958</u>.

217. Cooney, Thomas V.: **Motions and Vertical-Tail Loads Experienced by Jet Transport Aircraft in Rough Air.** NASA Conference on Some Problems Related to Aircraft Operations, <u>November 5–6, 1958</u>.

218. Jordan, Gareth H.; and McLeod, Norman J.: **Boundary-Layer Noise at Subsonic and Supersonic Speeds.** NASA Conference on Some Problems Related to Aircraft Operations, <u>November 5–6, 1958</u>, 87H29996.

Presents results of flight surveys of boundary-layer and engine noise levels in an attempt to establish the contribution and relative importance of boundary-layer and engine noise on the noise environment of aircraft in flight. The two airplanes used were the B-47A and the Douglas 558-2.

219. Armstrong, Neil A.: **Future Range and Flight Test Area Needs for Hypersonic and Orbital Vehicles.** Society of Experimental Test Pilots, Vol. 3 No. 2, (see F70-0705), <u>Winter 1959</u>.

This paper points out some of the desirable and mandatory area and control requirements for the flight testing of such vehicles up to and including those of orbital velocity with indications of the needs of operational military and air carrier organizations.

1959 Technical Publications

220. Nugent, Jack: **Lift and Drag of a Swept-Wing Fighter Airplane at Transonic and Supersonic Speeds.** NASA Memo 10-1-58H, <u>January 1959</u>, 87H25781.

Lift and drag measurements were made during a flight investigation of a swept-wing fighter airplane in the basic configuration and in a slats-locked-closed configuration over a Mach number range from about 0.63 to about 1.44. Negligible drag-coefficient difference existed between the basic configuration and the slats-locked-closed configuration over a comparable test range. For the basic configuration at zero lift the supersonic drag-coefficient level was about three times as great as the subsonic drag-coefficient level, which was about 0.01.

221. Matranga, Gene J.: **Roll Utilization of an F-100A Airplane During Service Operational Flying.** NASA Memo 12-1-58H, <u>January 1959</u>, 87H25787.

An instrumented North American F-100A fighter airplane was flown by Air Force pilots at Nellis Air Force Base, Nev., during 20 hours of service operational flying which included air-to-air gunnery, air-to-ground gunnery and bombing, aircraft combat maneuvering, and acrobatic-type maneuvers. During this investigation altitudes up to 50,000 feet and Mach numbers up to 1.22 were realized. In this paper the roll utilization for the various maneuvers performed and the roll utilization at supersonic speeds are analyzed.

222. Walker, Joseph A.: **Outline of the X-15 Project.** Presented at the IAS Meeting, San Francisco, California, <u>January 15, 1959</u>.

This paper presents a brief discussion of the following phases of this project: history, cost, research objectives, protection and escape of the pilot, description of the aircraft, industry participation, flight-test range, role of the pilots, and flight testing.

223. Williams, Walter C.: **X-15 Airplane as a Research Tool.** Presented at the IAS 20th Annual Meeting, New York, <u>January 26–29, 1959</u>, IAS Report, pp. 59–79.

224. Messing, Wesley E.: **Residual Fuel Expulsion From a Simulated 50,000-Pound-Thrust Liquid-Propellant Rocket Engine Having a Continuous Rocket-Type Igniter.** NASA Memo 2-1-59H, <u>February 1959</u>, 87H25790.

Tests were conducted to determine the starting characteristics of a simulated 50,000-pound-thrust rocket engine with a quantity of fuel lying dormant in the main thrust chamber. Ignition was alcohol-water and anhydrous ammonia was used as the residual fuel. The igniter successfully expelled the maximum amount of residual fuel (3 1/2 gal) in 2.9 seconds when the igniter was equipped with a sonic discharge nozzle. When the igniter was equipped with a supersonic exhaust nozzle, a slightly less effective expulsion rate was encountered.

225. Weil, Joseph: **Summary of Planned X-15 Entry Research.** NASA Conference on Review of NASA Research Related to Control Guidance and Navigation of Space Vehicles, NASA Ames Research Center, <u>February 25–27, 1959</u>.

226. Drake, Hubert M.: **Energy Management Requirements of Entry Vehicles.** NASA Conference on Review of NASA Research Related to Control Guidance and Navigation of Space Vehicles, NASA Ames Research Center, <u>February 25–27, 1959</u>.

227. Finch, Thomas W.: **Flight and Analog Studies of Approach and Landing Characteristics of Low L/D Configurations.** NASA Conference on Review of NASA Research Related to Control Guidance and Navigation of Space Vehicles, NASA Ames Research Center, <u>February 25–27, 1959</u>.

228. Fischel, Jack: **Use of Air-Launched Techniques in Space Research.** NASA Conference on Review of NASA Research Related to Control Guidance and Navigation of Space Vehicles, NASA Ames Research Center, <u>February 25–27, 1959</u>.

229. Holleman, Euclid C.: **Utilization of Pilot During the Boost Stage of Multistaged Vehicles.** NASA Conference on Review of NASA Research Related to Control Guidance and Navigation of Space Vehicles, NASA Ames Research Center, <u>February 25–27, 1959</u>.

230. Boslaugh, David L.: **Investigation of Precise Attitude Control—Simulator Program.** NASA Conference on Review of NASA Research Related to Control Guidance and Navigation of Space Vehicles, NASA Ames Research Center, <u>February 25–27, 1959</u>.

231. Funk, Jack; and Cooney, T. V.: **Some Effects of Yaw Damping on Airplane Motions and Vertical-Tail Loads in Turbulent Air.** NASA Memo 2-17-59L, <u>March 1959</u>.

Results of analytical and flight studies are presented to indicate the effect of yaw damping on the airplane motions and vertical-tail loads in rough air. The analytical studies indicate a rapid reduction in the airplane motions and the loads on the vertical tail as the damping is increased up to the point of damping the lateral motions to 1/2 amplitude in one cycle. Flight measurements indicate that a yaw damper reduces the loads on the vertical tail due to turbulent air and that the pilot could provide a significant amount of lateral damping.

232. McKay, J. B.: **Problems Associated with High-Speed Flight.** NASA TM X-56245. Presented at the Air Force Academy Instructors Workshop, Moore AFB, Mission, Texas, <u>18 March 1959</u>, 1959, 65N83273.

233. Armstrong, Neil A.: **Test Pilot's View on Space Ventures.** American Society of Mechanical Engineers Meeting in Los Angeles, California, <u>March 11, 1959</u>.

234. Andrews, William H.; and Rediess, Herman A.: **Flight-Determined Stability and Control Derivatives of a Supersonic Airplane With a Low-Aspect-Ratio Unswept Wing and a Tee-Tail.** NASA Memo 2-2-59H, April 1959, 87H25794.

The longitudinal and lateral directional stability and control derivatives have been determined in the trim angle-of-attack range between Mach numbers of 0.88 and 2.08. The static and dynamic lateral directional derivatives were determined by the time-vector method, modified by using yawing velocity as a reference instead of sideslip angle. Generally, the flight data compared favorably with existing published and unpublished wind-tunnel data.

235. Fischel, Jack; Butchart, Stanley P.; Robinson, Glenn H.; and Tremant, Robert A.: **Flight Studies of Problems Pertinent to Low-Speed Operation of Jet Transports.** NASA Memo 3-1-59H, April 1959, 87H25799.

The specific areas investigated include those of the take-off and landing, and relation of these maneuvers to the 1 g stall speed and stalling characteristics. The take-off studies included evaluation of the factors affecting the take-off speed and attitude, including the effects of premature rotation and of overrotation on ground run required. The approach and landing studies pertained to such factors as: desirable lateral-directional damping characteristics; lateral-control requirements; space-positioning limitations during approach under VFR or IFR conditions and requirements for glide-path controls; and evaluation of factors affecting the pilot's choice of landing speeds. Specific recommendations and some indication of desirable characteristics for the jet transports are advanced to alleviate possible operational difficulties or to improve operational performance in the low-speed range.

236. Butchart, Stanley P.; Fischel, Jack; Tremant, Robert A.; and Robinson, Glenn H.: **Flight Studies of Problems Pertinent to High-Speed Operation of Jet Transports.** NASA Memo 3-2-59H, April 1959, 87H25803.

Some of the specific areas investigated include: (1) an overall evaluation of longitudinal stability and control characteristics at transonic speeds, with an assessment of pitch-up characteristics, (2) the effect of buffeting on airplane operational speeds and maneuvering, (3) the desirable lateral-directional damping characteristics, (4) the desirable lateral-control characteristics, (5) an assessment of overspeed and speed-spread requirements, including the upset maneuver, and (6) an assessment of techniques and airplane characteristics for rapid descent and slow-down. The results presented include pilot's evaluation of the various problem areas and specific recommendations for possible improvement of jet-transport operations in the cruising speed range.

237. Bellman, Donald R.: **A Summary of Flight-Determined Transonic Lift and Drag Characteristics of Several Research Airplane Configurations.** NASA Memo 3-3-59H, April 1959, 87H25804.

Flight-determined lift and drag data from transonic flights of seven research airplane configurations of widely varying characteristics are presented and compared with wind-tunnel and rocket-model data. The effects of some of the basic configuration differences on the lift and drag characteristics are demonstrated.

238. Williams, Walter C.: **Pilot Considerations in the X-15 Research Airplane Program.** Presented at the Annual Meeting of the American Psychiatric Association, Philadelphia, Pennsylvania, April 29, 1959.

This report briefly discusses the aircraft, the pilots working space and environment, the pilots selected for flights, simulator programs, and the monitoring of the pilot's physical condition during flight.

239. Taillon, Norman V.: **Flow Characteristics About Two Thin Wings of Low Aspect Ratio Determined From Surface Pressure Measurements Obtained in Flight at Mach Numbers from 0.73 to 1.90.** NASA Memo 5-1-59H, May 1959, 87H25805.

The effects of Mach number and angle of attack on the flow about the X-3 wing (4.5-percent thickness ratio, aspect ratio 3.09) and the X-1E wing (4-percent thickness ratio, aspect ratio 4.0) as determined from surface pressure measurements are presented. The effect of the flow behavior on the section normal-force and moment coefficients of the two wings is also discussed. The detailed survey of pressures from which the data were selected is available in tabular form from the National Aeronautics and Space Administration.

240. Martin, James A.: **Determination of Local Skin Friction by Means of Surface Total-Pressure Probes.** OTP-1959, May 1959, 87H30092.

Work by J. F. Naleid has further extended the method of Preston to the case of compressible flow with adverse pressure gradient and zero heat transfer. Tests were performed at M = 2.

241. Finch, Thomas W.: **Results of the First X-15 Flight.** Presented at the IAS Summer Meeting, Los Angeles, California, June 17, 1959.

242. McTigue, J. G.; Overton, J. D.; and Petty, G., Jr.: **Two Techniques for Detecting Boundary-Layer Transition in Flight at Supersonic Speeds and at Altitudes**

Above 20,000 Feet. NASA TN D-18, <u>August 1959</u>, 78N78571, 87H26761.

The location of transition was measured on a supersonic fighter-type airplane by resistance-thermometer and sublimation techniques. Application of these techniques required the use of only the external surface without disturbing the internal structure. Agreement between the two methods as achieved throughout this program is discussed. Also presented are possible extensions of the program to higher Mach numbers.

243. Matranga, Gene J.; and Armstrong, Neil A.: **Approach and Landing Investigation at Lift-Drag Ratios of 2 to 4 Utilizing a Straight-Wing Fighter Airplane.** NASA TM X-31, <u>August 1959</u>, 87H25161, 62N71855.

A series of landings were performed with a straight-wing fighter airplane to evaluate the effect of low lift-drag ratios on landing. Landings with peak lift-drag ratios as low as 3 were achieved by altering the airplane configuration (extending speed brakes, flaps, and gear and reducing throttle setting).

244. McKay, James M.: **Measurements of Ground-Reaction Forces and Vertical Acceleration at the Center of Gravity of a Transport Airplane Taxiing Over Obstacles.** NASA TN D-22, <u>September 1959</u>, 89N70669, 87H26775.

Results are presented of the effects of ground speed and obstacle width on the vertical and rearward drag ground-reaction forces, the vertical acceleration at the center of gravity of the airplane, the shock-strut displacement, and the dynamic response of the upper mass of the airplane structure. The obstacles were 3.0 inches in height and 1 and 4 feet in width, and the investigation covered a range of ground speeds from 12 to 86 knots.

245. Saltzman, Edwin J.: **Flight Investigation of the Effect of Distributed Roughness of Skin Drag of a Full-Scale Airplane.** NASA TM X-36, <u>September 1959</u>, 87H25176.

The change in drag caused by the addition of two sizes of distributed sand-type roughness to the wings and tail surfaces of a delta-wing airplane has been measured at Mach numbers near 0.8 and 1.1. The largest roughness, 0.006-inch mean effective diameter, caused an increase in drag comparable to the increase predicted by the low-speed drag law for a rough plate. The increase in drag caused by the addition of the smallest roughness, 0.002-inch mean effective diameter, was less than half that predicted by the low-speed drag law for a rough plate.

246. Day, Richard E.; and Reisert, Donald: **Flight Behavior of the X-2 Research Airplane to a Mach Number of 3.20 and a Geometric Altitude of 126,200 Feet.** NASA TM X-137, <u>September 1959</u>, 87H25418.

Flight-test data obtained with the X-2 research airplane are presented for the maximum performance flights. An analysis is made of the instability leading to the loss of the airplane.

247. Finch, Thomas W.; and Matranga, Gene J.: **Launch, Low-Speed, and Landing Characteristics Determined from the First Flight of the North American X-15 Research Airplane.** NASA TM X-195, <u>September 1959</u>, 62N72019, 87H25292.

The primary areas of emphasis in the results of the first flight of the X-15 research airplane are the launch and landing characteristics. The launch characteristics were satisfactory and, in general, were qualitatively predicted by wind-tunnel studies. The landing characteristics were predicted qualitatively by analog and flight program, and the recommended technique of extending the flaps and gear at a minimum altitude appears to be a satisfactory method of landing the X-15 airplane.

248. Marcy, W. L.: **Flight Investigation of Loads on a Tee-Tail at Transonic and Supersonic Speeds.** NASA TM X-57, <u>September 1959</u>, 71N73446, 87H25224

Horizontal- and vertical-tail loads were measured on a supersonic fighter airplane. Lift-curve slopes, spanwise centers of load, and interference effects are shown for Mach numbers from 0.81 to 2.06 at altitudes from 20,000 to 55,000 feet. Flight results agreed well with wind-tunnel data and theoretical calculations. It was concluded that calculations of a preliminary-design type are adequate for the prediction of loads on tee-tails at small angles of attack and sideslip up to a Mach number of 2.

249. Jordan, Gareth H.: **Some Aspects of Shock-Wave Generation by Supersonic Airplanes.** AGARD Report 251, Flight Test Panel of AGARD, Aachen, Germany, <u>September 21–25, 1959</u>.

250. Keener, Earl R.: **Pressure Measurements Obtained in Flight at Transonic Speeds for a Conically Cambered Delta Wing.** NASA TM X-48, <u>October 1959</u>, 87H25203, 65N12688.

Pressures were obtained over the wing of the Convair JF-102A airplane at Mach numbers up to 1.19. The wing has aspect and taper ratios of 2.08 and 0.023, respectively, and incorporates two fences, a reflexed tip, and an elevon-control surface. Wing Reynolds number varied between 23 X 10 sup 6 and 58 X 10 sup 6. The results are analyzed with regard to the effects of camber on the distribution of leading-edge pressures, on the span-load distribution, and on the flow-separation characteristics. Tabulated data are available upon request from the National Aeronautics and Space Administration.

E-2551

JF-102A Airplane

251. Nugent, Jack: **Interaction of Nonsteady Twin-Inlet Flow and Airplane Directional Motions at a Mach Number of Approximately 1.9.** NASA TM X-54, <u>October 1959</u>, 87H25217, 71N73436.

Flight tests of a twin-duct propulsion system performed at a Mach number of about 1.9 have indicated a direct interaction between an asymmetric shock configuration at the inlets and airplane directional motion. The asymmetric shock configuration was produced at reduced mass flows and was aggravated by sideslip angle. Installation of a duct splitter plate at the engine face alleviated, but did not eliminate, the interaction phenomenon.

252. Matranga, Gene J.; and Menard, Joseph A.: **Approach and Landing Investigation at Lift-Drag Ratios of 3 to 4 Utilizing a Delta-Wing Interceptor Airplane.** NASA TM X-125, <u>October 1959</u>, 87H25396.

A series of landings was performed with a delta-wing interceptor airplane, having an average test wing loading of 35 pounds per square foot, to evaluate the effect of landing at low lift-drag ratios. Landings with peak effective lift-drag ratios as low as 3.75 were achieved by altering the airplane configuration. The reduction in lift-drag ratio resulted in an increase in the pertinent flare parameters. The pilot also flew several calculated landing patterns which he reported were easy and comfortable to fly.

253. McKay, James M.: **Measurements Obtained During the First Landing of the X-15 Research Airplane.** NASA TM X-207, <u>October 1959</u>, 87H25342, 62N72031.

One purpose of the first glide first of the X-15 research airplane was to evaluate the effectiveness of the landing-gear system. Some results are presented of the landing-approach characteristics, the impact period, and the runout phase of the landing maneuver.

254. Walker, Joseph A.: **Some Concepts of Pilot's Presentation.** Presented at the SETP Symposium, <u>October 8–10, 1959</u>, OTP-1959, CC-H-149, 1959, 87H30656.

Contents include a discussion of the pilot's instrument presentation and control system. The X-15 is used as an example.

255. Finch, Thomas W.: **X-15 Flight Test Program and Significant Flight Results.** Scientific Advisory Board Panel on Aerospace Sciences, <u>October 23, 1959</u>.

256. Day, Richard E.: **Training Considerations During the X-15 Development.** Presented to the National Security Industrial Association Training Advisory Committee Meeting, Los Angeles, California, <u>November 17, 1959</u>, NASA CC-H-157 OTP-1959, 1959.

This paper reviews briefly some of the early uses of pilot training aids in research investigations. A pertinent flight trajectory of the X-15 research airplane is summarized and the various training aids that have been, and are being, used in preparing the pilot for flying this trajectory are indicated.

257. Campbell, George S.; and Weil, Joseph: **The Interpretation of Nonlinear Pitching Moments in Relation to the Pitch-Up Problem.** NASA TN D-193, <u>December 1959</u>, 89N70901, 87H26510.

Equations are presented for calculating the dynamic behavior of airplanes having arbitrarily nonlinear aerodynamic characteristics. Application of the methods derived is directed toward a study of some of the factors affecting the severity of pitch-up motions encountered by airplanes having regions of reduced stability: pitching-moment shape, control movement, dynamic pressure, airplane moment of inertia, and aerodynamic damping. Brief consideration is also given to the effectiveness of automatic stabilization devices in reducing pitch-up severity.

258. Love, James E.; and Stillwell, Wendell H.: **The Hydrogen-Peroxide Rocket Reaction-Control System for the X-1B Research Airplane.** NASA TN D-185, <u>December 1959</u>, 89N70595, 87H26473.

A fixed-thrust on-off H_2O_2-rocket reaction-control system was installed in the X-1B research airplane as a means of control at high altitude. The design considerations, fabrication, installation, and ground testing of this system are described. The operational characteristics and some problems associated with system operations are discussed.

259. Beeler, De Elroy: **The Supersonic Transport. A Technical Summary.** OTP-1959, <u>1959</u>.

Contents: State of the art - performance. Some noise problems of the supersonic transport. Structures and materials problems associated with supersonic transports. Structural loads on supersonic transports. Flying qualities of supersonic transports. Runway and braking requirements. Airway traffic control and operations. Variable geometry for transports. Effect of variable sweep on structural weight. Possible performance improvements. Proposed ground-simulation studies and flight investigation pertinent to the supersonic transport.

260. Walker, Joseph A.: **Piloting Research Aircraft.** OTP-1959, <u>1959</u>, 87H29770.

This paper cites some examples of control problems gained from the experience of the author in flying advanced research and production aircraft at the NACA High-Speed Flight Station.

1960 Technical Publications

261. Anon.: **Aerodynamic and Landing Measurements Obtained During the First Powered Flight of the North American X-15 Research Airplane.** NASA TM X-269, <u>January 1960</u>, 62N72093.

The first powered flight of the North American X-15 research airplane was performed on September 17, 1959. A Mach number of 2.1 and an altitude of 52,000 feet were attained. Static and dynamic maneuvers were performed to evaluate the characteristics of the airplane as subsonic and supersonic speeds. Data from these maneuvers as well as from the launch and landing phases are presented, discussed, and compared with predicted values.

262. Larson, Terry J.; and Washington, Harold P.: **Summary of Rawinsonde Measurements of Temperatures, Pressure Heights, and Winds Above 50,000 Feet Along a Flight-Test Range in the Southwestern United States.** NASA TN D-192, <u>January 1960</u>, 89N70968, 87H26504

Yearly, seasonal, diurnal, and 24-hour variations of temperatures, pressure heights, and winds in the 100-millibar to 2-millibar pressure range from rawinsonde data of four stations along a flight-test range in the southwestern United States are presented. This range, referred to as High Range, extends from Edwards, Calif., to Wendover, Utah, to accommodate flight operations of the X-15 and other high-performance craft. Comparisons of average temperatures and pressure heights are made with those of the U.S. Extension to the ICAO Standard Atmosphere.

263. Reed, Robert D.: **Vertical-Tail Loads Measured in Flight on Four Airplane Configurations at Transonic and Supersonic Speeds.** NASA TN D-215, <u>February 1960</u>, 89N70902, 87H26629.

Aerodynamic loads were obtained from the X-5 airplane, an F-100 with a small vertical tail, F-100 with a large vertical tail, and the X-1E airplane. Effects of sideslip angle, rudder deflection, and Mach number are presented for trim flight at altitudes from 40,000 feet to 70,000 feet and at Mach numbers from 0.70 to 2.08. Comparisons are made with simple theoretical methods of estimating the loads. Also, the total directional stability for each airplane as calculated by use of vertical-tail loads is shown.

264. Walker, Joseph A.: **A Pilot's Look at the X-15 Program.** Presented at the IAS, Texas Section, Dallas, Texas, <u>April 28–30, 1960</u>. OTP-1960

265. Armstrong, N. A.: **X-15 Operations: Electronics and the Pilot.** *Astronautics*, vol. 5, no. 5, <u>May 1960</u>, pp. 42–43, 76–78.

Electronic equipment figures prominently in X-15 flight and ground systems, but this hypersonic vehicle is an instrument of the pilot, depending on him for control and flight success.

266. Bellman, Donald R.; and Toll, Thomas A.: **Aeronautical Operating Problems—Supersonic Transport.** Presented at the NASA Conference, <u>June 2–3, 1960</u>.

267. Weil, Joseph; and Matranga, Gene J.: **Review of Techniques Applicable to the Recovery of Lifting Hypervelocity Vehicles.** NASA TM X-67563. Presented at the Joint Conference on Lifting Manned Hypervelocity and Reentry Vehicles, Part 1, pp. 313–328. Langley Research Center, April 11–14, 1960. Also Scientific Advisory Board, Boeing, Seattle, Washington, and IAS Symposium on Recovery of Space Vehicles, Los Angeles, California, <u>August 31–September 1, 1960</u>, (see N72-70963 06-99), 72N70983.

268. Walker, Harold J.; and Wolowicz, Chester H.: **Theoretical Stability Derivatives for the X-15 Research Airplane at Supersonic and Hypersonic Speeds Including a Comparison With Wind-Tunnel Results.** NASA TM X-287, <u>August 1960</u>, 87H25655, 65N24060, #.

The hypersonic small-disturbance theory for lifting surfaces and the second-order shock-expansion method for bodies of revolution are employed in conjunction with the results from slender-body and linear theory to predict the longitudinal and lateral-directional stability and control derivatives for angles of attack from 0 degrees to 25 degrees and for Mach numbers extending well beyond the airplane design limit. The results are compared with available wind-tunnel data at Mach numbers from approximately 2 to 7 and with the limiting values given by Newtonian theory. Good agreement is obtained for the most part, but several notable differences are found among the lateral-directional derivatives at high angles of attack.

269. Holleman, E. C.; and Sadoff, M.: **Simulation Requirements for the Development of Advanced Manned Military Aircraft.** NASA TM X-54672, Presented at the IAS National Meeting, San Diego, California, August 3, 1960, 75N72588.

The present state of the art of the piloted flight simulator leaves no major deterrent to the mechanization of required simulators for the design of present or future manned military airplanes. The fixed-base simulator with adequate presentation and controls is completely satisfactory for the investigation of a wide range of airplane problems. However, there are some areas which require some form of motion stimulus. Other areas remain where simulator requirements are not yet resolved, but work is continuing to better define these simulator requirements.

270. Fischel, Jack: **The X-15 Flight Research Program in Relation to the Development of Advance Military Aircraft.** Presented at the IAS National Meeting, San Diego, California, August 1–3, 1960.

271. Bikle, Paul F.: **Initial Remarks About the X-15 Flight Research Program.** Presented at the 3rd Annual West Coast Meeting of American Astronautics Society, Seattle, Washington, August 9, 1960.

272. Day, Richard E.: **Training Aspects of the X-15 Program.** In *The Training of Astronauts*, Report of a Working Group Conference: Panel on Psychology, Armed Forces-NRC Committee on Bio-Astronautics, Woods Hole, Massachusetts, August 29–30, 1960, pp. 5–14, 62N12371.

Various training aids in the development of the X-15 program are presented. Future flight data obtained in more critical control areas will afford the unique opportunity to assess the true value of these training aids for the X-15 and to establish training requirements for future vehicles.

273. Baker, Thomas F. **Dyna-Soar I—Flight-Data Objectives.** Presented at the IAS Symposium on Recovery of Space Vehicles, Los Angeles, California, August 31– September 1, 1960.

274. Nugent, Jack; and Powers, Bruce G.: **Flight Tests of a Twin-Duct Induction System for a Mach Number Range of 0.78 to 2.07.** NASA TM X-281, September 1960, 87H25628.

Time histories of several airplane, engine, and induction-system parameters are presented for maneuvers made at altitude of 26,000 feet, 40,000 feet, and 55,000 feet over a Mach number range of 0.78 to 2.07. A time history of a push-down-turn maneuver at 40,000 feet is also presented. Comparisons of the data were made to show the effects of angle of attack. Mach number, altitude, and duct bypass area on the induction system parameters.

275. Weil, Joseph; and Matranga, Gene J.: **Review of Techniques Applicable to the Recovery of Lifting Hypervelocity Vehicles.** NASA TM X-334, September 1960, 87H26028.

A general review of piloting problems concerned with the recovery phase of lifting hypervelocity vehicles is presented. A short discussion is offered pertinent to the maneuvering capabilities and piloting techniques applicable to the initial approach phase of gliders with low lift-drag ratios. The principal emphasis concerns factors affecting the final approach and landing operation of these gliders. The results of general flight studies as well as recent experience obtained in the approach and landing of the X-15 research airplane are reviewed. Finally, a definition of the limits of piloted flared landings is developed.

276. Tambor, Ronald: **Flight Investigation of the Lift and Drag Characteristics of a Swept-Wing, Multijet, Transport-Type Airplane.** NASA TN-D-30, (Corrected Copy), September 1960.

The lift and drag characteristics of a Boeing KC-135 airplane were determined during maneuvering flight over the Mach number range from 0.70 to 0.85 for the airplane in the clean configuration at an altitude of 26,000 feet. Data were also obtained over the speed range of 130 knots to 160 knots at 9,000 feet for various flap deflections with gear down.

277. Stillwell, W. H.; and Larson, T. J.: **Measurement of the Maximum Speed Attained by the X-15 Airplane Powered With Interim Rocket Engines.** NASA TN D-615 September 1960, 62N71189, 87H27079.

On August 4, 1960 a flight was made with the X-15 airplane to achieve the maximum speed possible with two interim engines. Presented are the details of the techniques utilized to determine the maximum Mach number (3.31 plus or minus 0.04) and speed (2,196 mph plus or minus 35) attained.

278. Wolowicz, C. H.; Drake, H. M.; Videan, E. N.; Morris, G. J.; and Stickle, J. W.: **Simulator Investigation of Controls and Display Required for Terminal Phase of Coplanar, Orbital Rendezvous.** NASA TN D-511, October 1960, 62N71085, 87H27353.

A simulator study was made of presentations and control requirements for a manned astrovehicle employed for the interception of artificial satellites during the terminal phase of an orbital rendezvous. Two oscilloscope and one direct-visual-observation presentation and three control modes were investigated. The study was considered in terms of a manned interceptor having a home berth at a manned space station which is in circular orbit 500 miles above the earth. Interceptions were restricted to coplanar conditions.

279. Stillwell, W. H.; and Larson, T. J.: **Measurement of the Maximum Altitude Attained by the X-15 Airplane Powered With Interim Rocket Engines.** NASA TN D-623, October 1960, 62N71197, 87H27097.

On August 12, 1960, an X-15 flight was made to achieve essentially the maximum altitude expected to be possible with the interim rocket engines. Presented are the details of the techniques utilized to determine the maximum geometric altitude of this flight (136,500 ft plus or minus 600).

280. Beeler, De E.: **The X-15 Research Program.** AGARD Report 289, Tenth Annual General Assembly of AGARD, Istanbul, Turkey, October 3–8, 1960.

Brief summary of the research program which led to the X-15 aircraft, and some of the early flight tests. Includes flight regimes, mission, research areas, shock-wave patterns at hypersonic speeds, simulator support, stability derivatives, control effectiveness derivatives, drag characteristics power-off, heat transfer, wing temperature station, wing pressure distribution midspan station, wing loads, maximum speed and altitude, and damping.

281. White, R. M.; and Walker, Joseph A.: **X-15 Program Status Report, Parts 1 and 2.** Proceedings from SETP Annual Symposium, Vol. 5, No. 2, October 7, 1960.

Contains a brief resume of four flights leading to, and including, the maximum speed flight of the X-15 with the interim engine, then discusses some of the results to date, and concludes with a summary of the intended flight program with the design XLR-99 engine.

282. Johnson, Clinton T.: **Investigation of the Characteristics of 6-Foot Drogue-Stabilization Ribbon Parachutes at High Altitudes and Low Supersonic Speeds.** NASA TM X-448, November 1960, 87H25617.

Performance data are presented for two types of ribbon parachutes. The parachutes were forcibly deployed from an air-launched test vehicle at altitudes from 55,000 feet to 70,000 feet and at Mach numbers between 0.92 and 1.52. Opening shock, steady-state drag performance, and canopy-porosity effects are evaluated with respect to Mach number and dynamic pressure.

283. Smith, Harriet J.: **Experimental and Calculated Flow Fields Produced by Airplanes Flying at Supersonic Speeds.** NASA TN D-621, November 1960, 62N71195, 87H27094.

Results are presented of a flight investigation conducted to survey the flow field generated by airplanes flying at supersonic speeds. The pressure signatures of an F-100, an F-104, and a B-58 airplane, representing widely varying configurations, at distances from 120 to 425 feet from the generating aircraft and at Mach numbers from 1.2 to 1.8 are shown. Calculations made by using Whitham's method gave good agreement with experimental results. A procedure for calculating the F(y) function used in Whitham's method is also given.

284. Andrews, W. H.; and Holleman, E. C.: **Experience With a Three-Axis Side-Located Controller During a Static and Centrifuge Simulation of the Piloted Launch of a Manned Multistage Vehicle.** NASA TN D-546, November 1960, 62N71120, 87H26912.

The control problems associated with piloting multistaged vehicles to orbital conditions were investigated with static and dynamic simulators. A three-axis controller was used for primary control. Presented are design details of the controller, pilot opinions concerning its operation, and other data pertinent to the design and use of a controller of this type.

285. Saltzman, Edwin J.: **Preliminary Full-Scale Power-Off Drag of the X-15 Airplane for Mach Numbers From 0.7 to 3.1.** NASA TM X-430, December 1960, 87H25514, 62N72254.

These drag data provide preliminary means of appraising present methods of extrapolating wind-tunnel drag results to full scale at Mach numbers up to 3. Estimated drag values based on wind-tunnel measurements are included. Free-stream Reynolds numbers range from 13.9 x 10 (sup) 6 to 28 x 10 (sup) 6, based on the mean aerodynamic chord.

286. Holleman, E. C.: **Utilization of the Pilot During Boost Phase of the Step 1 Mission.** In its Joint Conference on Lifting Manned Hypervelocity and Reentry Vehicles, Part 2 1960, pp. 261–272, (see N72-71002 06-99), 72N71021.

287. Baker, T. F.; Russell, H. G.; and Schofield, B. L.: **Dyna-Soar Step 1 Flight Test Program.** In Joint Conference on Lifting Manned Hypervelocity and Reentry Vehicles, Part 2, 1960, pp. 311–324, (see N72-71002 06-99), 72N71025.

288. Truszynski, G. M.; and Lindfors, P. O.: **Instrumentation and Communications Considerations.** In its Joint Conference on Lifting Manned Hypervelocity and Reentry Vehicles, Part 2, 1960, pp. 325–334, (see N72-71002 06-99), 72N71026.

289. Holleman, Euclid C.; Armstrong, Neil A.; and Andrews, William H.: **Utilization of the Pilot in the Launch**

and Injection of a Multistage Orbital Vehicle. Presented at the IAS 28th Annual Meeting, New York, New York, January 25–27, 1960, 87H30992.

The Flight Research Center has conducted fixed-base and centrifuge simulator programs to investigate the capabilities of the pilot in providing control and guidance during launch. For the centrifuge program an attempt was made to minimize the adverse effects of acceleration on the pilot by designing a molded seat and three-axis controller that were functionally independent of acceleration. The effects of staging acceleration environment on the pilot's performance were determined to 15g, and the control task associated with two- and four-stage vehicle launches were investigated.

290. Thompson, Milton O.: **Piloting Aspect of Project ALSOR.** For publication in SETP newsletter, 1960.

The ALSOR program is inclined toward providing current information in a reliable and efficient manner to support the X-15 program.

1961 Technical Publications

291. Reed, Robert D.; and Watts, Joe D.: **Skin and Structural Temperatures Measured on the X-15 Airplane During a Flight to a Mach Number of 3.3.** NASA TM X-468, January 1961, 87H25738.

A survey of skin and structural temperatures was obtained on the X-15 airplane during a flight to a Mach number of 3.3. Fuselage, wing, horizontal-tail, and vertical-tail temperatures are presented to show temperature variations on the external surfaces and temperature differences between the skin and internal structure. The maximum temperature recorded was 440 °F on an unsupported skin area on the lower vertical tail. Temperature differences of 400 °F were recorded between the external skin and internal spar webs on the wing. Local external temperature differences caused by the heat-sink effect of the supporting structure were as great as 220 °F. Temperature indicating paint aided in identifying the location of areas of concentrated heating on the lower surface of the wing.

292. Matranga, Gene J.: **Launch Characteristics of the X-15 Research Airplane as Determined in Flight.** NASA TN D-723, February 1961, 62N71297, 87H27349.

The first 16 air launches of the X-15 airplane demonstrated the feasibility of air launch from an asymmetric position under the wing of the B-52 carrier airplane. Use of the stability augmentation system markedly reduced the launch transients. Reasonable agreement exists between flight and predicted data.

E-4942

X-15 Launch From a B-52 Airplane

293. Holleman, Euclid C.; and Reisert, Donald: **Controllability of the X-15 Research Airplane With Interim Engines During High-Altitude Flights.** NASA TM X-514, March 1961, 87H25871.

A peak geometric altitude of 136,500 feet with a minimum dynamic pressure of 10.6 lb/sq. ft. was attained with only the aerodynamic controls available to the pilot for controlling and stabilizing the airplane. Aerodynamic control was adequate throughout the flight, but at minimum dynamic pressure the airplane was lightly damped, which made precise control difficult. Because of the transient nature of the trajectory and the negligible load factors associated with the airplane oscillation, the pilot did not object to the poor dynamic characteristics of the airplane under these conditions and could satisfactorily control the airplane along the trajectory.

294. McKay, J. M.; and Scott, B. J.: **Landing-Gear Behavior During Touchdown and Runout for 17 Landings of the X-15 Research Airplane.** NASA TM X-518, March 1961, 63N12563, #.

Data are presented for the pretouchdown conditions, the impact period, and the runout phase of the landing for vertical velocities up to 9.5 feet per second and true ground speeds between 145 knots and 238 knots. The dynamic response of the airplane during the impact period is presented in the form of time histories of shock strut force and displacement, main-gear and nose-gear drag forces, upper-mass acceleration, horizontal-tail setting, horizontal-tail load, airplane angle of attack, and pitching velocity. Also included is the variation of the coefficient of friction of the main-gear skid with ground speed during the runout of a typical landing.

295. Day, Richard E.: **X-15 Simulation and the X-15 Flight Program.** Presented to the National Academy of Sciences, Panel on Acceleration Stress, ARC, March 11, 1961.

A general discussion of the role played by various simulators in the development of the X-15 program.

296. Banner, R. D.; and *Kinsler, M. R.: **Status of X-15 Aerodynamic-Heating Studies.** ARS Paper-1629-61. Presented at the ARS Missile and Space Vehicle Testing Conference, Los Angeles, California, March 13–16, 1961, 63N15312.

One of the primary purposes of the X-15 program is to obtain full-scale aerodynamic-heating information that can be used to establish the adequacy of current theoretical methods and model tests. In conjunction with this purpose, a special flight was performed which maximized the heating rates and minimized the transient flight conditions. This flight reached a Mach number of 3.1. Results indicated a reasonable agreement between measured heat transfer data and simple theoretical predictions. Boundary-layer-transition data were obtained which pointed out a continuing problem of prediction that should probably be treated with conservatism until more detailed information is obtained.

*North American Aviation, Downey, California.

297. Reisert, Donald; and Adkins, Elmor J.: **Flight and Operational Experiences With Pilot-Operated Reaction Controls.** ARS Paper-1674-61. Presented at the ARS Missile and Space Vehicle Testing Conference, Los Angeles, California, March 13–16, 1961.

298. Finch, Thomas W.: **X-15 Flight Program.** Presented at The ARS Missile and Space Vehicle Testing Conference, Los Angeles, California, March 13–16, 1961.

This paper discusses a number of program phases that have been completed, including the contractor's flight program and the Government research program utilizing an interim-engine configuration giving an indication of its experiences and a description of future program plans.

299. Taylor, Lawrence W., Jr.; and Smith, John W.: **An Analytical Approach to the Design of an Automatic Discontinuous Control System.** NASA TN D-630, April 1961, 62N71204, 87H27116.

The design of a attitude-stabilization system for a vehicle experiencing negligible external moments is investigated analytically. A discontinuous control system employing a linear switching function and having a neutral zone and time delays is studied and equations are developed to generalize and optimize the system's transient and limit-cycle performance. Example systems which can minimize power required, attitude error, and angular-velocity error within a specified period of operation are included

300. Kordes, Eldon E.; and Noll, Richard B.: **Flight Experience of Panel Flutter.** ARS Lifting Reentry Vehicles, Structures, Materials, and Design Conference, Palm Springs, California, April 4–6, 1961.

Presents X-15 panel flutter data and compares with flutter boundary established by wind tunnel tests.

301. Weil, Joseph: **Application of Analytical Techniques to Flight Evaluations in Critical Control Areas.** AGARD Report No. 369, AGARD Specialist Meeting on Aircraft Stability and Control, Brussels, Belgium, April 10–14, 1961.

Flight data can be dangerously misleading in the absence of careful interpretation. This report discusses test results pertinent to a variety of typical flight-control problem areas of the current generation of airplanes. The results presented were obtained from flight investigations of many research and operational aircraft at the NASA Flight Research Center over the past 10 years. The report considers basic stability problems such as pitch-up, roll coupling, and marginal directional stability. Development of augmentation systems and control system evaluations are also discussed in some detail. Throughout the report, the importance of coordinating flight and similar results are very much stressed and it is shown that in many areas even the most painstaking interpretation of flight data can lead to possible disaster if flight tests are not adequately supported by simulator studies using realistic stability and control derivatives.

302. Weil, Joseph; and Adkins, E. J.: **Review of Selected X-15 Development and Operating Experiences.** Presented at the ISA Aero-Space Instrumentation Symposium, Dallas, Texas, April 30–May 4, 1961.

This paper reviews the flight-control simulation experiences of X-15 systems and components. The roll of simulators and auxiliary aircraft is discussed, with emphasis on pilot training and the development of flight procedures necessary to obtain the maximum research return on the investment.

303. Weil, Joseph; and Adkins, E. J.: **Utilization of Aircraft as Systems and Flight Control Test Beds.** Presented at the ISA Aero-Space Instrumentation Symposium, Dallas, Texas, May 4, 1961.

304. Taylor, Lawrence W., Jr.; and Day, Richard E.: **Flight Controllability Limits and Related Human Transfer Functions as Determined From Simulator and Flight Tests.** NASA TN D-746, May 1961, 87H27401.

A simulator study and limited flight tests were performed to determine the levels of static stability and damping necessary for pilot control of the pitch, roll, and yaw attitudes of a vehicle for a the pilot to control the airplane at conditions that were otherwise uncontrollable. The influence on the controllability limits of the more important aerodynamic coefficients and other factors, such as learning and interruption of the pilot's display, was also investigated. Information concerning human transfer functions applicable to marginally controllable tasks is presented which should aid in assessing the controllability of any specific configuration.

305. Matranga, Gene J.: **Analysis of X-15 Landing Approach and Flare Characteristics Determined From the First 30 Flights.** NASA TN D-1057, <u>July 1961</u>, 62N71631, 87H27661.

This paper presents lift, drag, and angle-of-attack data for various approach and landing configurations. The conditions and problems encountered during the approach pattern and the flare to touchdown are discussed. The value of flight simulations of the approach and flare maneuvers is assessed.

306. Saltzman, Edwin J.: **Preliminary Base Pressures Obtained From the X-15 Airplane at Mach Numbers From 1.1 to 3.2.** NASA TN D-1056, <u>August 1961</u>, 62N71630, 87H27659.

Base pressure measurements have been made on the fuselage, 10 degrees-wedge vertical fin, and side fairing of the X-15 airplane. Data are presented for Mach numbers between 1.1 and 3.2 for both powered and unpowered flight. Comparisons are made with data for small-scale-model tests, semiempirical estimates, and theory.

307. Jordan, G. H.; McLeod, N. J.; and Ryan, B. M.: **Review of Flight Measurements of Sonic Booms and Effects of Shock Waves on Other Aircraft.** Presented at 5th Annual Symposium of the Society of Experimental Test Pilots, Beverly Hills, California, <u>September 29–30, 1961</u>, 63N81390.

308. Andrews, William H.; Cooney, Thomas V.; and Fischel, Jack: **Contributions from the X-15 Flight Test Program Relating to Design and Development of the Supersonic Transport.** SETP 62-9686. Presented at 5th Annual Symposium of the Society of Experimental Test Pilots, Beverly Hills, California, <u>September 29–30, 1961.</u>

Discussion of information and experience gained with the X-15 which is applicable to supersonic transport design, and of means by which future data may be provided. Extensive treatment is given to (1) structural heating, including temperature, temperature gradients, and temperature effects on structures; (2) structural dynamics, including a brief resume of flutter experience with the X-15; and (3) augmentation systems, including fundamental problems experienced and the reliability of the system. The air-data-sensing systems employed in the X-15 and the related system-measurement accuracies obtained are covered. The

reliability of the subsystems and the maintenance of such items as the environmental control system and the hydraulic system are discussed. Future programs involving fundamental studies requiring specialized instrumentation not presently installed in the X-15 are considered.

309. Taylor, Lawrence W., Jr.: **Analysis of a Pilot-Airplane Lateral Instability Experienced With the X-15 Airplane.** NASA TN D-1059, <u>November 1961</u>, 62N71633, 87H27667.

By using an experimentally developed human transfer function for the pilot and system-analysis methods, the pilot-airplane lateral instability observed with the X-15 airplane is analyzed. The methods used adequately explain the lateral-control problem and can be used to predict the problem. The calculated area of lateral-control difficulty agreed with that determined on the X-15 piloted flight simulator and with flight data.

310. Beeler, De E.: **Recent X-15 Flight Results.** Flight Mechanics Panel, Paris, France, <u>November 21–24, 1961</u>.

311. Anon.: **Research-Airplane-Committee Report on Conference on the Progress of the X-15 Project.** NASA TM X-57072, <u>1961</u>, (see N71-75444), 71N75443.

This document is a compilation of the papers presented at the Conference on the Progress of the X-15 Project held at the NASA Flight Research Center, Edwards Air Force Base, California, November 20–21, 1961. This conference was held by the Research Airplane Committee of the U.S. Air Force, the U.S. Navy, and the National Aeronautics and Space Administration to report on the technical status of this research airplane. The papers were presented by members of the staffs of North American Aviation, Inc.; Aeronautical Systems Division, U.S. Air Force; Air Force Flight Test Center; and National Aeronautics and Space Administration.

312. Beeler, D. E.; and Toll, T. A.: **Status of X-15 Research Program.** Research-Airplane-Committee Report on Conference on the Progress of the X-15 Project, Edwards AFB, California, <u>November 20–21, 1961</u>, pp. 1–10, 71N-75444.

313. Banner, R. D.; Kuhl, A. E.; and Quinn, R. D.: **Preliminary Results of Aerodynamic Heating Studies on the X-15.** Research-Airplane-Committee Report on Conference on the Progress of the X-15 Project, <u>1961</u>, pp. 11–28, (see N71-75443), 71N75445. (See also 341.)

The results of the preliminary flight heat-transfer studies on the X-15 airplane are presented, together with a discussion of the manner in which the data have been obtained, a comparison of measured and calculated turbulent heat-transfer coefficients, a correlation of the model test results and the flight results for turbulent heat transfer; some information on boundary-layer transition, and a comparison of measured and calculated skin temperatures at several locations on the airplane.

314. Kordes, Eldon E.; Reed, Robert D.; and *Dawdy, Alpha L.: **Structural Heating Experiences of the X-15.** Research-Airplane-Committee Report on Conference on the Progress of the X-15 Project, 1961, pp. 29–45, (see N71-75443), 71N75446.

The expected structural temperatures and their effect on the development and design of the X-l5 airplane structure have been described in previous conferences, and Banner, Kuhl, and Quinn (paper no. 2) have discussed in detail the many factors affecting the heat input to the structure. The purpose of the present paper is to show the magnitude of structural temperatures measured during the flight program and to describe structural problems that have developed due to structural heating.

*North American Aviation, Inc., Downey, California.

315. Jordan, G. H.; McLeod, N. J.; and *Guy, L. D.: **Structural Dynamic Experiences of the X-15** Research-Airplane-Committee Report on Conference on the Progress of the X-15 Project, 1961, pp. 47–59, (see N71-75443), 71N75447.

This paper reviews the structural dynamics problems that influenced the design of the structure and discusses the experiences that have been encountered during the flight tests.

*NASA Langley Research Center, Hampton, Virginia.

316. McKay, J. M.; and Kordes, E. E.: **Landing Loads and Dynamics of the X-15 Airplane.** Research-Airplane-Committee Report on Conference on the Progress of the X-15 Project, 1961, pp. 61–71, (see N71-75443), 71N75448. (See also 342.)

Because the landing-gear configuration represents a marked departure from previously used configurations, the present paper has been prepared to report on the landing loads experience of the X-15 A further purpose of this paper is to review the dynamics of landing and to present results of a recent theoretical study of the effects of various parameters on the landing loads.

317. Keener, E. R.; and Pembo, C.: **Aerodynamic Forces on Components of the X-15.** Research-Airplane-Committee Report on Conference on the Progress of the X-15 Project, 1961, pp. 73–82, (see N71-75443), 71N75449. (See also 343.)

An attempt has been made in the flight research program to verify some of the force measurements with both pressure and strain-gage measurements. This paper presents a summary of the flight force data obtained to date. The data are compared with the wind-tunnel results and with some of the more familiar theoretical methods and approximations.

318. *Hopkins, E. J.; **Fetterman, D. E., Jr.; and Saltzman, E. J.: **A Comparison of Full-Scale X-15 Lift and Drag Characteristics with Wind-Tunnel Results and Theory.** Research-Airplane-Committee Report on Conference on the Progress of the X-15 Project, 1961, pp. 83–98, (see N71-75443), 71N75450. (See also 344.)

Data on the lift and drag characteristics of the X-15 airplane obtained in flight are shown to be in agreement with wind-tunnel-model data for Mach numbers up to 5. Existing theoretical methods are indicated to be adequate for estimating the X-l5 minimum drag but underestimated the drag due to lift and overestimated the maximum lift-drag ratio. Two-dimensional theory is shown to be adequate for predicting the base pressures behind surfaces having very blunt trailing edges) such as those on the vertical tail of the X-l5.

*NASA Ames Research Center, Moffett Field, California.
**NASA Langley Research Center, Hampton, Virginia.

319. Walker, H. J.; and Wolowicz, C. H.: **Stability and Control Derivative Characteristics of the X-15.** Research-Airplane-Committee Report on Conference on the Progress of the X-15 Project, 1961, pp. 99–112, (see N71-75443), 71N75451. (See also 345.)

The flight-determined derivative characteristics are compared with the predictions from wind-tunnel tests and theory for Mach numbers extending to 5.5 and angles of attack up to 17 degrees. With few exceptions, the predictions were found generally to be in good agreement with the flight data. Areas of deficient stability and control are briefly discussed.

320. White, R. M.; Robinson, G. H.; and Matranga, G. J.: **Resume of X-15 Handling Qualities.** Research-Airplane-Committee Report on Conference on the Progress of the X-15 Project, 1961, pp. 113–130, (see N71-75443), 71N75452. (See also 346)

The handling qualities of the X-15 research airplane have been assessed from pilot's opinions, with verification in many cases by data acquired during flights. Areas of interest covered are the launch, climbout, ballistic, reentry, and landing phases of flights made to date.

321. Petersen, F. S.; Rediess, H. A.; and Weil, J.: **Lateral Directional Control Characteristics.** Research-Airplane-

Committee Report on Conference on the Progress of the X-15 Project, 1961, pp. 131–154, (see N71-75443), 71N75453. (See also 347.)

The deterioration of lateral directional controllability with roll damper off and the pilot performing a lateral control task is explained. The problem area was defined by fixed-base and airborne simulators and verified by closed-loop analysis in which a human transfer function represents the pilot. A parameter which will predict the problem area for the X-15 airplane is developed. The means considered to alleviate the control problem in the X-15 airplane are also discussed.

322. Hoey, R. G.; and Day, R. E.: **X-15 Mission Planning and Operational Procedures.** Research-Airplane-Committee Report on Conference on the Progress of the X-15 Project, 1961, pp. 155–169, (see N71-75443), 71N75454.

The philosophy of the X-15 flight-test program thus far has been to expand the flight envelope to the maximum speed and design altitude as rapidly as practical and simultaneously to obtain as much detailed research data on the hypersonic environment as possible. The envelope expansion program has been performed on an incremental performance basis; that is, each successive flight is designed to go to a slightly higher speed or altitude than the previous flight, thus permitting a reasonable extrapolation of flight-test data from one flight to the next and also building a backlog of pilot experience. The mission planning and operational procedures associated with the program are discussed in this paper. The effect on flight planning of systems reliability, stability limitations, and ranging considerations are also discussed. General piloting techniques and pilot training are mentioned.

323. Taylor, L. W., Jr.; and Merrick, G. B.: **X-15 Stability Augmentation System.** Research-Airplane-Committee Report on Conference on the Progress of the X-15 Project, 1961, pp. 171–182, (see N71-75443), 71N75455.

This paper describes the basic damper system currently installed in the X-15, discusses some of the problems encountered during its development and flight testing, and reviews briefly the system reliability.

324. *Johannes, R. P.; Armstrong, N. A.; and Hays, T. C.: **Development of X-15 Self-Adaptive Flight-Control System.** Research-Airplane-Committee Report on Conference on the Progress of the X-15 Project, 1961, pp. 183–194, (see N71-75443), 71N75456.

In-house studies conducted at Wright-Patterson Air Force Base in 1956 convinced the Flight Control Laboratory, Aeronautical Systems Division, of the theoretical feasibility of designing a self-adaptive flight-control system. As the name implies, such a system would automatically adapt itself in order to provide essentially constant damping and

frequency of the aircraft in combination with the control system as the vehicle encountered flight conditions of varying aerodynamic control-surface effectiveness. To this end a number of study contracts were awarded in 1957 which soon led to flight-test programs testing adaptive concepts in F-94 airplanes by the Massachusetts Institute of Technology and the Minneapolis Honeywell Regulator Company. Minneapolis-Honeywell continued this effort with a company funded flight-test program for testing the system in an F-101A airplane.

*Aeronautical Systems Division, U.S. Air Force.

325. *Mace, W. D.; and Ball, J. L.: **Flight Characteristics of X-15 Hypersonic Flow-Direction Sensor.** Research-Airplane-Committee Report on Conference on the Progress of the X-15 Project, 1961, pp. 195–201, (see N71-75443), 71N75457.

The purpose of this paper is to discuss the experience that has been obtained through the use of the nulling ball-nose flow direction sensor during flight testing of the airplane.

*NASA Langley Research Center, Hampton, Virginia.

326. *Leiby, R. G.; Bellman, D. R.; and DeMar, N. E.: **XLR99 Engine Operating Experience.** Research-Airplane-Committee Report on Conference on the Progress of the X-15 Project, 1961, pp. 215–226, (see N71-75443), 71N75459.

XLR99-RM-1 rocket engine, which was developed specifically for the X-15 airplane, is the largest rocket engine designed from the outset for use in a manned vehicle to be completely controlled by the crew. In order to provide the desired safety and controllability required by the X-15 mission, many unique features were included in the design. Delays in the development of the engine required that the initial X-15 flights be made with an interim engine. However, the first flight with the XLR99 was made in November 1960, and the engine has been used in government flight operations since February 1961. Since the first flight, fifteen flights have been made with the XLR99. This paper summarizes the XLR99 operating experience during the flight program.

*Air Force Flight Test Center, Edwards AFB, California.

327. *Rowen, B.; *Richardson, R. N.; and Layton, G. P., Jr.: **Bioastronautics Support of the X-15 Program.** Research-Airplane-Committee Report on Conference on the Progress of the X-15 Project, 1961, pp. 255–264, (see N71-75443), 71N75461.

The techniques of air-to-ground telemetry have been used in research aircraft testing since the start of the X-1 program in 1946. It became apparent during the development of the

X-type research aircraft that personnel responsible for aerospace medical support of the pilot were not taking full advantage of the progress in telemetry systems to monitor for medical purposes the pilot and his environment during flight. One of the research objectives of the X-15 program is to obtain the pilot's physiological response to flight at increased speed and altitude. This objective is accomplished with the pilot wearing a full pressure suit; therefore, this garment and biomedical data acquisition equipment, techniques, and results are discussed in this paper.

*Air Force Flight Test Center, Edwards AFB, California.

328. Love, J. E.; and Palmer, J. R.: **Operational Reliability Experiences with the X-15 Aircraft.** Research-Airplane-Committee Report on Conference on the Progress of the X-15 Project, 1961, pp. 277–287, (see N71-75443), 71N75463.

It is the purpose of this paper to describe a comprehensive picture of X-15 operational reliability. The curves and text presented are based on actual parts failure records, flight logs, and the daily repair work sheets. It is therefore not only a picture of the reliability with regard to safety in flight, but also in view of ground preparation time and cost. Repeated system and component failures have resulted in many costly delays.

329. Walker, J. A.: **A Pilot's Impression of the X-15 Program.** Research-Airplane-Committee Report on Conference on the Progress of the X-15 Project, 1961, pp. 303–312, (see N71-75443), 71N75465.

It is the intent of this paper to be critical of the X-15 because of its deficiencies or problems. It should rather be kept in mind that many compromises had to be accepted in the design of the X-15 to get on the job, and rightly so, because there are some questions which still have not been resolved.

330. Bikle, P. F.; and *Pezda, E. F.: **Future Plans for the X-15.** Research-Airplane-Committee Report on Conference on the Progress of the X-15 Project, 1961, pp. 329–333, (see N71-75443), 71N75467.

This third X-15 conference has given us an opportunity to review and evaluate, in considerable detail, the progress that has been achieved in the flight research program to date. Figures 1 and 2 have been selected as a summary of the areas thus far explored. Similar results have been discussed in detail in the papers presented. Although it is not possible, in any one or two figures, to show the desired information for all the varied areas of interest in the program, these plots of altitude and angle of attack against velocity do represent two of the many parameters of interest, and the shaded areas demonstrate roughly the progress that has been made. It appears that most of the work originally planned is nearly completed, with perhaps 50 percent of the aerodynamics,

structures, heating, and bioastronautics information already obtained.

*Aeronautical Systems Division, U.S. Air Force.

1962 Technical Publications

331. Yancey, R. B.; Rediess, H. A.; and Robinson, G. H.: **Aerodynamic-Derivative Characteristics of the X-15 Research Airplane as Determined From Flight Tests for Mach Numbers from 0.6 to 3.4.** Wolowicz, C. H.: **Appendix A–Approximate Equations for Determining** $C_{n_\beta}, C_{l_\beta},$ **and** $(C_{n_r} - C_{n_\beta})$. NASA TN D-1060, January 1962, 62N10089, #, 87H27669.

Lateral, directional, and longitudinal stability and control derivatives are determined from flight tests of the X-15 airplane with the low-power LR11 rocket engine. Approximate relationships are developed for determining the derivatives C sub n sub Beta, C sub l sub Beta, and (C sub n sub r - C sub n sub derivative of Beta) and for isolating the effects of stability augmentation. Wind-tunnel predictions are compared with the flight-determined derivatives.

332. Kordes, Eldon E.; and Noll, Richard B.: **Theoretical Flutter Analysis of Flat Rectangular Panels in Uniform Coplanar Flow with Arbitrary Direction.** NASA TN D-1156, January 1962, 62N10092, #, 87H27601.

Numerical calculations show that small variations in flow direction have a marked effect on the flutter of simply supported rectangular panels. The results of the calculations also show that the critical flutter mode changes at small flow angles when the length-width ratio is less than 1. Flutter conditions for a given panel at different flow angles can be compared on a common basis by use of a dynamic-pressure-parameter ratio referenced to flow conditions of an aligned panel.

333. Roman, James A.: **Biomedical Monitoring In-Flight**. *Lectures in Aerospace Medicine*, School of Aerospace Medicine, Aerospace Medical Division, Brooks AFB, Texas, January 8–12, 1962, pp. 97–114, 62N14203.

334. Kordes, Eldon E.; and Noll, Richard B.: **Flight Flutter Results for Flat Rectangular Panels.** NASA TN D-1058, February 1962, 62N10043, #, 87H27664.

Panel-flutter data obtained from several different aircraft during supersonic flight are presented and compared with a previously established flutter boundary based on results from wind-tunnel tests. The flight data were obtained for rectangular panels aligned with the flow and for rectangular panels swept at 52 degrees. Some results of a flutter analysis of swept, flat, rectangular panels are presented and used to compare the flight results with the flutter boundary for aligned panels.

335. Bellman, Donald R.; and Washington, Harold P.: **Preliminary Performance Analysis of Air Launching Manned Orbital Vehicles.** NASA TM X-636, H-229, February 1962, 72N71616, 87H26325.

A preliminary performance analysis was made to determine the capability of large subsonic and supersonic bombers for air launching manned hypersonic and satellite vehicles. The bombers considered now exist or are being developed in the United States. Four booster configurations were used in the calculations, with a winged vehicle of the Dyna-Soar type as the payload. Comparisons were made on the basis of vacuum specific impulse, burnout velocity, ratio of payload weight to launch-package gross weight, and structural weight.

336. Taylor, Lawrence W., Jr.; and *Merrick, G. B.: **X-15 Airplane Stability Augmentation System.** NASA TN D-1157, March 1962, 62N10587, 87H27604, #.

The basic damper system currently installed in the airplane is described. Some of the problems encountered during the development and flight testing of the system are discussed, and the reliability of the system is reviewed briefly.

*North American Aviation, Inc., Inglewood, California.

337. Jordan, Gareth H.; McLeod, Norman J.; and Guy, Lawrence D.: **Structural Dynamics Experiences of the X-15 Airplane.** NASA TN D-1158, March 1962, 62N10586, 87H27606, #.

The structural dynamic problems anticipated during the design of the X-15 airplane are reviewed briefly, and the actual flight experiences with the airplane are described. The noise environment, acoustic fatigue problems, and panel-flutter experiences are discussed. Where these problems led to structural modifications, the modifications are described.

338. Hoey, Robert G.; and Day, Richard E.: **Mission Planning and Operational Procedures for the X-15 Airplane.** NASA TN D-1159, March 1962, 62N10585, 87H27608, #.

Mission-planning methods and techniques used for the X-15 airplane envelope-expansion flight-test program are discussed. Use of the six-degree-of-freedom, ground-based simulator is indicated for prediction of performance, stability and controllability; development of piloting techniques and pilot training; evaluation of, and practice for, all possible emergency conditions; and energy management development. Other pilot-training devices and the role of the ground-monitoring station are also described. Predicted trajectory data and actual flight results are compared. The initial reasons and the final justifications for conducting the X-15 envelope expansion by performance increment are presented.

339. McLeod, Norman J.: **Flight-Determined Aerodynamic-Noise Environment of an Airplane Nose Cone Up to a Mach Number of 2.** NASA TN D-1160, March 1962, 62N10644, 87H27611, #.

The aerodynamic-noise environment was measured at one point on the surface of a 24.5 degrees included-angle cone and at three internal positions. The data were obtained in flight for Mach numbers from 0.8 to 2, free-stream dynamic pressures from approximately 200 lb sq ft to 1,000 lb sq ft, and at altitudes of about 26,000 feet and 40,000 feet. The over-all noise levels and spectrum analysis of representative selected data are presented.

340. Matranga, Gene J.; Dana, William H.; and Armstrong, Neil A.: **Flight Simulated Off-the-Pad Escape and Landing Maneuvers for a Vertically Launched Hypersonic Glider.** NASA TM X-637, March 1962, 66N33330, 87H26328, #.

A series of subsonic maneuvers was flown with an airplane having a maximum lift-drag ratio of 4.7. No particularly difficult piloting or maneuvering problems were encountered. A reduction of the pilot's visibility from the cockpit did not appreciably impair his navigation capabilities, but did adversely affect his performance of the escape and landing maneuvers.

341. Banner, Richard D.; Kuhl, Albert E.; and Quinn, Robert D.: **Preliminary Results of Aerodynamic Heating Studies on the X-15 Airplane.** NASA TM X-638, March 1962, 66N29468, 87H26332, #. (See also 313.)

The results of the preliminary flight heat-transfer studies on the X-15 airplane are presented, together with a discussion of the manner in which the data have been obtained, a comparison of measured and calculated turbulent heat-transfer coefficients, a correlation of the model test results and the flight results for turbulent heat transfer, some information on boundary-layer transition, and a comparison of measured and calculated skin temperatures at several locations on the airplane.

342. McKay, James M.; and Kordes, Eldon E.: **Landing Loads and Dynamics of the X-15 Airplane.** NASA TM X-639, March 1962, 63N12564, 87H26336, #. (See also 313.)

The loads, accelerations, and displacements of the X-15 airplane and landing-gear system measured during landing impact are discussed. The measured quantities are related to the initial touchdown conditions and are compared with data from a theoretical analysis to determine the effects of variations in such parameters as elevator position, skid coefficient of friction, main-gear location, and initial touchdown conditions beyond the range of the experimental data.

343. Keener, Earl R.; and Pembo, Chris: **Aerodynamic Forces on Components of the X-15 Airplane.** NASA TM X-712, March 1962, 65N23920, 87H25526, #. (See also 317.)

Aerodynamic force data on the components of the X-15 airplane have been obtained by both pressure and strain-gage measurements in flights covering a Mach number range up to 6.04, altitudes up to about 217,000 feet, and angles of attack up to 15 degrees. Comparison of the flight data with wind-tunnel data shows generally good agreement for the flight conditions covered.

344. Hopkins, Edward J.; Fetterman, David E. Jr.; and Saltzman, Edwin J.: **Comparison of Full-Scale Lift and Drag Characteristics of the X-15 Airplane With Wind-Tunnel Results and Theory.** NASA TM X-713, March 1962, 65N23921, 87H25527. (See also 318.)

Comparisons are made between the minimum drag characteristics of the full-scale X-15 airplane and wind-tunnel model data and theory extrapolated to flight Reynolds numbers for Mach numbers of 2.5 and 3.0. Similar comparisons are made for drag due to lift and maximum lift-drag ratio for Mach numbers up to about 5. Speed-brake drag and base-drag results are presented up to Mach numbers of 5.5 and 6, respectively.

345. Walker, Harold J.; and Wolowicz, Chester H.: **Stability and Control Derivative Characteristics of the X-15 Airplane.** NASA TM X-714, March 1962, 65N23922, 87H25529, #. (See also 319.)

The flight-determined derivative characteristics are compared with the predictions from wind-tunnel tests and theory for Mach numbers extending to 5.5 and angles of attack up to 17 degrees. With few exceptions, the predictions were found generally to be in good agreement with the flight data. Areas of deficient stability and control are briefly discussed.

346. *White, Robert M.; Robinson, Glenn H.; and Matranga, Gene J.: **Resume of Handling Qualities of the X-15 Airplane.** NASA TM X-715, March 1962, 65N23923, 87H25530, #. (See also 320.)

A summary of handling qualities is presented as assessed from pilot opinion and flight data. Segments of the flight profile which were evaluated include the launch, climbout, semiballistic flight, atmosphere entry, and landing. Longitudinal controllability is compared with results from current studies of reentry-type vehicles.

*Air Force Flight Test Center, Edwards AFB, California,

347. Petersen, Forrest S.; Rediess, Herman A.; and Weil, Joseph: **Lateral-Directional Control of the X-15 Airplane.** NASA TM X-726, March 1962, 65N23924, 87H25533, #. (See also 321.)

The deterioration of lateral-directional controllability with roll damper off and the pilot performing a lateral-control task is discussed. The problem area was defined by fixed-base and airborne simulators and verified by closed-loop analysis in which a human transfer function represents the pilot. A parameter which predicts the problem area for the X-15 airplane is developed. The means considered to alleviate the control problem in the X-15 airplane are also discussed.

348. Taylor, Lawrence W., Jr.; Samuels, James L.; and Smith, John W.: **Simulator Investigation of the Control Requirements of a Typical Hypersonic Glider.** NASA TM X-635, H-226, March 1962, 72N71506, 87H26322.

The handling qualities of a typical hypersonic glider were investigated with a flight simulator at Mach numbers of 0.26, 1.0, 3.5, 8, and 20 over an angle-of-attack range of 0° to 50°. Inasmuch as flight conditions influencing the control of the glider can be expected to change relatively slowly, a five-degree-of-freedom mechanization was used. Pilots assessed the controllability of the glider without augmentation with fixed gain dampers, and with on adaptive control system. The investigation was limited to aerodynamic control.

349. Kordes, Eldon E.; Reed, Robert D.; and Dawdy, Alpha L.: **Structural Heating Experiences on the X-15 Airplanes.** NASA TM X-711. Prepared in cooperation with North American Aviation, Inc., Inglewood, California, March 1962, 71N75350, 87H25525.

A survey of maximum structural temperatures measured on the X-15 airplane during speed flights up to a Mach number of 6 is presented. Structural problems caused by local hot spots and discontinuities are described. Structural modifications in the affected areas to eliminate the problems are discussed.

350. Walker, J. A.: **The X-15 Program.** Presented at The Institute of Aerospace Sciences meeting, St. Louis, Missouri, April 30–May 2, 1962, 62N12923, #.

The high-temperature structural design approach utilized for the X-15 configuration has been successful; no major design deficiencies were encountered nor major modifications required. With but few exceptions, the local thermal problems encountered have not affected primary structural areas. In general, the aerodynamic derivatives extracted from flight-test data have confirmed the estimated derivatives obtained from wind-tunnel evaluations at hypersonic speeds. The aerodynamic flight control system and the simple stability augmentation system of the X-15 airplane have proved to be good technical designs. The airplane can be flown with satisfactory handling qualities through the range of dynamic pressures from about 1,500 lb/sq ft to below 100 lb/sq ft through the range of Mach numbers from 6.0 to subsonic landing conditions. Although only limited flight experience has been gained with the reaction control system, its basic design appears to be completely adequate. This type of system apparently provides an adequate means of attitude control for future space vehicles. Pilot transition from aerodynamic controls to reaction controls has been accomplished without problems.

351. Drake, H. M.: **Crew Safety and Survival Aspects of the Lunar-Landing Mission.** Presented at IAS Meeting on Man's Progress in the Conquest of Space, St. Louis, Missouri, April 30–May 2, 1962, 62N12866, #.

Some of the safety and survival aspects of the manned lunar-landing mission are examined. The conditions requiring abort to the earth, lunar orbit, and lunar surface are determined. Some of the possible design requirements to permit abort to lunar orbit or surface are indicated. Lunar orbital and surface survival kits are described, and the stationing of such kits in lunar orbit and at the intended landing site is proposed.

352. Weil, Joseph: **Review of the X-15 Program.** NASA TN D-1278, June 1962, 62N13289, 87H27936, #.

The X-15 project is reviewed from its inception in 1954 through 1961. Some of the more important historical aspects of the program are noted, but major emphasis is placed on the significant research results.

353. Fichter, W. B.; and Kordes, E. E.: **Response of Multiweb Beams to Static and Dynamic Loading.** NASA TN D-1258, May 1962, 62N11650, #.

354. Drake, H. M.: **Survey of FRC Recovery Research** Presented to Meeting on Space Vehicle Landing and Recovery Research and Technology, (see N73-70937 04-99), July 11, 1962, 73N70943.

355. Horton, V. W.: **Manned Paraglider Flight Tests.** Presented to Meeting on Space Vehicle Landing and Recovery Research and Technology, (see N73-70937 04-99), July 11, 1962, 73N70944.

356. Armstrong, Neil A.; and Holleman, Euclid C.: **A Review of In-Flight Simulation Pertinent to Piloted Space Vehicles.** AGARD Report 403, 21st Flight Mechanics Panel Meeting, Paris, France, July 9–11, 1962.

This paper shows how the environment of actual flight may be used to simulate many phase of manned space exploration. A number of simulations using conventional, modified, and specially built aircraft are discussed in relation to the portion of space flight to which they are generally applicable, that is, the launch, orbital, entry, or the landing approach phase.

357. Holleman, Euclid C.; and Armstrong, Neil A.: **Pilot Utilization During Boost.** Presented at the Inter-Center Technical Conference on Control Guidance and Navigation Research for Manned Lunar Missions, Ames Research Center, Moffett Field, California, July 24–25, 1962, 63X14567.

The capabilities of the pilot as the controller of an aircraft have been well documented, but relatively few investigators have considered the use of the pilot as the primary controller of a vertical launch vehicle. This role in the launch of a multistage vehicle has received increased interest recently. Figure 1 summarizes the studies in this area made to date. Of necessity, these programs utilized simulators to represent the launch vehicle. Some investigators used a human centrifuge to simulate the acceleration representative of these vehicles.

358. Taylor, Lawrence W., Jr.; and Adkins, Elmor J.: **Recent X-15 Flight Test Experience With the MH-96 Adaptive Control System.** Presented at the Inter-Center Technical Conference on Control Guidance and Navigation Research for Manned Lunar Missions, Ames Research Center, Moffett Field, California, July 24–25, 1962.

359. Matranga, Gene J.; and Bellman, Donald R.: **Concept of a Free-Flying Lunar Landing and Take-Off Research Vehicle.** Presented at the Inter-Center Technical Conference on Control Guidance and Navigation Research for Manned Lunar Missions, Ames Research Center, Moffett Field, California, July 24–25, 1962.

360. Layton, Garrison P.; and Thompson, Milton O.: **Summary of Low-Speed Paraglider Flight Investigations. Part 1, Performance and Control Characteristics, Part 2, Flare and Landing.** Presented at the Inter-Center Technical Conference on Control Guidance and Navigation Research for Manned Lunar Missions, Ames Research Center, July 24–25, 1962.

361. Kordes, Eldon E.: **Experience With the X-15 Airplane in Relation to Problems of Reentry Vehicles.** 3rd Congress of the International Council of the Aeronautical Sciences, Stockholm, Sweden, August 27–September 1, 1962. 62N12630.

This paper discusses some of the results obtained from the flight program of the X-15 research airplane that have application to the design philosophy of future glide reentry vehicles. Experiences in the areas of panel flutter, landing dynamics, flight control systems, and aerodynamic and structural heating are described; and some of the problems that have developed are discussed briefly. A bibliography of papers published on the X-15 flight program is included.

362. Walker, J. A.: **I Fly the X-15.** *National Geographic*, Vol. 122, No. 3, September 1962, pp. 428–450.

363. Armstrong, N. A.; Walker, J. A.; Petersen, F. S.; and White, R. M.: **The X-15 Flight Program.** *NASA Proceedings* *of the Second National Conference on the Peaceful Uses of Space*, Seattle, Washington, May 8–10, 1962, November 1962, pp. 263–271, 63N11158.

This paper reviews the philosophy of the X-15 airplane, describes its concept in operation, and prophesies its future. The X-15 was the first design to require rocket reaction control within its design envelope. The flight and landing of the X-15 are reviewed. Some of the follow-on uses of the X-15 include guidance-instrument experiments. precise determination of atmospheric density at extreme altitude, measurement of size and quantity of micrometeorites in near space, and determination of the intensity of ultraviolet and infrared rays in near space.

364. Veatch, Donald W.: **X-20 Instrumentation Sensors.** Paper for the X-20A (Dyna-Soar) Symposium, November 5–7, 1962.

365. Martin, J. A.: **The Record-Setting Research Airplanes.** Reproduced from *Aerospace Engineering*, Vol. 21, No. 12, December 1962, pp. 49–54, 63N13571.

The first compilation of all available data on the unofficial records of the rocket airplanes is presented. The maximum Mach number, true velocity, and the altitude obtained by the X-1-1, D-558-II, X-1A, X-2, and X-15 airplanes are given in tabular form. Also, the physical characteristics of these airplanes are given and include wing spans, wing sweep, launch weight, and landing weight.

366. Tremant, R. A.: **Operational Experiences and Characteristics of the X-15 Flight Control System.** NASA TN D-1402, December 1962, 63N11123, #.

X-15 flight and simulator experiences with the manual flight control and stability augmentation system for the period from December 1958 to January 1962 are presented. The flight data extend to a Mach number of 6.04 and an altitude of 217,000 feet, and the simulator data cover the design flight envelope. The characteristics of the manual flight control system and the stability augmentation system are discussed, in conjunction with pilot evaluation, operational problems, modifications, and reliability. Pertinent X-15 flight history is included.

1963 Technical Publications

367. Horton, V. W.; and Messing, W. E.: **Some Operational Aspects of Using a High-Performance Airplane as a First-Stage Booster for Air-Launching Solid-Fuel Sounding Rockets.** NASA TN D-1279, January 1963, 63N12192, #.

Five test vehicles were air-launched from an F-104A airplane to investigate some of the operational aspects and the practicability of using the energy input of the airplane as a first-stage booster for sounding rockets. A launch maneuver and launcher system were developed and matched to the airplane's capabilities so that suitable repeatability of launch parameters was attained.

368. Larson, T. J.; and Webb, L. D.: **Calibrations and Comparisons of Pressure-Airspeed-Altitude Systems of the X-15 Airplane From Subsonic to High Supersonic Speeds.** NASA TN D-1724, February 1963, 63N12951, #.

The X-15 flight calibration data to define static-pressure position errors are presented for two types of pressure-sensing configurations: a standard NACA pitot-static tube attached to a nose boom, and two manifolded flush static-pressure ports on the ogive nose. The position-error calibrations are presented up to $M = 3.31$ for the standard nose boom installation and up to $M = 4$ for the flush static system. Presented also are stagnation-pressure errors sensed by a pitot probe ahead of the canopy. Methods used to determine the position errors are described. The nose-boom configuration is shown to be superior from the standpoint of position error and ease of calibration for the available data range.

369. Holleman, Euclid C.; and Wilson, Warren, S.: **Flight-Simulator Requirements for High-Performance Aircraft Based on X-15 Experience.** ASME Paper 63-AHGT-81, ASME Aviation and Space, Hydraulics, and Gas Turbine Conference and Products Show, Los Angeles, California, March 3–7, 1963, 63A17579.

Review of the simulation experience acquired during the design and flight testing of the X-15 research airplane. Discussed are the problems encountered and the use of simulators in their solution, with particular reference to the X-15 fixed-base simulator. Simulator techniques which may be used in the supersonic-transport program, such as a variable-stability airborne simulator, are suggested.

370. Row, Perry V.; and Fischel, Jack: **Operational Flight-Test Experience With the X-15 Airplane.** AIAA Paper 63-075, AIAA Space Flight Testing Conference, Cocoa Beach, Florida, March 18–20, 1963, 63A15995.

Review of the experience of the NASA Flight Research Center in coping with the problems of component and system checkout and operational flight procedures in an advanced flight research program. The operational evolution of the most troublesome and the most important systems on the North American X-15 is discussed, and operational and research data are presented. Procedures now being utilized and those that will be applied to newer systems are also discussed. The use of a flight simulator to check out several flight systems and to practice normal and emergency operational procedures is assessed. Finally, the flight operational techniques evolved for ground monitoring of flight systems data and flight-trajectory information to provide pilot backup support are described. Evidence is introduced to show how these techniques have facilitated the rapid expansion of the flight envelope and have aided in achievement of research objectives.

371. Layton, G. P., Jr.; and Thompson, M. O.: **Preliminary Flight Evaluation of Two Unpowered Manned Paragliders.** NASA TN D-1826, April 1963, 63N14429, #.

Towed and free-flight tests were made with unpowered, manned paragliders to study the performance, stability, and control characteristics of a typical paraglider. The paragliders used had maximum lift-drag ratios greater than 3.5 and wing loadings of approximately 4.0 lb/sq ft. The airspeed range was limited by the rearward center-of-pressure shift at angles of attack above and below trim angle of attack. Performance data obtained from flight tests are presented and compared with analytical results. Center-of-gravity shift, accomplished by tilting the wing relative to the fuselage, was used for control. This method of control was adequate for towed and free flight as well as for flare and landing. The pilot's evaluation of the vehicle's handling qualities, and a discussion of development problems are presented.

372. Walker, J. A.; and Weil, J.: **The X-15 Program.** *Proceedings of AIAA 2nd Manned Space Flight Meeting,* AD-400711, April 22–24, 1963, pp. 295–307, 63A19019, 63N23237.

Review of the important operational problems encountered in the flights of the North American X-15 aircraft. The history of the project is considered, outlining the design development and the flight tests, including aerodynamic configurations, mode of operation, flight program, and performance. Summarized is the operational experience, such as the structural and thermostructural problems, and the rocket engines, auxiliary-power-unit, and the control and guidance systems experience. The piloting aspects of the X-15 mission are described, including the boost, entry, and landing techniques.

373. Noll, R. B.; and Halasey, R. L.: **Theoretical Investigation of the Slideout Dynamics of a Vehicle Equipped With a Tricycle Skid-Landing-Gear System.** NASA TN D-1828, May 1963, 63N16298, #.

The equations-of-motion for the slideout of a vehicle equipped with a tricycle skid-type landing-gear system are presented and reduced to three degrees of freedom. A comparison of the results of numerical calculations for the three-degree-of-freedom slideout of the X-15 research

vehicle with flight-test results shows that the theoretical analysis of the slideout can adequately predict the slideout distance, the direction of lateral displacement, and the approximate lateral displacement. A numerical study of the slideout equations indicates that the velocity at which the aerodynamic influence on the vehicle becomes negligible can be predicted.

374. Ferguson, T. J.: **Flight Research Center Instrumentation Program.** NASA Goddard Space Flight Center *Proceedings of the Optical Communications and Tracking Symposium,* (see N68-84351), June 1963, 68N84355.

375. Row, Perry V.; and Fischel, Jack: **X-15 Flight Experience.** *Astronautics and Aerospace Engineering,* Vol. 1, June 1963, pp. 25–32, 63A17556.

Survey of the operational aspects of the X-15 aircraft development program. Discussed are the major structural problems encountered, such as landing-gear overloading, panel flutter, side-fairing buckling, wing leading-edge skin buckling, windshield heat damage, and internal heat damage. It is shown how the X-15 was made operational for the simplest of tasks and was then built up to the maximum demands in discrete progressive steps. Accidents in the program, and their causes, are examined.

376. Matranga, G. J.; Washington, H. P.; Chenoweth, P. L.; and Young, W. R.: **Handling Qualities and Trajectory Requirements for Terminal Lunar Landing, as Determined From Analog Simulation.** NASA TN D-1921, August 1963, 63N19606, #.

A six-degree-of-freedom analog study was performed to aid in defining handling qualities and trajectory potential for terminal lunar landing. Results showed that, for a maneuvering task in the pitch mode and a random-motion-correction task in the roll and yaw modes, the pilots preferred rate or attitude command with control accelerations of about 10 deg/sec and reasonable artificial damping. Also, to consistently perform successful landings, the pilots generally used thrust-to-weight ratios throttled between a minimum value of 0.8 lunar g and maximum value of 1.8 lunar g.

377. Watts, J. D.; and Banas, R. P.: **X-15 Structural Temperature Measurements and Calculations for Flights to Maximum Mach Numbers of Approximately 4, 5, and 6.** NASA TM X-883, H-315, August 1963, 72N73396.

Structural temperatures on the X-l5 airplane were measured continuously during three performance-envelope expansion flights to maximum Mach numbers of approximately 4, 5, and 6. Tabulations of temperature time histories, representing all surfaces and some wing internal structure, are presented for these flights. Methods of predicting surface temperature levels and gradients are described, and the resulting calculations are compared with measured temperatures.

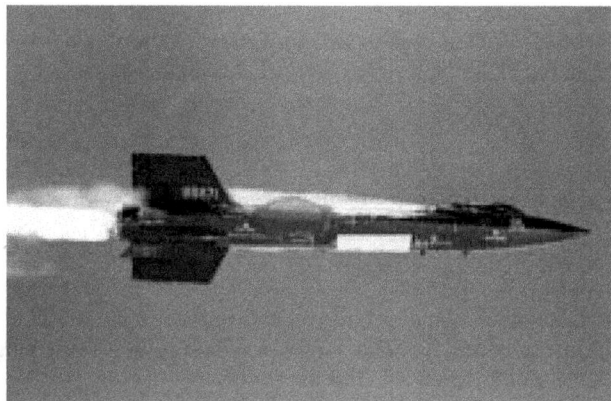

EC88-0180-1

X-15 Airplane

378. Videan, Edward N.; Banner, Richard D.; and Smith, John P.: **The Application of Analog and Digital Computer Techniques in the X-15 Flight Research Program.** Presented at the International Symposium on Analog and Digital Techniques Applied to Aeronautics, Liege, Belgium, September 9–12, 1963.

This paper is limited, however, to the particular area of computer application to research flight planning and system implementation. Two systems are described, one analog and one digital, which support the flight planning and system implementation. Today, because of changing flight test requirements, a relatively sophisticated and complete simulation system is considered necessary to carry on a flight research program.

379. Thompson, Milton O.: **Preliminary Results of the Lifting-Body Flight Program.** NASA TM X-56005. Presented at the 7th Annual SETP Symposium, Beverly Hills, California, September 27–28, 1963.

This paper covers the design, construction, preflight, and initial flight testing of the NASA Flight Research Center's M-2 lifting-body vehicle. The paper also discusses the concept of lifting-body utilization and the reasons for construction of a lightweight vehicle.

380. Noll, R. B.; Jarvis, C. R.; Pembo, C.; Lock, W. P.; and Scott, B. J.: **Aerodynamic and Control-System Contributions to the X-15 Airplane Landing-Gear Loads.** NASA TN D-2090, October 1963, 63N22117, #.

The effects of the X-15 manual flight control and stability augmentation systems on the horizontal-tail load, and the effect of wing-flap position on the wing load during touchdown are investigated. Methods for significantly reducing the maximum total load on the main gear during

landings are described. Data from typical X-15 landings and from landings in which modified touchdown techniques were used are presented and compared.

381. Weil, Joseph: **Piloted Flight Simulation at the NASA Flight Research Center.** Presented at IEEE 10th Annual East Coast Conference on Aerospace and Navigation Electronics, Baltimore, Maryland, October 21–23, 1963.

382. Nugent, Jack: **The X-15 Advanced Air-Breathing Engine Program.** Presented at Bumblebee Composite Design Research Panel, November 1963.

383. Horton, V. W.; Layton, G. P., Jr.; and Thompson, M. O.: **Exploratory Flight Tests of Advanced Piloted Spacecraft Concepts.** NASA TM X-51360. Presented at the AIAA, AFFTC, and NASA FRC Testing of Manned Flight Systems Conference, Edwards, California, December 4–6, 1963, 65N89037.

384. Sisk, T. R.; and Andrews, W. H.: **Utilization of Existing Aircraft in Support of Supersonic-Transport Research Programs.** NASA TM X-51360. Presented at the AIAA, AFFTC, and NASA FRC Testing of Manned Flight Systems Conference, Edwards, California, December 4–6, 1963, pp. 67–76, 64N12881.

The supersonic transport will not necessarily be derivative of a previous military airplane, as are the current family of jet transports. Therefore, full-scale test data and operational experience for this vehicle will be limited, and in some areas nonexistent. In an attempt to fill this void, the NASA Flight Research Center has initiated several programs utilizing existing high-performance aircraft to investigate some of the problems predicted in the supersonic-transport operational environment. This paper discusses three of these programs: a minimum-flight-speed investigation utilizing an F5D aircraft, and Air Traffic Control (ATC) compatibility program utilizing an A-5A aircraft, and specific vehicle research on the XB-70 aircraft.

385. Rediess, H. A.; and Deets, D. A.: **An Advanced Method for Airborne Simulation.** NASA TM X-51360. Presented at the AIAA, AFFTC, and NASA FRC Testing of Manned Flight Systems Conference, Edwards, California, December 4–6, 1963, pp. 33–39, 64N12880. (See also 406.)

The NASA Flight Research Center has conducted and sponsored studies leading to the design and developments of a general-purpose airborne simulator (GPAS) to support the supersonic-transport program and to perform general research. This paper presents some of the results of these studies. The response feedback, and the model-control concepts for an airborne simulator are discussed and evaluated. The model-following performance of the system designed for the GPAS, and, other results believed generally applicable are also presented.

386. Larson, T. J.; and Montoya, E. J.: **Stratosphere and Mesosphere Density-Height Profiles Obtained With the X-15 Airplane.** NASA TM X-51734, <u>1963</u>, 65N33708, #.

Density-height profiles in the stratosphere and mesosphere were obtained from impact-pressure, velocity,. and altitude measurements made on six X-l5 research airplane flights. A form of the Rayleigh pilot formula was used for density computations. Because of pressure-instrumentation limitations and pressure lag, the maximum altitude for reasonably accurate density determination was considered to be about 65 km. Good agreement was obtained between temperatures calculated from faired density-height profiles of two X-l5 flights and temperatures measured by rocketsondes launched near the times of flight from the Pacific Missile Range, Point Mugu, California.

1964 Technical Publications

387. Pyle, J. S.: **Comparison of Flight Pressure Measurements With Wind-Tunnel Data and Theory for the Forward Fuselage of the X-15 Airplane at Mach Numbers From 0.8 to 6.0.** NASA TN D-2241, <u>January 1964</u>, 64N12961, #.

The results of flight pressure measurements on the forward fuselage of the X-15 airplane are presented for angles of attack from O degrees to 15 degrees and Mach numbers from 0.8 to 6.0. Comparisons of flight and wind-tunnel data showed good agreement, and theoretical calculations predicted flight pressure measurements reasonably well.

388. Holleman, E. C.; and Adkins, E. J.: **Contributions of the X-15 Program to Lifting Entry Technology.** NASA TM X-51359. Presented at the AIAA Aerospace Sciences Meeting, New York, <u>January 20–24, 1964</u>, 65N89079. (See also 389.)

Entries from altitudes greater than 350,000 ft with the X-15 airplane have provided piloting experience and verification of predicted control characteristics and operational techniques. The airplane re-enters as a glider and duplicates several phases in the recovery of higher-performance vehicles, for example, transition from near-zero dynamic pressure to aerodynamic flight, and the terminal-area ranging and landing. During entries, reaction controls have been used to surprisingly high dynamic pressures. Rate command control provided satisfactory control, and hold modes were appreciated by the pilots for secondary control modes. With conservatively planned flights, the pilots have had no problem controlling range to base with contact navigation. Landmarks have been observed from above 300,000 ft and 160 miles range. The approach and landing of the low-lift-drag-ratio X-15 airplane has become routine, with relatively small dispersion in touchdown and slideout distance. The speed brakes have been an important control for regulation of

ranging for landing; however, the pilots indicated that faster-acting speed brakes would allow more flexible operation.

389. Holleman, E. C.; and Adkins, E. J.: **Contributions of the X-15 Program to Lifting Entry Technology.** AIAA Paper 64-17, <u>January 1964</u>, 64N15273. (See also 388.)

390. Drake, H. M.: **Aerodynamic Testing Using Special Aircraft.** NASA TM X-51605. Presented at AIAA Aerodynamic Testing Conference, Washington, D. C., <u>March 9–10, 1964</u>, 65N88557, 65N35225, #. (See also 391.)

In this paper some of the recent applications of special aircraft to aerodynamic testing are reviewed and something of the complementary relationship such testing bears to theory and to research in ground facilities is indicated. Some of the primary reasons for flight research are to verify theory, ground facilities, and design. Encounter new or overlooked problems. Investigate flight in the true environment. Establish crew-vehicle integration and requirements. Study the atmosphere, earth, and space.

391. Drake, H. M.: **Aerodynamic Testing Using Special Aircraft.** American Institute of Aeronautics and Astronautics Aerodynamics Testing Conference, <u>March 10, 1964</u>, pp. 78–188, 64N17019. (See also 390.)

392. Quinn, R. D.; and Kuhl, A. E.: **Comparison of Flight-Measured and Calculated Turbulent Heat Transfer on the X-15 Airplane at Mach Numbers From 2.5 to 6.0 at Low Angles of Attack.** NASA TM X-939, H-332, <u>March 1964</u>, 72N73498.

Turbulent heat-transfer data obtained on the X-l5 airplane for a flight to a Mach number of 6.0 are presented and compared with calculated values. Calculated boundary-layer thicknesses and Mach number profiles in the shear layer are also presented. Comparisons between measured and calculated heat-transfer coefficients show that the calculated heat-transfer coefficients are from 30 to 60 percent higher than the measured values when bluntness effects are included in estimates of the local Mach number at the edge of the boundary layer.

393. Fischel, Jack; and Toll, Thomas A.: **The X-15 Project: Results and New Research.** *Astronautics & Aeronautics*, <u>March 1964</u>, pp. 20–28.

394. Chenoweth, P. L.; and Dana, W. H.: **Flight Evaluation of Wide-Angle Overlapping Monoculars for Providing Pilot's Field of Vision.** NASA TN D-2265, <u>April 1964</u>, 64N17753, #.

A qualitative evaluation was made of the effectiveness of wide-angle, overlapping monoculars as the sole source of outside visual reference during takeoffs, aerial maneuvers, visual navigation, and approaches and landings in a light observation aircraft. The evaluation was made during the day and at night and in air conditions which varied from no turbulence to severe turbulence.

395. Holleman, E. C.: **Piloting Performance During the Boost of the X-15 Airplane to High Altitude.** NASA TN D-2289, April 1964, 64N19002, #.

396. Gray, W. E., Jr.: **NASA Flight Research Center Handling-Qualities Program on General-Aviation Aircraft.** NASA TM X-56004, April 21, 1964, 65N35235, #.

397. Jarvis, C. R.; and Adkins, E. J.: **Operational Experience With X-15 Reaction Controls.** NASA TM X-56002. Presented at the SAE-ASME Symposium on Position, Attitude and Thrust Vector Control, April 21, 1964, 64N20683, #.

The four reaction-control-system configurations investigated during the X-15 program include a proportional acceleration command system, on-off proportional rate command and attitude hold systems, and a rate-sensing on-off stability augmentation system. Each of the systems is described briefly, and development problems encountered in hardware design, component compatibility, and systems integration are discussed. The practical aspects of system design and operation are emphasized. Flight experience with each system is also discussed. Flight data showing the results of open-loop and closed-loop control during critical X-15 reentry maneuvers are presented.

398. Sanderson, K. C.: **The X-15 Flight Test Instrumentation.** NASA TM X-56000. *Flight Test Instrumentation*, Vol. 3, pp. 267–290, proceedings of the Third International Symposium, (see TL 671.7 I54 V. 3), April 21, 1964, 1964, 64N19899, #.

The basic instrumentation philosophy for the X-15 program was dictated primarily by two factors. First, if the X-15 were to successfully fulfill its mission of providing timely research data, it had to be built and instrumented quickly. Second, the instrumentation had to be accurate and reliable. The philosophy adopted was as follows: Onboard recording would be used, selected parameters would be telemetered and displayed to ground monitors in real time, continuous ground radar tracking provided instrumentation system would have to be flexible, maximum use of off-the-shelf instrumentation components and systems.

399. Wall, D. E.: **A Study of Hypersonic Aircraft.** NASA TM X-56001, April 24, 1964, 64N20549, #. (See also 400.)

A study is being made at the NASA Flight Research Center to determine the gross characteristics of future hypersonic aircraft, without the refinement of configuration optimization. The characteristics defined by this study are to be used as a guide in assessing the need for future hypersonic flight research.

400. Wall, D. E.: **A Study of Hypersonic Aircraft.** NASA TM X-51641, 1964, 65N35263, #. (See also 399.)

401. Taylor, L. W., Jr.; and Adkins, E. J.: **Adaptive Flight Control Systems—Pro and Con.** NASA TM X-56008. Presented at the AIAA Specialists Meeting, Los Angeles, California, April 28, 1964, 64N27261, #.

In light of difficulties posed by the X-15, the adaptive flight control system was developed and has been most successful. Although several problems were encountered during the development of the MH-96 adaptive system, and emphasis on them in this paper tends to paint a dark picture, these problems were solved on the ground before the first flight, except for some insignificant details which affected only the periphery functions of the MH-96 even during the early flights. There is a saying that "a bird in hand is worth two in the bush." For adaptive flight control system concepts, we would put the ratio at about 10. An adaptive control system which has been successfully demonstrated in the X-15 is worth about 10 proposed new adaptive concepts which have not been exposed to the idiosyncrasies of control-system hardware.

402. Kordes, E. E.; and Tanner, C. S.: **Preliminary Results of Boundary-Layer Noise Measured on the X-15 Airplane.** NASA TM X-56003, May 1, 1964, 65N35284, #.

In order to provide detailed information on boundary-layer noise over a wide range of controlled flight conditions, the NASA Flight Research Center is conducting a boundary-layer-noise research program with the X-l5 airplane. This paper describes the program and presents some of the preliminary results.

403. Thompson, M. O.: **Aerospace Medical and Bioengineering Considerations in Lifting-Body and Research-Aircraft Operations.** NASA TM X-56005. Presented at the 35th Aerospace Medical Association Annual Meeting, Miami Beach, Florida, May 11–14, 1964, 64N22440, #.

The lifting-body vehicle we have flown at the Flight Research Center is the M-2 rather than the M-l; thus, it is this vehicle I shall discuss. For those who may not be familiar with the M-2 or the lifting-body concept, I shall describe it briefly. As the name implies, a lifting body is a vehicle with a body shape, rather than wings, which generates lift at an angle or attack. The only irregularities or protuberances in the body shape are the surfaces required for aerodynamic control. Figure 1 compares the advantages or the three configurations having reentry capability, that is, the ballistic or semiballistic, the lifting body, and the winged vehicle. The energy footprints or the vehicles, or landing areas available to each, can be estimated. For operational usage, a lifting reentry vehicle appears to be highly desirable because of its versatility for reentry from a number of orbit planes or the capability for recovery at a number of landing sites within the United States.

404. Maher, J. F., Jr.; Ottinger, C. W.; and Capasso, V. N., Jr.: **YLR99-RM-1 Rocket Engine Operating Experience in the X-15 Aircraft.** NASA TN D-2391, July 1964, 64N25810, #.

This paper describes the unique operating experience obtained during the first 50 government flights with the YLR99 engine installed in the X-15 aircraft, with emphasis on problem areas of the engine and their effects on the X-15 program.

405. Powers, B. G.; and Matheny, N. W.: **Flight Evaluation of Three Techniques of Demonstrating the Minimum Flying Speed of a Delta-Wing Airplane.** NASA TN D-2337, July 1964, 64N24966, #.

A flight test program was conducted with an F5D airplane to evaluate three techniques for demonstrating the minimum flying speed of a delta-wing aircraft: The Civil Air Regulations stall-speed demonstration, the 1 g demonstration, and the constant-rate-of-climb demonstration. The Civil Air Regulation stall-speed demonstration currently used for civil transport aircraft was found to be inadequate for demonstrating the minimum speed of a delta-wing airplane, because this type of airplane does not have a well-defined stall point near maximum lift coefficient. The 1 g minimum speed, which is based on maintaining a constant 1 g normal acceleration, was difficult to determine precisely, especially when buffeting was present. The constant-rate-of-climb minimum-speed maneuvers, which are based on the ability to maintain a constant rate of climb, were reasonably easy to perform and were unaffected by the aircraft buffet characteristics. The level-flight minimum speed obtained from the constant-rate-of-climb techniques was found to be the most rational minimum speed for a delta-wing aircraft. The applicability of these techniques to other types of aircraft was shown in limited tests on a sweptwing airplane.

406. Rediess, H. A.; and Deets, D. A.: **An Advanced Method for Airborne Simulation.** NASA RP 337. Reprinted from *J. Aircraft*, Vol. 1, No. 4, July–August 1964, pp. 185–190. Presented at the AIAA, AFFTC, and NASA FRC Testing of Manned Flight Systems Conference, Edwards AFB, California, December 4–6, 1963, 64N31214. (See also 385.)

In a general discussion of airborne simulation, it is observed that the motion of a specific aircraft cannot be matched completely with an airborne simulator, except at certain specific conditions, if the number of independent control devices for angular and linear motion is less than the number of corresponding degrees of freedom to be stimulated. However, airborne simulators can be valuable research and pilot-training tools through proper choice of the motion parameters to be matched and by tailoring the program to the particular simulator used.

407. Fischel, J.; and Webb, L. D.: **Flight-Informational Sensors, Display, and Space Control of the X-15 Airplane for Atmospheric and Near-Space Flight Missions.** NASA TN D-2407, August 1964, 64N26629, #.

This paper presents pertinent information obtained during the X-15 program and discusses its use by the pilot in performing a variety of atmospheric and near-space flight missions.

408. Saltzman, Edwin J.: **Base Pressure Coefficients Obtained From the X-15 Airplane for Mach Numbers Up to 6.** NASA TN D-2420, August 1964, 64N27122, #.

Base pressure measurements were made on the vertical fin, side fairing, fuselage, and wing trailing edge of the X-15. Data are presented between Mach numbers of 0.8 and 6. Power-off and power-on data are included and compared with wind-tunnel measurements and theory.

409. Hughes, D. L.; Powers, B. G.; and Dana, W. H.: **Flight Evaluation of Some Effects of the Present Air Traffic Control System on Operation of a Simulated Supersonic Transport.** NASA TN D-2219, November 1964, 64N33082, #.

An exploratory flight program was conducted to investigate the effect of the present Air Traffic Control system on the operation of a simulated supersonic transport in the Los Angeles terminal area. The climb and descent portions of a representative supersonic transport flight profile were flown with an A-5A airplane. In addition, en route problems were explored within the speed and altitude data were obtained, as well as flight-crew opinions and ground-personnel comments.

410. Yancey, R. B.: **Flight Measurements of Stability and Control Derivatives of the X-15 Research Airplane to a Mach Number of 6.02 and an Angle of Attack of 25 Degrees** NASA TN D-2532, November 1964, 65N10638, #.

Flight tests of the X-15 airplane provided data from which longitudinal, lateral, and directional stability and control derivations were determined over a Mach number range from 0.60 to 6.02 and over an angle-of-attack range from -2.7 degrees to 25 degrees. The data were obtained with the lower rudder on and off, speed brakes open and closed, and power on and off. The longitudinal derivatives show the expected trends of increasing levels through the transonic region and diminishing levels as the Mach number increases in the supersonic region. A high level of longitudinal stability is indicated by the flight data.

411. Holleman, E. C.; and Adkins, E. J.: **Contributions of the X-15 Program to Lifting Entry Technology.** *J. Aircraft*, Vol. 1, No. 6, November–December 1964.

Entries from altitudes greater than 350,000 ft with the X-15 airplane have provided piloting experience and verification of predicted control characteristics and operational techniques. The airplane re-enters as a glider and duplicates several phases in the recovery of higher-performance vehicles, for example, transition from near-zero dynamic pressure to aerodynamic flight, and the terminal-area ranging and landing. During entries, reaction controls have been used to surprisingly high dynamic pressures. Rate command control provided satisfactory control, and hold modes were appreciated by the pilots for secondary control modes. With conservatively planned flights, the pilots have had no problem controlling range to base with contact navigation. Landmarks have been observed from above 300,000 ft and 160 miles range. The approach and landing of the low-lift-drag-ratio X-15 airplane has become routine, with relatively small dispersion in touchdown and slideout distance. The speed brakes have been an important control for regulation of ranging for landing; however, the pilots indicated that faster-acting speed brakes would allow more flexible operation.

412. Thompson, M. O.: **General Review of Piloting Problems Encountered During Simulation and Flights of the X-15.** NASA TM X-56884, Society of Experimental Test Pilots Ninth Annual Report. Presented at the SETP Symposium, Beverly Hills, California, 1964, 66N83857.

413. Fischel, J.; and Toll, T. A.: **The X-15 Project—Results and New Research.** NASA RP 186, 1964, 64N22066.

414. Fischel, J.; and Toll, T. A.: **The X-15 Research Aircraft—Research Accomplished and Planned.** NASA TM X-51485, 1964, 65N89070.

415. Winglade, R. L.: **Current Research on Advanced Cockpit Display Systems.** NASA TM X-56010, 1964, 65N20814, #.

Current cockpit-display philosophy is discussed in terms of the pilot's informational requirements. Pilots scan patterns obtained through the use of an eye-position camera and a ground-based simulator are depicted for a conventional display system and for two advanced concepts. Preliminary results of some flight-test and ground-simulation evaluations of advanced concepts, such as totally integrated displays and indirect pilot viewing systems, are discussed.

416. Montoya, Earl J.; and Larson, Terry J.: **Stratosphere and Mesosphere Densities Measured With the X-15 Airplane.** NASA RP 499, NASA TM X-56009, 1964. (See also *Geophysical Research*, Vol. 69, No. 4, pp. 5123–5130, 1964.)

Density-height profiles in the stratosphere and mesosphere were obtained from measurements of impact pressure, velocity, and altitude on six X-15 research airplane flights. A form of the Rayleigh pilot formula was used for density computations. Because of pressure-instrumentation limitations and pressure lag, the maximum altitude for reasonably accurate density determination was considered to be about 65 km. Temperatures calculated from faired density-height profiles of two X-l5 flights agreed well with temperatures measured by rocketsondes launched near the times of flight from the Pacific Missile Range, Point Mugu, California.

1965 Technical Publications

417. Pyle, J. S.: **Flight-Measured Wing Surface Pressures and Loads for the X-15 Airplane at Mach Numbers From 1.2 to 6.0.** NASA TN D-2602, January 1965, 65N14854, #.

418. Roman, James: **Long-Range Program to Develop Medical Monitoring In Flight—The Flight Research Program-I.** *Aerospace Medicine*, Vol. 36, No. 6, June 1965.

NASA's Flight Research Center is conducting a long-range program designed to advance the state of the art in biomedical monitoring. Better knowledge of the physiological parameters used in monitoring the crew is one of major aims of the program. An instrumentation-development phase and a phase involving development of computer techniques for handling medical flight data both contribute to the overall program. The physiological-parameters-research phase and the instrumentation-development phase have yielded significant results after one year of operation.

419. Jarvis, C. R.; and Lock, W. P.: **Operational Experience With the X-15 Reaction Control and Reaction Augmentation Systems.** NASA TN D-2864, June 1965, 65N25725, #.

This paper describes the X-15 reaction control system and discusses the system characteristics, operational experiences, and development problems. Data are presented from X-15 high-altitude flights during which both the manual control and reaction augmentation systems were operated.

420. Cary, J. P.; and Keener, E. R.: **Flight Evaluation of the X-15 Ball-Nose Flow-Direction Sensor as an Air-Data System.** NASA TN D-2923, July 1965, 65N27945, #.

This paper assesses the suitability of the modified ball-nose system for obtaining Mach number and pressure altitude from pressure measurements at Mach numbers up to 5.3, altitudes up to 130,000 feet, and Reynolds number from 0.1 to 1.6×10 to the 6th per foot. The results are compared with experimental and theoretical results for spheres.

421. Pyle, J. S.: **Flight Pressure Distributions on the Vertical Stabilizers and Speed Brakes of the X-15 Airplane at Mach Numbers From 1 to 6.** NASA TN D-3048, September 1965, 65N34437, #.

This paper, the third in series on the X-15 surface-pressure distributions, presents flight-measured pressure distributions for the upper and lower vertical stabilizers with the speed brakes opened and closed. Data are shown for Mach numbers from 1 to 6 and angles of attack from 0 degree to 15 degree. Comparisons are made with wind-tunnel data and theory.

422. Smith, H. J.: **Evaluation of the Lateral-Directional Stability and Control Characteristics of the Lightweight M2-F1 Lifting Body at Low Speeds.** NASA TN D-3022, September 1965, 65N33839, #.

This paper summarizes the lateral-directional stability and control characteristics investigated during the flight tests and compares some wind-tunnel data with the flight values. Performance data from the tests are reported.

EC-64-404

M2-F1 Lifting Body Vehicle

423. Horton, V. W.; Eldredge, R. C.; and Klein, R. E.: **Flight-Determined Low-Speed Lift and Drag Characteristics of the Lightweight M2-F1 Lifting Body.** NASA TN D-3021, September 1965, 65N33357, #.

The low-speed lift and drag characteristics of a manned, lightweight M-2 lifting-body vehicle were determined in unpowered free-flight tests at angles of attack from 0 degrees to 22 degrees (0.38 radian) and at calibrated airspeeds from 61 knots to 113 knots (31.38 to 58.13 meters/second). Flight data are compared with results from full-scale wind-tunnel tests of the same vehicle.

424. Bellman, D. R.; and Matranga, G. J.: **Design and Operational Characteristics of a Lunar-Landing**

Research Vehicle. NASA TN D-3023, September 1965, 65N33549, #.

This paper represents the significant technical details and research capabilities of a free-flight lunar-landing simulator as they existed at the time of the initial flights of the vehicle. The lunar-landing research vehicle (LLRV) consists of a pyramid-shaped structural frame with four truss-type legs. A pilot's platform extends forward between two legs, and an electronics platform is similarly located, extending rearward. A jet engine is mounted vertically in a gimbal ring at the center of the vehicle. The LLRV is instrumented for research purposes. The data obtained are converted to digital form transmitted to a ground tape recorder by means of an 80-channel pulse-code-modulation type (PCM) telemetry system. Each channel can be read every 0.005 second, if desired.

ECN-535

Lunar Landing Research Vehicle (LLRV)

425. Banas, R. P.: **Comparison of Measured and Calculated Turbulent Heat Transfer in a Uniform and Nonuniform Flow Field on the X-15 Upper Vertical Fin at Mach Numbers of 4.2 and 5.3.** NASA TM X-1136, H-382, September 1965, 72N73703.

Turbulent heat-transfer coefficients and measured local static pressures were obtained in flight on the X-15 upper vertical fin with both a sharp and a blunt leading edge. The data are compared with calculated values. Calculated and measured Mach number profiles in the shear layer are also presented. Heat-transfer coefficients were obtained from measured skin temperatures at free-stream Mach numbers of approximately 4.2 and 5.3 and free-stream Reynolds numbers between $1.8 \times 10(6)$ and $2.5 \times 10(6)$ per foot. Comparisons of measured and calculated heat-transfer coefficients obtained in both a uniform flow field and a nonuniform flow field show that the heat-transfer coefficients calculated by Eckert's reference-temperature method were from 32 percent to 57 percent higher than the measured values.

426. Anon.: **Progress of the X-15 Research Airplane Program.** NASA-SP-90, USAF, USN, and NASA Conference on Progress of the X-15 Research Airplane Program, Edwards AFB, California October 7, 1965, 73N71303.

427. Love, J. E.; and Fischel, J.: **Status of X-15 Program.** NASA SP-90, (see N73-71303 05-99), 1965, pp. 1–15, 73N71304.

This paper briefly reviews the significant activities and present status of the project in order to aid you in properly relating the information presented during this conference to the total X-15 program. A comprehensive bibliography of information related to the X-15 program is included at the end of this paper.

428. Banner, R. D.; and Kuhl, A. E.: **A Summary of X-15 Heat Transfer and Skin Friction Measurements.** NASA SP-90, (see N73-71303 05-99), 1965, pp. 17–26, 73N71305. (See also 449.)

429. Lewis, T. L.; and McLeod, N. J.: **Flight Measurements of Boundary Layer Noise on the X-15.** NASA SP-90, (see N73-71303 05-99), 1965, pp. 27–33, 73N71306. (See also 451.)

Boundary-layer-noise data measured in flight over a Mach number range from 1.0 to 5.4 and at altitudes from 45,000 feet to 105,000 feet are presented. The data were obtained at four locations on the X-l5 (selected to provide varied boundary-layer conditions). The highest recorded noise level was 150 decibels. Boundary-layer parameters were measured at one location and are used to present the noise data in a nondimensional form for comparison with data from flat-plate wind-tunnel studies by other experimenters.

430. McKay, J. M.; and Noll, R. B.: **A Summary of the X-15 Landing Loads.** NASA SP-90, (see N73-71303 05-99), 1965, pp. 35–43, 73N71307. (See also 447.)

The purpose of this paper is to review the present status of the X-15 landing-gear loads, to discuss the parameters which affect these loads, and to show additional modifications that might be made to improve the landing gear system.

431. Taylor, L. W., Jr.; Robinson, G. H.; and Iliff, K. W.: **A Review of Lateral Directional Handling Qualities Criteria as Applied to the X-15.** NASA SP-90, (see N73-71303 05-99), 1965, pp. 45–60, 73N71308.

The lateral-directional handling qualities of the X-15 have been extensively surveyed in terms of pilot ratings and vehicle response characteristics throughout the operational envelope of the airplane. Results are reviewed for two vertical-tail configurations as well as for dampers on and off, and significant problem areas are discussed in relation to the basic stability and control parameters and the influence of the pilot's control. These results are used to assess the validity and limitations of some of the lateral-directional handling-qualities design criteria currently in use. Finally, a new and more generally applicable criterion recently proposed by the NASA Flight Research Center is described and similarly assessed against a broad range of test conditions available with the X-l5 vehicles.

432. Holleman, E. C.: **Control Experiences of the X-15 Pertinent to Lifting Entry.** NASA SP-90, (see N73-71303 05-99), 1965, pp. 61–73, 73N71309. (See also 448.)

The purpose of this paper is to discuss the flight experiences obtained in recovering the X-15 airplanes from high altitude with conventional and adaptive controls, and to place these experiences in proper perspective relative to future lifting entry programs.

433. Burke, M. E.; and Basso, R. J.: **Resume of X-15 Experience Related to Flight Guidance Research.** NASA SP-90, (see N73-71303 05-99), 1965, pp. 75–84, 73N71310.

The purpose of this paper is twofold. The first is to present a resume of the experience gained to date in using these two systems, and the second is to discuss a planned guidance research program that will be implemented in the near future on the X-15.

434. Adkins, E. J.; and Armstrong, J. G.: **Development and Status of the X-15-2 Airplane.** NASA SP-90, (see N73-71303 05-99), 1965, pp. 103–115, 73N71313.

The original X-15-2 airplane has been extensively modified to provide a Mach 8 configuration. The modifications included jettisonable tanks for additional propellants which would provide the increased performance and consequently would provide a realistic environment for the development and evaluation of a hypersonic air-breathing propulsion system. This paper summarizes the development and initial evaluation of the modified airplane.

435. Watts, J. D.; Cary, J. P.; and *Dow, M. B.: **Advanced X-15-2 Thermal Protection System.** NASA SP-90, (see N73-71303 05-99), 1965, pp. 117–125, 73N71314.

The use of silicone-based elastomeric ablative material for the advanced X-15-2 thermal protection system is discussed and results of candidate ablator evaluation tests in arc facilities and on X-15 flights at Mach 5 are presented.

*NASA Langley Research Center, Hampton, Virginia.

436. Bikle, P. F.; and *McCollom, J. S.: **X-15 Research Accomplishments and Future Plans.** NASA SP-90, (see N73-71303 05-99), 1965, pp. 133–139, 73N71316.

The purpose of this paper is twofold: first to review the overall achievements of the X-15 project with proper emphasis on the highlight of the papers presented and second, to indicate future X-15 plans, both the definitely planned and approved programs and several proposals that are not presently approved but are believed to offer the potential of an excellent return on investment.

*U.S. Air Force, Aeronautical Systems Division.

437. Matranga, G. J.; and Walker, J. A.: **An Investigation of Terminal Lunar Landing With the Lunar Landing Research Vehicle.** NASA TM X-74475. Presented at AIAA Manned Space Flight Meeting, St. Louis, Missouri, October 11–13, 1965, 77N74066.

438. Wolowicz, C. H.; and Gossett, T. D.: **Operational and Performance Characteristics of the X-15 Spherical, Hypersonic Flow-Direction Sensor.** NASA TN D-3070, November 1965, 66N10603, #.

The basic design concepts, operational experiences (malfunctions, system characteristics, and system improvements), and flight-data measurements of the sensor are discussed and analyzed. The accuracy of the sensor in measuring angle of attack and angle of sideslip is assessed on the basis of an analysis of flight data and comparisons of these data with X-15 flight data determined from vane-type nose-boom installations and X-15 wind-tunnel data. Some practical limitations in the use of the sensor for extreme altitude applications are also considered.

439. Love, J. E.; and Young, W. R.: **Component Performance and Flight Operations of the X-15 Research Airplane Program.** NASA TM X-74527. Presented at the Annual Symposium on Reliability, San Francisco, California, January 25–27, 1966, November 1965, 77N74609.

This paper discusses and analyzes the system and component failures that have occurred during the X-15 program. Component performance is expressed in terms of its effect upon the entire operation, that is, as a failure rate per flight. Three representative systems are discussed: the engine system, the auxiliary power system, and the propellant system. Failures of shelf-stock components prior to their installation on the flight vehicles are also examined.

440. McTigue, J. G.; and Thompson, M. O.: **Lifting-Body Research Vehicles in a Low-Speed Flight Test Program.** NASA TM X-57412. Presented at ASSET/ Advanced Lifting Reentry Technological Symposium, Miami, Florida, 14–16 December 1965, December 1965, 76N70924.

The lightweight M-2 flight test program has demonstrated the capability of a pilot to control lightweight lifting body during approach, flare, and landing. Further investigation is needed, however. Areas that are important, and that being investigated, include the use of optical landing systems, night and instrument capability, and thrust-augmented flare. A serious effort is required to reduce the complexity of the aerodynamic control system to prevent the lifting reentry vehicle from being seriously compromised in weight.

441. Stillwell, Wendell H.: **X-15 Research Results With a Selected Bibliography**, NASA-SP-60, 1965, 65N20162, #.

Contents include X-15 aircraft development concept, flight research, aerodynamic characteristics of supersonic-hypersonic flight, hypersonic structure, flying laboratory, and bibliography.

442. Sisk, T. R.; Irwin, K. S.; and McKay, J. M.: **Review of the XB-70 Flight Program.** NASA SP-83, NASA Conference on Aircraft Operating Problems, May 10–12, 1965, 1965, 65N31120.

Although the major NASA research effort is directed toward XB-70-2, which will not enter its flight program until the summer of 1965, a limited amount of information is available from the early flights of the XB-70-1 airplane. Initial take-off and landing performance data have generally substantiated predictions and indicate no unforeseen problems for this class of vehicle. Vertical velocities at impact are of the same order of magnitude as those being experienced by present-day subsonic jets. The XB-70 distances from brake release to lift-off graphically illustrate the advantage of the increased thrust-weight ratio of the supersonic cruise vehicle. The landing loads are well within the design limits up to the highest vertical velocities encountered to date, and recorded data show the response at the pilot station to be somewhat greater than that recorded at the center of gravity. Persistent shaking has been encountered in flight at subsonic speed. The cause of the excitation is not known at present but the oscillation does not appear to be conventional buffeting. The oscillation occurrence drops off appreciably at supersonic speeds and can be correlated with atmospheric turbulence. The stability and control characteristics at subsonic speeds appear satisfactory with stability augmentation on and off. A longitudinal trim discrepancy from predictions has been noted in the transonic region which appears to be decreasing with increasing supersonic speed. The supersonic handling qualities are considered adequate with stability augmentation off; however, sensitive lateral control has resulted in small pilot-induced oscillations.

EC-16695

XB-70A Airplane

443. Andrews, W. H.; Butchart, S. P.; Sisk, T. R.; and Hughes, D. L.: **Flight Tests Related to Jet-Transport Upset and Turbulent-Air Penetration.** NASA SP-83, NASA Conference on Aircraft Operating Problems, May 10–12, 1965, <u>1965</u>, 65N31114.

A flight program, utilizing a Convair 880 and a Boeing 720 airplane, was conducted in conjunction with wind-tunnel and simulator programs to study problems related to jet-transport upsets and operation in a turbulent environment. During the handling-qualities portion of the program the basic static stability of the airplanes was considered to be satisfactory and the lateral-directional damping was considered to be marginal without damper augmentation. An evaluation of the longitudinal control system indicated that this system can become marginal in effectiveness in the high Mach number and high dynamic-pressure range of the flight envelope. From the upset and recovery phase of the program it was apparent that retrimming the stabilizer and spoiler deployment were valuable tools in effecting a positive recovery; however, if these devices are to be used safely, it appears that a suitable g-meter should be provided in the cockpit because the high control forces in recovery tend to reduce the pilot's sensitivity to the actual acceleration loads. During the turbulence penetrations the pilot noted that the measured vibrations of 4 to 6 cps in the cockpit considerably disrupted their normal scan pattern and suggested that an improvement should be made in the seat cushion and restraint system. Also it was observed that the indicator needles on the flight instruments were quite stable in the turbulent environment.

444. Beeler, De E.: **NASA Flight Research Center Technical Programs.** NASA-Western University Conference at JPL, Jet Propulsion Laboratory, Pasadena, California, <u>November 8–9, 1965</u>.

445. Tanner, C. S.; and McLeod, N. J.: **Preliminary Measurements of Take-Off and Landing Noise From a New Instrumented Range.** <u>1965</u>, 65N31110.

This paper describes the NASA noise-survey instrumentation system presently in use at Edwards Air Force Base, California, and presents preliminary noise data from an F-104 airplane. Also presented are noise measurements of the XB-70 and 707-131B airplanes obtained with essentially the same equipment at another location. The difference between measured noise levels for the XB-70 and 707 is illustrated and comparisons of perceived noise levels are made. The adequacy of noise predictions is discussed briefly.

1966 Technical Publications

446. Jenkins, J. M.; and Sefic, W. J.: **Experimental Investigation of Thermal-Buckling Characteristics of Flanged, Thin-Shell Leading Edges.** NASA TN D-3243, <u>January 1966</u>, 66N15493, #.

The thermal-buckling behavior of a wide range of flanged, thin-shell leading-edge specimens was investigated. Specimens of varying geometry were subjected to temperature-rise up to 50 degrees F per sec (27.7 degrees per sec) and maximum heating rates up to 19.6 Btu/ft 2-sec (222.4 kW/m2). The specimens investigated were constructed of 2024-T3 aluminum, SAE 4130 steel, or Inconel X-750. Regions of stable structural behavior were established on the basis of leading-edge dimensional and thermal-load parameters. Two types buckling were observed in the flanges of most of the specimens. The results of the experiments provide thermal-buckling information from which a variety of flanged, thin-shell leading-edge geometries may be selected that are free of unstable structural behavior while under the influence of severe thermal loadings.

447. McKay, J. M.; and Noll, R. B.: **A Summary of the X-15 Landing Loads.** NASA TN D-3263, <u>February 1966</u>, 66N15644, #. (See also 430.)

The dynamic response of the X-15 airplane at touchdown is reviewed briefly to show the unusual landing characteristics resulting from the airplane configuration. The effect of sinking speed is discussed, as well as the influence of the horizontal-stabilizer load, wing, lift, and increased landing weight on the landing characteristics. Consideration is given to some factors providing solutions to these problems, such as cutout of the stability augmentation damper at gear contact, pilot manipulation of the stabilizer, the use of a stick pusher at touchdown, and a proposed third skid installed in the unjettisoned portion of the lower ventral fin. Studies to determine the effect on the main-landing-gear loads of relocating the X-15 nose gear are discussed.

448. Holleman, E. C.: **Control Experiences of the X-15 Pertinent to Lifting Entry.** NASA TN D-3262, February 1966, 66N15643, #. (See also 432.)

In the program to expand the flight envelope of the X-15 airplane, flights to and entries from altitudes up to 350,000 feet have been accomplished. During these entries, flight-control experience was obtained with four different control-system configurations having varying degrees of complexity. The high steady acceleration and rapidly changing aerodynamic environment did not affect the pilot's capability to control the entry. All the control systems evaluated were judged by the pilots to be satisfactory for the control of the X-15 entry from the design altitude. Entries have been made that presented more severe control problems than predicted for entries of advanced vehicles at higher velocities.

449. Banner, R. D.; and Kuhl, A. E.: **A Summary of X-15 Heat Transfer and Skin Friction Measurements.** NASA TM X-1210, Second Annual NASA-University Conference on Manual Control, M.I.T., Cambridge, Massachusetts, February 28–March 2, 1966, February 1966, 71N72665. (See also 428.)

Measured local Mach numbers and heat transfer obtained on the lower surface of the X-l5 wing and bottom centerline of the fuselage at angles of attack up to 18° and on the vertical fin with both a sharp and a blunt leading edge are summarized and compared with calculations using Eckert's reference-temperature method. Direct measurements of skin friction on the surface of the sharp-leading-edge vertical fin are also presented. It is shown that both the heat-transfer and skin-friction data can be predicted by neglecting the effect of wall temperature in the calculation of the reference temperature by Eckert's method. Uncertainties in level and trend of Reynolds analogy factor with Mach number are discussed, and a planned flight investigation is described.

450. Smith, Harriet J.: **Human Describing Functions Measured in Flight and on Simulators.** NASA SP-128, Second Annual NASA-University Conference on Manual Control, M.I.T., Cambridge, Massachusetts, February 28–March 2, 1966. (See also 476, 507.)

Comparisons have been made between human describing functions measured in flight and on the ground using two different types of ground simulators. A T-33 variable-stability airplane was used for the in-flight measurements. The ground tests were conducted in the T-33 airplane on the ground with simulated instrument flight and also on a general-purpose analog computer in conjunction with a contact analog display. For this study a multiple-degree-of-freedom controlled element was used in a single-loop compensatory tracking task. The input disturbance in each case consisted of the sum of 10 sine waves with a cutoff frequency of 1.5 radians per second. The results of this investigation indicate no significant difference between the average describing functions measured in flight and those measured in a fixed-base simulator. However, the variance was found to be considerably higher in the flight data. The system open-loop describing functions measured in the fixed-base simulator agreed well with the results of an investigation by McRuer in which the tracking task was similar, although the controlled-element dynamics were different. The average linear coherence was also close to the values found in this same investigation. Contrary to the results of previous investigations, the linear-correlation functions ρ were always equal to 1.

451. Lewis, T. L.; and McLeod, N. J.: **Flight Measurements of Boundary-Layer Noise on the X-15.** NASA TN D-3364, March 1966, 66N19602, #. (See also 429.)

This paper was included in a classified report entitled "Fourth Conference on Progress of the X-15 Research Airplane Program," Flight Research Center, Oct. 7, 1965. NASA SP-90, 1965 [see chronological numbers 425 through 435]. An appendix has been added to describe the instrumentation, and its frequency response, that was used in obtaining the data.

452. Saltzman, E. J.; and Garringer, D. J.: **Summary of Full-Scale Lift and Drag Characteristics of the X-15 Airplane.** NASA TN D-3343, March 1966, 66N19345, #.

Full-scale power-off flight lift and drag characteristics of the X-15 airplane are summarized for Mach numbers from 0.65 to 6.0 and for free-stream Reynolds numbers from 0.2×10^6 to 2.8×10^6 per foot. Comparisons are made between flight results and the wind-tunnel data that most nearly simulate the full-scale flight conditions. The apparent effect of a sting support on the base pressure of an X-15 wind-tunnel model was propagated onto the vertical-fin base at least one sting diameter above and about one-half sting diameter forward of the sting-model intercept at Mach numbers between 2.5 and 3.5. For the X-15, the effect amounts to from 8 to 15 percent of the base drag between these Mach numbers. For some future vehicles and missions, proper accounting of this interference effect may be necessary to adequately predict the full-scale transonic and supersonic performance. Specifically conducted wind-tunnel-model drag studies, when extrapolated to full-scale Reynolds numbers by the T' (reference temperature) method, accurately predicted the full-scale zero-lift drag minus base drag of the X-15 at Mach numbers of 2.5 and 3.0.

453. Wilson, R. J.: **Drag and Wear Characteristics of Various Skid Materials on Dissimilar Lakebed Surfaces During the Slideout of the X-15 Airplane.** NASA TN D-3331, <u>March 1966</u>, 66N18172, #.

An investigation was made to determine the coefficients of friction and the wear characteristics for X-15 landing gear skids of various materials. Data are presented for skids made of 4130 steel, with and without cermet coating, and Inconel X for several lakebed-surface conditions. The mean coefficient of friction on a dry-hard surface was found to be 0.30 for 4130 steel skids, 0.36 for 4130 steel skids with cermet coating, and 0.35 for Inconel X surface was 0.46; for Inconel skids on a damp surface the mean value was 0.25. Flight data are compared with experimental ground-tow test data on natural and simulated lakebed surfaces. Also included is the variation of skid wear with slideout distance.

454. Wolowicz, C. H.: **Analysis of an Emergency Deceleration and Descent of the XB-70-1 Airplane Due to Engine Damage Resulting From Structural Failure.** NASA TM X-1195, <u>March 1966</u>, 66N21099, #.

An emergency on flight 12 of the XB-70-1 airplane at a Mach number of 2.6 and a pressure altitude of 63,000 feet provided unusual operational, handling qualities, and stability and control data of interest to the supersonic-transport designer. Failure of the wing apex, its ingestion into the right inlet duct, and subsequent damage to the engines produced a steadily deteriorating propulsion situation, which led to resonant vibrations in the relatively flexible fuselage and subsequent stability and control problems in attempting to deal with the vibrations. The results of an analysis of this emergency may be useful in developing adequate operational margins and procedures in the design of the supersonic transport.

455. Barber, Marvin R.; Haise, Fred W.; and Jones, Charles K.: **An Evaluation of General Aviation Aircraft Flying Qualities.** SAE-Paper-660219, Business Aircraft Conference, Wichita, Kansas, <u>March 30–April 1, 1966</u>.

456. Holleman, E. C.: **Summary of High-Altitude and Entry Flight Control Experience With the X-15 Airplane.** NASA TN D-3386, <u>April 1966</u>, 66N21041, #.

This paper summarizes the high-altitude X-15 flight experience, which culminated in a flight to an altitude of 354,200 feet. Discussed are the basis stability, control, and handling characteristics of the airplane, the cockpit displays, and the operational techniques that enabled it to be successfully flown to and recovered from high altitudes without special piloting aids other than stability augmentation. Flight experience to moderately high altitude

with the airplane equipped with interim rocket engines is discussed.

457. Taylor, L. W., Jr.; and Iliff, K. W.: **Recent Research Directed Toward the Prediction of Lateral-Directional Handling Qualities.** NASA TM X-59621, AGARD paper R-531 presented at AGARD 28th Meeting of the Flight Mechanics Panel, Paris, France, May 10–11, 1966, <u>May 1966</u>, 67N23242, #.

A survey of lateral-directional handling qualities has been made for the purpose of developing; a technique for predicting pilot ratings. This survey was made by obtaining pilot ratings of lateral control on a fixed-base simulator in conjunction with a color contact analog display. The effect of five lateral-directional handling qualities parameters were studied by systematically varying them over a wide range. Forty-five charts comprise the results of this survey. However these have been condensed into three charts to provide a rapid means for hand computing the pilot ratings. For more accurate predictions a digital computer program was written which incorporated the data from all 45 charts.

458. Berry, D. T.; and Deets, D. A.: **Design, Development, and Utilization of a General Purpose Airborne Simulator.** NASA TM X-74543, AGARD Paper 529. Presented at AGARD 28th Flight Mechanics Panel, Paris, France, May 10–11 1966. <u>May 1966</u>, 77N74646.

459. Patten, C. W.; Ramme, F. B.; and Roman, J. A.: **Dry Electrodes for Physiological Monitoring.** NASA TN D-3414, <u>May 1966</u>, 66N25548, #.

A method for very rapid application of electrocardiogram electrodes by spraying a conductive mixture is described. The electrodes are also suitable for electroencephalograms. All required equipment and the application procedure are described in detail. The finished electrode is dry and is less than 0.01-inch thick. Electrical and operational factors are not considered.

460. Sadoff, Melvin; Bray, Richard S.; and Andrews, William H.: **Summary of NASA Research on Jet Transport Control Problems in Severe Turbulence.** *Journal of Aircraft*, Vol. 3, No. 3, <u>May–June 1966</u>.

461. Andrews, W. H.: **Summary of Preliminary Data Derived From the XB-70 Airplanes.** NASA TM X-1240, Washington, NASA, <u>June 1966</u>, 66N28013, #.

Preliminary data obtained during the initial flight-envelope expansion of the XB-70 airplanes are presented in the areas of stability and control, general performance, propulsion-system inlet operation, structural thermal response, internal noise, runway noise, and sonic boom.

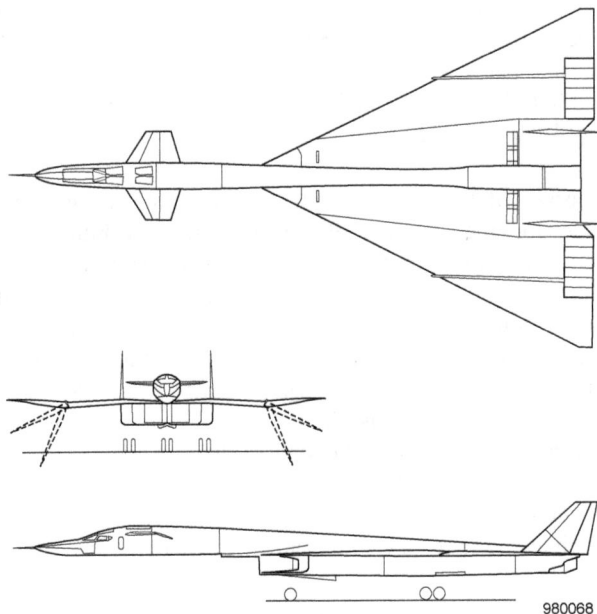

XB-70A Airplane, Three-View Drawing

462. Palitz, M.: **Measured and Calculated Flow Conditions on the Forward Fuselage of the X-15 Airplane and Model at Mach Numbers From 3.0 to 8.0.** NASA TN D-3447, June 1966, 66N26849, #.

Early analyses of X-15 flight heat-transfer data were based on calculated values of the local-flow conditions. The resultant differences between measured and predicted heat transfer were thought to be partially due to an incomplete knowledge of the local fluid properties. Subsequently, a flight investigation was made to determine the extent and character of the local flow on the X-15 airplane in order to aid in the interpretation of the measured heat-transfer data. The results of the flow-field investigation on the forebody of the X-15 are presented and analyzed in this paper.

463. Larson, Terry J.; and Covington, Alan: **A Technique for Measuring Mesospheric Densities With the X-15 Research Airplane.** Presented at the Fourth Aerospace Sciences Meeting, Los Angeles, California, June 27–29, 1966.

Atmospheric-density measurements for altitudes between 30 kilometers and 74 kilometers were obtained during flights with the X-15 research airplane in the southwestern United States. The pilot-pressure method used to derive the densities is discussed in terms of its applicability to X-15 trajectory and instrumentation characteristics. The use of radar tracking to derive X-15 velocity and altitude is described, as well as the

manner in which rawinsonde and rocketsonde data are applied. Flow-angularity effects were avoided by measuring stagnation pressures on a spherical flow-direction sensor, which maintains continuous alignment of the pilot-pressure port with the local flow vector. The quality of the data was further enhanced by applying semiempirical lag corrections to the pressure measurements. The measured density and derived temperature data from the X-15 agree well with rawinsonde data at low altitudes and with Arcas rocketsonde data at higher altitudes.

464. Jenkins, J. M.: **A Pretensioning Concept for Relief of Critical Leading-Edge Thermal Stress.** NASA TN D-3507, July 1966, 66N30079, #.

This paper introduces an analytical concept designed to relieve problems arising from the chordwise temperature gradients by reducing the magnitude of critical compressive stress in a leading edge. The reduction is accomplished by adding an internal column that applies an internal load to the ends of the leading edge. Equations that define the behavior of a pretensioned leading edge are developed and applied to a mathematical model to demonstrate the mechanics of using the concept.

465. Powers, B. G.: **A Parametric Study of Factors Influencing the Deep-Stall Pitch-Up Characteristics of T-Tail Transport Aircraft.** NASA TN D-3370, August 1966, 66N32326, #.

This paper presents the results of the program, in which the transport-type aircraft were investigated. A series of stall maneuvers was made with deceleration rates into the stall of 1, 3, and 5 knots per second, with recovery initiated over a range of angle attack. The relative effects of the shape of the pitching-moment curves in the deep-stall region as well as in the initial-stall region were determined in terms of angle-of-attack overshoot and altitude losses during recovery.

466. Roman, James: **Flight Research Program-III High Impedance Electrode Techniques.** *Aerospace Medicine*, Vol. 37, No. 8, August 1966.

This paper describes electrode techniques designed for large-scale flight physiological data collection on a routine basis. Large-scale data collection requires both smaller demands on crew time and less interference with crew comfort than could be achieved by former methods. The resistive components of electrode impedance appears to be related primarily to the extent of skin preparation. For any one method of skin preparation, both resistance and capacitance appear to be primarily a function of electrode area. Motion artifacts are not caused by changes in electrode impedance. Dry electrodes showing a resistive component in excess of 50,000 ohms can be used to obtain tracings of quality comparable, and in some cases superior to those obtained with larger wet electrodes.

467. Quinn, R. D.; and Palitz, M.: **Comparison of Measured and Calculated Turbulent Heat Transfer on the X-15 Airplane at Angles of Attack Up to 19.0 Degrees.** NASA TM X-1291, September 1966, 73N70599.

468. Barber, Marvin R.; and Haise, Fred W., Jr.: **Handling Qualities Evaluation of Seven General Aviation Aircraft.** *Symposium Proceedings, Society of Experimental Test Pilots,* Vol. 8, No. 2, September 23–24, 1966.

469. Mallick, Donald L.; Kluever, Emil E.; and Matranga, Gene J.: **Flight Results With a Non-Aerodynamic, Variable Stability, Flying Platform.** *Symposium Proceedings, Society of Experimental Test Pilots,* Vol. 8, No. 2, September 23–24, 1966.

470. Thompson, Milton O.; Peterson, Bruce A.; and *Gentry, J. R.: **Manned Lifting-Body Flight Testing.** NASA TM X-59042. Presented at the SETP 10th Symposium, Los Angeles, California, September 1966.

*Air Force Flight Test Center, Edwards, California.

This paper describes the Joint NASA-Air Force lifting-body flight test program and the three research vehicles, the M2-F2, the HL-10 and the SV-5P. These three vehicles are representative of manned maneuverable reentry spacecraft capable of horizontal landing.

471. Jarvis, C. R.: **Operational Experience With the Electronic Flight Control Systems of a Lunar-Landing Research Vehicle.** NASA TN D-3689, October 1966, 66N39536, #.

Two research vehicles were delivered to the NASA Flight Research Center in the Spring of 1964. After delivery, several months were devoted to checking systems and installing research instrumentation. During this period, many problems were encountered which required extensive modifications to the vehicle and its systems. Subsequent development flight testing disclosed additional problems and resulted in further modifications. This paper discusses the nature of these problems and the performance of the flight control systems during the early flights.

472. Layton, G. P., Jr.; and Dana, W. H.: **Flight Tests of a Wide-Angle, Indirect Optical Viewing System in a High-Performance Jet Aircraft.** NASA TN D-3690, October 1966, 66N38800, #.

A wide-angle, indirect optical viewing system was qualitatively evaluated in an F-104B aircraft as a means of providing visual reference to the pilot. Safe and acceptable performance using the indirect viewing system was demonstrated for all phases of daytime visual flight. Landings were performed in both the conventional and low lift-drag-ratio configurations. When the horizon was in the field of view, aircraft attitude sensing with the optics was satisfactory about all axes except pitch attitude in climbing flight. This degraded pitch-attitude sensing was due to the poor resolution at the bottom of the field and the lack of view to the sides. A night flight was also performed. The system, in its present form, was considered unacceptable for this use because of large light losses and degraded resolution. It was evident in the study that additional view directly to the side is required for performing circling approaches.

473. Love, J. E.; and Young, W. R.: **Survey of Operation and Cost Experience of the X-15 Airplane as a Reusable Space Vehicle.** NASA TN D-3732, November 1966, 67N11328, #.

The X-15 airplane has been flown more than 150 times in an environment similar to that anticipated for many of the reusable space vehicles being studied. Data are presented on X-15 development and operational costs, turnaround time, and refurbishment cycles, based upon actual operation of the aircraft. For example, 27 flights were accomplished in 1964 at a total cost of $16,268,000, or an average cost of more than $602,000 per flight. It is believed that information from the X-15 program will be helpful in feasibility studies of the reusable-vehicle concept, inasmuch as the X-15 operation is more directly comparable than any other operational program to the reusable systems being considered.

474. Barber, M. R.; Jones, C. K.; Sisk, T. R.; and Haise, F. W.: **An Evaluation of the Handling Qualities of Seven General-Aviation Aircraft.** NASA TN D-3726, November 1966, 66N39905, #.

A review of existing criteria indicated that the criteria have not kept pace with aircraft development in the areas of dutch roll, adverse yaw, effective dihedral, and allowable trim changes with gear, flaps, and power. This study indicated that criteria should be specified for control-system friction and control-surface float. Furthermore, this program suggests a method of quantitatively evaluating the handling qualities of aircraft by the use of a pilot-workload factor.

475. Roman, James; and *Brigden, Wayne H.: **Flight Research Program: V. Mass Spectrometer in Medical Monitoring.** *Aerospace Medicine,* Vol. 37, No. 12, December 1966.

Mass spectrometers, traditionally large and complicated instruments, have been miniaturized and greatly simplified for the National Space Program. This recent development opens new areas to medicine and to space medicine in particular. The principles of operation of mass spectrometers will soon be important to those engaged in physiological research or in medical monitoring. They are discussed in this paper. A summary of flight test data obtained with a small mass spectrometer in a jet aircraft is presented.

*Volt Technical Corporation, NASA Field Team, Edwards, California.

476. Smith, H. J.: **Human Describing Functions Measured in Flight and on Simulators.** *Manual Control,* (see N67-15859), <u>1966</u>, pp. 279–290, 67N15871. (See also 450, 507.)

477. Smith, R. H.; and Schweikhard, W. G.: **Initial Flight Experience With the XB-70 Air-Induction System.** NASA SP-124, (see N75-71754 05-98), <u>1966</u>, pp. 185–194, 75N71767.

The preliminary results and developmental problems from flight tests of the XB-70 air-induction system are briefly reviewed. The system is generally satisfactory, is adequately matched to the engine flow requirements, and can be controlled for the various flight ranges. Inlet unstarts at cruise Mach number constitute a new problem for high supersonic aircraft seriously affecting the dynamics of the inlet and airframe.

478. *Rolls, L. S.; *Snyder, C. T.; and Schweikhard, W. G.: **Flight Studies of Ground Effects on Airplanes With Low-Aspect-Ratio Wings.** NASA SP-124, (see N75-71754 05-98), <u>1966</u>, pp. 285–295, 75N71774.

The ground effects on two aircraft with low-aspect-ratio delta wings, the F5D-l and the XB-70A, were measured in flight tests. In a companion program, both small and full-scale models and several wind tunnels were used to document the ground effects for the F5D-l. These flight tests indicated ground effects were not a problem in landing either of these vehicles. The limited wind-tunnel program indicated that scale effects were not of first-order importance in defining ground effects, and that wind-tunnel tests provide reasonable agreement with the values in flight. A simulation study, using a fixed-cockpit projection-type simulator, performed in conjunction with these studies indicated levels of moment and lift changes which would be unsatisfactory from the pilot's viewpoint; however, some possible alleviating features were noted.

*Ames Research Center, Moffett Field, California.

479. Wolowicz, Chester H.: **Considerations in the Determination of Stability and Control Derivatives and Dynamic Characteristics From Flight Data.** AGARD Report 549, Part I, <u>1966.</u>

This report is the handbook on the determination of stability and control characteristics from flight test. It describes several axis systems, axis transformations, the equations of motions and their limitations, techniques used to determine the mass characteristics of the airplane, the installation and behavior of flight instrumentation, flight test techniques, and the theory and limitations of techniques used to determine the stability and control characteristics from flight data. This report brings all the factors together in the determination of stability and control and provide a ready reference of

pertinent information. It is a greatly expanded version of AGARD 224, *Stability-Derivative Determination From Flight Data,* by Chester H. Wolowicz and Euclid C. Holleman.

1967 Technical Publications

480. Wilson, R. J.: **Statistical Analysis of Landing Contact Conditions of the X-15 Airplane.** NASA TN D-3801, <u>January 1967</u>, 67N14935, #.

The landing contact conditions and slideout distances for 135 landings of the X-l5 research airplane are discussed. The conditions are similar to those that might he experienced by future lifting-body reentry vehicles or other flight vehicles with low lift-drag ratios. Results are presented in the form of histograms for frequency distributions, and Pearson Type III probability curves for the landing contact conditions of vertical velocity, calibrated airspeed, true ground speed, rolling velocity, roll angle, distance from intended touchdown point, and slideout distance.

481. Garringer, D. J.; and Saltzman, E. J.: **Flight Demonstration of a Skin-Friction Gage to a Local Mach Number of 4.9.** NASA TN D-3830, February 1967, <u>February 1967</u>, 67N17173.

A small, commercially available skin-friction gage was flight tested on the X-15 airplane. The Reynolds number range investigated extended from 3.8×10^6 to 10×10^6, and local Mach numbers ranged from 0.7 to 4.9. The ratio of wall-to-recovery temperature varied from about 0.4 to 1.4. The gage, its cooling system, and the supporting instrumentation performed well. Turbulent skin-friction values measured in flight for a wide range of wall-to-recovery temperature ratios are similar in level to adiabatic flat-plate and wind tunnel results for corresponding Mach numbers and Reynolds numbers. Thus, for the present tests the influence of wall-to-recovery temperature ratio appears to be less than estimated by turbulent theory.

482. Jarvis, Calvin R.: **Fly-By-Wire Control System Experience With a Free-Flight Lunar-Landing Research Vehicle.** AIAA Paper 67-273, AIAA Flight Test, Simulation, and Support Conference, Cocoa Beach, Florida, <u>February 6–8, 1967.</u>

483. Matranga, Gene J.; Mallick, Donald L.; and Kluever, Emil E.: **An Assessment of Ground and Flight Simulators for the Examination of Manned Lunar Landing.** AIAA Paper 67-238, AIAA Flight Test, Simulation, and Support Conference, Cocoa Beach, Florida, <u>February 6–8, 1967.</u>

484. Roman, James, Perry, John J.; Carpenter, Lewis R.; and *Awni, Shiban: **Flight Research Program: VI. Heart Rate and Landing Error in Restricted Field of View Landing.** *Aerospace Medicine*, Vol. 38, No. 3, February 1967.

Two pilots were instrumented for electrocardiogram in a T-33 jet aircraft in the course of eleven flights in which pilot horizontal field of view was varied from 360 degrees to 5.7 degrees. Landing error was recorded in terms of distance from the desired touchdown point. A high degree of correlation was found to exist between heart rate and landing error. There was no significant correlation between heart rate and field of view, nor was there significant correlation between field of view and landing error for the fields of view tested. At the 5.7 degree field of view the monocular fields of view did not overlap, so that only one eye could be used. Landing error did not increase significantly when only one eye was used. This finding has implications with respect to aeromedical standards.

*Computing and Software, Incorporated, Panorama City, California.

485. Roman, James; *Older, Harry; and **Jones, Walton L.: **Flight Research Program: VII. Medical Monitoring of Navy Carrier Pilots in Combat.** *Aerospace Medicine*, Vol. 38, No. 2, February 1967.

The feasibility of medical monitoring in combat was demonstrated by instrumenting ten dive-bombing missions from a Navy attack aircraft carrier operating in the Gulf of Tonkin. Nine missions suitable for data analysis were obtained. The results were remarkable primarily for the low heart rates seen on these opposed missions. The overall heart rate for 18 hours of data was 87.6 beats per minute. The heart rates at launch and recovery were substantially higher than the bombing heart rates, in spite of the significant normal acceleration experienced during the bomb runs. The difference between launch or recovery, and bombing was statistically highly significant. Comparisons between the first and the second combat missions of the day for the same pilots on the same day showed heart rate to be substantially lower on the second mission. The difference was statistically significant. The pilots were of an unusually high experience level, and the data presented could not be considered representative for a pilot group of average combat experience, or average carrier operations experience.

*Consultant to NASA, Washington, D. C.
**NASA Headquarters, Washington, D. C.

486. Gord, P. R.: **Measured and Calculated Structural Temperature Data From Two X-15 Airplane Flights With Extreme Aerodynamic Heating Conditions.** NASA TM X-1358, H-442, March 1967, 74N71363.

This paper presents structural temperature data from two flights of the X-15 airplane in which extreme aerodynamic-heating conditions were experienced. These flights, shown on the X-15 flight envelope represent the extremes of maximum dynamic pressure and maximum altitude achieved during X-15 flights to date. The temperature data recorded are presented in tabulated form for 103 locations of the airplane.

487. Taylor, L. W., Jr.: **A Comparison of Human Response Modeling in the Time and Frequency Domains.** NASA TM X-59750. Presented at the USC and NASA Conference on Manual Control, Los Angeles, California, March 1–3 1967, (previously announced as N68-25276), 1967, 68N37735. (See also 511.)

Frequency and time domain methods of analyzing human control response while performing compensatory tracking tasks are reviewed. Sample linear model results using these methods are compared and discussed. The inherent requirement of constraining the freedom of the form of the pilot models is also discussed. The constraint in the frequency domain consists of smoothing with respect to frequency; whereas, the constraint for the time domain model is more natural and meaningful in that it consists simply of limiting the memory of the pilot model. The linear models determined by both methods were almost identical.

488. Jarvis, C. R.: **Flight-Test Evaluation of an On-Off Rate Command Attitude Control System of a Manned Lunar-Landing Research Vehicle.** NASA TN D-3903, April 1967, 67N23293, #.

This paper deals specifically with the evaluation of the capability of an on-off rate command attitude control system to provide satisfactory control for maneuvering a vehicle in a lunar-gravity environment. Control boundaries, based on pilot ratings, are established from fixed-base simulator studies that define satisfactory valued of rate dead band, controller sensitivity, and angular acceleration. These boundaries are then compared to flight results obtained with the LLRV. Results are presented for both Earth and lunar-oriented operation.

489. Adkins, Elmor J.: **X-15 Research Program Accomplishments and Plans.** Presented at the AIAA Symposium of Hypersonic Flight, Los Angeles, California, April 27, 1967.

490. Saltzman, Edwin J.; and Hintz, John: **Flight Evaluation of Splitter-Plate Effectiveness in Reducing Base Drag at Mach Numbers From 0.65 to 0.90.** NASA TM X-1376, May 1967, 67N26558, #.

An experiment has been conducted to determine the effectiveness of a splitter plate in reducing base drag at subsonic speeds. The test configuration was a "fin-like" shape mounted on the under belly of a F-104 which may be representative of blunt-trailing-edge stabilizing surfaces of future hypersonic aircraft or reentry vehicles. The test chord Reynolds numbers, up to 36.2×10^6, are believed to be representative of chord Reynolds numbers for the terminal, subsonic phase of a lifting-body reentry. The splitter plate which extended into the wake a distance of 1 base width, reduced the negative base pressure coefficients between 30 percent and 40 percent. This increment in base pressure coefficient was as large as obtained on a two-dimensional wind-tunnel model at the higher comparable Mach numbers and about 12 percent lower at the lower comparable Mach numbers, even though the flight results represented higher Reynolds numbers and contained outboard end (three-dimensional) effects.

491. Szalai, K. J.: **The Influence of Response Feedback Loops on the Lateral-Directional Dynamics of a Variable-Stability Transport Aircraft.** NASA TN D-3966, Washington, NASA, May 1967, Refs, May 1967, 67N26545.

Several response feedback loops are analyzed to determine their effects on the lateral-directional dynamics of a variable-stability transport aircraft. The response feedback system feeds back response variables such as sideslip angle or roll rate as rudder or aileron commands, or both, thus altering the various transfer functions which describe the dynamic characteristics of the aircraft. The range of the feedback gain for which approximate expressions are valid describing the effect of a particular loop is noted. The root-locus method is used to show the dutch roll, roll, and spiral modes are influenced as a function of feedback gain. Expressions are developed which directly relate feedback gains to some response parameter, such as dutch roll frequency, damping ratio, or roll and spiral mode time constants. The expansion to multiloop systems is discussed, along with limitations of the response feedback system from the standpoint of operating a variable-stability aircraft.

492. Lytton, L. E.: **Evaluation of a Vertical-Scale, Fixed-Index Instrument Display Panel for the X-15 Airplane.** NASA TN D 3967, May 1967, 67N25037,#.

A comparative evaluation was performed on an analog simulator to compare pilot performance when using the operational X-15 instrument panel and a panel incorporating vertical-scale, fixed-index flight instruments. The purpose of the evaluation was to provide experiential evidence to complement pilot opinion concerning the acceptability of the vertical-scale panel for use in the X-15 airplane. This evidence was obtained in the form of a wide variety of performance measures for 16 subjects, for two different representative mission profiles, and over three trials or runs

for each profile. The data were subjected to both parametric and nonparametric statistical analysis.

493. Love, James E.; and Young, William, R.: **Operational Experience of the X-15 Airplane as a Reusable Vehicle System.** Presented at SAE 2nd Annual Space Technology Conference, Palo Alto, California, May 9–11, 1967.

494. Wilson, R. J.; and Larson, R. R.: **Statistical Analysis of Landing-Contact Conditions for the XB-70 Airplane.** NASA TN D-4007, June 1967, 67N27617, #.

Landing-contact conditions for 71 landings of the XB-70 airplanes are analyzed. Some of the conditions are similar to those that may be experienced by future supersonic vehicles. Results are presented as frequency histograms and cumulative frequency distributions in terms of probability. The landing-contact parameters examined include vertical velocity; indicated airspeed; angles of roll, pitch, attack, and sideslip; and rolling and pitching velocities.

495. Perry, J. J.; Dana, W. H.; and Bacon, D. C., Jr.: **Flight Investigation of the Landing Task in a Jet Trainer With Restricted Fields of View.** NASA TN D-4018, June 1967, 67N27294, #.

A total of 155 landings were made in a T-33A jet aircraft in order to determine the relationship between the pilot's field of view and his performance of the landing maneuver. The field of view was reduced from unrestricted to a minimum of 0.10 radian (5.7 degrees) horizontal and 0.52 radian (30 degrees) vertical. The pilot's task was to fly a 180 power-on pattern and final approach and land the aircraft on a predetermined point on the runway. Also, power-off 360 degrees overhead and straight-in approaches were performed by one of the pilots. The quality of the performance of the power-on task was measured by recording touchdown error. Pilot comments were obtained for all flights.

496. Lewis, Charles E., Jr.; Jones, Walton L.; *Austin, Frank; and Roman, James: **Flight Research Program: IX. Medical Monitoring of Carrier Pilots in Combat – II.** *Aerospace Medicine*, Vol. 38, No. 6, June 1967.

Cardiorespiratory functioning in flight was monitored on Naval aviators flying bombing missions against heavily defended targets in North Vietnam. Thirty-one missions suitable for data analysis were obtained. Continuous records of ECG, respiratory rate, acceleration and voice were recorded in flight. Both day and night missions were monitored. The pilots studied were of an unusually high experience level, averaging 1,952 total flying hours and 104 combat missions per man. The overall combat heart rate was 94.9 bpm. Overall bombing heart rate was 112.3 bpm, including day and night bombing; frequently in bad weather. Overall respiratory rate was 22.9 breaths per minute. In a comparison study on Marine reserve pilots, gravitational stress was determined to be of importance in elevating the bombing heart rate observed in this combat study. The stresses of combat flying, particularly the element of risk, is clearly shown to be ineffectual in evoking cardiovascular response in the group studied.

*Capt., U. S. Marine Corps.

497. Taylor, L. W., Jr.; and Balakrishnan, A. V.: **Identification of Human Response Models in Manual Control Systems.** NASA TM X-60204. Presented at the IFAC Symposium on the Probl. of Identification of Automatic Control Systems, Prague, June 12–17, 1967, <u>1967</u>, 68N25712, #.

Frequency domain and time domain methods of analysis are reviewed with their regard to their application toward identifying pilot models. The models would subsequently be used to study the stability and performance of a man-machine system in which the human controller performs a compensatory tracking task. Sample linear model results are compared and discussed. The inherent requirement constraining the freedom of the form of the pilot model is also discussed.

498. Noll, R. B.; and McKay, J. M.: **Theoretical Dynamic Analysis of the Landing Loads on a Vehicle With a Tricycle Landing Gear.** NASA TN D-4075, <u>August 1967</u>, 67N32394, #.

A theoretical analysis is presented for the landing dynamics of a vehicle equipped with a tricycle landing-gear system. The equations are simplified in order to provide a more convenient yet adequate analysis for most vehicles. The adequacy of the simplified analysis for simulating the landing dynamics and loads of a vehicle is illustrated by comparing results of calculations with flight-test data from the X-15 research airplane. The feasibility of using the modified analysis for investigating off-design landing contingencies is demonstrated by examples of studies performed for the X-15.

499. Pyle, J. S.; and Swanson, R. H.: **Lift and Drag Characteristics of the M2-F2 Lifting Body During Subsonic Gliding Flight.** NASA TM X-1431, <u>August 1967</u>, 71N70184.

The subsonic flight lift and drag characteristics of the M2-F2 lifting-body configuration are presented at angles of attack from –4 degrees to 16 degrees. Flight results are compared with data obtained from full-scale wind-tunnel tests on the flight vehicle and with M2-F1 flight results.

ECN-1088

M2-F2 Lifting Body

500. Beeler, De E.: **Optimization of Aircraft Performance and Mission Completion Through Research on the Pilot and Aircraft as an Overall System.** *Aerospace Proceedings 1966*, Royal Aeronautical Society, Centenary Congress and International Council of the Aeronautical Sciences, Congress, 5th, London, England, September 12–16, 1966, Vol. 2, (see A66-42492), <u>1967</u>, pp. 909–930, 68A19806.

The philosophies and findings of the research aeroplane programme are in many respects directly applicable to the requirements for the development of successful future high-performance aircraft. One of the lessons could be the importance of an experimental or prototype aircraft as a basic requirement to the successful development of proposed aircraft of the future.

501. Gaidsick, H. G.; Layton, G. P., Jr.; and Dana, W. H.: **Indirect Pilot Viewing for Reentry Vehicles and SSTs.** *Space/Aeronautics*, Vol. 48, <u>September 1967</u>, pp. 118–121, 68A14761.

Indirect pilot viewing systems for reentry vehicles and SST, discussing overlapping monoculars and panoramic display.

502. *McDonald, R. T.; and Roman, J.: **Development of Respiration-Rate Transducers for Aircraft Environments.** NASA TN D-4217, <u>November 1967</u>, 67N39753, #.

Two types of sensors for monitoring respiration rate in aircraft environments have been developed: a low-pressure pneumotachometer designed to monitor the pilot's respiration rate in aircraft that have a low-pressure breathing-oxygen supply, and a high-pressure pneumotachometer designed to monitor the pilot's respiration rate in aircraft with a high-pressure breathing-oxygen supply. For both pneumotachometers, the sensor is placed in series with the oxygen supply line and the pilot s oxygen line. The sensor detects gas flow that accompanies inspiration.

*Northrop Corporation, Hawthorne, California.

503. Kordes, E. E.; and Love, B. J.: **Preliminary Evaluation of XB-70 Airplane Encounters With High-Altitude Turbulence.** NASA TN D-4209, November 1967, 67N39719, #.

Measurements of airplane response to clear-air turbulence were obtained during supersonic flights of the XB-70 airplanes to an altitude of 74,000 feet (22,555 meters) over the Western United States. In general, the results for 75,757 miles (121,919 kilometers) of operation above 40,000 feet (12,192 meters) altitude show that turbulence was encountered an average of 7.2 percent of the miles flown between 40,000 feet (12,192 meters) and 65,000 feet (19,812 meters) and an average of 3.3 percent of the miles flown above 65,000 feet (19,812 meters) with less than 1 percent of the turbulent areas exceeding 100 miles (160.93 kilometers) in length. Power-spectral-density estimates of the acceleration response to turbulence show that the structural modes contribute an appreciable amount to the total response.

504. Montoya, E. J.; and Palitz, M.: **Wind-Tunnel Investigation of the Flow Field Beneath the Fuselage of the X-15 Airplane at Mach Numbers From 4 to 8.** NASA TM X-1469, November 1967, 68N11147, #.

Wind-tunnel data were obtained on the local flow field beneath the fuselage of a model of the X-15 airplane approximately 5 to 8 fuselage diameters aft of the model nose from the model surface to the bow shock. Multiple-tube rakes, model surface pressure orifices, and a cone probe were used to survey the flow field. The cone probe was used to obtain Mach numbers in the flow field up to a free-stream Mach number of 6 and to obtain flow angularity up to a Mach number of 8. Test results were obtained at free-stream Mach numbers from 4 to 8 and angles of attack from −3 degrees to 20 degrees and were compared with theory and flight data.

505. Roman, J.; and Sato, R. N.: **A Useful Modification of the Wright Spirometer.** NASA TN D-4234, NASA, November 1967, 68N10057, #.

The Wright spirometer is a useful gas flowmeter for physiological use, in that it is small and reliable. However, data collected with this device must be reduced manually, and the calibration curve is nonlinear at low flow values. The instrument was modified by fitting the output shaft with a spooked wheel that interrupts the light beam between a low-power light source and a photonsensor. This modification provides a digital electrical output that can be computer-reduced, permitting correction of the data for the nonlinearity of the calibration curve. The power drain is 96 milliwatts, which is small enough to be drawn from the battery supplies of most self-contained miniature tape recorders.

506. Taylor, L. W., Jr.; and Smith, J. W.: **An Analysis of the Limit-Cycle and Structural-Resonance Characteristics of the X-15 Stability Augmentation System.** NASA TN D-4287, December 1967, 68N11545, #.

This paper considers in some detail the limit-cycle and structural-resonance problems by using nonlinear mathematical models in the analysis of the system stability. The results of the analysis are compared with results obtained from ground flight tests. Limit cycle calculations involved multiple, nonseparable, nonlinear elements which demonstrate the use of describing functions.

507. Smith, H. J.: **Human Describing Functions Measured in Flight and on Simulators.** *IEEE Transactions on Human Factors in Electronics*, Vol. HFE-8, December 1967, pp. 264–268, 68A20662. (See also 450, 476.)

Human describing functions measured in flight and on simulators, noting difference in variances.

508. Thompson, M. O.; Weil, J.; and Holleman, E. C.: **An Assessment of Lifting Reentry Flight Control Requirements During Abort, Terminal Glide, and Approach and Landing Situations.** NASA TM X-59119. Presented at Specialists meeting on Stability and Control, Cambridge, England, September 20–23, 1966, 1967, 68N27404.

The results of the X-15 research airplane and M-2 lifting body flight programs and various simulation programs are summarized for pertinence to the control requirements for manned lifting reentry. Piloted reentries have been successfully accomplished with several degrees of control-system sophistication and at a variety of reentry conditions some more severe than expected during orbital reentry.

509. Walker, H. J.; and Thompson, M. O.: **Handling Qualities of Hypersonic Cruise Aircraft.** *Conference on Hypersonic Aircraft Technology*, 1967, pp. 155–169, 74N73060.

510. Reed, R. D.: **Flight Testing of Advanced Spacecraft Recovery Concepts Using the Aeromodeler's Approach.** NASA Langley Research Center Inter-Agency Flexible Wing Technology Meeting, 1967, 86N72377. (See also 522.)

Model flight investigations are being conducted at the NASA Flight Research Center to explore various spacecraft terminal-landing concepts. Modern model-airplane equipment and procedures have contributed to many successful flights on radio-controlled experimental gliding parachute models launched from a large radio-controlled launch model. In addition, three flights of a similar large-scale parachute model were made with the aid of a helicopter. Launches took place approximately 1000 feet above the ground with the radio-controlled launch model and 4000 feet above the ground with the helicopter. Studies were made of parawing deployment transients, steering control, and model landing impact. Experiments with parawings in combination with the aerodynamically stable lifting-body payloads revealed potential directional-coupling characteristics at full-scale conditions. Also, approximately 20 tests on advanced variable-geometry free-flight and radio-controlled bodies provided some insight into low-speed stability and control characteristics with conventional wings "stowed" and "extended." The information obtained was primarily qualitative, based on movies of the flight tests. Control inputs were recorded to provide some quantitative data on parawing turning rates as a function of control input.

511. Taylor, L. W., Jr.: **A Comparison of Human Response Modeling in the Time and Frequency Domains.** *Three-D Annual NASA University Conference on Manual Control*, <u>1967</u>, pp. 137–153, (see N68-15901 06-05), 68N15910, #. (See also 487.)

Frequency and time-domain methods of analyzing human control response while performing compensatory tracking tasks are reviewed. Sample linear model results using these methods are compared and discussed. The inherent requirement of constraining the freedom of the form of the pilot models is also discussed. The constraint in the frequency domain consists of smoothing with respect to frequency; whereas, the constraint for the time domain model is more natural and meaningful in that it consists simply of limiting the memory of the pilot model. The linear models determined by both methods were almost identical.

512. Taylor, L. W., Jr.: **Relationships Between Fourier and Spectral Analyses.** *Three-D Annual NASA University Conference on Manual Control*, <u>1967</u>, pp. 183–186, (see N68-15901 06-05), 68N15913, #.

About 2-1/2 years ago the Flight Research Center was preparing to analyze human response data for a joint NASA-USAF-Cornell program using a ground based simulator and the variable-stability T-33 airplane. A decision to use expressions of the cross- and power-spectral density functions involving Fourier transforms instead of the cross- and auto-correlation functions led to certain simplifications which raised some questions.

513. Fischel, J.; and Gee, S. W.: **Aeronautical Flight-Control Systems Research.** NASA SP-154, <u>1967</u>, (see N68-33169 20-30), pp. 245–259, 68N33186.

The primary flight control system configuration now being used, an electromechanical-hydraulic combination, has proved to be fairly reliable; however, this system is complex and has several inherent undesirable features and attendant problems. The increasing complexity of flight control systems resulting from the increased performance of future aircraft can be best resolved electrically by a fly-by-wire system. Consideration should be given to the integration and simplification of display parameters to alleviate pilot effort and for the display of new parameters providing essential information for improved flight control by the pilot. When this is accomplished, we can look toward completely automatic control and, possibly, remote control.

514. Gee, S. W.: **A Review of Avionics Requirements for General Aviation.** NASA SP-154, *Aerospace Electronic Systems Technology*, <u>1967</u>, (see N68-33169 20-30), pp. 261–272, 68N33187, #.

1968 Technical Publications

515. Taylor, L. W., Jr.: **Nonlinear, Time-Domain Models of Human Controllers.** NASA TM X-60996. Presented at Hawaii International Conference on System Sciences, Honolulu, Hawaii, January 29–30, 1968, <u>January 1968</u>, also *Journal of Optimization Theory and Applications*, January 1968, 68N28920, #.

This paper presents results of analyses and discusses the method of selecting maximum memory time and order of the nonlinear model. In addition, there was discussion and results of orthogonal expansion of the weighting functions for reasons for data compression and reduced computation.

516. Dana, W. H.: **From the Pilot's Seat.** *Science News*, <u>February 24, 1968</u>, pp. 188–189.

517. Thompson, M. O.; and Dana, W. H.: **Flight Simulation of Night Landings of Lifting Entry Vehicles.** AIAA Paper 68-259. Presented at the 2nd AIAA Flight Test, Simulation and Support Conference, Los Angeles, California, March 25–27, 1968, <u>March 1968</u>, 68A23680, #.

As part of an evaluation of the operational capabilities of lifting entry vehicles, night approaches and landings were performed in fighter aircraft configured to provide a maximum L/D ratio of approximately 3.0. These approaches were performed to a lighted runway and to a dry lake bed illuminated by airborne parachute flares. Approach patterns were 270 degree overhead patterns begun at altitudes of 30,000 to 45,000 ft. Approach pattern control was accomplished by the pilot. Moonlight varied from full moon to no moon. Each night flight was paired with an identical flight flown the preceding afternoon. The approaches are compared with one another and with their daytime counterparts using radar tracking plots and touch-down miss distance as evaluation criteria. Landing-site comparison (runway or lake bed) is by pilot comment. Effects of moonlight on pattern control are discussed. Spot landing miss distances for the entire program are presented as evidence of the feasibility of night landings in lifting entry vehicles.

518. Bogue, R. K.; and Webb, L. D.: **Advanced Air Data Sensing Techniques.** NASA TM X-61115, <u>1968</u>, 68N37326, #. (See also 519.)

Determination of the feasibility of using a fluidic-type temperature sensor for measuring total temperature on an aircraft traveling at hypersonic speeds within the atmosphere. Problem areas that do not severely limit the application but do require further study to assess the total effect of each problem in the system operation were revealed. A partial total-temperature time history of X-15 flight 53 (Oct. 3, 1967) up to peak Mach number is shown, together with radar measurements of the X-15 Mach number and altitude, in addition to the data obtained from the shielded thermocouple sensor and the fluidic sensor.

519. Bogue, R. K.; and Webb, L. D.: **Advanced Air Data Sensing Techniques.** Presented at the International Aerospace Instrumentation Symposium, 5th, Cranfield, Beds., England, March 25–28, 1968, *Proceedings*, 14 refs., (A69-16747 05-14), <u>1968</u>, pp. 66–75, 69A16755, #. (See also 518.)

520. Taillon, N. V.: **A Method for the Surface Installation and Fairing of Static-Pressure Orifices on a Large Supersonic-Cruise Airplane.** NASA TM X-1530, <u>March 1968</u>, 68N19341, #.

A method for installing and fairing static-pressure orifices on the wing surface of a supersonic airplane without penetrating the skin is described. Orifice discs were fixed to pressure tubes which were, in turn, attached to the ferrous skin by welded straps. The assembly was faired over with a temperature-resistant aerodynamic smoothing compound hand-milled flush with the orifices. Some deviation from the mold line is inherent in the method; however, analytical estimates indicate that the effect on local aerodynamic pressures is negligible for this installation. The smoothing compound has been found to be operationally suitable at a Mach number of 3.

521. Van Leynseele, F. J.: **Evaluation of Lateral-Directional Handling Qualities of Piloted Reentry Vehicles Utilizing a Fixed Base Simulation.** NASA TN D-4410, <u>March 1968</u>, 68N19226, #.

A simulator investigation was conducted to evaluate the lateral-directional handling qualities of piloted vehicles. The lateral-directional parameters were chosen to represent a sample of dynamic characteristics typical of reentry-vehicle configurations. The evaluations were made by using a three-degree-of-freedom fixed-base simulator with a pseudo-outside world visual display (contact analog). The investigation showed that the pilots preferred the ratio of the roll transfer function numerator frequency to the dutch roll frequency to be unity, independent of the magnitude of bank angle to sideslip angle ratio. They objected to an excessive amount of sideslip angle excitation with ailerons when the ratio of the roll transfer function numerator frequency to the dutch roll frequency differed from unity, the bank angle to sideslip angle ratio was low, and the yawing moment due to aileron was large.

522. Reed, R. D.: **Flight Testing of Advanced Spacecraft Recovery Concepts Using the Aeromodeler's Approach.** AIAA Paper 68-242. Presented at the 2nd AIAA and Flight Test Simulation and Support Conference, Los Angeles, California, March 25–27, 1968, <u>March 1968</u>, 68A23665, #. (See also 510.)

523. Lasagna, P. L.; and McLeod, N. J.: **Preliminary Measured and Predicted XB-70 Engine Noise.** NASA TM X-1565, <u>April 1968</u>, 68N21834, #.

This paper presents measured and predicted noise levels and computed perceived noise levels for the XB-70 airplane during takeoffs, a landing, and a flyby at Edwards Air Force Base, Calif. The SAE jet-noise prediction method was used to predict noise levels for comparison with measured values.

524. Carpenter, R.; and Roman, J.: **Recording and Signal-Conditioning Techniques and Equipment Used in a 1,000-Flight Biomedical Study.** NASA TN D-4487, <u>April 1968</u>, 68N21538, #.

The NASA Flight Research Center recently concluded a biomedical monitoring program involving 1,000 flights in high-performance aircraft by students of the USAF Aerospace Research Pilot School and by NASA aerospace research pilots. To permit accurate and reliable data acquisition of electrocardiogram (ECG), respiration rate, and normal acceleration, it was necessary to design and develop a means of reliably recording and transcribing flight medical data in a format compatible with computer reduction. Signal conditioners and interconnecting harnesses were designed and fabricated, and guidelines were established for the construction of a five-channel analog tape recorder to record these data while the recorder is being carried on the pilot with minimum interference or discomfort. The equipment operated reliably and enabled satisfactory data acquisition of biomedical information both in extended biomedical instrumentation studies and in remote-site medical monitoring.

525. Carpenter, R.; and Roman, J.: **FM Handling and Analog-to-Digital Conversion of Biomedical Data From a**

1,000-Flight Study. NASA TN D-4488, <u>April 1968</u>, 68N21537.

To collect, process, and analyze FM-recorded biomedical data from 1,000 flights in high-performance aircraft and test vehicles, it was necessary to devise a handling facility that would prepare these data in a standard format for high-speed-computer processing. The handling system designed maintains the very high signal-to-noise radio inherent in the original data-acquisition equipment, provides push-button control for converting the medical information into a standard format for digital processing at either four or eight times faster than the original record speed, and provides an effective number of quality-control checkpoints. The system is described in detail, and system design considerations are discussed in relation to preventing data degradation in both FM handling and digital conversion.

526. Ehernberger, L. J.: **Meteorological Aspects of High-Altitude Turbulence Encountered by the XB-70 Airplane.** NASA TM X-61114, <u>1968</u>, 68N37298, #. (See also 527.)

This paper discusses the preliminary results of a study of meteorological features associated with turbulence encountered by the XB-70 airplane at flight levels above 40,000 feet (12,200 meters). Also, three of the larger temperature transients encountered during level flight at high altitudes are described. This study was conducted at the NASA Flight Research Center, Edwards, California, and covers XB-70 airplane flights made between April 1965 and March 1966 over the Western United States.

527. Ehernberger, L. J.: **Meteorological Aspects of High-Altitude Turbulence Encountered by the XB-70 Airplane.** *Proceedings*, 3rd National Conference On Aerospace Meteorology, New Orleans, Louisiana, May 6–9, 1968, (A68-35067 17-20), pp. 515–522. Boston, Massachusetts, American Meteorological Society, Conference Sponsored by the American Meteorological Society, the American Institute of Aeronautics and Astronautics, and the Institute of Environmental Sciences, <u>1968</u>, 68A35132, #. (See also 526.)

528. Wolowicz, C. H.; Strutz, L. W.; Gilyard, G. B.; and Matheny, N. W.: **Preliminary Flight Evaluation of the Stability and Control Derivatives and Dynamic Characteristics of the Unaugmented XB-70-1 Airplane Including Comparisons With Predictions.** NASA TN D-4578, <u>May 1968</u>, 68N24498, #.

Stability and control characteristics of the XB-70-1 airplane were evaluated from data obtained during the early phases of the flight-test program at Mach numbers extending to 2.56 and altitudes to 64,700 feet (19,700 meters). This report summarizes the results of the evaluation and compares the flight-determined derivatives with those obtained from wind-tunnel tests and with estimated effects of aeroelasticity.

529. Powers, B. G.: **A Review of Transport Handling-Qualities Criteria in Terms of Preliminary XB-70 Flight Experience.** NASA TM X-1584, <u>May 1968</u>, 68N23901, #.

A preliminary flight evaluation of handling qualities of the unaugmented XB-70 airplane was made during the initial flight test and envelope-expansion program. The evaluations consisted of pilot ratings and comments on the longitudinal and lateral-directional characteristics. The pilot ratings were compared with several current handling-qualities criteria for transport aircraft to establish the applicability of these criteria to this class of airplane.

530. Sisk, T. R.; Matheny, N. W.; Kier, D. A.; and Manke, J. A.: **A Preliminary Flying-Qualities Evaluation of a Variable-Sweep Fighter-Type Aircraft.** NASA TM X-1583, H-509, <u>May 1968</u>, 75N70035.

An evaluation of F-111A airplane number 6 (S/N 63-9771) consisting of 9 pilot-familiarization flights and 14 data-acquisition flights extending to Mach numbers approaching 1.9 at 47,500 feet (14,478 meters) altitude and 1.1 at 10,000 feet (3048 meters) altitude were completed. This preliminary evaluation allowed the assessment of flight-control-system and airplane response characteristics as various wing sweeps over the normal operating envelope of the aircraft with stability augmentation on and off. Augmentation-off flight is considered to be outside the normal flight environment of an operational aircraft and to be an emergency condition.

531. Watts, Joe D.; and Olinger, Frank V.: **Heat Transfer Effects of Surface Protuberances on the X-15 Airplane.** NASA TM X-1566, H-507, <u>May 1968</u>, 75N70033.

Heat-transfer effects of separated flow were investigated in flight tests of two protuberance configurations on the X-15 airplane. The 0.20-inch forward-and-aft-facing step and the 0.20-inch-amplitude sine-wave oriented at a right angle to the stream direction resulted in local heat-transfer variation of 0.09 to 2.23 and 0.34 to 2.03 times the smooth surface value, respectively.

532. Webb, L. D.: **Characteristics and Use of X-15 Air-Data Sensors.** NASA TN D-4597, <u>June 1968</u>, 68N25317, #.

The uses, techniques of correlation, and analysis of flight-guidance and air-data sensors that have been flown on the X-15 airplane are examined. Methods by which meteorological balloons and high altitude rocketsondes were used to define the atmospheric envelope around the X-15 airplane are discussed. The application of onboard sensor data, meteorological data, and radar in obtaining altitude, velocity, Mach number, and dynamic pressure is explained.

533. Holleman, E. C.: **Stability and Control Characteristics of the M2-F2 Lifting Body Measured During 16 Glide Flights.** NASA TM X-1593, June 1968, 70N78443.

Sixteen glide flights with the M2-F2 lifting-body research vehicle were analyzed to obtain a measure of some of the static and dynamic stability and control and handling characteristics for a Mach number range of 0.4 to 0.7. The vehicle was statically and dynamically stable in the regions in which it was predicted to be stable. The upper flap was about twice as effective as the lower flap as a pitch control. The flight stability and control results agreed reasonably well with the wind-tunnel predicted characteristics. The M2-F2 handling qualities with dampers on and rudder-to-aileron interconnect operative were rated satisfactory for the M2-F2 research mission by the four pilots in the program. The predicted unacceptable handling characteristics of the basic vehicle were observed in flight. Various handling-qualities criteria predicted handling that was in general agreement with the actual pilot evaluation for the M2-F2 vehicle. The vehicle has the lift capability and maneuverability for satisfactory approach and landing as a glider at a selected landing site. The approach and landing piloting task was demanding and required detailed preparation and practice for the flight and complete concentration during the maneuver.

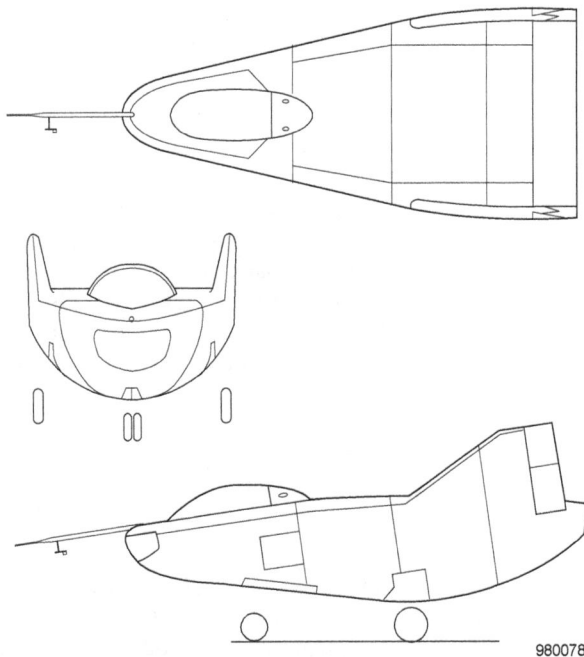

980078

M2-F2 Lifting Body Three-View Drawing

534. Wolowicz, Chester H.; and Wykes, John H.: **Stability Derivatives of an Elastic Airplane From Flight Test.** 1968 Seminar on Elastic Airplane Stability, Control, and Response, University of Kansas, June 12, 1968.

535. Smith, R. H.; Bellman, D. R.; and Hughes, D. L.: **Preliminary Flight Investigation of Dynamic Phenomena Within Air Breathing Propulsion Systems of Supersonic Aircraft.** AIAA Paper 68-593. Presented at the 4th AIAA Propulsion Joint Specialist Conference, Cleveland, Ohio, June 10–14, 1968, June 1968, 68A33790, #.

Many of the aerodynamic conditions that contribute to the propulsion system problems of aircraft are dynamic and require higher response instrumentation than is generally used for flight-test work. Such problems become increasingly prominent as aircraft advance into the supersonic speed region where the function and control of the inlet and engine become more critical. At the NASA Flight Research Center, the F-111A airplane and the XB-70A airplane, both capable of flying at Mach numbers greater than 2, have been instrumented to measure pressure fluctuations in the propulsion-system airstream at frequencies as high as 200 hertz. This paper presents design and development details of the two instrumentation systems as well as their characteristics as shown by laboratory tests. Temperature effects on the pressure transducers and means for their compensation and correction are discussed. XB-70A flight results for compressor-face pressures are included.

536. Beaulieu, W.; Campbell, R.; and Burcham, W.: **Measurement of the XB-70A Propulsion Performance Incorporating the Gas Generator Method.** AIAA Paper 68-594, Propulsion Joint Specialist Conference, Cleveland, Ohio, June 10–14, 1968, June 1968, 68A33791. (See also 578.)

Propulsion performance of XB-70A aircraft calculated by gas generator method.

537. Burke, M. E.: **X-15 Analog and Digital Inertial Systems Flight Experience.** NASA TN D-4642, July 1968, 68N29404, #.

Two different types of inertial flight data systems, an analog system and a digital system, have been used during the X-15 program to provide primary flight information for the X-15 pilot. This use has afforded an opportunity to compare the two mechanization concepts in the same operating environment. The two systems, although having basically different computers, use similar inertial measurement units. Equation mechanization is different primarily because of the difference in computers. The development problems on the analog system were considerably more complex than those with the digital system, inasmuch as the analog it could be refined. These development problems ultimately brought about the redesign of analog system and utilization of the digital system.

538. Burcham, F. W., Jr.: **Wind-Tunnel Calibration of a 40 Deg Conical Pressure Probe at Mach Numbers From 3.5 to 7.4.** NASA TN D-4678, July 1968, 68N28801, #.

A wind-tunnel calibration of a 40° included-angle flow-field cone probe was made over a Mach number range of 3.5 to 7.4. The cone probe was designed and fabricated by the NASA Flight Research Center to obtain flow-field data on the X-15 airplane. Estimated accuracy of the calibration was ±2 percent in Mach number and ±0.2 degree in flow angularity at a Mach number of 7.4. Reynolds number effects were negligible over the test range of 0.65 million to 3.25 million per foot (0.20 million to 1. 0 million per meter). A rake designed for flight on the X-15 was used to mount two cone probes. Slightly different calibrations resulted for the two cones because of differences in the cone afterbody configurations.

539. Carpenter, L. R.; Lewis, C. E., Jr.; and McDonald, R. T.: **Electrocardiograph Transmitted by RF and Telephone Links in Emergency Situations.** FRC-10031, July 1968, 68B10233.

540. Roman, J.; Larmie, F. M.; and Figarola, T. R.: **A Simple Laboratory Method for Reduction of Rhythm and Rate in Large-Scale Monitoring of Electrocardiogram.** NASA TN D-4751, August 1968, 68N32100, #.

A laboratory system for rapid reduction of large amounts of continuously recorded ECG information has been developed. The system consists of a 60-times-real-time playback device which generates one pulse for each cardiac cycle, appropriate signal conditioning and logic circuitry, and a counting and printing system. Practical means for culling out noisy information, at 60 times real time, are provided.

541. McLain, L. J.; and Palitz, M.: **Flow-Field Investigations on the X-15 Airplane and Model Up to Hypersonic Speeds.** NASA TN D-4813, September 1968, 68N35173, #.

Flight-measured impact pressures and local Mach numbers near the surface of the rear-lower-fuselage centerline, wing lower surface, and upper vertical tail of the X-15 airplane are presented and compared with calculated results and wind-tunnel data. In addition, wind-tunnel-derived total pressures in the rear-lower-fuselage flow field are presented. The flight measurements are presented over a free-stream Mach number range of 1 to 5.7 and an angle-of-attack range of 0 degree to 20 degrees. The wind-tunnel measurements cover a Mach number range of 4.0 to 8.0.

542. Ehernberger, L. J.: **Atmospheric Conditions Associated With Turbulence Encountered by the XB-70 Airplane Above 40,000 Feet Altitude.** NASA TN D-4768, September 1968, 68N33416, #.

High altitude atmospheric turbulence has been encountered by the XB-70 airplane during flight tests over the Western United States. The encounters from 36 flights were used to obtain a preliminary assessment of the meteorological features associated with high altitude turbulence. This study used data from an NACA VGH recorder carried on the airplane and from rawinsonde observations made near turbulence encounters at altitudes above 40,000 feet (12,200 meters). These data showed that turbulence of significant intensity at high altitudes is related to wind velocity, vertical and wind shear, and the vertical temperature gradient. These findings are in general agreement with various turbulence-generating disturbances suggested previously in the literature. It is also indicated that the disturbances causing high-altitude turbulence can originate in both the lower atmosphere and the stratosphere.

543. Saltzman, Edwin J.; Goecke, Sheryll A.; and Pembo, Chris: **Base Pressure Measurements on the XB-70 Airplane at Mach Numbers From 0.4 to 3.0.** NASA TM X-1612, September 1968, 71N17132, #.

Full-scale flight base pressure coefficients obtained from the XB-70 propulsion package are compared with predicted values based on a combination of cold jet flow wind tunnel models and data from a two-engine side-by-side jet, full-scale aircraft. At cruise mach numbers the base pressures of the full-scale aircraft were higher than predicted, resulting in a favorable increment of about 2 percent in terms of lift-drag ratio. At low supersonic speeds near a Mach number of 1.2, the negative base pressure coefficients were about three times larger than predicted, which would result in a significant lift-drag-ratio decrement. The investigation showed that the net calculated effect of underestimating the base drag a low supersonic climbout speeds, even though overestimating the base drag at cruise, can seriously reduce the range potential of the aircraft, depending on several operational factor that can influence transonic excess thrust. The trend of this range decrement (with respect to the transonic excess thrust) emphasizes the need for a base drag prediction based on models with a higher degree of similitude throughout the transonic and supersonic range.

544. Taylor, Lawrence W.; and Iliff, Kenneth W.: **A Modified Newton-Raphson Method for Determining Stability Derivatives From Flight Data.** Second International Conference on Computing Methods in Optimization Problems, San Remo, Italy, September 9–13, 1968.

This paper presents the formulation of least squares and the Newton-Raphson method. The results are compared and discussed. The work reported was done jointly by the authors and Dr. A. V. Balakrishnan of the University of California at Los Angeles. Example solutions are included that show not only the quality of the fitted solution but also a comparison of the estimated coefficients with values obtained by other techniques.

545. Kordes, Eldon E.: **Status of Structural-Response and Modal-Suppression Programs on the XB-70.** Langley Meeting on Aircraft Response to Turbulence, NASA Langley Research Center, Hampton, Virginia, September 24–25, 1968.

The XB-70 flight program has provided an excellent opportunity to study the dynamic response of a large flexible aircraft under full-scale conditions up to a Mach number of 3 at 70,000 feet altitude The purpose of this paper is to describe some of the research being carried out on the XB-70 in the area of turbulence, turbulence encountered, and airplane response and to present some preliminary results obtained 50 far in the program.

546. Mallick, Donald L.; Kluever, Emil E.; and Matranga, Gene J.: **Flight Results Obtained With a Non-Aerodynamic, Variable Stability, Flying Platform.** NASA TM X-59039. Presented at 10th Symposium and Banquet, Los Angeles, California, September 23, 1968.

547. Wilson, R. J.; and McKay, J. M.: **Landing Loads and Accelerations of the XB-70-1 Airplane.** NASA TN D-4836, October 1968, 68N36073, #.

Data are presented on landing-contact conditions for the first 48 landings of the XB-70-1 airplane. Landing weights varied from 419, 800 pounds (190,400 kilograms) to 274,600 pounds (124,600 kilograms), Vertical velocities at touchdown ranged from 5.26 feet/second (1.603 meters/second) to 1.49 feet/second (0.454 meter/second). Maximum indicated airspeed was 195.0 knots, with a minimum of 167.3 knots.

548. Watts, Joe D.: **Flight Experience With Shock Impingement and Interference Heating on the X-15-2 Research Airplane.** NASA TM X-1669, October 1968, 92N70863, #.

Severe structural melting damage due to complex shock impingement and interference effects on local aerodynamic heating was experienced on a flight of the X-15-2 research airplane to a maximum Mach number of 6.7. Measured flight temperature data and observed structural damage resulting from shock impingement and interference heating on the airplane and its ablative coating were analyzed in the light of hypersonic wind-tunnel results. The best approximations of the flight results were made by increasing the undisturbed pylon leading-edge heat-transfer coefficient by a factor of 9 and the undisturbed heat-transfer coefficient in the two interference zones by a factor of 7. The calculated effect of increased heat transfer due to interference in radiation-equilibrium temperature is presented for selected hypersonic cruise conditions.

549. Fulton, F. L., Jr.: **Lessons From the XB-70 as Applied to the Supersonic Transport.** NASA TM X-56014. Presented at the 21st Annual International Air Safety Seminar, Anaheim, California, October 7–11, 1968. 1968, 68N35734, #.

The lessons from the XB-70A program that have been selected for discussion are only a few of the things that have been learned during the program. These things will certainly apply to the supersonic transport (SST). In some cases they will apply to any large airplane, and in a few cases they will apply to almost any airplane. The XB-70 is a very valuable research airplane; there is no other airplane in the world of similar size that can fly in the same speed environment. Many of its design features were pushing the state of the art; therefore, both positive and negative results were obtained, providing validation or correlation of design prediction techniques. It also provided information on operational factors applicable to a large supersonic aircraft The program has been expensive in money, time, and personal sacrifice, but if the knowledge gained from the XB-70A test program makes it possible to avoid even one catastrophic SST accident, the program will more than pay for itself.

550. Richardson, R. B.; and Harney, P. F.: **Flight and Laboratory Testing of a Double Sideband FM Telemetry System.** NASA TM X-56015. *Proceedings of the International Telemetering Conference,* Los Angeles, California, October 8–11, 1968, 1968, pp. 581–596, 69A19132.

Double sideband suppressed carrier FM telemetry system as airborne data recorder, discussing noise, environmental conditions, laboratory and flight tests.

551. Kordes, Eldon E.: **XB-70 Contributions to Environmental Technology of the Supersonic Transport.** Presented at the 1968 ASME Transportation Engineering Conference, Washington, D.C., October 27–30, 1968.

552. Wilson, E. J.: **Use of Strain Gages for Measurements of Flight Loads in a High-Temperature Environment.** *Proceedings, Instrument Society Of America, 5th Annual Test Measurement Symposium,* New York, New York, October 28–31, 1968, 1968, pp. 555 1 to 555 5, 69A31277.

Strain gages to measure flight loads in high temperature environment, discussing selection, calibration techniques and performance characteristics.

553. Reed, R. D.: **Can the R/C'er Contribute to Aeronautical Research?** *R/C Modeler,* Vol. 5, No. 10, October 1968, pp. 28–35.

554. Taylor, Lawrence W., Jr.; Iliff, Kenneth W.; and Powers, Bruce G.: **A Comparison of Newton-Raphson and Other Methods for Determining Stability Derivatives From Flight Data.** Third Technical Workshop on Dynamic

Stability Problems, Ames Research Center, Moffett Field, California, November 4–7, 1968. (See also 562.)

This paper presents the formulation of least squares, Shinbrot, and Newton-Raphson methods as applied to the problem of determining stability derivatives from flight data. The results are compared and discussed. The work reported was done jointly by the authors and Dr. A. V. Balakrishnan of the University of California at Los Angeles. Example solutions are included that show not only the quality of the fitted solution but also a comparison of the estimated coefficients with values obtained by other methods.

555.   McTigue, J. G.; and Ryan, B. M.: **Lifting-Body Research Vehicles in a Low-Speed Flight Test Program.** *New York Academy of Sciences, International Congress on Subsonic Aeronautics,* New York, New York, April 3–6, 1967, *New York Academy of Sciences, Annals,* Vol. 154, November 1968, pp. 1014–1032, 69A15571.

The potential advantages offered by the lifting-body concept for entry and landing prompted the NASA Flight Research Center at Edwards, Calif., to initiate a multiphased flight study to determine the handling qualities and maneuvering required to flare and land this class of vehicles. This paper discusses the background of the program, the objectives, and the results obtained to date.

556.   Kock, B. M.; and Painter, W. D.: **Investigation of the Controllability of the M2-F2 Lifting-Body Launch From the B-52 Carrier Airplane.** NASA TM X-1713, December 1968, 71N15004, #.

The launch characteristics of the M2-F2 lifting body after release from the B-52 carrier airplane were studied by using analytical methods and simulators to predict launch safety and to determine the piloting requirements during launch. The predicted launch characteristics and the flight results are compared.

557.   Jenkins, J. M.; Tang, M. H.; and Pearson, G. P. E.: **Vertical-Tail Loads and Control-Surface Hinge-Moment Measurements on the M2-F2 Lifting Body During Initial Subsonic Flight Tests.** NASA TM X-1712, December 1968, 71N15003, #.

Subsonic aerodynamic load characteristics are presented for the right vertical tail and the control surfaces on the M2-F2 lifting-body vehicle. The effects of vehicle attitude and control-surface deflection on the vertical-tail loads are determined. Coefficients defining the effects of angle of attack, angle of sideslip, upper-flap deflection, and rudder deflection on flight-measured vertical-tail loads are presented in terms of linear equations. Portions of two maneuver time histories are included to illustrate the magnitude of each of these effects. The effects of angle of attack and control-surface deflection on the flight-measured rudder, upper-flap, and lower flap hinge moments are discussed. The measured loads data are presented in aerodynamic-coefficient form. Large vertical-tail loads were measured during flight tests. Flight-measured control-surface hinge-moment data are compared with wind-tunnel data obtained from full-scale vehicle tests.

558.   McLeod, N. J.; Lasagna, P. L.; and Putnam, T. W.: **Predicted and Measured XB-70 Ground-To-Ground Engine Noise.** NASA SP-189. Presented in program of NASA Research Relating to Noise Alleviation of Large Subsonic Jet Aircraft, 1968, pp. 423–434, 69N11569, #.

Measurements have been made of XB-70 engine noise during ground runs. The effect of engine power settings and engine spacing on the noise spectra during the ground runs is presented. Some of the data obtained during the ground runs were analyzed to determine the amplitude variation, and the effect of averaging time was determined. The SAE method was used to predict the noise levels for various test conditions, and comparisons of predicted and measured spectra are presented. Tests indicate some limitations for the SAE prediction method. During ground operation of the XB-70 airplane, the amplitude variations in the acoustic data during quasi-stable engine thrust indicate that similar variations might occur when flyover noise spectra are being measured. Atmospheric attenuation predictions were greater than the measured attenuation for the high-frequency octave bands at the specific conditions of these tests.

1969 Technical Publications

559.   Taylor, L. W., Jr.; Smith, H. J.; and Iliff, K. W.: **Experience Using Balakrishnan's Epsilon Technique to Compute Optimum Flight Profiles.** AIAA Paper 69-75. Presented at the 7th AIAA Aerospace Sciences Meeting, New York, New York, January 20–22, 1969, 70A28088, 69A18058. (See also 589, 605.)

A technique for computing optimum profiles is developed which differs from the classical gradient method in that a term representing the constraint of satisfying the equations of motion is included in the cost function to be minimized. Although the number of unknown independent functions is increased to include the state variables, the dimensionally of the gradient of the modified cost is greatly reduced, resulting in considerable savings in complexity and time. The unknown control and state variables are expressed in s functional expansion to facilitate solution by means of Newton's method. The effects of weighting terms and the number of functions on the convergence properties are discussed. Comparisons are made of solutions using the classical gradient method, dynamic programming, and Balakrishnan's epsilon technique.

560. *Newell, F. D.; and Smith, H. J.: **Human Transfer Characteristics in Flight and Ground Simulation for a Roll Tracking Task.** NASA TN D-5007, February 1969, 69N17814.

Pilot transfer characteristics for three pilots have been measured in flight and in ground-based simulators for a compensatory roll tracking task with small bank-angle disturbances. The forcing function, in each case, consisted of the sum-of-ten-sine-waves with a bandwidth of 15 radians per second. A variable-stability T-33 airplane was used to obtain the flight measurements. Ground-based simulator measurements were obtained with both the T-33 airplane and a general-purpose simulator which used a contact-analog color display. Three different controlled elements were used, two of which were simple single-degree-of-freedom controlled elements that had been studied previously. The third was a multiple-degree-of-freedom element representative of an airplane with good handling qualities and was considered and controlled as a single-degree-of-freedom configuration in roll.

*Cornell Aeronautical Laboratory, Inc., Buffalo, New York.

561. Montoya, E. J.; and Nugent, J.: **Wind-Tunnel Force and Pressure Tests of Rocket-Engine Nozzle Extensions on the 0.0667-Scale X-15-2 Model at Supersonic and Hypersonic Speeds.** NASA TM X-1759, March 1969, 69N20873, #.

Wind-tunnel force and pressure test results of nozzle extensions on the 0.0667-scale X-15-2 model over the free-stream Mach number range from 2.3 to 8.0 at angles of attack from −5 degree to 18 degree and Reynolds numbers of 2.0×10 (to the 6th) per foot and 3.4×10 (to the 6th) per foot (1.12×107 per meter) are presented. The effects of the presence of an aft-mounted ramjet shape and control-surface deflections are shown.

562. Taylor, L. W., Jr.; Iliff, K. W.; and Powers, B. G.: **A Comparison of Newton-Raphson and Other Methods for Determining Stability Derivatives From Flight Data.** AIAA Paper 69-315, 3rd AIAA and FTSS Conference, Houston, Texas, March 10–12, 1969, 69A22379, #. (See also 554.)

A new technique of determining stability derivatives from flight data is formulated and compared with the simple equations, analog matching, least squares, and Shinbrot

methods of analysis. It is shown that the new technique, termed Newton-Raphson, is superior to the others whether flight data or a statistical model is used. Although the new method uses the Newton-Raphson technique, it is also similar to quasilinearization. The Newton-Raphson technique has been developed to enable the use of a priori (wind tunnel) information and to automatically adjust bias terms and initial conditions to compensate for errors. The technique has been successfully applied to the X-15, XB-70, F-111, and HL-10 vehicles and has application to many other system identification problems.

563. Quinn, Robert D.; and Olinger, Frank V.: **Heat-Transfer Measurements Obtained on the X-15 Airplane Including Correlations With Wind-Tunnel Results.** NASA TM X-1705, NAS 1.15:X-1705, March 1969, 92N70607.

Heat transfer measurements were obtained on the X-15 airplane from two flights under quasi-steady conditions at a freestream Mach number of 5.1 and an angle of attack of 2.0 degrees, and a freestream Mach number of 4.98 and an angle of attack of 16.3 degrees. These measurements were made at corresponding freestream Reynolds numbers of 2.45×10 (exp 6) and 1.31×10 (exp 6) per foot. Experimental heat transfer coefficients derived from temperatures obtained from 200 recording thermocouples on the skin of the airplane are tabulated. Correlations with wind tunnel results show that the wind tunnel data are in fair to good agreement with the flight data obtained on the wing, ventral tail, and vertical tail at low angles of attack but are generally in poor agreement with high angle of attack data and the low angle of attack fuselage data.

564. Wagner, C. A.: **Visual Simulation Image Generation Using a Flying-Spot Scanner.** NASA TN D-5151, April 1969, 69N23194, #.

This paper analyzes the flying-spot scanner television camera used as a video signal generator for visual flight simulation. A description of the technique is included as well as a detailed theoretical analysis of the quality of the video that can be produced. A commercially available flying-spot scanner designed for flight simulation was tested, and its capabilities are presented. Discussion is limited to the television camera; display devices such as monitors are not discussed. The flying-spot scanner was found to be a low-cost device which can simulate all motions of an aircraft except roll. Large excursions at high rates are easily achieved. It is limited to a relatively small field of view, a fixed forward visibility, and simulation of flat terrain. The quality of the video is adequate over a moderate range of altitudes; a very high and very low altitudes result in poor performance. Possible approaches to increasing the useful altitude range are discussed.

565. Mallick, D. L.; and Fulton, F. L., Jr.: **Flight Crew Preparation and Training for the Operation of Large Supersonic Aircraft.** FAUSST VII Meeting, Paris, France, March 3–7, 1969.

566. Bellman, D. R.; and Hughes, D. L.: **The Flight Investigation of Pressure Phenomena in the Air Intake of an F-111A Airplane.** AIAA Paper 69-488. Presented at the 5th AIAA Propulsion Joint Specialist Conference, U. S. Airforce Academy, Colorado Springs, Colorado, June 9–13, 1969, June 1969, 69A32706, #.

ECN-2092

F-111A Aardvark Airplane

567. Painter, W. D.; and Kock, B. M.: **Operational Experiences and Characteristics of the M2-F2 Lifting Body Flight Control System.** NASA TM X-1809, June 1969, 71N14526, #.

Flights of the M2-F2 lifting body demonstrated that the manual control system and the stability augmentation system met the operational flight control requirements for the test vehicle. The regions of pilot-induced oscillation predicted from ground simulation were encountered in flight. The pilots considered the control system to be adequate for the M2-F2 flight envelope flown. Limit-cycle data obtained during ground tests agreed with flight results. Structural frequencies of the vehicle control surfaces were never sustained in flight as a result of filtering in the stability augmentation system.

568. Taylor, Lawrence W., Jr.; Smith, Harriet J.; and Iliff, Kenneth W.: **A Comparison of Minimum Time Profiles for the F-104 Using Balakrishnan's Epsilon Technique and the Energy Method.** Presented by Dr. A. V. Balakrishnan at Symposium on Optimization, Nice, France, June 29–July 5, 1969. (See also 649.)

Balakrishnan's epsilon technique is used to compute minimum time profiles for the F-104 airplane. This technique differs from the classical gradient method in that a quadratic penalty on the error in satisfying the equations of motion is included in the cost function to be minimized as a means of eliminating the requirement of satisfying the equations of motion. Although the number of unknown independent functions is increased to include the state variables, the evaluation of the gradient of the modified cost is simplified, resulting in considerable computational savings. The unknown control and state variables are approximated by a functional expansion with unspecified coefficients which are determined by means of Newton's method. Typically 8 to 10 iterations are required for convergence when using the epsilon technique. Comparisons are made of solutions obtained by using this technique and the energy method.

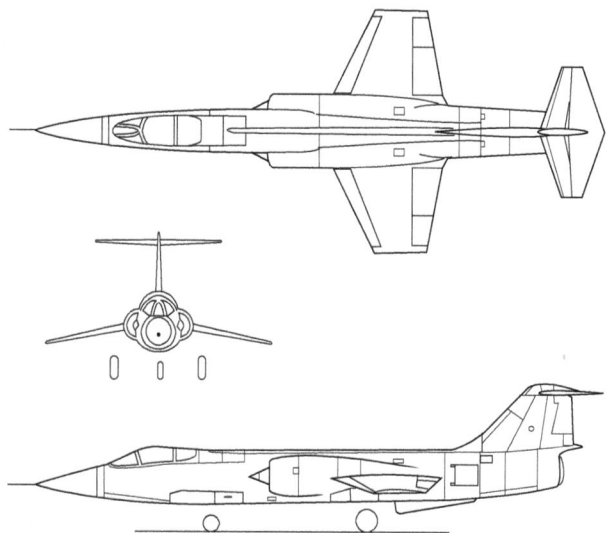

980064

F-104 Airplane, Three-View Drawing

569. Lock, W. P.; and Gee, S. W.: **Flight Investigation of a Fluidic Autopilot System.** NASA TN D-5298, July 1969, 69N30946, #.

A flight investigation was made of an experimental fluidic flight control system capable of various modes of operation, including altitude hold, heading hold, wings leveler and turn control. The fluidic control system was tested in each mode at two flight conditions: cruise at 5000 feet, and cruise at 10,000 feet. Although stability problems were encountered early in the program, stable performance was achieved in each control mode for the flight conditions tested. High reliability was demonstrated, in that there were no failures with fluidic elements themselves. Failures were experienced, however, with the mechanical portion of the mechanical fluidic components.

570. Gaidsick, H. G.; Dana, W. H.; and McCracken, R. C.: **Evaluation of an Indirect Viewing System for Lifting-Body Terminal-Area Navigation and Landing Tasks.** NASA TN D-5299, July 1969, 69N29730, #.

A short-eyed-relief optical system, consisting of two monocular periscopes with overlapping fields of view, was mounted in an F-104B airplane to evaluate the feasibility of using this type of indirect viewing system in place of normal vision for performing simulated lifting-body approaches and landings. Three approach techniques were used in the study. Performance was evaluated by measuring touchdown distance from a marked touchdown point and rate of sink and airspeed at touchdown. Results obtained with the optics system were compared with normal-vision results. The ability of the pilots to perform the simulated lifting-body tasks was not noticeably reduced with the optics system. The workload and other pilot acceptance factors, however, indicated that this particular system required improvement in design, even though the pilots could readily adapt to its use.

571. Swaroop, R.; West, K. A.; and Lewis, C. E., Jr.: **A Simple Technique for Automatic Computer Editing of Biodata.** NASA TN D-5275, July 1969, 69N29592, #.

Before any data are statistically analyzed, it is always necessary to edit the data to some extent. Furthermore, when large quantities of data are collected, the editing must performed by automatic means. One common task in the editing process is the identification of observations which deviate markedly from the rest of the sample, commonly known outliers. A simple statistical technique for identifying the outliers and the necessary computer program is presented in this report. The program requires as input only the data set, sample size, and preselected levels of significance which outliers are to be identified. It is assumed that the data set is a random sample of size larger than two from a normal population. Two examples are presented to illustrate applications of the described technique.

572. Layton, Garrison P., Jr.: **Interim Results of the Lifting-Body Flight-Test Program.** NASA TM X-1827. Presented at AIAA Entry Vehicle Systems and Technology Meeting, Hampton, Virginia, December 3–5, 1968. July 1969, 71N14527, #.

The significant results of the joint NASA/U. S. Air Force lifting-body flight-test program are presented in general terms, based on 16 M2-F2 glide flights, 14 HL-10 flights and wind-tunnel tests of the X-24A flight vehicle. The lifting-body flight-test program has demonstrated that lifting reentry vehicles can be maneuvered to an unpowered landing from

initial conditions representing the entry of the terminal area for a reentry vehicle.

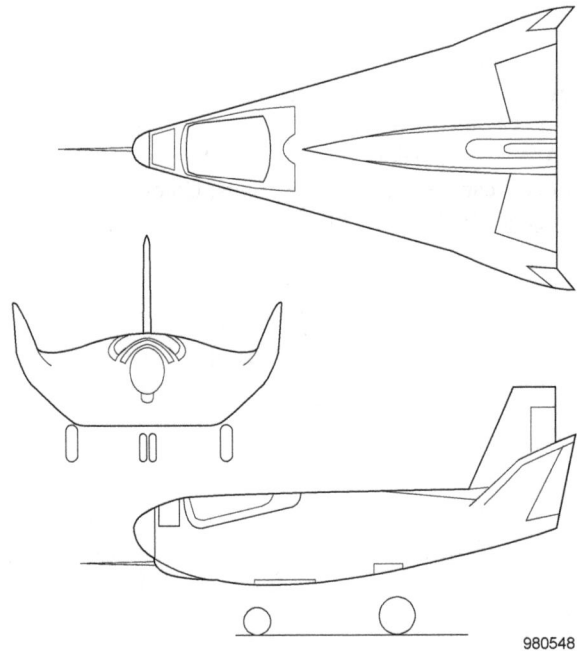

HL-10 Lifting Body, Three-View Drawing

573. Borek, R. W.; and Richardson, R. B.: **Flight and Laboratory Tests of an "L-Band" Telemetry RF System.** *Telemetry Journal*, Vol. 4, July 1969, pp. 21–24, 69A35996.

Laboratory and flight tests of airborne solid state UHF telemetry transmitter, discussing miniaturized coaxial hardware from RF power conservation viewpoint.

574. Taylor, L. W., Jr.; and Iliff, K. W.: **Fixed-Base Simulator Pilot Rating Surveys for Predicting Lateral-Directional Handling Qualities and Pilot Rating Variability.** NASA TN D-5358, August 1969, 69N35762, #.

Pilot ratings of lateral-directional handling qualities were collected for a wide range of simplified aircraft characteristics through the use of a simple fixed-base simulator with a color contact analog display. The results of the general survey were obtained with an engineer as the subject and are contained in 45 plots involving five parameters. The survey results show that the handling qualities for the specific simulations used were, in general, optimum. The results of the general survey are used in an empirical method for predicting lateral-directional pilot ratings for most airplane configurations and flight conditions. In another survey, utilizing the same simulation, ratings were obtained from many pilots in order to study the variability in pilot ratings among pilots and the differences in pilot rating that result from changes in mission. The standard deviation of individual pilot ratings ranged from 1. 0 at the "good" end of the scale to 2. 0 in the middle of the scale. Ratings for specific missions were generally numerically higher (more adverse) than those for the general mission for the same vehicle characteristic.

575. Jenkins, J. M.; DeAngelis, V. M.; Friend, E. L.; and Monaghan, R. C.: **Flight Measurements of Canard Loads, Canard Buffeting, and Elevon and Wing Tip Hinge Moments on the XB-70 Aircraft Including Comparisons With Predictions.** NASA TN D-5359, August 1969, 69N32284, #.

During a flight-test program with the XB-70 airplane, canard, elevon, and wingtip flight load measurements were made in the Mach number range from 0.40 to 3.00. The data are compared with the manufacturer's rigid and aeroelastic predictions, wind-tunnel airfoil data, or results obtained from flight tests of other applicable aircraft. The magnitudes of the flight loads and the variation of surface loads with angle of attack or surface deflection corresponded generally with predictions. Canard buffeting was experienced at subsonic speeds. The characteristics of this effect are examined on the basis of the results of in-flight tuft studies and the analysis of flight-measured bending-moment data.

576. Kotfilia, R. P.; and Painter, W. D.: **Design, Development, and Flight Test Experience With Lifting Body Stability Augmentation Systems.** AIAA Paper 69-887. Presented at the AIAA Guidance, Control and Flight Mechanics Conference, Princeton, New Jersey, August 18–20, 1969, 69A39413, #.

The aerodynamic characteristics of lifting body research vehicles tested thus far require stability augmentation systems (SAS) to improve the handling qualities of the vehicles in some areas of the flight envelope. The design goals for such a system are performance, reliability, and ease of testing. Validation of these goals requires realistic test criteria that establish vehicle-SAS performance based on ground tests. This paper describes the design of the SAS for the X-24A vehicle and the ground test techniques that were used for this validation. Test criteria and procedures are established for various ground tests, such as frequency response, limit cycle, and structural resonance. Ground test results are compared with subsequent flight test data obtained in the joint NASA-USAF lifting body flight research program.

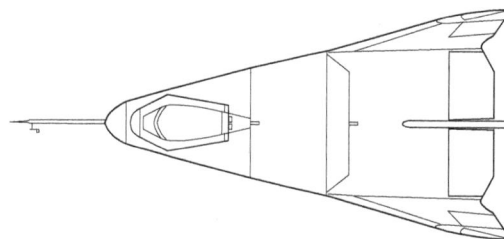

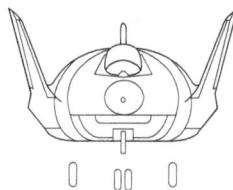

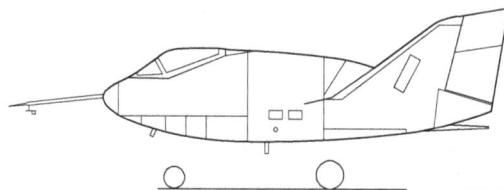

X-24A Lifting Body, Three-View Drawing

577. Rediess, H. A.; and *Whitaker, H. P.: **A New Model Performance Index for the Engineering Design of Flight Control Systems.** AIAA Paper 69-885. Presented at the AIAA Guidance, Control, and Flight Mechanics Conference, Princeton, Jew Jersey, August 18–20, 1969, 69A39410, #.

The theory and application of a new performance index, the Model PI, that brings engineering design specifications into the analytical design process is presented. A parameter optimization design procedure is established that starts with practical engineering specifications and uses the Model PI as a synthesis tool to obtain a satisfactory design. The Model P1 represents a new criterion for approximating one dynamical system by another, based on a novel geometrical representation of linear autonomous systems. It is shown to be an effective performance index in designing practical systems and to be substantially more efficient to use than a comparable model-referenced integral squared error performance index. The design procedure is demonstrated by designing a lateral-directional stability augmentation system for the X-15 aircraft.

*Massachusetts Institute of Technology, Cambridge, Massachusetts.

578. Beaulieu, W.; Campbell, R.; and Burcham, W.: **Measurement of XB-70 Propulsion Performance Incorporating the Gas Generator Method.** *J. Aircraft,* Vol. 6, No. 4, July–August 1969, 9A37152. (See also 536.)

Propulsion performance of XB-70A aircraft calculated by gas generator method.

579. Sefic, W. J.; and Anderson, K. F.: **NASA High Temperature Loads Calibration Laboratory.** NASA TM X-1868, September 1969, 69N36224, #.

The NASA High Temperature Loads Calibration Laboratory and the equipment it contains for simulating the loading and heating of aircraft or their components are described. Particular emphasis is placed on various fail-safe devices which are built into the equipment to minimize the possibility of damage to flight vehicles. The data-acquisition system is described. This system involves on-site pickup of data and signal conditioning coupled with conversion from analog to digital data and transmission to a central area for recording on magnetic tape and distribution to real-time displays. Instrumentation available in the facility for measuring load, position, and strain is also discussed.

580. Fields, R. A.; and Vano, A.: **Evaluation of an Infrared Heating Simulation of a Mach 4.63 Flight on an X-15 Horizontal Stabilizer.** NASA TN D-5403, September 1969, 69N35949, #.

Temperatures recorded on the X-15 horizontal stabilizer during a Mach 4.63 flight were simulated in the laboratory. A liquid-nitrogen evaporative cooler was used to cool the structure to a prelaunch condition; the heating was provided by an infrared heating system with closed-loop control. The simulated flight produced temperatures from approximately – 50 degrees F (228 degrees K) to 750 degrees F (672 degrees K). The simulation was evaluated by comparing flight-measured temperatures with those measured during the simulation.

581. Lewis, C. E., Jr.; and Krier, G. E.: **Flight Research Program: XIV—Landing Performance in Jet Aircraft After the Loss of Binocular Vision.** *Aerospace Medicine,* Vol. 40, September 1969, pp. 957–963, 69A41675.

Landing performance in T-33A aircraft with loss of binocular vision is compared to performance with both eyes.

582. *Lipana, J. G.; *Fletcher, J.; *Brown, W.; and *Cohen, G.: **Effects of Various Respiratory Maneuvers on the Physiological Response to Angular Acceleration.** *Aerospace Medicine,* Vol. 40, September 1969, pp. 976–980, 69A41679.

The effects of breath holding, Ml, Valsalva and Mueller's maneuvers were studied on healthy males during static condition at various postures and during pure axis rotations. The subject was seated inside a hollow spherical simulator (ARTS). Rotation was at the rate of 6 rpm with the axis of rotation through the body. Heart rates, EGG, blood pressures, respiratory rates, voice and TV were monitored via telemetry.

*Systems Research Laboratories, Inc., City, State.

583. Adkins, E. J.; McLeod, N. J.; and Lasagna, P. L.: **Variation in Engine Noise for Two Landing-Approach Configurations of a Jet Transport Aircraft.** NASA TM X-1896, October 1969, 69N38104, #.

A limited flight investigation was conducted to determine the effect of reduced flap deflections on power required and the resulting engine noise for a subsonic jet transport aircraft. Noise levels were measured during level flight at an altitude of 400 feet (122 meters) at approach speeds. Data were obtained during flybys with flap deflections of 50 degrees and 36 degree. The maximum overall sound pressure level (OASPL) from flybys with 36 degree of flap deflection averaged 3 decibels (ref. 0.00002 newtons/meter^2) lower than for flybys with 50 degree of flap deflection. Buffet intensity was reduced by the use of lower-flap deflections.

584. Fisher, D. F.: **Flight-Measured Aerodynamic Drag of Two Large External Tanks Attached to the X-15-2 Airplane at Mach Numbers of 1.6 to 2.3.** NASA TM X-1895, October 1969, 69N38065, #.

Full-scale power-on flight lift and drag measurements were made on the X-15-2 airplane just before and just after two large external fuel tanks were ejected. By subtracting the drag of the airplane after the tank ejection from the drag of the airplane before tank ejection, the incremental drag due to the tanks was determined. Analysis of the data showed that the percentage increase of incremental drag due to the tanks was almost equal to the percentage increase in cross-sectional area caused by the tanks. A buildup drag estimate based on free-stream conditions agreed well with the flight data; whereas, the wind tunnel data, although they had the same general trend of the tank drag coefficient with Mach number, were lower than both the estimate and the flight data.

E-17242

XB-70 and X-15-2 on Ramp

585. Irwin, K. S.; and Andrews, W. H.: **Summary of XB-70 Airplane Cockpit Environmental Data.** NASA TN D-5449, October 1969, 69N38010, #.

Thermal, acoustical, and acceleration environmental data were obtained for the crew compartment of the XB-70 airplane during the 186-flight-hour airworthiness test program. More than 20 hours were flown at Mach numbers greater than 2.5. Temperature levels, gradients, and time histories are presented for the cockpit walls, floor, and windshields. Heat transfer through the walls and along the floor produced no crew discomfort. Thermal radiation from the hot inner windshield would have been objectionable to the crew if they had not been protected by insulated flight suits and helmets with faceplates. The acoustical environment of the crew compartment was similar to that of other military turbojet bomber aircraft. At Mach 3 the sound-pressure level in the XB-70 cockpit, primarily generated by onboard electrical and environmental equipment, was 90 decibels, which is about 10 decibels higher than that measured on a present subsonic jet transport. Subsonically, the cockpit noise levels exceeded military specification limits by as much as 10 decibels at frequencies above 400 hertz. At cruise conditions the cockpit noise levels exceeded the supersonic transport internal-noise-level design criteria in the frequency range above 300 hertz. Acceleration data for the XB-70 crew compartment and center of gravity are presented for taxi, takeoff, subsonic buffet, and atmospheric-turbulence conditions. The long, flexible fuselage produced unpleasant ride characteristics in the crew compartment under vibrational situations. However, flight control was always maintained, even in heavy turbulence.

586. McTigue, J. G.; and Layton, G. P., Jr.: **Lifting Body Flight Tests and Analysis.** SAE Paper 69-0662. Presented at the Society of Automotive Engineers, National Aeronautic and Space Engineering and Manufacturing Meeting, Los Angeles, California, October 6–10, 1969, 70A15840.

Reusable lifting entry vehicle flight tests, investigating handling qualities and subsonic-transonic aerodynamics of M2-F2, M2-F3, HL-10 and X-24A.

ECN-2353

X-24A, M2-F3, and HL-10 Lifting Bodies

587. Tang, M. H.; and DeAngelis, V. M.: **Fin Loads and Control-Surface Hinge Moments Measured in Full-Scale Wind-Tunnel Tests on the X-24A Flight Vehicle.** NASA TM X-1922, H-580, November 1969, 71N14501, #.

Tests were conducted on the full-scale X-24A lifting-body in the 40- by 80-Foot Wind Tunnel at the NASA Ames Research Center. One purpose of the tests was to measure aerodynamic loads on the stabilizing fins and hinge moments on all the control surfaces. The tests were conducted at dynamic pressures of 60, 80, and 100 lb/ft^2 (2870, 3830, and 4790 N/m^2). The effects of variations in rudder deflections, flap deflection, and angles of attack and sideslip were studied. Also, limited tests were performed with a simulated ablative surface on the aerodynamic characteristics. Detailed results of the wind-tunnel tests are given in the form of load coefficients and hinge-moment coefficients. The results are compared with data from tests performed in other wind tunnels on small-scale models.

588. Quinn, Robert D.; and Olinger, Frank V.: **Flight-Measured Heat Transfer and Skin Friction at a Mach Number of 5.25 and at Low Wall Temperatures.** NASA TM X-1921, H-579, NAS 1.15:X-1921, November 1969, 92N70606, #.

Turbulent skin friction and heat transfer coefficients were measured simultaneously on a test panel installed on the sharp leading edge upper vertical tail of the X-15 airplane at wall to recovery temperature ratios of 0.218 to 0.333 and at a nominal free stream Reynolds number of $1.54 \times 10(\exp 6)$ per foot. The data were obtained from one flight at a nominal free stream Mach number of 5.25. Reynolds analogy factors were derived from skin friction and heat transfer measurements. The measured data are compared with values predicted by various theories.

589. Taylor, Lawrence W., Jr.; Smith, Harriet J.; and Iliff, Kenneth W.: **Experiences Using Balakrishnan's Epsilon Technique to Compute Optimum Flight Profiles.** Fourth NASA Inter-Center Control Systems Conference, Boston, Massachusetts, November 4–5, 1969. (See also 559, 605.)

A technique for computing optimum profiles is developed which differs from the classical gradient method in that a term representing the constraint of satisfying the equations of motion is included in the cost function to be minimized. Although the number of unknown independent functions is increased to include the state variables, the dimensionally of the gradient of the modified cost is greatly reduced, resulting in considerable savings in complexity and time. The unknown control and state variables are expressed in s functional expansion to facilitate solution by means of Newton's method. The effects of weighting terms and the number of functions on the convergence properties are discussed. Comparisons are made of solutions using the classical gradient method, dynamic programming, and Balakrishnan's epsilon technique.

590. Deets, Dwain A.: **Optimal Regulator of Conventional Setup Techniques for a Model Following Simulator Control System.** Fourth NASA Inter-Center Control Systems Conference, Boston, Massachusetts, November 4–5, 1969. (See also 969.)

This paper compares the optimal regulator technique for determining simulator control system gains with the conventional servo analysis approach. Practical considerations associated with airborne motion simulation using a model-following system provided the basis for comparison. The simulation fidelity specifications selected were important in evaluating the relative advantages of the two methods. Frequency responses for a JetStar aircraft following a roll mode model were calculated digitally to illustrate the various cases. A technique for generating forward loop lead in the optimal regulator model-following problem was developed which increases the flexibility of that approach. In this study it appeared to be the only way in which the optimal regulator method could meet the fidelity specifications.

591. Rediess, Herman A.: **Linear Optimal Control Via a Model Performance Index.** Fourth NASA Inter-Center Control Systems Conference, Boston, Massachusetts, November 4–5, 1969.

592. Iliff, K. W.; and Taylor, L. W., Jr.: **A Modified Newton-Raphson Method for Determining Stability Derivatives From Flight Data.** *Computing Methods in Optimization Problems—2, Proceedings of the Second International Conference,* San Remo, Italy, September 9–13, 1968, 1969, pp. 353-364, 70A19272.

===

1970 Technical Publications

593. Thompson, M. O.; and Welsh, J. R.: **Flight Test Experience With Adaptive Control Systems.** AGARD-CP-58, Paper 11. *Advanced Control System Concepts.* January 1970, pp. 139–147, 70N23037, #.

594. Taylor, L. W., Jr.: **Nonlinear Time-Domain Models of Human Controllers.** *Journal of Optimization Theory and Applications,* Vol. 5, January 1970, pp. 23–38, 70A26396.

Human controllers nonlinear time domain mathematical model for analyzing compensatory tracking task data.

595. Berry, D. T.; and Powers, B. G.: **Handling Qualities of the XB-70 Airplane in the Landing Approach.** NASA TN D-5676, H-587, February 1970, 70N19804, #.

Approaches and landings during the XB-70 program were performed at various approach speeds, glide-slope angles, gross weights, runway offsets, and operational conditions. Representative time histories, pilot comments, and pilot ratings were obtained from these maneuvers. Stability and control data and limited correlations with predictions and handling-qualities criteria were also obtained. The XB-70 flight experience indicated that the height of the cockpit above the runway in combination with nose-high landing attitudes and high approach speeds made the landing task more difficult than that for current subsonic jet transports. Three-degree glide slopes were considered unsatisfactory at the 200-knot indicated airspeed approaches required by the XB-70 The high rate of descent reduced the time available to accomplish the flare and, therefore, increased the possibility of a hard landing. Large changes in lift due to elevon deflection were satisfactory because of the high control effectiveness. Laterally, the aircraft was sensitive to turbulence. Lateral-offset maneuvers simulating breakout from an overcast were not difficult; however, because of the higher approach speeds, excessive runway distances would be covered prior to touchdown and the adverse yaw accompanying aileron deflection was considered excessive. Sidestep maneuvering performance was adequately predicted by a simple technique.

596. Burcham, F. W., Jr.; and Nugent, J.: **Local Flow Field Around a Pylon-Mounted Dummy Ramjet Engine on the X-15-2 Airplane for Mach Numbers From 2.0 to 6.7.** NASA TN D-5638, H-566, February 1970, 70N18035, #.

The flow field around a pylon-mounted dummy ramjet engine on the X-15-2 airplane was surveyed at Mach numbers from 2.0 to 6.7 in preparation for flight tests of a hydrogen-burning hypersonic ramjet engine. Impact pressures, local Mach number, and flow angularity were determined and compared with wind-tunnel data and theoretical calculations. The wing, camera fairing, and side fairing of the X-15-2 generated shock waves which impinged on the dummy ramjet and pylon. However, a region free of significant shock-wave impingement on the ramjet inlet existed for flight at a free-stream angle of attack of 5 degree or less for free-stream Mach numbers from 3. 0 to 8.0. In flight regions free of shock-wave impingement, impact pressure, local Mach number, and angle of attack generally showed good agreement with wind-tunnel data. Shock-wave locations determined from impact-pressure data and wind-tunnel schlieren photograph data showed good agreement. Strong flow-interference effects occurred at the pylon-fuselage intersection. The separated-flow region and the resulting separation shock wave remained within 10 inches (25.4 centimeters) of the fuselage surface in front of the pylon for all flight conditions. The extent of separated flow was sensitive to angle of attack and extremely sensitive to small deviations from 0 degree in angle of sideslip.

EC88-180-2

X-15 Airplane With Dummy Ramjet

597. Gee, S. W.; Kock, B. M.; and Schofield, B. L.: **Operational Experiences With Unpowered Terminal Area Instrument Approaches.** *Proceedings, Inst. of Navigation, National Space Meeting on Space Navigation - Theory and Practice in the Post Apollo Era,* NASA Ames Research Center, Moffett Field, California, February 17–19, 1970, 1970, pp. 211–223, 70A30465, #.

598. Putnam, T. W.; and Smith, R. H.: **XB-70 Compressor-Noise Reduction and Propulsion-System Performance for Choked Inlet Flow.** NASA TN D-5692, H-578, March 1970, 70N20484, #.

An investigation was conducted with the XB-70 airplane attached to a thrust stand to observe compressor-radiated noise and propulsion-system performance as the inlet throat area was reduced to form an aerodynamically choked flow. The anticipated compressor-noise reduction was not experienced. Tests at constant engine speed settings disclosed only minor noise reductions as a result of choking the inlet. Additional tests were performed with the inlet fixed full open and the engines set at successively higher speeds from 60-percent to 57-percent rpm. These tests disclosed considerable noise reduction (10 decibels) in the compressor-blade passing frequencies at engine settings above 80-percent rpm. Thus, it was concluded that most of the noise reduction expected for the throat-closing tests, which were done at engine settings of 87-percent rpm and higher, had already occurred and that only slight additional suppression could he expected when the throat area was decreased to choke the flow. Choking the flow resulted in thrust losses due to decreased total-pressure recovery and airflow in the inlet. These test results suggest that major noise reduction may be obtained without a full-choked flow and the concurrent propulsion-system performance loss.

599. Wykes, J. H.; and Kordes, E. E.: **Analytical Design and Flight Tests of a Modal Suppression System on the XB-70 Airplane: Part 1 - Design Analysis, Part 2 - Flight Tests.** AGARD-CP-46, Paper 22. *Aeroelastic Effects From a Flight Mech. Standpoint,* March 1970, (see N70-29401 15-02), 70N29423, #.

A control system designed to damp the structural motion of flexible airframes was flight tested on the XB-70 airplane, a flexible, low-aspect-ratio supersonic configuration. Even though the system—known as ILAF (Identical Location of Accelerometer and Force)—was an exploratory device and was not developed as an optimum system, the flight tests provided valuable information applicable to aircraft of the supersonic-transport type. This paper reviews the design processes and presents some preliminary results obtained from flight data.

600. Szalai, K. J.; and Deets, D. A.: **An Airborne Simulator Program to Determine If Roll-Mode Simulation Should Be a Moving Experience.** AIAA Paper 70-351. Presented at the AIAA Visual and Motion Simulation Technology Conference, Cape Canaveral, Florida, March 16–18, 1970, 70A24202, #.

Motion and visual cue influences on pilot performance and opinion in roll motion tasks were investigated in an airborne simulator flight program. Human describing functions were obtained from a compensatory tracking task for three roll damping conditions (low, medium, and high) for each of three simulator configurations (fixed base, IFR; moving base, IFR; and moving base, VFR). In addition, the pilots made handling qualities evaluations of the nine different cases. The gross effects of motion and visual stimuli, as determined by pilot comments and ratings, were compared with the conclusions drawn from compensatory tracking task results. The quantitative results from the tracking task experiment showed definite motion cue influences. However, the handling qualities experiment indicated that motion was not necessary to obtain valid results. It was concluded that the quantitative results from tracking task are not adequate to establish the need for motion in a handling qualities research simulator.

601. Sisk, Thomas R.; Enevoldson, Einar K.; and Krier, Gary E.: **Factors Affecting Tracking Precision.** Presented at AIAA Fighter Airplane Conference, St. Louis, Missouri, March 5–7, 1970.

A tracking study conducted at the Flight Research Center on three aircraft has demonstrated that the degradation in tracking precision due solely to buffet intensity is on the order of 5 to 6 mils for buffet intensity levels to 0.2, and it is believed that these trends are generally applicable to other fighter aircraft. Also, the results of this study indicate that only a portion of the buffet-free normal-force coefficient attained with maneuver flaps on the F-104 aircraft may be utilized if tracking precision is to be maintained because of the introduction of wing rock. Finally, it has been demonstrated that certain stability and control or handling-qualities factors can degrade tracking precision to an equal or greater degree than buffet intensity.

602. Evans, Robert D., Jr.: **Development and Testing of a Triaxial Angular Accelerometer for High-Performance Aerospace Vehicles.** Presented at the 6th International Aerospace Instrumentation Symposium, Cranfield, England, March 23–26, 1970.

603. Fields, R. A.: **A Study of the Accuracy of a Flight-Heating Simulation and Its Effect on Load Measurement.** NASA TN D-5741, H-597, April 1970, 70N24320, #.

A series of laboratory heating tests simulating the flight heating on an X-15 horizontal stabilizer was conducted. The initial test simulated, as nearly as reasonably possible, the temperatures that were recorded during an X-15 flight to a Mach number of 4.63. Ten additional heating tests were conducted during which inaccuracies were introduced into the flight-heating simulation. The objective of these tests was to establish the effect of the inaccuracies on the strain-gage responses and ensuing load measurements. Strain-gage-bridge responses from all tests were reviewed and compared with those calculated for a stabilizer load of 6000 pounds force (26,700 newtons). The tests were shown to be useful for selecting bridges for use in load-equation derivations and for selecting the equations that yield load measurements with the lowest overall error.

604. Andrews, W. H.; Robinson, G. H.; Krier, G. E.; and Drinkwater, F. J., III: **Flight-Test Evaluation of the Wing Vortex Wake Generated by Large Jet-Transport Aircraft.** *FAA Comp. of Work Papers Concerning Wake Turbulence Tests*, (see N70-40911 23-02), April 1970, 70N40912, #.

605. Taylor, L. W., Jr.; Smith, H. J.; and Iliff, K. W.: **Experience Using Balakrishnan's Epsilon Technique to Compute Optimum Flight Profiles.** AIAA Paper 69-75. Presented at the 7th AIAA Aerospace Sciences Meeting, New York, New York, January 20–22, 1969. *Journal of Aircraft*, Vol. 7, No. 2, March–April 1970, (see A69-18058), April 1970, pp. 182–187, 70A28088, #. (See also 559, 589.)

A technique for computing optimum profiles is developed which differs from the classical gradient method in that a term representing the constraint of satisfying the equations of motion is included in the cost function to be minimized. Although the number of unknown independent functions is increased to include the state variables, the dimensionally of the gradient of the modified cost is greatly reduced, resulting in considerable savings in complexity and time. The unknown control and state variables are expressed in a functional expansion to facilitate solution by means of

Newton's method. The effects of weighting terms and the number of functions on the convergence properties are discussed. Comparisons are made of solutions using the classical gradient method, dynamic programming, and Balakrishnan's epsilon technique.

606. Berry, D. T.; and Powers, B. G.: **Flying Qualities of a Large, Supersonic Aircraft in Cruise and Landing Approach.** AIAA Paper 70-566. Presented at the AIAA Atmospheric Flight Mechanics Conference, Tullahoma, Tennessee, May 13–15, 1970, 70A29031, #.

XB-70 handling-qualities flight-test experience is reviewed and its implications for handling qualities criteria are analyzed. Pilot ratings, pilot comments, and flight-determined handling qualities parameters are presented. Results throughout the entire flight envelope are considered, but emphasis is placed on high-speed supersonic cruise and landing approach.

607. Fischel, Jack; and Friend, Edward L.: **Preliminary Assessment of Effects of Wing Flaps on High Subsonic Flight Buffet Characteristics on Three Airplanes.** Presented at the American Institute of Aeronautics and Astronautics, Atmospheric Flight Mechanics Conference, Tullahoma, Tennessee, May 13–15, 1970.

608. Lane, James W.; and Evans, Robert D.: **A High Altitude Altimeter Utilizing a Vibrating Diaphragm Transducer.** Presented at the ISA 16th National Aeronautics Institute Symposium, Seattle, Washington, May 11–13, 1970.

609. Saltzman, Edwin J.; and Fisher, David F.: **Some Turbulent Boundary-Layer Measurements Obtained From the Forebody of an Airplane at Mach Numbers Up to 1.72.** NASA TN D-5838, H-567, June 1970, 70N29908, #.

Boundary-layer-profile data were obtained from the smooth undersurface of the A-5A airplane fuselage during the demonstration of sensors for measuring boundary-layer characteristics. The data represent Mach numbers from 0.51 to 1.72. angles of attack up to 7°, and Reynolds numbers up to 74 million. The data are interpreted in terms of local skin friction and momentum thickness, and the velocity profiles from which these data are derived are tabulated. Local transformed friction coefficients obtained from a Clauser type of determination from velocity profiles were close to the incompressible values of Karman-Schoenherr when presented as a function of momentum thickness Reynolds number. Turbulent momentum thickness values were significantly influenced by angle of attack. The flight values of momentum thickness for angles of attack near 6° and 7° were lower than the flat plate values, approaching the level for slender cones. At angles of attack near 0° and 1°, momentum thickness from flight was higher than flat plate values. The aircraft nose boom and the protuberances on the boom are believed to be major reasons for the additional thickness at low angles of attack.

ECN-231

A-5A Vigilante Airplane

610. Kier, D. A.: **Flight Comparison of Several Techniques for Determining the Minimum Flying Speed for a Large, Subsonic Jet Transport.** NASA TN D-5806, H-590, June 1970, 70N28674, #.

A flight investigation was conducted to define the minimum flying speed for a large, subsonic jet transport by using three techniques: (1) the Federal Aviation Regulations (FAR) Part 25 demonstration technique; (2) a flight-path 1-g-break technique; and (3) a constant-rate-of-climb technique. The effect of thrust on minimum speed is analyzed. Results indicate that the flight-path 1-g-break technique was the best overall technique. The constant-rate-of-climb technique, or minimum level-flight speed, though highly affected by the deceleration dynamics of the maneuver, was found to be an acceptable alternate for the 1-g-break technique. The FAR demonstration technique, when analyzed by two current analysis methods, was found to yield the least conservative results. However, if the analysis were based on actual airplane maximum lift capability, the technique would yield acceptable results.

611. Gallagher, R. J.: **Investigation of a Digital Simulation of the XB-70 Inlet and Its Application to Flight-Experienced Free-Stream Disturbances at Mach Numbers of 2.4 to 2.6.** NASA TN D-5827, H-585, June 1970, 70N28343, #.

The capability of a digital inlet simulation program to predict both the performance of the started XB-70 inlet system at free-stream Mach numbers of 2.4 to 2.6 and the dynamic aspects of an inlet unstart at these Mach numbers was analyzed. The simulation-predicted performance was compared with flight measurements, and reasonable agreement was obtained for started and unstarting inlet modes. The agreement between empty-fill (buzz) simulations and flight data was less precise. This was attributed to the need for additional information on the boundary-layer-separation process during this mode of inlet operation. The

simulation program was used to determine the reaction of the started inlet over a range of performance levels to free-stream temperature gradients in smooth air and in clear-air turbulence. Atmospheric-temperature variations were found to be nearly as significant as severe turbulence for operation of that type of inlet. Unstart margins for the manually controlled XB-70 inlet in the presence of these disturbances were obtained thorough use of the simulation program.

612. Martin, R. A.: **Dynamic Analysis of XB-70-1 Inlet Pressure Fluctuations During Takeoff and Prior to a Compressor Stall at Mach 2.5.** NASA TN D-5826, H-595, June 1970, 70N28273, #.

Instrumentation in the left inlet of the XB-70-1 airplane was used to record high-response total- and static-pressure data from 0 to 200 hertz during takeoff and immediately prior to a compressor stall at Mach 2.5 and an altitude of 63,100 feet (19,200 meters). Since the statistical assumptions of stationarity, randomness, and normality were found to be approximately valid for the inlet pressure data, random data-analysis techniques were applied. Values of mean turbulence parameter as high as 12 percent were obtained during takeoff and from 14 percent to as high as 31 percent prior to stall. The flight inlet turbulence-producing mechanism, namely, normal-shock boundary-layer interaction, can he simulated successfully in ground test facilities up to at least 40 hertz as evident in the pressure-wave power spectra; however, higher turbulence values were experienced in flight than in model tests by an engine compressor prior to stall.

613. Rediess, Herman A.: **Is Modern Control Theory Relevant to Flight Control Systems? — A Design Challenge.** Presented at the Joint Automatic Control Conference, Atlanta, Georgia, June 22–23, 1970.

614. Burcham, F. W., Jr.; and Hughes, D. L.: **Analysis of In-Flight Pressure Fluctuations Leading to Engine Compressor Surge in an F-111A Airplane for Mach Numbers to 2.17.** AIAA Paper 70-624. Presented at the 6th AIAA Propulsion Joint Specialist Conference, San Diego, California, June 15–19, 1970, 70A33543, #.

615. Jarvis, C. R.; Loschke, P. C.; and Enevoldson, E. K.: **Evaluation of the Effect of a Yaw-Rate Damper on the Flying Qualities of a Light Twin-Engine Airplane.** NASA TN D-5890, H-584, July 1970, 70N32770, #.

A flight-test program was conducted with a light twin-engine airplane to determine the effect of a parallel yaw damper and aileron-to-rudder interconnect on the flying qualities of this class of aircraft. Both quantitative and qualitative results are presented for several flight tasks and conditions, including flight in turbulence. Airplane handling qualities and ride qualities are summarized. The effect of the yaw damper on the stall and post-stall motions of the test airplane and the motions resulting from sudden engine failure are also discussed.

616. Kordes, E. E.: **Secondary Structures and Mechanisms — Design Trouble Area for the Space Shuttle.** TM X-52876, *Space Transportation System Technology Symposium*, Vol. 3, July 1970, pp. 93–99, 70N42983, #.

The design of secondary structures and mechanisms for a reusable space shuttle can produce problems as serious as those involved in designing the primary structure and thermal protection system. Several events involving failure of secondary structures during the X-15 flight program have been selected to illustrate potential problem areas. Similar problems may be expected on future reusable vehicles until additional research provided adequate design information in these areas.

617. Capasso, V. N., Jr.: **Space Shuttle Related Maintenance Experience With the X-15 Aircraft.** NASA TM X-52876. *Proceedings, Space Transportation System Technology Symposium*, Vol. 5, July 1970, pp. 33–44, 70N39605, #.

This paper discusses the maintenance activity between X-15 flights and the number and types of repair items which would be related to space shuttle requirements. The increased size and complexity of the shuttle systems will magnify the number of repair items, making the required turnaround time difficult or impossible to achieve unless careful consideration is given to problem prevention and access for system repair and maintainability.

618. Schofield, B. L.; Gaidsick, H. G.; and Gee, S. W.: **Experience With Unpowered Terminal-Area Instrument Approaches.** NASA TM X-52876. *Proceedings, Space Transportation System Technology Symposium*, Vol. 6, July 1970, (see N70-40951 23-31), pp. 133–147, 70N40960.

The first part of this paper will discuss a terminal-area guidance technique recently developed by the Air Force Flight Test Center around the F-111A inertial navigation system. The results of flying under instrument flight rules using this guidance scheme will be reported as will the results of ground controlled approaches (GCA) using an NB-52B airplane in an unpowered, low L/D configuration. The latter portion of this paper will discuss a circular approach guidance scheme under development at the NASA Flight Research Center.

619. Thompson, M. O.: **Lifting-Body Progress Report.** NASA TM X-66712. Presented at the ELDO/NASA Space Transportation Systems Briefing, Bonn, July 7–8, 1970, 71N18428, #.

620. Montoya, L. C.: **Drag Characteristics Obtained From Several Configurations of the Modified X-15-2 Airplane Up to Mach 6.7.** NASA TM X-2056, H-598, August 1970, 70N35693, #.

Flight tests were made with and without the lower ventral fin, dummy ramjet (including the modified fixed ventral fin), and ablative coating over the entire wetted area. Data were obtained at Mach numbers from 0. 5 to 6.7 and free-stream Reynolds numbers from approximately 1.7×10 (to the 8th) to 3.6×10 (to the 7th) based on fuselage length. Angle of attack ranged from 0 degree to 11 degrees, dynamic pressure from about 300 lb/ft^2 (14,364 N/m^2) to 770 lb/ft^2 (36,868 N/m square), and altitude from approximately 3000 ft (914 m) to 102.000 ft (31,090 m). Supersonic flight results showed an increase in drag coefficient caused by the ablative coating of 0.008 at a lift coefficient of 0 and 0.022 at a lift coefficient of 0.3. At subsonic speeds the average increase in drag coefficient was about 0.013 for lift coefficients of 0.3 and 0.4. The flight incremental increase in drag coefficient due to the ablative coating showed good agreement with compressible predicted values at low lift coefficients. The average incremental increase in drag coefficient caused by the lower ventral fin and dummy ramjet was about 0.010 at subsonic speeds at a lift coefficient of about 0.3. The flight incremental increase in drag coefficient of the lower ventral fin between Mach 3.8 and 4.9 was about 0.006 at a lift coefficient of 0.1 and 0.014 at a lift coefficient of 0.3.

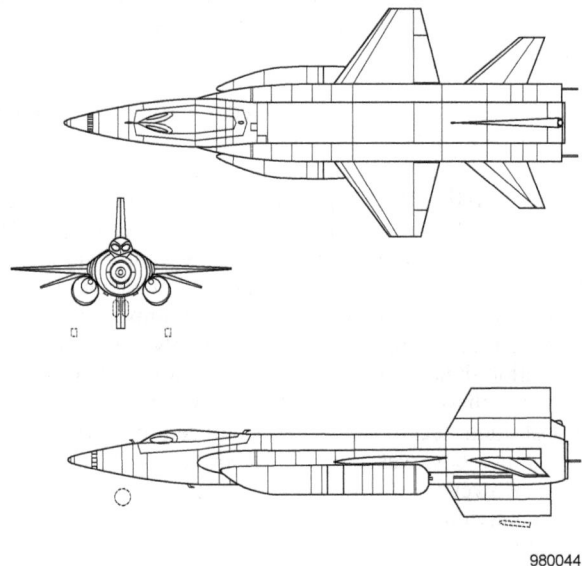

980044

X-15-2 Airplane, Three-View Drawing

621. Holleman, E. C.: **Flight Investigation of the Roll Requirements for Transport Airplanes in Cruising Flight.** NASA TN D-5957, H-616, September 1970, 70N38625, #.

An airborne simulator provided a wide range of maximum roll control power (0.05 to 3.5 rad/sec square) and time constants (0.1 to 10 sec) for pilot evaluation and rating. Roll criteria were developed and compared favorably with previously reported criteria. Maximum roll angular acceleration, maximum roll rate, roll time constant, time to bank. and bank-angle change in a given time all appear to be effective roll-criteria parameters. Steady-state roll rates of about 20 deg/sec and roll time constants of 1.8 seconds or less were required for satisfactory pilot ratings. With experienced test pilots, valid evaluation of single-degree-of-freedom roll response ran be obtained with a fixed-base simulator.

622. Andrews, W. H.: **Flight-Test Evaluation of the Wing Vortex Wake Generated by Large Jet-Transport Aircraft.** Presented at the Wake Turbulence Meeting, Seattle, Washington, September 1–3, 1970. (See *Aircraft Wake Turbulence and Its Detection*, Plenum Press, 1971.)

623. Lewis, C. E., Jr.; and Rezek, T. W.: **A Miniature Respiratory Minute Volume Sensor for the Flight Environment.** *Space Life Sciences,* Vol. 2, September 1970, pp. 206–218, 70A44840.

624. Carpenter, Richard: **Description of an Energy Absorbing Seat Designed for Medium-Velocity Impacts.** Presented at Annual Safety and Risk Management Conference, Lewis Research Center, September 30–October 1, 1970.

625. Baker, P. A.; Schweikhard, W. G.; and Young, W. R.: **Flight Evaluation of Ground Effect on Several Low-Aspect-Ratio Airplanes.** NASA TN D-6053, H-550, October 1970, 70N42738, #.

A constant-angle-of-attack-approach technique was used to measure ground effect on several low-aspect-ratio aircraft. The flight results were compared with results from constant-altitude flybys, wind-tunnel studies, and theoretical prediction data. It was found that the constant-angle of-attack technique provided data that were consistent with data obtained from constant-altitude flybys and required fewer runs to obtain the same amount of data. The test results from an F5D-1 airplane modified with an ogee wing, a prototype F5D-1 airplane, two XB-70 airplanes, and an F-104A airplane indicate that theory and wind-tunnel results adequately predict the trends caused by ground effect as a function of height and aspect ratio. However, the magnitude of these predictions did not always agree with the flight-measured results. In addition, there was consistent evidence that the aircraft encountered ground effect at a height above one wing span.

626. Wagner, C. A.: **Frequency Responses and Other Characteristics of Six Fast-Decay Phosphors Applicable to Flying-Spot Scanners.** NASA TN D-6036, H-609, October 1970, 70N42118, #.

Several tests were conducted on six fast-decay phosphors to measure their characteristics applicable to flying-spot scanners. P-16, P-24, P-36, P-37, and P-SP phosphors are currently available in production cathode-ray tubes; P-X42 is an experimental phosphor. A pulse test measured rise and decay times, and two scanning tests measured frequency responses. Screen noise, burn and aging resistance, and variation of light output as a function of electron beam dwell time were also measured. The frequency responses of P-16, P-37, and P-SP phosphors did not vary during the tests. The frequency response of P-36 phosphor varied with electron beam dwell time, and the frequency response of P-24

phosphor varied with both dwell time and beam current. The bandwidths (frequencies at which the gain is 0.1) were as follows: P-16, 22 megahertz; P-24, 12 megahertz; P-36, 12 megahertz; P-37, 34 megahertz; P-SP, 21 megahertz. The bandwidth of P-X42 phosphor, too high to measure with the equipment used, was estimated to be in excess of 100 megahertz. However, this phosphor produced relatively little light and had a screen that was too noisy to be useful in flying-spot scanners.

627. Anon.: **Flight Test Results Pertaining to the Space Shuttlecraft Symposium Papers.** NASA TM X-2101, October 1970, 71N10101, #.

This compilation consists of papers presented at the NASA Symposium on Flight Test Results Pertaining to the Space Shuttlecraft, held at the NASA Flight Research Center, Edwards, Calif, on June 30, 1970. The symposium was divided into the following sessions: Lifting Body Flight Test Results and Additional Space Shuttle Oriented Studies. Papers were presented by representatives from the NASA Flight Research Center and the U. S. Air Force Flight Test Center. A list of attendees is included.

628. McTigue, J. G.: **Background and Current Status of the Lifting Body Program.** NASA TM X-2101, October 1970, pp. 1–10, 71N10102, #.

The purpose of this paper is to present the results from the flight-test program and the correlations of these data with predictions. Evaluations and impressions of the lifting body vehicles' overall handling qualities will also be presented by several of the pilots in the program. Finally, future plans for the lifting body flight program will be discussed.

629. Kempel, R. W.; Strutz, L. W.; and *Kirsten, P.: **Stability and Control Derivatives of the Lifting Body Vehicles.** NASA TM X-2101, October 1970, pp. 11–27, 71N10103, #.

In this paper the more important longitudinal and lateral-directional aerodynamic stability and control derivatives obtained from flight are compared with small- and full-scale wind-tunnel results where applicable. Significant trends and important differences are pointed out, and the implications discussed.

*Air Force Flight Test Center, Edwards, California.

630. Manke, J. A.; *Retelle, J. P.; and Kempel, R. W.: **Assessment of Lifting Body Vehicle Handling Qualities.** NASA TM X-2101, October 1970, pp. 29–41, 71N10104, #. (See also 659.)

Handling qualities have always been vitally important to the pilot. Before the current series of lifting body flight tests, there was speculation and concern about how this class of wingless vehicle would handle. The general behavior of the three lifting bodies in flight is described in broad terms in this paper, and some specific examples of behavior that may be of special interest from the pilot's viewpoint are presented. In addition, comments are offered concerning simulation requirements.

*Air Force Flight Test Center, Edwards, California.

631. Pyle, J. S.; and *Ash, L. G.: **Performance Characteristics of the Lifting Body Vehicle.** NASA TM X-2101, October 1970, pp. 43–58, 71N10105, #.

Flight and wind-tunnel lift and drag data obtained on three lifting body vehicles has been compared. With the exception of the drag-due-to-lift factor, the flight and small-scale wind-tunnel results generally agree; however, it is extremely important that the model contours match the flight vehicle and the flow on the model be carefully observed, because minor separation problems on the model may become severe on the full-scale vehicle in flight. The full-scale wind-tunnel results obtained with the flight vehicle generally predicted higher zero-lift drag coefficients and lower drag-due-to-lift factors than were observed during the flight tests.

*Air Force Flight Test Center, Edwards, California.

632. Tang, M. H.: **Correlation of Flight-Test Loads With Wind-Tunnel Predicted Loads on Three Lifting Body Vehicles.** NASA TM X-2101, October 1970, pp. 59-72, 71N10106, #.

An essential area of research with the unique M2-F2, HL-10, and X-24A lifting body configurations is the assessment of the ability to predict flight loads from wind-tunnel tests. Flight measurements and correlation with predictions are necessary in verifying the structural integrity of existing vehicles and establishing the groundwork for weight savings on future vehicles of similar shapes. As part of the overall lifting body flight investigation at the Flight Research Center, detailed aerodynamic-load studies are being made on each of the three vehicles. This paper presents the preliminary results from these studies.

633. Dana, W. H.; and *Gentry, J. R.: **Pilot Impressions of Lifting Body Vehicles.** NASA TM X-2101, October 1970, pp. 73–88, 71N10107, #.

Piloting aspects of the lifting body vehicles are discussed in this paper by two of the pilots assigned to the flight program. Subjects discussed include: approach, landing, and energy management considerations; field of view requirements; stability considerations; and vehicle riding qualities, including the effects of turbulence. Remarks pertinent to the various subject areas are made by each pilot.

*Air Force Flight Test Center, Edwards, California.

634. Layton, G. P., Jr.: **Summary of Primary Results of the Lifting Body Program.** NASA TM X-2101, October 1970, pp. 89–97, 71N10108, #.

This summary paper will point out results of the lifting body program that have a bearing on the design of a large space shuttle vehicle. The initial program objectives, the primary program results, and the pertinence of these results to the shuttle will be outlined, as will the future direction of the program.

635. Kock, B. M.; and Fulton, F. L., Jr.: **Approach and Landing Studies.** NASA TM X-2101, October 1970, pp. 99–108, 71N10109, #.

This paper will discuss the application of recent approach and landing studies to the proposed space shuttle. These studies were conducted basically in two areas: powered approaches with the HL-10 lifting body, and unpowered types of approaches with shuttle-size vehicles, the B-52 and CV-990 airplanes.

636. Holleman, E. C.: **Rationale for Proposed Flying-Qualities Specifications.** NASA TM X-2101, October 1970, pp. 127–145, 71N10111, #.

The NASA Flight Research Center is reviewing the applicability of flying-qualities experience to the shuttle mission for the purpose of preparing a shuttle flying-qualities specification. This paper is a progress report on this review; the result presented are, of course, preliminary.

637. Thompson, M. O.: **Flight Test Results Pertaining to the Space Shuttlecraft — Final Remarks and Future Plans.** NASA TM X-2101, October 1970, pp. 147–151, 71N10112, #.

This paper sums up the flight test results pertaining to the space shuttlecraft symposium held at the Flight Research Center. Additional remarks by the author discuss future plans to continue work on unpowered approach and landing techniques and the feasibility of a lifting entry.

638. Carpenter, Lewis R.: **Biotechnology Problems Relative to the Space Shuttle Vehicle.** Presented at AIAA 7th Annual Meeting and Technology Display, Houston, Texas, October 19–22, 1970.

639. Egger, R. L.; and Wilson, E. J.: **Design and Operation of a 1500 F Thermal-Null Strain Gage.** *Instrument Society of America, Annual Conference, 25th, Philadelphia, Pennsylvania, Oct. 26–29, 1970, Proceedings: Part 2*, 1970, pp. 631.1–631.6, 71A22721.

High temperature thermal null strain gage with sensing unit and electronic control unit to measure mechanical strain in terms of induced thermal strain.

640. Roman, J.; Lewis, C. E., Jr.; and Allen, W. H.: **Hazards of the G-Suit in Lower Extremity Thrombophlebitis.** *Aerospace Medicine*, Vol. 41, October 1970, pp. 1198–1199, 70A45347.

Trauma is widely accepted as an etiologic factor in venous thrombosis and thrombophlebitis of the lower extremities. Because of the frequent participation of military pilots and test pilots in athletic activities, the incidence of venous thrombosis of the extremities may be expected to be significant in this population. This group is likely to fly high performance vehicles and, therefore, likely to use the g-suit. On theoretical grounds, use of the g-suit in the face of recent venous thrombosis in the lower extremities should be hazardous. This problem is considered in this paper.

641.   Thompson, M. O.: **A Progress Report on the Lifting Body Flight Test Program.** *Proceedings, Space Technology and Earth Problems, American Astronautical Society, Symposium,* Las Cruces, New Mexico, October 23–25, 1969, <u>1970</u>, pp. 23–27, 71A14819.

642.   Wilson, E. J.: **Installation and Testing of Strain Gages for High-Temperature Aircraft Applications.** Presented at the Society for Experimental Stress Analysis, Fall Meeting, Boston, Massachusetts, <u>October 18–22, 1970</u>, 71A13781, #.

643.   Burke, M. E.: **Flight Research Experience With Guidance and Control Computers Related to General Applications.** NASA TM X-66491, <u>November 1970</u>, 71N12610, #.

Several guidance and control research programs involving the X-15 and F-104 airplanes are discussed, with the discussion oriented toward airborne digital computer utilization. An analog and a digital systems mechanization are compared, and the performance advantages of the digital system are pointed out. The flexibility of the digital computer as a research tool is indicated, as are advantages of decentralized computers. Application of a general purpose computer to the solution of strapdown system equations was successful in the laboratory in preparation for a flight program. The effects of input-output mechanizations on software complexity are discussed. The utility of a general purpose digital computer is shown by its flexibility in being used for various research tasks. This utility is degraded, however, by the effort required to write programs in machine language for real-time applications.

644.   Arnaiz, H. H.; and Schweikhard, W. G.: **Validation of the Gas Generator Method of Calculating Jet-Engine Thrust and Evaluation of XB-70-1 Airplane Engine Performance at Ground Static Conditions.** NASA TN D-7028, H-596, <u>December 1970</u>, 71N13419, #.

Deficiencies in established techniques of measuring aircraft thrust in flight led to the application of the gas generator method of calculating engine thrust to the XB-70-1 airplane. A series of tests on a ground static-thrust stand was performed on the airplane to establish at ground static conditions the accuracy of this method, to measure the installed thrust of the YJ93-GE-3 engine, and to determine the effect of instrumentation errors and nonuniform flows at the engine compressor face on the thrust calculation. Tests

with an aerodynamically choked inlet, an opened inlet-bypass system, and varying combinations of operating engines were also conducted. Results showed that the accuracy of the gas generator method was ±2 percent for the normal operation of the XB-70-1 airplane at ground static conditions and for the upper 70 percent of the engine's throttle range. They also showed that the effect of individual instrument errors on the thrust calculation was reduced because of the large number of measurements and that abnormally high inlet flow distortion affects the thrust calculation. When corrected for inlet losses, the installed thrust of the YJ93-GE-3 engine agreed favorably with the engine manufacturer's uninstalled estimated thrust for all power settings except those at the low end.

645.   Rediess, H. A.; and Whitaker, H. P.: **A New Model Performance Index for Engineering Design of Flight Control Systems.** AIAA Paper 69-885, presented at AIAA Guidance, Control, and Flight Mechanics Conference, Princeton, New Jersey, <u>August 18–20, 1969</u>, 71A12682, #. (Also *J. Aircraft*, Vol. 7, No. 21, December 1970, pp. 542–549, A69-39410.)

Model performance index /Pi/ providing criterion for approximating one dynamic flight control system by another based on geometrical representation of linear autonomous systems.

646.   *Allison, R. D.; Lewis, C. E.; and Rezek, T. W.: **Vascular Dynamics — Impedance Plethysmograph Study During a Standardized Tilt Table Procedure.** *Space Life Sciences*, Vol. 2, <u>December 1970</u>, pp. 361–393, 71A17958.

A study, using the four-electrode impedance plethysmograph system, was completed to evaluate simultaneous variations in conduction of upper and lower body segments relative to displacement of blood volume during change in body position. Measurements of cardiac output were compared with simultaneous results by dye dilution methods as a means of ascending the use of impedance technique to determine cardiac output during tilt table studies. Two groups, 48 healthy private pilots and 22 patients with diabetes mellitus, were tested and the results were compared.

*Scott and White Clinic, Temple, Texas.

647.   Dana, W. H.; and Gentry, G.: **Flying the Lifting Bodies.** *Flight International*, Vol. 98, <u>December 31, 1970</u>, pp. 1016–1020, 71A16680.

648.   Taylor, L. W., Jr.: **Nonlinear Time-Domain Models of Human Controllers.** NASA SP-215, <u>1970</u>, pp. 49–65, 70N30880.

This paper presents some of the results of subsequent analyses and discusses the method of selecting the maximum memory time and the order of the non-linear model. In addition, some results of orthogonal expansion of the weighting functions for reasons of data compression and reduction computation are presented and discussed.

649. Taylor, L. W., Jr.; Smith, H. J.; and Iliff, K. W.: **A Comparison of Minimum Time Profiles for the F-104 Using Balakhrishnan's Epsilon Technique and the Energy Method.** *Proceedings, International Federation For Information Processing, Symposium On Optimization,* Nice, France, June 29–July 5, 1969, 1970, pp. 327–335, 71A28831. (See also 568.)

Balakrishnan's epsilon technique is used to compute minimum time profiles for the F-104 airplane. This technique differs from the classical gradient method in that a quadratic penalty on the error in satisfying the equations of motion is included in the coat function to be minimized as a means of eliminating the requirement of satisfying the equation of motion. Although the number of unknown independent functions is increased to include the state variables, the evaluation of the gradient of the modified cost is simplified, resulting in considerable computational savings. The unknown control and state variables are approximated by 3 functional expansion with unspecified coefficients which are determined by means of Newton's Method. Typically 8 to 10 iterations are required for convergence when using the epsilon technique. Comparisons are made of solutions obtained by using this technique and the energy method.

E-6213

F-104 Airplane

===

1971 Technical Publications

650. Lasagna, P. L.; and Putnam, T. W.: **Engine Exhaust Noise During Ground Operation of the XB-70 Airplane.** NASA TN D-7043, H-599, January 1971, 71N15820, #.

XB-70 engine noise was measured from 90 to 1600 from the airplane heading at a radius of 500 feet (152 meters). Overall sound pressure levels, perceived noise levels, and normalized spectra are presented for jet exhaust velocities up to 3300 feet/second (1006 meters/second), various engine spacings, and various numbers of adjacent engines operating. The direction of propagation of maximum noise levels moved from 135 degree to 120 degree as either the jet velocity was

increased or the number of adjacent engines operating was increased. As the distance between two operating engines became greater, the overall sound pressure level increased as the angle between the microphone position and the exhaust axis decreased. The overall sound pressure level agreed best with the SAE prediction levels at an angle of 120 degree for exhaust velocities between 1500 feet/second (457 meters/second) and 3000 feet/second (914 meters/second). The SAE method adequately estimated the noise spectrum of the XB-70 airplane for subsonic exhaust flow and underestimated the high-frequency spectral levels for supersonic flow. Some shielding of the high frequencies was observed when two or more adjacent engines were operating in supersonic exhaust flow conditions. The noise spectrum shape was independent of jet exhaust velocity for the XB-70 engines with supersonic flow.

651. Carpenter, R.; Thompson, M. O.; and *Bowers, J. H.: **Instrumentation and Drop-Testing Techniques for Investigating Flight Vehicles and Personnel Protective Systems.** NASA TM X-2149, H-621, January 1971, 71N14780, #.

A vehicle and flight systems dynamic impact laboratory, with appropriate instrumentation, was constructed recently at the NASA Flight Research Center. The purpose of the laboratory is to investigate energy-absorbing characteristics of various flight vehicle configurations and personnel protection and restraint systems during low-energy impacting. The laboratory was designed to permit investigation of a large range of horizontal and vertical impact velocities that would occur in low-level crash situations. It has provided acquisition of dynamic structural data on both vehicle configurations and personnel restraint systems.

*Northrop Corporation, Field Teams at Flight Research Center, Edwards, California.

652. Rediess, Herman A.; Mallick, Donald L.; and Berry, Donald T.: **Recent Flight Test Results on Minimum Longitudinal Handling Qualities for Transport Aircraft.** Presented at FAUSST VIII Meeting, Washington, D.C., January 1971.

653. Pecoraro, Joseph N.; and Carpenter, Lewis R.: **Shuttle: Life Support, Protective Systems, and Crew Systems Interface Technology.** *Astronautics and Aeronautics,* Vol. 9, February 1971, pp. 58–63.

654. Pyle, J. S.: **Lift and Drag Characteristics of the HL-10 Lifting Body During Subsonic Gliding Flight.** NASA TN D-6263, March 1971, 71N18867, #.

Subsonic lift and drag data obtained during the HL-10 lifting body glide flight program are presented for four configurations for angles of attack from 5.0 to 26.0 and Mach numbers from 0.35 to 0.62. These flight data, where applicable, are compared with results from small-scale wind-tunnel tests of an HL-10 model, full-scale wind-tunnel results obtained with the flight vehicle, and flight results for the M2–F2 lifting body. The lift and drag characteristics obtained from the HL-10 flight results showed that a severe flow problem existed on the upper surface of the vehicle during the first flight test. This problem was corrected by modifying the leading edges of the tip fins. The vehicle attained lift-drag ratios as high as 4.0 during the landing flare (performed with the landing gear up), which is approximately 14 percent higher than demonstrated by the M2-F2 vehicle in similar maneuvers.

ECN-2203

HL-10 Lifting Body With B-52 Flyover

655. Larson, T. J.; and Schweikhard, W. G.: **Verification of Takeoff Performance Predictions for the XB-70 Airplane.** NASA TM X-2215, H-574, March 1971, 71N18509, #.

XB-70 airplane standardized takeoff data are compared with simple predictions based on aerodynamic and engine estimates. Effects of atmospheric and aircraft variables on takeoff distance are evaluated. Although experimentation with various techniques for aircraft rotation to lift-off attitudes was limited, the effect of the pilot techniques used are discussed and compared. Predictions of distance from brake release to initiation of rotation as 5 functions of velocity were found to he accurate to approximately 100 feet (30 meters). Because of the significant drag at the high aircraft attitudes required for takeoff, the standardized ground roll distance for a given velocity was increased nominally by 400 feet (120 meters) over the distance which would occur with no increase in drag. Standardized performance during climb from lift-off to a height of 35 feet (10.7 meters) with all engines operating was marginal because of low longitudinal accelerations, resulting from high induced drag at lift-off

attitude. Additional work is required to include rotation variables in standardizing test data and in more fully defining the rotation effects on performance from a limited number of takeoff tests.

656. Staff of the Flight Research Center: **Experience With the X-15 Adaptive Flight Control System.** NASA TN D-6208, H-618, March 1971, 71N18422, #.

The X-15 adaptive flight control system is briefly described, and system development and flight-test experiences in the X-15 research airplane are discussed. Airplane handling qualities with the system and system reliability are also discussed.

657. McLeod, N. J.: **Acoustic Attenuation Determined Experimentally During Engine Ground Tests of the XB-70 Airplane and Comparison With Predictions.** NASA TM X-2223, H-633, March 1971, 71N17951, #.

Acoustic data obtained during ground runs of the XB-70 airplane enabled the attenuation of sound to be determined for ground-to-ground propagation over distances of 500 feet (152 meters) and 1000 feet (305 meters) for one set of atmospheric conditions. The considerable scatter in the experimentally determined attenuations seemed to be associated with variations in the wind parameters. For downwind propagation, reducing the predicted acoustic-attenuation values obtained from the Society of Automotive Engineers, Inc., APP 866 by 50 percent for octave bands above 1000 hertz resulted in good agreement between the present experimentally determined and predicted values. Previous investigators recommended the modification to the predicted attenuation values and obtained similar results. Some unexplained differences remain between the experimentally determined and modified predicted attenuation values, indicating that additional research is required.

658. Gee, S. W.; Gaidsick, H. G.; and Enevoldson, E. K.: **Flight Evaluation of Angle of Attack as a Control Parameter in General-Aviation Aircraft.** NASA TN D-6210, H-603, March 1971, 71N18442, #.

The use of angle-of-attack information for a pilot's display in a general-aviation airplane was investigated to determine whether this form of information would improve performance and flight safety. An angle-of-attack system consisting of a wing-mounted vane, an electronic computer unit, and a display instrument was installed and flight tested in a typical twin-engine, general-aviation airplane. The flight-test maneuvers were limited to the low-speed flight region where the benefits of angle-of-attack presentation were likely to be greatest. Some of the expected advantages of this parameter, such as visual indication of stall margin and its independence of gross weight and flap position, were realized; however, certain aerodynamic characteristics of the airplane, such as the phugoid and directional-control capability, were found to limit and tended to negate some of the expected advantages. As a result. this use of angle of attack did not show a significant improvement in performance and flight safety.

659. Manke, J. A.; Kempel, R. W.; and *Retelle, J. P.: **Assessment of Lifting Body Vehicle Handling Qualities.** AIAA Paper 71-310, AIAA Space Shuttle Development Testing and Operations Conference, Phoenix, Arizona, March 15–17, 1971, 71A22622, #. (See also 630.)

Before the current series of lifting body flight tests, there was speculation and concern about how this class of wingless vehicle would handle. The general behavior of the three lifting bodies in flight is described in broad terms in this paper, and some specific examples of behavior that may be of special interest from the pilot's viewpoint are presented.

*USAF, Flight Test Center, Edwards AFB, California.

660. Burcham, F. W., Jr.: **An Investigation of Two Variations of the Gas Generator Method to Calculate the Thrust of the Afterburning Turbofan Engines Installed in an F-111A Airplane.** NASA TN D-6297, H-643, April 1971, 71N22614, #.

The NASA Flight Research Center investigated two variations of the gas generator method for calculating the net thrust of the afterburning turbofan engines installed in an F-111A airplane. An influence coefficient study and two ground thrust tests were performed. It was found that the gas generator method can be successfully applied to an afterburning turbofan engine. At static conditions with two engines operating, ±2 percent accuracy can be achieved for most power settings using either the method based primarily on nozzle total pressure and area (PTA) or the method based primarily on nozzle total temperature and weight flow (TTW). For in-flight conditions the influence coefficient results indicated that the accuracy of the TTW method was about ±3 percent, whereas the accuracy of the PTA method was about ±5 percent for a military power setting. With either calculation method, additional errors in calculated thrust of ±2 percent could result from high inlet flow distortion. If accurate thrust values are required, both thrust calculation methods should be used.

661. Holleman, E. C.; and Gilyard, G. B.: **In-Flight Evaluation of the Lateral Handling of a Four-Engine Jet Transport During Approach and Landing.** NASA TN D-6339, H-642, May 1971, 71N25537, #.

As part of a program to document the stability, control, and flying qualities of jet transport airplanes, the lateral handling of a typical jet transport was evaluated during up-and-away and approach flight in the landing configuration. Sidestep maneuvers to a landing were performed with several levels of lateral control power in smooth-air conditions. A roll control power capability of about 15 deg/sec^2 was required for

satisfactory lateral control, but 61-meter (200-foot) lateral offsets to the runway could be safely corrected with very low levels of lateral control power, approximately 2 to 5 deg/sec^2, using altered piloting techniques. The pilot evaluation results were in general agreement with results from other studies.

662. Tang, M. H.: **Vertical-Fin Loads and Rudder Hinge-Moment Measurements on a 1/8 Scale Model of the M2-F3 Lifting Body Vehicle at Mach Numbers From 0.50 to 1.30.** NASA TM X-2286, H-650, May 1971, 71N24581, #.

Outboard-fin loads and rudder hinge-moment measurements were obtained from a 1/8-scale model of the M2-F3 lifting body vehicle tested in the Ames Research Center's 11-Foot Transonic Wind Tunnel. The tests were conducted at Mach 0.50 to 1.30. The effects of variations in rudder deflection, upper flap deflection, lower-flap deflection, and angles of attack and sideslip were studied. The left-outboard-fin loads increased with increase in angle of attack, Mach number, rudder deflection, lower-flap deflection, and negative sideslip and decreased with increasing upper-flap deflection. The rudder hinge moment increased with increase in rudder deflection and, generally, with Mach number.

E-21533

M2-F3 Lifting Body

663. Goecke, S. A.: **Comparison of Wind Tunnel and Flight-Measured Base Pressures From the Sharp-Leading-Edge Upper Vertical Fin of the X-15 Airplane for Turbulent Flow at Mach Numbers From 1.5 to 5.0.** NASA TN D-6348, H-602, May 1971, 71N23922, #.

Pressures measured at six locations on the base of the sharp-leading edge upper vertical fin of the X-15 airplane during the power-off portion of eight flights are compared with previous flight data obtained from a blunt-leading-edge fin, theory, and wind-tunnel data. The flight and wind-tunnel base pressure ratios for the Mach number range from 1.5 to 5.0 are presented as a linearized function of turbulent boundary-layer height and base width by using a Mach-number-dependent factor derived in the study. The resulting curve seems to provide another criterion for determining whether flow is laminar or turbulent. The difference between base pressure and free-stream pressure for any specific Mach number of the study is found to be a linear function of both free-stream pressure and dynamic pressure. Data from the sharp-leading-edge upper vertical fin agree with data from the blunt-leading-edge upper vertical fin. The flight data show the variation in pressure across the base to be negligible.

664. Ehernberger, L. J.; and Wilson, R. J.: **Analysis of Subjective Ratings for the XB-70 Airplane Response to Atmospheric Turbulence and Controlled Inputs.** *Proceedings, Royal Aeronautical Society, International Conference on Atmospheric Turbulence,* London, England, May 18–21, 1971, <u>1971</u>, 71A29774, #.

This paper presents the XB-70 crew's subjective evaluation of the turbulence response in comparison with measured accelerations; evaluates the turbulence response of the crew station and other fuselage locations; and examines the crew's reaction to controlled sinusoidal excitations of the airframe during flight. During the XB-70 flight tests, turbulence data were obtained as turbulence was encountered during scheduled flights; no flights were scheduled solely to obtain turbulence information.

665. Carpenter, R.: **Evaluation of an Energy Absorbing Crew Seat Integrated With a Rocket Extraction System.** *Space Shuttle Technology Conference,* Vol. 2, <u>May 3, 1971</u>, pp. 19–34, 71N35268, #.

Consideration has been given to equipping the scaled prototype shuttle vehicle with a lightweight energy absorbing seat integrated with a crew extraction rocket. Such a system would provide protection for low velocity vehicle impacts and also offer a means of escape during higher velocity conditions. This system has been developed and fabricated at the Flight Research Center (FRC). The energy absorbing seat has been tested in a dynamic impact laboratory will satisfactory results. The escape system has been evaluated by extracting dummies by tractor rockets from a typical cockpit configuration. These tests indicate unsatisfactory performance during high roll rates.

666. Wilson, E. J.: **Installation and Testing of Strain Gages for High-Temperature Aircraft Applications.** *Proceedings, Strain Gages and Extreme Environments, Society for Experimental Stress Analysis, Technical Session,* Huntsville, Alabama, May 19, 1970, <u>May 1971</u>, pp. 1–10, 71A30681, #.

Survey of a research program conducted to define the optimal selection, installation, and calibration criteria for strain gages used in aircraft flight-load measurements in a high-temperature environment caused by aerodynamic heating. Tests have been made to determine apparent strain, hysteresis, gage factor, insulation resistance, and attachment methods. The necessity of an evaluation program to select the optimum strain gage for specific applications, strain-gage-installation procedures, fatigue problems associated with weldable gages, and new strain-measurement concepts are discussed. Data from laboratory tests to determine the performance characteristics of bonded and weldable strain gages for high-temperature applications are presented.

667. Marshall, R. T.: **Flight Determined Acceleration and Climb Performance of an F-104G Airplane for Use in an Optimum Flight Path Computer Program.** NASA TN D-6398, H-636, <u>June 1971</u>, 71N27002, #.

A flight-test investigation was conducted to determine the standard-day performance characteristics (excess thrust, fuel flow, and climb potential) at maximum afterburner power for an F-104G airplane. The tests were conducted at Mach numbers from 0.5 to 2.0 and at altitudes from 5000 feet (1524 meters) to 50,000 feet 15,240 meters). The standard-day excess thrust and fuel-flow data obtained from the investigation were used to define a computer model of the performance of the test airplane. In addition, the climb-potential (specific excess power) data obtained from the flight tests were compared with the available predicted climb-potential data. From the comparisons, it was found that the predicted data for the "average" F-104G airplane did not represent the performance of the test airplane as accurately as required for the computation of meaningful flight trajectories. Therefore, to compute meaningful flight trajectories for the test airplane, the flight-derived model should be used.

668. Burcham, F. W., Jr.: **Use of the Gas Generator Method to Calculate the Thrust of an Afterburning Turbofan Engine.** AIAA Paper 71-680. Presented at the 7th AIAA and Society of Automotive Engineers, Propulsion Joint Specialist Conference, Salt Lake City, Utah, <u>June 14–18, 1971</u>, 71A30744, #.

The feasibility of using the gas generator method to calculate the thrust of an afterburning turbofan engine was investigated. The NASA Flight Research Center's F-111A airplane, powered by TF30 afterburning turbofan engines, was used. Two variations of the gas generator method were utilized, one based primarily on the exhaust nozzle total pressure and area and the other on the nozzle total temperature and weight flow. An influence coefficient study was performed for static and flight conditions. Results showed that the accuracy of the two calculation methods was about equal at static conditions, but for flight conditions the total temperature and weight flow calculation was superior. Two ground thrust stand tests were also performed, and the thrust calculated by using both methods was compared to the measured thrust; results using either method were generally within ±3 percent except at low power settings. High inlet flow distortion caused an additional scatter of as much as ±2 percent.

669. Wilson, R. J.; Love, B. J.; and Larson, R. R.: **Evaluation of Effects of High-Altitude Turbulence Encounters on the XB-70 Airplane.** NASA TN D-6457, H-631, July 1971, 71N30718, #.

A turbulence response investigation was conducted with the XB-70 airplane. No special turbulence penetration techniques, speeds, or other restrictions were specified for the investigation, nor were any flights made solely to obtain turbulence data. During 79 flights, turbulence was encountered, and recorded on a VGH recorder, 6.2 percent of the total flight distance at supersonic speeds above an altitude of 12,192 meters (40,000 feet). Geographical locations are given for selected turbulence encounters. For 22 flights the airplane was instrumented to measure true gust velocities and the structural acceleration response to turbulence. The turbulence intensities measured were very low in comparison with those measured at high altitudes in other investigations. Acceleration response spectra, frequency response transfer functions, and coherence functions were computed from three turbulence encounters at Mach numbers of 0.88, 1.59, and 2.35. Results are compared with calculated studies. Frequencies from the vertical and lateral structural modes, dominant in the airplane acceleration responses, were compared with the natural frequencies of the human body in the vertical and lateral directions.

670. Saltzman, Edwin J.: **In-Flight Use of Traversing Boundary-Layer Probes.** NASA TN D-6428, H-640, July 1971, 71N28872, #.

Two prototype traversing boundary-layer pitot probes were demonstrated in flight. A motor-operated screw-driven type of probe was used on two jet aircraft for defining boundary layers at profile edge Mach numbers from 0.2 to 2.2. The other type of traversing probe was motor driven through a Scotch yoke mechanism and was operated on several flights of the X-15 airplane. The highest free-stream Mach number reached during this series of flights was 5.6. The mechanical and electrical features of these probes are described, and photographs and conceptual drawings are included. Problems encountered during the development of the devices are described, and the solutions that were found are explained. Boundary-layer profile data are presented in several forms, and local friction coefficients derived from the profile through a Clauser type of determination are shown.

671. Swaroop, R.; and Winter, W. R.: **A Statistical Technique for Computer Identification of Outliers in Multivariate Data.** NASA TN D-6472, H-657, August 1971, 71N31371, #.

A statistical technique and the necessary computer program for editing multivariate data are presented. The technique is particularly useful when large quantities of data are collected and the editing must be performed by automatic means. One task in the editing process is the identification of outliers, or observations which deviate markedly from the rest of the sample. A statistical technique, and the related computer program, for identifying the outliers in univariate data was presented in NASA TN D-5275. The current report is a multivariate analog which considers the statistical linear relationship between the variables in identifying the outliers. The program requires as inputs the number of variables, the data set, and the level of significance at which outliers are to be identified. It is assumed that the data are from a multivariate normal population and the sample size is at least two greater than the number of variables. Although the technique has been used primarily in editing biodata, the method is applicable to any multivariate data encountered in engineering and the physical sciences.

672. Saltzman, E. J.; and Bellman, D. R.: **A Comparison of Some Aerodynamic Drag Factors as Determined in Full-Scale Flight With Wind-Tunnel and Theoretical Results.** NASA TM X-67413, AGARD-CP-83-71, Paper 15. *Facilities and Tech. for Aerodyn. Testing at Transonic Speeds and High Reynolds Number*, August 1971, pp. 16-1 to 16-9, 72N11869, #.

Reliable techniques for defining flight values of overall aircraft drag and turbulent skin friction, and the drag associated with local regions of separated flow are reported. Selected results from these studies are presented for several types of aircraft, including the X-15, the XB-70, lifting bodies, and military interceptors. These flight results are compared with predictions derived from windtunnel models or, for friction, with the Karman-Schoenherr relationship. The flight experiments have defined the turbulent skin friction to Reynolds numbers somewhat above 10 to the 8th power, the overall drag of two airplanes, base pressure coefficients for aircraft and for an aft-facing step immersed in a thick boundary layer. A flight application of a splitter plate for reducing base drag is discussed along with examples of the drag associated with afterbody flow separation for shapes having relatively large afterbody closure angles.

673. Kempel, R. W.: **Analysis of a Coupled Roll Spiral Mode, Pilot Induced Oscillation Experienced With the M2-F2 Lifting Body.** NASA TN D-6496, H-633, September 1971, 71N33307, #.

During the 16 glide flights of the M2-F2 lifting body vehicle, severe lateral pilot-induced oscillations occurred on three occasions in the low-angle-attack, final-approach, preflare situation. These oscillations were analyzed qualitatively to determine the type and similarity and by a systems analysis to determine the root cause. The analysis was complemented by a piloted simulator study, which verified the results. The systems analysis revealed the presence of a coupled roll-spiral mode which caused the pilots to generate a closed-loop lateral instability in the low-angle-of-attack, preflare flight region. A systems analysis, a piloted simulator study, and flight data showed that the addition of a fixed center fin lessened the pilot-induced-oscillation tendencies in the critical flight region.

674. Martin, R. A.; and Hughes, D. L.: **Comparisons of In-Flight F-111A Inlet Performance for On and Off Scheduled Inlet Geometry at Mach Numbers of 0.68 to 2.18.** NASA TN D-6490, H-654, September 1971, 71N33211, #.

675. Wilson, E. J.: **Strain Gage and Thermocouple Installation on a Research Airplane.** Presented at the Western Regional Strain Gage Committee Meeting, Tempe, Arizona, September 20–21, 1971.

Strain gages with modified Karman filaments and backings of glass-fiber-reinforced epoxy resin matrices were selected use on a YF-12 aircraft. The gages were installed with an epoxy adhesive and are being used in a flight-loads measurements program. Individual laboratory performance tests indicated that the gages would be capable of operating at expected flight temperature.

676. Tang, M. H.; and Pearson, G. P. E.: **Flight-Measured HL-10 Lifting Body Center Fin Loads and Control Surface Hinge Moments and Correlation With Wind-Tunnel Predictions.** NASA TM X-2419, H-669, October 1971, 71N38700, #.

Subsonic, transonic, and supersonic aerodynamic loads data are presented for the center fin and the control surfaces of the HL-10 lifting body vehicle. The effects of variations in angle of attack, angle of sideslip, aileron deflection, rudder deflection, and Mach number on the center fin loads are presented in terms of coefficient slopes. The effects of vehicle attitude, control surface deflection, Mach number, and rocket engine operation on the outboard and inboard tip fin flaps, rudder, elevon flap, and elevon hinge-moment coefficients are discussed. The flight test aerodynamic loads are compared with full-scale and small-scale wind-tunnel data.

677. Szalai, K. J.: **Validation of a General Purpose Airborne Simulator for Simulation of Large Transport Aircraft Handling Qualities.** NASA TN D-6431, H-591, October 1971, 71N37823, #.

A flight simulation program was conducted to validate the general purpose airborne simulator (GPAS) for handling-qualities studies of large transport aircraft in cruise. Pilots compared flying qualities of the XB-70-1 with those simulated on the GPAS during consecutive flights of the two vehicles. In addition, various handling-qualities parameters and time histories for the XB-70 and the airborne simulator were compared to assess simulator fidelity. The GPAS was shown to be capable of accurate and realistic simulation of the XB-70 at two flight conditions (Mach 1.2 at 12,200 meters (40,000 feet) altitude and Mach 2.35 at 16,800 meters (55,000 feet) attitude. In-flight changes to the programmed model were required to obtain a satisfactory simulation from the pilot's point of view. In most instances, these changes were necessary to improve model

representation of the XB-70 rather than to correct for possible simulator-introduced distortions.

678. Szalai, K. J.: **Motion Cue and Simulation Fidelity Aspects of the Validation of a General Purpose Airborne Simulator.** NASA TN D-6432, H-648, October 1971, 71N36672, #.

In the validation of the general purpose airborne simulator, certain motion and visual cues could not be duplicated because the airborne simulator could not be independently controlled in six degrees of freedom. According to pilot opinion (NASA TN D-6431), however, the XB-70 airplane at two flight conditions had been simulated satisfactorily. Because of the dependence of simulation results on simulator configuration, two areas were investigated after the validation program was completed. The first was the effect of mismatched cues on observed handling qualities. Experiments which varied lateral acceleration at the pilot's location and yaw rate, while keeping constant the lateral-directional dynamics displayed on the pilot's instruments, showed pilot sensitivity to directional motion cues to be different for the simulation of two XB-70 flight conditions. A technique for allowing consecutive evaluations of moving- and fixed-base configurations in flight was used successfully to determine motion cue effects. The second area investigated was the measurement and description of simulation fidelity. In-flight frequency-response measurement of the model-following system were taken to examine model-following fidelity for directly matched variables such as sideslip and roll rate as well as uncontrolled parameters such as lateral acceleration.

679. Carpenter, R.; and Roman, J.: **Digital Automatic Data Reduction Techniques Used in a 1000-Flight Biomedical Study.** NASA TN D-6601, H-651, December 1971, 72N12059, #.

Techniques developed to automatically process a large quantity of physiological data obtained during a 1000-flight study are described. To reduce this data reliably, a study program was conducted using physiological data from X-15 flights as a data source for experimenting with signal enhancement and noise elimination techniques. The techniques include an automatic means for counting heart rates, averaging electrocardiogram waveforms, plotting histograms of heart rate versus frequency, and counting respiration rates. These techniques were used to reduce more than 2000 hours of physiological data recorded in flight.

680. Kempel, R. W.; and Thompson, R. C.: **Flight-Determined Aerodynamic Stability and Control Derivatives of the M2-F2 Lifting Body Vehicle at Subsonic Speeds.** NASA TM X-2413, H-520, December 1971, 72N11900, #.

Aerodynamic derivatives were obtained for the M2-F2 lifting body flight vehicle in the subsonic flight region between

Mach numbers of 0.41 and 0.64 and altitudes of 7000 feet to 45,000 feet. The derivatives were determined by a flight time history curve-fitting process utilizing a hybrid computer. The flight-determined derivatives are compared with wind-tunnel and predicted values. Modal-response characteristics, calculated from the flight derivatives, are presented.

681. Lewis, T. L.; and Banner, R. D.: **Boundary Layer Transition Detection on the X-15 Vertical Fin Using Surface-Pressure-Fluctuation Measurements.** NASA TM X-2466, H-660, <u>December 1971</u>, 72N12994, #.

A flush-mounted microphone on the vertical fin of an X-15 airplane was used to investigate boundary layer transition phenomenon during flights to peak altitudes of approximately 70,000 meters. The flight results were compared with those from wind tunnel studies, skin temperature measurements, and empirical prediction data. The Reynolds numbers determined for the end of transition were consistent with those obtained from wind tunnel studies. Maximum surface-pressure-fluctuation coefficients in the transition region were about an order of magnitude greater than those for fully developed turbulent flow. This was also consistent with wind tunnel data. It was also noted that the power-spectral-density estimates of the surface-pressure fluctuations were characterized by a shift in power from high frequencies to low frequencies as the boundary layer changed from turbulent to laminar flow. Large changes in power at the lowest frequencies appeared to mark the beginning of transition.

682. Burcham, F. W., Jr.; and Bellman, D. R.: **A Flight Investigation of Steady State and Dynamic Pressure Phenomena in the Air Inlets of Supersonic Aircraft.** NASA TM X-67495, AGARD-CP-91-71, Paper 24. UDC-533.697. *Inlets and Nozzles for Aerospace Eng.*, (see N72-16685 07-28), <u>December 1971</u>, 72N16709, #.

The difficulty of achieving adequate inlet performance and stability and avoiding engine compressor stalls at supersonic speeds has led to the investigation of pressure phenomena in the inlets of several supersonic aircraft. Results of tests with the F-111A airplane are presented showing the inlet steady state and dynamic performance. The inlet total pressure distortion that causes compressor stall is discussed, and the requirement for high response instrumentation is demonstrated. A duct resonance encountered at Mach numbers near 2.0 is analyzed and shown to be due to a normal shock oscillation at the duct fundamental frequency. Another type of resonance, in the engine fan duct, is shown to be a possible cause of reduced engine stall margin in afterburning operation. Plans for a comprehensive inlet study of the YF-12 airplane are discussed including flight tests and full scale, 1/3 scale, and 1/12 scale wind tunnel tests.

683. Lipana, J. G.; *Masters, R. L.; and Winter, W. R.: **An Operating Environmental Health Program.** *Proceedings of the Annual Conference of NASA Clinic*

Directors, Environmental Health Officers and Medical Program Advisors, <u>1971</u>, pp. 204–223, 73N17093.

Some concepts of an operational program for medical and environmental health are outlined. Medical services of this program are primarily concerned with emergency care, laboratory examinations, advice to private physician with patient permission, medical monitoring activities, and suggestions for treatment or control of the malfunction.

*Lovelace Foundation for Medical Education and Research, Albuquerque, New Mexico.

684. Barber, M. R.; and Fischel, J.: **General Aviation: the Seventies and Beyond.** NASA SP-292. *Vehicle Technology for Civil Aviation*, <u>1971</u>, pp. 317–332, 72N13013, #.

The possible advancements in general aviation through the applications of technology during the next decade are discussed in terms of aircraft performance, utility, safety, and public acceptance.

685. Burcham, F. W., Jr.; Calogeras, J. E.; Meyer, C. L.; Povolny, J. H.; and Rudey, R. A.: **Effects of Engine Inlet Disturbances on Engine Stall Performance.** NASA SP-259. *Aircraft Propulsion*, <u>1971</u>, (see N72-19451 09-28), pp. 313–341, 71N19461, #.

686. Gee, S. W.; and Burke, M. E.: **NASA Flight Research Center Fly by Wire Flight Test Program.** *Proceedings of the Space Shuttle Integrated Electron. Conference*, Vol. 1, <u>1971</u>, (see N71 33051 20-31), pp. 365–391, 71N33066, #.

687. Andrews, W. H.; Robinson, G. H.; and Larson, R. R.: **Aircraft Response to the Wing Trailing Vortices Generated by Large Jet Transports.** NASA SP-270. *NASA Aircraft Safety and Operating Probl.*, Vol. 1, <u>1971</u>, (see N71 30756 18-02), pp. 115–126, 71N30765, #.

688. Loschke, P. C.; Barber, M. R.; Jarvis, C. R.; and Enevoldson, E. K.: **Handling Qualities of Light Aircraft With Advanced Control Systems and Displays.** NASA SP–270, in *NASA Aircraft Safety and Operating Probl.*, Vol. 1, <u>1971</u>, (see N71 30756 18-02), pp. 189–206, 71N30771, #.

Flight tests to determine the benefits of advanced control systems and displays on the handling qualities of general aviation aircraft, primarily during ILS (Instrument Landing System) approaches in turbulence, have shown that very significant benefits can be achieved. The use of a flight-director display and an attitude-command control system in combination was shown to transform a typical light aircraft into a flying machine that borders on being perfect from a handling-qualities standpoint during ILS approaches in turbulent air. The singular use of either the flight director display or the attitude-command control system provided significant benefits. A rate-command control system was found to provide significantly less benefit than attitude-command control system.

1972 Technical Publications

689. Anon.: **Supercritical Wing Technology: A Report on Flight Evaluations.** NASA SP-301, 1972, 77N85474.

The papers in this compilation were presented at the NASA Symposium on "Supercritical Wing Technology: A Progress Report on Flight Evaluations," held at the NASA Flight Research Center, Edwards, Calif, on February 29, 1972. The purpose of the symposium was to present timely information on flight results obtained with the F-8 and T-2C supercritical wing configurations, discuss comparisons with wind-tunnel predictions, and project follow-on flight programs planned for the F-8 and F-111 (TACT) airplanes. Papers were presented by representatives of the NASA Flight Research Center, the NASA Langley Research Canter, and North American Rockwell-Columbus Division.

690. Andrews, W. H.: **Status of the F-8 Supercritical Wing Program.** NASA SP-301, 1972, (see N77-85474 24-02), pp. 49–58 , 77N85478.

This paper discusses the modifications incorporated in the test airplane and the status of the program. The flight program of the F-8 supercritical wing test-bed airplane has proceeded in an orderly manner, particularly in view of the difficulties of testing in the transonic speed range in either wind tunnels or flight. An attempt has been made to acquire accurate data from precise state-of-the-art instrumentation and test techniques.

EC73-3468

F-8 Supercritical Wing Airplane

691. Pyle, J. S.: **Preliminary Lift and Drag Characteristics of the F-8 Supercritical Wing Airplane.**

NASA SP-301, 1972, (see N77 85474 24-02), pp. 59–70, 77N85479.

This paper reviews the lift and drag results obtained from the first series of flights with the F-8 supercritical wing configuration. To concentrate on the performance of the wing and eliminate extraneous effects of the fuselage and propulsion system, the internal drag and base drag components have been removed from the flight and wind-tunnel data. Although removing these variables provides for the best comparison of the wind-tunnel and flight wing drag, which is the immediate purpose of this paper, it is somewhat unreal for purposes of assessing the ability of a designer to use wind-tunnel results to predict the absolute drag level of a complete airplane.

692. Montoya, L. C.; and Banner, R. D.: **F-8 Supercritical Wing Pressure Distribution Evaluation.** NASA SP-301, 1972, (see N77 85474 24-02), pp. 71–84, 77N85480.

Pressure measurements were made on the F-8 Supercritical Wing in flight. This paper presents some of these data, compares them with Langley 8-foot wind-tunnel results, and relates the measurements to the drag and buffet characteristics of the complete configuration.

693. DeAngelis, V. M.; and Banner, R. D.: **Buffet Characteristics of the F-8 Supercritical Wing Airplane.** NASA SP-301, 1972, (see N77 85474 24-02), pp. 85–96, 77N85481.

Airplane and wing structural response measurements were made to show the buffet characteristics of the F-8 Supercritical Wing Flight Program at transonic speeds. This paper presents some of the preliminary results of that investigation. Wing structural response was used to sense the buffet of the wing, and these data are compared with wind-tunnel-model data and the wing flow characteristics at transonic speeds.

694. McMurtry, T. C.; Matheny, N. W.; and Gatlin, D. H.: **Piloting and Operational Aspects of the F-8 Supercritical Wing Airplane.** NASA SP-301, 1972, (see N77-85474 24-02), pp. 97–110, 77N85482.

This paper considers both the overall handling characteristics of the test vehicle and the correlation of flight data with wind-tunnel results. It should be pointed out that the basic intent of the program is to validate the wing concept and design approach. An effort was made to achieve acceptable handling qualities; however, time and cost constraints made it impossible to optimize them.

695. Weil, J.; and *Dingeldein, R. C.: **Summary and Future Plans.** NASA SP-301, 1972, (see N77-85474 24-02), pp. 121–133, 77N85484.

A summary of where we have been and where we think we may be going in supercritical wing proof-of-concept flight testing.

*NASA Langley Research Center, Hampton, Virginia.

696. Bellman, D. R.; Burcham, F. W., Jr.; and Taillon, N. V.: **Techniques for the Evaluation of Air-Breathing Propulsion Systems in Full-Scale Flight.** NASA TM X-68305, AGARD-CP-85, Paper 7. *Flight Test Tech.* (see N72 20976 12-02), February 1972, 72N20983, #.

Techniques for evaluating air breathing propulsion systems in full scale flight are discussed. Examples of flight test techniques being used to measure the performance of turbojet propulsion systems are presented. Included are the determination of jet engine thrust, the study of inlet pressure phenomena, the measurement of exhaust nozzle characteristics, and the use of tufts at supersonic speeds. A flow diagram of a gas generator method of thrust calculation is illustrated.

697. Layton, G. P., Jr.; and Thompson, M. O.: **Lifting Body Flight-Test Techniques.** NASA TM X-68306, AGARD-CP-85, Paper 10. *Flight Test Tech.,* (see N72-20976 12-02), February 1972, 72N20986, #.

Specific techniques and procedures for conducting flight tests of lifting body type aircraft are presented. The characteristics of the aircraft in transonic and supersonic flight regions were investigated. The data collection and analysis techniques with which the flight results were analyzed are outlined. Included are analog and digital matching techniques for derivative extractions and a method for extracting lift and drag data. Problems encountered in the flight test program and methods for solving these problems are discussed.

698. Sisk, Thomas R.: **A Proposed Flight-Test Technique to Assess Fighter Aircraft Maneuverability.** Presented at Air-to-Air Combat Analysis and Simulator Symposium, Kirkland AFB, New Mexico, February 29–March 2, 1972.

Recent emphasis on air-to-air combat has led the National Aeronautics and Space Administration to intensify research into methods for improving the transonic maneuverability of fighter aircraft. As a part of this effort, the Flight Research Center has been conducting flight programs utilizing various aircraft to determine the factors affecting tracking precision and to investigate ways of improving transonic maneuverability. Fixed-reticle gunsights and cameras have been installed in various aircraft, and closed-loop tracking maneuvers have been performed throughout the transonic Mach range to the maximum load factor capability of each aircraft. Analysis of the gun camera film in conjunction with airplane response parameters from onboard instrumentation has been found to provide excellent means of assessing the overall maneuvering capability of different aircraft and alternate configurations of the same aircraft. A flight technique for evaluating aircraft agility (i.e., combined performance and handling qualities) has grown out of these studies and is proposed for consideration in assisting in the air superiority evaluation task. An agility index is suggested for use with early design data.

699. Fields, R. A.; Olinger, F. V.; and Monaghan, R. C.: **Experimental Investigation of Mach 3 Cruise Heating Simulations on a Representative Wing Structure for Flight Loads Measurement.** NASA TN D-6749, H-676, March 1972, 72N19922, #.

Radiant heating experiments were performed in the laboratory on an instrumented multispar wing structure to investigate: (1) how accurately the structural temperatures of a Mach 3 cruise-flight profile could be simulated, (2) what the effects of the heating and heating inaccuracies would be on the responses of strain-gage bridges installed on the structure, and (3) how these responses would affect flight loads measurements. Test temperatures throughout the structure agreed well with temperatures calculated for a Mach 3 profile. In addition, temperatures produced by two identical tests were repeatable to less than ± 6 K deg. Thermally induced strain-gage-bridge responses were large enough to be detrimental to a high-speed flight loads program with a goal of establishing aerodynamic loads (exclusive of thermal loads). It was shown that heating simulation can be used effectively for thermal calibration (that is, to provide corrections for a high-temperature environment), and that thermal calibration may not be needed if the simulation data are used to carefully select bridges and load equations.

700. Iliff, K. W.; and Taylor, L. W., Jr.: **Determination of Stability Derivatives From Flight Data Using a Newton-Raphson Minimization Technique.** NASA TN D-6579, H-626, March 1972, 72N19659, #.

A modified Newton-Raphson or quasilinearization minimization technique for determining stability derivatives from flight data was developed and compared with simple-equations, analog-matching, least-squares, and Shinbrot methods of analysis. For the data analyzed, the solutions computed by using the estimates obtained from the Newton-Raphson technique fit the data and determined coefficients adequately. A further modification to include a priori information was found to be useful. A model statistically similar to the flight data was analyzed using the same methods (excluding analog matching), and the Newton-Raphson technique was found to yield superior estimates. An approximate Cramer-Rao bound was compared with the error covariance matrix of the model and was found to provide information about the reliability of the individual estimates obtained. The technique was successfully applied to data obtained from a light airplane, a large supersonic airplane, and a lifting body vehicle. It was shown that the reliability of the estimates of a given coefficient obtained from these vehicles depends upon the data analyzed.

701. Kock, B. M.; Fulton, F. L.; and Drinkwater, F. J., III: **Low-Lift-to-Drag-Ratio Approach and Landing Studies Using a CV-990 Airplane.** NASA TN D-6732, H-672, March 1972, 72N19022, #.

The results are presented of a flight-test program utilizing a CV-990 airplane, flow in low-lift-to-drag-ratio (L/D) configurations, to simulate terminal area operation, approach, and landing of large unpowered vehicles. The results indicate that unpowered approaches and landings are practical with vehicles of the size and performance characteristics of the proposed shuttle vehicle. Low L/D landings provided touchdown dispersion patterns acceptable for operation on runways of reasonable length. The dispersion pattern was reduced when guidance was used during the final approach. High levels of pilot proficiency were not required for acceptable performance.

702. Hughes, D. L.; Holzman, J. K.; and Johnson, H. J.: **Flight-Determined Characteristics of an Air Intake System on an F-111A Airplane.** NASA TN D-6679, H-661, March 1972, 72N18996, #.

Flow phenomena of the F-111A air intake system were investigated over a large range of Mach number, altitude, and angle of attack. Boundary-layer variations are shown for the fuselage splitter plate and inlet entrance stations. Inlet performance is shown in terms of pressure recovery, airflow, mass-flow ratio, turbulence factor, distortion factor, and power spectral density. The fuselage boundary layer was found to be not completely removed from the upper portion of the splitter plate at all Mach numbers investigated. Inlet boundary-layer ingestion started at approximately Mach 1.6 near the translating spike and cone. Pressure-recovery distribution at the compressor face showed increasing distortion with increasing angle of attack and increasing Mach number. The time-averaged distortion-factor value approached 1300, which is near the distortion tolerance of the engine at Mach numbers above 2.1.

703. Larson, R. R.: **Statistical Analysis of Landing Contact Conditions for Three Lifting Body Research Vehicles.** NASA TN D-6708, H-684, March 1972, 72N18895, #.

The landing contact conditions for the HL-10, M2-F2/F3, and the X-24A lifting body vehicles are analyzed statistically for 81 landings. The landing contact parameters analyzed are true airspeed, peak normal acceleration at the center of gravity, roll angle, and roll velocity. Ground measurement parameters analyzed are lateral and longitudinal distance from intended touchdown, lateral distance from touchdown to full stop, and rollout distance. The results are presented in the form of histograms for frequency distributions and cumulative frequency distribution probability curves with a Pearson Type 3 curve fit for extrapolation purposes.

704. Andrews, W. H.; Robinson, G. H.; and Larson, R. R.: **Exploratory Flight Investigation of Aircraft Response to the Wing Vortex Wake Generated by Jet Transport Aircraft.** NASA TN D-6655, H-671, March 1972, 72N18003, #.

The effect of intercepting wing tip vortices generated by large jet transports, including jumbo jets, over separation distances from 1 nautical mile to 15 nautical miles is evaluated on the basis of the response of a vortex probe airplane in the roll mode. The vortex probe test aircraft included a representative general aviation airplane, an executive jet, a fighter, and light and medium weight jet transports. The test conditions and airplane configurations were comparable to those normally used during takeoff, landing, or holding pattern operations. For flight safety the tests were performed at altitudes from 9500 feet to 12,500 feet. In addition to an evaluation of the probe airplane response, a flight test technique is suggested for determining minimum separation distance, using as variable the ratio of vortex-induced roll acceleration to maximum lateral control acceleration and the gross weight of the generating aircraft.

705. Nugent, J.; Sakamoto, G. M.; and Webb, L. D.: **Flight-Test Results From Two Total Temperature Probes for Air-Data Measurements Up to 2014 K (3625 R).** NASA TN D-6748, H-668, March 1972, 72N20399, #.

An experimental temperature probe package containing a fluidic oscillator temperature probe and a shielded thermocouple temperature probe was tested during several X-15 flights. The X-15 flights provided greatly varying test conditions, including a wide range of rapidly changing total temperatures and Mach numbers which extended from subsonic to hypersonic speeds. Within restricted ranges of free-stream Mach number, free-stream unit weight flow, and local stagnation pressure, both probes yielded ramp outputs of temperature parallel to ramp inputs of free-stream total temperature. Within these ranges both probes were used to determine total temperature in the Mach 6 temperature environment. Because ambient temperature was known, both probes were used to estimate velocity and Mach number.

706. Loschke, P. C.; Barber, M. R.; Jarvis, C. R.; and *Enevoldson, E. K.: **Flight Evaluations of the Effect of Advanced Control Systems and Displays on the Handling Qualities of a General Aviation Airplane.** SAE Paper 720316, March 1972, 72A25580.

Flight tests have shown that, by means of improved displays and advanced control systems, it is possible to transform a typical light airplane into a flying machine that borders on being perfect from a handling-qualities standpoint. A flight-director display and an attitude-command control system used in combination transformed a vehicle with poor handling qualities during ILS approaches in turbulent air into a vehicle with extremely good handling qualities. The attitude-command control system also improved the ride qualities of the airplane. A rate-command control system was less beneficial than an attitude-command control system. Although this paper deals primarily with general aviation aircraft, the results presented pertain to other types of aircraft. Short-takeoff-and-landing (STOL) aircraft would be a natural application of the control systems because, as a result of their low speeds, they encounter many of the handling-qualities problems noted on light aircraft. The improved ride qualities should be of interest to all airline operations, and for STOL aircraft in particular, because of their prolonged exposure to low-altitude turbulence.

707. Carpenter, R.; and Manke, J.: **Flight Experiments to Determine Visibility Requirements for Approaches and Landings.** Presented at the AIAA and NASA, Space Shuttle Operations, Maintenance, and Safety Technology Conference, Cocoa Beach, Florida, March 29, 1972, 72A31697, #.

Some of the effects of horizontal visual restriction on the front cockpit of a T-33 aircraft were studied. These studies are pertinent to the establishment of guidelines that will be used in canopy design for limited visibility situations. Results of the study revealed that runway extension lines are helpful for restricted visibility situations. The superiority of a 300-foot runway over a 200-foot runway was greater than expected from geometric considerations. It was also shown that practice learning has a noticeable effect on performance. Finally, visibility restrictions that force a pilot into shallow glides should be avoided, and the available visibility should be sufficient to provide adequate information so that the pilot can solve the lateral-directional and pitch tasks simultaneously.

708. Webb, L. D.; and Washington, H. P.: **Flight Calibration of Compensated and Uncompensated Pitot-Static Airspeed Probes and Application of the Probes to Supersonic Cruise Vehicles.** NASA TN D-6827, H-665, May 1972, 72N24016, #.

Static pressure position error calibrations for a compensated and an uncompensated XB-70 nose boom pitot static probe were obtained in flight. The methods (Pacer, acceleration-deceleration, and total temperature) used to obtain the position errors over a Mach number range from 0.5 to 3.0 and an altitude range from 25,000 feet to 70,000 feet are discussed. The error calibrations are compared with the position error determined from wind tunnel tests, theoretical analysis, and a standard NACA pitot static probe. Factors which influence position errors, such as angle of attack, Reynolds number, probe tip geometry, static orifice location, and probe shape, are discussed. Also included are examples showing how the uncertainties caused by position errors can affect the inlet controls and vertical altitude separation of a supersonic transport.

709. Taylor, L. W., Jr.; and Iliff, K. W.: **Systems Identification Using a Modified Newton-Raphson**

Method: **A FORTRAN Program.** NASA TN D-6734, L-8028, May 1972, 72N22581, #.

A FORTRAN program is offered which computes a maximum likelihood estimate of the parameters of any linear, constant coefficient, state space model. For the case considered, the maximum likelihood estimate can be identical to that which minimizes simultaneously the weighted mean square difference between the computed and measured response of a system and the weighted square of the difference between the estimated and a priori parameter values. A modified Newton-Raphson or quasilinearization method is used to perform the minimization which typically requires several iterations. A starting technique is used which insures convergence for any initial values of the unknown parameters. The program and its operation are described in sufficient detail to enable the user to apply the program to his particular problem with a minimum of difficulty.

710. Gilyard, G. B.: **Flight-Determined Derivatives and Dynamic Characteristics of the CV-990 Airplane.** NASA TN D-6777, H-693, May 1972, 72N23027, #.

Flight-determined longitudinal and lateral-directional stability and control derivatives are presented for the CV-990 airplane for various combinations of Mach number, altitude, and flap setting throughout the flight envelope up to a Mach number of 0.87. Also presented are the dynamic characteristics of the aircraft calculated from the flight-obtained derivatives and the measured phugoid characteristics. The derivative characteristics were obtained from flight records of longitudinal and lateral-directional transient oscillation maneuvers by using a modified Newton-Raphson digital derivative determination technique. Generally the derivatives exhibited consistent variation with lift coefficient in the low-speed data and with Mach number and altitude in the high-speed data. Many also varied with flap deflection, notably spoiler effectiveness and directional stability.

711. Holleman, E. C.; and Gilyard, G. B.: **In-Flight Pilot Evaluations of the Flying Qualities of a Four-Engine Jet Transport.** NASA TN D-6811, H-680, May 1972, 72N22026, #.

The flying qualities of the CV-990 jet transport were evaluated over the normal operating flight envelope and in smooth air to provide baseline data for transport airplanes. Pilot ratings of airplane handling characteristics for specific test conditions and configurations from approach to normal cruise were compared with various flying qualities criteria. In general, the CV-990 flying qualities were evaluated as satisfactory, and the evaluations supported transport flying qualities criteria. The dutch roll damping was rated more satisfactory than was predicted by the flying qualities criteria. The pilots found rudder coordination for the yaw generated during high roll rates very difficult. They preferred to control with roll and pitch controls and to use the yaw damper to provide the required rudder coordination.

712. *Leverett, S. D., Jr.; *Davis, H. M., Jr.; and Winter, W. R.: **Physiological Response in Pilot/Back-Seat Man During Aerial Combat Maneuvers in F-4E Aircraft.** *Aerospace Medical Association, 43rd Annual Scientific Meeting,* Bal Harbour, Florida, May 8–11, 1972, *Preprints, 1972,* (see A72-28251 12-04), pp. 192–193, 72A28317, #.

Comparison of objective/subjective physiological data between the pilot and the back-seat man during training within the G maneuvering envelope. It appears that the psychological requirements for the pilot to be mentally alert and physiologically adapted to a continually changing environment places additional responsibility on him to the extent the physiological signs monitored are indicative of a high stress condition and are increased by a significant amount over the back-seat man who is, in most instances, riding passively.

*USAF School of Aerospace Medicine, Brooks AFB, Texas.

713. Painter, W. D.; and Sitterle, G. J.: **Ground and Flight Test Methods for Determining Limit Cycle and Structural Resonance Characteristics of Aircraft Stability Augmentation Systems.** NASA TN D-6867, H-682, June 1972, 72N26017, #.

Performance criteria and test techniques are applied to stability augmentation systems (SAS) during ground testing to predict objectionable limit cycles and preclude structural resonance during flight. Factors that give rise to these problems, means of suppressing their effects, trade-offs to be considered, and ground test methods that have been developed are discussed. SAS performance predicted on the basis of these tests is compared with flight data obtained from three lifting body vehicles and the X-15 research airplane. Limit cycle and structural resonance test criteria, based upon ground and flight experience and data, were successfully applied to these vehicles. The criteria used were: The limit cycle amplitude (SAS gain multiplied by peak-to-peak angular rate) shall not exceed 0.5 deg for the highest product of control power and SAS gain that will be used in flight; the maximum in-flight SAS gain should never exceed 50 percent of the value at which a structural resonance can be sustained during ground test.

714. Wolowicz, C. H.; and Yancey, R. B.: **Longitudinal Aerodynamic Characteristics of Light, Twin-Engine, Propeller-Driven Airplanes.** NASA TN D-6800, H-646, June 1972, 72N26006, #.

Representative state-of-the-art analytical procedures and design data for predicting the longitudinal static and dynamic stability and control characteristics of light, propeller-driven airplanes are presented. Procedures for predicting drag characteristics are also included. The procedures are applied to a twin-engine, propeller-driven airplane in the clean configuration from zero lift to stall conditions. The calculated characteristics are compared with wind-tunnel and flight data. Included in the comparisons are level-flight trim characteristics, period and damping of the short-period oscillatory mode, and windup-turn characteristics. All calculations are documented.

715. Bikle, P.: **Sailplane Performance Measured in Flight.** Presented at the 12th OSTIV Congress, Alpine, Texas, 1970, *Aero-Revue,* June 1972, pp. 333–338, 72A34215. (Also published in *Technical Soaring,* January 1972, Vol. 1, No. 3.)

Description of the T-6, a modified HP-14 sailplane, the performance data obtained, and the test techniques, as well as the comparison tests and results obtained for seven other sailplanes. These are the Kestrel, Cirrus, Phoebus C, 16.5-m Diamant, Phoebus A, BG-12, and 1-26. The T-6 is of all-metal construction, has a shoulder-high wing, a retractable gear, simple hinged flaps with no speed brakes or tail parachute, and is of medium aspect ratio and wing loading.

716. Putnam, T. W.; and Lasagna, P. L.: **Externally Blown Flap Impingement Noise.** AIAA Paper 72-664, June 1972, 72A35961, #. (See also 737.)

An investigation of externally blown flap impingement noise was conducted using a full-scale turbofan engine and aircraft wing. The noise produced with a daisy nozzle installed on the engine exhaust system was greater than that produced by a conical nozzle at the same thrust. The daisy nozzle caused the jet velocity to decay about 35 percent at the flap. The presence of the wing next to the conical nozzle increased the noise, as did increasing the flap deflection. Compared with the conical nozzle, the daisy nozzle produced slightly less noise at a flap deflection of 60 deg but produced more noise at the lower flap deflections tested.

717. Powers, B. G.: **Statistical Survey of XB-70 Airplane Responses and Control Usage With an Illustration of the Application to Handling Qualities Criteria.** NASA TN D-6872, H-663, July 1972, 72N27013, #.

The magnitude and frequency of occurrence of aircraft responses and control inputs during 27 flights of the XB-70 airplane were measured. Exceedance curves are presented for the airplane responses and control usage. A technique is presented which makes use of these exceedance curves to establish or verify handling qualities criteria. This technique can provide a means of incorporating current operational experience in handling qualities requirements for future aircraft.

718. Smith, J. P.: **Research Aircraft Simulators.** Western Simulator Council, Los Angeles, California, July 27, 1972.

719. Friend, E. L.; and Sefic, W. J.: **Flight Measurements of Buffet Characteristics of the F-104 Airplane for Selected Wing-Flap Deflections.** NASA TN D-6943, H-666, <u>August 1972</u>, 72N30004, #.

A flight program was conducted on the F-104 airplane to investigate the effects of moderate deflections of wing leading- and trailing-edge flaps on the buffet characteristics at subsonic and transonic Mach numbers. Selected deflections of the wing leading and trailing-edge flaps, individually and in combination, were used to assess buffet onset, intensity, and frequency; lift curves; and wing-rock characteristics for each configuration. Increased deflection of the trailing-edge flap delayed the buffet onset and buffet intensity rise to a significantly higher airplane normal-force coefficient. Deflection of the leading-edge flap produced some delay in buffet onset and the resulting intensity rise at low subsonic speeds. Increased deflection of the trailing-edge flap provided appreciable lift increments in the angle-of-attack range covered, whereas the leading-edge flap provided lift increments only at high angles-of-attack. The pilots appreciated the increased maneuvering envelope provided by the flaps because of the improved turn capability.

720. Edwards, J. W.: **Analysis of an Electrohydraulic Aircraft Control Surface Servo and Comparison With Test Results.** NASA TN D-6928, H-629, <u>August 1972</u>, 72N30002, #.

An analysis of an electrohydraulic aircraft control-surface system is made in which the system is modeled as a lumped, two-mass, spring-coupled system controlled by a servo valve. Both linear and nonlinear models are developed, and the effects of hinge-moment loading are included. Transfer functions of the system and approximate literal factors of the transfer functions for several cases are presented. The damping action of dynamic pressure feedback is analyzed. Comparisons of the model responses with results from tests made on a highly resonant rudder control-surface servo indicate the adequacy of the model. The effects of variations in hinge-moment loading are illustrated.

721. Anon.: **Basic Research Review for the NASA OAST Research Council.** NASA TM-74910, <u>August 2, 1972</u>, 77N84624.

In preparing this report on the basic research activities included in the flight research programs at this Center, it became apparent that many elements of the multi-disciplinary programs would be reported because of the difficulty of isolating basic research. Furthermore, in reporting the progress during the past year, it was felt that some cognizance and response should be given to the comments and suggestions of the Office of Aeronautics and Space Technology (OAST) Research Council after the last annual review. Details of the present day flight research programs at the Flight Research Center, including basic research elements, are presented in this review.

722. Deets, D. A.; and Szalai, K. J.: **Design and Flight Experience With a Digital Fly-By-Wire Control System Using Apollo Guidance System Hardware on an F-8 Aircraft.** AIAA Paper 72-881, presented at the AIAA Guidance and Control Conference, Stanford, California, <u>August 14–16, 1972</u>, 72A40060, #.

This paper discusses the design and initial flight tests of the first digital fly-by-wire system to be flown in an aircraft. The system, which used components from the Apollo guidance system, was installed in an F-8 aircraft. A lunar module guidance computer is the central element in the three-axis, single-channel, multimode, digital, primary control system. An electrohydraulic triplex system providing unaugmented control of the F-8 aircraft is the only backup to the digital system. Emphasis is placed on the digital system in its role as a control augmentor, a logic processor, and a failure detector. A sampled-data design synthesis example is included to demonstrate the role of various analytical and simulation methods. The use of a digital system to implement conventional control laws was shown to be practical for flight. Logic functions coded as an integral part of the control laws were found to be advantageous. Verification of software required an extensive effort, but confidence in the software was achieved. Initial flight results showed highly successful system operation, although quantization of pilot's stick and trim were areas of minor concern from the piloting standpoint.

ECN-3276

F-8 Digital Fly-by-Wire Airplane

723. Edwards, J. W.: **Flight Test Experience in Digital Control of a Remotely Piloted Vehicle.** AIAA Paper 72-883, presented at the AIAA Guidance and Control Conference, Stanford, California, <u>August 14–16, 1972</u>.

724. Strutz, L. W.: **Flight-Determined Derivatives and Dynamic Characteristics for the HL-10 Lifting Body Vehicle at Subsonic and Transonic Mach Numbers.** NASA TN D-6934, H-708, <u>September 1972</u>, 72N30903, #.

The HL-10 lifting body stability and control derivatives were determined by using an analog-matching technique and compared with derivatives obtained from wind-tunnel results. The flight derivatives were determined as a function of angle of attack for a subsonic configuration at Mach 0.7 and for a transonic configuration at Mach 0.7, 0.9, and 1.2. At an angle of attack of 14 deg, data were obtained for a Mach number range from 0.6 to 1.4. The flight and wind-tunnel derivatives were in general agreement, with the possible exception of the longitudinal and lateral damping derivatives. Some differences were noted between the vehicle dynamic response characteristics calculated from flight-determined derivatives and those predicted by the wind-tunnel results. However, the only difference the pilots noted between the response of the vehicle in flight and the response of a simulator programmed with wind-tunnel-predicted data was that the damping generally was higher in the flight vehicle.

725. Schweikhard, William G.; and Montoya, E. J.: **Research Instrumentation Requirements for Flight/Wind-Tunnel Tests of the YF-12 Propulsion System and Related Experience.** Presented at the Symposium on Instrumentation for Airbreathing Propulsion, Naval Postgraduate School, Monterey, California, September 19–21, 1972.

726. Smith, Ronald H.; and Burcham, Frank W., Jr.: **Instrumentation for In-Flight Determination of Steady State and Dynamic Inlet Performance in Supersonic Aircraft.** Presented at the Symposium on Instrumentation for Airbreathing Propulsion, Naval Postgraduate School, Monterey, California, September 19–21, 1972. (See also 819.)

Advanced instrumentation and techniques for in-flight measurements of air inlet performance of the XB-70, F-111A, and YF-12 supersonic airplanes were developed and evaluated in flight tests at the NASA Flight Research Center. A compressor face rake with in-flight zeroing capability was flown on the F-111A and found to give excellent steady state as well as high frequency response pressure data. The severe temperature environment of the YF-12 necessitated development of special high temperature transducers. Mounting these transducers to give the required 500-hertz frequency response required some special rake designs. Vibration test requirements necessitated some modifications to the rakes. The transducers and rakes were evaluated in flight tests and were found to function properly. Preliminary data have been obtained from the YF-12 propulsion program in flights that began in May 1972. One example shows the terminal shock wave effects on cowl surface pressures during bypass and spike motions.

727. Gilyard, G. B.; Berry, D. T.; and Belte, D.: **Analysis of a Lateral-Directional Airframe/Propulsion System Interaction of a Mach 3 Cruise Aircraft.** AIAA Paper 72-961, presented at the 2nd AIAA Flight Mechanics Conference, Palo Alto, California, September 11–13, 1972, 72A42348, #.

Mach 3 flight data from a YF-12 airplane are analyzed to determine the causes of the significant reduction in dutch roll damping induced by automatic inlet operation. Two stability derivative extraction techniques, the time vector and the modified Newton-Raphson, were applied to the flight data to determine the forces and moments resulting from the variable geometry of the engine inlet. The sideslip angle measurement, which is fed to the inlet for terminal shock stabilization, was found to have a sensor time lag of approximately 0.5 second. These results are then included in a root locus analysis of the overall airframe/propulsion system.

728. Lewis, T. L.; and Dods, J. B., Jr.: **Wind Tunnel Measurements of Surface Pressure Fluctuations at Mach Numbers of 1.6, 2.0, and 2.5 Using 12 Different Transducers.** NASA TN D-7087, H-700, October 1972, 72N33387, #.

The turbulent boundary layer on the wall of a 9 by 7 foot wind tunnel was measured with 12 different transducers at Mach numbers of 1.6, 2.0, and 2.5. The results indicated that the wall surface-pressure-fluctuation field was more homogeneous at a Mach number of 2.5 than at Mach numbers of 1.6 or 2.0. A comparison of power-spectral-density data at Mach 2.5 with a summary of similar data (Mach 0.1 to 3.45) showed good agreement. The measurement uncertainty was greatest when frequencies were low and the surface-pressure-fluctuation field was homogeneous. The uncertainty at higher frequencies increased as the surface-pressure-fluctuation field became more inhomogeneous. Since transducer mounting effects and system noise levels were determined not to have contributed appreciably to measurement uncertainties, the result was attributed to an interaction between the surface-pressure-fluctuation field and the transducers. Corcos' correction for size effects improved the comparison between transducers at the high frequencies, but did not eliminate an apparent size effect at the lower frequencies.

729. Holleman, E. C.; and Powers, B. G.: **Flight Investigation of the Roll Requirements for Transport Airplanes in the Landing Approach.** NASA TN D-7062, H-711, October 1972, 72N33019, #.

An in-flight evaluation of transport roll characteristics in the landing approach was made with a general purpose airborne simulator. The evaluation task consisted of an instrument approach with a visual correction for a (200-foot) lateral offset. Pilot evaluations and ratings were obtained for approaches made at 140 knots and 180 knots indicated airspeed with variations of wheel characteristics, maximum roll rate, and roll time constant.

730. Wolowicz, C. H.; and Yancey, R. B.: **Lateral-Directional Aerodynamic Characteristics of Light, Twin-Engine, Propeller Driven Airplanes.** NASA TN D-6946, H-694, October 1972, 73N11016, #.

Analytical procedures and design data for predicting the lateral-directional static and dynamic stability and control characteristics of light, twin engine, propeller driven airplanes for propeller-off and power-on conditions are reported. Although the consideration of power effects is limited to twin engine airplanes, the propeller-off considerations are applicable to single engine airplanes as well. The procedures are applied to a twin engine, propeller driven, semi-low-wing airplane in the clean configuration through the linear lift range. The calculated derivative characteristics are compared with wind tunnel and flight data. Included in the calculated characteristics are the spiral mode, roll mode, and dutch roll mode over the speed range of the airplane.

731. Gee, S. W.; and Wolf, T. D.: **NASA Ride Quality Program at the Flight Research Center.** *Symposium on Vehicle Ride Quality*, October 1972, (see N73-10012 01-02), pp. 247–251, 73N10025.

A flight test program to determine the effects of low frequency vibrations on passengers in short haul aircraft is discussed. The objective of the program is to accumulate flight test data on aircraft ride quality in terms of vehicle motion and acceleration and human responses. The subjects discussed are: (1) test procedures, (2) data processing, and (3) the program schedule.

732. *Wells, T. L.; *Canon, R. F.; *Rolls, G. C.; and Wilson, E. J.: **Development of a High Temperature Fatigue Sensor.** *Proceedings, Instrument Society of America, 27th Annual Conference, Part 2*, New York, New York, October 9–12, 1972, 1972, 73A22504.

An experimental program was conducted to extend the Tracor Safety Gauge (patent pending) to elevated temperature service. The Safety Gauge is based on a conductive composite device which can be fabricated to function as a fatigue sensor that undergoes an irreversible resistance increase which results from cumulative strain damage. Prototype sensors were developed which appear capable of 1000 deg F operation for short periods of time (approaching one hour); however, bonding difficulties currently limit their use to about 775 deg F. The resistance change of the sensor was generally on the order of 400% or greater as the fatigue life of a titanium alloy (Ti-5Al-2.5Sn) test specimen was approached.

*Tracor, Inc., Austin, Texas.

733. Robinson, G. H.; and Larson, R. R.: **A Flight Evaluation of Methods for Predicting Vortex Wake Effects on Trailing Aircraft.** NASA TN D-6904, H-712, November 1972, 73N12033, #.

The results of four current analytical methods for predicting wing vortex strength and decay rate are compared with the results of a flight investigation of the wake characteristics of several large jet transport aircraft. An empirical expression defining the strength and decay rate of wake vortices is developed that best represents most of the flight-test data. However, the expression is not applicable to small aircraft that would be immersed in the vortex wake of large aircraft.

734. Wolowicz, C. H.; Iliff, K. W.; and Gilyard, G. B.: **Flight Test Experience in Aircraft Parameter Identification.** AGARD-CP-119, Paper 23. *Stability and Control*, November 1972, 73N17012.

An automatic method for determining stability and control derivatives from flight data is presented. The technique, a modification of the Newton-Raphson method for derivative extraction, has a priori provision that makes use of initial estimates of the derivatives and provides a means of checking the validity of the results. Recommendations for applications of the method are included.

735. Hughes, D. L.: **Survey of Wing and Flap Lower-Surface Temperatures and Pressures During Full-Scale Ground Tests of an Externally Blown Flap System.** NASA SP-320, 1972 (see N73-32934 24-02), 73N32947.

Full-scale ground tests of an externally blown flap system were made using the wing of an F-111B airplane and a CF700 engine. Pressure and temperature distributions were determined on the undersurface of the wing, vane, and flap for two engine exhaust nozzles (conical and daisy) at several engine power and engine/wing positions. The tests were made with no airflow over the wing. The leading-edge wing sweep angle was fixed at 26 deg, the angle of incidence between the engine and the wing was fixed at 3 deg, and the tests were conducted with the flap retracted, extended and deflected 35 deg, and extended and deflected 60 deg. The integrated local pressures on the undersurface of the flap produced loads approximately three times as great at the 60 deg flap position as at the 35 deg flap position. With both nozzle configurations, more than 90 percent of the integrated pressure loads were contained within plus or minus 20 percent of the flap span centered around the engine exhaust centerline. The maximum temperature recorded on the flaps was 218 C (424 F) for the conical nozzle and 180 C (356 F) for the daisy nozzle.

736. Gee, S. W.; Barber, M. R.; and McMurtry, T. C.: **A Flight Evaluation of Curved Landing Approaches.** NASA SP-320, 1972, pp. 245–258, 73N32953.

The development of STOL technology for application to operational short-haul aircraft is accompanied by the requirement for solving problems in many areas. One of the most obvious problems is STOL aircraft operations in the terminal area. The increased number of terminal operations needed for an economically viable STOL system as compared with the current CTOL system and the incompatibility of STOL and CTOL aircraft speeds are positive indicators of an imminent problem. The high cost of aircraft operations, noise pollution, and poor short-haul service are areas that need improvement. A potential solution to some of the operational problems lies in the capability of making curved landing approaches under both visual and instrument flight conditions.

737.   Lasagna, P. L.; and Putnam, T. W.: **Externally Blown Flap Impingement Noise.** NASA SP-320, 1972, pp. 427–441, 73N32964. (See also 716.)

Tests of the noise produced by the impingement of the jet exhaust on the wing and flap for an externally blown flap system were conducted with a CF700 turbofan engine and an F-111B wing panel. The noise produced with a daisy nozzle installed on the engine was greater than that produced by a conical nozzle at the same thrust. The presence of the wing next to the test nozzles increased the noise, as did increasing the flap deflection angle. Compared with the conical nozzle, the daisy nozzle produced slightly less noise at a flap deflection of 60 deg but produced more noise at the lower flap deflections tested. Tests showed that the single-slotted flap deflected 60 deg, produced less noise than the double-slotted flaps. Also, maintaining the maximum distance between the exit nozzle and flap system resulted in a minor reduction in noise.

738.   Kier, D. A.; Powers, B. G.; Grantham, W. D.; and Nguyen, L. T.: **Simulator Evaluation of the Flying Qualities of Externally Blown Flap and Augmentor Wing Transport Configurations.** NASA SP-320, 1972, (see N73-32934 24-02), pp. 157–800 , 73N32948.

Concurrent simulations of powered-lift STOL transport aircraft having either an externally blown flap configuration or an augmentor wing configuration were conducted. The following types of simulators of varying sophistication were used: (1) a simple fixed-base simulation with a simple visual display, (2) a more complex fixed-base simulation using a realistic transport cockpit and a high-quality visual display, and (3) a six-degree-of-freedom motion simulator that had a realistic transport cockpit and a sophisticated visual display. The unaugmented flying qualities determined from these simulations were rated as unacceptable for both the externally blown flap and augmentor wing configurations. The longitudinal, lateral-directional, and single-engine-failure characteristics were rated satisfactory with extensive augmentation, including pitch and roll command systems, flight-path (or speed) augmentation, turn coordination, and effective yaw damping. However, the flare and landing characteristics from any approach glide-path angle in excess of 4 deg were rated as unsatisfactory but acceptable.

739.   Carpenter, R.; and Winter, W. R.: **A Flight-Rated Liquid-Cooled Garment for Use Within a Full-Pressure Suit.** NASA SP-302 (see N72-27106 18-05), 1972, 72N27121.

A flight rated liquid cooled garment system for use inside a full pressure suit has been designed, fabricated, and tested. High temperature tests with this system have indicated that heat is absorbed at a rate decreasing from 224 kg-cal/hr to 143 kg-cal/hr over a 40-min period. The first 30 min are very comfortable; thereafter a gradual heat load builds that results in mild sweating at the end of the 40-min period. In flight tests during hot weather when this cooling system was worn under a regulation flight suit, the pilot reported that temperatures were comfortable and that the garment prevented sweating.

740.   Dorsch, R. G.; Lasagna, P. L.; Maglieri, D. J.; and Olsen, W. A.: **Flap Noise.** NASA SP-311, 1972, (see N73-12012 03-02), pp. 259–290, 73N12024.

Externally-blown-flap noise research can be summarized by the following remarks: With lower-surface blowing, the sources of the flap noise are beginning to be understood and the noise scaling laws have been established. Further, progress has been made on suppressing the flap interaction noise at the large flap deflections used during landing. Recent small-scale noise tests of configurations using external upper-surface blowing indicate that engine-over-the-wing configurations may be promising.

1973 Technical Publications

741.   Hughes, D. L.: **Pressures and Temperatures on the Lower Surfaces of an Externally Blown Flap System During Full-Scale Ground Tests.** NASA TN D-7138, H-729, January 1973, 73N14984, #.

Full-scale ground tests of an externally blown flap system were made using the wing of an F-111B airplane and a CF700 engine. Pressure and temperature distributions were determined on the undersurface of the wing, vane, and flap for two engine exhaust nozzles (conical and daisy) at several engine power levels and engine/wing positions. The test were made with no airflow over the wing. The wing sweep angle was fixed at 26 deg; and the angle of incidence between the engine and the wing was fixed at 3 deg; and the flap was in the retracted, deflected 35 deg, and deflected 60 deg positions. The pressure load obtained by integrating the local pressures on the undersurface of the flap, F_p was approximately three times greater at the 60 deg flap position than at the 35 deg flap position. At the 60 deg flap position, F_p was between 40 percent and 55 percent of the engine thrust over the measured range of thrust. More than 90 percent of F_p was contained within plus or minus 20 percent of the flap span centered around the engine exhaust centerline with both nozzle configurations. Maximum temperatures recorded on the flaps were 218 C (424 F) and 180 C (356 F) for the conical and daisy nozzles, respectively,

742. Holzman, J. K.; and Payne, G. A.: **Design and Flight Testing of a Nullable Compressor Face Rake.** NASA TN D-7162, H-733, January 1973, 73N16247, #.

A compressor face rake with an internal valve arrangement to permit nulling was designed, constructed, and tested in the laboratory and in flight at the NASA Flight Research Center. When actuated by the pilot in flight, the nullable rake allowed the transducer zero shifts to be determined and then subsequently removed during data reduction. Design details, the fabrication technique, the principle of operation, brief descriptions of associated digital zero-correction programs and the qualification tests, and test results are included. Sample flight data show that the zero shifts were large and unpredictable but could be measured in flight with the rake. The rake functioned reliably and as expected during 25 hours of operation under flight environmental conditions and temperatures from 230 K (–46 F) to greater than 430 K (314 F). The rake was nulled approximately 1000 times. The in-flight zero-shift measurement technique, as well as the rake design, was successful and should be useful in future applications, particularly where accurate measurements of both steady-state and dynamic pressures are required under adverse environmental conditions.

743. Gilyard, G. B.: **Explicit Determination of Lateral-Directional Stability and Control Derivatives by Simultaneous Time Vector Analysis of Two Maneuvers.** NASA TM X-2722, H-751, February 1973, 73N16010, #.

An extension of the time vector technique for determining stability and control derivatives from flight data is formulated. The technique provides for explicit determination of derivatives by means of simultaneous analysis of two maneuvers which differ by a dependent control input. The control derivatives for the dependent input are also explicitly determined. This extended technique is preferable to the application of the time vector method to single maneuvers in that no estimates of derivatives are required. An example illustrating the application of the technique is given.

744. Marshall, R. T.; and Schweikhard, W. G.: **Modeling of Airplane Performance From Flight-Test Results and Validation With an F-104G Airplane.** NASA TN D-7137, H-723, February 1973, 73N16008, #.

A technique of defining an accurate performance model of an airplane from limited flight-test data and predicted aerodynamic and propulsion system characteristics is developed. With the modeling technique, flight-test data from level accelerations are used to define a 1g performance model for the entire flight envelope of an F-104G airplane.

The performance model is defined in terms of the thrust and drag of the airplane and can be varied with changes in ambient temperature or airplane weight. The model predicts the performance of the airplane within 5 percent of the measured flight-test data. The modeling technique could substantially reduce the time required for performance flight testing and produce a clear definition of the thrust and drag characteristics of an airplane.

745. Montoya, E. J.: **Wind-Tunnel Calibration and Requirements for In-Flight Use of Fixed Hemispherical Head Angle-of-Attack and Angle-of-Sideslip Sensors.** NASA TN D-6986, H-702, March 1973, 73N18014, #.

Wind-tunnel tests were conducted with three different fixed pressure-measuring hemispherical head sensor configurations which were strut-mounted on a nose boom. The tests were performed at free-stream Mach numbers from 0.2 to 3.6. The boom-angle-of-attack range was –6 to 15 deg, and the angle-of-sideslip range was –6 to 6 deg. The test Reynolds numbers were from 3.28 million to 65.6 million per meter. The results were used to obtain angle-of-attack and angle-of-sideslip calibration curves for the configurations. Signal outputs from the hemispherical head sensor had to be specially processed to obtain accurate real-time angle-of-attack and angle-of-sideslip measurements for pilot displays or aircraft systems. Use of the fixed sensors in flight showed them to be rugged and reliable and suitable for use in a high temperature environment.

746. Lewis, T. L.; Dods, J. B., Jr.; and Hanly, R. D.: **Measurements of Surface-Pressure Fluctuations on the XB-70 Airplane at Local Mach Numbers Up to 2.45.** NASA TN D-7226, H-714, March 1973, 73N18013, #.

Measurements of surface-pressure fluctuations were made at two locations on the XB-70 airplane for nine flight-test conditions encompassing a local Mach number range from 0.35 to 2.45. These measurements are presented in the form of estimated power spectral densities, coherence functions, and narrow-band-convection velocities. The estimated power spectral densities compared favorably with wind-tunnel data obtained by other experimenters. The coherence function and convection velocity data supported conclusions by other experimenters that low-frequency surface-pressure fluctuations consist of small-scale turbulence components with low convection velocity.

747. McKay, J. M.; Kordes, E. E.; and *Wykes, J. H.: **Flight Investigation of XB-70 Structural Response to Oscillatory Aerodynamic Shaker Excitation and Correlation With Analytical Results.** NASA TN D-7227, H-713, April 1973, 73N24892, #.

The low frequency symmetric structural response and damping characteristics of the XB-70 airplane were measured at four flight conditions: heavyweight at a Mach number of

0.87 at an altitude of 7620 meters (25,000 feet); lightweight at a Mach number of 0.86 at an altitude of 7620 meters (25,000 feet); a Mach number of 1.59 at an altitude of 11,918 meters (39.100 feet); and a Mach number of 2.38 and an altitude of 18,898 meters (62,000 feet). The flight data are compared with the response calculated by using early XB-70 design data and with the response calculated with mass, structural, and aerodynamic data updated to reflect as closely as possible the airplane characteristics at three of the flight conditions actually flown.

*North American Rockwell Corp., Los Angeles, California.

748.   Barber, M. R.: **Application of Advanced Control System and Display Technology to General Aviation.** SAE Paper 730321. Presented at the Society of Automotive Engineers, Business Aircraft Meeting, Wichita, Kansas, April 3–6, 1973, 73A34679.

This paper reviews NASA's progress in research directed toward providing the technology necessary for the application of advanced control systems and displays to general aviation aircraft, and its plans for this effort in the future. Flight evaluations of such systems as wing levelers, fluidic autopilots, yaw dampers, and angle of attack displays have been made, and test conditions and major results of some of this work are reported. Potentially valuable systems evaluated thus far are an attitude command control system and a flight-director display. As presently configured, both are prohibitively expensive for us in general aviation, however, and efforts are underway to apply technology to the goal of reducing their cost. Perhaps the most promising development in this area is called separate surface stability augmentation and plans for its implementation and flight testing are described.

749.   Gee, S. W.; and *Servais, N. A.: **Development of a Low-Cost Flight Director System for General Aviation.** SAE Paper 730331. Presented at the Society of Automotive Engineers, Business Aircraft Meeting, Wichita, Kansas, April 3–6, 1973, 73A34684.

The NASA Flight Research Center awarded a contract to Astronautics Corporation of America to develop a low-cost flight director system for general aviation. The system that was designed is expected to cost the consumer less than $3,000, a reduction of nearly 70 percent in the total cost of available systems. The features that permit lower cost without excessive degradation in performance are use of belt drives, high-volume-production standard parts, single-box construction including gyros, and post-plate construction techniques.

*Astronautics Corporation, of America, Milwaukee, Wisconsin.

750.   *Roskam, J.; Barber, M. R.; and Loschke, P. C.: **Separate Surfaces for Automatic Flight Controls.** SAE

Paper 730304. Presented at the Society of Automotive Engineers, Business Aircraft Meeting, Wichita, Kansas, April 3–6, 1973, 73A34665.

The purpose of this paper is to describe an investigation of separate surface stability augmentation systems for general aviation aircraft. The program objective were twofold: first, a wind tunnel program to determine control effectiveness of separate surfaces in the presence of main surfaces, and hinge moment feedback from separate surfaces via the main surfaces to the pilot; second, a theoretical study to determine the minimum performance of actuators and sensors that can be tolerated, the best slaving gains to be used with separate surfaces, and control authority needed for proper operation under direct pilot control, under autopilot control, and in failure situations. On the basis of the results obtained, it has been concluded that separate surface systems are feasible and advantageous for use in general aviation aircraft.

*Kansas, University, Lawrence, Kansas.

751.   Goecke, S. A.: **Flight-Measured Base Pressure Coefficients for Thick Boundary-Layer Flow Over an Aft-Facing Step for Mach Numbers From 0.4 to 2.5.** NASA TN D-7202, H-740, May 1973, 73N24317, #.

A 0.56-inch thick aft-facing step was located 52.1 feet from the leading edge of the left wing of an XB-70 airplane. A boundary-layer rake at a mirror location on the right wing was used to obtain local flow properties. Reynolds numbers were near 10 to the 8th power, resulting in a relatively thick boundary-layer. The momentum thickness ranged from slightly thinner to slightly thicker than the step height. Surface static pressures forward of the step were obtained for Mach numbers near 0.9, 1.5, 2.0, and 2.4. The data were compared with thin boundary-layer results from flight and wind-tunnel experiments and semiempirical relationships. Significant differences were found between the thick and the thin boundary-layer data.

752.   Johnson, H. J.; and Montoya, E. J.: **Local Flow Measurements at the Inlet Spike Tip of a Mach 3 Supersonic Cruise Airplane.** NASA TN D-6987, H-722, May 1973, 73N24037, #.

The flow field at the left inlet spike tip of a YF-12A airplane was examined using at 26 deg included angle conical flow sensor to obtain measurements at free-stream Mach numbers from 1.6 to 3.0. Local flow angularity, Mach number, impact pressure, and mass flow were determined and compared with free-stream values. Local flow changes occurred at the same time as free-stream changes. The local flow usually approached the spike centerline from the upper outboard side because of spike cant and toe-in. Free-stream Mach number influenced the local flow angularity; as Mach number increased above 2.2, local angle of attack increased and local sideslip angle decreased. Local Mach number was generally

3 percent less than free-stream Mach number. Impact-pressure ratio and mass flow ratio increased as free-stream Mach number increased above 2.2, indicating a beneficial forebody compression effect. No degradation of the spike tip instrumentation was observed after more than 40 flights in the high-speed thermal environment encountered by the airplane. The sensor is rugged, simple, and sensitive to small flow changes. It can provide accurate inputs necessary to control an inlet.

753. Edwards, John W.: **Flight Test of a Remotely Piloted Vehicle Using a Remote Digital Computer for Control Augmentation.** Presented at the Symposium on Applications of Control Theory to Modern Weapons Systems, California City, California, May 9–10, 1973.

754. Wilson, E. J.: **Strain Gage Installation on the YF-12 Aircraft.** Presented at the Society for Experimental Stress Analysis, Spring Meeting, Los Angeles, California, May 13–18, 1973, 73A35444.

A flight-loads measurement program on the YF-12 aircraft required the mounting of 101 strain-gauge bridges in the fuselage, fuel tanks, control surfaces, and three stations on the left wing. The sensors were to be installed primarily on titanium and were required to operate between –70 and +600 F. Strain gauges with modified Karman filaments and backings of glass-fiber reinforced epoxy resin matrices were selected and were installed with an epoxy adhesive. Attention is given to the calibration, mounting, and performance of the sensors in flight-load measurements.

755. Fisher, D. F.; and Saltzman, E. J.: **Local Skin Friction Coefficients and Boundary Layer Profiles Obtained in Flight From the XB-70-1 Airplane at Mach Numbers Up to 2.5.** NASA TN D-7220, H-710, June 1973, 73N25276, #.

Boundary-layer and local friction data for Mach numbers up to 2.5 and Reynolds numbers up to 3.6×10 to the 8th power were obtained in flight at three locations on the XB-70-1 airplane: the lower forward fuselage centerline (nose), the upper rear fuselage centerline, and the upper surface of the right wing. Local skin friction coefficients were derived at each location by using (1) a skin friction force balance, (2) a Preston probe, and (3) an adaptation of Clauser's method which derives skin friction from the rake velocity profile. These three techniques provided consistent results that agreed well with the von Karman-Schoenherr relationship for flow conditions that are quasi-two-dimensional. At the lower angles of attack, the nose-boom and flow-direction vanes are believed to have caused the momentum thickness at the nose to be larger than at the higher angles of attack. The boundary-layer data and local skin friction coefficients are tabulated. The wind-tunnel-model surface-pressure distribution ahead of the three locations and the flight surface-pressure distribution ahead of the wing location are included.

756. Tang, M. H.; and Pearson, G. P. E.: **Flight-Measured X-24A Lifting Body Control Surface Hinge Moments and Correlation With Wind Tunnel Predictions.** NASA TM X-2816, H-748, June 1973, 73N25049, #.

Control-surface hinge-moment measurements obtained in the X-24A lifting body flight-test program are compared with results from wind-tunnel tests. The effects of variations in angle of attack, angle of sideslip, rudder bias, rudder deflection, upper-flap deflection, lower-flap deflection, Mach number, and rocket-engine operation on the control-surface hinge moments are presented. In-flight motion pictures of tufts attached to the inboard side of the right fin and the rudder and upper-flap surfaces are discussed.

ECN-2006

X-24A Lifting Body

757. Rediess, Herman A.: **A Survey of Parameter Identification Applications on Aircraft Flight Testing.** Presented at the Joint Automatic Control Conference, Columbus, Ohio, June 20–22, 1973.

758. Burcham, F. W.; Hughes, D. L.; and Holzman, J. K.: **Steady-State and Dynamic Pressure Phenomena in the Propulsion System of an F-111A Airplane.** NASA TN D-7328, H-741, July 1973, 73N29806, #.

Flight tests were conducted with two F-111A airplanes to study the effects of steady-state and dynamic pressure phenomena on the propulsion system. Analysis of over 100 engine compressor stalls revealed that the stalls were caused by high levels of instantaneous distortion. In 73 percent of these stalls, the instantaneous circumferential distortion parameter, k_θ, exhibited a peak just prior to stall higher than any previous peak. The K_θ parameter was a better indicator of stall than the distortion factor, k_d, and the maximum-minus-minimum distortion parameter, d, was poor indicator of stall. Inlet duct resonance occurred in both F-111A airplanes and is believed to have been caused by oscillations of the normal shock wave from an internal to an external position. The inlet performance of the two airplanes was similar in terms of pressure recovery, distortion, and turbulence, and there was good agreement between flight and wind-tunnel data up to a Mach number of approximately 1.8.

759. Wolowicz, C. H.; and Yancey, R. B.: **Comparisons of Predictions of the XB-70-1 Longitudinal Stability and Control Derivatives With Flight Results for Six Flight Conditions.** NASA TM X-2881, H-773, <u>August 1973</u>, 73N30940, #.

Preliminary correlations of flight-determined and predicted stability and control characteristics of the XB-70-1 reported in NASA TN D-4578 were subject to uncertainties in several areas which necessitated a review of prediction techniques particularly for the longitudinal characteristics. Reevaluation and updating of the original predictions, including aeroelastic corrections, for six specific flight-test conditions resulted in improved correlations of static pitch stability with flight data. The original predictions for the pitch-damping derivative, on the other hand, showed better correlation with flight data than the updated predictions. It appears that additional study is required in the application of aeroelastic corrections to rigid model wind-tunnel data and the theoretical determination of dynamic derivatives for this class of aircraft.

760. Wilson, R. J.; Cazier, F. W., Jr.; and Larson, R. R.: **Results of Ground Vibration Tests on a YF-12 Airplane.** NASA TM X-2880, H-736, <u>August 1973</u>, 73N29944, #.

Ground vibration tests were conducted on a YF-12 airplane. To approximate a structural free-free boundary condition during the tests, each of the landing gears was supported on a support system designed to have a low natural frequency. The test equipment and the procedures used for the ground vibration tests are described. The results are presented in the form of frequency response data, measured mode lines, and elastic mode shapes for the wing/body, rudder, and fuselage ventral fin. In the frequency range between 3.4 cps and 28.8 cps, nine symmetrical wing/body modes, six antisymmetrical wing/body modes, two rudder modes, and one ventral fin mode were measured.

761. Wolf, T. D.; and McCracken, R. C.: **Ground and Flight Experience With a Strapdown Inertial Measuring Unit and a General Purpose Airborne Digital Computer.** NASA TM X-2848, H-735, <u>August 1973</u>, 73N29713, #.

Ground and flight tests were conducted to investigate the problems associated with using a strapdown inertial flight data system. The objectives of this investigation were to develop a three axis inertial attitude reference system, to evaluate a self-alignment technique, and to examine the problem of time-sharing a general purpose computer for the several tasks required of it. The performance of the strapdown platform/computer system that was developed was sufficiently accurate for the tasks attempted. For flights on the order of 45 minutes duration, attitude angle errors of $\pm$ .035 radian ($\pm$ 2 deg) in all axes were observed. Laboratory tests of the self-alignment technique gave accuracies of $\pm$.00075 radian in pitch and roll axes and $\pm$ 0.0045 radian in the yaw axis. Self-alignment flight results were inconsistent, since a stable solution was not obtained on windy days because of aircraft rocking motions.

762. Putnam, T. W.: **Investigation of Coaxial Jet Noise and Inlet Choking Using an F-111A Airplane.** NASA TN D-7376, H-685, <u>August 1973</u>, 73N28989, #.

Measurements of engine noise generated by an F-111A airplane positioned on a thrustmeasuring platform were made at angles of 0 deg to 160 deg from the aircraft heading. Sound power levels, power spectra, and directivity patterns are presented for jet exit velocities between 260 feet per second and 2400 feet per second. The test results indicate that the total acoustic power was proportional to the eighth power of the core jet velocity for core exhaust velocities greater than 300 meters per second (985 feet per second) and that little or no mixing of the core and fan streams occurred. The maximum sideline noise was most accurately predicted by using the average jet velocity for velocities above 300 meters per second (985 feet per second). The acoustic power spectrum was essentially the same for the single jet flow of afterburner operation and the coaxial flow of the nonafterburning condition. By varying the inlet geometry and cowl position, reductions in the sound pressure level of the blade passing frequency on the order of 15 decibels to 25 decibels were observed for inlet Mach numbers of 0.8 to 0.9.

763. Monaghan, R. C.; and Fields, R. A.: **Experiments to Study Strain Gage Load Calibrations on a Wing Structure at Elevated Temperatures.** NASA TN D-7390, H-763, <u>August 1973</u>, 73N28883, #.

Laboratory experiments were performed to study changes in strain-gage bridge load calibrations on a wing structure heated to temperatures of 200 F, 400 F, and 600 F. Data were also obtained to define the experimental repeatability of strain-gage bridge outputs. Experiments were conducted to establish the validity of the superposition of bridge outputs due to thermal and mechanical loads during a heating simulation of Mach 3 flight. The strain-gage bridge outputs due to load cycle at each of the above temperature levels were very repeatable. A number of bridge calibrations were found to change significantly as a function of temperature. The sum of strain-gage bridge outputs due to individually applied thermal and mechanical loads compared well with that due to combined or superimposed loads. The validity of superposition was, therefore, established.

128

764. Monaghan, R. C.; and Friend, E. L.: **Effects of Flaps on Buffet Characteristics and Wing-Rock Onset of an F-8C Airplane at Subsonic and Transonic Speeds.** NASA TM X-2873, H-742, August 1973, 73N27905, #.

Wind-up-turn maneuvers were performed to establish the values of airplane normal force coefficient for buffet onset, wing-rock onset, and buffet loads with various combinations of leading- and trailing-edge flap deflections. Data were gathered at both subsonic and transonic speeds covering a range from Mach 0.64 to Mach 0.92. Buffet onset and buffet loads were obtained from wingtip acceleration and wing-root bending-moment data, and wing-rock onset was obtained from airplane roll rate data. Buffet onset, wing-rock onset, and buffet loads were similarly affected by the various combinations of leading- and training-edge flaps. Subsonically, the 12 deg leading-edge-flap and trailing-edge-flap combination was most effective in delaying buffet onset, wing-rock onset, and equivalent values of buffet loads to a higher value of airplane normal force coefficient. This was the maximum flap deflection investigated. Transonically, however, the optimum leading-edge flap position was generally less than 12 deg.

765. Gee, S. W.; and McCracken, R. C.: **Preliminary Flight Evaluation of a Painted Diamond on a Runway for Visual Indication of Glide Slope.** NASA TM X-2849, H-739, August 1973, 73N27027, #.

A diamond sized to appear equidimensional when viewed from a 3.6 deg slide slope was painted on the end of a small general aviation airport runway, and a series of flights was made to evaluate its usage as a piloting aid. The pilots could detect and fly reasonably close to the glide slope projected by the diamond. The flight path oscillations that were recorded during approaches using the diamond were not significantly different from the oscillations that were recorded without the diamond; the difference that did exist could be attributed to converging on a known projected glide slope in one case, and flying an unknown, random glide slope in the other. The results indicated that the diamond would be effective as a means of intercepting and controlling a predetermined glide slope. Other advantages of the diamond were positive runway identification and greater aim point visibility. The major disadvantage was a tendency to overconcentrate on the diamond and consequently to neglect cockpit instruments and airport traffic.

766. Berry, D. T.; and Gilyard, G. B.: **Airframe/ Propulsion System Interactions - An Important Factor in Supersonic Aircraft Flight Control.** AIAA Paper 73-831. Presented at the AIAA Guidance and Control Conference, Key Biscayne, Florida, August 20–22, 1973, 73A40501, #.

The demands of supersonic flight have resulted in propulsion system features that have a significant influence on aircraft flight control. Data from a Mach 3 cruise airplane show that airframe/propulsion system interactions can reduce phugoid and dutch-roll damping, increase vehicle sensitivity to atmospheric disturbances, alter the effective static and dynamic stability of the aircraft, and produce moments as strong as aerodynamic controls. In turn, these effects can lead to large aircraft excursions or high pilot workload, or both, and place increased demands on stability augmentation systems and aerodynamic controls. A need to integrate flight control and propulsion control in advanced vehicles is indicated.

767. *Johnson, W. A.; and Rediess, H. A.: **Study of Control System Effectiveness in Alleviating Vortex Wake Upsets.** AIAA Paper 73-833. Presented at the AIAA Guidance and Control Conference, Key Biscayne, Florida, August 20–22, 1973, 73A38776.

The problem of an airplane being upset by encountering the vortex wake of a large transport on takeoff or landing is currently receiving considerable attention. This paper describes the technique and results of a study to assess the effectiveness of automatic control systems in alleviating vortex wake upsets. A six-degree-of-freedom nonlinear digital simulation was used for this purpose. The analysis included establishing the disturbance input due to penetrating a vortex wake from an arbitrary position and angle. Simulations were computed for both a general aviation airplane and a commercial jet transport. Dynamic responses were obtained for the penetrating aircraft with no augmentation and with various command augmentation systems. The results of this preliminary study indicate that it is feasible to use an automatic control system to alleviate vortex encounter upsets.

*Systems Technology, Inc., Hawthorne, California.

768. Wolowicz, C. H.; and Yancey, R. B.: **Summary of Stability and Control Characteristics of the XB-70 Airplane.** NASA TM X-2933, H-781, October 1973, 73N31958, #.

The stability and control characteristics of the XB-70 airplane were evaluated for Mach numbers up to 3.0 and altitudes up to 21,300 meters (70,000 feet). The airplane's inherent longitudinal characteristics proved to be generally satisfactory. In the lateral-directional modes, the airplane was characterized by light wheel forces, low static directional stability beyond approximately 2 deg of sideslip, adverse yaw response to aileron inputs throughout the entire Mach number range, and negative effective dihedral with wingtips full down. At subsonic Mach numbers, with the flight augmentation control system off, the light wheel forces and adverse yaw response to aileron inputs caused the pilots to minimize use of the ailerons. At supersonic Mach numbers, with the augmentation system off, the adverse yaw due to aileron and the negative effective dihedral were conducive to pilot-induced oscillations.

769. Armistead, K. H.; and Webb, L. D.: **Flight Calibration Tests of a Nose-Boom-Mounted Fixed Hemispherical Flow-Direction Sensor.** NASA TN D-7461, H-779, October 1973, 73N31956, #.

Flight calibrations of a fixed hemispherical flow angle-of-attack and angle-of-sideslip sensor were made from Mach numbers of 0.5 to 1.8. Maneuvers were performed by an F-104 airplane at selected altitudes to hemispherical sensor with that from a standard angle-of-attack vane. The hemispherical flow-direction sensor measured differential pressure at two angle-of-attack ports and two angle-of-sideslip ports in diametrically opposed positions. Stagnation pressure was measured at a center port. The results of these tests showed that the calibration curves for the hemispherical flow-direction sensor were linear for angles of attack up to 13 deg. The overall uncertainty in determining angle of attack from these curves was plus or minus 0.35 deg or less. A Mach number position error calibration curve was also obtained for the hemispherical flow-direction sensor. The hemispherical flow-direction sensor exhibited a much larger position error than a standard uncompensated pitot-static probe.

770. Powers, B. G.; and Kier, D. A.: **Simulator Evaluation of the Low-Speed Flying Qualities of an Experimental STOL Configuration With an Externally Blown Flap Wing on an Augmentor Wing.** NASA TN D-7454, H-780, October 1973, 73N31951, #.

The low-speed flying qualities of an experimental STOL configuration were evaluated by using a fixed-base six-degree-of-freedom simulation. The configuration had either an externally blown flap (EBF) wing or an augmentor wing (AW). The AW configuration was investigated with two tails, one sized for the AW configuration and a larger one sized for the EBF configuration. The emphasis of the study was on the 70-knot approach task. The stability and control characteristics were compared with existing criteria. Several control systems were investigated for the normal four-engine condition and for the engine-out transient condition. Minimum control and stall speeds were determined for both the three- and four-engine operation.

771. Lock, W. P.; Kordes, E. E.; McKay, J. M.; and *Wykes, J. H.: **Flight Investigation of a Structural Mode Control System for the XB-70 Aircraft.** NASA TN D-7420, H-732, October 1973, 73N31950, #.

A flight investigation of a structural mode control system termed identical location of accelerometer and force (ILAF) was conducted on the XB-70-1 airplane. During the first flight tests, the ILAF system encountered localized structural vibration problems requiring a revision of the compensating network. After modification, successful structural mode control that did not adversely affect the rigid body dynamics was demonstrated. The ILAF system was generally more effective in supersonic than subsonic flight, because the conditions for which the system was designed were more nearly satisfied at supersonic speeds. The results of a turbulence encounter at a Mach number of 1.20 and an altitude of 9754 meters indicated that the ILAF system was effective in reducing the vehicle's response at this flight condition. An analytical study showed that the addition of a small canard to the modal suppression system would greatly improve the automatic control of the higher frequency symmetric modes.

*North American Rockwell Corp., Los Angeles, California.

772. Washington, H. P.; and Gibbons, J. T.: **Analytical Study of Takeoff and Landing Performance for a Jet STOL Transport Configuration With Full-Span, Externally Blown, Triple-Slotted Flaps.** NASA TN D-7441, H-709, October 1973, 73N31939, #.

Takeoff and landing performance characteristics and field length requirements were determined analytically for a jet STOL transport configuration with full-span, externally blown, tripleslotted flaps. The configuration had a high wing, high T-tail, and four pod-mounted high-bypass-ratio turbofan engines located under and forward of the wing. One takeoff and three approach and landing flap settings were evaluated. The effects of wing loading, thrust-to-weight ratio, weight, ambient temperature, altitude on takeoff and landing field length requirements are discussed.

773. Sim, A. G.: **Results of a Feasibility Study Using the Newton-Raphson Digital Computer Program to Identify Lifting Body Derivatives From Flight Data.** NASA TM X-56017, October 1973, 74N11814, #.

A brief study was made to assess the applicability of the Newton-Raphson digital computer program as a routine technique for extracting aerodynamic derivatives from flight tests of lifting body types of vehicles. Lateral-direction flight data from flight tests of the HL-10 lifting body research vehicle were utilized. The results in general, show the computer program to be a reliable and expedient means for extracting derivatives for this class of vehicles as a standard procedure. This result was true even when stability augmentation was used. As a result of the study, a credible set of HL-10 lateral-directional derivatives was obtained from flight data. These derivatives are compared with results from wind-tunnel tests.

774. Pyle, J. S.; and Saltzman, E. J.: **Review of Drag Measurements From Flight Tests of Manned Aircraft**

With Comparisons to Wind-Tunnel Predictions. AGARD-CP-124, Paper 26. *AGARD Aerodyn. Drag,* October 1973, pp. 25-1 to 25-12, 74N14735.

In-flight studies of the overall and local components of drag of many types of aircraft were conducted. The primary goal of these studies was to evaluate wind-tunnel and semiempirical prediction methods. Some evaluations are presented in this paper which may be summarized by the following observations: Wind-tunnel predictions of overall vehicle drag can be accurately extrapolated to flight Reynolds numbers, provided that the base drag is removed and the boattail areas on the vehicle are small. The addition of ablated roughness to lifting body configurations causes larger losses in performance and stability than would be expected from the added friction drag due to the roughness. Successful measurements of skin friction have been made in flight to Mach numbers above 4. A reliable inflatable deceleration device was demonstrated in flight which effectively stabilizes and decelerates a lifting aircraft at supersonic speeds.

775. Borek, R. W.: **Development of AIFTDS-4000, a Flight-Qualified, Flexible, High-Speed Data Acquisition System.** NASA TM X-56018. International Telemetering Conference, Washington, D.C., October 9–11, 1973, 73N32087, #.

The NASA flight research center has developed a prototype data acquisition system which integrates an airborne computer with a high-speed pulse code modulation system. The design of the airborne integrated flight test data system (AIFTDS) is the result of experience with airborne pulse code modulation data systems. The AIFTDS-4000 has proved the premise on which it was designed: that the needs and requirements of data acquisition system users can be integrated to produce a highly flexible system that will be more useful than existing systems.

776. Berry, D. T.; and Gilyard, G. B.: **Some Stability and Control Aspects of Airframe/Propulsion System Interactions on the YF-12 Airplane.** ASME Paper 73-WA/ AERO-4. Presented at the American Society of Mechanical Engineers, Winter Annual Meeting, Detroit, Michigan, November 11–15, 1973, 74A13246, #.

Airframe/propulsion system interactions can strongly affect the stability and control of supersonic cruise aircraft. These interactions generate forces and moments similar in magnitude to those produced by the aerodynamic controls, and can cause significant changes in vehicle damping and static stability. This in turn can lead to large aircraft excursions or high pilot workload, or both. For optimum integration of an airframe and its jet propulsion system, these phenomena may have to be taken into account.

777. Lewis, C. E., Jr.; Swaroop, R.; McMurtry, T. C.; *Blakeley, W. R.; and **Masters, R. L.: **Landing Performance by Low-Time Private Pilots After the Sudden Loss of Binocular Vision — Cyclops II.** *Aerospace Medicine,* Vol. 44, No. 11, November 1973, pp. 1241–1245, 74A13530.

Study of low-time general aviation pilots, who, in a series of spot landings, were suddenly deprived of binocular vision by patching either eye on the downwind leg of a standard, closed traffic pattern. Data collected during these landings were compared with control data from landings flown with normal vision during the same flight. The sequence of patching and the mix of control and monocular landings were randomized to minimize the effect of learning. No decrease in performance was observed during landings with vision restricted to one eye, in fact, performance improved. This observation is reported at a high level of confidence (p less than 0.001). These findings confirm the previous work of Lewis and Krier and have important implications with regard to aeromedical certification standards.

*New Mexico University, Albuquerque, New Mexico.
**Lovelace Foundation For Medical Education and Research, Albuquerque, New Mexico.

778. Burcham, F. W., Jr.; Holzman, J. K.; and Reukauf, P. J.: **Preliminary Results of Flight Tests of the Propulsion System of the YF-12 Airplane at Mach Numbers to 3.0.** AIAA Paper 73-1314. Presented at the AIAA and 9th Society of Automotive Engineers Propulsion Conference, Las Vegas, Nevada, November 5–7, 1973, 74A12951, #.

Flight tests of the propulsion system of a YF-12 airplane were made which included off-schedule inlet operation and deliberately induced unstarts and compressor stalls. The tests showed inlet/engine compatibility to be good through most of the flight envelope. The position of the terminal shock wave could be determined from throat static pressure profiles or from root-mean-square levels of throat static pressure fluctuations. A digital simulation of the control system showed an oscillation of the forward bypass doors to be caused by hysteresis in the bypass door actuator linkages.

779. *Webb, W. L.; and Reukauf, P. J.: **Development of a Turbine Inlet Gas Temperature Measurement and Control System Using a Fluidic Temperature Sensor.** AIAA Paper 73-1251. Presented at the 9th AIAA and Society of Automotive Engineers, Propulsion Conference, Las Vegas, Nevada, November 5–7, 1973, 74A11272, #. (See also 811.)

*United Aircraft Corp., Pratt and Whitney Aircraft Division, West Palm Beach, Florida.

780. Pyle, J. S.; Phelps, J. R.; and Baron, R. S.: **Performance of a Ballute Decelerator Towed Behind a Jet Airplane.** NASA TM X-56019, H-815, <u>December 1973</u>, 74N14760, #.

An F-104B airplane was modified to investigate the drag and stability characteristics of a ballute decelerator in the wake of an asymmetrical airplane. Decelerator deployments were initiated at a Mach number of 1.3 and an altitude of 15,240 meters (50,000 feet) and terminated when the airplane had decelerated to a Mach number of 0.5. The flight tests indicated that the decelerator had a short inflation time with relatively small opening forces. The drag levels attained with the subject decelerator were less than those obtained with other high-speed decelerators behind a symmetrical tow vehicle. The ballute demonstrated good stability characteristics behind the testbed airplane.

781. Sim, A. G.: **Flight-Determined Stability and Control Characteristics of the M2-F3 Lifting Body Vehicle.** NASA TN D-7511, H-791, <u>December 1973</u>, 74N12534, #.

Flight data were obtained over a Mach number range from 0.4 to 1.55 and an angle-of-attack range from –2 deg to 16 deg. Lateral-directional and longitudinal derivatives, reaction control rocket effectiveness, and longitudinal trim information obtained from flight data and wind-tunnel predictions are compared. The effects of power, configuration change, and speed brake are discussed.

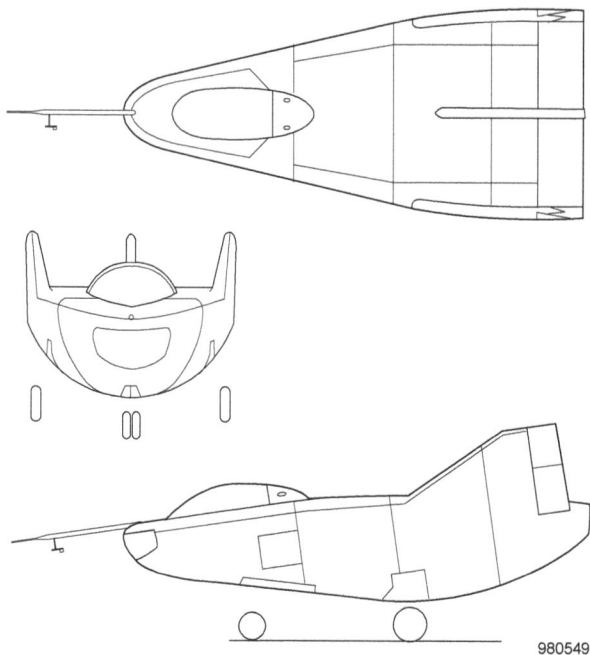

980549

M2-F3 Lifting Body, Three-View Drawing

782. McMurtry, T. C.; Gee, S. W.; and Barber, M. R.: **A Flight Evaluation of Curved Landing Approaches.** *Society of Experimental Test Pilots,* Technical Review, Vol. 11, No. 3, <u>1973</u>, pp. 5–17, 73A28901.

A potential solution to some of the operational problems of STOL aircraft operations in the terminal area lies in the capability of making curved landing approaches under both visual and instrument flight conditions. Tests are described which were conducted with a twin-engine, light weight, general aviation aircraft. The advanced control system mode utilized during the curved approaches was an attitude command control system. Four curved patterns were investigated using a steep glide slope: two display configurations, and two flight control modes. When using the flight director display, curved approaches were not significantly different in difficulty and work load than straight approaches.

783. Peterson, B. A.; Krier, G. E.; and *Jarvis, C. R.: **Development and Flight Test of a Digital Fly-By-Wire F-8 Airplane.** *Society of Experimental Test Pilots,* Technical Review, Vol. 11, No. 2, <u>1973</u>, pp. 57–71, 73A22180.

The objective of the F-8 digital fly-by-wire program is to establish a technology base for the implementation of advanced flight control systems. The central element is the Apollo Lunar Guidance Computer (LGC). This versatile computer ran over 2000 hours in support of fly-by-wire without a failure. Difficulties encountered in the first flights were corrected rapidly and simply by changes in the erasable software memory. Control-configured vehicles offer significant weight-saving possibilities.

* NASA, Washington, D.C.

784. Iliff, K. W.: **Identification and Stochastic Control With Application to Flight Control in Turbulence.** UCLA-ENG-7340 (Ph.D. dissertation), <u>1973</u>, 74N17383.

The problem is dealt with of adaptive control of an aircraft in atmospheric turbulence. The problem is approached by first identifying the unknown coefficients and then applying optimal control theory to the system so determined. The theory developed is general enough to apply to any linear system with unknown coefficients and state noise. The bulk of the development concerns the identification problem and several methods are studied. In particular, what may be called stochastic identification method, taking into account the unknown state noise, is studied. The identification and control theory is first verified on simulated data. It is shown that the methods that accounted for the state noise are adequate where the assumptions hold. The optimal control results agree well with theory in achieving the desired minimization.

785. Montoya, L. C.; Brauns, D. A.; and Cissell, R. E.: **Flight Experience With a Pivoting Traversing Boundary-Layer Probe.** NASA TM X-56022, January 1974, 74N16102, #.

A pivoting traversing boundary layer probe was evaluated in flight on an F-104 airplane. The evaluation was performed at free stream Mach numbers from 0.8 to 2.0. The unit is described, and operating problems and their solutions are discussed. Conventional boundary layer profiles containing variations in flow angle within the viscous layer are shown for free stream Mach numbers of 0.8, 1.6, and 2.0. Although the unit was not optimized for size and weight, it successfully measured simultaneously flow angularity, probe height, and pitot pressure through the boundary layer.

786. Painter, W. D.; and Sitterle, G. J.: **HL-10 Lifting Body Flight Control System Characteristics and Operational Experience.** NASA TM X-2956, H-704, January 1974, 74N14753, #.

A flight evaluation was made of the mechanical hydraulic flight control system and the electrohydraulic stability augmentation system installed in the HL-10 lifting body research vehicle. Flight tests performed in the speed range from landing to a Mach number of 1.86 and the altitude range from 697 meters (2300 feet) to 27,550 meters (90,300 feet) were supplemented by ground tests to identify and correct structural resonance and limit-cycle problems. Severe limit-cycle and control sensitivity problems were encountered during the first flight. Stability augmentation system structural resonance electronic filters were modified to correct the limit-cycle problem. Several changes were made to control stick gearing to solve the control sensitivity problem. Satisfactory controllability was achieved by using a nonlinear system. A limit-cycle problem due to hydraulic fluid contamination was encountered during the first powered flight, but the problem did not recur after preflight operations were improved.

787. Kempel, R. W.; and Manke, J. A.: **Flight Evaluation of HL-10 Lifting Body Handling Qualities at Mach Numbers From 0.30 to 1.86.** NASA TN D-7537, H-757, January 1974, 74N14535, #.

The longitudinal and lateral-directional handling qualities of the HL-10 lifting body vehicle were evaluated in flight at Mach numbers up to 1.86 and altitudes up to approximately 27,450 meters (90,000 feet). In general, the vehicle's handling qualities were considered to be good. Approximately 91 percent of the pilot ratings were 3.5 or better, and 42.4 percent were 2.0. Handling qualities problems were encountered during the first flight due to problems with the control system and vehicle aerodynamics. Modifications of the flight vehicle corrected all deficiencies, and no other significant handling qualities problems were encountered.

788. Love, J. E.; *Fox, W. J.; and **Wicklund, E. J.: **Flight Study of a Vehicle Operational Status and Monitoring System.** NASA TN D-7546, H-789, January 1974, 74N13725, #.

An analog onboard monitoring system was installed on a YF-12 airplane as the first phase of a program to monitor the engine inlet and portions of the airplane's electrical and fuel management subsystems in flight. The system provided data which were considered to form a suitable base for diagnostic test logic and decision criteria for the rest of the program. The data were also adequate for the purpose of maintaining the engine inlet and identifying malfunctions within it. The investigation showed that the requirements of an onboard monitoring system should be considered during the original design of the system to be monitored.

*Lockheed-California Co., Burbank, California.
**Honeywell, Inc., Minneapolis, Minnesota.

789. Putnan, T. W.: **Flight Experience With the Decelerating Noise Abatement Approach.** NASA TM X-56020, January 1974, 74N12720, #.

The noise of older aircraft can be reduced in two principal ways: retrofitting the aircraft with a quiet propulsion system, and changing the flight operational procedures used in flying the aircraft. The former approach has already proved to be expensive, time consuming, and difficult to implement even though low-noise propulsion system technology exists. The latter method seems to hold promise of being less expensive and easier to implement. One operational technique which might reduce the noise beneath the landing approach path is the decelerating approach. This technique requires intercepting the 3 deg approach path at a relatively high speed with the aircraft in the cruise configuration, then reducing the thrust to idle and allowing the aircraft to decelerate along the 3 deg approach path. As the appropriate airspeed is achieved, the landing flaps and landing gear are deployed for a normal flare and landing. Because the engines, which are the predominant noise source on landing approach, are at idle thrust, a significant reduction in the noise beneath the approach path should be realized.

790. Jarvis, C. R.: **A Digital Fly-By-Wire Technology Development Program Using an F-8C Test Aircraft.** AIAA Paper 74-28, Twelfth AIAA Aerospace Sciences Meeting, Washington, D.C., January 30–February 1, 1974, pp. 11, January 1974, 74A20755, #.

A digital fly-by-wire flight control system has been installed in an F-8C test airplane and has undergone extensive ground and flight testing as part of an overall program to develop digital fly-by-wire technology. This is the first airplane to fly with a digital fly-by-wire system as its primary means of control and with no mechanical reversion capability. Forty-two test flights were made for a total flight time of 57 hours. Six pilots participated in the evaluation. This paper presents an overview of the digital fly-by-wire program and discusses some of the flight-test results.

791. Taillon, N. V.: **Flight-Test Investigation of the Aerodynamic Characteristics and Flow Interference Effects About the Aft Fuselage of the F-111A Airplane.** NASA TN D-7563, H-717, February 1974, 74N18657, #.

Static pressure measurements were made on the aft fuselage of an F-111A airplane to determine local flow characteristics and engine/airframe interaction effects. Data were obtained over the Mach number range from 0.5 to 2.0. Aspiration effects associated with low ejector nozzle expansion ratios reduced the local pressure coefficients particularly on the interfairing but also extending to the trailing edge of the nacelle. The presence of afterbodies also affected the behavior of the air flowing into and about the ejector nozzle. Pressures about the aft fuselage were improved by an increase in primary nozzle area at a supersonic speed. A comparison of wind-tunnel and flight-test results showed generally good agreement, although there was a large disparity in pressure level about the ejector nozzle. However, the shape of the data curves and the local flow behavior were basically similar.

792. Larson, T. J.; and Schweikhard, W. G.: **A Simplified Flight-Test Method for Determining Aircraft Takeoff Performance That Includes Effects of Pilot Technique.** NASA TN D-7603, H-802, February 1974, 74N16717, #.

A method for evaluating aircraft takeoff performance from brake release to air-phase height that requires fewer tests than conventionally required is evaluated with data for the XB-70 airplane. The method defines the effects of pilot technique on takeoff performance quantitatively, including the decrease in acceleration from drag due to lift. For a given takeoff weight and throttle setting, a single takeoff provides enough data to establish a standardizing relationship for the distance from brake release to any point where velocity is appropriate to rotation. The lower rotation rates penalized takeoff performance in terms of ground roll distance; the lowest observed rotation rate required a ground roll distance that was 19 percent longer than the highest. Rotations at the minimum rate also resulted in lift-off velocities that were approximately 5 knots lower than the highest rotation rate at any given lift-off distance.

793. Saltzman, E. J.; and Meyer, R. R., Jr.: **Drag Reduction Obtained by Rounding Vertical Corners on a Box-Shaped Ground Vehicle.** NASA TM X-56023, March 1974, 74N17703, #.

A box-shaped ground vehicle was used to simulate the aerodynamic drag of delivery vans, trucks, and motor homes.

A coast-down method was used to define the drag of this vehicle in a configuration with all square corners and a modified configuration with the four vertical corners rounded. The tests ranged in velocity from 30 miles per hour to 65 miles per hour, and Reynolds numbers ranged from $4.4 \times 1,000,000$ to 1.0×10 to the 7th power based on vehicle length. The modified configuration showed a reduction in aerodynamic drag of about 40 percent as compared to the square cornered configuration.

794. Holleman, E. C.: **Initial Results From Flight Testing a Large, Remotely Piloted Airplane Model.** NASA TM X-56024, March 1974, 74N18671, #.

The first four flights of a remotely piloted airplane model showed that a flight envelope can be expanded rapidly and that hazardous flight tests can be conducted safely with good results. The flights also showed that aerodynamic data can be obtained quickly and effectively over a wide range of flight conditions, clear and useful impressions of handling and controllability of configurations can be obtained, and present computer and electronic technology provide the capability to close flight control loops on the ground, thus providing a new method of design and flight test for advanced aircraft.

795. Anon.: **Parameter Estimation Techniques and Applications in Aircraft Flight Testing.** NASA TN D-7647, H-806, Aircraft Symposium, Edwards, California, April 24–25, 1973, 74N25569, #.

Technical papers were presented by selected representatives from industry, universities, and various Air Force, Navy, and NASA installations. The topics covered included the newest developments in identification techniques, the most recent flight-test experience, and the projected potential for the near future.

796. Rediess, H. A.: **An Overview of Parameter Estimation Techniques and Applications in Aircraft Flight Testing.** NASA TN D-7647, H-806. *Parameter Estimation Tech. and Appl. in Aircraft Flight Testing*, April 1974, pp. 1–18, (see N74-25569 15-02), 74N25570.

Parameter estimation is discussed as it applies to aircraft flight testing, and an overview of the symposium is presented. The evolution of techniques used in flight testing is reviewed briefly, and it is pointed out how the changing character of the aircraft tested and the availability of advanced data systems have promoted this evolution. Recent advances in optimal estimation theory have stimulated widespread interest and activity in parameter estimation. The framework of these advanced techniques is outlined to set the stage for subsequent papers. The session topics are introduced and related to the requirements of flight-test research.

797. Iliff, K. W.: **Identification of Aircraft Stability and Control Derivatives in the Presence of Turbulence.**

NASA TN D-7647, H-806. *Parameter Estimation Tech. and Appl. in Aircraft Flight Testing*, April 1974, pp. 77–114, (see N74-25569 15-02), 74N25575.

A maximum likelihood estimator for a linear system with state and observation noise is developed to determine stability and control derivatives from flight data obtained in the presence of turbulence. The formulation for the longitudinal short-period mode is presented briefly, including a special case that greatly simplifies the problem if the measurement noise on one signal is negligible. The effectiveness and accuracy of the technique are assessed by applying it first to simulated flight data, in which the true parameter values and state noise are known, then to actual flight data obtained in turbulence. The results are compared with data obtained in smooth air and with wind-tunnel data. The complete maximum likelihood estimator, which accounts for both state and observation noise, is shown to give the most accurate estimate of the stability and control derivatives from flight data obtained in turbulence. It is superior to the techniques that ignore state noise and to the simplified method that neglects the measurement noise on the angle-of-attack signal.

798. Gilyard, G. B.: **Determination of Propulsion-System-Induced Forces and Moments of a Mach 3 Cruise Aircraft.** NASA TN D-7647, H-806. *Parameter Estimation Tech. and Appl. in Aircraft Flight Testing*, April 1974, pp. 369–374, (see N74-25569 15-02), 74N25591.

During the joint NASA/USAF flight research program with the YF-12 airplane, the Dutch roll damping was found to be much less during automatic inlet operation than during fixed inlet operation at Mach numbers greater than 2.5 and with the yaw stability augmentation system off. It was concluded that the significant reduction in dutch roll damping was due to the forces and moments induced by the variable-geometry features of the inlet. Two stability-derivative extraction techniques were applied to the flight data; the recently developed Newton-Raphson technique and the time vector method. These techniques made it possible to determine the forces and moments generated by spike and bypass door movement.

799. Matheny, N. W.: **Flight Investigation of Approach and Flare From Simulated Breakout Altitude of a Subsonic Jet Transport and Comparison With Analytical Models.** NASA TN D-7645, H-803, April 1974, 74N19672, #.

Satisfactory and optimum flare windows are defined from pilot ratings and comments. Maximum flare normal accelerations, touchdown rates of sink, and total landing maneuver time increments are summarized as a function of approach airspeed margin (with respect to reference airspeed) and flare initiation altitude. The effects of two thrust management techniques are investigated. Comparisons are made with predictions from three analytical models and the results of a simulator study. The approach speed margin was found to have a greater influence on the flare initiation altitude than the absolute airspeed. The optimum airspeed was between the reference airspeed and the reference airspeed plus 10 knots. The optimum flare initiation altitude range for unrestricted landings was from 11 meters to 20 meters (36 feet to 66 feet), and the landing time in the optimum window was 8 seconds. The duration of the landing maneuver increased with increasing flare initiation altitude and with increasing speed margins on the approach.

800. Weirather, L. H.: **Transducers.** AGARDOGRAPH-160-VOL-1. *Flight Test Instrumentation Ser.*, Vol. 1, April 1974, (see N74-25933 15-14), 74N25937.

The use of transducers in the measuring channels of flight test instrumentation systems is discussed. Emphasis is placed on transducers with an electrical output. The physical effects used for producing the electrical outputs are defined. Diagrams of the various types of transducers are included to show the operating principles.

801. Reed, R. D.: **RPRVs—The First and Future Flights; Remotely Piloted Research Vehicle.** *Astronautics and Aeronautics*, Vol. 12, April 1974, pp. 26–42, 74A26410, #.

The merits of the RPRV (remotely piloted research vehicle) concept are discussed, along with its historical background and development culmination in the 3/8-scale F-15. The use of RPRVs is shown to be especially attractive when testing must be done at low cost, or in quick response to demand, or when hazardous testing must assure the safety of proceeding to manned vehicles.

ECN-4891

F-15 Spin Research Vehicle

802. Schweikhard, W. G.; and Berry, D. T.: **Cooperative Airframe/Propulsion Control for Supersonic Cruise Aircraft.** SAE Paper 740478, Society of Automotive Engineers, Air Transportation Meeting, Dallas, Texas, April 30–May 2, 1974, 74A34998.

Interactions between propulsion systems and flight controls have emerged as a major control problem on supersonic cruise aircraft. This paper describes the nature and causes of these interactions and the approaches to predicting and solving the problem. Integration of propulsion and flight control systems appears to be the most promising solution if the interaction effects can be adequately predicted early in the vehicle design. Significant performance, stability, and control improvements may be realized from a cooperative control system.

803. Deets, D. A.; and Szalai, K. J.: **Design and Flight Experience With a Digital Fly-By-Wire Control System in an F-8 Airplane.** AGARD CP-137. *Advances in Control Systems*, May 1974, (see N74-31429 21-02), 74N31450.

A digital fly-by-wire flight control system was designed, built, and for the first time flown in an airplane. The system, which uses components from the Apollo guidance system, is installed in an F-8 airplane as the primary control system. A lunar module guidance computer is the central element in the three-axis, single-channel, multimode, digital control system. A triplex electrical analog system which provides unaugmented control of the airplane is the only backup to the digital system. Flight results showed highly successful system operation, although the trim update rate was inadequate for precise trim changes, causing minor concern. The use of a digital system to implement conventional control laws proved to be practical for flight. Logic functions coded as an integral part of the control laws were found to be advantageous. Although software verification required extensive effort, confidence in the software was achieved.

804. Smith, R. H.; and Bauer, C. A.: **Atmospheric Effects on the Inlet System of the YF-12 Aircraft.** *Proceedings, Eleventh National Conference on Environmental Effects on Aircraft and Propulsion Systems*, Trenton, New Jersey, U.S. Naval Air Propulsion Test Center, May 21–23, 1974, 1974, 74A39744, #.

Flights of a YF-12 airplane were performed over a wide range of operating conditions so that detailed comparisons could be made with data from tests on scale models in NASA ground facilities. Extensive flight instrumentation for inlet performance comparisons provided flight data that also lend insight into supersonic inlet operation during atmospheric turbulence. Pressure and flow direction measurements near the inlet gave results different from conventional accelerometer data normally used for flight determination of turbulence severity. A nonturbulent atmospheric temperature excursion during an XB-70 flight caused inlet duct pressure

variations as extreme as those experienced during heavy turbulence on the YF-12 airplane.

805. Loschke, P. C.; Barber, M. R.; Enevoldson, E. K.; and McMurtry, T. C.: **Flight Evaluation of Advanced Control Systems and Displays on a General Aviation Airplane.** NASA TN D-7703, H-783, June 1974, 74N27499, #.

A flight-test program was conducted to determine the effect of advanced flight control systems and displays on the handling qualities of a light twin-engined airplane. A flight-director display and an attitude-command control system, used separately and in combination, transformed a vehicle with poor handling qualities during ILS approaches in turbulent air into a vehicle with good handling qualities. The attitude-command control system also improved the ride qualities of the airplane. A rate-command control system made only small improvements to the airplane's ILS handling qualities in turbulence. Both the rate- and the attitude-command control systems reduced stall warning in the test airplane, increasing the likelihood of inadvertent stalls. The final approach to the point of flare was improved by both the rate- and the attitude-command control systems. However, the small control wheel deflections necessary to flare were unnatural and tended to cause overcontrolling during flare. Airplane handling qualities are summarized for each control-system and display configuration.

806. Nugent, J.; and Holzman, J. K.: **Flight-Measured Inlet Pressure Transients Accompanying Engine Compressor Surges on the F-111A Airplane.** NASA TN D-7696, H-804, June 1974, 74N26251, #.

Two F-111A airplanes were subjected to conditions that caused engine compressor surges and accompanying duct hammershock pressure transients. Flight speed ranged from Mach 0.71 to Mach 2.23, and altitude varied from approximately 3200 meters to 14,500 meters. A wide range of compressor pressure ratios was covered. Stabilized free-stream, engine, and duct conditions were established before each compressor surge. Dynamic pressure instrumentation at the compressor face and in the duct recorded the pressure transients associated with the surges. Hammershock pressures were analyzed with respect to the stabilized conditions preceding the compressor surges. The hammershock transients caused large pressure rises at the compressor face and in the duct. Hammershock pressure ratios at the compressor face were not affected by free-stream Mach number or altitude but were functions of engine variables, such as compressor pressure ratio. The maximum hammershock pressure ratio of approximately 1.83 occurred at a compressor pressure ratio of approximately 21.7.

807. Lasagna, P. L.; and Putnam, T. W.: **Preliminary Measurements of Aircraft Aerodynamic Noise.** AIAA Paper 74-572, Seventh AIAA Fluid and Plasma Dynamics

Conference, Palo Alto, California, June 17–19, 1974, 74A34332, #.

Flight measurements of aerodynamic noise were made on an AeroCommander airplane with engines off and a JetStar airplane with engines at both idle power and completely shut off. The overall sound level for these airplanes in the landing configuration varied as the sixth power of the aircraft velocity. For the JetStar airplane, the overall sound level decreased as the inverse square of the distance in the lateral direction. The aerodynamic noise was approximately 11 decibels below the FAR Part 36 noise level for the JetStar airplane. The landing gear were a significant contributor to aerodynamic noise for both aircraft.

ECN-2478

C-140 JetStar Airplane

808. Montoya, L. C.; Economu, M. A.; and Cissell, R. E.: **Use of a Pitot-Static Probe for Determining Wing Section Drag in Flight at Mach Numbers From 0.5 to Approximately 1.0.** NASA TM X-56025, H-844, July 1974, 74N29370, #.

The use of a pitot-static probe to determine wing section drag at speeds from Mach 0.5 to approximately 1.0 was evaluated in flight. The probe unit is described and operational problems are discussed. Typical wake profiles and wing section drag coefficients are presented. The data indicate that the pitot-static probe gave reliable results up to speeds of approximately 1.0.

809. Anon.: **Advanced Control Technology and Its Potential for Future Transport Aircraft.** NASA TM X-70240, Advanced Control Technology Symposium, Los Angeles, California, July 9–11, 1974, 74X10214, #.

This document is a compilation of papers prepared for a symposium on advanced control technology sponsored by the National Aeronautics and Space Administration. This symposium focuses national attention on recent advances in control technology and the impact it should have on future transport aircraft. These technical papers present work performed by the Government and industry. The topics covered include recent flight-test results of advanced control

technology programs, such as fly-by-wire, digital control, and control configured vehicles; important applications of advanced control systems to such vehicles as the space shuttle orbiter, the Lockheed C-5A, and the Boeing 747; advanced and integrated propulsion control systems; and case studies of the benefits of applying active control technology to transport aircraft. Also included are several papers on the design, testing, and reliability of advanced control systems directed primarily toward the technical specialist.

810. Rediess, Herman A.; Kordes, Eldon E.; and Edwards, John W.: **A Remotely Augmented Approach to Flight Testing of Advanced Control Technology.** NASA Advanced Control Technology Symposium, Los Angeles, California, July 9–11, 1974.

811. *Webb, W. L.; and Reukauf, P. J.: **Development of a Turbine Inlet Gas Temperature Measurement and Control System Using a Fluidic Temperature Sensor.** *Journal of Aircraft*, Vol. 11, No. 7, July 1974, pp. 422–427. (See also 779.)

A fluidic turbine engine gas temperature measurement and control system was developed for use on a Pratt & Whitney Aircraft J58 engine. This paper includes the criteria used for material selection, system design, and system performance. It was found that the fluidic temperature sensor had the durability for flight test under conditions existing in the YF-12 airplane. As a result of turbine inlet gas temperatures fluctuations, over-all engine-control system performance cannot be adequately evaluated without a multiple-gas sampling system.

*United Aircraft Corp., Pratt and Whitney Aircraft Div., West Palm Beach, Florida.

812. Gilyard, G. B.; Smith, J. W.; and *Falkner, V. L.: **Flight Evaluation of a Mach 3 Cruise Longitudinal Autopilot.** AIAA Paper 74-910, AIAA Mechanics and Control of Flight Conference, Anaheim, California, August 5–9, 1974, 74A37890, #.

At high Mach numbers (approximately 3) and altitudes greater than 70,000 feet, the original altitude and Mach hold modes of the YF-12 autopilot produced aircraft excursions that were erratic or divergent or both. Data analysis and simulator studies showed that static pressure port sensitivity to angle of attack had a detrimental effect on the performance of both altitude and Mach hold modes. Good altitude hold performance was obtained when a high-passed pitch rate feedback was added to compensate for angle-of-attack sensitivity and the altitude error and integral altitude gains were reduced. Good Mach hold performance was obtained with the removal of angle-of-attack sensitivity.

*Honeywell, Inc., Minneapolis, Minnesota.

813. Layton, G. P.: **NASA Flight Research Center Scale F-15 Remotely Piloted Research Vehicle Program.** *Advancements in Flight Test Engineering; Proceedings of the Fifth Annual Symposium*, Anaheim, California, August 7–9, 1974, (see A74-43601 22-02), 74A43603. (See also 814.)

The NASA Flight Research Center undertook a remotely piloted research vehicle (RPRV) program with a 3/8-scale model of an F-15 aircraft to determine the usefulness of the RPRV testing technique in high-risk flight testing such as spin testing. The results of the first flights of the program are presented. The program has shown that the RPRV technique, including the use of a digital control system, is a viable method for obtaining flight research data. Also presented are some negative aspects that have been learned about the RPRV technique in terms of model size, command frequency, and launch technique.

814. Layton, G. P.: **NASA Flight Research Center Scale F-15 Remotely Piloted Research Vehicle Program.** *Soc. of Flight Test Engr. Advan. in Flight Test Eng.*, 1974, (see N75-10910 02-05), 75N10912. (See also 813.)

A remotely piloted research vehicle (RPRV) program was conducted with a 3/8-scale model of an F-15 airplane to determine the usefulness of the RPRV testing technique in high risk flight testing such as spin testing. The results of the first flights of the program are presented. The program has shown that the RPRV technique, including the use of a digital control system, is a viable method for obtaining flight research data. Also presented are some negative aspects that have been learned about the RPRV technique in terms of model size, command frequency, and launch technique.

815. Iliff, K. W.: **An Aircraft Application of System Identification in the Presence of State Noise.** Presented at NATO Advantageous Study Institute, New Directions in Signal Processing in Communications and Control, Darlington, England, August 5–17, 1974, (AD-A001936 AFOSR-74-1756TR), 75N19234, #. (See also 872.)

A maximum likelihood estimator for a linear system with state and observation noise is developed to determine unknown aircraft coefficients from flight data in the presence of turbulence (state noise). The formulation of the algorithm is presented briefly. The linear equations for an aircraft in atmospheric turbulence are defined. The effectiveness and accuracy of the technique are assessed by first applying it to simulated flight data, in which the true parameter values are known, then to actual flight data obtained in turbulence. A complete set of aircraft coefficients is obtained as well as an estimate of the turbulence time history. The validity of the estimated state noise and of the estimated coefficients is tested. The feasibility of using the algorithm for defining an adaptive control law to alleviate the effects of turbulence on the aircraft is discussed.

816. Berry, D. T.; and Gilyard, G. B.: **Some Stability and Control Aspects of Airframe/Propulsion System Interactions on the YF-12 Airplane.** *Journal of Engineering for Industry, Transactions of the ASME,* August 1974.

Airframe/propulsion system interactions can strongly affect the stability and control of supersonic cruise aircraft. These interactions generate forces and moments similar in magnitude to those produced by the aerodynamic controls, and can cause significant changes in vehicle damping and static stability. This in turn can lead to large aircraft excursions or high pilot workload, or both. For optimum integration of an airframe and its jet propulsion system, these phenomena may have to be taken into account.

817. DeMarco, D. M.: **A Dynamic Pressure Generator for Checking Complete Pressure Sensing Systems Installed on an Airplane.** NASA TM X-56026, September 1974, 74N31923, #.

A portable dynamic pressure generator, how it operates, and a test setup on an airplane are described. The generator is capable of providing a sinusoidal pressure having a peak-to-peak amplitude of 3.5 N/sq cm (5 psi) at frequencies ranging from 100 hertz to 200 hertz. A typical power spectral density plot of data from actual dynamic pressure fluctuation tests within the air inlet of the YF-12 airplane is presented.

818. Barber, M. R.; and *Tymczyszyn, J. J.: **Recent Wake Turbulence Flight Test Programs.** *Society of Experimental Test Pilots, Technical Review*, Vol. 12, No. 2, 1974, pp. 52–68, 75A24805.

In early flight tests the size and intensity of the wake vortexes generated by aircraft ranging in size from the Learjet to the C-5A and the B-747 were studied to determine the effects of aircraft configuration, weight, and speed. Early problems were related to vortex marking, the measurement of separation distance, and test techniques. Recent tests conducted with B-747 showed that vortexes were alleviated by reducing the deflection of the outboard flaps. It was found that a more rapid dissipation of the vortex system can be obtained through alterations in the span lift distribution.

*FAA, Washington, D.C.

819. Smith, R. H.; and Burcham, F. W., Jr.: **Instrumentation for In-Flight Determination of Steady-State and Dynamic Inlet Performance in Supersonic Aircraft.** *Instrumentation for Airbreathing Propulsion; Proceedings of the Symposium*, Monterey, California, September 19–21, 1972. Cambridge, Massachusetts, MIT Press, 1974, pp. 41–58, 74A28286. (See also 726.)

Advanced instrumentation and techniques for in-flight measurements of air inlet performance of the XB-70,

F-111A, and YF-12 supersonic airplanes were developed and evaluated in flight tests at the NASA Flight Research Center. A compressor face rake with in-flight zeroing capability was flown on the F-111A and found to give excellent steady state as well as high frequency response pressure data. The severe temperature environment of the YF-12 necessitated development of special high temperature transducers. Mounting these transducers to give the required 500-hertz frequency response required some special rake designs. Vibration test requirements necessitated some modifications to the rakes. The transducers and rakes were evaluated in flight tests and were found to function properly. Preliminary data have been obtained from the YF-12 propulsion program in flights that began in May 1972. One example shows the terminal shock wave effects on cowl surface pressures during bypass and spike motions.

820. Green, K. S.; and Putnam, T. W.: **Measurements of Sonic Booms Generated by an Airplane Flying at Mach 3.5 and 4.8.** NASA TM-X-3126, H-838, October 1974, 74N34486, #.

Sonic booms generated by the X-15 airplane flying at Mach numbers of 3.5 and 4.8 were measured. The experimental results agreed within 12 percent with results obtained from theoretical methods. No unusual phenomena related to overpressure were encountered. Scaled data from the X-15 airplane for Mach 4.8 agreed with data for an SR-71 airplane operating at lower Mach numbers and similar altitudes. The simple technique used to scale the data on the basis of airplane lift was satisfactory for comparing X-15 and SR-71 sonic boom signatures.

821. Gilyard, G. B.; and Belte, D.: **Flight-Determined Lag of Angle-of-Attack and Angle-of-Sideslip Sensors in the YF-12A Airplane From Analysis of Dynamic Maneuvers.** NASA TN D-7819, H-767, October 1974, 74N34460, #.

Magnitudes of lags in the pneumatic angle-of-attack and angle-of-sideslip sensor systems of the YF-12A airplane were determined for a variety of flight conditions by analyzing stability and control data. The three analysis techniques used are described. An apparent trend with Mach number for measurements from both of the differential-pressure sensors showed that the lag ranged from approximately 0.15 second at subsonic speed to 0.4 second at Mach 3. Because Mach number was closely related to altitude for the available flight data, the individual effects of Mach number and altitude on the lag could not be separated clearly. However, the results indicated the influence of factors other than simple pneumatic lag.

822. Saltzman, E. J.; Meyer, R. R., Jr.; and Lux, D. P.: **Drag Reductions Obtained by Modifying a Box-Shaped Ground Vehicle.** NASA TM X-56027, October 1974, 74N34449, #.

A box-shaped ground vehicle was used to simulate the aerodynamic drag of high volume transports, that is, delivery vans, trucks, or motor homes. The coast-down technique was used to define the drag of the original vehicle, having all square corners, and several modifications of the vehicle. Test velocities ranged up to 65 miles per hour, which provided maximum Reynolds numbers of 1 times 10 to the 7th power based on vehicle length. One combination of modifications produced a reduction in aerodynamic drag of 61 percent as compared with the original square-cornered vehicle.

823. Wolowicz, C. H.; and Yancey, R. B.: **Experimental Determination of Airplane Mass and Inertial Characteristics.** NASA TR R-433, H-814, October 1974, 75N10062, #.

Current practices are evaluated for experimentally determining airplane center of gravity, moments of inertia, and products of inertia. The techniques discussed are applicable to bodies other than airplanes. In pitching- and rolling-moment-of-inertia investigations with the airplane mounted on and pivoted about knife edges, the nonlinear spring moments that occur at large amplitudes of oscillation can be eliminated by using the proper spring configuration. The single-point suspension double-pendulum technique for obtaining yawing moments of inertia, products of inertia, and the inclination of the principal axis provides accurate results from yaw-mode oscillation data, provided that the sway-mode effects are minimized by proper suspension rig design. Rocking-mode effects in the data can be isolated.

824. Schweikhard, W. G.: **Test Techniques, Instrumentation, and Data Processing.** AGARD Lecture Series No. 72, *Distortion Induced Eng. Instability*, November 7–15, 1974, (see N75-12954 04-07), 75N12960.

Procedures for determining the effects of dynamic distortion on engine stability are analyzed. The test techniques, methods and types of instrumentation, and data processing functions are described. The advantages and limitations of various methods are reported. It is emphasized that ground facility tests are only a simulation of the flight environment, that instrumentation provides only a partial representation of the physical phenomena, and that poorly organized data processing procedures can impede and even distort the final result.

825. Bellman, D. R.; and Kier, D. A.: **HiMAT—A New Approach to the Design of Highly Maneuverable Aircraft.** SAE Paper 740859, Society of Automotive Engineers, National Aerospace Engineering and Manufacturing Meeting, San Diego, California, October 1–3, 1974, 75A16921.

Needed improvements in the maneuvering performance of combat aircraft appear to be possible through the simultaneous application of advances in various disciplines in such a way that they complement one another and magnify the benefits derived. The highly maneuverable aircraft technology (HiMAT) program is being conducted to investigate such multidisciplinary concepts. The program has three phases: preliminary studies, conceptual design studies, and the final design and construction of a test airplane. Work is now in the second phase. The test airplane will be a scaled model flown by a remotely piloted research vehicle technique. This paper outlines the HiMAT program and indicates the types of concepts being considered.

826. Reukauf, P. J.; Schweikhard, W. G.; and *Arnaiz, H.: **Flight-Test Techniques for Obtaining Valid Comparisons of Wind-Tunnel and Flight Results From Tests on a YF-12 Mixed-Compression Inlet.** AIAA Paper 74-1195, Tenth AIAA Society of Automotive Engineers, Propulsion Conference, San Diego, California, October 21–23, 1974, 75A11301, #.

The ability to predict the inlet characteristics of high-speed propulsion systems from wind-tunnel test results is being studied by the NASA Flight Research Center in a flight program on the YF-12 aircraft. The obvious requirement for matching geometry, instrumentation, and test conditions has led to the development of special flight test techniques, hardware, and systems. This paper describes this development, the technical and operational problems encountered and their solutions and the compromises that were found to be necessary.

827. Love, J. E.: **Flight Test Results of an Automatic Support System on Board a YF-12A Airplane.** *Automatic Support Systems for Advanced Maintainability Symposium,* San Diego, California, October 30–November 1, 1974, Institute of Electrical and Electronics Engineers, Inc., 1974, pp. 211–220, 75A35272.

An automatic support system concept that isolated faults in an existing nonavionics subsystem was flight tested up to a Mach number of 3. The adaptation of the automated support concept to an existing system (the jet engine automatic inlet control system) caused most of the problems one would expect to encounter in other applications. These problems and their solutions are discussed. Criteria for integrating automatic support into the initial design of new subsystems are included in the paper. Cost effectiveness resulted from both the low maintenance of the automated system and the man-hour saving resulting from the real time diagnosis of the monitored subsystem.

828. Larson, T. J.: **Compensated and Uncompensated Nose Boom Static Pressures Measured From Two Air Data Systems on a Supersonic Airplane.** NASA TM X-3132, H-835, November 1974, 79N77423.

Two static-pressure-measuring air data systems that were used on the YF-12 airplane for supersonic flight testing were compared. One system consisted of a nose boom pitot-static probe with two sets of static-pressure orifices designed for static-pressure error compensation, two air data computers, and a photopanel for recording. The other system consisted of an identical nose boom probe and a third set of static-pressure orifices not designed for error compensation, pressure transducers for direct pressure measurements instead of air data computers, and 5 pulse code modulation system for recording. The comparisons showed that the uncompensated static-pressure orifices provided more accurate air data measurements than either set of compensated static-pressure sources. Whereas the uncompensated static-pressure source was relatively insensitive to angle of attack, the compensated sources were characterized by a position error at supersonic speeds that increased with angle of attack and Mach number. Pitot-static measurements acquired by using air data computers that incorporate cams for static error compensation provide reference data that are less accurate than similar measurements made by pressure transducers.

829. Deets, D. A.; and Edwards, J. W.: **A Remotely Augmented Vehicle Approach to Flight Testing RPV Control Systems.** NASA TM X-56029, H-870, November 1974, 75N10936, #.

A remotely augmented vehicle concept for flight testing advanced control systems was developed as an outgrowth of a remotely piloted research vehicle (RPV) program in which control laws are implemented through telemetry uplink and computer which provides the control law computations. Some advantages of this approach are that the cost of one control system facility is spread over a number of RPV programs, and control laws can be changed quickly as required, without changing the flight hardware. The remotely augmented vehicle concept is described, and flight test results from a subscale F-15 program are discussed. Suggestions of how the concept could lead to more effective testing of RPV control system concepts, and how it is applicable to a military RPV reconnaissance mission are given.

830. Ehernberger, L. J.: **High Altitude Turbulence Encountered by the Supersonic YF-12A Airplane.** *Sixth Annual Conference on Aerospace and Aeronautical Meteorology,* El Paso, Texas, November 12–15, 1974, pp. 305–312, (see A75-35351 16-47), 75A35409, #.

The present work describes the turbulence experienced by the YF-12A airplane on the basis of airplane acceleration data obtained at altitudes above 12.2 km. Data presented include the subjective intensities reported by the air crew, the portion of flight distance in turbulence, the variation of turbulence with season, and the thickness and length of turbulence patches as determined along the flight path. Compared with that experienced by subsonic jets below 12.2 km, turbulence above 12.2 km was mild, but the crew was more sensitive to gust accelerations during supersonic flight at altitudes above 12.2 km than during subsonic flight at lower altitudes. About 6–8% of the distance traveled was in turbulence between 12.2 and 16.8 km, as compared to less than 1% above 18.3 km.

High-altitude turbulence increased by a factor of three from summer to winter. Turbulence patches were 0.4 km thick and 10 km long on the average.

831. Montoya, L. C.; and Steers, L. L.: **Aerodynamic Drag Reduction Tests on a Full-Scale Tractor-Trailer Combination With Several Add-On Devices.** NASA TM X-56028, Reduction of Aerodynamic Drag of Trucks Conference, Pasadena, California, October 10–11, 1974, December 1974, 75N12900, #. (See also 832.)

Aerodynamic drag tests were performed on a conventional cab-over-engine tractor with a 45-foot trailer and five commercially available or potentially available add-on devices using the coast-down method. The tests ranged in velocity from approximately 30 miles per hour to 65 miles per hour and included some flow visualization. A smooth, level runway at Edwards Air Force Base was used for the tests, and deceleration measurements were taken with both accelerometers and stopwatches. An evaluation of the drag reduction results obtained with each of the five add-on devices is presented.

832. Montoya, L. C.; and Steers, L. L.: **Aerodynamic Drag Reduction Tests on a Full-Scale Tractor-Trailer Combination With Several Add-On Devices.** Presented at the Reduction of Aerodynamic Drag of Trucks Conference, Pasadena, California, October 10–11, 1974. *Proceedings of the Conference Workshop*, (available from the National Science Foundation, RANN Document Center, Washington, D.C.) December 1974, pp. 63–88. (See also 831.)

833. Schweikhard, W. G.; and Montoya, E. J.: **Research Instrumentation Requirements for Flight/Wind-Tunnel Tests of the YF-12 Propulsion System and Related Flight Experience.** *Instrumentation for Airbreathing Propulsion; Proceedings of the Symposium*, Monterey, California, September 19–21, 1972, MIT Press, Cambridge Massachusetts, 1974, pp. 19–39, (see A74-28283 12-14), 74A28285.

Description of the requirements for a comprehensive flight and wind-tunnel propulsion research program to examine the predictability of inlet performance, evaluate the effects of high-frequency pressure phenomena on inlets, and investigate improved control concepts in order to cope with airframe interactions. This program is unique in that it requires precise similarity of the geometry of the flight vehicle and tunnel modes; the test conditions, including local flow at the inlet; and instrumentation. Although few wind-tunnel instrumentation problems exist, many problems emerge during flight tests because of the thermal environment. Mach 3 flight temperatures create unique problems with transducers, connectors, and wires. All must be capable of withstanding continuous 1000 F temperatures, as well as the mechanical stresses imposed by vibration and thermal cycling.

1975 Technical Publications

834. Barber, M. R.; Kurkowski, R. L.; Garodz, L. J.; Robinson, G. H.; Smith, H. J.; Jacobsen, R. A.; Stinnett, G. W., Jr.; McMurtry, T. C.; Tymczyszyn, J. J.; and Devereaux, R. L.: **Flight Test Investigation of the Vortex Wake Characteristics Behind a Boeing 727 During Two-Segment and Normal ILS Approaches (A Joint NASA/FAA Report).** NASA TM X-62398, FAA-NA-151, January 1975, 75N17340, #.

Flight tests were performed to evaluate the vortex wake characteristics of a Boeing 727 aircraft during conventional and two-segment instrument landing approaches. Smoke generators were used for vortex marking. The vortex was intentionally intercepted by a Lear Jet and a Piper Comanche aircraft. The vortex location during landing approach was measured using a system of phototheodolites. The tests showed that at a given separation distance there are no readily apparent differences in the upsets resulting from deliberate vortex encounters during the two types of approaches. The effect of the aircraft configuration on the extent and severity of the vortices is discussed.

835. Ehernberger, L. J.; and Love, B. J.: **High Altitude Gust Acceleration Environment as Experienced by a Supersonic Airplane.** NASA TN D-7868, H-836, January 1975, 75N13791, #.

High altitude turbulence experienced at supersonic speeds is described in terms of gust accelerations measured on the YF-12A airplane. The data were obtained during 90 flights at altitudes above 12.2 kilometers (40,000 feet). Subjective turbulence intensity ratings were obtained from air crew members. The air crew often rated given gust accelerations as being more intense during high altitude supersonic flight than during low altitude subsonic flight. The portion of flight distance in turbulence ranged from 6 percent to 8 percent at altitudes between 12.2 kilometers and 16.8 kilometers (40,000 feet and 55,000 feet) to less than 1 percent at altitudes above 18.3 kilometers (60,000 feet). The amount of turbulence varied with season, increasing by a factor of 3 or more from summer to winter. Given values of gust acceleration were less frequent, on the basis of distance traveled, for supersonic flight of the YF-12A airplane at altitudes above 12.2 kilometers (40,000 feet) than for subsonic flight of a jet passenger airplane at altitudes below 12.2 kilometers (40,000 feet). The median thickness of high altitude turbulence patches was less than 400 meters (1300 feet); the median length was less than 16 kilometers (10 miles). The distribution of the patch dimensions tended to be log normal.

836. Rediess, H. A.; and Szalai, K. J.: **Status and Trends in Active Control Technology.** NASA SP-372,

January 1975, pp. 273–322, (see N75-29001 20-01), 75N29015.

The emergence of highly reliable fly-by-wire flight control systems makes it possible to consider a strong reliance on automatic control systems in the design optimization of future aircraft. This design philosophy has been referred to as the control configured vehicle approach or the application of active control technology. Several studies and flight tests sponsored by the Air Force and NASA have demonstrated the potential benefits of control configured vehicles and active control technology. The present status and trends of active control technology are reviewed and the impact it will have on aircraft designs, design techniques, and the designer is predicted.

837. Smith, J. W.; and Berry, D. T.: **Analysis of Longitudinal Pilot-Induced Oscillation Tendencies of YF-12 Aircraft.** NASA TN D-7900, H-805, February 1975, 75N16560, #.

Aircraft flight and ground tests and simulator studies were conducted to explore pilot-induced oscillation tendencies. Linear and nonlinear calculations of the integrated flight control system's characteristics were made to analyze and predict the system's performance and stability. The investigations showed that the small-amplitude PIO tendency was caused by the interaction of the pilot with a combination of the aircraft's short-period poles and the structural first bending mode zeros. It was found that the large-amplitude PIOs were triggered by abrupt corrective control actions by the pilot, which caused the stability augmentation system servo to position and rate limit. The saturation in turn caused additional phase lag, further increasing the tendency of the overall system to sustain a PIO.

838. Anon.: **Description and Flight Test Results of the NASA F-8 Digital Fly-By-Wire Control System.** NASA TN D-7843, H-853. Presented at the NASA Symposium on Advanced Control Technol., Los Angeles, California, July 9–11, 1974, February 1975, 75N18245, #.

A NASA program to develop digital fly-by-wire (DFBW) technology for aircraft applications is discussed. Phase I of the program demonstrated the feasibility of using a digital fly-by-wire system for aircraft control through developing and flight testing a single channel system, which used Apollo hardware, in an F-8C airplane. The objective of Phase II of the program is to establish a technology base for designing practical DFBW systems. It will involve developing and flight testing a triplex digital fly-by-wire system using state-of-the-art airborne computers, system hardware, software, and redundancy concepts. The papers included in this report describe the Phase I system and its development and present results from the flight program. Man-rated flight software and the effects of lightning on digital flight control systems are also discussed.

839. Jarvis, C. R.: **An Overview of NASA's Digital Fly-By-Wire Technology Development Program.** NASA TN D-7843, H-853, *Description and Flight Test Results of the NASA F-8 Digital Fly-by-Wire Control System,* February 1975, pp. 1–12, (see N75-18245 10-08), 75N18246. (See also 898.)

The feasibility of using digital fly-by-wire systems to control aircraft was demonstrated by developing and flight testing a single channel system, which used Apollo hardware, in an F-8C test airplane. This is the first airplane to fly with a digital fly-by-wire system as its primary means of control and with no mechanical reversion capability. The development and flight test of a triplex digital fly-by-wire system, which will serve as an experimental prototype for future operational digital fly-by-wire systems, is underway.

840. Deets, D. A.: **Design and Development Experience With a Digital Fly-By-Wire Control System in an F-8C Airplane.** NASA TN D-7843, H-853. *Description and Flight Test Results of the NASA F-8 Digital Fly-by-Wire Control System,* February 1975, pp. 13–40, (see N75-18245 10-08), 75N18247. (See also 899.)

To assess the feasibility of a digital fly-by-wire system, the mechanical flight control system of an F-8C airplane was replaced with a digital system and an analog backup system. The Apollo computer was used as the heart of the primary system. This paper discusses the experience gained during the design and development of the system and relates it to active control systems that are anticipated for future civil transport applications.

841. Lock, W. P.; Petersen, W. R.; and *Whitman, G. B.: **Mechanization of and Experience With a Triplex Fly-By-Wire Backup Control System.** NASA TN D-7843, H-853. *Description and Flight Test Results of the NASA F-8 Digital Fly-by-Wire Control System,* February 1975, pp. 41–72, (see N75-18245 10-08), 75N18248. (See also 900.)

A redundant three-axis analog control system was designed and developed to back up a digital fly-by-wire control system for an F-8C airplane. Forty-two flights, involving 58 hours of flight time, were flown by six pilots. The mechanization and operational experience with the backup control system, the problems involved in synchronizing it with the primary system, and the reliability of the system are discussed. The backup control system was dissimilar to the primary system, and it provided satisfactory handling through the flight envelope evaluated. Limited flight tests of a variety of control tasks showed that control was also satisfactory when the backup control system was controlled by a minimum-displacement (force) side stick. The operational reliability of the F-8 digital fly-by-wire control system was satisfactory, with no unintentional downmodes to the backup control system in flight. The ground and flight reliability of the system's components is discussed.

*Sperry Flight Systems Div., Phoenix, Arizona.

842. *Plumer, J. A.; **Malloy, W. A.; and Craft, J. B.: **The Effects of Lightning on Digital Flight Control Systems.** NASA TN D-7843, H-853. *Description and Flight Test Results of the NASA F-8 Digital Fly-by-Wire Control System,* February 1975, pp. 73–92, (see N75-18245 10-08), 75N18249. (See also 905.)

Present practices in lightning protection of aircraft deal primarily with the direct effects of lightning, such as structural damage and ignition of fuel vapors. There is increasing evidence of troublesome electromagnetic effects, however, in aircraft employing solid-state microelectronics in critical navigation, instrumentation and control functions. The potential impact of these indirect effects on critical systems such as digital fly-by-wire (DFBW) flight controls has been studied by several recent research programs, including an experimental study of lightning-induced voltages in the NASA F8 DFBW airplane. The results indicate a need for positive steps to be taken during the design of future fly-by-wire systems to minimize the possibility of hazardous effects from lightning.

*General Electric Research and Development, Schenectady, New York.
**General Motors Corp., Detroit, Michigan.

843. Szalai, K. J.: **Flight Test Experience With the F-8 Digital Fly-By-Wire System.** NASA TN D-7843, H-853. *Description and Flight Test Results of the NASA F-8 Digital Fly-by-Wire Control System,* February 1975, pp. 127–180, (see N75-18245 10-08),75N18251. (See also 901.)

Flight test results of the F-8 digital fly-by-wire (DFBW) control system are presented and the implications for application to active control technology (ACT) are discussed. The F-8 DFBW system has several of the attributes of proposed ACT systems, so the flight test experience is helpful in assessing the capabilities of those systems. Topics of discussion include the predicted and actual flight performance of the control system, assessments of aircraft flying qualities and other piloting factors, software management and control, and operational experience.

844. Krier, G. E.: **A Pilot's Opinion of the F-8 Digital Fly-By-Wire Airplane.** NASA TN D-7843, H-853. *Description and Flight Test Results of the NASA F-8 Digital Fly-by-Wire Control System,* February 1975, pp. 181–195, (see N75-18245 10-08), 75N18252. (See also 902.)

The handling qualities of the F-8 digital fly-by-wire airplane are evaluated by using the Cooper-Harper rating scale. The reasons for the ratings are given, as well as a short description of the flying tasks. It was concluded that the handling qualities of the airplane were good in most situations, although occasional ratings of unsatisfactory were given.

845. Nugent, J.; Couch, L. M.; and Webb, L. D.: **Exploratory Wind Tunnel Tests of a Shock-Swallowing Air Data Sensor at a Mach Number of Approximately 1.83.** NASA TM X-56030, March 1975, 75N20329, #.

The test probe was designed to measure free-stream Mach number and could be incorporated into a conventional airspeed nose boom installation. Tests were conducted in the Langley 4-by 4-foot supersonic pressure tunnel with an approximate angle of attack test range of –5 deg to 15 deg and an approximate angle of sideslip test range of + or –4 deg. The probe incorporated a variable exit area which permitted internal flow. The internal flow caused the bow shock to be swallowed. Mach number was determined with a small axially movable internal total pressure tube and a series of fixed internal static pressure orifices. Mach number error was at a minimum when the total pressure tube was close to the probe tip. For four of the five tips tested, the Mach number error derived by averaging two static pressures measured at horizontally opposed positions near the probe entrance were least sensitive to angle of attack changes. The same orifices were also used to derive parameters that gave indications of flow direction.

846. Steers, S. T.; and Iliff, K. W.: **Effects of Time-Shifted Data on Flight Determined Stability and Control Derivatives.** NASA TN D-7830, H-849, March 1975, 75N18244, #.

Flight data were shifted in time by various increments to assess the effects of time shifts on estimates of stability and control derivatives produced by a maximum likelihood estimation method. Derivatives could be extracted from flight data with the maximum likelihood estimation method even if there was a considerable time shift in the data. Time shifts degraded the estimates of the derivatives, but the degradation was in a consistent rather than a random pattern. Time shifts in the control variables caused the most degradation, and the lateral-directional rotary derivatives were affected the most by time shifts in any variable.

847. Putnam, T. W.; Lasagna, P. L.; and *White, K. C.: **Measurements and Analysis of Aircraft Airframe Noise.** AIAA Paper 75-510, presented at the American Institute of Aeronautics and Astronautics, Second Annual Aero-Acoustics Conference, Hampton, Virginia, March 1975, 75A25776, #. (Also *Aeroacoustics: STOL Noise; Airframe and Airfoil Noise,* Vol. 45, *Progress in Astronautics and Aeronautics,* March 1975.)

Flyover measurements of the airframe noise of AeroCommander, JetStar, CV-990, and B-747 aircraft are presented. Data are shown for both cruise and landing configurations. Correlations between airframe noise and aircraft parameters are developed and presented. The landing approach airframe noise for the test aircraft was approximately 10 EPNdB below present FAA certification requirements.

*NASA Ames Research Center, Moffett Field, California.

848. Sanderson, K. C.: **A New Flight Test Data System for NASA Aeronautical Flight Research.** *Proceedings, London Royal Aeronautical Society, Eighth International Aerospace Instrumentation Symposium*, Cranfield, Beds., England, March 24–27, 1975, (see A75-28765 12-06), 75A28774, #.

The airborne integrated flight test data system (AIFTDS) is described. This system integrates an airborne digital computer with a high-bit-rate pulse code modulation system. Its design was influenced by in-house technical experience with similar modules and by the multiproject environment in which it was expected to operate. The present work describes events leading to the development of the system, reviews factors that influenced the objectives for the system and the resulting design, and describes the elements themselves. Block diagrams supplement the text.

849. Edwards, J. W.; and Deets, D. A.: **Development of a Remote Digital Augmentation System and Application to a Remotely Piloted Research Vehicle.** NASA TN D-7941, H-854, April 1975, 75N20293, #.

A cost-effective approach to flight testing advanced control concepts with remotely piloted vehicles is described. The approach utilizes a ground based digital computer coupled to the remotely piloted vehicle's motion sensors and control surface actuators through telemetry links to provide high bandwidth feedback control. The system was applied to the control of an unmanned 3/8-scale model of the F-15 airplane. The model was remotely augmented; that is, the F-15 mechanical and control augmentation flight control systems were simulated by the ground-based computer, rather than being in the vehicle itself. The results of flight tests of the model at high angles of attack are discussed.

850. Smith, H. J.: **A Flight Test Investigation of the Rolling Moments Induced on a T-37B Airplane in the Wake of a B-747 Airplane.** NASA TM X-56031, April 1975, 75N20221, #.

A flight test investigation of the B-747 vortex wake characteristics was conducted using a T-37B as a probe aircraft. The primary purpose of the program was the validation of the results of B-747 model tests which predicted significant alleviation of the vortex strength when only the inboard flaps were deflected. Measurements of the vortex-induced rolling moments of the probe aircraft showed that the predicted alleviation did occur. The effects of landing gear extension, increased lift coefficient, idle thrust, and sideslip were investigated, and all had an adverse effect on the alleviated condition as evidenced by increased induced rolling moments of the T-37B probe aircraft. Idle thrust also increased the strength of the B-747 wake vortexes with both inboard and outboard flaps extended.

851. Maine, R. E.; and Iliff, K. W.: **A FORTRAN Program for Determining Aircraft Stability and Control Derivatives From Flight Data.** NASA TN D-7831, H-856, April 1975, 75N25621, #.

A digital computer program written in FORTRAN IV for the estimation of aircraft stability and control derivatives is presented. The program uses a maximum likelihood estimation method, and two associated programs for routine, related data handling are also included. The three programs form a package that can be used by relatively inexperienced personnel to process large amounts of data with a minimum of manpower. This package was used to successfully analyze 1500 maneuvers on 20 aircraft, and is designed to be used without modification on as many types of computers as feasible. Program listings and sample check cases are included.

852. Montoya, L. C.; and Lux, D. P.: **Comparisons of Wing Pressure Distribution From Flight Tests of Flush and External Orifices for Mach Numbers From 0.50 to 0.97.** NASA TM X-56032, April 1975, 75N22275, #.

Wing pressure distributions obtained in flight with flush orifice and external tubing orifice installations for Mach numbers from 0.50 to 0.97 are compared. The procedure used to install the external tubing orifice is discussed. The results indicate that external tubing orifice installations can give useful results.

853. Bennett, D. L.: **Evaluation of a Hemispherical Head Flow Direction Sensor for Inlet Duct Measurements.** NASA TM X-3232, H-862, May 1975, 75N22277, #.

A hemispherical head flow direction sensor was tested in a wind tunnel to evaluate its effectiveness for measuring dynamic duct flow direction angles of plus and minus 27 degrees. The tests were conducted at Reynolds numbers of 3.8 million per meter (1.0 million per foot) and 4.92 million per meter (1.5 million per foot) and at Mach numbers from 0.30 to 0.70. The design criteria for the probe are discussed and the wind tunnel results are presented. Three techniques for deriving the flow angles are described.

854. Iliff, K. W.; and Maine, R. E.: **Practical Aspects of Using a Maximum Likelihood Estimator.** AGARD CP-172. *Methods for Aircraft State and Parameter Identification*, May 1975, (see N75-29997 21-01), 75N30013.

The application of a maximum likelihood estimator to flight data is discussed and procedures to facilitate routine analysis of a large amount of flight data are proposed. Flight data were used to demonstrate the proposed procedures. Modeling considerations are discussed for the system to be identified, including linear aerodynamics, instrumentation, and data time shifts, and aerodynamic biases for the specific types of maneuvers to be analyzed. Data editing to eliminate common data acquisition problems, and a method of identifying other problems are considered. The need for careful selection of the maneuver or portions of the maneuver to be analyzed is pointed out. Uncertainty levels (analogous to Cramer-Rao bounds) are discussed as a way of recognizing significant new information.

855. Pyle, J. S.; and Steers, L. L.: **Flight Determined Lift and Drag Characteristics of an F-8 Airplane Modified With a Supercritical Wing With Comparison to Wind-Tunnel Results.** NASA TM X-3250, H-843, June 1975, 79N33159, #.

Flight measurements obtained with a TF-8A airplane modified with a supercritical wing are presented for altitudes from 7.6 kilometers (25,000 feet) to 13.7 kilometers (45,000 feet), Mach numbers from 0.6 to 1.2, and Reynolds numbers from 0.8×10 to the 7th power to 2.3×10 to the 7th power. Flight results for the airplane with and without area-rule fuselage fairings are compared. The techniques used to determine the lift and drag characteristics of the airplane are discussed. Flight data are compared with wind-tunnel model results, where applicable.

856. Hedgley, D. R., Jr.: **An Algorithm and Computer Program to Locate Real Zeros of Real Polynomials.** NASA TN D-8009, H-855, June 1975, 75N25651, #.

A method for reliably extracting real zeros of real polynomials using an expanded two-point secant and bisection method is formed into an algorithm for a digital computer, and a computer program based on this algorithm is presented. The results obtained with the program show that the proposed method compares favorably with the Laguerre, Newton-Raphson, and Jenkins-Traub methods when the polynomial has all real zeros, and is more efficient when the polynomial has complex zeros.

857. Szalai, K. J.; and Deets, D. A.: **F-8 Digital Fly-By-Wire Flight Test Results Viewed From an Active Controls Perspective.** *Impact of Active Control Technologies on Airplane Design*, June 1975, (see N75-30027 21-01), 75N30049.

The results of the NASA F-8 digital fly-by-wire flight test program are presented, along with the implications for active controls applications. The closed loop performance of the digital control system agreed well with the sampled-data system design predictions. The digital fly-by-wire mechanization also met pilot flying qualities requirements. The advantages of mechanizing the control laws in software became apparent during the flight program and were realized without sacrificing overall system reliability. This required strict software management. The F-8 flight test results are shown to be encouraging in light of the requirements that must be met by control systems for flight-critical active controls applications.

858. Kempel, R. W.; Dana, W. H.; and Sim, A. G.: **Flight Evaluation of the M2-F3 Lifting Body Handling Qualities**

at Mach Numbers From 0.30 to 1.61. NASA TN D-8027, H-852, July 1975, 75N27015, #.

Percentage distributions of 423 pilot ratings obtained from 27 flights are used to indicate the general level of handling qualities of the M2-F3 lifting body. Percentage distributions are compared on the basis of longitudinal and lateral-directional handling qualities, control system, control system status, and piloting task. Ratings of longitudinal handling qualities at low speed were slightly better than those for transonic and supersonic speed. The ratings of lateral-directional handling qualities were unaffected by speed and configuration. Specific handling qualities problems are discussed in detail, and comparisons are made with pertinent handling qualities criteria.

859. Smith, H. J.: **Flight-Determined Stability and Control Derivatives for an Executive Jet Transport.** NASA TM X-56034, H-901, July 1975, 76N11105, #.

A modified maximum likelihood estimation (MMLE) technique which included a provision for including a priori information about unknown parameters was used to determine the aerodynamic derivatives of the Lockheed JetStar airplane. Two hundred sixty-five maneuvers were performed with the JetStar airplane, which was modified to include direct lift controls, to obtain lateral-directional and longitudinal derivatives. Data were obtained at altitudes of 3048 meters, 6096 meters, and 9144 meters (10,000 feet, 20,000 feet, and 30,000 feet) and over an angle of attack range from approximately 3 deg to 13 deg and a Mach number range from 0.25 to 0.75. Side force generators were installed and tested in 87 maneuvers to determine their effectiveness and their effect on the other derivatives. Lateral-directional data for four flight conditions were analyzed without using a priori information to assess the effect of this feature on the results. The MMLE method generally gave consistent (repeatable) estimates of the derivatives, with the exception of the rolling moment due to yaw rate, which showed large variances.

860. Steers, L. L.; Montoya, L. C.; and Saltzman, E. J.: **Aerodynamic Drag Reduction Tests on a Full-Scale Tractor-Trailer Combination and a Representative Box-Shaped Ground Vehicle.** SAE Paper 750703, presented at the Society of Automotive Engineers, West Coast Meeting, Seattle, Washington, August 11–14, 1975, 76A14479.

Aerodynamic drag tests were performed on a tractor-trailer combination and a box-shaped ground vehicle using the coast-down method on a smooth, nearly level runway. The tractor-trailer tests included an investigation of drag reduction add-on devices that are commercially available or under development. The box-shaped vehicle was modified by rounding the corners and sealing the undercarriage. The tests ranged in velocity from approximately 35 miles per hour to 65 miles per hour for the tractor-trailer combination and included fuel consumption measurements and one set of measurements of drive shaft torque. This paper presents the results for both vehicles, showing the effects of the various modifications on the aerodynamic drag. The effects of variation in the aerodynamic drag of the tractor-trailer combination on fuel consumption are also presented.

861. Arnaiz, H. H.: **Techniques for Determining Propulsion System Forces for Accurate High Speed Vehicle Drag Measurements in Flight.** AIAA Paper 75-964, presented at the AIAA Aircraft Systems and Technology Meeting, Los Angeles, California, August 4–7, 1975, 75A41689, #.

As part of a NASA program to evaluate current methods of predicting the performance of large, supersonic airplanes, the drag of the XB-70 airplane was measured accurately in flight at Mach numbers from 0.75 to 2.5. This paper describes the techniques used to determine engine net thrust and the drag forces charged to the propulsion system that were required for the in-flight drag measurements. The accuracy of the measurements and the application of the measurement techniques to aircraft with different propulsion systems are discussed. Examples of results obtained for the XB-70 airplane are presented.

862. Putnam, T. W.: **Review of Aircraft Noise Propagation.** NASA TM X-56033, September 1975, 75N32119, #.

The current state of knowledge about the propagation of aircraft noise was reviewed. The literature on the subject is surveyed and methods for predicting the most important and best understood propagation effects are presented. Available empirical data are examined and the data's general validity is assessed. The methods used to determine the loss of acoustic energy due to uniform spherical spreading, absorption in a homogeneous atmosphere, and absorption due to ground cover are presented. A procedure for determining ground induced absorption as a function of elevation angle between source and receiver is recommended. Other factors that affect propagation, such as refraction and scattering due to turbulence, which were found to be less important for predicting the propagation of aircraft noise, are also evaluated.

863. Shafer, M. F.: **Stability and Control Derivatives of the T-37B Airplane.** NASA TM X-56036, September 1975, 76N14137, #.

Subsonic stability and control derivatives were determined by a modified maximum likelihood estimator from flight data for the longitudinal and lateral-directional modes of the T-37B airplane. Data from two flights, in which 166 stability and control maneuvers were performed, were used in the determination. The configurations investigated were: zero flaps, gear up; half flaps, gear up; full flaps, gear up; and zero flaps, gear down.

864. Reukauf, P. J.; Burcham, F. W., Jr.; and Holzman, J. K.: **Status of a Digital Integrated Propulsion/Flight Control System for the YF-12 Airplane.** AIAA Paper 75-1180, presented at the AIAA Institute of Aeronautics and Astronautics and Society of Automotive Engineers, Eleventh Annual Propulsion Conference, Anaheim, California, September 29–October 1, 1975, 76A10252, #.

The NASA Flight Research Center is engaged in a program with the YF-12 airplane to study the control of interactions between the airplane and the propulsion system. The existing analog air data computer, autothrottle, autopilot, and inlet control system are to be converted to digital systems by using a general purpose airborne computer and interface unit. First, the existing control laws will be programmed in the digital computer and flight tested. Then new control laws are to be derived from a dynamic propulsion model and a total force and moment aerodynamic model to integrate the systems. These control laws are to be verified in a real time simulation and flight tested.

865. Garodz, L. J.: **Flight Test Investigation of the Vortex Wake Characteristics Behind a Boeing 727 During Two-Segment and Normal ILS Approaches.** NASA TM X-72908, FAA-NA-75-151, AD-A018366. Joint study with National Aviation Facilities Experimental Center, Atlantic City, New Jersey, October 1975, 76N14046, #.

A series of flight tests were performed to evaluate the vortex wake characteristics of a Boeing 727 (B727-200) aircraft during conventional and two-segment ILS approaches. Flights of the B727, equipped with smoke generators for vortex marking, were flown wherein its vortex wake was intentionally encountered by a Lear Jet model 23 (LR-23) or a Piper Twin Comanche (PA-30); and its vortex location during landing approach was measured using a system of

ECN-3831

B-727 Airplane With Wingtip Smoke Generators

photo-theodolites. The tests showed that at a given separation distance there were no differences in the upsets resulting from deliberate vortex encounters during the two types of approaches. Timed mappings of the position of the landing configuration vortices showed that they tended to descend approximately 91 meters (300 feet) below the flight path of the B727. The flaps of the B727 have a dominant effect on the character of the trailed wake vortex. The clean wing produces a strong, concentrated vortex. As the flaps are lowered, the vortex system becomes more diffuse. Pilot opinion and roll acceleration data indicate that 4.5 nautical miles would be a minimum separation distance at which roll control could be maintained during parallel encounters of the B727's landing configuration wake by small aircraft.

866. Burcham, F. W., Jr.; Putnam, T. W.; Lasagna, P. L.; and Parish, O. O.: **Measured Noise Reductions Resulting From Modified Approach Procedures for Business Jet Aircraft.** NASA TM X-56037, November 1975, 76N32973, #.

Five business jet airplanes were flown to determine the noise reductions that result from the use of modified approach procedures. The airplanes tested were a Gulfstream 2, JetStar, Hawker Siddeley 125-400, Sabreliner-60 and LearJet-24. Noise measurements were made 3, 5, and 7 nautical miles from the touchdown point. In addition to a standard 3 deg glide slope approach, a 4 deg glide slope approach, a 3 deg glide slope approach in a low-drag configuration, and a two-segment approach were flown. It was found that the 4 deg approach was about 4 EPNdB quieter than the standard 3 deg approach. Noise reductions for the low-drag 3 deg approach varied widely among the airplanes tested, with an average of 8.5 EPNdB on a fleet-weighted basis. The two-segment approach resulted in noise reductions of 7 to 8 EPNdB at 3 and 5 nautical miles from touchdown, but only 3 EPNdB at 7 nautical miles from touchdown when the airplanes were still in level flight prior to glide slope intercept. Pilot ratings showed progressively increasing workload for the 4 deg, low-drag 3 deg, and two-segment approaches.

867. Gee, S. W.; Wolf, T. D.; and Rezek, T. W.: **Passenger Ride Quality Response to an Airborne Simulator Environment.** NASA TM X-3295, DOT-TSC-OST-75-40. *The 1975 Ride Quality Symposium,* November 1975, pp. 373–385, (see N76-16754 07-53), 76N16770.

The present study was done aboard a special aircraft able to effect translations through the center of gravity with a minimum of pitch and roll. The aircraft was driven through controlled motions by an on-board analog computer. The input signal was selectively filtered Gaussian noise whose power spectra approximated that of natural turbulence. This input, combined with the maneuvering capabilities of this aircraft, resulted in an extremely realistic simulation of turbulent flight. The test flights also included varying bank angles during turns. Subjects were chosen from among NASA Flight Research Center personnel. They were all volunteers, were given physical examinations, and were queried about their attitudes toward flying before final selection. In profile, they were representative of the general flying public. Data from this study include (1) a basis for comparison with previous commercial flights, that is, motion dominated by vertical acceleration, (2) extension to motion dominated by lateral acceleration, and (3) evaluation of various bank angles.

868. Kordes, E. E.; and *Curtis, A. R.: **Results of NASTRAN Modal Analyses and Ground Vibration Tests on the YF-12A Airplane.** ASME Paper 75-WA/AERO-8, presented at the American Society of Mechanical Engineers, Winter Annual Meeting, Houston, Texas, November 30–December 4, 1975, 76A21855, #.

The YF-12A aircraft, a delta-winged vehicle powered by two jet engines, was utilized in an investigation of the structural dynamic characteristics of a large, flexible, supersonic research vehicle. A large NASA structural analysis (NASTRAN) finite-element model was used to compute the ten lowest frequency symmetric and ten lowest frequency antisymmetric modes for the YF-12A aircraft. The results of the analysis were compared with experimental data obtained in a ground vibration test conducted with the completed aircraft. It was found that the finite-element structural model employed provides an adequate prediction of the dynamic behavior of the aircraft structure in the case of basic wing and body modes.

*Lockheed-California Co., Burbank, California.

869. Manke, J. A.; and *Love, M. V.: **X-24B Flight Test Program.** Presented at the Nineteenth Society of Experimental Test Pilots Symposium, Beverly Hills, California, September 24–27, 1975, *Society of Experimental Test Pilots, Technical Review,* Vol. 12, No. 4, 1975, pp. 129–154, 76A18659.

The X-24B is an air launched, rocket powered research aircraft. A number of its design features constitute a tradeoff between aerodynamics and heating considerations. A vehicle description is given and test program objectives are discussed along with operational procedures and aspects of energy management. Attention is also given to X-24B handling qualities, approach and landing, wind tunnel data and simulation, and proposed X-24C vehicle requirements.

*USAF, Edwards AFB, California.

X-24B Lifting Body

EC75-4642

870. *Hoffman, E. L.; **Payne, L.; and Carter, A. L.: **Fabrication Methods for YF-12 Wing Panels for the Supersonic Cruise Aircraft Research Program.** *Materials Review '75, Proceedings of the Seventh National Technical Conference,* Albuquerque, New Mexico, October 14–16, 1975, pp. 68–82, 76A15157.

Advanced fabrication and joining processes for titanium and composite materials are being investigated by NASA to develop technology for the Supersonic Cruise Aircraft Research (SCAR) Program. With Lockheed-ADP as the prime contractor, full-scale structural panels are being designed and fabricated to replace an existing integrally stiffened shear panel on the upper wing surface of the NASA YF-12 aircraft. The program involves ground testing and Mach 3 flight testing of full-scale structural panels and laboratory testing of representative structural element specimens. Fabrication methods and test results for weldbrazed and Rohrbond titanium panels are discussed. The fabrication methods being developed for boron/aluminum, Borsic/aluminum, and graphite/polyimide panels are also presented.

*NASA Langley Research Center, Hampton, Virginia.
**Lockheed-California Co., Sunland, California.

871. Saltzman, E. J.: **Use of a Pitot Probe for Determining Wing Section Drag in Flight.** NASA CR-145627. *Kansas University Proceedings of the NASA, Industry, University, General Aviation Drag Reduction Workshop,* 1975, pp. 171–189, (see N76-10997 02-01), 76N11010.

A wake traversing probe was used to obtain section drag and wake profile data from the wing of a sailplane. The transducer sensed total pressure defect in the wake as well as freestream total pressure on both sides of the sensing element when the probe moved beyond the wake. Profiles of wake total pressure defects plotted as a function of distance above and below the trailing edge plane were averaged for calculating section drag coefficients for flights at low dynamic pressures.

PIK-20E Sailplane

EC91-504-1

872. Iliff, Kenneth W.: **An Airplane Application of System Identification in the Presence of State Noise.** *New Directions in Signal Processing in Communications and Control,* NATO Advanced Study Institutes Series, Series E: Applied Sciences - No. 12, 1975. (See also 815.)

A maximum likelihood estimator for a linear system with state and observation noise is developed to determine unknown aircraft coefficients from flight data in the presence of turbulence (state noise). The formulation of the algorithm is presented briefly. The linear equations for an aircraft in atmospheric turbulence are defined. The effectiveness and accuracy of the technique are assessed by first applying it to simulated flight data, in which the true parameter values are known, then the actual flight data obtained in turbulence. A complete set of aircraft coefficients is obtained as well as an estimate of the turbulence time history. The validity of the estimated state noise and of the estimated coefficients is tested. The feasibility of using the algorithm for defining an adaptive control law to alleviate the effects of turbulence on the aircraft is discussed.

1976 Technical Publications

873. *Jacobsen, R. T.; *Stewart, R. B.; **Crain, R. W., Jr.; †Rose, G. L.; and Myers, A. F.: **A Method for the Selection of a Functional Form for a Thermodynamic Equation of State Using Weighted Linear Least Squares Stepwise Regression.** *Proceedings, Cryogenic Engineering Conference,* Kingston, Ontario, Canada, July 22–25, 1975, pp. 532–537, Plenum Press, New York, New York, 1976, 77A42171.

A method was developed for establishing a rational choice of the terms to be included in an equation of state with a large number of adjustable coefficients. The methods presented were developed for use in the determination of an equation of state for oxygen and nitrogen. However, a general application of the methods is possible in studies involving the determination of an optimum polynomial equation for fitting a large number of data points. The data considered in the least squares problem are experimental thermodynamic pressure-density-temperature data. Attention is given to a description of stepwise multiple regression and the use of stepwise regression in the determination of an equation of state for oxygen and nitrogen.

*University of Idaho, Moscow, Idaho.
**Washington State University, Pullman, Washington.
†McKellip Engineering, Inc., Boise, Idaho.

874. Edwards, J. W.: **A FORTRAN Program for the Analysis of Linear Continuous and Sample-Data Systems.** NASA TM X-56038, January 1976, 76N18823, #.

A FORTRAN digital computer program which performs the general analysis of linearized control systems is described. State variable techniques are used to analyze continuous, discrete, and sampled data systems. Analysis options include the calculation of system eigenvalues, transfer functions, root loci, root contours, frequency responses, power spectra, and transient responses for open- and closed-loop systems. A flexible data input format allows the user to define systems in a variety of representations. Data may be entered by inputting explicit data matrices or matrices constructed in user written subroutines, by specifying transfer function block diagrams, or by using a combination of these methods.

875. Holleman, E. C.: **Summary of Flight Tests to Determine the Spin and Controllability Characteristics of a Remotely Piloted, Large-Scale (3/8) Fighter Airplane Model.** NASA TN D-8052, H-889, January 1976, 76N17156, #.

An unpowered, large, dynamically scaled airplane model was test flown by remote pilot to investigate the stability and controllability of the configuration at high angles of attack. The configuration proved to be departure/spin resistant; however, spins were obtained by using techniques developed on a flight support simulator. Spin modes at high and medium high angles of attack were identified, and recovery techniques were investigated. A flight support simulation of the airplane model mechanized with low speed wind tunnel data over an angle of attack range of ± 90 deg. and an angle of sideslip range of ± 40 deg. provided insight into the effects of altitude, stability, aerodynamic damping, and the operation of the augmented flight control system on spins. Aerodynamic derivatives determined from flight maneuvers were used to correlate model controllability with two proposed departure/spin design criteria.

876. Iliff, K. W.; Maine, R. E.; and Shafer, M. F.: **Subsonic Stability and Control Derivatives for an Unpowered, Remotely Piloted 3/8-Scale F-15 Airplane Model Obtained From Flight Test.** NASA TN D-8136, H-905, January 1976, 76N15176, #.

In response to the interest in airplane configuration characteristics at high angles of attack, an unpowered remotely piloted 3/8-scale F-15 airplane model was flight tested. The subsonic stability and control characteristics of this airplane model over an angle of attack range of –20 to 53 deg are documented. The remotely piloted technique for obtaining flight test data was found to provide adequate stability and control derivatives. The remotely piloted technique provided an opportunity to test the aircraft mathematical model in an angle of attack regime not previously examined in flight test. The variation of most of the derivative estimates with angle of attack was found to be consistent, particularly when the data were supplemented by uncertainty levels.

877. White, K. C.; Lasagna, P. L.; and Putnam, T. W.: **Preliminary Measurements of Aircraft Airframe Noise With the NASA CV-990 Aircraft.** NASA TM X-73116, A-6506, January 1976, 76N26145, #.

Flight tests were conducted in a CV-990 jet transport with engines at idle power to investigate aircraft airframe noise. Test results showed that airframe noise was measured for the aircraft in the landing configuration. The results agreed well with the expected variation with the fifth power of velocity. For the aircraft in the clean configuration, it was concluded that airframe noise was measured only at higher airspeeds with engine idle noise present at lower speeds. The data show that landing gear and flaps make a significant contribution to airframe noise.

878. Hedgley, D. R., Jr.: **An Exact Transformation From Geocentric to Geodetic Coordinates for Nonzero Altitudes.** NASA TR R-458, H-909, March 1976, 76N19836, #.

An exact method for the nonzero altitude transformation from geocentric to geodetic coordinates is derived. The method is mathematically general and should serve as a primary standard.

879. Albers, J. A.: **Status of the NASA YF-12 Propulsion Research Program.** NASA TM X-56039, H-935, March 1976, 76N19152, #.

The YF-12 research program was initiated to establish a technology base for the design of an efficient propulsion system for supersonic cruise aircraft. The major technology areas under investigation in this program are inlet design analysis, propulsion system steady-state performance, propulsion system dynamic performance, inlet and engine control systems, and airframe/propulsion system interactions. The objectives, technical approach, and status of the YF-12 propulsion program are discussed. Also discussed are the results obtained to date by the NASA Ames, Lewis, and Dryden research centers. The expected technical results and proposed future programs are also given. Propulsion system configurations are shown.

880. Sim, Alex G.: **A Correlation Between Flight Determined Derivatives and Wind-Tunnel Data for the X-24B Research Aircraft.** NASA TM SX-3371, March 1976, (republished as NASA TM-113084, August 1997).

Longitudinal and lateral-directional estimates of the aerodynamic derivatives of the X-24B research aircraft were obtained from flight by using a modified maximum likelihood estimation method. Data were obtained over a mach number range from 0.35 to 1.72 and over an angle of attack range from 3.5° to 15.7°. Data are presented for a subsonic and transonic configuration. The flight derivatives were generally consistent and documented the aircraft well. The correlation between flight data and the wind-tunnel predictions is presented and discussed.

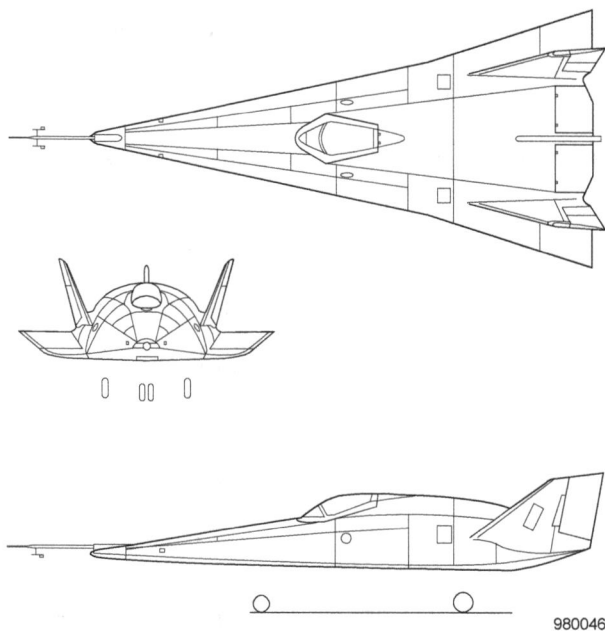

980046

X-24B Lifting Body, Three-View Drawing

881. Iliff, K. W.; and Maine, R. E.: **Practical Aspects of a Maximum Likelihood Estimation Method to Extract Stability and Control Derivatives From Flight Data.** NASA TN D-8209, H-908, April 1976, 76N23272, #.

A maximum likelihood estimation method was applied to flight data and procedures to facilitate the routine analysis of a large amount of flight data were described. Techniques that can be used to obtain stability and control derivatives from aircraft maneuvers that are less than ideal for this purpose are described. The techniques involve detecting and correcting the effects of dependent or nearly dependent variables, structural vibration, data drift, inadequate instrumentation, and difficulties with the data acquisition system and the mathematical model. The use of uncertainty levels and multiple maneuver analysis also proved to be useful in improving the quality of the estimated coefficients. The

procedures used for editing the data and for overall analysis are also discussed.

882. Petersen, K. L.: **Evaluation of an Envelope-Limiting Device Using Simulation and Flight Test of a Remotely Piloted Research Vehicle.** NASA TN D-8216, H-914, April 1976, 76N21218, #.

The operating characteristics of a nonlinear envelope-limiting device were investigated at extreme flight conditions by using a real time digital aircraft spin simulation and flight tests of a scale model remotely piloted research vehicle. A digital mechanization of the F-15 control system, including the stall inhibiter, was used in the simulation and in the control system of the scale model. The operational characteristics of the stall inhibiter and the effects of the stall inhibiter on the spin susceptibility of the airplane were investigated.

883. Kurkowski, R. L.; Barber, M. R.; and Garodz, L. J.: **Characteristics of Wake Vortex Generated by a Boeing 727 Jet Transport During Two-Segment and Normal ILS Approach Flight Paths.** NASA TN D-8222, A-6208, April 1976, 76N21175, #.

A series of flight tests was conducted to evaluate the vortex wake characteristics of a Boeing 727 (B727-200) aircraft during conventional and two-segment ILS approaches. Twelve flights of the B727, which was equipped with smoke generators for vortex marking, were flown and its vortex wake was intentionally encountered by a Lear Jet model 23 (LR-23) and a Piper Twin Comanche (PA-30). Location of the B727 vortex during landing approach was measured using a system of photo-theodolites. The tests showed that at a given separation distance there were no readily apparent differences in the upsets resulting from deliberate vortex position of the landing configuration vortices showed that they tended to descend approximately 91 m (300 ft) below the flight path of the B727. The flaps of the B727 have a dominant effect on the character of the trailed wake vortex. The clean wing produces a strong, concentrated vortex but as the flaps are lowered, the vortex system becomes more diffuse. Pilot opinion and roll acceleration data indicate that 4.5 nmi would be a minimum separation distance at which roll control of light aircraft (less than 5,670 kg (12,500 lb) could be maintained during parallel encounters of the B727's landing configuration wake. This minimum separation distance is generally in scale with results determined from previous tests of other aircraft using the small roll control criteria.

884. Putnam, T. W.; and Burcham, F. W.: **Business Jet Approach Noise Abatement Techniques—Flight Test Results.** SAE Paper 760463, presented at the Society of Automotive Engineers, Business Aircraft Meeting, Wichita, Kansas, April 6, 1976, 76A31961.

Operational techniques for reducing approach noise from business jet aircraft were evaluated in flight by measuring the noise generated by five such aircraft during modified approaches. Approaches with 4-deg glide slopes were approximately 4.0 EPNdB quieter than approaches with standard 3-deg glide slopes. Noise reductions for low-drag 3-deg approaches varied widely among the airplanes tested; the fleet-weighted reduction was 8.5 EPNdB. Two-segment approaches resulted in noise reductions of 7.0 EPNdB to 8.5 EPNdB 3 nautical miles and 5 nautical miles from touchdown. Pilot workload increased progressively for the 4-deg, low-drag 3-deg, and two-segment approach.

885. *Lockenour, J. L.; and Layton, G. P.: **RPRV Research Focus on HiMAT.** *Astronautics and Aeronautics*, Vol. 14, April 1976, pp. 36–41, 76A25721, #.

A review is presented of the F-15 Remotely Piloted Research Vehicle (RPRV) project. The F-15 RPRV is air-launched from a B-52 at 50,000 ft. Following launch a series of research maneuvers are performed during an unpowered descent to a recovery altitude. Another RPRV program considered is the Highly Maneuverable Aircraft Technology (HiMAT) program. This program is designed to use RPRVs to speed the technology transition from wind tunnel to flight and to reduce the cost of aeronautical experiments. It is pointed out that HiMAT will make extensive use of composite materials.

*USAF, Flight Dynamics Laboratory, Wright-Patterson AFB, Ohio.

886. Layton, G. P.: **A New Experimental Flight Research Technique: The Remotely Piloted Airplane.** AGARD CP-187. *Flight/Ground Testing Facilities Correlation*, April 1976, (see N76-25266 16-09), 76N25287.

The results obtained so far with a remotely piloted research vehicle (RPRV) using a 3/8 scale model of an F-15 airplane, to determine the usefulness of the RPRV testing technique in high risk flight testing, including spin testing, were presented. The program showed that the RPRV technique, including the use of a digital control system, is a practical method for obtaining flight research data. The spin, stability, and control data obtained with the 3/8-scale model also showed that predictions based on wind-tunnel tests were generally reasonable.

887. Gee, Shu W.: **Model Aircraft Technology Applications at NASA.** *R/C Modeler Magazine*, April 1976.

888. Montoya, Earl J.: **Aeronautics.** Presented at NASA Symposium on Aeronautics and Space Technology, New Mexico State University, Las Cruces, New Mexico, April 21–23, 1976.

This paper compares the NASA organization to the National Football League and the importance to both of training.

889. Sakamoto, G. M.: **Aerodynamic Characteristics of a Vane Flow Angularity Sensor System Capable of Measuring Flight Path Accelerations for the Mach Number Range From 0.40 to 2.54.** NASA TN D-8242, H-900, May 1976, 76N23257, #.

The aerodynamic characteristics of the angle of attack vane and the angle of sideslip vane are summarized. The test conditions ranged in free stream Mach number from 0.40 to 2.54, in angle of attack from –2 deg to 22 deg, in angle of sideslip from –2 deg to 12 deg, and in Reynolds number from 590,000 per meter to 1.8 million per meter. The results of the wind tunnel investigation are compared with results obtained with similar vane configurations. Comparisons with a NACA vane configuration are also made. In addition, wind tunnel-derived upwash for the test installation is compared with analytical predictions.

890. *Gillingham, K. K.; and Winter, W. R.: **Physiologic and Anti-G Suit Performance Data From YF-16 Flight Tests.** *Aviation, Space, and Environmental Medicine*, Vol. 47, June 1976, pp. 672–673, 76A37075.

Biomedical data were collected during high-G portions of 11–16 test flights. Test pilots monitored revealed increased respiratory rate and volume, decreased tidal volume, and increased heart rate at higher G levels, with one pilot exhibiting various cardiac arrhythmias. Anti-G suit inflation and pressurization lags varied inversely with G-onset rate, and suit pressurization slope was near the design value.

*USAF, School of Aerospace Medicine, Brooks AFB, Texas.

891. Iliff, K. W.: **Maximum Likelihood Estimates of Lift and Drag Characteristics Obtained From Dynamic Aircraft Maneuvers.** *Proceedings, 3rd AIAA Atmospheric Flight Mechanics Conference*, Arlington, Texas, June 7–9, 1976, pp. 137–150, (see A76-36901 17-08), 76A36916, #.

A maximum likelihood estimation method for obtaining lift and drag characteristics from dynamic flight maneuvers was investigated. This paper describes the method and compares the estimates of lift and drag obtained by using the method with estimates obtained from wind-tunnel tests and from established methods for obtaining estimates from flight data. In general, the lift and drag coefficients extracted from dynamic flight maneuvers by the maximum likelihood estimation technique are in good agreement with the estimates obtained from the wind-tunnel tests and the other methods. When maneuvers that met the requirements of both flight methods were analyzed, the results of each method were nearly the same. The maximum likelihood estimation technique showed promise in terms of estimating lift and drag characteristics from dynamic flight maneuvers. Further studies should be made to assess the best mathematical model and the most desirable type of dynamic maneuver to get the highest quality results from this technique.

892. Petersen, K. L.: **Remotely Piloted Research Vehicle Evaluation of Advanced Control System Effects on Spins.** *Proceedings, 3rd AIAA Atmospheric Flight Mechanics Conference*, Arlington, Texas, June 7–9, 1976, pp. 55–64, (see A76-36901 17-08), 76A36907, #.

Special functions of an advanced control system were investigated for effects on spin entries and recoveries utilizing a 3/8-scale model of the F-15 airplane as a remotely piloted research vehicle (RPRV). Telemetry uplinks and downlinks were used with a ground-based digital computer to mechanize the RPRV control system for spin tests in flight. Results from the model RPRV flight tests and from a real time digital spin simulation were used to evaluate the F-15 stall inhibiter and an automatic spin recovery system developed for the RPRV model.

893. Iliff, K. W.: **Estimation of Characteristics and Stochastic Control of an Aircraft Flying in Atmospheric Turbulence.** *Proceedings, 3rd AIAA Atmospheric Flight Mechanics Conference*, Arlington, Texas, June 7–9, 1976, pp. 26–38, (see A76-36901 17-08), 76A36905, #.

An adaptive control technique to improve the flying qualities of an aircraft in turbulence was investigated. The approach taken was to obtain maximum likelihood estimates of the unknown coefficients of the aircraft system and then, using these estimates along with the separation principle, to define the stochastic optimal control. The maximum likelihood estimation technique that accounted for the effects of turbulence provided good estimates of the unknown coefficients and of the turbulence. The assessment of the stochastic optimal control based on the maximum likelihood estimates showed that the desired effects were attained for the regulator problem of minimizing pitch angle and the tracking problem of requiring normal acceleration to follow the pilot input.

894. Burcham, F. W., Jr.; and *Batterton, P. G.: **Flight Experience With a Digital Integrated Propulsion Control System on an F-111E Airplane.** AIAA Paper 76-653, presented at 12th AIAA and SAE Annual Propulsion Conference, Palo Alto, California, July 26–29, 1976, 76A42411, #.

A digital integrated propulsion control system (IPCS) installed in the left side of an F-111 E aircraft was tested in flight. The F-111 aircraft was selected for the IPCS program because it incorporated a variable geometry inlet and an afterburning turbofan engine and had two engines, one of which could remain in the normal configuration to ensure flight safety. Flight data were compared with results of tests run in an altitude test chamber. The digital system was found

to be capable of duplicating the standard engine and inlet control systems. Instabilities such as inlet buzz and afterburner rumble were detected and controlled. The usefulness of an altitude chamber for developing a software and testing hardware was proven. The flexibility of IPCS was demonstrated when an autothrottle, an in-flight thrust calculation, and a coannular noise study capability were added at the end of the flight tests.

*NASA Lewis Research Center, Cleveland, Ohio.

F-111E IPCS Airplane ECN-4359

895. *Hersh, A. S.; Putnam, T. W.; Lasagna, P. L.; and Burcham, F. W., Jr.: **Semi-Empirical Airframe Noise Prediction Model.** AIAA Paper 76-527, presented at 3rd AIAA Annual Aero-Acoustics Conference, Palo Alto, California, July 20–23, 1976, (see also NASA TM-56041.) 76A38052, #. (See also 912.)

A semi-empirical maximum overall sound pressure level (OASPL) airframe noise model was derived. The noise radiated from aircraft wings and flaps was modeled by using the trailing-edge diffracted quadrupole sound theory derived by Ffowcs Williams and Hall. The noise radiated from the landing gear was modeled by using the acoustic dipole sound theory derived by Curle. The model was successfully correlated with maximum OASPL flyover noise measurements obtained at the NASA Dryden Flight Research Center for three jet aircraft—the Lockheed JetStar, the Convair 990, and the Boeing 747 aircraft.

*Hersh Acoustical Engineering, Chatsworth, California.

896. Anon.: **Advanced Control Technology and Its Potential for Future Transport Aircraft.** NASA TM X-3409, H-904. Presented at a Symposium on Adv. Control Technol., Los Angeles, California, July 9–11, 1974, August 1976, 76N31135, #.

897. *Lange, R. H.; and Deets, D. A.: **Study of an ACT Demonstrator With Substantial Performance Improvements Using a Redesigned JetStar.** NASA TM X-3409. *NASA Dryden Flight Research Center Advanced Control Technol. and Its Potential for Future Transport*

152

Aircraft, <u>August 1976</u>, pp. 3–35, (see N76-31135 22-01), 76N31159.

The feasibility was studied of modifying a JetStar airplane into a demonstrator of benefits to be achieved from incorporating active control concepts in the preliminary design of transport type aircraft. Substantial benefits are shown in terms of fuel economy and community noise by virtue of reduction in induced drag through use of a high aspect ratio wing which is made possible by a gust alleviation system. An intermediate configuration was defined which helps to isolate the benefits produced by active controls technology from those due to other configuration variables.

*Lockheed-Georgia Company, Marietta, Georgia.

898. Jarvis, C. R.: **An Overview of NASA's Digital Fly-By-Wire Technology Development Program**. NASA TM X-3409. *NASA Dryden Flight Research Center Advanced Control Technol. and Its Potential for Future Transport Aircraft*, <u>August 1976</u>, pp. 93–103, (see N76-31135 22-01), 76N31140. (See also 839.)

The feasibility of using digital fly by wire systems to control aircraft was demonstrated by developing and flight testing a single channel system, which used Apollo hardware, in an F-8C test airplane. This is the first airplane to fly with a digital fly by wire system as its primary means of control and with no mechanical reversion capability. The development and flight test of a triplex digital fly by wire system, which will serve as an experimental prototype for future operational digital fly by wire systems, are underway.

899. Deets, D. A.: **Design and Development Experience With a Digital Fly-By-Wire Control System in an F-8C Airplane**. NASA TM X-3409. *NASA Dryden Flight Research Center Advanced Control Technol. and Its Potential for Future Transport Aircraft*, <u>August 1976</u>, pp. 105–132, (see N76-31135 22-01), 76N31141. (See also 840.)

To assess the feasibility of a digital fly by wire system, the mechanical flight control system of an F-8C airplane was replaced with a digital primary system and an analog backup system. The Apollo computer was used as the heart of the primary system. This paper discusses the experience gained during the design and development of the system and relates it to active control systems that are anticipated for future civil transport applications.

900. Lock, W. P.; Petersen, W. R.; and *Whitman, G. B.: **Mechanization of and Experience With a Triplex Fly-By-Wire Backup Control System**. NASA TM X-3409. *NASA Dryden Flight Research Center Advanced Control Technol. and Its Potential for Future Transport Aircraft*, <u>August 1976</u>, pp. 133–163, (see N76-31135 22-01), 76N31142. (See also 841.)

A redundant three axis analog control system was designed and developed to back up a digital fly by wire control system for an F-8C airplane. The mechanization and operational experience with the backup control system, the problems involved in synchronizing it with the primary system, and the reliability of the system are discussed. The backup control system was dissimilar to the primary system, and it provided satisfactory handling through the flight envelope evaluated. Limited flight tests of a variety of control tasks showed that control was also satisfactory when the backup control system was controlled by a minimum displacement (force) side stick. The operational reliability of the F-8 digital fly by wire control system was satisfactory, with no unintentional downmodes to the backup control system in flight. The ground and flight reliability of the system's components is discussed.

*Sperry Flight Systems Div., Phoenix, Arizona.

901. Szalai, K. J.: **Flight Test Experience With the F-8 Digital Fly-By-Wire System**. NASA TM X-3409. *NASA Dryden Flight Research Center Advanced Control Technology and Its Potential for Future Transport Aircraft*, <u>August 1976</u>, pp. 199–252, (see N76-31135 22-01), 76N31144. (See also 843.)

Flight test results of the F-8 digital fly by wire control system are presented and the implications for application to active control technology are discussed. The F-8 DFBW system has several of the attributes of proposed ACT systems, so the flight test experience is helpful in assessing the capabilities of those systems. Topics of discussion include the predicted and actual flight performance of the control system, assessments of aircraft flying qualities and other piloting factors, software management and control, and operational experience.

902. Krier, G. E.: **A Pilot's Opinion of the F-8 Digital Fly-By-Wire Airplane**. NASA TM X-3409. *NASA Dryden Flight Research Center Advanced Control Technol. and Its Potential for Future Transport Aircraft*, <u>August 1976</u>, pp. 253–267, (see N76-31135 22-01), 76N31145. (See also 844.)

The handling qualities of the F-8 digital fly by wire airplane are evaluated by using the Cooper-Harper rating scale. The reasons for the ratings are given, as well as a short description of the flying tasks. It was concluded that the handling qualities of the airplane were good in most situations, although occasional ratings of unsatisfactory were given.

903. Berry, D. T.; and Schweikhard, W. G.: **Potential Benefits of Propulsion and Flight Control Integration for Supersonic Cruise Vehicles**. NASA TM X-3409. *NASA Dryden Flight Research Center Advanced Control Technol. and Its Potential for Future Transport Aircraft*, <u>August 1976</u>, pp. 433–452, (see N76-31135 22-01), 76N31152.

Typical airframe/propulsion interactions such as Mach/altitude excursions and inlet unstarts are reviewed. The improvements in airplane performance and flight control that can be achieved by improving the interfaces between propulsion and flight control are estimated. A research program to determine the feasibility of integrating propulsion and flight control is described. This program includes analytical studies and YF-12 flight tests.

904. Anon.: **The ACT Transport: Panacea for the 80's Or Designer's Illusion (Panel Discussion).** NASA TM X-3409. *NASA Dryden Flight Research Center Advanced Control Technol. and Its Potential for Future Transport Aircraft,* August 1976, pp. 805–827, (see N76-31135 22-01), 76N31169.

A panel discussion was held which attempted to make an objective and pragmatic assessment of the standing of active control technology. The discussion focused on the standing of active control technology relative to civil air transport applications, the value as opposed to the cost of the projected benefits, the need for research, development, and demonstration, the role of government and industry in developing the technology, the major obstacles to its implementation, and the probable timing of the full utilization of active control technology in commercial transportation. An edited transcription of the prepared statements of the panel members and the subsequent open discussion between the panel and the audience is presented.

905. *Plumer, J. A.; **Malloy, W. A.; and Craft, J. B.: **The Effects of Lightning on Digital Flight Control Systems.** NASA TM X-3409. *NASA Dryden Flight Research Center Advanced Control Technol. and Its Potential for Future Transport Aircraft,* August 1976, pp. 989–1008, (see N76-31135 22-01), 76N31176. (See also 842.)

Present practices in lightning protection of aircraft deal primarily with the direct effects of lightning, such as structural damage and ignition of fuel vapors. There is increasing evidence of troublesome electromagnetic effects, however, in aircraft employing solid-state microelectronics in critical navigation, instrumentation and control functions. The potential impact of these indirect effects on critical systems such as digital fly by wire (DFBW) flight controls was studied. The results indicate a need for positive steps to be taken during the design of future fly by wire systems to minimize the possibility of hazardous effects from lightning.

*General Electric, Corporate Research and Development, Schenectady, New York.
**General Motors Corporation, Detroit, Michigan.

906. Szalai, K. J.; *Felleman, P. G.; **Gera, J.; and †Glover, R. D.: **Design and Test Experience With a Triply Redundant Digital Fly-By-Wire Control System.** AIAA Paper 76-1911. *Proceedings, Guidance and Control Conference,* San Diego, California, August 16–18, 1976, 76A41491, #.

A triplex digital fly-by-wire flight control system was developed and then installed in a NASA F-8C aircraft to provide fail-operative, full authority control. Hardware and software redundancy management techniques were designed to detect and identify failures in the system. Control functions typical of those projected for future actively controlled vehicles were implemented. This paper describes the principal design features of the system, the implementation of computer, sensor, and actuator redundancy management, and the ground test results. An automated test program to verify sensor redundancy management software is also described.

*Draper Laboratory, Incorporated, Cambridge, Massachusetts.
**NASA Langley Research Center, Hampton, Virginia.
†NASA Johnson Space Center, Houston, Texas.

907. Gee, S. W.; *Jenks, G. E.; *Roskam, J.; and **Stone, R. L.: **Flight Test Evaluation of a Separate Surface Attitude Command Control System on a Beech 99 Airplane.** AIAA Paper 76-1991. *Proceedings, Guidance and Control Conference,* San Diego, California, August 16–18, 1976, 76A41489. (See also 914.)

A joint NASA/university/industry program was conducted to flight evaluate a potentially low cost separate surface implementation of attitude command in a Beech 99 airplane. Saturation of the separate surfaces was the primary cause of many problems during development. Six experienced professional pilots made simulated instrument flight evaluations in light-to-moderate turbulence. They were favorably impressed with the system, particularly with the elimination of control force transients that accompanied configuration changes. For ride quality, quantitative data showed that the attitude command control system resulted in all cases of airplane motion being removed from the uncomfortable ride region.

*University of Kansas, Lawrence, Kansas.
**Beech Aircraft Corp., Wichita, Kansas.

908. Schweikhard, W. G.; Gilyard, G. B.; *Talbot, J. E.; and *Brown, T. W.: **Effects of Atmospheric Conditions on the Operating Characteristics of Supersonic Cruise Aircraft.** IAF Paper 76-112, presented at the International Astronautical Federation, Twenty-Seventh International Astronautical Congress, Anaheim, California, October 10–16, 1976, 77A10912, #.

Since for maximum range a supersonic transport must cruise near its maximum Mach number, accurate flight control is needed, especially when severe atmospheric transients are encountered. This paper describes atmospheric transients that have been encountered by the XB-70, YF-12, and Concorde aircraft during supersonic flights and the ensuing responses of the aircraft propulsion and flight control systems. It was found that atmospheric conditions affected these supersonic cruise vehicles in much the same way, with minor differences according to the type of propulsion and flight control system. Onboard sensors are sufficiently accurate to provide data on the atmosphere, including turbulence over the route, that are accurate enough for entry in the climatic record and for use as inputs to the control systems. Nominal atmospheric transients can be satisfactorily controlled, but some problems remain for extreme cases.

*British Aircraft Company, Bristol, England.

909.   Baer, J. L.; Holzman, J. K.; and Burcham, F. W., Jr.: **Procedures Used in Flight Tests of an Integrated Propulsion Control System on an F-111E Airplane.** SAE Paper 760933, presented at the Society of Automotive Engineers, Aerospace Engineering and Manufacturing Meeting, San Diego, California, November 29–December 2, 1976, 77A28238.

A digital integrated propulsion control system (IPCS) was tested on an F-111E airplane. The IPCS provided full authority control of the left inlet and the TF30 afterburning engine. Supersonic test conditions were of primary interest. The operational procedures and maneuvers developed for IPCS evaluation, displays for test monitoring and data acquisition, flight safety, and problems encountered are discussed. The software refinements that made modifications to standard flight test procedures necessary are described. The flexibility of digital control and the ways software was used to overcome hardware deficiencies are discussed. Application of these procedures to a typical IPCS flight is described.

910.   Enevoldson, E.: **The X-24B, Spot Landing.** *Soaring,* Vol. 40, No. 11, November 1976.

911.   Foster, J. D.; and Lasagna, P. L.: **Flight-Test Measurement of the Noise Reduction of a Jet Transport Delayed Flap Approach Procedure.** NASA TM X-73172, A-6775, December 1976, 77N20078, #.

A delayed flap approach procedure was flight tested using the NASA CV-990 airplane to measure and analyze the noise produced beneath the flight path. Three other types of landing approaches were also flight tested to provide a comparison of the noise reduction benefits to the delayed flap approach. The conventional type of approach was used as a baseline to compare the effectiveness of the other approaches. The decelerating approach is a variation of the delayed flap approach. A detailed comparison of the ground perceived noise generated during the approaches is presented. For this comparison, the measured noise data were normalized to compensate for variations in aircraft weight and winds that occurred during the flight tests. The data show that the

reduced flap approach offers some noise reduction, while the delayed flap and decelerating approaches offer significant noise reductions over the conventional approach.

912.   *Hersh, A. S.; Burcham, F. W., Jr.; Putnam, T. W.; and Lasagna, P. L.: **Semiempirical Airframe Noise Prediction Model and Evaluation With Flight Data.** NASA TM X-56041, H-951, December 1976, 77N13791, #. (See also 895.)

A semiempirical maximum overall sound pressure level (OASPL) airframe noise model was derived. Noise radiated from aircraft wings was modeled on the trailing edge diffractes quadrupole sound theory. The acoustic dipole sound theory was used to model noise from the landing gear. The model was correlated with maximum OASPL flyover noise measurements obtained for three jet aircraft. One third octave band sound pressure level flyover data was correlated and interpreted.

*Hersh Acoustical Engineering, Westlake Village, California.

913.   Berry, D. T.; and Gilyard, G. B.: **A Review of Supersonic Cruise Flight Path Control Experience With the YF-12 Aircraft.** NASA SP-416. *Aircraft Safety and Operating Problems,* 1976, pp. 147–164, (see N77-18081 09-03), 77N18089, #.

Flight research with the YF-12 aircraft indicates that solutions to many handling qualities problems of supersonic cruise are at hand. Airframe/propulsion system interactions in the dutch roll mode can be alleviated by the use of passive filters or additional feedback loops in the propulsion and flight control systems. Mach and altitude excursions due to atmospheric temperature fluctuations can be minimized by the use of a cruise autothrottle. Autopilot instabilities in the altitude hold mode have been traced to angle of attack-sensitive static ports on the compensated nose boom. For the YF-12, the feedback of high-passed pitch rate to the autopilot resolves this problem. Manual flight path control is significantly improved by the use of an inertial rate of climb display in the cockpit.

914.   Gee, S. W.; *Jenks, G. E.; *Roskam, J.; and **Stone, R. L.: **Flight Test Evaluation of a Separate Surface Attitude Command Control System on a Beech 99 Airplane.** NASA SP-416. *Aircraft Safety and Operating Problems,* 1976, pp. 121–146, (see N77-18081 09-03), 77N18088, #. (See also 907.)

A joint NASA/university/industry program was conducted to flight evaluate a potentially low cost separate surface implementation of attitude command in a Beech 99 airplane. Saturation of the separate surfaces was the primary cause of many problems during development. Six experienced professional pilots who made simulated instrument flight evaluations experienced improvements in airplane handling qualities in the presence of turbulence and a reduction in pilot workload. For ride quality, quantitative data show that the attitude command control system results in all cases of airplane motion being removed from the uncomfortable ride region.

*University of Kansas, Lawrence, Kansas.
**Beech Aircraft Corp., Wichita, Kansas.

915. Albers, J. A.; and Olinger, F. V.: **YF-12 Propulsion Research Program and Results.** NASA CP-001. *Proceedings of the SCAR Conf., Part 1*, 1976, pp. 417–456, (see N77-17996 09-01), 77N18017, #.

The objectives and status of the propulsion program, along with the results acquired in the various technology areas, are discussed. The instrumentation requirements for and experience with flight testing the propulsion systems at high supersonic cruise are reported. Propulsion system performance differences between wind tunnel and flight are given. The effects of high frequency flow fluctuations (transients) on the stability of the propulsion system are described, and shock position control is evaluated.

916. Reukauf, P. J.; and Burcham, F. W., Jr.: **Propulsion System/Flight Control Integration for Supersonic Aircraft.** NASA CP-001. *Proceedings of the SCAR Conf., Part 1*, 1976, pp. 281–302, (see N77-17996 09-01), 77N18010, #.

Digital integrated control systems are studied. Such systems allow minimization of undesirable interactions while maximizing performance at all flight conditions. One such program is the YF-12 cooperative control program. The existing analog air data computer, autothrottle, autopilot, and inlet control systems are converted to digital systems by using a general purpose airborne computer and interface unit. Existing control laws are programmed and tested in flight. Integrated control laws, derived using accurate mathematical models of the airplane and propulsion system in conjunction with modern control techniques, are tested in flight. Analysis indicates that an integrated autothrottle autopilot gives good flight path control and that observers are used to replace failed sensors.

917. Berry, D. T.; Mallick, D. L.; and Gilyard, G. B.: **Handling Qualities Aspects of NASA YF-12 Flight Experience.** NASA CP-001. *Proceedings of the SCAR Conf., Part 1*, 1976, pp. 193–214, (see N77-17996 09-01), 77N18007, #.

The handling qualities of the YF-12 airplane as observed during NASA research flights over the past five years were reviewed. Aircraft behavior during takeoff, acceleration, climb, cruise, descent, and landing are discussed. Pilot comments on the various flight phases and tasks are presented. Handling qualities parameters such as period, damping, amplitude ratios, roll-yaw coupling, and flight path response sensitivity are compared to existing and proposed handling qualities criteria. The influence of the propulsion systems, stability augmentation, autopilot systems, atmospheric gusts, and temperature changes are also discussed. YF-12 experience correlates well with flying qualities criteria, except for longitudinal short period damping, where existing and proposed criteria appear to be more stringent than necessary.

918. Gillingham, K. K.; and Winter, W. R.: **Physiologic and Anti-G Suit Performance Data From YF-16 Flight Tests.** NASA TM X-74617, AD-A032357, 1976, 77N77316, #.

919. Donlan, C. J.; and Weil, J.: **Characteristics of Swept Wings at High Speeds**, 30 January 1952. *Collected Works of Charles J. Donlan*, 1976, (see N77-29059 20-01), 77N29078, #.

Some results of recent swept wing investigations are presented, that were undertaken to determine the effects of thickness and thickness distribution, camber and twist, nose-flap deflection, and devices or fixes for improving the wing pitching moment characteristics at high lift coefficients.

920. Montoya, E. J.; and *Faye, A. E., Jr.: **NASA Participation in the AMST Program.** *NASA Langley Res. Center Powered-Lift Aerodyn. and Acoustics*, 1976, pp. 465–478, (see N78-24046 15-02), 78N24075, #.

The objectives of the NASA Advanced Medium STOL Transport Experiments Program are discussed and several of the NASA experiments currently implemented and conducted on the YC-14 and YC-15 prototype aircraft are described. Emphasis is placed on experiments related to powered lift aerodynamics and acoustics.

*NASA Ames Research Center, Moffett Field, California.

921. *Bales, T. T.; *Hoffman, E. L.; *Payne, L.; and Carter, A. L.: **Fabrication and Evaluation of Advanced Titanium and Composite Structural Panels.** *NASA Proceedings of the SCAR Conf., Part. 2*, 1976, (see N77-18019 09-01), 77N18034, #.

Advanced manufacturing methods for titanium and composite material structures are being developed and evaluated. The focus for the manufacturing effort is the fabrication of full-scale structural panels which replace an existing shear panel on the upper wing surface of the NASA YF-12 aircraft. The program involves design, fabrication, ground testing, and Mach 3 flight service of full-scale structural panels and laboratory testing of representative structural element specimens.

*Lockheed, California Co., Burbank, California.

1977 Technical Publications

922. Parish, O. O.; and Putnam, T. W.: **Equations for the Determination of Humidity From Dewpoint and Psychrometric Data.** NASA TN D-8401, H-937, January 1977, 77N16859, #.

A general expression based on the Claperon-Clausius differential equation that relates saturation vapor pressure, absolute temperature, and the latent heat of transformation was derived that expresses saturation vapor pressure as a function of absolute temperature. This expression was then used to derive general expressions for vapor pressure, absolute humidity, and relative humidity as functions of either dewpoint and ambient temperature or psychrometric parameters. Constants for all general expressions were then evaluated to give specific expressions in both the international system of units and U.S. customary units for temperatures above and below freezing.

923. Wilner, D. O.: **Results of a Remote Multiplexer/Digitizer Unit Accuracy and Environmental Study.** NASA TM X-56043, January 1977, 77N15368, #.

A remote multiplexer/digitizer unit (RMDU), a part of the airborne integrated flight test data system, was subjected to an accuracy study. The study was designed to show the effects of temperature, altitude, and vibration on the RMDU. The RMDU was subjected to tests at temperatures from –54 C (–65 F) to 71 C (160 F), and the resulting data are presented here, along with a complete analysis of the effects. The methods and means used for obtaining correctable data and correcting the data are also discussed.

924. *Hallock, J. N.; *Burnham, D. C.; **Tombach, I. H.; †Brashears, M. R.; †Zalay, A. D.; and Barber, M. R.: **Ground-Based Measurements of the Wake Vortex Characteristics of a B-747 Aircraft in Various Configurations.** AIAA Paper 77-9, presented at the American Institute of Aeronautics and Astronautics, Fifteenth Aerospace Sciences Meeting, Los Angeles, California, January 24–26, 1977, 77A19770, #.

A Boeing 747 aircraft flew 54 passes at low level over ground-based sensors. Vortex velocities were measured by a laser-Doppler velocimeter, an array of monostatic acoustic sounders, and an array of propeller anemometers. Flow visualization of the wake was achieved using smoke and balloon tracers. Preliminary results were obtained on the initial downwash field, the time for merging of the multiple vortices, the velocity fields, vortex decay, and the effects of spoilers and differential flap settings on the dissipation and structure of vortices.

*U.S. Department of Transportation, Transportation Systems Center, Cambridge, Massachusetts.

**AeroVironment, Incorporated, Pasadena, California.
†Lockheed Missiles and Space Company, Incorporated, Huntsville, Alabama.

ECN-4242

B-747 Airplane With Smoke Generators

925. Jenkins, Jerald M.; **Problems Associated With Attaching Strain Gages to Titanium Alloy Ti-6Al-4V.** NASA TM X-56044, February 1977.

Weldable strain gages have shown excellent high temperature characteristics for supersonic cruise aircraft application. The spotwelding attachment method, however, has resulted in serious reductions in the fatigue life of titanium alloy (Ti-6Al-4V) fatigue specimens. The reduction is so severe that the use of weldable strain gages on operational aircraft must be prohibited. The cause of the fatigue problem is thought to be a combination of the microstructure changes in the material caused by spotwelding and the presence of the flange of the stain gage. Brazing, plating, and plasma spraying were investigated as substitutes for spotwelding. The attachment of a flangeless gage by plasma spraying provided the most improvement in the fatigue life of the titanium.

926. Burcham, F. W., Jr.; Lasagna, P. L.; and Kurtenbach, F. J.: **Static and Flyover Noise Measurements of an Inverted Profile Exhaust Jet.** ASME Paper 77-GT-81, presented at the American Society of Mechanical Engineers, Gas Turbine Conference and Products Show, Philadelphia, Pennsylvania, March 27–31, 1977, 77A28592, #.

Tests using a TF30 mixed flow afterburning turbofan engine in an F-111 airplane were conducted to study the noise characteristics of an inverted velocity profile jet. Full-authority digital engine control allowed the inverted profile jet to be compared to a uniform jet of equal thrust statically and in flight. An exhaust velocity survey showed that the ratio of the outer to inner stream velocities was 1.37; therefore, only small noise reductions were expected. At static conditions, the inverted profile jet was approximately 3 decibels quieter than the uniform jet at peak noise angles. During a flyover it was approximately 1 decibel quieter.

927. Edwards, J. W.; *Ashley, H.; and *Breakwell, J. V.: **Unsteady Aerodynamic Modeling for Arbitrary Motions.** AIAA Paper 77-451, presented at the Eighteenth Structures, Structural Dynamics and Materials Conference, March 21–23, 1977, and Dynamics Specialist Conference, San Diego, California, March 24–25, 1977, *Technical Papers*, Vol. B, 1977, (see A77-25778 10-01), 77A25808, #. (See also 932.)

A study is presented on the unsteady aerodynamic loads due to arbitrary motions of a thin wing and their adaptation for the calculation of response and true stability of aeroelastic modes. In an Appendix, the use of Laplace transform techniques and the generalized Theodorsen function for two-dimensional incompressible flow is reviewed. New applications of the same approach are shown also to yield airloads valid for quite general small motions. Numerical results are given for the two-dimensional supersonic case. Previously proposed approximate methods, starting from simple harmonic unsteady theory, are evaluated by comparison with exact results obtained by the present approach. The Laplace inversion integral is employed to separate the loads into "rational" and "nonrational" parts, of which only the former are involved in aeroelastic stability of the wing. Among other suggestions for further work, it is explained how existing aerodynamic computer programs may be adapted in a fairly straightforward fashion to deal with arbitrary transients.

*Stanford University, Stanford, California.

928. Kordes, E. E.: **Influence of Structural Dynamics on Vehicle Design—Government View.** AIAA Paper 77-438, presented at the Structures, Structural Dynamics and Materials Conference, March 21–23, 1977, and Dynamics Specialist Conference, San Diego, California, March 24–25, 1977, *Technical Papers*, Vol. B, (A77-25778 10-01), 1977, 77A25798, #.

Dynamic design considerations for aerospace vehicles are discussed, taking into account fixed wing aircraft, rotary wing aircraft, and launch, space, and reentry vehicles. It is pointed out that space vehicles have probably had the most significant design problems from the standpoint of structural dynamics, because their large lightweight structures are highly nonlinear. Examples of problems in the case of conventional aircraft include the flutter encountered by high performance military aircraft with external stores. A description is presented of a number of examples which illustrate the direction of present efforts for improving aircraft efficiency. Attention is given to the results of studies

on the structural design concepts for the arrow-wing supersonic cruise aircraft configuration and a system study on low-wing-loading, short haul transports.

929. Szalai, K. J.; *Felleman, P. G.; **Gera, J.; and †Glover, R. D.: **Design and Test Experience With a Triply Redundant Digital Fly-By-Wire Control System.** *Integrity in Electron. Flight Control Systems,* AGARD AG-224, paper 21, April 1977, (see N77-25055 16-01), 77N25076, #.

A triplex digital fly-by-wire flight control system was developed and then installed in a NASA F-8C aircraft to provide fail-operative, full authority control. Hardware and software redundancy management techniques were designed to detect and identify failures in the system. Control functions typical of those projected for future actively controlled vehicles were implemented. The principal design features of the system, the implementation of computer, sensor and actuator redundancy management, and the ground test results are described. An automated test program to verify sensor redundancy management software is also described.

*Draper Laboratory, Inc., Cambridge, Massachusetts.
**NASA Langley Research Center, Hampton, Virginia.
†NASA Johnson Space Center, Houston, Texas.

930. Bartoli, F.: **An Advanced Airborne Data Acquisition System.** *Flight Test Techniques*, AGARD CP 223, paper 23, April 1977, (see N77-24107 15-05), 77N24130, #.

The development and features of and user experience with an advanced airborne data acquisition system are described. The system consists of as many as 16 high speed pulse code modulation data acquisition units which are integrated with an airborne computer and a cockpit display unit. The data acquisition units may be operated without the computer. Operation without the computer is termed stand-alone operation. Computer integrated operation is intended for large-scale projects, and stand-alone operation is designed for small-scale projects. The cockpit display unit, which is part of the computer operated system, displays computed real time data in engineering units. An example of the cost reduction experienced by a major aircraft company by using the advanced data acquisition system is given.

931. *Newsom, B. D.; *Goldenrath, W. L.; *Sandler, H.; and Winter, W. R.: **Tolerance of Females to +Gz Centrifugation Before and After Bedrest.** *Aviation, Space, and Environmental Medicine*, Vol. 48, April 1977, pp. 327–331, 77A30881.

Because women may be included as passengers in the proposed Space Shuttle System, experiments were conducted on 12 female subjects aged 24-35 yr. to investigate the +Gz tolerance of women and the possible degradation of this tolerance after a period of weightlessness as simulated by bedrest. Over a 1-week period, each subject was exposed to +Gz levels starting at +2 Gz and increasing by 0.5 Gz increments to a gray-out point. This point was determined by peripheral vision loss with a standard lightbar and by reverse blood flow in the temporal artery. Ultimately, each woman was subjected to three runs at the +3 Gz level for about 55 min long each, separated by 5-min rest periods. Eight subjects with the best tolerance times were selected for 14 days of bedrest in a horizontal position; the other four being ambulatory controls. Tests before bedrest, immediately following, and 5 days later showed that average +Gz tolerance decreased by 67% after bedrest.

*NASA Ames Research Center, Moffett Field, California.

932. Edwards, J. W.: **Unsteady Aerodynamic Modeling for Arbitrary Motions.** *AIAA Journal*, Vol. 15, April 1977, pp. 593–595, 77A29910, #. (See also 927.)

Results indicating that unsteady aerodynamic loads derived under the assumption of simple harmonic motions executed by airfoil or wing can be extended to arbitrary motions are summarized. The generalized Theodorsen (1953) function referable to loads due to simple harmonic oscillations of a wing section in incompressible flow, the Laplace inversion integral for unsteady aerodynamic loads, calculations of root loci of aeroelastic loads, and analysis of generalized compressible transient airloads are discussed.

933. Arnaiz, H. H.: **Flight-Measured Lift and Drag Characteristics of a Large, Flexible, High Supersonic Cruise Airplane.** NASA TM X-3532, H-913, May 1977, 77N24100, #.

Flight measurements of lift, drag, and angle of attack were obtained for the XB-70 airplane, a large, flexible, high supersonic cruise airplane. This airplane had a length of over 57 meters, a takeoff gross mass of over 226,800 kilograms, and a design cruise speed of Mach 3 at an altitude of 21,340 meters. The performance measurements were made at Mach numbers from 0.72 to 3.07 and altitudes from approximately 7620 meters to 21,340 meters. The measurements were made to provide data for evaluating the techniques presently being used to design and predict the performance of aircraft in this category. Such performance characteristics as drag polars, lift-curve slopes, and maximum lift-to-drag ratios were derived from the flight data. The base drag of the airplane, changes in airplane drag with changes in engine power setting at transonic speeds, and the magnitude of the drag components of the propulsion system are also discussed.

934. Montoya, L. C.; and Banner, R. D.: **F-8 Supercritical Wing Flight Pressure, Boundary Layer, and Wake Measurements and Comparisons With Wind Tunnel Data.** NASA TM X-3544, H-850, June 1977, 77N29098, #.

Data for speeds from Mach 0.50 to Mach 0.99 are presented for configurations with and without fuselage area-rule additions, with and without leading-edge vortex generators, and with and without boundary-layer trips on the wing. The wing pressure coefficients are tabulated. Comparisons between the airplane and model data show that higher second velocity peaks occurred on the airplane wing than on the model wing. The differences were attributed to wind tunnel wall interference effects that caused too much rear camber to be designed into the wing. Optimum flow conditions on the outboard wing section occurred at Mach 0.98 at an angle of attack near 4 deg. The measured differences in section drag with and without boundary-layer trips on the wing suggested that a region of laminar flow existed on the outboard wing without trips.

935. Jacobs, P. F.; Flechner, S. G.; and Montoya, L. C.: **Effect of Winglets on a First-Generation Jet Transport Wing. 1: Longitudinal Aerodynamic Characteristics of a Semispan Model at Subsonic Speeds.** NASA TN D-8473, L-11354, June 1977, 78N20064, #.

The effects of winglets and a simple wing-tip extension on the vectors behind the wing tip of a first generation jet transport wing were investigated in the Langley 8-foot transonic pressure tunnel using a semi-span model. The test was conducted at Mach numbers of 0.30, 0.70, 0.75, 0.78, and 0.80. At a Mach number of 0.30, the configurations were tested with combinations of leading- and trailing-edge flaps.

936. Montoya, L. C.; Flechner, S. G.; and Jacobs, P. F.: **Effect of Winglets on a First-Generation Jet Transport Wing. 2: Pressure and Spanwise Load Distributions for a Semispan Model at High Subsonic Speeds.** NASA TN D-8474, L-11026, July 1977, 78N20065, #.

Pressure and spanwise load distributions on a first-generation jet transport semispan model at high subsonic speeds are presented for the basic wing and for configurations with an upper winglet only, upper and lower winglets, and a simple wing-tip extension. Selected data are discussed to show the general trends and effects of the various configurations.

937. Montoya, L. C.; Jacobs, P. F.; and Flechner, S. G.: **Effect of Winglets on a First-Generation Jet Transport Wing. 3: Pressure and Spanwise Load Distributions for a Semispan Model at Mach 0.30.** NASA TN D-8478, L-11370, June 1977, 78N20063, #.

Pressure and spanwise load distributions on a first-generation jet transport semispan model at a Mach number of 0.30 are given for the basic wing and for configurations with an upper winglet only, upper and lower winglets, and a simple wing-tip extension. To simulate second-segment-climb lift conditions, leading- and/or trailing-edge flaps were added to some configurations.

938. Jenkins, J. M.; and Kuhl, A. E.: **A Study of the Effect of Radical Load Distributions on Calibrated Strain Gage Load Equations.** NASA TM-56047, H-984, July 1977, 77N27430, #.

For several decades, calibrated strain gages have been used to measure loads on airplanes. The accuracy of the equations used to relate the strain gage measurements to the applied loads has been based primarily on the results of the load calibration. An approach is presented for studying the effect of widely varying load distributions on strain gage load equations. The computational procedure provides a link between the load calibration and the load to be measured in flight. A matrix approach to equation selection is presented, which is based on equation standard error, load distribution, and influence coefficient plots of the strain gage equations, and is applied to a complex, delta-wing structure.

939. Jenkins, J. M.; Kuhl, A. E.; and Carter, A. L.: **The Use of a Simplified Structural Model as an Aid in the Strain Gage Calibration of a Complex Wing.** NASA TM-56046, H-959, July 1977, 77N27429, #.

The use of a relatively simple structural model to characterize the load responses of strain gages located on various spars of a delta wing is examined. Strains measured during a laboratory load calibration of a wing structure are compared with calculations obtained from a simplified structural analysis model. Calculated and measured influence coefficient plots that show the shear, bending, and torsion characteristics of typical strain gage bridges are presented. Typical influence coefficient plots are shown for several load equations to illustrate the derivation of the equations from the component strain gage bridges. A relatively simple structural model was found to be effective in predicting the general nature of strain distributions and influence coefficient plots. The analytical processes are shown to be an aid in obtaining a good load calibration. The analytical processes cannot, however, be used in lieu of an actual load calibration of an aircraft wing.

940. *Brilliant, H. M.; and Bauer, C. A.: **Comparison of Estimated With Measured Maximum Instantaneous Distortion Using Flight Data From an Axisymmetric Mixed Compression Inlet.** AIAA Paper 77-876, presented at the American Institute of Aeronautics and Astronautics and Society of Automotive Engineers, Thirteenth Propulsion Conference, Orlando, Florida, July 11–13. 1977, 77A38570, #.

YF-12C flight-measured inlet dynamic distortion data are compared with predictions made on the basis of the method reported by Melick et al. (1976). The YF-12C aircraft is a twin engine aircraft capable of speeds above 3. The inlets have a translating spike to control the inlet throat area. A bypass system is used to control the terminal shock of the inlet for operation in the mixed compression mode. The dynamic data were obtained with the aid of 24 high frequency response total pressure sensors. The model of Melick et al. is discussed along with the computer program used to implement the model. It is found that the predictions of maximum instantaneous distortion are within 20 percent of the measured values, which had been obtained at Mach numbers of 1.8, 2.1, 2.5, and 3.0.

*U.S. Air Force Academy, Colorado Springs, Colorado.

ECN-3516

YF-12C Airplane

941. *Rawlings, K., III; *Cooper, J. M.; and Hughes, D. L.: **Dynamic Test Techniques—Concepts and Practices.** *The Many Disciplines of Flight Test, Proceedings of the Seventh Annual Symposium*, Eastsound, Orcas Island, Washington, August 4–6, 1976, Society of Flight Test Engineers, pp. 25-1 to 25-20, (see A77-38003 17-05), 77A38026.

An initial investigation of dynamic flight test analysis techniques indicated that a strict, comprehensive force-moment accounting system would be necessary. An implementation of the longitudinal force-moment accounting system provided excellent results in accounting for small lift/drag and tail deflection changes. Attention is given to gross thrust calculation, instrumentation, maneuvers, and aspects of data correlation. The results of the studies demonstrate that it is possible to generate a lift/drag model which is capable of predicting performance from nearly any maneuver.

*USAF, Flight Test Center, Edwards AFB, California.

942. *Johnson, H. J.; and Painter, W. D.: **The Development and Flight Test of an Electronic Integrated Propulsion Control System.** *The Many Disciplines of Flight Test, Proceedings of the Seventh Annual Symposium,* Eastsound, Orcas Island, Washington, August 4–6, 1976, Society of Flight Test Engineers, pp. 12-1 to 12-19, (see A77-38003 17-05), 77A38013.

Advanced technical features of the electronic integrated propulsion control system (IPCS) and flight evaluation tests of IPCS (F-111E with TF30-P-9 engines as test vehicle) are described. Nine baseline flight tests and 15 IPCS flight tests were conducted. Instrumentation, data acquisition and data processing systems, software maintenance procedures, flight test procedures, flight safety criteria, flight test results, and ground and flight testing of the aircraft system are described. Advantages conferred by IPCS include faster accelerations (both gas generator and afterburner performance), better thrust and flight control, reduced flight idle thrust, reduced engine ground trim, extended service ceiling, automatic stall detection, and stall recovery detection.

*Boeing Commercial Airplane Co., Seattle, Washington.

943. Maine, R. E.: **Maximum Likelihood Estimation of Aerodynamic Derivatives for an Oblique Wing Aircraft From Flight Data.** AIAA Paper 77-1135, presented at the Atmospheric Flight Mechanics Conference, Hollywood, Florida, August 8–10, 1977, pp. 124–133, (see A77-43151 20-08), 77A43166, #.

There are several practical problems in using current techniques on 5-degree-of-freedom equations to estimate the stability and control derivatives of oblique wing aircraft from flight data. A technique has been developed to estimate these derivatives by separating the analysis of the longitudinal and lateral-directional motion without neglecting cross-coupling effects. This technique was used on flight data from a remotely piloted oblique wing aircraft. The results demonstrated that the relatively simple approach developed was adequate to obtain high quality estimates of the aerodynamic derivatives of such aircraft.

ECN-5209

Oblique Wing Research Vehicle

944. Iliff, K. W.; and Maine, R. E.: **Further Observations on Maximum Likelihood Estimates of Stability and Control Characteristics Obtained From Flight Data.** AIAA Paper 77-1133, presented at the Atmospheric Flight Mechanics Conference, Hollywood, Florida, August 8–10, 1977, *Technical Papers*, pp. 100–112, (see A77-43151 20-08), 77A43164, #.

A maximum likelihood estimation method for flight test data is described. Flight results based on 3000 maneuvers from 30 aircraft on the effect of resolution and sampling rate on the estimates, on understanding the discrepancies previously observed in the magnitude of the Cramer-Rao bounds, on the scale effects on the derivative estimates obtained from dynamic aircraft flight maneuvers, and on the analysis of lateral-directional maneuvers obtained in turbulence, are presented.

945. Edwards, J. W.; *Breakwell, J. V.; and *Bryson, A. E., Jr.: **Active Flutter Control Using Generalized Unsteady Aerodynamic Theory.** AIAA Guidance and Control Conference, Hollywood, Florida, August 8–10, 1977, *Technical Papers*, pp. 172–185, 77A42772, #. (See also 970.)

This paper describes the application of generalized unsteady aerodynamic theory to the problem of active flutter control. The controllability of flutter modes is investigated. It is shown that the response of aeroelastic systems is composed of a portion due to a rational transform and a portion due to a

161

nonrational transform. The oscillatory response characteristic of flutter is due to the rational portion, and a theorem is given concerning the construction of a linear, finite-dimensional model of this portion of the system. The resulting rational model is unique and does not require state augmentation. Active flutter control designs using optimal regulator synthesis are presented.

*Stanford University, Stanford, California.

946. *Hartmann, G.; *Stein, G.; and Petersen, K.: **Flight Data Processing With the F-8 Adaptive Algorithm.** AIAA Paper 77-1042, AIAA Guidance and Control Conference, Hollywood, Florida, *Technical Papers*, (see A77-42751 20-35), August 8–10, 1977, pp. 53–60, 77A42758, #.

An explicit adaptive control algorithm based on maximum likelihood estimation of parameters has been designed for NASA's DFBW F-8 aircraft. To avoid iterative calculations, the algorithm uses parallel channels of Kalman filters operating at fixed locations in parameter space. This algorithm has been implemented in NASA/DFRC's Remotely Augmented Vehicle (RAV) facility. Real-time sensor outputs (rate gyro, accelerometer and surface position) are telemetered to a ground computer which sends new gain values to an on-board system. Ground test data and flight records were used to establish design values of noise statistics and to verify the ground-based adaptive software. The software and its performance evaluation based on flight data are described.

*Honeywell, Inc., Minneapolis, Minnesota.

947. Andrews, W. H.; and McMurtry, T. C.: **Space Shuttle Orbiter Approach and Landing Program Status.** *Flight Test Technology, Proceedings of the Eighth Annual Symposium*, Washington, D.C., Society of Flight Test Engineers, (see A78-19426 06-01), August 10–12, 1977, pp. 2-1 to 2-14, 78A19428.

The approach and landing test (ALT) phase of the Space Shuttle program aims at assessing the Orbiter's subsonic aerodynamic flight and landing characteristics along with the support equipment, ground facilities, and the approximate hardware and software to be used in the terminal phase of orbital missions. The program also evaluates the performance of the Shuttle carrier aircraft (SCA) as related to the transport of the Orbiter to the launch sites during the stages of Space Shuttle operations. Results are presented for the SCA inert Orbiter flight testing and the program plans up to the completion of the ALT program. Emphasis is placed on testing the airworthiness of the mated B-747 Shuttle carrier aircraft and Orbiter, checkout of the Orbiter systems in captive flight, and launching the Orbiter with and without the tail cone installed. Major program milestones before the first manned orbital flight are summarized in graphic form.

ECN77-8608

Space Shuttle Enterprise Launch From B-747 Airplane

948. Andrews, W. H.: **Space Shuttle Orbiter Approach and Landing Program Status.** AIAA Paper 77-1204, presented at the American Institute of Aeronautics and Astronautics, Aircraft Systems and Technology Meeting, Seattle, Washington, August 22–24, 1977, 77A44314, #.

The space shuttle approach and landing test (ALT) program is being conducted in four phases. The first phase, completed in March of 1977, consisted of verifying the airworthiness of the mated B-747 shuttle carrier aircraft and orbiter. The second phase consists of checking the orbiter systems in captive flight. The third phase is to be confined to launching the orbiter with and without the tail cone installed to evaluate the final landing phase of the shuttle operations through the verification of the automatic landing system. The fourth and final phase of the program is to document the mated configuration's performance relative to the ferry operations to be conducted between the return from the orbiter's landing sites and launch sites. This paper presents the results of the SCA inert orbiter flight testing and the program plans up to the completion of the ALT program.

949. DeAngelis, V. M.; and Monaghan, R. C.: **Buffet Characteristics of the F-8 Supercritical Wing Airplane.** NASA TM-56049, H-945, September 1977, 77N32080, #.

The buffet characteristics of the F-8 supercritical wing airplane were investigated. Wing structural response was used to determine the buffet characteristics of the wing and these characteristics are compared with wind tunnel model data and the wing flow characteristics at transonic speeds. The wingtip accelerometer was used to determine the buffet onset boundary and to measure the buffet intensity characteristics of the airplane. The effects of moderate trailing edge flap deflections on the buffet onset boundary are presented. The supercritical wing flow characteristics were determined from wind tunnel and flight static pressure measurements and from a dynamic pressure sensor mounted on the flight test airplane in the vicinity of the shock wave that formed on the upper surface of the wing at transonic speeds. The comparison of the airplane's structural response data to the supercritical flow characteristics includes the effects of a leading edge vortex generator.

950. Megna, Vincent A.; and Szalai, Kenneth J.: **Multi-Flight Computer Redundancy Management for Digital Fly-By-Wire Aircraft Control.** IEEE COMPCON 77, September 1977.

951. Sefic, Walter J.; and Carter, Alan L.: **Loads Calibration Experience With a Reentry Wing Structure.** Presented at Fall Meeting, Western Regional Strain Gage Committee, Society for Experimental Stress Analysis, September 28, 1977.

952. Jenkins, Jerald M.; and Kuhl, Albert E.: **Recent Loads Calibration Experience With a Delta Wing Airplane.** Presented at Fall Meeting, Western Regional Strain Gage Committee, Society for Experimental Stress Analysis, September 28, 1977.

953. Tang, Ming H.; and Fields, Roger A.: **Analysis of a Loads Calibration of a Hypersonic Cruise Wing Test Structure.** Presented at Fall Meeting, Western Regional Strain Gage Committee, Society for Experimental Stress Analysis, September 28, 1977.

954. Steers, L. L.; and Saltzman, E. J.: **Reduced Truck Fuel Consumption Through Aerodynamic Design.** *Journal of Energy*, Vol. 1, No. 5, September–October 1977, pp. 312–318, 77A48572, #.

Full-scale fuel consumption and drag tests were performed on a conventional cab-over-engine tractor-trailer combination and a version of the same vehicle with significant forebody modifications. The modified configuration had greatly increased radii on all front corners and edges of the tractor and a smooth fairing of the modified tractor top and sides extending to the trailer. Concurrent highway testing of the two configurations showed that the modified design used 20% to 24% less fuel than the baseline configuration at 88.5 km/hr (55 mph) with near-calm wind conditions. Coastdown test results showed that the modified configuration reduced the drag coefficient by 0.43 from the baseline value of 1.17 at 88.5 km/hr (55 mph) in calm wind conditions.

ECN-4724

Low-Drag Truck

955. Fulton, F. L., Jr.: **Shuttle Carrier Aircraft Flight Tests.** Society of Experimental Test Pilots, Twenty-First Annual Symposium, Beverly Hills, California, Society of Experimental Test Pilots, *Technical Review*, Vol. 13, No. 4, October 12–15, 1977, pp. 191–204, 78A28464.

Since the Space Shuttle will need to be transported from its place of assembly to the launch site, a method has been developed whereby the Shuttle rides piggyback on a modified Boeing 747, called the Shuttle carrier aircraft (SCA). This paper describes tests of the SCA in its mated configuration. Tests include flutter, found to decrease when fiberglass and wood fairings were added to the base of each supporting pylon; stability and control, found to be acceptable after damping with control pulses; noise and buffet, found high but acceptable; and climb, in which drag was marked but acceptable with the special rated thrust (SRT) power setting. Simulated launch maneuvers were undertaken at an airspeed of 273 KCAS. Transport of the Shuttle takes place with the

Shuttle tail cone on, at a cruise speed of 288 KCAS at an altitude of 22,000 feet.

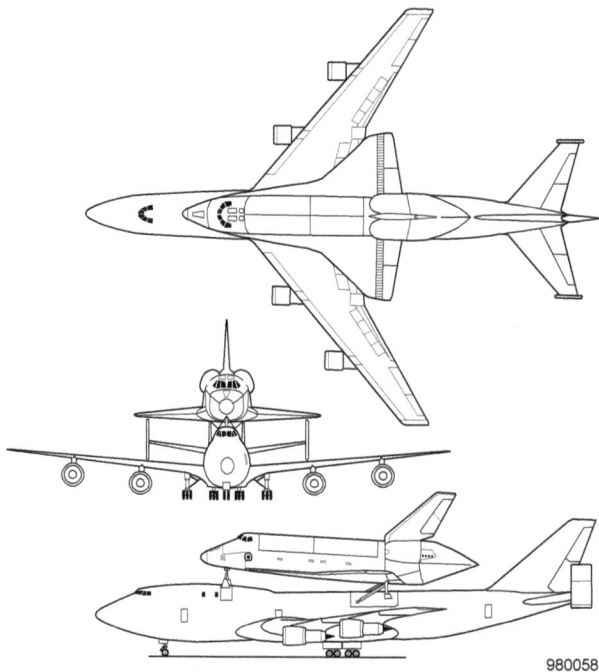

Space Shuttle Mated to B-747, Three-View Drawing

956.   Brown, S. R.; and Szalai, K. J.: **Flight Experience With a Fail-Operational Digital Fly-By-Wire Control System.** AIAA Paper 77-1507, presented at the Second Digital Avionics Systems Conference, Los Angeles, California, November 2–4, 1977, *Collection of Technical Papers,* 1977, pp. 186–199, (see A78-12226 02-04), 78A12253, #.

The NASA Dryden Flight Research Center is flight testing a triply redundant digital fly-by-wire (DFBW) control system installed in an F-8 aircraft. The full-time, full-authority system performs three-axis flight control computations, including stability and command augmentation, autopilot functions, failure detection and isolation, and self-test functions. Advanced control law experiments include an active flap mode for ride smoothing and maneuver drag reduction. This paper discusses research being conducted on computer synchronization, fault detection, fault isolation, and recovery from transient faults. The F-8 DFBW system has demonstrated immunity from nuisance fault declarations while quickly identifying truly faulty components.

957.   Powers, B. G.: **Phugoid Characteristics of a YF-12 Airplane With Variable-Geometry Inlets Obtained in Flight Tests at a Mach Number of 2.9.** NASA TP-1107, H-953, December 1977, 78N12100, #.

Flight tests were conducted with the YF-12 airplane to examine the airplane's longitudinal characteristics at a Mach number of approximately 2.9. Phugoid oscillations as well as short period pulses were analyzed with the variable geometry engine inlets in the fixed and the automatic configurations. Stability and control derivatives for the velocity and altitude degrees of freedom and the standard short period derivatives were obtained. Inlet bypass door position was successfully used to represent the total inlet system, and the effect of the inlets on the velocity and altitude derivatives was determined. The phugoid mode of the basic airplane (fixed inlet configuration) had neutral damping, and the height mode was stable. With the addition of the inlets in the automatic configuration, the phugoid mode was slightly divergent and the height mode was divergent with a time to double amplitude of about 114 seconds. The results of the derivative estimation indicated that the change in the height mode characteristics was primarily the result of the change in the longitudinal force derivative with respect to velocity.

958.   Jenkins, J. M.; Kuhl, A. E.; and Carter, A. L.: **Strain Gage Calibration of a Complex Wing.** *Journal of Aircraft,* Vol. 14, December 1977, pp. 1192–1196, 78A16182, #.

Modern complex structural arrangements have complicated the task of measuring flight loads with calibrated strain gages. This paper examines the use of a relatively simple structural model to characterize the load responses of strain gages located on various spars of a delta wing. Strains measured during a laboratory load calibration of a wing structure are compared with calculations obtained from a simplified NASA structural analysis (NASTRAN) model. Calculated and measured influence coefficient plots that show the shear, bending, and torsion characteristics of typical strain-gage bridges are presented. Typical influence coefficient plots are given for several load equations to illustrate the derivation of the equations from the component strain-gage bridges. A relatively simple structural model was found to be effective in predicting the general nature of strain distributions and influence coefficient plots. The analytical processes are shown to be useful in obtaining a good load calibration. The analytical processes cannot, however, be used in lieu of an actual load calibration of an aircraft wing.

959.   Iliff, Kenneth W.: **Maximum Likelihood Estimation of Lift and Drag From Dynamic Aircraft Maneuvers.** *Journal of Aircraft,* Vol. 14, No. 12, December 1977, pp. 1175–1181.

A maximum likelihood estimation method for obtaining lift and drag characteristics from dynamic flight maneuvers was investigated. This paper describes the method and compares the estimates of lift and drag obtained by using the method with estimates obtained from wind-tunnel tests and from established methods for obtaining estimates from flight data. In general, the lift and drag coefficients extracted from dynamic flight maneuvers by the maximum likelihood estimation technique are in good agreement with the estimates obtained from the wind-tunnel tests and the other methods. When maneuvers that met the requirements of both flight methods were analyzed, the results of each method were nearly the same. The maximum likelihood estimation technique showed promise in terms of estimating lift and drag characteristics from dynamic flight maneuvers. Further studies should be made to assess the best mathematical model and the most desirable type of dynamic maneuver to get the highest quality results from this technique.

960. Smougur, T.; Morgan, T.; Sears, W.; Dana, W.; Enevoldson, E.; Melvin, J.; and *Tays, M.: **Joint Testing of the RAF High Altitude Protective Ensemble.** SAFE Association, Fifteenth Annual Symposium, Las Vegas, Nevada, December 5–8, 1977, *Proceedings*, pp. 243–245, (see A79-14401 03-03), 79A14434.

The "get-me-down" capability from flight above 50,000 ft for the unencumbering RAF partial pressure clothing for use in F-104 and F-15 aircraft is tested. The equipment assembly tested includes a sleeveless Jerkin pressure vest, a G-suit and an RAF P/Q oronasal mask. The test program consists of six coordinated efforts: laboratory evaluation, orientation/ training of NASA test pilots, quantification of aerodynamic suction effects on cockpit altitude, definition of protective envelope, suit/aircraft integration, and in-flight test and evaluation. It is suggested that the RAF ensemble or equivalent would be the only currently available item that would be acceptable to tactical crews. The Jerkin ensemble appears to meet both the pilot's physiological and functional requirements.

*USAF, Aerospace Medical Div., Holloman AFB, New Mexico.

961. *Jacobsen, R. A.; and Barber, M. R.: **Flight Test Techniques for Wake-Vortex Minimization Studies.** *NASA Wake Vortex Minimization*, 1977, pp. 193–220, (see N78-12017 03-02), 78N12022, #.

Flight test techniques developed for use in a study of wake turbulence and used recently in flight studies of wake minimization methods are discussed. Flow visualization was developed as a technique for qualitatively assessing minimization methods and is required in flight test procedures for making quantitative measurements. The quantitative techniques are the measurement of the upset dynamics of an aircraft encountering the wake and the measurement of the wake velocity profiles. Descriptions of the instrumentation and the data reduction and correlation methods are given.

*NASA Ames Research Center, Moffett Field, California.

962. Barber, M. R.; Hastings, E. C., Jr.; Champine, R. A.; and *Tymczyszyn, J. J.: **Vortex Attenuation Flight Experiments.** *NASA Wake Vortex Minimization*, 1977, pp. 369–403, (see N78-12017 03-02), 78N12028, #.

Flight tests evaluating the effects of altered span loading, turbulence ingestion, combinations of mass and turbulence ingestion, and combinations of altered span loading turbulence ingestion on trailed wake vortex attenuation were conducted. Span loadings were altered in flight by varying the deflections of the inboard and outboard flaps on a B-747 aircraft. Turbulence ingestion was achieved in flight by mounting splines on a C-54G aircraft. Mass and turbulence ingestion was achieved in flight by varying the thrust on the B-747 aircraft. Combinations of altered span loading and turbulence ingestion were achieved in flight by installing a spoiler on a CV-990 aircraft and by deflecting the existing spoilers on a B-747 aircraft. The characteristics of the attenuated and unattenuated vortexes were determined by probing them with smaller aircraft. Acceptable separation distances for encounters with the attenuated and unattenuated vortexes are presented.

*FAA, Los Angeles, California.

963. Albers, J. A.: **Inlet Operating Flow Field of the YF-12 Aircraft and Effects of This Flow Field on Inlet Performance.** *NASA Lewis Research Center Inlet Workshop*, 1977, pp. 383–396, (see N86-72197 18-01), 86N72222.

964. Albers, J. A.; and Washington, H. P.: **Technique for Determining Inlet Forces and Inlet Airframe Interactions on the F-15 Aircraft.** NASA Lewis Research Center Inlet Workshop, 1977, pp. 615–631, (see N86-72197 18-01), 86N72235.

ECN-5000

F-15 Airplane

965. Edwards, John William: **Unsteady Aerodynamic Modeling and Active Aeroelastic Control.** AZ 41 E95, NASA Grant NG L-05-020-007, Stanford University, Stanford, California, <u>1977</u>.

1978 Technical Publications

966. Painter, W. D.; and Caw, L. J.: **Design and Physical Characteristics of the Transonic Aircraft Technology (TACT) Research Aircraft.** NASA TM-56048, H-976, <u>January 1978</u>, 79N14014, #.

The Transonic Aircraft Technology (TACT) research program provided data necessary to verify aerodynamic concepts, such as the supercritical wing, and to gain the confidence required for the application of such technology to advanced high performance aircraft. An F-111A aircraft was employed as the flight test bed to provide full scale data. The data were correlated extensively with predictions based on data obtained from wind tunnel tests. An assessment of the improvement afforded at transonic speeds in drag divergence, maneuvering performance, and airplane handling qualities by the use of the supercritical wing was included in the program. Transonic flight and wind tunnel testing techniques were investigated, and specific research technologies evaluated were also summarized.

967. Ko, W. L.: **Finite Element Microscopic Stress Analysis of Cracked Composite Systems.** *Journal of Composite Materials*, Vol. 12, <u>January 1978</u>, pp. 97–115, 78A28851.

This paper considers the stress concentration problems of two types of cracked composite systems: (1) a composite system with a broken fiber (a penny-shaped crack problem), and (2) a composite system with a cracked matrix (an annular crack problem). The cracked composite systems are modeled with triangular and trapezoidal ring finite elements. Using NASTRAN (NASA Structural Analysis) finite element computer program, the stress and deformation fields in the cracked composite systems are calculated. The effect of fiber-matrix material combination on the stress concentrations and on the crack opening displacements is studied.

968. Taylor, L. W., Jr.; and Smith, H. J.: **A New Formulation for the Epsilon Method Applied to the Minimum-Time-to-Climb Problem.** NASA CP-007. *NASA Washington Fourth Inter-Center Control Systems Conference,* <u>January 1978</u>, pp. 423–434, (see N78-23010 13-99), 78N23028, #.

Balakrishnan's epsilon technique is used to compute minimum-time profiles for the F-104 airplane. This technique differs from the classical gradient method in that a quadratic penalty on the error in satisfying the equation of motion is included in the cost function to be minimized as a means of eliminating the requirement of satisfying the equations of motion. Although the number of unknown independent functions is increased to include the state variables, the evaluation of the gradient of the cost function is simplified, resulting in considerable computational savings, thereby making it appear feasible to use the epsilon method for real-time application.

969. Deets, D. A.: **Optimal Regulator or Conventional Setup Techniques for a Model Following Simulator Control System.** NASA CP-007. *NASA Washington Fourth Inter-Center Control Systems Conf.*erence, <u>January 1978</u>, pp. 237–252, (see N78-23010 13-99), 78N23020, #. (See also 590.)

Optimal regulator technique was compared for determining simulator control system gains with the conventional servo analysis approach. Practical considerations, associated with airborne motion simulation using a model-following system, provided the basis for comparison. The simulation fidelity specifications selected were important in evaluating the relative advantages of the two methods. Frequency responses for a JetStar aircraft following a roll mode model were calculated digitally to illustrate the various cases. A technique for generating forward loop lead in the optimal regulator model-following problem was developed which increases the flexibility of that approach. It appeared to be the only way in which the optimal regulator method could meet the fidelity specifications.

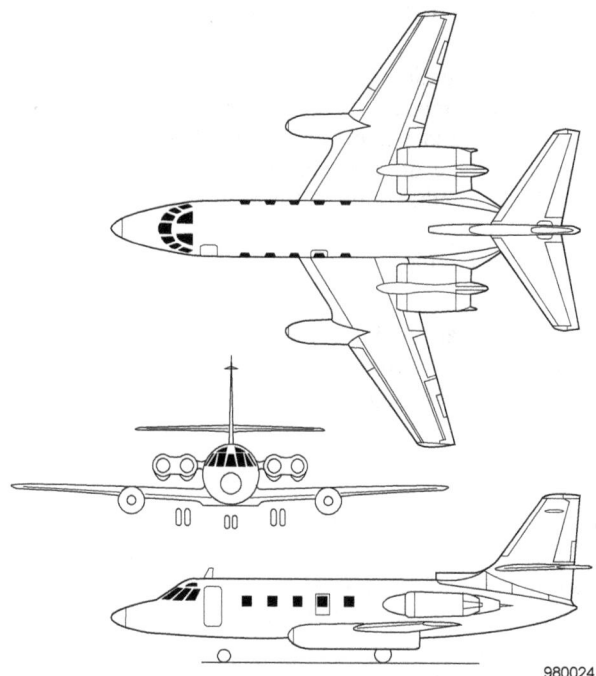

980024

JetStar Airplane, Three-View Drawing

970. Edwards, J. W.; Breakwell, J. V.; and Bryson, A. E., Jr.: **Active Flutter Control Using Generalized Unsteady**

Aerodynamic Theory. *Journal of Guidance and Control,* January–February 1978. Vol 1, No. 1, pp. 32–40. (See also 945.)

971. Powers, B. G.: **Analytical Study of Ride Smoothing Benefits of Control System Configurations Optimized for Pilot Handling Qualities.** NASA TP-1148, H-922, February 1978, 78N18076, #.

An analytical study was conducted to evaluate the relative improvements in aircraft ride qualities that resulted from utilizing several control law configurations that were optimized for pilot handling qualities only. The airplane configuration used was an executive jet transport in the approach configuration. The control law configurations included the basic system, a rate feedback system, three command augmentation systems (rate command, attitude command, and rate command/attitude hold), and a control wheel steering system. Both the longitudinal and lateral directional axes were evaluated. A representative example of each control law configuration was optimized for pilot handling qualities on a fixed base simulator. The root mean square airplane responses to turbulence were calculated, and predictions of ride quality ratings were computed by using three models available in the literature.

972. Meyer, R. R., Jr.: **Effect of Winglets on a First-Generation Jet Transport Wing. 4: Stability Characteristics for a Full-Span Model at Mach 0.30.** NASA TP-1119, L-11705, February 1978, 78N17997, #.

The static longitudinal and lateral directional characteristics of a 0.035 scale model of a first generation jet transport were obtained with and without upper winglets. The data were obtained for take off and landing configurations at a free stream Mach number of 0.30. The results generally indicated that upper winglets had favorable effects on the stability characteristics of the aircraft.

973. Sheridan, A. E.; and Grier, S. J.: **Drag Reduction Obtained by Modifying a Standard Truck.** NASA TM-72846, H-977, February 1978, 78N20457, #.

A standard two-axle truck with a box-shaped cargo compartment was tested to determine whether significant reductions in aerodynamic drag could be obtained by modifying the front of the cargo compartment. The coastdown method was used to determine the total drag of the baseline vehicle, which had a square-cornered cargo box, and of several modified configurations. Test velocities ranged from 56.3 to 94.6 kilometers per hour (35 to 60 miles per hour). At 88.5 kilometers per hour (55 miles per hour), the aerodynamic drag reductions obtained with the modified configurations ranged from 8 to 30 percent.

974. Matheny, N. W.; and Gatlin, D. H.: **Flight Evaluation of the Transonic Stability and Control Characteristics of an Airplane Incorporating a Supercritical Wing.** NASA TP-1167, H-916, February 1978, 78N20140, #.

A TF-8A airplane was equipped with a transport type supercritical wing and fuselage fairings to evaluate predicted performance improvements for cruise at transonic speeds. A comparison of aerodynamic derivatives extracted from flight and wind tunnel data showed that static longitudinal stability, effective dihedral, and aileron effectiveness, were higher than predicted. The static directional stability derivative was slower than predicted. The airplane's handling qualities were acceptable with the stability augmentation system on. The unaugmented airplane exhibited some adverse lateral directional characteristics that involved low Dutch roll damping and low roll control power at high angles of attack and roll control power that was greater than satisfactory for transport aircraft at cruise conditions. Longitudinally, the aircraft exhibited a mild pitchup tendency. Leading edge vortex generators delayed the onset of flow separation, moving the pitchup point to a higher lift coefficient and reducing its severity.

975. Gee, S. W.; Carr, P. C.; Winter, W. R.; and Manke, J. A.: **Development of Systems and Techniques for Landing an Aircraft Using Onboard Television.** NASA TP-1171, H-973, February 1978, 78N20114, #.

A flight program was conducted to develop a landing technique with which a pilot could consistently and safely land a remotely piloted research vehicle (RPRV) without outside visual reference except through television. Otherwise, instrumentation was standard. Such factors as the selection of video parameters, the pilot's understanding of the television presentation, the pilot's ground cockpit environment, and the operational procedures for landing were considered. About 30 landings were necessary for a pilot to become sufficiently familiar and competent with the test aircraft to make powered approaches and landings with outside visual references only through television. When steep approaches and landings were made by remote control, the pilot's workload was extremely high. The test aircraft was used as a simulator for the F-15 RPRV, and as such was considered to be essential to the success of landing the F-15 RPRV.

976. Iliff, K. W.; Maine, R. E.; and Steers, S. T.: **Flight-Determined Stability and Control Coefficients of the F-111A Airplane.** NASA TM-72851, March 1978, 78N18075, #.

A complete set of linear stability and control derivatives of the F-111A airplane was determined with a modified maximum likelihood estimator. The derivatives were determined at wing sweep angles of 26 deg, 35 deg, and 58 deg. The flight conditions included a Mach number range of 0.63 to 1.43 and an angle of attack range of 2 deg to 15 deg. Maneuvers were performed at normal accelerations from 0.9g to 3.8g during steady turns to assess the aeroelastic effects on the stability and control characteristics. The derivatives generally showed consistent trends and reasonable agreement with the wind tunnel estimates. Significant Mach effects were observed for Mach numbers as low as 0.82. No large effects attributable to aeroelasticity were noted.

977. Ko, William L.: **Traverse Diffusivity of Dual Phase Composites,** *Fiber Science and Technology*, Vol. II, No. 2, <u>March 1978</u>, pp. 157–162.

This paper compares the exact and approximate theories developed for predicting the traverse diffusivity of dual phase composite systems containing a rectangular lattice of uniform parallel circular cylindrical inclusions. Due to the difficulties in obtaining an explicit exact mathematical expression for the diffusivity of the composite system, approximations or mathematical models are usually introduced in the calculation of the diffusivity of the composite. The two most common approximate theories used in estimating the transverse diffusivity (or conductivity) of the composite systems are described.

978. Iliff, Kenneth W.: **Identification and Stochastic Control of an Aircraft Flying in Turbulence.** *Journal of Guidance and Control*, Vol. 1, No. 2, <u>March–April 1978</u>. Also published (in Russian) *Rocket Technology and Cosmonautics*, <u>June 1979</u>, pp. 150–159.

An adaptive control technique to improve the flying qualities of an aircraft in turbulence was investigated. The approach taken was to obtain maximum likelihood estimates of the unknown coefficients of the aircraft system and then, using these estimates along with the separation principle, to define the stochastic optimal control. The maximum likelihood estimation technique that accounts for the effects of turbulence provided good estimates of the unknown coefficients and of the turbulence. The assessment of the stochastic optimal control based on the maximum likelihood estimates showed that the desired effects were attained for the regulator problem of minimizing pitch angle and the tracking problem of requiring normal acceleration to follow the pilot input.

979. Hedgley, D. R.: **An Efficient Algorithm for Choosing the Degree of a Polynomial to Approximate Discrete Nonoscillatory Data.** NASA TM-72854, H-1010, <u>April 1978</u>, 78N21839, #.

An efficient algorithm for selecting the degree of a polynomial that defines a curve that best approximates a data set was presented. This algorithm was applied to both oscillatory and nonoscillatory data without loss of generality.

980. Gilyard, G. B.; and Smith, J. W.: **Results From Flight and Simulator Studies of a Mach 3 Cruise Longitudinal Autopilot.** NASA TP-1180, H-940, <u>April 1978</u>, 78N21160, #.

At Mach numbers of approximately 3.0 and altitudes greater than 21,300 meters, the original altitude and Mach hold modes of the YF-12 autopilot produced aircraft excursions that were erratic or divergent, or both. Flight data analysis and simulator studies showed that the sensitivity of the static pressure port to angle of attack had a detrimental effect on the performance of the altitude and Mach hold modes. Good altitude hold performance was obtained when a high passed pitch rate feedback was added to compensate for angle of attack sensitivity and the altitude error and integral altitude gains were reduced. Good Mach hold performance was obtained when the angle of attack sensitivity was removed; however, the ride qualities remained poor.

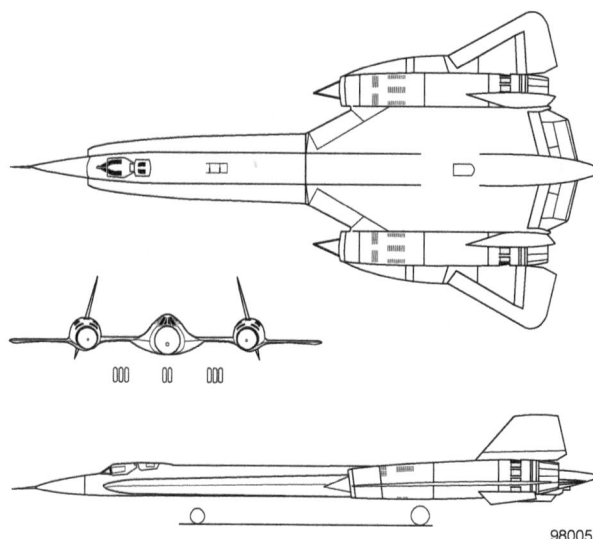

980055

YF-12A Airplane, Three-View Drawing

981. *Siemers, P. M., III; and Larson, T. J.: **The Space Shuttle Orbiter and Aerodynamic Testing.** AIAA Paper 78-790, Tenth Annual Aerodynamic Testing Conference, San Diego, California, <u>April 19–21, 1978</u>, *Technical Papers,* pp. 145–158, (A78-32326 12-09),78A32347, #.

The concept of utilizing the Space Shuttle Orbiter as an aerodynamic flight research vehicle is discussed. The orbiter's planned flight frequency and its complex flight control system provide an unprecedented flight research potential. This paper defines the orbiter's flight environment and applicable baseline systems, their capabilities and limitations, as well as those instrument systems required to augment the baseline capability. These required systems, which are being developed under NASA's Orbiter Experiments Program (OEX) are the Aerodynamic Coefficient Identification Package (ACIP), Shuttle Entry Air Data System (SEADS), and the Shuttle Upper Atmosphere Mass Spectrometer (SUMS). Finally, the need for and capability of launching payloads from the orbiter to extend the research potential beyond the orbiter configuration and/or environment is defined.

*NASA Langley Research Center, Space Systems Div., Hampton, Virginia.

982. Powers, S. G.: **Flight-Measured Pressure Characteristics of Aft-Facing Steps in High Reynolds Number Flow at Mach Numbers of 2.20, 2.50, and 2.80 and Comparison With Other Data.** NASA TM-72855, H-956, May 1978, 78N25055, #.

The YF-12 airplane was studied to determine the pressure characteristics associated with an aft-facing step in high Reynolds number flow for nominal Mach numbers of 2.20, 2.50, and 2.80. Base pressure coefficients were obtained for three step heights. The surface static pressures ahead of and behind the step were measured for the no-step condition and for each of the step heights. A boundary layer rake was used to determine the local boundary layer conditions. The Reynolds number based on the length of flow ahead of the step was approximately 10 to the 8th power and the ratios of momentum thickness to step height ranged from 0.2 to 1.0. Base pressure coefficients were compared with other available data at similar Mach numbers and at ratios of momentum thickness to step height near 1.0. In addition, the data were compared with base pressure coefficients calculated by a semiempirical prediction method. The base pressure ratios are shown to be a function of Reynolds number based on momentum thickness. Profiles of the surface pressures ahead of and behind the step and the local boundary layer conditions are also presented.

983. Monaghan, R. C.: **Flight-Measured Buffet Characteristics of a Supercritical Wing and a Conventional Wing on a Variable-Sweep Airplane.** NASA TP-1244, H-991, May 1978, 78N23056, #.

Windup-turn maneuvers were performed to assess the buffet characteristics of the F-111A aircraft and the same aircraft with a supercritical wing, which is referred to as the F-111 transonic aircraft technology (TACT) aircraft. Data were gathered at wing sweep angles of 26, 35, and 58 deg for Mach numbers from 0.60 to 0.95. Wingtip accelerometer data were the primary source of buffet information. The analysis was supported by wing strain-gage and pressure data taken in flight, and by oil-flow photographs taken during tests of a wind tunnel model. In the transonic speed range, the overall buffet characteristics of the aircraft having a supercritical wing are significantly improved over those of the aircraft having a conventional wing.

ECN-3945

F-111 TACT Airplane

984. Jenkins, Jerald M.; Fields, Roger A.; and Sefic, Walter J.: **Effect of Elevated Temperature on the Calibrated Strain Gages of the YF-12A Wing.** Presented at the Society of Experimental Stress Analysis, Spring Meeting, Wichita, Kansas, May 14–19, 1978.

985. Larson, Terry J.; and Schweikhard, William G.: **Use of the Shuttle Entry Air Data Pressure System at Subsonic Speeds.** Presented at the Second Biennial Air Data Systems Conference, Colorado Springs, Colorado, May 1–5, 1978.

The purpose of this paper is to show that, in limited wind-tunnel tests of a 0.1-scale shuttle model, SEADS, when combined with auxiliary flush static-pressure measurements aft of the nose cap, can provide accurate air data system. The SEADS pressure data are from tests made in NASA Lewis Research Center's 10- by 10-Foot Supersonic Wind Tunnel; the auxiliary flush static-pressure data are partly from those tests and partly from tests in the NASA Ames Research Center's Fourteen-Foot Transonic Wind Tunnel.

986. Reed, R. D.: **High-Flying Mini-Sniffer RPV—Mars Bound.** *Astronautics and Aeronautics*, Vol. 16, June 1978, pp. 26–39, 78A38521, #.

The Mini-Sniffer is a small unmanned survey aircraft developed by NASA to conduct turbulence and atmospheric pollution measurements from ground level to an altitude of 90,000 ft. Carrying a 25-lb air sampling apparatus, the Mini-Sniffer typically cruises for one hour at 70,000 ft before being remotely piloted back to earth. A hydrazine monopropellant engine powers the craft, while a PCM telemetering system and a radar transponder provide control functions.

Development of a high-performance low-Reynolds-number airfoil could make the research craft suitable for a low-altitude terrain-following mission on Mars.

Mini-Sniffer RPV   ECN-4898

987. *Peterson, J. B., Jr.; and Fisher, D. F.: **Flight Investigation of Insect Contamination and Its Alleviation**. NASA CP-2036-PT-1. *NASA CTOL Transport Technol.*, June 1978, pp. 357–373, (see N78-27046 18-01), 78N27067, #.

An investigation of leading edge contamination by insects was conducted with a JetStar airplane instrumented to detect transition on the outboard leading edge flap and equipped with a system to spray the leading edge in flight. The results of airline type flights with the JetStar indicated that insects can contaminate the leading edge during takeoff and climbout. The results also showed that the insects collected on the leading edges at 180 knots did not erode at cruise conditions for a laminar flow control airplane and caused premature transition of the laminar boundary layer. None of the superslick and hydrophobic surfaces tested showed any significant advantages in alleviating the insect contamination problem. While there may be other solutions to the insect contamination problem, the results of these tests with a spray system showed that a continuous water spray while encountering the insects is effective in preventing insect contamination of the leading edges.

*NASA Langley Research Center, Hampton, Virginia.

988. Nugent, J.; Taillon, N. V.; and *Pendergraft, O. C., Jr.: **Status of a Nozzle-Airframe Study of a Highly Maneuverable Fighter.** AIAA Paper 78-990, presented at American Institute of Aeronautics and Astronautics and Society of Automotive Engineers, Fourteenth Joint Propulsion Conference, Las Vegas, Nevada, July 25–27, 1978, 78A48470, #.

NASA is sponsoring a research program that uses coordinated wind tunnel and flight tests to investigate nozzle-airframe flow interactions. The program objective is to compare transonic flight and wind tunnel measurements over a wide Reynolds number range. The paper discusses the progress of the program and the coordination of the wind tunnel and flight tests with regard to program elements, model-airplane differences, instrument locations, and test conditions. The real-time feedback techniques used to obtain steady flight conditions are presented. Available wind tunnel results are presented for the jet effects model showing the influence of the rear-end geometry and test variables on nozzle drag. Available flight results show the effect of the variable inlet ramp angle and angle of attack on fuselage pressures and upper surface boundary layers.

*NASA Langley Research Center, Hampton, Virginia.

989. *Lucas, E. J.; **Fanning, A. E.; and Steers, L. L.: **Comparison of Nozzle and Afterbody Surface Pressures From Wind Tunnel and Flight Test of the YF-17 Aircraft.** AIAA Paper 78-992, presented at American Institute of Aeronautics and Astronautics and Society of Automotive Engineers, Fourteenth Joint Propulsion Conference, Las Vegas, Nevada, July 25–27, 1978, 78A43540, #.

Results are reported from the initial phase of an effort to provide an adequate technical capability to accurately predict the full scale, flight vehicle, nozzle-afterbody performance of future aircraft based on partial scale, wind tunnel testing. The primary emphasis of this initial effort is to assess the current capability and identify the cause of limitations on this capability. A direct comparison of surface pressure data is made between the results from an 0.1-scale model wind tunnel investigation and a full-scale flight test program to evaluate the current subscale testing techniques. These data were acquired at Mach numbers 0.6, 0.8, 0.9, 1.2, and 1.5 on four nozzle configurations at various vehicle pitch attitudes. Support system interference increments were also documented during the wind tunnel investigation. In general, the results presented indicate a good agreement in trend and level of the surface pressures when corrective increments are applied for known effects and surface differences between the two articles under investigation.

*ARO, Inc., Arnold Air Force Station, Tennessee.
**USAF, Aero Propulsion Laboratory, Wright-Patterson AFB, Ohio.

EC76-5270

YF-17 Airplane

990. Brownlow, J.: **A Statistical Package for Computing Time and Frequency Domain Analysis.** NASA TM-56045, H-981, August 1978, 78N29843, #.

The spectrum analysis (SPA) program is a general purpose digital computer program designed to aid in data analysis. The program does time and frequency domain statistical analyses as well as some preanalysis data preparation. The capabilities of the SPA program include linear trend removal and/or digital filtering of data, plotting and/or listing of both filtered and unfiltered data, time domain statistical characterization of data, and frequency domain statistical characterization of data.

991. *Morosow, G.; **Dublin, M.; and Kordes, E. E.: **Needs and Trends in Structural Dynamics.** *Astronautics and Aeronautics*, Vol. 16, July–August 1978, pp. 90–94, 78A43364, #.

The paper discusses dynamic analyses and testing of aerospace vehicles and the application of such analyses and testing to nonaerospace fields. Items covered in the section on dynamic analyses of aerospace vehicles include self-induced and forced oscillatory loads, approaches to dynamic modeling and analysis, nonlinear analyses, and integrated dynamics design and optimization. Items covered in the section on the dynamic testing of aerospace vehicles include integrated test philosophy, test facilities, and ways of improving performance and reducing costs. The nonaerospace applications that are discussed include ground and water transportation, medicine, and nuclear power plants.

*Martin Marietta Aerospace, Bethesda, Maryland.
**General Dynamics Corp., Pomona, California.

992. Fisher, D. F.; and *Peterson, J. B., Jr.: **Flight Experience on the Need and Use of Inflight Leading Edge Washing for a Laminar Flow Airfoil.** AIAA Paper 78-1512, presented at American Institute of Aeronautics and Astronautics, Aircraft Systems and Technology Conference, Los Angeles, California, August 21–23, 1978, 78A47947, #.

An investigation of leading-edge contamination by insects was conducted at the NASA Dryden Flight Research Center with a JetStar airplane instrumented to detect transition on the outboard leading-edge flap and equipped with a system to wash the leading edge in flight. The results of airline-type flights with the JetStar indicated that insects can contaminate the leading edge during take-off and climbout at large jet airports in the United States. The results also showed that the insects collected on the leading edges at 180 knots did not erode at cruise conditions for a laminar flow control airplane and caused premature transition of the laminar boundary layer. None of the superslick and hydrophobic surfaces tested showed any significant advantages in alleviating the insect contamination problem. While there may be other solutions to the insect contamination problem, the results of these tests with a washer system showed that a continuous water spray while encountering the insects is effective in preventing insect contamination of the leading edges.

*NASA Langley Research Center, Hampton, Virginia.

993. Montoya, L. C.; Bikle, P. F.; and Banner, R. D.: **Section Drag Coefficients From Pressure Probe Traverses of a Wing Wake at Low Speeds.** AIAA Paper 78-1479, presented at the American Institute of Aeronautics and Astronautics, Aircraft Systems and Technology Conference, Los Angeles, California, August 21–23, 1978, 78A47924, #. (See also 1035.)

This paper reviews the techniques used to increase data reliability and to minimize certain bias errors during a series of wing profile drag measurements performed in flight on a sailplane airfoil. Unresolved questions concerning errors in the use of total probes in this and other studies are discussed.

994. Sisk, T. R.: **A Technique for the Assessment of Fighter Aircraft Precision Controllability.** AIAA Paper 78-1364, Atmospheric Flight Mechanics Conference, Palo Alto, California, August 7–9, 1978, *Technical Papers,* pp. 253–265, (see A78-46526 20-08), 78A46553, #.

Today's emerging fighter aircraft are maneuvering as well at normal accelerations of 7 to 8 g's as their predecessors did at 4 to 5 g's. This improved maneuvering capability has significantly expanded their operating envelope and made the task of evaluating handling qualities more difficult. This paper describes a technique for assessing the precision controllability of highly maneuverable aircraft, a technique that was developed to evaluate the effects of buffet intensity on gunsight tracking capability and found to be a useful tool for the general assessment of fighter aircraft handling qualities. It has also demonstrated its usefulness for evaluating configuration and advanced flight control system refinements. This technique is believed to have application to future aircraft dynamics and pilot-vehicle interface studies.

995. Maine, R. E.; and Iliff, K. W.: **Maximum Likelihood Estimation of Translational Acceleration Derivatives From Flight Data.** AIAA Paper 78-1342, Atmospheric Flight Mechanics Conference, Palo Alto, California, August 7–9, 1978, *Technical Papers,* pp. 121–131, (see A78-46526 20-08), 78A46539, #. (See also 1069.)

This paper shows that translational acceleration derivatives, such as pitching moment due to rate of change of angle of attack, can be estimated from flight data with the use of appropriately designed maneuvers. No new development of estimation methodology is necessary to analyze these maneuvers. Flight data from a T-37B airplane were used to verify that rate of change of angle of attack could be estimated from rolling maneuvers.

996. Anon.: **YF-12 Experiments Symposium.** NASA CP-2054-VOL-1, H-1059. *Proceedings of the YF-12 Experiments Symposium,* Edwards, California, September 13–15, 1978, 78N32055, #. (See also N78-32056 through N78-32065.)

Papers presented by personnel from the Dryden Flight Research Center, the Lewis Research Center, and the Ames Research Center are presented. Topics cover propulsion system performance, inlet time varying distortion, structures, aircraft controls, propulsion controls, and aerodynamics. The reports were based on analytical studies, laboratory experiments, wind tunnel tests, and extensive flight research with two YF-12 airplanes.

997. Kock, B. M.: **Overview of the NASA YF-12 Program.** NASA CP-2054-VOL-1. *NASA YF-12 Experiments Symposium,* Vol. 1, August 1978, pp. 3–25, (see N78-32055 23-02), 78N32056, #.

The history of NASA's interest in supersonic research and the agency's contribution to the development of the YF-12 aircraft is reviewed as well as the program designed to use that aircraft as a test bed for supersonic cruise research. Topics cover elements of the program, project organization, and major accomplishments.

998. Jenkins, J. M.; and Kuhl, A. E.: **Recent Load Calibrations Experience With the YF-12 Airplane.** NASA CP-2054-VOL-1. *NASA YF-12 Experiments Symposium,* Vol. 1, August 1978, pp. 47–72, (see N78-32055 23-02), 78N32057, #.

The use of calibrated strain gages to measure wing loads on the YF-12A airplane is discussed as well as structural configurations relative to the thermal environment and resulting thermal stresses. A thermal calibration of the YF-12A is described to illustrate how contaminating thermal effects can be removed from loads equations. The relationship between ground load calibrations and flight measurements is examined for possible errors, and an analytical approach to accommodate such errors is presented.

999. Meyer, R. R., Jr.; and DeAngelis, V. M.: **Flight-Measured Aerodynamic Loads on a 0.92 Aspect Ratio Lifting Surface.** NASA CP-2054-VOL-1. *NASA YF-12 Experiments Symposium,* Vol. 1, August 1978, pp. 73–91, (see N78-32055 23-02), 78N32058, #.

Ventral fin loads, expressed as normal force coefficients, bending moment coefficients, and torque coefficients, were measured during flight tests of a YF-12A airplane. Because of the proximity of the ventral fin to the ailerons, the aerodynamic loads presented were the result of both sideslip loads and aileron crossflow loads. Aerodynamic data obtained from strain gage loads instrumentation and some flight pressure measurements are presented for several Mach numbers ranging from 0.70 to 2.00. Selected wind tunnel data and results of linear theoretical aerodynamic calculations are presented for comparison.

1000. Gilyard, G. B.; and Smith, J. W.: **Flight Experience With Altitude Hold and Mach Hold Autopilots on the YF-12 Aircraft at Mach 3.** NASA CP-2054-VOL-1. *NASA YF-12 Experiments Symposium,* Vol. 1, August 1978, pp. 97–119, (see N78-30255 23-02), 78N32059, #.

The altitude hold mode of the YF-12A airplane was modified to include a high-pass-filtered pitch rate feedback along with optimized inner loop altitude rate proportional and integral gains. An autothrottle control system was also developed to control either Mach number or KEAS at the high-speed flight conditions. Flight tests indicate that, with the modified system, significant improvements are obtained in both altitude and speed control, and the combination of altitude and autothrottle hold modes provides the most stable aircraft platform thus far demonstrated at Mach 3 conditions.

1001. Rezek, T. W.: **Pilot Workload Measurement and Experience on Supersonic Cruise Aircraft.** NASA CP-2054-VOL-1. *NASA YF-12 Experiments Symposium,* Vol. 1, August 1978, pp. 121–134, (see N78-32055 23-02), 78N32060, #.

Aircraft parameters and physiological parameters most indicative of crew workload were investigated. Recommendations were used to form the basis for a continuing study in which variations of the interval between heart beats are used as a measure of nonphysical workload. Preliminary results are presented and current efforts in further defining this physiological measure are outlined.

1002. Ehernberger, L. J.: **The YF-12 Gust Velocity Measuring System.** NASA CP-2054-VOL-1. *NASA YF-12 Experiments Symposium*, Vol. 1, August 1978, pp. 135–154, (see N78-32055 23-02), 78N32061, #.

A true gust velocity measuring system designed to alleviate complications resulting from airframe flexibility and from the high-speed, high-temperature environment of supersonic cruise aircraft was evaluated on a YF-12 airplane. The system uses fixed vanes on which airflow direction changes produce differential pressure variations that are measured. Airframe motions, obtained by postflight integration of recorded angular rate and linear acceleration data, are removed from the flow angle data. An example of turbulence data obtained at high-altitude, supersonic flight conditions is presented and compared with previous high-altitude turbulence measurements obtained with subsonic aircraft and with turbulence criteria contained in both military and civil design specifications for supersonic cruise vehicles. Results of these comparisons indicate that the YF-12 turbulence sample is representative of turbulence present in the supersonic cruise environment.

1003. Powers, S. G.: **Flight-Measured Pressure Characteristics of Aft-Facing Steps in Thick Boundary Layer Flow for Transonic and Supersonic Mach Numbers.** NASA CP-2054-VOL-1. *NASA YF-12 Experiments Symposium*, Vol. 1, August 1978, pp. 201–226, (see N78-32055 23-02), 78N32063, #.

Aft-facing step base pressure flight data were obtained for three step heights for nominal transonic Mach numbers of 0.80, 0.90, and 0.95, and for supersonic Mach numbers of 2.2, 2.5, and 2.8 with a Reynolds number, based on the fuselage length ahead of the step, of about 10 to the 8th power. Surface static pressures were measured ahead of the step, behind the step, and on the step face (base), and a boundary layer rake was used to obtain boundary layer reference conditions. A comparison of the data from the present and previous experiments shows the same trend of increasing base pressure ratio (decreasing drag) with increasing values of momentum thickness to step height ratios. However, the absolute level of these data does not always agree at the supersonic Mach numbers. For momentum thickness to height ratios near 1.0, the differences in the base pressure ratios appear to be primarily a function of Reynolds number based on the momentum thickness. Thus, for Mach numbers above 2, the data analyzed show that the base pressure ratio decreases (drag increases) as Reynolds number based on momentum thickness increases for a given momentum thickness and step height.

1004. Fisher, D. F.: **Boundary Layer, Skin Friction, and Boattail Pressure Measurements From the YF-12 Airplane at Mach Numbers Up to 3.** NASA CP-2054-VOL-1. *NASA YF-12 Experiments Symposium*, Vol. 1, August 1978, pp. 227–258, (see N78-32055 23-02), 78N32064, #.

In-flight measurements of boundary layer and skin friction data were made on YF-12 airplanes for Mach numbers between 2.0 and 3.0. Boattail pressures were also obtained for Mach numbers between 0.7 and 3.0 with Reynolds numbers up to four hundred million. Boundary layer data measured along the lower fuselage centerline indicate local displacement and momentum thicknesses can be much larger than predicted. Skin friction coefficients measured at two of five lower fuselage stations were significantly less than predicted by flat plate theory. The presence of large differences between measured boattail pressure drag and values calculated by a potential flow solution indicates the presence of vortex effects on the upper boattail surface. At both subsonic and supersonic speeds, pressure drag on the longer of two boattail configurations was equal to or less than the pressure drag on the shorter configuration. At subsonic and transonic speeds, the difference in the drag coefficient was on the order of 0.0008 to 0.0010. In the supersonic cruise range, the difference in the drag coefficient was on the order of 0.002. Boattail drag coefficients are based on wing reference area.

1005. Quinn, R. D.; and Gong, L.: **In-Flight Compressible Turbulent Boundary Layer Measurements on a Hollow Cylinder at a Mach Number of 3.0.** NASA CP-2054-VOL-1. *NASA YF-12 Experiments Symposium*, Vol. 1, August 1978, pp. 259–286, (see N78-32055 23-02), 78N32065, #.

Skin temperatures, shearing forces, surface static pressures, and boundary layer pitot pressures and total temperatures were measured on a hollow cylinder 3.04 meters long and 0.437 meter in diameter mounted beneath the fuselage of the YF-12A airplane. The data were obtained at a nominal free stream Mach number of 3.0 and at wall-to-recovery temperature ratios of 0.66 to 0.91. The free stream Reynolds number had a minimal value of 4.2 million per meter. Heat transfer coefficients and skin friction coefficients were derived from skin temperature time histories and shear force measurements, respectively. Boundary layer velocity profiles were derived from pitot pressure measurements, and a Reynolds analogy factor of 1.11 was obtained from the measured heat transfer and skin friction data. The skin friction coefficients predicted by the theory of van Driest were in excellent agreement with the measurements.

Theoretical heat transfer coefficients, in the form of Stanton numbers calculated by using a modified Reynolds analogy between skin friction and heat transfer, were compared with measured values. The measured velocity profiles were compared to Coles' incompressible law-of-the-wall profile.

ECN-4777

YF-12 Airplane With "Coldwall" Experiment

1006. Monaghan, Richard C.: **Flight Measured Buffet Characteristics.** Presented at the Symposium on Transonic Aircraft Technology, Lancaster, California, August 15–17, 1978.

Windup-turn maneuvers were performed to assess the buffet characteristics of the F-111A aircraft and the same aircraft with a supercritical wing, which is referred to as the F-1ll transonic aircraft technology (TACT) aircraft. Data were gathered at wing sweep angles of 26 degree, 35 degree, and 58 degree for Mach numbers from 0.60 to 0.95. Wingtip accelerometer data were the primary source of buffet information. The analysis was supported by wing strain-gage and fuselage accelerometer data. Buffet intensity rise boundaries in the form of plots of aircraft normal-force coefficient as a function of Mach number, as well as individual buffet intensity curves at specific Mach numbers, are presented for each aircraft. In the transonic speed range, the overall buffet characteristics of the aircraft having a supercritical wing are significantly improved over those of the aircraft having a conventional wing. At subsonic speeds or at the aft wing sweep position where the supercritical wing is off design, the two aircraft have similar buffet characteristics.

1007. Sakamoto, Glenn M.; and Friend, Edward L.: **Agility Evaluation.** Presented at the Symposium on

Transonic Aircraft Technology, Lancaster, California, August 15–17, 1978.

This paper present the results of a study conducted with the F-111 transonic aircraft technology (TACT) airplane to assess the improvement in maneuverability afforded by a supercritical wing when installed on an F-111A aircraft. The study evaluated the aerodynamic performance, maneuver performance, and precision controllability of both the basic F-111A and the F-111 TACT aircraft over the transonic Mach number region at three wing-sweep positions. The aerodynamic performance evaluation showed that the supercritical wing significantly improved the buffet characteristics of the F-111A airplane at high subsonic and transonic Mach numbers. Wing rock was experienced on both aircraft, with the F-111 TACT airplane having the higher onset boundaries. The maneuver performance evaluation showed the F-111 TACT airplane to have higher drag-rise Mach number as well as improved transonic sustained turn performance. The supercritical wing did not alter the F-111A airplane's basic precision controllability. The agility analysis demonstrated that the supercritical wing improved the F-111A airplane's maneuverability.

1008. Maine, R. E.: **Aerodynamic Derivatives for an Oblique Wing Aircraft Estimated From Flight Data by Using a Maximum Likelihood Technique.** NASA TP-1336, H-1003, October 1978, 78N33054, #.

There are several practical problems in using current techniques with five degree of freedom equations to estimate the stability and control derivatives of oblique wing aircraft from flight data. A technique was developed to estimate these derivatives by separating the analysis of the longitudinal and lateral directional motion without neglecting cross coupling effects. Although previously applied to symmetrical aircraft, the technique was not expected to be adequate for oblique wing vehicles. The application of the technique to flight data from a remotely piloted oblique wing aircraft is described. The aircraft instrumentation and data processing were reviewed, with particular emphasis on the digital filtering of the data. A complete set of flight determined stability and control derivative estimates is presented and compared with predictions. The results demonstrated that the relatively simple approach developed was adequate to obtain high quality estimates of the aerodynamic derivatives of such aircraft.

1009. Tang, M. H.; Sefic, W. J.; and Sheldon, R. G.: **Comparison of Concurrent Strain Gage- and Pressure Transducer-Measured Flight Loads on a Lifting Reentry Vehicle and Correlation With Wind Tunnel Predictions.** NASA TP-1331, H-1035, October 1978, 78N33053, #.

Concurrent strain gage and pressure transducer measured flight loads on a lifting reentry vehicle are compared and correlated with wind tunnel-predicted loads. Subsonic, transonic, and supersonic aerodynamic loads are presented for the left fin and control surfaces of the X-24B lifting reentry vehicle. Typical left fin pressure distributions are shown. The effects of variations in angle of attack, angle of sideslip, and Mach number on the left fin loads and rudder hinge moments are presented in coefficient form. Also presented are the effects of variations in angle of attack and Mach number on the upper flap, lower flap, and aileron hinge-moment coefficients. The effects of variations in lower flap hinge moments due to changes in lower flap deflection and Mach number are presented in terms of coefficient slopes.

1010. Sim, A. G.; and Curry, R. E.: **Flight-Determined Stability and Control Derivatives for the F-111 TACT Research Aircraft.** NASA TP-1350, H-1004, <u>October 1978</u>, 79N10068, #.

A flight investigation was conducted to provide a stability and control derivative data base for the F-111 transonic aircraft technology research aircraft. Longitudinal and lateral-directional data were obtained as functions of Mach number, angle of attack, and wing sweep. For selected derivatives, the flight results were correlated with derivatives calculated based on vehicle geometry. The validity of the angle of attack measurement was independently verified at a Mach number of 0.70 for angles of attack between 3 and 10 degrees.

1011. Curry, R. E.: **Utilization of the Wing-Body Aerodynamic Analysis Program.** NASA TM-72856, H-1071, <u>October 1978</u>, 79N10020, #.

The analysis program was used to investigate several aircraft characteristics. The studies performed included vehicle stability analysis, determination of upwash angle, identification of nonpotential flow, launch dynamics, and wake vortex upset loads. The techniques and are discussed. When possible, computed results are compared with experimental data.

1012. Ko, W. L.: **Effect of Crack Size on the Natural Frequencies of a Cracked Plate.** *International Journal of Fracture*, Vol. 14, <u>October 1978</u>, pp. R273–R275, 79A20012.

Results are presented for a finite element modal analysis of a centrally cracked rectangular plate made of linearly elastic material. The objective is to assess the effect of crack size on the natural vibration frequencies of the cracked plate. Only the in-plane vibration modes are studied. The results presented are finite-element mesh-size dependent. Namely, shrinking the mesh size, especially in the crack tip region,

would change the magnitudes of the natural frequencies, and the trends would be the same as shown in the present note.

1013. *Hamer, M. J.; and Kurtenbach, F. J.: **A Simplified Gross Thrust Computing Technique for an Afterburning Turbofan Engine.** *Why Flight Test, Proceedings of the Ninth Annual SFTE Symposium*, Arlington, Texas, <u>October 4–6, 1978</u>, pp. 22-1 to 22-20, (see A79-50426 22-01), 79A50440.

A simplified gross thrust computing technique extended to the F100-PW-100 afterburning turbofan engine is described. The technique uses measured total and static pressures in the engine tailpipe and ambient static pressure to compute gross thrust. Empirically evaluated calibration factors account for three-dimensional effects, the effects of friction and mass transfer, and the effects of simplifying assumptions for solving the equations. Instrumentation requirements and the sensitivity of computed thrust to transducer errors are presented. NASA altitude facility tests on F100 engines (computed thrust versus measured thrust) are presented, and calibration factors obtained on one engine are shown to be applicable to the second engine by comparing the computed gross thrust. It is concluded that this thrust method is potentially suitable for flight test application and engine maintenance on production engines with a minimum amount of instrumentation.

*Computing Devices Co., Ottawa, Canada.

1014. Iliff, K. W.; Maine, R. E.; and Montgomery, T. D.: **Considerations in the Analysis of Flight Test Maneuvers.** *Why Flight Test, Proceedings of the Ninth Annual SFTE Symposium*, Arlington, Texas, <u>October 4–6, 1978</u>, pp. 10-1 to 10-36, (see A79-50426 22-01), 79A50433.

This paper discusses the application of a maximum likelihood estimator to dynamic flight-test data. The information presented is based on the experience in the past twelve years at the NASA Dryden Flight Research Center of estimating stability and control derivatives from over 3,000 maneuvers from 32 aircraft. The overall approach to the analysis of dynamic flight-test data is discussed. Detailed requirements for data and instrumentation are discussed and several examples of the types of problems that may be encountered are presented.

1015. Jenkins, J. M.; Schuster, L. S.; and Carter, A. L.: **Correlation of Predicted and Measured Thermal Stresses on a Truss-Type Aircraft Structure.** NASA TM-72857, H-1074, <u>November 1978</u>, 79N11995, #.

A test structure representing a portion of a hypersonic vehicle was instrumented with strain gages and thermocouples. This test structure was then subjected to laboratory heating representative of supersonic and hypersonic flight conditions. A finite element computer model of this structure was developed using several types of elements with the NASA structural analysis (NASTRAN) computer program. Temperature inputs from the test were used to generate predicted model thermal stresses and these were correlated with the test measurements.

1016. Burcham, F. W., Jr.: **Propulsion-Flight Control Integration Technology.** AGARD-AG-234, *Active Controls in Aircraft Design*, November 1978, (see N79-16864 08-08), 79N16872, #.

The propulsion-flight control integration technology (PROFIT) concept to be implemented on a high performance supersonic twin-engine aircraft which will make possible the evaluation of a wide variety of integrated control concepts is discussed. The aircraft's inlet, engine, and flight control systems are to be integrated with a digital computer. The airplane control hardware is to be modified to provide the necessary capability for control research; software will be used to provide flexibility in the control integration capability. The background for flight and propulsion control system development and probable future trends are described. Examples of integrated control research that have application to future aircraft designs are also presented.

1017. Deets, D. A.; and *Crother, C. A.: **Highly Maneuverable Aircraft Technology.** AGARD AG-234, *Active Controls in Aircraft Design*, November 1978, (see N79-16864 08-08), 79N16871, #.

A remotely piloted research vehicle (RPRV) with active controls designed to develop high maneuverable aircraft technologies (HiMAT) is described. The HiMAT RPRV is the central element in a new method to bring advanced aircraft technologies to a state of readiness. The RPRV is well into the construction phase, with flight test evaluations planned. The closely coupled canard-wing vehicle includes relaxed static stability, direct force control, and a digital active control system. Nonlinearities in the aerodynamics led to unusual demands on the active control systems. For example, the longitudinal static margin is 10-percent negative at low angles of attack, but increases to 30-percent negative at high angles of attack and low Mach numbers. The design procedure followed and experiences encountered as they relate to the active control features are discussed. Emphasis is placed on the aspects most likely to be encountered in the design of a full-scale operational vehicle. In addition, a brief overview of the flight control system features unique to the RPRV operation is presented.

*Rockwell International Corp., Los Angeles, California.

ECN-14280

HiMAT RPRV

1018. Hartmann, G. L.; Stein, G.; Szalai, K. J.; Brown, S. R.; and Petersen, K. L.: **F-8 Active Control.** AGARD AG-234, paper 6, Active Controls in Aircraft Design, November 1978, (see N79-16864 08-08), 79N16870, #.

An advanced flight control research program conducted with a modified F-8C aircraft is described. Key technologies investigated include system redundancy management and active control laws. Two control law packages proposed for flight test are discussed. The first is the control configured vehicle package which incorporates command augmentation, boundary control, ride smoothing, and maneuver flap functions. The second package is an adaptive control law based on a parallel channel maximum likelihood estimation algorithm. The design, implementation, and flight test experience with both sets of control laws are described.

1019. Iliff, K. W.: **Estimation of Aerodynamic Characteristics From Dynamic Flight Test Data.** AGARD CP-235, Dynamic Stability Parameters, November 1978, (see N79-15061 06-08), 79N15075, #.

Significant effort was spent in estimating unknown aircraft coefficients, such as stability and control derivatives from dynamic flight maneuvers. The techniques used to estimate these coefficients are becoming increasingly complex; however, these techniques make it possible to obtain estimates of coefficients that in the past were nearly impossible to obtain. A survey of the investigations that were undertaken to obtain estimates of coefficients from dynamic flight maneuvers is presented. One method, the maximum likelihood estimation technique, is described briefly and some of the successful applications of the technique are presented. Possible techniques for analyzing responses obtained in the stall/spin regime are discussed. Recent data obtained in the stall/spin flight regime are presented along with a discussion of how some basic results can be obtained with simple analysis techniques.

1020. Szalai, K. J.; Jarvis, C. R.; Krier, G. E.; *Megna, V. A.; *Brock, L. D.; and *O'Donnell, R. N.: **Digital Fly-By-Wire Flight Control Validation Experience.** NASA TM-72860, R-1164, H-1080, <u>December 1978</u>, 79N14109, #.

The experience gained in digital fly-by-wire technology through a flight test program being conducted by the NASA Dryden Flight Research Center in an F-8C aircraft is described. The system requirements are outlined, along with the requirements for flight qualification. The system is described, including the hardware components, the aircraft installation, and the system operation. The flight qualification experience is emphasized. The qualification process included the theoretical validation of the basic design, laboratory testing of the hardware and software elements, systems level testing, and flight testing. The most productive testing was performed on an iron bird aircraft, which used the actual electronic and hydraulic hardware and a simulation of the F-8 characteristics to provide the flight environment. The iron bird was used for sensor and system redundancy management testing, failure modes and effects testing, and stress testing in many cases with the pilot in the loop. The flight test program confirmed the quality of the validation process by achieving 50 flights without a known undetected failure and with no false alarms.

*Charles Draper Laboratory, Cambridge, Massachusetts, Inc.

1021. *Burnham, D. C.; *Hallock, J. N.; **Tombach, I. H.; †Brashears, M. R.; and Barber, M. R.: **Ground-Based Measurements of the Wake Vortex Characteristics of a B-747 Aircraft in Various Configurations.** NASA TM-80474, AD-A067588, <u>December 1978</u>, 79N26016, #.

A Boeing 747 aircraft flew 54 passes at low altitude over ground based sensors. Vortex velocities were measured by a laser Doppler velocimeter, an array of monostatic acoustic sounders, and an array of propeller anemometers. Flow visualization of the wake was achieved using smoke and balloon tracers and was recorded photographically. Data were obtained on vortex velocity fields, vortex decay, and the effects of spoilers and differential flap settings on the dissipation and structure of the vortices.

*Transportation Systems Center, Cambridge, Massachusetts.
**AeroVironment, Inc., Pasadena, California.
†Lockheed Missiles and Space Co., Huntsville, Alabama.

1022. Friend, E. L.; and Sakamoto, G. M.: **Flight Comparison of the Transonic Agility of the F-111A Airplane and the F-111 Supercritical Wing Airplane.** NASA TP-1368, H-985, <u>December 1978</u>, 79N13056, #.

A flight research program was conducted to investigate the improvements in maneuverability of an F-111A airplane equipped with a supercritical wing. In this configuration the aircraft is known as the F-111 TACT (transonic aircraft technology) airplane. The variable-wing-sweep feature permitted an evaluation of the supercritical wing in many configurations. The primary emphasis was placed on the transonic Mach number region, which is considered to be the principal air combat arena for fighter aircraft. An agility study was undertaken to assess the maneuverability of the F-111A aircraft with a supercritical wing at both design and off-design conditions. The evaluation included an assessment of aerodynamic and maneuver performance in conjunction with an evaluation of precision controllability during tailchase gunsight tracking tasks.

1023. Burcham, F. W., Jr.; Lasagna, P. L.; and *Oas, S. C.: **Measurements and Predictions of Flyover and Static Noise of a TF30 Afterburning Turbofan Engine.** NASA TP-1372, H-1017, <u>December 1978</u>, 79N13045, #.

The noise of the TF30 afterburning turbofan engine in an F-111 airplane was determined from static (ground) and flyover tests. A survey was made to measure the exhaust temperature and velocity profiles for a range of power settings. Comparisons were made between predicted and measured jet mixing, internal, and shock noise. It was found that the noise produced at static conditions was dominated by jet mixing noise, and was adequately predicted by current methods. The noise produced during flyovers exhibited large contributions from internally generated noise in the forward arc. For flyovers with the engine at nonafterburning power, the internal noise, shock noise, and jet mixing noise were accurately predicted. During flyovers with afterburning power settings, however, additional internal noise believed to be due to the afterburning process was evident; its level was as much as 8 decibels above the nonafterburning internal noise. Power settings that produced exhausts with inverted velocity profiles appeared to be slightly less noisy than power settings of equal thrust that produced uniform exhaust velocity profiles both in flight and in static testing.

*Boeing Co. Airplane Co., Seattle, Washington.

1024. Kurtenbach, F. J.: **Comparison of Calculated and Altitude-Facility-Measured Thrust and Airflow of Two Prototype F100 Turbofan Engines.** NASA TP-1373, H-1015, <u>December 1978</u>, 79N13044, #.

A comparison is made of the facility performance data for the two engines with an engine performance model, and it provides corrections that can be applied to the model so that it represents the test engines accurately over the flight envelope. Test conditions ranged from Mach numbers of 0.80 to 2.00 and altitudes from 4020 meters to 15,240 meters. Two distortion screens were used to determine the effect of distortion on airflow. Reynolds number effects were also determined. Engine hysteresis is documented, as is an attempt to determine engine degradation. The calibrated engine model had a twice standard deviation accuracy of approximately 1.24 percent for corrected airflow and 2.38 percent for gross thrust.

1025. Brenner, M. J.; Iliff, K. W.; and Whitman, R. K.: **Effect of Sampling Rate and Record Length on the Determination of Stability and Control Derivatives.** NASA TM-72858, H-1077, December 1978, 79N12096, #.

Flight data from five aircraft were used to assess the effects of sampling rate and record length reductions on estimates of stability and control derivatives produced by a maximum likelihood estimation method. Derivatives could be extracted from flight data with the maximum likelihood estimation method even if there were considerable reductions in sampling rate and/or record length. Small amplitude pulse maneuvers showed greater degradation of the derivative maneuvers than large amplitude pulse maneuvers when these reductions were made. Reducing the sampling rate was found to be more desirable than reducing the record length as a method of lessening the total computation time required without greatly degrading the quantity of the estimates.

1026. *Siegel, W. H.; Fields, R. A.; and **Easley, J. T.: **Experimental Investigation of the Buckling Characteristics of a Beaded Skin Panel for a Hypersonic Aircraft—Including Comparisons With Finite Element and Classical Analyses.** ASME Paper 78-WA/AERO-3, presented at the American Society of Mechanical Engineers, Winter Annual Meeting, San Francisco, California, December 10–15, 1978, 79A19717, #.

Results of a compression test of a beaded panel intended for a proposed hypersonic aircraft are presented. The panel was tested to failure at room temperature to determine its buckling characteristics, in particular, to study the buckling caused by pure compression. The boundary conditions of the panel simulated as nearly as possible a wing mounted condition. Strain, out-of-plane deflection, and load data were measured, and elastic buckling strength as well as mode shapes of the panel were determined. Application of the moire technique is described.

*University of California, Berkley, California and Lawrence Livermore Laboratory, Livermore, California.
**University of Kansas, Lawrence, Kansas.

1027. Montoya, L. C.; *Flechner, S. G.; and *Jacobs, P. F.: **Effect of an Alternate Winglet on the Pressure and Spanwise Load Distributions of a First Generation Jet Transport Wing.** NASA TM-78786, L-12519, December 1978, 79N14012, #.

Pressure and spanwise load distributions on a first-generation jet transport semispan model at subsonic speeds are presented. The wind tunnel data were measured for the wing with and without an alternate winglet. The results show that the winglet affected outboard wing pressure distributions and increased the spanwise loads near the tip.

*NASA Langley Research Center, Hampton, Virginia.

1028. Szalai, Kenneth J.: **The F-8 Digital Fly-By-Wire Program.** A Status Report to the Winter Meeting of the ASME, December 13, 1978.

1029. Gee, S. W.; and Brown, Samuel R.: **Flight Tests of a Radio-Controlled Airplane Mode With a Free-Wing, Free-Canard Configuration.** NASA TM-72853, H-1008, 1978, 78N18042, #.

Flight characteristics, controllability, and potential operating problems were investigated in a radio-controlled airplane model in which the wing is so attached to the fuselage that it is free to pivot about a spanwise axis forward of its aerodynamic center and is subject only to aerodynamic pitching moments imposed by lift and drag forces and a control surface. A simple technique of flying the test vehicle in formation with a pickup truck was used to obtain trim data. The test vehicle was flown through a series of maneuvers designed to permit evaluation of certain characteristics by observation. The free-wing free-canard concept was determined to be workable. Stall/spin characteristics were considered to be excellent, and no effect on longitudinal stability was observed when center of gravity changes were made. Several problems were encountered during the early stages of flight testing, such as aerodynamic lockup of the free canard and excessive control sensitivity. Lack of onboard instrumentation precluded any conclusions about gust alleviation or ride qualities.

1030. *Dunham, R. E., Jr.; Barber, M. R.; and Croom, D. R.: **Wake Vortex Technology.** NASA CP-2036-PT-2. *NASA CTOL Transport Technology*, 1978, pp. 757–771, (see N78-29046 20-01), 78N29055, #.

A brief overview of the highlights of NASA's wake vortex minimization program is presented. The significant results of this program are summarized as follows: (1) it is technically feasible to reduce significantly the rolling upset created on a trailing aircraft; (2) the basic principles or methods by which reduction in the vortex strength can be achieved have been identified; and (3) an analytical capability for investigating aircraft vortex wakes has been developed.

*NASA Langley Research Center, Hampton, Virginia.

1031. Ko, W. L.: **An Orthotropic Sandwich Plate Containing a Part-Through Crack Under Mixed Mode Deformation.** *Engineering Fracture Mechanics*, Vol. 10, No. 1, 1978, pp. 15–23, 78A23567.

1032. Fields, R. A.: **Dryden Flight Research Center Hot Structures Research.** *Recent Advan. in Structures for Hypersonic Flight*, NASA CP-2065, Part 2, 1978, pp. 707–750, (see N79-21435 12-39), 79N21441, #.

The facilities, testing techniques, and design methods are described for NASA Dryden Flight Research Center. High temperature strain gage technology, realistic flight hardware fabrication, and structural analysis are discussed. A considerable amount of experimental work on hot structure concepts for hypersonic vehicles was performed; all the work is not complete, and there are still problem areas that need to be resolved.

1033. Shideler, J. L.; Fields, R. A.; and Reardon, L. F.: **Tests of Beaded and Tubular Structural Panels.** *Recent Advan. in Structures for Hypersonic Flight*, NASA CP-2065, Part 2, 1978, pp. 538–576, (see N79-21435 12-39), 79N21436, #.

Two efficient concepts built from curved elements were identified, and a data base for tubular panels was developed. The tubular panel failure modes were understood, and the data base for these panels indicated that their performance can be predicted. The concepts are currently being tested in a realistic builtup structure; 157 room temperature tests and 67 hot tests were made with no structural failures, although all of these tests were not at the design load of the structure.

1034. Lux, D. P.: **In-Flight Three-Dimensional Boundary Layer and Wake Measurements From a Swept Supercritical Wing.** NASA CP-2045-PT-2. *NASA Langley Res. Center Advanced Technology Airfoil Res.*, Vol. 1, Part 2, 1978, pp. 643–655, (see N79-19989 11-01), 79N20002, #.

Three-dimensional boundary layer and wake velocity profiles were measured in flight on the supercritical wing of the F-111 transonic aircraft technology aircraft. These data, along with pressure distributions, were obtained to establish a data base with which data obtained by three-dimensional analytical techniques could be correlated. Only a brief summary of the total data base is given. The data presented represented one chord station at a wing leading-edge sweep angle of 26 deg. They cover an angle of attack range from 6 degs to 9 degs at free-stream Mach numbers from 0.85 to 0.90. A brief discussion of the techniques used to obtain the boundary layer and wake profiles is included.

1035. Montoya, L. C.; *Bikle, P. F.; and Banner, R. D.: **Section Drag Coefficients From Pressure Probe Transverses of a Wing Wake at Low Speeds.** NASA CP-2045-PT-2. *NASA Langley Res. Center Advanced Technol. Airfoil Res.*, Vol. 1, Part 2, 1978, pp. 601–621, (see N79-19989 11-01), 79N20000, #. (See also 993.)

An in-flight wing wake section drag investigation was conducted using traversing pitot and static probes. The primary objective was to develop measurement techniques and improve the accuracy of in-flight wing profile drag measurements for low values of dynamic pressure and Reynolds number. Data were obtained on a sailplane for speeds from about 40 knots to 125 knots at chord Reynolds numbers between 1,000,000 and 3,000,000. Tests were conducted with zero flap deflection, deflected flaps, and various degrees of surface roughness, and for smooth and rough atmospheric conditions. Several techniques were used

to increase data reliability and to minimize certain bias errors. A discussion of the effects of a total pressure probe in a pressure gradient, and the effects of discrete turbulence levels, on the data presented and other experimental results is also included.

*Soaring Society of America, Santa Monica, California.

1979 Technical Publications

1036. Rediess, H. A.: **Avionics and Controls Research and Technology.** NASA CP-2061, January 1979, 79N15898.

The workshop provided a forum for industry and universities to discuss the state-of-the-art, identify the technology needs and opportunities, and describe the role of NASA in avionics and controls research.

1037. Webb, L. D.; Whitmore, S. A.; and *Janssen, R. L.: **Preliminary Flight and Wind Tunnel Comparisons of the Inlet/Airframe Interaction of the F-15 Airplane.** AIAA Paper 79-0102, presented at the American Institute of Aeronautics and Astronautics, Seventeenth Annual Aerospace Sciences Meeting, New Orleans, Louisiana, January 15–17, 1979, 79A23513, #.

Preliminary flight and wind tunnel comparison data are presented for the F-15 inlet/airframe interactions program. Test conditions and instrumentation for both the model and the aircraft are described. Flight and wind tunnel inlet drag data (for a 0-deg angle of attack and Mach numbers of 0.6, 0.9, and 1.2), derived by using nearly identical pressure integration equations, are compared. The effects of a movable cowl, movable ramps, and other system components on pressure flow fields along the airframe are discussed. Excellent agreement between wind tunnel and flight pressure-integrated drags is found at all three Mach numbers. The wind tunnel data show good agreement for pressure-integrated and force-balance-measured inlet drag, except at Mach 0.6. Flight-measured pressure-integrated inlet lift is lower than that measured in the wind tunnel.

1038. *Stevens, C. H.; *Spong, E. D.; Nugent, J.; and **Neumann, H. E.: **Reynolds Number, Scale, and Frequency Content Effects on F-15 Inlet Instantaneous Distortion.** AIAA Paper 79-0104, presented at the American Institute of Aeronautics and Astronautics, Seventeenth Annual Aerospace Sciences Meeting, New Orleans, Louisiana, January 15–17, 1979, 79A19533, #.

An inlet instantaneous distortion study program sponsored by NASA was recently completed using an F-15 fighter aircraft. Peak distortion data from subscale inlet model wind tunnel tests are shown to be representative of full-scale flight test peak distortion. The effects on peak distortion are investigated for engine presence, Reynolds number, scale and frequency content. Data are presented which show that: (1) the effect of engine presence on total pressure recovery, peak distortion, and turbulence is small but favorable, (2) increasing the Reynolds number increases total pressure recovery, decreases peak distortion, and decreases turbulence, and (3) increasing the filter cutoff frequency increases the calculated values of both peak distortion and turbulence.

*McDonnell Douglas Corp., St. Louis, Missouri.
**NASA Lewis Research Center, Cleveland, Ohio.

1039. Rawlings, K., III; Cooper, J. M.; and Hughes, D. L.: **Dynamic Test Techniques—Concepts and Practices.** *Society of Flight Test Engineers, Journal*, Vol. 1, January 1979, pp. 10–20, 79A50164.

The concepts involved in dynamic performance testing represent a philosophy of developing a single, coherent performance model using thrust and drag modeling. It is shown that if all thrust drag interactions, maneuver rates, and instrumentation are taken into consideration, it is possible to generate a lift/drag model which is capable of predicting performance from nearly any maneuver. Although this capability is dependent on the ability to calculate gross thrust adequately, the engines can be calibrated through static thrust runs and the thrust computation procedures verified in flight. The capability of generating a consistent lift/drag model in considerably less time than conventional performance methods is demonstrated.

1040. Hedgley, D. R.: **A Characterization of the Real Zeros of a Particular Transcendental Function.** NASA TP-1420, H-1065, March 1979, 79N18679, #.

The real zeros of the transcendental function $y = ax + be^{cx}$ are characterized, and the results should alleviate the difficulty of determining their existence, location, and number.

1041. Jenkins, J. M.; Fields, R. A.; and Sefic, W. J.: **Elevated-Temperature Effects on Strain Gages on the YF-12A Wing.** Presented at the Society for Experimental Stress Analysis, Spring Meeting, Wichita, Kansas, May 14–18, 1978, *Experimental Mechanics*, Vol. 19, March 1979, pp. 81–86, 79A26400.

A general study is made of the effects of structural heating on calibrated-strain-gage load measurements on the wing of a supersonic airplane. The primary emphasis is on temperature-induced effects as they relate to slope changes and thermal shifts of the applied load/strain relationships. These effects are studied by using the YF-12A airplane, a structural computer model, and subsequent analyses. Such topics as the thermal environment of the structure, the variation of load paths at elevated temperature, the thermal response characteristics of load equations, elevated-temperature load-measurement approaches, the thermal calibration of wings,

and the correlation of strains are discussed. Ways are suggested to measure loads with calibrated strain gages in the supersonic environment.

1042. Iliff, K. W.; Maine, R. E.; and Montgomery, T. D.: **Important Factors in the Maximum Likelihood Analysis of Flight Test Maneuvers.** NASA TP-1459, H-1076, April 1979, 79N22113, #.

The information presented is based on the experience in the past 12 years at the NASA Dryden Flight Research Center of estimating stability and control derivatives from over 3500 maneuvers from 32 aircraft. The overall approach to the analysis of dynamic flight test data is outlined. General requirements for data and instrumentation are discussed and several examples of the types of problems that may be encountered are presented.

1043. Jenkins, J. M.: **Correlation of Predicted and Measured Thermal Stresses on an Advanced Aircraft Structure With Similar Materials.** NASA TM-72862, H-1086, April 1979, 79N20989, #.

A laboratory heating test simulating hypersonic heating was conducted on a heat-sink type structure to provide basic thermal stress measurements. Six NASTRAN models utilizing various combinations of bar, shear panel, membrane, and plate elements were used to develop calculated thermal stresses. Thermal stresses were also calculated using a beam model. For a given temperature distribution there was very little variation in NASTRAN calculated thermal stresses when element types were interchanged for a given grid system. Thermal stresses calculated for the beam model compared similarly to the values obtained for the NASTRAN models. Calculated thermal stresses compared generally well to laboratory measured thermal stresses. A discrepancy of significance occurred between the measured and predicted thermal stresses in the skin areas. A minor anomaly in the laboratory skin heating uniformity resulted in inadequate temperature input data for the structural models.

1044. Tanner, R. R.; and Montgomery, T. D.: **Stability and Control Derivative Estimates Obtained From Flight Data for the Beech 99 Aircraft.** NASA TM-72863, H-1081, April 1979, 79N20134, #.

Lateral-directional and longitudinal stability and control derivatives were determined from flight data by using a maximum likelihood estimator for the Beech 99 airplane. Data were obtained with the aircraft in the cruise configuration and with one-third flap deflection. The estimated derivatives show good agreement with the predictions of the manufacturer.

1045. Burcham, F. W., Jr.: **Measurements and Predictions of Flyover and Static Noise of an**

Afterburning Turbofan Engine in an F-111 Airplane. AIAA Paper 79-7018, *Proceedings of the Fourth International Symposium on Air Breathing Engines*, Orlando, Florida, April 1–6, 1979, pp. 133–145, (see A79-29376 11-07), 79A29391, #.

The noise of the TF30 afterburning turbofan engine in an F-111 airplane was determined from static (ground) and flyover tests. Exhaust temperatures and velocity profiles were measured for a range of power settings. Comparisons were made between predicted and measured jet mixing, internal, and shock noise. It was found that the noise produced at static conditions was dominated by jet mixing noise, and was adequately predicted by current methods. The noise produced during flyovers exhibited large contributions from internally generated noise in the forward arc. For flyovers with the engine at nonafterburning power, the internal noise, shock noise, and jet mixing noise were accurately predicted. During flyovers with afterburning power settings, however, additional internal noise believed to be due to the afterburning process was evident; its level was as much as 8 decibels above the nonafterburning internal noise.

1046. Edwards, J. W.: **Applications of Laplace Transform Methods to Airfoil Motion and Stability Calculations.** AIAA Paper 79-0772, *Technical Papers on Structures and Materials*, Twentieth Structures, Structural Dynamics, and Materials Conference, St. Louis, Missouri, April 4–6, 1979, pp. 465–481, (see A79-29002 11-39), 79A29050, #.

This paper reviews the development of generalized unsteady aerodynamic theory and presents a derivation of the generalized Possion integral equation. Numerical calculations resolve questions concerning subsonic indicial lift functions and demonstrate the generation of Kutta waves at high values of reduced frequency, subsonic Mach number, or both. The use of rational function approximations of unsteady aerodynamic loads in aeroelastic stability calculations is reviewed, and a reformulation of the matrix Pade approximation technique is given. Numerical examples of flutter boundary calculations for a wing which is to be flight tested are given. Finally, a simplified aerodynamic model of transonic flow is used to study the stability of an airfoil exposed to supersonic and subsonic flow regions.

1047. Ko, W. L.: **Elastic Constants for Superplastically Formed/Diffusion-Bonded Sandwich Structures.** AIAA Paper 79-0756, *Technical Papers on Dynamics and Loads*, Twentieth Structures, Structural Dynamics, and Materials Conference, St. Louis, Missouri, April 4–6, 1979, pp. 188–207, (see A79-28251 10-39), 79A28271, #. (See also 1102.)

Formulae and the associated graphs are presented for contrasting the effective elastic constants for a superplastically formed/diffusion-bonded (SPF/DB) corrugated sandwich core and a honeycomb sandwich core.

The results used in the comparison of the structural properties of the two types of sandwich cores are under conditions of equal sandwich density. It was found that the stiffness in the thickness direction of the optimum SPF/DB corrugated core (i.e., triangular truss core) was lower than that of the honeycomb core, and that the former had higher transverse shear stiffness than the latter.

1048. *Davis, R. E.; *Champine, R. A.; and Ehernberger, L. J.: **Meteorological and Operational Aspects of 46 Clear Air Turbulence Sampling Missions With an Instrument B-57B Aircraft. Volume 1: Program Summary.** NASA TM-80044, May 1979, 79N25667, #.

The results of 46 clear air turbulence (CAT) probing missions conducted with an extensively instrumented B-57B aircraft are summarized. Turbulence samples were obtained under diverse conditions including mountain waves, jet streams, upper level fronts and troughs, and low altitude mechanical and thermal turbulence. CAT was encouraged on 20 flights comprising 77 data runs. In all, approximately 4335 km were flown in light turbulence, 1415 km in moderate turbulence, and 255 km in severe turbulence during the program. The flight planning, operations, and turbulence forecasting aspects conducted with the B-57B aircraft are presented.

*NASA Langley Research Center, Hampton, Virginia.

ECN-21064

B-57B Airplane

1049. Sisk, T. R.; and Matheny, N. W.: **Precision Controllability of the F-15 Airplane.** NASA TM-72861, H-1073, May 1979, 79N23979, #.

A flying qualities evaluation conducted on a preproduction F-15 airplane permitted an assessment to be made of its precision controllability in the high subsonic and low transonic flight regime over the allowable angle of attack range. Precision controllability, or gunsight tracking, studies were conducted in windup turn maneuvers with the gunsight in the caged pipper mode and depressed 70 mils. This evaluation showed the F-15 airplane to experience severe buffet and mild-to-moderate wing rock at the higher angles of attack. It showed the F-15 airplane radial tracking precision to vary from approximately 6 to 20 mils over the load factor range tested. Tracking in the presence of wing rock essentially doubled the radial tracking error generated at the lower angles of attack. The stability augmentation system affected the tracking precision of the F-15 airplane more than it did that of previous aircraft studied.

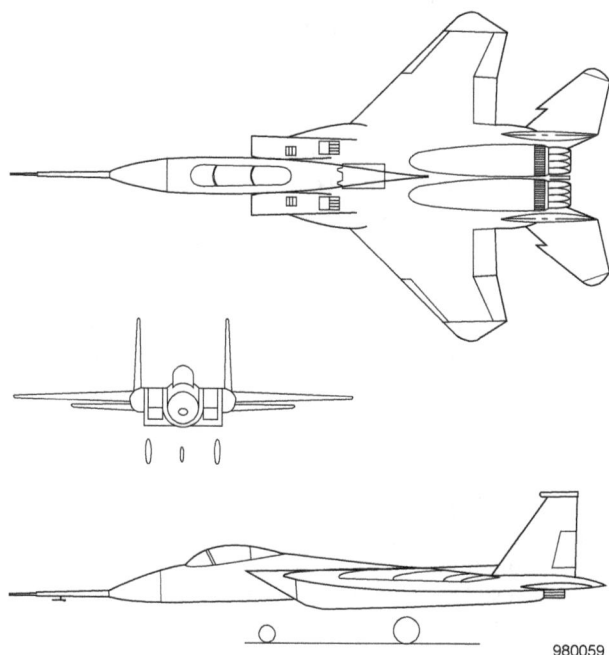

F-15 Aircraft, Three-View Drawing.

1050. Stoll, F.; Tremback, J. W.; and Arnaiz, H. H.: **Effect of Number of Probes and Their Orientation on the Calculation of Several Compressor Face Distortion Descriptors.** NASA TM-72859, H-1070, May 1979, 79N23087, #.

A study was performed to determine the effects of the number and position of total pressure probes on the calculation of five compressor face distortion descriptors. This study used three sets of 320 steady state total pressure measurements that were obtained with a special rotating rake apparatus in wind tunnel tests of a mixed-compression inlet. The inlet was a one third scale model of the inlet on a YF-12 airplane, and it was tested in the wind tunnel at representative flight conditions at Mach numbers above 2.0. The study shows that large errors resulted in the calculation of the distortion descriptors even with a number of probes that were considered adequate in the past. There were errors as large as 30 and -50 percent in several distortion descriptors for a configuration consisting of eight rakes with five equal-area-weighted probes on each rake.

1051. Saltzman, E. J.: **Reductions in Vehicle Fuel Consumption Due to Refinements in Aerodynamic Design.** *Learning To Use Our Environment; Proceedings of the Twenty-Fifth Annual Technical Meeting*, Seattle, Washington, April 30–May 2, 1979, pp. 63–68, Institute of Environmental Sciences, Prospect, Illinois (see A79-50326 22-42), 79A50335.

Over-the-highway fuel consumption and coastdown drag tests were performed on cab-over-engine, van type trailer trucks and modifications of these vehicles incorporating refinements in aerodynamic design. In addition, 1/25-scale models of these configurations, and derivatives of these configurations were tested in a wind tunnel to determine the effects of wind on the magnitude of the benefits that aerodynamic refinements can provide. The results of these tests are presented for a vehicle incorporating major redesign features and for a relatively simple add-on modification. These results include projected fuel savings on the basis of annual savings per vehicle year as well as probable nationwide fuel savings.

1052. Borek, Robert W.: **Practical Considerations in the Selection of Electrical Connectors for Aircraft Instrumentation Systems.** AGARD *Short Course on Flight Test Instrumentation*, Cranfield, England, May 7–18, 1979.

1053. Iliff, Kenneth W.; and Maine, Richard E.: **Observation on Maximum Likelihood Estimation of Aerodynamic Characteristics From Flight Data.** *Journal of Guidance and Control*, Vol. 2, No. 3, May–June 1979. (Also in *Rocket Technology and Cosmonautics*, September 1979, pp. 152–160, [in Russian].)

This paper discusses the application of a maximum likelihood estimation method in flight test data. The results are based on 11 years' experience of estimating stability and control derivatives from 3000 maneuvers from 30 aircraft. Flight results are presented from recent studies on understanding the discrepancies previously observed in the magnitude of the Cramer-Rao bounds, on the scale effects on the derivative estimates obtained from dynamic aircraft flight maneuvers, and on the analysis of lateral-directional maneuvers obtained in turbulence.

1054. *Ashworth, G. R.; Putnam, T. W.; Dana, W. H.; Enevoldson, E. K.; and Winter, W. R.: **Flight Test Evaluation of an RAF High Altitude Partial Pressure Protective Assembly.** NASA TM-72864, June 1979, 79N24654, #.

A partial pressure suit was evaluated during tests in an F-104 and F-15 as a protective garment for emergency descents. The garment is an pressure jerkin and modified anti-g suit combined with an oronasal mask. The garment can be donned and doffed at the aircraft to minimize thermal buildup. The oronasal mask was favored by the pilots due to its immobility

182

on the face during high g-loading. The garment was chosen to provide optimum dexterity for the pilot, which is not available in a full pressure suit, while protecting the pilot at altitudes up to 18,288 meters, during a cabin decompression, and subsequent aircraft descent. During cabin decompressions in the F-104 and F-15, cabin pressure altitude was measured at various aircraft angles of attack, Mach numbers, and altitudes to determine the effect of the aerodynamic slipstream on the cabin altitude.

*System Development Corp., Edwards, California.

1055. Jenkins, J. M.: **Correlation of Predicted and Measured Thermal Stresses on an Advanced Aircraft Structure With Dissimilar Materials.** NASA TM-72865, H-1092, June 1979, 79N27088, #.

Additional information was added to a growing data base from which estimates of finite element model complexities can be made with respect to thermal stress analysis. The manner in which temperatures were smeared to the finite element grid points was examined from the point of view of the impact on thermal stress calculations. The general comparison of calculated and measured thermal stresses is quite good and there is little doubt that the finite element approach provided by NASTRAN results in correct thermal stress calculations. Discrepancies did exist between measured and calculated values in the skin and the skin/frame junctures. The problems with predicting skin thermal stress were attributed to inadequate temperature inputs to the structural model rather than modeling insufficiencies. The discrepancies occurring at the skin/frame juncture were most likely due to insufficient modeling elements rather than temperature problems.

1056. Kurtenbach, F. J.: **Evaluation of a Simplified Gross Thrust Calculation Technique Using Two Prototype F100 Turbofan Engines in an Altitude Facility.** NASA TP-1482, H-1061, June 1979, 79N26057, #.

The technique which relies on afterburner duct pressure measurements and empirical corrections to an ideal one dimensional flow analysis to determine thrust is presented. A comparison of the calculated and facility measured thrust values is reported. The simplified model with the engine manufacturer's gas generator model are compared. The evaluation was conducted over a range of Mach numbers from 0.80 to 2.00 and at altitudes from 4020 meters to 15,240 meters. The effects of variations in inlet total temperature from standard day conditions were explored. Engine conditions were varied from those normally scheduled for flight. The technique was found to be accurate to a twice standard deviation of 2.89 percent, with accuracy a strong function of afterburner duct pressure difference.

1057. Wilner, D. O.: **AIFTDS Stand-Alone RMDU Flight Test Report.** NASA TM-72866, H-1099, July 1979, 79N28167, #.

The remote multiplexer/digitizer unit for the airborne integrated flight test data system was subjected to a flight test environment in order to study its dynamic response and that of its associated instrumentation circuitry during an actual flight test. The shielding schemes and instrumentation used are described and the data obtained are analyzed.

1058. Rediess, H. A.; and McIver, D. E.: **Avionics and Controls Research and Technology.** NASA CP-2061, L-12498, 1979, 79N15898, #.

The workshop provided a forum for industry and universities to discuss the state-of-the-art, identify the technology needs and opportunities, and describe the role of NASA in avionics and controls research.

1059. Wolowicz, C. H.; Brown, J. S., Jr.; and Gilbert, W. P.: **Similitude Requirements and Scaling Relationships as Applied to Model Testing.** NASA TP-1435, H-1022, August 1979, 79N30176, #.

The similitude requirements for the most general test conditions are presented. These similitude requirements are considered in relation to the scaling relationships, test technique, test conditions (including supersonic flow), and test objectives. Particular emphasis is placed on satisfying the various similitude requirements for incompressible and compressible flow conditions. For free flying models tests, the test velocities for incompressible flow are scaled from Froude number similitude requirements and those for compressible flow are scaled from Mach number similitude requirements. The limitations of various test techniques are indicated, with emphasis on the free flying model.

1060. Petersen, K. L.: **Flight Control Systems Development of Highly Maneuverable Aircraft Technology/HiMAT/Vehicle.** AIAA Paper 79-1789, presented at the American Institute of Aeronautics and Astronautics, Aircraft Systems and Technology Meeting, New York, New York, August 20–22, 1979, 79A47878, #.

The highly maneuverable aircraft technology (HiMAT) program was conceived to demonstrate advanced technology concepts through scaled-aircraft flight tests using a remotely piloted technique. Closed-loop primary flight control is performed from a ground-based cockpit, utilizing a digital computer and up/down telemetry links. A backup flight control system for emergency operation resides in an onboard computer. The onboard systems are designed to provide fail-operational capabilities and utilize two microcomputers, dual uplink receiver/decoders, and redundant hydraulic actuation and power systems. This paper discusses the design and validation of the primary and backup digital flight control systems as well as the unique pilot and specialized systems interfaces.

1061. *Hartmann, G.; *Stein, G.; and Powers, B.: **Flight Test Experience With an Adaptive Control System Using**

a Maximum Likelihood Parameter Estimation Technique. AIAA Paper 79-1702, *Collection of Technical Papers*, Guidance and Control Conference, Boulder, Colorado, August 6–8, 1979, (see A79-45351 19-12), 79A45357, #.

The flight test performance of an adaptive control system for the F-8 DFBW aircraft is summarized. The adaptive system is based on explicit identification of surface effectiveness parameters which are used for gain scheduling in a command augmentation system. Performance of this control law under various design parameter variations is presented. These include variations in test signal level, sample rate, and identification channel structure. Flight performance closely matches analysis and simulation predictions from previous references.

*Honeywell, Inc., Minneapolis, Minnesota.

1062. *Lorincz, D. J.; and Friend, E. L.: **Water Tunnel Visualization of the Vortex Flows of the F-15.** AIAA Paper 79-1649, *Collection of Technical Papers*, Atmospheric Flight Mechanics Conference for Future Space Systems, Boulder, Colorado, August 6–8, 1979, (see A79-45302 19-01), 79A45325, #.

Flow visualization studies were conducted in a diagnostic water tunnel to provide details of the wing, glove, and forebody vortex flow fields of the F-15 aircraft over a range of angles of attack and sideslip. Both the formation and breakdown of the vortex flow as a function of angle of attack and sideslip are detailed for the basic aircraft configuration. Additional tests showed that the wing upper surface vortex flows were sensitive to variations in an inlet mass flow ratio and an inlet cowl cross-sectional shape, were tested in addition to the basic forebody. Asymmetric forebody vortices were observed at zero sideslip and high angles of attack on each forebody. A large nose boom was added to each of the three forebodies, and it was observed that the turbulent wake shed from the boom disrupted the forebody vortices.

*Northrop Corp., Hawthorne, California.

1063. Smith, J. W.: **Analysis of a Lateral Pilot-Induced Oscillation Experienced on the First Flight of the YF-16 Aircraft.** NASA TM-72867, September 1979, 79N31220, #.

In order to compare and assess potential improvements, two control systems were modeled; the original first flight or prototype aircraft system, and a modification of the prototype system, which essentially reduced the overall gain for the takeoff and landing phase. In general, the overall system gain reduction of the modified flight control system was sufficient to avoid lateral pilot-induced oscillation tendencies. Lowering the system gain reduced the tendency to rate saturate, which resulted in correspondingly higher critical pilot gains for the same control input.

1064. Walker, H. J.: **Performance Evaluation Method for Dissimilar Aircraft Designs.** NASA RP-1042, H-1064, September 1979, 79N30139, #.

A rationale is presented for using the square of the wingspan rather than the wing reference area as a basis for nondimensional comparisons of the aerodynamic and performance characteristics of aircraft that differ substantially in planform and loading. Working relationships are developed and illustrated through application to several categories of aircraft covering a range of Mach numbers from 0.60 to 2.00. For each application, direct comparisons of drag polars, lift-to-drag ratios, and maneuverability are shown for both nondimensional systems. The inaccuracies that may arise in the determination of aerodynamic efficiency based on reference area are noted. Span loading is introduced independently in comparing the combined effects of loading and aerodynamic efficiency on overall performance. Performance comparisons are made for the NACA research aircraft, lifting bodies, century-series fighter aircraft, F-111A aircraft with conventional and supercritical wings, and a group of supersonic aircraft including the B-58 and XB-70 bomber aircraft. An idealized configuration is included in each category to serve as a standard for comparing overall efficiency.

1065. Jenkins, J. M.: **Criteria for Representing Circular Arc and Sine Wave Spar Webs by Non-Curved Elements.** NASA TM-72869, H-1106, October 1979, 79N33499, #.

The basic problem of how to simply represent a curved web of a spar in a finite element structural model was addressed. The ratio of flat web to curved web axial deformations and longitudinal rotations were calculated using NASTRAN models. Multiplying factors were developed from these calculations for various web thicknesses. These multiplying factors can be applied directly to the area and moment of inertia inputs of the finite element model. This allows the thermal stress relieving configurations of sine wave and circular arc webs to be simply accounted for in finite element structural models.

1066. Jenkins, J. M.: **Effect of Element Density on the NASTRAN Calculated Mechanical and Thermal Stresses of a Spar.** NASA TM-72868, H-1104, October 1979, 79N32151, #.

A NASTRAN model of a spar was examined to determine the sensitivity of calculated axial thermal stresses and bending stresses to changes in element density of the model. The thermal stresses calculated with three different element densities resulted in drastically differing values. The position of the constraint also significantly affected the value of the calculated thermal stresses. Mechanical stresses calculated from an applied loading were insensitive to element density.

1067. Cooper, D. W.; and *James, R.: **Shuttle Orbiter Radar Cross-Sectional Analysis.** NASA TM-72870, H-1095, October 1979, 80N10276, #.

Theoretical and model simulation studies on signal to noise levels and shuttle radar cross section are described. Premission system calibrations, system configuration, and postmission system calibration of the tracking radars are described. Conversion of target range, azimuth, and elevation into radar centered east north vertical position coordinates are evaluated. The location of the impinging rf energy with respect to the target vehicles body axis triad is calculated. Cross section correlation between the two radars is presented.

*James and Associates, Lancaster, California.

1068. *Muirhead, V. U.; and Saltzman, E. J.: **Reduction of Aerodynamic Drag and Fuel Consumption for Tractor-Trailer Vehicles.** *Journal of Energy,* Vol. 3, No. 5, September–October 1979, pp. 279–284, 80A16948, #.

Wind-tunnel tests were performed on a scale model of a cab-over-engine tractor-trailer vehicle and several modifications of the model. Results from two of the model configurations were compared with full-scale drag data obtained from similar configurations during coast-down tests. Reductions in fuel consumption derived from these tests are presented in terms of fuel quantity and dollar savings per vehicle year, based on an annual driving distance of 160,900 km (100,000 mi). The projected savings varied from 13,001 (3435) to 25,848 (6829) liters (gallons) per year which translated to economic savings from $3435 to about $6829 per vehicle year for an operating speed of 88.5 km/h (55 mph) and wind speeds near the national average of 15.3 km/h (9.5 mph). The estimated cumulative fuel savings for the entire U.S. fleet of cab-over-engine tractor, van-type trailer combinations ranged from 4.18 million kl (26.3 million bbl) per year for a low-drag configuration to approximately twice that amount for a more advanced configuration.

*Kansas University, Lawrence, Kansas.

1069. Maine, Richard E.; and Iliff, Kenneth W.: **Maximum Likelihood Estimation of Translational Acceleration Derivatives From Flight Data.** *Journal of Aircraft,* Vol. 16, No. 10, pp. 674–679, October 1979. (See also 995.)

This paper shows that translational acceleration derivatives, such as pitching moment due to rate of change of angle of attack, $C_{m_{\dot{\alpha}}}$, can be estimated from flight data with the use of appropriately design maneuvers. No new development of estimation methodology is necessary to analyze these maneuvers. Flight data from a T-37B airplane were used to verify that $C_{m_{\dot{\alpha}}}$, could be estimated from rolling maneuvers.

1070. Steers, L. L.: **Flight-Measured Afterbody Pressure Coefficients From an Airplane Having Twin Side-By-Side Jet Engines for Mach Numbers From 0.6 to 1.6.** NASA TP-1549, H-1066, November 1979, 80N11035, #.

Afterbody pressure distribution data were obtained in flight from an airplane having twin side-by-side jet exhausts. The data were obtained in level flight at Mach numbers from 0.60 to 1.60 and at elevated load factors for Mach numbers of 0.60, 0.90, and 1.20. The test altitude varied from 2300 meters (7500 feet) to 15,200 meters (50,000 feet) over a speed range that provided a matrix of constant Mach number and constant unit Reynolds number test conditions. The results of the full-scale flight afterbody pressure distribution program are presented in the form of plotted pressure distributions and tabulated pressure coefficients with Mach number, angle of attack, engine nozzle pressure ratio, and unit Reynolds number as controlled parameters.

1071. Iliff, K. W.: **Aircraft Identification Experience.** *AGARD Lecture Series No. 104* on Parameter Identification, AGARD LS-104, paper 6, November 1979, (see N80-19094 10-05), 80N19100, #.

Important aspects of estimating the unknown coefficients of the aircraft equations of motion from dynamic flight data are presented. The primary topic is the application of the maximum likelihood estimation technique. Basic considerations that must be addressed in the estimation of stability and control derivatives from conventional flight maneuvers are discussed. Some complex areas of estimation (such as estimation in the presence of atmospheric turbulence, estimation of acceleration derivatives, and analysis of maneuvers where both kinematic and aerodynamic coupling are present) are also discussed.

1072. Swaroop, R.; Brownlow, J. D.; and Winter, William R.: **Extreme Mean and Its Applications.** NASA TM-81346, December 1979, 80N13863, #.

Extreme value statistics obtained from normally distributed data are considered. An extreme mean is defined as the mean of p-th probability truncated normal distribution. An unbiased estimate of this extreme mean and its large sample distribution are derived. The distribution of this estimate even for very large samples is found to be nonnormal. Further, as the sample size increases, the variance of the unbiased estimate converges to the Cramer-Rao lower bound. The computer program used to obtain the density and distribution functions of the standardized unbiased estimate, and the confidence intervals of the extreme mean for any data are included for ready application. An example is included to demonstrate the usefulness of extreme mean application.

1073. Sefic, W. J.: **Friction Characteristic of Steel Skids Equipped With Skegs on a Lakebed Surface.** NASA TM-81347, H-1111, <u>December 1979</u>, 80N13027, #.

The coefficient of friction was determined for steel skids with and without skegs. The addition of a 1.27 centimeter deep skeg caused the coefficient of friction to increase from an average value of .36 to .53, a 47 percent increase over the flat skid. The addition of a .64 centimeter deep skeg increased the friction coefficient from .36 to .46, a 16 percent increase over the flat skid. Comparisons are made with data for similar test conditions obtained during the X-15 program.

1074. Carr, P. C.; and Gilbert, W. P.: **Effects of Fuselage Forebody Geometry on Low-Speed Lateral-Directional Characteristics of Twin-Tail Fighter Model at High Angles of Attack.** NASA TP-1592, L-13270, <u>December 1979</u>, 80N13002, #.

Low-speed, static wind-tunnel tests were conducted to explore the effects of fighter fuselage forebody geometry on lateral-directional characteristics at high angles of attack and to provide data for general design procedures. Effects of eight different forebody configurations and several add-on devices (e.g., nose strakes, boundary-layer trip wires, and nose booms) were investigated. Tests showed that forebody design features such as fineness ratio, cross-sectional shape, and add-on devices can have a significant influence on both lateral-directional and longitudinal aerodynamic stability. Several of the forebodies produced both lateral-directional symmetry and strong favorable changes in lateral-directional stability. However, the same results also indicated that such forebody designs can produce significant reductions in longitudinal stability near maximum lift and can significantly change the influence of other configuration variables. The addition of devices to highly tailored forebody designs also can significantly degrade the stability improvements provided by the clean forebody.

1980 Technical Publications

1075. Fields, R. A.; Reardon, L. F.; and Siegel, W. H.: **Loading Tests of a Wing Structure for a Hypersonic Aircraft.** NASA TP-1596, H-1046, <u>January 1980</u>, 80N15068, #.

Room-temperature loading tests were conducted on a wing structure designed with a beaded panel concept for a Mach 8 hypersonic research airplane. Strain, stress, and deflection data were compared with the results of three finite-element structural analysis computer programs and with design data. The test program data were used to evaluate the structural concept and the methods of analysis used in the design. A force stiffness technique was utilized in conjunction with load conditions which produced various combinations of panel shear and compression loading to determine the failure envelope of the buckling critical beaded panels The

force-stiffness data did not result in any predictions of buckling failure. It was, therefore, concluded that the panels were conservatively designed as a result of design constraints and assumptions of panel eccentricities. The analysis programs calculated strains and stresses competently. Comparisons between calculated and measured structural deflections showed good agreement. The test program offered a positive demonstration of the beaded panel concept subjected to room-temperature load conditions.

1076. Lasagna, P. L.; Mackall, K. G.; Burcham, F. W., Jr.; and Putnam, T. W.: **Landing Approach Airframe Noise Measurements and Analysis.** NASA TP-1602, <u>January 1980</u>, 80N15028, #.

Flyover measurements of the airframe noise produced by the AeroCommander, JetStar, CV-990, and B-747 airplanes are presented for various landing approach configurations. Empirical and semiempirical techniques are presented to correlate the measured airframe noise with airplane design and aerodynamic parameters. Airframe noise for the jet-powered airplanes in the clean configuration (flaps and gear retracted) was found to be adequately represented by a function of airplane weight and the fifth power of airspeed. Results show the airframe noise for all four aircraft in the landing configuration (flaps extended and gear down) also varied with the fifth power of airspeed, but this noise level could not be represented by the addition of a constant to the equation for clean-configuration airframe noise.

1077. *Dougherty, N. S., Jr.; and *Fisher, D. F.: **Boundary-Layer Transition on a 10-Deg Cone—Wind Tunnel/Flight Correlation.** AIAA Paper 80-0154. Presented at AIAA 18th Aerospace Sciences Meeting, Pasadena, California, <u>January 14–16, 1980</u>, 80A22737, #.

Boundary-layer transition location measurements were made on a 10-deg sharp cone in 23 wind tunnels of the US and Europe and in flight. The data were acquired at subsonic, transonic, and supersonic Mach numbers over a range of unit Reynolds numbers to obtain an improved understanding of wind tunnel flow quality influence. Cone surface microphone measurements showed Tollmien-Schlichting waves present. Transition location defined by pitot probe measurements showed transition Reynolds number to be correlatable to cone surface disturbance amplitude within ±20 percent for the majority of tunnel and flight data.

*ARO, Inc., Arnold Air Force Station, Tennessee.

1078. *Bangert, L. H.; Burcham, F. W., Jr.; and Mackall, K. G.: **YF-12 Inlet Suppression of Compressor Noise—First Results.** AIAA Paper 80-0099. Presented at AIAA 18th Aerospace Sciences Meeting, Pasadena, California, <u>January 14–16, 1980</u>, 80A34537, #.

An aeroacoustic test program was performed with a YF-12 aircraft at aerodynamic data that could determine the cause of inlet noise suppression observed earlier. The first results of the test program are presented here. There was no indication that the flow was close to choking. The data indicated significant reduction in sound pressure level (SPL) across the strut and bypass region at frequencies near the blade passing. Far-field data showed that the maximum sound pressure level near the blade-passing frequency was at zero degrees from the inlet centerline.

*Lockheed-California Co., Burbank, California.

1079. Plant, T. J.; Nugent, J.; and Davis, R. A.: **Flight-Measured Effects of Boattail Angle and Mach Number on the Nozzle Afterbody Flow of a Twin-Jet Fighter.** AIAA Paper 80-0110. Presented at AIAA 18th Aerospace Sciences Meeting, Pasadena, California, <u>January 14–16, 1980</u>, 80A23009, #.

The paper presents the flight-measured nozzle afterbody surface pressures and engine exhaust nozzle pressure-area integrated axial force coefficients on a twin-jet fighter for varying boattail angles. The objective of the tests was to contribute to a full-scale flight data base applicable to the nozzle afterbody drag of advanced tactical fighter concepts. The data were acquired during the NASA F-15 Propulsion/Airframe Interactions Flight Research Program. Nozzle boattail angles from 7.7 deg to 18.1 deg were investigated. Results are presented for cruise angle of attack at Mach numbers from 0.6 to 2.0 at altitudes from 20,000 to 45,000 feet. The data show the nozzle axial force coefficients to be a strong function of nozzle boattail angle and Mach number.

1080. Ko, W. L.: **Structural Properties of Superplastically Formed/Diffusion-Bonded Orthogonally Corrugated Core Sandwich Plates.** AIAA Paper 80-0304. Presented at AIAA 18th Aerospace Sciences Meeting, Pasadena, California, <u>January 14–16, 1980</u>, 80A18305, #. (See also 1196.)

This paper describes a new superplastically formed/diffusion-bonded (SPF/DB) orthogonally corrugated sandwich structure, and presents formulae and the associated plots for evaluating the effective elastic constants for the core of this new sandwich structure. Comparison of structural properties of this new sandwich structure with the conventional honeycomb core sandwich structure was made under the condition of equal sandwich density. It was found that the SPF/DB orthogonally corrugated sandwich core has higher transverse shear stiffness than the conventional honeycomb sandwich core. However, the former has lower stiffness in the sandwich core thickness direction than the latter.

1081. Maine, R. E.; and Iliff, K. W.: **Estimation of the Accuracy of Dynamic Flight-Determined Coefficients.** AIAA Paper 80-0171. Presented at AIAA 18th Aerospace

Sciences Meeting, Pasadena, California, <u>January 14–16, 1980</u>, 80A17700, #.

This paper discusses means of assessing the accuracy of maximum likelihood parameter estimates obtained from dynamic flight data. The commonly used analytical predictors of accuracy are compared from both statistical and simplified geometric standpoints. Emphasizing practical considerations, such as modeling error, the accuracy predictions are evaluated with real and simulated data. Improved computations of the Cramer-Rao bound to correct large discrepancies caused by colored noise and modeling error are presented. This corrected Cramer-Rao bound is the best available analytical predictor of accuracy. Engineering judgment, aided by such analytical tools, is the final arbiter of accuracy estimation.

1082. Arnaiz, H. H.; *Peterson, J. B., Jr.; and **Daugherty, J. C.: **Wind-Tunnel/Flight Correlation Study of Aerodynamic Characteristics of a Large Flexible Supersonic Cruise Airplane (XB-70-1). 3: A Comparison Between Characteristics Predicted From Wind-Tunnel Measurements and Those Measured in Flight.** NASA TP-1516, H-1079, <u>March 1980</u>, 80N17986, #.

A program was undertaken by NASA to evaluate the accuracy of a method for predicting the aerodynamic characteristics of large supersonic cruise airplanes. This program compared predicted and flight-measured lift, drag, angle of attack, and control surface deflection for the XB-70-1 airplane for 14 flight conditions with a Mach number range from 0.76 to 2.56. The predictions were derived from the wind-tunnel test data of a 0.03-scale model of the XB-70-1 airplane fabricated to represent the aeroelastically deformed shape at a 2.5 Mach number cruise condition. Corrections for shape variations at the other Mach numbers were included in the prediction. For most cases, differences between predicted and measured values were within the accuracy of the comparison. However, there were significant differences at transonic Mach numbers. At a Mach number of 1.06 differences were as large as 27 percent in the drag coefficients and 20 deg in the elevator deflections. A brief analysis indicated that a significant part of the difference between drag coefficients was due to the incorrect prediction of the control surface deflection required to trim the airplane.

*NASA Langley Research Center, Hampton, Virginia.
**NASA Ames Research Center, Moffett Field, California.

1083. McWithey, R. R.; Royster, D. M.; and Ko, W. L.: **Compression Panel Studies for Supersonic Cruise Vehicles.** NASA TP-1617, L-13525, NAS 1.60:1617, <u>March 1980</u>, 83N28099, #.

Results of analytical and experimental studies are summarized for titanium, boron fiber reinforced aluminum matrix composite, Borsic fiber reinforced aluminum matrix composite, and titanium sheathed Borsic fiber reinforced aluminum matrix composite stiffened panels. The results indicate that stiffened panels with continuous joints (i.e., brazed, diffusion bonded or adhesive bonded joints) are more structurally efficient than geometrically similar panels with discrete joints (i.e., spotwelded or bolted joints). In addition, results for various types of fiber reinforced aluminum matrix stiffened panels indicate that titanium sheathed Borsic fiber reinforced aluminum matrix composite panels are the most structurally efficient. Analytical results are also presented for graphite fiber reinforced polyimide matrix composite stiffened panels and superplastically formed and diffusion bonded titanium sandwich panels.

1084. Ehernberger, L. J.: **Clear Air Turbulence: Historical Comments.** NASA CP-2139, FAA-RD-80-67. *NASA Marshall Space Flight Center Proceedings Fourth Annual Workshop on Meteorological and Environmental Inputs to Aviation Systems,* March 1980 (see N81-14555 05-47), pp. 71–81, 81N14562, #.

The basic reference material for gust design criteria are cited. The status of clear air turbulence meteorology (forecasting and detection) is discussed. The directions of further research technology is indicated.

1085. Smith, J. W.; and Edwards, J. W.: **Design of a Nonlinear Adaptive Filter for Suppression of Shuttle Pilot-Induced Oscillation Tendencies.** NASA TM-81349, H-1119, April 1980, 80N21355, #.

Analysis of a longitudinal pilot-induced oscillation (PIO) experienced just prior to touchdown on the final flight of the space shuttle's approach landing tests indicated that the source of the problem was a combination of poor basic handling qualities aggravated by time delays through the digital flight control computer and rate limiting of the elevator actuators due to high pilot gain. A nonlinear PIO suppression (PIOS) filter was designed and developed to alleviate the vehicle's PIO tendencies by reducing the gain in the command path. From analytical and simulator studies it was shown that the PIOS filter, in an adaptive fashion, can attenuate the command path gain without adding phase lag to the system. With the pitch attitude loop of a simulated shuttle model closed, the PIOS filter increased the gain margin by a factor of about two.

1086. Ko, W. L.: **Elastic Constants for Superplastically Formed/Diffusion-Bonded Corrugated Sandwich Core.** NASA TP-1562, H-1094, May 1980, 80N23677, #.

Formulas and associated graphs for evaluating the effective elastic constants for a superplastically formed/diffusion bonded (SPF/DB) corrugated sandwich core, are presented. A comparison of structural stiffnesses of the sandwich core and a honeycomb core under conditions of equal sandwich core density was made. The stiffness in the thickness direction of the optimum SPF/DB corrugated core (that is, triangular truss core) is lower than that of the honeycomb

core, and that the former has higher transverse shear stiffness than the latter.

1087. Sisk, T. R.; and Matheny, N. W.: **Precision Controllability of the YF-17 Airplane.** NASA TP-1677, H-1089, May 1980, 80N23327, #.

A flying qualities evaluation conducted on the YF-17 airplane permitted assessment of its precision controllability in the transonic flight regime over the allowable angle of attack range. The precision controllability (tailchase tracking) study was conducted in constant-g and windup turn tracking maneuvers with the command augmentation system (CAS) on, automatic maneuver flaps, and the caged pipper gunsight depressed 70 mils. This study showed that the YF-17 airplane tracks essentially as well at 7 g's to 8 g's as earlier fighters did at 4 g's to 5 g's before they encountered wing rock. The pilots considered the YF-17 airplane one of the best tracking airplanes they had flown. Wing rock at the higher angles of attack degraded tracking precision, and lack of control harmony made precision controllability more difficult. The revised automatic maneuver flap schedule incorporated in the airplane at the time of the tests did not appear to be optimum. The largest tracking errors and greatest pilot workload occurred at high normal load factors at low angles of attack. The pilots reported that the high-g maneuvers caused some tunnel vision and that they found it difficult to think clearly after repeated maneuvers.

1088. Larson, T. J.; Flechner, S. G.; and Siemers, P. M., III: **Wind Tunnel Investigation of an All Flush Orifice Air Data System for a Large Subsonic Aircraft.** NASA TP-1642, H-1085, May 1980, 80N23304, #.

The results of a wind tunnel investigation on an all flush orifice air data system for use on a KC-135A aircraft are presented. The investigation was performed to determine the applicability of fixed all flush orifice air data systems that use only aircraft surfaces for orifices on the nose of the model (in a configuration similar to that of the shuttle entry air data system) provided the measurements required for the determination of stagnation pressure, angle of attack, and angle of sideslip. For the measurement of static pressure, additional flush orifices in positions on the sides of the fuselage corresponding to those in a standard pitot-static system were required. An acceptable but less accurate system, consisting of orifices only on the nose of the model, is defined and discussed.

1089. Swaroop, R.; Brownlow, J. D.; Ashworth, G. R.; and Winter, W. R.: **Bivariate Normal, Conditional and Rectangular Probabilities: A Computer Program With Applications.** NASA TM-81350, May 1980, 80N24099, #.

Some results for the bivariate normal distribution analysis are presented. Computer programs for conditional normal probabilities, marginal probabilities, as well as joint probabilities for rectangular regions are given: routines for computing fractile points and distribution functions are also presented. Some examples from a closed circuit television experiment are included.

1090. Ko, W. L.: **Elastic Stability of Superplastically Formed/Diffusion-Bonded Orthogonally Corrugated Core Sandwich Plates.** AIAA Paper 80-0683. Presented at 21st AIAA Structures, Structural Dynamics and Materials Conference, Seattle, Washington, <u>May 12–14, 1980</u>, pp. 167–176, 80A35005, #.

The paper concerns the elastic buckling behavior of a newly developed superplastically formed/diffusion-bonded (SPF/DB) orthogonally corrugated core sandwich plate. Uniaxial buckling loads were calculated for this type of sandwich plate with simply supported edges by using orthotropic sandwich plate theory. The buckling behavior of this sandwich plate was then compared with that of an SPF/DB unidirectionally corrugated core sandwich plate under conditions of equal structural density. It was found that the buckling load for the former was considerably higher than that of the latter.

1091. Reed, R. D.: **Flight Research Techniques Utilizing Remotely Piloted Research Vehicles.** AGARD LS-108, Paper 8, *Aircraft Assessment and Acceptance Testing,* (ISBN-02-835-0266-3), <u>May 1980</u>, (see N80-31329 22-01), AD-A088530, 80N31337, #.

The use of the remotely piloted research vehicle (RPRV) in aeronautical research is surveyed. The flight test experience that has been acquired with several types of RPRV's including those with a pilot in the loop is emphasized. The approaches utilized range from the simplest and least expensive of vehicles, such as the Minisniffer, to the sophisticated highly maneuverable aircraft technology (HiMAT) RPRV. The advantages and disadvantages of RPRV's are discussed, as well as safety considerations. The ground rules set early in a program can profoundly affect program cost effectiveness and timeliness.

1092. Bender, G. L.; Arnaiz, H.; Ottomeyer, D.; Woratschek, R.; Higgins, L.; and Tulloch, J. S.: **Preliminary Airworthiness Evaluation AH-1S Helicopter With Ogee Tip Shape Rotor Blades.** AD-A089625, USAAEFA-77-25, <u>May 1980</u>, 81N10061, #.

The United States Army Aviation Engineering Flight Activity conducted a Preliminary Airworthiness Evaluation of the AH-1S helicopter with OGEE tip-shape main rotor blades to determine if any improvement in performance or handling qualities resulted from replacing the K747 blades. Additionally, the acoustics signature of the OGEE blades were measured by the US Army Research and Technology Laboratories (Aeromechanics Lab). Tests were conducted at Edwards Air Force Base (elevation 2302 feet) and Coyote Flats (elevation 9980 feet), California from 1 November 1979 through 8 April 1980. Forty-five test flights were flown for a total of 36.6 productive hours (63.2 total hours). Both hover and level flight performance were degraded by installation of OGEE tip-shape main rotor blades. Low-speed handling qualities were unaffected by the OGEE blades. Other handling qualities tests were not accomplished. Results of acoustics tests will be reported by the laboratories under a separate cover.

1093. Larson, T. J.; and *Siemers, P. M., III: **Subsonic Tests of an All-Flush-Pressure-Orifice Air Data System.** NASA TP-1871, H-1122. Presented at the 1980 Air Data Systems Conference, Colorado, Springs, Colorado, May 1980, <u>June 1981</u>, 81N26144, #.

The use of an all-flush-pressure-orifice array as a subsonic air data system was evaluated in flight and wind tunnel tests. Two orifice configurations were investigated. Both used orifices arranged in a cruciform pattern on the airplane nose. One configuration also used orifices on the sides of the fuselage for a source of static pressure. The all-nose-orifice configuration was similar to the shuttle entry air data system (SEADS). The flight data were obtained with a KC-135A airplane. The wind tunnel data were acquired with a 0.035-scale model of the KC-135A airplane. With proper calibration, several orifices on the vertical centerline of the vehicle's nose were found to be satisfactory for the determination of total pressure and angle of attack. Angle of sideslip could be accurately determined from pressure measurements made on the horizontal centerline of the aircraft. Orifice pairs were also found that provided pressure ratio relationships suitable for the determination of Mach number. The accuracy that can be expected for the air data determined with SEADS during subsonic orbiter flight is indicated.

*NASA Langley Research Center, Hampton, Virginia.

1094. Ko, W. L.: **Comparison of Structural Behavior of Superplastically Formed/Diffusion-Bonded Sandwich Structures and Honeycomb Core Sandwich Structures.** NASA TM-81348, <u>June 1980</u>, 80N23685, #.

A superplasticity formed/diffusion-bonded (SPF/DB) orthogonally corrugated core sandwich structure is discussed and its structural behavior is compared to that of a conventional honeycomb core sandwich structure. The stiffness and buckling characteristics of the two types of sandwich structures are compared under conditions of equal structural density. It is shown that under certain conditions, the SPF/DB orthogonally corrugated core sandwich structure is slightly more efficient than the optimum honeycomb core (square-cell core) sandwich structure. However, under different conditions, this effect can be reversed.

1095. Ko, W. L.: **Mode I Fracture Behavior of Nonlinear Materials.** *International Journal of Fracture,* Vol. 16, <u>June 1980</u>, pp. 207–219, 80A39939, #.

A finite element analysis is presented for the Mode I fracture behavior of cracked plates (stationary crack) made of different nonlinear materials (elastoplastic or elastic locking). The assumed stress-strain behavior of the nonlinear materials was piecewise linear. For each given "stationary" crack size, the corresponding critical remote tensile stress was calculated based on the maximum crack-tip stress failure criterion. It was found that in the log-log plots of the critical remote stress versus critical crack length, the fracture data of the piecewise linear materials obey a "stepwise-linear-inverse-square-root" fracture law. It is also shown how the fracture data of the piecewise linear materials can be fitted by proper piecewise graphical shifting of the classical "inverse-square-root" fracture curve for the linearly elastic materials.

1096. Myers, A. F.; and Sheets, S. G.: **Qualification of HiMAT Flight Systems.** *Proceedings, Seventh Annual Technical Symposium of the Association for Unmanned Vehicle Systems,* Dayton, Ohio, June 16–18, 1980, pp. 1–10, 81A22603, #.

The highly maneuverable aircraft technology (HiMAT) remotely piloted research vehicle is discussed with emphasis on the advanced composite and metallic structures, digital fly-by-wire controls, and digitally implemented integrated propulsion control systems. Techniques used to qualify the systems for flight are examined. Computation and simulation of the HiMAT system are investigated in relation to Cyber-Varian simulation. The techniques used in flight qualification are complicated by ground based flight critical systems and severe onboard volume constraints imposed by the scale design.

1097. Bennett, George; Enevoldson, Einar; Gera, Joe; and Patton, Jim: **Pilot Evaluation of Sailplane Handling Qualities.** *Technical Soaring,* Vol. 5, No. 4, June 1980, pp. 3–14.

1098. Gilyard, G. B.; and Burken, J. J.: **Development and Flight Test Results of an Autothrottle Control System at Mach 3 Cruise.** NASA TP-1621, H-1090, July 1980, 80N26328, #.

Flight test results obtained with the original Mach hold autopilot designed the YF-12C airplane which uses elevator control and a newly developed Mach hold system having an autothrottle integrated with an altitude hold autopilot system are presented. The autothrottle tests demonstrate good speed control at high Mach numbers and high altitudes while simultaneously maintaining control over altitude and good ride qualities. The autothrottle system was designed to control either Mach number or knots equivalent airspeed (KEAS). Excellent control of Mach number or KEAS was obtained with the autothrottle system when combined with altitude hold. Ride qualities were significantly better than with the conventional Mach hold system.

1099. *McRae, D. S.; Fisher, D. F.; and **Peake, D. J.: **A Computational and Experimental Study of High Reynolds Number Viscous/Inviscid Interaction About a Cone at High Angle of Attack.** AIAA Paper 80-1422. Presented at 13th AIAA Fluid and Plasma Dynamics Conference, Snowmass, Colorado, July 14–16 1980, 80A44492, #.

The flow over a 5 deg problem for the flow over aircraft forebodies. A computational method utilizing the conically symmetric Navier-Stokes equations is used to obtain theoretical flow results which are compared with experimental data from the Ames Research Center 6- by 6-Foot Wind Tunnel and with results from a cone model sting mounted on an F-15 aircraft. The computed results agree well with the wind-tunnel data but less well with the flight data. Modification of the algebraic turbulence model was necessary to reflect an apparent lower turbulence level in flight than was present in the wind tunnel.

*USAF, Flight Dynamics Laboratory, Wright-Patterson AFB, Ohio.
**NASA Ames Research Center, Moffett Field, California.

1100. Pool, A.; Sanderson, K. C.; and *Ferrell, K. R.: **Helicopter Flight Test Instrumentation.** AGARD-AG-160-VOL-10, AD-A089909, July 1980, 80N33406.

The helicopter characteristics with which instrumentation must contend with are discussed. Typical tests that are conducted are outlined. Major aircraft components and systems which may be instrumented are listed and suggestions are made for sensors, locations, and installation. Instrumentation requirements are summarized. A sample instrumentation management technique is also presented.

*Army Aviation Research and Development Command, Edwards AFB, California.

1101. *Wuest, W.; Pool, A.; and Sanderson, K. C.: **Pressure and Flow Measurement.** AGARD-AG-160-VOL-11, AD-A090961, July 1980, 80N33407.

The evolution of flight test instrumentation systems during the last decade reflects the radical changes of electronic measuring techniques. Nevertheless the basic principles of measurement methods are essentially unchanged and the sensors for flow and pressure measurements have experienced only slight changes. The fundamentals of flow and pressure measurements are explained from the viewpoint of flight test instrumentation. An overview of modern instrumentation is given with important applications to altitude measurement, vertical and horizontal speed measurement, boundary layer, wake and engine flow measurement. The scope of this manual is to give self consistent information on the different techniques and systems and to give references for a more detailed study of special techniques.

*DFVLR, Goettingen, West Germany.

1102. Ko, William L.: **Elastic Constants for Superplastically Formed/Diffusion-Bonded Sandwich Structures.** *AIAA Journal*, Vol. 18, No. 8, pp. 986–987, August 1980. (See also 1047.)

Formulas for evaluating the effective elastic constants for a superplastically formed/diffusion-bonded (SPF/DB) unidirectionally corrugated sore sandwich structure like that shown in Fig. 1 are presented. This structure is formed by diffusion bonding three superplastic alloy sheets (two face sheets and one core sheet) in the selected areas and the superplastically expanding the multiple sheet pack inside a die cavity by using gas pressure. Thus, this structure is slightly different from the conventional corrugated-core sandwich structure because the corrugation leg does not have uniform thickness. Because of superplastic expansion, the diagonal segment of the corrugation leg is always thinner than the flat segment (crest or trough) of the corrugation leg, which has a thickness that is nearly the pre-expansion thickness. Thus, the results given by Ref. 2 for a corrugated-core sandwich plate cannot be used in the present structure without considerable modification.

1103. Balakrishnan, A. V.; and Edwards, J. W.: **Calculation of the Transient Motion of Elastic Airfoils Forced by Control Surface Motion and Gusts.** NASA TM-81351, H-1125, August 1980, 80N32329, #.

The time-domain equations of motion of elastic airfoil sections forced by control surface motions and gusts were developed for the case of incompressible flow. Extensive use was made of special functions related to the inverse transform of Theodorsen's function. Approximations for the special cases of zero stream velocity, small time, large and time are given. A numerical solution technique for the solution of the general case is given. Examples of the exact transient response of an airfoil are presented.

1104. *Nguyen, L. T.; *Gilbert, W. P.; Gera, J.; Iliff, K. W.; and Enevoldson, E. K.: **Application of High-Alpha Control System Concepts to a Variable-Sweep Fighter Airplane.** AIAA Paper 80-1582. AIAA Atmospheric Flight Mechanics Conference, Danvers, Massachusetts, August 11–13, 1980, 80A50098, #.

The use of control system design to enhance high-angle-of-attack flying qualities and departure/spin resistance has become an accepted and widely used approach for modern fighter aircraft. NASA and the Navy are currently conducting a joint research program to investigate the application of this technology to the F-14. The paper discusses the results of this program within the context of its contributions to advancing high-alpha control system technology. General topics covered include (1) analysis and design tools, (2) control system design approach, and (3) flight test approach and results.

*NASA Langley Research Center, Hampton, Virginia.

1105. *Hoyt, C. E.; Kempel, R. W.; and Larson, R. R.: **Backup Flight Control System for a Highly Maneuverable Remotely Piloted Research Vehicle.** AIAA Paper 80-1761. Presented at AIAA Guidance and Control Conference, Danvers, Massachusetts, August 11–13, 1980, pp. 283–289, 80A45548, #.

NASA is currently conducting flight tests of a remotely piloted subscale advanced fighter configuration as part of the Highly Maneuverable Aircraft Technology (HiMAT) program. This paper describes the initial development, user modification, and flight test experience of a back-up control system (BCS) contained within one of two onboard microprocessors. The development of the BCS proceeded in two distinct steps: the initial contractor development of control laws and logic to satisfy BCS design objectives, and user modifications required to satisfy operational requirements. A brief resume of flight qualification procedures and pilot comments is presented.

*Teledyne Ryan Aeronautical, San Diego, California.

1106. *Travassos, R. H.; *Gupta, N. K.; Iliff, K. W.; and Maine, R.: **Determination of an Oblique Wing Aircraft's Aerodynamic Characteristics.** AIAA Paper 80-1630. Presented at AIAA Atmospheric Flight Mechanics Conference, Danvers, Massachusetts, August 11–13, 1980. pp. 608–618, 80A45918, #.

In this paper, the integration of wind tunnel and flight test procedures are studied for specifying aerodynamic model forms. A procedure is described which employs a stepwise regression method to systematically determine model structures and F-ratio statistics to rank the importance of each aerodynamic coefficient within a given model. Application of this technique and wind tunnel procedures to an oblique-wing aircraft indicate that the aircraft's measured and estimated response are in good agreement at both small and large wing skew angles.

*Systems Control, Inc., Palo Alto, California.

1107. Shafer, M. F.: **Low Order Equivalent Models of Highly Augmented Aircraft Determined From Flight Data Using Maximum Likelihood Estimation.** AIAA Paper 80-1627. Presented at AIAA Atmospheric Flight Mechanics Conference, Danvers, Massachusetts, August 11–13, 1980, pp. 572–582, 80A45915, #. (See also 1220.)

This paper presents the results of a study of the feasibility of using low order equivalent mathematical models of a highly augmented aircraft, the F-8 digital fly-by-wire (DFBW), for flying qualities research. Increasingly complex models were formulated and evaluated using flight data and maximum likelihood estimation techniques. The aircraft actuator was modeled alone first. Next the equivalent derivatives were used to model the longitudinal unaugmented F-8 DFBW aircraft dynamics. The most complex model incorporated a pure time shift of the pilot input, a first order lag, and the basic longitudinal airframe model. This same model was then implemented for the F-8 DFBW aircraft in a highly augmented mode. Excellent matching of the dynamics resulted for this model, indicating that low order equivalent models which are good representations of the highly augmented F-8 DFBW aircraft can be formulated with these methods.

1108. Berry, D. T.; Powers, B. G.; Szalai, K. J.; and Wilson, R. J.: **A Summary of an In-Flight Evaluation of Control System Pure Time Delays During Landing Using the F-8 DFBW Airplane.** AIAA Paper 80-1626. Presented at AIAA Atmospheric Flight Mechanics Conference, Danvers, Massachusetts, <u>August 11–13, 1980</u>, pp. 561–571, 80A45914, #. (See also 1197.)

An in-flight investigation of the effect of pure time delays on low L/D space shuttle type landing tasks was undertaken. The results indicate that the sensitivity of the pilot ratings to changes in pure time delay in pitch is strongly affected by the task and only slightly affected by changes in control system augmentation mode. Low L/D spot landings from a lateral offset were twice as sensitive to pure time delay as normal low L/D landings. For comparison purposes, formation flying was also investigated, and was found to be less sensitive to time delay than the landing tasks.

1109. Maine, R. E.; and Iliff, K. W.: **Formulation and Implementation of a Practical Algorithm for Parameter Estimation With Process and Measurement Noise.** AIAA Paper 80-1603. Presented at AIAA Atmospheric Flight Mechanics Conference, Danvers, Massachusetts, <u>August 11–13, 1980</u>, pp. 397–411, 80A45896, #. (See also 1184, 1209.)

A new formulation is proposed for the problem of parameter estimation of dynamic systems with both process and measurement noise. The formulation gives estimates that are maximum likelihood asymptotically in time. The means used to overcome the difficulties encountered by previous formulations are discussed. It is then shown how the proposed formulation can be efficiently implemented in a computer program. A computer program using the proposed formulation is available in a form suitable for routine application. Examples with simulated and real data are given to illustrate that the program works well.

1110. Powers, B. G.: **Experience With an Adaptive Stick-Gain Algorithm to Reduce Pilot-Induced-Oscillation Tendencies.** AIAA Paper 80-1571. Presented at Atmospheric Flight Mechanics Conference, Danvers, Massachusetts, <u>August 11–13, 1980</u>, pp. 142–154, 80A45870, #

As part of a program to improve the approach and landing characteristics of the Space Shuttle, the NASA Dryden Flight Research Center has developed an adaptive algorithm that varies the longitudinal stick gearing to reduce the Shuttle's tendency for pilot-induced oscillation (PIO). This paper describes the algorithm, which is known as the PIO suppresser, and discusses some of the tradeoffs involved in optimizing the system. The results of fixed-base, moving-base, and in-flight simulations of the PIO suppresser are presented.

1111. Iliff, K. W.: **Stall/Spin Flight Results for the Remotely Piloted Spin Research Vehicle.** AIAA Paper 80-1563. Presented at AIAA Atmospheric Flight Mechanics Conference, Danvers, Massachusetts, <u>August 11–13, 1980</u>, pp. 62–75, 80A45862, #.

The unmanned, remotely piloted, unpowered, spin research vehicle was used to evaluate the effects of the nose boom and of a wind tunnel-designed nose strake on the vehicle's stall/spin characteristics. The flight-determined directional stability derivatives and the attempted spin entries indicated that the vehicle with a nose strake had increased resistance to departure and spin. The acquisition of high quality steady spin data for this vehicle was made possible by the remotely piloted technique. The zero control smooth spin modes were found to be highly repeatable for a given configuration and to vary with forebody configuration. Several spin recovery techniques, including a nose parachute, are also evaluated.

1112. Myers, A.: **Simulation Use in the Development and Validation of HiMAT Flight Software.** AGARD CP-272, Paper 22. *AGARD Advan. in Guidance and Control Systems Using Digital Tech.*, (ISBN-92-835-0247-7), <u>August 1980</u>, AD-A076146, 80N14039, #.

The use of real time simulation in the development and validation of flight software for the highly maneuverable aircraft technology (HiMAT) remotely piloted research vehicle is described. Four simulations are interfaced with varying amounts of actual flight hardware to produce dynamic system operation.

1113. Larson, T. J.; and *Siemers, P. M., III: **Use of Nose Cap and Fuselage Pressure Orifices for Determination of Air Data for Space Shuttle Orbiter Below Supersonic Speeds.** NASA TP-1643, H-1096, <u>September 1980</u>, 80N32389, #.

Wind tunnel pressure measurements were acquired from orifices on a 0.1 scale forebody model of the space shuttle orbiter that were arranged in a preliminary configuration of the shuttle entry air data system (SEADS). Pressures from those and auxiliary orifices were evaluated for their ability to provide air data at subsonic and transonic speeds. The orifices were on the vehicle's nose cap and on the sides of the forebody forward of the cabin. The investigation covered a Mach number range of 0.25 to 1.40 and an angle of attack range from 4 deg. to 18 deg. An air data system consisting of nose cap and forebody fuselage orifices constitutes a complete and accurate air data system at subsonic and transonic speeds. For Mach numbers less than 0.80 orifices confined to the nose cap can be used as a complete and accurate air data system. Air data systems that use only flush pressure orifices can be used to determine basic air data on other aircraft at subsonic and transonic speeds.

*NASA Langley Research Center, Hampton, Virginia.

1114. Tang, M. H.: **A Modified T-Value Method for Selection of Strain Gages for Measuring Loads.** NASA TM-85464. Presented at Western Regional Gage Comm. Soc. for Expt. Stress Analysis, China, Lake, California, September 16–17, 1980. 1980, 84N75770.

1115. Szalai, K. J.; Larson, R. R.; and Glover, R. D.: **Flight Experience With Flight Control Redundancy Management.** AGARD LS 109, Paper 8. *Fault Tolerance Design and Redundancy Management Tech.*, (ISBN-92-835-0274-4), September 1980, (see N81-11266 02-31), (AD-A090849, 81N11274, #.

Flight experience with both current and advanced redundancy management schemes was gained in recent flight research programs using the F-8 digital fly by wire aircraft. The flight performance of fault detection, isolation, and reconfiguration (FDIR) methods for sensors, computers, and actuators is reviewed. Results of induced failures as well as of actual random failures are discussed. Deficiencies in modeling and implementation techniques are also discussed. The paper also presents comparison off multisensor tracking in smooth air, in turbulence, during large maneuvers, and during maneuvers typical of those of large commercial transport aircraft. The results of flight tests of an advanced analytic redundancy management algorithm are compared with the performance of a contemporary algorithm in terms of time to detection, false alarms, and missed alarms. The performance of computer redundancy management in both iron bird and flight tests is also presented.

1116. Andrews, W. H.; Sim, A. G.; Monaghan, R. C.; Felt, L. R.; McMurtry, T. C.; and *Smith, R. C.: **AD-1 Oblique Wing Aircraft Program.** SAE Paper 801180. Society of Automotive Engineers, Aerospace Congress and Exposition, Los Angeles, California, October 13–16, 1980, 81A34193.

The oblique wing concept for super- and subsonic transport was assessed by analysis and wind tunnel radio control model and remotely piloted vehicle testing. A one-sixth scale wind tunnel model and a low speed manned oblique wing research airplane (AD-1) were developed. Model wind tunnel test data on dynamic structural response characteristics were used in a simulator to develop the control system. The airplane is of simple design with fiber glass skin, weight of approximately 2100 lbs and speeds of up to 175 knots at altitudes up to 15,000 ft. Flight testing will investigate handling and flying qualities, oblique wing flight control characteristics,

aeroelastic wing design and will compare actual with predicted aerodynamic characteristics. Nineteen flights were made at 12,000 to 13,000 feet with speeds of 100-160 knots. Flutter clearance as a function of wing sweep angle is now under investigation.

*NASA Ames Research Center, Moffett Field, California

ECN-13302B

AD-1 Oblique Wing Airplane

1117. Maine, R. E.; and Iliff, K. W.: **User's Manual for MMLE3, a General FORTRAN Program for Maximum Likelihood Parameter Estimation.** NASA TP-1563, H-1084, November 1980, 81N12744, #.

A user's manual for the FORTRAN IV computer program MMLE3 is described. It is a maximum likelihood parameter estimation program capable of handling general bilinear dynamic equations of arbitrary order with measurement noise and/or state noise (process noise). The theory and use of the program is described. The basic MMLE3 program is quite general and, therefore, applicable to a wide variety of problems. The basic program can interact with a set of user written problem specific routines to simplify the use of the program on specific systems. A set of user routines for the aircraft stability and control derivative estimation problem is provided with the program.

1118. Quinn, R. D.; and Gong, L.: **In-Flight Boundary-Layer Measurements on a Hollow Cylinder at a Mach Number of 3.0.** NASA TP-1764, H-1101, November 1980, 81N12361, #.

Skin temperatures, shear forces, surface static pressures, boundary layer pitot pressures, and boundary layer total temperatures were measured on the external surface of a hollow cylinder that was 3.04 meters long and 0.437 meter in diameter and was mounted beneath the fuselage of the YF-12A airplane. The data were obtained at a nominal free stream Mach number of 3.0 (a local Mach number of 2.9) and at wall to recovery temperature ratios of 0.66 to 0.91. The local Reynolds number had a nominal value of 4,300,000 per meter. Heat transfer coefficients and skin friction coefficients were derived from skin temperature time histories and shear force measurements, respectively. In addition, boundary layer velocity profiles were derived from pitot pressure measurements, and a Reynolds analogy factor was obtained from the heat transfer and skin friction measurements. The measured data are compared with several boundary layer prediction methods.

1119. Tang, M. H.; and Sheldon, R. G.: **A Modified T-Value Method for Selection of Strain Gages for Measuring Loads on a Low Aspect Ratio Wing.** NASA TP-1748, H-1108, November 1980, 81N12066, #.

A technique which may be useful for selecting strain gages for use in load equations is described. The technique is an adaptation of the previously used T-value method and is applied to a multispar structure. The technique, called the modified T-value method, is used to reduce the number of strain gages used in a load equation from twelve to two. A parallel reduction is made by calculating relative equation accuracies from three applied load distributions. The equations developed from the modified T-value method proved to be accurate more consistently than the T-value method.

1120. Jenkins, J. M.: **The Effect of Thermal Stresses on the Integrity of Three Built-Up Aircraft Structures.** NASA TM-81352, H-1138, November 1980, 81N12064, #.

A Mach 6 flight was simulated in order to examine heating effects on three frame/skin specimens. The specimens included: a titanium truss frame with a lockalloy skin; a stainless steel z-frame with a lockalloy skin; and a titanium z-frame with a lockalloy skin. Thermal stresses and temperature were measured on these specimens for the purpose of examining their efficiency, performance, and integrity. Measured thermal stresses were examined with respect to material yield strengths, buckling criteria, structural weight, and geometric locations. Principal thermal stresses were studied from the standpoint of uniaxial stress assumptions. Measured thermal stresses were compared to predicted values.

1121. *Runyan, L. J.; and Steers, L. L.: **Boundary Layer Stability Analysis of a Natural Laminar Flow Glove on the F-111 TACT Airplane.** Viscous Flow Drag Reduction Symposium, Dallas, Texas, *Technical Papers*, November 7–8, 1979, pp. 17–32, 81A26503, #.

A natural laminar flow airfoil has been developed as a part of the aircraft energy efficiency program. A NASA flight program incorporating this airfoil into partial wing gloves on the F-111 TACT airplane was scheduled to start in May, 1980. In support of this research effort, an extensive boundary layer stability analysis of the partial glove has been conducted. The results of that analysis show the expected effects of wing leading-edge sweep angle, Reynolds number, and compressibility on boundary layer stability and transition. These results indicate that it should be possible to attain on the order of 60% laminar flow on the upper surface and 50% laminar flow on the lower surface for sweep angles of at least 20 deg, chord Reynolds numbers of 25×10 to the 6th and Mach numbers from 0.81 to 0.85.

*Boeing Commercial Airplane Co., Seattle, Washington.

1122. Anon.: **Research and Technology Accomplishments.** NASA TM-102949, NAS 1.15:102949, 1980, 90N70764.

1123. Andrews, W. H.: **The Oblique Wing-Research Aircraft.** *Society of Experimental Test Pilots Tech. Rev.*, Vol. 15, No. 1, 1980 (see N80-33337 24-01), pp. 4–5, 80N33338.

The AD-1 airplane was designed as a low cost, low speed manned research tool to evaluate the flying qualities of the oblique wing concept. The airplane is constructed primarily of foam and fiberglass and incorporates simplicity in terms of the onboard systems. There are no hydraulics, the control system is cable and torque tube, and the electrical systems consist of engine driven generators which power the battery for engine start, cockpit gages, trim motors, and the onboard data system. The propulsion systems consist of two Microturbo TRS-18 engines sea level trust rated at 220 pounds. The airplane weighs approximately 2100 pounds and has a performance potential in the range of 200 knots and an altitude of 15,000 feet.

1981 Technical Publications

1124. Kurtenbach, F. J.; and Burcham, F. W., Jr.: **Flight Evaluation of a Simplified Gross Thrust Calculation Technique Using an F100 Turbofan Engine in an F-15 Airplane.** NASA TP-1782, H-1118, January 1981, 81N15000, #.

A simplified gross thrust calculation technique was evaluated in flight tests on an F-15 aircraft using prototype F100-PW-100 engines. The technique relies on afterburner duct pressure measurements and empirical corrections to an ideal one-dimensional analysis to determine thrust. In-flight gross thrust calculated by the simplified method is compared to gross thrust calculated by the engine manufacturer's gas generator model. The evaluation was conducted at Mach numbers from 0.6 to 1.5 and at altitudes from 6000 meters to 13,700 meters. The flight evaluation shows that the simplified gross thrust method and the gas generator method agreed within plus or minus 3 percent. The discrepancies between the data generally fell within an uncertainty band derived from instrumentation errors and recording system resolution.

1125. *Peake, D. J.; Fisher, D. F.; and **McRae, D. S.: **Flight Experiments With a Slender Cone at Angle of Attack.** AIAA Paper 81-0337, Presented at the 19th AIAA Aerospace Sciences Meeting, St. Louis, Missouri, January 1981, 81A20761, #.

The three-dimensional leeward separation about a 5 deg semi-angle cone at an 11 deg angle of attack was investigated in flight, in the wind tunnel, and by numerical computations. The test conditions were Mach numbers of 0.6, 1.5, and 1.8 at Reynolds numbers between 7 and 10 million based on free-stream conditions and a 30-inch wetted length or surface. The surface conditions measured included mean static and fluctuating pressures; skin friction magnitudes and separation line positions were obtained using obstacle blocks. The mean static pressures from flight and wind tunnel were in good agreement. The computed results gave the same distributions, but were slightly more positive in magnitude. The experimentally measured primary and secondary separation line locations compared closely with computed results. There were substantial differences in level and in trend between the surface root-mean-square pressure fluctuations obtained in flight and in the wind tunnel, due, it is thought, to a relatively high acoustic disturbance level in the tunnel compared with the quiescent conditions in flight.

*3-D Flowz, Inc., Moffett Field, California.
**USAF, Moffett Field, California.

1126. Ehernberger, L. J.; and Guttman, N. B.: **Climatological Characteristics of High Altitude Wind Shear and Lapse Rate Layers.** NASA TM-81353, H-1132, February 1981, 81N18608, #.

Indications of the climatological distribution of wind shear and temperature lapse and inversion rates as observed by rawinsonde measurements over the western United States are recorded. Frequencies of the strongest shear, lapse rates, and inversion layer strengths were observed for a 1 year period of record and were tabulated for the lower troposphere, the upper troposphere, and five altitude intervals in the lower stratosphere. Selected bivariate frequencies were also tabulated. Strong wind shears, lapse rates, and inversion are observed less frequently as altitude increases from 175 millibars to 20 millibars. On a seasonal basis the

frequencies were higher in winter than in summer except for minor stratospheric wind reversal in the spring and fall.

1127. Monaghan, R. C.: **Description of the HiMAT Tailored Composite Structure and Laboratory Measured Vehicle Shape Under Load.** NASA TM-81354, H-1144, February 1981, 81N18047, #.

The aeroelastically tailored outer wing and canard of the highly maneuverable aircraft technology (HiMAT) vehicle are closely examined and a general description of the overall structure of the vehicle is provided. Test data in the form of laboratory measured twist under load and predicted twist from the HiMAT NASTRAN structural design program are compared. The results of this comparison indicate that the measured twist is generally less than the NASTRAN predicted twist. These discrepancies in twist predictions are attributed, at least in part, to the inability of current analytical composite materials programs to provide sufficiently accurate properties of matrix dominated laminates for input into structural programs such as NASTRAN.

1128. Jarvis, C. R.; and Szalai, K. J.: **Ground and Flight Test Experience With a Triple Redundant Digital Fly by Wire Control System.** NASA CP-2172. *NASA Langley Research Center Advan. Aerodyn. and Active Controls,* February 1981, (see N81 19001 10-01), pp. 67–84, 81N19006, #.

A triplex digital fly by wire flight control system was developed and installed in an F-8C aircraft to provide fail operative, full authority control. Hardware and software redundancy management techniques were designed to detect and identify failures in the system. Control functions typical of those projected for future actively controlled vehicles were implemented.

1129. Steers, L. L.: **Natural Laminar Flow Flight Experiment.** NASA CP-2172. *NASA Langley Research Center Advan. Aerodyn. and Active Controls,* February 1981, (see N81-19001 10-01), pp. 135–144, 81N19010, #.

A supercritical airfoil section was designed with favorable pressure gradients on both the upper and lower surfaces. Wind tunnel tests were conducted in the Langley 8 Foot Transonic Pressure Tunnel. The outer wing panels of the F-111 TACT airplane were modified to incorporate partial span test gloves having the natural laminar, flow profile. Instrumentation was installed to provide surface pressure data as well as to determine transition location and boundary layer characteristics. The flight experiment encompassed 19 flights conducted with and without transition fixed at several locations for wing leading edge sweep angles which varied from 10 to 26 at Mach numbers from 0.80 to 0.85 and altitudes of 7620 meters and 9144 meters. Preliminary results indicate that a large portion of the test chord experienced laminar flow.

1130. Montoya, L. C.: **KC-135 Winglet Flight Results.** NASA CP-2172. *NASA Langley Research Center Advan. Aerodyn. and Active Controls*, <u>February 1981</u>, (see N81-19001 10-01), pp. 145–156, 81N19011, #.

Three KC-135 winglet configurations were flight tested for cant/incidence angles of 15 deg/–4 deg, 15 deg/–2 deg, and 0 deg/–4 deg, as well as the basic wing. The flight results for the 15 deg/–4 deg and basic wing configurations confirm the wind tunnel predicted 7% incremental decrease in total drag at cruise conditions. The 15 deg/–4 configuration flight measured wing and winglet pressure distributions, loads, stability and control, flutter, and buffet also correlate well with predicted values. The only unexpected flight results as compared with analytical predictions is a flutter speed decrease for the 0 deg/–4 deg configuration. The 15 deg/–2 deg configuration results show essentially the same incremental drag reduction as the 15 deg/–4 deg configuration; however, the flight loads are approximately 30% higher for the 15 deg/–2 deg configuration. The drag data for the 0 deg/–4 deg configuration show only a flight drag reduction.

KC-135 Airplane With Winglets ECN-11484

1131. Harney, P. F.: **Diversity Techniques for Omnidirectional Telemetry Coverage of the HiMAT Research Vehicle.** NASA TP-1830, H-1133, <u>March 1981</u>, 81N20074, #.

The highly maneuverable aircraft technology (HiMAT) remotely piloted research vehicle (RPRV) was flight tested and a number of technological advances applicable to future fighter aircraft were demonstrated. The aircraft control system uses airborne and ground-based computers which communicate via uplink and downlink telemetry. Antenna radiation patterns are normally much less than ideal for continuous reception or transmission for all aircraft attitudes. After flight qualification and testing on other aircraft, a frequency diversity concept and an antenna diversity concept were implemented on the HiMAT vehicle to obtain omnidirectional telemetry coverage.

1132. Maine, R. E.: **User's Manual for SYNC: A FORTRAN Program for Merging and Time-Synchronizing Data.** NASA TM-81355, <u>March 1981</u>, 81N19793, #.

The FORTRAN 77 computer program SYNC for merging and time synchronizing data is described. The program SYNC reads one or more input files which contain either synchronous data frames or time-tagged data points, which can be compressed. The program decompresses and time synchronizes the data, correcting for any channel time skews. Interpolation and hold last value synchronization algorithms are available. The output from SYNC is a file of time synchronized data frames at any requested sample rate.

1133. *Weaver, E. A.; Ehernberger, L. J.; **Gary, B. L.; †Kurkowski, R. L.; ††Kuhn, P. M.; and ††Stearns, L. P.: **The 1979 Clear Air Turbulence Flight Test Program.** NASA Langley Research Center, CP-2178, *The 1980 Aircraft Safety and Operating Problems*, *Part 1*, <u>March 1981</u>, (see N81-19035 10-03), pp. 293–311, 81N19050, #.

The flight experiments for clear air turbulence (CAT) detection and measurement concepts are described. The test were conducted over the western part of the United States during the winter season of 1979 aboard NASA's Galileo 2 flying laboratory. A carbon dioxide pulsed Doppler lidar and an infrared radiometer were tested for the remote detection and measurement of CAT. Two microwave radiometers were evaluated for their ability to provide encounter warning and altitude avoidance information.

*NASA Marshall Space Flight Center, Huntsville, Alabama.
**NASA Jet Propulsion Laboratory, Pasadena, California.
†NASA Ames Research Center, Moffett Field, California.
††National Oceanic and Atmospheric Administration, Department of Commerce, Washington, D. C.

1134. *Chambers, J. R.; and Iliff, K. W.: **Estimation of Dynamic Stability Parameters From Drop Model Flight**

Tests. AGARD LS-114. Presented at the NATO, *AGARD Lecture Series on Dynamic Stability Parameters*, Moffett Field, California, March 2–5, 1981, and Rhode-Saint-Genese, Belgium, March 16–19, 1981, 81A35551, #. (See also 1141.)

A recent NASA application of a remotely-piloted drop model to studies of the high angle-of-attack and spinning characteristics of a fighter configuration has provided an opportunity to evaluate and develop parameter estimation methods for the complex aerodynamic environment associated with high angles of attack. The paper discusses the overall drop model operation including descriptions of the model, instrumentation, launch and recovery operations, piloting concept, and parameter identification methods used. Static and dynamic stability derivatives were obtained for an angle-of-attack range from –20 deg to 53 deg. The results of the study indicated that the variations of the estimates with angle of attack were consistent for most of the static derivatives, and the effects of configuration modifications to the model (such as nose strakes) were apparent in the static derivative estimates. The dynamic derivatives exhibited greater uncertainty levels than the static derivatives, possibly due to nonlinear aerodynamics, model response characteristics, or additional derivatives.

*NASA Langley Research Center, Hampton, Virginia.

1135. Barber, M. R.; and *Tymczyszyn, J. J.: **Wake Vortex Attenuation Flight Tests: A Status Report.** NASA Langley Research Center, CP-2178, *The 1980 Aircraft Safety and Operating Problems*, *Part 2*, March 1981, (see N81-19056 10-03), pp. 387–408, 81N19057, #. (See also 1201.)

Flight tests were conducted to evaluate the magnitude of aerodynamic attenuation of the wake vortices of large transport aircraft that can be achieved through the use of static spoiler deflection and lateral control oscillation. These methods of attenuation were tested on Boeing B-747 and Lockheed L-1011 commercial transport aircraft. Evaluations were made using probe aircraft, photographic and visual observations, and ground based measurements of the vortex velocity profiles. The magnitude of attenuation resulting from static spoiler deflection was evaluated both in and out of ground effect. A remotely piloted QF-86 drone aircraft was used to probe the attenuated vortices in flight in and out of ground effect, and to make landings behind an attenuated B-747 airplane at reduced separation distances.

*FAA, Los Angeles, California.

ECN-7848

L-1011 Airplane With Smokers

1136. Maine, Richard E.; and Iliff, Kenneth W.: **Use of Cramer-Rao Bounds on Flight Data With Colored Residuals.** *Journal of Guidance and Control*, Vol. 4, No. 2, pp. 207–213, March–April 1981.

This paper discusses the use of the Cramer-Rao bound as a means of assessing the accuracy of maximum likelihood parameter estimates obtained from dynamic flight data. Emphasizing practical considerations such as modeling error, the Cramer-Rao bound is evaluated with real and simulated data. Improved computations of the bound to correct large discrepancies caused by colored noise and modeling error are presented. This corrected Cramer-Rao bound is the best available analytical predictor of accuracy.

1137. Borek, R. W.: **Practical Aspects of Instrumentation Installation in Support of Subsystem Testing.** AGARD CP-299, Paper 25. *AGARD Subsystem Testing and Flight Test Instr.*, (ISBN-92-835-0290-6), April 1981, (see N81-29065 20-01), AD-A101016, 81N29090, #.

Some of the problems associated with using military specification MIL-W-5088H as a guideline for wire gage selection are discussed. Examples of proper use of this specification as a criterion for interfacing wire bundles and connectors are provided. The quantitative results of 22 projects that have used the technique known as sneak analysis are reviewed and examples are given.

1138. Redin, P. C.: **Application of a Performance Modeling Technique to an Airplane With Variable Sweep Wings.** NASA TP-1855, H-1131, May 1981, 81N24048, #.

A performance modeling concept previously applied to an F-104F G and a YF-12C airplane was applied to an F-111A airplane. This application extended the concept to an airplane with variable sweep wings. The performance model adequately matched flight test data for maneuvers flown at different wing sweep angles at maximum afterburning and intermediate power settings. For maneuvers flown at less than intermediate power, including dynamic maneuvers, the performance model was not validated because the method used to correlate model and in-flight power setting was not adequate. Individual dynamic maneuvers were matched successfully by using adjustments unique to each maneuver.

1139. Jenkins, J. M.: **A Comparison of Laboratory Measured Temperatures With Predictions for a Spar/Skin Type Aircraft Structure.** NASA TM-81359, May 1981, 81N23067, #

A typical spar/skin aircraft structure was heated nonuniformly in a laboratory and the resulting temperatures were measured. The heat transfer NASTRAN computer program was used to provide predictions. Calculated temperatures based on a thermal model with conduction, radiation, and convection features compared closely to measured spar temperatures. Results were obtained without the thermal conductivity, specific heat, or emissivity with temperature. All modes of heat transfer (conduction, radiation, and convection) show to affect the magnitude and distribution of structural temperatures.

1140. Carter, A. L.; and Sims, R. L.: **Comparison of Theoretical Predictions of Orbiter Airloads With Wind Tunnel and Flight Test Results for a Mach Number of 0.52.** NASA TM-81358, May 1981, 81N23066, #.

The measurement and prediction of wing airloads for space shuttle orbiter 101 during approach and landing tests is discussed. Strain gage instrumentation, calibration, and flight data processing are covered along with wind tunnel and simulator results. The generation of theoretical predictions using the FLEXSTAB computer program is described, and the results are compared to experimental measurements.

1141. *Chambers, J. R.; and Iliff, K. W.: **Estimation of Dynamic Stability Parameters From Drop Model Flight Tests.** AGARD LS-114, *AGARD Dyn. Stability Parameters*, May 1981, (see N81-31105 22-01), 81N31116, #. (See also 1134.)

The overall remotely piloted drop model operation, descriptions, instrumentation, launch and recovery operations, piloting concept, and parameter identification methods are discussed. Static and dynamic stability derivatives were obtained for an angle attack range from –20 deg to 53 deg. It is indicated that the variations of the estimates with angle of attack are consistent for most of the static derivatives, and the effects of configuration modifications to the model were apparent in the static derivative estimates.

*NASA Langley Research Center, Hampton, Virginia.

1142. Ehernberger, L. J.: **Aspects of Clear Air Turbulence Severity Forecasting and Detection.** *Proceedings, 1st International Conference on Aviation Weather Systems*, Montreal, Canada, May 4–6, 1981. pp. 146–152, 82A45823.

Factors influencing the accuracy of the forecasts of incidences of clear air turbulence (CAT) are discussed, along with techniques for improved verification. Descriptive ranking terms for the intensity of CAT events, ranging from light to extreme, are developed, and meteorological parameters used for predictions are reviewed, including jetstream core location, vertical and horizontal wind shears, stable layers, tropopause height, trough speed, 500-mb vorticity, surface fronts, pressure centers and cyclogenesis, and wind speeds near mountain ridges. Methods of remote detection of CAT, particularly by using radiometry sensitive to the IR water vapor band, are noted to have had some success in detecting actual CAT events and decreasing false alarms. Statistical aspects of CAT encounter severity are discussed, including the establishment of confidence intervals for thresholds of detection of CATs of varying intensities.

1143. Borek, Robert W.: **Some Practical Aspects of Minimizing the Weight and Volume of Airborne Instrumentation Systems.** Fourth AGARD/DUT/CIT Special Course on Flight Test Instrumentation, Delft, the Netherlands, May 11–22, 1981.

1144. Maine, R. E.: **Programmer's Manual for MMLE3, a General FORTRAN Program for Maximum Likelihood Parameter Estimation.** NASA TP-1690, H-1105, June 1981, 81N27813, #.

The MMLE3 is a maximum likelihood parameter estimation program capable of handling general bilinear dynamic equations of arbitrary order with measurement noise and/or state noise (process noise). The basic MMLE3 program is quite general and, therefore, applicable to a wide variety of problems. The basic program can interact with a set of user written problem specific routines to simplify the use of the program on specific systems. A set of user routines for the aircraft stability and control derivative estimation problem is provided with the program. The implementation of the program on specific computer systems is discussed. The structure of the program is diagrammed, and the function and operation of individual routines is described. Complete listings and reference maps of the routines are included on microfiche as a supplement. Four test cases are discussed; listings of the input cards and program output for the test cases are included on microfiche as a supplement.

1145. *Mancuso, R. L.; *Endlich, R. M.; and Ehernberger, L. J.: **An Objective Isobaric/Isentropic Technique for Upper Air Analysis.** *Monthly Weather Review*, Vol. 109, June 1981, pp. 1326–1334, 81A43360.

An objective meteorological analysis technique is presented whereby both horizontal and vertical upper air analyses are performed. The process used to interpolate grid-point values from the upper-air station data is the same as for grid points on both an isobaric surface and a vertical cross-sectional plane. The nearby data surrounding each grid point are used in the interpolation by means of an anisotropic weighting scheme, which is described. The interpolation for a grid-point potential temperature is performed isobarically; whereas wind, mixing-ratio, and pressure height values are interpolated from data that lie on the isentropic surface that passes through the grid point. Two versions (A and B) of the technique are evaluated by qualitatively comparing computer analyses with subjective handdrawn analyses. The objective products of version A generally have fair correspondence with the subjective analyses and with the station data, and depicted the structure of the upper fronts, tropopauses, and jet streams fairly well. The version B objective products correspond more closely to the subjective analyses, and show the same strong gradients across the upper front with only minor smoothing.

*SRI International Atmospheric Science Center, Menlo Park, California.

1146. Sim, Alex G.: **Althaus on Airfoils.** *Astronautics & Aeronautics*, Vol. 19, No. 6, June 1981.

Book review of Profilpolaren fur Den Modelflug-WindKanalmessungen an Profilen im Kristischen Reynoldszahlbereich (Polars for Airfoils for Model Airplanes-Wind Tunnel Measurements on Airfoils at Critical Reynolds Numbers) by Dieter Althaus.

1147. Maine, R. E.; and Iliff, K. W.: **The Theory and Practice of Estimating the Accuracy of Dynamic Flight-Determined Coefficients.** NASA-RP-1077, H-1128, July 1981, 81N27865, #.

Means of assessing the accuracy of maximum likelihood parameter estimates obtained from dynamic flight data are discussed. The most commonly used analytical predictors of accuracy are derived and compared from both statistical and simplified geometrics standpoints. The accuracy predictions are evaluated with real and simulated data, with an emphasis on practical considerations, such as modeling error. Improved computations of the Cramer-Rao bound to correct large discrepancies due to colored noise and modeling error are presented. The corrected Cramer-Rao bound is shown to be the best available analytical predictor of accuracy, and several practical examples of the use of the Cramer-Rao bound are given. Engineering judgment, aided by such analytical tools, is the final arbiter of accuracy estimation.

1148. Weil, J.; and Powers, Bruce G.: **Correlation of Predicted and Flight Derived Stability and Control Derivatives With Particular Application to Tailless Delta Wing Configurations.** NASA TM-81361, July 1981, 81N26154, #.

Flight derived longitudinal and lateral-directional stability and control derivatives were compared to wind-tunnel derived values. As a result of these comparisons, boundaries representing the uncertainties that could be expected from wind-tunnel predictions were established. These boundaries provide a useful guide for control system sensitivity studies prior to flight. The primary application for this data was the space shuttle, and as a result the configurations included in the study were those most applicable to the space shuttle. The configurations included conventional delta wing aircraft as well as the X-15 and lifting body vehicles.

1149. Hughes, D. L.: **Comparison of Three Thrust Calculation Methods Using In-Flight Thrust Data.** NASA TM-81360, H-1141, July 1981, 81N30111, #.

The gross thrust of an experimental airplane was determined by each method using the same flight maneuvers and generally the same data parameters. Coefficients determined from thrust stand calibrations for each of the three methods were then extrapolated to cruise flight conditions. The values of total aircraft gross thrust calculated by the three methods for cruise flight conditions agreed within ±3 percent. The disagreement in the values of thrust calculated by the different techniques manifested itself as a bias in the data. There was little scatter (0.5 percent) for the thrust levels examined in flight.

1150. *Barrett, W. J.; *Rembold, J. P.; Burcham, F. W.; and Myers, L.: **Flight Test of a Full Authority Digital Electronic Engine Control System in an F-15 Aircraft.** AIAA Paper 81-1501. Presented at the 17th AIAA, SAE, and ASME Joint Propulsion Conference, Colorado Springs, Colorado, July 27–29, 1981, 81A40912, #. (See also 1242.)

The Digital Electronic Engine Control (DEEC) system considered is a relatively low cost digital full authority control system containing selectively redundant components and fault detection logic with capability for accommodating faults to various levels of operational capability. The DEEC digital control system is built around a 16-bit, 1.2 microsecond cycle time, CMOS microprocessor, microcomputer system with approximately 14 K of available memory. Attention is given to the control mode, component bench testing, closed loop bench testing, a failure mode and effects analysis, sea-level engine testing, simulated altitude engine testing, flight testing, the data system, cockpit, and real time display.

*United Technologies Corp., Government Products Div., West Palm Beach, Florida.

1151. Anon.: **Preliminary Analysis of STS-1 Entry Flight Data.** NASA TM-81363, August 1981, 81N29153, #.

A preliminary analysis of data acquired during the first shuttle orbiter reentry is presented. Heating levels were higher than predicted. Variations in measured versus predicted lift to drag ratio and trim are discussed, as are plots showing time histories of control surface and jet activity. The confidence felt in the stability and control derivatives is only fair. Confidence in the derivatives extracted for Mach numbers below 3.5 is especially weak, because these derivatives were affected by sideslip data contaminated by wind and turbulence, nonindependent rudder motions, and buffet. The sources of the data used are described. Recommendations are presented for changes to the Aerodynamic Data Book, and for planning future flights.

1152. Ayers, T. G.; and Hallissy, J. B.: **Historical Background and Design Evolution of the Transonic Aircraft Technology Supercritical Wing.** NASA TM-81356, H-1148, August 1981, 81N32116, #.

Two dimensional wind tunnel test results obtained for supercritical airfoils indicated that substantial improvements in aircraft performance at high subsonic speeds could be achieved by shaping the airfoil to improve the supercritical flow above the upper surface. Significant increases in the drag divergence Mach number, the maximum lift coefficient for buffer onset, and the Mach number for buffet onset at a given lift coefficient were demonstrated for the supercritical airfoil, as compared with a NACA 6 series airfoil of comparable thickness. These trends were corroborated by results from three dimensional wind tunnel and flight tests. Because these indicated extensions of the buffet boundaries could provide significant improvements in the maneuverability of a fighter airplane, an exploratory wind tunnel investigation was initiated which demonstrated that significant aerodynamic improvements could be achieved from the direct substitution of a supercritical airfoil on a variable wing sweep multimission airplane model.

1153. Sims, R. L.: **User's Manual for FSLIP-3, FLEXSTAB Loads Integration Program.** NASA TM-81364, H-1158, August 1981, 81N30815, #.

The FSLIP program documentation and user's manual is presented. As a follow on program to the FLEXSTAB computer analysis system, the primary function of this FORTRAN IV program is to integrate panel pressure coefficients computed by FLEXSTAB to obtain total shear,

bending, and torque airloads on various surfaces, summed relative to user specified axes. The program essentially replaces the ALOADS module in FLEXSTAB with expanded capabilities and flexibility. As such, FSLIP is generalized to work on any FLEXSTAB model or other pressure data if in a compatible format.

1154. Berry, D. T.: **Flying Qualities Criteria and Flight Control Design.** AIAA Paper 81-1823. *Guidance and Control Conference,* Albuquerque, New Mexico, August 19–21, 1981, pp. 411–415, (see A81-44076 21-12), 81A44127, #.

Despite the application of sophisticated design methodology, newly introduced aircraft continue to suffer from basic flying qualities deficiencies. Two recent meetings, the DOD/NASA Workshop on Highly Augmented Aircraft Criteria and the NASA Dryden Flight Research Center/Air Force Flight Test Center/AIAA Pilot Induced Oscillation Workshop, addressed this problem. An overview of these meetings is provided from the point of view of the relationship between flying qualities criteria and flight control system design. Among the items discussed are flying qualities criteria development, the role of simulation, and communication between flying qualities specialists and control system designers.

1155. Walker, H. J.: **Analytic Study of Orbiter Landing Profiles.** NASA TM-81365, H-1160, September 1981, 82N10001, #.

A broad survey of possible orbiter landing configurations was made with specific goals of defining boundaries for the landing task. The results suggest that the center of the corridors between marginal and routine represents a more or less optimal preflare condition for regular operations. Various constraints used to define the boundaries are based largely on qualitative judgments from earlier flight experience with the X-15 and lifting body research aircraft. The results should serve as useful background for expanding and validating landing simulation programs. The analytic approach offers a particular advantage in identifying trends due to the systematic variation of factors such as vehicle weight, load factor, approach speed, and aim point. Limitations such as a constant load factor during the flare and using a fixed gear deployment time interval, can be removed by increasing the flexibility of the computer program. This analytic definition of landing profiles of the orbiter may suggest additional studies, including more configurations or more comparisons of landing profiles within and beyond the corridor boundaries.

1156. Borek, R. W.; *Pool, A.; and Sanderson, K. C.: **Practical Aspects of Instrumentation System Installation, Volume 13.** NASA TM-84067, AGARD-AG-160, Vol 13, September 1981, 82N13140, #.

A review of factors influencing installation of aircraft flight test instrumentation is presented. Requirements, including such factors as environment, reliability, maintainability, and system safety are discussed. The assessment of the mission profile is followed by an overview of electrical and mechanical installation factors with emphasis on shock/vibration isolation systems and standardization of the electric wiring installation, two factors often overlooked by instrumentation engineers. A discussion of installation hardware reviews the performance capabilities of wiring, connectors, fuses and circuit breakers, and a guide to proper selections is provided. The discussion of the installation is primarily concerned with the electrical wire routing, shield terminations and grounding. Also included are some examples of installation mistakes that could affect system accuracy. System verification procedures and special considerations such as sneak circuits, pyrotechnics, aircraft antenna patterns, and lightning strikes are discussed.

*National Aerospace Lab., Amsterdam, the Netherlands.

1157. Enevoldson, E. K.; Horton, and V. W.: **"Light Bar" Attitude Indicator.** *Proceedings of 5th Advanced Aircrew Display Symposium,* Patuxent River, Maryland, September 15–16, 1981, (see A83-16126 04-06), pp. 251–261, 83A16136, #.

The development and evaluation of a light bar attitude indicator to help maintain proper aircraft attitude during high altitude night flying is described. A standard four-inch ADI was modified to project an artificial horizon across the instrument panel for pitch and roll information. A light bulb was put in the center of the ADI and a thin slit cut on the horizon, resulting in a thin horizontal sheet of light projecting from the instrument. The intensity of the projected beam is such that it can only be seen in a darkened room or at night. The beam on the instrument panel of the T-37 jet trainer is shown, depicting various attitudes. The favorable comments of about 50 pilots who evaluated the instrument are summarized, including recommendations for improving the instrument. Possible uses for the instrument to ease the pilot task are listed. Two potential problems in using the device are the development of pilot complacency and an upright-inverted ambiguity in the instrument.

1158. Thompson, M. O.; and Horton, V. W.: **Exploratory Flight Test of Advanced Piloted Spacecraft—Circa 1963.** *Technical Review,* presented at the 25th Society of Experimental Test Pilots Symposium, Beverly Hills, California, September 23–26, 1981, Vol. 16, No. 2, 1981, pp. 229–248, 82A14941, #.

The NASA early experimental program for parawing and lifting body spacecraft recovery concepts is discussed. Simple hand drawings, in-house construction, and crude drop tests were used in lieu of a thorough stress analysis. The parawing (Parasev) was controlled by manually shifting the center of gravity with respect to the center of pressure; the craft would take off while being towed at 40 KIAS. The M-2 lifting body was originally constructed with a 3/32 in.

mahogany skin by a glider manufacturer and employed general aviation aircraft nose and main wheel assemblies. A minimum altitude of 200 ft was found acceptable for release of the parasev, allowing the pilot time to adjust for transients incurred at the tow release. A small landing assist rocket was furnished for the M-2/F-2 and X-24A lifting bodies to enhance stability, and landings at a maximum lift/drag ratio of 2.8 were successfully completed. The data gained were eventually applied in the development of the Shuttle.

Parasev Vehicle   E-8009

1159. Myers, A. F.; Earls, M. R.; and *Callizo, L. A.: **HiMAT Onboard Flight Computer System Architecture and Qualification.** AIAA Paper 81-2107. *Technical Papers,* presented at AIAA 3rd Computers in Aerospace Conference, San Diego, California, October 26–28, 1981, pp. 41–54, 82A10082, #. (See also 1268.)

Two highly maneuverable aircraft technology (HiMAT) remotely piloted research vehicles (RPRV's) are being flight tested at NASA Dryden Flight Research Center, Edwards, California, to demonstrate and evaluate a number of technological advances applicable to future fighter aircraft. Closed-loop primary flight control is performed from a ground-based cockpit utilizing a digital computer and up/down telemetry links. A backup flight control system for emergency operation resides in one of two onboard computers. Other functions of the onboard computer system are uplink processing, downlink processing, engine control, failure detection, and redundancy management. This paper describes the architecture, functions, and flight qualification of the HiMAT onboard flight computer systems.

*Rockwell International Corp., Los Angeles, California.

1160. Anon.: **Report on Research and Technology-FY 1981.** NASA TM-81367, November 1981, 82N14047, #.

More than 65 technical reports, papers, and articles published by personnel and contractors at the Dryden Flight Research Center are listed. Activities performed for the Offices of Aeronautics and Space Technology, Space and Terrestrial Applications, Space Transportation Systems, and Space Tracking and Data Systems are summarized. Preliminary stability and control derivatives were determined for the shuttle orbiter at hypersonic speeds from the data obtained at reentry. The shuttle tile tests, spin research vehicle nose shapes flight investigations, envelope expansion flights for the Ames tilt rotor research aircraft, and the AD-1 oblique wing programs were completed as well as the KC-135 winglet program.

1161. Sims, R. L.; and Carter, A. L.: **Comparison of Wind Tunnel and Theoretical Aeroelastic Predictions With Flight Measured Airloads for the B-1 Aircraft.** AIAA Paper 81-2387. AIAA, SETP, SFTE, SAE, ITEA, and IEEE, 1st Flight Testing Conference, Las Vegas, Nevada, November 11–13, 1981, 82A14393, #.

An aeroelastic analysis of the B-1 aircraft was generated using the FLEXSTAB computer program. Relatively simple aerodynamic and structural models were employed. Theoretical wing and horizontal stabilizer airloads were compared to wind tunnel predictions and flight data measured during quasi-steady pitch maneuvers at Mach numbers of 0.85 and 1.2 with the wing in the 67.5 degree full aft sweep position. The basic objective was to evaluate the usefulness of the FLEXSTAB program for pre-flight airloads analysis of large flexible aircraft. Significant aeroelastic increments were noted between rigid and flexible vehicle results. FLEXSTAB predicted airloads for the outer wing panel were in good agreement with measured data for both rigid airloads and elastic increments. FLEXSTAB results for the horizontal stabilizer were useful for defining general aeroelastic trends, but absolute load levels were not well predicted due to theoretical limitations and difficulties encountered in modeling the complex B-1 configuration. Overall, the FLEXSTAB program is viewed as a useful integrated tool for static aeroelastic analysis in support of flight programs.

1162. McMurtry, T. C.; Sim, A. G.; and Andrews, W. H.: **AD-1 Oblique Wing Aircraft Program.** AIAA Paper 81-2354. AIAA, SETP, SFTE, SAE, ITEA, and IEEE, 1st Flight Testing Conference, Las Vegas, Nevada, November 11–13, 1981, 82A14390, #.

A NASA program for evaluation of the handling and flying characteristics of the AD-1 oblique wing aircraft is discussed. The vehicle was flown to compare wind tunnel predictions with aerodynamic data, explore the control system requirements, and obtain a preliminary assessment of the aeroelastic effects. The fiberglass sandwich skin aircraft is designed for 8 g positive and 4 g negative loading at

175 knots, while the wing pivot can withstand 25 g loading. Flight monitoring was accomplished with a 41 channel pulse code modulation system for telemetry and by averaging of pilot ratings. Maneuvering tests are outlined, noting that pilot ratings indicated acceptable handling at up to 50 deg sweep. It is concluded that acceptable flying qualities can be achieved with a 60 deg sweep, and that aeroelastic tailoring can be used to satisfy cruise design technology.

1163. Bohn-Meyer, M.; and *Jiran, F.: **Techniques for Modifying Airfoils and Fairings on Aircraft Using Foam and Fiberglass.** AIAA Paper 81-2445. AIAA, SETP, SFTE, SAE, ITEA, and IEEE, 1st Flight Testing Conference, Las Vegas, Nevada, November 11–13, 1981, 82A14383, #.

The concept of using foam and fiberglass reinforced plastic to modify airfoils and fairings was applied successfully to high-speed aircraft at NASA Dryden Flight Research Center. An on-aircraft installation method was used to modify an F-15 wing glove and wing leading edge and an F-104 flap trailing edge in support of the Shuttle tile airload tests. A combination of methods, both an on-aircraft installation and an off-aircraft fabrication for installation on the aircraft, was used to modify a section of an F-111 supercritical wing with a natural laminar flow airfoil. Techniques, methods, problem areas, and recommendations are presented which indicate that using foam and fiberglass to modify airfoils and fairings on high-speed aircraft is a viable means of quickly developing airfoils and fairings with desired aerodynamic characteristics with little risk to the parent or carrier aircraft.

*Fred Jiran Glider Repairs, Mojave, California.

1164. Saltzman, E. J.; and Ayers, T. G.: **A Review of Flight-to-Wind Tunnel Drag Correlation.** AIAA Paper 81-2475. AIAA, SETP, SFTE, SAE, ITEA, and IEEE, 1st Flight Testing Conference, Las Vegas, Nevada, November 11–13, 1981, 82A14382, #.

Comparisons are made of wind-tunnel-model and flight drag data for various configurations representing aircraft from the mid-1940s to the 1970s. Discrepancies between model and flight data such as Reynolds number effects, wall interference, and aeroelastic problems are discussed. Sting support effects and the inability of models to simulate surface deflections for longitudinal trim are also studied. A wind tunnel-to-flight correlation of turbulent friction drag confirms the incompressible Karman-Schoenherr variation of turbulent skin friction with Reynolds number and the T' method for accounting compressibility effects. NASA tested 10 deg cone research indicates that model tests which are affected by tunnel noise may require the lower disturbance level environment available in flight, and it is concluded that new cryogenic facilities will improve the fidelity of model simulations of full-scale flight flow phenomena.

1165. DeAngelis, V. M.: **In-Flight Deflection Measurement of the HiMAT Aeroelastically Tailored Wing.** AIAA Paper 81-2450. AIAA, SETP, SFTE, SAE, ITEA, and IEEE, 1st Flight Testing Conference, Las Vegas, Nevada, November 11–13, 1981, 82A14381, #. (See also 1229.)

An electro-optical flight deflection measurement system was developed for NASA for use on the highly maneuverable aircraft technology (HiMAT) remotely piloted research vehicle (RPRV) to provide a means of evaluating the performance of the HiMAT's aeroelastically tailored composite wing and canard. A description of the flight deflection measurement system is presented from a user's viewpoint and includes the general method of operation, system capabilities and limitations, method of installation on the HiMAT vehicle, and calibration of targets. Also included is a general description of the HiMAT RPRV and its design goals. Preliminary flight deflection and bending moment data were obtained at Mach 0.8 and were extrapolated to the Mach 0.9 maneuver design condition for comparison to NASTRAN predictions and ground loads test results. The preliminary flight test results tended to agree with the results obtained from the static ground loads tests, that is, that the NASTRAN model overpredicted the streamwise twist of the composite outer wing panel.

1166. Swann, M. R.; Duke, E. L.; Enevoldson, E. K.; and Wolf, T. D.: **Experience With Flight Test Trajectory Guidance.** AIAA Paper 81-2504. AIAA, SETP, SFTE, SAE, ITEA, and IEEE, 1st Flight Testing Conference, Las Vegas, Nevada, November 11–13, 1981, 82A14379, #. (See also 1276.)

A system that provides the test pilot with flight test trajectory guidance is presently evolving at the NASA Dryden Flight Research Facility. In use, this system has resulted in discernible improvements in the ease and accuracy with which pilots have approached and maintained the desired flight test conditions or trajectories. This paper describes the use of the guidance system in several past flight programs at Dryden, including the F-111 TACT program, the F-15 airframe/propulsion system interaction program, the F-15 cone transition and boundary layer experiments, and the Space Shuttle tiles flight test program.

1167. Bever, G. A.: **The Development and Use of a Computer-Interactive Data Acquisition and Display System in a Flight Environment.** AIAA Paper 81-2371. AIAA, SETP, SFTE, SAE, ITEA, and IEEE, 1st Flight Testing Conference, Las Vegas, Nevada, November 11–13, 1981, 82A13946, #.

The flight test data requirements at the NASA Dryden Flight Research Center increased in complexity, and more advanced instrumentation became necessary to accomplish mission goals. This paper describes the way in which an airborne computer was used to perform real-time calculations on critical flight test parameters during a flight test on a winglet-equipped KC-135A aircraft. With the computer, an airborne flight test engineer can select any sensor for airborne display in several formats, including engineering units. The computer is able to not only calculate values derived from the sensor outputs but also to interact with the data acquisition system. It can change the data cycle format and data rate, and even insert the derived values into the pulse code modulation (PCM) bit stream for recording.

1168. Meyer, R. R., Jr.; Jarvis, C. R.; and *Barneburg, J.: **In-Flight Aerodynamic Load Testing of the Shuttle Thermal Protection System.** AIAA Paper 81-2468. AIAA, SETP, SFTE, SAE, ITEA, and IEEE, 1st Flight Testing Conference, Las Vegas, Nevada, November 11–13, 1981, 82A13932, #.

To contribute to the certification of the structural integrity of the Space Shuttle orbiter's thermal protection system (TPS) before the first Shuttle flight, in-flight aerodynamic load tests of six simulated areas of the orbiter were conducted. The tests were performed on an F-104 and F-15 aircraft. This paper describes the test approach, techniques used, and results. Two areas of the orbiter TPS were redesigned and retested as a result of these tests. No TPS failures due to air-loads occurred in the areas that were evaluated in the flight tests during the Shuttle's first flight.

*NASA Johnson Space Center, Houston, Texas.

1169. Baer-Riedhart, J. L.: **The Development and Flight Test Evaluation of an Integrated Propulsion Control System for the HiMAT Research Airplane.** AIAA Paper 81-2467. AIAA, SETP, SFTE, SAE, ITEA, and IEEE, 1st Flight Testing Conference, Las Vegas, Nevada, November 11–13, 1981, 82A13931, #.

The Highly Maneuverable Aircraft Technology airplane is a .44-scale version of an advanced fighter design. It is remotely piloted from a ground cockpit and is powered by a J85-GE-21 turbojet engine. The engine is electronically controlled by a digital computer onboard the airplane to operate at selected engine operation modes. The HiMAT design and development philosophy emphasized high-risk, low-cost and minimum testing, and also required that no single failure would cause loss of the vehicle. This philosophy generated unique requirements for design, computer simulation methods, specialized test techniques, and support systems which are discussed in this paper.

1170. Gera, J.; Wilson, R. J.; Enevoldson, E. K.; and *Nguyen, L. T.: **Flight Test Experience With High-Alpha Control System Techniques on the F-14 Airplane.** AIAA Paper 81-2505. AIAA, SETP, SFTE, SAE, ITEA, and IEEE, 1st Flight Testing Conference, Las Vegas, Nevada, November 11–13, 1981, 82A13906, #.

Improved handling qualities of fighter aircraft at high angles of attack can be provided by various stability and control augmentation techniques. NASA and the U.S. Navy are conducting a joint flight demonstration of these techniques on an F-14 airplane. This paper reports on the flight test experience with a newly designed lateral-directional control system which suppresses such high angle of attack handling qualities problems as roll reversal, wing rock, and directional divergence while simultaneously improving departure/spin resistance. The technique of integrating a piloted simulation into the flight program was used extensively in this program. This technique had not been applied previously to high angle of attack testing and required the development of a valid model to simulate the test airplane at extremely high angles of attack.

*NASA Langley Research Center, Hampton, Virginia.

1171. Ko, W. L.; Quinn, R. D.; Gong, L.; Schuster, L. S.; and Gonzales, D.: **Preflight Reentry Heat Transfer Analysis of Space Shuttle.** AIAA Paper 81-2382. AIAA, SETP, SFTE, SAE, ITEA, and IEEE, 1st Flight Testing Conference, Las Vegas, Nevada, November 11–13, 1981, 82A13882, #.

Preflight predictions of the structural temperature distributions during entry are compared with data from the initial Shuttle flight. Finite element thermal analysis programming was used to model the heat flow on Shuttle structures and actual gas properties of air were employed in the analyses of aerodynamic heating. Laminar, separated, and turbulent heat fluxes were calculated for varying locations on the craft using velocity-attitude and angle-of-attack projections taken from the nominal STS-1 trajectory. Temperature time histories of the first flight are compared with laminar and turbulent flow assumptions and an unpredicted rapid cooling 1800 sec into entry is credited to inaccurate assumptions of structural heat dissipative properties or flow conditions in that time phase of the flight; additional discrepancies in descriptions of heating of the upper fuselage are attributed to a lack of knowledge of the complex flow patterns existing over that area of the Shuttle body.

1172. Iliff, K. W.; Maine, R. E.; and *Cooke, D. R.: **Selected Stability and Control Derivatives From the First Space Shuttle Entry.** AIAA Paper 81-2451. AIAA, SETP, SFTE, SAE, ITEA, and IEEE, 1st Flight Testing Conference, Las Vegas, Nevada, November 11–13, 1981, 82A13880, #. (See also 1267.)

Primary stability and control derivative estimates garnered from the first Shuttle entry are reported. The craft was the first vehicle to maneuver over a wide range of hypersonic velocities, yielding data on flight characteristics from previously unexplored regimes. The flight envelope was confined to entry and safe landing, with no additional maneuvers to gain control data. Data for a Mach number range of 25–1.5 and altitudes of 515,000–50,000 ft are provided, and functional ranges of the Shuttle control surfaces and attitude jets are outlined. On-board systems gathered data on aerodynamic coefficient identification, flight condition and Euler angles, and jet chamber pressures. A maximum likelihood estimation program, which contained unknown stability and control derivatives, was used for control; a control input determined the value of the unknown derivatives, and the input and spacecraft response were measured. Longitudinal and lateral directional maneuvers and their derivative estimates are described, noting wind contamination of the sideslip measurements below Mach 3. Further maneuvering and stability tests are projected for subsequent flights.

*NASA Johnson Space Center, Houston, Texas.

1173. Burcham, F. W., Jr.; Myers, L. P.; Nugent, J.; Lasagna, P. L.; and Webb, L. D.: **Recent Propulsion System Flight Tests at the NASA Dryden Flight Research Center.** AIAA Paper 81-2438. AIAA, SETP, SFTE, SAE, ITEA, and IEEE, 1st Flight Testing Conference, Las Vegas, Nevada, November 11–13, 1981, 82A13874, #.

The article presents a summary of the propulsion system tests conducted on a number of aircraft at the NASA Dryden Flight Research Center. The tests included digital engine control systems, engine-inlet compatibility, inlet-airframe interactions, nozzle-boattail drag and advanced turboprop acoustics. Among the aircraft evaluated were the F-15, HiMAT, F-14, and the JetStar.

1174. Matheny, N. W.; and *Panageas, G. N.: **HiMAT Aerodynamic Design and Flight Test Experience.** AIAA Paper 81-2433. AIAA, SETP, SFTE, SAE, ITEA, and IEEE, 1st Flight Testing Conference, Las Vegas, Nevada, November 11–13, 1981, 82A13871, #.

Consideration is given to the design phase of the highly maneuverable aircraft technology program. Design objectives are examined, noting full-scale design and the remotely piloted research vehicle. Attention is given to subsonic, transonic, and supersonic design. Design results are discussed with reference to aerodynamic efficiency, aeroelastic tailoring, and the flight test program.

*Rockwell International Corp., North American Aircraft Div., Los Angeles, California.

1175. Petersen, K. L.: **Flight Experience With a Remotely Augmented Vehicle Flight Test Technique.** AIAA Paper 81-2417. AIAA, SETP, SFTE, SAE, ITEA, and

IEEE, 1st Flight Testing Conference, Las Vegas, Nevada, November 11–13, 1981, 82A13857, #.

A flight technique which uses the remotely augmented vehicle (RAV) concept is developed to flight test advanced control law concepts. The design, development and flight test validation of a RAV system mechanized on a digital fly-by-wire aircraft are described, and future applications are discussed. Flight experiments investigate complete inner loop, low sample rate, and adaptive control system mechanisms. The technique, which utilizes a ground-based FORTRAN programmable digital computer and up and down telemetry links is found to provide the flexibility necessary to effectively investigate alternate control law mechanisms in flight.

1176. Hedgley, D. R.: **Solution to the Hidden-Line Problem**. *Astronautics and Aeronautics*, Vol. 19, November 1981, 82A12803, #.

It is pointed out that realistic three-dimensional renderings of solid objects or surfaces by computers have long been needed. The NASA Dryden Flight Research Center will soon publish a report and the computer program on an algorithm that solves for hidden lines. The computer program is written in FORTRAN IV and its size is approximately 35N + 9500 words, where N is the number of elements. A number of pictures are presented which were drawn by a computer using the algorithm.

1177. *Williams, D. A.; Pool, A.; and Sanderson, K. C.: **AGARD Flight Test Instrumentation Series. Volume 14: The Analysis of Random Data.** AGARD-AG-160-VOL-14, November 1981, 82N21099, #.

*Cranfield Institute of Technology, Bedford, U. K.

1178. Smith, J. W.: **Analysis of a Longitudinal Pilot-Induced Oscillation Experienced on the Approach and Landing Test of the Space Shuttle.** NASA TM-81366, December 1981, 82N13149, #.

During the final free flight (FF-5) of the shuttle's approach and landing tests, the vehicle experienced pilot-induced oscillations near touchdown. The light test data showed that pilot inputs to the hand controller reached peak-to-peak amplitudes of 20 deg at a frequency between 3 and 3.5 radians per second. The controller inputs were sufficient to exceed the priority rate limit set in the pitch axis. A nonlinear analytical study was conducted to investigate the combined effects of pilot input, rate limiting, and time delays. The frequency response of the total system is presented parametrically as a function of the three variables. In general, with no dead time, for controller inputs of 5 deg or less, the total system behaves in a linear fashion. For 10 deg of

controller input, independent of the delay time, the elevon loop will be rate saturated above a frequency of 4 radians per second.

1179. Sefic, W. J.: **NASA Dryden Flight Loads Research Facility.** NASA TM-81368, December 1981, 82N15079, #.

The Dryden Flight Loads Research Facility (NASA) and the associated equipment for simulating the loading and heating of aircraft or their components are described. Particular emphasis is placed on various fail-safe devices which are built into the equipment to minimize the possibility of damage to flight vehicles. The equipment described includes the ground vibration and moment of inertia equipment, the data acquisition system, and the instrumentation available in the facility for measuring load, position, strain, temperature, and acceleration.

1180. Kelley, W. W.; and Enevoldson, E. K.: **Limited Evaluation of an F-14A Airplane Utilizing an Aileron-Rudder Interconnect Control System in the Landing Configuration.** NASA TM-81972, December 1981, 82N13148, #.

A flight test was conducted for preliminary evaluation of an aileron-rudder interconnect (ARI) control system for the F-14A airplane in the landing configuration. Two ARI configurations were tested in addition to the standard F-14 flight control system. Results of the flight test showed marked improvement in handling qualities when the ARI systems were used. Sideslip due to adverse yaw was considerably reduced, and airplane turn rate was more responsive to pilot lateral control inputs. Pilot comments substantiated the flight data and indicated that the ARI systems were superior to the standard control system in terms of pilot capability to make lateral offset corrections and heading changes on final approach.

1181. *Kalev, I.: **Cyclic Plasticity Models and Application in Fatigue Analysis.** Presented at 3rd Nonlinear Finite Element Analysis and ADINA Conference, Cambridge, Massachusetts, June 10–12, 1981. *Computers and Structures*, Vol. 13, October–December 1981, pp. 709–716, 81A38340.

An analytical procedure for prediction of the cyclic plasticity effects on both the structural fatigue life to crack initiation and the rate of crack growth is presented. The crack initiation criterion is based on the Coffin-Manson formulae extended for multiaxial stress state and for inclusion of the mean stress effect. This criterion is also applied for the accumulated damage ahead of the existing crack tip which is assumed to be related to the crack growth rate. Three cyclic plasticity models, based on the concept of combination of several yield surfaces, are employed for computing the crack growth rate of a crack plane stress panel under several cyclic loading conditions.

*National Research Council, Washington, D. C.

1182. Lasagna, P.; and Mackall, K.: **Acoustic Flight Testing of Advanced Design Propellers on a JetStar Aircraft.** NASA CP-2208, *NASA Langley Research Center Advan. Aerodyn.: Selected NASA Res.,* December 1981, (see N84-27660 18-01), pp. 1–10, 84N27661, #.

Advanced turboprop-powered aircraft have the potential to reduce fuel consumption by 15 to 30 percent as compared with an equivalent technology turbofan-powered aircraft. An important obstacle to the use of advanced design propellers is the cabin noise generated at Mach numbers up to .8 and at altitudes up to 35,000 feet. As part of the NASA Aircraft Energy Efficiency Program, the near-field acoustic characteristics on a series of advanced design propellers are investigated. Currently, Dryden Flight Research Center is flight testing a series of propellers on a JetStar airplane. The propellers used in the flight test were previously tested in wind tunnels at the Lewis Research Center. Data are presented showing the narrow band spectra, acoustic wave form, and acoustic contours on the fuselage surface. Additional flights with the SR-3 propeller and other advanced propellers are planned in the future.

ECN-15662

C-140 JetStar Propeller Testbed

1183. Montoya, L. C.; Steers, L. L.; and Trujillo, B.: **F-111 TACT Natural Laminar Flow Glove Flight Results.** NASA CP-2208, *NASA Langley Research Center Advan. Aerodyn.: Selected NASA Res.,* December 1981, (see N84-27660 18-01), pp. 11–20, 84N27662, #.

Improvements in cruise efficiency on the order of 15 to 40% are obtained by increasing the extent of laminar flow over lifting surfaces. Two methods of achieving laminar flow are being considered, natural laminar flow and laminar flow control. Natural laminar flow (NLF) relies primarily on airfoil shape while laminar flow control involves boundary layer suction or blowing with mechanical devices. The extent of natural laminar flow that could be achieved with consistency in a real flight environment at chord Reynolds numbers in the range of $30 \times 10(6)$ power was evaluated. Nineteen flights were conducted on the F-111 TACT airplane having a NLF airfoil glove section. The section consists of a supercritical airfoil providing favorable pressure gradients over extensive portions of the upper and lower surfaces of the wing. Boundary layer measurements were obtained over a range of wing leading edge sweep angles at Mach numbers from 0.80 to 0.85. Data were obtained for natural transition and for a range of forced transition locations over the test airfoil.

1184. Maine, Richard E.; and Iliff, Kenneth W.: **Formulation and Implementation of a Practical Algorithm for Parameter Estimation With Process and Measurement Noise.** *SIAM Journal on Applied Mathematics,* Vol. 41, No. 3, December 1981, (See also 1109, 1209.)

A new formulation is proposed for the problem of parameter estimation of dynamic systems with both process and measurement noise. The formulation gives estimates that are maximum likelihood asymptotically in time. The means used to overcome the difficulties encountered by previous formulations are discussed. It is then shown how the proposed formulation can be efficiently implemented in a computer program. A computer program using the proposed formulation is available in a form suitable for routine application. Examples with simulated and real data are given to illustrate that the program works well.

1982 Technical Publications

1185. *Kelly, G. L.; *Berthold, G.; and Abbott, L.: **Implementation of the DAST ARW II Control Laws Using an 8086 Microprocessor and an 8087 Floating-Point Coprocessor.** *Mini and Microcomputers in Control and Measurement, Proceedings of the International Symposium,* San Francisco, California, Acta Press, Anaheim, California and Calgary, Alberta, Canada, 1982, pp. 58–60, 83A11910.

A 5 MHZ single-board microprocessor system which incorporates an 8086 CPU and an 8087 Numeric Data Processor is used to implement the control laws for the NASA Drones for Aerodynamic and Structural Testing, Aeroelastic Research Wing II. The control laws program was executed in 7.02 msec, with initialization consuming 2.65 msec and the control law loop 4.38 msec. The software emulator execution times for these two tasks were 36.67 and 61.18, respectively, for a total of 97.68 msec. The space, weight and cost reductions achieved in the present, aircraft control application of this combination of a 16-bit microprocessor with an 80-bit floating point coprocessor may be obtainable in other real time control applications.

*University of Kansas, Lawrence, Kansas.

EC80-14090

Firebee DAST RPV

1186.   Anon.: **KC-135 Winglet Program Review.** NASA CP-2211, H-1165, NAS 1.55:2211. Symposium held at Edwards, California, September 16, 1981, <u>January 1982</u>, 84N27686, #.

1187.   Barber, M. R.; and *Selegan, D.: **KC-135 Winglet Program Overview.** NASA CP-2211, KC-135 Winglet Program Rev., (see N84-27686 18-02), <u>January 1982</u>, pp. 1–46, 84N27687, #.

A joint NASA/USAF program was conducted to accomplish the following objectives: (1) evaluate the benefits that could be achieved from the application of winglets to KC-135 aircraft; and (2) determine the ability of wind tunnel tests and analytical analysis to predict winglet characteristics. The program included wind-tunnel development of a test winglet configuration; analytical predictions of the changes to the aircraft resulting from the application of the test winglet; and finally, flight tests of the developed configuration. Pressure distribution, loads, stability and control, buffet, fuel mileage, and flutter data were obtained to fulfill the objectives of the program.

*AFWAL, Wright-Patterson AFB, Ohio.

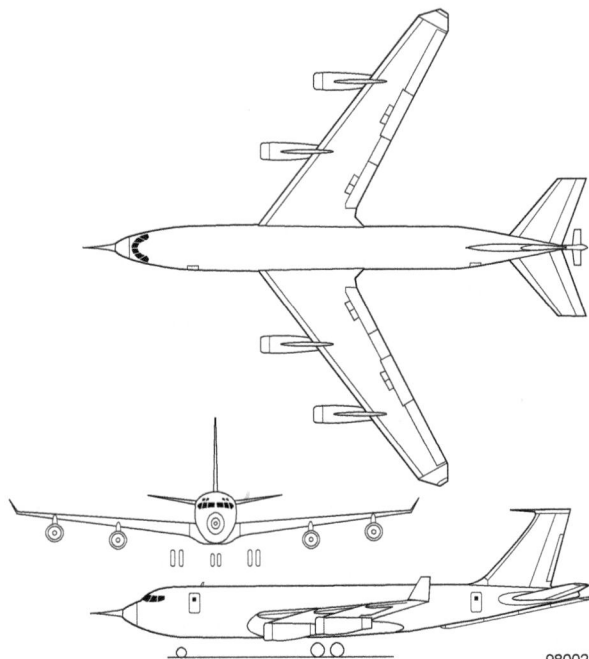

980025

KC-135 Airplane, Three-View Drawing

1188.   Montoya, L. C.; *Jacobs, P.; *Flechner, S.; and Sims, R.: **KC-135 Wing and Winglet Flight Pressure Distributions, Loads, and Wing Deflection Results With Some Wind Tunnel Comparisons.** NASA CP-2211, KC-135 Winglet Program Rev., (see N84-27686 18-02), <u>January 1982</u>, pp. 47–102, 84N27688, #.

A full-scale winglet flight test on a KC-135 airplane with an upper winglet was conducted. Data were taken at Mach numbers from 0.70 to 0.82 at altitudes from 34,000 feet to 39,000 feet at stabilized flight conditions for wing/winglet configurations of basic wing tip, 15/–4 deg, 15/–2 deg, and 0/–4 deg winglet cant/incidence. An analysis of selected pressure distribution and data showed that with the basic wing tip, the flight and wind tunnel wing pressure distribution data showed good agreement. With winglets installed, the effects on the wing pressure distribution were mainly near the tip. Also, the flight and wind tunnel winglet pressure distributions had some significant differences primarily due to the oilcanning in flight. However, in general, the agreement was good. For the winglet cant and incidence configuration presented, the incidence had the largest effect on the winglet pressure distributions. The incremental flight wing deflection data showed that the semispan wind tunnel model did a reasonable job of simulating the aeroelastic effects at the wing tip. The flight loads data showed good agreement with predictions at the design point and also substantiated the predicted structural penalty (load increase) of the 15 deg cant/–2 deg incidence winglet configuration.

*NASA Langley Research Center, Hampton, Virginia.

1189. Lux, D. P.: **In-Flight Lift and Drag Measurements on a First Generation Jet Transport Equipped With Winglets.** NASA CP-2211, KC-135 Winglet Program Rev., (see N84-27686 18-02), January 1982, pp. 103–116, 84N27689, #.

A KC-135A aircraft equipped with wing tip winglets was flight tested to demonstrate and validate the potential performance gain of the winglet concept as predicted from analytical and wind tunnel data. Flight data were obtained at cruise conditions for Mach numbers of 0.70, 0.75, and 0.80 at a nominal altitude of 36,000 ft. and winglet configurations of 15 deg cant/–4 deg incidence, 0 deg cant/–4 deg incidence, and baseline. For the Mach numbers tested the data show that the addition of winglets did not affect the lifting characteristics of the wing. However, both winglet configurations showed a drag reduction over the baseline configuration, with the best winglet configuration being the 15 deg cant/–4 deg incidence configuration. This drag reduction due to winglets also increased with increasing lift coefficient. It was also shown that a small difference exists between the 15 deg cant/–4 deg incidence flight and wind tunnel predicted data. This difference was attributed to the pillowing of the winglet skins in flight which would decrease the winglet performance.

1190. Kehoe, M. W.: **KC-135A Winglet Flight Flutter Program.** NASA CP-2211, H-1169, KC-135 Winglet Program Rev., (see N84-27686 18-02), January 1982, pp. 171–188, 84N27692, #.

The evaluation techniques, results and conclusions for the flight flutter testing conducted on a KC-135A airplane configured with and without winglets are discussed. Test results are presented for the critical symmetric and antisymmetric modes for a fuel distribution that consisted of 10,000 pounds in each wing main tank and empty reserve tanks. The results indicated that a lightly damped oscillation was experienced for a winglet configuration of a 0 deg cant and –4 deg incidence. The effects of cant and incidence angle variation on the critical modes are also discussed. Lightly damped oscillations were not encountered for any other winglet cant and incidence angles tested.

1191. *Dougherty, N. S., Jr.; and Fisher, D. F.: **Boundary-Layer Transition Correlation on a Slender Cone in Wind Tunnels and Flight for Indications of Flow Quality.** NASA TM-84732, NAS 1.15:84732, AD-A111328, AEDC TR-81-26, Arnold AFB, Tennessee, February 1982, 82N25228, #.

Boundary layer transition location measurements were made on a 10 deg sharp cone in 23 wind tunnels in the United States and Europe and in flight. The data were acquired at subsonic, transonic, and supersonic Mach numbers over a range of unit Reynolds numbers in an effort to obtain an improved understanding of the effect of wind tunnel flow quality on transition location. The data indicate that the transition

mechanism in both wind tunnels in flight is associated with the formation of Tollmien-Schlichting waves in the laminar boundary layer. However, the location of the end of transition was found to be primarily a function of the noise under the laminar boundary of the cone surface and, within + or –20 percent, independent of Mach number and unit Reynolds number.

*ARO, Inc., Tullahoma, Tennessee.

1192. Hedgley, D. R., Jr.: **User's Guide for SKETCH.** NASA TM-81369, H-1169, February 1982, 82N17878, #.

A user's guide for the computer program SKETCH is presented. The removal of hidden lines from images of solid objects is a problem in computer graphics which is solved by SKETCH.

1193. Hedgley, D. R., Jr.: **A General Solution to the Hidden-Line Problem.** NASA RP-1085, H-1162, NAS 1.61:1085, March 1982, 82N21907, #.

The requirements for computer-generated perspective projections of three dimensional objects has escalated. A general solution was developed. The theoretical solution to this problem is presented. The method is very efficient as it minimizes the selection of points and comparison of line segments and hence avoids the devastation of square-law growth.

1194. *Elfstrom, G. M.; *Kostopoulos, C.; **Peake, D. J.; and Fisher, D. F.: **The Obstacle Block as a Device to Measure Turbulent Skin Friction in Compressible Flow.** AIAA Paper 82-0589. Presented at 12th Aerodynamic Testing Conference, Williamsburg, Virginia, (see A82-24651 10-09), March 22–24, 1982, pp. 131–138, 82A24664, #.

The obstacle block, developed as an alternative to the Preston tube for indirectly measuring skin friction on smooth surfaces in incompressible flows, is examined as a device for compressible flows as well. The block, which is congruent with a surface static pressure orifice, has a geometry which is easily specified and thus has a universal calibration. Data from two independent studies are used to establish such a calibration using "wall" variables, valid for Mach numbers up to about 3. Various aspects concerning practical application of the device are examined, such as sensitivity to yaw and the minimum permissible axial spacing between blocks. Several examples showing the utility of the device are given.

*National Aeronautical Establishment, High Speed Aero Laboratory, Ottawa, Canada.
**NASA Ames Research Center, Moffett Field, California.

1195. Smith, Harriet J.; and Enevoldson, Einar: **The Application of a Six-Degree-of-Freedom Piloted Simulation in Support of the F-14 Flight Research**

Program. Presented at the SES-SFTF Symposium on Simulation Aircraft Test and Evaluation, Naval Air Test Center, Maryland, March 16–17, 1982.

1196. Ko, W. L.: **Structural Properties of Superplastically Formed/Diffusion-Bonded Orthogonally Corrugated Core Sandwich Plates.** *AIAA Journal*, Vol. 20, No. 4, April 1982, (see AIAA 80-0304), pp. 536–543, 80A18305, #. (See also 1080.)

A new orthogonally corrugated sandwich structure that can be fabricated by using the superplastic forming-diffusion bonding (SPF-DB) process is described. Formulas and the associated plots for evaluating the effective elastic constants and the bending stiffness for the core of this new sandwich structure are presented. The structural properties of this sandwich structure are compared with the conventional honeycomb core sandwich structure under the conditions of equal sandwich density. The SPF-DB orthogonally corrugated sandwich core has higher traverse shear stiffness than the conventional honeycomb sandwich core, but has lower stiffness in the sandwich core-thickness direction.

1197. Berry, D. T.; Powers, B. G.; Szalai, K. J.; and Wilson, R. J.: **In-Flight Evaluation of Control System Pure Time Delays.** *J. of Aircraft*, Vol. 19, No. 4, April 1982 (see AIAA 80-1626), pp. 318–323. (See also 1108.)

1198. Glover, R. D.: **Aircraft Interrogation and Display System: A Ground Support Equipment for Digital Flight Systems.** NASA TM-81370, NAS 1.15:81370, April 1982, 82N21175, #.

A microprocessor-based general purpose ground support equipment for electronic systems was developed. The hardware and software are designed to permit diverse applications in support of aircraft flight systems and simulation facilities. The implementation of the hardware, the structure of the software, describes the application of the system to an ongoing research aircraft project are described.

1199. Berry, D. T.: **Flying Qualities—A Costly Lapse in Flight-Control Design.** *Astronautics and Aeronautics*, Vol. 20, April 1982, pp. 54–57, 82A28280, #.

Generic problems in advanced aircraft with advanced control systems which suffer from control sensitivity, sluggish response, and pilot-induced oscillation tendencies are examined, with a view to improving techniques for eliminating the problems in the design phase. Results of two NASA and NASA/AIAA workshops reached a consensus that flying qualities criteria do not match control system development, control system designers are not relying on past experience in their field, ground-based simulation is relied on too heavily, and communications between flying qualities and control systems engineers need improvement. A summation is offered in that hardware and software have

outstripped the pilot's capacity to use the capabilities which new aircraft offer. The flying qualities data base is stressed to be dynamic, and continually redefining the man/machine relationships.

1200. Dittmar, J. H.; and Lasagna, P. L.: **A Preliminary Comparison Between the SR-3 Propeller Noise in Flight and in a Wind Tunnel.** NASA TM-82805, NAS 1.15:82805. Presented at 103rd Meeting of the Acoust. Soc. of Am., Chicago, Illinois, April 27–30, 1982, 82N21998, #.

The noise generated by supersonic-tip-speed propellers is addressed. Models of such propellers were tested for acoustics in the Lewis 8-by-6-foot wind tunnel. One of these propeller models, SR-3, was tested in flight on the JetStar airplane and noise data were obtained. Preliminary comparisons of the maximum blade passing tone variation with helical tip Mach number taken in flight with those taken in the tunnel showed good agreement when corrected to the same test conditions. This indicated that the wind tunnel is a viable location for measuring the noise of these propeller models. Comparisons of the directivities at 0.6 and 0.7 axial Mach number showed reasonable agreement. At 0.75 and 0.8 axial Mach number the tunnel directivity data fell off more towards the front than did the airplane data. A possible explanation for this is boundary layer refraction which could be different in the wind tunnel from that in flight. This may imply that some corrections should be applied to both the airplane and wind tunnel data at the forward angles. At and aft of the peak noise angle the boundary layer refraction does not appear to be significant and no correction appears necessary.

1201. Barber, M. R.; and *Tymczyszyn, J. J.: **Wake Vortex Attenuation Flight Tests—A Status Report.** Presented at the 13th Annual Symposium of the Society of Experimental Test Pilots, Rottach-Egern, West Germany. Published in *Cockpit*, Vol. 17, April–June 1982, pp. 6–26, 83A11806. (See also 1135.)

*FAA, Los Angeles, California.

1202. *Shideler, J. L.; **Swegle, A. R.; and Fields, R. A.: **Development of René 41 Honeycomb Structure as an Integral Cryogenic Tankage/Fuselage Concept for Future Space Transportation Systems.** AIAA Paper 82-0653. Presented at AIAA, ASME, ASCE, and AHS 23rd Structures, Structural Dynamics and Materials Conference, New Orleans, Louisiana, May 10–12, 1982, pp. 66–75, 82A30084, #. (See also 1203, 1342.)

The status of the structural development of an integral cryogenic-tankage/hot-fuselage concept for future space transportation systems is reviewed. The concept comprises a honeycomb sandwich structure that serves the combined functions of containing the cryogenic fuel, supporting the vehicle loads, and protecting the spacecraft from entry heating. The inner face sheet is exposed to cryogenic temperature of –423 F during boost; the outer face sheet, which is slotted to reduce thermal stress, is exposed to a maximum temperature of 1400 F during a high-altitude gliding entry. Attention is given to the development of a fabrication process for a Rene 41 honeycomb sandwich panel with a core density of less than 1 percent that is consistent with desirable heat treatment processes for high strength.

*NASA Langley Research Center, Hampton, Virginia.
**Boeing Aerospace Co., Seattle, Washington.

1203. *Shideler, J. L.; *Swegle, A. R.; and Fields, R. A.: **Development of René 41 Honeycomb Structure as an Integral Cryogenic Tankage/Fuselage Concept for Future Space Transportation Systems.** NASA TM-83306, NAS 1.15:83306, Presented at the 23rd AIAA, ASME, ASCE, and AHS Structural, Structural Dynamics and Materials Conference, New Orleans, Louisiana, May 10–12, 1982, June 1982, 82N30328, #. (See also 1202, 1342.)

The status of the structural development of an integral cryogenic-tankage/hot-fuselage concept for future space transportation systems (STS) is discussed. The concept consists of a honeycomb sandwich structure which serves the combined functions of containment of cryogenic fuel, support of vehicle loads, and thermal protection from an entry heating environment. The inner face sheet is exposed to a cryogenic (LH2) temperature of –423 F during boost; and the outer face sheet, which is slotted to reduce thermal stress, is exposed to a maximum temperature of 1400 F during a high altitude, gliding entry. A fabrication process for a Rene' 41 honeycomb sandwich panel with a core density less than 1 percent was developed which is consistent with desirable heat treatment processes for high strength.

*NASA Langley Research Center, Hampton, Virginia.
**Boeing Aerospace Co., Seattle, Washington.

1204. Fisher, D. F.; and *Dougherty, N. S., Jr.: **In-Flight Transition Measurement on a 10 Deg Cone at Mach Numbers From 0.5 to 2.0.** NASA TP-1971, H-1117, NAS 1.60:1971, June 1982, 82N26227, #.

Boundary layer transition measurements were made in flight on a 10 deg transition cone tested previously in 23 wind tunnels. The cone was mounted on the nose of an F-15 aircraft and flown at Mach numbers room 0.5 to 2.0 and altitudes from 1500 meters (5000 feet) to 15,000 meters (50,000 feet), overlapping the Mach number/Reynolds number envelope of the wind tunnel tests. Transition was detected using a traversing pitot probe in contact with the surface. Data were obtained near zero cone incidence and adiabatic wall temperature. Transition Reynolds number was found to be a function of Mach number and of the ratio of wall temperature to adiabatic all temperature. Microphones mounted flush with the cone surface measured free-stream disturbances imposed on the laminar boundary layer and

identified Tollmien-Schlichting waves as the probable cause of transition. Transition Reynolds number also correlated with the disturbance levels as measured by the cone surface microphones under a laminar boundary layer as well as the free-stream impact.

*ARO, Inc., Tullahoma, Tennessee.

1205. Baer-Riedhart, J. L.: **Evaluation of a Simplified Gross Thrust Calculation Method for a J85-21 Afterburning Turbojet Engine in an Altitude Facility.** AIAA Paper 82-1044. Presented at 18th AIAA, SAE and ASME Joint Propulsion Conference, Cleveland, Ohio, June 21–23, 1982, 82A34978, #.

A simplified gross thrust calculation method was evaluated on its ability to predict the gross thrust of a modified J85-21 engine. The method used tailpipe pressure data and ambient pressure data to predict the gross thrust. The method's algorithm is based on a one-dimensional analysis of the flow in the afterburner and nozzle. The test results showed that the method was notably accurate over the engine operating envelope using the altitude facility measured thrust for comparison. A summary of these results, the simplified gross thrust method and requirements, and the test techniques used are discussed in this paper.

1206. Myers, L. P.; Mackall, K. G.; Burcham, F. W., Jr.; and *Walter, W. A.: **Flight Evaluation of a Digital Electronic Engine Control System in an F-15 Airplane.** AIAA Paper 82-1080. Presented at 18th AIAA, SAE and ASME Joint Propulsion Conference, Cleveland, Ohio, June 21–23, 1982, 82A37683, #.

Benefits provided by a full-authority digital engine control are related to improvements in engine efficiency, performance, and operations. An additional benefit is the capability of detecting and accommodating failures in real time and providing engine-health diagnostics. The digital electronic engine control (DEEC), is a full-authority digital engine control developed for the F100-PW-100 turbofan engine. The DEEC has been flight tested on an F-15 aircraft. The flight tests had the objective to evaluate the DEEC hardware and software over the F-15 flight envelope. A description is presented of the results of the flight tests, which consisted of nonaugmented and augmented throttle transients, airstarts, and backup control operations. The aircraft, engine, DEEC system, and data acquisition and reduction system are discussed.

*United Technologies Corp., Pratt and Whitney Aircraft Group, West Palm Beach, Florida.

1207. Mackall, K. G.; Lasagna, P. L.; *Dittmar, J. H.; and Walsh, K.: **In-Flight Acoustic Results From an Advanced-Design Propeller at Mach Numbers to 0.8.** AIAA Paper 82-1120. Presented at 18th AIAA, SAE and ASME Joint

Propulsion Conference, Cleveland, Ohio, June 21–23, 1982, 82A35017, #.

Acoustic data for the advanced-design SR-3 propeller at Mach numbers to 0.8 and helical tip Mach numbers to 1.14 are presented. Several advanced-design propellers, previously tested in wind tunnels at the Lewis Research Center, are being tested in flight at the Dryden Flight Research Facility. The flight-test propellers are mounted on a pylon on the top of the fuselage of a JetStar airplane. Instrumentation provides near-field acoustic data for the SR-3. Acoustic data for the SR-3 propeller at Mach numbers up to 0.8, for propeller helical tip Mach numbers up to 1.14, and comparison of wind tunnel to flight data are included. Flowfield profiles measured in the area adjacent to the propeller are also included.

*NASA Lewis Research Center, Cleveland, Ohio.

1208. Webb, L. D.; and Nugent, J.: **Selected Results of the F-15 Propulsion Interactions Program.** AIAA Paper 82-1041. Presented at 18th AIAA, SAE and ASME Joint Propulsion Conference, Cleveland, Ohio, June 21–23, 1982, 82A34976, #.

A better understanding of propulsion system/airframe flow interactions could aid in the reduction of aircraft drag. For this purpose, NASA and the United States Air Force have conducted a series of wind-tunnel and flight tests on the F-15 airplane. This paper presents a correlation of flight test data from tests conducted at the NASA Dryden Flight Research Facility of the Ames Research Center, with data obtained from wind-tunnel tests. Flights were made at stabilized Mach numbers around 0.6, 0.9, 1.2, and 1.5 with accelerations up to near Mach number 2. Wind-tunnel tests used a 7.5 percent-scale F-15 inlet/airframe model. Flight and wind-tunnel pressure coefficients showed good agreement in most cases. Correlation of interaction effects caused by changes in cowl angle, angle-of-attack, and Mach number are presented. For the afterbody region, the pressure coefficients on the nozzle surfaces were influenced by boattail angles and Mach number. Boundary-layer thickness decreased as angle of attack increased above 4 deg.

1209. Maine, R. E.; and Iliff, K. W.: **Formulation of a Practical Algorithm for Parameter Estimation With Process and Measurement Noise.** *Identification and System Parameter Estimation 1982. Proceedings of the Sixth IFAC Symposium*, Washington, DC, Vol. 2, June 7–11, 1982, pp. 1139–1144, 84A18611. (See also 1109, 1184.)

A new formulation is proposed for the problem of parameter estimation in dynamic systems with both process and measurement noise. The formulation applies to continuous-time state space system models with discrete-time measurements. Previous formulations of this problem encountered several theoretical and practical difficulties which are overcome by the new formulation. The most important element of the new formulation is a reparameterization of the unknown noise covariances. A computer program that implements the new formulation is available.

1210. Meyer, R. R., Jr.: **A Unique Flight Test Facility — Description and Results.** *Proceedings, 13th International Council of the Aeronautical Sciences Congress, and AIAA Aircraft Systems and Technology Conference*, Seattle, Washington, Vol. 1, August 22–27, 1982, pp. 433–448, 82A40925, #. (See also 1223.)

The Dryden Flight Research Facility has developed a unique research facility for conducting aerodynamic and fluid mechanics experiments in flight. A low aspect ratio fin, referred to as the flight test fixture (FTF), is mounted on the underside of the fuselage of an F-104G aircraft. The F-104/FTF facility is described, and the capabilities are discussed. The capabilities include (1) a large Mach number envelope (0.4 to 2.0), including the region through Mach 1.0; (2) the potential ability to test articles larger than those that can be tested in wind tunnels; (3) the large chord Reynolds number envelope (greater than 40 million); and (4) the ability to define small increments in friction drag between two test surfaces. Data are presented from experiments that demonstrate some of the capabilities of the FTF, including the shuttle thermal protection system airload tests, instrument development, and base drag studies. Proposed skin friction experiments and instrument evaluation studies are also discussed.

1211. Kempel, R. W.: **Flight Experience With a Backup Flight-Control System for the HiMAT Research Vehicle.** AIAA Paper 82-1541. Presented at AIAA Guidance and Control Conference, San Diego, California, August 9–11, 1982, 82A40429, #.

The NASA Dryden Flight Research Facility is conducting flight tests of two remotely piloted, subscale, advanced fighter configurations; the tests are part of the Highly Maneuverable Aircraft Technology (HiMAT) project. Closed-loop primary flight control is performed from a ground-based cockpit and digital computer in conjunction with an up/down telemetry link. A significant feature of these vehicles is an on-board, digitally active, backup control system designed to recover the vehicle in the event of a transfer from primary control. Automatic transfers occur upon certain critical ground or airborne system malfunctions. Control modes are provided that enable a ground or airborne controller to guide the vehicle to a safe landing. This paper describes the features, operational development, and flight evaluation of the HiMAT backup flight control system.

1212. Shafer, M. F.: **Flight-Determined Correction Terms for Angle of Attack and Sideslip.** AIAA Paper 82-1374. Presented in 9th AIAA Atmospheric Flight Mechanics Conference, San Diego, California, August 9–11, 1982, 82A40290, #.

The effects of local flow, upwash, and sidewash on angle of attack and sideslip (measured with boom-mounted vanes) were determined for subsonic, transonic, and supersonic flight using a maximum likelihood estimator. The correction terms accounting for these effects were determined using a series of maneuvers flown at a large number of flight conditions in both augmented and unaugmented control modes. The correction terms provide improved angle-of-attack and sideslip values for use in the estimation of stability and control derivatives. In addition to detailing the procedure used to determine these correction terms, this paper discusses various effects, such as those related to Mach number, on the correction terms. The use of maneuvers flown in augmented and unaugmented control modes is also discussed.

1213. *Gupta, N. K.; and Iliff, K. W.: **Identification of Aerodynamic Indicial Functions Using Flight Data.** AIAA Paper 82-1375. Presented in 9th AIAA Atmospheric Flight Mechanics Conference, San Diego, California, August 9–11, 1982, 82A39136, #.

It is pointed out that the use of indicial function representation provides a model superior to the aerodynamic derivative model. Specific derivatives can be approximated from the indicial models. The model can also be used to compute equivalent stability and control parameters not usually available from flight data. It is shown that derivatives regarding the angle-of-attack and the side slip angle can be derived directly from the indicial functions without any identifiability problem. Attention is given to the pitch moment coefficient, linear indicial function representation, the identification problem for the pitch moment equation, the identifiability of linear systems, parametric representations of the indicial functions, an identification technique, angle-of-attack and pitch rate dynamics in the pitch plane, multivariate linear models, nonlinear aerodynamic indicial functions, measurement system accuracy, and poststall and spin-entry data from a scaled research vehicle.

*Integrated Systems, Inc., Palo Alto, California.

1214. Iliff, K. W.; and Maine, R. E.: **NASA Dryden's Experience in Parameter Estimation and Its Uses in Flight Test.** AIAA Paper 82-1373. Presented in 9th AIAA Atmospheric Flight Mechanics Conference, San Diego, California, August 9–11, 1982, 82A39135, #. (See also 1294.)

An explanation of the parameter estimation method used at the Dryden Flight Research Facility is presented, and an overview is provided of experience related to the employment of this method, taking into account the utilization of this experience in flight tests. According to a definition of the aircraft parameter estimation problem, the system investigated is assumed to be modeled by a set of dynamic equations containing unknown parameters. To

determine the values of the unknown parameters, the system is excited by a suitable input, and the input and actual system response are measured. The values of the unknown parameters are then inferred, based on the requirement that the model response to the given input match the actual system response. Examples of parameter estimation in flight test are discussed, giving attention to the F-14 fighter, the HiMAT (high maneuverable aircraft technology) vehicle, and the Space Shuttle.

1215. Curry, R. E.; and Sim, A. G.: **Unique Flight Characteristics of the AD-1 Oblique-Wing Research Airplane.** AIAA Paper 82-1329. Presented at 9th AIAA Atmospheric Flight Mechanics Conference, San Diego, California, August 9–11, 1982, 82A39106, #. (See also 1257.)

Flight characteristics associated with an oblique-wing airplane have been studied with limited scope and complexity using the AD-1 research vehicle. The AD-1 is a low-speed, low-cost, manned airplane with an aeroelastically tailored wing that can be pivoted 0 to 60 deg asymmetrically. Results of the flight tests include aerodynamic parameter extraction, verification of the aeroelastic wing design criteria, trim requirements, stall characteristics, and an evaluation of the handling qualities and basic control system requirements. Some of the unique characteristics of these results that pertain to the oblique-wing design are presented.

1216. Maine, R. E.; and Iliff, K. W.: **Selected Stability and Control Derivatives From the First Three Space Shuttle Entries.** AIAA Paper 82-1318. Presented at the 9th AIAA Atmospheric Flight Mechanics Conference, San Diego, California, August 9–11, 1982, 82A39096, #.

Stability and control derivative estimates obtained from the first three Space Shuttle entries are presented. The derivative estimates were obtained using the established modified maximum likelihood estimation program (MMLE3). The method of analysis used by the MMLE3 program is reviewed, the Shuttle configuration and data system are described, and the various types of maneuvers analyzed from the three entries are illustrated. Finally, the paper presents selected derivative results and compares them with predictions. Most of the flight-derived estimates agreed fairly well with predictions, considering the lack of experience in these new flight regimes. The most notable exception was the aerodynamic interference caused by firing the reaction control jets in the atmosphere. The flight results showed this interference to be considerably smaller than predicted.

1217. *Bailey, R. E.; *Smith, R. E.; and Shafer, M. F.: **An In-Flight Investigation of Pilot-Induced Oscillation Suppression Filters During the Fighter Approach and Landing Task.** *Flight Testing Technology: A State-of-the-Art Review; Proceedings of the Thirteenth Annual SETP*

Symposium, New York, New York, September 19–22, 1982, pp. 185–191, A84-44451.

An investigation of pilot-induced oscillation suppression (PIOS) filters was performed using the USAF/Flight Dynamics Laboratory variable stability NT-33 aircraft, modified and operated by Calspan. This program examined the effects of PIOS filtering on the longitudinal flying qualities of fighter aircraft during the visual approach and landing task. Forty evaluations were flown to test the effects of different PIOS filters. Although detailed analyses were not undertaken, the results indicate that PIOS filtering can improve the flying qualities of an otherwise unacceptable aircraft configuration (Level 3 flying qualities). However, the ability of the filters to suppress pilot-induced oscillations appears to be dependent upon the aircraft configuration characteristics. Further, the data show that the filters can adversely affect landing flying qualities if improperly designed. The data provide an excellent foundation from which detail analyses can be performed.

*Calspan Advanced Technology Center, Buffalo, New York.

1218. Duke, E. L.: **Automated Flight Test Maneuvers— The Development of a New Technique.** *Flight Testing Technology: A State-of-the-Art Review; Proceedings of the Thirteenth Annual SETP Symposium*, New York, New York, September 19–22, 1982, pp. 101–119, 84A44464, #.

A new flight test technique using a maneuver autopilot is being applied at the Dryden Flight Research Facility of the NASA Ames Research Center. The flight test maneuver autopilot (FTMAP) is designed to provide precise, repeatable control of an aircraft during certain prescribed maneuvers so that a large quantity of high quality test data can be obtained with a minimum of flight time. This paper discusses the control algorithms, the flight test application, and the preliminary flight demonstration results of the FTMAP.

1219. Harney, P. F.: **Real-Time Data Display for AFTI/F-16 Flight Testing.** *ITC/USA/'82; Proceedings of the International Telemetering Conference*, San Diego, California, September 28–30, 1982, pp. 13–33, (see A84-32401 14-32), 84A32403. (See also 1225.)

Advanced fighter technologies to improve air to air and air to surface weapon delivery and survivability is demonstrated. Real time monitoring of aircraft operation during flight testing is necessary not only for safety considerations but also for preliminary evaluation of flight test results. The complexity of the AFTI/F-16 aircraft requires an extensive capability to accomplish real time data goals; that capability and the resultant product are described. Previously announced in STAR as N83-13095.

EC92-10061-10

AFTI F-16 Airplane

1220. Shafer, M. F.: **Low Order Equivalent Models of Highly Augmented Aircraft Determined From Flight Data Using Maximum Likelihood Estimation.** *Journal of Guidance, Control and Dynamics*, Vol. 5, No. 5, September–October 1982, (see AIAA Paper 80-1627), pp. 504–511. (See also 1107.)

This paper presents the results of a study of the feasibility of using low order equivalent mathematical models of a highly augmented aircraft, the F-8 digital fly-by-wire (DFBW), for flying qualities research. Increasingly complex models were formulated and evaluated using flight data and maximum likelihood estimation techniques. The airframe was first modeled alone. Next, equivalent derivatives were used to model the longitudinal unaugmented F-8 DFBW aircraft dynamics. The most complex model of the unaugmented aircraft incorporated a pure time shift of the pilot input, a first order lag, and the basic longitudinal airframe model. This same model was then implemented for the F-8 DFBW aircraft in a highly augmented mode. Excellent matching of the dynamics resulted for this model, indicating that low order equivalent models that are good representations of the highly augmented F-8 DFBW aircraft can be formulated with these methods.

1221. Murray, J. E.: **User's Manual for THPLOT, A FORTRAN 77 Computer Program for Time History Plotting.** NASA TM-81374, NAS 1.15:81374, October 1982, 83N12881, #.

A general purpose FORTRAN 77 computer program (THPLOT) for plotting time histories using Calcomp pen plotters is described. The program is designed to read a time history data file and to generate time history plots for selected time intervals and/or selected data channels. The capabilities of the program are described. The card input required to define the plotting operation is described and examples of card input and the resulting plotted output are given. The examples are followed by a description of the printed output, including both normal output and error messages. Lastly, implementation of the program is described. A complete listing of the program with reference maps produced by the CDC FTN 5.0 compiler is included.

1222. *Peake, D. J.; Fisher, D. F.; and **McRae, D. S.: **Flight, Wind Tunnel and Numerical Experiments With a Slender Cone at Incidence.** *AIAA Journal,* Vol. 20, No.10, October 1982.

The three-dimensional leeward separation about a 5 deg semi-angle cone at an 11 deg incidence was investigated in flight, in the wind tunnel, and by numerical computations. The test conditions were Mach numbers of 0.6, 1.5, and 1.8 at Reynolds numbers between 7 and 10 million based on free-stream conditions and a 76.2 cm (30-in.) length of surface. The surface conditions measured included those of fluctuating pressures and mean static, as well as recovery pressures generated by obstacle blocks to provide skin friction and separation line positions. The mean static pressures from flight and wind tunnel were in reasonably good agreement. The computed results gave the same distributions, but were slightly more positive in magnitude. The experimentally measured primary and secondary separation line locations compared closely with computed results. There were substantial differences in level between the surface root-mean-square pressure fluctuations obtained in flight and in the wind tunnel, due, it is thought, to a relatively high acoustic disturbance level in the tunnel compared with the quiescent conditions in flight.

*NASA Ames Research Center, Moffett Field, California.
**North Carolina State University, Raleigh, North Carolina.

1223. Meyer, R. R., Jr.: **A Unique Flight Test Facility: Description and Results.** NASA TM-84900, NAS 1:15:84900. ICAS Paper 82-5.3.3. Presented at 13th Congr. of the ICAS/AIAA Aircraft Systems and Technology Conference, Seattle, Washington, August 22–27, 1982, November 1982, 83N13124, #. (See also 1210.)

The Dryden Flight Research Facility has developed a unique research facility for conducting aerodynamic and fluid mechanics experiments in flight. A low aspect ratio fin, referred to as the flight test fixture (FTF), is mounted on the underside of the fuselage of an F-104G aircraft. The F-104G/FTF facility is described, and the capabilities are discussed. The capabilities include (1) a large Mach number envelope (0.4 to 2.0), including the region through Mach 1.0; (2) the potential ability to test articles larger than those that can be tested in wind tunnels; (3) the large chord Reynolds number envelope (greater than 40 million); and (4) the ability to define small increments in friction drag between two test surfaces. Data are presented from experiments that

demonstrate some of the capabilities of the FTF, including the shuttle thermal protection system airload tests, instrument development, and base drag studies. Proposed skin friction experiments and instrument evaluation studies are also discussed.

1224. Roncoli, R. B.: **A Flight Test Maneuver Autopilot for a Highly Maneuverable Aircraft.** NASA TM-81372, H-1176, NAS 1.15:81372. Presented at the AIAA Region 6, 32nd Annual Student Conference, Irvine, California, April 28–May 1, 1982, November 1982, 83N13115, #.

A flight test maneuver autopilot (FTMAP) is currently being flown to increase the quality and quantity of the data obtained in the flight testing of the highly maneuverable aircraft technology (HiMAT) remotely piloted research vehicle (RPRV). The FTMAP resides in a ground-based digital computer and was designed to perform certain prescribed maneuvers precisely, while maintaining critical flight parameters within close tolerances. The FTMAP operates as a non-flight-critical outer loop controller and augments the vehicle primary flight control system. The inputs to the FTMAP consist of telemetry-downlinked aircraft sensor data. During FTMAP operation, the FTMAP computer replaces normal pilot inputs to the aircraft stick and throttle positions. The FTMAP maneuvers include straight-and-level flight, level accelerations and decelerations, pushover pullups, and windup turns. The pushover pullups can be executed holding throttle or Mach number fixed. The windup turns can be commanded by either normal acceleration or angle of attack. The operational procedures, control mode configuration, and initial simulation results are discussed.

1225. Harney, P. F.: **Real-Time Data Display for AFTI/F-16 Flight Testing.** NASA TM-84899, NAS 1.15:84899, November 1982, 83N13095, #. (See also 1219.)

Advanced fighter technologies to improve air to air and air to surface weapon delivery and survivability is demonstrated. Real time monitoring of aircraft operation during flight testing is necessary not only for safety considerations but also for preliminary evaluation of flight test results. The complexity of the AFTI/F-16 aircraft requires an extensive capability to accomplish real time data goals; that capability and the resultant product are described.

1226. Carter, A. L.: **Strain Gage Load Measurement on the Shuttle Orbiter.** NASA TM-84898, NAS 1.15:84898. Presented at SESA 1982 Fall Meeting, Hartford, Connecticut, November 7–12, 1982, 83N12135, #.

This paper describes the application of the calibrated strain gage load measurement method to the shuttle orbiter. Descriptions of instrumentation and calibration are included, along with comparisons of measured results with wind tunnel and FLEXSTAB analytical predictions.

1227. Fisher, D. F.; and *Dougherty, N. S., Jr.: **Flight and Wind-Tunnel Correlation of Boundary-Layer Transition on the AEDC Transition Cone.** NASA TM-84902, NAS 1.15:84902. Presented at the AGARD Flight Mechanics Panel Symposium, Cesme, Turkey, October 11–14, 1982, November 1982, 83N14433, #. (See also 1243.)

Transition and fluctuating surface pressure data were acquired on a 10 deg included angle cone, using the same instrumentation and technique over a wide range of Mach and Reynolds numbers in 23 wind tunnels and in flight. Transition was detected with a traversing pitot-pressure probe in contact with the surface. The surface pressure fluctuations were measured with microphones set flush in the cone surface. Good correlation of end of transition Reynolds number RE(T) was obtained between data from the lower disturbance wind tunnels and flight up to a boundary layer edge Mach number, M(e) = 1.2. Above M(e) = 1.2, however, this correlation deteriorates, with the flight Re(T) being 25 to 30% higher than the wind tunnel Re(T) at M(e) = 1.6. The end of transition Reynolds number correlated within ± 20% with the surface pressure fluctuations, according to the equation used. Broad peaks in the power spectral density distributions indicated that Tollmien-Schlichting waves were the probable cause of transition in flight and in some of the wind tunnels.

*Rockwell International Corp., Huntsville, Alabama.

1228. Saltzman, Edwin J.: **A Summary of NASA Dryden's Truck Aerodynamic Research.** SAE Paper 821284. Presented at SAE Truck & Bus Meeting and Exposition, Indianapolis, Indiana, November 8–11, 1982.

A combination of subscale wind tunnel model tests and full-scale coast down and highway fuel consumption tests have been conducted on baseline and low-drag tractor-trailer configurations. Fuel savings calculated for the low-drag configuration, based on the model drag data or the full-scale drag data, correlate quite well with fuel savings obtained from the over-the-roads tests at highway speeds. Subscale drag test for flow-vane and boattail devices provided drag reductions of about 48 percent and 15 percent, respectively, for bus- or motor-home-type vehicles. Full-scale boattail drag data are also presented.

1229. DeAngelis, V. M.: **In-Flight Deflection Measurement of the HiMAT Aeroelastically Tailored Wing.** Presented at 1st AIAA, SETP, SFTE, SAE, ITEA, and IEEE Flight Testing Conference, Las Vegas, Nevada, November 11–13, 1981. *Journal of Aircraft*, Vol. 19, December 1982, pp. 1088–1094, 83A13167, #. (See also 1165.)

1230. Gong, L.; Quinn, R. D.; and Ko, W. L.: **Reentry Heating Analysis of Space Shuttle With Comparison of**

Flight Data. NASA CP-2216. *NASA Langley Research Center Computational Aspects of Heat Transfer in Struct.,* 1982, (see N82-23473 14-34), pp. 271–294, 82N23490, #.

Surface heating rates and surface temperatures for a space shuttle reentry profile were calculated for two wing cross sections and one fuselage cross section. Heating rates and temperatures at 12 locations on the wing and 6 locations on the fuselage are presented. The heating on the lower wing was most severe, with peak temperatures reaching values of 1240 C for turbulent flow and 900 C for laminar flow. For the fuselage, the most severe heating occurred on the lower glove surface where peak temperatures of 910 C and 700 C were calculated for turbulent flow and laminar flow, respectively. Aluminum structural temperatures were calculated using a finite difference thermal analyzer computer program, and the predicted temperatures are compared to measured flight data. Skin temperatures measured on the lower surface of the wing and bay 1 of the upper surface of the wing agreed best with temperatures calculated assuming laminar flow. The measured temperatures at bays two and four on the upper surface of the wing were in quite good agreement with the temperatures calculated assuming separated flow. The measured temperatures on the lower forward spar cap of bay four were in good agreement with values predicted assuming laminar flow.

1231. Ko, W. L.; Quinn, R. D.; and Gong, L.: **Reentry Heat Transfer Analysis of the Space Shuttle Orbiter.** NASA CP-2216, *NASA Langley Research Center Computational Aspects of Heat Transfer in Struct.,* 1982, (see N82-23473 14-34), pp. 295–325, 82N23491, #.

A structural performance and resizing finite element thermal analysis computer program was used in the reentry heat transfer analysis of the space shuttle. Two typical wing cross sections and a midfuselage cross section were selected for the analysis. The surface heat inputs to the thermal models were obtained from aerodynamic heating analyses, which assumed a purely turbulent boundary layer, a purely laminar boundary layer, separated flow, and transition from laminar to turbulent flow. The effect of internal radiation was found to be quite significant. With the effect of the internal radiation considered, the wing lower skin temperature became about 39 C (70 F) lower. The results were compared with fight data for space transportation system, trajectory 1. The calculated and measured temperatures compared well for the wing if laminar flow was assumed for the lower surface and bay one upper surface and if separated flow was assumed for the upper surfaces of bays other than bay one. For the fuselage, good agreement between the calculated and measured data was obtained if laminar flow was assumed for the bottom surface. The structural temperatures were found to reach their peak values shortly before touchdown. In addition, the finite element solutions were compared with those obtained from the conventional finite difference solutions.

1983 Technical Publications

1232. Burcham, F. W., Jr.; Myers, L. P.; and *Zeller, J. R.: **Flight Evaluation of Modifications to a Digital Electronic Engine Control System in an F-15 Airplane.** NASA TM-83088, NAS 1.15:83088, AIAA Paper 83-0537. Presented at AIAA 21st Aerospace Sciences Meeting, Reno, Nevada, January 10–13, 1983. 1983, 83N22201, #. (See also 1233.)

The third phase of a flight evaluation of a digital electronic engine control system in an F-15 has recently been completed. It was found that digital electronic engine control software logic changes and augmentor hardware improvements resulted in significant improvements in engine operation. For intermediate to maximum power throttle transients, an increase in altitude capability of up to 8000 ft was found, and for idle to maximum transients, an increase of up to 4000 ft was found. A nozzle instability noted in earlier flight testing was investigated on a test engine at NASA Lewis Research Center, a digital electronic engine control software logic change was developed and evaluated, and no instability occurred in the Phase 3 flight evaluation. The backup control airstart modification was evaluated, and gave an improvement of airstart capability by reducing the minimum airspeed for successful airstarts by 50 to 75 knots.

*NASA Lewis Research Center, Cleveland, Ohio.

1233. Burcham, F. W., Jr.; Myers, L. P.; and *Zeller, J. R.: **Flight Evaluation of Modifications to a Digital Electronic Engine Control System in an F-15 Airplane.** AIAA Paper 83-0537. Presented at AIAA 21st Aerospace Sciences Meeting, Reno, Nevada, January 10–13, 1983, 83A19593, #. (See also 1232.)

The third phase of a flight evaluation of a digital electronic engine control system in an F-15 has recently been completed. It was found that digital electronic engine control software logic changes and augmentor hardware improvements resulted in significant improvements in engine operation. For intermediate to maximum power throttle transients, an increase in altitude capability of up to 8000 ft was found, and for idle to maximum transients, an increase of up to 4000 ft was found. A nozzle instability noted in earlier flight testing was investigated on a test engine at NASA Lewis Research Center, a digital electronic engine control software logic change was developed and evaluated, and no instability occurred in the Phase 3 flight evaluation. The backup control airstart modification was evaluated, and gave an improvement of airstart capability by reducing the minimum airspeed for successful airstarts by 50 to 75 knots.

*NASA Lewis Research Center, Cleveland, Ohio.

EC83-25819

Dryden Flight Research Facility Aircraft, circa 1983, (front row), Lockheed F-104, (2nd row), Rockwell International HiMAT, Piper PA-30, Volmer Ultralight, (3rd row), Schweizer 1-36, Lockheed F-104, Northrop T-38, Lockheed F-104, (4th row) Eiri-Avion PIK-20E, Grumman F-14, Lockheed C-140 JetStar, Vought F-8 DFBW, (5th row) General Dynamics F-111E IPCS, Martin B-57B, McDonnell-Douglas F-15, Douglas C-47, (back row) Boeing 720 CID, Boeing 747 SCA, and Boeing B-52

1234. Gilyard, G. B.; and Edwards, J. W.: **Real-Time Flutter Analysis of an Active Flutter-Suppression System on a Remotely Piloted Research Aircraft.** NASA TM-84901, NAS 1.15:84901, January 1983, 83N18710, #. (See also 1244.)

Flight flutter-test results of the first aeroelastic research wing (ARW-1) of NASA's drones for aerodynamic and structural testing program are presented. The flight-test operation and the implementation of the active flutter-suppression system are described as well as the software techniques used to obtain real-time damping estimates and the actual flutter testing procedure. Real-time analysis of fast-frequency aileron excitation sweeps provided reliable damping estimates. The open-loop flutter boundary was well defined at two altitudes; a maximum Mach number of 0.91 was obtained. Both open-loop and closed-loop data were of exceptionally high quality. Although the flutter-suppression system provided augmented damping at speeds below the flutter boundary, an error in the implementation of the system resulted in the system being less stable than predicted. The vehicle encountered system-on flutter shortly after crossing the open-loop flutter boundary on the third flight and was lost. The aircraft was rebuilt. Changes made in real-time test techniques are included.

1235. *Wiederholt, J. V.; and Pahle, J. W.: **The Design of a Human-Powered Vehicle.** AIAA Paper 83-0649. Presented at AIAA 21st Aerospace Sciences Meeting, Reno, Nevada, January 10–13, 1983, 83A16816, #.

Human power applied through a bicycle is perhaps the most efficient means of transport available today. Aerodynamic drag, however, limits the speed possible from the man/bicycle combination. An aerodynamically efficient body enclosing the system can reduce the drag and permit increased speeds. A study was conducted to determine an efficient body design for a high-speed bicycle. Wind tunnel and potential flow studies were conducted to evaluate the drag and lift characteristics of proposed shell designs. A proposed bicycle/shell design is presented.

*General Dynamics Corp., Convair Div., San Diego, California.

1236. Mackall, D. A.; Ishmael, S. D.; and *Regenie, V. A.: **Qualification of the Flight-Critical AFTI/F-16 Digital Flight Control System.** AIAA Paper 83-0060. Presented at AIAA 21st Aerospace Sciences Meeting, Reno, Nevada, January 10–13, 1983, 83A16492, #. (See also 1253.)

Qualification considerations for assuring the safety of a life-critical digital flight control system include four major areas: systems interactions, verification, validation, and configuration control. The AFTI/F-16 design, development, and qualification illustrate these considerations. In this paper,

qualification concepts, procedures, and methodologies are discussed and illustrated through specific examples.

*Systems Control Technology, Inc., Edwards, California.

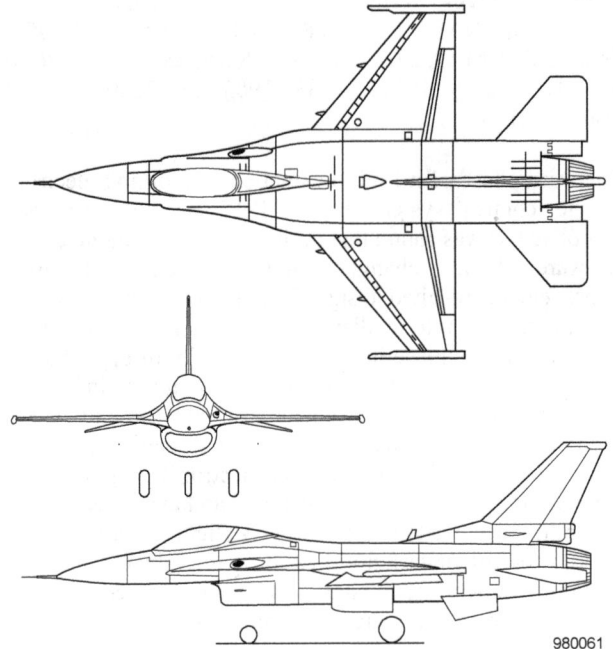

F-16 Airplane, Three-View Drawing

1237. Duke, E. L.; Jones, F. P.; and Roncoli, R. B.: **Development of a Flight Test Maneuver Autopilot for a Highly Maneuverable Aircraft.** AIAA Paper 83-0061. Presented at AIAA 21st Aerospace Sciences Meeting, Reno, Nevada, January 10–13, 1983, 83A16493, #.

This paper details the development of a flight test maneuver autopilot for a highly maneuverable aircraft. This newly developed flight test technique is being applied at the Dryden Flight Research Facility of the NASA Ames Research Center. The flight test maneuver autopilot (FTMAP) is designed to increase the quantity and quality of the data obtained in flight test. The vehicle with which it is being used is the highly maneuverable aircraft technology (HiMAT) vehicle. This paper describes the HiMAT vehicle systems, maneuver requirements, FTMAP development process, and flight results.

1238. *Butler, G. F.; *Corbin, M. J.; *Mepham, S.; Stewart, J. F.; and Larson, R. R.: **NASA/RAE Collaboration on Nonlinear Control Using the F-8C Digital Fly-By-Wire Aircraft.** AGARD CP-321. *AGARD Advances in Guidance and Control Systems*, January 1983, (see N83 22093 12-01), 83N22109, #. (See also 1239.)

A cooperative advanced digital research experiment (CADRE) was established by the National Aeronautics and

Space Administration (NASA) and the Royal Aircraft Establishment (RAE), in which nonlinear control algorithms developed by the RAE were tested on the F-8C digital fly-by-wire (DFBW) aircraft based at the Dryden Flight Research Facility. In the initial phase of the collaboration, some variable-gain algorithms, referred to collectively as variable integral control to optimize response (VICTOR) algorithms, were fight tested. With VICTOR, various measures available within the control system are used to vary gains and time-constants within the closed loop and thereby enhance the control capability of the system, while reducing the adverse effects of sensor noise on the control surfaces. A review of design procedures for VICTOR and results of preliminary flight tests are presented. the F-8C aircraft is operated in the remotely augmented vehicle (RAV) mode, with the control laws implemented as FORTRAN programs on a ground-based computer. Pilot commands and sensor information are telemetered to the ground, where the data are processed to form surface commands which are then telemetered to the ground, where the data are processed to form surface commands which are then telemetered back to the aircraft. The RAV mode represents a single-string (simplex) system and is therefore vulnerable to a hardover since comparison monitoring is not possible. Hence, extensive error checking is conducted on both the ground and airborne computers to prevent the development of potentially hazardous situations. Experience with the RAV monitoring and validation procedures is described.

*Royal Aircraft Establishment, Farnborough, U. K.

1239. *Butler, G. F.; *Corbin, M. J.; *Mepham, S.; Stewart, J. F.; and Larson, R. R.: **NASA/RAE Collaboration on Nonlinear Control Using the F-8C Digital Fly-By-Wire Aircraft.** NASA TM-84296, NAS 1.15:84296, February 1983, 83N23316, #. (See also 1238.)

Design procedures are reviewed for variable integral control to optimize response (VICTOR) algorithms and results of preliminary flight tests are presented. The F-8C aircraft is operated in the remotely augmented vehicle (RAV) mode, with the control laws implemented as FORTRAN programs on a ground-based computer. Pilot commands and sensor information are telemetered to the ground, where the data are processed to form surface commands which are then telemetered back to the aircraft. The RAV mode represents a singlestring (simplex) system and is therefore vulnerable to a hardover since comparison monitoring is not possible. Hence, extensive error checking is conducted on both the ground and airborne computers to prevent the development of potentially hazardous situations. Experience with the RAV monitoring and validation procedures is described.

*Royal Aircraft Establishment, Farnborough, U. K.

1240. Jenkins, J. M.: **A Study of the Effect of Apparent Strain on Thermal Stress Measurement for Two Types of Elevated Temperature Strain Gages.** NASA TM-84904, NAS 1.15:84904, February 1983, 83N18719, #.

A weldable type strain gage was used to measure low level thermal stress in an elevated temperature environment. Foil strain gages used in a comparative manner reveal that the apparent strain of weldable strain gages is not sufficiently known to acquire accurate low level thermal stress data. Apparent strain data acquired from coupon tests reveals a large scatter in apparent strain characteristics among the weldable strain gages. It is concluded that apparent strain data for individual weldable strain gages must be required prior to installation if valid thermal stress data is to be obtained through the temperature range of room temperature to 755 K (900 F).

1241. Curry, R. E.: **Limited Flight Test Experience With a Laser Transit Velocimeter.** NASA TM-84896, NAS 1.15.84896, February 1983, 83N17507, #.

Limited flight testing of a laser transit velocimeter provided insight into the problems associated with the use of such instruments for flight research. Although the device tested was not designed for flight application, it had certain features such as fiber optics and low laser power which are attractive in the airborne environment. During these tests, operation of the velocimeter was limited by insufficient concentrations of light-scattering particles and background light interference. Normal operation was observed when these conditions were corrected by utilizing cloud particles and flying at night. A comparison between the laser flow velocity measurements and corresponding pressure measurements is presented and shows a coarse correlation. Statistical bias due to turbulence in the flow is suspected to have affected the laser measurements.

1242. *Barrett, W. J.; *Rembold, J. P.; Burcham, F. W., Jr.; and Myers, L. P.: **Digital Electronic Engine Control System—F-15 Flight Test.** AIAA 81-1501. Presented at 17th AIAA, SAE, and ASME Joint Propulsion Conference, Colorado Springs, Colorado. *J. Aircraft*, Vol. 20, February 1983, pp. 134–141, 83A18406, #. (See also 1150.)

*United Technologies Corp., Pratt and Whitney Aircraft Group, West Palm Beach, Florida.

1243. Fisher, D. F.; and *Dougherty, N. S., Jr.: **Flight and Wind-Tunnel Correlation of Boundary-Layer Transition on the AEDC Transition Cone.** AGARD CP-339, Paper 6, *AGARD Ground/Flight Test Tech. and Correlation*, February 1983, (see 83N30357), 83N30363, #. (See also 1227.)

Transition and fluctuating surface pressure data were acquired on a 10 degree included angle cone, using the same instrumentation and technique over a wide range of Mach and Reynolds numbers in 23 wind tunnels and in flight. Transition was detected with a traversing pitot pressure probe in contact with the surface. The surface pressure fluctuations were measured with microphones set flush in the cone surface. Good correlation of end of transition Reynolds number Re (sub T) was obtained between data from the lower disturbance wind tunnels and flight up to a boundary layer edge Mach number, M (sub e) = 1.2. Above M (sub e) = 1.2, however, this correlation deteriorates, with the flight Re (sub T) being 25 to 30% higher than the wind tunnel Re (sub T) at M (sub e) = 1.6. The end of transition Reynolds number correlated within ±20% with the surface pressure fluctuations. Broad peaks in the power spectral density distributions indicated that Tollmien-Schlichting waves were the probable cause of transition in flight and in some of the wind tunnels.

*Rockwell International, Los Angeles, California.

1244. Gilyard, G. B.; and Edwards, J. W.: **Real-Time Flutter Analysis of an Active Flutter-Suppression System on a Remotely Piloted Research Aircraft.** AGARD CP-339, Paper 23. *AGARD Ground/Flight Test Tech. and Correlation*, February 1983, (see 83N30357), 83N30380, #. (See also 1234.)

Flight-test results of the first three flights of an aeroelastic research wing are described. The flight flutter-test technique used to obtain real-time damping estimates from fast-frequency sweep data was obtained and the open-loop flutter boundary determined. Nyquist analyses of sweep maneuvers appear to provide additional valuable information about flutter suppression system operation, both in terms of phase-margin estimates and as a means of evaluating maneuver quality. An error in implementing the flutter-suppression system required in a one-half nominal gain configuration, which caused the wing to be unstable at lower Mach numbers than anticipated, and the vehicle experienced closed-loop flutter on its third flight. Real-time flutter-testing procedures were improved.

1245. Jenkins, J. M.; and Montoya, C. A.: **Experimental Creep Data for a Built-Up Aluminum/Titanium Structure Subjected to Heating and Loading.** NASA TM-84906, NAS 1.15:84906, March 1983, 83N22629, #.

Experimental creep, temperature, and strain data resulting from a laboratory experiment on a built-up aluminum/titanium structure are presented. The structure and the experiment are described in detail. A heating and loading experiment lasting approximately six hours is conducted on a test structure. Considerable creep strain resulted from compressive stresses in the heated skin. Large residual stresses were found after the experiment was completed. The residual stresses in the substructure frames were large enough to preclude further cycles of creep experiments with this built-up structure because of concern that the frame webs would buckle.

1246. Licata, S. J.; and Burcham, F. W., Jr.: **Airstart Performance of a Digital Electronic Engine Control System in an F-15 Airplane.** NASA TM-84908, NAS 1.15:84908, April 1983, 83N22203, #.

The airstart performance of the F100 engine equipped with a digital electronic engine control (DEEC) system was evaluated in an F-15 airplane. The DEEC system incorporates closed-loop airstart logic for improved capability. Spooldown and jet fuel starter-assisted airstarts were made over a range of airspeeds and altitudes. All jet fuel starter-assisted airstarts were successful, with airstart time varying from 35 to 60 sec. All spooldown airstarts at airspeeds of 200 knots and higher were successful; airstart times ranged from 45 sec at 250 knots to 135 sec at 200 knots. The effects of altitude on airstart success and time were small. The flight results agreed closely with previous altitude facility test results. The DEEC system provided successful airstarts at airspeeds at least 50 knots lower than the standard F100 engine control system.

1247. Painter, W. D.: **Flight Testing of Unique Aircraft Configurations.** *AIAA Student Journal,* Vol. 21, Spring 1983, pp. 2–7, 84A43889, #.

Some historical developments of flight testing of unique aircraft configurations by NASA and the military sector are documented. Several test aircraft are outlined including the M2-F1 (which was the first Space Shuttle concept ever demonstrated, and contributed to the present design), the X-15, the Flying Wing, the Lunar Landing Research Vehicle, the Oblique Wing Research Aircraft, and the Space Shuttle Enterprise. Future test aircraft such as the forward swept wing X-29A Advanced Technology Demonstrator Aircraft, and the X-Wing vehicle are also mentioned. It is noted that the logical preliminary to flight testing is flight simulation, and that flight testing itself is the vital final component of the development, and seems to be the most direct approach to aircraft evaluations.

EC86-33555-2

X-Wing Airplane

1248. Nugent, J.; Plant, T. J.; Davis, R. A.; and Taillon, N. V.: **Pressures Measured in Flight on the Aft Fuselage and External Nozzle of a Twin-Jet Fighter.** NASA TP-2017, H-1161, NAS 1.60:2017, May 1983, 83N25665, #.

Fuselage, boundary layer, and nozzle pressures were measured in flight for a twin jet fighter over a Mach number range from 0.60 to 2.00 at test altitudes of 6100, 10,700, and 13,700 meters for angles of attack ranging from 0 deg to 7 deg. Test data were analyzed to find the effects of the propulsion system geometry. The flight variables, and flow interference. The aft fuselage flow field was complex and showed the influence of the vertical tail, nacelle contour, and the wing. Changes in the boattail angle of either engine affected upper fuselage and lower fuselage pressure coefficients upstream of the nozzle. Boundary layer profiles at the forward and aft locations on the upper nacelles were relatively insensitive to Mach number and altitude. Boundary layer thickness decreased at both stations as angle of attack increased above 4 deg. Nozzle pressure coefficient was influenced by the vertical tail, horizontal tail boom, and nozzle interfairing; the last two tended to separate flow over the top of the nozzle from flow over the bottom of the nozzle. The left nozzle axial force coefficient was most affected by Mach number and left nozzle boattail angle. At Mach 0.90, the nozzle axial force coefficient was 0.0013.

1249. Dittmar, J. H.; Lasagna, P. L.; and Mackall, K. G.: **A Preliminary Comparison Between the SR-6 Propeller Noise in Flight and in a Wind Tunnel.** NASA TM-83341, NAS 1.15:83341. Presented at 105th Meeting of the Acoustical Society of America, Cincinnati, Ohio, May 9–13, 1983, 1983, 83N24287, #.

High speed turboprops offer an attractive candidate for aircraft because of their high propulsive efficiency. However, one of the possible problems associated with these propellers is their high noise level at cruise condition that may create a cabin environment problem. Models of these propellers were tested for acoustics in the 8 by 6-foot wind tunnel and on the Jet Star airplane. Comparisons between the airplane and wind tunnel data for the SR-6 propeller are shown. The comparison of maximum blade passing tone variation with helical tip Mach number between the tunnel and flight data was good when corrected to the same test conditions. Directivity comparisons also showed fairly good agreement. These good comparisons indicate that the wind tunnel is a viable location for measuring the blade passage tone noise of these propellers.

1250. Anderson, S. B.; Enevoldson, E. K.; and Nguyen, L. T.: **Pilot Human Factors in Stall/Spin Accidents of Supersonic Fighter Aircraft.** NASA TM-84348, NAS 1.15:84348. Presented at AGARD Conference Flight Mechanics System Design Lessons from Operational Experience, Athens, Greece, May 10–13, 1983, May 1983, 83N26846, #. (See also 1275.)

A study has been made of pilot human factors related to stall/spin accidents of supersonic fighter aircraft. The military specifications for flight at high angles of attack are examined. Several pilot human factors problems related to stall/spin are discussed. These problems include (1) unsatisfactory nonvisual warning cues; (2) the inability of the pilot to quickly determine if the aircraft is spinning out of control, or to recognize the type of spin; (3) the inability of the pilot to decide on and implement the correct spin recovery technique; (4) the inability of the pilot to move, caused by high angular rotation; and (5) the tendency of pilots to wait too long in deciding to abandon the irrecoverable aircraft. Psycho-physiological phenomena influencing pilot's behavior in stall/spin situations include (1) channelization of sensory inputs, (2) limitations in precisely controlling several muscular inputs, (3) inaccurate judgment of elapsed time, and (4) disorientation of vestibulo-ocular inputs. Results are given of pilot responses to all these problems in the F-14A, F-16/AB, and F/A-18A aircraft. The use of departure spin resistance and automatic spin prevention systems incorporated on recent supersonic fighters are discussed. These systems should help to improve the stall/spin accident record with some compromise in maneuverability.

1251. Chiles, H. R.: **Capture and Real-Time Display of Selected Space Shuttle Reentry Data.** *Proceedings, 29th International Instrumentation Symposium,* Albuquerque, New Mexico, May 2–6, 1983, pp. 643–660, (see A85-2955 12-35), 85A29574.

Because the flight planning for the orbital flight test (OFT) flights of the NASA Space Shuttle required several months, there was very little time to analyze data from one flight before it was necessary to start final planning for the next flight. Real-time and selected immediate postflight data display of the reentry data minimized the postflight computer analysis time required so that the rigid time restraints imposed by the program could be met. This paper describes the methods used to decommutate and provide real-time and immediate postflight data display of selected Space Shuttle reentry data.

1252. Harney, P.; Clifton, W.; and *Johnson, D. A.: **Instrumentation and Data Processing for AFTI/F-16 Flight Testing.** *NAECON 1983; Proceedings of the National Aerospace and Electronics Conference,* Vol 2, Dayton, Ohio, May 17–19, 1983, pp. 1404–1409, (see A84-16526 05-01), 84A16690.

The primary objective of the advanced fighter technology integration/F-16 (AFTI/F-16) development program is to demonstrate advanced fighter technologies to improve weapon delivery and aircraft survivability. Instrumentation and data processing for monitoring aircraft operation during flight testing is necessary not only for safety-of-flight considerations but also for rapid evaluation of flight test results. The complexity of the AFTI/F-16 aircraft necessitates an extensive capability to accomplish data goals; this paper describes that capability and the resultant product.

*General Dynamics Corp., Fort Worth, Texas.

1253. Mackall, D. A.; Regenie, V. A.; and Gordoa, M.: **Qualification of the Flight-Critical AFTI/F-16 Digital Flight Control System.** *NAECON 1983; Proceedings of the National Aerospace and Electronics Conference,* Dayton, Ohio, May 17–19, 1983, (See also 1236.)

1254. Iliff, K. W.: **Parameter Estimation for Aircraft Problems.** Presented at the SIAM National Meeting, Symposium on System Identification, Denver, Colorado, June 6–8, 1983.

1255. Lasagna, P. L.; Mackall, K. G.; and Cohn, R. B.: **In-Flight Acoustic Test Results for the SR-2 and SR-3 Advanced-Design Propellers.** AIAA Paper 83-1214. Presented at 19th AIAA, SAE, and ASME Joint Propulsion Conference, Seattle, Washington, June 27–29, 1983, 83A36286, #.

Several advanced-design propellers, previously tested in the wind tunnel at the Lewis Research Center, have been tested in flight at the Dryden Flight Research Facility. The flight-test propellers were mounted on a pylon on the top of the fuselage of a JetStar airplane. Acoustic data for the advanced-design SR-2 and SR-3 propellers at Mach numbers to 0.8 and helical-tip Mach numbers to 1.15 are presented; maximum blade-passage frequency sound-pressure levels are also compared.

1256. *Keller, T. L.; *Wurtele, M. G.; and Ehernberger, L. J.: **Numerical Simulation of the Atmosphere During a CAT Encounter.** Presented at the 9th Conference on Aerospace and Aeronautical Meteorology, Omaha, Nebraska, June 6–9, 1983, pp. 316–319, preprints, American Meteorological Society, Boston, Massachusetts, (see A83-38701 17-47), 83A38764.

In an attempt to determine whether clear air turbulence (CAT) which caused a brief, intense turbulence encounter to a jetliner might have been related to gravity waves generated by a line of thunderstorms, local sounding data taken within two hours of the incident have been used as input to a numerical model designed to simulate stratified flow over obstacles. In the model a rigid obstacle at the lower boundary acted as the source of the gravity waves. The model results show a large amplitude disturbance localized over the obstacle at and above flight level, in regions where CAT would be expected. Stratification studies have been conducted, varying the height and shape of the obstacle and the input wind profile. The success of the experiment leads to the conclusion that atmospheric gravity wave simulation can be useful in understanding and possibly avoiding CAT.

*University of California, Los Angeles, California.

1257. Curry, R. E.; and Sim, A. G.: **Unique Flight Characteristics of the AD-1 Oblique-Wing Research Airplane.** AIAA Paper 82-1329. AIAA 9th Atmospheric Flight Mechanics Conference, San Diego, California, August 9–11, 1982. Also *J. of Aircraft,* Vol. 20, June 1983, pp. 564–568, 83A32588, #. (See also 1215.)

1258. *Deckert, J. C.; and Szalai, K. J.: **Analytic Redundancy Management for Flight Control Sensors.** AGARD AG-272, Paper 9. *AGARD Advan. in Sensors and their Integration Into Aircraft Guidance and Control Systems,* (ISBN-92-835-1451-3), June 1983, (see N83-34891 23-01), AD-A13290, 83N34900, #.

The formulation and flight test results of an algorithm to detect and isolate the first failure of any one of 12 duplex control sensor signals (24 in all) being monitored are reviewed. The technique uses like signal differences for fault detection while relying upon analytic redundancy relationships among unlike quantities to isolate the faulty sensor. The fault isolation logic utilizes the modified sequential probability ratio test, which explicitly accommodates the inevitable, irreducible low frequency errors present in the analytic redundancy residuals. In addition, the algorithm used sensor output selftest, which takes advantage of the duplex sensor structure by immediately removing a hard failed sensor from control calculations and analytic redundancy relationships while awaiting a definitive fault isolation decision via analytic redundancy. This study represents a proof of concept demonstration of a methodology that is applied to duplex or higher flight control sensor configurations and, in addition, can monitor the health of one simplex signal per analytic redundancy relationship.

*Draper Laboratory, Cambridge, Massachusetts.

1259. Rezek, T. W.: **Unmanned Vehicle Systems Experiences at the Dryden Flight Research Facility; Remotely Piloted Vehicles.** NASA TM-84913, H-1192, NAS 1.15:84913, AUVS-83 Symposium Unmanned Systems: Confidence for the 80's, Salt Lake City, Utah, June 28–30, 1983, June 1983, 83N27978, #.

An overview is presented of the remotely piloted research vehicle (RPRV) activities at the NASA Dryden Flight Research Facility from their beginning to the present. The development of RPRV's as flight test tools is discussed, and system configuration is presented. Solutions derived from human factors experience related to flight activities and pilot responses have contributed to overall system capability. The development and use of visual displays, which are a critical feature of successful RPRV flights, are discussed as well as directions for future RPRV efforts.

1260. Stewart, Alphonzo J.: **NASA Ames-Dryden Flight Research Facility Battery Systems Laboratory.** NASA TM-84905, August 1983.

This document discusses the development of the Dryden Flight Research Facility Battery Systems laboratory. This laboratory processes nickel-cadmium and silver-zinc batteries used in the various flight research vehicles flown at the Dryden facility. Described is the evolvement of the original manually operated lead-acid battery facility to the present computerized laboratory. Described also are the equipment and present capabilities of the laboratory, which can process both sealed and wet vented cells that range in capacity from 0.5 to 200 A-hr.

1261. Duke, E. L.; and Lux, D. P.: **The Application and Results of a New Flight Test Technique.** AIAA Paper 83-2137. Presented at AIAA Atmospheric Flight Mechanics Conference, Gatlinburg, Tennessee, August 15–17, 1983, 83A41959, #.

The application of a flight test maneuver auto-pilot test technique for collecting aerodynamic and structural flight research data on a highly maneuverable aircraft is described. This newly developed flight test technique was applied at the Dryden Flight Research Facility of the NASA Ames Research Center on the highly maneuverable aircraft technology (HiMAT) vehicle. A primary flight experiment was done to verify the design techniques used to develop the HiMAT aerodynamics and structures. This required the collection of large quantities of high-quality pressure distribution, loads, and deflection data. The effectiveness of the flight test technique is illustrated with a flight test example comparing various pressure distribution measurements.

1262. *Bailey, R. E.; Stewart, J. F.; Smith, R. E.; and Shafer, M. F.: **Flight Test Experience With Pilot-Induced-Oscillation Suppressor Filters.** AIAA Paper 83-2107. Presented at AIAA Atmospheric Flight Mechanics Conference, Gatlinburg, Tennessee, August 15–17, 1983, 83A41936, #. (See also 1297.)

Digital flight control systems are popular for their flexibility, reliability, and power; however, their use sometimes results in deficient handling qualities, including pilot-induced oscillation (PIO), which can require extensive redesign of the control system. When redesign is not immediately possible, temporary solutions, such as the PIO suppression (PIOS) filter developed for the Space Shuttle, have been proposed. To determine the effectiveness of such PIOS filters on more conventional, high-performance aircraft, three experiments were performed using the NASA F-8 digital fly-by-wire and USAF/Calspan NT-33 variable-stability aircraft. Two types of PIOS filters were evaluated, using high-gain, precision tasks (close formation, probe-and-drogue refueling, and precision touch-and-go landing) with a time delay or a first-order lag added to make the aircraft prone to PIO. Various configurations of the PIOS filter were evaluated in the flight programs, and most of the PIOS filter configurations reduced the occurrence of PIOs and improved the handling qualities of the PIO-prone aircraft. These experiments also confirmed

the influence of high-gain tasks and excessive control system time delay in evoking pilot-induced oscillations.

*Grumman Aerospace Corp., Bethpage, New York.

1263. Whitmore, S. A.: **Reconstruction of the Shuttle Reentry Air Data Parameters Using a Linearized Kalman Filter.** AIAA Paper 83-2097. Presented at AIAA Atmospheric Flight Mechanics Conference, Gatlinburg, Tennessee, August 15–17, 1983, 83A41926, #.

This paper presents the reconstruction of the space shuttle's wind-relative reentry trajectory for the orbital flights. The technique uses a linearized Kalman filter (LKF) to merge high and low-frequency inertial and wind-relative data to obtain enhanced high-frequency results that closely follow expected mean levels. Two verifications are presented. First, wind trajectories resulting from the reconstruction are compared with analytically predicted values. There is close comparison. Second, the frequency characteristics are investigated using system identification techniques. The stability and control model generated using the LKF trajectory shows good agreement between measured and predicted spacecraft response for both high and low frequencies.

1264. *Walker, R. A.; *Gupta, N. K.; and Gilyard, G. B.: **Algorithms for Real-Time Flutter Identification.** AIAA Paper 83-2223. Presented at AIAA Guidance and Control Conference, Gatlinburg, Tennessee, August 15–17, 1983, pp. 432–440, (see A83-41659 19-63), 83A41703, #.

The work reported here addresses the important algorithm issues necessary to achieve a real-time flutter monitoring system; namely, the guidelines for choosing appropriate model forms, reduction of the parameter convergence transient, handling multiple modes, the effect of overparameterization, and estimate accuracy predictions, both online and for experiment design. An approach for efficiently computing continuous-time flutter parameter Cramer-Rao estimate error bounds has been developed. This enables a convincing comparison of theoretical and simulation results, as well as off-line studies in preparation for a flight test. Theoretical predictions, simulation and flight test results from the NASA/Dryden Drones for Aerodynamic and Structural Test (DAST) Program are compared.

*Integrated Systems, Inc., Palo Alto, California.

1265. Larson, R. R.; Smith, R. E.; and Krambeer, K. D.: **Flight-Test Results Using Nonlinear Control With the F-8C Digital Fly-By-Wire Aircraft.** AIAA Paper 83-2174. Presented at AIAA Guidance and Control Conference, Gatlinburg, Tennessee, August 15–17, 1983, pp. 97–110, (see A83-41659 19-63), 83A41669, #.

The design and operation of the cooperative advanced digital research experiment (CADRE) to develop nonlinear pitch flight control algorithms is described, and the results of an in-flight evaluation using the F-8C digital fly-by-wire (DFBW) research aircraft are presented. The CADRE controller is described, including the initial filter, linear command prefilter, nonlinear command prefilter, and gain scheduling. The variable-integral control-to-optimize response of the controller is considered, and CADRE parameter combinations are addressed. The remotely-augmented-vehicle interface used in the DFBW aircraft experiment is discussed. The distant-tracking and close-formation tracking evaluation tasks for the aircraft are described along with evaluation configurations, and the test results are presented and discussed. The latter indicate that a nonlinear adaptive controller is a feasible control tracking task.

1266. Putnam, T. W.; Burcham, F. W., Jr.; and Kock, B. M.: **Flight Testing the Digital Electronic Engine Control (DEEC) A Unique Management Experience.** *Proceedings, Flight Testing Today: Innovative Management and Technology; SETP Fourteenth Annual Symposium*, Newport Beach, California, August 15–19, 1983, pp. 2.2-1 to 2.2-6, 85A28636.

The concept for the DEEC had its origin in the early 1970s. At that time it was recognized that the F100 engine performance, operability, reliability, and cost could be substantially improved by replacing the original mechanical/supervisory electronic control system with a full-authority digital control system. By 1978, the engine manufacturer had designed and initiated the procurement of flight-qualified control system hardware. As a precursor to an integrated controls program, a flight evaluation of the DEEC system on the F-15 aircraft was proposed. Questions regarding the management of the DEEC flight evaluation program are discussed along with the program elements, the technical results of the F-15 evaluation, and the impact of the flight evaluation on after-burning turbofan controls technology and its use in and application to military aircraft. The lessons learned through the conduct of the program are discussed.

1267. Iliff, K. W.; Maine, R. E.; and *Cooke, D. R.: **Space Shuttle Stability and Control Derivatives Estimated From the First Entry.** AIAA Paper 81-2451. Presented at the 1st AIAA, SETP, SFTE, SAE, ITEA, and IEEE Flight Testing Conference, Las Vegas, Nevada, November 11–13, 1981. *Journal of Guidance, Control, and Dynamics*, Vol. 6, July–August 1983, pp. 264–271, 83A37065, #. (See also 1172.)

*NASA Johnson Space Center, Houston, Texas.

1268. Myers, A. F.; Earls, M. R.; and *Callizo, L. A.: **HiMAT Onboard Flight Computer System Architecture and Qualification.** *Journal of Guidance, Control, and Dynamics*, Vol. 6, July–August 1983, pp. 231–238, (see A82-10082), 83A37061, #. (See also 1159.)

*Rockwell International Corp., Los Angeles, California.

1269. Rezek, T. W.: **Preliminary Experience With a Stereoscopic Video System in a Remotely Piloted Aircraft Application.** NASA TM-84909, H-1185, NAS 1.15:84909, September 1983, 84N22557, #.

Remote piloting video display development at the Dryden Flight Research Facility of NASA's Ames Research Center is summarized, and the reasons for considering stereo television are presented. Pertinent equipment is described. Limited flight experience is also discussed, along with recommendations for further study.

1270. Painter, W. D.; and *Camp, D. W.: **NASA B-57B Severe Storms Flight Program.** *1983 Report to the Aerospace Profession; Proceedings of the Twenty-Seventh SETP Symposium*, Beverly Hills, California, September 28–October 1, 1983, pp. 292–313, (see A84-16157 05-05), 84A16174. (See also 1293.)

Plots of winds encountered in-flight are presented for a severe turbulence case from JAWS flight 7 (near Denver on the afternoon of July 15, 1982). During the flight the B-57B showed a 30-knot increase in airspeed over a distance of about 426 ft and then a more gradual decrease of 40 to 50 knots over a distance of about 3.2 miles. This suspected outflow feature was associated with downdraft in excess of 20 knots. The horizontal wind direction changed almost 180 deg during the pass through the feature, and the intensity of velocity differences decreased for all three components within the downdraft. Calculated probability density functions for u, v, and w showed a jagged character; and distributions for Delta-u, Delta-v, and Delta-w were distinctly non-Gaussian. Based on skewness and kurtosis values, the data could probably best be modeled by a Pearson type VII (Student's t) distribution.

*NASA Marshall Space Flight Center, Systems Dynamics Laboratory, Huntsville, Alabama.

1271. Myers, L. P.; and Burcham, F. W., Jr.: **Comparison of Flight Results With Digital Simulation for a Digital Electronic Engine Control in an F-15 Airplane.** NASA TM-84903, NAS 1.15.84903, October 1983, 84N14144, #.

Substantial benefits of a full authority digital electronic engine control on an air breathing engine were demonstrated repeatedly in simulation studies, ground engine tests, and engine altitude test facilities. A digital engine electronic control system showed improvements in efficiency, performance, and operation. An additional benefit of full authority digital controls is the capability of detecting and correcting failures and providing engine health diagnostics.

1272. Ishmael, S. D.; and McMonagle, D. R.: **AFTI/F-16 Flight Test Results and Lessons.** NASA TM-84920, NAS 1.15:84920. Presented at the 27th Symposium of the SETP,

Beverly Hills, California, September 28–October 1, 1983, October 1983, 84N15159, #. (See also 1273.)

The advanced fighter technology integration (AFTI) F-16 aircraft is a highly complex digital flight control system integrated with advanced avionics and cockpit. The use of dissimilar backup modes if the primary system fails requires the designer to trade off system simplicity and capability. The tradeoff is evident in the AFTI/F-16 aircraft with its limited stability and fly by wire digital flight control systems when a generic software failure occurs the backup or normal mode must provide equivalent envelop protection during the transition to degraded flight control. The complexity of systems like the AFTI/F-16 system defines a second design issue, which is divided into two segments: (1) the effect on testing, (2) and the pilot's ability to act correctly in the limited time available for cockpit decisions. The large matrix of states possible with the AFTI/F-16 flight control system illustrates the difficulty of both testing the system and choosing real time pilot actions. The third generic issue is the possible reductions in the user's reliability expectations where false single channel information can be displayed at the pilot vehicle interface while the redundant set remains functional.

1273. Ishmael, S. D.; and *McMonagle, D. R.: **AFTI/F-16 Flight Test Results and Lessons.** *1983 Report to the Aerospace Profession; Proceedings of the Twenty-Seventh SETP Symposium*, Beverly Hills, California, September 28–October 1, 1983, (see A84-16157 05-05), 84A16167, pp. 158–184. (See also 1272.)

The AFTI/F-16 flight test program is summarized, and several design issues of general interest are addressed. A brief description is given of the test vehicle, its flight control modes, and the flight envelopes in which testing was performed. Flight test results are summarized by addressing benefits experienced in flight control task-tailoring, handling qualities in mission tasks, aircraft structure considerations, digital flight control system performance, and human factors. Finally, several design issues relevant to future fighter aircraft are examined, including degraded flight control, system complexity, simplex information in redundant systems, and single failure propagation in redundant systems.

*USAF Flight Test Center, Edwards AFB, California.

1274. Schneider, E. T.; and Meyer, R. R., Jr.: **Real-Time Pilot Guidance System for Improved Flight-Test Maneuvers.** *1983 Report to the Aerospace Profession; Proceedings of the Twenty-Seventh SETP Symposium*, Beverly Hills, California, September 28– October 1, 1983, pp. 57–72, (see A84-16157 05-05), 84A16161. (See also 1284.)

The real-time pilot display uplink development at the Dryden Flight Research Facility is described, with a focus on recent F-104 studies. A nose boom gathers data on the Mach number, pressure altitude, and angle of attack. The system provides the pilot with guidance to improve maneuver accuracy and fly more complex trajectories. The uplink presents the pilot with computed differences between a reference flight path and actual flight state conditions, using a downlink to the ground where engineering computations are performed, feedback is transmitted, and corrections are applied. Details of the flight test trajectories and data from test results are provided for level turns, constant thrust turns, dynamic pressure trajectories, constant radar altitude accelerations and decelerations, and a Reynolds number trajectory. The system has proved capable of reducing pilot workload and saving fuel by decreasing the flight time necessary to obtain specific data.

1275. *Anderson, S. B.; Enevoldson, E. K.; and **Nguyen, L. T.: **Pilot Human Factors in Stall/Spin Accidents of Supersonic Fighter Aircraft.** AGARD CP-347. *AGARD Flight Mech. and System Design Lessons From Operational Experience*, (see N84-15076 06-01), October 1983, 84N15102, #. (See also 1250.)

A study has been made of pilot human factors related to stall/spin accidents of supersonic fighter aircraft. The military specifications for flight at high angles of attack are examined. Several pilot human factors problems related to stall/spin are discussed. These problems include: (1) unsatisfactory nonvisual warning cues; (2) the inability of the pilot to quickly determine if the aircraft is spinning out of control, or to recognize the type of spin; (3) the inability of the pilot to decide on and implement the correct spin recovery technique; (4) the inability of the pilot to move, caused by high angular rotation; and (5) the tendency of pilots to wait too long in deciding to abandon the irrecoverable aircraft. Psycho-physiological phenomena influencing pilot's behavior in stall/spin situations include: (1) channelization of sensor inputs, (2) limitations in precisely controlling several muscular inputs, (3) inaccurate judgment of elapsed time, and (4) disorientation of vestibulo-ocular inputs. Results are given of pilot responses to all these problems in the F-14A, F-16/AB, and F/A-18A aircraft. The use of departure spin resistance and automatic spin prevention systems incorporated on recent supersonic fighters are discussed. These systems should help to improve the stall/spin accident record with some compromise in maneuverability.

*NASA Ames Research Center, Moffett Field, California.
**NASA Langley Research Center, Hampton, Virginia.

1276. Duke, E. L.; Swann, M. R.; Enevoldson, E. K.; and Wolf, T. D.: **Experience With Flight Test Trajectory Guidance.** AIAA Paper 81-2504. AIAA, SETP, SFTE, SAE,

ITEA, and IEEE 1st Flight Testing Conference, Las Vegas, Nevada, November 11–13, 1981. *Journal of Guidance, Control, and Dynamics*, (ISSN 0731-5090), Vol. 6, September–October 1983, October 1983, pp. 393–398, 83A45470, #. (See also 1166.)

1277. Painter, W. D.: **AD-1 Oblique Wing Research Aircraft Pilot Evaluation Program.** AIAA Paper 83-2509, Aircraft Design, Systems and Technology Meeting, Fort Worth, Texas, October 17–19, 1983, 84A10573, #.

A flight test program of a low cost, low speed, manned, oblique wing research airplane was conducted at the NASA Dryden Flight Research Facility in cooperation with NASA Ames Research Center between 1979 and 1982. When the principal purpose of the test program was completed, which was to demonstrate the flight and handling characteristics of the configuration, particularly in wing-sweep-angle ranges from 45 to 60 deg, a pilot evaluation program was conducted to obtain a qualification evaluation of the flying qualities of an oblique wing aircraft. These results were documented for use in future studies of such aircraft.

1278. Evans, M. B.; and Schilling, L. J.: **Simulations Used in the Development and Flight Test of the HiMAT Vehicle.** AIAA Paper 83-2505. Aircraft Design, Systems and Technology Meeting, Fort Worth, Texas, October 17–19, 1983, October 1983, 83A48355, #.

Real-time simulations have been essential in the flight-test program of the highly maneuverable aircraft technology (HiMAT) remotely piloted research vehicle at the Dryden Flight Research Facility of NASA Ames Research Center. The HiMAT project makes extensive use of simulations in design, development, and qualification for flight, pilot training, and flight planning. Four distinct simulations, each with varying amounts of hardware in the loop, were developed for the HiMAT project. The use of simulations has been the key to flight qualification of the HiMAT vehicle. Specifically, they are useful in detecting anomalous behavior of the flight software and hardware at the various stages of development, verification, and validation.

1279. Burcham, Frank W., Jr.; Myers, Lawrence P.; and Walsh, Kevin R.: **Flight Evaluation Results for a Digital Electronic Engine Control in an F-15 Airplane.** NASA TM 84918, AIAA Paper 83-2703. AIAA, AHS, IES, SETP, SFTE, and DGLR 2nd Flight Testing Conference, Las Vegas, Nevada, November 16–18, 1983, October 1983, 84A12310, #. (See also 1289, 1441.)

A digital electronic engine control (DEEC) system on an F100 engine in an F-15 airplane was evaluated in flight. Thirty flights were flown in a four-phase program from June 1981 to February 1983. Significant improvements in the operability and performance of the F100 engine were developed as a result of the flight evaluation: the augmentor envelope was increased by 15,000 ft, the airstart envelope was improved by 75 knots, and the need to periodically trim the engine was eliminated. The hydromechanical backup control performance was evaluated and was found to be satisfactory. Two system failures were encountered in the test program; both were detected and accommodated successfully. No transfers to the backup control system were required, and no automatic transfers occurred. As a result of the successful DEEC flight evaluation, the DEEC system has entered the full-scale development phase.

1280. Glover, R. D.: **Application Experience With the NASA Aircraft Interrogation and Display System—A Ground-Support Equipment for Digital Flight Systems.** *Proceedings, 5th Digital Avionics Systems Conference,* Seattle, Washington, October 31–November 3, 1983, pp. 17.3.1 to 17.3.10, (see A84-26701 11-06), 84A26777, #.

The NASA Dryden Flight Research Facility has developed a microprocessor-based, user-programmable, general-purpose aircraft interrogation and display system (AIDS). The hardware and software of this ground-support equipment have been designed to permit diverse applications in support of aircraft digital flight-control systems and simulation facilities. AIDS is often employed to provide engineering-units display of internal digital system parameters during development and qualification testing. Such visibility into the system under test has proved to be a key element in the final qualification testing of aircraft digital flight-control systems. Three first-generation 8-bit units are now in service in support of several research aircraft projects, and user acceptance has been high. A second-generation design, extended AIDS (XAIDS), incorporating multiple 16-bit processors, is now being developed to support the forward swept wing aircraft project (X-29A). This paper outlines the AIDS concept, summarizes AIDS operational experience, and describes the planned XAIDS design and mechanization.

1281. Abbott, L. W.: **Operational Characteristics of the Dispersed Sensor Processor Mesh.** *Proceedings, 5th Digital Avionics Systems Conference,* Seattle, Washington, October 31–November 3, 1983, pp. 9.4.1–9.4.8, 84A26737, #.

The dispersed sensor processing mesh (DSPM) is part of an experimental system used to pursue a proof of concept for an advanced fault-tolerant communication strategy. The DSPM experiments incorporate sensors and effectors into an ultra-reliable nodal network in which a central bus controller performs algorithms to grow and maintain the network. The experiments demonstrate that DSPM is an achievable communication network that can sustain failures and continue to function properly. The results of the experiment give insights into the unique characteristics of the DSPM network and the network's capacity to limit physical damage propagation, limit damaged-data propagation, and to survive cyclic communication paths. This paper describes the concept, mechanization, and performance of the DSPM system in a real-time flight-critical environment.

1282. Petersen, K. L.; and Flores, C., Jr.: **Software Control and System Configuration Management—A Process That Works.** *Proceedings, 5th Digital Avionics Systems Conference,* Seattle, Washington, October 31–November 3, 1983, pp. 4.5.1–4.5.8, 84A26713, #. (See also 1345.)

A comprehensive software control and system configuration management process for flight-crucial digital control systems of advanced aircraft has been developed and refined to insure efficient flight system development and safe flight operations. Because of the highly complex interactions among the hardware, software, and system elements of state-of-the-art digital flight control system designs, a systems-wide approach to configuration control and management has been used. Specific procedures are implemented to govern discrepancy reporting and reconciliation, software and hardware change control, systems verification and validation testing, and formal documentation requirements. An active and knowledgeable configuration control board reviews and approves all flight system configuration modifications and revalidation tests. This flexible process has proved effective during the development and flight testing of several research aircraft and remotely piloted research vehicles with digital flight control systems that ranged from relatively simple to highly complex, integrated mechanizations.

1283. Stewart, J. F.; and Bauer, C. A.: **A Project Management System for the X-29A Flight Test Program.** AIAA Paper 83-2712. AIAA, AHS, IES, SETP, SFTE, and DGLR 2nd Flight Testing Conference, Las Vegas, Nevada, November 16–18, 1983, November 1983, 84A15850, #.

The project-management system developed for NASA's participation in the X-29A aircraft development program is characterized from a theoretical perspective, as an example of a system appropriate to advanced, highly integrated technology projects. System-control theory is applied to the analysis of classical project-management techniques and structures, which are found to be of closed-loop multivariable type; and the effects of increasing project complexity and integration are evaluated. The importance of information flow, sampling frequency, information holding, and delays is stressed. The X-29A system is developed in four stages: establishment of overall objectives and requirements, determination of information processes (block diagrams) definition of personnel functional roles and relationships, and development of a detailed work-breakdown structure. The resulting system is shown to require a greater information flow to management than conventional methods. Sample block diagrams are provided.

X-29A Airplane   EC 85-33297-23

1284. Meyer, R. R., Jr.; and Schneider, E. T.: **Real-Time Pilot Guidance System for Improved Flight-Test Maneuvers.** AIAA Paper 83-2747. AIAA, AHS, IES, SETP, SFTE, and DGLR 2nd Flight Testing Conference, Las Vegas, Nevada, November 16–18, 1983, November 1983, 84A15188, #. (See also 1274.)

The Dryden Flight Research Facility has developed a pilot trajectory guidance system that is intended to increase the accuracy of flight-test data and decrease the time required to achieve and maintain desired test conditions, or both. The system usually presented to the pilot computed differences between reference or desired and actual flight state conditions. The pilot then used a cockpit display as an aid to acquire and hold desired test conditions. This paper discusses various flight-test maneuvers and the quality of data obtained using the guidance system. Some comparisons are made between the quality of maneuvers obtained with and without the system. Limited details of the guidance system and algorithms used are included. In general, the guidance system improved the quality of the maneuvers and trajectories flown, as well as allowing trajectories to be flown that would not have been possible without the system. This system has moved from the developmental stage to full operational use in various Dryden research and test aircraft.

1285. Trujillo, B. M.; Meyer, R. R., Jr.; and *Sawko, P. M.: **In-Flight Load Testing of Advanced Thermal Protection Systems.** AIAA Paper 83-2704. AIAA, AHS, IES, SETP, SFTE, and DGLR 2nd Flight Testing Conference, Las Vegas, Nevada, November 16–18, 1983, November 1983, 84A15187, #. (See also 1291.)

NASA Ames Research Center has conducted in-flight airload testing of some advanced thermal protection systems (TPS) at the Dryden Flight Research Center. The two flexible TPS materials tested, felt reusable surface insulation (FRSI) and advanced flexible reusable surface insulation (AFRSI), are currently certified for use on the Shuttle orbiter. The objectives of the flight tests were to evaluate the performance of FRSI and AFRSI at simulated launch airloads and to provide a data base for future advanced TPS flight tests. Five TPS configurations were evaluated in a flow field which was representative of relatively flat areas without secondary flows. The TPS materials were placed on a fin, the Flight Test Fixture (FTF), that is attached to the underside of the fuselage of an F-104 aircraft. This paper describes the test approach and techniques used and presents the results of the advanced TPS flight test. There were no failures noted during post-flight inspections of the TPS materials which were exposed to airloads 40 percent higher than the design launch airloads.

*NASA Ames Research Center, Moffett Field, California.

1286. Ko, W. L.; and Schuster, L. S.: **Pre-Flight Transient Dynamic Analysis of B-52 Carrying Space Shuttle Solid Rocket Booster Drop-Test Vehicle.** AIAA Paper 83-2698. AIAA, AHS, IES, SETP, SFTE, and DGLR 2nd Flight Testing Conference, Las Vegas, Nevada, November 16–18, 1983, <u>November 1983</u>, 84A13725, #. (See also 1296.)

This paper concerns the transient dynamic analysis of the B-52 aircraft carrying the Space Shuttle solid-rocket booster drop-test vehicle (SRB/DTV). The NASA structural analysis (NASTRAN) finite-element computer program was used in the analysis. The B-52 operating conditions considered for analysis were (1) landing and (2) braking on aborted takeoff runs. The transient loads for the B-52 pylon front and rear hooks were calculated. The results can be used to establish the safe maneuver envelopes for the B-52 carrying the SRB/DTV in landings and brakings.

1287. Putnam, T. W.: **X-29 Flight Research Program.** AIAA Paper 83-2687. AIAA, AHS, IES, SETP, SFTE, and DGLR 2nd Flight Testing Conference, Las Vegas, Nevada, November 16–18, 1983, <u>November 1983</u>, 84A13724, #. (See also 1298, 1373.)

The X-29A aircraft is the first manned, experimental high-performance aircraft to be fabricated and flown in many years. The approach for expanding the X-29 flight envelope and collecting research data is described including the methods for monitoring wing divergence, flutter, and aeroservoelastic coupling of the aerodynamic forces with the structure and the flight-control system. Examples of the type of flight data to be acquired are presented along with types of aircraft maneuvers that will be flown. A brief description of the program management structure is also presented and the program schedule is discussed.

1288. Wilner, D. O.; and Bever, G. A.: **An Automated Stall-Speed Warning System.** AIAA Paper 83-2705. AIAA, AHS, IES, SETP, SFTE, and DGLR 2nd Flight Testing Conference, Las Vegas, Nevada, November 16–18, 1983, <u>November 1983</u>, 84A12311, #. (See also 1308.)

The NASA Dryden Flight Research Facility embarked upon a project with the United States Army Aviation Engineering Flight Activity (USAAEFA) to develop and test a stall-speed warning system. NASA designed and built an automated stall-speed warning system which presents both airspeed and stall speed to the pilot. The airspeed and stall speed are computed in real time by monitoring the basic aerodynamic parameters (dynamic pressure, horizontal and vertical accelerations, and pressure altitude) and other parameters (elevator and flap positions, engine torques, and fuel flow). In addition, an aural warning at predetermined stall margins is presented to the pilot through a voice synthesizer. Once the system was designed and installed in the aircraft, a flight-test program of less than 20 hr was anticipated to determine the stall-speed software coefficients. These coefficients would then be inserted in the system's software and then test flown over a period of about 10 hr for the purposes of evaluation.

1289. Burcham, F. W., Jr.; Myers, L. P.; and Walsh, K. R.: **Flight Evaluation Results for a Digital Electronic Engine Control in an F-15 Airplane.** AIAA Paper 83-2703. AIAA, AHS, IES, SETP, SFTE, and DGLR 2nd Flight Testing Conference, Las Vegas, Nevada, November 16–18, 1983, <u>November 1983</u>, 84A12310, #. (See also 1279, 1441.)

A digital electronic engine control (DEEC) system on an F100 engine in an F-15 airplane was evaluated in flight. Thirty flights were flown in a four-phase program from June 1981 to February 1983. Significant improvements in the operability and performance of the F100 engine were developed as a result of the flight evaluation: the augmentor envelope was increased by 15,000 ft, the airstart envelope was improved by 75 knots, and the need to periodically trim the engine was eliminated. The hydromechanical backup control performance was evaluated and was found to be satisfactory. Two system failures were encountered in the test program; both were detected and accommodated successfully. No transfers to the backup control system were required, and no automatic transfers occurred. As a result of the successful DEEC flight evaluation, the DEEC system has entered the full-scale development phase.

1290. Johnson, J. B.; and Nelson, J.: **Flight Evaluation of the DEEC Secondary Control Air-Start Capability.** NASA TM-84910, H-1186, NAS 1.15:84910, <u>December 1983</u>, 84N18203, #.

The air-start capability of a secondary engine control (SEC) was tested for a DEEC-equipped F100 engine and installed in an F-15 airplane. Two air-start schedules were tested. The first was referred to as the group I schedule; the second or revised schedule was the group II start schedule. Using the group I start schedule, an airspeed of 300 knots was required to ensure successful 40- and 25-percent SEC-mode air starts. If N2 were less than 40 percent, a stall would occur when the start bleeds closed 40 sec after initiation of the air start. All

JFS-assisted air starts were successful with the group start schedule. For the group II schedule, the time between pressurization and start-bleed closure ranged between 50 and 72 sec depending on altitude. All air starts were successful above 225 knots given a 75-knot reduction in required airspeed for a successful air start. Spooldown air starts of 40 percent were successful at 200 knots at altitudes up to 10,650 m and at 175 knots at altitudes up to 6100 m. Idle rpm was lower than the desired 65 percent for air starts at higher altitudes and lower airspeeds. All JSF-assisted air starts were successful.

1291. Trujillo, B. M.; Meyer, R., Jr.; and Sawko, P. M.: **In-Flight Load Testing of Advanced Shuttle Thermal Protection Systems.** NASA TM-86024, H-1212, NAS 1.15:86024, AIAA Paper 83-2704. Presented at the 2nd AIAA Flight Test Conference, Las Vegas, Nevada, November 16–18, 1983, <u>December 1983</u>, 84N17250, #. (See also 1285.)

NASA Ames Research Center has conducted in-flight airload testing of some advanced thermal protection systems (TPS) at the Dryden Flight Research Center. The two flexible TPS materials tested, felt reusable surface insulation (FRSI) and advanced flexible reusable surface insulation (AFRSI), are currently certified for use on the Shuttle orbiter. The objectives of the flight tests were to evaluate the performance of FRSI and AFRSI at simulated launch airloads and to provide a data base for future advanced TPS flight tests. Five TPS configurations were evaluated in a flow field which was representative of relatively flat areas without secondary flows. The TPS materials were placed on a fin, the Flight Test fixture (FTF), that is attached to the underside of the fuselage of an F-104 aircraft. This paper describes the test approach and techniques used and presents the results of the advanced TPS flight test. There were no failures noted during post-flight inspections of the TPS materials which were exposed to airloads 40 percent higher than the design launch airloads.

1292. Stewart, J. F.; and Bauer, C. A.: **Project Management Techniques for Highly Integrated Programs.** NASA TM-86023, H-1211, NAS 1.15:86023. Second Flight Test Conference, Las Vegas, Nevada, November 16–18, 1983, <u>December 1983</u>, 84N14965, #.

The management and control of a representative, highly integrated high-technology project, in the X-29A aircraft flight test project is addressed. The X-29A research aircraft required the development and integration of eight distinct technologies in one aircraft. The project management system developed for the X-29A flight test program focuses on the dynamic interactions and the intercommunication among components of the system. The insights gained from the new conceptual framework permitted subordination of departments to more functional units of decision making, information processing, and communication networks. These processes were used to develop a project management system for the X-29A around the information flows that minimized the effects inherent in sampled-data systems and exploited the closed-loop multivariable nature of highly integrated projects.

1293. Painter, W. D.; and *Camp, D. W.: **NASA B-57B Severe Storms Flight Program.** NASA TM-84921, NAS 1.15:84921, H-1196, <u>December 1983</u>, 84N14129, #. (See also 1270.)

The B-57B Severe Storms Flight Program gathers data to characterize atmosphere anomalies such as wind shear, turbulence, and microbursts at altitudes up to 1000 feet (300 meters). These data are used to enhance the knowledge of atmospheric processes, to improve aviation safety, to develop systems technology and piloting technique for avoiding hazards and to increase the understanding of the causes of related aircraft accidents. The NASA Dryden Flight Research Facility B-57B aircraft has participated in several severe storms data collection programs such as the Joint Airport Weather Studies (JAWS) located in Denver, Colorado area, Operation Rough Rider located in the Norman, Oklahoma area with the National Severe Storms Laboratory, and mountain and desert turbulence in the Edwards Air Force Base, California area. Flight data are presented from flights which encountered the wind shear, turbulence and microburst anomalies. These flight results are discussed and some conclusions are made relating to these atmospheric anomalies.

*NASA Marshall Space Flight Center, Systems Dynamics Laboratory, Huntsville, Alabama.

1294. Iliff, K. W.; and Maine, R. E.: **Uses of Parameter Estimation in Flight Test.** *Journal of Aircraft,* (ISSN 0021-8669), Vol. 20, <u>December 1983</u>, pp. 1043–1049, 84A14734, #. (See also 1214.)

1295. Maine, R. E.; and Iliff, K. W.: **Formulation of a Practical Parameter Estimation With Process and Measurement Noise.** IFAC Identification and System Parameter Estimation, 1982, Pergamon Press, <u>1983</u>.

A new formulation is proposed for the problem of parameter estimation in dynamic systems with both process and measurement noise. The formulation applies to continuous-time state space system models with discrete-time measurements. Previous formulations of this problem encountered several theoretical and practical difficulties which are overcome by the new formulation. The most important element of the new formulation is a reparameterization of the unknown noise covariances. A computer program that implements the new formulation is available.

1984 Technical Publications

1296. Ko, W. L.; and Schuster, L. S.: **Preflight Transient Dynamic Analyses of B-52 Aircraft Carrying Space Shuttle Solid Rocket Booster Drop-Test Vehicle.** NASA TM-84925, H-1197, NAS 1.15:84925. Presented at the AIAA 2nd Flight Test Conference, Las Vegas, Nevada, November 16–18, 1983, (see A84-13725), January 1984, 84N15588, #. (See also 1286.)

This paper concerns the transient dynamic analysis of the B-52 aircraft carrying the Space Shuttle solid rocket booster drop test vehicle (SRB/DTV). The NASA structural analysis (NASTRAN) finite element computer program was used in the analysis. The B-52 operating conditions considered for analysis were (1) landing and (2) braking on aborted takeoff runs. The transient loads for the B-52 pylon front and rear hooks were calculated. The results can be used to establish the safe maneuver envelopes for the B-52 carrying the SRB/DTV in landings and brakings.

1297. Shafer, M. F.; Smith, R. E.; Stewart, J. F.; and *Bailey, R. E.: **Flight Test Experience With Pilot-Induced-Oscillation Suppression Filters.** NASA TM-86028, H-1216, NAS 1.15:86028, AIAA Paper 83-2107. Presented at the AIAA Atmospheric Flight Mechanics Conference, Gatlinburg, Tennessee, August 15–17, 1983, (see A83-41936), January 1984, 84N16213, #. (See also 1262.)

Digital flight control systems are popular for their flexibility, reliability, and power; however, their use sometimes results in deficient handling qualities, including pilot-induced oscillation (PIO), which can require extensive redesign of the control system. When redesign is not immediately possible, temporary solutions, such as the PIO suppression (PIOS) filter developed for the Space Shuttle, have been proposed. To determine the effectiveness of such PIOS filters on more conventional, high-performance aircraft, three experiments were performed using the NASA F-8 digital fly-by-wire and USAF/Calspan NT-33 variable-stability aircraft. Two types of PIOS filters were evaluated, using high-gain, precision tasks (close formation, probe-and-drogue refueling, and precision touch-and-go landing) with a time delay or a first-order lag added to make the aircraft prone to PIO. Various configurations of the PIOS filter were evaluated in the flight programs, and most of the PIOS filter configurations reduced the occurrence of PIOs and improved the handling qualities of the PIO-prone aircraft. These experiments also confirmed the influence of high-gain tasks and excessive control system time delay in evoking pilot-induced oscillations.

*Grumman Aerospace Corp., Bethpage, New York.

1298. Putnam, T. W.: **X-29 Flight-Research Program.** NASA TM-86025, H-1213, NAS 1.15:86025. Presented at the AIAA 2nd Flight Test Conference, Las Vegas, Nevada,

November 16–18, 1983, (see A84-13724), January 1984, 84N16168, #. (See also 1287, 1373.)

The X-29A aircraft is the first manned, experimental high-performance aircraft to be fabricated and flown in many years. The approach for expanding the X-29 flight envelope and collecting research data is described including the methods for monitoring wind divergence, flutter, and aeroservoelastic coupling of the aerodynamic forces with the structure and the flight-control system. Examples of the type of flight data to be acquired are presented along with types of aircraft maneuvers that will be flown. A brief description of the program management structure is also presented and the program schedule is discussed.

1299. Curry, R. E.; Meyer, R. R., Jr.; and O'Connor, M.: **The Use of Oil for In-Flight Flow Visualization.** NASA TM-84915, H-1195, NAS 1.15:84915. Presented at the 14th Annual Symposium of the Soc. of Flight Test Engr., Newport Beach, California, August 15–19, 1983, January 1984, 84N14122, #.

Oil was used to visualize inflight aerodynamic characteristics such as boundary layer transition, shock wave location, regions of separated flow, and surface flow direction. The technique, which is similar to wind tunnel oil-flow testing, involves an oil mixture to test aircraft before takeoff. After takeoff, the airplane climbs immediately to the test altitude and photographs are taken. The developmental experience is summarized, several examples of inflight oil-flow photographs are presented and discussed, and an approach for potential users of the technique is presented.

1300. Meyer, R. R., Jr.; and Schneider, E. T.: **Real-Time Pilot Guidance System for Improved Flight Test Maneuvers.** NASA TM-84922, H-1204, NAS 1.15:84922. Presented at the AIAA 2nd Flight Test Conference, Las Vegas, Nevada, November 16–18, 1983, January 1984, 84N16176, #.

The Dryden Flight Research Facility of the NASA Ames Research Center has developed a pilot trajectory guidance system that increases the accuracy of flight-test data and decreases the time required to achieve and maintain desired test conditions. The system usually presented to the pilot computed differences between reference or desired and actual flight state conditions. The pilot then used a cockpit display as an aid to acquire and hold desired test conditions. This paper discusses various flight-test maneuvers and the quality of data obtained using the guidance system. Some comparisons are made between the quality of maneuvers obtained with and without the system. Limited details of the guidance system and algorithms used are included. In general, the guidance system improved the quality of the maneuvers and trajectories flown, as well as allowing trajectories to be flown that would not have been possible without the system. This system has moved from the developmental stage to full operational use in various Dryden research and test aircraft.

1301. Painter, Weneth D.: **Flight Testing as a Design Driver.** NASA TM-101101, NAS 1.15:101101. Presented at the AIAA Session, Anaheim, California, January 26, 1984, <u>1984</u>, 89N70898.

1302. Budd, G. D.: **Locally Linearized Longitudinal and Lateral-Directional Aerodynamic Stability and Control Derivatives for the X-29A Aircraft.** NASA TM-84919, H-1203, NAS 1.26:84919, <u>January 1984</u>, 86N23566, #.

The locally linearized longitudinal and lateral-directional aerodynamic stability and control derivatives for the X-29A aircraft were calculated for altitudes ranging from sea level to 25 deg. Several other parameters were also calculated, including 5 deg aerodynamic force and moment coefficients, control face position, normal acceleration, static margin, and reference angle of attack.

1303. Ishmael, S. D.; Regenie, V. A.; and Mackall, D. A.: **Design Implications From AFTI/F-16 Flight Test.** NASA TM-86026, H-1213, NAS 1.15:86026. Presented at IEE/AIAA 5th Digital Avionics Systems Conference, Seattle, Washington, October 31–November 3, 1983, <u>January 1984</u>, 84N14157, #.

Advanced fighter technologies are evolving into highly complex systems. Flight controls are being integrated with advanced avionics to achieve a total system. The advanced fighter technology integration (AFTI) F-16 aircraft is an example of a highly complex digital flight control system integrated with advanced avionics and cockpit. The architecture of these new systems involves several general issues. The use of dissimilar backup modes if the primary system fails requires the designer to tradeoff system simplicity and capability. This tradeoff is evident in the AFTI/F-16 aircraft with its limited stability and fly-by-wire digital flight control systems. In case of a generic software failure, the backup or normal mode must provide equivalent envelope protection during the transition to degraded flight control. The complexity of systems like the AFTI/F-16 system defines a second design issue, which can be divided into two segments: the effect on testing, and the pilot's ability to act correctly in the limited time available for cockpit decisions. The large matrix of states possible with the AFTI/F-16 flight control system illustrates the difficulty of both testing the system and choosing real-time pilot actions.

1304. Moore, A. L.: **The Western Aeronautical Test Range of NASA Ames Research Center.** NASA TM-85924, H-1280, NAS 1.15:85924, AIAA Paper 85-0316. Presented at the 23rd AIAA Aerospace Sciences Meeting, Reno, Nevada, January 14–17, 1984, <u>January 1984</u>, 85N15756, #. (See also 1387.)

An overview of the Western Aeronautical Test Range (WATR) of NASA Ames Research Center (ARC) is presented in this paper. The three WATR facilities are discussed, and three WATR elements—mission control centers, communications systems, real-time processing and display systems, and tracking systems—are reviewed. The relationships within the NASA WATR, with respect to the NASA aeronautics program, are also discussed.

1305. *Brooks, B. M.; and Mackall, K. G.: **Measurement and Analysis of Acoustic Flight Test Data for Two Advanced Design High Speed Propeller Models.** AIAA Paper 84-0250. American Institute of Aeronautics and Astronautics, 22nd Aerospace Sciences Meeting, Reno, Nevada, January 9–12, 1984, <u>January 1984</u>, 84A20049, #.

The recent test program, in which the SR-2 and SR-3 Prop-Fan models were acoustically tested in flight, is described and the results of analysis of noise data acquired are discussed. The trends of noise levels with flight operating parameters are shown. The acoustic benefits of the SR-3 design with swept blades relative to the SR-2 design with straight blades are shown. Noise data measured on the surface of a small-diameter microphone boom mounted above the fuselage and on the surface of the airplane fuselage are compared to show the effects of acoustic propagation through a boundary layer. Noise level estimates made using a theoretically based prediction methodology are compared with measurements.

*United Technologies Corp., Hamilton Standard Div., Windsor Locks, Connecticut.

1306. Powers, B. G.: **Space Shuttle Pilot-Induced-Oscillation Research Testing.** NASA TM-86034, H-1227, NAS 1.15:86034, <u>February 1984</u>, 84N20566, #. (See also 1381.)

The simulation requirements for investigation of pilot-induced-oscillation (PIO) characteristics during the landing phase are discussed. Orbiters simulations and F-8 digital fly-by-wire aircraft tests are addressed.

1307. Jenkins, J. M.: **Effect of Creep in Titanium Alloy Ti-6Al-4V at Elevated Temperature on Aircraft Design and Flight Test.** NASA TM-86033, H-1228, NAS 1.15:86033, <u>February 1984</u>, 84N18685, #.

Short-term compressive creep tests were conducted on three titanium alloy Ti-6Al-4V coupons at three different stress levels at a temperature of 714 K (825 F). The test data were compared to several creep laws developed from tensile creep tests of available literature. The short-term creep test data did not correlate well with any of the creep laws obtained from available literature. The creep laws themselves did not correlate well with each other. Short-term creep does not appear to be very predictable for titanium alloy Ti-6Al-4V. Aircraft events that result in extreme, but short-term temperature and stress excursions for this alloy should be approached cautiously. Extrapolations of test data and creep laws suggest a convergence toward predictability in the longer-term situation.

1308. Wilner, D. O.; and Bever, G. A.: **An Automated Stall-Speed Warning System.** NASA TM-84917, H-1209, NAS 1.15:84917, AIAA Paper 83-2705-REV. Presented at the AIAA 2nd Flight Test Conference, Las Vegas, Nevada, November 16–18, 1983, February 1984, 84N20520, #. (See also 1288.)

The development and testing of a stall-speed warning system for the OV-1C was examined. NASA designed and built an automated stall-speed warning system which presents both airspeed and stall speed to the pilot. The airspeed and stall speed are computed in real time by monitoring the basic aerodynamic parameters (dynamic pressure, horizontal and vertical accelerations, and pressure altitude) and other parameters (elevator and flap positions, engine torques, and fuel flow). In addition, an aural warning at predetermined stall margins is presented to the pilot through a voice synthesizer. Once the system was designed and installed in the aircraft, a flight-test program of less than 20 hrs was anticipated to determine the stall-speed software coefficients. These coefficients would then be inserted in the system's software and then test flown over a period of about 10 hr for the purpose of evaluation.

OV-1C Aircraft   EC83-22719

1309. Larson, T. J.: **Evaluation of a Flow Direction Probe and a Pitot-Static Probe on the F-14 Airplane at High Angles of Attack and Sideslip.** NASA TM-84911, H-1189, NAS 1.15:84911, March 1984, 84N20514, #.

The measurement performance of a hemispherical flow-angularity probe and a fuselage-mounted pitot-static probe was evaluated at high flow angles as part of a test program on an F-14 airplane. These evaluations were performed using a calibrated pitot-static noseboom equipped with vanes for reference flow direction measurements, and another probe incorporating vanes but mounted on a pod under the fuselage nose. Data are presented for angles of attack up to 63, angles of sideslip from –22 deg to 22 deg, and for Mach numbers from approximately 0.3 to 1.3. During maneuvering flight, the hemispherical flow-angularity probe exhibited flow angle errors that exceeded 2 deg. Pressure measurements with the pitot-static probe resulted in very inaccurate data above a Mach number of 0.87 and exhibited large sensitivities with flow angle.

1310. Mackall, D. A.: **AFTI/F-16 Digital Flight Control System Experience.** NASA CP-2296. NASA Langley Research Center *NASA Aircraft Controls Research*, 1983, (see N84-20567 11-08), March 1984, pp. 469–487, 84N20592, #.

The Advanced Fighter Technology Integration (AFTI) F-16 program is investigating the integration of emerging technologies into an advanced fighter aircraft. The three major technologies involved are the triplex digital flight control system; decoupled aircraft flight control; and integration of avionics, pilot displays, and flight control. In addition to investigating improvements in fighter performance, the AFTI/F-16 program provides a look at generic problems facing highly integrated, flight-crucial digital controls. An overview of the AFTI/F-16 systems is followed by a summary of flight test experience and recommendations.

1311. Berry, D. T.: **Flying Qualities Criteria for Superaugmented Aircraft.** NASA CP-2296. NASA Langley Research Center *NASA Aircraft Controls Research*, 1983, (see N84-20567 11-08), March 1984, pp. 25–36, 84N20569, #.

An overview of Dryden superaugmented aircraft flying qualities research is presented. This includes F-8 digital fly by wire flight experiments, orbiter flying qualities, shuttle improvements, AFTI/F-16, flying qualities and control system alternatives, Vertical Motion Simulator Shuttle evaluation and Total in Flight Simulator pitch rate criteria.

1312. Iliff, K. W.; and Maine, R. E.: **Practical Aspects of Modeling Aircraft Dynamics From Flight Data.** NASA CP-2296. NASA Langley Research Center *NASA Aircraft Controls Research*, 1983, (see N84-20567 11-08), March 1984, pp. 135–154, 84N20575, #.

The purpose of parameter estimation, a subset of system identification, is to estimate the coefficients (such as stability and control derivatives) of the aircraft differential equations of motion from sampled measured dynamic responses. In the past, the primary reason for estimating stability and control derivatives from flight tests was to make comparisons with wind tunnel estimates. As aircraft became more complex, and as flight envelopes were expanded to include flight regimes that were not well understood, new requirements for the derivative estimates evolved. For many years, the flight determined derivatives were used in simulations to aid in flight planning and in pilot training. The simulations were particularly important in research flight test programs in which an envelope expansion into new flight regimes was required. Parameter estimation techniques for estimating stability and control derivatives from flight data became more sophisticated to support the flight test programs. As knowledge of these new flight regimes increased, more complex aircraft were flown. Much of this increased complexity was in sophisticated flight control systems. The design and refinement of the control system required higher fidelity simulations than were previously required.

1313. *Camp, D.; *Campbell, W.; **Frost, W.; †Murrow, H.; and Painter, W.: **NASA's B-57B Gust Gradient Program.** AIAA Paper 83-0208. Presented at the AIAA 21st Aerospace Sciences Meeting, Reno, Nevada, January 10–13, 1983. *Journal of Aircraft*, (ISSN 0021-8669), Vol. 21, March 1984, pp. 175–182, 84A24103, #.

The B-57B Gust Gradient Program is a joint effort of NASA Headquarters, Marshall Space Flight Center, Dryden Flight Research Facility, Langley Research Center, and Ames Research Center. The primary program goal is to measure spanwise variations of turbulent gusts across an airflow. To this end, the NASA B-57B aircraft was equipped with three component gust probes on each wing tip and on the nose. Early results of flights done in conjunction with the Joint Airport Weather Studies (JAWS) project are described.

*NASA Marshall Space Flight Center, Huntsville, Alabama.
**Tennessee University, Space Institute, Tullahoma, Tennessee.
†NASA Langley Research Center, Hampton, Virginia.

1314. Anon.: **Digital Electronic Engine Control (DEEC) Flight Evaluation in an F-15 Airplane.** NASA CP-2298, H-1201, NAS 1.55:2298. *Conference Proceedings*, March 1984, (see N86-25343 through N86-25356), 86N25342, #.

Flight evaluation in an F-15 aircraft by digital electronic engine control (DEEC) was investigated. Topics discussed include: system description, F100 engine tests, effects of inlet distortion on static pressure probe, flight tests, digital electronic engine control fault detection and accommodation flight evaluation, flight evaluation of a hydromechanical backup control, augmentor transient capability of an F100 engine, investigation of nozzle instability, real time in flight thrust calculation, and control technology for future aircraft propulsion systems. It is shown that the DEEC system is a powerful and flexible controller for the F100 engine.

1315. Kock, B.: **Digital Electronic Engine Control F-15 Overview.** *Digital Electronic Engine Control (DEEC) Flight Evaluation in an F-15 Airplane*, NASA CP-2298, Paper 1, (see N86-25342 16-07), March 1984, pp. 1–14, 86N25343, #.

A flight test evaluation of the digital electronic engine control (DEEC) system was conducted. An overview of the flight program is presented. The roles of the participating parties, the system, and the flight program objectives are described. The test program approach is discussed, and the engine performance benefits are summarized. A description of the follow-on programs is included.

1316. Putnam, T. W.: **Digital Electronic Engine Control History.** *Digital Electronic Engine Control (DEEC) Flight Evaluation in an F-15 Airplane*, NASA CP-2298, Paper 2, (see N86-25342 16-07), March 1984, pp. 15–31, 86N25344, #.

Full authority digital electronic engine controls (DEECs) were studied, developed, and ground tested because of projected benefits in operability, improved performance, reduced maintenance, improved reliability, and lower life cycle costs. The issues of operability and improved performance, however, are assessed in a flight test program. The DEEC on a F100 engine in an F-15 aircraft was demonstrated and evaluated. The events leading to the flight test program are chronicled and important management and technical results are identified.

1317. Myers, L. P.: **F-15 Digital Electronic Engine Control System Description.** *Digital Electronic Engine Control (DEEC) Flight Evaluation in an F-15 Airplane*, NASA CP-2298, Paper 3, (see N86-25342 16-07), March 1984, pp. 33–53, 86N25345, #.

A digital electronic engine control (DEEC) was developed for use on the F100-PW-100 turbofan engine. This control system has full authority control, capable of moving all the controlled variables over their full ranges. The digital computational electronics and fault detection and accommodation logic maintains safe engine operation. A hydromechanical backup control (BUC) is an integral part of the fuel metering unit and provides gas generator control at a reduced performance level in the event of an electronics failure. The DEEC's features, hardware, and major logic diagrams are described.

1318. Hughes, D. L.; and Mackall, K. G.: **Effects of Inlet Distortion on a Static Pressure Probe Mounted on the Engine Hub in an F-15 Airplane.** *Digital Electronic Engine Control Flight Evaluation in an F-15 Airplane*, NASA CP-2298, Paper 5, (see N86-25342 16-07), March 1984, pp. 73–89, 86N25347, #.

Problems encountered in obtaining good engine face pressure data were studied. A single static measurement located upstream of the engine hub in the stream flow was found to provide a pressure signal suitable for engine control. Two identical probes for measuring fan inlet static (PS2) pressure were designed and mounted on the hub of the left F100-PW-100 turbofan engine installed in the F-15 test aircraft for flight evaluation. The probe is used as a static pressure sensor for a digital engine control system.

1319. Myers, L. P.: **Flight Testing the Digital Electronic Engine Control in the F-15 Airplane.** *Digital Electronic Engine Control (DEEC) Flight Evaluation in an F-15 Airplane*, NASA CP-2298, Paper 6, (see N86-25342 16-07), March 1984, pp. 91–105, 86N25348, #.

The digital electronic engine control (DEEC) is a full-authority digital engine control developed for the F100-PW-100 turbofan engine which was flight tested on an F-15 aircraft. The DEEC hardware and software throughout the F-15 flight envelope was evaluated. Real-time data reduction and data display systems were implemented. New test techniques and stronger coordination between the propulsion test engineer and pilot were developed which produced efficient use of test time, reduced pilot work load, and greatly improved quality data. The engine pressure ratio (EPR) control mode is demonstrated. It is found that the nonaugmented throttle transients and engine performance are satisfactory.

1320. Baer-Riedhart, J. L.: **Digital Electronic Engine Control Fault Detection and Accommodation Flight Evaluation.** *Digital Electronic Engine Control (DEEC) Flight Evaluation in an F-15 Airplane*, NASA CP-2298, Paper 7, (see N86-25342 16-07), March 1984, pp. 107–126, 86N25349, #.

The capabilities and performance of various fault detection and accommodation (FDA) schemes in existing and projected engine control systems were investigated. Flight tests of the digital electronic engine control (DEEC) in an F-15 aircraft show discrepancies between flight results and predictions based on simulation and altitude testing. The FDA methodology and logic in the DEEC system, and the results of the flight failures which occurred to date are described.

1321. Burcham, F. W., Jr.: **Airstart Performance of a Digital Electronic Engine Control System on an F100 Engine.** *Digital Electronic Engine Control (DEEC) Flight Evaluation in an F-15 Airplane*, NASA CP-2298, Paper 8, (see N86-25342 16-07), March 1984, pp. 127–139, 86N25350, #.

The digital electronic engine control (DEEC) system installed on an F100 engine in an F-15 aircraft was tested. The DEEC system incorporates a closed-loop air start feature in which the fuel flow is modulated to achieve the desired rate of compressor acceleration. With this logic the DEEC

equipped F100 engine can achieve air starts over a larger envelope. The DEEC air start logic, the test program conducted on the F-15, and its results are described.

1322. Walsh, K. R.; and Burcham, F. W.: **Flight Evaluation of a Hydromechanical Backup Control for the Digital Electronic Engine Control System in an F100 Engine.** *Digital Electronic Engine Control (DEEC) Flight Evaluation in an F-15 Airplane*, NASA CP-2298, Paper 9, (see N86-25342 16-07), March 1984, pp. 141–155, 86N25351, #.

The backup control (BUC) features, the operation of the BUC system, the BUC control logic, and the BUC flight test results are described. The flight test results include: (1) transfers to the BUC at military and maximum power settings; (2) a military power acceleration showing comparisons between flight and simulation for BUC and primary modes; (3) steady-state idle power showing idle compressor speeds at different flight conditions; and (4) idle-to-military power BUC transients showing where compressor stalls occurred for different ramp rates and idle speeds. All the BUC transfers which occur during the DEEC flight program are initiated by the pilot. Automatic transfers to the BUC do not occur.

1323. Johnson, J. B.: **Backup Control Airstart Performance on a Digital Electronic Engine Control-Equipped F100-Engine.** *Digital Electronic Engine Control (DEEC) Flight Evaluation in an F-15 Airplane*, NASA CP-2298, Paper 10, (see N86-25342 16-07), March 1984, pp. 157–170, 86N25352, #.

The air start capability of a backup control (BUC) was tested for a digital electronic engine control (DEEC) equipped F100 engine, which was installed in an F-15 aircraft. Two air start schedules were tested. Using the group 1 start schedule, based on a 40 sec timer, an air speed of 300 knots was required to ensure successful 40 and 25% BUC mode spooldown airstarts. If core rotor speed (N2) was less than 40% a stall would occur when the start bleed closed, 40 sec after initiation of the air start. All jet fuel starter (JFS) assisted air starts were successful with the group 1 start schedule. For the group 2 schedule, the time between pressurization and start bleed closure ranged between 50 sec and 72 sec. Idle rpms was lower than the desired 65% for air starts at higher altitudes and lower air speeds.

1324. Burcham, F. W., Jr.; and Pai, G. D.: **Augmentor Transient Capability of an F100 Engine Equipped With a Digital Electronic Engine Control.** *Digital Electronic Engine Control (DEEC) Flight Evaluation in an F-15 Airplane*, NASA CP-2298, Paper 11, (see N86-25342 16-07), March 1984, pp. 171–199, 86N25353, #.

An F100 augmented turbofan engine equipped with digital electronic engine control (DEEC) system was evaluated. The engine was equipped with a specially modified augmentor to provide improved steady state and transient augmentor capability. The combination of the DEEC and the modified augmentor was evaluated in sea level and altitude facility tests and then in four different flight phases in an F-15 aircraft. The augmentor configuration, logic, and test results are presented.

1325. Burcham, F. W., Jr.; and *Zeller, J. R.: **Investigation of a Nozzle Instability on an F100 Engine Equipped With a Digital Electronic Engine Control.** *Digital Electronic Engine Control (DEEC) Flight Evaluation in an F-15 Airplane,* NASA CP-2298, Paper 12, (see N86-25342 16-07), March 1984, pp. 201–214, 86N25354, #.

An instability in the nozzle of the F100 engine, equipped with a digital electronic engine control (DEEC), was observed during a flight evaluation on an F-15 aircraft. The instability occurred in the upper left hand corner (ULMC) of the flight envelope during augmentation. The instability was not predicted by stability analysis, closed-loop simulations of the engine, or altitude testing of the engine. The instability caused stalls and augmentor blowouts. The nozzle instability and the altitude testing are described. Linear analysis and nonlinear digital simulation test results are presented. Software modifications on further flight test are discussed.

*NASA Lewis Research Center, Cleveland, Ohio

1326. *Ray, R. J.; and Myers, L. P.: **Real-Time In-Flight Thrust Calculation on a Digital Electronic Engine Control-Equipped F100 Engine in an F-15 Airplane.** *Digital Electronic Engine Control (DEEC) Flight Evaluation in an F-15 Airplane,* NASA CP-2298, Paper 13, (see N86-25342 16-07), March 1984, pp. 231–247, 86N25355, #.

Computer algorithms which calculate in-flight engine and aircraft performance real-time are discussed. The first step was completed with the implementation of a real-time thrust calculation program on a digital electronic engine control (DEEC) equipped F100 engine in an F-15 aircraft. The in-flight thrust modifications that allow calculations to be performed in real-time, to compare results to predictions, are presented.

*California Polytechnic State Univ., San Luis Obispo, California.

1327. Evans, M. B.; and Schilling, L. J.: **The Role of Simulation in the Development and Flight Test of the HiMAT Vehicle.** NASA TM-84912, H-1190, NAS 1.15:84912, April 1984, 84N21537, #.

Real time simulations have been essential in the flight test program of the highly maneuverable aircraft technology (HiMAT) remotely piloted research vehicle at NASA Ames

Research Center's Dryden Flight Research Facility. The HiMAT project makes extensive use of simulations in design, development, and qualification for flight, pilot training, and flight planning. Four distinct simulations, each with varying amounts of hardware in the loop, were developed for the HiMAT project. The use of simulations in detecting anomalous behavior of the flight software and hardware at the various stages of development, verification, and validation has been the key to flight qualification of the HiMAT vehicle.

1328. Anon.: **Peripheral Vision Horizon Display (PVHD).** NASA-CP-2306, H-1232, NAS 1.55:2306. Conference held at Edwards, California, March 15–16, 1983, April 1984, 85N10044, #.

1329. Bever, G. A.: **The Development of an Airborne Instrumentation Computer System for Flight Test.** NASA TM-86036, H-1233, NAS 1.15:86036. Presented at the AGARD Flight Mech. Panel Symposium on Flight Test Tech., Lisbon, April 2–5, 1984, April 1984, 84N20521, #. (See also 1344.)

Instrumentation interfacing frequently requires the linking of intelligent systems together, as well as requiring the link itself to be intelligent. The airborne instrumentation computer system (AICS) was developed to address this requirement. Its small size, approximately 254 by 133 by 140 mm (10 by 5 1/4 by 5 1/2 in), standard bus, and modular board configuration give it the ability to solve instrumentation interfacing and computation problems without forcing a redesign of the entire unit. This system has been used on the F-15 aircraft digital electronic engine control (DEEC) and its follow on engine model derivative (EMD) project and in an OV-1C Mohawk aircraft stall speed warning system. The AICS is presently undergoing configuration for use on an F-104 pace aircraft and on the advanced fighter technology integration (AFTI) F-111 aircraft.

1330. Layton, G. P.: **A Review of Recent Developments in Flight Test Techniques at the Ames Research Center, Dryden Flight Research Facility.** NASA TM-86039, H-1237, NAS 1.15:86039. Presented at the Canadian Aeronautics and Space Inst. (CASI) Flight Test Symposium, Cold Lake, Alberta, April 11–12, 1984, 84N20515, #.

New flight test techniques in use at Ames Dryden are reviewed. The use of the pilot in combination with ground and airborne computational capabilities to maximize data return is discussed, including the remotely piloted research vehicle technique for high-risk testing, the remotely augmented vehicle technique for handling qualities research, and use of ground computed flight director information to fly unique profiles such as constant Reynolds number profiles through the transonic flight regime. Techniques used for checkout and design verification of systems-oriented aircraft are discussed, including descriptions of the various simulations, iron bird setups, and vehicle tests. Some newly developed techniques to support the aeronautical research disciplines are discussed, including a new approach to position-error determination, and the use of a large skin friction balance for the measurement of drag caused by various excrescences.

1331. Anon.: **NASA Ames-Dryden T-37 Demonstration Comments.** NASA CP-2306. *Peripheral Vision Horizon Display (PVHD)*, (see N85-10044 01-06), April 1984, pp. 111–112, 85N10056, #.

A homemade peripheral vision horizon device (PVHD) made from an eight-ball attitude indicator, with a slit cut at the equator of the eight ball, and a light source at its center that was used on a T-37 for several years is discussed. The instrument produced a sharp white line about one-fourth of an inch that extended completely across the cockpit from about the left to the right quarter panels. The line remained parallel to the real horizon during all maneuvers. Its brightness and vertical distance from the horizon were adjustable in flight, as was the lateral center-of-rotation in later flights. Flight demonstrations were done on visual flight rules (VFR) moonless nights and over terrain with few lights. Pilot responses were mostly favorable to enthusiastic, with no negative reactions. Problem areas noted were the upright-inverted ambiguity; one pilot recovered inverted following an unusual attitude exercise and a general deterioration in the naturalness of cueing at bank angles greater than 60 deg or pitch attitudes greater than 30 deg.

1332. Kehoe, M. W.: **Highly Maneuverable Aircraft Technology (HiMAT) Flight-Flutter Test Program.** NASA TM-84907, H-1183, NAS 1.15:84907, May 1984, 86N27290, #.

The highly maneuverable aircraft technology (HiMAT) vehicle was evaluated in a joint NASA and Air Force flight test program. The HiMAT vehicle is a remotely piloted research vehicle. Its design incorporates the use of advanced composite materials in the wings, and canards for aeroelastic tailoring. A flight-flutter test program was conducted to clear a sufficient flight envelope to allow for performance, stability and control, and loads testing. Testing was accomplished with and without flight control-surface dampers. Flutter clearance of the vehicle indicated satisfactory damping and damping trends for the structural modes of the HiMAT vehicle. The data presented include frequency and damping plotted as a function of Mach number.

1333. Sarrafian, S. K.: **Evaluation of HiMAT Aircraft Landing Approach Lateral Control Gearing Using Simulation and a Visual Display.** NASA TM-84916, H-1205, NAS 1.15:84916, May 1984, 84N27743, #.

The utility of a visual display when studying the influence of changes in lateral stick gearing gains on the Highly Maneuverable Aircraft Technology (HiMAT) vehicle handling qualities during simulated approaches and landings is investigated. The visual display improved the validity of the simulation and provided improved roll response cues for the HiMAT aircraft landing approach. A range of acceptable constant lateral stick gearing gains is found that provides adequate maneuverability and allows for precision moments.

1334. Schneider, E. T.; and Enevoldson, E. K.: **Modernizing Engine Displays.** *Proceedings, 6th Advanced Aircrew Display Symposium*, Patuxent River, Maryland, May 15–16, 1984, (see A85-38951 18-06), 1984, pp. 96–125, 85A38956, #.

The introduction of electronic fuel control to modern turbine engines has a number of advantages, which are related to an increase in engine performance and to a reduction or elimination of the problems associated with high angle of attack engine operation from the surface to 50,000 feet. If the appropriate engine display devices are available to the pilot, the fuel control system can provide a great amount of information. Some of the wealth of information available from modern fuel controls are discussed in this paper. The considered electronic engine control systems in their most recent forms are known as the Full Authority Digital Engine Control (FADEC) and the Digital Electronic Engine Control (DEEC). Attention is given to some details regarding the control systems, typical engine problems, the solution of problems with the aid of displays, engine displays in normal operation, an example display format, a multipage format, flight strategies, and hardware considerations.

1335. Haering, E. A., Jr.; and Burcham, F. W., Jr.: **Minimum Time and Fuel Flight Profiles for an F-15 Airplane With a Highly Integrated Digital Electronic Control (HIDEC) System.** NASA TM-86042, H-1242, NAS 1.15:86042, June 1984, 86N23587, #.

A simulation study was conducted to optimize minimum time and fuel consumption paths for an F-15 airplane powered by two F100 Engine Model Derivative (EMD) engines. The benefits of using variable stall margin (uptrim) to increase performance were also determined. This study supports the NASA Highly Integrated Digital Electronic Control (HIDEC) program. The basis for this comparison was minimum time and fuel used to reach Mach 2 at 13,716 m (45,000 ft) from the initial conditions of Mach 0.15 at 1524 m (5000 ft). Results were also compared to a pilot's estimated minimum time and fuel trajectory determined from the F-15 flight manual and previous experience. The minimum time trajectory took 15 percent less time than the pilot's estimate for the standard EMD engines, while the minimum fuel trajectory used 1 percent less fuel than the pilot's estimate for the minimum fuel trajectory. The F-15 airplane with EMD engines and uptrim, was 23 percent faster than the pilot's estimate. The minimum fuel used was 5 percent less than the estimate.

F-15 HiDEC Aircraft

ECN-18899

1336. Myers, L. P.; and Burcham, F. W., Jr.: **Preliminary Flight Test Results of the F100 EMD Engine in an F-15 Airplane.** NASA TM-85902, H-1247, NAS 1.15:85902. Presented at the 20th AIAA, ASME, and SAE Joint Propulsion Conference, Cincinnati, Ohio, June 11–13, 1984, June 1984, 84N24588, #. (See also 1337.)

A flight evaluation of the F100 Engine Model Derivative (EMD) is conducted. The F100 EMD is an advanced version of the F100 engine that powers the F15 and F16 airplanes. The F100 EMD features a bigger fan, higher temperature turbine, a Digital Electronic Engine Control system (DEEC), and a newly designed 16 segment afterburner, all of which results in a 15 to 20 percent increase in sea level thrust. The flight evaluations consist of investigation of performance (thrust, fuel flow, and airflow) and operability (transient response and airstart) in the F-15 airplane. The performance of the F100 EMD is excellent. Aircraft acceleration time to Mach 2.0 is reduced by 23 percent with two F100 EMD engines. Several anomalies are discovered in the operability evaluations. A software change to the DEEC improved the throttle, and subsequent Cooper Harper ratings of 3 to 4 are obtained. In the extreme upper left hand corner of the flight enveloped, compressor stalls occur when the throttle is retarded to idle power. These stalls are not predicted by altitude facility tests or stability for the compressor.

1337. Myers, L. P.; and Burcham, F. W., Jr.: **Preliminary Flight Test Results of the F100 EMD Engine in an F-15 Airplane.** AIAA Paper 84-1332. AIAA, SAE, and ASME, 20th Joint Propulsion Conference, Cincinnati, Ohio, June 11–13, 1984, 84A35176, #. (See also 1336.)

An assessment is given of results from a 17-flight evaluation of the F100 Engine Model Derivative (EMD) powerplant in

an F-15 fighter. The EMD variant of the F100 engine incorporates a larger fan, a higher temperature turbine, a digital control system, and a 16-segment afterburner. These modifications result in a 15 to 20 percent increase in thrust which is exhibited in the reduction of F-15 acceleration time to Mach 2.0 by 23 percent. The only uncorrected shortcoming of the engine upon completion of the 17-flight test course was the occurrence of compressor stalls at the throttle's idle setting. These stalls had not been predicted by either ground facility tests or compressor stability assessments.

1338. Burcham, F. W., Jr.; and Haering, E. A., Jr.: **Highly Integrated Digital Engine Control System on an F-15 Airplane.** NASA TM-86040, H-1240, NAS 1.15:86040. Presented at the 20th AIAA, ASM, and SAE Joint Propulsion Conference, Cincinnati, Ohio, June 11–13, 1984, 84N24587, #. (See also 1339.)

The Highly Integrated Digital Electronic Control (HIDEC) program will demonstrate and evaluate the improvements in performance and mission effectiveness that result from integrated engine/airframe control systems. This system is being used on the F-15 airplane. An integrated flightpath management mode and an integrated adaptive engine stall margin mode are implemented into the system. The adaptive stall margin mode is a highly integrated mode in which the airplane flight conditions, the resulting inlet distortion, and the engine stall margin are continuously computed; the excess stall margin is used to uptrim the engine for more thrust. The integrated flightpath management mode optimizes the flightpath and throttle setting to reach a desired flight condition. The increase in thrust and the improvement in airplane performance is discussed.

1339. Burcham, F. W., Jr.; and Haering, E. A., Jr.: **Highly Integrated Digital Engine Control System on an F-15 Airplane.** AIAA Paper 84-1259. Presented at the 20th AIAA, ASME, and SAE Joint Propulsion Conference, Cincinnati, Ohio, June 11–13, 1984, 84A35149, #. (See also 1338.)

The highly integrated digital electronic control (HIDEC) program will demonstrate and evaluate the improvements in performance and mission effectiveness that result from integrated engine-airframe control systems. This system is being used on the F-15 airplane at the Dryden Flight Research Facility of NASA Ames Research Center. An integrated flightpath management mode and an integrated adaptive engine stall margin mode are being implemented into the system. The adaptive stall margin mode is a highly integrated mode in which the airplane flight conditions, the resulting inlet distortion, and the engine stall margin are continuously computed; the excess stall margin is used to uptrim the engine for more thrust. The integrated flightpath management mode optimizes the flightpath and throttle setting to reach a desired flight condition. The increase in thrust and the improvement in airplane performance is discussed in this paper.

1340. Gong, L.; Ko, W. L.; and Quinn, R. D.: **Thermal Response of Space Shuttle Wing During Reentry Heating.** NASA TM-85907, H-1254, NAS 1.15:85907. Presented at the 19th AIAA Thermophysics Conference, Snowmass, Colorado, June 25–28, 1984, 84N27785, #. (See also 1341.)

A structural performance and resizing (SPAR) finite element thermal analysis computer program was used in the heat transfer analysis of the space shuttle orbiter that was subjected to reentry aerodynamic heatings. One wing segment of the right wing (WS 240) and the whole left wing were selected for the thermal analysis. Results showed that the predicted thermal protection system (TPS) temperatures were in good agreement with the space transportation system, trajectory 5 (STS-5) flight-measured temperatures. In addition, calculated aluminum structural temperatures were in fairly good agreement with the flight data up to the point of touchdown. Results also showed that the internal free convection had a considerable effect on the change of structural temperatures after touchdown.

1341. Gong, L.; Ko, W. L.; and Quinn, R. D.: **Thermal Response of Space Shuttle Wing During Reentry Heating.** AIAA Paper 84-1761. AIAA 19th Thermophysics Conference, Snowmass, Colorado, June 25–28, 1984, 84A40813, #. (See also 1340.)

A structural performance and resizing (SPAR) finite element thermal analysis computer program was used in the heat transfer analysis of the Space Shuttle Orbiter that was subjected to reentry aerodynamic heatings. One wing segment of the right wing (WS 240) and the whole left wing were selected for the thermal analysis. Results showed that the predicted thermal protection system (TPS) temperatures were in good agreement with the space transportation system, trajectory 5 (STS-5) flight-measured temperatures. In addition, calculated aluminum structural temperatures were in fairly good agreement with flight data up to the point of touchdown. Results also showed that the internal free convection has a considerable effect on the change of structural temperatures after touchdown.

1342. *Shideler, J. L.; **Swegle, A. R.; and Fields, R. A.: **Honeycomb Sandwich Structure for Future Space Transportation Systems With Integral Cryogenic Tankage.** *Journal of Spacecraft and Rockets,* (ISSN 0022-4650), Vol. 21, May–June 1984, June 1984, (see A82-30084), pp. 246–252, 84A36556, #. (See also 1202, 1203.)

*NASA Langley Research Center, Hampton, Virginia.
**Boeing Aerospace Co., Seattle, Washington.

1343. Cho, T. K.; and Burcham, F. W., Jr.: **Preliminary Flight Evaluation of F100 Engine Model Derivative Airstart Capability in an F-15 Airplane.** NASA TM-86031, H-1200, NAS 1.15:86031, July 1984, 84N28792, #.

A series of airstarts was conducted in an F-15 airplane with two prototype F100 engine model derivative (EMD) engines equipped with digital electronic engine control (DEEC) systems. The airstart envelope and time required for airstarts were defined. The success of an airstart is most heavily dependent on airspeed. Spooldown airstarts at 200 knots and higher were all successful. Spooldown airstart times ranged from 53 sec at 250 knots to 170 sec at 175 knots. Jet fuel starter (JFS) assisted airstarts were conducted at 175 knots at two altitudes, and airstart times were 50 and 60 sec, significantly faster than unassisted airstart. The effect of altitude on airstarts was small. In addition, the airstart characteristics of the two test engines were found to closely resemble each other. The F100 EMD airstart characteristics were very similar to the DEEC equipped F100 engine tested previously. Finally, the time required to spool down from intermediate power compressor rotor speed to a given compressor rotor speed was found to be a strong function of altitude and a weaker function of airspeed.

1344. Bever, G. A.: **The Development of an Airborne Instrumentation Computer System for Flight Test.** AGARD CP-373, Paper 25. *AGARD Flight Test Tech.*, (see N84-34396 24-01), July 1984, 84N34421, #. (See also 1329.)

Instrumentation interfacing frequently requires the linking of intelligent systems together, as well as requiring the link itself to be intelligent. The airborne instrumentation computer system (AICS) was developed to address this requirement. Its small size, approximately 254 by 133 by 140 mm (10 by 51/4 by 51/2 in), standard bus, and modular board configuration give it the ability to solve instrumentation interfacing and computation problems without forcing a redesign of the entire unit. This system has been used on the F-15 aircraft digital electronic engine control (DEEC) and its follow on engine model derivative (EMD) project and in an OV-1C Mohawk aircraft stall speed warning system. The AICS is presently undergoing configuration for use on an F-104 pace aircraft and on the advanced fighter technology integration (AFTI) F-111 aircraft.

1345. Petersen, K. L.; and Flores, C., Jr.: **Software Control and System Configuration Management: A Systems-Wide Approach.** NASA TM-85908, H-1256, NAS 1.15:85908. Presented at IEEE/AIAA 5th Digital Avionics Systems Conference, Seattle, Washington, October 31– November 3, 1983, August 1984, 84N31112, #. (See also 1282.)

A comprehensive software control and system configuration management process for flight-crucial digital control systems of advanced aircraft has been developed and refined to insure efficient flight system development and safe flight operations. Because of the highly complex interactions among the hardware, software, and system elements of state-of-the-art digital flight control system designs, a systems-wide approach to configuration control and management has been used. Specific procedures are implemented to govern discrepancy reporting and reconciliation, software and hardware change control, systems verification and validation testing, and formal documentation requirements. An active and knowledgeable configuration control board reviews and approves all flight system configuration modifications and revalidation tests. This flexible process has proved effective during the development and flight testing of several research aircraft and remotely piloted research vehicles with digital flight control systems that ranged from relatively simple to highly complex, integrated mechanizations.

1346. Sim, A. G.: **Flight Characteristics of a Manned, Low-Speed, Controlled Deep Stall Vehicle.** NASA TM-86041, H-1242, NAS 1.15:86041. Presented at the AIAA Atmospheric Flight Mechanics Conference, Seattle, Washington, <u>August 21–23, 1984</u>, 84N29863, #. (See also 1353.)

A successful manned, low speed, controlled deep stall flight research program was conducted at NASA Ames Research Center's Dryden Flight Research Facility. Piloting techniques were established that enabled the pilot to attain and stabilize on an angle of attack in the 30 deg to 72 deg range. A flight determined aerodynamic data base was established for angles of attack as high as 72 deg. Poor lateral directional flying qualities were encountered at angles of attack above 60 deg. Insight into the high angle of attack lateral directional dynamics was gained through a basic root locus analysis.

1347. Bowers, A. H.: **X-29A Longitudinal and Directional Force and Moment Supplemental Transonic Wind Tunnel Test Results.** NASA TM-85909, H-1257, NAS 1.15:85909, <u>August 1984</u>, 87N10861, #.

Aerodynamic data from NASA Ames Research Center's 11-Foot Transonic Wind Tunnel are plotted for the 1/8-scale X-29A forward-swept wing aircraft model. Eleven configurations were tested to provide supplemental data to investigate single surface failure modes, complex nonlinearities, and model buildup. These data can be used for control system refinements, pilot training, flight planning, and aerodynamic model validation. Data are presented as corrected wind tunnel data without analysis to document results that are being used for the aerodynamic model.

1348. Crawford, D. B.; and Burcham, F. W., Jr.: **Effect of Control Logic Modifications on Airstart Performance of F100 Engine Model Derivative Engines in an F-15 Airplane.** NASA TM-85900, H-1243, NAS 1.15:85900, <u>August 1984</u>, 84N29879, #.

A series of airstarts were conducted in an F-15 airplane with two prototype Pratt and Whitney F100 Engine Model Derivative engines equipped with Digital Electronic Engine Control (DEEC) systems. The airstart envelope and the time required for airstarts were defined. Comparisons were made between the original airstart logic, and modified logic which was designed to improve the airstart capability. Spooldown airstarts with the modified logic were more successful at lower altitudes than were those with the original logic. Spooldown airstart times ranged from 33 seconds at 250 knots to 83 seconds at 175 knots. The modified logic improved the airstart time from 31% to 53%, with the most improved times at slower airspeeds. Jet fuel starter (JFS)-assisted airstarts were conducted at 7000 m and airstart times were significantly faster than unassisted airstarts. The effect of altitude on airstart times was small.

1349. Gupta, K. K.: **Numerical Formulation for a Higher Order Plane Finite Dynamic Element.** *International Journal for Numerical Methods in Engineering,* (ISSN 0029-5981), Vol. 20, <u>August 1984,</u> pp. 1407–1414, 84A48285.

The paper describes the development of an eight-node plane rectangular finite dynamic element and presents detailed descriptions of the associated numerical formulation involving the higher order dynamic correction terms pertaining to the related stiffness and inertia matrices. Numerical test results of free vibration analyses are presented in detail for the newly developed eight-node element and also the corresponding four-node element in order to make a clear comparison of the relative efficiencies of the corresponding finite element and dynamic element procedures. Such results indicate a superior pattern of solution convergence of the presently developed dynamic element.

1350. *Berthe, C. J.; *Chalk, C. R.; and Sarrafian, S.: **An In-Flight Investigation of Pitch Rate Flight Control Systems and Application of Frequency Domain and Time Domain Predictive Criteria.** AIAA Paper 84-1897. *Technical Papers,* AIAA Guidance and Control Conference, Seattle, Washington, August 20–22, 1984, (A84-43401 21-63). New York, American Institute of Aeronautics and Astronautics, <u>1984</u>, pp. 731–742, 84A43482.

The degree of attitude control provided by current integral-proportional pitch rate command-type control systems, while a prerequisite for flared landing, is insufficient for "Level 1" performance. The pilot requires "surrogate" feedback cues to precisely control flight path in the landing flare. Monotonic stick forces and pilot station vertical acceleration are important cues which can be provided by means of angle-of-attack and pitch rate feedback in order to achieve conventional short period and phugoid characteristics. Integral-proportional pitch rate flight control systems can be upgraded to Level 1 flared landing performance by means of lead/lag and washout prefilters in the command path. Strong pilot station vertical acceleration cues can provide Level 1 flared landing performance even in the absence of monotonic stick forces.

*Calspan Advanced Technology Center, Buffalo, New York.

1351. Sarrafian, S. K.: **Simulator Evaluation of a Remotely Piloted Vehicle Lateral Landing Task Using a Visual Display.** AIAA Paper 84-2095. Presented at the Atmospheric Flight Mechanics Conference, Seattle, Washington, <u>August 21–23, 1984</u>, pp. 218–230, 84A42348, #. (See also 1352, 1464.)

A simulator evaluation of a remotely piloted research vehicle was conducted at NASA Ames Research Center's Dryden Flight Research Facility to determine the utility of a visual display when studying the influence of changes in the lateral-stick gearing gains during landing approaches. The test vehicle used in this study was a highly maneuverable aircraft technology (HiMAT) aircraft, which is a 0.44-scale version of an envisioned small, single-seat fighter airplane. Handling qualities ratings and comments obtained from pilots using a simulated visual display of a runway scene and a simulated instrument landing system (ILS) display were compared with the results of actual flight tests. The visual display was found to provide an adequate representation of the test vehicle in a visual landing approach, and it improved the roll response cues provided to the pilot. The handling qualities ratings and comments for flight and simulation visual landing approaches correlated well. The ILS simulation results showed reduced correlation compared with the flight results for ILS approaches. Handling qualities criteria for remotely piloted research vehicles are also discussed in this paper.

1352. Sarrafian, S. K.: **Simulator Evaluation of a Remotely Piloted Vehicle Lateral Landing Task Using a Visual Display.** NASA TM-85903, H-1246, NAS 1.15:85903. AIAA Atmospheric Flight Mechanics Conference, Seattle, Washington, <u>August 21–23, 1984</u>, 84N29885, #. (See also 1351, 1464.)

A simulator evaluation of a remotely piloted research vehicle was conducted at NASA Ames Research Center's Dryden Flight Research Facility to determine the utility of a visual display when studying the influence of changes in the lateral stick gearing gains during landing approaches. The test vehicle used in this study was a highly maneuverable aircraft technology (HiMAT) aircraft, which is a 0.44 scale version of an envisioned small, single seat fighter airplane. Handling qualities ratings and comments obtained from pilots using a simulated visual display of a runway scene and a simulated instrument landing system (ILS) display were compared with the results of actual flight tests. The visual display was found to provide an adequate representation of the test vehicle in a visual landing approach, and it improved the roll response cues provided to the pilot. The handling qualities ratings and comments for flight and simulation visual landing approaches correlated well. The ILS simulation results

showed reduced correlation compared with the flight results for ILS approaches. Handling qualities criteria for remotely piloted research vehicles are also discussed in this paper.

1353. Sim, A. G.: **Flight Characteristics of a Manned, Low-Speed, Controlled Deep Stall Vehicle.** AIAA Paper 84-2074. Presented at the Atmospheric Flight Mechanics Conference, Seattle, Washington, <u>August 21–23, 1984</u>, (A84-42326 20-01), pp. 50–56, 84A42330, #. (See also 1346.)

A successful manned, low-speed, controlled deep stall flight research program was conducted at NASA Ames Research Center's Dryden Flight Research Facility. Piloting techniques were established that enabled the pilot to attain and stabilize on an angle of attack in the 30 to 72 deg range. A flight-determined aerodynamic data base was established for angles of attack as high as 72 deg. Poor lateral-directional flying qualities were encountered at angles of attack above 60 deg. Insight into the high angle-of-attack, lateral-directional dynamics was gained through a basic root-locus analysis.

1354. Shafer, M. F.: **Flight Investigation of Various Control Inputs Intended for Parameter Estimation.** NASA TM-85901. Presented at the Atmospheric Flight Mechanics Conference, Seattle, Washington, <u>August 21–23, 1984</u>, 84A42329, #. (See also 1355.)

NASA's F-8 digital fly-by-wire aircraft has been subjected to stability and control derivative assessments, leading to the proposal of improved control inputs for more efficient control derivative estimation. This will reduce program costs by reducing flight test and data analysis requirements. Inputs were divided into sinusoidal types and cornered types. Those with corners produced the best set of stability and control derivatives for the unaugmented flight control system mode. Small inputs are noted to have provided worse derivatives than larger ones.

1355. Shafer, M. F.: **Flight Investigation of Various Control Inputs Intended for Parameter Estimation.** AIAA Paper 84-2073. Presented at the Atmospheric Flight Mechanics Conference, Seattle, Washington, <u>August 21–23, 1984</u>, pp. 33–49, 84A42329, #. (See also 1354.)

NASA's F-8 digital fly-by-wire aircraft has been subjected to stability and control derivative assessments, leading to the proposal of improved control inputs for more efficient control derivative estimation. This will reduce program costs by reducing flight test and data analysis requirements. Inputs were divided into sinusoidal types and cornered types. Those with corners produced the best set of stability and control derivatives for the unaugmented flight control system mode. Small inputs are noted to have provided worse derivatives than larger ones.

1356. Iliff, K. W.; and Maine, R. E.: **More Than You May Want to Know About Maximum Likelihood Estimation.** AIAA Paper 84-2070. Presented at the Atmospheric Flight Mechanics Conference, Seattle, Washington, August 21–23, 1984, pp. 1–24, 84A42327, #. (See also 1383.)

A discussion is undertaken concerning the maximum likelihood estimator and the aircraft equations of motion it employs, with attention to the application of the concepts of minimization and estimation to a simple computed aircraft example. Graphic representations are given for the cost functions to help illustrate the minimization process. The basic concepts are then generalized, and estimations obtained from flight data are evaluated. The example considered shows the advantage of low measurement noise, multiple estimates at a given condition, the Cramer-Rao bounds, and the quality of the match between measured and computed data.

1357. Privoznik, C. M.; Berry, D. T.; and Bartoli, A. G.: **Measurements of Pilot Time Delay as Influenced by Controller Characteristics and Vehicles Time Delays.** NASA CP-2341. Twentieth Annual Conference on Manual Control, Vol. 1, (see N85-14487 05-54), September 1984, pp. 210–221, 85N14500, #.

A study to measure and compare pilot time delay when using a space shuttle rotational hand controller and a more conventional control stick was conducted at NASA Ames Research Center's Dryden Flight Research Facility. The space shuttle controller has a palm pivot in the pitch axis. The more conventional controller used was a general-purpose engineering simulator stick that has a pivot length between that of a typical aircraft center stick and a sidestick. Measurements of the pilot's effective time delay were obtained through a first-order, closed-loop, compensatory tracking task in pitch. The tasks were implemented through a space shuttle cockpit simulator and a critical task tester device. The study consisted of 450 data runs with four test pilots and one nonpilot, and used three control stick configurations and two system delays. Results showed that the heavier conventional stick had the lowest pilot effective time delays associated with it, whereas the shuttle and light conventional sticks each had similar higher pilot time delay characteristics. It was also determined that each control stick showed an increase in pilot time delay when the total system delay was increased.

1358. Whitmore, S. A.; Larson, T. J.; and Ehernberger, L. J.: **Air Data Position-Error Calibration Using State Reconstruction Techniques.** NASA TM-86029, H-1217, NAS 1.15:86029, September 1984, 84N32384, #.

During the highly maneuverable aircraft technology (HiMAT) flight test program recently completed at NASA Ames Research Center's Dryden Flight Research Facility, numerous problems were experienced in airspeed calibration.

This necessitated the use of state reconstruction techniques to arrive at a position-error calibration. For the HiMAT aircraft, most of the calibration effort was expended on flights in which the air data pressure transducers were not performing accurately. Following discovery of this problem, the air data transducers of both aircraft were wrapped in heater blankets to correct the problem. Additional calibration flights were performed, and from the resulting data a satisfactory position-error calibration was obtained. This calibration and data obtained before installation of the heater blankets were used to develop an alternate calibration method. The alternate approach took advantage of high-quality inertial data that was readily available. A linearized Kalman filter (LKF) was used to reconstruct the aircraft's wind-relative trajectory; the trajectory was then used to separate transducer measurement errors from the aircraft position error. This calibration method is accurate and inexpensive. The LKF technique has an inherent advantage of requiring that no flight maneuvers be specially designed for airspeed calibrations. It is of particular use when the measurements of the wind-relative quantities are suspected to have transducer-related errors.

1359. Schuster, L. S.: **NASTRAN/FLEXSTAB Procedure for Static Aeroelastic Analysis.** NASA TM-8489, NAS 1.15:84897, September 1984, 86N28076, #.

Presented is a procedure for using the FLEXSTAB External Structural Influence Coefficients (ESIC) computer program to produce the structural data necessary for the FLEXSTAB Stability Derivatives and Static Stability (SD&SS) program. The SD&SS program computes trim state, stability derivatives, and pressure and deflection data for a flexible airplane having a plane of symmetry. The procedure used a NASTRAN finite-element structural model as the source of structural data in the form of flexibility matrices. Selection of a set of degrees of freedom, definition of structural nodes and panels, reordering and reformatting of the flexibility matrix, and redistribution of existing point mass data are among the topics discussed. Also discussed are boundary conditions and the NASTRAN substructuring technique.

1360. Gupta, K. K.: **Development of Numerical Procedures for Analysis of Complex Structures.** *Proceedings, 3rd International Conference on Space Structures,* University of Surrey, Guildford, Surrey, England, September 4–14, 1984. Publishers, Elsevier Applied Science, London and New York, 1984, pp. 394–399, 85A24948.

The paper is concerned with the development of novel numerical procedures for the solution of static, stability, free vibration and dynamic response analysis of large, complex practical structures. Thus, details of numerical algorithms evolved for dynamic analysis of usual non-rotating and also rotating structures as well as finite dynamic elements are presented in the paper. Furthermore, the article provides some description of a general-purpose computer program STARS specifically developed for efficient analysis of complex practical structures.

1361. Duke, E. L.; and Jones, F. P.: **Computer Control for Automated Flight Test Maneuvering.** *Journal of Aircraft*, (ISSN 0021-8669), Vol. 21, October 1984, pp. 776–782, 84A49088, #.

The application of an experimental flight test maneuver autopilot test technique for collecting aerodynamic and structural flight research data on a highly maneuverable aircraft is described in this paper. This technique, which was developed to increase the quality and quantity of data obtained during flight test, was applied to the highly maneuverable aircraft technology (HiMAT) vehicle. A primary flight experiment was to verify the design techniques used to develop the HiMAT aerodynamics and structures. This required the performance of maneuvers for collection of large quantities of high-quality pressure distribution, loads, and wing and canard deflection data. Flight data obtained while executing these research maneuvers are presented to demonstrate the effectiveness of this new technique.

1362. *Pendergraft, O. C., Jr.; and Nugent, J.: **Results of a Wind Tunnel/Flight Test Program to Compare Afterbody/Nozzle Pressures on a 1/12 Scale Model and an F-15 Aircraft.** SAE Paper 841543. *Advances in Aerospace Propulsion*; *Proceedings of the Aerospace Congress and Exposition*, Long Beach, California, October 15–18, 1984 (A85-39057 18-07), 1984, pp. 101–110, 85A39066.

In 1975 NASA Dryden Flight Research Facility received the No. 2 prototype F-15 aircraft from the USAF to conduct the F-15 Propulsion/Airframe Interactions Program. About the same time, NASA Langley Research Center acquired a 1/12 1scale F-15 propulsion model, whose size made it suitable for detailed afterbody/nozzle static pressure distribution studies. Close coordination between Langley and Dryden assured identical orifice locations and nozzle geometries on the model and aircraft. This paper discusses the sequence of the test programs and how retesting the model after completion of the flight tests greatly increased the ability to match hardware and test conditions. The experience gained over the past decade from involvement in the program should prove valuable to any future programs attempting to match wind tunnel and flight test conditions and hardware.

*NASA Langley Research Center, Hampton, Virginia.

1363. Wrin, J. W.; and *Sullivan, A.: **New Antenna Feed Revitalizes Space Shuttle Tracker at NASA Edwards**. ITC/USA/'84. *Proceedings, International Telemetering Conference*, Las Vegas, Nevada, (see A86-13201 03-32), October 22–25, 1984, pp. 787–799, 86A13261.

An account is given of the upgrading of a 12-ft-diameter single-channel monopulse tracking system, which had been relegated to slaved backup status at NASA Edwards, to support research flights for Ames Dryden Research Center and for tracking orbital passes of the Space Shuttle and

Shuttle landings both at Edwards and at White Sands. The improved system is now a stand-alone telemetry tracking system. A new conical scanning feed (known as Radscan) replaces the single channel monopulse feed in the upgraded system. Where previously the system would not autotrack at elevation angles below 5 degrees, it now automatically acquires the Space Shuttle when it appears on the horizon and autotracks from approximately 2 degrees in elevation to touchdown, and does so virtually unattended.

*Electro-Magnetic Processes, Inc., Chatsworth, California.

1364. Szalai, K. J.: **Role of Research Aircraft in Technology Development.** NASA TM-85913, H-1265, NAS 1.15:85913. Presented at the AIAA, AHS, and ASEE Aircraft Design Systems and Operation Meeting, October 31–November 2, 1984, San Diego, California, 1984, 85N10932, #. (See also 1365.)

The United States's aeronautical research program has been rich in the use of research aircraft to explore new flight regimes, develop individual aeronautical concepts, and investigate new vehicle classes and configurations. This paper reviews the NASA supercritical wing, digital fly-by-wire, HiMAT, and AD-1 oblique-wing flight research programs, and draws from these examples general conclusions regarding the role and impact of research aircraft in technology development. The impact of a flight program on spinoff technology is also addressed. The secondary, serendipitous results are often highly significant. Finally, future research aircraft programs are examined for technology trends and expected results.

1365. Szalai, K. J.: **Role of Research Aircraft in Technology Development.** AIAA Paper 84-2473. Presented at the AIAA, AHS, and ASEE Aircraft Design Systems and Operation Meeting, San Diego, California, October 31–November 2, 1984, 85A16106, #. (See also 1364.)

NASA supercritical wing technology, and the digital fly-by-wire program are discussed as used on the F-8 research aircraft. Furthermore, the Highly Maneuverable Aircraft Technology (HiMAT) program, using a 0.44-scale, 3500 lb jet-powered remotely piloted research aircraft, is analyzed. Highly accurate data on aerodynamic and structural loads and deflection data were obtained from model flight tests. In addition, an oblique-wing technology is discussed through the example of the piloted AD-1 research aircraft, noting the low cost of the experiment. Other topics include: integrated system technology; generic forces of the research aircraft program; and aeronautical technology application trends.

1366. Painter, W. D.; and *Erickson, R. E.: **Rotor Systems Research Aircraft Airplane Configuration Flight-Test Results.** NASA TM-85911, H-1263, NAS 1.15:85911. Presented at the AIAA, AHS, and ASEE

Aircraft Design Systems and Operation Meeting, October 31–November 2, 1984, San Diego, California, October 1984, 85N10034, #. (See also 1374.)

The rotor systems research aircraft (RSRA) has undergone ground and flight tests, primarily as a compound aircraft. The purpose was to train pilots and to check out and develop the design flight envelope. The preparation and flight test of the RSRA in the airplane, or fixed-wind, configuration are reviewed and the test results are discussed.

*NASA Ames Research Center, Moffett Field, California.

RSRA Airplane

ECN-30043

1367. Gupta, K. K.: **STARS: A General-Purpose Finite Element Computer Program for Analysis of Engineering Structures.** NASA-RP-1129, H-1224, NAS 1.61:1129, October 1984, 85N11378, #.

STARS (Structural Analysis Routines) is primarily an interactive, graphics-oriented, finite-element computer program for analyzing the static, stability, free vibration, and dynamic responses of damped and undamped structures, including rotating systems. The element library consists of one-dimensional (1-D) line elements, two-dimensional (2-D) triangular and quadrilateral shell elements, and three-dimensional (3-D) tetrahedral and hexahedral solid elements. These elements enable the solution of structural problems that include truss, beam, space frame, plane, plate, shell, and solid structures, or any combination thereof. Zero, finite, and interdependent deflection boundary conditions can be implemented by the program. The associated dynamic response analysis capability provides for initial deformation and velocity inputs, whereas the transient excitation may be either forces or accelerations. An effective in-core or out-of-core solution strategy is automatically employed by the

program, depending on the size of the problem. Data input may be at random within a data set, and the program offers certain combination of free and fixed formats. Interactive graphics capabilities enable convenient display of nodal deformations, mode shapes, and element stresses.

1368. Myers, L. P.; and Burcham, F. W., Jr.: **Propulsion Control Experience Used in the Highly Integrated Digital Electronic Control (HIDEC) Program.** NASA TM-85914, H-1267, NAS 1.15:85914. Presented at the SAE Aerospace Congress and Exposition, Long Beach, California, October 15–18, 1984, 84N33415, #.

The highly integrated digital electronic control (HIDEC) program will integrate the propulsion and flight control systems on an F-15 airplane at NASA Ames Research Center's Dryden Flight Research Facility. Ames-Dryden has conducted several propulsion control programs that have contributed to the HIDEC program. The digital electronic engine control (DEEC) flight evaluation investigated the performance and operability of the F100 engine equipped with a full-authority digital electronic control system. Investigations of nozzle instability, fault detection and accommodation, and augmentor transient capability provided important information for the HIDEC program. The F100 engine model derivative (EMD) was also flown in the F-15 airplane, and airplane performance was significantly improved. A throttle response problem was found and solved with a software fix to the control logic. For the HIDEC program, the F100 EMD engines equipped with DEEC controls will be integrated with the digital flight control system. The control modes to be implemented are an integrated flightpath management mode and an integrated adaptive engine control system mode. The engine control experience that will be used in the HIDEC program is discussed.

1369. Cazier, F. W., Jr.; and Kehoe, M. W.: **Ground Vibration Test of F-16 Airplane With Initial Decoupler Pylon.** NASA TM-86259, L-15782, NAS 1.15:86259, October 1984, 84N34439, #.

A ground vibration test was conducted on an F-16 airplane loaded on each wing with a 370-gal tank mounted on a standard pylon, a GBU-8 store mounted on a decoupler pylon, and an AIM-9J missile mounted on a wing-tip launcher. The decoupler pylon is a passive wing/store flutter-suppression device. The test was conducted prior to initial flight tests to determine the modal frequencies, mode shapes, and structural damping coefficients. The data presented include frequency response plots, force effect plots, and limited mode shape data.

1370. Sim, A. G.; and Curry, R. E.: **Flight-Determined Aerodynamic Derivatives of the AD-1 Oblique-Wing Research Airplane.** NASA TP-2222, H-1179, NAS 1.60:2222, October 1984, 87N10871.

The AD-1 is a variable-sweep oblique-wing research airplane that exhibits unconventional stability and control characteristics. In this report, flight-determined and predicted stability and control derivatives for the AD-1 airplane are compared. The predictions are based on both wind tunnel and computational results. A final best estimate of derivatives is presented.

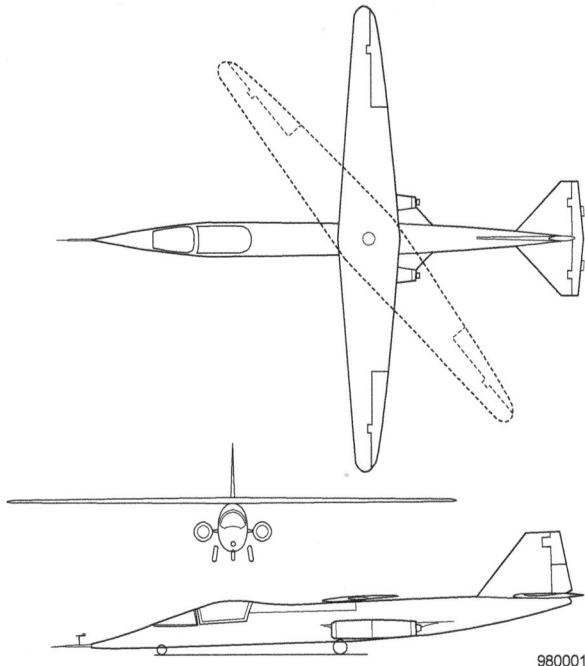

AD-1 Airplane, Three-View Drawing

1371. Curry, R. E.; and Sim, A. G.: **In-Flight Total Forces, Moments and Static Aeroelastic Characteristics of an Oblique-Wing Research Airplane.** NASA TP-2224, H-1181, NAS 1.60:2224, October 1984, 87N10103, #.

A low-speed flight investigation has provided total force and moment coefficients and aeroelastic effects for the AD-1 oblique-wing research airplane. The results were interpreted and compared with predictions that were based on wind tunnel data. An assessment has been made of the aeroelastic wing bending design criteria. Lateral-directional trim requirements caused by asymmetry were determined. At angles of attack near stall, flow visualization indicated viscous flow separation and spanwise vortex flow. These effects were also apparent in the force and moment data.

1372. Powers, B. G.: **Active Control Technology Experience With the Space Shuttle in the Landing Regime.** NASA TM-85910, H-1260, NAS 1.15:85910. Presented at the AGARD Flight Mechanics Panel Symposium on Active Control Systems, Toronto, October 15–18, 1984, 85N10071, #. (See also 1394, 1395.)

The shuttle program took on the challenge of providing a manual landing capability for an operational vehicle returning from orbit. Some complex challenges were encountered in developing the longitudinal flying qualities required to land the orbiter manually in an operational environmental. Approach and landing test flights indicated a tendency for pilot-induced oscillation near landing. Changes in the operational procedures reduced the difficulty of the landing task, and an adaptive stick filter was incorporated to reduce the severity of any pilot-induced oscillatory motions. Fixed-base, moving-base, and in-flight simulations were used for the evaluations, and in general, flight simulation was the only reliable means of assessing the low-speed longitudinal flying qualities problems. Overall, the orbiter control system and operational procedures have produced a good capability for routinely performing precise landings in a large, unpowered vehicle with a low lift-to-drag ratio.

1373. Putnam, T. W.: **The X-29 Flight-Research Program.** AIAA Student Journal (ISSN 0001-1452), Vol. 22, Fall 1984, pp. 2–12, 39, 85A13895. (See also 1287, 1298.)

The X-29 experimental aircraft, which is a technology integration and evaluation platform for such features as static longitudinal instability, sweptforward wings and three-surface longitudinal control, offers an opportunity to validate the entire aircraft design process through careful correlation and comparison of flight test results with wind tunnel results and design predictions. Attention is presently given to the design features of the aircraft, which encompass supercritical airfoils, digital flight control, and aeroelastically tailored composite wings, as well as to the flight test program that was formulated to investigate the interactions and relative merits of these design features, in light of data gathered by carefully positioned sensors.

1374. Painter, W. D.; and *Erickson, R. E.: **Rotor Systems Research Aircraft Airplane Configuration Flight-Test Results.** AIAA Paper 84-2465. AIAA, AHS, ASEE Aircraft Design Systems and Operations Meeting, San Diego, California, October 31–November 2, 1984, 85A13551, #. (See also 1366.)

The Rotor Systems Research Aircraft (RSRA) has been undergoing ground and flight tests by Ames Research Center since late 1979, primarily as a compound aircraft. The purpose was to train pilots and to check out and develop the design flight envelope established by the Sikorsky Aircraft Company. This paper reviews the preparation and flight test of the RSRA in the airplane, or fixed-wing, configuration and discusses the results of that test.

*NASA Ames Research Center, Moffett Field, California.

1375. Bowers, A. H.; and Sim, A. G.: **A Comparison of Wortmann Airfoil Computer-Generated Lift and Drag Polars With Flight and Wind Tunnel Results.** NASA TM-86035, H-1231, NAS 1.15:86035, November 1984, 85N12868, #.

Computations of drag polars for a low-speed Wortmann sailplane airfoil are compared with both wind tunnel and flight test results. Excellent correlation was shown to exist between computations and flight results except when separated flow regimes were encountered. Smoothness of the input coordinates to the PROFILE computer program was found to be essential to obtain accurate comparisons of drag polars or transition location to either the flight or wind tunnel flight results.,

1376. Webb, L. D.; Andriyich-Varda, D.; and Whitmore, S. A.: **Flight and Wind-Tunnel Comparisons of the Inlet-Airframe Interaction of the F-15 Airplane.** NASA TP-2374, H-1175, NAS 1.60:2374, November 1984, 85N12884, #.

The design of inlets and nozzles and their interactions with the airplane which may account for a large percentage of the total drag of modern high performance aircraft is discussed. The inlet/airframe interactions program and the flight tests conducted is described. Inlet drag and lift data from a 7.5% wind-tunnel model are compared with data from an F-15 airplane with instrumentation to match the model. Pressure coefficient variations with variable cowl angles, capture ratios, examples of flow interactions and angles of attack are for Mach numbers of 0.6, 0.9, 1.2, and 1.5 are presented.

1377. Gupta, K. K.: **Development of a Solid Hexahedron Finite Dynamic Element.** *International Journal for Numerical Methods in Engineering*, (ISSN 0029-5981), Vol. 20, November 1984, pp. 2143–2150, 85A16262.

This paper presents the pertinent details of a newly developed solid rectangular hexahedron finite dynamic element, involving the derivation of the higher order stiffness and inertia dynamic correction matrices. Numerical results of a test case are also presented which indicate that adoption of the dynamic elements significantly improves the solution convergence, when compared with the related performance of the corresponding finite elements.

1378. Abbott, L. W.: **Test Experience on an Ultrareliable Computer Communication Network.** NASA TM-85915, H-1268, NAS 1.15:85915. Presented at the AIAA and IEEE 6th Digital Avionics Conference, Baltimore, December 3–6, 1984, 85N13514, #. (See also 1382.)

The dispersed sensor processing mesh (DSPM) is an experimental, ultra-reliable, fault-tolerant computer communications network that exhibits an organic-like ability

to regenerate itself after suffering damage. The regeneration is accomplished by two routines—grow and repair. This paper discusses the DSPM concept for achieving fault tolerance and provides a brief description of the mechanization of both the experiment and the six-node experimental network. The main topic of this paper is the system performance of the growth algorithm contained in the grow routine. The characteristics imbued to DSPM by the growth algorithm are also discussed. Data from an experimental DSPM network and software simulation of larger DSPM-type networks are used to examine the inherent limitation on growth time by the growth algorithm and the relationship of growth time to network size and topology.

1379. Putnam, T. W.; and *Robinson, M. R.: **Closing the Design Loop on HiMAT (highly maneuverable aircraft technology).** NASA TM-85923, NAS 1.15:85923, (see NA 84-1893). Presented at the 14th Congress of the International Council of the Aeronautical Sciences, Toulouse, France, September 9–14, 1984, December 1984, 85N14836, #.

The design methodology used in the HiMAT program and the wind tunnel development activities are discussed. Selected results from the flight test program are presented and the strengths and weaknesses of testing advanced technology vehicles using the RPV concept is examined. The role of simulation on the development of digital flight control systems and in RPVs in particular is emphasized.

*Rockwell International, Los Angeles, California.

1380. Hallion, R. P.: **On the Frontier: Flight Research at Dryden 1946—1981.** NASA SP-4303, NAS 1.21:4303, (see LC-83-14136), 1984, 85N17934, #.

The history of flight research at the NASA Hugh L. Dryden Flight Research Center is recounted. The period of emerging supersonic flight technology (1944 to 1959) is reviewed along with the era of flight outside the Earth's atmosphere (1959 to 1981). Specific projects such as the X-15, Gemini, Apollo, and the space shuttle are addressed. The flight chronologies of various aircraft and spacecraft are given.

1381. Powers, B. G.: **Space Shuttle Pilot-Induced-Oscillation Research Testing.** AGARD AG-262, Paper 1. *AGARD Ground and Flight Testing for Aircraft Guidance and Control*, (see N85-22350 13-01), (original language document was announced as N84-20566), (ISBN-92-835-1482-3), December 1984, 85N22351, #. (See also 1306.)

The simulation requirements for investigation of pilot-induced-oscillation (PIO) characteristics during the landing phase are discussed. Orbiters simulations and F-8 digital fly-by-wire aircraft tests are addressed.

1382. Abbott, L. W.: **Test Experience on an Ultrareliable Computer Communication Network.** AIAA Paper 84-2649. *Proceedings, Sixth Digital Avionics Systems Conference*, Baltimore, Maryland, December 3–6, 1984, (see A85-17801 06-01), 1984, pp. 233–238, 85A17836, #. (See also 1378.)

The dispersed sensor processing mesh (DSPM) is an experimental, ultrareliable, fault-tolerant computer communications network that exhibits an organic-like ability to regenerate itself after suffering damage. The regeneration is accomplished by two routines - grow and repair. This paper discusses the DSPM concept for achieving fault tolerance and provides a brief description of the mechanization of both the experiment and the six-node experimental network. The main topic of this paper is the system performance of the growth algorithm contained in the grow routine. The characteristics imbued to DSPM by the growth algorithm are also discussed. Data from an experimental DSPM network and software simulation of larger DSPM-type networks are used to examine the inherent limitation on growth time by the growth algorithm and the relationship of growth time to network size and topology.

1985 Technical Publications

1383. Iliff, K. W.; and Maine, R. E.: **More Than You Want to Know About Maximum Likelihood Estimation.** NASA TM-85905, H-1252, NAS 1.15.85905, AIAA Paper 84-2070. Presented at the AIAA Atmospheric Flight Mech. Conference, Seattle, Washington, August 21–23, 1984, January 1985, 85N15752, #. (See also 1356.)

The maximum likelihood estimator has been used to extract stability and control derivatives from flight data for many years. Most of the literature on aircraft estimation concentrates on new developments and applications, assuming familiarity with basic estimation concepts. Some of these basic concepts are presented. The maximum likelihood estimator is briefly discussed and the aircraft equations of motion that the estimator uses. The basic concepts of minimization and estimation are examined for a simple computed aircraft example. The cost functions that are to be minimized during estimation are defined and discussed. Graphic representations of the cost functions are given to help illustrate the minimization process. Finally, the basic concepts are generalized, and estimation from flight data is discussed. Some of the major conclusions for the computed example are also developed for the analysis of flight data.

1384. Burcham, F. W., Jr.; Myers, L. P.; and Ray, R. J.: **Predicted Performance Benefits of an Adaptive Digital Engine Control System of an F-15 Airplane.** NASA TM-85916, H-1269, NAS 1.15:85916, January 1985, 85N15729, #. (See also 1385.)

The highly integrated digital electronic control (HIDEC) program will demonstrate and evaluate the improvements in performance and mission effectiveness that result from integrating engine-airframe control systems. Currently this is accomplished on the NASA Ames Research Center's F-15 airplane. The two control modes used to implement the systems are an integrated flightpath management mode and in integrated adaptive engine control system (ADECS) mode. The ADECS mode is a highly integrated mode in which the airplane flight conditions, the resulting inlet distortion, and the available engine stall margin are continually computed. The excess stall margin is traded for thrust. The predicted increase in engine performance due to the ADECS mode is presented in this report.

1385. Burcham, F. W., Jr.; Myers, L. P.; and Ray, R. J.: **Predicted Performance Benefits of an Adaptive Digital Engine Control System on an F-15 Airplane.** AIAA Paper 85-0255. Presented at the American Institute of Aeronautics and Astronautics, 23rd Aerospace Sciences Meeting, Reno, Nevada, January 14–17, 1985, 85A19801, #. (See also 1384.)

The highly integrated digital electronic control (HIDEC) program will demonstrate and evaluate the improvements in performance and mission effectiveness that result from integrating engine-airframe control systems. Currently this is accomplished on the NASA Ames Research Center's F-15 airplane. The two control modes used to implement the systems are an integrated flightpath management mode and an integrated adaptive engine control system (ADECS) mode. The ADECS mode is a highly integrated mode in which the airplane flight conditions, the resulting inlet distortion, and the available engine stall margin are continually computed. The excess stall margin is traded for thrust. The predicted increase in engine performance due to the ADECS mode is presented in this report.

1386. Powers, B. G.: **Low-Speed Longitudinal Orbiter Qualities.** NASA CP-2342-PT-1. *NASA Johnson Space Center Space Shuttle Technical Conference*, Part 1, (see N85-16889 08-12), January 1985, pp. 143–150, 85N16905, #.

The shuttle program took on the challenge of providing a manual landing capability for an operational vehicle returning from orbit. Some complex challenges were encountered in developing the longitudinal flying qualities required to land the orbiter manually in an operational environment. Approach and landing test flights indicated a tendency for pilot-induced oscillation near landing. Changes in the operational procedures reduced the difficulty of the landing task, and an adaptive stick filter was incorporated to reduce the severity of any pilot-induced oscillatory motions. Fixed-base, moving base, and in-flight simulations were used for the evaluations, and in general, flight simulation was the only reliable means of assessing the low-speed longitudinal flying qualities problems. Overall, the orbiter control system and operational procedures have produced a good capability to routinely perform precise landings with a large, unpowered vehicle with a low lift-to-drag ratio.

1387. Moore, A. L.: **The Western Aeronautical Test Range of NASA Ames Research Center.** AIAA Paper 85-0316. Presented at the American Institute of Aeronautics and Astronautics, 23rd Aerospace Sciences Meeting, Reno, Nevada, January 14–17, 1985, 85A19678, #. (See also 1304.)

An overview of the Western Aeronautical Test Range (WATR) of NASA Ames Research Center (ARC) is presented in this paper. The three WATR facilities are discussed, and three WATR elements—mission control centers, communications systems, real-time processing and display systems, and tracking systems—are reviewed. The relationships within the NASA WATR, with respect to the NASA aeronautics program, are also discussed.

1388. Curry, R. E.; and Bowers, A. H.: **Ground-Effect Analysis of a Jet Transport Airplane.** AIAA Paper 85-0307. Presented at the American Institute of Aeronautics and Astronautics, 23rd Aerospace Sciences Meeting, Reno, Nevada, January 14–17, 1985, 85A19677, #. (See also 1389.)

An analysis of the ground effect of a jet transport airplane has been made. Data were obtained from recent flight tests primarily using the constant angle-of-attack approach technique. Reasonable results were obtained for ground-effect pitching moment and lift increments. These were compared with data from other sources, including computations, wind tunnel, and previous flight tests. A recommended ground-effect model was developed from the results. A brief simulator study was conducted to determine the sensitivity of a particular configuration to this ground-effect model and its associated uncertainty.

1389. Curry, R. E.; and Bowers, A. H.: **Ground-Effect Analysis of a Jet Transport Airplane.** NASA TM-85920, H-1273, NAS 1.15:85920, AIAA Paper 85-0307. Presented at the 23rd AIAA Aerospace Sciences Meeting, Reno, Nevada, January 14–17, 1985, (A85-19677), 85N15687, #. (See also 1388.)

An analysis of the ground effect of a jet transport airplane has been made. Data were obtained from recent flight tests primarily using the constant angle-of-attack approach technique. Reasonable results were obtained for ground-effect pitching moment and lift increments. These were compared with data from other sources, including computations, wind tunnel, and previous flight test. A recommended ground-effect model was developed from the results. A brief simulator study was conducted to determine the sensitivity of a particular configuration to this ground-effect model and its associated uncertainty.

1390. Maine, R. E.; Iliff, K. W.; and Bogue, R. K.: **Identification of Dynamic Systems.** AGARD-AG-300-VOL-2, ISBN-92-835-1488-2, AD-A154031, January 1985, 85N25249, #. (See also 1391.)

The problem of estimating parameters of dynamic systems is addressed. The theoretical basis of system identification and parameter estimations is presented in a manner that is complete and rigorous, yet understandable with minimum prerequisites. Emphasis is on maximum likelihood and related knowledge of stochastic processes or functional analysis. No previous background in statistics is assumed. The treatment emphasizes unification of the various areas in estimation theory and practice. For example, the theory of estimation in dynamic systems is treated as a direct outgrowth of the static system theory. Topics covered include: basic concept and definitions, numerical optimization methods; probability; statistical estimators; estimation in static systems; stochastic processes; state estimation in dynamic systems; output error, filter error, and equation error methods of parameter estimation in dynamic systems; and the accuracy of the estimates.

1391. Maine, R. E.; and Iliff, K. W.: **Identification of Dynamic Systems, Theory and Formulation.** NASA RP-1138, H-1255, NAS 1.61:1138, AGARDOGRAPH-300 February 1985, 85N19784, #. (See also 1390.)

The problem of estimating parameters of dynamic systems is addressed in order to present the theoretical basis of system identification and parameter estimation in a manner that is complete and rigorous, yet understandable with minimal prerequisites. Maximum likelihood and related estimators are highlighted. The approach used requires familiarity with calculus, linear algebra, and probability, but does not require knowledge of stochastic processes or functional analysis. The treatment emphasizes unification of the various areas in estimation in dynamic systems is treated as a direct outgrowth of the static system theory. Topics covered include basic concepts and definitions; numerical optimization methods; probability; statistical estimators; estimation in static systems; stochastic processes; state estimation in dynamic systems; output error, filter error, and equation error methods of parameter estimation in dynamic systems, and the accuracy of the estimates.

1392. Sim, Alex G.; and Curry, Robert E.: **Flight Characteristics of the AD-1 Oblique-Wing Research Aircraft.** NASA TP-2223, H-1180, NAS 1.60:2223, March 1985, 87N18570, #.

The AD-1 is a low-speed oblique-wing research airplane. This report reviews the vehicle's basic flight characteristics, including many aerodynamic, stability, and control effects that are unique to an oblique-wing configuration. These effects include the change in sideforce with angle of attack, moment changes with angle of attack and load factor, initial stall on the trailing wing, and inertial coupling caused by a roll-pitch cross product of inertia. An assessment of the handling qualities includes pilot ratings and comments. Ratings were generally satisfactory through 30 deg of wing sweep but degraded with increased sweep. A piloted simulation study indicated that a basic rate feedback control system could be used to improve the handling qualities at higher wing sweeps.

1393. Ko, W. L.: **Impacts of Space Shuttle Thermal Protection System Tile on F-15 Aircraft Vertical Tile.** NASA TM-85904, H-1248, NAS 1.15:85904, March 1985, 85N21245, #.

Impacts of the space shuttle thermal protection system (TPS) tile on the leading edge and the side of the vertical tail of the F-15 aircraft were analyzed under different TPS tile orientations. The TPS tile-breaking tests were conducted to simulate the TPS tile impacts. It was found that the predicted tile impact forces compare fairly well with the tile-breaking forces, and the impact forces exerted on the F-15 aircraft vertical tail were relatively low because a very small fraction of the tile kinetic energy was dissipated in the impact, penetration, and fracture of the tile. It was also found that the oblique impact of the tile on the side of the F-15 aircraft vertical tail was unlikely to dent the tail surface.

1394. Powers, B. G.: **Active Control Technology Experience With the Space Shuttle in the Landing Regime.** AGARD-CP-384, Paper 17. *AGARD Active Control Systems: Review, Evaluation and Projections*, (ISBN-92-835-0375-9), (see N85-27883 17-08), March 1985, AD-A155853, 85N27900, #. (See also 1372, 1395.)

The shuttle program took on the challenge of providing a manual landing capability for an operational vehicle returning from orbit. Some complex challenges were encountered in developing the longitudinal flying qualities required to land the orbiter manually in an operational environment. Approach and landing test flights indicated a tendency for pilot-induced oscillation near landing. Changes in the operational procedures reduced the difficulty of the landing task, and an adaptive stick filter was incorporated to reduce the severity of any pilot-induced oscillatory motions. Fixed-base, moving-base, and in-flight simulations were used for the evaluations, and in general, flight simulation has been the only reliable means of assessing the low-speed longitudinal flying qualities problems. Overall, the orbiter control system and operational procedures have produced a good capability for routinely performing precise landings in a large, unpowered vehicle with a low lift-to-drag ratio.

1395. Powers, B. G.: **Active Control Technology Experience With the Space Shuttle in the Landing Regime.** AGARD-AR-220. *AGARD Tech. Evaluation Report on the Flight Mech. Symposium on Active Control Systems*, Paper 17, (ISBN-92-835-1493-9), (see N85-26730 16-08), March 1985, AD-A154472, 85N26747, #. (See also 1372, 1394.)

An interesting description was provided of the development of the shuttle flight control systems. Of particular concern was a tendency to excite PIO during the landing phase. Both ground based and in-flight simulation were used to study the problem. It was found that in-flight simulation was the only reliable method to use in the study of PIO. Two of the major contributions to the PIO problem were found to be system time delay and the lack of a clear motion cue at the pilot's location following a pitch up command. The PIO problem was solved by reducing the demands of the piloting task and introducing an adaptive stick gain limiter.

1396. Meyer, Robert R., Jr.; and Jennett, Lisa A.: **In-Flight Surface Oil-Flow Photographs With Comparisons to Pressure Distribution and Boundary-Layer Data**, NASA TP-2395, H-1184, NAS 1.60:2395, April 1985, 87N20966, #.

Upper surface oil-flow photographs were obtained at transonic speeds on an F-111 transonic aircraft technology (TACT) aircraft, which had been fitted with a natural laminar-flow airfoil section. The oil-flow photographs were interpreted with regard to shock and boundary-layer characteristics and compared to results obtained from pressure distributions and boundary-layer measurements. Results indicated that flow phenomena (such as shock location and strength) and chord location of boundary-layer characteristics (such as transition location) could be correctly identified from the oil-flow photographs.

1397. Harney, P. F.; Craft, J. B., Jr.; and Johnson, R. G.: **Remote Control of an Impact Demonstration Vehicle.** NASA TM-85925, H-1282, NAS 1.15:85925, Paper-542. Presented at the 31st International Instrumentation Symposium of the Instrument Soc. of Am., San Diego, California, May 6–9, 1985, April 1985, 85N23797, #.

Uplink and downlink telemetry systems were installed in a Boeing 720 aircraft that was remotely flown from Rogers Dry Lake at Edwards Air Force Base and impacted into a designated crash site on the lake bed. The controlled impact demonstration (CID) program was a joint venture by the National Aeronautics and Space Administration (NASA) and the Federal Aviation Administration (FAA) to test passenger survivability using antimisting kerosene (AMK) to inhibit postcrash fires, improve passenger seats and restraints, and improve fire-retardant materials. The uplink telemetry system was used to remotely control the aircraft and activate onboard systems from takeoff until after impact. Aircraft systems for remote control, aircraft structural response, passenger seat and restraint systems, and anthropomorphic dummy responses were recorded and displayed by the downlink stems. The instrumentation uplink and downlink systems are described.

B-720 Controlled Impact Demonstrator

1398. Iliff, K W.; and Maine, R. E.: **Maximum Likelihood Estimation With Emphasis on Aircraft Flight Data.** *JPL Proc. of the Workshop on Identification and Control of Flexible Space Struct.*, Vol. 3, (see N85-31195 20-18), April 1985, pp. 197–246, 85N31208, #.

Accurate modeling of flexible space structures is an important field that is currently under investigation. Parameter estimation, using methods such as maximum likelihood, is one of the ways that the model can be improved. The maximum likelihood estimator has been used to extract stability and control derivatives from flight data for many years. Most of the literature on aircraft estimation concentrates on new developments and applications, assuming familiarity with basic estimation concepts. Some of these basic concepts are presented. The maximum likelihood estimator and the aircraft equations of motion that the estimator uses are briefly discussed. The basic concepts of minimization and estimation are examined for a simple computed aircraft example. The cost functions that are to be minimized during estimation are defined and discussed. Graphic representations of the cost functions are given to help illustrate the minimization process. Finally, the basic concepts are generalized, and estimation from flight data is discussed. Specific examples of estimation of structural dynamics are included. Some of the major conclusions for the computed example are also developed for the analysis of flight data.

1399. *Berkhout, J.; *Osgood, R.; and Berry, D.: **Pilot Usage of Decoupled Flight Path and Pitch Controls.** *Proceedings, 3rd Annual Symposium on Aviation Psychology*, Columbus, Ohio, April 22–25, 1985, (see A86-29851 13-53), 1985, pp. 39–46, 86A29854, #.

Data from decoupled flight maneuvers have been collected and analyzed for four AFTI-F-16 pilots operating this aircraft's highly augmented fly-by-wire control system, in order to obtain spectral density, cross spectra, and Bode amplitude data, as well as coherences and phase angles for the two longitudinal axis control functions of each of 50 20-sec epochs. The analysis of each epoch yielded five distinct plotted parameters for the left hand twist grip and right hand sidestick controller output time series. These two control devices allow the left hand to generate vertical translation, direct lift, or pitch-pointing commands that are decoupled from those of the right hand. Attention is given to the control patterns obtained for decoupled normal flight, air-to-air gun engagement decoupled maneuvering, and decoupled air-to-surface bombing run maneuvering.

*South Dakota University, Vermillion, South Dakota.

1400. Iliff, K. W.: **Extraction of Aerodynamic Parameters for Aircraft at Extreme Flight Conditions.** NASA TM-86730, H-1290, NAS 1.15:86730, NASA CP-386. Presented at the AGARD Symposium on Unsteady Aerodyn. Fundamentals and Appl. to Aircraft Dyn., Goettingen, West Germany, May 6–9, 1985, 85N29686, #. (See also 1439.)

The maximum likelihood estimator has been used to extract stability and control derivatives from flight data for many years. Most of the literature on aircraft estimation concentrates on new developments and applications, assuming familiarity with basic concepts. This paper briefly discusses the maximum likelihood estimator and the aircraft equations of motion that the estimator uses. The current strength and limitations associated with obtaining flight-determined aerodynamic coefficients in extreme flight conditions is assessed. The importance of the careful combining of wind tunnel results (or calculations) and flight results and the thorough evaluation of the mathematical model is emphasized. The basic concepts of minimization and estimation are examined for a simple computed aircraft example, and the cost functions that are to be minimized during estimation are defined and discussed. Graphic representations of the cost functions are given to help illustrate the minimization process. Finally, the basic concepts are generalized, and estimation of stability and control derivatives from flight data is discussed.

1401. Whitmore, S. A.: **Formulation and Implementation of Nonstationary Adaptive Estimation Algorithm With Applications to Air-Data Reconstruction.** NASA TM-86727, H-1285, NAS 1.15:86727. Presented at the IEEE

Natl. Aerospace and Electron. Conference, Dayton, Ohio, May 20–24, 1985, 85N26699, #. (See also 1402.)

The dynamics model and data sources used to perform air-data reconstruction are discussed, as well as the Kalman filter. The need for adaptive determination of the noise statistics of the process is indicated. The filter innovations are presented as a means of developing the adaptive criterion, which is based on the true mean and covariance of the filter innovations. A method for the numerical approximation of the mean and covariance of the filter innovations is presented. The algorithm as developed is applied to air-data reconstruction for the space shuttle, and data obtained from the third landing are presented. To verify the performance of the adaptive algorithm, the reconstruction is also performed using a constant covariance Kalman filter. The results of the reconstructions are compared, and the adaptive algorithm exhibits better performance.

1402. Whitmore, S. A.: **Formulation and Implementation of Nonstationary Adaptive Estimation Algorithm With Applications to Air-Data Reconstruction.** *NAECON 1985: Proceedings, National Aerospace and Electronics Conference*, Vol. 1, Dayton, Ohio, May 20–24, 1985, 1985, pp. 291–298, (A86-28326 12-04) 86A28365, #. (See also 1401.)

The dynamics model and data sources used to perform air-data reconstruction are discussed, as well as the Kalman filter. The need for adaptive determination of the noise statistics of the process is indicated. The filter innovations are presented as a means of developing the adaptive criterion, which is based on the true mean and covariance of the filter innovations. A method for the numerical approximation of the mean and covariance of the filter innovations is presented. The algorithm as developed is applied to air-data reconstruction for the Space Shuttle, and data obtained from the third landing are presented. To verify the performance of the adaptive algorithm, the reconstruction is also performed using a constant covariance Kalman filter. The results of the reconstructions are compared, and the adaptive algorithm exhibits better performance.

1403. Larson, T. J.; and Ehernberger, L. J.: **A Constant Altitude Flight Survey Method for Mapping Atmospheric Ambient Pressures and Systematic Radar Errors.** *NAECON 1985: Proceedings of the National Aerospace and Electronics Conference*, Dayton, Ohio, May 20–24, 1985, Vol. 2, (see A86-28326 12-04), 1985, pp. 1519–1526, 86A28507, #. (See also 1404.)

The flight test technique described uses controlled survey runs to determine horizontal atmospheric pressure variations and systematic altitude errors that result from space positioning measurements. The survey data can be used not

only for improved air data calibrations, but also for studies of atmospheric structure and space positioning accuracy performance. The examples presented cover a wide range of radar tracking conditions for both subsonic and supersonic flight to an altitude of 42,000 ft.

1404. Larson, T. J.; and Ehernberger, L. J.: **A Constant Altitude Flight Survey Method for Mapping Atmospheric Ambient Pressures and Systematic Radar Errors.** NASA TM-86733, H-1304, NAS 1.15:86733. Presented at the IEEE National Aerospace and Electronics Conference, Dayton, Ohio, May 20–24, 1985, June 1985, 85N29951, #. (See also 1403.)

The flight test technique described uses controlled survey runs to determine horizontal atmospheric pressure variations and systematic altitude errors that result from space positioning measurements. The survey data can be used not only for improved air data calibrations, but also for studies of atmospheric structure and space positioning accuracy performance. The examples presented cover a wide range of radar tracking conditions for both subsonic and supersonic flight to an altitude of 42,000 ft.

1405. *Menon, P. K. A.; *Saberi, H. A.; *Walker, R. A.; and Duke, E. L.: **Flight Test Trajectory Controller Synthesis With Constrained Eigenstructure Assignment.** *1985 American Control Conference Proceedings*, Vol. 3, Boston, Massachusetts, June 19–21, 1985, (see A86-35326 15-63), IEEE, New York, New York, 1985, pp. 1181–1186, 86A35404. (See also 1551.)

The design of a maneuver eigenvalue/eigenvector assignment is examined. The aircraft considered was a high-performance fighter with a command augmentation system engaged in all three axes. Attention is given to difficulties encountered in the generation of the desired eigenvalues and eigenvectors. It is found that this approach demands several iterations to converge to a satisfactory result, and does not appear to easily yield suitable insight for the output feedback design of high-order multivariable systems which will be used at other operating points. It is concluded that this technique could be made more attractive by generating gradients of the eigensystem between flight conditions, and including this information in the single-point design technique.

*Integrated Systems, Inc., Palo Alto, California.

1406. Myers, L. P.; Baer-Riedhart, J. L.; and *Maxwell, M. D.: **Fault Detection and Accommodation Testing on an F100 Engine in an F-15 Airplane.** NASA TM-86735, H-1293, NAS 1.15:86735, Paper 85-1294. Presented at the AIAA, SAE, ASME, and ASEG 21st Joint Propulsion Conference, Monterey, California, July 8–10, 1985, 85N29962, #. (See also 1407.)

The fault detection and accommodation (FDA) methodology for digital engine-control systems may range from simple comparisons of redundant parameters to the more complex and sophisticated observer models of the entire engine system. Evaluations of the various FDA schemes are done using analytical methods, simulation, and limited-altitude-facility testing. Flight testing of the FDA logic has been minimal because of the difficulty of inducing realistic faults in flight. A flight program was conducted to evaluate the fault detection and accommodation capability of a digital electronic engine control in an F-15 aircraft. The objective of the flight program was to induce selected faults and evaluate the resulting actions of the digital engine controller. Comparisons were made between the flight results and predictions. Several anomalies were found in flight and during the ground test. Simulation results showed that the inducement of dual pressure failures was not feasible since the FDA logic was not designed to accommodate these types of failures.

*Pratt and Whitney Aircraft, West Palm Beach, Florida.

1407. Myers, L. P.; Baer-Riedhart, J. L.; and *Maxwell, M. D.: **Fault Detection and Accommodation Testing on an F100 Engine in an F-15 Airplane.** AIAA Paper 85-1294 AIAA, SAE, ASME, and ASEE, 21st Joint Propulsion Conference, Monterey, California, <u>July 8-10, 1985</u>, 85A40830, #. (See also 1406.)

The fault detection and accommodation (FDA) methods that can be used for digital engine control systems are presently subjected to a flight test program in the case of the F-15 fighter's F100 engine electronic controls, inducing selected faults and then evaluating the resulting digital engine control responses. In general, flight test results were found to compare well with both ground tests and predictions. It is noted that the inducement of dual-pressure failures was not feasible, since FDA logic was not designed to accommodate them.

*United Technologies Corporation, Pratt and Whitney Aircraft Group, West Palm Beach, Florida.

1408. *Yonke, W. A.; **Terrell, L. A.; and Meyers, L. P.: **Integrated Flight/Propulsion Control—Adaptive Engine Control System Mode.** AIAA Paper 85-1425 AIAA, SAE, ASME, and ASEE, 21st Joint Propulsion Conference, Monterey, California, <u>July 8-10, 1985</u>, 85A39772, #.

The adaptive engine control system mode (ADECS), which is developed and tested on an F-15 aircraft with PW1128 engines using the NASA sponsored highly integrated digital electronic control program, is examined. The operation of the ADECS mode, as well as the basic control logic, the avionic architecture, and the airframe/engine interface are described. By increasing engine pressure ratio (EPR) additional thrust is

obtained at intermediate power and above. To modulate the amount of EPR uptrim and to prevent engine stall, information from the flight control system is used. The performance benefits, anticipated from control integration are shown for a range of flight conditions and power settings. It is found that at higher altitudes, the ADECS mode can increase thrust as much as 12 percent, which is used for improved acceleration, improved turn rate, or sustained turn angle.

*McDonnell Aircraft Co., St. Louis, Missouri.
**United Technologies Corporation, Pratt and Whitney Group, West Palm Beach, Florida.

1409. Felt, L. R.; and Kehoe, M. W.: **Flight Flutter Testing at Ames-Dryden.** Proceedings, Society of Flight Test Engineers 16th Annual Symposium, Seattle, Washington, July 29–August 2, 1985, (see A86-47776 23-05), <u>1985</u>, pp. 6.6-1 to 6.6-36, 86A47802.

Over the past several years the NASA Ames-Dryden Flight Research Facility at Edwards Air Force Base has developed a variety of flight flutter and ground test techniques which have been applied to an assortment of new or modified aerospace research vehicles. This paper presents a summary of these techniques and the experiences gained from these applications. Topics discussed include the roles of ground vibration testing, flight flutter testing, wind tunnel flutter model testing, predictive analyses, and aeroservoelastic considerations. Data are presented for a wide variety of aircraft, including remotely piloted vehicles, modern fighters with relaxed static stability and highly augmented flight control systems, aircraft modified for laminar flow control experiments, a glider modified for deep stall tests, and aircraft with skewed or forward swept wings. The conclusions include a brief discussion of future directions in flight flutter testing at Ames-Dryden.

1410. Kempel, R. W.; and Horton, T. W.: **Flight Test Experience and Controlled Impact of a Large, Four-Engine Remotely Piloted Airplane.** Proceedings, Society of Flight Test Engineers 16th Annual Symposium, Seattle, Washington, July 29–August 2, 1985, (see A86-47776 23-05), <u>1985</u>, pp. 2.1-1 to 2.1-14, 86A47781. (See also 1421.)

A controlled impact demonstration (CID) program using a large, four engine, remotely piloted transport airplane was conducted. Closed loop primary flight control was performed from a ground based cockpit and digital computer in conjunction with an up/down telemetry link. Uplink commands were received aboard the airplane and transferred through uplink interface systems to a highly modified Bendix PB-20D autopilot. Both proportional and discrete commands were generated by the ground pilot. Prior to flight tests, extensive simulation was conducted during the development of ground based digital control laws. The control laws included primary control, secondary control, and racetrack and final approach guidance. Extensive ground checks were performed on all remotely piloted systems. However, manned flight tests were the primary method of verification and validation of control law concepts developed from simulation. The design development, and flight testing of control laws and the systems required to accomplish the remotely piloted mission are discussed.

1411. *Gupta, N. K.; and Iliff, K. W.: **Identification of Unsteady Aerodynamics and Aeroelastic Integro-Differential Systems.** NASA TM-86749, H-1313, NAS 1.15:86749, <u>August 1985</u>, 85N32851, #.

The problem of estimating integro-differential models based on test or simulation data is dealt with. The identification techniques proposed for estimating parameters in models described by differential equations need to be considerably extended to deal with the integral terms. Conditions under which the integral terms may be approximated by algebraic values are discussed. The integro-differential models discussed are related to indicial models proposed by aerodynamicists to describe unsteady flow.

*Integrated Systems, Inc., Palo Alto, California.

1412. *Gupta, N. K.; and Iliff, K. W.: **Identification of Integro-Differential Systems for Application to Unsteady Aerodynamics and Aeroelasticity.** AIAA Paper 85-1763. *Technical Papers, 12th Atmospheric Flight Mechanics Conference,* Snowmass, Colorado, August 19–21, 1985, (see A85-43826 21-08), <u>1985</u>, pp. 10–21, 85A43828, #.

Integro-differential equations for unsteady aerodynamic and aeroelastic phenomena are identified by means of several approaches. When the product of the frequency of motion and maximum time delay is much smaller than unity, the integral term can be approximated by a constant; when greater than unity, however, approximation of the integral is not possible. Approximations of integro-differential models are needed to obtain identifiability. While the least-squares method may be used for model determination, the maximum likelihood technique is needed for accurate parameter estimation. High angle of attack and post stall/spin regions appear to have characteristics that can be satisfied by indicial models.

*Integrated Systems, Inc., Palo Alto, California.

1413. Regenie, V. A.; and Duke, E. L.: **Design of an Expert-System Flight Status Monitor.** NASA TM-86739, H-1300, NAS 1.15:86739, AIAA Paper 85-1980. AIAA Guidance and Control Conference, Snowmass, Colorado, August 19–21, 1985, <u>August 1985</u>, (see A85-45975), 85N32794, #. (See also 1414.)

The modern advanced avionics in new high-performance aircraft strains the capability of current technology to safely monitor these systems for flight test prior to their generalized use. New techniques are needed to improve the ability of systems engineers to understand and analyze complex systems in the limited time available during crucial periods of the flight test. The Dryden Flight Research Facility of NASA's Ames Research Center is involved in the design and implementation of an expert system to provide expertise and knowledge to aid the flight systems engineer. The need for new techniques in monitoring flight systems and the conceptual design of an expert-system flight status monitor is discussed. The status of the current project and its goals are described.

1414. Regenie, V. A.; and Duke, E. L.: **Design of an Expert-System Flight Status Monitor.** AIAA Paper 85-1908. AIAA Guidance, Navigation and Control Conference, Snowmass, Colorado, <u>August 19–21, 1985</u>, 85A45975, #. (See also 1413.)

The present technology used to monitor systems in flight tests is not advanced enough for the modern avionics in high performance aircraft. Research is being conducted at NASA's Dryden Flight Research Facility to design an expert system to monitor test flights. The expert system is to automatically detect any problems in the flight control system (FCS), interpret the problem from the information contained in its knowledge base, inform the systems engineer, and recommend solutions. The data is to be downlinked from the aircraft to the control room. The expert system will lessen the responsibilities of the engineers by providing them with fast, expert advice. Time is the most critical factor in flight testing and the expert system will be able to quickly recognize discrepancies and provide corrections. A demonstration of the expert system, not operating in real time, has already been tested.

1415. Duke, E. L.; and Antoniewicz, R. F.: **Development and Validation of a General Purpose Linearization Program for Rigid Aircraft Models.** NASA TM-86737, H-1295, NAS 1.15:86737, AIAA Paper 85-1891. Presented at the AIAA Guidance, Navigation, and Control Conference, Snowmass, Colorado, August 19–21, 1985, <u>August 1985</u>, 85N32122, #. (See also 1416.)

A FORTRAN program that provides the user with a powerful and flexible tool for the linearization of aircraft models is discussed. The program LINEAR numerically determines a linear systems model using nonlinear equations of motion and a user-supplied, nonlinear aerodynamic model. The system model determined by LINEAR consists of matrices for both the state and observation equations. The program has been designed to allow easy selection and definition of the state, control, and observation variables to be used in a particular model. Also, included in the report is a comparison of linear and nonlinear models for a high performance aircraft.

1416. Duke, E. L.; and Antoniewicz, R. F.: **Development and Validation of a General Purpose Linearization Program for Rigid Aircraft Models.** AIAA Paper 85-1891. Presented at the AIAA Guidance, Navigation and Control Conference, Snowmass, Colorado, <u>August 19–21, 1985</u>, 85A45976, #. (See also 1415.)

This paper discusses a FORTRAN program that provides the user with a powerful and flexible tool for the linearization of aircraft models. The program LINEAR numerically determines a linear systems model using nonlinear equations of motion and a user-supplied, nonlinear aerodynamic model. The system model determined by LINEAR consists of matrices for both the state and observation equations. The program has been designed to allow easy selection and definition of the state, control, and observation variables to be used in a particular model. Also, included in the report is a comparison of linear and nonlinear models for a high-performance aircraft.

1417. Putnam, T. W.; Burcham, F. W., Jr.; *Andries, M. G.; and *Kelly, J. B.: **Performance Improvements of a Highly Integrated Digital Electronic Control System for an F-15 Airplane.** NASA TM-86748, H-1312, NAS 1.15:86748, AIAA Paper 85-1876. Presented at the AIAA Guidance and Control Conference, Snowmass, Colorado, <u>August 19–21, 1985</u>, 85N32120, #.

The NASA highly integrated digital electronic control (HIDEC) program is structured to conduct flight research into the benefits of integrating an aircraft flight control system with the engine control system. A brief description of the HIDEC system installed on an F-15 aircraft is provided. The adaptive engine control system (ADECS) mode is described in detail, together with simulation results and analyses that show the significant excess thrust improvements achievable with the ADECS mode. It was found that this increased thrust capability is accompanied by reduced fan stall margin and can be realized during flight conditions where engine face distortion is low. The results of analyses and simulations also show that engine thrust response is improved and that fuel consumption can be reduced. Although the performance benefits that accrue because of airframe and engine control integration are being demonstrated on an F-15 aircraft, the principles are applicable to advanced aircraft such as the advanced tactical fighter and advanced tactical aircraft.

*Pratt and Whitney Aircraft, West Palm Beach, Florida.

1418. Chiles, H. R.; and Johnson, J. B.: **Development of a Temperature-Compensated Hot-Film Anemometer System for Boundary-Layer Transition Detection on**

High-Performance Aircraft. NASA TM-86732, H-1292, NAS 1.15:86732. Presented at ICIASF '85—Eleventh International Congress on Instrumentation in Aerospace Simulation Facilities, Stanford, California, August 26–28, 1985, <u>August 1985</u>, pp. 86–91, 85N33121, #. (See also 1419.)

A hot-film constant-temperature anemometer (CTA) system was flight-tested and evaluated as a candidate sensor for determining boundary-layer transition on high-performance aircraft. The hot-film gage withstood an extreme flow environment characterized by shock waves and high dynamic pressures, although sensitivity to the local total temperature with the CTA indicated the need for some form of temperature compensation. A temperature-compensation scheme was developed and two CTAs were modified and flight-tested on the F-104/Flight Test Fixture (FTF) facility at a variety of Mach numbers and altitudes, ranging from 0.4 to 1.8 and 5,000 to 40,000 ft respectively.

1419. Chiles, H. R.; and Johnson, J. B.: **Development of a Temperature-Compensated Hot-Film Anemometer System for Boundary-Layer Transition Detection on High-Performance Aircraft.** *ICIASF' 85—Eleventh International Congress on Instrumentation in Aerospace Simulation Facilities*, Stanford, California, <u>August 26–28, 1985</u>, pp. 86–91, 86A38236, #. (See also 1418.)

A hot-film constant-temperature anemometer (CTA) system was flight-tested and evaluated as a candidate sensor for determining boundary-layer transition on high-performance aircraft. The hot-film gage withstood an extreme flow environment characterized by shock waves and high dynamic pressures, although sensitivity to the local total temperature with the CTA indicated the need for some form of temperature compensation. A temperature-compensation scheme was developed and two CTAs were modified and flight-tested on the F-104/Flight Test Fixture (FTF) facility at a variety of Mach numbers and altitudes, ranging from 0.4 to 1.8 and 5,000 to 40,000 ft respectively.

1420. Kehoe, M. W.; and Ellison, J. F.: **Flutter Clearance of the Schweizer 1-36 Deep-Stall Sailplane.** NASA TM-85917, REPT-85136, NAS 1.15:85917, <u>August 1985</u>, 85N33118, #.

A Schweizer 1-36 sailplane was modified for a controlled, deep-stall flight program. This modification allowed the horizontal stabilizer to pivot as much as 70 deg leading edge down. Ground vibration and flutter testing were accomplished on the sailplane with the horizontal stabilizer in the normal flight and deep-stall flight positions. Test results indicated satisfactory damping levels and trends for the structural modes of the sailplane. The modified sailplane was demonstrated to be free of aeroelastic instabilities to 83 KEAS with the horizontal stabilizer in the normal flight position and to 39 KEAS with the horizontal stabilizer in the deep-stall flight position. This flight envelope was adequate for the controlled, deep-stall flight experiments.

ECN-26847

Schweizer 1-36 Sailplane

ECN-31808

B-720 Controlled Impact Demonstrator

1421. Kempel, R. W.; and Horton, T. W.: **Flight Test Experience and Controlled Impact of a Large, Four-Engine, Remotely Piloted Airplane.** NASA TM-86738, H-1298, NAS 1.15:86738. Presented at the SFTE 16th Annual Symposium, Seattle, Washington, July 29–August 2, 1985, August 1985, 85N33123, #. (See also 1410.)

A controlled impact demonstration (CID) program using a large, four engine, remotely piloted transport airplane was conducted. Closed loop primary flight control was performed from a ground based cockpit and digital computer in conjunction with an up/down telemetry link. Uplink commands were received aboard the airplane and transferred through uplink interface systems to a highly modified Bendix PB-20D autopilot. Both proportional and discrete commands were generated by the ground pilot. Prior to flight tests, extensive simulation was conducted during the development of ground based digital control laws. The control laws included primary control, secondary control, and racetrack and final approach guidance. Extensive ground checks were performed on all remotely piloted systems. However, manned flight tests were the primary method of verification and validation of control law concepts developed from simulation. The design, development, and flight testing of control laws and the systems required to accomplish the remotely piloted mission are discussed.

1422. Mackall, D. A.: **Qualification Needs for Advanced Integrated Aircraft.** NASA TM-86731, H-1291, NAS 1.15:86731. AIAA Conference, Snowmass, Colorado, August 19–21, 1985, 1985, 85N33119, #. (See also 1423.)

In an effort to achieve maximum aircraft performance, designers are integrating aircraft systems. The characteristics of aerodynamics, vehicle structure, and propulsion systems are being integrated and controlled through embedded, often flight critical, electronic systems. The qualification needs for such highly integrated aircraft systems are addressed. Based on flight experience with research aircraft, a set of test capabilities is described which allows for complete and efficient qualification of advanced integrated aircraft.

1423. Mackall, D. A.: **Qualification Needs for Advanced Integrated Aircraft.** AIAA Paper 85-1865. *Technical Papers,* presented at the Guidance, Navigation and Control Conference, Snowmass, Colorado, August 19–21, 1985, (see A85-45876 22-08), 1985, pp. 152–164, 85A45894, #. (See also 1422.)

In an effort to achieve maximum aircraft performance, designers are integrating aircraft systems. The characteristics of aerodynamics, vehicle structure, and propulsion systems are being integrated and controlled through embedded, often flight-critical, electronic systems. This paper addresses the qualification needs for such highly integrated aircraft systems. Based on flight experience with research aircraft, a set of test capabilities is described which allows for complete and efficient qualification of advanced integrated aircraft.

1424. Sarrafian, S. K.; and Powers, B. G.: **Application of Frequency Domain Handling Qualities Criteria to the Longitudinal Landing Task.** NASA TM-86728, H-1288, NAS 1.15:86728, AIAA Paper 85-1848. Presented at the AIAA Guidance, Navigation, and Control Conference, Snowmass, Colorado, August 19–21, 1985, August 1985, 85N33124, #. (See also 1425, 1658.)

Under NASA sponsorship, an in-flight simulation of the longitudinal handling qualities of several configurations for the approach and landing tasks was performed on the USAF/AFWAL Total In-Flight Simulator by the Calspan Corporation. The basic configuration was a generic transport airplane with static instability. The control laws included proportional plus integral gain loops to produce pitch-rate and angle-of-attack feedback loops. The evaluation task was a conventional visual approach to a flared touchdown at a designated spot on the runway with a lateral offset. The general conclusions were that the existing criteria are based on pitch-attitude response and that these characteristics do not adequately discriminate between the good and bad configurations of this study. This paper describes the work that has been done to further develop frequency-based criteria in an effort to provide better correlation with the observed data.

1425. Sarrafian, S. K.; and Powers, B. G.: **Application of Frequency Domain Handling Qualities Criteria to the Longitudinal Landing Task.** AIAA Paper 85-1848. *Technical Papers,* presented at the Guidance, Navigation and Control Conference, Snowmass, Colorado, August 19–21, 1985, (see A85-45876 22-08), pp. 1–12, 85A45877, #. (See also 1424, 1658.)

Three frequency-domain handling qualities criteria have been applied to the observed data to correlate the actual pilot ratings assigned to generic transport configurations with stability augmentation during the longitudinal landing task. The criteria are based on closed-loop techniques using pitch attitude, altitude rate at the pilot station, and altitude at the pilot station as dominating control parameters during this task. It is found that most promising results are obtained with altitude control performed by closing an inner loop on pitch attitude and closing an outer loop on altitude.

1426. *Alag, G. S.; and Duke, E. L.: **Development of Control Laws for a Flight Test Maneuver Autopilot for an F-15 Aircraft.** NASA TM-86736, H-1294, NAS 1.15:86736. Presented at the AIAA Guidance Navigation and Control Conference, Snowmass, Colorado, August 19–21, 1985, August 1985, 85N33122, #. (See also 1427, 1515.)

An autopilot can be used to provide precise control to meet the demanding requirements of flight research maneuvers with high-performance aircraft. The development of control laws within the context of flight test maneuver requirements is discussed. The control laws are developed using eigensystem assignment and command generator tracking.

The eigenvalues and eigenvectors are chosen to provide the necessary handling qualities, while the command generator tracking enables the tracking of a specified state during the maneuver. The effectiveness of the control laws is illustrated by their application to an F-15 aircraft to ensure acceptable aircraft performance during a maneuver.

*Western Michigan University, Kalamazoo, Michigan.

1427. *Alag, G. S.; and Duke, E. L.: **Development of Control Laws for a Flight Test Maneuver Autopilot for an F-15 Aircraft.** AIAA. Paper 85-1859. *Technical Papers,* presented at the Guidance, Navigation and Control Conference, Snowmass, Colorado, August 19–21, 1985, (see A85-45876 22-08), pp. 105–110, 85A45888, #. (See also 1426, 1515.)

An autopilot can be used to provide precise control to meet the demanding requirements of flight research maneuvers with high-performance aircraft. This paper presents the development of control laws within the context of flight test maneuver requirements. The control laws are developed using eigensystem assignment and command generator tracking. The eigenvalues and eigenvectors are chosen to provide the necessary handling qualities, while the command generator tracking enables the tracking of a specified state during the maneuver. The effectiveness of the control laws is illustrated by their application to an F-15 aircraft to ensure acceptable aircraft performance during a maneuver.

*Western Michigan University, Kalamazoo, Michigan.

1428. Berry, D. T.: **In-Flight Evaluation of Pure Time Delays in Pitch and Roll.** AIAA Paper 85-1852. *Technical Papers,* presented at the Guidance, Navigation and Control Conference, Snowmass, Colorado, August 19–21, 1985, (see A85-45876 22-08), pp. 39–46, 85A45881, #. (See also 1527.)

An in-flight investigation of the effect of pure time delays in pitch and roll was undertaken. The evaluation tasks consisted of low lift-to-drag-ratio landings of various levels of difficulty and formation flying. The results indicate that the effect of time delay is strongly dependent on the task. In the pitch axis, in calm air, spot landings from a lateral offset were most strongly influenced by time delay. In the roll axis, in calm air, formation flying was most strongly influenced by time delay. However, when landings were made in turbulence, flying qualities in pitch were only slightly degraded, whereas in roll they were severely degraded.

1429. *Abernethy, Robert B.; **Adams, Gary R.; †Steurer, John W.; ††Ascough, John C.; Baer-Riedhart, Jennifer L.; ‡Balkcom, George H.; and ‡‡Biesiadny, Thomas: **Uncertainty of In-Flight Thrust Determination.** SAE-AIR-1678. *In-Flight Thrust Determination and Uncertainty,* Society of Automotive Engineers, Inc., 1986, (A88-15226 04-05), November 1985, pp. 243–338, 88A15228.

Methods for estimating the measurement error or uncertainty of in-flight thrust determination in aircraft employing conventional turbofan/turbojet engines are reviewed. While the term in-flight thrust determination is used synonymously with in-flight thrust measurement, in-flight thrust is not directly measured but is determined or calculated using mathematical modeling relationships between in-flight thrust and various direct measurements of physical quantities. The in-flight thrust determination process incorporates both ground testing and flight testing. The present text is divided into the following categories: measurement uncertainty methodology and in-flight thrust measurement processes.

*Pratt and Whitney, East Hartford, Connecticut.
**USAF Wright-Patterson AFB, Ohio.
†McDonnell Douglas Co., St. Louis, Missouri.
††Royal Aircraft Establishment, Farnborough, England.
‡General Dynamics Corporation, St. Louis, Missouri.
‡‡NASA Lewis Research Center, Cleveland, Ohio.

1430. Jenkins, J. M.; *Taylor, A. H.; and **Sakata, I. F.: **A Comparison of Measured and Calculated Thermal Stresses in a Hybrid Metal Matrix Composite Spar Cap Element.** NASA TM-86729, H-1289, NAS 1.15:86729, September 1985, 86N11525, #.

A hybrid spar of titanium with an integrally brazed composite, consisting of an aluminum matrix reinforced with boron-carbide-coated fibers, was heated in an oven and the resulting thermal stresses were measured. Uniform heating of the spar in an oven resulted in thermal stresses arising from the effects of dissimilar materials and anisotropy of the metal matrix composite. Thermal stresses were calculated from a finite element structural model using anisotropic material properties deduced from constituent properties and rules of mixtures. Comparisons of calculated thermal stresses with measured thermal stresses on the spar are presented. It was shown that failure to account for anisotropy in the metal matrix composite elements would result in large errors in correlating measured and calculated thermal stresses. It was concluded that very strong material characterization efforts are required to predict accurate thermal stresses in anisotropic composite structures.

*NASA Langley Research Center, Hampton, Virginia.
**Lockheed California Co., Burbank, California.

1431. Ishmael, S. D.; and *Wierzbanowski, T.: **X-29 Initial Flight Test Results.** *Proceedings, Society of Experimental Test Pilots, 29th Symposium,* Beverly Hills, California, September 25–28, 1985, (see A86-44936 21-05), pp. 95–113, 86A44942.

It is announced that the X-29 forward-swept-wing (FSW) aircraft has been built, with flight testing under way and proceeding smoothly. The X-29 is a single-seat, single-engine supersonic aircraft that blends an optimized FSW, a close-coupled near-coplanar canard, an F-5A forward fuselage module employing two side-mounted engine inlets, and a new aft fuselage. An F404-GE-400 engine with afterburner provides about 16,000 lb of thrust. The X-29 was designed to be near neutrally stable in the supersonic region to minimize drag; it becomes highly unstable transonically and subsonically, which dictates the use of a computerized fly-by-wire flight control system capable of stabilizing the aircraft. The X-29 advanced technology demonstrator began flight testing on December 14, 1984; by September 26, 1985, its envelope had been expanded to 0.75 Mach, 350 knots estimated airspeed, and 30,000 feet altitude. The aircraft has flown with very few problems and aerodynamic, structural, and control system results have correlated well with predictions. Areas where prediction and performance are not so well correlated are noted.

*USAF Flight Test Center, Edwards AFB, California.

1432. Kehoe, M. W.; Cazier, F. W., Jr.; and Ellison, J. F.: **Ground Vibration Test of the Laminar Flow Control JetStar Airplane.** NASA TM-86398, L-15949, NAS 1.15:86398, October 1985, 86N13321, #.

A ground vibration test was conducted on a Lockheed JetStar airplane that had been modified for the purpose of conducting laminar flow control experiments. The test was performed prior to initial flight flutter tests. Both sine-dwell and single-point-random excitation methods were used. The data presented include frequency response functions and a comparison of mode frequencies and mode shapes from both methods.

1433. Beckner, C.; and Curry, R. E.: **Water Tunnel Flow Visualization Using a Laser.** NASA TM-86743, H-1307, NAS 1.15:86743. Presented at the 3rd AIAA Applied Aerodynamics Conference, Colorado Springs, October 1985, 86N11206, #. (See also 1434.)

Laser systems for flow visualization in water tunnels (similar to the vapor screen technique used in wind tunnels) can provide two-dimensional cross-sectional views of complex flow fields. This parametric study documents the practical application of the laser-enhanced visualization (LEV) technique to water tunnel testing. Aspects of the study include laser power levels, flow seeding (using fluorescent dyes and embedded particulates), model preparation, and photographic techniques. The results of this study are discussed to provide potential users with basic information to aid in the design and setup of an LEV system.

1434. Curry, R. E.; and Beckner, C.: **Water Tunnel Flow Visualization Using a Laser.** AIAA Paper 85-5016. Third AIAA Applied Aerodynamics Conference, Colorado Springs, Colorado, October 14–16, 1985, 86A11064, #. (See also 1433.)

Laser systems for flow visualization in water tunnels (similar to the vapor screen technique used in wind tunnels) can provide two-dimensional cross-sectional views of complex flow fields. This parametric study documents the practical application of the laser-enhanced visualization (LEV) technique to water tunnel testing. Aspects of the study include laser power levels, flow seeding (using fluorescent dyes and embedded particulates), model preparation, and photographic techniques. The results of this study are discussed to provide potential users with basic information to aid in the design and setup of an LEV system.

1435. Ko, W. L.; and Schuster, L. S.: **Stress Analyses of B-52 Pylon Hooks.** NASA TM-84924, H-1221, NAS 1.15:84924, October 1985, 86N11524, #.

The NASTRAN finite element computer program was used in the two dimensional stress analysis of B-52 carrier aircraft pylon hooks: (1) old rear hook (which failed), (2) new rear hook (improved geometry), (3) new DAST rear hook (derated geometry), and (4) front hook. NASTRAN model meshes were generated by the aid of PATRAN-G computer program. Brittle limit loads for all the four hooks were established. The critical stress level calculated from NASTRAN agrees reasonably well with the values predicted from the fracture mechanics for the failed old rear hook.

1436. Duke, E. L.; and Regenie, V. A.: **Expert Systems Development and Application.** NASA TM-86746, H-1310, NAS 1.15:86746. IEEE Symposium on Expert Systems in Government, McLean, Virginia, October 23–25, 1985, 86N11194, #.

Current research in the application of expert systems to problems in the flight research environment is discussed. In what is anticipated to be a broad research area, a real time expert system flight status monitor has been identified as the initial project. This real time expert system flight status monitor is described in terms of concept, application, development, and schedule.

1437. Duke, E. L.; and Regenie, V. A.: **Description of an Experimental Expert System Flight Status Monitor.** NASA TM-86791, H-1317, NAS 1.15:86791, AIAA Paper 85-6042-CP. Presented at the 5th AIAA Computers in Aerospace Conference, Long Beach, California, October 21–23, 1985, 86N11195, #.

This paper describes an experimental version of an expert system flight status monitor being developed at the Dryden Flight Research Facility of the NASA Ames Research Center. This experimental expert system flight status monitor (ESSFSM) is supported by a specialized knowledge acquisition tool that provides the user with a powerful and easy-to-use documentation and rule construction tool. The EESFSM is designed to be a testbed for concepts in rules, inference mechanisms, and knowledge structures to be used in a real-time expert system flight status monitor that will monitor the health and status of the flight control system of state-of-the-art, high-performance, research aircraft.

1438. Hughes, D. L.; Ray, R. J.; and Walton, J. T.: **Net Thrust Calculation Sensitivity of an Afterburning Turbofan Engine to Variations in Input Parameters.** AIAA Paper 85-4041. Presented at the AIAA, AHS, and ASEE, Aircraft Design Systems and Operations Meeting, Colorado Springs, Colorado, October 14–16, 1985, 86A10969, #.

The calculated value of net thrust of an aircraft powered by a General Electric F404-GE-400 afterburning turbofan engine was evaluated for its sensitivity to various input parameters. The effects of a 1.0-percent change in each input parameter on the calculated value of net thrust with two calculation methods are compared. This paper presents the results of these comparisons and also gives the estimated accuracy of the overall net thrust calculation as determined from the influence coefficients and estimated parameter measurement accuracies.

1439. Iliff, K. W.: **Extraction of Aerodynamic Parameters for Aircraft at Extreme Flight Conditions.** AGARD-CP-386 Paper 24. *AGARD Unsteady Aerodynamics-Fundamentals and Applications to Aircraft Dynamics*, (ISBN-92-835-0382-1), (see N86-27224 18-02), AD-A165045, November 1985, 86N27248, #. (See also 1400.)

The maximum likelihood estimator was used to extract stability and control derivatives from flight data for many years. Most of the literature on aircraft estimation concentrates on new development and applications, assuming familiarity with basic concepts. The maximum likelihood estimator and the aircraft equations of motion that the estimator uses are discussed. The current strength and limitations associated with obtaining flight-determined aerodynamic coefficients in extreme flight conditions are assessed. The importance of the careful combining of wind tunnel results (or calculations) and flight results and the thorough evaluation of the mathematical model is emphasized. The basic concepts of minimization and estimation are examined for a simple computed aircraft example, and the cost functions that are to be minimized during estimation are defined and discussed. Graphic representations of the cost functions are given to help illustrate the minimization process. Finally, the basic concepts are generalized, and estimation of stability and control derivatives from flight data is discussed.

1440. [*]Abernethy, Robert B.; [**]Adams, Gary R.; [†]Ascough, John C.; Baer-Riedhart, Jennifer L.; [††]Balkcom, George H.; [‡]Biesiadny, Thomas: **In-Flight Thrust Determination.** SAE-AIR-1703, *In-Flight Thrust*

256

Determination and Uncertainty, (see A88-15226 04-05), 1986, <u>November 1985</u>, 88A15227.

The major aspects of processes that may be used for the determination of in-flight thrust are reviewed. Basic definitions are presented as well as analytical and ground-test methods for gathering data and calculating the thrust of the propulsion system during the flight development program of the aircraft. Test analysis examples include a single-exhaust turbofan, an intermediate-cowl turbofan, and a mixed-flow afterburning turbofan.

*Pratt and Whitney, East Hartford, Connecticut.
**USAF Wright-Patterson AFB, Ohio.
†Royal Aircraft Establishment, Farnborough, England.
††General Dynamics Corporation, St. Louis, Missouri.
‡NASA Lewis Research Center, Cleveland, Ohio.

1441. Burcham, F. W., Jr.; Myers, L. P.; and Walsh, K. R.: **Flight Evaluation of a Digital Electronic Engine Control in an F-15 Airplane.** *Journal of Aircraft*, Vol. 22, December 1985, (see A84-12310), <u>December 1985</u>, pp. 1072–1078, 86A17784, #. (See also 1279, 1289.)

1442. Webb, L. D.: **Mach Number and Flow-Field Calibration at the Advanced Design Propeller Location on the JetStar Airplane.** NASA TM-84923, H-1222, NAS 1.15:84923, <u>December 1985</u>, 86N16197, #.

Advanced design propellers on a JetStar aircraft were tested at NASA Ames Research Center's Dryden Flight Research Facility. A calibration of the flow field at the test location to obtain local Mach number and flow direction was performed. A pitot-static probe and flow direction vane installation was installed and tested at Mach 0.3 to 0.8 and altitudes from 3000 m (10,000 ft) to 9100 m (30,000 ft). Local Mach number and flow direction relationships were obtained and related to their noseboom counterparts. Effects of varying angles of sideslip to + or –3 deg. were investigated.

1443. Hughes, D. L.; Myers, L. P.; and Mackall, K. G.: **Effects of Inlet Distortion on a Static Pressure Probe Mounted on the Engine Hub in an F-15 Airplane.** NASA TP-2411, H-1182, NAS 1.60:2411, <u>1985</u>, 85N22394, #.

An inlet static pressure (PS2) probe was mounted on the hub of an F100 engine in an F-15 airplane. Flight test results showed that for low distortion conditions, the ratio of engine-face total pressure to static pressure agreed well with previous altitude facility data. Off-schedule operation of the inlet third ramp angle caused increased distortion of the inlet airflow during steady-state flight conditions. Data are shown for inlet third ramp excursions leading to engine stall. The relationships of inlet face total to static pressure ratio as a function of several distortion descriptors are also described.

1444. Walsh, K. R.: **Flow Field Survey Near the Rotational Plane of an Advanced Design Propeller on a JetStar Airplane** NASA TM-86037, H-1226, NAS 1.15:86037, <u>December 1985</u>, 86N16196, #.

An investigation was conducted to obtain upper fuselage surface static pressures and boundary layer velocity profiles below the centerline of an advanced design propeller. This investigation documents the upper fuselage velocity flow field in support of the in-flight acoustic tests conducted on a JetStar airplane. Initial results of the boundary layer survey show evidence of an unusual flow disturbance, which is attributed to the two windshield wiper assemblies on the aircraft. The assemblies were removed, eliminating the disturbances from the flow field. This report presents boundary layer velocity profiles at altitudes of 6096 and 9144 m (20,000 and 30,000 ft) and Mach numbers from 0.6 to 0.8, and it investigated the effects of windshield wiper assemblies on these profiles. Because of the unconventional velocity profiles that were obtained with the assemblies mounted, classical boundary layer parameters, such as momentum and displacement thicknesses, are not presented. The effects of flight test variables (Mach number and angles of attack and sideslip) and an advanced design propeller on boundary layer profiles—with the wiper assemblies mounted and removed—are presented.

1445. Ko, W. L.: **Stress Concentration Around a Small Circular Hole in the HiMAT Composite Plate.** NASA TM-86038, H-1235, NAS 1.15:86038, <u>December 1985</u>, 86N15350, #.

Anisotropic plate theory is used to calculate the anisotropic stress concentration factors for a composite plate (AS/3501-5 graphite/epoxy composite, single ply or laminated) containing a circular hole. This composite material is used on the highly maneuverable aircraft technology (HiMAT) vehicle. It is found that the anisotropic stress concentration factor could be greater or less than 3 (the stress concentration factor for isotropic materials), and that the locations of the maximum tangential stress points could shift with the change of fiber orientation with respect to the loading axis. The effect of hole size on the stress concentration factor is examined using the Point Stress Criterion and the Averaged Stress Criterion. The predicted stress concentration factors based on the two theories compared fairly well with the measured values for the hole size 0.3175 cm (1/8 in). It is also found that through the lamination process, the stress concentration factor could be reduced drastically, indicating an improvement in structural performance.

1446. *Alag, G. S.; and Duke, E. L.: **Development of a Flight Test Maneuver Autopilot for an F-15 Aircraft.** NASA TM-86799, H-1328, NAS 1.15:86799. Presented at the IEEE Conference on Decision and Control, <u>December 11, 1985</u>, 86N14275, #.

An autopilot can be used to provide precise control to meet the demanding requirements of flight research maneuvers with high-performance aircraft. This paper presents the development of control laws for a flight test maneuver autopilot for an F-15 aircraft. A linear quadratic regulator approach is used to develop the control laws within the context of flight test maneuver requirements by treating the maneuver as a finite time tracking problem with regulation of state rates. Results are presented to show the effectiveness of the controller in insuring acceptable aircraft performance during a maneuver.

*Western Michigan University, Kalamazoo, Michigan.

1447. *Hall, Robert M. Capt.; and Del Frate, John H.: **Interactions Between Forebody and Wing Vortices.** AFWAL TM-85-252, 1985.

A water tunnel study examining the influence of fuselage cross section on forebody-wing interactions was carried out in the NASA Ames-Dryden water tunnel for a 55 degree, cropped delta-wing model. The fuselage cross-sections studied included two chines with included chine angles of 7.5 and 90.0 degrees. The third fuselage was circular. Planview and sideview photographs showing the forebody vortices interacting with the main wing vortices by means of injected colored dye are presented for zero and non-zero sideslip angles. It is found that the stronger the forebody vortex, the more energy is imparted to the wing vortex system and, as a consequence, the wing vortex system is more able to resist bursting. In sideslip, however, the chine-shaped configurations showed very large differences in burst locations between the windward and leeward wing panels.

*USAF, Wright Aeronautical Laboratory, Dayton, Ohio.

1986 Technical Publications

1448. Veatch, Donald W.; and Bogue, Rodney K.: **Analog Signal Conditioning for Flight-Test Instrumentation.** NASA RP-1159, H-1191, NAS 1.61:1159. Presented at the AGARD Flight Mechanics Panel, Flight-test Techniques Working Group, AGARDograph 160, Flight-Test Instrumentation Series, January 1986, 87N29533, #. (See also 1467.)

The application of analog signal conditioning to flight-tests data acquisition systems is discussed. Emphasis is placed on practical applications of signal conditioning for the most common flight-test data-acquisition systems. A limited amount of theoretical discussion is included to assist the reader in a more complete understanding of the subject matter. Nonspecific signal conditioning, such as amplification, filtering, and multiplexing, is discussed. Signal conditioning for various specific transducers and data terminal devices is also discussed to illustrate signal conditioning that is unique to particular types of transducers. The purpose is to delineate for the reader the various signal-conditioning technique options, together with tradeoff considerations, for commonly encountered flight-test situations.

1449. Berry, D. T.: **A Flightpath Overshoot Flying Qualities Metric for the Landing Task.** NASA TM-86795, H-1322, NAS 1.15:86795. Presented at the AIAA 24th Aerospace Sciences Meeting, Reno, Nevada, January 1986, 86N14276, #. (See also 1450, 1539.)

An analysis was conducted of the attitude and flightpath angle response of configurations used in the Total In-Flight Simulator (TIFS) pitch-rate command systems program. The results show poor correlation between pilot ratings and attitude response and indicate that attitude was not a major influence in the results. A strong correlation was found to exist, however, between the amount of flightpath angle peak overshoot and the pilot ratings. This correlation is similar to the best correlations that have been obtained in recent closed-loop and time-domain analyses, but has the advantage of greatly simplified implementation and interpretation.

1450. Berry, D. T.: **A Flightpath Overshoot Flying Qualities Metric for the Landing Task.** AIAA Paper 86-0334. Presented at the AIAA 24th Aerospace Sciences Meeting, Reno, Nevada, January 6–9, 1986, 86A19820, #. (See also 1449, 1539.)

An analysis was conducted of the attitude and flightpath angle response of configurations used in the Total In-Flight Simulator (TIFS) pitch-rate command systems program. The results show poor correlation between pilot ratings and attitude response and indicate that attitude was not a major influence in the results. A strong correlation was found to exist, however, between the amount of flightpath angle peak overshoot and the pilot ratings. This correlation is similar to the best correlations that have been obtained in recent closed-loop and time-domain analyses but has the advantage of greatly simplified implementation and interpretation.

1451. Cox, T. H.; and Gilyard, G. B.: **Ground Vibration Test Results for Drones for Aerodynamic and Structural Testing (DAST)/Aeroelastic Research Wing (ARW-1R) Aircraft.** NASA TM-85906, H-1261, NAS 1.15:85906, January 1986, 86N19312, #.

The drones for aerodynamic and structural testing (DAST) project was designed to control flutter actively at high subsonic speeds. Accurate knowledge of the structural model was critical for the successful design of the control system. A ground vibration test was conducted on the DAST vehicle to determine the structural model characteristics. This report presents and discusses the vibration and test equipment, the test setup and procedures, and the antisymmetric and symmetric mode shape results. The modal characteristics were subsequently used to update the structural model employed in the control law design process.

1452. Deets, D. A.; Lock, W. P.; and *Megna, V. A.: **Flight Test of a Resident Backup Software System.** NASA TM-86807, H-1338, NAS 1.15:86807, January 1986, 86N19325, #. (See also 1572.)

A new fault-tolerant system software concept employing the primary digital computers as host for the backup software portion has been implemented and flight tested in the F-8 digital fly- by-wire airplane. The system was implemented in such a way that essentially no transients occurred in transferring from primary to backup software. This was accomplished without a significant increase in the complexity of the backup software. The primary digital system was frame synchronized, which provided several advantages in implementing the resident backup software system. Since the time of the flight tests, two other flight vehicle programs have made a commitment to incorporate resident backup software similar in nature to the system described in this paper.

* Draper Laboratory, Cambridge, Massachusetts.

1453. *Disbrow, J. D.; Duke, E. L.; and Regenie, V. A.: **Development of a Knowledge Acquisition Tool for an Expert System Flight Status Monitor.** NASA TM-86802, H-1332, NAS 1.15:86802, AIAA Paper 86-0240. Presented at the AIAA 24th Aerospace Sciences Meeting, Reno, Nevada, January 1986, 86N16944, #. (See also 1454.)

Two of the main issues in artificial intelligence today are knowledge acquisition dion and knowledge representation. The Dryden Flight Research Facility of NASA's Ames Research Center is presently involved in the design and implementation of an expert system flight status monitor that will provide expertise and knowledge to aid the flight systems engineer in monitoring today's advanced high-performance aircraft. The flight status monitor can be divided into two sections: the expert system itself and the knowledge acquisition tool. The knowledge acquisition tool, the means it uses to extract knowledge from the domain expert, and how that knowledge is represented for computer use is discussed. An actual aircraft system has been codified by this tool with great success. Future real-time use of the expert system has been facilitated by using the knowledge acquisition tool to easily generate a logically consistent and complete knowledge base.

* Systems Control Technology, Inc., Palo Alto, California.

1454. *Disbrow, J. D.; Duke, E. L.; and Regenie, V. A.: **Development of a Knowledge Acquisition Tool for an Expert System Flight Status Monitor.** AIAA Paper 86-0240. Presented at the AIAA 24th Aerospace Sciences

Meeting, Reno, Nevada, January 6–9, 1986, 86A19764, #. (See also 1453.)

Two of the main issues in artificial intelligence today are knowledge acquisition and knowledge representation. The Dryden Flight Research Facility of NASA's Ames Research Center is presently involved in the design and implementation of an expert system flight status monitor that will provide expertise and knowledge to aid the flight systems engineer in monitoring today's advanced high-performance aircraft. The flight status monitor can be divided into two sections: the expert system itself and the knowledge acquisition tool. This paper discusses the knowledge acquisition tool, the means it uses to extract knowledge from the domain expert, and how that knowledge is represented for computer use. An actual aircraft system has been codified by this tool with great success. Future real-time use of the expert system has been facilitated by using the knowledge acquisition tool to easily generate a logically consistent and complete knowledge base.

*Systems Control Technology, Inc., Palo Alto, California.

1455. Gera, J.: **Dynamics and Controls Flight Testing of the X-29A Airplane.** NASA TM-86803, H-1333, NAS 1.15:86803, AIAA Paper 86-0167. Presented at AIAA 24th Aerospace Sciences Meeting, Reno, Nevada, January 1986, 86N19313, #. (See also 1456.)

A brief description of the flight control system of the X-29A forward-swept-wing flight demonstrator is followed by a discussion of the flight test techniques and procedures in the area of flight dynamics and control. These techniques, which evolved during the initial few months of flight testing, are based on integrating flight testing with simulation and analysis on a flight-by-flight basis. A limited amount of flight test results in dynamic stability and handling qualities is also presented.

1456. Gera, J.: **Dynamics and Controls Flight Testing of the X-29A Airplane.** AIAA Paper 86-0167. Presented at the AIAA 24th Aerospace Sciences Meeting, Reno, Nevada, January 6–9, 1986, 86A19728, #. (See also 1455.)

A brief description of the flight control system of the X-29A forward-swept-wing flight demonstrator is followed by a discussion of the flight test techniques and procedures in the area of flight dynamics and control. These techniques, which evolved during the initial few months of flight testing, are based on integrating flight testing with simulation and analysis on a flight-by-flight basis. A limited amount of flight test results in dynamic stability and handling qualities is also presented.

1457. Moore, A. L.: **The Role of a Real-Time Flight Support Facility in Flight Research Programs.** NASA TM-86805, H-1335, NAS 1.15:86805, AIAA Paper 86-0166.

Presented at the AIAA 24th Aerospace Sciences Meeting, Reno, Nevada, January 1986, 86N19330, #. (See also 1458.)

This paper presents some of the approaches taken by the NASA Western Aeronautical Test Range (WATR) of Ames Research Center to satisfy the ever-increasing real-time requirements of research projects such as the F-14, F-15, advanced fighter technology integration (AFTI) F-16, YAV-8B, and the X-29A. The approaches include the areas of data acquisition, communications (video and audio), real-time processing and display, data communications, and tracking.

1458. Moore, A. L.: **The Role of a Real-Time Flight Support Facility in Flight Research Programs.** AIAA Paper 86-0166. Presented at the AIAA 24th Aerospace Sciences Meeting, Reno, Nevada, January 6–9, 1986, 86A19727, #. (See also 1457)

This paper presents some of the approaches taken by the NASA Western Aeronautical Test Range (WATR) of Ames Research Center to satisfy the ever-increasing real-time requirements of research projects such as the F-14, F-15, advanced fighter technology integration (AFTI) F-16, YAV-8B, and the X-29A. The approaches include the areas of data acquisition, communications (video and audio), real-time processing and display, data communications, and tracking.

1459. *Menon, P. K. A.; *Walker, R. A.; and Duke, E. L.: **Flight Test Maneuver Modeling and Control.** AIAA Paper 86-0426. Presented at the AIAA 24th Aerospace Sciences Meeting, Reno, Nevada, January 6–9, 1986, 86A19868, #. (See also 1694.)

The use of automated flight test schemes decrease the aircraft flight testing time and pilot work load while enhancing the data quality. Two major elements involved in developing such an automated technique are maneuver modeling to generate command histories from the maneuver specifications and the synthesis of control systems to track these command histories. This paper describes the maneuver modeling for eight flight test trajectories. The control system synthesis with Kosut's suboptimal minimum error excitation linear quadratic regulator approach is presented. The closed-loop simulation results are given.

*Integrated Systems, Inc., Palo Alto, California.

1460. Barber, R.: **CID Flight/Impact.** NASA CP-2395 NASA Langley Research Center Full-Scale Transport Controlled Impact Demonstration, (see N86-21933 12-39), January 1986, pp. 17–28, 86N21935, #.

The planned versus the actual results of the controlled impact demonstration of a transport aircraft are discussed. Remote control systems, site selection, manned flight tests, and wreckage distribution are discussed.

1461. Privoznik, C. M.; and Berry, D. T.: **Comparison of Pilot Effective Time Delay for Cockpit Controllers Used on Space Shuttle and Conventional Aircraft.** NASA TM-86030, H-1222, NAS 1.15:86030, February 1986, 86N19324, #.

A study was conducted at the Dryden Flight Research Facility of NASA Ames Research Center (Ames-Dryden) to compare pilot effective time delay for the space shuttle rotational hand controller with that for conventional stick controllers. The space shuttle controller has three degrees of freedom and nonlinear gearing. The conventional stick has two degrees of freedom and linear gearing. Two spring constants were used, allowing the conventional stick to be evaluated in both a light and a heavy configuration. Pilot effective time delay was obtained separately for pitch and roll through first-order, closed-loop, compensatory tracking tasks. The tasks were implemented through the space shuttle cockpit simulator and a critical task tester device. A total of 900 data runs were made using four test pilots and one nonpilot (engineer) for two system delays in pitch and roll modes. Results showed that the heavier conventional control stick had the lowest pilot effective time delays. The light conventional control stick had pilot effective time delays similar to those of the shuttle controller. All configurations showed an increase in pilot effective time delay with an increase in total system delay.

1462. VanNorman, M.; and Mackall, D. A.: **Development Experience With a Simple Expert System Demonstrator for Pilot Emergency Procedures.** NASA TM-85919, H-1272, NAS 1.15:85919, February 1986, 86N23603, #.

Expert system techniques, a major application area of artificial intelligence (AI), are examined in the development of pilot associate to handle aircraft emergency procedures. The term pilot associate is used to describe research involving expert systems that can assist the pilot in the cockpit. The development of expert systems for the electrical system and flight control system emergency procedures are discussed. A simple, high-level expert system provides the means to choose which knowledge domain is needed. The expert systems were developed on a low-cost, FORTH-based package, using a personal computer.

1463. Putnam, T. W.; Petersen, K. L.; Ishmael, S. D.; and Sefic, W. J.: **X-29 Flight—Acid Test for Design Predictions.** *Aerospace America* (ISSN 0740-722X), Vol. 24, February 1986, pp. 40–42, 86A31333, #.

The X-29 flight test data are being disseminated to interested industrial and military users as fast as it becomes available. The aircraft is extensively instrumented with accelerometers and pressure sensors and optical sensors for measuring wing deflection. The thoroughness of preflight preparations permitted a rapid advance through initial test checkpoints, which have both confirmed many predictions and revealed several discrepancies. The flight envelope had been expanded to Mach 1.1 and an altitude of 40,000 ft by December 1985. Notably, the X-29 has provided in-flight data which could not be faithfully depicted in a simulator, e.g., flare procedures during landing, and has shown that the stability adjustments, although adequate for controlling the aircraft, are not rapid enough to offer a satisfactory margin of harmony. The tests are now being performed in the transonic regime, where supercritical airfoil and forward swept wing drag reduction become significant factors.

1464.   Sarrafian, S. K.: **Simulator Evaluation of a Remotely Piloted Vehicle Visual Landing Task.** *Journal of Guidance, Control, and Dynamics*, (ISSN 0731-5090), Vol. 9, January–February 1986, pp. 80–84, 86A20238, #. (See also 1351, 1352.)

1465.   Quinn, R. D.; and Fields, R. A.: **Comparison of Measured and Calculated Temperatures for a Mach 8 Hypersonic Wing Test Structure.** NASA TM-85918, H-1271, A-85137, NAS 1.15:85918, March 1986, 86N22563, #.

Structural temperatures were measured on a hypersonic wing test structure during a heating test that simulated a Mach 8 thermal environment. Measured data are compared to design calculations and temperature predictions obtained from a finite-difference thermal analysis.

1466.   Arnold, R. J.; Epstein, C. S.; and Bogue, R. K.: **Store Separation Flight Testing.** AGARD-AG-300-VOL-5, ISBN-92-845-1523-4, AD-A171301, April 1986, 86N30727, #.

This volume in the AGARD Flight Test Techniques Series treats stores separation testing from the overall systems standpoint. All aspects of testing are described from the time of identification of a particular aircraft/store requirement through all steps leading to the establishment of a satisfactory employment envelope. Considerable emphasis is placed on the planning and execution of the flight test phase of the stores clearance program, including the definition of a basic structure, and a set of procedures which will maximize the safe and efficient execution of such a program.

1467.   Veatch, D. W.; and Bogue, R.: **Analogue Signal Conditioning for Flight Test Instrumentation.** AGARD-AG-160-VOL-17, ISBN-92-835-1520-X, AD-A171303, April 1986, 86N29816, #. (See also 1448.)

The application of analog signal conditioning to flight-test data-acquisition systems is discussed. Emphasis is placed on practical applications of signal conditioning for the most common flight-test data-acquisition systems. A limited amount of theoretical discussion is included to assist the reader in a more complete understanding of the subject matter. Nonspecific signal conditioning, such as amplification, filtering, and multiplexing, is discussed. Signal

conditioning for various specific transducers and data terminal devices is also discussed to illustrate signal conditioning that is unique to particular types of transducers. The purpose is to delineate for the reader the various signal-conditioning technique options, together with tradeoff considerations, for commonly encountered flight-test situations.

1468.   Burcham, F. W., Jr.; Trippensee, G. A.; Fisher, D. F.; and Putnam, T. W.: **Summary of Results of NASA F-15 Flight Research Program.** NASA TM-86811, H-1341, NAS 1.15:86811, AIAA Paper 86-9761. Presented at the AIAA 3rd Flight Testing Conference, Las Vegas, Nevada, April 2–4, 1986, 86N26277, #. (See 1469.)

NASA conducted a multidisciplinary flight research program on the F-15 airplane. The program began in 1976 when two preproduction airplanes were obtained from the U.S. Air Force. Major projects involved stability and control, handling qualities, propulsion, aerodynamics, propulsion controls, and integrated propulsion-flight controls. Several government agencies and aerospace contractors were involved. In excess of 330 flights were flown, and over 85 papers and reports were published. This document describes the overall program, the projects, and the key results. The F-15 was demonstrated to be an excellent flight research vehicle, producing high-quality results.

1469.   Burcham, F. W., Jr.; Trippensee, G. A.; Fisher, D. F.; and Putnam, T. W.: **Summary of Results of NASA F-15 Flight Research Program.** AIAA Paper 86-9761. Presented at the AIAA, AHS, CASI, DGLR, IES, ISA, ITEA, SETP, and SFTE, 3rd Flight Testing Conference, Las Vegas, Nevada, April 2–4, 1986, 86A37064, #. (See also 1468.)

NASA conducted a multidisciplinary flight research program on the F-15 airplane. The program began in 1976 when two preproduction airplanes were obtained from the U.S. Air Force. Major projects involved stability and control, handling qualities, propulsion, aerodynamics, propulsion controls, and integrated propulsion-flight controls. Several government agencies and aerospace contractors were involved. In excess of 330 flights were flown, and over 85 papers and reports were published. This document describes the overall program, the projects, and the key results. The F-15 was demonstrated to be an excellent flight research vehicle, producing high-quality results.

1470.   *Davis, R. E.; *Fischer, M. C.; Fisher, D. F.; and Young, R.: **Cloud Particle Effects on Laminar Flow in the NASA LEFT Program—Preliminary Results.** AIAA Paper 86-9811. Presented at the AIAA, AHS, CASI, DGLR, IES, ISA, ITEA, SETP, and SFTE, 3rd Flight Testing Conference, Las Vegas, Nevada, April 2–4, 1986, 86A32138, #.

Laminar flow offers the promise of significant fuel savings on future commercial transport aircraft, but laminar flow can be lost while encountering clouds or haze at cruise conditions. To quantify the effect of cloud particles on laminar flow during typical airline operating conditions, and evaluate candidate cloud particle detection instrument concepts for future laminar flow aircraft, two types of cloud particle detectors are being flown aboard a NASA JetStar aircraft in the Leading Edge Flight Test (LEFT) program. The instrumentation is described, and preliminary results and conclusions are presented.

*NASA Langley Research Center, Hampton, Virginia.

1471. Bosworth, J. T.; and *West, J. C.: **Real-Time Open-Loop Frequency Response Analysis of Flight Test Data.** AIAA Paper 86-9738. Presented at the AIAA, AHS, CASI, DGLR, IES, ISA, ITEA, SETP, and SFTE, 3rd Flight Testing Conference, Las Vegas, Nevada, April 2–4, 1986, 86A32084, #.

A technique has been developed to compare the open-loop frequency response of a flight test aircraft real time with linear analysis predictions. The result is direct feedback to the flight control systems engineer on the validity of predictions and adds confidence for proceeding with envelope expansion. Further, gain and phase margins can be tracked for trends in a manner similar to the techniques used by structural dynamics engineers in tracking structural modal damping.

*USAF Flight Test Center, Edwards AFB, California.

1472. *Cazier, F. W., Jr.; and Kehoe, M. W.: **Flight Test of a Decoupler Pylon for Wing/Store Flutter Suppression.** AIAA Paper 86-9730. Presented at the AIAA, AHS, CASI, DGLR, IES, ISA, ITEA, SETP, and SFTE, 3rd Flight Testing Conference, Las Vegas, Nevada, April 2–4, 1986, 86A32077, #. (See also 1494.)

The decoupler pylon is a NASA concept of passive wing-store flutter suppression achieved by providing a low store-pylon pitch frequency. Flight tests where performed on an F-16 airplane carrying on each wing an AIM-9J wingtip missile, a GBU-8 bomb near midspan, and an external fuel tank. Baseline flights with the GBU-8 mounted on a standard pylon established that this configuration is characterized by an antisymmetric limited amplitude flutter oscillation within the operational envelope. The airplane was then flown with the GBU-8 mounted on the decoupler pylon. The decoupler pylon successfully suppressed wing-store flutter throughout the flight envelope. A 37-percent increase in flutter velocity over the standard pylon was demonstrated. Maneuvers with load factors to 4g were performed. Although the static store displacements during maneuvers were not sufficiently large to be of concern, a store pitch alignment system was tested and performed successfully. One GBU-8 was ejected demonstrating that weapon separation from the decoupler pylon is normal. Experience with the present decoupler pylon

design indicated that friction in the pivoting mechanism could affect its proper functioning as a flutter suppressor.

*NASA Langley Research Center, Hampton, Virginia.

1473. Sefic, W. J.; and *Cutler, W.: **X-29A Advanced Technology Demonstrator Program Overview.** AIAA Paper 86-9727. Presented at the AIAA, AHS, CASI, DGLR, IES, ISA, ITEA, SETP, and SFTE, 3rd Flight Testing Conference, Las Vegas, Nevada, April 2–4, 1986, 86A32076, #.

The present discussion of the X-29A forward-swept wing experimental aircraft's functional flight program and concept evaluation program gives attention to the program management structure for a test team that encompasses NASA, the U.S. Air Force, and the prime contractor for the X-29A. The preflight, flight-functional, envelope-expansion and flight research test objectives of the program are also noted, together with the qualitative characterizations obtained to date for both a limited envelope flight control system and one for an expanded envelope.

*Grumman Corporation, Grumman Aircraft Systems Div., Bethpage, New York.

1474. *Cazier, F. W., Jr.; and Kehoe, M. W.: **Ground Vibration Test of an F-16 Airplane With Modified Decoupler Pylons.** NASA TM-87634, L-16065, NAS 1.15:87634, April 1986, 86N24685, #.

The decoupler pylon is a passive wing/store flutter suppression device. It was modified to reduce friction following initial flight tests. A ground vibration test was conducted on an F-16 aircraft loaded on each wing with a one-half-full (center bay empty) 370-gallon fuel tank mounted on a standard pylon, a GBU-8 store mounted on the decoupler pylon, and an AIM-9J missile mounted on a wingtip launcher. The test was conducted prior to flight tests with the modified pylon to determine modal frequencies, mode shapes, and structural damping coefficients. Data presented include frequency response plots, mode shape plots, and limited force-effect plots.

*NASA Langley Research Center, Hampton, Virginia.

1475. Duke, E. L.: **Combining and Connecting Linear, Multi-Input, Multi-Output Subsystem Models.** NASA TM-85912, H-1264, NAS 1.15:85912, April 1986, 86N25166, #.

The mathematical background for combining and connecting linear, multi-input, multi-output subsystem models into an overall system model is provided. Several examples of subsystem configurations are examined in detail. A description of a MATRIX (sub x) command file to aid in the process of combining and connecting these subsystem models is contained.

1476. Walton, James T.; and Burcham, Frank W., Jr.: **Augmentor Performance of an F100 Engine Model Derivative Engine in an F-15 Airplane.** NASA TM-86745, H-1309, NAS 1.15:86745, May 1986, 88N23805, #.

The transient performance of the F100 engine model derivative (EMD) augmentor was evaluated in an F-15 airplane. The augmentor was a newly designed 16-segment augmentor. It was tested with a segment-1 spray-ring with 90 deg fuel injection, and later with a modified segment-1 spray-ring with centerline fuel injection. With the 90 deg injection, no-lights occurred at high altitudes with airspeeds of 175 knots or less; however, the results were better than when using the standard F100-PW-100 engine. With the centerline fuel injection, all transients were successful to an altitude of 15,500 meters and an airspeed of 150 knots: no failures to light, blowouts, or stalls occurred. For a first flight evaluation, the augmentor transient performance was excellent.

1477. Sefic, W. J.; and Maxwell, C. M.: **X-29A Technology Demonstrator Flight Test Program Overview.** NASA TM-86809, H-1347, NAS 1.15:86809, ISA-504. Presented at the ISA Aerospace Industries/Test Measurement Symposium, Seattle, Washington, May 5–8, 1986, May 1986, 86N26328, #.

An overview of the X-29A functional flight program and concept evaluation program is presented, including some of the unique and different preparations for the first flight. Included are a discussion of the many organizational responsibilities and a description of the program management structure for the test team. Also discussed are preflight ground, flight functional envelope expansion, and flight research test objectives and qualitative results to date for both a limited-envelope flight control system and an expanded-envelope system. The aircraft, including the instrumentation system and measurements, is described. In addition, a discussion is included regarding the use of major support facilities, such as ground and flight simulators, the NASA Western Aeronautical Test Range and mission control center, and the Grumman automated telemetry station. An overview of the associated real-time and postflight batch data processing software approaches is presented. The use of hardware-in-the-loop simulation for independent verification and validation and mission planning and practice is discussed. Also included is a description of the flight-readiness review, the airworthiness and flight safety review, work scheduling, technical briefings, and preflight and postflight crew briefings. The configuration control process used on the X-29A program is described, and its relationship to both simulation and aircraft operations is discussed. An X-29A schedule overview is presented with an outline of a proposed follow-on program.

1478. Ko, W. L.; Shideler, J. L.; and Fields, R. A.: **Buckling Behavior of Rene 41 Tubular Panels for a Hypersonic Aircraft Wing.** NASA TM-86798, H-1327, NAS 1.15:86798, AIAA Paper 86-0978. Presented at the AIAA/ASME/ASCE/AHS 27th Structures, Structural Dynamics and Materials Conference, San Antonio, Texas, May 19–21, 1986, 86N26653, #. (See also 1479.)

The buckling characteristics of Rene 41 tubular panels for a hypersonic aircraft wing were investigated. The panels were repeatedly tested for buckling characteristics using a hypersonic wing test structure and a universal tension/compression testing machine. The nondestructive buckling tests were carried out under different combined load conditions and in different temperature environments. The force/stiffness technique was used to determine the buckling loads of the panel. In spite of some data scattering, resulting from large extrapolations of the data fitting curve (because of the termination of applied loads at relatively low percentages of the buckling loads), the overall test data correlate fairly well with theoretically predicted buckling interaction curves. Also, the structural efficiency of the tubular panels was found to be slightly higher than that of beaded panels.

1479. Ko, W. L.; Fields, R. A.; and *Shideler, J. L.: **Buckling Behavior of Rene 41 Tubular Panels for a Hypersonic Aircraft Wing.** AIAA Paper 86-0978. *Technical Papers*, presented at the 27th Structures, Structural Dynamics and Materials Conference, San Antonio, Texas, May 19–21, 1986, Part 1, (see A86-38801 18-39), 1986, pp. 517–544, 86A38857, #. (See also 1478.)

The buckling characteristics of Rene 41 tubular panels for a hypersonic aircraft wing were investigated. The panels were repeatedly tested for buckling characteristics using a hypersonic wing test structure and a universal tension/compression testing machine. The nondestructive buckling tests were carried out under different combined load conditions and in different temperature environments. The force/stiffness technique was used to determine the buckling loads of the panels. In spite of some data scattering resulting from large extrapolations of the data-fitting curve (because of the termination of applied loads at relatively low percentages of the buckling loads), the overall test data correlate fairly well with theoretically predicted buckling interaction curves. Also, the structural efficiency of the tubular panels was found to be slightly higher than that of beaded panels.

*NASA Langley Research Center, Hampton, Virginia.

1480. Duke, E. L.; Regenie, V. A.; Brazee, M.; and *Brumbaugh, R. W.: **An Engineering Approach to the Use of Expert Systems Technology in Avionics Applications.** NASA TM-88263, H-1364, NAS 1.15:88263. Presented at the IEEE National Aerospace and Electronics Conference

(NAECON), Dayton, Ohio, May 19–23, 1986, <u>May 1986</u>, 86N24687, #.

The concept of using a knowledge compiler to transform the knowledge base and inference mechanism of an expert system into a conventional program is presented. The need to accommodate real-time systems requirements in applications such as embedded avionics is outlined. Expert systems and a brief comparison of expert systems and conventional programs are reviewed. Avionics applications of expert systems are discussed before the discussions of applying the proposed concept to example systems using forward and backward chaining.

*PRC Kentron, Edwards, California.

1481. Dana, W. H.; *Smith, W. B.; and **Howard, J. D.: **Pilot Vehicle Interface on the Advanced Fighter Technology Integration F-16.** *NAECON 1986: Proceedings of the National Aerospace and Electronics Conference,* Dayton, Ohio, May 19–23, 1986, Vol. 2, (see A87-16726 05-01), <u>1986</u>, pp. 595–607, 87A16787.

This paper focuses on the work load aspects of the pilot vehicle interface in regard to the new technologies tested during AMAS Phase II. Subjects discussed in this paper include: a wide field-of-view head-up display; automated maneuvering attack system/sensor tracker system; master modes that configure flight controls and mission avionics; a modified helmet mounted sight; improved multifunction display capability; a voice interactive command system; ride qualities during automated weapon delivery; a color moving map; an advanced digital map display; and a g-induced loss-of-consciousness and spatial disorientation autorecovery system.

*General Dynamics Corporation, Fort Worth, Texas.
**USAF Flight Test Center, Edwards AFB, California.

1482. Maine, Richard E.; and Iliff, Kenneth W.: **Application of Parameter Estimation to Aircraft Stability and Control: The Output-Error Approach.** NASA RP-1168, H-1299, NAS 1.61:1168, <u>June 1986</u>, 87N29499, #.

The practical application of parameter estimation methodology to the problem of estimating aircraft stability and control derivatives from flight test data is examined. The primary purpose of the document is to present a comprehensive and unified picture of the entire parameter estimation process and its integration into a flight test program. The document concentrates on the output-error method to provide a focus for detailed examination and to allow us to give specific examples of situations that have arisen. The document first derives the aircraft equations of motion in a form suitable for application to estimation of stability and control derivatives. It then discusses the issues that arise in adapting the equations to the limitations of

analysis programs, using a specific program for an example. The roles and issues relating to mass distribution data, preflight predictions, maneuver design, flight scheduling, instrumentation sensors, data acquisition systems, and data processing are then addressed. Finally, the document discusses evaluation and the use of the analysis results.

1483. *Alag, G. S.; Kempel, R. W.; and Pahle, J. W.: **Decoupling Control Synthesis for an Oblique-Wing Aircraft.** NASA TM-86801, H-1339, NAS 1.15:86801. Presented at the American Control Conference, Seattle, Washington, <u>June 18–20, 1986</u>, 86N26339, #. (See also 1484.)

Interest in oblique-wing aircraft has surfaced periodically since the 1940's. This concept offers some substantial aerodynamic performance advantages but also has significant aerodynamic and inertial cross-coupling between the aircraft longitudinal and lateral-directional axes. This paper presents a technique for synthesizing a decoupling controller while providing the desired stability augmentation. The proposed synthesis procedure uses the concept of a real model-following control system. Feedforward gains are selected on the assumption that perfect model-following conditions are satisfied. The feedback gains are obtained by using eigensystem assignment, and the aircraft is stabilized by using partial state feedback. The effectiveness of the control laws developed in achieving the desired decoupling is illustrated by application to linearized equations of motion of an oblique-wing aircraft for a given flight condition.

*Western Michigan University, Kalamazoo, Michigan.

1484. *Alag, G. S.; Kempel, R. W.; and Pahle, J. W.: **Decoupling Control Synthesis for an Oblique-Wing Aircraft.** *Proceedings, 1986 American Control Conference,* Seattle, Washington, June 18–20, 1986, Vol. 1, (see A87-13301 03-63), N86-26339, <u>1986</u>, pp. 472–480, 87A13342. (See also 1483.)

Interest in oblique-wing aircraft has surfaced periodically since the 1940's. This concept offers some substantial aerodynamic performance advantages but also has significant aerodynamic and inertial cross-coupling between the aircraft longitudinal and lateral-directional axes. This paper presents a technique for synthesizing a decoupling controller while providing the desired stability augmentation. The proposed synthesis procedure uses the concept of a real model-following control system. Feedforward gains are selected on the assumption that perfect model-following conditions are satisfied. The feedback gains are obtained by using eigensystem assignment, and the aircraft is stabilized by using partial state feedback. The effectiveness of the control laws developed in achieving the desired decoupling is illustrated by application to linearized equations of motion of an oblique-wing aircraft for a given flight condition.

*Western Michigan University, Kalamazoo, Michigan.

1485. Burken, J. J.; *Alag, G. S.; and Gilyard, G. B.: **Aeroelastic Control of Oblique-Wing Aircraft.** NASA TM-86808, H-1346, NAS 1.15:86808. Presented at the 5th American Control Conference, Seattle, Washington, June 18–20, 1986, June 1986, 86N26340, #. (See also 1486.)

The U.S. Navy and NASA are currently involved in the design and development of an unsymmetric-skew-wing aircraft capable of 65 deg wing sweep and flight at Mach 1.6. A generic skew-wing aircraft model was developed for 45 deg wing skew at a flight condition of Mach 0.70 and 3048 m altitude. At this flight condition the aircraft has a wing flutter mode. An active implementable control law was developed using the linear quadratic Gaussian design technique. A method of modal residualization was used to reduce the order of the controller used for flutter suppression.

* Western Michigan University, Kalamazoo, Michigan.

1486. Burken, J. J.; Gilyard, G. B.; and *Alag, G. S.: **Aeroelastic Control of Oblique-Wing Aircraft.** *Proceedings, 5th American Control Conference,* Seattle, Washington, June 18–20, 1986, Vol. 1, (see A87-13301 03-63), pp. 463–471, 87A13341, #. (See also 1485.)

The U.S. Navy and NASA are currently involved in the design and development of an unsymmetric-skew-wing aircraft capable of 65 deg wing sweep and flight at Mach 1.6. A generic skew-wing aircraft model was developed for 45 deg wing skew at a flight condition of Mach 0.70 and 3048 m altitude. At this flight condition the aircraft has a wing flutter mode. An active implementable control law was developed using the linear quadratic Gaussian design technique. A method of modal residualization was used to reduce the order of the controller used for flutter suppression.

*Western Michigan University, Kalamazoo, Michigan.

1487. Deets, Dwain A.; DeAngelis, V. Michael; and Lux, David P.: **HiMAT Flight Program: Test Results and Program Assessment Overview.** NASA TM-86725, H-1283, NAS 1.15:86725, June 1986, 88N10026, #.

The Highly Maneuverable Aircraft Technology (HiMAT) program consisted of design, fabrication of two subscale remotely piloted research vehicles (RPRVs), and flight test. This technical memorandum describes the vehicles and test approach. An overview of the flight test results and comparisons with the design predictions are presented. These comparisons are made on a single-discipline basis, so that aerodynamics, structures, flight controls, and propulsion controls are examined one by one. The interactions between the disciplines are then examined, with the conclusions that the integration of the various technologies contributed to total vehicle performance gains. An assessment is made of the subscale RPRV approach from the standpoint of research data quality and quantity, unmanned effects as compared with

manned vehicles, complexity, and cost. It is concluded that the RPRV technique, as adopted in this program, resulted in a more complex and costly vehicle than expected but is reasonable when compared with alternate ways of obtaining comparable results.

1488. Ray, R. J.; and Myers, L. P.: **Test and Evaluation of the HIDEC Engine Uptrim Algorithm.** NASA TM-88262, H-1363, NAS 1.15:88262. Presented at the AIAA, ASME, SAE, and ASEE 22nd Joint Propulsion Conference, Huntsville, Alabama, June 16–18, 1986, July 1986, 86N28088, #. (See also 1489.)

The highly integrated digital electronic control (HIDEC) program will demonstrate and evaluate the improvements in performance and mission effectiveness that result from integrated engine-airframe control systems. Performance improvements will result from an adaptive engine stall margin mode, a highly integrated mode that uses the airplane flight conditions and the resulting inlet distortion to continuously compute engine stall margin. When there is excessive stall margin, the engine is uptrimmed for more thrust by increasing engine pressure ratio (EPR). The EPR uptrim logic has been evaluated and implemented into computer simulations. Thrust improvements over 10 percent are predicted for subsonic flight conditions. The EPR uptrim was successfully demonstrated during engine ground tests. Test results verify model predictions at the conditions tested.

1489. Ray, R. J.; and Myers, L. P.: **Test and Evaluation of the HIDEC Engine Uptrim Algorithm.** AIAA Paper 86-1676. Presented at the AIAA, ASME, SAE, and ASEE, 22nd Joint Propulsion Conference, Huntsville, Alabama, June 16–18, 1986, 86A42787, #. (See also 1488.)

The highly integrated digital electronic control (HIDEC) program will demonstrate and evaluate the improvements in performance and mission effectiveness that result from integrated engine-airframe control systems. Performance improvements will result from an adaptive engine stall margin mode, a highly integrated mode that uses the airplane flight conditions and the resulting inlet distortion to continuously compute engine stall margin. When there is excessive stall margin, the engine is uptrimmed for more thrust by increasing engine pressure ratio (EPR). The EPR uptrim logic has been evaluated and implement into computer simulations. Thrust improvements over 10 percent are predicted for subsonic flight conditions. The EPR uptrim was successfully demonstrated during engine ground tests. Test results verify model predictions at the conditions tested.

1490. *Emery, A. F.; *Abrous, A.; and Hedgley, D. R., Jr.: **Specular and Direct Radiative Loads on Space Structure.** AIAA Paper 86-1355. Presented at the AIAA and ASME 4th Joint Thermophysics and Heat Transfer Conference, Boston, Massachusetts, June 2–4, 1986, 86A49599, #.

The use of special models for trusses, and of fast graphical computational techniques, are discussed to reduce the computation times of intersurface radiation loads and specularly reflected radiation. The conditions under which the One-Dimensional approximation can be used, and the computation of the obstructed view factors for arbitrary surfaces, including the One-Dimensional surface, are considered using both contour and double area integration. The Adaptive Ray Tracing method is found to be very fast for surface configurations and obstruction densities typical of space structures, and it is shown to be best suited to views of J from I which are relatively simple and cover only a few subareas of S.

*University of Washington, Seattle, Washington.

1491. *Landy, R. J.; *Yonke, W. A.; and Stewart, J. F.: **Development of HiDEC Adaptive Engine Control Systems.** ASME Paper 86-GT-252. Presented at the ASME 31st International Gas Turbine Conference and Exhibit, Duesseldorf, West Germany, June 8–12, 1986, 86A48278, #.

The purpose of NASA's Highly Integrated Digital Electronic Control (HIDEC) flight research program is the development of integrated flight propulsion control modes, and the evaluation of their benefits aboard an F-15 test aircraft. HIDEC program phases are discussed, with attention to the Adaptive Engine Control System (ADECS I); this involves the upgrading of PW1128 engines for operation at higher engine pressure ratios and the production of greater thrust. ADECS II will involve the development of a constant thrust mode which will significantly reduce turbine operating temperatures.

*McDonnell Aircraft Co., St. Louis, Missouri.

1492. Regenie, Victoria A.; Chacon, Claude V.; and Lock, Wilton P.: **Experience With Synchronous and Asynchronous Digital Control Systems.** AIAA Paper 86-2239. Presented at the AIAA Guidance, Navigation, and Control Conference, Williamsburg, Virginia, August 18–20, 1986, (see N86-29866), June 1986, 87A40274, #. (See also 1510.)

Flight control systems have undergone a revolution since the days of simple mechanical linkages; presently the most advanced systems are full-authority, full-time digital systems controlling unstable aircraft. With the use of advanced control systems, the aerodynamic design can incorporate features that allow greater performance and fuel savings, as can be seen on the new Airbus design and advanced tactical fighter concepts. These advanced aircraft will be and are relying on the flight control system to provide the stability and handling qualities required for safe flight and to allow the pilot to control the aircraft. Various design philosophies have been proposed and followed to investigate system architectures for these advanced flight control systems. One

major area of discussion is whether a multichannel digital control system should be synchronous or asynchronous. This paper addressed the flight experience at the Dryden Flight Research Facility of NASA's Ames Research Center with both synchronous and asynchronous digital flight control systems. Four different flight control systems are evaluated against criteria such as software reliability, cost increases, and schedule delays.

1493. Del Frate, J. H.: **Water Tunnel Results of Leading-Edge Vortex Flap Tests on a Delta Wing Vehicle.** NASA CP-2416. NASA *Langley Research Center Vortex Flow Aerodynamics*, Vol. 1, (see N86-27190 18-02), July 1986, pp. 379–389, 86N27208, #.

A water tunnel flow visualization test on leading edge vortex flaps was conducted at the flow visualization facility of the NASA Ames Research Center's Dryden Flight Research Facility. The purpose of the test was to visually examine the vortex structures caused by various leading edge vortex flaps on the delta wing of an F-106 model. The vortex flaps tested were designed analytically and empirically at the NASA Langley Research Center. The three flap designs were designated as full-span gothic flap, full-span untapered flap, and part-span flap. The test was conducted at a Reynolds number of 76,000/m (25,000/ft). This low Reynolds number was used because of the 0.076-m/s (0.25-ft/s) test section flow speed necessary for high quality flow visualization. However, this low Reynolds number may have influenced the results. Of the three vortex flaps tested, the part-span flap produced what appeared to be the strongest vortex structure over the flap area. The full-span gothic flap provided the next best performance.

1494. Cazier, F. W., Jr.; and Kehoe, M. W.: **Flight Test of a Decoupler Pylon for Wing/Store Flutter Suppression.** NASA TM-87767, NAS 1.15:87767. Presented at the AIAA Third Flight Testing Conference, Las Vegas, Nevada, April 2–4, 1986, July 1986, 86N29814, #. (See also 1472.)

The decoupler pylon is a NASA concept of passive wing-store flutter suppression achieved by providing a low store-pylon pitch frequency. Flight tests were performed on an F-16 aircraft carrying on each wing an AIM-9J wingtip missile, a GBU-8 bomb near midspan, and an external fuel tank. Baseline flights with the GBU-8 mounted on a standard pylon established that this configuration is characterized by an antisymmetric limited amplitude flutter oscillation within the operational envelope. The airplane was then flown with the GBU-8 mounted on the decoupler pylon. The decoupler pylon successfully suppressed wing-store flutter throughout the flight envelope. A 37-percent increase in flutter velocity over the standard pylon was demonstrated. Maneuvers with load factors to 4g were performed. Although the static store displacements during maneuvers were not sufficiently large to be of concern, a store pitch alignment system was tested and performed successfully. One GBU-8 was ejected demonstrating that weapon separation from the decoupler pylon is normal. Experience with the present decoupler pylon design indicated that friction in the pivoting mechanism could affect its proper functioning as a flutter suppressor.

1495. Maine, R. E.; and Murray, J. E.: **Application of Parameter Estimation to Highly Unstable Aircraft.** NASA TM-88266, H-1365, NAS 1.15:88266, AIAA Paper 86-2020-CP. Presented at the AIAA Atmospheric Flight Mechanics Conference, Williamsburg, Virginia, August 18–20, 1986, 86N28078, #. (See also 1496, 1651.)

The application of parameter estimation to highly unstable aircraft is discussed. Included are a discussion of the problems in applying the output error method to such aircraft and demonstrates that the filter error method eliminates these problems. The paper shows that the maximum likelihood estimator with no process noise does not reduce to the output error method when the system is unstable. It also proposes and demonstrates an ad hoc method that is similar in form to the filter error method, but applicable to nonlinear problems. Flight data from the X-29 forward-swept-wing demonstrator is used to illustrate the problems and methods discussed.

1496. Maine, R. E.; and Murray, J. E.: **Application of Parameter Estimation to Highly Unstable Aircraft.** AIAA Paper 86-2020. *Technical Papers*, presented at the Atmospheric Flight Mechanics Conference, Williamsburg, Virginia, August 18–20, 1986, (see A86-47651 23-08), 1986, pp. 25–36, 86A47655, #. (See also 1495, 1651.)

This paper discusses the application of parameter estimation to highly unstable aircraft. It includes a discussion of the problems in applying the output error method to such aircraft and demonstrates that the filter error method eliminates these problems. The paper shows that the maximum likelihood estimator with no process noise does not reduce to the output error method when the system is unstable. It also proposes and demonstrates an ad hoc method that is similar in form to the filter error method, but applicable to nonlinear problems. Flight data from the X-29 forward-swept-wing demonstrator is used to illustrate the problems and methods discussed.

1497. Kehoe, M. W.: **Modified U.S. Army U-8F Ground Vibration Test.** NASA TM-86741, H-1297, NAS 1.15:86741, August 1986, 86N30723, #.

The Dryden Flight Research Facility of NASA Ames Research Center conducted a ground vibration test on a modified U.S. Army U-8F airplane. Modifications included new engines, propellers, and engine-mounted truss assemblies. The ground vibration test was conducted using sine dwell, single-point random, and impact excitations. The test was performed to determine modal frequencies, mode shapes, and structural damping coefficients of the airframe and propeller with full and empty fuel tanks. The data

presented include frequency response plots, rigid-body and structural modal frequencies, and mode shapes.

1498. Anderson, K. F.; Wrin, J. W.; and *James, R.: **A Radar Data Processing and Enhancement System.** NASA TM-88274, H-1377, NAS 1.15:88274. Presented at the IRIG Electronic Trajectory Measurements Group Meeting, El Paso, Texas, August 6, 1986, 86N29884, #.

This report describes the space position data processing system of the NASA Western Aeronautical Test Range. The system is installed at the Dryden Flight Research Facility of NASA Ames Research Center. This operational radar data system (RADATS) provides simultaneous data processing for multiple data inputs and tracking and antenna pointing outputs while performing real-time monitoring, control, and data enhancement functions. Experience in support of the space shuttle and aeronautical flight research missions is described, as well as the automated calibration and configuration functions of the system.

*GMD Systems, Lancaster, California.

1499. *Alag, G. S.; Burken, J. J.; and Gilyard, G. B.: **Eigensystem Synthesis for Active Flutter Suppression on an Oblique-Wing Aircraft.** NASA TM-88275, H-1359, NAS 1.15:88275, AIAA Paper 86-2243-CP. Presented at the AIAA Guidance, Navigation and Control Conference, Williamsburg, Virginia, August 18–20, 1986, 1986, 86N29868, #. (See also 1500, 1602.)

The application of the eigensystem synthesis technique to place the been practical for active flutter suppression, primarily because of the availability of only one control surface (aileron) for flutter suppression. The oblique-wing aircraft, because of its configuration, provides two independent surfaces (left and right ailerons), making the application of eigensystem synthesis practical. This paper presents the application of eigensystem synthesis using output feedback for the design of an active flutter suppression system for an oblique-wing aircraft. The results obtained are compared with those obtained by linear quadratic Gaussian techniques.

*Western Michigan University, Kalamazoo, Michigan.

1500. *Alag, G. S.; Burken, J. J.; and Gilyard, G. B.: **Eigensystem Synthesis for Active Flutter Suppression on an Oblique-Wing Aircraft.** AIAA Paper 86-2243. *Technical Papers*, presented at the Guidance, Navigation and Control Conference, Williamsburg, Virginia, August 18–20, 1986, (see A86-47401 23-63), pp. 812–817, 86A47491, #. (See also 1499, 1602.)

The application of the eigensystem synthesis technique to place the closed-loop eigenvalues and shape the closed-loop eigenvectors has not been practical for active flutter suppression, primarily because of the availability of only one control surface (aileron) for flutter suppression. The oblique-wing aircraft, because of its configuration, provides two independent surfaces (left and right ailerons), making the application of eigensystem synthesis practical. This paper presents the application of eigensystem synthesis using output feedback for the design of an active flutter suppression system for an oblique-wing aircraft. The results obtained are compared with those obtained by linear quadratic Gaussian techniques.

*Western Michigan University, Kalamazoo, Michigan.

1501. *Alag, G. S.; Kempel, R. W.; Pahle, J. W.; Bresina, J. J.; and Bartoli, F.: **Model-Following Control for an Oblique-Wing Aircraft**. NASA TM-88269, H-1362, NAS 1.15:88269, AIAA Paper 86-2244CP. Presented at the AIAA Conference on Guidance and Control, Williamsburg, Virginia, August 18–20, 1986, August 1986, 86N29867, #. (See also 1502.)

A variable-skew oblique wing offers a substantial aerodynamic performance advantage for aircraft missions that require both high efficiency in subsonic flight and supersonic dash or cruise. The most obvious characteristic of the oblique-wing concept is the asymmetry associated with wing-skew angle which results in significant aerodynamic and inertial cross-coupling between the aircraft longitudinal and lateral-directional axes. A technique for synthesizing a decoupling controller while providing the desired stability augmentation. The proposed synthesis procedure uses the concept of explicit model following. Linear quadratic optimization techniques are used to design the linear feedback system. The effectiveness of the control laws developed in achieving the desired decoupling is illustrated for a given flight condition by application to linearized equations of motion, and also to the nonlinear equations of six degrees of freedom of motion with nonlinear aerodynamic data.

*Western Michigan University, Kalamazoo, Michigan.

1502. *Alag, G. S.; Kempel, R. W.; Pahle, J. W.; Bresina, J. J.; and Bartoli, F.: **Model-Following Control for an Oblique-Wing Aircraft**. AIAA Paper 86-2244. *Technical Papers*, presented at the Guidance, Navigation and Control Conference, Williamsburg, Virginia, August 18–20, 1986, (see A86-47401 23-63), pp. 818–827, 86A47492, #. (See also 1501.)

A variable-skew oblique wing offers a substantial aerodynamic performance advantage for aircraft missions that require both high efficiency in subsonic flight and supersonic dash or cruise. The most obvious characteristic of the oblique-wing concept is the asymmetry associated with

wing-skew angle which results in significant aerodynamic and inertial cross-coupling between the aircraft longitudinal and lateral-directional axes. This paper presents a technique for synthesizing a decoupling controller while providing the desired stability augmentation. The proposed synthesis procedure uses the concept of explicit model following. Linear quadratic optimization techniques are used to design the linear feedback system. The effectiveness of the control laws developed in achieving the desired decoupling is illustrated for a given flight condition by application to linearized equations of motion, and also to the nonlinear equations of six degrees of freedom of motion with nonlinear aerodynamic data.

*Western Michigan University, Kalamazoo, Michigan.

1503. Smith, R. E.; and Sarrafian, S. K.: **Effect of Time Delay on Flying Qualities: An Update**. NASA TM-88264, H-1351, NAS 1.15:88264. Proposed for presentation at the AIAA Guidance, Navigation and Control Conference, Williamsburg, Virginia, August 18–20, 1986, August 1986, 86N28092, #. (See also 1504, 1526.)

Flying qualities problems of modern, full-authority electronic flight control systems are most often related to the introduction of additional time delay in aircraft response to a pilot input. These delays can have a significant effect on the flying qualities of the aircraft. Time delay effects are reexamined in light of recent flight test experience with aircraft incorporating new technology. Data from the X-29A forward-swept-wing demonstrator, a related preliminary in-flight experiment, and other flight observations are presented. These data suggest that the present MIL-F-8785C allowable-control system time delay specifications are inadequate or, at least, incomplete. Allowable time delay appears to be a function of the shape of the aircraft response following the initial delay. The cockpit feel system is discussed as a dynamic element in the flight control system. Data presented indicate that the time delay associated with a significant low-frequency feel system does not result in the predicted degradation in aircraft flying qualities. The impact of the feel system is discussed from two viewpoints: as a filter in the control system which can alter the initial response shape and, therefore, the allowable time delay, and as a unique dynamic element whose delay contribution can potentially be discounted by special pilot loop closures.

1504. Smith, R. E.; and Sarrafian, S. K.: **Effect of Time Delay on Flying Qualities—An Update**. AIAA Paper 86-2202. *Technical Papers*, presented at the Guidance, Navigation and Control Conference, Williamsburg, Virginia, August 18–20, 1986, (see A86-47401 23-63), pp. 711–720, 86A47482, #. (See also 1503, 1526.)

Flying qualities problems of modern, full-authority electronic flight control systems are most often related to the introduction of additional time delay in aircraft response to a pilot input. These delays can have a significant effect on the flying qualities of the aircraft. This paper reexamines time delay effects in light of recent flight test experience with aircraft incorporating new technology. Data from the X-29A forward-swept-wing demonstrator, a related preliminary in-flight experiment, and other flight observations are presented. These data suggest that the present MIL-F-8785C allowable-control system time delay specifications are inadequate or, at least, incomplete. Allowable time delay appears to be a function of the shape of the aircraft response following the initial delay. The cockpit feel system is discussed as a dynamic element in the flight control system. Data presented indicate that the time delay associated with a significant low-frequency feel system does not result in the predicted degradation in aircraft flying qualities. The impact of the feel system is discussed from two viewpoints: as a filter in the control system which can alter the initial response shape and, therefore, the allowable time delay, and as a unique dynamic element whose delay contribution can potentially be discounted by special pilot loop closures.

1505. Cazier, F. W., Jr.; and Kehoe, M. W.: **Flight Test of Passive Wing/Store Flutter Suppression.** NASA TM-87766, NAS 1.15:87766. Presented at the 1986 Aircraft/ Stores Compatibility Symposium, Wright-Patterson AFB, Ohio, April 8–10, 1986, August 1986, 86N31568, #.

Flight tests were performed on an F-16 airplane carrying on each wing an AIM-9J wingtip missile, a GBU-8 bomb near midspan, and an external fuel tank. Baseline flights with the GBU-8 mounted on a standard pylon established that this configuration is characterized by an antisymmetric limited amplitude flutter oscillation within the operational envelope. The airplane was then flown with GBU-8 mounted on the decoupler pylon. The decoupler pylon is a NASA concept of passive wing-store flutter suppression achieved by providing a low store-pylon pitch frequency. The decoupler pylon successfully suppressed wing-store flutter throughout the flight envelope. A 37 percent increase in flutter velocity over the standard pylon was demonstrated. Maneuvers with load factors to 4g were performed. Although the static store displacements during maneuvers were not sufficiently large to be of concern, a store pitch alignment system was tested and performed successfully. One GBU-8 was ejected demonstrating that weapon separation from the decoupler pylon is normal.

1506. Powers, B. G.; and Sarrafian, S. K.: **Simulation Studies of Alternate Longitudinal Control Systems for the Space Shuttle Orbiter in the Landing Regime.** NASA TM-86815, H-1356, NAS 1.15:86815. Presented at the AIAA Atmospheric Flight Mechanics Conference, Williamsburg, Virginia, August 18–20, 1986, 1986, 86N28091, #. (See also 1507.)

Simulations of the space shuttle orbiter in the landing task were conducted by the NASA Ames-Dryden Flight Research Facility using the Ames Research Center vertical motion simulator (VMS) and the total in-flight simulator (TIFS) variable-stability aircraft. Several new control systems designed to improve the orbiter longitudinal response characteristics were investigated. These systems improved the flightpath response by increasing the amount of pitch-rate overshoot. Reduction in the overall time delay was also investigated. During these evaluations, different preferences were noted for the baseline or the new systems depending on the pilot background. The trained astronauts were quite proficient with the baseline system and found the new systems to be less desirable than the baseline. On the other hand, the pilots without extensive flight training with the orbiter had a strong preference for the new systems. This paper presents the results of the VMS and TIFS simulations. A hypothesis is presented regarding the control strategies of the two pilot groups and how this influenced their control systems preferences. Interpretations of these control strategies are made in terms of open-loop aircraft response characteristics as well as pilot-vehicle closed-loop characteristics.

1507. Powers, B. G.; and Sarrafian, S. K.: **Simulation Studies of Alternate Longitudinal Control Systems for the Space Shuttle Orbiter in the Landing Regime.** AIAA Paper 86-2127. *Technical Papers*, presented at the Atmospheric Flight Mechanics Conference, Williamsburg, Virginia, August 18–20, 1986, (see A86-47651 23-08), pp. 182–192, 86A47673, #. (See also 1506.)

Simulations of the Space Shuttle Orbiter in the landing task were conducted by the NASA Ames-Dryden Flight Research Facility using the Ames Research center vertical motion simulation (VMS) and the total in-flight simulator (TIFS) variable-stability aircraft. Several new control systems designed to improve the orbiter longitudinal response characteristics were investigated. These systems improved the flightpath response by increasing the amount of pitch-rate overshoot. Reduction in the overall time delay was also investigated. During these evaluations, different preferences were noted for the baseline or the new systems depending on the pilot background. The trained astronauts were quite proficient with the baseline system and found the new systems to be less desirable than the baseline. On the other hand, the pilots without extensive flight training with the Orbiter had a strong preference for the new systems. This paper presents the results of the VMS and TIFS simulations. A hypothesis is presented regarding the control strategies of the two pilot groups and how this influenced their control system preferences. Interpretations of these control strategies are made in terms of open-loop aircraft response characteristics as well as pilot-vehicle closed-loop characteristics.

1508. Berry, D. T.; and Sarrafian, S. K.: **Validation of a New Flying Quality Criterion for the Landing Task.** NASA TM-88261, H-1357, NAS 1.15:88261, AIAA Paper 86-2126-CP. Presented at the AIAA Atmospheric Flight Mechanics Conference, Williamsburg, Virginia, August 18–20, 1986, <u>1986</u>, 86N26341, #. (See also 1509.)

A strong correlation has been found to exist between flight path angle peak overshoot and pilot ratings for the landing task. The use of flightpath overshoot as a flying quality metric for landing is validated by correlation with four different in-flight simulation programs and a ground simulation study. Configurations tested were primarily medium-weight generic transports. As a result of good correlation with this extensive data base, criterion boundaries are proposed for landing based on the flight path peak overshoot metric.

1509. Berry, D. T.; and Sarrafian, S. K.: **Validation of a New Flying Quality Criterion for the Landing Task.** AIAA Paper 86-2126. *Technical Papers*, presented at the Atmospheric Flight Mechanics Conference, Williamsburg, Virginia, <u>August 18–20, 1986</u>, (see A86-47651 23-08), pp. 175–181, 86A47672, #. (See also 1508.)

A strong correlation has been found to exist between flight path angle peak overshoot and pilot ratings for the landing task. The use of flight path overshoot as a flying quality metric for landing is validated by correlation with four different in-flight simulation programs and a ground simulation study. Configurations tested were primarily medium-weight generic transports. As a result of good correlation with this extensive data base, criterion boundaries are proposed for landing based on the flight path peak overshoot metric.

1510. Regenie, V. A.; Chacon, C. V.; and Lock, W. P.: **Experience With Synchronous and Asynchronous Digital Control Systems.** NASA TM-88271, H-1372, NAS 1.15:88271, AIAA Paper 86-2239-CP. Presented at the AIAA Guidance, Navigation and Control Conference, Williamsburg, Virginia, <u>August 18–20, 1986</u>, 86N29866, #. (See also 1492.)

Flight control systems have undergone a revolution since the days of simple mechanical linkages; presently the most advanced systems are full-authority, full-time digital systems controlling unstable aircraft. With the use of advanced control systems, the aerodynamic design can incorporate features that allow greater performance and fuel savings, as can be seen on the new Airbus design and advanced tactical fighter concepts. These advanced aircraft will be and are relying on the flight control system to provide the stability and handling qualities required for safe flight and to allow the pilot to control the aircraft. Various design philosophies have been proposed and followed to investigate system

architectures for these advanced flight control systems. One major area of discussion is whether a multichannel digital control system should be synchronous or asynchronous. This paper addressed the flight experience at the Dryden Flight Research Facility of NASA's Ames Research Center with both synchronous and asynchronous digital flight control systems. Four different flight control systems are evaluated against criteria such as software reliability, cost increases, and schedule delays.

1511. Larson, R. R.: **Flight Control System Development and Flight Test Experience With the F-111 Mission Adaptive Wing Aircraft.** NASA TM-88265, H-1366, NAS 1.15:88265, AIAA Paper 86-2237-CP. Presented at the AIAA Guidance, Navigation, and Control Conference, Williamsburg, Virginia, August 18–20, 1986, <u>1986</u>, 86N29813, #. (See also 1512.)

The wing on the NASA F-111 transonic aircraft technology airplane was modified to provide flexible leading and trailing edge flaps. This wing is known as the mission adaptive wing (MAW) because aerodynamic efficiency can be maintained at all speeds. Unlike a conventional wing, the MAW has no spoilers, external flap hinges, or fairings to break the smooth contour. The leading edge flaps and three-segment trailing edge flaps are controlled by a redundant fly-by-wire control system that features a dual digital primary system architecture providing roll and symmetric commands to the MAW control surfaces. A segregated analog backup system is provided in the event of a primary system failure. This paper discusses the design, development, testing, qualification, and flight test experience of the MAW primary and backup flight control systems.

1512. Larson, R. R.: **Flight Control System Development and Flight Test Experience With the F-111 Mission Adaptive Wing Aircraft.** AIAA Paper 86-2237. *Technical Papers*, presented at the Guidance, Navigation and Control Conference, Williamsburg, Virginia, <u>August 18–20, 1986</u>, (see A86-47401 23-63), pp. 784–801, 86A47489, #. (See also 1511.)

The wing on the NASA F-111 transonic aircraft technology airplane was modified to provide flexible leading and trailing edge flaps. This wing is known as the mission adaptive wing (MAW) because aerodynamic efficiency can be maintained at all speeds. Unlike a conventional wing, the MAW has no spoilers, external flap hinges, or fairings to break the smooth contour. The leading edge flaps and three-segment trailing edge flaps are controlled by a redundant fly-by-wire control system that features a dual digital primary system architecture providing roll and symmetric commands to the MAW control surfaces. A segregated analog backup system is provided in the event of a primary system failure. This paper discusses the design, development, testing, qualification, and flight test experience of the MAW primary and backup flight control systems.

EC85-33205-07

F-111 Mission Adaptive Wing Airplane

1513. Trujillo, B. M.: **Determination of Lift and Drag Characteristics of Space Shuttle Orbiter Using Maximum Likelihood Estimation Technique.** AIAA Paper 86-2225. *Technical Papers*, presented at the Atmospheric Flight Mechanics Conference, Williamsburg, Virginia, <u>August 18–20, 1986</u>, (see A86-47651 23-08), pp. 390–351, 86A47688, #.

This paper presents the technique and results of maximum likelihood estimation used to determine lift and drag characteristics of the Space Shuttle Orbiter. Maximum likelihood estimation uses measurable parameters to estimate nonmeasurable parameters. The nonmeasurable parameters for this case are elements of a nonlinear, dynamic model of the orbiter. The estimated parameters are used to evaluate a cost function that computes the differences between the measured and estimated longitudinal parameters. The case presented is a dynamic analysis. This places less restriction on pitching motion and can provide additional information about the orbiter such as lift and drag characteristics at conditions other than trim, instrument biases, and pitching moment characteristics. In addition, an output of the analysis is an estimate of the values for the individual components of lift and drag that contribute to the total lift and drag. The results show that maximum likelihood estimation is a useful tool for analysis of Space Shuttle Orbiter performance and is also applicable to parameter analysis of other types of aircraft.

1514. *Roy, R. H.; *Walker, R. A.; and Gilyard, G. B.: **Real-Time Flutter Identification With Close Mode**

Resolution. AIAA Paper 86-2019. *Technical Papers*, presented at the Atmospheric Flight Mechanics Conference, Williamsburg, Virginia, <u>August 18–20, 1986</u>, (see A86-47651 23-08), pp. 20–24, 86A47654, #.

Real-time flutter prediction including close modes can be effectively estimated from turbulence or on-board excitation with an Extended Kalman Filter (EKF) approach. A physically based model form enables prediction of the damping rate as well as damping, giving a time to instability estimate with its variance. The approach is recursive and can operate asynchronously to drop data outliers and hence is quite robust. Its speed is reasonable for on-line application but can also be used effectively as an off-line analysis tool for application to any modal testing situation.

*Integrated Systems, Inc., Palo Alto, California.

1515. *Alag, G. S.; and Duke, E. L.: **Development of Control Laws for a Flight Test Maneuver Autopilot.** *Journal of Guidance, Control, and Dynamics* (ISSN 0731-5090), Vol. 9, July–August 1986, pp. 441–445, (see A85-45888), <u>August 1986</u>, 86A46460, #. (See also 1426, 1427.)

*Western Michigan University, Kalamazoo, Michigan.

1516. Meyer, Robert R., Jr.; and Covell, Peter F.: **Effects of Winglets on a First-Generation Jet Transport Wing. 7: Sideslip Effects on Winglet Loads and Selected Wing Loads at Subsonic Speeds for a Full-Span Model.** NASA TP-2619, H-1193, NAS 1.60:2619, <u>September 1986</u>, 88N18567, #.

The effect of sideslip on winglet loads and selected wing loads was investigated at high and low subsonic Mach numbers. The investigation was conducted in two separate wind tunnel facilities, using two slightly different 0.035-scale full-span models. Results are presented which indicate that, in general, winglet loads as a result of sideslip are analogous to wing loads caused by angle of attack. The center-of-pressure locations on the winglets are somewhat different than might be expected for an analogous wing. The spanwise center of pressure for a winglet tends to be more inboard than for a wing. The most notable chordwise location is a forward center-of-pressure location on the winglet at high sideslip angles. The noted differences between a winglet and an analogous wing are the result of the influence of the wing on the winglet.

1517. Duke, Eugene L.; Jones, Frank P.; and Roncoli, Ralph B.: **Development and Flight Test of an Experimental Maneuver Autopilot for a Highly Maneuverable Aircraft.** NASA TP-2618, H-1258, NAS 1.60:2618, <u>September 1986,</u> 88N21153, #.

This report presents the development of an experimental flight test maneuver autopilot (FTMAP) for a highly maneuverable aircraft. The essence of this technique is the application of an autopilot to provide precise control during required flight test maneuvers. This newly developed flight test technique is being applied at the Dryden Flight Research Facility of NASA Ames Research Center. The FTMAP is designed to increase the quantity and quality of data obtained in test flight. The technique was developed and demonstrated on the highly maneuverable aircraft technology (HiMAT) vehicle. This report describes the HiMAT vehicle systems, maneuver requirements, FTMAP development process, and flight results.

1518. Smith, Rogers E.; and *Schroeder, Kurt C.: **Flight Testing the X-29.** *1986 Report to the Aerospace Profession: Proceedings of the Thirtieth SETP Symposium*, Beverly Hills, California, September 24–27, 1986, (see A87-47835 21-05), 1986, pp. 116–134, 87A47841.

A testing status report is presented for the X-29 forward-swept-wing experimental aircraft, which integrates such advanced technologies as an aeroelastically tailored composite wing, a thin supercritical airfoil, three-surface pitch control, discrete variable camber, full-authority close-coupled canards, static instability, and digital fly-by-wire flight controls. X-29 flight test results to date raise several issues pertinent to the design of future combat aircraft flight control systems; for example, they bring into question the current MIL-8785C requirements on control system time delays.

*Grumman Corporation, Bethpage, New York.

1519. *Birk, Frank T.; and Smith, Rogers E.: **Mission Adaptive Wing Test Program.** *1986 Report to the Aerospace Profession: Proceedings of the Thirtieth SETP Symposium*, Beverly Hills, California, September 24–27, 1986, (see A87-47835 21-05), 1986, pp. 86–100, 87A47839.

With the completion of the F-111 test-bed Mission Adaptive Wing (MAW) test program's manual flight control system, emphasis has been shifted to flight testing of MAW automatic control modes. These encompass (1) cruise camber control, (2) maneuver camber control, (3) maneuver load control, and (4) maneuver enhancement and load alleviation control. The aircraft is currently cleared to a 2.5-g maneuvering limit due to generally higher variable-incidence wing pivot loads than had been anticipated, especially at the higher wing-camber settings. Buffet is noted to be somewhat higher than expected at the higher camber settings.

*USAF Flight Test Center, Edwards AFB, California.

1520. Whitmore, S. A.; and *Leondes, C. T.: **Formulation and Implementation of a Practical Algorithm for Non-Stationary Adaptive State Estimation.** *International Journal of Control* (ISSN 0020-7179), Vol. 44, September 1986, pp. 767–775, 87A12066.

Background information on the Kalman filter is given first. A discussion of the filter parameters and their a priori determination follows. The discussion points out the need for adaptive determination of the process noise statistics. The filter innovations are presented as a means for developing the adaptive criteria. The criteria center around the estimation of the true mean and covariance of the filter innovations. A method for the numerical approximation of the mean and covariance of a locally stationary random process is presented. The definition of a local stationarity is presented. Local stationarity allows for the separation of the process statistics into a stationary component and a time-varying component. The separation method is discussed. A method for estimating the stationary and time-varying components is presented. As an example of its application to real problems, the algorithm is applied to the problem to the problem of reentry trajectory estimation for the Space Shuttle. Both the adaptive algorithm and the steady-state Kalman filter are applied to the problem. The results of the reconstructions are presented. The adaptive algorithm exhibits superior performance.

*University of California, Los Angeles, California.

1521. Ko, William L.; Quinn, Robert D.; and Gong, Leslie: **Effects of Forced and Free Convections on Structural Temperatures of Space Shuttle Orbiter During Reentry Flight.** NASA TM-86800, H-1414, NAS 1.15:86800, AIAA Paper 87-1600. Presented at the AIAA 22nd Thermophysics Conference, Honolulu, Hawaii, June 8–10, 1987, Revised October 1986, 88N10275, #. (See also 1567.)

Structural performance and resizing (SPAR) finite element thermal analysis computer programs was used in the heat transfer analysis of the space shuttle orbiter wing subjected to reentry aerodynamic heating. With sufficient external forced convective cooling near the end of the heating cycle, the calculated surface temperatures of the thermal protection system (TPS) agree favorable with the flight data for the entire flight profile. However, the effects of this external forced convective cooling on the structural temperatures were found to be negligible. Both free and forced convection elements were introduced to model the internal convection effect of the cool air entering the shuttle interior. The introduction of the internal free convection effect decreased the calculated wing lower skin temperatures by 20° F, 1200 sec after touchdown. If the internal convection is treated as forced convection, the calculated wing lower skin temperatures after touchdown can be reduced to match the flight measured data. By reducing the TPS thicknesses to certain thicknesses to account for the TPS gap heating, the calculated wing lower skin temperatures prior to touchdown can be raised to agree with the flight data perfectly.

1522. Iliff, Kenneth W.; and Maine, Richard E.: **Bibliography for Aircraft Parameter Estimation.** NASA

TM-86804, H-1358, NAS 1.15:86804, October 1986, 87N29498, #.

An extensive bibliography in the field of aircraft parameter estimation has been compiled. This list contains definitive works related to most aircraft parameter estimation approaches. Theoretical studies as well as practical applications are included. Many of these publications are pertinent to subjects peripherally related to parameter estimation, such as aircraft maneuver design or instrumentation considerations.

1523. Duke, E. L.; Regenie, V. A.; and Deets, D. A.: **Rapid Prototyping Facility for Flight Research in Artificial-Intelligence-Based Flight Systems Concepts.** NASA TM-88268, H-1367, NAS 1.15:88268, October 1986, 87N12273, #. (See also 1701.)

The Dryden Flight Research Facility of the NASA Ames Research Facility of the NASA Ames Research Center is developing a rapid prototyping facility for flight research in flight systems concepts that are based on artificial intelligence (AI). The facility will include real-time high-fidelity aircraft simulators, conventional and symbolic processors, and a high-performance research aircraft specially modified to accept commands from the ground-based AI computers. This facility is being developed as part of the NASA-DARPA automated wingman program. This document discusses the need for flight research and for a national flight research facility for the rapid prototyping of AI-based avionics systems and the NASA response to those needs.

1524. *Waggoner, E. G.; Jennett, L. A.; and **Bates, B. L.: **X-29 Flight Test Program Including Wind Tunnel and Computational Support.** SAE Paper 861642. Presented at the SAE Aerospace Technology Conference and Exposition, Long Beach, California, October 13–16, 1986, 87A32584.

A cooperative effort has been defined between NASA-Ames/ Dryden Flight Research Facility and NASA-Langley Research Center in support of the X-29A Advanced Technology Demonstrator. The effort involves three phases: flight testing, wind-tunnel testing in the National Transonic Facility, and computational support of each experimental phase. These efforts are primarily aimed at understanding the complex flow phenomena and component interactions associated with the X-29A. Each phase of the effort is discussed in detail and initial data comparisons are presented. In summary, the synergistics effects of the complementary phases are identified, which will enhance the understanding of the unique aerodynamics of the X-29A.

*NASA Langley Research Center, Hampton, Virginia.
**Vigyan Research Associates, Inc., Hampton, Virginia.

1525. Deets, D. A.; and *Brown, L. E.: **Wright Brothers Lectureship in Aeronautics: Experience With HiMAT**

Remotely Piloted Research Vehicle—An Alternate Flight Test Approach. AIAA Paper 86-2754. Presented at the AIAA, AHS, and ASEE, Aircraft Systems, Design and Technology Meeting, Dayton, Ohio, October 20–22, 1986, 87A17963, #.

The highly maneuverable aircraft technology (HiMAT) program explored the various and complex interactions of advanced technologies, such as aeroelastic tailoring, close-coupled canard, and relaxed static stability. A 0.44-subscale remotely piloted research vehicle (RPRV) of a hypothetical fighter airplane was designed and flight-tested to determine the effects of these interactions and to define the design techniques appropriate for advanced fighter technologies. Flexibility and high maneuverability were provided by flight control laws implemented in ground-based computers and telemetered to the vehicle control system during flight tests. The high quality of the flight-measured data and their close correlation with the analytical design modeling proved that the RPRV is a viable and cost-effective tool for developing aerodynamic, structure, and control law requirements for highly maneuverable fighter airplanes of the future.

**Rockwell International Corporation, North American Aircraft Operations Div., El Segundo, California.

1526. Smith, R. E.; and Sarrafian, S. K.: **Effect of Time Delay on Flying Qualities—An Update.** *Technical Papers,* presented at the Guidance, Navigation and Control Conference, Williamsburg, Virginia, August 18–20, 1986, pp. 711–720. *Journal of Guidance, Control, and Dynamics,* (ISSN 0731-5090), Vol. 9, September–October 1986, (A86-47482), October 1986, pp. 578–584, 87A17758, #. (See also 1503, 1504.)

1527. Berry, D. T.: **In-Flight Evaluation of Incremental Time Delays in Pitch and Roll.** *Journal of Guidance, Control, and Dynamics,* (ISSN 0731-5090), Vol. 9, September–October 1986, (see A85-45881), pp. 573–577, 87A17757, #. (See also 1428.)

1528. Powers, B. G.: **Space Shuttle Longitudinal Landing Flying Qualities.** *Journal of Guidance, Control, and Dynamics,* (ISSN 0731-5090), Vol. 9, September–October 1986, pp. 566–572, 87A17756, #.

The Space Shuttle program took on the challenge of providing a manual landing capability for an operational vehicle returning from orbit. Some complex challenges were encountered in developing the longitudinal flying qualities required to land the Orbiter manually in an operational environment. Approach and landing test flights indicated a tendency of pilot-induced oscillation near landing. Changes in the operational procedures reduced the difficulty of the landing task, and an adaptive stick filter was incorporated to reduce the severity of any pilot-induced oscillatory motions. Fixed-base, moving-base, and in-flight simulations were used for the evaluations. Overall, the Orbiter control system and operational procedures produced a good capability to perform routinely precise landings with a large, unpowered vehicle that has a low lift-to-drag ratio.

1529. Ehernberger, L. J.: **High Altitude Turbulence for Supersonic Cruise Vehicles.** AAS Paper 86-418. Presented at Aerospace Century XXI: Space Sciences, Applications, and Commercial Developments; *Proceedings of the Thirty-third Annual AAS International Conference*, Boulder, Colorado, October 26–29, 1986, (see A88-35123 13-12), (see N87-23100), pp. 1391–1405, 88A35140. (See also 1563.)

The characteristics of high altitude turbulence and its associated meteorological features are reviewed. Findings based on data from NASA flight research programs with prototype military aircraft, the XB-70 and YF-12A, are emphasized. An example of detailed numerical atmospheric simulations, which may provide greatly increased understanding of these earlier turbulence observations, is presented. Comparisons between observation and numerical simulation should help to delineate the limitations of analysis techniques and improve our understanding of atmospheric processes in the stratosphere.

1530. *Erickson, G. E.; **Peake, D. J.; Del Frate, J.; *Skow, A. M.; and *Malcolm, G. N.: **Water Facilities in Retrospect and Prospect: An Illuminating Tool for Vehicle Design.** NASA TM-89409, A-87021, NAS 1.15:89409, November 1986, 87N13403, #. (See also 1569.)

Water facilities play a fundamental role in the design of air, ground, and marine vehicles by providing a qualitative, and sometimes quantitative, description of complex flow phenomena. Water tunnels, channels, and tow tanks used as flow-diagnostic tools have experienced a renaissance in recent years in response to the increased complexity of designs suitable for advanced technology vehicles. These vehicles are frequently characterized by large regions of steady and unsteady three-dimensional flow separation and ensuing vortical flows. The visualization and interpretation of the complicated fluid motions about isolated vehicle components and complete configurations in a time and cost effective manner in hydrodynamic test facilities is a key element in the development of flow control concepts, and, hence, improved vehicle designs. A historical perspective of the role of water facilities in the vehicle design process is presented. The application of water facilities to specific aerodynamic and hydrodynamic flow problems is discussed, and the strengths and limitations of these important experimental tools are emphasized.

*Eidetics International, Inc., Torrance, California.
**Ames Research Center, Moffett Field, California.

1531. Powers, Sheryll Goecke; *Huffman, Jarrett K.; and *Fox, Charles H., Jr.: **Flight and Wind-Tunnel Measurements Showing Base Drag Reduction Provided by a Trailing Disk for High Reynolds Number Turbulent Flow for Subsonic and Transonic Mach Numbers.** NASA TP-2638, H-1281, NAS 1.60:2638, November 1986, 88N14299, #.

The effectiveness of a trailing disk, or trapped vortex concept, in reducing the base drag of a large body of revolution was studied from measurements made both in flight and in a wind tunnel. Pressure data obtained for the flight experiment, and both pressure and force balance data were obtained for the wind tunnel experiment. The flight test also included data obtained from a hemispherical base. The experiment demonstrated the significant base drag reduction capability of the trailing disk to Mach 0.93 and to Reynolds numbers up to 80 times greater than for earlier studies. For the trailing disk data from the flight experiment, the maximum decrease in base drag ranged form 0.08 to 0.07 as Mach number increased from 0.70 to 0.93. Aircraft angles of attack ranged from 3.9 to 6.6 deg for the flight data. For the trailing disk data from the wind tunnel experiment, the maximum decrease in base and total drag ranged from 0.08 to 0.05 for the approximately 0 deg angle of attack data as Mach number increased from 0.30 to 0.82.

*NASA Langley Research Center, Hampton, Virginia.

1532. Ko, William L.; *Shideler, John L.; and Fields, Roger A.: **Buckling Characteristics of Hypersonic Aircraft Wing Tubular Panels.** NASA TM-87756, L-16128, NAS 1.15:87756, December 1986, 89N13816, #.

The buckling characteristics of Rene 41 tubular panels installed as wing panels on a hypersonic wing test structure (HWTS) were determined nondestructively through use of a force/stiffness technique. The nondestructive buckling tests were carried out under different combined load conditions and different temperature environments. Two panels were subsequently tested to buckling failure in a universal tension compression testing machine. In spite of some data scattering because of large extrapolations of data points resulting from termination of the test at a somewhat low applied load, the overall test data correlated fairly well with theoretically predicted buckling interaction curves. The structural efficiency of the tubular panels was slightly higher than that of the beaded panels which they replaced.

*NASA Langley Research Center, Hampton, Virginia.

1533. *Wagner, R. D.; Fisher, D. F.; *Fischer, M. C.; *Bartlett, D. W.; and Meyer, R. R., Jr.: **Laminar Flow Integration: Flight Tests Status and Plans.** NASA CP 2397. *Langley Symposium on Aerodynamics*, Vol. 1, (see N88-14926 07-01), December 1986, pp. 485–518, 88N14952, #.

Under the Aircraft Energy Efficiency - Laminar Flow Control Program, there are currently three flight test programs under way to address critical issues concerning laminar flow technology application to commercial transports. The Leading-Edge Flight Test (LEFT) with a JetStar aircraft is a cooperative effort with the Ames/Dryden Flight Research Facility to provide operational experience with candidate leading-edge systems representative of those that might be used on a future transport. In the Variable Sweep Transition Flight Experiment (VSTFE), also a cooperative effort between Langley and Ames/Dryden, basic transition data on an F-14 wing with variable sweep will be obtained to provide a data base for laminar flow wing design. Finally, under contract to the Boeing Company, the acoustic environment on the wing of a 757 aircraft will be measured and the influence of engine noise on laminar flow determined with a natural laminar flow glove on the wing. The status and plans for these programs are reported.

*NASA Langley Research Center, Hampton, Virginia.

1534. Johnson, J. Blair; and *Sandlin, Doral R.: **Comparison of Theoretical and Flight-Measured Local Flow Aerodynamics for a Low-Aspect-Ratio Fin.** NASA TM-86806, H-1336, NAS 1.15:86806, December 1986, 87N15941, #.

Flight test and theoretical aerodynamic data were obtained for a flight test fixture mounted on the underside of an F-104G aircraft. The theoretical data were generated using two codes: a two-dimensional transonic code called code H, and a three-dimensional subsonic and supersonic code called wing-body. Pressure distributions generated by the codes for the flight test fixture, as well as compared with the flight-measured data. The two-dimensional code pressure distributions compared well except at the minimum pressure point and the trailing edge. Shock locations compared well except at high transonic speeds. However, the two-dimensional code did not adequately predict the displacement thickness of the flight test fixture. The three-dimensional code pressure distributions compared well except at the trailing edge of the flight test fixture.

*California Polytechnic State University, San Luis Obispo, California.

1535. Ko, William L.; Quinn, Robert D.; and Gong, Leslie: **Finite-Element Reentry Heat-Transfer Analysis of Space Shuttle Orbiter.** NASA TP-2657, H-1236, NAS 1.60:2657, December 1986, 87N29795, #.

A structural performance and resizing (SPAR) finite-element thermal analysis computer program was used in the heat-transfer analysis of the space shuttle orbiter subjected to reentry aerodynamic heating. Three wing cross sections and one midfuselage cross section were selected for the thermal

analysis. The predicted thermal protection system temperatures were found to agree well with flight-measured temperatures. The calculated aluminum structural temperatures also agreed reasonably well with the flight data from reentry to touchdown. The effects of internal radiation and of internal convection were found to be significant. The SPAR finite-element solutions agreed reasonably well with those obtained from the conventional finite-difference method.

1536. Maine, R. E.; and Iliff, K. W.: **Identification of Dynamic Systems—Applications to Aircraft. Part 1: the Output Error Approach.** AGARD-AG-300-VOL-3-PT-1, ISBN-92-835-1540-4, AD-A178766, December 1986, 87N21913, #.

This document examines the practical application of parameter estimation methodology to the problem of estimating aircraft stability and control derivatives from flight test data. The primary purpose of the document is to present a comprehensive and unified picture of the entire parameter estimation process and its integration into the flight test program. The document concentrates on the output-error method to provide a focus for detailed examination and to allow us to give specific examples of situations that have arisen in our experience. The document first derives the aircraft equations of motion in a form suitable for application to estimation of stability and control derivatives. It then discusses the issues that arise in adapting the equations to the limitations of analysis programs, using a specific program for an example. The document then addresses the roles and issues relating to mass distribution data, preflight predictions, maneuver design, flight scheduling, instrumentation sensors, data acquisition systems, and data processing. Finally, the document discusses evaluation and use of the analysis results.

1537. Walton, James T.; and Burcham, Frank W., Jr.: **Exhaust-Gas Pressure and Temperature Survey of F404-GE-400 Turbofan Engine.** NASA TM-88273, H-1375, NAS 1.15:88273, December 1986, 88N20307, #.

An exhaust-gas pressure and temperature survey of the General Electric F404-GE-400 turbofan engine was conducted in the altitude test facility of the NASA Lewis Propulsion System Laboratory. Traversals by a survey rake were made across the exhaust-nozzle exit to measure the pitot pressure and total temperature. Tests were performed at Mach 0.87 and a 24,000-ft altitude and at Mach 0.30 and a 30,000-ft altitude with various power settings from intermediate to maximum afterburning. Data yielded smooth pressure and temperature profiles with maximum jet temperatures approximately 1.4 in. inside the nozzle edge and maximum jet temperatures from 1 to 3 in. inside the edge. A low-pressure region located exactly at engine center was noted. The maximum temperature encountered was 3800 R.

1538. Gupta, K. K.: **Formulation of Numerical Procedures for Dynamic Analysis of Spinning Structures.** *International Journal for Numerical Methods in Engineering* (ISSN 0029-5981), Vol. 23, December 1986, pp. 2347–2357, 87A29025.

The paper presents the descriptions of recently developed numerical algorithms that prove to be useful for the solution of the free vibration problem of spinning centrifugal forces in a finite element owing to any specified spin rate is derived in detail. This is followed by a description of an improved eigenproblem solution procedure that proves to be economical for the free vibration analysis of spinning structures. Numerical results are also presented which indicate the efficacy of the currently developed procedures.

1539. Berry, Donald T.: **A Flight-Path-Overshoot Flying Qualities Metric for the Landing Task.** *Journal of Guidance, Control, and Dynamics* (ISSN 0731-5090), Vol. 9, November–December 1986, pp. 609–613, 87A23976, #. (See also 1449, 1450.)

1987 Technical Publications

1540. Glover, Richard D.: **Design and Initial Application of the Extended Aircraft Interrogation and Display System: Multiprocessing Ground Support Equipment for Digital Flight Systems.** NASA TM-86740, H-1296, NAS 1.15:86740, January 1987, 87N16820, #.

A pipelined, multiprocessor, general-purpose ground support equipment for digital flight systems has been developed and placed in service at the NASA Ames Research Center's Dryden Flight Research Facility. The design is an outgrowth of the earlier aircraft interrogation and display system (AIDS) used in support of several research projects to provide engineering-units display of internal control system parameters during development and qualification testing activities. The new system, incorporating multiple 16-bit processors, is called extended AIDS (XAIDS) and is now supporting the X-29A forward-swept-wing aircraft project. This report describes the design and mechanization of XAIDS and shows the steps whereby a typical user may take advantage of its high throughput and flexible features.

1541. Hicks, John W.; *Kania, Jan; **Pearce, Robert; and **Mills, Glen: **Challenges in Modeling the X-29 Flight Test Performance.** NASA TM-88282, H-1395, NAS 1.15:88282. Presented at the AIAA 25th Aerospace Sciences Meeting, Reno, Nevada, January 12–15, 1987, January 1987, (see A87-22402), 87N20991, #. (See also 1542.)

Presented are methods, instrumentation, and difficulties associated with drag measurement of the X-29A aircraft. The

initial performance objective of the X-29A program emphasized drag polar shapes rather than absolute drag levels. Priorities during the flight envelope expansion restricted the evaluation of aircraft performance. Changes in aircraft configuration, uncertainties in angle-of-attack calibration, and limitations in instrumentation complicated the analysis. Limited engine instrumentation with uncertainties in overall in-flight thrust accuracy made it difficult to obtain reliable values of coefficient of parasite drag. The aircraft was incapable of tracking the automatic camber control trim schedule for optimum wing flaperon deflection during typical dynamic performance maneuvers; this has also complicated the drag polar shape modeling. The X-29A was far enough off the schedule that the developed trim drag correction procedure has proven inadequate. However, good drag polar shapes have been developed throughout the flight envelope. Preliminary flight results have compared well with wind tunnel predictions. A more comprehensive analysis must be done to complete performance models. The detailed flight performance program with a calibrated engine will benefit from the experience gained during this preliminary performance phase.

* Air Force Flight Test Center, Edwards AFB, California.
** Grumman Aerospace Corporation, Edwards, California.

1542. Hicks, John W.; *Kania, Jan; **Pearce, Robert; and **Mills, Glen: **Challenges in Modeling the X-29A Flight Test Performance.** AIAA Paper 87-0081. Presented at the AIAA 25th Aerospace Sciences Meeting, Reno, Nevada, January 12–15, 1987, 87A22402, #. (See also 1541.)

The paper presents the methods, instrumentation, and difficulties associated with drag measurement of the X-29A aircraft. The initial performance objective of the X-29A program emphasized drag polar shapes rather than absolute drag levels. Priorities during the flight envelope expansion restricted the evaluation of aircraft performance. Changes in aircraft configuration, uncertainties in angle-of-attack calibration, and limitations in instrumentation complicated the analysis. Limited engine instrumentation with uncertainties in overall in-flight thrust accuracy made it difficult to obtain reliable values of coefficient of parasite drag. The aircraft was incapable of tracking the automatic camber control trim schedule for optimum wing flaperon deflection during typical dynamic performance maneuvers; this has also complicated the drag polar shape modeling. The X-29A was far enough off the schedule that the developed trim drag correction procedure has proven inadequate. Despite these obstacles, good drag polar shapes have been developed throughout the flight envelope. Preliminary flight results have compared well with wind tunnel predictions. A more comprehensive analysis must be done to complete the performance models. The detailed flight performance program with a calibrated engine will benefit from the experience gained during this preliminary performance phase.

*USAF Flight Test Center, Edwards AFB, California.
**Grumman Aerospace Corporation, Edwards, California.

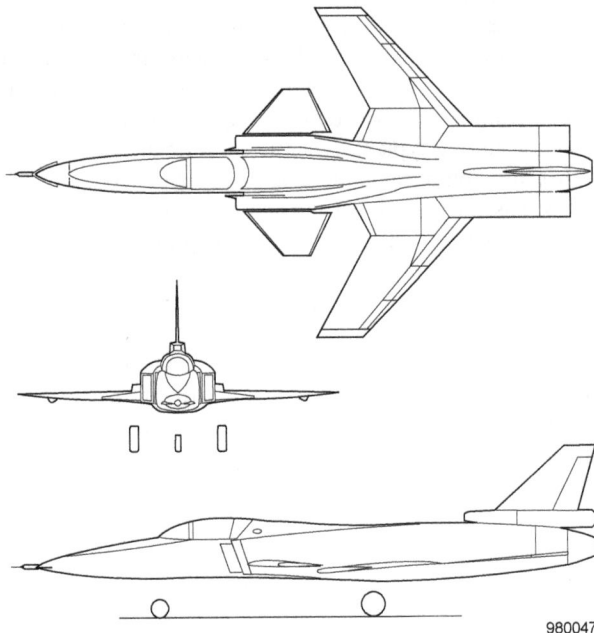

980047

X-29A Airplane, Three-View Drawing

1543. Iliff, Kenneth W.: **Aircraft Parameter Estimation**. NASA TM-88281, H-1394, NAS 1.15:88281. Presented at the AIAA 25th Aerospace Sciences Meeting, Reno, Nevada, January 1987, 87N19376, #. (See also 1544, 1743.)

The aircraft parameter estimation problem is used to illustrate the utility of parameter estimation, which applies to many engineering and scientific fields. Maximum likelihood estimation has been used to extract stability and control derivatives from flight data for many years. This paper presents some of the basic concepts of aircraft parameter estimation and briefly surveys the literature in the field. The maximum likelihood estimator is discussed, and the basic concepts of minimization and estimation are examined for a simple simulated aircraft example. The cost functions that are to be minimized during estimation are defined and discussed. Graphic representations of the cost functions are given to illustrate the minimization process. Finally, the basic concepts are generalized, and estimation from flight data is discussed. Some of the major conclusions for the simulated example are also developed for the analysis of flight data from the F-14, highly maneuverable aircraft technology (HiMAT), and space shuttle vehicles.

1544. Iliff, Kenneth W.: **Aircraft Parameter Estimation**. AIAA Paper 87-0623, Presented at the AIAA 25th Aerospace

Sciences Meeting, Reno, Nevada, January 12–15, 1987, 87A22745, #. (See also 1543, 1743.)

The aircraft parameter estimation problem is used to illustrate the utility of parameter estimation, which applies to many engineering and scientific fields. Maximum likelihood estimation has been used to extract stability and control derivatives from flight data for many years. This paper presents some of the basic concepts of aircraft parameter estimation and briefly surveys the literature in the field. The maximum likelihood estimator is discussed, and the basic concepts of minimization and estimation are examined for a simple simulated aircraft example. The cost functions that are to be minimized during estimation are defined and discussed. Graphic representations of the cost functions are given to illustrate the minimization process. Finally, the basic concepts are generalized, and estimation from flight data is discussed. Some of the major conclusions for the simulated examples are also developed for the analysis of flight data from the F-14, highly maneuverable aircraft technology (HiMAT), and Space Shuttle vehicles.

1545. Bauer, Jeffrey E.; *Crawford, David B.; *Andrisani, Dominick, II; and Gera, Joseph: **Real-Time Comparison of X-29A Flight Data and Simulation Data**. AIAA Paper 87-0344. Presented at the AIAA 25th Aerospace Sciences Meeting, Reno, Nevada, January 12–15, 1987, 87A22570, #. (See also 1690.)

This paper presents a technique for comparing, in real time, the flight test time histories for X-29A aircraft with time histories computed from linearized mathematical models. Such a comparison allows the flight test personnel to verify that the aircraft is performing as predicted, to determine regions of nonlinear behavior, and to increase the rate of envelope expansion. The types of mathematical modeling and equipment required, the procedure used, and actual flight test results are discussed.

*Purdue University, West Lafayette, Indiana.

1546. Hicks, John W.; Cooper, James M., Jr.; and Sefic, Walter J.: **Flight Test Techniques for the X-29A Aircraft**. AIAA Paper 87-0082. Presented at the AIAA 25th Aerospace Sciences Meeting, Reno, Nevada, January 12–15, 1987, 87A22403, #. (See also 1547.)

The X-29A advanced technology demonstrator is a single-seat, single-engine aircraft with a forward-swept wing. The aircraft incorporates many advanced technologies being considered for this country's next generation of aircraft. This unusual aircraft configuration, which had never been flown before, required a precise approach to flight envelope expansion. This paper describes the real-time analysis methods and flight test techniques used during the envelope expansion of the X-29A aircraft, including new and innovative techniques that provided for a safe, efficient envelope expansion. The use of integrated test blocks in the expansion program and in the overall flight test approach is discussed.

1547. Hicks, John W.; Cooper, James M., Jr.; and Sefic, Walter J.: **Flight Test Techniques for the X-29A Aircraft.** NASA TM-88289, H-1401, NAS 1.15:88289, AIAA Paper 87-0082. Presented at the AIAA 25th Aerospace Sciences Meeting, Reno, Nevada, January 12–15, 1987, (see A87-22403), February 1987, 87N21908, #. (See also 1546.)

The X-29A advanced technology demonstrator is a single-seat, single-engine aircraft with a forward-swept wing. The aircraft incorporates many advanced technologies being considered for this country's next generation of aircraft. This unusual aircraft configuration, which had never been flown before, required a precise approach to flight envelope expansion. This paper describes the real-time analysis methods and flight test techniques used during the envelope expansion of the X-29A aircraft, including new and innovative approaches.

1548. Hedgley, David R., Jr.: **A General Solution to the Silhouette Problem.** NASA TP-2695, H-1348, NAS 1.60:2695, February 1987, 88N14629, #.

In displaying computer-generated graphics, it is advantageous to have the facility to render any subset of polygons as a silhouette with respect to itself. While the silhouette problem has been addressed before, there has been no completely general solution. In this report, the silhouette problem for calligraphic drawings is solved for the most general case. This solution offers all possible combinations of silhouette and non-silhouette specifications for an arbitrary solid. It allows the flexibility to enhance the clarity of any three-dimensional scene presented in two dimensions.

1549. Johnson, J. Blair; Larson, Terry J.; and Ficke, Jules M.: **Digital Program for Calculating Static Pressure Position Error.** NASA TM-86726, H-1284, NAS 1.15:86726, February 1987, 87N16821, #.

A computer program written to calculate the static pressure position error of airspeed systems contains five separate methods for determining position error, of which the user may select from one to five at a time. The program uses data from both the test aircraft and the ground-based radar to calculate the error. In addition, some of the methods require rawinsonde data or an atmospheric analysis, or both. The program output lists the corrections to Mach number, altitude, and static pressure that are due to position error. Reference values such as angle of attack, angle of sideslip, indicated Mach number, indicated pressure altitude, stagnation pressure, and total temperature are also listed.

1550. Larson, Richard R.: **AFTI/F-111 MAW Flight Control System and Redundancy Management**

Description. NASA TM-88267, H-1368, NAS 1.15:88267, February 1987, 87N16819, #.

The wing on the NASA F-111 transonic aircraft technology (TACT) airplane was modified to provide flexible leading and trailing edge flaps; this modified wing is known as the mission adaptive wing (MAW). A dual digital primary fly-by-wire flight control system was developed with analog backup reversion for redundancy. This report discusses the functions, design, and redundancy management of the flight control system for these flaps.

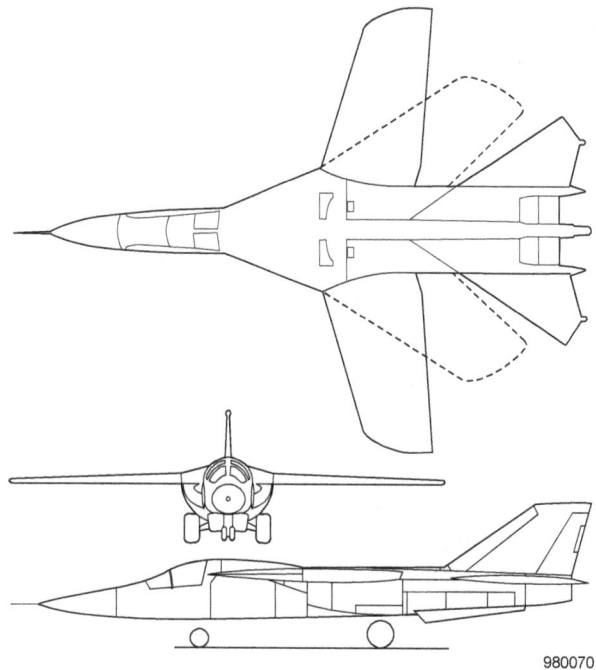

AFTI F-111 MAW Airplane, Three-View Drawing

1551. *Menon, P. K. A.; *Badgett, M. E.; *Walker, R. A.; and Duke, E. L.: **Nonlinear Flight Test Trajectory Controllers for Aircraft.** *Journal of Guidance, Control, and Dynamics,* (ISSN 0731-5090), Vol. 10, January–February 1987, February 1987, pp. 67–72, 87A28910, #. (See also 1405.)

Flight test trajectory control systems are designed to enable the pilot to follow complex trajectories for evaluating an aircraft within its known flight envelope and to explore the boundaries of its capabilities. Previous design approaches were based on linearized aircraft models necessitating a large amount of data storage along with gain schedules. In this paper, the synthesis of nonlinear flight test trajectory controllers for a fixed-wing aircraft is described. This approach uses singular perturbation theory and the recently developed theory of prelinearizing transformations. These controllers do not require gain scheduling for satisfactory operation, can be used in arbitrarily nonlinear maneuvers, and are mechanized with a direct, noniterative analytic solution.

*Integrated Systems, Inc., Palo Alto, California.

1552. Ko, William L.; and Jenkins, Jerald M.: **Thermal Stress Analysis of Space Shuttle Orbiter Wing Skin Panel and Thermal Protection System.** NASA TM-88276, H-1382, NAS 1.15:88276, March 1987, 87N23994, #.

Preflight thermal stress analysis of the space shuttle orbiter wing skin panel and the thermal protection system (TPS) was performed. The heated skin panel analyzed was rectangular in shape and contained a small square cool region at its center. The wing skin immediately outside the cool region was found to be close to the state of elastic instability in the chordwise direction based on the conservative temperature distribution. The wing skin was found to be quite stable in the spanwise direction. The potential wing skin thermal instability was not severe enough to tear apart the strain isolation pad (SIP) layer. Also, the preflight thermal stress analysis was performed on the TPS tile under the most severe temperature gradient during the simulated reentry heating. The tensile thermal stress induced in the TPS tile was found to be much lower than the tensile strength of the TPS material. The thermal bending of the TPS tile was not severe enough to cause tearing of the SIP layer.

1553. Nugent, Jack; and Pendergraft, Odis C., Jr.: **Comparison of Wind Tunnel and Flight Test Afterbody and Nozzle Pressures for a Twin-Jet Fighter Aircraft at Transonic Speeds.** NASA TP-2588, H-1214, NAS 1.60:2588, March 1987, 88N10765, #.

Afterbody and nozzle pressures measured on a 1/12-scale model and in flight on a twin-jet fighter aircraft were compared as Mach number varied from 0.6 to 1.2, Reynolds number from 17.5 million to 302.5 million, and angle of attack from 1 to 7 deg. At Mach 0.6 and 0.8, nozzle pressure coefficient distributions and nozzle axial force coefficients agreed and showed good recompression. At Mach 0.9 and 1.2, flow complexity caused a loss in recompression for both flight and wind tunnel nozzle data. The flight data exhibited less negative values of pressure coefficient and lower axial force coefficients than did the wind tunnel data. Reynolds number effects were noted only at these Mach numbers. Jet temperature and mass flux ratio did not affect the comparisons of nozzle axial flow coefficient. At subsonic speeds, the levels of pressure coefficient distributions on the upper fuselage and lower nacelle surfaces for flight were less negative than those for the model. The model boundary layer thickness at the aft rake station exceeded that for the forward rake station and increased with increasing angle of attack. The flight boundary layer thickness at the aft rake station was less than that for the forward rake station and decreased with increasing angle of attack.

1554. Budd, Gerald D.: **Predicted Pitching Moment Characteristics of X-29A Aircraft.** NASA TM-88284, H-1398, NAS 1.15:88284, March 1987, 89N18418, #.

The predicted pitching moment characteristics of the X-29A aircraft are presented for angles of attack from 0 to 20 deg. and Mach numbers of 0.2, 0.6, 0.9, 1.2, and 1.5 for altitudes of sea level, 4572 m (15,000 ft), 9144 m (30,000 ft), and 12,192 m (40,000 ft). These data are for both rigid and flexible aircraft and for the full range of control-surface positions. The characteristics were extracted from a nonlinear, symmetric, flexibilized wind tunnel data base.

1555. Baer-Riedhart, Jennifer L.; and *Landy, Robert J.: **Highly Integrated Digital Electronic Control: Digital Flight Control, Aircraft Model Identification, and Adaptive Engine Control.** NASA TM-86793, H-1318, NAS 1.15:86793, AIAA Paper 85-1877. Presented at the AIAA Guidance and Control Conference, Snowmass, Colorado, August 19–21, 1985, March 1987, 87N23619, #.

The highly integrated digital electronic control (HIDEC) program at NASA Ames Research Center, Dryden Flight Research Facility is a multiphase flight research program to quantify the benefits of promising integrated control systems. McDonnell Aircraft Company is the prime contractor, with United Technologies Pratt and Whitney Aircraft, and Lear Siegler Incorporated as major subcontractors. The NASA F-15A testbed aircraft was modified by the HIDEC program by installing a digital electronic flight control system (DEFCS) and replacing the standard F100 (Arab 3) engines with F100 engine model derivative (EMD) engines equipped with digital electronic engine controls (DEEC), and integrating the DEEC's and DEFCS. The modified aircraft provides the capability for testing many integrated control modes involving the flight controls, engine controls, and inlet controls. This paper focuses on the first two phases of the HIDEC program, which are the digital flight control system/ aircraft model identification (DEFCS/AMI) phase and the adaptive engine control system (ADECS) phase.

*McDonnell Aircraft Co., St. Louis, Missouri.

1556. Larson, Terry J.; Whitmore, Stephen A.; Ehernberger, L. J.; Johnson, J. Blair; and Siemers, Paul M., III: **Qualitative Evaluation of a Flush Air Data System at Transonic Speeds and High Angles of Attack.** NASA TP-2716, H-1277, NAS 1.60:2716, April 1987, 87N29497, #.

Flight tests were performed on an F-14 aircraft to evaluate the use of flush pressure orifices on the nose section for obtaining air data at transonic speeds over a large range of flow angles. This program was part of a flight test and wind tunnel program to assess the accuracies of such systems for general use on aircraft. It also provided data to validate algorithms developed for the shuttle entry air data system designed at NASA Langley. Data were obtained for Mach numbers between 0.60 and 1.60, for angles of attack up to 26.0 deg, and for sideslip angles up to 11.0 deg. With careful calibration, a flush air data system with all flush orifices can provide accurate air data information over a large range of flow angles. Several orifices on the nose cap were found to be suitable for determination of stagnation pressure. Other orifices on the nose section aft of the nose cap were shown to be suitable for determination of static pressure. Pairs of orifices on the nose cap provided the most sensitive measurements for determining angles of attack and sideslip, although orifices located farther aft on the nose section could also be used.

1557. Jenkins, Jerald M.: **Inelastic Strain Analogy for Piecewise Linear Computation of Creep Residues in Built-Up Structures.** NASA TM-86813, H-1355, NAS 1.15:86813, April 1987, 87N23995, #.

An analogy between inelastic strains caused by temperature and those caused by creep is presented in terms of isotropic elasticity. It is shown how the theoretical aspects can be blended with existing finite-element computer programs to exact a piecewise linear solution. The creep effect is determined by using the thermal stress computational approach, if appropriate alterations are made to the thermal expansion of the individual elements. The overall transient solution is achieved by consecutive piecewise linear iterations. The total residue caused by creep is obtained by accumulating creep residues for each iteration and then resubmitting the total residues for each element as an equivalent input. A typical creep law is tested for incremental time convergence. The results indicate that the approach is practical, with a valid indication of the extent of creep after approximately 20 hr of incremental time. The general analogy between body forces and inelastic strain gradients is discussed with respect to how an inelastic problem can be worked as an elastic problem.

1558. Gupta, Kajal K.; and *Lawson, Charles L.: **Implementation of a Block Lanczos Algorithm for Eigenproblem Solution of Gyroscopic Systems.** NASA TM-88290 H-1404 NAS 1.15:88290 AIAA Paper 87-0946-CP. Presented at the AIAA Dynamics Specialty Conference, Monterey, California, April 1987, 87N19753, #. (See also 1559.)

The details of implementation of a general numerical procedure developed for the accurate and economical computation of natural frequencies and associated modes of any elastic structure rotating along an arbitrary axis are described. A block version of the Lanczos algorithm is derived for the solution that fully exploits associated matrix sparsity and employs only real numbers in all relevant computations. It is also capable of determining multiple roots and proves to be most efficient when compared to other, similar, existing techniques.

*Harvey Mudd College, Claremont, California.

1559. Gupta, K. K.; and *Lawson, C. L.: **Implementation of a Block Lanczos Algorithm for Eigenproblem Solution of Gyroscopic Systems.** AIAA Paper 87-0946. *Technical Papers, Part 2b*, presented at the 28th Structures, Structural Dynamics and Materials Conference, Monterey, California, April 6–8, 1987 and AIAA Dynamics Specialists Conference, Monterey, California, April 9–10, 1987, (see A87-33654 14-39), pp. 919–924, 87A33744, #. (See also 1558.)

This paper describes the details of implementation of a general numerical procedure developed for the accurate and economical computation of natural frequencies and associated modes of any elastic structure rotating along an arbitrary axis. A block version of the Lanczos algorithm is derived for the solution that fully exploits associated matrix sparsity and employs only real numbers in all relevant computations. It is also capable of determining multiple roots and proves to be most efficient when compared to other, similar, existing techniques.

*Harvey Mudd College, Claremont, California.

1560. Gupta, K. K.; Brenner, M. J.; and Voelker, L. S.: **Integrated Aeroservoelastic Analysis Capability With X-29A Analytical Comparisons.** AIAA Paper 87-0907. *Technical Papers, Part 2b*, presented at the 28th Structures, Structural Dynamics and Materials Conference, Monterey, California, April 6–8, 1987, and AIAA Dynamics Specialists Conference, Monterey, California, April 9–10, 1987, (see A87-33654 14-39), 1987, pp. 636–647, 87A33716, #. (See also 1686.)

An extension of the program STARS (a general-purpose structural analysis program) has been developed; this extension implements a complete aeroservoelastic analysis capability. Previous capabilities included finite-element modeling as well as statics, buckling, vibration, dynamic response, and flutter analyses. This paper presents a description and the formulation of STARS in its current state along with example dynamic, aeroelastic, and aeroservoelastic analyses pertaining to the X-29A aircraft. These examples include vibration analysis results as well as flutter analysis results obtained by the conventional k method and the velocity root-contour solution. Finally, selected open- and closed-loop aeroservoelastic analysis results based on a hybrid formulation are compared to illustrate, using the calculated frequency responses, the interactions of structures, aerodynamics, and flight controls.

1561. Kehoe, Michael W.: **Aircraft Ground Vibration Testing at NASA Ames-Dryden Flight Research Facility.** *Proceedings, 5th International Modal Analysis Conference*, London, England, April 6–9, 1987, Vol. 1 (see A88-50789 21-39), (see N87-27655), 1987, pp. 728–736, 88A50831, #. (See also 1571.)

At the NASA Ames Research Center's Dryden Flight Research Facility at Edwards Air Force Base, California, a variety of ground vibration test techniques has been applied to an assortment of new or modified aerospace research vehicles. This paper presents a summary of these techniques and the experience gained from various applications. The role of ground vibration testing in the qualification of new and modified aircraft for flight is discussed. Data are presented for a wide variety of aircraft and component tests, including comparison of sine-dwell, single-input random, and multiple-input random excitation methods on a JetStar airplane.

1562. Whitmore, Stephen A.; Heeg, Jennifer; Larson, Terry J.; Ehernberger, L. J.; Hagen, Floyd W.; and Deleo, Richard V.: **High-Angle-of-Attack Pneumatic Lag and Upwash Corrections for a Hemispherical Flow Direction Sensor.** NASA TM-86790, H-1314, NAS 1.15:86790, May 1987, 87N23616, #.

As part of the NASA F-14 high angle of attack flight test program, a nose mounted hemispherical flow direction sensor was calibrated against a fuselage mounted movable vane flow angle sensor. Significant discrepancies were found to exist in the angle of attack measurements. A two fold approach taken to resolve these discrepancies during subsonic flight is described. First, the sensing integrity of the isolated hemispherical sensor is established by wind tunnel data extending to an angle of attack of 60 deg. Second, two probable causes for the discrepancies, pneumatic lag and upwash, are examined. Methods of identifying and compensating for lag and upwash are presented. The wind tunnel data verify that the isolated hemispherical sensor is sufficiently accurate for static conditions with angles of attack up to 60 deg and angles of sideslip up to 30 deg. Analysis of flight data for two high angle of attack maneuvers establishes that pneumatic lag and upwash are highly correlated with the discrepancies between the hemispherical and vane type sensor measurements.

1563. Ehernberger, L. J.: **High Altitude Turbulence for Supersonic Cruise Vehicles.** NASA TM-88285, H-1399, AAS-86-418, NAS 1.15:88285. Presented at the 33rd Annual Meeting of the American Astronautical Society, Boulder, Colorado, October 26–29, 1986, May 1987, 87N23100, #. (See also 1529.)

The characteristics of high altitude turbulence and its associated meteorological features are reviewed. Findings based on data from NASA flight research programs with prototype military aircraft, the XB-70 and YF-12A, are emphasized. An example of detailed numerical atmospheric simulations, which may provide greatly increased understanding of these earlier turbulence observations, is presented. Comparisons between observation and numerical simulation should help to delineate the limitations of analysis techniques and improve our understanding of atmospheric processes in the stratosphere.

1564. Ko, William L.: **Prediction of Service Life of Aircraft Structural Components Using the Half-Cycle Method.** NASA TM-86812, H-1352, NAS 1.15:86812, May 1987, 87N23009, #.

The service life of aircraft structural components undergoing random stress cycling was analyzed by the application of fracture mechanics. The initial crack sizes at the critical stress points for the fatigue-crack growth analysis were established through proof load tests. The fatigue-crack growth rates for random stress cycles were calculated using the half-cycle method. A new equation was developed for calculating the number of remaining flights for the structural components. The number of remaining flights predicted by the new equation is much lower than that predicted by the conventional equation.

1565. *Yonke, W. A.; *Landy, R. J.; and Stewart, J. F.: **HiDEC Adaptive Engine Control System Flight Evaluation Results.** ASME Paper 87-GT-257. ASME 32nd International Gas Turbine Conference and Exhibition, Anaheim, California, May 31–June 4, 1987, May 1987, 88A11137, #.

An integrated flight propulsion control mode, the Adaptive Engine Control System (ADECS), has been developed and flight tested on an F-15 aircraft as part of the NASA Highly Integrated Digital Electronic Control program. The ADECS system realizes additional engine thrust by increasing the engine pressure ratio (EPR) at intermediate and afterburning power, with the amount of EPR uptrim modulated using a predictor scheme for angle-of-attack and sideslip angle. Substantial improvement in aircraft and engine performance was demonstrated, with a 16 percent rate of climb increase, a 14 percent reduction in time to climb, and a 15 percent reduction in time to accelerate. Significant EPR uptrim capability was found with angles-of-attack up to 20 degrees.

*McDonnell Aircraft Company, St. Louis, Missouri.

1566. Myers, Lawrence P.; and Walsh, Kevin R.: **Preliminary Flight Results of an Adaptive Engine Control System of an F-15 Airplane.** AIAA Paper 87-1847, AIAA, SAE, ASME, and ASEE, 23rd Joint Propulsion Conference, San Diego, California, June 29–July 2, 1987, June 1987, 87A45247, #.

Results of the flight demonstration of the adaptive engine control system (ADECS), an integrated flight and propulsion control system, are reported. The ADECS system provides additional engine thrust by increasing engine pressure ratio (EPR) at intermediate and afterburning power, with the amount of EPR uptrim modulated in accordance with the maneuver requirements, flight conditions, and engine information. As a result of EPR uptrimming, engine thrust has increased by as much as 10.5 percent, rate of climb has increased by 10 percent, and the time to climb from 10,000 to 40,000 ft has been reduced by 12.5 percent. Increases in acceleration of 9.3 and 13 percent have been obtained at intermediate and maximum power, respectively. No engine anomalies have been detected for EPR increases up to 12 percent.

1567. Ko, William L.; Quinn, Robert D.; and Gong, Leslie: **Effects of Forced and Free Convections on Structural Temperatures of Space Shuttle Orbiter During Reentry Flight.** AIAA Paper 87-1600. AIAA 22nd Thermophysics Conference, Honolulu, Hawaii, <u>June 8–10, 1987</u>, (see N87-11968), 87A43104, #. (See also 1521.)

Structural performance and resizing (SPAR) finite-element thermal analysis computer program was used in the heat transfer analysis of the Space Shuttle Orbiter wing subjected to reentry aerodynamic heating. With sufficient external forced convective cooling near the end of the heating cycle, the calculated surface temperatures of the thermal protection system (TPS) agree favorably with the flight data for the entire flight profile. However, the effects of this external forced convective cooling on the structural temperatures were found to be negligible. Both free convection and forced convection elements were introduced to model the internal convection effect of the cool air entering the Shuttle interior. The introduction of the internal free convection effect decreased the calculated wing lower skin temperatures by 20° F at most, 1200 sec after touchdown. If the internal convection is treated as forced convection, the calculated wing lower skin temperatures after touchdown can be reduced to match the flight-measured data very closely. By reducing the TPS thicknesses to certain effective thickness to account for the TPS gap heating, the calculated wing lower skin temperatures prior to touchdown can be raised to agree with the flight data perfectly.

1568. *Dowden, Donald J.; and Bessette, Denis E.: **Advanced Fighter Technology Integration (AFTI)/F-16 Automated Maneuvering Attack System Final Flight Test Results.** SAE Paper 871348. Presented at the SAE Aerospace Vehicle Conference, Washington, DC, <u>June 8–10, 1987</u>, 88A14372.

The AFTI F-16 Automated Maneuvering Attack System has undergone developmental and demonstration flight testing over a total of 347.3 flying hours in 237 sorties. The emphasis of this phase of the flight test program was on the development of automated guidance and control systems for air-to-air and air-to-ground weapons delivery, using a digital flight control system, dual avionics multiplex buses, an advanced FLIR sensor with laser ranger, integrated flight/fire-control software, advanced cockpit display and controls, and modified core Multinational Stage Improvement Program avionics.

*USAF Flight Test Center, Edwards AFB, California.

1569. *Erickson, Gary E.; **Peake, David J.; Del Frate, John; *Skow, Andrew M.; and *Malcolm, Gerald N.: **Water Facilities in Retrospect and Prospect: An Illuminating Tool for Vehicle Design.** AGARD-CP-413, Paper 1. *AGARD Aerodynamic and Related Hydrodynamic Studies Using Water Facilities,* (ISBN-92-835-0419-4) (see N88-23125 16-34), <u>June 1987</u>, AD-A199357, 88N23126, #. (See also 1530.)

Water facilities play a fundamental role in the design of air, ground, and marine vehicles by providing a qualitative, and sometimes quantitative, description of complex flow phenomena. Water tunnels, channels, and tow tanks used as flow-diagnostic tools have experienced a renaissance in recent years in response to the increased complexity of designs suitable for advanced technology vehicles. These vehicles are frequently characterized by large regions of steady and unsteady 3-D flow separation and ensuing vortical flows. The visualization and interpretation of the complicated fluid motions about isolated vehicle components and complete configurations in a time and cost effective manner in hydrodynamic test facilities is a key element in the development of flow control concepts, and, hence, improved vehicle designs. A historical perspective of the role of water facilities in the vehicle design process is presented. The application of water facilities to specific aerodynamic and hydrodynamic flow problems is discussed, and the strengths and limitations of these important experimental tools are emphasized.

*Eidetics International, Inc., Torrance, California.
**Ames Research Center, Moffett Field, California.

1570. Iliff, K. W.: **Aircraft Parameter Estimation: A Successful Application.** *Proceedings of CONCOM.* The First International Conference in Communication and Control Systems, Washington, D. C., <u>June 18–20, 1987</u>.

1571. Kehoe, Michael W.: **Aircraft Ground Vibration Testing at NASA Ames-Dryden Flight Research Facility**, NASA TM-88272, H-1374, NAS 1.15:88272. Presented at the 5th International Modal Analysis Conference, London, England, April 6–9, 1987 <u>July 1987</u>, 87N27655, #. (See also 1561.)

At the NASA Ames Research Center's Dryden Flight Research Facility at Edwards Air Force Base, California, a variety of ground vibration test techniques has been applied to an assortment of new or modified aerospace research vehicles. This paper presents a summary of these techniques and the experience gained from various applications. The role of ground vibration testing in the qualification of new and modified aircraft for flight is discussed. Data are presented for a wide variety of aircraft and component tests, including comparisons of sine-dwell, single-input random, and multiple-input random excitation methods on a JetStar airplane.

1572. Deets, Dwain A.; Lock, Wilton P.; and *Megna, Vincent A.: **Flight Test of a Resident Backup Software System.** AGARD AG-249, *Fault Tolerant Considerations and Methods for Guidance and Control Systems,* (see N88-10796 02-08), <u>July 1987</u>, 88N10805, #. (See also 1452.)

A new fault-tolerant system software concept employing the primary digital computers as host for the backup software portion has been implemented and flight tested in the F-8 digital fly-by-wire airplane. The system was implemented in such a way that essentially no transients occurred in transferring from primary to backup software. This was accomplished without a significant increase in the complexity of the backup software. The primary digital system was frame synchronized, which provided several advantages in implementing the resident backup software system. Since the time of the flight tests, two other flight vehicle programs have made a commitment to incorporate resident backup software similar in nature to the system described here.

*Draper, Charles Stark Lab., Inc., Cambridge, Massachusetts.

1573. Gera, Joseph; and Bosworth, John T.: **Dynamic Stability and Handling Qualities Tests on a Highly Augmented, Statically Unstable Airplane.** NASA TM-88297, H-1422, NAS 1.15:88297, AIAA Paper 87-2258-CP. Presented at the AIAA Guidance, Navigation and Control Conference, Monterey, California, August 17–19, 1987 and at SFTE 18th Annual Symposium, Amsterdam, Netherlands, September 28–October 2, 1987, <u>August 1987</u>, 87N26920, #. (See also 1574, 1585.)

Initial envelope clearance and subsequent flight testing of a new, fully augmented airplane with an extremely high degree of static instability can place unusual demands on the flight test approach. Previous flight test experience with these kinds of airplanes is very limited or nonexistent. The safe and efficient flight testing may be further complicated by a multiplicity of control effectors that may be present on this class of airplanes. This paper describes some novel flight test and analysis techniques in the flight dynamics and handling qualities area. These techniques were utilized during the initial flight envelope clearance of the X-29A aircraft and were largely responsible for the completion of the flight controls clearance program without any incidents or significant delays.

1574. Gera, Joseph; and Bosworth, John T.: **Dynamic Stability and Handling Qualities Tests on a Highly Augmented, Statically Unstable Airplane.** AIAA Paper 87-2258. *Technical Papers,* presented at the AIAA Guidance, Navigation and Control Conference, Monterey, California, <u>August 17–19, 1987</u>, Vol. 1, (see A87-50401 22-08), pp. 170–182, 87A50421, #. (See also 1573, 1585.)

Novel flight test and analysis techniques in the flight dynamics and handling qualities area are described. These techniques were utilized at NASA Ames-Dryden during the initial flight envelope clearance of the X-29A aircraft. It is shown that the open-loop frequency response of an aircraft with highly relaxed static stability can be successfully computed on the ground from telemetry data. Postflight closed-loop frequency response data were obtained from pilot-generated frequency sweeps and it is found that the current handling quality requirements for high-maneuverability aircraft are generally applicable to the X-29A.

1575. Ko, William L.; and Olona, Timothy: **Effect of Element Size on the Solution Accuracies of Finite-Element Heat Transfer and Thermal Stress Analyses of Space Shuttle Orbiter.** NASA TM-88292, H-1409, NAS 1.15:88292. Presented at the 5th International Conference on Numerical Methods in Thermal Problems, Montreal, Quebec, June 24–July 3, 1987, <u>August 1987</u>, 88N18971, #. (See also 1576, 1609.)

The effect of element size on the solution accuracies of finite-element heat transfer and thermal stress analyses of space shuttle orbiter was investigated. Several structural performance and resizing (SPAR) thermal models and NASA structural analysis (NASTRAN) structural models were set up for the orbiter wing midspan bay 3. The thermal model was found to be the one that determines the limit of finite-element fineness because of the limitation of computational core space required for the radiation view factor calculations. The thermal stresses were found to be extremely sensitive to a slight variation of structural temperature distributions. The minimum degree of element fineness required for the thermal model to yield reasonably accurate solutions was established. The radiation view factor computation time was found to be insignificant compared with the total computer time required for the SPAR transient heat transfer analysis.

1576. Ko, William L.; and Olona, Timothy: **Effect of Element Size on the Solution Accuracies of Finite-Element Heat Transfer and Thermal Stress Analyses of Space Shuttle Orbiter.** *Proceedings of the 5th International Conference on Numerical Methods in Thermal Problems,* Montreal, Quebec, June 24–July 3, 1987, Vol. 5, Part 2, <u>July 1987</u>, pp. 1112–1130. (See also 1575, 1609.)

1577. Burcham, Frank W., Jr.; and Ray, Ronald J.: **The Value of Early Flight Evaluation of Propulsion Concepts Using the NASA F-15 Research Airplane.** NASA TM-100408, H-1419, NAS 1.15:100408, AIAA Paper 87-2877. Presented at the AIAA, AHS, and ASEE Aircraft Design, Systems and Operations Meeting, St. Louis, Missouri, September 13–16, 1987, <u>September 1987</u>, 87N26913, #. (See also 1578.)

The value of early flight evaluation of propulsion and propulsion control concepts was demonstrated on the NASA F-15 airplane in programs such as highly integrated digital electronic control (HIDEC), the F100 engine model derivative (EMD), and digital electronic engine control (DEEC). (In each case, the value of flight demonstration was conclusively demonstrated.) This paper described these programs, and discusses the results that were not expected, based on ground test or analytical prediction. The role of flight demonstration in facilitating transfer of technology from the laboratory to operational airplanes is discussed.

1578. Burcham, Frank W., Jr.; and Ray, Ronald J.: **The Value of Early Flight Evaluation of Propulsion Concepts Using the NASA F-15 Research Airplane.** AIAA Paper 87-2877. Presented at the AIAA, AHS, and ASEE, Aircraft Design, Systems and Operations Meeting, St. Louis, Missouri, September 14–16, 1987, 88A14258, #. (See also 1577.)

The value of early flight evaluation of propulsion and propulsion control concepts was demonstrated on the NASA F-15 airplane in programs such as highly integrated digital electronic control (HIDEC), the F100 engine model derivative (EMD), and digital electronic engine control (DEEC). (In each case, the value of flight demonstration was conclusively demonstrated.) This paper describes these programs, and discusses the results that were not expected, based on ground test or analytical prediction. The role of flight demonstration in facilitating transfer of technology from the laboratory to operational airplanes is discussed.

1579. Hicks, John W.; and Matheny, Neil W.: **Preliminary Flight Assessment of the X-29A Advanced Technology Demonstrator.** NASA TM-100407, H-1427, NAS 1.15:100407, AIAA Paper 87-2949. Presented at the AIAA, AHS, and ASEE Aircraft Design, Systems and Operations Meeting, St. Louis, Missouri, September 13–16, 1987, September 1987, 87N26906, #. (See also 1580.)

Several new technologies integrated on the X-29A advanced technology demonstrator are being evaluated for the next generation of fighter aircraft. Some of the most noteworthy ones are the forward-swept wing, digital fly-by-wire flight control system, close-coupled wing-canard configuration, aeroelastically tailored composite wing skins, three-surface pitch control configuration, and a highly unstable airframe. The expansion of the aircraft 1-g and maneuver flight envelopes was recently completed over a two-year period in 84 flights. Overall flight results confirmed the viability of the aircraft design, and good agreement with preflight predictions was obtained. The individual technologies' operational workability and performance were confirmed. This paper deals with the flight test results and the preliminary evaluation of the X-29A design and technologies. A summary of the primary technical findings in structural static loads, structural dynamic characteristics,

flight control system characteristics, aerodynamic stability and control, and aerodynamic performance is presented.

1580. Hicks, John W.; and Matheny, Neil W.: **Preliminary Flight Assessment of the X-29A Advanced Technology Demonstrator.** AIAA Paper 87-2949. Presented at the AIAA, AHS, and ASEE, Aircraft Design, Systems and Operations Meeting, St. Louis, Missouri, September 14–16, 1987, 88A14284, #. (See also 1579.)

Several new technologies integrated on the X-29A advanced technology demonstrator are being evaluated for the next generation of fighter aircraft. Some of the most noteworthy ones are the forward-swept wing, digital fly-by-wire flight control system, close-coupled wing-canard configuration, aeroelastically tailored composite wing skins, three-surface pitch control configuration, and a highly unstable airframe. The expansion of the aircraft 1-g and maneuver flight envelopes was recently completed over a two-year period in 84 flights. Overall flight results confirmed the viability of the aircraft design, and good agreement with preflight predictions was obtained. The individual technologies' operational workability and performance were confirmed. This paper deals with the flight test results and the preliminary evaluation of the X-29A design and technologies. A summary of the primary technical findings in structural static loads, structural dynamic characteristics, flight control system characteristics, aerodynamic stability and control, and aerodynamic performance is presented.

1581. Murray, James E.; and Maine, Richard E.: **The pEst Version 2.1 User's Manual.** NASA TM-88280, H-1390, NAS 1.15:88280, September 1987, 87N28317, #.

This report is a user's manual for version 2.1 of pEst, a FORTRAN 77 computer program for interactive parameter estimation in nonlinear dynamic systems. The pEst program allows the user complete generality in defining the nonlinear equations of motion used in the analysis. The equations of motion are specified by a set of FORTRAN subroutines; a set of routines for a general aircraft model is supplied with the program and is described in the report. The report also briefly discusses the scope of the parameter estimation problem the program addresses. The report gives detailed explanations of the purpose and usage of all available program commands and a description of the computational algorithms used in the program.

1582. Kehoe, Michael W.: **Flutter Clearance of the F-14 Variable-Sweep Transition Flight Experiment Airplane, Phase 1.** NASA TM-88287, H-1402, NAS 1.15:88287, September 1987, 87N27663, #.

An F-14 airplane was modified to become the test bed aircraft for the variable sweep transition flight experiment (VSTFE) program. The latter is a laminar flow program designed to measure the effects of wing sweep on boundary layer transition from laminar to turbulent flow. The airplane was modified by adding an upper surface foam-fiberglass glove over a portion of the left wing. Ground vibration and flight flutter testing were accomplished to clear a sufficient flight envelope to conduct the laminar flow experiments. Flight test data indicated satisfactory damping levels and damping trends for the elastic structural modes of the airplane. The data presented include frequency and damping as functions of Mach number.

1583. *Chin, J.; Chacon, V.; and Gera, J.: **X-29A Flight Control System Performance During Flight Test.** AIAA Paper 87-2878. Presented at the AIAA, AHS, and ASEE, Aircraft Design, Systems and Operations Meeting, St. Louis, Missouri, September 14–16, 1987, 88A14259, #.

An account is given of flight control system performance results for the X-29A forward-swept wing 'Advanced Technology Demonstrator' fighter aircraft, with attention to its software and hardware components' achievement of the requisite levels of system stability and desirable aircraft handling qualities. The Automatic Camber Control Logic is found to be well integrated with the stability loop of the aircraft. A number of flight test support software programs developed by NASA facilitated monitoring of the X-29A's stability in real time, and allowed the test team to clear the envelope with confidence.

*Grumman Aerospace Corporation, Aircraft Systems Division, Bethpage, New York.

1584. Hunter, H. J.; and Bogue, R. K.: **Developmental Airdrop Testing Techniques and Devices.** AGARD-AG-300-VOL-6, ISBN-92-835-1559-5, AD-A18962, September 1, 1987, 88N12481, #.

The practical aspects of planning, conducting, and reporting on developmental airdrop tests made from cargo transport type aircraft are presented. Typical cargo aircraft aerial delivery systems, parachute extraction systems, and special devices and rigging techniques are described in detail. Typical instrumentation systems for obtaining aircraft and parachute systems force data are also described and piloting techniques for various airdrop methods are briefly discussed. A scenario of a typical parachute tow test is used to demonstrate the application of these techniques and the use of challenge and response checklists among the flight crew members. Finally the use of reports is discussed and appendices are included with many useful charts and calculations that are readily applicable in research and development airdrop testing.

1585. Gera, Joseph; and Bosworth, John T.: **Dynamic Stability and Handling Qualities Tests on a Highly Augmented, Statically Unstable Airplane.** *Proceedings, Society of Flight Test Engineers, 18th Annual Symposium,* Amsterdam, the Netherlands, September 28–October 2,

1987, (see A88-51450 22-05), 1987, pp. 2-1 to 2-13, 88A51452, #. (See also 1573, 1574.)

This paper describes some novel flight tests and analysis techniques in the flight dynamics and handling qualities area. These techniques were utilized during the initial flight envelope clearance of the X-29A aircraft and were largely responsible for the completion of the flight controls clearance program without any incidents or significant delays. The resulting open-loop and closed-loop frequency responses and the time history comparison using flight and linear simulation data are discussed.

1586. Dana, William H.: **A History of the X-15 Program.** *Proceedings, 1987 Report to the Aerospace Profession; Society of Experimental Test Pilots, 31st Symposium,* Beverly Hills, California, September 23–26, 1987, (see A88-51426 22-05), 1987, pp. 257–272, 88A51440.

The present historical account of the X-15 hypersonic research aircraft development program, which began in 1952 with the determination by NACA's Committee on Aeronautics to attempt speeds of Mach 10–12 and altitudes of 12–50 miles. While the technical proposal adopted by the program in 1954 reduced speed requirements to Mach 6.6, representing the state-of-the-art capability in high temperature structures, the X-15 would ultimately reach a speed of Mach 6.7. The structural material employed was Inconel X, an Ni-Cr alloy slightly heavier than steel. The X-15 program studied problems in exoatmospheric flight control, structural heating, control in weightlessness, and atmospheric reentry. The last flights were conducted in 1968.

1587. Smolka, James W.: **HiDEC F-15 Adaptive Engine Control System Flight Test Results.** *Proceedings, 1987 Report to the Aerospace Profession, Society of Experimental Test Pilots, 31st Symposium,* Beverly Hills, California, September 23–26, 1987, (see A88-51426 22-05), 1987, pp. 114–137, 88A51433.

NASA-Ames' Highly Integrated Digital Electronic Control (HIDEC) flight test program aims to develop fully integrated airframe, propulsion, and flight control systems. The HIDEC F-15 adaptive engine control system flight test program has demonstrated that significant performance improvements are obtainable through the retention of stall-free engine operation throughout the aircraft flight and maneuver envelopes. The greatest thrust increase was projected for the medium-to-high altitude flight regime at subsonic speed which is of such importance to air combat. Adaptive engine control systems such as the HIDEC F-15's can be used to upgrade the performance of existing aircraft without resort to expensive reengining programs.

1588. DeAngelis, V. Michael; and *Fodale, Robert: **Electro-Optical Flight Deflection Measurement System.** *Proceedings, Society of Flight Test Engineers, 18th Annual*

Symposium, Amsterdam, the Netherlands, September 28–October 2, 1987, (see A88-51450 22-05), 1987, pp. 22-1 to 22-14, 88A51470, #.

This paper describes an electro-optical flight-deflection measurement system (FDMS) developed for use on highly-maneuverable-aircraft-technology (HiMAT) RPV flight research program. The FDMS provides in-flight measurements of the aircraft structural deflections and magnetic-tape recordings for automated data processing. The capabilities and limitations, requirements for installation on an aircraft, analytical considerations, and typical flight data acquired from the HiMAT research program are examined. The flight data indicate that the background light is the major obstacle to acquiring high-quality data and that the relationship between the target displacement and the output of the FDMS is nonlinear; however, the nonlinear effects can be minimized with judicious planning of the installation of the FDMS on the aircraft. Excellent flight deflection data were obtained from both the HiMAT and X-29A flight research program with very little data lost as a result of encounters with severe background light.

*Grumman Aerospace Corporation, Bethpage, New York.

1589. Maine, Richard E.: **Manual for GetData Version 3.1: A FORTRAN Utility Program for Time History Data.** NASA TM-88288, H-1403, NAS 1.15:88288, October 1987, 88N10520, #.

This report documents version 3.1 of the GetData computer program. GetData is a utility program for manipulating files of time history data, i.e., data giving the values of parameters as functions of time. The most fundamental capability of GetData is extracting selected signals and time segments from an input file and writing the selected data to an output file. Other capabilities include converting file formats, merging data from several input files, time skewing, interpolating to common output times, and generating calculated output signals as functions of the input signals. This report also documents the interface standards for the subroutines used by GetData to read and write the time history files. All interface to the data files is through these subroutines, keeping the main body of GetData independent of the precise details of the file formats. Different file formats can be supported by changes restricted to these subroutines. Other computer programs conforming to the interface standards can call the same subroutines to read and write files in compatible formats.

1590. Ko, William L.; and Fields, Roger A.: **Thermal Stress Analysis of Space Shuttle Orbiter Subjected to Reentry Aerodynamic Heating.** NASA TM-88286, H-1400, NAS 1.15:88286, October 1987, 88N10389, #.

A structural performance and resizing (SPAR) finite-element computer program and NASA structural analysis (NASTRAN) finite-element computer programs were used in the thermal stress analysis of the space shuttle orbiter subjected to reentry aerodynamic heating. A SPAR structural model was set up for the entire left wing of the orbiter, and NASTRAN structural models were set up for: (1) a wing segment located at midspan of the orbiter left wing, and (2) a fuselage segment located at midfuselage. The thermal stress distributions in the orbiter structure were obtained and the critical high thermal stress regions were identified. It was found that the thermal stresses induced in the orbiter structure during reentry were relatively low. The thermal stress predictions from the whole wing model were considered to be more accurate than those from the wing segment model because the former accounts for temperature and stress effects throughout the entire wing.

1591. *Jackson, L. Robert; *Dixon, Sidney C.; *Tenney, Darrel R.; Carter, Alan L.; and **Stephens, Joseph R.: **Hypersonic Structures and Materials—A Progress Report.** *Aerospace America* (ISSN 0740-722X), Vol. 25, October 1987, pp. 24, 25, and 28–30, 88A16748, #.

The weight of a hypersonic, airbreathing SSTO vehicle may be more critical than for any previous aerospace craft; an evaluation is accordingly made of the development status and applicability of intermetallic compounds, metal-matrix composites, carbon-carbon composites, ceramics, and ceramic-matrix composites applicable to SSTO craft primary structures. Aerothermal, aerothermoelastic, and acoustic loads are high because the airbreathing SSTO vehicle must follow a high dynamic pressure trajectory in order to achieve the requisite propulsive efficiency. Attention is given to the prospects for integral cryogenic tankage and actively hydrogen-cooled airframe and engine structures.

*NASA Langley Research Center, Hampton, Virginia.
**NASA Lewis Research Center, Cleveland, Ohio.

1592. *Zamanzadeh, Behzad; *Trover, William F.; and Anderson, Karl F.: **DACS II—A Distributed Thermal/Mechanical Loads Data Acquisition and Control System.** *ITC/USA/'87; Proceedings of the International Telemetering Conference*, San Diego, California, October 26–29, 1987, (see A88-33626 13-32), 1987, pp. 737–752, 88A33689, #.

A distributed data acquisition and control system has been developed for the NASA Flight Loads Research Facility. The DACS II system is composed of seven computer systems and four array processors configured as a main computer system, three satellite computer systems, and 13 analog input/output systems interconnected through three independent data networks. Up to three independent heating and loading tests can be run concurrently on different test articles or the entire system can be used on a single large test such as a full scale hypersonic aircraft. Thermal tests can include up to 512 independent adaptive closed loop control channels. The control system can apply up to 20 MW of heating to a test specimen while simultaneously applying independent mechanical loads. Each thermal control loop is capable of heating a structure at rates of up to 150° F per second over a temperature range of –300 to +2500° F. Up to 64 independent mechanical load profiles can be commanded along with thermal control. Up to 1280 analog inputs monitor temperature, load, displacement and strain on the test specimens with real time data displayed on up to 15 terminals as color plots and tabular data displays. System setup and operation is accomplished with interactive menu-driver displays with extensive facilities to assist the users in all phases of system operation.

*Teledyne Controls, Los Angeles, California.

1593. Jenkins, Jerald M.: **Comparison of Measured Temperatures, Thermal Stresses and Creep Residues With Predictions on a Built-Up Titanium Structure.** NASA TM-86814, H-1354, NAS 1.15:86814, <u>November 1987</u>, 88N12125, #.

Temperature, thermal stresses, and residual creep stresses were studied by comparing laboratory values measured on a built-up titanium structure with values calculated from finite-element models. Several such models were used to examine the relationship between computational thermal stresses and thermal stresses measured on a built-up structure. Element suitability, element density, and computational temperature discrepancies were studied to determine their impact on measured and calculated thermal stress. The optimum number of elements is established from a balance between element density and suitable safety margins, such that the answer is acceptably safe yet is economical from a computational viewpoint. It is noted that situations exist where relatively small excursions of calculated temperatures from measured values result in far more than proportional increases in thermal stress values. Measured residual stresses due to creep significantly exceeded the values computed by the piecewise linear elastic strain analogy approach. The most important element in the computation is the correct definition of the creep law. Computational methodology advances in predicting residual stresses due to creep require significantly more viscoelastic material characterization.

1594. Gong, Leslie; Ko, William L.; Quinn, Robert D.; and Richards, W. Lance: **Comparison of Flight-Measured and Calculated Temperatures on the Space Shuttle Orbiter.** NASA TM-88278, H-1384, NAS 1.15:88278, <u>November 1987</u>, 88N12029, #.

Structural temperatures and thermal protection system surface temperatures were measured on the space shuttle during the flight of STS 5. The measured data are compared with values calculated at wing stations 134, 240, and 328 and at fuselage station 877. The theoretical temperatures were calculated using the structural performance and resizing finite element thermal analysis program. The comparisons show that the calculated temperatures are, generally, in good agreement with the measured data.

1595. Ko, William L.: **Accuracies of Southwell and Force/Stiffness Methods in the Prediction of Buckling Strength of Hypersonic Aircraft Wing Tubular Panels.** NASA TM-88295, H-1415, NAS 1.15:88295, <u>November 1987</u>, 88N17090, #.

Accuracies of the Southwell method and the force/stiffness (F/S) method are examined when the methods were used in the prediction of buckling loads of hypersonic aircraft wing tubular panels, based on nondestructive buckling test data. Various factors affecting the accuracies of the two methods were discussed. Effects of load cutoff point in the nondestructive buckling tests on the accuracies of the two methods were discussed in great detail. For the tubular panels under pure compression, the F/S method was found to give more accurate buckling load predictions than the Southwell method, which excessively overpredicts the buckling load. It was found that the Southwell method required a higher load cutoff point, as compared with the F/S method. In using the F/S method for predicting the buckling load of tubular panels under pure compression, the load cutoff point of approximately 50 percent of the critical load could give reasonably accurate predictions.

1596. Trippensee, Gary A.; and Lux, David P.: **X-29A Forward-Swept-Wing Flight Research Program Status.** NASA TM-100413, H-1432, NAS 1.15:100413. Presented at the SAE International Pacific Air and Space Technology Conference, Melbourne, Australia, November 13–17, 1987, <u>November 1987</u>, 88N17644, #. (See also 1597.)

The X-29A aircraft is a fascinating combination of integrated technologies incorporated into a unique research aircraft. The X-29A program is multiple agency program with management and other responsibilities divided among NASA, DARPA, the U.S. Air Force, and the Grumman Corporation. An overview of the recently completed X-29A flight research program, objectives achieved, and a discussion of its future is presented. Also discussed are the flight test approach expanding the envelope, typical flight maneuvers performed, X-29A program accomplishments, lessons learned for the Number One aircraft, and future plans with the Number Two aircraft. A schedule for both aircraft is presented. A description of the unique technologies incorporated into the X-29A aircraft is given, along with descriptions of the onboard instrumentation system. The X-29A aircraft research program has proven highly successful. Using high fly rates from a very reliable experimental aircraft, the program has consistently met or exceeded its design and research goals.

1597. Trippensee, Gary A.; and Lux, David P.: **X-29A Forward-Swept-Wing Flight Research Program Status.**

SAE Paper 872418. *Proceedings, International Pacific Air and Space Technology Conference*, Melbourne, Australia, November 13–17, 1987, (see A89-10627 01-01), <u>1988</u>, pp. 181–188, 89A10640, #. (See also 1596.)

The X-29A aircraft is a fascinating combination of integrated technologies incorporated into a unique research aircraft. The X-29A program is a multiple agency program with management and other responsibilities divided among NASA, DARPA, the U.S. Air Force, and the Grumman Corporation. An overview of the recently completed X-29A flight research program, objectives achieved, and a discussion of its future is presented. Also discussed are the flight test approach expanding the envelope, typical flight maneuvers performed, X-29A program accomplishments, lessons learned for the Number One aircraft, and future plans with the Number Two aircraft. A schedule for both aircraft is presented. A description of the unique technologies incorporated into the X-29A aircraft is given, along with descriptions of the onboard instrumentation system. The X-29A aircraft research program has proven highly successful. Using high fly rates from a very reliable experimental aircraft, the program has consistently met or exceeded its design and research goals.

1598. Fisher, David F.; and *Fischer, Michael C.: **Development Flight Tests of JetStar LFC Leading-Edge Flight Test Experiment**. NASA CP-2487. *NASA Langley Research Center, Research in Natural Laminar Flow and Laminar-Flow Control, Part 1*, (see N90-12503 04-02) <u>December 1987</u>, pp. 117–140, 90N12509, #.

The overall objective of the flight tests on the JetStar aircraft was to demonstrate the effectiveness and reliability of laminar flow control under representative flight conditions. One specific objective was to obtain laminar flow on the JetStar leading-edge test articles for the design and off-design conditions. Another specific objective was to obtain operational experience on a Laminar Flow Control (LFC) leading-edge system in a simulated airline service. This included operational experience with cleaning requirements, the effect of clogging, possible foreign object damage, erosion, and the effects of ice particle and cloud encounters. Results are summarized.

*NASA Langley Research Center, Hampton, Virginia.

1599. Meyer, Robert R.; Trujillo, Bianca M.; and *Bartlett, Dennis W., **F-14 VSTFE and Results of the Cleanup Flight Test Program**, NASA CP-2487, *NASA Langley Research Center, Research in Natural Laminar Flow and Laminar-Flow Control, Part 3*, (see N90-12539 04-02), <u>December 1987</u>, pp. 819–844, 90N12547, #.

Flight transition data applicable to swept wings at high subsonic speeds are needed to make valid assessments of the potential for natural laminar flow or laminar flow control for transports of various sizes at various cruise speeds. NASA initiated the variable sweep transition flight experiment (VSTFE) to help establish a boundary layer transition data base for use in laminar flow wing design. The carrier vehicle for this experiment is an F-14, which has variable sweep capability. The variable sweep outer panels of the F-14 were modified with natural laminar flow gloves to provide not only smooth surfaces but also airfoils that can produce a wide range of pressure distributions for which transition location can be determined. The VSTFE program is briefly described and some preliminary glove I flight results are presented.

*NASA Langley Research Center, Hampton, Virginia.

EC87-0100-4

F-14 VSTFE Airplane

1600. *Maddalon, Dal V.; Fisher, David F.; Jennett, Lisa A.; and *Fischer, Michael C.: **Simulated Airline Service Experience With Laminar-Flow Control Leading-Edge Systems**. NASA CP-2487. *Research in Natural Laminar Flow and Laminar-Flow Control, Part 1*, (see N90-12503 04-02), <u>December 1987</u>, pp. 195–218, 90N12512, #.

The first JetStar leading edge flight test was made November 30, 1983. The JetStar was flown for more than 3 years. The titanium leading edge test articles today remain in virtually the same condition as they were in on that first flight. No degradation of laminar flow performance has occurred as a result of service. The JetStar simulated airline service flights have demonstrated that effective, practical leading edge systems are available for future commercial transports. Specific conclusions based on the results of the simulated airline service test program are summarized.

*NASA Langley Research Center, Hampton, Virginia.

EC87-165-1

Deicing JetStar Laminar Flow Leading Edge, Flight Test Experiment

1601. Duke, Eugene L.; Patterson, Brian P.; and Antoniewicz, Robert F.: **User's Manual for LINEAR, a FORTRAN Program to Derive Linear Aircraft Models.** NASA TP-2768, H-1259, NAS 1.60:2768, December 1987, 88N21740, #.

This report documents a FORTRAN program that provides a powerful and flexible tool for the linearization of aircraft models. The program LINEAR numerically determines a linear system model using nonlinear equations of motion and a user-supplied nonlinear aerodynamic model. The system model determined by LINEAR consists of matrices for both state and observation equations. The program has been designed to allow easy selection and definition of the state, control, and observation variables to be used in a particular model.

1602. *Alag, Gurbux S.; and Burken, John J.: **Eigensystem Synthesis for Active Flutter Suppression on an Oblique-Wing Aircraft.** *Journal of Guidance, Control, and Dynamics* (ISSN 0731-5090), Vol. 10, November–December 1987, (see A86-47491), December 1987, pp. 535–539, 88A22607, #. (See also 1499, 1500.)

*Western Michigan University, Kalamazoo, Michigan.

1988 Technical Publications

1603. Ko, William L.: **Delamination Stresses in Semicircular Laminated Composite Bars.** NASA TM-4026, H-1417, NAS 1.15:4026, January 1988, 88N20375, #.

Using anisotropic elasticity theory, delamination stresses in a semicircular laminated composite curved bar subjected to end forces and end moments were calculated, and their radial locations determined. A family of design curves was presented, showing variation of the intensity of delamination stresses and their radial locations with different geometry and different degrees of anisotropy of the curved bar. The effect of anisotropy on the location of peak delamination stress was found to be small.

1604. *Kempel, Robert W.; **McNeill, Walter E.; and Maine, Trindel A.: **Oblique-Wing Research Airplane Motion Simulation With Decoupling Control Laws.** AIAA Paper 88-0402. Presented at the AIAA 26th Aerospace Sciences Meeting, Reno, Nevada, January 11–14, 1988, 88A22296, #.

A large piloted vertical motion simulator was used to assess the performance of a preliminary decoupling control law for an early version of the F-8 oblique wing research demonstrator airplane. Evaluations were performed for five discrete flight conditions, ranging from low-altitude subsonic Mach numbers to moderate-altitude supersonic Mach numbers. Asymmetric sideforce as a function of angle of attack was found to be the primary cause of both the lateral acceleration noted in pitch and the tendency to roll into left turns and out of right turns. The flight control system was shown to be effective in generally decoupling the airplane and reducing the lateral acceleration in pitch maneuvers.

*PRC Kentron, Inc., Edwards, California.
**NASA Ames Research Center, Moffett Field, California.

1605. Glover, Richard D.: **Concept of a Programmable Maintenance Processor Applicable to Multiprocessing Systems.** NASA TM-100406, H-1425, NAS 1.15:100406, February 1988, 88N17333, #.

A programmable maintenance processor concept applicable to multiprocessing systems has been developed at the NASA Ames Research Center's Dryden Flight Research Facility. This stand-alone-processor is intended to provide support for system and application software testing as well as hardware diagnostics. An initial mechanization has been incorporated into the extended aircraft interrogation and display system (XAIDS) which is multiprocessing general-purpose ground support equipment. The XAIDS maintenance processor has

EC88-0042-01

Dryden Flight Research Facility Aircraft, circa 1988, (front row) Grumman X-29A, (2nd row) AD-1, Piper PA-30, Rockwell International HiMAT, (3rd row) Lockheed F-104, Vought F-8 DFBW, General Dynamics AFTI F-16, Northrop T-38, (4th row) two McDonnell Douglas F/A-18's, (5th row) General Dynamics AFTI F-111 MAW, McDonnell F-15, Sikorsky RSRA, (back row) Boeing B-52, Lockheed C-140 JetStar, Boeing 747 SCA.

independent terminal and printer interfaces and a dedicated magnetic bubble memory that stores system test sequences entered from the terminal. This report describes the hardware and software embodied in this processor and shows a typical application in the check-out of a new XAIDS.

1606. Powers, Sheryll Goecke: **Influence of Base Modifications on In-Flight Base Drag in the Presence of Jet Exhaust for Mach Numbers From 0.7 to 1.5.** NASA TP-2802, H-1408, NAS 1.60:2802, February 1988, 88N18881, #.

The use of external modifications in the base region to reduce the base drag of a blunt-base body in the presence of jet engine exhaust was investigated in flight. Base pressure data were obtained for the following configurations: (1) blunt base; (2) blunt base modified with splitter plate; and (3) blunt base modified with two variations of a vented cavity. Reynolds number based on the length of the aircraft ranged from 1.2 to 3.1 x 10 to the 8th. Mach number M ranges were 0.71 less than or = M less than or = 0.95 and 1.10 less than

or = M less than or = 1.51. The data were analyzed using the blunt base for a reference, or baseline condition. For 1.10 less than or = M less than or = 1.51, the reduction in base drag coefficient provided by the vented cavity configuration ranged from 0.07 to 0.05. These increments in base drag coefficient at M = 1.31 and 1.51 result in base drag reductions of 27 and 24 percent, respectively, when compared to the blunt base drag. For M less than 1, the drag increment between the blunt base and the modification is not significant.

1607. *Kuhn, Richard E.; Del Frate, John H.; and **Eshleman, James E.: **Ground Vortex Flow Field Investigation**. NASA CP-10008. *The 1987 Ground Vortex Workshop,* (see N89-10849 02-02), February 1988, pp. 61–90, 89N10852, #.

Flow field investigations were conducted at the NASA Ames-Dryden Flow Visualization Facility (water tunnel) to investigate the ground effect produced by the impingement of jets from aircraft nozzles on a ground board in a STOL operation. Effects on the overall flow field with both a stationary and a moving ground board were photographed and compared with similar data found in other references. Nozzle jet impingement angles, nozzle and inlet interaction, side-by-side nozzles, nozzles in tandem, and nozzles and inlets mounted on a flat plate model were investigated. Results show that the wall jet that generates the ground effect is unsteady and the boundary between the ground vortex flow field and the free-stream flow is unsteady. Additionally, the forward projection of the ground vortex flow field with a moving ground board is one-third less than that measured over a fixed ground board. Results also showed that inlets did not alter the ground vortex flow field.

*Kuhn (Richard E.), San Diego, California.
**Lockheed-California Co., Burbank, California.

1608. Johnson, J. Blair: **Preliminary In-Flight Boundary Layer Transition Measurements on a 45 Deg Swept Wing at Mach Numbers Between 0.9 and 1.8.** NASA TM-100412, H-1436, NAS 1.15:100412, March 1988, 88N20598, #.

A preliminary flight experiment was flown to generate a full-scale supersonic data base to aid the assessment of computational codes, to improve instrumentation for measuring boundary layer transition at supersonic speeds, and to provide preliminary information for the definition of follow-on programs. The experiment was conducted using an F-15 aircraft modified with a small cleanup test section on the right wing. Results are presented for Mach (M) numbers from 0.9 to 1.8 at altitudes from 25,000 to 55,000 ft. At M greater than or = 1.2, transition occurred near or at the leading edge for the clean configuration. The furthest aft that transition was measured was 20 percent chord at M = 0.9 and M = 0.97. No change in transition location was observed after the addition of a notch-bump on the leading edge of the inboard side of the test section which was intended to minimize attachment line transition problems. Some flow visualization was attempted during the flight experiment with both subliming chemicals and liquid crystals. However, difficulties arose from the limited time the test aircraft was able to hold test conditions and the difficulty of positioning the photo chase aircraft during supersonic test points. Therefore, no supersonic transition results were obtained.

1609. Ko, William L.; and Olona, Timothy: **Effect of Element Size on the Solution Accuracies of Finite-Element Heat Transfer and Thermal Stress Analyses of Space Shuttle Orbiter.** NASA CP-2505. Presented at the 16th NASTRAN Users Colloquium, Arlington, Virginia, April 25–29, 1988. (See also 1575, 1576.)

The effect of element size on the solution accuracies of finite-element heat transfer and thermal stress analyses of space shuttle orbiter was investigated. Several structural

performance and resizing (SPAR) thermal models and NASA structural analysis (NASTRAN) structural models were set up for the orbiter wing midspan bay 3. The thermal model was found to be the one that determines the limit of finite-element fineness because of the limitation of computational core space required for the radiation view factor calculations. The thermal stresses were found to be extremely sensitive to a slight variation of structural temperature distributions. The minimum degree of element fineness required for the thermal model to yield reasonably accurate solutions was established. The radiation view factor computation time was found to be insignificant compared with the total computer time required for the SPAR transient heat transfer analysis.

1610. Glover, Richard D.: **Aerospace Energy Systems Laboratory: Requirements and Design Approach.** NASA TM-100423, H-1448, NAS 1.15:100423. Presented at the ISA Aerospace Industries/Test Measurement Symposium, Albuquerque, New Mexico, May 2–5, 1988, May 1988, 88N24206, #. (See also 1641.)

The NASA Ames-Dryden Flight Research Facility at Edwards, California, operates a mixed fleet of research aircraft employing nickel-cadmium (NiCd) batteries in a variety of flight-critical applications. Dryden's Battery Systems Laboratory (BSL), a computerized facility for battery maintenance servicing, has developed over two decades into one of the most advanced facilities of its kind in the world. Recently a major BSL upgrade was initiated with the goal of modernization to provide flexibility in meeting the needs of future advanced projects. The new facility will be called the Aerospace Energy Systems Laboratory (AESL) and will employ distributed processing linked to a centralized data base. AESL will be both a multistation servicing facility and a research laboratory for the advancement of energy storage system maintenance techniques. This paper describes the baseline requirements for the AESL and the design approach being taken for its mechanization.

1611. Rhea, Donald C.; and Moore, Archie L.: **Development of a Mobile Research Flight Test Support Capability**, NASA TM-100428, H-1456, NAS 1.15:100428, AIAA Paper 88-2087. Presented at the 4th Flight Test Conference, San Diego, California, May 18–20, 1988, May 1988, 8N22883, #. (See also 1612.)

This paper presents the approach taken by the NASA Western Aeronautical Test Range (WATR) of the Ames Research Center to develop and utilize mobile systems to satisfy unique real-time research flight test requirements of research projects such as the advanced fighter technology integration (AFTI)F-16, YAV-8B Harrier, F-18 high-alpha research vehicle (HARV), XV-15, and the UH-60 Black Hawk. The approach taken is cost-effective, staff efficient, technologically current, and provides a safe and effective research flight test environment to support a highly complex set of real-time requirements including the areas of tracking and data acquisition, communications (audio and video) and real-time processing and display, postmission processing, and command uplink. The development of this capability has been in response to the need for rapid deployment at varied site locations with full real-time computations and display capability. This paper will discuss the requirements, implementation and growth plan for mobile systems development within the NASA Western Aeronautical Test Range.

EC80-13848

XV-15 Tilt Rotor Aircraft

1612. Rhea, Donald C.; and Moore, Archie L.: **Development of a Mobile Research Flight Test Support Capability.** AIAA Paper 88-2087. *Technical Papers*, presented at the AIAA 4th Flight Test Conference, San Diego, California, May 18–20, 1988, (see A88-38701 15-05), pp. 520–528, 88A38761, #. (See also 1611.)

This paper presents the approach taken by the NASA Western Aeronautical Test Range (WATR) of the Ames Research Center (ARC) to develop and utilize mobile systems to satisfy unique real-time research flight test requirements of research projects such as the advanced fighter technology integration (AFTI) F-16, YAV-8B Harrier, F-18 high-alpha research vehicle (HARV), XV-15, and the UH-60 Black Hawk. The approach taken is cost-effective, staff efficient, technologically current, and provides a safe and effective research flight test environment to support a highly complex set of real-time requirements including the areas of tracking and data acquisition, communications (audio and video) and real-time processing and display, postmission processing, and command uplink. The development of this capability has been in response to the need for rapid deployment at varied

site locations with full real-time commutation and display capability. This paper will discuss the requirements, implementation and growth plan for mobile systems development within the NASA Western Aeronautical Test Range.

1613. Kellogg, Gary V.; and Wagner, Charles A.: **Effects of Update and Refresh Rates on Flight Simulation Visual Displays.** NASA TM-100415, H-1439, NAS 1.15:100415, May 1988, 88N22033, #.

An experiment was performed to study the effects of update and refresh rates on dynamic calligraphic CRT displays, particularly those used for visual displays in flight simulators. A moving horizontal line was generated on a CRT and observed at various velocities. Observations were made with both one and two refreshes per update. The data gathered from these observations are presented on plots of refresh-update rate as a function of display velocity. The display velocity where picture degradation occurs can be found by using these plots. These velocities are related to actual simulated aircraft angular and linear velocities. Results show that a visual display updated at 30 Hz and refreshed at 60 Hz degrades at very low simulated aircraft angular and linear velocities. These velocities at which degradation occurs can be significantly increased by increasing the update rate of the visual display. Only minor improvements are possible by refreshing the display twice for each uptake. To display rapidly changing flight scenery without degradation, the display update rate must be far in excess of 60 Hz, typically several hundred Hz.

1614. Hammons, Kevin R.: **The PC/AT Compatible Computer as a Mission Control Center Display Processor at Ames-Dryden Flight Research Facility.** NASA TM-100426, H-1457, NAS 1.15:100426. Presented at the AIAA 4th Flight Test Conference, San Diego, California, May 18–20, 1988, May 1988, 88N21654, #. (See also 1615.)

Since 1982, the Western Aeronautical Test Range of the Ames-Dryden Flight Research Facility has been separating the data acquisition and processing function required on all telemetry pulse code modulation (PCM) data and the display processing function required in the flight research mission control centers (MCCs). These two functions historically have been done on the same set of super mini computers remote from the MCCs. Removing the display processing function from the realm of the superminis or telemetry-radar acquisition and processing system (TRAPS) and out into the MCCs will allow the research engineers the flexibility to configure their own display processing system to optimize performance during a flight research mission. Meanwhile, the TRAPS will have more time to acquire data. One of the processors chosen is an IBM PC/AT compatible rack-mounted personal computer. This class and type machine will not only allow the transfer of the display processing function into the MCCs, but also allow the research engineers a personalized set of analytic and display tools for use on their own unique sets of data.

1615. Hammons, Kevin R.: **The PC/AT Compatible Computer as a Mission Control Center Display Processor at Ames-Dryden Flight Research Facility.** AIAA Paper 88-2168. Presented at the AIAA 4th Flight Test Conference, San Diego, California, May 18–20, 1988, (see A88-38701 15-05), pp. 388–405, 88A38745, #. (See also 1614.)

The NASA Ames-Dryden Flight Research Facility's Western Aeronautical Test Range will assign the flight test data display processing function to Mission Control Centers in order to allow research engineers to flexibly configure their own display-processing system to optimize performance during a flight research mission. This will leave the Telemetry Radar Acquisition and Processing System more time to acquire data. One of the processors chosen to handle the display-processing function is an IBM PC/AT-compatible, rack-mounted PC giving engineers a personalized set of analytic and display tools, developed on the basis of off-the-shelf PC/AT-compatible engineering hardware and software items.

1616. Meyer, Robert R., Jr.; and *Barneburg, Jack: **In-Flight Rain Damage Tests of the Shuttle Thermal Protection System.** NASA TM-100438, H-1484, NAS 1.15:100438, AIAA Paper 88-2137. Presented at the 4th Flight Test Conference, San Diego, California, May 18–20, 1988, May 1988, 88N21241, #.

NASA conducted in-flight rain damage tests of the Shuttle thermal protection system (TPS). Most of the tests were conducted on an F-104 aircraft at the Dryden Flight Research Facility of NASA's Ames Research Center, although some tests were conducted by NOAA on a WP-3D aircraft off the eastern coast of southern Florida. The TPS components tested included LI900 and LI2200 tiles, advanced flexible reusable surface insulation, reinforced carbon-carbon, and an advanced tufi tile. The objective of the test was to define the damage threshold of various thermal protection materials during flight through rain. The test hardware, test technique, and results from both F-104 and WP-3D aircraft are described. Results have shown that damage can occur to the Shuttle TPS during flight in rain.

*NASA Lyndon B. Johnson Space Center, Houston, Texas.

EC90-224

F-104 Airplane With Flight Test Fixture

1617. Mackall, D. A.; Pickett, M. D.; Schilling, L. J.; and Wagner, C. A.: **The NASA Integrated Test Facility and Its Impact on Flight Research.** NASA TM-100418, H-1446, NAS 1.15:100418. Presented at the 4th Flight Test Conference, San Diego, California, May 18–20, 1988, May 1988, 88N21177, #. (See also 1618.)

The Integrated Test Facility (ITF), being built at NASA Ames-Dryden Flight Research Facility, will provide new test capabilities for emerging research aircraft. An overview of the ITF and the challenges being addressed by this unique facility are outlined. The current ITF capabilities, being developed with the X-29 Forward Swept Wing Program, are discussed along with future ITF activities.

1618. Mackall, D. A.; Pickett, M. D.; Schilling, L. J.; and Wagner, C. A.: **The NASA Integrated Test Facility and Its Impact on Flight Research.** AIAA Paper 88-2095. Presented at the AIAA 4th Flight Test Conference, San Diego, California, May 18–20, 1988, pp. 85–97, 88A38711, #. (See also 1617.)

NASA-Ames' Integrated Test Facility (ITF), when completed, will provide ground test facilities for the safe and efficient testing of advanced research aircraft with fully integrated flight control, propulsion systems, structures, and aerodynamic configurations. Flight test risk will be minimized through the reduction of differences between flight and ground test environments; the latter will involve the interfacing of real-time flight simulation with the actual aircraft through a simulation-interface device. The test process and the collection and management of test data will be automated. Attention is given to preliminary ITF results for the X-29 aircraft.

1619. Moore, Archie L.; and Harney, Constance D.: **Development of an Integrated Set of Research Facilities for the Support of Research Flight Test.** NASA TM-100427, H-1458, NAS 1.15:100427. AIAA Paper 88-2095. Presented at the AIAA 4th Flight Test Conference, San Diego, California, May 18–20, 1988, May 1988, (see A88-38701 15-05), 88N21169, #. (See also 1620.)

The Ames-Dryden Flight Research Facility (DFRF) serves as the site for high-risk flight research on many one-of-a-kind test vehicles like the X-29A advanced technology demonstrator, F-16 advanced fighter technology integration (AFTI), AFTI F-111 mission adaptive wing, and F-18 high-alpha research vehicle (HARV). Ames-Dryden is on a section of the historic Muroc Range. The facility is oriented toward the testing of high-performance aircraft, as shown by its part in the development of the X-series aircraft. Given the cost of research flight tests and the complexity of today's systems-driven aircraft, an integrated set of ground support experimental facilities is a necessity. In support of the research flight test of highly advanced test beds, the DFRF is developing a network of facilities to expedite the acquisition and distribution of flight research data to the researcher. The network consists of an array of experimental ground-based facilities and systems as nodes and the necessary telecommunications paths to pass research data and information between these facilities. This paper presents the status of the current network, an overview of current developments, and a prospectus on future major enhancements.

1620. Moore, Archie L.; and Harney, Constance D.: **Development of an Integrated Set of Research Facilities for the Support of Research Flight Test.** AIAA Paper 88-2096. Presented at the AIAA 4th Flight Test Conference, San Diego, California, May 18–20, 1988, pp. 98–111, 88A38712, #. (See also 1619.)

The Ames-Dryden Flight Research Facility (DFRF) serves as the site for the conduct of high-risk flight research on many one-of-a-kind test vehicles like the X-29A advanced technology demonstrator, F-16 advanced fighter technology integration (AFTI), AFTI F-111 mission adaptive wing, and F-18 high-alpha research vehicle (HARV). Ames-Dryden is on a section of the historic Muroc Range. The facility is oriented toward the testing of high-performance aircraft, as shown by its part in the development of the X-series aircraft. Given the cost of research flight test and the complexity of today's systems-driven aircraft, an integrated set of ground support experimental facilities is a necessity. In support of the research flight test of highly advanced test beds, the DFRF is developing a network of facilities to expedite the acquisition and distribution of flight research data to the researcher. This network consists of an array of experimental ground-based facilities and systems as nodes and the necessary telecommunications paths to pass research data and information between these facilities. This paper presents a status of the current network, an overview of current developments, and a prospectus on future major enhancements.

1621. Malone, Jacqueline C.; and Moore, Archie L.: **Western Aeronautical Test Range Real-Time Graphics Software Package MAGIC.** NASA TM-100425, H-1455, NAS 1.15:100425. Presented at the AIAA 4th Flight Test Conference, San Diego, California, May 18–20, 1988, May 1988, 88N20506, #.

The master graphics interactive console (MAGIC) software package used on the Western Aeronautical Test Range (WATR) of the NASA Ames Research Center is described. MAGIC is a resident real-time research tool available to flight researchers-scientists in the NASA mission control centers of the WATR at the Dryden Flight Research Facility at Edwards, California. The hardware configuration and capabilities of the real-time software package are also discussed.

1622. Comperini, Robert; and Rhea, Donald C.: **Development of an Interactive Real-Time Graphics System for the Display of Vehicle Space Positioning.** NASA TM-100429, H-1460, NAS 1.15:100429, AIAA Paper 88-2167. Presented at the 4th Flight Test Conference, San Diego, California, May 18–20, 1988, May 1988, 88N20344, #. (See also 1623.)

Outlined is a new approach taken by the NASA Western Aeronautical Test Range to display real-time space positioning data using computer-generated images that produce a graphic representation of an area map integrated with the research flight test aircraft track. This display system supports research flight test requirements of research projects such as the advanced fighter technology integration (AFTI) F-16, F-18 high alpha research vehicle (HARV), AFTI F-111 mission adaptive wing (MAW), F-15, and X-29A forward-swept wing. This paper will discuss the requirements, system configuration and capability, and future system applications.

1623. *Comperini, Robert; and Rhea, Donald C.: **Development of an Interactive Real-Time Graphics System for the Display of Vehicle Space Positioning.** AIAA Paper 88-2167. Presented at the 4th Flight Test Conference, San Diego, California, May 18–20, 1988, (see A88-38701 15-05), pp. 376–387, 88A38744, #. (See also 1622.)

This paper will outline a new approach taken by the NASA Western Aeronautical Test Range to display real-time space positioning data using computer-generated images that produce a graphic representation of an area map integrated with the research flight test aircraft track. This display system supports research flight test requirements of research projects such as the advanced fighter technology integration (AFTI) F-16, F-18 high alpha research vehicle (HARV), AFTI F-111 mission adaptive wing (MAW), F-15, and

X-29A forward-swept wing. This paper will discuss the requirements, system configuration and capability, and future system applications.

*Datamax Computer Systems, Inc., Edwards, California.

1624. Myers, Lawrence P.; and Walsh, Kevin R.: **Performance Improvements of an F-15 Airplane With an Integrated Engine-Flight Control System.** NASA TM-100431, H-1470, NAS 1.15:100431. Presented at the AIAA 4th Flight Test Conference, San Diego, California, May 18–20, 1988, May 1988, 88N21159, #. (See also 1625, 1907.)

An integrated flight and propulsion control system has been developed and flight demonstrated on the NASA Ames-Dryden F-15 research aircraft. The highly integrated digital control (HIDEC) system provides additional engine thrust by increasing engine pressure ratio (EPR) at intermediate and afterburning power. The amount of EPR uptrim is modulated based on airplane maneuver requirements, flight conditions, and engine information. Engine thrust was increased as much as 10.5 percent at subsonic flight conditions by uptrimming EPR. The additional thrust significantly improved aircraft performance. Rate of climb was increased 14 percent at 40,000 ft and the time to climb from 10,000 to 40,000 ft was reduced 13 percent. A 14 and 24 percent increase in acceleration was obtained at intermediate and maximum power, respectively. The HIDEC logic performed fault free. No engine anomalies were encountered for EPR increases up to 12 percent and for angles of attack and sideslip of 32 and 11 degrees, respectively.

1625. Myers, Lawrence P.; and Walsh, Kevin R.: **Performance Improvements of an F-15 Airplane With an Integrated Engine-Flight Control System.** AIAA Paper 88-2175. Presented at the AIAA 4th Flight Test Conference, San Diego, California, May 18–20, 1988, (see A88-38701 15-05), pp. 410–418, 88A38747, #. (See also 1624, 1907.)

An integrated flight and propulsion control system has been developed and flight demonstrated on the NASA Ames-Dryden F-15 research aircraft. The highly integrated digital control (HIDEC) system provides additional engine thrust by increasing engine pressure ratio (EPR) at intermediate and afterburning power. The amount of EPR uptrim is modulated based on airplane maneuver requirements, flight conditions, and engine information. Engine thrust was increased as much as 10.5 percent at subsonic flight conditions by uptrimming EPR. The additional thrust significantly improved aircraft performance. Rate of climb was increased 14 percent at 40,000 ft and the time to climb from 10,000 to 40,000 ft was reduced 13 percent. A 14 and 24 percent increase in acceleration was obtained at intermediate and maximum power, respectively. The HIDEC logic performed fault free.

No engine anomalies were encountered for EPR increases up to 12 percent and for angles of attack and sideslip of 32 and 11 deg, respectively.

1626. Chacon, Vince; and McBride, David: **Operational Viewpoint of the X-29A Digital Flight Control System.** NASA TM-100434, H-1467, NAS 1.15:100434. Presented at the ISA Aerospace Industries/Test Measurement Divisions 34th International Instrumentation Symposium, Albuquerque, New Mexico, May 2–5, 1988, May 1988, 88N21152, #.

In the past few years many flight control systems have been implemented as full-authority, full-time digital systems. The digital design has allowed flight control systems to make use of many enhanced elements that are generally considered too complex to implement in an analog system. Examples of these elements are redundant information exchanged between channels to allow for continued operation after multiple failures and multiple variable gain schedules to optimize control of the aircraft throughout its flight envelope and in all flight modes. The introduction of the digital system for flight control also created the problem of obtaining information from the system in an understandable and useful format. This paper presents how the X-29A was dealt with during its operations at NASA Ames-Dryden Flight Research Facility. A brief description of the X-29A control system, a discussion of the tools developed to aid in daily operations, and the troubleshooting of the aircraft are included.

1627. Ray, R. J.; Hicks, J. W.; and Alexander, R. I.: **Development of a Real-Time Aeroperformance Analysis Technique for the X-29A Advanced Technology Demonstrator.** NASA TM-100432, H-1471, NAS 1.15:100432. Presented at the AIAA 4th Flight Test Conference, San Diego, California, May 18–20, 1988, May 1988, 88N21151, #. (See also 1628, 1784.)

The X-29A advanced technology demonstrator has shown the practicality and advantages of the capability to compute and display, in real time, aeroperformance flight results. This capability includes the calculation of the in-flight measured drag polar, lift curve, and aircraft specific excess power. From these elements many other types of aeroperformance measurements can be computed and analyzed. The technique can be used to give an immediate postmaneuver assessment of data quality and maneuver technique, thus increasing the productivity of a flight program. A key element of this new method was the concurrent development of a real-time in-flight net thrust algorithm, based on the simplified gross thrust method. This net thrust algorithm allows for the direct calculation of total aircraft drag.

1628. Ray, R. J.; Hicks, J. W.; and *Alexander, R. I.: **Development of a Real-Time Aeroperformance Analysis Technique for the X-29A Advanced Technology**

Demonstrator. AIAA Paper 88-2145. *Technical Papers*, presented at the AIAA 4th Flight Test Conference, San Diego, California, May 18–20, 1988, (see A88-38701 15-05), pp. 323–337, 88A38738, #. (See also 1627, 1784.)

The X-29A advanced technology demonstrator has shown the practicality and advantages of the capability to compute and display, in real time, aeroperformance flight results. This capability includes the calculation of the in flight measured drag polar, lift curve, and aircraft specific excess power. From these elements, many other types of aeroperformance measurements can be computed and analyzed. The technique can be used to give an immediate postmaneuver assessment of data quality and maneuver technique, thus increasing the productivity of a flight program. A key element of this new method was the concurrent development of a real-time in flight net thrust algorithm, based on the simplified gross thrust method. This net thrust algorithm allows for the direct calculation of total aircraft drag.

*Computing Devices Co., Ottawa, Canada.

1629. Bohn-Meyer, Marta R.: **Constructing Gloved Wings for Aerodynamic Studies.** NASA TM-100440, H-1487, NAS 1.15:100440, AIAA Paper 88-2109. Presented at the AIAA 4th Flight Test Conference, San Diego, California, May 18–20, 1988, May 1988, 88N21128, #.

Recently, two aircraft from the Dryden Flight Research Facility were used in the general study of natural laminar flow (NLF). The first, an F-14A aircraft on short-term loan from the Navy, was used to investigate transonic natural laminar flow. The second, an F-15A aircraft on long-term loan from the Air Force, was used to examine supersonic NLF. These tests were follow-on experiments to the NASA F-111 NLF experiment conducted in 1979. Both wings of the F-14A were gloved, in a two-phased experiment, with full-span (upper surface only) airfoil shapes constructed primarily of fiberglass, foam, and resin. A small section of the F-15A right wing was gloved in a similar manner. Each glove incorporated provisions for instrumentation to measure surface pressure distributions. The F-14A gloves also had provisions for instrumentation to measure boundary layer profiles, acoustic environments, and surface pitot pressures. Discussions of the techniques used to construct the gloves and to incorporate the required instrumentation are presented.

1630. Fisher, David F.; Richwine, David M.; and Banks, Daniel W.: **Surface Flow Visualization of Separated Flows on the Forebody of an F-18 Aircraft and Wind-Tunnel Model.** NASA TM-100436, H-1481, NAS 1.15:100436, AIAA Paper 88-2112. Presented at the AIAA 4th Flight Test Conference, San Diego, California, May 18–20, 1988, May 1988, 88N21127, #.

A method of in-flight surface flow visualization similar to wind-tunnel-model oil flows is described for cases where photo-chase planes or onboard photography are not practical. This method, used on an F-18 aircraft in flight at high angles of attack, clearly showed surface flow streamlines in the fuselage forebody. Vortex separation and reattachment lines were identified with this method and documented using postflight photography. Surface flow angles measured at the 90 and 270 degrees meridians show excellent agreement with the wind tunnel data for a pointed tangent ogive with an aspect ratio of 3.5. The separation and reattachment line locations were qualitatively similar to the F-18 wind-tunnel-model oil flows but neither the laminar separation bubble nor the boundary-layer transition on the wind tunnel model were evident in the flight surface flows. The separation and reattachment line locations were in fair agreement with the wind tunnel data for the 3.5 ogive. The elliptical forebody shape of the F-18 caused the primary separation lines to move toward the leeward meridian. Little effect of angle of attack on the separation locations was noted for the range reported.

EC88-0212-002

F-18 HARV Surface Flow Visualization

1631. Duke, Eugene L.; Hewett, Marle D.; Brumbaugh, Randal W.; Tartt, David M.; Antoniewicz, Robert F.; and Agarwal, Arvind K.: **The Use of an Automated Flight Test Management System in the Development of a Rapid-Prototyping Flight Research Facility.** NASA TM-100435, H-1477, NAS 1.15:100435. Presented at the 4th Conference on Artificial Intelligence Applications, Long Beach, California, May 4–6, 1988, May 1988, 88N20896, #.

An automated flight test management system (ATMS) and its use to develop a rapid-prototyping flight research facility for artificial intelligence (AI) based flight systems concepts are described. The ATMS provides a flight test engineer with a set of tools that assist in flight planning and simulation. This system will be capable of controlling an aircraft during the flight test by performing closed-loop guidance functions, range management, and maneuver-quality monitoring. The rapid-prototyping flight research facility is being developed at the Dryden Flight Research Facility of the NASA Ames Research Center (Ames-Dryden) to provide early flight assessment of emerging AI technology. The facility is being developed as one element of the aircraft automation program which focuses on the qualification and validation of embedded real-time AI-based systems.

1632. Yergensen, Stephen; and Rhea, Donald C.: **Configuration Management Issues and Objectives for a Real-Time Research Flight Test Support Facility.** NASA TM-100437, H-1463, NAS 1.15:100437. Presented at the AIAA 4th Flight Test Conference, San Diego, California, May 18–20, 1988, May 1988, 88N20832, #. (See also 1633.)

Presented are some of the critical issues and objectives pertaining to configuration management for the NASA Western Aeronautical Test Range (WATR) of Ames Research Center. The primary mission of the WATR is to provide a capability for the conduct of aeronautical research flight test through real-time processing and display, tracking, and communications systems. In providing this capability, the WATR must maintain and enforce a configuration management plan which is independent of, but complimentary to, various research flight test project configuration management systems. A primary WATR objective is the continued development of generic research flight test project support capability, wherein the reliability of WATR support provided to all project users is a constant priority. Therefore, the processing of configuration change requests for specific research flight test project requirements must be evaluated within a perspective that maintains this primary objective.

1633. *Yergensen, Stephen; and Rhea, Donald C.: **Configuration Management Issues and Objectives for a Real-Time Research Flight Test Support Facility.** AIAA Paper 88-2200. *Technical Papers*, presented at the AIAA 4th Flight Test Conference, San Diego, California, May 18–20, 1988, (see A88-38701 15-05), pp. 495–503, 88A38757, #. (See also 1632.)

The Western Aeronautical Test Range (WATR) at NASA-Ames, whose primary function is the conduct of aeronautical research flight testing through real-time processing and display, tracking, and communications systems. The processing of WATR configuration change requests for specific research flight test projects must be conducted in such a way as to refrain from compromising the reliability of

WATR support to all project users. Configuration management's scope ranges from mission planning to operations monitoring and performance trend analysis.

*Datamax Computer Systems, Lancaster, California.

1634. Gupta, K. K.; and *Lawson, C. L.: **Development of a Block Lanczos Algorithm for Free Vibration Analysis of Spinning Structures.** *International Journal for Numerical Methods in Engineering,* (ISSN 0029-5981), Vol. 26, May 1988, pp. 1029–1037, 88A40117

This paper is concerned with the development of an efficient eigenproblem solution algorithm and an associated computer program for the economical solution of the free vibration problem of complex practical spinning structural systems. Thus, a detailed description of a newly developed block Lanczos procedure is presented in this paper that employs only real numbers in all relevant computations and also fully exploits sparsity of associated matrices. The procedure is capable of computing multiple roots and proves to be most efficient compared to other existing similar techniques.

*Harvey Mudd College, Claremont, California.

1635. Anderson, Bianca Trujillo; Meyer, Robert R., Jr.; and Chiles, Harry R.: **Techniques Used in the F-14 Variable-Sweep Transition Flight Experiment.** AIAA Paper 88-2110. *Technical Papers*, presented at the AIAA 4th Flight Test Conference, San Diego, California, May 18–20, 1988, (see A88-38701 15-05), pp. 529–548, 88A38762, #. (See also 1652, 1895.)

This paper discusses and evaluates the test measurement techniques used to determine the laminar-to-turbulent boundary-layer transition location in the F-14 variable-sweep transition flight experiment (VSTFE). The main objective of the VSTFE was to determine the effects of wing sweep on the laminar-to-turbulent transition location at conditions representative of transport aircraft. Four methods were used to determine the transition location: (1) a hot-film anemometer system, (2) two boundary-layer rakes, (3) surface pitot tubes, and (4) liquid crystals for flow visualization. Of the four methods, the hot-film anemometer system was the most reliable indicator of transition.

1636. Hicks, John W.; and Moulton, Bryan J.: **Effects of Maneuver Dynamics on Drag Polars of the X-29A Forward-Swept-Wing Aircraft With Automatic Wing Camber Control.** AIAA Paper 88-2144. *Technical Papers*, presented at the AIAA 4th Flight Test Conference, San Diego, California, May 18–20, 1988, (see A88-38701 15-05), pp. 312–322, 88A38737, #.

The camber control loop of the X-29A FSW aircraft was designed to furnish the optimum L/D for trimmed, stabilized flight. A marked difference was noted between automatic wing camber control loop behavior in dynamic maneuvers and in stabilized flight conditions, which in turn affected subsonic aerodynamic performance. The degree of drag level increase was a direct function of maneuver rate. Attention is given to the aircraft flight drag polar effects of maneuver dynamics in light of wing camber control loop schedule. The effect of changing camber scheduling to better track the optimum automatic camber control L/D schedule is discussed.

1637. Whitmore, Stephen A.: **Formulation of a General Technique for Predicting Pneumatic Attenuation Errors in Airborne Pressure Sensing Devices.** AIAA Paper 88-2085. *Technical Papers*, presented at the AIAA 4th Flight Test Conference, San Diego, California, May 18–20, 1988, (see A88-38701 15-05), pp. 40–50, 88A38707, #. (See also 1638.)

Presented is a mathematical model, derived from the Navier-Stokes equations of momentum and continuity, which may be accurately used to predict the behavior of conventionally mounted pneumatic sensing systems subject to arbitrary pressure inputs. Numerical techniques for solving the general model are developed. Both step and frequency response lab tests were performed. These data are compared against solutions of the mathematical model. The comparisons show excellent agreement. The procedures used to obtain the lab data are described. In-flight step and frequency response data were obtained. Comparisons with numerical solutions of the mathematical model show good agreement. Procedures used to obtain the flight data are described. Difficulties encountered with obtaining the flight data are discussed.

1638. Whitmore, Stephen A.: **Formulation of a General Technique for Predicting Pneumatic Attenuation Errors in Airborne Pressure Sensing Devices.** NASA TM-100430, H-1462, NAS 1.15:100430. Presented at the AIAA 4th Flight Test Conference, San Diego, California, May 18–20, 1988, May 1988, 88N20302, #. (See also 1637.)

Presented is a mathematical model derived from the Navier-Stokes equations of momentum and continuity, which may be accurately used to predict the behavior of conventionally mounted pneumatic sensing systems subject to arbitrary pressure inputs. Numerical techniques for solving the general model are developed. Both step and frequency response lab tests were performed. These data are compared with solutions of the mathematical model and show excellent agreement. The procedures used to obtain the lab data are described. In-flight step and frequency response data were obtained. Comparisons with numerical solutions of the math model show good agreement. Procedures used to obtain the flight data are described. Difficulties encountered with obtaining the flight data are discussed.

1639. Kehoe, Michael W.: **Aircraft Flight Flutter Testing at the NASA Ames-Dryden Flight Research**

Facility. AIAA Paper 88-2075. *Technical Papers*, presented at the AIAA 4th Flight Test Conference, San Diego, California, May 18–20, 1988, (see A88-38701 15-05), pp. 1–14, 88A38702, #. (See also 1640.)

Many parameter identification techniques have been used at the NASA Ames Research Center, Dryden Flight Research Facility at Edwards Air Force Base to determine the aeroelastic stability of new and modified research vehicles in flight. This paper presents a summary of each technique used with emphasis on fast Fourier transform methods. Experiences gained from application of these techniques to various flight test programs are discussed. Also presented are data-smoothing techniques used for test data distorted by noise. Data are presented for various aircraft to demonstrate the accuracy of each parameter identification technique discussed.

1640. Kehoe, Michael W.: **Aircraft Flight Flutter Testing at the NASA Ames-Dryden Flight Research Facility.** NASA TM-100417, H-1445, NAS 1.15:100417. Presented at the AIAA 4th Flight Test Conference, San Diego, California, May 18–20, 1988, May 1988, 88N20301, #. (See also 1639.)

Many parameter identification techniques have been used at the NASA Ames Research Center, Dryden Research Facility at Edwards Air Force Base to determine the aeroelastic stability of new and modified research vehicles in flight. This paper presents a summary of each technique used with emphasis on fast Fourier transform methods. Experiences gained from application of these techniques to various flight test programs are discussed. Also presented are data-smoothing techniques used for test data distorted by noise. Data are presented for various aircraft to demonstrate the accuracy of each parameter identification technique discussed.

1641. Glover, Richard D.: **Aerospace Energy Systems Laboratory—Requirements and Design Approach.** *Proceedings, 34th International Instrumentation Symposium*, Albuquerque, New Mexico, May 2–6, 1988, (see A89-27651 10-35), pp. 359–367, 89A27669, #. (See also 1610)

The NASA Ames/Dryden Flight Research Facility operates a mixed fleet of research aircraft employing NiCd batteries in a variety of flight-critical applications. Dryden's Battery Systems Laboratory (BSL), a computerized facility for battery maintenance servicing, has evolved over two decades into one of the most advanced facilities of its kind in the world. Recently a major BSL upgrade was initiated with the goal of modernization to provide flexibility in meeting the needs of future advanced projects. The new facility will be called the Aerospace Energy Systems Laboratory (AESL) and will employ distributed processing linked to a centralized data base. AESL will be both a multistation servicing facility and a research laboratory for the advancement of energy storage system maintenance techniques. This paper describes the baseline requirements for the AESL and the design approach being taken for its mechanization.

1642. Chiles, Harry R.: **The Design and Use of a Temperature-Compensated Hot-Film Anemometer System for Boundary-Layer Flow Transition Detection on Supersonic Aircraft.** NASA TM-100421, H-1451, NAS 1.15:100421. Presented at the Aerospace Industries/ Test Measurement Symposium, Albuquerque, New Mexico, May 2–5, 1988, <u>May 1988</u>, 88N20304, #. (See also 1643.)

An airborne temperature-compensated hot-film anemometer system has been designed, fabricated, and used to obtain in-flight airfoil boundary-layer flow transition data by the NASA Ames-Dryden Flight Research Facility. Salient features of the anemometer include near constant sensitivity over the full flight envelope, installation without coaxial wiring, low-noise outputs, and self-contained signal conditioning with dynamic and steady-state outputs. The small size, low-power dissipation, and modular design make the anemometer suitable for use in modern high-performance research aircraft. Design of the temperature-compensated hot-film anemometer and its use for flow transition detection on a laminar flow flight research project are described. Also presented are data gathered in flight which is representative of the temperature-compensated hot-film anemometer operation at subsonic, transonic, and supersonic flight conditions.

1643. Chiles, Harry R.: **The Design and Use of a Temperature-Compensated Hot-Film Anemometer System for Boundary-Layer Flow Transition Detection on Supersonic Aircraft.** *Proceedings, 34th International Instrumentation Symposium,* Albuquerque, New Mexico, <u>May 2–6, 1988</u>, (see A89-27651 10-35), pp. 347–358, 89A27668, #. (See also 1642.)

1644. Nesel, Michael C.; and Hammons, Kevin R.: **Real-Time Flight Test Data Distribution and Display.** NASA TM-100424, H-1454, NAS 1.15:100424, REPT-314-50, REPT-314-60, AIAA Paper 88-2216. Presented at the 4th Flight Test Conference, San Diego, California, <u>May 18–20, 1988</u>, 88N22050, #.

Enhancements to the real-time processing and display systems of the NASA Western Aeronautical Test Range are described. Display processing has been moved out of the telemetry and radar acquisition processing systems super-minicomputers into user/client interactive graphic workstations. Real-time data is provided to the workstations by way of Ethernet. Future enhancement plans include use of fiber optic cable to replace the Ethernet.

1645. Powers, Sheryll Goecke: **Flight Tests of External Modifications Used to Reduce Blunt Base Drag.** NASA TM-100433, H-1472, NAS 1.15:100433, AIAA

Paper 88–2553. Presented at the AIAA 6th Applied Aerodynamics Conference, Williamsburg, Virginia, June 6–8, 1988, <u>1988</u>, 88N20279, #. (See also 1646, 1873.)

The effectiveness of a trailing disk (the trapped vortex concept) in reducing the blunt base drag of an 8-in diameter body of revolution was studied from measurements made both in flight and in full-scale wind-tunnel tests. The experiment demonstrated the significant base drag reduction capability of the trailing disk to Mach 0.93. The maximum base drag reduction obtained from a cavity tested on the flight body of revolution was not significant. The effectiveness of a splitter plate and a vented-wall cavity in reducing the base drag of a quasi-two-dimensional fuselage closure was studied from base pressure measurements made in flight. The fuselage closure was between the two engines of the F-111 airplane; therefore, the base pressures were in the presence of jet engine exhaust. For Mach numbers from 1.10 to 1.51, significant base drag reduction was provided by the vented-wall cavity configuration. The splitter plate was not considered effective in reducing base drag at any Mach number tested.

1646. Powers, Sheryll Goecke: **Flight Tests of External Modifications Used to Reduce Blunt Base Drag.** AIAA Paper 88-2553. *Technical Papers,* presented at the AIAA 6th Applied Aerodynamics Conference, Williamsburg, Virginia, <u>June 6–8, 1988</u>, (see A88-40701 16-02), pp. 615–628, 88A40763, #. (See also 1645, 1873.)

The effectiveness of a trailing disk (the trapped vortex concept) in reducing the blunt base drag of an 8-in diameter body of revolution was studied from measurements made both in flight and in full-scale wind-tunnel tests. The experiment demonstrated the significant base drag reduction capability of the trailing disk to Mach 0.93. The maximum base drag reduction obtained from a cavity tested on the flight body of revolution was not significant. The effectiveness of a splitter plate and a vented-wall cavity in reducing the base drag of a quasi-two-dimensional fuselage closure was studied from base pressure measurements made in flight. The fuselage closure was between the two engines of the F-111 airplane; therefore, the base pressures were in the presence of jet engine exhaust. For Mach numbers from 1.10 to 1.51, significant base drag reduction was provided by the vented-wall cavity configuration. The splitter plate was not considered effective in reducing base drag at any Mach number tested.

1647. Kempel, Robert W.; and Earls, Michael R.: **Flight Control Systems Development and Flight Test Experience With the HiMAT Research Vehicles.** NASA TP-2822, H-1428, NAS 1.60:2822, <u>June 1988</u>, 89N15929, #.

Two highly maneuverable aircraft technology (HiMAT) remotely piloted vehicles were flown a total of 26 flights. These subscale vehicles were of advanced aerodynamic configuration with advanced technology concepts such as composite and metallic structures, digital integrated propulsion control, and ground (primary) and airborne (backup) relaxed static stability, digital fly-by-wire control systems. Extensive systems development, checkout, and flight qualification were required to conduct the flight test program. The design maneuver goal was to achieve a sustained 8-g turn at Mach 0.9 at an altitude of 25,000 feet. This goal was achieved, along with the acquisition of high-quality flight data at subsonic and supersonic Mach numbers. Control systems were modified in a variety of ways using the flight-determined aerodynamic characteristics. The HiMAT program was successfully completed with approximately 11 hours of total flight time.

1648. Putnam, Terrill W.; and Ayers, Theodore G.: **Flight Research and Testing.** NASA TM-100439, H-1483, NAS 1.15:100439. Presented at the Transonic Symposium, Hampton, Virginia, April 1988, June 1988, 88N26361, #. (See also 1692.)

Flight research and testing form a critical link in the aeronautic R and D chain. Brilliant concepts, elegant theories, and even sophisticated ground tests of flight vehicles are not sufficient to prove beyond doubt that an unproven aeronautical concept will actually perform as predicted. Flight research and testing provide the ultimate proof that an idea or concept performs as expected. Ever since the Wright brothers, flight research and testing have been the crucible in which aeronautical concepts have advanced and been proven to the point that engineers and companies have been willing to stake their future to produce and design new aircraft. This is still true today, as shown by the development of the experimental X-30 aerospace plane. The Dryden Flight Research Center (Ames-Dryden) continues to be involved in a number of flight research programs that require understanding and characterization of the total airplane in all the aeronautical disciplines, for example the X-29. Other programs such as the F-14 variable-sweep transition flight experiment have focused on a single concept or discipline. Ames-Dryden also continues to conduct flight and ground based experiments to improve and expand the ability to test and evaluate advanced aeronautical concepts. A review of significant aeronautical flight research programs and experiments is presented to illustrate both the progress made and the challenges to come.

1649. *Hewett, Marle D.; *Tartt, David M.; Duke, Eugene L.; Antoniewicz, Robert F.; and **Brumbaugh, Randal W.: **The Development of an Automated Flight Test Management System for Flight Test Planning and Monitoring.** *Proceedings, 1st International Conference on Industrial and Engineering Applications of Artificial Intelligence and Expert Systems,* Tullahoma, Tennessee, June 1–3, 1988, (see A89-27601 10-66), 1988, pp. 324–333, 89A27613.

The development of an automated flight test management system (ATMS) as a component of a rapid-prototyping flight

research facility for AI-based flight systems concepts is described. The rapid-prototyping facility includes real-time high-fidelity simulators, numeric and symbolic processors, and high-performance research aircraft modified to accept commands for a ground-based remotely augmented vehicle facility. The flight system configuration of the ATMS includes three computers: the TI explorer LX and two GOULD SEL 32/27s.

*Sparta, Inc., Laguna Hills, California.
**PRC Kentron, Inc., Edwards, California.

1650. Ko, William L.: **Solution Accuracies of Finite Element Reentry Heat Transfer and Thermal Stress Analyses of Space Shuttle Orbiter.** *International Journal for Numerical Methods in Engineering,* (ISSN 0029-5981), Vol. 25, June 1988, pp. 517–543, 88A48632.

Accuracies of solutions (structural temperatures and thermal stresses) obtained from different thermal and structural FEMs set up for the Space Shuttle Orbiter (SSO) are compared and discussed. For studying the effect of element size on the solution accuracies of heat-transfer and thermal-stress analyses of the SSO, five SPAR thermal models and five NASTRAN structural models were set up for wing midspan bay 3. The structural temperature distribution over the wing skin (lower and upper) surface of one bay was dome shaped and induced more severe thermal stresses in the chordwise direction than in the spanwise direction. The induced thermal stresses were extremely sensitive to slight variation in structural temperature distributions. Both internal convention and internal radiation were found to have equal effects on the SSO.

1651. Maine, Richard E.; and Murray, James E.: **Application of Parameter Estimation to Highly Unstable Aircraft.** *Journal of Guidance, Control, and Dynamics,* (ISSN 0731-5090), Vol. 11, May–June 1988, (see A86-47655), pp. 213–219, 88A43204, #. (See also 1495, 1496.)

1652. Anderson, Bianca Trujillo; Meyer, Robert R., Jr.; and Chiles, Harry R.: **Techniques Used in the F-14 Variable-Sweep Transition Flight Experiment.** NASA TM-100444, H-1461, NAS 1.15:100444, AIAA Paper 88-2110. Presented at the 4th AIAA Flight Test Conference, San Diego, California, May 18–20, 1988, July 1988, 88N30093, #. (See also 1635, 1895.)

This paper discusses and evaluates the test measurement techniques used to determine the laminar-to-turbulent boundary layer transition location in the F-14 variable-sweep transition flight experiment (VSTFE). The main objective of the VSTFE was to determine the effects of wing sweep on the laminar-to-turbulent transition location at conditions representative of transport aircraft. Four methods were used to determine the transition location: (1) a hot-film anemometer system; (2) two boundary-layer rakes; (3) surface pitot tubes; and (4) liquid crystals for flow visualization. Of the four methods, the hot-film anemometer system was the most reliable indicator of transition.

1653. Duke, Eugene L.: **Application of Flight Systems Methodologies to the Validation of Knowledge-Based Systems.** NASA TM-100442, H-1493, NAS 1.15:100442. Presented at the Space Operations Automation and Robotics (SOAR) Workshop, Dayton, Ohio, July 20–23, 1988, July 1988, 88N25207, #. (See also 1680.)

Flight and mission-critical systems are verified, qualified for flight, and validated using well-known and well-established techniques. These techniques define the validation methodology used for such systems. In order to verify, qualify, and validate knowledge-based systems (KBS's), the methodology used for conventional systems must be addressed, and the applicability and limitations of that methodology to KBS's must be identified. The author presents an outline of how this approach to the validation of KBS's is being developed and used at the Dryden Flight Research Facility of the NASA Ames Research Center.

1654. Jenkins, Jerald M.: **A Comparison of Experimental and Calculated Thin-Shell Leading-Edge Buckling Due to Thermal Stresses.** NASA TM-100416, H-1440, NAS 1.15:100416, July 1988, 88N23999, #.

High-temperature thin-shell leading-edge buckling test data are analyzed using NASA structural analysis (NASTRAN) as a finite element tool for predicting thermal buckling characteristics. Buckling points are predicted for several combinations of edge boundary conditions. The problem of relating the appropriate plate area to the edge stress distribution and the stress gradient is addressed in terms of analysis assumptions. Local plasticity was found to occur on the specimen analyzed, and this tended to simplify the basic problem since it effectively equalized the stress gradient from loaded edge to loaded edge. The initial loading was found to be difficult to select for the buckling analysis because of the transient nature of thermal stress. Multiple initial model loadings are likely required for complicated thermal stress time histories before a pertinent finite element buckling analysis can be achieved. The basic mode shapes determined from experimentation were correctly identified from computation.

1655. Carr, Peter C.; and *McKissick, Burnell T.: **Analysis Procedures and Subjective Flight Results of a Simulator Validation and Cue Fidelity Experiment.** NASA TM-88270, H-1371, NAS 1.15:88270, July 1988, 88N24634, #.

A joint experiment to investigate simulator validation and cue fidelity was conducted by the Dryden Flight Research Facility of NASA Ames Research Center (Ames-Dryden)

and NASA Langley Research Center. The primary objective was to validate the use of a closed-loop pilot-vehicle mathematical model as an analytical tool for optimizing the tradeoff between simulator fidelity requirements and simulator cost. The validation process includes comparing model predictions with simulation and flight test results to evaluate various hypotheses for differences in motion and visual cues and information transfer. A group of five pilots flew air-to-air tracking maneuvers in the Langley differential maneuvering simulator and visual motion simulator and in an F-14 aircraft at Ames-Dryden. The simulators used motion and visual cueing devices including a g-seat, a helmet loader, wide field-of-view horizon, and a motion base platform.

*NASA Langley Research Center, Hampton, Virginia.

1656. Schuster, Lawrence S.; and Lokos, William A.: **Current Flight Test Experience Related to Structural Divergence of Forward-Swept Wings.** NASA TM-100445, H-1500, NAS 1.15:100445. Presented at the 1988 International Symposium of Flight Test Engineers, Arlington, Texas, August 14–18, 1988, August 1988, 88N24633, #. (See also 1657.)

Flight testing the X-29A forward-swept wing aircraft has required development of new flight test techniques to accomplish subcritical extrapolations to the actual structural divergence dynamic pressure of the aircraft. This paper provides current experience related to applying these techniques to analysis of flight data from the forward-swept wing in order to assess the applicability of these techniques to flight test data. The measurements required, maneuvers flown, and flight test conditions are described. Supporting analytical predictions for the techniques are described and the results using flight data are compared to these predictions. Use of the results during envelope expansion and the resulting modifications to the techniques are discussed. Some of the analysis challenges that occurred are addressed and some preliminary conclusions and recommendations are made relative to the usefulness of these techniques in the flight test environment.

1657. Schuster, Lawrence S.; and Lokos, William A.: **Current Flight Test Experience Related to Structural Divergence of Forward-Swept Wings.** *Proceedings, Society of Flight Test Engineers, 19th Annual Symposium,* Arlington, Texas, August 14–18, 1988, (see A89-45126 19-05), pp. V-2.1 to V-2.10, 89A45141. (See also 1656.)

Flight testing the X-29A forward-swept wing aircraft has required development of new flight test techniques to accomplish subcritical extrapolations to the actual structural divergence dynamic pressure of the aircraft. This paper provides current experience related to applying these techniques to analysis of flight data from the forward-swept wing in order to assess the applicability of these techniques to flight test data. The measurements required, maneuvers flown, and flight test conditions are described. Supporting analytical predictions for the techniques are described and the results using flight data are compared to these predictions. Use of the results during envelope expansion and the resulting modifications to the techniques are discussed. Some of the analysis challenges that occurred are addressed and some preliminary conclusions and recommendations are made relative to the usefulness of these techniques in the flight test environment.

1658. Sarrafian, Shahan K.; and Powers, Bruce G.: **Application of Frequency-Domain Handling Qualities Criteria to the Longitudinal Landing Task.** *Journal of Guidance, Control, and Dynamics* (ISSN 0731-5090), Vol. 11, July–August 1988, Abridged, (see A85-45877), pp. 291–292, 88A46702, #. (See also 1424, 1425.)

1659. *Bailey, Randall E.; Powers, Bruce G.; and Shafer, Mary F.: **Interaction of Feel System and Flight Control System Dynamics on Lateral Flying Qualities.** AIAA Paper 88-4327. Presented at the AIAA Atmospheric Flight Mechanics Conference, Minneapolis, Minnesota, August 15–17, 1988, 88A50620, #.

An investigation of feel system and flight control system dynamics on lateral flying qualities was conducted using the variable stability USAF NT-33 aircraft. Experimental variations in feel system natural frequency, force-deflection gradient, control system command architecture type, flight control system filter frequency, and control system delay were made. The experiment data include pilot ratings using the Cooper-Harper (1969) rating scale, pilot comments, and tracking performance statistic. Three test pilots served as evaluators. The data indicate that as the feel system natural frequency is reduced lateral flying qualities degrade. At the slowest feel system frequency, the closed-loop response becomes nonlinear with a 'bobweight' effect apparent in the feel system. Feel system influences were essentially independent of the control system architecture. The flying qualities influence due to the feel system was different than when the identical dynamic system was used as a flight control system element.

*Calspan Advanced Technology Center, Buffalo, New York.

1660. *Zerweckh, S. H.; *Von Flotow, A. H.; and Murray, J. E.: **Flight Testing a Highly Flexible Aircraft—Case Study on the MIT Light Eagle.** AIAA Paper 88-4375. *Technical Papers*, presented at the AIAA Atmospheric Flight Mechanics Conference, Minneapolis, Minnesota, August 15–17, 1988, (see A88-50576 21-01), pp. 405–414, 88A50613, #. (See also 1774.)

This paper describes the techniques developed for a flight test program of a human powered aircraft, the application of these techniques in the winter of 1987/88 and the results of the flight testing. A system of sensors, signal conditioning and data recording equipment was developed and installed in the aircraft. Flight test maneuvers which do not exceed the aircraft's limited capability were developed and refined in an iterative sequence of test flights. The test procedures were adjusted to yield maximum data quality from the point of view of estimating lateral and longitudinal stability derivatives. Structural flexibility and unsteady aerodynamics are modeled in an ad hoc manner, capturing the effects observed during the test flights. A model with flexibility-extended equations of motion is presented. Results of maneuvers that were flown are compared with the predictions of that model and analyzed. Finally the results of the flight test program are examined critically, especially with respect to future applications, and suggestions are made in order to improve maneuvers for parameter estimation of very flexible aircraft.

*MIT, Cambridge, Massachusetts.

1661. Berry, Donald T.: **Longitudinal Long-Period Dynamics of Aerospace Craft.** AIAA Paper 88-4358. *Technical Papers*, presented at the AIAA Atmospheric Flight Mechanics Conference, Minneapolis, Minnesota, August 15–17, 1988, (see A88-50576 21-01), pp. 254–264, 88A50601, #. (See also 1846.)

Linear analyses are performed to examine the generic aspects of aerospace vehicle longitudinal long-period or trajectory modes of motion. The influence of Mach number, dynamic pressure, thrust-to-drag ratio, and propulsion system thrust laws on the longitudinal trajectory modes is presented in terms of phugoid frequency and damping and height mode stability. The results of these analyses are compared to flying qualities requirements where possible, and potential deficiencies in both the vehicle and the criteria are noted. A preliminary look at possible augmentation schemes to improve potential deficiencies is also presented. Interpretation of the practical consequences of the results is aided by typical time histories. Results indicate that propulsion system characteristics are the dominant influence on the longitudinal long-period flight dynamics of hypersonic aerospace craft. However, straightforward augmentation systems demonstrated the potential to accommodate these influences if the effects are included in the design process. These efforts may be hampered by a lack of design criteria for hypersonic aircraft.

1662. *Zeis, Joseph E., Jr.; Lambert, Heather H.; **Calico, Robert A.; and **Gleason, Daniel: **Angle of Attack Estimation Using an Inertial Reference Platform.** AIAA Paper 88-4351. *Technical Papers*, presented at the AIAA Atmospheric Flight Mechanics Conference, Minneapolis, Minnesota, August 15–17, 1988, (see A88-50576 21-01), pp. 180–190, 88A50595, #.

This paper presents the mathematical development and flight test results of an angle of attack estimation system based on inertial navigation system inputs. The estimator uses these inputs to determine the coefficient of lift required at any instant inflight. Angle of attack is then modeled through a regression analysis based on coefficient of lift, altitude and Mach. Overall correlation of the estimator as tested was generally within 0.5 degrees through 17 degrees angle of attack on an F-15A aircraft. A robustness analysis indicates that the system can be used adequately in maneuvering flight.

*USAF Edwards AFB, California.
**USAF Institute of Technology, Wright-Patterson AFB, Ohio.

1663. Duke, Eugene L.; Antoniewicz, Robert F.; and Krambeer, Keith D.: **Derivation and Definition of a Linear Aircraft Model.** NASA RP-1207, H-1391, NAS 1.61:1207, August 1988, 89N15123, #.

A linear aircraft model for a rigid aircraft of constant mass flying over a flat, nonrotating earth is derived and defined. The derivation makes no assumptions of reference trajectory or vehicle symmetry. The linear system equations are derived and evaluated along a general trajectory and include both aircraft dynamics and observation variables.

1664. *Wagner, R. D.; *Maddalon, D. V.; and Fisher, D. F.: **Laminar Flow Control Leading Edge Systems in Simulated Airline Service.** *Proceedings, ICAS, 16th Congress,* Vol. 2, Jerusalem, Israel, August 28–September 2, 1988, (see A89-13501 03-05), pp. 1014–1023, 89A13604, #. (See also 1764.)

The feasibility of two candidate leading-edge flow laminarization systems applicable to airline service was tested using representative airline operational conditions with respect to air traffic, weather, and airport insect infestation. One of the systems involved a perforated Ti alloy suction surface with about 1 million 0.0025-in. diameter holes drilled by electron beam, as well as a Krueger-type flap that offered protective shielding against insect impingement; the other supplied surface suction through a slotted Ti alloy skin with 27 spanwise slots on the upper and lower surface.

*NASA Langley Research Center, Hampton, Virginia.

1665. Curry, Robert E.; and *Richwine, David M.: **An Airborne System for Vortex Flow Visualization on the F-18 High-Alpha Research Vehicle.** AIAA Paper 88-4671. Presented at the AIAA, NASA, and AFWAL, Conference on Sensors and Measurement Techniques for Aeronautical Applications, Atlanta, Georgia, September 7–9, 1988, 88A53830, #.

A flow visualization system for the F-18 high-alpha research vehicle is described which allows direct observation of the separated vortex flows over a wide range of flight conditions. The system consists of a smoke generator system, on-board photographic and video systems, and instrumentation. In the present concept, smoke is entrained into the low-pressure

vortex core, and vortex breakdown is indicated by a rapid diffusion of the smoke. The resulting pattern is observed using photographic and video images and is correlated with measured flight conditions.

*PRC Systems Services, Edwards, California.

1666. *Hamory, Philip J.: **Flight Systems Design Issues for a Research-Oriented Hypersonic Vehicle.** *Proceedings, 1st International Conference on Hypersonic Flight in the 21st Century,* Grand Forks, North Dakota, September 20–23, 1988, (see A89-54326 24-15), pp. 455–468, 89A54371.

The impact of flight system design for a research-oriented hypersonic vehicle is examined. The design requirements of the vehicle are discussed, including strong onboard processing capability, integrated propulsion and flight controls, and analytic redundancy management. Consideration is given to tradeoffs between synchronization and asynchronization, distributed and centralized architectures, and digital and analog backup systems. A research-oriented hypersonic vehicle structure is proposed which uses nodal network architecture to maximize flight system effectiveness in controlling various tasks.

*Datamax Computer Systems, Inc., Edwards, California.

1667. Antoniewicz, Robert F.; Duke, Eugene L.; and Patterson, Brian P.: **User's Manual for Interactive LINEAR: A FORTRAN Program to Derive Linear Aircraft Models.** NASA TP-2835, H-1443, NAS 1.60:2835, September 1988, 89N16437, #.

An interactive FORTRAN program that provides the user with a powerful and flexible tool for the linearization of aircraft aerodynamic models is documented in this report. The program LINEAR numerically determines a linear system model using nonlinear equations of motion and a user-supplied linear or nonlinear aerodynamic model. The nonlinear equations of motion used are six-degree-of-freedom equations with stationary atmosphere and flat, nonrotating earth assumptions. The system model determined by LINEAR consists of matrices for both the state and observation equations. The program has been designed to allow easy selection and definition of the state, control, and observation variables to be used in a particular model.

1668. Fisher, David F.; and Meyer, Robert R., Jr.: **Flow Visualization Techniques for Flight Research.** NASA TM-100455, H-1524, NAS 1.15:100455. Presented at the 73rd AGARD Symposium of Flight Mechanics, Panel on Flight Test Techniques, Edwards AFB, California, October 17–20, 1988, 89N11719, #. (See also 1710.)

In-flight flow visualization techniques used at the Dryden Flight Research Facility of NASA Ames Research Center

(Ames-Dryden) and its predecessor organizations are described. Results from flight tests which visualized surface flows using flow cones, tufts, oil flows, liquid crystals, sublimating chemicals, and emitted fluids have been obtained. Off-surface flow visualization of vortical flow has been obtained from natural condensation and two methods using smoke generator systems. Recent results from flight tests at NASA Langley Research Center using a propylene glycol smoker and an infrared imager are also included. Results from photo-chase aircraft, onboard and postflight photography are presented.

1669. Garbinski, Charles; Redin, Paul C.; and Budd, Gerald D.: **User's Manual for EZPLOT Version 5.5: a FORTRAN Program for 2-Dimensional Graphic Display of Data.** NASA TM-88293, H-1410, NAS 1.15:88293, October 1988, 89N12269, #.

EZPLOT is a computer applications program that converts data resident on a file into a plot displayed on the screen of a graphics terminal. This program generates either time history or x-y plots in response to commands entered interactively from a terminal keyboard. Plot parameters consist of a single independent parameter and from one to eight dependent parameters. Various line patterns, symbol shapes, axis scales, text labels, and data modification techniques are available. This user's manual describes EZPLOT as it is implemented on the Ames Research Center, Dryden Research Facility ELXSI computer using DI-3000 graphics software tools.

1670. Hernandez, Francisco J.; and Burcham, Frank W., Jr.: **Flight Measured and Calculated Exhaust Jet Conditions for an F100 Engine in an F-15 Airplane.** NASA TM-100419, H-1449, NAS 1.15:100419, October 1988, 89N13435, #.

The exhaust jet conditions, in terms of temperature and Mach number, were determined for a nozzle-aft end acoustic study flown on an F-15 aircraft. Jet properties for the F100 EMD engines were calculated using the engine manufacturer's specification deck. The effects of atmospheric temperature on jet Mach number, M10, were calculated. Values of turbine discharge pressure, PT6M, jet Mach number, and jet temperature were calculated as a function of aircraft Mach number, altitude, and power lever angle for the test day conditions. At a typical test point with a Mach number of 0.9, intermediate power setting, and an altitude of 20,000 ft, M10 was equal to 1.63. Flight measured and calculated values of PT6M were compared for intermediate power at altitudes of 15500, 20500, and 31000 ft. It was found that at 31000 ft, there was excellent agreement between both, but for lower altitudes the specification deck overpredicted the flight data. The calculated jet Mach numbers were believed to be accurate to within 2 percent.

1671. Ko, William L.; Quinn, Robert D.; and Gong, Leslie: **Effect of Internal Convection and Internal**

Radiation on the Structural Temperatures of Space Shuttle Orbiter. NASA TM-100414, H-1466, NAS 1.15:100414, October 1988, 89N23819, #.

Structural performance and resizing of the finite-element thermal analysis computer program was used in the reentry heat transfer analysis of the space shuttle orbiter. One midfuselage cross section and one midspan wing segment were selected to study the effects of internal convection and internal radiation on the structural temperatures. The effect of internal convection was found to be more prominent than that of internal radiation in the orbiter thermal analysis. Without these two effects, the calculated structural temperatures at certain stations could be as much as 45 to 90 percent higher than the measured values. By considering internal convection as free convection, the correlation between the predicted and measured structural temperatures could be improved greatly.

1672. *Granaas, Michael M.; and Rhea, Donald C.: **The Psychology of Computer Displays in the Modern Mission Control Center.** NASA TM-100451, H-1507, NAS 1.15:100451, October 1988, 90N22213, #. (See also 1673.)

Work at NASA's Western Aeronautical Test Range (WATR) has demonstrated the need for increased consideration of psychological factors in the design of computer displays for the WATR mission control center. These factors include color perception, memory load, and cognitive processing abilities. A review of relevant work in the human factors psychology area is provided to demonstrate the need for this awareness. The information provided should be relevant in control room settings where computerized displays are being used.

* South Dakota University, Vermillion, South Dakota.

1673. *Granaas, Michael M.: **The Psychology of Computer Displays in the Modern Mission Control Center.** AIAA Paper 88-2065. *Technical Papers*, presented at the 15th Aerodynamic Testing Conference, San Diego, California, May 18–20, 1988, (see A88-37907 15-09), pp. 446–448, 88A37951, #. (See also 1672.)

Work at NASA's Western Aeronautical Test Range (WATR) has demonstrated the need for increased consideration of psychological factors in the design of computer displays for the WATR mission control center. These factors include memory load, color perception, and cognitive processing abilities. A review of relevant work in the human factors psychology area is provided to demonstrate the need for this awareness. The information provided should be relevant in control room settings where computerized displays are being used.

*South Dakota University, Vermillion, South Dakota.

1674. Hicks, John W.; and Petersen, Kevin L.: **Real-Time Flight Test Analysis and Display Techniques for the X-29A Aircraft.** NASA TM-101692, H-1520, NAS 1.15:101692. Presented at the 73rd AGARD Symposium on Flight Test Techniques, Flight Mechanics Panel, Edwards AFB, California, October 17–20, 1988, November 1988, 89N13424, #. (See also 1714.)

The X-29A advanced technology demonstrator flight envelope expansion program and the subsequent flight research phase gave impetus to the development of several innovative real-time analysis and display techniques. These new techniques produced significant improvements in flight test productivity, flight research capabilities, and flight safety. These techniques include real-time measurement and display of in-flight structural loads, dynamic structural mode frequency and damping, flight control system dynamic stability and control response, aeroperformance drag polars, and aircraft specific excess power. Several of these analysis techniques also provided for direct comparisons of flight-measured results with analytical predictions. The aeroperformance technique was made possible by the concurrent development of a new simplified in-flight net thrust computation method. To achieve these levels of on-line flight test analysis, integration of ground and airborne systems was required. The capability of NASA Ames Research Center, Dryden Flight Research Facility's Western Aeronautical Test Range was a key factor in enabling implementation of these methods.

1675. Nissim, E.; and Burken, John J.: **Control Surface Spanwise Placement in Active Flutter Suppression Systems.** NASA TP-2873, H-1492, NAS 1.60:2873, November 1988, 89N16196, #.

A method is developed that determines the placement of an active control surface for maximum effectiveness in suppressing flutter. No specific control law is required by this method which is based on the aerodynamic energy concept. It is argued that the spanwise placement of the active controls should coincide with the locations where maximum energy per unit span is fed into the system. The method enables one to determine the distribution, over the different surfaces of the aircraft, of the energy input into the system as a result of the unstable fluttering mode. The method is illustrated using three numerical examples.

1676. Kempel, Robert W.; McNeill, Walter E.; Gilyard, Glenn B.; and Maine, Trindel A.: **A Piloted Evaluation of an Oblique-Wing Research Aircraft Motion Simulation With Decoupling Control Laws.** NASA TP-2874, H-1430, NAS 1.60:2874, November 1988, 89N15930, #.

The NASA Ames Research Center developed an oblique-wing research plane from NASA's digital fly-by-wire airplane. Oblique-wing airplanes show large cross-coupling in control and dynamic behavior which is not present on conventional symmetric airplanes and must be compensated for to obtain acceptable handling qualities. The large vertical motion simulator at NASA Ames-Moffett was used in the piloted evaluation of a proposed flight control system designed to provide decoupled handling qualities. Five discrete flight conditions were evaluated ranging from low altitude subsonic Mach numbers to moderate altitude supersonic Mach numbers. The flight control system was effective in generally decoupling the airplane. However, all participating pilots objected to the high levels of lateral acceleration encountered in pitch maneuvers. In addition, the pilots were more critical of left turns (in the direction of the trailing wingtip when skewed) than they were of right turns due to the tendency to be rolled into the left turns and out of the right turns. Asymmetric side force as a function of angle of attack was the primary cause of lateral acceleration in pitch. Along with the lateral acceleration in pitch, variation of rolling and yawing moments as functions of angle of attack caused the tendency to roll into left turns and out of right turns.

1677. Horton, Timothy W.; and Kempel, Robert W.: **Flight Test Experience and Controlled Impact of a Remotely Piloted Jet Transport Aircraft.** NASA TM-4084, H-1447, NAS 1.15:4084, November 1988, 89N15910, #.

The Dryden Flight Research Center Facility of NASA Ames Research Center (Ames-Dryden) and the FAA conducted the controlled impact demonstration (CID) program using a large, four-engine, remotely piloted jet transport airplane. Closed-loop primary flight was controlled through the existing onboard PB-20D autopilot which had been modified for the CID program. Uplink commands were sent from a ground-based cockpit and digital computer in conjunction with an up-down telemetry link. These uplink commands were received aboard the airplane and transferred through uplink interface systems to the modified PB-20D autopilot. Both proportional and discrete commands were produced by the ground system. Prior to flight tests, extensive simulation was conducted during the development of ground-based digital control laws. The control laws included primary control, secondary control, and racetrack and final approach guidance. Extensive ground checks were performed on all remotely piloted systems; however, piloted flight tests were the primary method and validation of control law concepts developed from simulation. The design, development, and flight testing of control laws and systems required to accomplish the remotely piloted mission are discussed.

1678. Mackall, Dale A.: **Development and Flight Test Experiences With a Flight-Crucial Digital Control System.** NASA TP-2857, H-1344, NAS 1.60:2857, November 1988, 89N24327, #.

Engineers and scientists in the advanced fighter technology integration (AFTI) F-16 program investigated the integration of emerging technologies into an advanced fighter aircraft. AFTI's three major technologies included: flight-crucial

305

digital control, decoupled aircraft flight control, and integration of avionics, flight control, and pilot displays. In addition to investigating improvements in fighter performance, researchers studied the generic problems confronting the designers of highly integrated flight-crucial digital control. An overview is provided of both the advantages and problems of integration digital control systems. Also, an examination of the specification, design, qualification, and flight test life-cycle phase is provided. An overview is given of the fault-tolerant design, multimoded decoupled flight control laws, and integrated avionics design. The approach to qualifying the software and system designs is discussed, and the effects of design choices on system qualification are highlighted.

1679. Webb, Lannie D.; *McCain, William E.; and *Rose, Lucinda A.: **Measured and Predicted Pressure Distributions on the AFTI/F-111 Mission Adaptive Wing.** NASA TM-100443, H-1495, NAS 1.15:100443, AIAA Paper 88-2555. Presented at the 6th Applied Aerodynamics Conference, Williamsburg, Virginia, June 6–8, 1988, November 1988, 89N15908, #.

Flight tests have been conducted using an F-111 aircraft modified with a mission adaptive wing (MAW). The MAW has variable-camber leading and trailing edge surfaces that can change the wing camber in flight, while preserving smooth upper surface contours. This paper contains wing surface pressure measurements obtained during flight tests at Dryden Flight Research Facility of NASA Ames Research Center. Upper and lower surface steady pressure distributions were measured along four streamwise rows of static pressure orifices on the right wing for a leading-edge sweep angle of 26 deg. The airplane, wing, instrumentation, and test conditions are discussed. Steady pressure results are presented for selected wing camber deflections flown at subsonic Mach numbers up to 0.90 and an angle-of-attack range of 5 to 12 deg. The Reynolds number was 26 million, based on the mean aerodynamic chord. The MAW flight data are compared to MAW wind tunnel data, transonic aircraft technology (TACT) flight data, and predicted pressure distributions. The results provide a unique database for a smooth, variable-camber, advanced supercritical wing.

*PRC Systems Services Co., Edwards, California.

1680. Duke, Eugene L.: **Application of Flight Systems Methodologies to the Validation of Knowledge-Based Systems.** NASA CP-3019. NASA Lyndon B. Johnson Space Center, 2nd Annual Workshop on Space Operations Automation and Robotics (SOAR 1988), (see N89-19817 12-59), November 1988, pp. 107–121, 89N19832, #. (See also 1653.)

Flight and mission-critical systems are verified, qualified for flight, and validated using well-known and well-established techniques. These techniques define the validation methodology used for such systems. In order to verify, qualify, and validate knowledge-based systems (KBS's), the methodology used for conventional systems must be addressed, and the applicability and limitations of that methodology to KBS's must be identified. An outline of how this approach to the validation of KBS's is being developed and used is presented.

1681. Voracek, David F.; and Morales, Adolfo M.: **The Effects of Excitation Waveforms and Shaker Moving Mass on the Measured Modal Characteristics of a 2- by 5-Foot Aluminum Plate.** NASA TM-100446, H-1502, NAS 1.15:100446, December 1988, 89N15109, #.

Ground vibration tests were conducted to compare and to investigate the effects of five excitation waveforms and the shaker moving mass (equipment and armature used to attach the shaker to the structure) on the experimental modal characteristics of a 2- by 5-ft aluminum plate using fast Fourier transform techniques. The five types of excitation waveforms studied were sine dwell, random, impact, sine sweep, and impulsive sine. The results showed that the experimental modal frequencies for all types of excitation were within 3 percent, while the modal damping data exhibited greater scatter. The sets of mode shapes obtained by the five types of excitation were consistent. The results of the shaker moving mass investigation on the 2- by 5-ft aluminum plate showed that modal frequency decreases and modal damping remains relatively constant with an increase in shaker moving mass. The generalized mass of the structure appears to decrease with an increase in shaker moving mass. In addition, it was seen that having a shaker near a node line can reduce some of the effects of the added shaker moving mass on the frequencies and the damping.

1682. Duke, E. L.: **LINEAR—Derivation and Definition of a Linear Aircraft Model.** ARC-12422, 1988, 94M10035.

The Derivation and Definition of a Linear Model program, LINEAR, provides the user with a powerful and flexible tool for the linearization of aircraft aerodynamic models. LINEAR was developed to provide a standard, documented, and verified tool to derive linear models for aircraft stability analysis and control law design. Linear system models define the aircraft system in the neighborhood of an analysis point and are determined by the linearization of the nonlinear equations defining vehicle dynamics and sensors. LINEAR numerically determines a linear system model using nonlinear equations of motion and a user supplied linear or nonlinear aerodynamic model. The nonlinear equations of motion used are six-degree-of-freedom equations with stationary atmosphere and flat, nonrotating earth assumptions. LINEAR is capable of extracting both linearized engine effects, such as net thrust, torque, and gyroscopic effects and including these effects in the linear system model. The point at which this linear model is defined is determined either by completely specifying the state and control variables, or by specifying an analysis point on a trajectory and directing the program to determine the control variables and the remaining state variables. The system model determined by LINEAR consists of matrices for both the state and observation equations. The program has been designed to provide easy selection of state, control, and observation variables to be used in a particular model. Thus, the order of the system model is completely under user control. Further, the program provides the flexibility of allowing alternate formulations of both the state and observation equations. Data describing the aircraft and the test case is input to the program through a terminal or formatted data files. All data can be modified interactively from case to case. The aerodynamic model can be defined in two ways: a set of nondimensional stability and control derivatives for the flight point of interest, or a full non-linear aerodynamic model as used in simulations. LINEAR is written in FORTRAN and has been implemented on a DEC VAX computer operating under VMS with a virtual memory requirement of approximately 296K of 8 bit bytes. Both an interactive and batch version are included. LINEAR was developed in 1988.

1989 Technical Publications

1683. Rhea, Donald C.; Hammons, Kevin R.; Malone, Jacqueline C.; and Nesel, Michael C.: **Development and Use of Interactive Displays in Real-Time Ground Support Research Facilities.** NASA TM-101694, H-1529, NAS 1.15:101694. Presented at the AIAA 27th Aerospace Meeting, Reno, Nevada, January 9–12, 1989, January 1989, 9N14683, #.

The NASA Western Aeronautical Test Range (WATR) is one of the world's most advanced aeronautical research flight test support facilities. A variety of advanced and often unique real-time interactive displays has been developed for use in the mission control centers (MCC) to support research flight and ground testing. These displays consist of applications operating on systems described as real-time interactive graphics super workstations and real-time interactive PC/AT compatible workstations. This paper reviews these two types of workstations and the specific applications operating on each display system. The applications provide examples that demonstrate overall system capability applicable for use in other ground-based real-time research/test facilities.

1684. *Granaas, Michael M.; and Rhea, Donald C.: **Techniques for Optimizing Human-Machine Information Transfer Related to Real-Time Interactive Display Systems.** NASA TM-100450, H-1506, NAS 1.15:100450, AIAA Paper 89-0151. Presented at the 27th AIAA Aerospace Sciences Meeting, Reno, Nevada, January 9–12, 1989, January 1989, 90N11441, #. (See also 1685.)

In recent years the needs of ground-based researcher-analysts to access real-time engineering data in the form of processed information has expanded rapidly. Fortunately, the capacity to deliver that information has also expanded. The development of advanced display systems is essential to the success of a research test activity. Those developed at the National Aeronautics and Space Administration (NASA), Western Aeronautical Test Range (WATR), range from simple alphanumerics to interactive mapping and graphics. These unique display systems are designed not only to meet basic information display requirements of the user, but also to take advantage of techniques for optimizing information display. Future ground-based display systems will rely heavily not only on new technologies, but also on interaction with the human user and the associated productivity with that interaction. The psychological abilities and limitations of the user will become even more important in defining the difference between a usable and a useful display system. This paper reviews the requirements for development of real-time displays; the psychological aspects of design such as the layout, color selection, real-time response rate, and interactivity of displays; and an analysis of some existing WATR displays.

*South Dakota University, Vermillion, South Dakota.

1685. *Granaas, Michael M.; and Rhea, Donald C.: **Techniques for Optimizing Human-Machine Information Transfer Related to Real-Time Interactive Display Systems.** AIAA Paper 89-0151. Presented at the AIAA, 27th Aerospace Sciences Meeting, Reno, Nevada, January 9–12, 1989, 89A25134, #. (See also 1684.)

The requirements for the development of real-time displays are reviewed. Of particular interest are the psychological aspects of design such as the layout, color selection, real-time response rate, and the interactivity of displays. Some existing Western Aeronautical Test Range displays are analyzed.

*South Dakota University, Vermillion, South Dakota.

1686. Gupta, K. K.; Brenner, M. J.; and Voelker, L. S.: **Integrated Aeroservoelastic Analysis Capability With X-29A Comparisons.** Journal of Aircraft (ISSN 0021-8669), Vol. 26, (see A87-33716), January 1989, pp. 84–90, 89A24311, #. (See also 1560.)

1687. Kehoe, Michael W.; and Voracek, David F.: **Ground Vibration Test Results of a JetStar Airplane Using Impulsive Sine Excitation.** NASA TM-100448, H-1504, NAS 1.15:100448. Presented at the 7th International Modal Analysis Conference, Las Vegas, Nevada, January 30–February 2, 1989, February 1989, 89N15909, #. (See also 1744.)

Structural excitation is important for both ground vibration and flight flutter testing. The structural responses caused by this excitation are analyzed to determine frequency, damping, and mode shape information. Many excitation waveforms have been used throughout the years. The use of impulsive sine (sin omega t)/omega t as an excitation waveform for ground vibration testing and the advantages of using this waveform for flight flutter testing are discussed. The ground vibration test results of a modified JetStar airplane using impulsive sine as an excitation waveform are compared with the test results of the same airplane using multiple-input random excitation. The results indicated that the structure was sufficiently excited using the impulsive sine waveform. Comparisons of input force spectrums, mode shape plots, and frequency and damping values for the two methods of excitation are presented.

1688. Gilyard, Glenn B.: **The Oblique-Wing Research Aircraft: A Test Bed for Unsteady Aerodynamic and Aeroelastic Research**. NASA CP-3022. NASA Langley Research Center, *Transonic Unsteady Aerodynamics and Aeroelasticity, Part 2*, (see N89-19247 12-02), February 1989, pp. 395–414, 89N19253, #.

The advantages of oblique wings have been the subject of numerous theoretical studies, wind tunnel tests, low speed flight models, and finally a low speed manned demonstrator, the AD-1. The specific objectives of the OWRA program are: (1) to establish the necessary technology base required to translate theoretical and experimental results into practical mission oriented designs; (2) to design, fabricate and flight test an oblique wing aircraft throughout a realistic flight envelope, and (3) to develop and validate design and analysis tools for asymmetric aircraft configurations. The preliminary design phase of the project is complete and has resulted in a wing configuration for which construction is ready to be initiated.

1689. Smith, John P.; Schilling, Lawrence J.; and Wagner, Charles A.: **Simulation at Dryden Flight Research Facility From 1957 to 1982**. NASA TM-101695, H-1530, NAS 1.15:101695. Presented at the SES/SFTE Simulation-Aircraft Test and Evaluation Symposium, Patuxent River, Maryland, March 16–17, 1982, February 1989, 89N20983, #.

The Dryden Flight Research Facility has been a leader in developing simulation as an integral part of flight test research. The history of that effort is reviewed, starting in 1957 and continuing to the present time. The contributions of the major program activities conducted at Dryden during this 25-year period to the development of a simulation philosophy and capability is explained.

1690. Bauer, Jeffrey E.; *Crawford, David B.; *Andrisani, Dominick, II; and Gera, Joseph: **Real-Time Comparison of X-29A Flight Data and Simulation Data**. *Journal of Aircraft* (ISSN 0021-8669), Vol. 26, February 1989, pp. 117–123, 89A27736, #. (See also 1545.)

*Purdue University, West Lafayette, Indiana.

1691. Ko, William L.: **Application of Fracture Mechanics and Half-Cycle Theory to the Prediction of**

Fatigue Life of Aerospace Structural Components. *International Journal of Fracture, Structural Integrity: Theory and Experiment*, vol 39, March 1989, pp. 45–62, (see A89-51259 22-39), Kluwer Academic Publishers, Doredrecht, the Netherlands, 89A51263.

The service life of aircraft structural components undergoing random stress cycling was analyzed by the application of fracture mechanics. The initial crack sizes at the critical stress points for the fatigue crack growth analysis were established through proof load tests. The fatigue crack growth rates for random stress cycles were calculated using the half-cycle method. A new equation was developed for calculating the number of remaining flights for the structural components. The number of remaining flights predicted by the new equation is much lower than that predicted by the conventional equation. This report describes the application of fracture mechanics and the half-cycle method to calculate the number of remaining flights for aircraft structural components.

1692. Putnam, Terrill W.; and Ayers, Theodore G.: **Flight Research and Testing**. NASA CP-3020. NASA Langley Research Center, *Transonic Symposium: Theory, Application, and Experiment*, Vol. 1, Part 1, (see N89-20925 14-02), March 1989, pp. 33–59, 89N20927, #. (See also 1648.)

Flight research and testing form a critical link in the aeronautic research and development chain. Brilliant concepts, elegant theories, and even sophisticated ground tests of flight vehicles are not sufficient to prove beyond a doubt that an unproven aeronautical concept will actually perform as predicted. Flight research and testing provide the ultimate proof that an idea or concept performs as expected. Ever since the Wright brothers, flight research and testing were the crucible in which aeronautical concepts were advanced and proven to the point that engineers and companies are willing to stake their future to produce and design aircraft. This is still true today, as shown by the development of the experimental X-30 aerospace plane. The Dryden Flight Research Center (Ames-Dryden) continues to be involved in a number of flight research programs that require understanding and characterization of the total airplane in all the aeronautical disciplines, for example the X-29. Other programs such as the F-14 variable-sweep transition flight experiment have focused on a single concept or discipline. Ames-Dryden also continues to conduct flight and ground based experiments to improve and expand the ability to test and evaluate advanced aeronautical concepts. A review of significant aeronautical flight research programs and experiments is presented to illustrate both the progress being made and the challenges to come.

1693. *Davis, Richard E.; *Maddalon, Dal V.; *Wagner, Richard D.; Fisher, David F.; and Young, Ronald: **Evaluation of Cloud Detection Instruments and Performance of Laminar-Flow Leading-Edge Test**

Articles During NASA Leading-Edge Flight-Test Program. NASA TP-2888, L-16509, NAS 1.60:2888, April 1989, 91N24199, #.

Summary evaluations of the performance of laminar-flow control (LFC) leading edge test articles on a NASA JetStar aircraft are presented. Statistics, presented for the test articles' performance in haze and cloud situations, as well as in clear air, show a significant effect of cloud particle concentrations on the extent of laminar flow. The cloud particle environment was monitored by two instruments, a cloud particle spectrometer (Knollenberg probe) and a charging patch. Both instruments are evaluated as diagnostic aids for avoiding laminar-flow detrimental particle concentrations in future LFC aircraft operations. The data base covers 19 flights in the simulated airline service phase of the NASA Leading-Edge Flight-Test (LEFT) Program.

*NASA Langley Research Center, Hampton, Virginia.

1694. *Menon, P. K. A.; **Walker, R. A.; and Duke, E. L.: **Flight-Test Maneuver Modeling and Control.** *Journal of Guidance, Control, and Dynamics* (ISSN 0731-5090), Vol. 12, March–April 1989, (see A86-19868), April 1989, pp. 195–200, 89A31461, #. (See also 1459.)

*Georgia Institute of Technology, Atlanta, Georgia.
**FMC Central Engineering Laboratory, Santa Clara, California.

1695. Johnson, Jeff: **Flutter Testing of Modern Aircraft.** *AIAA Student Journal* (ISSN 0001-1460), Vol. 27, Spring 1989, pp. 6–11, 89A51221, #.

Structural dynamicists avoid aircraft structural flutter through the use of flutter analyses, wind tunnel tests, ground-vibration tests, and flight flutter testing. FEM and unsteady aerodynamics models are often employed in analyses whose results' accuracies are verified by wind tunnel test results. Ground-vibration testing is used to ascertain an airframe's resonant modes of vibration and their associated frequencies and damping rates; these data are then compared to the FEM analysis results. Flutter wind tunnel testing serves the same purpose for unsteady aerodynamic analysis as ground vibration testing does for the vibration analysis. Finally, flight flutter testing ensures that no flutter is present at any point in the envelope.

1696. Nissim, E.: **Design of Control Laws for Flutter Suppression Based on the Aerodynamic Energy Concept and Comparisons With Other Design Methods.** AIAA Paper 89-1212. Presented at the AIAA, ASME, ASCE, AHS, and ASC, 30th Structures, Structural Dynamics and Materials Conference, Mobile, Alabama, April 3–5, 1989, 89A31100, #. (See also 1812.)

The aerodynamic energy method is used in this paper to synthesize control laws for NASA's Drone for Aerodynamic and Structural Testing-Aerodynamic Research Wing 1 (DAST-ARW1) mathematical model. The performance of these control laws in terms of closed-loop flutter dynamic pressure, control surface activity, and robustness is compared against other control laws that appear in the literature and relate to the same model. A control law synthesis technique that makes use of the return difference singular values is developed in this paper. it is based on the aerodynamic energy approach and is shown to yield results superior to those given in the literature and based on optimal control theory. Nyquist plots are presented together with a short discussion regarding the relative merits of the minimum singular value as a measure of robustness, compared with the more traditional measure of robustness involving phase and gain margins.

1697. Nissim, E.; and Gilyard, G. B.: **Method for Experimental Determination of Flutter Speed by Parameter Identification.** AIAA Paper 89-1324. *Technical Papers, Part 3*, presented at the AIAA, ASME, ASCE, AHS, and ASC, 30th Structures, Structural Dynamics and Materials Conference, Mobile, Alabama, April 3–5, 1989, (see A89-30651 12-39), 1989, pp. 1427–1441, 89A30801, #. (See also 1705.)

A method for flight flutter testing is proposed which enables one to determine the flutter dynamic pressure from flights flown far below the flutter dynamic pressure. The method is based on the identification of the coefficients of the equations of motion at low dynamic pressures, followed by the solution of these equations to compute the flutter dynamic pressure. The initial results of simulated data reported in the present work indicate that the method can accurately predict the flutter dynamic pressure, as described. If no insurmountable difficulties arise in the implementation of this method, it may significantly improve the procedures for flight flutter testing.

1698. Nissim, E.: **Effect of Control Surface Mass Unbalance on the Stability of a Closed-Loop Active Control System.** AIAA Paper 89-1211. *Technical Papers, Part 1*, presented at the AIAA, ASME, ASCE, AHS, and ASC, 30th Structures, Structural Dynamics and Materials Conference, Mobile, Alabama, April 3–5, 1989, (see A89-30651 12-39), pp. 476–486, 89A30700, #. (See also 1742.)

An inertial energy approach similar to the aerodynamic energy method for flutter suppression is used to investigate the effects of mass-unbalanced control surfaces on the stability of a closed-loop system. It is demonstrated that a spanwise section for sensor location can be obtained which ensures minimum sensitivity to the mode shapes of the aircraft. Leading-edge control is characterized by a compatibility between inertial stabilization and aerodynamic stabilization that trailing-edge control lacks.

1699. Nissim, E.; and Burken, J. J.: **Control Surface Spanwise Placement in Active Flutter Suppression Systems.** NASA Langley Research Center, *Recent Advances* *in Multidisciplinary Analysis and Optimization*, Part 2, (see N89-25173 19-05), <u>April 1989</u>, pp. 919–934, 89N25195, #.

All flutter suppression systems require sensors to detect the movement of the lifting surface and to activate a control surface according to a synthesized control law. Most of the work performed to date relates to the development of control laws based on predetermined locations of sensors and control surfaces. These locations of sensors and control surfaces are determined either arbitrarily, or by means of a trial and error procedure. The aerodynamic energy concept indicates that the sensors should be located within the activated strip. Furthermore, the best chordwise location of a sensor activating a T.E. control surface is around the 65 percent chord location. The best chordwise location for a sensor activating a L.E. surface is shown to lie upstream of the wing (around 20 percent upstream of the leading edge), or alternatively, two sensors located along the same chord should be used.

1700. *Brumbaugh, Randal W.; and Duke, Eugene L.: **Real-Time Application of Knowledge-Based Systems.** NASA Langley Research Center, *Recent Advances in Multidisciplinary Analysis and Optimization*, Part 1, (see N89-25146 19-05), <u>April 1989</u>, pp. 357–371, 89N25163, #.

The Rapid Prototyping Facility (RPF) was developed to meet a need for a facility which allows flight systems concepts to be prototyped in a manner which allows for real-time flight test experience with a prototype system. This need was focused during the development and demonstration of the expert system flight status monitor (ESFSM). The ESFSM was a prototype system developed on a LISP machine, but lack of a method for progressive testing and problem identification led to an impractical system. T he RPF concept was developed, and the ATMS designed to exercise its capabilities. The ATMS Phase 1 demonstration provided a practical vehicle for testing the RPF, as well as a useful tool. ATMS Phase 2 development continues. A dedicated F-18 is expected to be assigned for facility use in late 1988, with RAV modifications. A knowledge-based autopilot is being developed using the RPF. This is a system which provides elementary autopilot functions and is intended as a vehicle for testing expert system verification and validation methods. An expert system propulsion monitor is being prototyped. This system provides real-time assistance to an engineer monitoring a propulsion system during a flight.

*PRC Systems Services Co., Hampton, Virginia.

1701. Duke, Eugene L.; *Brumbaugh, Randal W.; and *Disbrow, James D.: **A Rapid Prototyping Facility for Flight Research in Advanced Systems Concepts.** *Computer* (ISSN 0018-9162), Vol. 22, <u>May 1989</u>, (see N87-12273), pp. 61–66, 89A41698. (See also 1523.)

The Dryden Flight Research Facility of the NASA Ames Research Facility of the NASA Ames Research Center is developing a rapid prototyping facility for flight research in flight systems concepts that are based on artificial intelligence (AI). The facility will include real-time high-fidelity aircraft simulators, conventional and symbolic processors, and a high-performance research aircraft specially modified to accept commands from the ground-based AI computers. This facility is being developed as part of the NASA-DARPA automated wingman program. This document discusses the need for flight research and for a national flight research facility for the rapid prototyping of AI-based avionics systems and the NASA response to those needs.

*PRC Systems Services, McLean, Virginia.

1702. *Bonnema, Kenneth L.; and Lokos, William A.: **AFTI/F-111 Mission Adaptive Wing Flight Test Instrumentation Overview.** *Proceedings, 35th International Instrumentation Symposium*, Orlando, Florida, <u>May 1–4, 1989</u>, (see A91-19651 06-35), pp. 809–840, 91A19710, #.

The AFTI F-111 Mission Adaptive Wing (MAW) development is described together with the flight test demonstration program. The program developed a smooth variable camber wing and flight control system capable of adjusting the wing's airfoil shape in flight in response to pilot input and flight condition, in order to maximize the aerodynamic efficiency in all areas of flight envelope. This paper examines the instrumentation requirements and the systems implemented and presents the results of flight tests. These results demonstrate the practicality, airworthiness, maintainability, and performance benefits of the smooth variable camber wing system.

*USAF Wright Aeronautical Laboratories, Wright-Patterson AFB, Ohio.

1703. *Butler, G. F.; *Graves, A. T.; **Disbrow, J. D.; and Duke, E. L.: **An American Knowledge Base in England—Alternate Implementations of an Expert System Flight Status Monitor.** *NAECON 89: Proceedings of the IEEE National Aerospace and Electronics Conference*, Dayton, Ohio, May 22–26, 1989, Vol. 1, (see A90-30676 12-01), <u>1989</u>, pp. 428–434, 90A30719.

A joint activity between the Dryden Flight Research Facility of the NASA Ames Research Center (Ames-Dryden) and the Royal Aerospace Establishment (RAE) on knowledge-based systems has been agreed. Under the agreement, a flight status monitor knowledge base developed at Ames-Dryden has been implemented using the real-time AI (artificial intelligence) toolkit MUSE, which was developed in the UK. Here, the background to the cooperation is described and the details of the flight status monitor and a prototype MUSE implementation are presented. It is noted that the capabilities of the expert-system flight status monitor to monitor data downlinked from the flight test aircraft and to generate information on the state and health of the system for the test engineers provides increased safety during flight testing of new systems. Furthermore, the expert-system flight status monitor provides the systems engineers with ready access to the large amount of information required to describe a complex aircraft system.

*Royal Aerospace Establishment, Farnborough, England.
**PRC System Services, Edwards, California.

1704. Reardon, Lawrence F.: **Evaluation of a Strain-Gage Load Calibration on a Low-Aspect-Ratio Wing Structure at Elevated Temperature.** NASA TP-2921, H-1331, NAS 1.60:2921, June 1989, 89N28034, #.

The environmental aspect of elevated temperature and its relationship to the science of strain gage calibrations of aircraft structures are addressed. A section of a wing designed for a high-speed aircraft structure was used to study this problem. This structure was instrumented with strain gages calibrated at both elevated and room temperatures. Load equations derived from a high-temperature load calibration were compared with equations derived from an identical load calibration at room temperature. The implications of the high temperature load calibration were studied from the viewpoint of applicability and necessity. Load equations derived from the room temperature load calibration resulted in generally lower equation standard errors than equations derived from the elevated temperature load calibration. A distributed load was applied to the structure at elevated temperature and strain gage outputs were measured. This applied load was then calculated using equations derived from both the room temperature and elevated temperature calibration data. It was found that no significant differences between the two equation systems existed in terms of computing this applied distributed load, as long as the thermal shifts resulting from thermal stresses could be identified. This identification requires a heating of the structure. Therefore, it is concluded that for this structure, a high temperature load calibration is not required. However, a heating of the structure is required to determine thermal shifts.

1705. *Nissim, E.; and Gilyard, Glenn B.: **Method for Experimental Determination of Flutter Speed by Parameter Identification.** NASA TP-2923, H-1510, NAS 1.60:2923, June 1989, 89N26844, #. (See also 1697.)

A method for flight flutter testing is proposed which enables one to determine the flutter dynamic pressure from flights flown far below the flutter dynamic pressure. The method is based on the identification of the coefficients of the equations of motion at low dynamic pressures, followed by the solution of these equations to compute the flutter dynamic pressure. The initial results of simulated data reported in the present work indicate that the method can accurately predict the flutter dynamic pressure, as described. If no insurmountable difficulties arise in the implementation of this method, it may significantly improve the procedures for flight flutter testing.

*National Research Council Fellow, Technion - Israel Institute of Technology, Haifa, Israel.

1706. Martin, C. Wayne; Lung, S. F.; and Gupta, K. K.: **A Three-Node C Deg Element for Analysis of Laminated Composite Sandwich Shells.** NASA TM-4125, H-1479, NAS 1.15:4125, June 1989, 89N27213, #.

A three-node flat shell element with C deg rotation fields has been developed for analysis of arbitrary composite shells. The element may consist of any number of orthotropic layers, each layer having different material properties and angular orientation. The formulation includes coupling between bending and extension, which is essential for analysis of unsymmetric laminates. Shearing deflections are included, since laminated and sandwich construction frequently results in shear stiffness much smaller than bending stiffness. Formulation of the element is straightforward, and calculation of its stiffness matrix is simple and fast. Convergence of solutions with mesh refinement is uniform for both thin and thick shells and is insensitive to element shape, although not as rapid as some other elements that lack one or more capabilities of the newly developed element. An experimental verification of the shall element is reported in the appendix.

1707. *Maddalon, D. V.; *Land, C. K.; **Collier, F. S.; and Montoya, L. C.: **Transition Flight Experiments on a Swept Wing With Suction.** AIAA Paper 89-1893. Presented at the AIAA 20th Fluid Dynamics, Plasma Dynamics and Lasers Conference, Buffalo, New York, June 12–14, 1989, 89A42115, #.

Flight experiments were conducted on a 30 degree swept wing with a perforated leading edge by systematically varying the location and amount of suction over a range of Mach number and Reynolds number. Suction was varied chordwise ahead of the front spar from either the front or rear direction by sealing spanwise perforated strips. Transition from laminar to turbulent flow was due to leading edge turbulence contamination or crossflow disturbance growth and/or Tollmien-Schlichting disturbance growth, depending on the test configuration, flight condition, and suction location. A state-of-the-art linear stability theory which accounts for body and streamline curvature and compressibility was used to study the boundary layer stability as suction location and magnitude varied. N-factor correlations with transition location were made for various suction configurations.

*NASA Langley Research Center, Hampton, Virginia.
**High Technology Corporation, Hampton, Virginia.

1708. *Williams, Peggy S.; *Menon, P. K. A.; Antoniewicz, Robert F.; and Duke, Eugene L.: **Study of a Pursuit-Evasion Guidance Law for High Performance Aircraft.** *Proceedings, 1989 8th American Control*

Conference, Pittsburgh, Pennsylvania, June 21–23, 1989, Vol. 3, (see A89-53951 24-63), pp. 2469–2474, 89A54084.

The study of a one-on-one aircraft pursuit-evasion guidance scheme for high-performance aircraft is discussed. The research objective is to implement a guidance law derived earlier using differential game theory in conjunction with the theory of feedback linearization. Unlike earlier research in this area, the present formulation explicitly recognizes the two-sided nature of the pursuit-evasion scenario. The present research implements the guidance law in a realistic model of a modern high-performance fighter aircraft. Also discussed are the details of the guidance law, implementation in a highly detailed simulation of a high-performance fighter, and numerical results for two engagement geometries. Modifications of the guidance law for onboard implementation is also discussed.

*Georgia Institute of Technology, Atlanta, Georgia.

1709. Glover, Richard D.; and O'Neill-Rood, Nora: **The Aerospace Energy Systems Laboratory: Hardware and Software Implementation**. NASA TM-101706, H-1518, NAS 1.15:101706. Presented at the 5th iRUG International Conference, Schaumberg, Illinois, November 14–15, 1988, July 1989, 90N10610, #.

For many years NASA Ames Research Center, Dryden Flight Research Facility has employed automation in the servicing of flight critical aircraft batteries. Recently a major upgrade to Dryden's computerized Battery Systems Laboratory was initiated to incorporate distributed processing and a centralized database. The new facility, called the Aerospace Energy Systems Laboratory (AESL), is being mechanized with iAPX86 and iAPX286 hardware running iRMX86. The hardware configuration and software structure for the AESL are described.

1710. Fisher, David F.; and Meyer, Robert R., Jr.: **Flow Visualization Techniques for Flight Research**. AGARD-CP-452, Paper 18. *Flight Test Techniques*. Presented at the 73rd AGARD Symposium of Flight Mechanics, Panel on Flight Test Techniques, Edwards AFB, California, October 17–20, 1988 (ISBN-92-835-0509-3) (see N90-10860 02-05), July 1989, AD-A213795, 90N10878, #. (See also 1668.)

In-flight flow visualization techniques used at the Dryden Flight Research Facility of NASA Ames Research Center (Ames-Dryden) and its predecessor organizations are described. Results from flight tests which visualized surface flows using flow cones, tufts, oil flows, liquid crystals, sublimating chemicals, and emitted fluids were obtained. Off-surface flow visualization of vortical flow was obtained from natural condensation and two methods using smoke generator systems. Recent results from flight tests at NASA Langley Research Center using a propylene glycol smoker and an infrared imager are also included. Results from

photo-chase aircraft, onboard and postflight photography are presented.

1711. *Disbrow, James D.; Duke, Eugene L.; and Ray, Ronald J.: **Preliminary Development of an Intelligent Computer Assistant for Engine Monitoring**. AIAA Paper 89-2539. Presented at the AIAA, ASME, SAE, and ASEE, 25th Joint Propulsion Conference, Monterey, California, July 10–13, 1989, 89A46910, #. (See also 1719.)

As part of the F-18 high-angle-of-attack vehicle program, an AI method has been developed for the real-time monitoring of the propulsion system and for the identification of recovery procedures for the F404 engine. The aim of the development program is to provide enhanced flight safety and to reduce the duties of the propulsion engineers. As telemetry data is received, the results are continually displayed in a number of different color graphical formats. The system makes possible the monitoring of the engine state and the individual parameters. Anomaly information is immediately displayed to the engineer.

*PRC Systems Services, Inc., Edwards, California.

1712. Conners, Timothy R.: **Measurement Effects on the Calculation of In-Flight Thrust for an F404 Turbofan Engine**. AIAA Paper 89-2364. Presented at the AIAA, ASME, SAE, and ASEE, 25th Joint Propulsion Conference, Monterey, California, July 10–13, 1989, 89A46777, #. (See also 1731.)

A study has been performed that investigates parameter measurement effects on calculated in-flight thrust for the General Electric F404-GE-400 afterburning turbofan engine which powered the X-29A forward-swept wing research aircraft. Net-thrust uncertainty and influence coefficients were calculated and are presented. Six flight conditions were analyzed at five engine power settings each. Results were obtained using the mass flow-temperature and area-pressure thrust calculation methods, both based on the commonly used gas generator technique. Thrust uncertainty was determined using a common procedure based on the use of measurement uncertainty and influence coefficients. The effects of data nonlinearity on the uncertainty calculation procedure were studied and results are presented. The advantages and disadvantages of using this particular uncertainty procedure are discussed. A brief description of the thrust-calculation technique along with the uncertainty calculation procedure is included.

1713. Ko, William L.; and Jackson, Raymond H.: **Multilayer Theory for Delamination Analysis of a Composite Curved Bar Subjected to End Forces and End Moments**. *Composite Structures 5: Proceedings of the Fifth International Conference*, Paisley, Scotland, July 24–26, 1989, (see A91-17376 05-39), Elsevier Applied Sciences, London, England and New York, New York, 1989, pp. 173–198, 91A17381. (See also 1729.)

A composite test specimen in the shape of a semicircular curved bar subjected to bending offers an excellent stress field for studying the open-mode delamination behavior of laminated composite materials. This is because the open-mode delamination nucleates at the midspan of the curved bar. The classical anisotropic elasticity theory was used to construct a 'multilayer' theory for the calculations of the stress and deformation fields induced in the multilayered composite semicircular curved bar subjected to end forces and end moments. The radial location and intensity of the open-mode delamination stress were calculated and were compared with the results obtained from the anisotropic continuum theory and from the finite element method. The multilayer theory gave more accurate predictions of the location and the intensity of the open-mode delamination stress than those calculated from the anisotropic continuum theory.

1714. Hicks, John W.; and Petersen, Kevin L.: **Real-Time Flight Test Analysis and Display Techniques for the X-29A Aircraft**. AGARD-CP-452, paper 6, *AGARD, Flight Test Techniques*, Presented at the 73rd AGARD Symposium of Flight Mechanics, Panel on Flight Test Techniques, Edwards AFB, California, October 17–20, 1988 (ISBN-92-835-0509-3), (see N90-10860 02-05), July 1989, AD-A213795, 90N10866, #. (See also 1674.)

The X-29A advanced technology demonstrator flight envelope expansion program and the subsequent flight research phase gave impetus to the development of several innovative real-time analysis and display techniques. These new techniques produced significant improvements in flight test productivity, flight research capabilities, and flight safety. These techniques include real-time measurement and display of in-flight structural loads, dynamic structural mode frequency and damping, flight control system dynamic stability and control response, aeroperformance drag polars, and aircraft specific excess power. Several of these analysis techniques also provided for direct comparisons of flight-measured results with analytical predictions. The aeroperformance technique was made possible by the concurrent development of a new simplified in-flight net thrust computation method. To achieve these levels of on-line flight test analysis, integration of ground and airborne systems was required. The capability of NASA Ames Research Center, Dryden Flight Research Facility's Western Aeronautical Test Range was a key factor to enable implementation of these methods.

1715. Curry, Robert E.; and Gilyard, Glenn B.: **Flight Evaluation of a Pneumatic System for Unsteady Pressure Measurements Using Conventional Sensors**. NASA TM-4131, H-1508, NAS 1.15:4131. Presented at the 4th AIAA Flight Test Conference, San Diego, California, May 18–20, 1988, August 1989, 90N14225, #.

A flight experiment was conducted to evaluate a pressure measurement system which uses pneumatic tubing and remotely located electronically scanned pressure transducer modules for in-flight unsteady aerodynamic studies. A parametric study of tubing length and diameter on the attenuation and lag of the measured signals was conducted. The hardware was found to operate satisfactorily at rates of up to 500 samples/sec per port in flight. The signal attenuation and lag due to tubing were shown to increase with tubing length, decrease with tubing diameter, and increase with altitude over the ranges tested. Measurable signal levels were obtained for even the longest tubing length tested, 4 ft, at frequencies up to 100 Hz. This instrumentation system approach provides a practical means of conducting detailed unsteady pressure surveys in flight.

1716. Hicks, John W.; and Huckabone, Thomas: **Preliminary Flight-Determined Subsonic Lift and Drag Characteristics of the X-29A Forward-Swept-Wing Airplane**. NASA TM-100409, H-1431, NAS 1.15:100409, August 1989, 91N29177, #.

The X-29A subsonic lift and drag characteristics determined, met, or exceeded predictions, particularly with respect to the drag polar shapes. Induced drag levels were as great as 20 percent less than wind tunnel estimates, particularly at coefficients of lift above 0.8. Drag polar shape comparisons with other modern fighter aircraft showed the X-29A to have a better overall aircraft aerodynamic Oswald efficiency factor for the same aspect ratio. Two significant problems arose in the data reduction and analysis process. These included uncertainties in angle of attack upwash calibration and effects of maneuver dynamics on drag levels. The latter problem resulted from significantly improper control surface automatic camber control scheduling. Supersonic drag polar results were not obtained during this phase because of a lack of engine instrumentation to measure afterburner fuel flow.

1717. Shafer, Mary F.; *Koehler, Ruthard; **Wilson, Edward M.; and [†]Levy, David R.: **Initial Flight Test of a Ground Deployed System for Flying Qualities Assessment**. NASA TM-101700, H-1554, NAS 1.15:101700, AIAA Paper 89-3359. Presented at the AIAA Atmospheric Flight Mechanics Conference, Boston, Massachusetts, August 14–16, 1989, August 1989, 91N15182, #. (See also 1718.)

In order to provide a safe, repeatable, precise, high-gain flying qualities task a ground deployed system was developed and tested at the NASA Ames Research Center's Dryden Flight Research Facility. This system, the adaptable target lighting array system (ATLAS), is based on the German Aerospace Research Establishment's ground attack test equipment (GRATE). These systems provide a flying-qualities task, emulating the ground-attack task with ground deployed lighted targets. These targets light in an unpredictable sequence and the pilot has to aim the aircraft at whichever target is lighted. Two flight-test programs were used to assess the suitability of ATLAS. The first program used the United States Air Force (USAF) NT-33A variability stability aircraft to establish that ATLAS provided a task suitable for use in flying qualities research. A head-up display (HUD) tracking task was used for comparison. The second program used the X-29A forward-swept wing aircraft to demonstrate that the ATLAS task was suitable for assessing the flying qualities of a specific experimental aircraft. In this program, the ground-attack task was used for comparison. All pilots who used ATLAS found it be highly satisfactory and thought it to be superior to the other tasks used in flying qualities evaluations. It was recommended that ATLAS become a standard for flying qualities evaluations.

*Deutsche Forschungs- und Versuchsanstalt fuer Luft- und aumfahrt, Brunswick, Federal Republic of Germany.
**Air Force Flight Test Center, Edwards AFB, California.
[†]Air Force Systems Command, Andrews AFB, Maryland.

1718. Shafer, Mary F.; *Koehler, Ruthard; **Levy, David R.; and [†]Wilson, Edward M.: **Initial Flight Test of a Ground Deployed System for Flying Qualities Assessment.** AIAA Paper 89-3359. Presented at the AIAA Atmospheric Flight Mechanics Conference, Boston, Massachusetts, August 14–16, 1989, (see A89-49051 21-01), pp. 106–112, 89A49063, #. (See also 1717.)

NASA Ames has developed a safe, repeatable, high-precision flying-qualities study system whose Adaptable Target Lighting Array System (ATLAS) furnishes a flying-qualities task that emulates a ground-attack mission with ground-deployed targets lighted in an unpredictable sequence; the pilot must aim the aircraft at whatever target is lighted. Two flight-test programs have been instituted to test the suitability of ATLAS. While the first of these uses a variable-stability aircraft to ascertain whether ATLAS has provided a suitable task for general flying qualities research, using an HUD-tracking task for comparison, the second employed the X-29A FSW research aircraft to demonstrate that ATLAS is appropriate for such research in the case of a specific aircraft.

*DLR, Institut fuer Flugmechanik, Brunswick, Federal Republic of Germany.
**USAF Systems Command, Andrews AFB, Maryland; DLR, Institut fuer Flugmechanik, Brunswick, Federal Republic of Germany.
[†]USAF Flight Test Center, Edwards AFB, California.

1719. *Disbrow, James D.; Duke, Eugene L.; and Ray, Ronald J.: **Preliminary Development of an Intelligent Computer Assistant for Engine Monitoring.** NASA TM-101702, H-1553, NAS 1.15:101702, (see A89-46910), August 1989, 90N22322, #. (See also 1711.)

As part of the F-18 high-angle-of-attack vehicle program, an AI method was developed for the real time monitoring of the propulsion system and for the identification of recovery procedures for the F404 engine. The aim of the development program is to provide enhanced flight safety and to reduce the duties of the propulsion engineers. As telemetry data is received, the results are continually displayed in a number of different color graphical formats. The system makes possible the monitoring of the engine state and the individual parameters. Anomaly information is immediately displayed to the engineer.

*PRC Systems Services Co., Edwards, California.

1720. Fisher, D. F.; Curry, R. E.; and Del Frate, J. H.: **In-Flight Flow Visualization Techniques on a Vortex-Lift Fighter Aircraft.** *Flow Visualization V.* Proceedings of the 5th International Symposium on Flow Visualization, August 21–25, 1989, Prague, Czechoslovakia, TA 357.I582, Hemisphere Publishing Corp., 1989, pp. 543–548,

Two unique methods of in-flight flow visualization have been used on a F-18 fighter aircraft at NASA Ames Research Center, Dryden Flight Research Facility. These methods were used to visualize vortical flow at high angle-of-attack flight conditions on the aircraft forebody and leading edge extensions. Surface flow visualization similar to oil flows in wind tunnels using an emitted fluid technique has been used to mark surface streamlines and lines of separation. Off-surface flow visualization using a smoke generator system and an array of onboard camera have been used to visualize vortex paths and vortex breakdown points.

1721. Earls, Michael R.; and Sitz, Joel R.: **Initial Flight Qualification and Operational Maintenance of X-29A Flight Software.** AIAA Paper 89-3596. *Technical Papers,* presented at the AIAA Guidance, Navigation and Control Conference, Boston, Massachusetts, August 14–16, 1989, Part 2, (see A89-52526 23-08), pp. 1392–1415, 89A52675, #. (See also 1730.)

This paper is predominantly a nontechnical discussion of some significant aspects of the initial flight qualification and operational maintenance of the flight control system software for the X-29A technology demonstrator. Flight qualification and maintenance of complex, embedded flight control system software poses unique problems. The X-29A technology demonstrator aircraft has a digital flight control system which incorporates functions generally considered too complex for analog systems. Organizational responsibilities, software assurance issues, tools, and facilities are discussed.

1722. Nissim, E.: **Modeling of Aerodynamic Forces in the Laplace Domain With Minimum Number of Augmented States for the Design of Active Flutter Suppression Systems.** AIAA Paper 89-3466. *Technical Papers,* presented at the AIAA Guidance, Navigation and Control Conference, Boston, Massachusetts, August 14–16, 1989, Part 1, (see A89-52526 23-08), pp. 332–352, 89A52561, #.

A method is proposed by which an aeroservoelastic problem is brought to a state-space form with a minimum number of augmented aerodynamic terms. The examples treated in this work relate to NASA's Drone for Aerodynamic and Structural Testing-Aerodynamic Research Wing 1 (DAST-ARW1) and to the YF-17 fighter model. It is shown that in all cases considered, the method yields a very good accuracy regarding the flutter parameters and the dynamic behavior of the systems, using only two augmented aerodynamic states. The method should prove useful in the design of lower order control laws based on optimal control theory.

1723. Bosworth, John T.; and Cox, Timothy H.: **A Design Procedure for the Handling Qualities Optimization of the X-29A Aircraft.** AIAA Paper 89-3428. *Technical Papers,* presented at the AIAA Guidance, Navigation and Control Conference, Boston, Massachusetts, August 14–16, 1989, Part 1, (see A89-52526 23-08), pp. 17–34, 89A52529, #. (See also 1732.)

The techniques used to improve the pitch-axis handling qualities of the X-29A wing-canard-planform fighter aircraft are reviewed. The aircraft and its FCS are briefly described, and the design method, which works within the existing FCS architecture, is characterized in detail. Consideration is given to the selection of design goals and design variables, the definition and calculation of the cost function, the validation of the mathematical model on the basis of flight-test data, and the validation of the improved design by means of nonlinear simulations. Flight tests of the improved design are shown to verify the simulation results.

1724. *Gaither, S. A.; *Agarwal, A. K.; *Shah, S. C.; and Duke, E. L.: **A Real-Time Expert System for Self-Repairing Flight Control.** AIAA Paper 89-3427. *Technical Papers*, presented at the AIAA Guidance, Navigation and Control Conference, Boston, Massachusetts, August 14–16, 1989, Part 1, (see A89-52526 23-08), pp. 10–16, 89A52528, #.

An integrated environment for specifying, prototyping, and implementing a self-repairing flight-control (SRFC) strategy is described. At an interactive workstation, the user can select paradigms such as rule-based expert systems, state-transition diagrams, and signal-flow graphs and hierarchically nest them, assign timing and priority attributes, establish blackboard-type communication, and specify concurrent execution on single or multiple processors. High-fidelity nonlinear simulations of aircraft and SRFC systems can be performed off-line, with the possibility of changing SRFC rules, inference strategies, and other heuristics to correct for control deficiencies. Finally, the off-line-generated SRFC can be transformed into highly optimized application-specific real-time C-language code. An application of this environment to the design of aircraft fault detection, isolation, and accommodation algorithms is presented in detail.

*Integrated Systems, Inc., Santa Clara, California.

1725. *Erickson, Gary E.; *Hall, Robert M.; *Banks, Daniel W.; Del Frate, John H.; and **Schreiner, John A.: **Experimental Investigation of the F/A-18 Vortex Flows at Subsonic Through Transonic Speeds.** AIAA Paper 89-2222. *Technical Papers,* presented at the AIAA 7th Applied Aerodynamics Conference, Seattle, Washington, July 31–August 2, 1989, (see A89-47626 21-02), pp. 519–594, 89A47678, #.

A subsonic-to-transonic speed wind tunnel study has been conducted to deepen understanding of the nature and possibilities for control of vortical flows associated with wing leading edge extensions (LEXs) on the F/A-18 aircraft; these vortical phenomena encompass vortex breakdown and vortex interactions with vertical stabilizers. Wind tunnel results were correlated with in-flight flow visualizations as well as handling-qualities trend data from a USN F-18 with LEX fences to improve the vertical tail buffet environment. Attention is given to the sensitivity of the vortex flows to Re and Mach numbers, reduced vertical tail excitation due to the presence of a LEX fence, and the interpretation of off-body flow visualizations.

*NASA Langley Research Center, Hampton, Virginia.
**NASA Ames Research Center, Moffett Field, California.

1726. Curry, Robert E.; Moulton, Bryan J.; and Kresse, John: **An In-Flight Investigation of Ground Effect on a Forward-Swept Wing Airplane.** NASA TM-101708, H-1573, NAS 1.15:101708. Presented at the AGARD Symposium on Aerodynamics of Combat Aircraft, Controls, and of Ground Effect, Madrid, Spain, October 2–5, 1989, September 1989, 90N14202, #. (See also 1766.)

A limited flight experiment was conducted to document the ground-effect characteristics of the X-29A research airplane. This vehicle has an aerodynamic platform which includes a forward-swept wing and close-coupled, variable incidence canard. The flight-test program obtained results for errors in the airdata measurement and for incremental normal force and pitching moment caused by ground effect. Correlations with wind-tunnel and computational analyses were made. The results are discussed with respect to the dynamic nature of the flight measurements, similar data from other configurations, and pilot comments. The ground-effect results are necessary to obtain an accurate interpretation of the vehicle's landing characteristics. The flight data can also be used in the development of many modern aircraft systems such as autoland and piloted simulations.

1727. Ko, W. L.; Carter, A. L.; Totton, W. W.; and Ficke, J. M.: **Application of Fracture Mechanics and Half-Cycle Method to the Prediction of Fatigue Life of B-52 Aircraft Pylon Components.** NASA TM-88277, H-1383, NAS 1.15:88277, September 1989, 90N13820, #.

Stress intensity levels at various parts of the NASA B-52 carrier aircraft pylon were examined for the case when the pylon store was the space shuttle solid rocket booster drop test vehicle. Eight critical stress points were selected for the pylon fatigue analysis. Using fracture mechanics and the half-cycle theory (directly or indirectly) for the calculations of fatigue-crack growth, the remaining fatigue life (number of flights left) was estimated for each critical part. It was found that the two rear hooks had relatively short fatigue life and that the front hook had the shortest fatigue life of all the parts analyzed. The rest of the pylon parts were found to be noncritical because of their extremely long fatigue life associated with the low operational stress levels.

1728. Richwine, David M.; Curry, Robert E.; and Tracy, Gene V.: **A Smoke Generator System for Aerodynamic Flight Research**. NASA TM-4137, H-1515, NAS 1.15:4137, September 1989, 90N13372, #.

A smoke generator system was developed for in-flight vortex flow studies on the F-18 high alpha research vehicle (HARV). The development process included conceptual design, a survey of existing systems, component testing, detailed design, fabrication, and functional flight testing. Housed in the forebody of the aircraft, the final system consists of multiple pyrotechnic smoke cartridges which can be fired simultaneously or in sequence. The smoke produced is ducted to desired locations on the aircraft surface. The smoke generator system (SGS) has been used successfully to identify vortex core and core breakdown locations as functions of flight condition. Although developed for a specific vehicle, this concept may be useful for other aerodynamic flight research which requires the visualization of local flows.

EC89-0096-206

F-18 HARV With Smoke

1729. Ko, William L.; and Jackson, Raymond H.: **Multilayer Theory for Delamination Analysis of a Composite Curved Bar Subjected to End Forces and End Moments**. NASA TM-4139, H-1490, NAS 1.15:4139. Presented at the 5th International Conference on Composite Structures, Paisley, Scotland, July 24–26, 1989, September 1989, 90N12669, #. (See also 1713.)

A composite test specimen in the shape of a semicircular curved bar subjected to bending offers an excellent stress field for studying the open-mode delamination behavior of laminated composite materials. This is because the open-mode delamination nucleates at the midspan of the curved bar. The classical anisotropic elasticity theory was used to construct a multilayer theory for the calculations of the stress and deformation fields induced in the multilayered composite semicircular curved bar subjected to end forces and end moments. The radial location and intensity of the open-mode delamination stress were calculated and were compared with the results obtained from the anisotropic continuum theory and from the finite element method. The multilayer theory gave more accurate predictions of the location and the intensity of the open-mode delamination stress than those calculated from the anisotropic continuum theory.

1730. Earls, Michael R.; and Sitz, Joel R.: **Initial Flight Qualification and Operational Maintenance of X-29A Flight Software**. NASA TM-101703, H-1558, NAS 1.15:101703, AIAA Paper 89-3596. Presented at the AIAA Guidance, Navigation and Control Conference, Boston, Massachusetts, August 14–16, 1989, September 1989, 90N10023, #. (See also 1721.)

A discussion is presented of some significant aspects of the initial flight qualification and operational maintenance of the flight control system software for the X-29A technology demonstrator. Flight qualification and maintenance of complex, embedded flight control system software poses unique problems. The X-29A technology demonstrator aircraft has a digital flight control system which incorporates functions generally considered too complex for analog systems. Organizational responsibilities, software assurance issues, tools, and facilities are discussed.

1731. Conners, Timothy R.: **Measurement Effects on the Calculation of In-Flight Thrust for an F404 Turbofan Engine**. NASA TM-4140, H-1556, NAS 1.15:4140, AIAA Paper 89-2364. Presented at the AIAA Joint Propulsion Conference, Monterey, California, July 10–14, 1989, (see A89-46777), September 1989, 90N11741, #. (See also 1712.)

A study was performed that investigates parameter measurement effects on calculated in-flight thrust for the General Electric F404-GE-400 afterburning turbofan engine which powered the X-29A forward-swept wing research aircraft. Net-thrust uncertainty and influence coefficients were calculated and are presented. Six flight conditions were analyzed at five engine power settings each. Results were obtained using the mass flow-temperature and area-pressure thrust calculation methods, both based on the commonly used gas generator technique. Thrust uncertainty was determined using a common procedure based on the use of measurement uncertainty and influence coefficients. The effects of data nonlinearity on the uncertainty calculation procedure were studied and results are presented. The advantages and disadvantages of using this particular uncertainty procedure are discussed. A brief description of the thrust-calculation technique along with the uncertainty calculation procedure is included.

1732. Bosworth, John T.; and Cox, Timothy H.: **A Design Procedure for the Handling Qualities Optimization of the X-29A Aircraft.** NASA TM-4142, H-1548, NAS 1.15:4142, AIAA Paper 89-3428. Presented at the Guidance, Navigation, and Control Conference, Boston, Massachusetts, August 14–16, 1989, (see A89-52529), September 1989, 90N11753, #. (See also 1723.)

A design technique for handling qualities improvement was developed for the X-29A aircraft. As with any new aircraft, the X-29A control law designers were presented with a relatively high degree of uncertainty in their mathematical models. The presence of uncertainties, and the high level of static instability of the X-29A caused the control law designers to stress stability and robustness over handling qualities. During flight test, the mathematical models of the vehicle were validated or corrected to match the vehicle dynamic behavior. The updated models were then used to fine tune the control system to provide fighter-like handling characteristics. A design methodology was developed which works within the existing control system architecture to provide improved handling qualities and acceptable stability with a minimum of cost in both implementation as well as software verification and validation.

1733. *Maddalon, D. V.; **Collier, F. S., Jr.; Montoya, L. C.; and †Putnam, R. J.: **Transition Flight Experiments on a Swept Wing With Suction.** Presented at the IUTAM 3rd Symposium on Laminar-Turbulent Transition, Toulouse, France, September 11–15, 1989, Preprints September 1989, 89A53830, #.

Flight boundary-layer transition experiments were conducted on a 30-degree swept wing with a perforated leading-edge suction panel. The transition location on the panel was changed by systematically varying the location and amount of suction. Transition from laminar to turbulent flow was due to leading-edge turbulence contamination or crossflow disturbance growth and/or Tollmien-Schlichting disturbance growth, depending on flight condition and suction variation.

Amplification factor correlations with transition location were made for various suction configurations using a state-of-the-art linear stability theory which accounts for body and streamline curvature and compressibility.

*NASA Langley Research Center, Hampton, Virginia.
**High Technology Corporation, Hampton, Virginia.
†PRC Kentron, Inc., Hampton, Virginia.

1734. Fisher, David F.; Del Frate, John H.; and *Richwine, David M.: **In-Flight Flow Visualization Characteristics of the NASA F-18 High Alpha Research Vehicle at High Angles of Attack.** SAE Paper 892222. Presented at the SAE Aerospace Technology Conference and Exposition, Anaheim, California, September 25–28, 1989, 90A45439. (See also 1857.)

Surface and off-surface flow visualization techniques have been used to visualize the three-dimensional separated flows on the NASA F-18 high alpha research vehicle at high angles of attack. Results near alpha = 25 deg to 26 deg and alpha = 45 deg to 49 deg are presented. Both the forebody and leading-edge extension (LEX) vortex cores and breakdown locations were visualized using smoke. Forebody and LEX vortex separation lines on the surface were defined using an emitted-fluid technique. A laminar separation bubble was also detected on the nose cone using the emitted fluid technique and was similar to that observed in the wind-tunnel test, but not as extensive. Regions of attached, separated, and vortical flow were noted on the wing and the leading-edge flap using tufts and flow cones, and compared well with limited wind-tunnel results.

*PRC System Services Co., Edwards, California.

1735. *Tartt, David M.; *Hewett, Marle D.; Duke, Eugene L.; Cooper, James M.; and **Brumbaugh, Randal W.: **The Development of a Flight Test Engineer's Workstation for the Automated Flight Test Management System.** *Proceedings, Society of Flight Test Engineers, 20th Annual Symposium,* Reno, Nevada, September 18–21, 1989, (see A91-20976 07-05), 1989, pp. 5.2-1 to 5.2-12, 91A20999.

The Automated Flight Test Management System (ATMS) is being developed as part of the NASA Aircraft Automation Program. This program focuses on the application of interdisciplinary state-of-the-art technology in artificial intelligence, control theory, and systems methodology to problems of operating and flight testing high-performance aircraft. The development of a Flight Test Engineer's Workstation (FTEWS) is presented, with a detailed description of the system, technical details, and future planned developments. The goal of the FTEWS is to provide flight test engineers and project officers with an automated computer environment for planning, scheduling, and performing flight test programs. The FTEWS system is an outgrowth of the development of ATMS and is an implementation of a component of ATMS on SUN workstations.

*Sparta, Inc., Laguna Hills, California.
**PRC Kentron, Inc., Edwards, California.

1736. *Kempel, Robert W.; **Phillips, Paul W.; Fullerton, C. Gordon; and Bresina, John J.: **AFTI/F-111 Airplane Mission Adaptive Wing Operational Flight Evaluation Technique Using Uplinked Pilot Command Cues**. *Proceedings, Society of Flight Test Engineers, 20th Annual Symposium*, Reno, Nevada, September 18–21, 1989, (see A91-20976 07-05), pp. 3.6-1 to 3.6-19, 91A20993.

NASA and the USAF have conducted a program to investigate aircraft performance improvements utilizing a mission adaptive wing (MAW). The MAW was designed and developed for the AFTI/F-111 variable-sweep aircraft to provide a hydraulically driven, smooth, and continuous variable camber of the trailing and leading edges as a function of maneuvering requirements or of flight conditions. The remotely augmented vehicle facility (RAV) at the NASA DFRF, as utilized in the MAW investigations, is described. The RAV was a dedicated, ground based, general purpose facility capable of receiving a data stream downlinked from a test vehicle, processing this data stream in a digital computer, and transmitting processed data back to the test vehicle. It is shown that this method of flight testing provides a technique that can evaluate highly dynamic maneuvers.

*PRC Systems Services, Aerospace Technologies Division, Edwards, California.
**USAF Flight Test Center, Edwards AFB, California.

1737. *Collier, F. S., Jr.; **Bartlett, D. W.; **Wagner, R. D.; **Tat, V. V.; and Anderson, B. T.: **Correlation of Boundary Layer Stability Analysis With Flight Transition Data**. Presented at the IUTAM 3rd Symposium on Laminar-Turbulent Transition, Toulouse, France, September 11–15, 1989, Springer-Verlag, Berlin and London, 1990, pp. 337–346, (see A91-39901 16-34), 91A39929.

Recently, NASA completed a boundary-layer transition flight test on an F-14 aircraft which has variable-sweep capability. Transition data were acquired for a wide variety of sweep angles, pressure distributions, Mach numbers, and Reynolds numbers. In this paper, the F-14 flight test is briefly described and N-factor correlations with measured transition locations are presented for one of two gloves flown on the F-14 wing in the flight program; a thin foam and fiberglass glove which provided a smooth sailplane finish on the basic F-14, modified NACA 6-series airfoil. For these correlations, an improved linear boundary-layer stability theory was utilized that accounts for compressibility and surface and streamline curvature effects for the flow past swept wings.

*High Technology Corporation, Hampton, Virginia.
**NASA Langley Research Center, Hampton, Virginia.

1738. Freudinger, Lawrence C.: **Flutter Clearance of the F-18 High-Angle-of-Attack Research Vehicle With Experimental Wingtip Instrumentation Pods**. NASA TM-4148, H-1528, NAS 1.15:4148, October 1989, 90N11732, #.

An F-18 aircraft was modified with wingtip instrumentation pods for use in NASA's high-angle-of-attack research program. Ground vibration and flight flutter testing were performed to atmospheric turbulence for structural excitation; the aircraft displayed no adverse aeroelastic trends within the envelope tested. The data presented in this report include mode shapes from the ground vibration and estimates of frequency and damping as a function of Mach number.

1739. Duke, E. L.; *Disbrow, J. D.; and **Butler, G. F.: **A Knowledge-Based Flight Status Monitor for Real-Time Application in Digital Avionics Systems**. NASA TM-101710, H-1568, NAS 1.15:101710. Presented at the MILCOMP'89 Conference, London, England, September 26–28, 1989, October 1989, 90N13995, #.

The Dryden Flight Research Facility of the National Aeronautics and Space Administration (NASA) Ames Research Center (Ames-Dryden) is the principal NASA facility for the flight testing and evaluation of new and complex avionics systems. To aid in the interpretation of system health and status data, a knowledge-based flight status monitor was designed. The monitor was designed to use fault indicators from the onboard system which are telemetered to the ground and processed by a rule-based model of the aircraft failure management system to give timely advice and recommendations in the mission control room. One of the important constraints on the flight status monitor is the need to operate in real time, and to pursue this aspect, a joint research activity between NASA Ames-Dryden and the Royal Aerospace Establishment (RAE) on real-time knowledge-based systems was established. Under this agreement, the original LISP knowledge base for the flight status monitor was reimplemented using the intelligent knowledge-based system toolkit, MUSE, which was developed under RAE sponsorship. Details of the flight status monitor and the MUSE implementation are presented.

*PRC Systems Services Co., Edwards, California.
**Royal Aerospace Establishment, Farnborough, England.

1740. Mackall, Dale A.; and *Allen, James G.: **A Knowledge-Based System Design/Information Tool for Aircraft Flight Control Systems**. NASA TM-101704, H-1546, NAS 1.15:101704. Presented at the 7th AIAA Computers in Aerospace Conference, Monterey, California, October 4–6, 1989, (see A90-10491), October 1989, 90N13990, #. (See also 1741, 1850.)

Research aircraft have become increasingly dependent on advanced control systems to accomplish program goals. These aircraft are integrating multiple disciplines to improve performance and satisfy research objectives. This integration is being accomplished through electronic control systems. Because of the number of systems involved and the variety of engineering disciplines, systems design methods and information management have become essential to program success. The primary objective of the system design/information tool for aircraft flight control system is to help transfer flight control system design knowledge to the flight test community. By providing all of the design information and covering multiple disciplines in a structured, graphical manner, flight control systems can more easily be understood by the test engineers. This will provide the engineers with the information needed to thoroughly ground test the system and thereby reduce the likelihood of serious design errors surfacing in flight. The secondary objective is to apply structured design techniques to all of the design domains. By using the techniques in the top level system design down through the detailed hardware and software designs, it is hoped that fewer design anomalies will result. The flight test experiences of three highly complex, integrated aircraft programs are reviewed: the X-29 forward-swept wing, the advanced fighter technology integration (AFTI) F-16, and the highly maneuverable aircraft technology (HiMAT) program. Significant operating anomalies and the design errors which cause them, are examined to help identify what functions a system design/information tool should provide to assist designers in avoiding errors.

*Draper Laboratory, Inc., Cambridge, Massachusetts.

1741. Mackall, Dale A.; and *Allen, James G.: **A Knowledge-Based System Design/Information Tool for Aircraft Flight Control Systems.** AIAA Paper 89-2978. *Technical Papers*, presented at the AIAA 7th Computers in Aerospace Conference, Monterey, California, October 3–5, 1989, Part 1, (see A90-10476 01-59), 1989, pp. 110–125, 90A10491, #. (See also 1740,1850.)

Flight test experiences of the X-29 forward-swept wing, the advanced fighter technology integration (AFTI) F-16, and the highly maneuverable aircraft technology (HiMAT) programs are reviewed. Significant operating anomalies in these programs and the design errors which caused them are examined. The functions which a system design/information

tool should provide to assist designers in avoiding errors are identified.

*Draper Laboratory, Inc., Cambridge, Massachusetts.

1742. *Nissim, E.: **Effect of Control Surface Mass Unbalance on the Stability of a Closed-Loop Active Control System**. NASA TP-2952, H-1534, NAS 1.60:2952, October 1989, 90N12042, #. (See also 1698.)

The effects on stability of inertial forces arising from closed-loop activation of mass-unbalanced control surfaces are studied analytically using inertial energy approach, similar to the aerodynamic energy approach used for flutter suppression. The limitations of a single control surface like a leading-edge (LE) control or a trailing-edge (TE) control are demonstrated and compared to the superior combined LE-TE mass unbalanced system. It is shown that a spanwise section for sensor location can be determined which ensures minimum sensitivity to the mode shapes of the aircraft. It is shown that an LE control exhibits compatibility between inertial stabilization and aerodynamic stabilization, and that a TE control lacks such compatibility. The results of the present work should prove valuable, both for the purpose of flutter suppression using mass unbalanced control surfaces, or for the stabilization of structural modes of large space structures by means of inertial forces.

*National Research Council Fellow, Technion - Israel Institute of Technology, Haifa, Israel.

1743. Iliff, Kenneth W.: **Parameter Estimation for Flight Vehicles.** *Journal of Guidance, Control, and Dynamics* (ISSN 0731-5090), Vol. 12, September–October 1989, pp. 609–622. (see A87-22745), October 1989, 89A51701, #. (See also 1543, 1544.)

1744. Kehoe, Michael W.; and Voracek, David F.: **Ground Vibration Test Results of a JetStar Airplane Using Impulsive Sine Excitation.** *Proceedings*, *7th International Modal Analysis Conference*, Las Vegas, Nevada, January 30–February 2, 1989, Vol. 1, (see A90-16955 05-39), (N89-15909), 1989, pp. 101–111, 90A16963, #. (See also 1687.)

Structural excitation is important for both ground vibration and flight flutter testing. The structural responses caused by this excitation are analyzed to determine frequency, damping, and mode shape information. Many excitation waveforms have been used throughout the years. The use of impulsive sine (sin omega t)/omega t as an excitation waveform for ground vibration testing and the advantages of using this waveform for flight flutter testing are discussed. The ground vibration test results of a modified JetStar airplane using impulsive sine as an excitation waveform are compared with the test results of the same airplane using multiple-input random excitation. The results indicated that the structure was sufficiently excited using the impulsive sine waveform. Comparisons of input force spectrums, mode shape plots, and frequency and damping values for the two methods of excitation are presented.

1745. Hudson, Larry D.: **Recent Experience With Elevated-Temperature Foil Strain Gages With Application to Thin-Gage Materials.** *Proceedings of the Hostile Environments and High Temperature Measurements Conference*, Kansas City, Missouri, November 6–8, 1989, (see A90-44483 20-35), 1989, pp. 68–81, 90A44492.

The effects of thin-gage materials on high-temperature strain measurements are discussed. Apparent strain test were performed using facesheet coupons, honeycomb coupons, and the panel with strain gages in an installed condition. The apparent strain results differed in each of the cases. The apparent strain curves from the panel tests are expected to provide the best correlation with analysis, assuming that the thermal strains are insignificant or that the thermal strains derived from the analysis of the apparent strain test performed on the panel can be used to correct the apparent strain curves.

1746. Bjarke, Lisa J.; and Ehernberger, L. J.: **An In-Flight Technique for Wind Measurement in Support of the Space Shuttle Program.** NASA TM-4154, H-1566, NAS 1.15:4154. Presented at the Society of Flight Test Engineers 20th Annual Symposium, Reno, Nevada, September 18–21, 1989, November 1989, 90N14224, #.

A technique to use an aircraft to measure wind profiles in the altitude range of 1,500 to 18,200 m was demonstrated at NASA Ames-Dryden. This demonstration was initiated to determine if an aircraft could measure wind profiles in support of space shuttle launches. The Jimsphere balloon is currently the device used to measure pre-launch wind profiles for the space shuttle. However, it takes approximately an hour for the Jimsphere to travel through the altitudes of interest. If these wind instruments could be taken with an aircraft closer to launch in a more timely manner and with the same accuracy as a Jimsphere balloon, some uncertainties in the measurements could be removed. The aircraft used for this investigation was an F-104G which is capable of flight above 18,000 m. It had conventional research instrumentation to provide air data and flow angles along with a ring laser gyro inertial navigation system (INS) to provide inertial and Euler angle data. During the course of 17 flights, wind profiles were measured in 21 climbs and 18 descents. Preliminary comparisons between aircraft measured wind profiles and Jimsphere measured profiles show reasonable agreement (within 3 m/sec). Most large differences between the profiles can usually be explained by large spatial or time differences

between the Jimsphere and aircraft measurements, the fact that the aircraft is not in a wings-level attitude, or INS shifts caused by aircraft maneuvering.

1747. Glover, Richard D.; and O'Neill-Rood, Nora: **The Aerospace Energy Systems Laboratory: A BITBUS Networking Application.** NASA TM-4149, H-1569, NAS 1.15:4149. Presented at the iRUG 6th International Conference, Bethesda, Maryland, November 13–14, 1989, November 1989, 90N14829, #.

The NASA Ames-Dryden Flight Research Facility developed a computerized aircraft battery servicing facility called the Aerospace Energy Systems Laboratory (AESL). This system employs distributed processing with communications provided by a 2.4-megabit BITBUS local area network. Customized handlers provide real time status, remote command, and file transfer protocols between a central system running the iRMX-II operating system and ten slave stations running the iRMX-I operating system. The hardware configuration and software components required to implement this BITBUS application are required.

1748. Neal, Bradford; and Sengupta, Upal: **The Implementation and Operation of a Variable-Response Electronic Throttle Control System for a TF-104G Aircraft.** NASA TM-101696, H-1542, NAS 1.15:101696, December 1989, 90N20086, #.

During some flight programs, researchers have encountered problems in the throttle response characteristics of high-performance aircraft. To study and to help solve these problems, the National Aeronautics and Space Administration Ames Research Center's Dryden Flight Research Facility (Ames-Dryden) conducted a study using a TF-104G airplane modified with a variable-response electronic throttle control system. Ames-Dryden investigated the effects of different variables on engine response and handling qualities. The system provided transport delay, lead and lag filters, second-order lags, command rate and position limits, and variable gain between the pilot's throttle command and the engine fuel controller. These variables could be tested individually or in combination. Ten research flights were flown to gather data on engine response and to obtain pilot ratings of the various system configurations. The results should provide design criteria for engine-response characteristics. The variable-response throttle components and how they were installed in the TF-104G aircraft are described. How the variable-response throttle was used in flight and some of the results of using this system are discussed.

1749. Sims, Robert; *McCrosson, Paul; *Ryan, Robert; and *Rivera, Joe: **X-29A Aircraft Structural Loads Flight**

Testing. NASA TM-101715, H-1574, NAS 1.15:101715. Presented at the 20th Annual Society of Flight Test Engineers Symposium, Reno, Nevada, September 18–21, 1989, December 1989, 90N19225, #.

The X-29A research and technology demonstrator aircraft has completed a highly successful multiphase flight test program. The primary research objective was to safely explore, evaluate, and validate a number of aerodynamic, structural, and flight control technologies, all highly integrated into the vehicle design. Most of these advanced technologies, particularly the forward-swept-wing platform, had a major impact on the structural design. Throughout the flight test program, structural loads clearance was an ongoing activity to provide a safe maneuvering envelope sufficient to accomplish the research objectives. An overview is presented of the technologies, flight test approach, key results, and lessons learned from the structural flight loads perspective. The overall design methodology was considered validated, but a number of structural load characteristics were either not adequately predicted or totally unanticipated prior to flight test. While conventional flight testing techniques were adequate to insure flight safety, advanced analysis tools played a key role in understanding some of the structural load characteristics, and in maximizing flight test productivity.

*Grumman Aerospace Corporation, Edwards, California.

1750. *Butler, G. F.; and Duke, E. L.: **NASA/RAE Cooperation on a Knowledge Based Flight Status Monitor.** AGARD-CP-455, Paper 7. *Advances in Techniques and Technologies for Air Vehicle Navigation and Guidance*, (ISBN-92-835-0535-2) (see N90-16731 09-04), December 1989, AD-A217512, 90N16738, #.

As part of a US/UK cooperative aeronautical research program, a joint activity between the Dryden Flight Research Facility of the NASA Ames Research Center (Ames-Dryden) and the Royal Aerospace Establishment (RAE) on Knowledge Based Systems was established. Under the agreement, a Flight Status Monitor Knowledge base developed at Ames-Dryden was implemented using the real-time IKBS toolkit, MUSE, which was developed in the UK under RAE sponsorship. The Flight Status Monitor is designed to provide on-line aid to the flight test engineer in the interpretation of system health and status by storing expert knowledge of system behavior in an easily accessible form. The background to the cooperation is described and the details of the Flight Status Monitor, the MUSE implementation are presented.

* Royal Aircraft Establishment, Farnborough, England.

1751. Hicks, John W.; and Matheny, Neil W.: **Flight Tests Confirm X-29 Technologies.** *Exxon Air World*, Vol. 41, No. 2, 1989, pp. 18–21, 89A48849.

Results of test flights of the X-29A which confirmed the viability of the aircraft design and obtained good agreement with preflight predictions are presented. In addition to a forward-swept wing, the features to be evaluated on the X-29 demonstrator were: a digital fly-by-wire flight control, a close-coupled wing-canard configuration, an aeroelastically tailored composite wing skin and a three-surface pitch control configuration. The X-29A advanced technology demonstrator is a single-seat, fighter-type aircraft, best known for its forward-swept wing with a thin supercritical airfoil. The key objectives in developing the technologies incorporated into the X-29A design included establishing new airframe-design freedoms and options, as well as demonstrating that adequate levels of dynamic stability can be achieved by controlling an unstable airframe with a close-coupled canard, symmetric flap, and strake-flap combination. The X-29A aircraft and its related systems performed well and are now in a flight research phase.

1752. Whitmore, Stephen Anthony: **Formulation and Verification of a Technique for Compensation of Pneumatic Attenuation Errors in Airborne Pressure Sensing Devices.** 1989, University of California at Los Angeles Ph.D. Thesis, 90N17084.

Recent advances in aircraft performance and maneuver capability have dramatically complicated the problem of flight control augmentation. With increasing regularity, aircraft system designs require that aerodynamic parameters derived from pneumatic measurements be used as control system feedbacks. These requirements necessitate that pneumatic data be measured with accuracy and fidelity. The emphasis here is on the development of a general numerical model for accurately predicting pneumatic attenuation errors in pressure sensing devices. Once the model was developed and verified, then techniques for inverting the model to provide a compensation algorithm were developed. A mathematical model, derived from the Navier-Strokes equations is used to predict the behavior of pneumatic configurations which are subjected to small but arbitrary inputs. Comparisons of the mathematical model to both lab and flight data indicate that its predictive capability is excellent. Two approaches for inverting the model to provide a compensation algorithm were developed. The first approach relied on the techniques of statistical deconvolution to develop a compensation model. The second technique overcame the difficulty of limited applicability inherent in the first approach by incorporating the dynamic model into the compensation routine using the techniques of Minimum Variance Estimation Theory. The latter algorithm has a broader range of applicability.

1990 Technical Publications

1753. Ko, William L.; Olona, Timothy; and Muramoto, Kyle M.: **Optimum Element Density Studies for Finite-Element Thermal Analysis of Hypersonic Aircraft Structures.** NASA TM-4163, H-1519, NAS 1.15:4163, January 1990, 90N17074, #.

Different finite element models previously set up for thermal analysis of the space shuttle orbiter structure are discussed and their shortcomings identified. Element density criteria are established for the finite element thermal modelings of space shuttle orbiter-type large, hypersonic aircraft structures. These criteria are based on rigorous studies on solution accuracies using different finite element models having different element densities set up for one cell of the orbiter wing. Also, a method for optimization of the transient thermal analysis computer central processing unit (CPU) time is discussed. Based on the newly established element density criteria, the orbiter wing midspan segment was modeled for the examination of thermal analysis solution accuracies and the extent of computation CPU time requirements. The results showed that the distributions of the structural temperatures and the thermal stresses obtained from this wing segment model were satisfactory and the computation CPU time was at the acceptable level. The studies offered the hope that modeling the large, hypersonic aircraft structures using high-density elements for transient thermal analysis is possible if a CPU optimization technique was used.

1754. Whitmore, Stephen A.; and *Leondes, Cornelius T.: **Compensating for Pneumatic Distortion in Pressure Sensing Devices.** NASA TM-101716, H-1586, NAS 1.15:101716. Presented at the AIAA 28th Aerospace Sciences Meeting, Reno, Nevada, January 8–11, 1990, January 1990, (see A90-19956), 90N19224, #. (See also 1755.)

EC90-280-1

Dryden Flight Research Facility Aircraft, circa 1990, (front row) McDonnell-Douglas F-18 HARV, (2nd row) Grumman X-29A, McDonnell-Douglas F-15, General Dynamics F-16XL-1, (3rd row) three McDonnell-Douglas F/A-18's (4th row) Northrop T-38, Lockheed F-104, (back row) Boeing B-52 With Orbital Sciences Corporation Pegasus® Rocket, Lockheed SR-71A, and Boeing 747 SCA

A technique of compensating for pneumatic distortion in pressure sensing devices was developed and verified. This compensation allows conventional pressure sensing technology to obtain improved unsteady pressure measurements. Pressure distortion caused by frictional attenuation and pneumatic resonance within the sensing system makes obtaining unsteady pressure measurements by conventional sensors difficult. Most distortion occurs within the pneumatic tubing which transmits pressure impulses from the aircraft's surface to the measurement transducer. To avoid pneumatic distortion, experiment designers mount the pressure sensor at the surface of the aircraft, (called in-situ mounting). In-situ transducers cannot always fit in the available space and sometimes pneumatic tubing must be run from the aircraft's surface to the pressure transducer. A technique to measure unsteady pressure data using conventional pressure sensing technology was developed. A pneumatic distortion model is reduced to a low-order, state-variable model retaining most of the dynamic characteristics of the full model. The reduced-order model is coupled with results from minimum variance estimation theory to develop an algorithm to compensate for the effects of pneumatic distortion. Both postflight and real-time algorithms are developed and evaluated using simulated and flight data.

*University of California, Los Angeles, California.

1755. Whitmore, Stephen A.; and *Leondes, Cornelius T.: **Compensating for Pneumatic Distortion in Pressure Sensing Devices.** AIAA Paper 90-0631. Presented at the AIAA 28th Aerospace Sciences Meeting, Reno, Nevada, January 8–11, 1990, 90A19956, #. (See also 1754.)

A general numerical technique for obtaining unsteady pressure measurements using conventional pressure sensing technology has been developed. A pneumatic distortion model, based on the Navier-Stokes equations of momentum and continuity, was reduced to a low-order, state-variable model retaining most of the dynamic characteristics of the full model. The reduced-order model is coupled with results from minimum variance estimation theory to develop an algorithm to compensate the effects of pneumatic distortion. Both postflight and real-time algorithms were developed and evaluated using simulated and flight data.

*University of California, Los Angeles, California.

1756. Haering, Edward A., Jr.: **Airdata Calibration of a High-Performance Aircraft for Measuring Atmospheric Wind Profiles.** NASA TM-101714, H-1580, NAS 1.15:101714, AIAA Paper 90-0230. Presented at the AIAA 28th Aerospace Sciences Meeting, Reno, Nevada, January 8–11, 1990, January 1990, 90N14228, #. (See also 1757, 1967.)

The research airdata system of an instrumented F-104 aircraft has been calibrated to measure winds aloft in support of the space shuttle wind measurement investigation at the National Aeronautics and Space Administration Ames Research Center Dryden Flight Research Facility. For this investigation, wind measurement accuracies comparable to those obtained from Jimsphere balloons were desired. This required an airdata calibration more accurate than needed for most aircraft research programs. The F-104 aircraft was equipped with a research pilot-static noseboom with integral angle-of-attack and flank angle-of-attack vanes and a ring-laser-gyro inertial reference unit. Tower fly-bys and radar acceleration-decelerations were used to calibrate Mach number and total temperature. Angle of attack and angle of sideslip were calibrated with a trajectory reconstruction technique using a multiple-state linear Kalman filter. The F-104 aircraft and instrumentation configuration, flight test maneuvers, data corrections, calibration techniques, and resulting calibrations and data repeatability are presented. Recommendations for future airdata systems on aircraft used to measure winds aloft are also given.

1757. Haering, Edward A., Jr.: **Airdata Calibration of a High-Performance Aircraft for Measuring Atmospheric Wind Profiles.** AIAA Paper 90-0230. Presented at the AIAA 28th Aerospace Sciences Meeting, Reno, Nevada, January 8–11, 1990, 90A19744, #. (See also 1756, 1967.)

The research airdata system of an instrumented F-104 aircraft has been calibrated to measure winds aloft in support of the Space Shuttle wind measurement investigation. The F-104 aircraft was equipped with a research pitot-static noseboom with integral angle-of-attack and flank angle-of-attack vanes and a ring-laser-gyro inertial reference unit. The F-104 aircraft and instrumentation configuration, flight test maneuvers, data corrections, calibration techniques, and resulting calibrations and data repeatability are presented. Recommendations for future airdata systems on aircraft used to measure winds aloft are also given.

1758. Whitmore, Stephen A.; Moes, Timothy R.; and *Larson, Terry J.: **Preliminary Results From a Subsonic High Angle-of-Attack Flush Airdata Sensing (Hi-FADS) System: Design, Calibration, and Flight Test Evaluation.** NASA TM-101713, H-1583, NAS 1.15:101713, AIAA Paper 90-0232. Presented at the 28th AIAA Aerospace Sciences Meeting, Reno, Nevada, January 8–11, 1990, January 1990, (see A90-19746), 90N16758, #. (See also 1759, 1984.)

A nonintrusive high angle-of-attack flush airdata sensing (Hi-FADS) system was installed and flight-tested on the F-18 high alpha research flight vehicle. The system is a matrix of 25 pressure orifices in concentric circles on the nose of the vehicle. The orifices determine angles of attack and sideslip, Mach number, and pressure altitude. Pressure was transmitted from the orifices to an electronically scanned pressure module by lines of pneumatic tubing. The Hi-FADS system was calibrated and demonstrated using dutch roll flight maneuvers covering large Mach, angle-of-attack, and sideslip ranges. Reference airdata for system calibration were generated by a minimum variance estimation technique blending measurements from two wingtip airdata booms with inertial velocities, aircraft angular rates and attitudes, precision radar tracking, and meteorological analyses. The pressure orifice calibration was based on identifying empirical adjustments to modified Newtonian flow on a hemisphere. Calibration results are presented. Flight test results used all 25 orifices or used a subset of 9 orifices. Under moderate maneuvering conditions, the Hi-FADS system gave excellent results over the entire subsonic Mach number range up to 55 deg angle of attack. The internal pneumatic frequency response of the system is accurate to beyond 10 Hz. Aerodynamic lags in the aircraft flow field caused some performance degradation during heavy maneuvering.

*Analytical Mechanics Associates, Inc., Hampton, Virginia.

1759. Whitmore, Stephen A.; Moes, Timothy R.: and *Larson, Terry J.: **Preliminary Results From a Subsonic High-Angle-of-Attack Flush Airdata Sensing (Hi-FADS) System—Design, Calibration, Algorithm Development, and Flight Test Evaluation.** AIAA Paper 90-0232. Presented at the AIAA 28th Aerospace Sciences Meeting, Reno, Nevada, January 8–11, 1990, 90A19746, #. (See also 1758, 1984.)

A nonintrusive high angle-of-attack flush airdata sensing (Hi-FADS) system was installed and flight-tested on the F-18 high alpha research vehicle. This paper discusses the airdata algorithm development and composite results expressed as airdata parameter estimates and describes the Hi-FADS system hardware, calibration techniques, and algorithm development. An independent empirical verification was performed over a large portion of the subsonic flight envelope. Test points were obtained for Mach numbers from 0.15 to 0.94 and angles of attack from –8.0 to 55.0 deg. Angles of sideslip ranged from –15.0 to 15.0 deg, and test altitudes ranged from 18,000 to 40,000 ft. The Hi-FADS system gave excellent results over the entire subsonic Mach number range up to 55 deg angle of attack. The internal pneumatic frequency response of the system is accurate to beyond 10 Hz.

*Analytical Mechanics Associates, Inc., Hampton, Virginia.

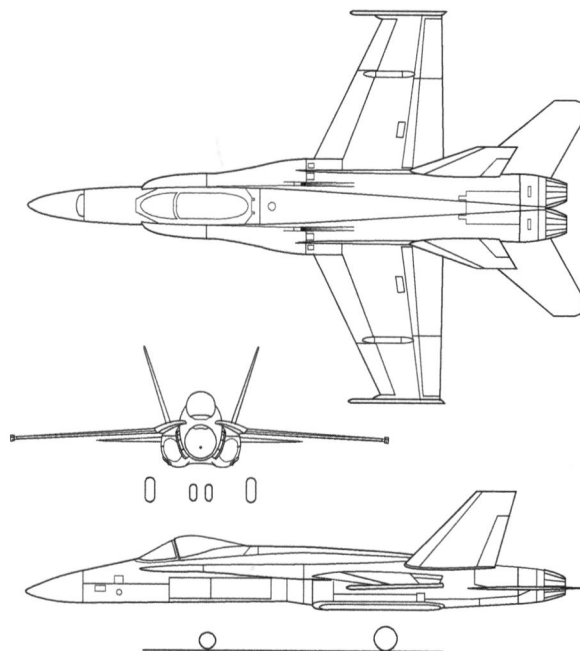

F-18 Airplane, Three-View Drawing

1760. Del Frate, John H.; and Zuniga, Fanny A.: **In-Flight Flow Field Analysis on the NASA F-18 High Alpha Research Vehicle With Comparisons to Ground Facility Data.** AIAA Paper 90-0231. Presented at the AIAA 28th Aerospace Sciences Meeting, Reno, Nevada, January 8–11, 1990, 90A19745, #.

In-flight flow visualization results of the vortical flow on the forebody and leading-edge extensions (LEX) of an F-18 research aircraft have been presented for angles of attack from 15.8 to 42.5 deg and for sideslip angles up to 7.5 deg. Water tunnel results using a 3-percent scale F-18 model and a variety of wind tunnel results are used for comparison and interpretation of the flight results. The LEX vortex core breakdown point moved forward with increasing angle of attack. For a constant angle of attack, the windward LEX vortex core breakdown moves forward and inboard with sideslip and the leeward vortex core breakdown moves aft and outboard. For a constant angle of attack, the windward location of interaction moved aft with increasing sideslip and the leeward interaction moved forward.

1761. Ko, William L.; and Jackson, Raymond H.: **Open-Mode Delamination Stress Concentrations in Horseshoe and Elliptic Composite Curved Bars Subjected to End Forces.** NASA TM-4164, H-1567, NAS 1.15:4164, January 1990, 90N16004, #.

The multilayer theory of anisotropic elasticity and a finite element method were used to analyze the open-mode delamination stress concentrations in horseshoe and elliptic laminated composite curved bars. Two types of laminations, solid laminations and sandwich laminations, were analyzed. It was found that the open-mode delamination stress concentration could be greatly increased in these two types of curved bars by decreasing their aspect ratios. The open-mode delamination stress concentration generated in the solid laminations was found to be far more severe than that generated in the sandwich laminations. The horseshoe curved bar may be used to determine both the open-mode delamination strength of solidly laminated composites and the open-mode debonding strength of sandwiched laminated composites. However, the elliptic curved bar is only good for determining the open-mode delamination strength of solidly laminated composites.

1762. Whitmore, Stephen A.; *Lindsey, William T.; Curry, Robert E.; and Gilyard, Glenn B.: **Experimental Characterization of the Effects of Pneumatic Tubing on Unsteady Pressure Measurements**. NASA TM-4171, H-1538, NAS 1.15:4171, March 1990, 90N27703, #.

Advances in aircraft control system designs have, with increasing frequency, required that air data be used as flight control feedback. This condition requires that these data be measured with accuracy and high fidelity. Most air data information is provided by pneumatic pressure measuring sensors. Typically unsteady pressure data provided by pneumatic sensing systems are distorted at high frequencies. The distortion is a result of the pressure being transmitted to the pressure sensor through a length of connective tubing. The pressure is distorted by frictional damping and wave reflection. As a result, air data provided all-flush, pneumatically sensed air data systems may not meet the frequency response requirements necessary for flight control augmentation. Both lab and flight test were performed at NASA-Ames to investigate the effects of this high frequency distortion in remotely located pressure measurement systems. Good qualitative agreement between lab and flight data are demonstrated. Results from these tests are used to describe the effects of pneumatic distortion in terms of a simple parametric model.

*Air Force, Wright Aeronautical Labs., Wright-Patterson AFB, Ohio.

1763. Johnson, Steven A.; and Fisher, David F.: **Water-Tunnel Study Results of a TF/A-18 and F/A-18 Canopy Flow Visualization**. NASA TM-101705, H-1570, NAS 1.15:101705, March 1990, 90N22532, #.

A water tunnel study examining the influence of canopy shape on canopy and leading edge extension flow patterns was initiated. The F/A-18 single-place canopy model and the TF/A-18 two place canopy model were the study subjects. Plan view and side view photographs showing the flow patterns created by injected colored dye are presented for 0 deg and 5 deg sideslip angles. Photographs taken at angle of attack and sideslip conditions correspond to test departure points found in flight test. Flight experience has shown that the TF/A-18 airplane departs in regions where the F/A-18 airplane is departure-resistant. The study results provide insight into the differences in flow patterns which may influence the resulting aerodynamics of the TF/A-18 and F/A-18 aircraft. It was found that at 0 deg sideslip, the TF/A-18 model has more downward flow on the sides of the canopy than the F/A-18 model. This could be indicative of flow from the leading edge extension (LEX) vortexes impinging on the sides of the wider TF/A-18 canopy. In addition, the TF/A-18 model has larger areas of asymmetric separated and unsteady flow on the LEXs and fuselage, possibly indicating a lateral and directional destabilizing effect at the conditions studied.

1764. *Wagner, R. D.; *Maddalon, D. V.; and Fisher, D. F.: **Laminar Flow Control Leading-Edge Systems in Simulated Airline Service**. *Journal of Aircraft* (ISSN 0021-8669), Vol. 27, (see A89-13604), March 1990, pp. 239–244, 90A26134, #. (See also 1664.)

*NASA Langley Research Center, Hampton, Virginia.

1765. Pahle, Joseph W.: **Output Model-Following Control Synthesis for an Oblique-Wing Aircraft**. NASA TM-100454, H-1522, NAS 1.15:100454, April 1990, 90N19241, #.

Recent interest in oblique-wing aircraft has focused on the potential aerodynamic performance advantage of a variable-skew oblique wing over a conventional or symmetric sweep wing. Unfortunately, the resulting asymmetric configuration has significant aerodynamic and inertial cross-coupling between the aircraft longitudinal and lateral-directional axes. Presented here is a decoupling control law synthesis technique that integrates stability augmentation, decoupling, and the direct incorporation of desired handling qualities into an output feedback controller. The proposed design technique uses linear quadratic regulator concepts in the framework of explicit model following. The output feedback strategy used is a suboptimal projection from the state space to the output space. Dynamics are then introduced into the controller to improve steady-state performance and increase system robustness. Closed-loop performance is shown by application of the control laws to the linearized equations of motion and nonlinear simulation of an oblique-wing aircraft.

1766. Curry, Robert E.; Moulton, Bryan J.; and Kresse, John: **An In-Flight Investigation of Ground Effect on a Forward-Swept Wing Airplane**. AGARD-CP-465, Paper 20. *Aerodynamics of Combat Aircraft Controls and of Ground Effects*, (see N90-28513 23-05), (ISBN-92-835-0555-7), April 1990, AD-A223680, 90N28533, #. (See also 1726.)

A limited flight experiment was conducted to document the ground effect characteristics of the X-29A research aircraft.

This vehicle has an aerodynamic platform which includes a forward-swept wing and close-coupled, variable incidence canard. The flight-test program obtained results for errors in the air data measurement and for incremental normal force and pitching moment caused by ground effect. Correlations with wind-tunnel and computational analyses were made. The results are discussed with respect to the dynamic nature of the flight measurements, similar data from other configurations, and pilot comments. The ground effect results are necessary to obtain an accurate interpretation of the vehicle's landing characteristics. The flight data can also be used in the development of many modern aircraft systems such as autoland and piloted simulation.

1767. *Larson, Terry J.; Moes, Timothy R.; and **Siemers, Paul M., III: **Wind-Tunnel Investigation of a Flush Airdata System at Mach Numbers From 0.7 to 1.4**. NASA TM-101697, H-1544, NAS 1.15:101697, April 1990, 90N18395, #.

Flush pressure orifices installed on the nose section of a 1/7 scale model of the F-14 airplane were evaluated for use as a flush airdata system (FADS). Wing-tunnel tests were conducted in the 11- by 11-ft Unitary Wind Tunnel at NASA Ames Research Center. A full-scale FADS of the same configuration was previously tested using an F-14 aircraft at the Dryden Flight Research Facility of NASA Ames Research Center (Ames-Dryden). These tests, which were published, are part of a NASA program to assess accuracies of FADS for use on aircraft. The test program also provides data to validate algorithms for the shuttle entry airdata system developed at the NASA Langley Research Center. The wind-tunnel test Mach numbers were 0.73, 0.90, 1.05, 1.20, and 1.39. Angles of attack were varied in 2 deg increments from -4 deg to 20 deg. Sideslip angles were varied in 4 deg increments from -8 deg to 8 deg. Airdata parameters were evaluated for determination of free-stream values of stagnation pressure, static pressure, angle of attack, angle of sideslip, and Mach number. These parameters are, in most cases, the same as the parameters investigated in the flight test program. The basic FADS wind-tunnel data are presented in tabular form. A discussion of the more accurate parameters is included.

*Analytical Mechanics Associates, Inc., Hampton, Virginia.
**NASA Langley Research Center, Hampton, Virginia.

1768. Ray, Ronald J.: **Evaluation of Various Thrust Calculation Techniques on an F404 Engine**, NASA TP-3001, H-1505, NAS 1.60:3001, April 1990, 90N25134, #.

In support of performance testing of the X-29A aircraft at the NASA-Ames, various thrust calculation techniques were developed and evaluated for use on the F404-GE-400 engine. The engine was thrust calibrated at NASA-Lewis. Results from these tests were used to correct the manufacturer's in-flight thrust program to more accurately calculate thrust for the specific test engine. Data from these tests were also used

to develop an independent, simplified thrust calculation technique for real-time thrust calculation. Comparisons were also made to thrust values predicted by the engine specification model. Results indicate uninstalled gross thrust accuracies on the order of 1 to 4 percent for the various in-flight thrust methods. The various thrust calculations are described and their usage, uncertainty, and measured accuracies are explained. In addition, the advantages of a real-time thrust algorithm for flight test use and the importance of an accurate thrust calculation to the aircraft performance analysis are described. Finally, actual data obtained from flight test are presented.

1769. Kehoe, Michael W.; *Laurie, Edward J.; and Bjarke, Lisa J.: **An In-Flight Interaction of the X-29A Canard and Flight Control System**. NASA TM-101718, H-1590, NAS 1.15:101718. Presented at the AIAA Dynamics Specialists Meeting, Long Beach, California, April 5–6, 1990, April 1990, 90N25973, #. (See also 1770.)

Many of today's high performance airplanes use high gain, digital flight control systems. These systems are liable to couple with the aircraft's structural dynamics and aerodynamics to cause an aeroservoelastic interaction. These interactions can be stable or unstable depending upon damping and phase relationships within the system. The details of an aeroservoelastic interaction experienced in flight by the X-29A forward-swept wing airplane. A 26.5-Hz canard pitch mode response was aliased by the digital sampling rate in the canard position feedback loop of the flight control system, resulting in a 13.5-Hz signal being commanded to the longitudinal control surfaces. The amplitude of this commanded signal increased as the wear of the canard seals increased, as the feedback path gains were increased, and as the canard aerodynamic loading decreased. The resultant control surface deflections were of sufficient amplitude to excite the structure. The flight data presented shows the effect of each component (structural dynamics, aerodynamics, and flight control system) for this aeroservoelastic interaction.

*Grumman Aerospace Corporation, Bethpage, New York.

1770. Kehoe, Michael W.; *Laurie, Edward J.; and Bjarke, Lisa J.: **An In-Flight Interaction of the X-29A Canard and Flight Control System**. AIAA Paper 90-1240. *Technical Papers*, presented at the AIAA Dynamics Specialists Conference, Long Beach, California, April 5–6, 1990, (see A90-26776 10-39), pp. 469–486, 90A26820, #. (See also 1769.)

This paper presents the details of an aeroservoelastic interaction experienced in flight by the X-29A forward-swept-wing aircraft. A 26.5-Hz canard pitch-mode response was aliased by the digital sampling rate in the canard-position feed-back loop of the flight-control system, resulting in a 13.5-Hz signal being commanded to the longitudinal control surfaces. The amplitude of this commanded signal increased as the wear of the canard seals increased, as the feedback path gains were increased, and as the canard aerodynamic loading decreased. The resultant control-surface deflections were of sufficient amplitude to excite the structure. The flight data presented shows the effect of each component (structural dynamics, aerodynamics, and flight-control system) for this aeroservoelastic interaction.

*Grumman Aerospace Corporation, Bethpage, New York.

1771. Kern, Lura E.; *Belle, Steve D.; and Duke, Eugene L.: **Effects of Simplifying Assumptions on Optimal Trajectory Estimation for a High-Performance Aircraft**. NASA TM-101721, H-1597, NAS 1.15:101721. Presented at the AIAA Atmospheric Flight Mechanics Conference, Boston Massachusetts, August 14–16, 1989, <u>April 1990</u>, 90N25142, #.

When analyzing the performance of an aircraft, certain simplifying assumptions, which decrease the complexity of the problem, can often be made. The degree of accuracy required in the solution may determine the extent to which these simplifying assumptions are incorporated. A complex model may yield more accurate results if it describes the real situation more thoroughly. However, a complex model usually involves more computation time, makes the analysis more difficult, and often requires more information to do the analysis. Therefore, to choose the simplifying assumptions intelligently, it is important to know what effects the assumptions may have on the calculated performance of a vehicle. Several simplifying assumptions are examined, the effects of simplified models to those of the more complex ones are compared, and conclusions are drawn about the impact of these assumptions on flight envelope generation and optimal trajectory calculation. Models which affect an aircraft are analyzed, but the implications of simplifying the model of the aircraft itself are not studied. The examples are atmospheric models, gravitational models, different models for equations of motion, and constraint conditions.

*PRC Inc., Edwards, California.

1772. *Urnes, James M.; Stewart, James; and **Eslinger, Robert: **Flight Demonstration of a Self Repairing Flight Control System in a NASA F-15 Fighter Aircraft**. AGARD-CP-456, Paper 20, *Fault Tolerant Design Concepts for Highly Integrated Flight Critical Guidance and Control Systems* (ISBN 92-835-0552-2), (see N91-12682 04-08), <u>April 1990</u>, AD-A223733, 91N12702, #.

Battle damage causing loss of control capability can compromise mission objectives and even result in aircraft loss. The Self Repairing Flight Control System (SRFCS) flight development program directly addresses this issue with a flight control system design that measures the damage and immediately refines the control system commands to preserve mission potential. The system diagnostics process detects in flight the type of faults that are difficult to isolate

post flight, and thus cause excessive ground maintenance time and cost. The control systems of fighter aircraft have the control power and surface displacement to maneuver the aircraft in a very large flight envelope with a wide variation in airspeed and g maneuvering conditions, with surplus force capacity available from each control surface. Digital flight control processors are designed to include built-in status of the control system components, as well as sensor information on aircraft control maneuver commands and response. In the event of failure or loss of a control surface, the SRFCS utilizes this capability to reconfigure control commands to the remaining control surfaces, thus preserving maneuvering response. Correct post-flight repair is the key to low maintainability support costs and high aircraft mission readiness. The SRFCS utilizes the large data base available with digital flight control systems to diagnose faults. Built-in-test data and sensor data are used as inputs to an Onboard Expert System process to accurately identify failed components for post-flight maintenance action. This diagnostic technique has the advantage of functioning during flight, and so is especially useful in identifying intermittent faults that are present only during maneuver g loads or high hydraulic flow requirements. A flight system was developed to test the reconfiguration and onboard maintenance diagnostics concepts on a NASA F-15 fighter aircraft.

*McDonnell-Douglas Astronautics Co., St. Louis, Missouri.
**Wright Research Development Center, Wright-Patterson AFB, Ohio.

1773. *Gilbert, William P.; *Nguyen, Luat T.; and Gera, Joseph: **Control Research in the NASA High-Alpha Technology Program**. AGARD-CP-465, *Aerodynamics of Combat Aircraft Controls and of Ground Effects*, (see N90-28513 23-05), <u>April 1990</u>, 90N28516, #.

NASA is conducting a focused technology program, known as the High-Angle-of-Attack Technology Program, to accelerate the development of flight-validated technology applicable to the design of fighters with superior stall and post-stall characteristics and agility. A carefully integrated effort is underway combining wind tunnel testing, analytical predictions, piloted simulation, and full-scale flight research. A modified F-18 aircraft has been extensively instrumented for use as the NASA High-Angle-of-Attack Research Vehicle used for flight verification of new methods and concepts. This program stresses the importance of providing improved aircraft control capabilities both by powered control (such as thrust-vectoring) and by innovative aerodynamic control concepts. The program is accomplishing extensive coordinated ground and flight testing to assess and improve available experimental and analytical methods and to develop new concepts for enhanced aerodynamics and for effective control, guidance, and cockpit displays essential for effective pilot utilization of the increased agility provided.

*NASA Langley Research Center Hampton, Virginia.

1774. *Zerweckh, S. H.; *Von Flotow, A. H.; and Murray, J. E.: **Flight Testing a Highly Flexible Aircraft—Case Study on the MIT Light Eagle.** *Journal of Aircraft* (ISSN 0021-8669), Vol. 27, April 1990, (see A88-50613), April 1990, pp. 342–349, 90A31284, #. (See also 1660.)

* MIT, Cambridge, Massachusetts.

1775. O'Neill-Rood, Nora; and Glover, Richard D.: **An Automated Calibration Laboratory for Flight Research Instrumentation: Requirements and a Proposed Design Approach.** NASA TM-101719, H-1594, NAS 1.15:101719. Presented at the 36th ISA International Instrumentation Symposium, Denver, Colorado, May 7–10, 1990, May 1990, 90N26564, #. (See also 1776.)

NASA's Dryden Flight Research Facility (Ames-Dryden), operates a diverse fleet of research aircraft which are heavily instrumented to provide both real time data for in-flight monitoring and recorded data for postflight analysis. Ames-Dryden's existing automated calibration (AUTOCAL) laboratory is a computerized facility which tests aircraft sensors to certify accuracy for anticipated harsh flight environments. Recently, a major AUTOCAL lab upgrade was initiated; the goal of this modernization is to enhance productivity and improve configuration management for both software and test data. The new system will have multiple testing stations employing distributed processing linked by a local area network to a centralized database. The baseline requirements for the new AUTOCAL lab and the design approach being taken for its mechanization are described.

1776. O'Neill-Rood, Nora; and Glover, Richard D.: **An Automated Calibration Laboratory—Requirements and Design Approach.** *Proceedings, 36th International Instrumentation Symposium*, Denver, Colorado, May 6–10, 1990, (see A91-51851 22-35), pp. 707–719, 91A51888. (See also 1775.)

NASA's Dryden Flight Research Facility (Ames-Dryden), operates a diverse fleet of research aircraft which are heavily instrumented to provide both real time data for in-flight monitoring and recorded data for postflight analysis. Ames-Dryden's existing automated calibration (AUTOCAL) laboratory is a computerized facility which tests aircraft sensors to certify accuracy for anticipated harsh flight environments. Recently, a major AUTOCAL lab upgrade was initiated; the goal of this modernization is to enhance productivity and improve configuration management for both software and test data. The new system will have multiple testing stations employing distributed processing linked by a local area network to a centralized database. The baseline requirements for the new AUTOCAL lab and the design approach being taken for its mechanization are described.

1777. Bauer, Jeffrey E.; and *Andrisani, Dominick: **Estimating Short-Period Dynamics Using an Extended Kalman Filter.** NASA TM-101722, H-1625, NAS 1.15:101722. Presented at the 5th Biannual Flight Test Conference, Ontario, California, May 21–24, 1990, 1990, 90N23392, #. (See also 1778.)

An extended Kalman filter (EKF) is used to estimate the parameters of a low-order model from aircraft transient response data. The low-order model is a state space model derived from the short-period approximation of the longitudinal aircraft dynamics. The model corresponds to the pitch rate to stick force transfer function currently used in flying qualities analysis. Because of the model chosen, handling qualities information is also obtained. The parameters are estimated from flight data as well as from a six-degree-of-freedom, nonlinear simulation of the aircraft. These two estimates are then compared and the discrepancies noted. The low-order model is able to satisfactorily match both flight data and simulation data from a high-order computer simulation. The parameters obtained from the EKF analysis of flight data are compared to those obtained using frequency response analysis of the flight data. Time delays and damping ratios are compared and are in agreement. This technique demonstrates the potential to determine, in near real time, the extent of differences between computer models and the actual aircraft. Precise knowledge of these differences can help to determine the flying qualities of a test aircraft and lead to more efficient envelope expansion.

*Purdue University, West Lafayette, Indiana.

1778. Bauer, Jeffrey E.; and *Andrisani, Dominick: **Estimating Short-Period Dynamics Using an Extended Kalman Filter.** AIAA Paper 90-1277. *Technical Papers*, presented at the AIAA, SFTE, DGLR, and SETP 5th Biannual Flight Test Conference, Ontario, California, May 22–24, 1990, (see A90-33886 14-05), pp. 135–169, 90A33901, #. (See also 1777.)

An extended Kalman filter is used to estimate the parameters of a low-order model from aircraft transient response data. The low-order model is a state-space model derived from the short-period approximation of the longitudinal aircraft dynamics. The model corresponds to the pitch rate to stick force transfer function currently used in flying qualities analysis. The parameters are estimated from flight data as well as from a 6-DOF nonlinear simulation of the aircraft. These two estimates are then compared, and the discrepancies noted. The low-order model is able to satisfactorily match both flight data and simulation data from a high-order computer simulation.

*Purdue University, West Lafayette, Indiana.

1779. Mackall, Dale; McBride, David; and Cohen, Dorothea: **Overview of the NASA Ames-Dryden Integrated Test Facility.** *Proceedings, 36th International Instrumentation Symposium*, Denver, Colorado, May 6–10, 1990, (see A91-51851 22-35), pp. 667–681, 91A51885.

An overview of the Integrated Test Facility (ITF) and the real-time systems being developed to operate it are outlined. The generic capabilities of the ITF real-time systems, the real-time data recording, and the remotely augmented vehicle (RAV) monitoring system are discussed. The benefits of applying simulation to aircraft-in-the-loop testing and the RAV monitoring system capabilities to the X-29A flight research program are considered.

1780. Schneider, Edward T.: **Piloted Simulator Assessments of Agility.** AIAA Paper 90-1306. Presented at the AIAA, SFTE, DGLR, and SETP 5th Biannual Flight Test Conference, Ontario, California, May 22–24, 1990, 90A36030, #.

NASA has utilized piloted simulators for nearly two decades to study high-angle-of-attack flying qualities, agility, and air-to-air combat. These studies have included assessments of an F-16XL aircraft equipped with thrust vectoring, an assessment of the F-18 HARV maneuvering requirements to assist in thrust vectoring control system design, and an agility assessment of the F-18. The F-18 agility assessment was compared with in-flight testing. Open-loop maneuvers such as 180-deg rolls to measure roll rate showed favorable simulator/in-flight comparison. Closed-loop maneuvers such as rolls to 90 deg with precision stops or certain maximum longitudinal pitching maneuvers showed poorer performance due to reduced aggressiveness of pilot inputs in flight to remain within flight envelope limits.

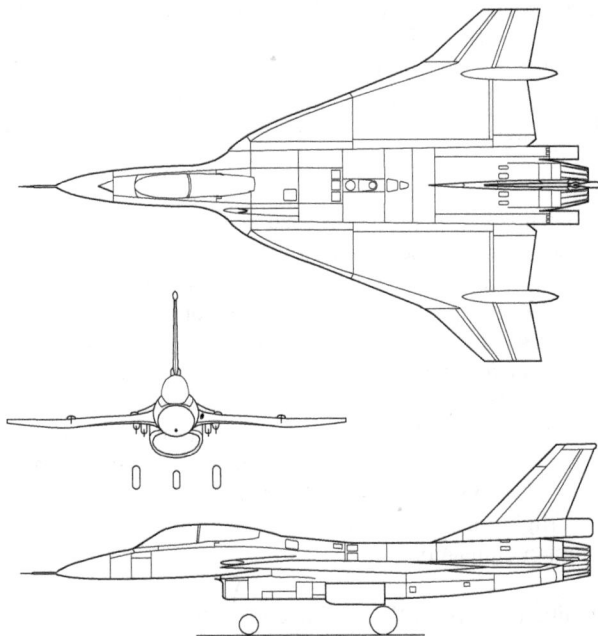

980060

F-16XL Airplane, Three-View Drawing

1781. Stewart, James F.; and Shuck, Thomas L.: **Flight-Testing of the Self-Repairing Flight Control System Using**

the F-15 Highly Integrated Digital Electronic Control Flight Research Facility. AIAA Paper 90-1321. Presented at the AIAA, SFTE, DGLR, and SETP 5th Biannual Flight Test Conference, Ontario, California, May 22–24, 1990, 90A34149, #. (See also 1796.)

Flight tests conducted with the self-repairing flight control system (SRFCS) installed on the NASA F-15 highly integrated digital electronic control aircraft are described. The development leading to the current SRFCS configuration is highlighted. Key objectives of the program are outlined: (1) to flight-evaluate a control reconfiguration strategy with three types of control surface failure; (2) to evaluate a cockpit display that will inform the pilot of the maneuvering capacity of the damaged aircraft; and (3) to flight-evaluate the onboard expert system maintenance diagnostics process using representative faults set to occur only under maneuvering conditions. Preliminary flight results addressing the operation of the overall system, as well as the individual technologies, are included.

1782. *Menon, P. K. A.; and Duke, E. L.: **Time-Optimal Aircraft Pursuit-Evasion With a Weapon Envelope Constraint.** *Proceedings, 1990 9th American Control Conference,* San Diego, California, May 23–25, 1990, Vol. 3, (see A91-30026 11-63), 1990, pp. 2337–2342, 91A30193. (See 1929.)

The optimal pursuit-evasion problem between two aircraft, including nonlinear point-mass vehicle models and a realistic weapon envelope, is analyzed. Using a linear combination of flight time and the square of the vehicle acceleration as the performance index, a closed-form solution is obtained in nonlinear feedback form. Due to its modest computational requirements, this guidance law can be used for onboard real-time implementation.

*NASA Ames Research Center, Moffett Field, California and Georgia Institute of Technology, Atlanta, Georgia.

1783. *Samuels, Jeffrey J.; and Payne, Gordon A.: **Preliminary Assessment of a Supersonic STOVL Flight Research and Demonstration Aircraft.** *Proceedings, AHS, 46th Annual Forum,* Washington, DC, May 21–23, 1990, Vol. 1, (see A91-17201 05-01), pp. 157–164, 91A17209.

NASA Ames has conducted a conceptual design study of a supersonic short takeoff and vertical landing (STOVL) flight research and demonstration aircraft sized according to current technology levels. The aircraft would provide the capability for demonstrating advanced technologies required for STOVL and would be instrumented to provide temperature, pressure, and noise data for power-induced-effects research. The propulsion concept for the single-engine aircraft studied operates in mixed flow without thrust augmentation during power-lift flight. The study aircraft is full scale to facilitate STOVL propulsion-system component validation and power-induced aerodynamics research. Performance is sufficient to permit investigation and validation of vertical landing and hover, accelerating and decelerating transitions, short takeoff, reduced-weight vertical takeoff, and supersonic flight. Mission and maneuver capability is sufficient to demonstrate the operational utility of this class of aircraft. Aircraft mission and technology sensitivities were also examined.

*NASA Ames Research Center, Moffett Field, California.

1784. Ray, Ronald J.; Hicks, John W.; and *Alexander, Russ I.: **Development of a Real-Time Aeroperformance Analysis Technique for the X-29A Advanced Technical Demonstrator.** *Journal of Aircraft* (ISSN 0021-8669), Vol. 27, July 1990, (see A88-38738), July 1990, pp. 660–667, 90A44738, #. (See also 1627, 1628.)

*Computing Devices Co., Ottawa, Canada.

1785. Anderson, Bianca Trujillo; and Meyer, Robert R., Jr.: **Effects of Wing Sweep on Boundary-Layer Transition for a Smooth F-14A Wing at Mach Numbers From 0.700 to 0.825.** NASA TM-101712, H-1531, NAS 1.15:101712, May 1990, 91N24556, #.

The results are discussed of the variable sweep transition flight experiment (VSTFE). The VSTFE was a natural laminar flow experiment flown on the swing wing F-14A aircraft. The main objective of the VSTFE was to determine the effects of wing sweep on boundary layer transition at conditions representative of transport aircraft. The experiment included the flight testing of two laminar flow wing gloves. Glove 1 was a cleanup of the existing F-14A wing. Glove 2, not discussed herein, was designed to provide favorable pressure distributions for natural laminar flow at Mach number (M) 0.700. The transition locations presented for glove 1 were determined primarily by using hot film sensors. Boundary layer rake data was provided as a supplement. Transition data were obtained for leading edge wing sweeps of 15, 20, 25, 30, and 35 degs, with Mach numbers ranging from 0.700 to 0.825, and altitudes ranging from 10,000 to 35,000 ft. Results show that a substantial amount of laminar flow was maintained at all the wing sweeps evaluated. The maximum transition Reynolds number of $13.7 \times 10(\exp 6)$ was obtained for the condition of 15 deg of sweep, M = 0.800, and an altitude of 20,000 ft.

1786. Anderson, Bianca Trujillo; and Meyer, Robert R., Jr.: **Effects of Wing Sweep on In-Flight Boundary-Layer Transition for a Laminar Flow Wing at Mach Numbers From 0.60 to 0.79.** NASA TM-101701, H-1565, NAS 1.15:101701, July 1990, 91N24555, #.

The variable sweep transition flight experiment (VSTFE) was conducted on an F-14A variable sweep wing fighter to examine the effect of wing sweep on natural boundary layer transition. Nearly full span upper surface gloves, extending to 60 percent chord, were attached to the F-14 aircraft's wings. The results are presented of the glove 2 flight tests. Glove 2 had an airfoil shape designed for natural laminar flow at a wing sweep of 20 deg. Sample pressure distributions and transition locations are presented with the complete results tabulated in a database. Data were obtained at wing sweeps of 15, 20, 25, 30, and 35 deg, at Mach numbers ranging from 0.60 to 0.79, and at altitudes ranging from 10,000 to 35,000 ft. Results show that a substantial amount of laminar flow was maintained at all the wing sweeps evaluated. The maximum transition Reynolds number obtained was $18.6 \times 10 (\exp 6)$ at 15 deg of wing sweep, Mach 0.75, and at an altitude of 10,000 ft.

1787. Burcham, Frank W., Jr.; Gilyard, Glenn B.; and Myers, Lawrence P.: **Propulsion System-Flight Control Integration and Optimization: Flight Evaluation and Technology Transition.** NASA TM-4207, H-1603, NAS 1.15:4207. Presented at the AIAA 26th Joint Propulsion Conference, Orlando, Florida, July 16–18, 1990, July 1990, 90N28551, #. (See also 1788.)

Integration of propulsion and flight control systems and their optimization offers significant performance improvements. Research programs were conducted which have developed new propulsion and flight control integration concepts, implemented designs on high-performance airplanes, demonstrated these designs in flight, and measured the performance improvements. These programs, first on the YF-12 airplane, and later on the F-15, demonstrated increased thrust, reduced fuel consumption, increased engine life, and improved airplane performance; with improvements in the 5 to 10 percent range achieved with integration and with no changes to hardware. The design, software and hardware developments, and testing requirements were shown to be practical.

1788. Burcham, Frank W., Jr.; Gilyard, Glenn B.; and Myers, Lawrence P.: **Propulsion System-Flight Control Integration-Flight Evaluation and Technology Transition.** AIAA Paper 90-2280. Presented at the AIAA, SAE, ASME, and ASEE, 26th Joint Propulsion Conference, Orlando, Florida, July 16–18, 1990, 90A42106, #. (See also 1787.)

Integration of propulsion and flight control systems and their optimization offering significant performance improvement are assessed. In particular, research programs conducted by NASA on flight control systems and propulsion system-flight control interactions on the YF-12 and F-15 aircraft are addressed; these programs have demonstrated increased thrust, reduced fuel consumption, increased engine life, and improved aircraft performance. Focus is placed on altitude control, speed-Mach control, integrated controller design, as well as flight control systems and digital electronic engine control. A highly integrated digital electronic control program is analyzed and compared with a performance seeking control program. It is shown that the flight evaluation and demonstration of these technologies have been a key part in the transition of the concepts to production and operational use on a timely basis.

1789. Freudinger, Lawrence C.; and Kehoe, Michael W.: **Flutter Clearance of the F-14A Variable-Sweep Transition Flight Experiment Airplane, Phase 2**. NASA TM-101717, H-1544, NAS 1.15:101717, July 1990, 90N25135, #.

An F-14A aircraft was modified for use as the test-bed aircraft for the variable-sweep transition flight experiment (VSTFE) program. The VSTFE program was a laminar flow research program designed to measure the effects of wing sweep on laminar flow. The airplane was modified by adding an upper surface foam and fiberglass glove to the right wing. An existing left wing glove had been added for the previous phase of the program. Ground vibration and flight flutter testing were accomplished to verify the absence of aeroelastic instabilities within a flight envelope of Mach 0.9 or 450 knots, calibrated airspeed, whichever was less. Flight test data indicated satisfactory damping levels and trends for the elastic structural modes of the airplane. Ground vibration test data are presented along with in-flight frequency and damping estimates, time histories and power spectral densities of in-flight sensors, and pressure distribution data.

1790. Sim, Alex G.: **Flight Characteristics of a Modified Schweizer SGS 1-36 Sailplane at Low and Very High Angles of Attack**. NASA TP-3022, H-1563, NAS 1.60:3022, July 1990, 91N10079, #.

A manned flight research program using a modified sailplane was conducted to very high angles of attack at the NASA-Ames. Piloting techniques were established that enabled the pilot to attain and stabilize on an angle of attack in the 30 to 72 deg range. Aerodynamic derivatives were estimated from the flight data for both low and very high angles of attack and are compared to wind tunnel data. In addition, limited performance and trim data are presented.

1791. Johnson, Steven A.: **A Simple Dynamic Engine Model for Use in a Real-Time Aircraft Simulation With Thrust Vectoring**. AIAA Paper 90-2166. Presented at the AIAA, SAE, ASME, and ASEE, 26th Joint Propulsion Conference, Orlando, Florida, July 16–18, 1990, 90A42054, #. (See also 1809.)

A simple dynamic engine model was developed for use in thrust vectoring control law development and real-time aircraft simulation. Engine dynamics were simulated using a throttle rate limiter and low-pass filter. This paper includes a description of a method to account for axial thrust loss resulting from thrust vectoring and the development of the simple dynamic engine model and its incorporation into the F-18 high alpha research vehicle (HARV) thrust vectoring simulation. The simple dynamic engine model was evaluated at Mach 0.2, 35,000-ft altitude and at Mach 0.7, 35,000-ft

altitude. The simple dynamic engine model is within 3 percent of the steady state response, and within 25 percent of the transient response of the complete nonlinear dynamic engine model.

1792. *Alag, Gurbux S.; and Gilyard, Glenn B.: **A Proposed Kalman Filter Algorithm for Estimation of Unmeasured Output Variables for an F100 Turbofan Engine**. AIAA Paper 90-1920. Presented at the AIAA, SAE, ASME, and ASEE, 26th Joint Propulsion Conference, Orlando, Florida, July 16–18, 1990, 90A40558, #. (See also 1808.)

To develop advanced control systems for optimizing aircraft engine performance, unmeasurable output variables must be estimated. The estimation has to be done in an uncertain environment and be adaptable to varying degrees of modeling errors and other variations in engine behavior over its operational life cycle. This paper presents an approach to estimate unmeasured output variables by explicitly modeling the effects of off-nominal engine behavior as biases on the measurable output variables. A state variable model accommodating off-nominal behavior is developed for the engine, and Kalman filter concepts are used to estimate the required variables. Results are presented from nonlinear engine simulation studies as well as the application of the estimation algorithm on actual flight data. The formulation presented has a wide range of application since it is not restricted or tailored to the particular application described in the paper.

*PRC Systems, Edwards, California.

1793. Maine, Trindel A.; Gilyard, Glenn B.; and Lambert, Heather H.: **A Preliminary Evaluation of an F100 Engine Parameter Estimation Process Using Flight Data**. AIAA Paper 90-1921. Presented at the AIAA, SAE, ASME, and ASEE, 26th Joint Propulsion Conference, Orlando, Florida, July 16–18, 1990, 90A40559, #. (See also 1794.)

The parameter estimation algorithm developed for the F100 engine is described. The algorithm is a two-step process. The first step consists of a Kalman filter estimation of five deterioration parameters, which model the off-nominal behavior of the engine during flight. The second step is based on a simplified steady-state model of the 'compact engine model' (CEM). In this step the control vector in the CEM is augmented by the deterioration parameters estimated in the first step. The results of an evaluation made using flight data from the F-15 aircraft are presented, indicating that the algorithm can provide reasonable estimates of engine variables for an advanced propulsion-control-law development.

1794. Maine, Trindel A.; Gilyard, Glenn B.; and Lambert, Heather H.: **A Preliminary Evaluation of an F100 Engine Parameter Estimation Process Using Flight Data**. NASA TM-4216, H-1602, NAS 1.15:4216. Presented at the AIAA,

SAE, ASME, and ASEE, 26th Joint Propulsion Conference, Orlando, Florida, July 16–18, 1990, (A90-40559), August 1990, 91N21446, #. (See also 1793.)

The parameter estimation algorithm developed for the F100 engine is described. The algorithm is a two-step process. The first step consists of a Kalman filter estimation of five deterioration parameters, which model the off-nominal behavior of the engine during flight. The second step is based on a simplified steady-state model of the compact engine model (CEM). In this step, the control vector in the CEM is augmented by the deterioration parameters estimated in the first step. The results of an evaluation made using flight data from the F-15 aircraft are presented, indicating that the algorithm can provide reasonable estimates of engine variables for an advanced propulsion control law development.

1795. Quinn, Robert D.; and Gong, Leslie: **Real-Time Aerodynamic Heating and Surface Temperature Calculations for Hypersonic Flight Simulation**. NASA TM-4222, H-1602, NAS 1.15:4222, August 1990, 90N28815, #.

A real-time heating algorithm was derived and installed on the Ames Research Center Dryden Flight Research Facility real-time flight simulator. This program can calculate two- and three-dimensional stagnation point surface heating rates and surface temperatures. The two-dimensional calculations can be made with or without leading-edge sweep. In addition, upper and lower surface heating rates and surface temperatures for flat plates, wedges, and cones can be calculated. Laminar or turbulent heating can be calculated, with boundary-layer transition made a function of free-stream Reynolds number and free-stream Mach number. Real-time heating rates and surface temperatures calculated for a generic hypersonic vehicle are presented and compared with more exact values computed by a batch aeroheating program. As these comparisons show, the heating algorithm used on the flight simulator calculates surface heating rates and temperatures well within the accuracy required to evaluate flight profiles for acceptable heating trajectories.

1796. Stewart, James F.; and Shuck, Thomas L.: **Flight-Testing of the Self-Repairing Flight Control System Using the F-15 Highly Integrated Digital Electronic Control Flight Research Facility**. NASA TM-101725, H-1635, NAS 1.15:101725, AIAA Paper 90-1321. Presented at the AIAA, SFTE, DGLR, and SETP 5th Biannual Flight Test Conference, Ontario, California, May 21–24, 1990, August 1990, 90N25144, #. (See also 1781.)

Flight tests conducted with the self-repairing flight control system (SRFCS) installed on the NASA F-15 highly integrated digital electronic control aircraft are described. The development leading to the current SRFCS configuration is highlighted. Key objectives of the program are outlined: (1) to flight-evaluate a control reconfiguration strategy with three types of control surface failure; (2) to evaluate a cockpit display that will inform the pilot of the maneuvering capacity of the damage aircraft; and (3) to flight-evaluate the onboard expert system maintenance diagnostics process using representative faults set to occur only under maneuvering conditions. Preliminary flight results addressing the operation of the overall system, as well as the individual technologies, are included.

1797. Fisher, David F.; *Banks, Daniel W.; and **Richwine, David M.: **F-18 High Alpha Research Vehicle Surface Pressures: Initial In-Flight Results and Correlation With Flow Visualization and Wind-Tunnel Data**. NASA TM-101724, H-1633, NAS 1.15:101724, AIAA Paper 90-3018. Presented at the AIAA 8th Applied Aerodynamics Conference, Portland, Oregon, August 20–22, 1990, August 1990, 91N19051, #. (See also 1798.)

Pressure distributions measured on the forebody and the leading-edge extensions (LEX's) of the NASA F-18 high alpha research vehicle (HARV) were reported at 10 and 50 degree angles of attack and at Mach 0.20 to 0.60. The results were correlated with HARV flow visualization and 6-percent scale F-18 wind-tunnel-model test results. The general trend in the data from the forebody was for the maximum suction pressure peaks to first appear at an angle of attack (alpha) of approximately 19 degrees and increase in magnitude with angle of attack. The LEX pressure distribution general trend was the inward progression and increase in magnitude of the maximum suction peaks up to vortex core breakdown and then the decrease and general flattening of the pressure distribution beyond that. No significant effect of Mach number was noted for the forebody results. However, a substantial compressibility effect on the LEX's resulted in a significant reduction in vortex-induced suction pressure as Mach number increased. The forebody primary and the LEX secondary vortex separation lines, from surface flow visualization, correlated well with the end of pressure recovery, leeward and windward, respectively, of maximum suction pressure peaks. The flight to wind-tunnel correlations were generally good with some exceptions.

*NASA Langley Research Center, Hampton, Virginia.
**PRC Inc., Edwards, California.

1798. Fisher, David F.; *Banks, Daniel W.; and **Richwine, David M.: **F-18 High Alpha Research Vehicle Surface Pressures—Initial In-Flight Results and Correlation With Flow Visualization and Wind-Tunnel Data**. AIAA Paper 90-3018. *Technical Papers*, presented at the AIAA 8th Applied Aerodynamics Conference, Portland, Oregon, August 20–22, 1990, Part 1, (see A90-45845 21-02), pp. 421–451, 90A45885, #. (See also 1797.)

Flight tests with the NASA F-18 high-alpha research vehicle (HARV) have yielded pressure distributions at angles of attack from 10 to 50 deg, at Mach 0.23 to 0.6, at five fuselage forebody stations and three on the leading-edge extensions

(LEXs). Correlations are made between these data and both previously obtained HARV flow visualizations and wind tunnel model test results. The general trend is one in which the forebody's maximum suction pressure peaks increase in magnitude, after their first appearance at alpha of about 19 deg, with increasing alpha. LEX pressure-distribution trends involve the inward progression of the maximum suction peaks, an increase in the magnitude of the maximum pressure peaks up to pressure core breakdown, and the decrease and general flattening of the pressure distribution beyond the LEX primary vortex breakdown.

*NASA Langley Research Center, Hampton, Virginia.
**PRC Inc., Edwards, California.

1799. Lokos, William A.: **Predicted and Measured In-Flight Wing Deformations of a Forward-Swept-Wing Aircraft.** *Proceedings, Society of Flight Test Engineers, 21st Annual Symposium*, Garden Grove, California, August 6–10, 1990, (see A92-35926 14-01), 1990, pp. 3.1-1 to 3.1-20, 92A35936.

An electrooptical flight-deflection measurement system (FDMS) is described in terms of its use in structural testing of the composite forward-swept wing of the X-29 aircraft. The wing deflected shapes measured using the present system are compared to the shapes predicted by NASTRAN and other codes as well as data from ground-test load measurements. The electrooptical FDMS is based on a control unit, two receivers, a target driver, and 12-16 IR LED targets. The FDMS determines the in-flight deflected wing shapes at a variety of altitudes at Mach 0.9, and the results are compared to the analytically predicted wing-twist distributions. The FDMS data describe the predicted increasing streamwise twist with increasing dynamic pressure and suggest that the streamwise twist is more prevalent at the inboard measurement station than at the wing tip. This hook shape is not represented in the predicted data, and suggestions are given for improving the modeling of the X-29 wing.

1800. Antoniewicz, Robert F.; Duke, Eugene L.; and *Menon, P. K. A.: **Flight Test of a Trajectory Controller Using Linearizing Transformations With Measurement Feedback.** AIAA Paper 90-3373. *Technical Papers*, presented at the AIAA Guidance, Navigation and Control Conference, Portland, Oregon, August 20–22, 1990, Part 1, (see A90-47576 21-08), pp. 518–532, 90A47631, #.

The design of nonlinear controllers has relied on the use of detailed aerodynamic and engine models that must be associated with the control law in the flight system implementation. Many of these controllers have been applied to vehicle flightpath control problems and have attempted to combine both inner- and outer-loop control functions in a single controller. This paper presents an alternate approach to the design of outer-loop controllers. The approach simplifies the outer-loop design problem by separating the inner-loop

(stabilization and control) from the outer-loop (guidance and navigation) functions. Linearizing transformations are applied using measurement feedback to eliminate the need for detailed aircraft models in outer-loop control applications. Also discussed is an implementation of the controller. This implementation was tested on a six-degree-of-freedom F-15 simulation and in flight on an F-15 aircraft. Proof of the concept is provided by flight test data which is presented and discussed.

*Georgia Institute of Technology, Atlanta, Georgia.

1801. *Hodgkinson, J.; *Potsdam, E. H.; and Smith, R. E.: **Interpreting the Handling Qualities of Aircraft With Stability and Control Augmentation.** AIAA Paper 90-2825. Presented at the AIAA 8th Atmospheric Flight Mechanics Conference, Portland, Oregon, August 20–22, 1990, 91A16285, #.

The general process of designing an aircraft for good flying qualities is first discussed. Lessons learned are pointed out, with piloted evaluation emerging as a crucial element. Two sources of rating variability in performing these evaluations are then discussed. First, the finite endpoints of the Cooper-Harper scale do not bias parametric statistical analyses unduly. Second, the wording of the scale does introduce some scatter. Phase lags generated by augmentation systems, as represented by equivalent time delays, often cause poor flying qualities. An analysis is introduced which allows a designer to relate any level of time delay to a probability of loss of aircraft control. This view of time delays should, it is hoped, allow better visibility of the time delays in the design process.

*Douglas Aircraft Co., Long Beach, California.

1802. Moes, Timothy R.; and Meyer, Robert R., Jr.: **In-Flight Investigation of Shuttle Tile Pressure Orifice Installations.** NASA TM-4219, H-1575, NAS 1.15:4219, September 1990, 90N28820, #.

To determine shuttle orbiter wing loads during ascent, wing load instrumentation was added to Columbia (OV-102). This instrumentation included strain gages and pressure orifices on the wing. The loads derived from wing pressure measurements taken during STS 61-C did not agree with those derived from strain gage measurements or with the loads predicted from the aerodynamic database. Anomalies in the surface immediately surrounding the pressure orifices in the thermal protection system (TPS) tiles were one possible cause of errors in the loads derived from wing pressure measurements. These surface anomalies were caused by a ceramic filler material which was installed around the pressure tubing. The filler material allowed slight movement of the TPS tile and pressure tube as the airframe flexed and bent under aerodynamic loads during ascent and descent. Postflight inspection revealed that this filler material had protruded from or receded beneath the surface, causing the orifice to lose its flushness. Flight tests were conducted at NASA Ames Research Center Dryden Flight Research Facility to determine the effects of any anomaly in surface flushness of the orifice installation on the measured pressures at Mach numbers between 0.6 and 1.4. An F-104 aircraft with a flight test fixture mounted beneath the fuselage was used for these flights. Surface flushness anomalies typical of those on the orbiter after flight (STA 61-C) were tested. Also, cases with excessive protrusion and recession of the filler material were tested. This report shows that the anomalies in STS 61-C orifice installations adversely affected the pressure measurements. But the magnitude of the affect was not great enough to account for the discrepancies with the strain gage measurements and the aerodynamic predictions.

1803. Ishmael, Stephen D.; Smith, Rogers E.; *Purifoy, Dana D.; and **Womer, Rodney K.: **X-29 High Angle of Attack.** *Proceedings, 1990 Report to the Aerospace Profession*: Society of Experimental Test Pilots, 34th Symposium, Beverly Hills, California, September 27–29, 1990, (see A92-16051 04-05), pp. 5–14, 92A16052.

Flight test program highlights are discussed for the X-29 high angle-of-attack (AOA) aircraft. The AOA envelope extended from 10 to 66 deg; the X-29 exhibited precise pitch control, allowing AOA to be maintained within 1 deg during stabilized points as well as permitting rapid recoveries from all AOAs. Attention is given to controllability degradation above 40-deg AOA due to asymmetric yawing moments. The use of this aircraft as a fundamental research tool which complements analytical methods is powerfully justified by the obviation of scaling effects.

*USAF Flight Test Center, Edwards AFB, California.
**Grumman Corporation, Point Mugu, California.

1804. Burcham, Frank W., Jr.; Gilyard, Glenn B.; and *Gelhausen, Paul A.: **Integrated Flight-Propulsion Control Concepts for Supersonic Transport Airplanes.** SAE Paper 901928. Presented at the SAE Aerospace Technology Conference and Exposition, Long Beach, California, October 1–4, 1990, September 1990, 91A48609. (See also 1819.)

Increased powerplant thrust and reduced fuel consumption are obtainable by controlling engine stall margins as a function of flight and engine operating conditions. An evaluation is presently conducted of the performance improvements obtainable by these means in SSTs. It is noted that inlet pressure recovery increases and inlet drag reductions are obtainable via inlet control system integration; the use of propulsion system forces and moments to augment the flight control and aircraft stabilization system can also reduce empennage areas, weights, and drag. Special control modes may be instituted for community noise minimization and emergency procedures.

*NASA Ames Research Center, Moffett Field, California.

1805. Chacon, Vince; Pahle, Joseph W.; and Regenie, Victoria A.: **Validation of the F-18 High Alpha Research Vehicle Flight Control and Avionics Systems Modifications.** NASA TM-101723, H-1632, NAS 1.15:101723. Presented at the IEEE, AIAA, and NASA 9th Digital Avionics Systems Conference, Virginia Beach, Virginia, October 15–18, 1990, October 1990, 90N28542, #. (See also 1806.)

The verification and validation process is a critical portion of the development of a flight system. Verification, the steps taken to assure the system meets the design specification, has become a reasonably understood and straightforward process. Validation is the method used to ensure that the system design meets the needs of the project. As systems become more integrated and more critical in their functions, the validation process becomes more complex and important. The tests, tools, and techniques which are being used for the validation of the high alpha research vehicle (HARV) turning vane control system (TVCS) are discussed and the problems and their solutions are documented. The emphasis of this paper is on the validation of integrated system.

1806. Chacon, Vince; Pahle, Joseph W.; and Regenie, Victoria A.: **Validation of the F-18 High Alpha Research Vehicle Flight Control and Avionics Systems Modifications.** *IEEE, AIAA, and NASA 9th Digital Avionics Systems Conference Proceedings*, Virginia Beach, Virginia, October 15–18, 1990, (see A91-54576 23-06), pp. 1–10, 91A54577. (See also 1805.)

The verification and validation process is a critical portion of the development of a flight system. Verification, the steps taken to assure the system meets the design specification, has become a reasonably understood and straightforward process. Validation is the method used to ensure that the system design meets the needs of the project. As systems become more integrated and more critical in their functions, the validation process becomes more complex and important. The tests, tools, and techniques which are being used for the validation of the high alpha research vehicle (HARV) turning valve control system (TVCS) are discussed, and their solutions are documented. The emphasis of this paper is on the validation of integrated systems.

1807. Del Frate, John H.; Fisher, David F.; and Zuniga, Fanny A.: **In-Flight Flow Visualization With Pressure Measurements at Low Speeds on the NASA F-18 High Alpha Research Vehicle.** NASA TM-101726, H-1651, NAS 1.15:101726. Presented at the AGARD Vortex Flow Aerodynamics Conference, Scheveningen, the Netherlands, October 1–4, 1990, October 1990, 90N28505, #. (See also 1868.)

In-flight results from surface and off-surface flow visualizations and from extensive pressure distributions document the vortical flow on the leading edge extensions (LEX) and forebody of the NASA F-18 high alpha research vehicle for low speeds and angles of attack up to 50 deg. Surface flow visualization data, obtained using the emitted fluid technique, were used to define separation lines and laminar separation bubbles. Off-surface flow visualization data, obtained by smoke injection, were used to document both the path of the vortex cores and the location of vortex core breakdown. The location of vortex core breakdown correlated well with the loss of suction pressure on the LEX and with the flow visualization results from ground facilities. Surface flow separation lines on the LEX and forebody corresponded well with the end of pressure recovery under the vortical flows. Correlation of the pressures with wind tunnel results show fair to good correlation.

1808. *Alag, Gurbux S.; and Gilyard, Glenn B.: **A Proposed Kalman Filter Algorithm for Estimation of Unmeasured Output Variables for an F100 Turbofan Engine**. NASA TM-4234, H-1639, NAS 1.15:4234. Presented at the AIAA, SAE, ASME, and ASEE Joint Propulsion Conference, Orlando, Florida, July 16–18, 1990, October 1990, 91N19099, #. (See also 1792.)

To develop advanced control systems for optimizing aircraft engine performance, unmeasurable output variables must be estimated. The estimation has to be done in an uncertain environment and be adaptable to varying degrees of modeling errors and other variations in engine behavior over its operational life cycle. This paper represented an approach to estimate unmeasured output variables by explicitly modeling the effects of off-nominal engine behavior as biases on the measurable output variables. A state variable model accommodating off-nominal behavior is developed for the engine, and Kalman filter concepts are used to estimate the required variables. Results are presented from nonlinear engine simulation studies as well as the application of the estimation algorithm on actual flight data. The formulation presented has a wide range of application since it is not restricted or tailored to the particular application described.

*PRC Inc., Edwards, California.

1809. Johnson, Steven A.: **A Simple Dynamic Engine Model for Use in a Real-Time Aircraft Simulation With Thrust Vectoring**. NASA TM-4240, H-1643, NAS 1.15:4240, AIAA Paper 90-2166. Presented at the AIAA, SAE, ASME, and ASEE Joint Propulsion Conference, Orlando, Florida, July 16–18, 1990, (see A90-42054), October 1990, 91N19079, #. (See also 1791.)

A simple dynamic engine model was developed at the NASA Ames Research Center, Dryden Flight Research Facility, for use in thrust vectoring control law development and real-time aircraft simulation. The simple dynamic engine model of the F404-GE-400 engine (General Electric, Lynn, Massachusetts) operates within the aircraft simulator. It was developed using tabular data generated from a complete nonlinear dynamic engine model supplied by the manufacturer. Engine dynamics were simulated using a

throttle rate limiter and low-pass filter. Included is a description of a method to account for axial thrust loss resulting from thrust vectoring. In addition, the development of the simple dynamic engine model and its incorporation into the F-18 high alpha research vehicle (HARV) thrust vectoring simulation. The simple dynamic engine model was evaluated at Mach 0.2, 35,000 ft altitude and at Mach 0.7, 35,000 ft altitude. The simple dynamic engine model is within 3 percent of the steady state response, and within 25 percent of the transient response of the complete nonlinear dynamic engine model.

1810. Sitz, Joel R.; and *Vernon, Todd H.: **Flight Control System Design Factors for Applying Automated Testing Techniques**. NASA TM-4242, H-1631, NAS 1.15:4242. Presented at the 9th Annual Digital Avionics System Conference, Virginia Beach, Virginia, October 15–18, 1990, (see A91-54610), October 1990, 93N30764, #. (See also 1811.)

Automated validation of flight-critical embedded systems is being done at ARC Dryden Flight Research Facility. The automated testing techniques are being used to perform closed-loop validation of man-rated flight control systems. The principal design features and operational experiences of the X-29 forward-swept-wing aircraft and F-18 High Alpha Research Vehicle (HARV) automated test systems are discussed. Operationally applying automated testing techniques has accentuated flight control system features that either help or hinder the application of these techniques. The paper also discusses flight control system features which foster the use of automated testing techniques.

*PRC Inc., Edwards, California.

1811. Sitz, Joel R.; and *Vernon, Todd H.: **Flight Control System Design Factors for Applying Automated Testing Techniques**. *Proceedings, IEEE, AIAA, and NASA 9th Digital Avionics Systems Conference*, Virginia Beach, Virginia, October 15–18, 1990, (see A91-54576 23-06), pp. 235–247, 91A54610. (See also 1810.)

The principal design features and operational experiences of the X-29 forward-swept-wing aircraft and F-18 high alpha research vehicle (HARV) automated test systems are discussed. It is noted that operational experiences in developing and using these automated testing techniques have highlighted the need for incorporating target system features to improve testability. Improved target system testability can be accomplished with the addition of nonreal-time and real-time features. Online access to target system implementation details, unobtrusive real-time access to internal user-selectable variables, and proper software instrumentation are all desirable features of the target system. Also, test system and target system design issues must be addressed during the early stages of the target system development. Processing speeds of up to 20 million instructions/s and the development of high-bandwidth reflective memory systems have improved the ability to integrate the target system and test system for the application of automated testing techniques. It is concluded that new methods of designing testability into the target systems are required.

*PRC Inc., Edwards, California.

1812. *Nissim, Eli: **Design of Control Laws for Flutter Suppression Based on the Aerodynamic Energy Concept and Comparisons With Other Design Methods.** NASA TP-3056, H-1549, NAS 1.60:3056, AIAA Paper 89-1212, (see A89-31100), October 1990, 91N10328, #. (See also 1696.)

The aerodynamic energy method is used to synthesize control laws for NASA's drone for aerodynamic and structural testing-aerodynamic research wing 1 (DAST-ARW1) mathematical model. The performance of these control laws in terms of closed-loop flutter dynamic pressure, control surface activity, and robustness is compared with other control laws that relate to the same model. A control law synthesis technique that makes use of the return difference singular values is developed. It is based on the aerodynamic energy approach and is shown to yield results that are superior to those results given in the literature and are based on optimal control theory. Nyquist plots are presented, together with a short discussion regarding the relative merits of the minimum singular value as a measure of robustness as compared with the more traditional measure involving phase and gain margins.

*National Research Council Fellow, Technion, Israel Institute of Technology, Haifa, Israel.

1813. *Ohlhorst, Craig W.; *Vaughn, Wallace L.; and Bresina, John J.: **NASA Langley Research Center National Aero-Space Plane Mission Simulation Profile Sets.** NASA TM-102670, NAS 1.15:102670, October 1990, 90N28541, #.

To provide information on the potential for long life service of oxidation resistant carbon-carbon (ORCC) materials in the National Aero-Space Plane (NASP) airframe environment, NASP ascent, entry, and cruise trajectories were analytically flown. Temperature and pressure profiles were generated for 20 vehicle locations. Orbital (ascent and entry) and cruise profile sets from four locations are presented along with the humidity exposure and testing sequences that are being used to evaluate ORCC materials. The four profiles show peak temperatures during the ascent leg of an orbital mission of 2800, 2500, 2000, and 1700 F. These profiles bracket conditions where carbon-carbon might be used on the NASP vehicle.

*NASA Langley Research Center, Hampton, Virginia.

1814. *Maglieri, Domenic J.; *Sothcott, Victor E.; and Hicks, John: **Influence of Vehicle Configuration and Flight Profile on X-30 Sonic Booms.** AIAA Paper 90-5224. Presented at the AIAA, 2nd International Aerospace Planes Conference, Orlando, Florida, October 29–31, 1990, 91A14450, #.

The role of vehicle configuration and the flight profile on sonic booms produced by the experimental NASP X-30 is investigated. Sonic boom signatures, overpressure levels, and footprints for X-30 are presented and compared with sonic boom measurements for F-104, SR-71, Concorde, XB-70, and STS Orbiter. Results show that the sonic boom signatures for X-30 fall within those of previous high-speed planes.

*Eagle Engineering, Inc., Hampton, Virginia.

1815. *Percy, Wendy C.; and Fields, Roger A.: **Buckling Analysis and Test Correlation of Hat Stiffened Panels for Hypersonic Vehicles.** AIAA Paper 90-5219. Presented at the AIAA 2nd International Aerospace Planes Conference, Orlando, Florida, October 29–31, 1990, 91A14445, #.

The paper discusses the design, analysis, and test of hat stiffened panels subjected to a variety of thermal and mechanical load conditions. The panels were designed using data from structural optimization computer codes and finite element analysis. Test methods included the grid shadow moire method and a single gage force stiffness method. The agreement between the test data and analysis provides confidence in the methods that are currently being used to design structures for hypersonic vehicles. The agreement also indicates that post buckled strength may potentially be used to reduce the vehicle weight.

*McDonnell Douglas Corporation, St. Louis, Missouri.

1816. *Chisholm, J. D.; *Nobbs, S. G.; and Stewart, J. F.: **Development of the HiDEC Inlet Integration Mode.** ASME, 34th International Gas Turbine and Aeroengine Congress and Exhibition, Toronto, Canada, June 4–8, 1989. *ASME, Transactions, Journal of Engineering for Gas Turbines and Power,* (ISSN 0022-0825), Vol. 112, October 1990, pp. 565–572, 91A13028, #.

The Highly Integrated Digital Electronic Control (HIDEC) development program conducted at NASA-Ames/Dryden will use an F-15 test aircraft for flight demonstration. An account is presently given of the HIDEC Inlet Integration mode's design concept, control law, and test aircraft implementation, with a view to its performance benefits. The enhancement of performance is a function of the use of Digital Electronic Engine Control corrected engine airflow computations to improve the scheduling of inlet ramp positions in real time; excess thrust can thereby be increased by 13 percent at Mach 2.3 and 40,000 ft. Aircraft supportability is also improved through the obviation of inlet controllers.

*McDonnell Aircraft Co., St. Louis, Missouri.

1817. DeAngelis, V. Michael; and Fields, Roger A.: **Techniques for Hot Structures Testing.** NASA TM-101727, H-1664, NAS 1.15:101727. Presented at the 1st Thermal Structures Conference, Charlottesville, Virginia, November 13–15, 1990, November 1990, (see A91-16035), 91N19080, #. (See also 1818.)

Hot structures testing have been going on since the early 1960's beginning with the Mach 6, X-15 airplane. Early hot structures test programs at NASA-Ames-Dryden focused on operational testing required to support the X-15 flight test program, and early hot structures research projects focused on developing lab test techniques to simulate flight thermal profiles. More recent efforts involved numerous large and small hot structures test programs that served to develop test methods and measurement techniques to provide data that promoted the correlation of test data with results from analytical codes. In November 1988 a workshop was sponsored that focused on the correlation of hot structures test data with analysis. Limited material is drawn from the workshop and a more formal documentation is provided of topics that focus on hot structures test techniques used at NASA-Ames-Dryden. Topics covered include the data acquisition and control of testing, the quartz lamp heater systems, current strain and temperature sensors, and hot structures test techniques used to simulate the flight thermal environment in the lab.

1818. DeAngelis, V. Michael; and Fields, Roger A.: **Techniques for Hot Structures Testing.** *Proceedings, 1st Thermal Structures Conference,* Charlottesville, Virginia, November 13–15, 1990, (see A91-16026 04-39), pp. 191–215, 91A16035 (See also 1817.)

Hot structures test techniques developed and applied by the Aerostructures Branch of the NASA Ames Research Center, Dryden Flight Research Facility, are presented. Topics covered include the data acquisition and control of testing, the quartz lamp heater systems, current strain and temperature sensors, and hot structures test techniques used to simulate the flight thermal environment in the laboratory.

1819. Burcham, Frank W., Jr.; Gilyard, Glenn B.; and Gelhausen, Paul A.: **Integrated Flight-Propulsion Control Concepts for Supersonic Transport Airplanes.** NASA TM-101728, H-1673, NAS 1.15:101728, SAE-901928. Presented at the Society of Automotive Engineers (SAE), Inc. Aerotech Conference, Long Beach, California, October 1–4, 1990, November 1990, 91N13460, #. (See also 1804.)

Integration of propulsion and flight control systems will provide significant performance improvements for supersonic transport airplanes. Increased engine thrust and reduced fuel consumption can be obtained by controlling engine stall margin as a function of flight and engine operating conditions. Improved inlet pressure recovery and decreased inlet drag can result from inlet control system integration. Using propulsion system forces and moments to augment the flight control system and airplane stability can reduce the flight control surface and tail size, weight, and drag. Special control modes may also be desirable for minimizing community noise and for emergency procedures. The overall impact of integrated controls on the takeoff gross weight for a generic high speed civil transport is presented.

1820. Ayers, T. G.: **The Need for a Hypersonic Demonstrator.** *Proceedings, European Symposium on the Future of High Speed Air Transport,* Strasbourg, France, November 6–8, 1989, (see A91-10951 01-01), Cepadues-Editions, Toulouse, France, 1990, pp. 290–296, 91A10977.

The requirement for research aircraft and demonstrator vehicles has been seriously challenged by tight budgets and erroneous impressions that aeronautical technology has matured to a point where the value added by flight research and/or demonstration is not sufficient to offset the costs. While this issue may be debatable with respect to subsonic/transonic speeds, such is not the case for high-speed (supersonic and hypersonic) operation. The aerodynamic performance, weight/payload fractions, and thermodynamic problems are such that small margins of error can be tantamount to the vehicle being unable to reach its design point or so inefficient as to render it useless. This paper addresses some of the critical design considerations and operational constraints which make it mandatory to carry out flight research and develop a demonstrator vehicle in order that the risks be reduced to an acceptable level to assure technology readiness for viable hypersonic flight.

1821. Ayers, T. G.: **NACA/NASA Supersonic Flight Research.** *Proceedings, European Symposium on the Future of High Speed Air Transport,* Strasbourg, France, November 6–8, 1989, (see A91-10951 01-01), Cepadues-Editions, Toulouse, France, 1990, pp. 34–41, 91A10953.

The use of experimental and testbed vehicles and their contributions to fundamental problem solving and overall vehicle characteristics are presented. A chronological description of aircraft from the first supersonic flight in the X-1 through the development of the F-100 series, the X-15, and the B-1 is given. One of the early significant contributions made was the development of the all-moving stabilizer that solved the problem associated with high-speed tuck and the trim requirements of entry into the supersonic regime. Some wind tunnel/flight drag characteristics studies associated with the B-1 bomber involving flexibility effects and wind tunnel effects are shown. Finally, the evolution of digital systems to enhance maintainability and reliability and to reduce the work load in the cockpit are described.

1822. *Teare, Wendy P.; and Fields, Roger A.: **Buckling Analysis and Test Correlation of High Temperature Structural Panels.** *Proceedings, 1st Thermal Structures Conference,* Charlottesville, Virginia, November 13–15, 1990, (see A91-16026 04-39), 1990, pp. 271–282, 91A16039.

This paper focuses on the design, analysis, and test of a high temperature structural panel, constructed of Ti-6-4, subjected to a variety of thermal and mechanical load conditions. A follow-on panel, constructed of TMC, is also discussed in less detail. The design constraints and test set-up are discussed, as well as the test methods that were used: the grid shadow moire method and a single gage force stiffness method. The agreement between the test data and analysis for this test program provides confidence in the methods that are currently being used to design structures for hypersonic vehicles. The agreement also suggests that postbuckled strength may potentially be used to reduce the vehicle weight.

*McDonnell Douglas Corporation, St. Louis, Missouri.

1823. Moes, Timothy R.; and Whitmore, Stephen A.: **A Preliminary Look at Techniques Used to Obtain Airdata From Flight at High Angles of Attack.** NASA TM-101729, H-1674, NAS 1.15:101729. Presented at the High Angle of Attack Technology Symposium, Hampton, Virginia, October 30– November 1, 1990, <u>December 1990</u>, 91N13453, #.

Flight research at high angles of attack has posed new problems for airdata measurements. New sensors and techniques for measuring the standard airdata quantities of static pressure, dynamic pressure, angle of attack, and angle of sideslip were subsequently developed. The ongoing airdata research supporting NASA's F-18 high alpha research program is updated. Included are the techniques used and the preliminary results. The F-18 aircraft was flown with three research airdata systems: a standard airdata probe on the right wingtip, a self-aligning airdata probe on the left wingtip, and a flush airdata system on the nose cone. The primary research goal was to obtain steady-state calibrations for each airdata system up to an angle of attack of 50 deg. This goal was accomplished and preliminary accuracies of the three airdata systems were assessed and are presented. An effort to improve the fidelity of the airdata measurements during dynamic maneuvering is also discussed. This involved enhancement of the aerodynamic data with data obtained from linear accelerometers, rate gyros, and attitude gyros. Preliminary results of this technique are presented.

1824. Voracek, David F.: **Monitoring Techniques for the X-29A Aircraft's High-Speed Rotating Power Takeoff Shaft.** NASA TM-101731, H-1680, NAS 1.15:101731. Presented at the 2nd International Machinery Monitoring and Diagnostic Conference, Los Angeles, California, October 22–25, 1990, <u>December 1990</u>, 91N19081, #.

The experimental X-29A forward swept-wing aircraft has many unique and critical systems that require constant monitoring during ground or flight operation. One such system is the power takeoff shaft, which is the mechanical link between the engine and the aircraft-mounted accessory drive. The X-29A power takeoff shaft operates in a range between 0 and 16,810 rpm, is longer than most jet engine

power takeoff shafts, and is made of graphite epoxy material. Since the X-29A aircraft operates on a single engine, failure of the shaft during flight could lead to loss of the aircraft. The monitoring techniques and test methods used during power takeoff shaft ground and flight operations are discussed. Test data are presented in two case studies where monitoring and testing of the shaft dynamics proved instrumental in discovering and isolating X-29A power takeoff shaft problems. The first study concerns the installation of an unbalanced shaft. The effect of the unbalance on the shaft vibration data and the procedure used to correct the problem are discussed. The second study deals with the shaft exceeding the established vibration limits during flight. This case study found that the vibration of connected rotating machinery unbalances contributed to the excessive vibration level of the shaft. The procedures used to identify the contributions of other rotating machinery unbalances to the power takeoff shaft unbalance are discussed.

1825. Davis, Steven B.: **Real-Time Application of Advanced Three-Dimensional Graphic Techniques for Research Aircraft Simulation.** NASA TM-101730, H-1642, NAS 1.15:101730, <u>December 1990</u>, 91N19742, #.

Visual aids are valuable assets to engineers for design, demonstration, and evaluation. Discussed here are a variety of advanced three-dimensional graphic techniques used to enhance the displays of test aircraft dynamics. The new software's capabilities are examined and possible future uses are considered.

1826. Whitmore, Stephen A.: **Formulation of a Minimum Variance Deconvolution Technique for Compensation of Pneumatic Distortion in Pressure Sensing Devices.** *Control and Dynamic Systems, Vol. 38— Advances in Aeronautical Systems,* (see A91-50618 21-66), <u>1990</u>, pp. 101–151, 91A50621.

Increasingly, aircraft system designs require that aerodynamic parameters feedbacks. Such high frequency pressure measurements' accuracy is compromised by pressure distortion due to frictional attenuation and pneumatic resonance within the sensing system. A pneumatic distortion model is here formulated and reduced to a low-order state-variable model which retains most of the full model's dynamic characteristics. This reduced-order model is coupled with standard results from minimum variance estimation theory to develop an algorithm to compensate for pneumatic-distortion effects.

1827. Ko, William L.: **Reentry Heat Transfer Analysis of Space Shuttle Orbiter.** Presented at the Symposium on Fluid Dynamics in honor of Professor Theodore Yao-Tsu Wu, California Institute of Technology, Pasadena California, August 17–18, 1989; published in *Engineering Science, Fluid Dynamics—A Symposium to Honor T. Y. Wu,* <u>1990</u>, pp. 209–225.

Reentry heat transfer analysis was performed on the space shuttle orbiter using the finite element method. Several different finite element models having different element densities were used in the analysis, and the solution accuracies and minimum element density requirements were examined in great detail. The effects of internal radiation and internal convection on orbiter structural temperatures were found to be considerable and cannot be neglected. A method of optimization of transient thermal analysis computation efficiencies was discussed, and an optimum element density level was established for analyzing the space shuttle-type structures. The studies formed the foundation for the thermal analysis of future hypersonic flight vehicles.

1991 Technical Publications

1828. Gupta, Kajal K.: **STARS: An Integrated General-Purpose Finite Element Structural, Aeroelastic, and Aeroservoelastic Analysis Computer Program**. NASA TM-101709-REV, H-1582-REV, NAS 1.15:101709-REV, revised January 1991, 91N21587, #.

The details of an integrated general-purpose finite element structural analysis computer program which is also capable of solving complex multidisciplinary problems is presented. Thus, the SOLIDS module of the program possesses an extensive finite element library suitable for modeling most practical problems and is capable of solving statics, vibration, buckling, and dynamic response problems of complex structures, including spinning ones. The aerodynamic module, AERO, enables computation of unsteady aerodynamic forces for both subsonic and supersonic flow for subsequent flutter and divergence analysis of the structure. The associated aeroservoelastic analysis module, ASE, effects aero-structural-control stability analysis yielding frequency responses as well as damping characteristics of the structure. The program is written in standard FORTRAN to run on a wide variety of computers. Extensive graphics, preprocessing, and postprocessing routines are also available pertaining to a number of terminals.

1829. Anon.: **Aerodynamic Heating / Aircraft Performance / Flight Tests / Hypersonic**. NASA-CP-3105, H-1622, NAS 1.55:3105. *Proceedings, X-15 First Flight 30th Anniversary Celebration Symposium*, Edwards, California, June 8, 1989. January 1991, 91N20071, #. (See also N91-20072 through N91-20077.)

A technical symposium and pilot's panel discussion were held on June 8, 1989, to commemorate the 30th anniversary of the first free flight of the X-15 rocket-powered research aircraft. The symposium featured technical presentations by former key government and industry participants in the advocacy, design, manufacturing, and flight research program activities. The X-15's technical contributions to the X-30 are cited. The panel discussion participants included seven of the eight surviving research pilots who flew the X-15 experimental aircraft to world altitude and speed records which still stand. Pilot's remarks include descriptions of their most memorable X-15 flight experience. The report also includes a historical perspective of the X-15.

1830. Williams, Walter C.: **X-15 Concept Evolution**. NASA CP-3105. *NASA Proceedings of the X-15 First Flight 30th Anniversary Celebration*, (see N91-20071 12-05), January 1991, pp. 11–26, 91N20072, #.

The historical events that led to the development of the X-15 research aircraft are presented. Some of the topics presented include: (1) manned airplane performance regions; (2) X-15 flight problems; (3) design characteristics for conceptual aircraft; (4) analysis of X-15 accident potential; (5) X-15 performance requirements; and (6) milestones in the development of the X-15.

1831. Storms, Harrison A., Jr.: **X-15 Hardware Design Challenges**. NASA CP-3105. *NASA Proceedings of the X-15 First Flight 30th Anniversary Celebration*, (see N91-20071 12-05), January 1991, pp. 27–53, 91N20073, #.

Historical events in the development of the X-15 hardware design are presented. Some of the topics covered include: (1) drivers that led to the development of the X-15; (2) X-15 space research objectives; (3) original performance targets; (4) the X-15 typical mission; (5) X-15 dimensions and weight; (5) the propulsion system; (6) X-15 development milestones; (7) engineering and manufacturing challenges; (8) the X-15 structure; (9) ballistic flight control; (10) landing gear; (11) nose gear; and (12) an X-15 program recap.

1832. Hallion, Richard P.: **X-15: The Perspective of History**. NASA CP-3105. *NASA Proceedings of the X-15 First Flight 30th Anniversary Celebration*, (see N91-20071 12-05), January 1991, pp. 54–93, 91N20074, #.

The linkages between the Apollo 11 voyage to Tranquility Base and the 199 flights of the X-15 aircraft are discussed. Accomplishments of the X-15 program and a history of aircraft developments that led up to the X-15 are presented.

1833. Donlan, Charles J.: **The Legacy of the X-15**. NASA CP-3105. *NASA Proceedings of the X-15 First Flight 30th Anniversary Celebration*, (see N91-20071 12-05), January 1991, pp. 94–102, 91N20075, #.

The X-15 established such widespread confidence in aerodynamic, thermal, and structural areas that new designs for operation aircraft for any speed regime could be expected to be successfully achieved if good use was made of all pertinent test facilities and analytical methods. This philosophy guided design of the space shuttle and is the real legacy of the X-15. The accomplishments and contributions attributable to the research and development work on the X-15 that influenced the formative years of the Space Shuttle Program are presented.

1834. Hoey, Robert G.: **X-15 Contributions to the X-30.** NASA CP-3105. *NASA Proceedings of the X-15 First Flight 30th Anniversary Celebration,* (see N91-20071 12-05), January 1991, pp. 103–121, 91N20076, #.

Some of the less publicized flight test results from the X-15 program that might relate to sustained high-speed flight in the atmosphere are presented. The topics covered include: (1) energy management and range considerations; (2) the advantages of pilot-in-the-loop and redundant-emergency systems; (3) a summary of some of the aerodynamic heating problems that were encountered; and (4) some comments on the advantages of an early flight test program and gradual expansion of the flight envelope.

1835. Ishmael, Stephen D.: **What Is the X-30.** NASA CP-3105. *NASA Proceedings of the X-15 First Flight 30th Anniversary Celebration,* (see N91-20071 12-05), January 1991, pp. 122–138, 91N20077, #.

The X-30 is envisioned to be a machine that is capable of exploring technology that is critical to single stage to orbit and to hypersonic cruise. The X-30 is comparable to a laboratory that will be able to investigate such things as the chemistry of supersonic combustion and the control of an of an integrated engine airframe, where the forebody of the airplane is the first compression surface for the propulsion. The X-30 is very ambitious; it follows a path that is pretty well established by such programs as the X-15. This document is limited to a discussion of what is anticipated in the flight tests of the X-30 as opposed to describing the entire vehicle.

1836. Fisher, David F.; Del Frate, John H.; and Zuniga, Fanny A.: **Summary of In-Flight Flow Visualization Obtained From the NASA High Alpha Research Vehicle.** NASA TM-101734, H-1686, NAS 1.15:101734. Presented at the High Angle of Attack Technology Symposium, Hampton, Virginia, October 30–November 1, 1990, January 1991, 91N19055, #.

A summary of the surface and off-surface flow visualization results obtained in flight on the F-18 high alpha research vehicle (HARV) is presented, highlighting the extensive 3-D vortical flow on the aircraft at angles of attack up to 50 degs. The emitted fluid technique, as well as tufts and flow cones, were used to document the surface flow. A smoke generator system injected smoke into the vortex cores generated by the forebody and leading edge extensions (LEXs). Documentation was provided by onboard still and video, by air-to-air, and by postflight photography. The surface flow visualization techniques revealed laminar separation bubbles near the forebody apex, lines of separation on the forebody and LEX, and regions of attached and separated flow on the wings and fins. The off-surface flow visualization techniques showed the path of the vortex cores on the forebody and LEX

as well as the LEX vortex core breakdown location. An interaction between the forebody and LEX vortices was noted. The flow over the surfaces of the vertical tail was categorized into regions of attached, unsteady, or separated flow using flow tufts.

1837. Ko, William L.; and Jackson, Raymond H.: **Thermal Behavior of a Titanium Honeycomb-Core Sandwich Panel.** NASA TM-101732, H-1661, NAS 1.15:101732, January 1991, 91N17433, #.

Finite element thermal stress analysis was performed on a rectangular titanium honeycomb-core sandwich panel which is subjected to thermal load with a temperature gradient across its depth. The distributions of normal stresses in the face sheets and the face-sheet/sandwich-core interfacial shear stresses are presented. The thermal buckling of the heated face sheet was analyzed by assuming the face sheet to be resting on an elastic foundation representing the sandwich core. Thermal buckling curves and thermal buckling load surface are presented for setting the limit for temperature gradient across the panel depth.

1838. Moes, Timothy R.; and Whitmore, Stephen A.: **Preliminary Results From an Airdata Enhancement Algorithm With Application to High-Angle-of-Attack Flight.** AIAA Paper 91-0672. Presented at the AIAA 29th Aerospace Sciences Meeting, Reno, Nevada, January 7–10, 1991, 91A19405, #. (See also 1843.)

A technique has been developed to improve the fidelity of airdata measurements during dynamic maneuvering. This technique is particularly useful for airdata measured during flight at high angular rates and high angles of attack. To support this research, flight tests using the F-18 high alpha research vehicle were conducted at the NASA Ames Research Center Dryden Flight Research Facility. A Kalman filter was used to combine information from research airdata, linear accelerometers, angular rate gyros, and attitude gyros to determine better estimates of airdata quantities such as angle of attack, angle of sideslip, airspeed, and altitude. This paper briefly develops the state and observation equations used by the Kalman filter and shows how the state and measurement covariance matrices were determined from flight data.

1839. Whitmore, Stephen A.; and Moes, Timothy R.: **The Effects of Pressure Sensor Acoustics on Airdata Derived From a High-Angle-of-Attack Flush Airdata Sensing (Hi-FADS) System.** AIAA Paper 91-0671. Presented at the AIAA 29th Aerospace Sciences Meeting, Reno, Nevada, January 7–10, 1991, 91A19404, #. (See also 1842.)

The accuracy of a prototype nonintrusive airdata system derived for high-angle-of-attack measurements was demonstrated for quasi-steady maneuvers as great as

55 degrees during phase one of the F-18 high alpha research vehicle flight test program. This system consists of a matrix of nine pressure ports arranged in annular rings on the aircraft nose, and estimates the complete airdata set utilizing flow modeling and nonlinear regression. Particular attention is paid to the effects of acoustical distortions within the individual pressure sensors of the Hi-FADS pressure matrix. A dynamic model to quantify these effects which describes acoustical distortion is developed and solved in closed form for frequency response.

1840. Geenen, Robert J.; Moulton, Bryan J.; and Haering, Edward A., Jr.: **A System for Testing Airdata Probes at High Angles of Attack Using a Ground Vehicle.** AIAA Paper 91-0088. Presented at the AIAA 29th Aerospace Sciences Meeting, Reno, Nevada, January 7–10, 1991, 91A19129, #.

A system to calibrate airdata probes at angles of attack between 0 and 90 deg was developed and tested at the NASA Ames Dryden Flight Research Facility. This system used a test fixture mounted to the roof of a ground vehicle and included an onboard instrumentation and data acquisition system for measuring pressures and flow angles. The data could be easily transferred to the facility mainframe computer for further analysis. The system was designed to provide convenient and inexpensive airdata probe calibrations for projects which require airdata at high angles of attack, such as the F-18 High Alpha Research Program. This type of probe was tested to 90 deg angle of attack in a wind tunnel and using the ground vehicle system. The results of both tests are in close agreement. An airdata probe with a swiveling pilot-static tube was also calibrated with the ground vehicle system. This paper presents the results of these tests and gives a detailed description of the test system.

1841. *Smith, R. H.; *Chisholm, J. D.; and Stewart, J. F.: **Optimizing Aircraft Performance With Adaptive, Integrated Flight/Propulsion Control.** ASME Paper 90-GT-252. Presented at the ASME, 35th International Gas Turbine and Aeroengine Congress and Exposition, Brussels, Belgium, June 11–14, 1990. *ASME, Transactions, Journal of Engineering for Gas Turbines and Power* (ISSN 0022-0825), Vol. 113, January 1991, pp. 87–94, 91A23644, #.

The Performance-Seeking Control (PSC) integrated flight/propulsion adaptive control algorithm presented was developed in order to optimize total aircraft performance during steady-state engine operation. The PSC multimode algorithm minimizes fuel consumption at cruise conditions, while maximizing excess thrust during aircraft accelerations, climbs, and dashes, and simultaneously extending engine service life through reduction of fan-driving turbine inlet temperature upon engagement of the extended-life mode. The engine models incorporated by the PSC are continually upgraded, using a Kalman filter to detect anomalous

operations. The PSC algorithm will be flight-demonstrated by an F-15 at NASA-Dryden.

*McDonnell Aircraft Co., St. Louis, Missouri.

1842. Whitmore, Stephen A.; and Moes, Timothy R.: **The Effects of Pressure Sensor Acoustics on Airdata Derived From a High-Angle-of-Attack Flush Airdata Sensing (Hi-FADS) System.** NASA TM-101736, H-1690, NAS 1.15:101736. Presented at the AIAA 29th Aerospace Sciences Meeting, Reno, Nevada, January 7–10, 1991, (see A91-19404), February 1991, 91N17060, #. (See also 1839.)

The accuracy of a nonintrusive high angle-of-attack flush airdata sensing (Hi-FADS) system was verified for quasi-steady flight conditions up to 55 deg angle of attack during the F-18 High Alpha Research Vehicle (HARV) Program. The system is a matrix of nine pressure ports arranged in annular rings on the aircraft nose. The complete airdata set is estimated using nonlinear regression. Satisfactory frequency response was verified to the system Nyquist frequency (12.5 Hz). The effects of acoustical distortions within the individual pressure sensors of the nonintrusive pressure matrix on overall system performance are addressed. To quantify these effects, a frequency-response model describing the dynamics of acoustical distortion is developed and simple design criteria are derived. The model adjusts measured Hi-FADS pressure data for the acoustical distortion and quantifies the effects of internal sensor geometries on system performance. Analysis results indicate that sensor frequency response characteristics very greatly with altitude, thus it is difficult to select satisfactory sensor geometry for all altitudes. The solution used presample filtering to eliminate resonance effects, and short pneumatic tubing sections to reduce lag effects. Without presample signal conditioning the system designer must use the pneumatic transmission line to attenuate the resonances and accept the resulting altitude variability.

1843. Moes, Timothy R.; and Whitmore, Stephen A.: **Preliminary Results From an Airdata Enhancement Algorithm With Application to High-Angle-of-Attack Flight.** NASA TM-101737, H-1691, NAS 1.15:101737. Presented at the AIAA 29th Aerospace Sciences Meeting, Reno, Nevada, January 7–10, 1990, (see A91-19405), February 1991, 91N19095, #. (See also 1838.)

A technique was developed to improve the fidelity of airdata measurements during dynamic maneuvering. This technique is particularly useful for airdata measured during flight at high angular rates and high angles of attack. To support this research, flight tests using the F-18 high alpha research vehicle (HARV) were conducted at NASA Ames Research Center, Dryden Flight Research Facility. A Kalman filter was used to combine information from research airdata, linear accelerometers, angular rate gyros, and attitude gyros to determine better estimates of airdata quantities such as angle of attack, angle of sideslip, airspeed, and altitude. The state and observation equations used by the Kalman filter are briefly developed and it is shown how the state and measurement covariance matrices were determined from flight data. Flight data are used to show the results of the technique and these results are compared to an independent measurement source. This technique is applicable to both postflight and real-time processing of data.

1844. *Walchli, Lawrence A.; and Smith, Rogers E.: **Flying Qualities of the X-29 Forward Swept Wing Aircraft.** AGARD CP-508, Paper 19. AGARD, *Flying Qualities*, (ISBN-92-835-0602-2), (see N91-23108 15-05), February 1991, AD-A235323, 91N23127, #.

An overview of the X-29 Forward Swept Wing Technology Demonstrator traces its development and test path during past years. Brief descriptions of the aircraft and its flight control system provide insight for evaluating this unique vehicle. The baseline flight control system provided a starting point for safe concept evaluation and envelope expansion for the aircraft. Subsequent up-dates resulted in performance levels favorably comparable to current fighter aircraft. Efforts are described for the current expansion of the X-29's capabilities into the high angle-of-attack (AOA) regime of flight. Control law changes have permitted all axis maneuvering to 40 deg AOA with pitch excursions to 66 deg, thereby exploiting the full potential of the X-29 forward swept wing configuration.

*Wright Research Development Center, Wright-Patterson AFB, Ohio.

1845. Hudson, Larry D.; and *Thompson, Randolph C.: **Single-Strain-Gage Force/Stiffness Buckling Prediction Techniques on a Hat-Stiffened Panel.** NASA TM-101733, H-1660, NAS 1.15:101733. Presented at the ASME Structures and Materials Conference, Dallas, Texas, November 25–30, 1990, February 1991, 91N19077, #.

Predicting the buckling characteristics of a test panel is necessary to ensure panel integrity developed on a hat-stiffened, monolithic titanium buckling panel. Thed was method is an adaptation of the original force/stiffness method which requires back-to-back gages. The single-gage method was developed because the test panel did not have back-to-back gages. The method was used to predict buckling loads and temperatures under various heating and loading conditions. The results correlated well with a finite element buckling analysis. The single-gage force/stiffness method was a valid real-time and post-test buckling prediction technique.

*PRC Inc., Edwards, California.

1846. Berry, Donald T.: **National Aerospace Plane Longitudinal Long-Period Dynamics.** *Journal of Guidance, Control, and Dynamics* (ISSN 0731-5090), Vol. 14, January–February 1991, (see A88-50601), February 1991, pp. 205–206, 91A22962, #. (See also 1661.)

1847. Bever, Glenn A.: **Digital Signal Conditioning for Flight Test Instrumentation.** NASA TM-101739, H-1695, NAS 1.15:101739, AGARDOGRAPH-160, Vol. 19, March 1991, 91N21135, #. (See also 1863.)

An introduction to digital measurement processes on aircraft is provided. Flight test instrumentation systems are rapidly evolving from analog-intensive to digital intensive systems, including the use of onboard digital computers. The topics include measurements that are digital in origin, as well as sampling, encoding, transmitting, and storing data. Particular emphasis is placed on modern avionic data bus architectures and what to be aware of when extracting data from them. Examples of data extraction techniques are given. Tradeoffs between digital logic families, trends in digital development, and design testing techniques are discussed. An introduction to digital filtering is also covered.

1848. Kehoe, Michael W.; and *Snyder, H. Todd: **Thermoelastic Vibration Test Techniques.** NASA TM-101742, H-1707, NAS 1.15:101742. Presented at the 9th International Modal Analysis Conference, Florence, Italy, April 14–18, 1991, April 1991, 91N19083, #. (See also 1849.)

The structural integrity of proposed high speed aircraft can be seriously affected by the extremely high surface temperatures and large temperature gradients throughout the vehicle's structure. Variations in the structure's elastic characteristics as a result of thermal effects can be observed by changes in vibration frequency, damping, and mode shape. Analysis codes that predict these changes must be correlated and verified with experimental data. The experimental modal test techniques and procedures used to conduct uniform, nonuniform, and transient thermoelastic vibration tests are presented. Experimental setup and elevated temperature instrumentation considerations are also discussed. Modal data for a 12 by 50 inch aluminum plate heated to a temperature of 475 F are presented. These data show the effect of heat on the plate's modal characteristics. The results indicated that frequency decreased, damping increased, and mode shape remained unchanged as the temperature of the plate was increased.

*PRC Inc., Edwards, California.

1849. Kehoe, Michael W.; and *Snyder, H. T.: **Thermoelastic Vibration Test Techniques.** *Proceedings, 9th International Modal Analysis Conference (IMAC)*, Florence, Italy, April 15–18, 1991, Vol. 2 (see A93-29227 10-39), (see N91-19083), 1991, pp. 1473–1484, 93A29293. (See also 1848.)

The structural integrity of proposed high speed aircraft can be seriously affected by the extremely high surface temperatures and large temperature gradients throughout the vehicle's structure. Variations in the structure's elastic characteristics as a result of thermal effects can be observed by changes in vibration frequency, damping, and mode shape. Analysis codes that predict these changes must be correlated and verified with experimental data. The experimental modal test techniques and procedures used to conduct uniform, nonuniform, and transient thermoelastic vibration tests are presented. Experimental setup and elevated temperature instrumentation considerations are also discussed. Modal data for a 12 by 50 inch aluminum plate heated to a temperature of 475 F are presented. These data show the effect of heat on the plate's modal characteristics. The results indicated that frequency decreased, damping increased, and mode shape remained unchanged as the temperature of the plate was increased.

*PRC Inc., Edwards, California.

1850. Mackall, Dale A.; and *Allen, James G.: **A Knowledge-Based System Design/Information Tool for Aircraft Flight Control Systems**. AGARD-CP-474, Paper 18. *Knowledge Based System Applications for Guidance and Control*, (ISBN-92-835-0610-3), (see N91-25121 17-04), April 1991, AD-A235715, 91N25139, #. (See also 1740, 1741.)

Research aircraft have become increasingly dependent on advanced electronic control systems to accomplish program goals. These aircraft are integrating multiple disciplines to improve performance and satisfy research objective. This integration is being accomplished through electronic control systems. Systems design methods and information management have become essential to program success. The primary objective of the system design/information tool for aircraft flight control is to help transfer flight control system design knowledge to the flight test community. By providing all of the design information and covering multiple disciplines in a structured, graphical manner, flight control systems can more easily be understood by the test engineers. This will provide the engineers with the information needed to thoroughly ground test the system and thereby reduce the likelihood of serious design errors surfacing in flight. The secondary object is to apply structured design techniques to all of the design domains. By using the techniques in the top level system design down through the detailed hardware and software designs, it is hoped that fewer design anomalies will result. The flight test experiences are reviewed of three highly complex, integrated aircraft programs: the X-29 forward swept wing; the advanced fighter technology integration (AFTI) F-16; and the highly maneuverable aircraft technology (HiMAT) program. Significant operating technologies, and the design errors which cause them, is examined to help identify what functions a system design/

information tool should provide to assist designers in avoiding errors.

*Draper Laboratory, Inc., Cambridge, Massachusetts.

1851. Voracek, David F.; and Clarke, Robert: **Buffet Induced Structural/Flight-Control System Interaction of the X-29A Aircraft.** NASA TM-101735, H-1687, NAS 1.15:101735, Paper-91-1053. Presented at the 32nd AIAA Structures, Structural Dynamics, and Materials Conference, Baltimore, Maryland, April 8–10, 1991, (see A91-32012), April 1991, 91N23133, #. (See also 1852, 2076.)

High angle-of-attack flight regime research is currently being conducted for modern fighter aircraft at the NASA Ames Research Center's Dryden Flight Research Facility. This flight regime provides enhanced maneuverability to fighter pilots in combat situations. Flight research data are being acquired to compare and validate advanced computational fluid dynamic solutions and wind-tunnel models. High angle-of-attack flight creates unique aerodynamic phenomena including wing rock and buffet on the airframe. These phenomena increase the level of excitation of the structural modes, especially on the vertical and horizontal stabilizers. With high gain digital flight-control systems, this structural response may result in an aeroservoelastic interaction. A structural interaction on the X-29A aircraft was observed during high angle-of-attack flight testing. The roll and yaw rate gyros sensed the aircraft's structural modes at 11, 13, and 16 Hz. The rate gyro output signals were then amplified through the flight-control laws and sent as commands to the flaperons and rudder. The flight data indicated that as the angle of attack increased, the amplitude of the buffet on the vertical stabilizer increased, which resulted in more excitation to the structural modes. The flight-control system sensors and command signals showed this increase in modal power at the structural frequencies up to a 30 degree angle-of-attack. Beyond a 30 degree angle-of-attack, the vertical stabilizer response, the feedback sensor amplitude, and control surface command signal amplitude remained relatively constant. Data are presented that show the increased modal power in the aircraft structural accelerometers, the feedback sensors, and the command signals as a function of angle of attack. This structural interaction is traced from the aerodynamic buffet to the flight-control surfaces.

1852. Voracek, David F.; and Clarke, Robert: **Buffet Induced Structural/Flight-Control System Interaction of the X-29A Aircraft.** AIAA Paper 91-1053. *Technical Papers*, presented at the AIAA, ASME, ASCE, AHS, and ASC 32nd Structures, Structural Dynamics, and Materials Conference, Baltimore, Maryland, April 8–10, 1991, Pt. 3, (see A91-31826 12–39), pp. 1779–1790, 91A32012, #. (See also 1851, 2076.)

High-alpha flight creates unique aerodynamic phenomena which increase the level of structural mode excitation; in conjunction with high-gain digital control systems, this structural response may result in an aeroservoelastic interaction. One such interaction has been observed during high-alpha flight testing of the X-29A. Data are presented which demonstrate the enhanced modal power in this aircraft's structural accelerometers, the feedback sensors, and the command signals as a function of alpha value. The structural interaction is traced from the aerodynamic buffet to the flight-control surfaces.

1853. Pahle, Joseph W.; Powers, Bruce; Regenie, Victoria; Chacon, Vince; *Degroote, Steve; and *Murnyak, Steven: **Research Flight-Control System Development for the F-18 High Alpha Research Vehicle**. NASA TM-104232, H-1715, NAS 1.15:104232. Presented at the High-Angle-of-Attack Technology Conference, Hampton, Virginia, October 30–November 1, 1990, <u>April 1991</u>, 91N22131, #.

The F-18 high alpha research vehicle was recently modified by adding a thrust vectoring control system. A key element in the modification was the development of a research flight control system integrated with the basic F-18 flight control system. Discussed here are design requirements, system development, and research utility of the resulting configuration as an embedded system for flight research in the high angle of attack regime. Particular emphasis is given to control system modifications and control law features required for high angle of attack flight. Simulation results are used to illustrate some of the thrust vectoring control system capabilities and predicted maneuvering improvements.

*McDonnell Aircraft Co., St. Louis, Missouri.

EC91-075-38

F-18 HARV With Thrust Vectoring

1854. *Snyder, H. Todd; and Kehoe, Michael W.: **Determination of the Effects of Heating on Modal Characteristics of an Aluminum Plate With Application to Hypersonic Vehicles**. NASA TM-4274, H-1688, NAS 1.15:4274, <u>April 1991</u>, 91N22111, #.

The structural integrity of proposed high speed aircraft can be seriously affected by the extremely high surface temperatures and large temperature gradients throughout the vehicle's structure. Variations in the structure's elastic characteristics as a result of thermal effects can be seen by changes in vibration characteristics. Analysis codes that predict these changes must be correlated and verified with experimental data. Analytical and experimental modal test results are given from uniform, nonuniform, and transient thermoelastic vibration tests of a 12 x 50 x 0.19 aluminum plate. The data show the effect of heat on the modal characteristics of the plate. The results showed that frequencies decreased, damping increased, and mode shapes remained unchanged as the temperature of the plate increased. Analytical predictions provided good correlation with experimental results.

*PRC Inc., Edwards, California.

1855. Bowers, Albion H.; Noffz, Gregory K.; *Grafton, Sue B.; *Mason, Mary L.; and **Peron, Lee R.: **Multiaxis Thrust Vectoring Using Axisymmetric Nozzles and Postexit Vanes on an F/A-18 Configuration Vehicle**. NASA TM-101741, H-1705, NAS 1.15:101741. Presented at the High-Angle-of-Attack Technology Conference, Hampton, Virginia, October 30–November 1, 1990, <u>April 1991</u>, 91N22083, #.

A ground-based investigation was conducted on an operational system of multiaxis thrust vectoring using postexit vanes around an axisymmetric nozzle. This thrust vectoring system will be tested on the NASA F/A-18 High Alpha Research Vehicle (HARV) aircraft. The system provides thrust vectoring capability in both pitch and yaw. Ground based data were gathered from two separate tests at NASA Langley Research Center. The first was a static test in the 16-foot Transonic Tunnel Cold-Jet Facility with a 14.25 percent scale model of the axisymmetric nozzle and the postexit vanes. The second test was conducted in the 30 by 60 foot wind tunnel with a 16 percent F/A-18 complete configuration model. Data from the two sets are being used to develop models of jet plume deflection and thrust loss as a function of vane deflection. In addition, an aerodynamic interaction model based on plume deflection angles will be developed. Results from the scale model nozzle test showed that increased vane deflection caused exhaust plume turning. Aerodynamic interaction effects consisted primarily of favorable interaction of moments and unfavorable interaction of forces caused by the vectored jet plume.

*NASA Langley Research Center, Hampton, Virginia.
**California Polytechnic State University, San Luis Obispo, California.

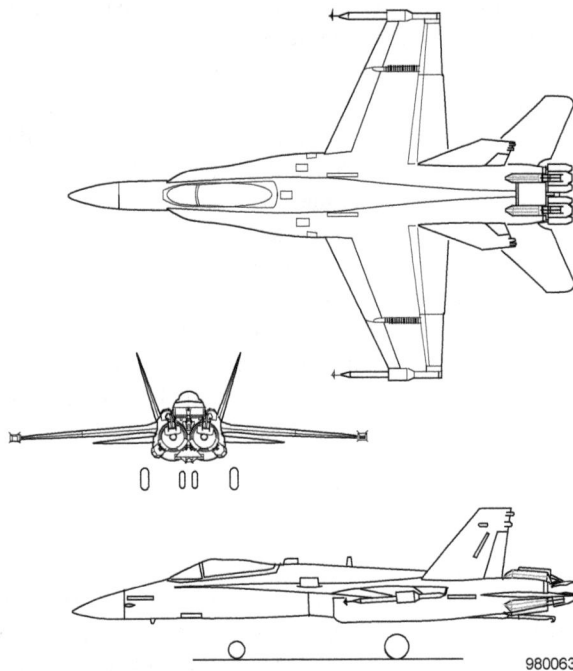

F-18 HARV With Thrust Vectoring, Three-View Drawing

1856. *Shelley, S.; *Allemang, R. J.; Freudinger, L.; and **Zhang, Q.: **Implementation of a Modal Filter on a Five Meter Truss Structure.** *Proceedings, 9th International Modal Analysis Conference (IMAC)*, Florence, Italy, April 15–18, 1991, Vol. 2, (see A93-29227 10–39), 1991, pp. 1036–1044, 93A29285.

Modal filtering is a spatial filtering technique which uses a weighted sum of a number of response measurements to extract the modal coordinates of the system from the physical response coordinates. No moving average or autoregressive calculations are required to implement the modal filter thus the modal coordinates may be calculated in real time. For practical implementation of the modal filter, the number and location of response locations must be chosen carefully. A modal filter is implemented on a five meter model space truss as a case study. The modal coordinates are extracted in real time using Hewlett Packard 3565 data acquisition and processing hardware. The effect of the number and location of response measurements on the performance of the modal filter is investigated. Applications of the modal filter to modal control and fast parameter identification are also discussed.

* University of Cincinnati, Ohio.
**RNUR, Rueil-Malmaison, France.

1857. Fisher, David F.; Del Frate, John H.; and *Richwine, David M.: **In-Flight Flow Visualization Characteristics of the NASA F-18 High Alpha Research Vehicle at High Angles of Attack.** NASA TM-4193, H-1576, NAS 1.15:4193, May 1991, 91N20055, #. (See also 1734.)

Surface and off-surface flow visualization techniques were used to visualize the 3-D separated flows on the NASA F-18 high alpha research vehicle at high angles of attack. Results near the alpha = 25 to 26 deg and alpha = 45 to 49 deg are presented. Both the forebody and leading edge extension (LEX) vortex cores and breakdown locations were visualized using smoke. Forebody and LEX vortex separation lines on the surface were defined using an emitted fluid technique. A laminar separation bubble was also detected on the nose cone using the emitted fluid technique and was similar to that observed in the wind tunnel test, but not as extensive. Regions of attached, separated, and vortical flow were noted on the wing and the leading edge flap using tufts and flow cones, and compared well with limited wind tunnel results (includes color photos).

*PRC Inc., Edwards, California.

1858. Gupta, K. K.; Brenner, M. J.; and Voelker, L. S.: **Development of an Integrated Aeroservoelastic Analysis Program and Correlation With Test Data.** NASA TP-3120, H-1543, NAS 1.60:3120, May 1991, 91N26113, #.

The details and results are presented of the general-purpose finite element STructural Analysis RoutineS (STARS) to perform a complete linear aeroelastic and aeroservoelastic analysis. The earlier version of the STARS computer program enabled effective finite element modeling as well as static, vibration, buckling, and dynamic response of damped and undamped systems, including those with pre-stressed and spinning structures. Additions to the STARS program include aeroelastic modeling for flutter and divergence solutions, and hybrid control system augmentation for aeroservoelastic analysis. Numerical results of the X-29A aircraft pertaining to vibration, flutter-divergence, and open- and closed-loop aeroservoelastic controls analysis are compared to ground vibration, wind-tunnel, and flight-test results. The open- and closed-loop aeroservoelastic control analyses are based on a hybrid formulation representing the interaction of structural, aerodynamic, and flight-control dynamics.

1859. Ko, William L.; and Jackson, Raymond H.: **Combined Compressive and Shear Buckling Analysis of Hypersonic Aircraft Structural Sandwich Panels.** NASA TM-4290, H-1694, NAS 1.15:4290, May 1991, 91N25422, #. (See also 1928.)

The combined-load (compression and shear) buckling equations were established for orthotropic sandwich panels by using the Rayleigh-Ritz method to minimize the panel total potential energy. The resulting combined-load buckling equations were used to generate buckling interaction curves for super-plastically-formed/diffusion-bonded titanium truss-core sandwich panels and titanium honeycomb-core sandwich panels having the same specific weight. The relative combined-load buckling strengths of these two types of sandwich panels are compared with consideration of their sandwich orientations. For square and nearly square panels of both types, the combined load always induces symmetric buckling. As the panel aspect ratios increase, antisymmetric buckling will show up when the loading is shear-dominated combined loading. The square panel (either type) has the highest combined buckling strength, but the combined load buckling strength drops sharply as the panel aspect ratio increases. For square panels, the truss-core sandwich panel has higher compression-dominated combined load buckling strength. However, for shear dominated loading, the square honeycomb-core sandwich panel has higher shear-dominated combined load buckling strength.

1860. Lambert, Heather H.: **A Simulation Study of Turbofan Engine Deterioration Estimation Using Kalman Filtering Techniques**. NASA TM-104233, H-1616, NAS 1.15:104233, June 1991, 91N25147, #.

Deterioration of engine components may cause off-normal engine operation. The result is an unnecessary loss of performance, because the fixed schedules are designed to accommodate a wide range of engine health. These fixed control schedules may not be optimal for a deteriorated engine. This problem may be solved by including a measure of deterioration in determining the control variables. These engine deterioration parameters usually cannot be measured directly but can be estimated. A Kalman filter design is presented for estimating two performance parameters that account for engine deterioration: high and low pressure turbine delta efficiencies. The delta efficiency parameters model variations of the high and low pressure turbine efficiencies from nominal values. The filter has a design condition of Mach 0.90, 30,000 ft altitude, and 47 deg power level angle (PLA). It was evaluated using a nonlinear simulation of the F100 engine model derivative (EMD) engine, at the design Mach number and altitude over a PLA range of 43 to 55 deg. It was found that known high pressure turbine delta efficiencies of –2.5 percent and low pressure turbine delta efficiencies of –1.0 percent can be estimated with an accuracy of + or –0.25 percent efficiency with a Kalman filter. If both the high and low pressure turbine are deteriorated, the delta efficiencies of –2.5 percent to both turbines can be estimated with the same accuracy.

1861. Bjarke, Lisa J.: **Flow Visualization Study of a 1/48-Scale AFTI/F111 Model to Investigate Horizontal Tail Flow Disturbances**. NASA TM-101698, H-1547, NAS 1.15:101698, June 1991, 91N24128, #.

During flight testing of the AFTI/F111 aircraft, horizontal tail buffet was observed. Flutter analysis ruled out any aeroelastic instability, so a water-tunnel flow visualization study was conducted to investigate possible flow disturbances on the horizontal tail which might cause buffet. For this study, a 1/48-scale model was used. Four different wing cambers and one horizontal tail setting were tested between 0 and 20 deg angle of attack. These wing cambers corresponded to the following leading training edge deflections: 0/2, 10/10, 10/2, and 0/10. Flow visualization results in the form of still photographs are presented for each of the four wing cambers between 8 and 12 deg angle of attack. In general, the horizontal tail experiences flow disturbances which become more pronounced with angle of attack or wing trailing-edge deflection.

1862. *Stephens, Craig A.; and **Hanna, Gregory J.: **Thermal Modeling and Analysis of a Cryogenic Tank Design Exposed to Extreme Heating Profiles**. AIAA Paper 91-1383. Presented at the AIAA 26th Thermophysics Conference, Honolulu, Hawaii, June 24–26, 1991, 91A43447, #.

A cryogenic test article, the Generic Research Cryogenic Tank, was designed to qualitatively simulate the thermal response of transatmospheric vehicle fuel tanks exposed to the environment of hypersonic flight. One-dimensional and two-dimensional finite-difference thermal models were developed to simulate the thermal response and assist in the design of the Generic Research Cryogenic Tank. The one-dimensional thermal analysis determined the required insulation thickness to meet the thermal design criteria and located the purge jacket to eliminate the liquefaction of air. The two-dimensional thermal analysis predicted the temperature gradients developed within the pressure-vessel wall, estimated the cryogen boiloff, and showed the effects the ullage condition has on pressure-vessel temperatures. The degree of ullage mixing, location of the applied high-temperature profile, and the purge gas influence on insulation thermal conductivity had significant effects on the thermal behavior of the Generic Research Cryogenic Tank. In addition to analysis results, a description of the Generic Research Cryogenic Tank and the role it will play in future thermal structures and transatmospheric vehicle research at the NASA Dryden Flight Research Facility is presented.

* PRC Inc., Edwards, California.
** Hanna Technology Resources, Boulder, Colorado.

1863. Bever, G. A.: **Digital Signal Conditioning for Flight Test, Volume 19.** AGARD-AG-160-VOL-19, (ISBN-92-835-0621-9), AD-A240140, June 1991, 91N26432, #. (See also 1847.)

Flight test instrumentation engineers are provided with an introduction to digital processes on aircraft. Flight test instrumentation systems are rapidly evolving from analog intensive to digital intensive systems, including the use of onboard digital computers. Topics include: measurements that are digital in origin, sampling, encoding, transmitting, and storing of data. Particular emphasis is placed on modern avionic data bus architectures and what to be aware of when extracting data from them. Some example data extractions are given. Tradeoffs between digital logic families, trends in digital development, and design testing techniques are discussed. An introduction to digital filtering is also covered.

1864. Gilyard, Glenn B.; Conley, Joseph L.; Le, Jeanette; and Burcham, Frank W., Jr.: **A Simulation Evaluation of a Four-Engine Jet Transport Using Engine Thrust Modulation for Flightpath Control.** AIAA Paper 91-2223. Presented at the AIAA, SAE, ASME, and ASEE, 27th Joint Propulsion Conference, Sacramento, California, June 24–26, 1991, 91A44162, #. (See also 1883.)

The use of throttle control laws to provide adequate flying qualities for flightpath control in the event of a total loss of conventional flight control surface use was evaluated. The results are based on a simulation evaluation by transport research pilots of a B-720 transport with visual display. Throttle augmentation control laws can provide flightpath control capable of landing a transport-type aircraft with up to moderate levels of turbulence. The throttle augmentation mode dramatically improves the pilots' ability to control flightpath for the approach and landing flight condition using only throttle modulation. For light turbulence, the average Cooper-Harper pilot rating improved from unacceptable to acceptable (a pilot rating improvement of 4.5) in going from manual to augmented control. The low frequency response characteristics of the engines require a considerably different piloting technique. The various techniques used by the pilots resulted in considerable scatter in the data. Many pilots readily adapted to a good piloting technique while some has difficulty. The research demonstrates a new and viable approach to providing an independent means of redundancy or increasing the redundancy capability of transport aircraft flightpath control.

1865. Lambert, H. H.; Gilyard, G. B.; *Chisholm, J. D.; and **Kerr, L. J.: **Preliminary Flight Evaluation of an Engine Performance Optimization Algorithm.** AIAA Paper 91-1998. Presented at the AIAA, SAE, ASME, and ASEE, 27th Joint Propulsion Conference, Sacramento, California, June 24–26, 1991, 91A44089, #. (See also 1892.)

A performance-seeking control (PSC) algorithm has undergone initial flight test evaluation in subsonic operation of a PW 1128-engine F-15; this algorithm is designed to optimize the quasi-steady performance of an engine for three primary modes: (1) minimum fuel consumption, (2) minimum fan-turbine inlet temperature (FTIT), and (3) maximum thrust. The flight test results have verified a thrust-specific fuel consumption reduction of 1 percent, up to 100 R decreases in FTIT, and increases of as much as 12 percent in maximum thrust. PSC technology promises to be of value in next-generation tactical and transport aircraft.

*McDonnell Aircraft Co., St. Louis, Missouri.
**Pratt and Whitney Group, West Palm Beach, Florida.

1866. *Flores, Jolen; *Tu, Eugene; Anderson, Bianca; and Landers, Stephen: **A Parametric Study of the Leading Edge Attachment Line for the F-16XL.** AIAA Paper 91-1621. Presented at the AIAA, 22nd Fluid Dynamics, Plasma Dynamics and Lasers Conference, Honolulu, Hawaii, June 24–26, 1991, 91A43555, #.

A three-dimensional Navier-Stokes code is used to computationally simulate the flow about a modified F-16XL. Transition mechanisms (e.g. attachment line location and crossflow instability) near the swept wing leading edge are analyzed in detail. Flow visualization is used to study the influence of angle-of-attack on the aforementioned transition mechanisms. Validation of the code is accomplished by comparison of numerically generated surface pressures with that obtained by in-flight experiments.

*NASA Ames Research Center, Moffett Field, California.

EC92-09032-2

F-16XL-1 With LFC Glove

1867. Burcham, F. W., Jr.; Fullerton, C. G.; Gilyard, Glenn B.; Wolf, Thomas D.; and Stewart, James F.: **A Preliminary Investigation of the Use of Throttles for Emergency Flight Control.** AIAA Paper 91-2222. Presented at the AIAA, SAE, ASME, and ASEE, 27th Joint Propulsion Conference, Sacramento, California, June 24–26, 1991, 91A41731, #. (See also 1881.)

A preliminary investigation was conducted regarding the use of throttles for emergency flight control of a multiengine aircraft. Several airplanes including a light twin-engine piston-powered airplane, jet transports, and a high performance fighter were studied during flight and piloted simulations. Simulation studies used the B-720, B-727, MD-11, and F-15 aircraft. Flight studies used the Lear 24, Piper PA-30, and F-15 airplanes. Based on simulator and flight results, all the airplanes exhibited some control capability with throttles. With piloted simulators, landings using manual throttles-only control were extremely difficult. An augmented control system was developed that converts conventional pilot stick inputs into appropriate throttle commands. With the augmented system, the B-720 and F-15 simulations were evaluated and could be landed successfully. Flight and simulation data were compared for the F-15 airplane.

ECN-2845

PA-30 Aircraft

1868. Del Frate, John H.; Fisher, David F.; and Zuniga, Fanny A.: **In-Flight Flow Visualization and Pressure Measurements at Low Speeds on the NASA F-18 High Alpha Research Vehicle**. AGARD-CP-494, Paper 13. *Vortex Flow Aerodynamics* (ISBN-92-835-0623-5), (see N92-12996 04–02), July 1991, AD-A244249, 92N13009, #. (See also 1807.)

Inflight results from surface and off surface flow visualizations and from extensive pressure distributions document the vortical flow on the leading edge extensions (LEXs) and forebody of the NASA F-18 high alpha research vehicle (HARV) for low speeds and angles of attack up to 50 deg. Surface flow visualization data, obtained using the emitted fluid technique, were used to define separation lines and laminar separation bubbles (LSB). Off surface flow visualization data, obtained by smoke injection, were used to document both the path of the vortex cores and the location

of vortex core breakdown. The location of vortex core breakdown correlated well with the loss of suction pressure on the LEX and with the flow visualization results from ground facilities. Surface flow separation lines on the LEX and forebody corresponded well with the end of pressure recovery under the vortical flows. Correlation of the pressures with wind tunnel results show fair to good correlation.

1869. *Hanna, Gregory J.; and **Stephens, Craig A.: **Predicted Thermal Response of a Cryogenic Fuel Tank Exposed to Simulated Aerodynamic Heating Profiles With Different Cryogens and Fill Levels**. AIAA Paper 91-4007. Presented at the ASME 1991 National Heat Transfer Conference, Minneapolis, Minnesota, July 28–31, 1991, 91A45461, #. (See also A-204)

A two-dimensional finite-difference thermal model was developed for the Generic Research Cryogenic Tank (GRCT). The model was used to predict the effects of heating profile, fill level, and cryogen type prior to experimental testing. These numerical predictions will assist in defining test scenarios, sensor locations, and venting requirements for the GRCT experimental tests. Boiloff rates, tank-wall and fluid temperatures, and wall heat fluxes were determined for 20 computational test cases. The test cases spanned three discrete fill levels and three heating profiles for hydrogen and nitrogen. Large temperature gradients developed in the vapor region of the tank when the vapor was allowed to stratify, but vapor mixing greatly reduced the top-to-bottom temperature gradient. The thermal response of the GRCT was qualitatively similar to anticipated transatmospheric vehicle (TAV) behavior. Nitrogen simulations deviated from hydrogen simulations in several key areas, particularly where the vapor heat capacity contributed to the system thermal response. The internal radiation and wall-to-vapor heat transfer effects were small compared with the effect of vapor mixing.

*Hanna Technology Resources, Boulder, Colorado.
**PRC Inc., Edwards, California.

1870. Ko, William L.; and Jackson, Raymond H.: **Compressive Buckling Analysis of Hat-Stiffened Panel**. NASA TM-4310, H-1724, NAS 1.15:4310, August 1991, 91N27592, #.

Buckling analysis was performed on a hat-stiffened panel subjected to uniaxial compression. Both local buckling and global buckling were analyzed. It was found that the global buckling load was several times higher than the buckling load. The predicted local buckling loads compared favorably with both experimental data and finite-element analysis.

1871. *Daysh, Colin; *Corbin, Malcolm; *Butler, Geoff; Duke, Eugene L.; **Belle, Steven D.; and **Brumbaugh, Randal W.: **A NASA/RAE Cooperation in the Development of a Real-Time Knowledge-Based**

Autopilot. NASA TM-104234, H-1727, NAS 1.15:104234. Presented at the Avionics Panel Symposium, Lisbon, Portugal, May 1991, <u>August 1991</u>, 91N32850, #. (See also 1885.)

As part of a US/UK cooperative aeronautical research program, a joint activity between the NASA Dryden Flight Research Facility and the Royal Aerospace Establishment on knowledge-based systems was established. This joint activity is concerned with tools and techniques for the implementation and validation of real-time knowledge-based systems. The proposed next stage of this research is described, in which some of the problems of implementing and validating a knowledge-based autopilot for a generic high-performance aircraft are investigated.

*Royal Aerospace Establishment, Farnborough, England.
**PRC Inc., Edwards, California.

1872. Schilling, Larry; and *Bolen, Dave: **NASA Ames-Dryden Integrated Test Facility: Presentation Outline.** NASA CP-10081. *Proceedings, Control Center Technology Conference,* NASA Johnson Space Center, (see N92-12010 03-14) <u>August 1991</u>, pp. 83–105, 92N12014, #.

The topics are presented in view graph form and include the following: (1) a Dryden overview; (2) the Integrated Tests Facility (ITF); (3) the ITF system architecture; (4) the computer aided system testing; and (5) the ITF system video.

*Computer Sciences Corporation, Moffett Field, California.

1873. Powers, Sheryll G.: **Flight Tests of External Modifications Used to Reduce Blunt Base Drag.** *Technical Papers,* presented at the AIAA 6th Applied Aerodynamics Conference, Williamsburg, Virginia, June 6–8, 1988, pp. 615–628. *Journal of Aircraft,* (ISSN 0021-8669), Vol. 28, August 1991, (see A88-40763), <u>August 1991</u>, pp. 517–525, 91A48821. (See also 1645, 1646.)

1874. Hicks, John W.: **Propulsion Modeling Techniques and Applications for the NASA Dryden X-30 Real-Time Simulator.** AIAA Paper 91-2937. *Technical Papers,* presented at the AIAA Flight Simulation Technologies Conference, New Orleans, Louisiana, <u>August 12–14, 1991</u>, (see A91-47801 20-01), pp. 210–223, 91A47824, #.

An overview is given of the flight planning activities to date in the current National Aero-Space Plane (NASP) program. The government flight-envelope expansion concept and other design flight operational assessments are discussed. The NASA Dryden NASP real-time simulator configuration is examined and hypersonic flight planning simulation propulsion modeling requirements are described. The major propulsion modeling techniques developed by the Edwards flight test team are outlined, and the application value of techniques for developmental hypersonic vehicles are discussed.

1875. Cohen, Dorothea; and Le, Jeanette H.: **The Role of the Remotely Augmented Vehicle (RAV) Laboratory in Flight Research.** AIAA Paper 91-2977. *Technical Papers,* presented at the AIAA Flight Simulation Technologies Conference, New Orleans, Louisiana, <u>August 12–14, 1991,</u> (see A91-47801 20–01), pp. 24–36, 91A47804, #. (See also 1882.)

This paper presents on overview of the unique capabilities and historical significance of the Remotely Augmented Vehicle (RAV) Laboratory at the NASA Dryden Flight Research Facility. The report reviews the role of the RAV Laboratory in enhancing flight test programs and efficient testing of new aircraft control laws. The history of the RAV Laboratory is discussed with a sample of its application using the X-29 aircraft. The RAV Laboratory allows for closed- or open-loop augmentation of the research aircraft while in flight using ground-based, high performance real-time computers. Telemetry systems transfer sensor and control data between the ground and the aircraft. The RAV capability provides for enhanced computational power, improved flight data quality, and alternate methods for the testing of control system concepts. The Laboratory is easily reconfigured to reflect changes within a flight program and can be adapted to new flight programs.

1876. Shafer, Mary F.: **In-Flight Simulation at the NASA Dryden Flight Research Facility.** AIAA Paper 91-2916. *Technical Papers,* presented at the AIAA Flight Simulation Technologies Conference, New Orleans, Louisiana, <u>August 12–14, 1991,</u> (see A91-47801 20-01), pp. 7–23, 91A47803, #. (See also 1942, 2075.)

An account of the in-flight simulation at the Dryden Flight Research Facility is presented and various aircraft and tests performed are discussed. In-flight simulation has been utilized for a variety of flying quality investigations including low-lift-to-drag ratio approach characteristics for vehicles like the X-15, the lifting bodies, and the Space Shuttle. Consideration is given to the effects of time delays on controllability of aircraft with digital flight-control systems, flight control systems for such aircraft as the X-29, and the causes and cures of pilot-induced oscillation in diverse aircraft.

1877. Ko, William L.; and Jackson, Raymond H.: **Combined-Load Buckling Behavior of Metal-Matrix Composite Sandwich Panels Under Different Thermal Environments.** NASA TM-4321, H-1714, NAS 1.15:4321, <u>September 1991</u>, 91N30563, #.

Combined compressive and shear buckling analysis was conducted on flat rectangular sandwich panels with the consideration of transverse shear effects of the core. The sandwich panel is fabricated with titanium honeycomb core and laminated metal matrix composite face sheets. The results show that the square panel has the highest combined load buckling strength, and that the buckling strength decreases sharply with the increases of both temperature and panel aspect ratio. The effect of layup (fiber orientation) on the buckling strength of the panels was studied in detail. The metal matrix composite sandwich panel was much more efficient than the sandwich panel with nonreinforced face sheets and had the same specific weight.

1878. Antoniewicz, Robert F.; Duke, Eugene L.; and *Menon, P. K. A.: **Application and Flight Test of Linearizing Transformations Using Measurement Feedback to the Nonlinear Control Problem.** NASA TP-3154, H-1629, NAS 1.60:3154, September 1991, 91N30154, #.

The design of nonlinear controllers has relied on the use of detailed aerodynamic and engine models that must be associated with the control law in the flight system implementation. Many of these controllers were applied to vehicle flight path control problems and have attempted to combine both inner- and outer-loop control functions in a single controller. An approach to the nonlinear trajectory control problem is presented. This approach uses linearizing transformations with measurement feedback to eliminate the need for detailed aircraft models in outer-loop control applications. By applying this approach and separating the inner-loop and outer-loop functions two things were achieved: (1) the need for incorporating detailed aerodynamic models in the controller is obviated; and (2) the controller is more easily incorporated into existing aircraft flight control systems. An implementation of the controller is discussed, and this controller is tested on a six degree-of-freedom F-15 simulation and in flight on an F-15 aircraft. Simulation data are presented which validates this approach over a large portion of the F-15 flight envelope. Proof of this concept is provided by flight-test data that closely matches simulation results. Flight-test data are also presented.

*Georgia Institute of Technology, Atlanta, Georgia.

1879. Sim, Alex G.: **Modeling, Simulation, and Flight Characteristics of an Aircraft Designed to Fly at 100,000 Feet.** NASA TM-104236, H-1731, NAS 1.15:104236, September 1991, 91N30153, #.

A manned real time simulation of a conceptual vehicle, the stratoplane, was developed to study the problems associated with the flight characteristics of a large, lightweight vehicle. Mathematical models of the aerodynamics, mass properties, and propulsion system were developed in support of the simulation and are presented. The simulation was at first conducted without control augmentation to determine the needs for a control system. The unaugmented flying qualities were dominated by lightly damped dutch roll oscillations. Constant pilot workloads were needed at high altitudes. Control augmentation was studied using basic feedbacks. For the longitudinal axis, flight path angle, and pitch rate feedback were sufficient to damp the phugoid mode and to provide good flying qualities. In the lateral directional axis,

bank angle, roll rate, and yaw rate feedbacks were sufficient to provide a safe vehicle with acceptable handling qualities. Intentionally stalling the stratoplane to very high angles of attack (deep stall) was studied as a means of enable safe and rapid descent. It was concluded that the deep stall maneuver is viable for this class of vehicle.

1880. Ray, Ronald J.; Hicks, John W.; and Wichman, Keith D.: **Real-Time In-Flight Engine Performance and Health Monitoring Techniques for Flight Research Application.** NASA TM-104239, H-1750, NAS 1.15:104239, September 1991, 91N30132, #. (See also 1916.)

Procedures for real time evaluation of the inflight health and performance of gas turbine engines and related systems were developed to enhance flight test safety and productivity. These techniques include the monitoring of the engine, the engine control system, thrust vectoring control system health, and the detection of engine stalls. Real time performance techniques were developed for the determination and display of inflight thrust and for aeroperformance drag polars. These new methods were successfully shown on various research aircraft at NASA-Dryden. The capability of NASA's Western Aeronautical Test Range and the advanced data acquisition systems were key factors for implementation and real time display of these methods.

1881. Burcham, F. W., Jr.; Fullerton, C. Gordon; Gilyard, Glenn B.; Wolf, Thomas D.; and Stewart, James F.: **A Preliminary Investigation of the Use of Throttles for Emergency Flight Control.** NASA TM-4320, H-1737, NAS 1.15:4320, AIAA Paper 91-2222. Presented at the 27th Joint Propulsion Conference, Sacramento, California, June 24–26, 1991, September 1991, 91N30130, #. (See also 1867.)

A preliminary investigation was conducted regarding the use of throttles for emergency flight control of a multiengine aircraft. Several airplanes including a light twin-engine piston-powered airplane, jet transports, and a high performance fighter were studied during flight and piloted simulations. Simulation studies used the B-720, B-727, MD-11, and F-15 aircraft. Flight studies used the Lear 24, Piper PA-30, and F-15 airplanes. Based on simulator and flight results, all the airplanes exhibited some control capability with throttles. With piloted simulators, landings using manual throttles-only control were extremely difficult. An augmented control system was developed that converts conventional pilot stick inputs into appropriate throttle commands. With the augmented system, the B-720 and F-15 simulations were evaluated and could be landed successfully. Flight and simulation data were compared for the F-15 airplane.

1882. Cohen, Dorothea; and Le, Jeanette H.: **The Role of the Remotely Augmented Vehicle (RAV) Laboratory in Flight Research.** NASA TM-104235, H-1728,

NAS 1.15:104235. Presented at the AIAA Flight Simulation Technologies Conference and Exhibit, New Orleans, Louisiana, August 12–14, 1991, September 1991, 91N30128, #. (See also 1875.)

An overview is presented of the unique capabilities and historical significance of the Remotely Augmented Vehicle (RAV) Lab at NASA-Dryden. The role is reviewed of the RAV Lab in enhancing flight test programs and efficient testing of new aircraft control laws. The history of the RAV Lab is discussed with a sample of its application using the X-29 aircraft. The RAV Lab allows for closed or open loop augmentation of the research aircraft while in flight using ground based, high performance real time computers. Telemetry systems transfer sensor and control data between the ground and the aircraft. The RAV capability provides for enhanced computational power, improved flight data quality, and alternate methods for the testing of control system concepts. The Lab is easily reconfigured to reflect changes within a flight program and can be adapted to new flight programs.

1883. Gilyard, Glenn B.; Conley, Joseph L.; Le, Jeanette; and Burcham, Frank W., Jr.: **A Simulation Evaluation of a Four-Engine Jet Transport Using Engine Thrust Modulation for Flightpath Control.** NASA TM-4324, H-1741, NAS 1.15:4324. Presented at the AIAA, ASME, SAE, and ASEE 27th Joint Propulsion Conference, Sacramento, California, June 24–26, 1991, September 1991, 91N29194, #. (See also 1864.)

The use of throttle control laws to provide adequate flying qualities for flight path control in the event of a total loss of conventional flight control surface use was evaluated. The results are based on a simulation evaluation by transport research pilots of a B-720 transport with visual display. Throttle augmentation control laws can provide flight path control capable of landing a transport-type aircraft with up to moderate levels of turbulence. The throttle augmentation mode dramatically improves the pilots' ability to control flight path for the approach and landing flight condition using only throttle modulation. For light turbulence, the average Cooper-Harper pilot rating improved from unacceptable to acceptable (a pilot rating improvement of 4.5) in going from manual to augmented control. The low frequency response characteristics of the engines require a considerably different piloting technique. The various techniques used by the pilot resulted in considerable scatter in data. Many pilots readily adapted to a good piloting technique while some had difficulty. A new viable approach is shown to provide independent means of redundancy of transport aircraft flight path control.

1884. Burcham, Frank W., Jr.; and Fullerton, C. Gordon: **Controlling Crippled Aircraft-With Throttles.** NASA TM-104238, H-1747, NAS 1.15:104238. Presented at the 44th International Air Safety Seminar, Singapore, November 12–14, 1991, September 1991, 91N29191, #.

A multiengine crippled aircraft, with most or all of the flight control system inoperative, may use engine thrust for control. A study was conducted of the capability and techniques for emergency flight control. Included were light twin engine piston powered airplanes, an executive jet transport, commercial jet transports, and a high performance fighter. Piloted simulations of the B-720, B-747, B-727, MD-11, C-402, and F-15 airplanes were studied, and the Lear 24, PA-30, and F-15 airplanes were flight tested. All aircraft showed some control capability with throttles and could be kept under control in up-and-away flight for an extended period of time. Using piloted simulators, landings with manual throttles-only control were extremely difficult. However, there are techniques that improve the chances of making a survivable landing. In addition, augmented control systems provide major improvements in control capability and make repeatable landings possible. Control capabilities and techniques are discussed.

1885. *Daysh, Colin; *Corbin, Malcolm; *Butler, Geoff; Duke, Eugene L.; **Belle, Steven D.; and **Brumbaugh, Randal W.: **A NASA/RAE Cooperation in the Development of a Real-Time Knowledge Based Autopilot.** AGARD-CP-499, Paper 11, *Machine Intelligence for Aerospace Electronic Systems*, (ISBN-92-835-0628-6) (see N92-12517 03–63), September 1991, AD-242025, 92N12528, #. (See also 1871.)

As part of a US/UK cooperative aeronautical research program, a joint activity between NASA-Ames and the Royal Aerospace Establishment on Knowledge Based Systems (KBS) was established. This joint activity is concerned with tools and techniques for the implementation and validation of real-time KBS. The proposed next stage of the research is described, in which some of the problems of implementing and validating a Knowledge Based Autopilot (KBAP) for a generic high performance aircraft will be studied.

*Royal Aerospace Establishment, Bedford, England.
**PRC Inc., Edwards, California.

1886. *Russell, P.; *Wegener, S.; **Langford, J.; †Anderson, J.; Lux, D.; and ††Hall, D. W.: **Advanced Aircraft for Atmospheric Research.** AIAA Paper 91-3162. Presented at the AIAA, AHS, and ASEE, Aircraft Design Systems and Operations Meeting, Baltimore, Maryland, September 23–25, 1991, 91A54076, #.

The development of aircraft for high-altitude research is described in terms of program objectives and environmental, technological limitations, and the work on the Perseus A aircraft. The need for these advanced aircraft is proposed in relation to atmospheric science issues such as greenhouse trapping, the dynamics of tropical cyclones, and stratospheric ozone. The implications of the study on aircraft design requirements is addressed with attention given to the basic categories of high-altitude, long-range, long-duration, and nap-of-the-earth aircraft. A strategy is delineated for a platform that permits unique stratospheric measurements and is a step toward a more advanced aircraft. The goal of Perseus A is to carry scientific air sampling payloads weighing at least 50 kg to altitudes of more than 25 km. The airfoils are designed for low Reynolds numbers, the structural weight is very low, and the closed-cycle power plant runs on liquid oxygen.

*NASA Ames Research Center, Moffett Field, California.
**Aurora Flight Sciences Corporation, Alexandria, Virginia.
†Harvard University, Cambridge, Massachusetts.
††David Hall Consulting, Sunnyvale, California.

EC91-0623-17

Perseus Vehicle.

1887. *Quast, Thomas; *Nelson, Robert C.; and Fisher, David F.: **A Study of High Alpha Dynamics and Flow Visualization for a 2.5-Percent Model of the F-18 HARV Undergoing Wing Rock.** AIAA Paper 91-3267. *Technical Papers*, presented at the AIAA 9th Applied Aerodynamics Conference, Baltimore, Maryland, September 23–25, 1991, Vol. 1, (see A91-53726 23–02), pp. 524–533, 91A53775, #.

Free-to-roll experiments and flow visualization studies have been conducted for a 2.5-percent model of the F-18 undergoing unsteady wing rock oscillations. Data have been acquired in the form of roll angle time histories as well as video recordings and 35 mm photography of the forebody and leading edge extension vortices. The time histories were differentiated to produce angular velocity and angular acceleration. From this the roll moment as a function of time and/or roll angle could be estimated. A thorough analysis of the data has revealed a genuine wing-rock phenomenon. Off-surface flow visualization was used to identify the forebody and LEX vortex core positions and their interaction in both static and dynamic configurations. A direct correlation between the dynamic data and visualized vortex activity during the wing-rock motion has been made.

*Notre Dame University, Notre Dame, Indiana.

1888. *Richwine, David M.; and Fisher, David F.: **In-Flight Leading-Edge Vortex Flow-Field Survey Measurements on a F-18 Aircraft at High Angle of Attack.** AIAA Paper 91-3248. *Technical Papers*, presented at the AIAA 9th Applied Aerodynamics Conference, Baltimore, Maryland, September 23–25, 1991, Vol. 1, (see A91-53726 23–02), pp. 346–369, 91A53759, #. (See also 1969.)

A rotating rake with 16 hemispherical-tipped five-hole probes was used to obtain flow-field measurements of the leading-edge-extension (LEX) vortex of the F-18 aircraft. The measurements were carried out under 1-g flight conditions at quasi-stabilized angles of attack of 10–52 deg and at Reynolds numbers based on a mean aerodynamic cord up to 16×10 to the 6th. Correlations with surface pressure, flow visualization, and computational fluid dynamics results are presented for angles of attack of 19 and 30 deg. (See also 1999.)

*PRC Inc., Edwards, California.

1889. *Foster, John V.; *Bundick, W. T.; and Pahle, Joseph W.: **Controls for Agility Research in the NASA High-Alpha Technology Program.** SAE Paper 912148. Presented at the SAE Aerospace Technology Conference and Exposition, Long Beach, California, September 23–26, 1991, 92A39984.

The research process being used to develop control law design methodologies and guidelines in the NASA High-Alpha Technology Program are discussed. This step-by-step process consists of four basic elements: (1) control law architecture definition and linear synthesis, (2) nonlinear batch simulation, (3) piloted simulation evaluation, and (4) flight test validation. This paper discusses the research tools being used in this effort and provides a status report on design methodologies and guidelines being developed for each of these elements.

*NASA Langley Research Center, Hampton, Virginia.

1890. Whitmore, Stephen A.: **Development of a Pneumatic High-Angle-of-Attack Flush Airdata Sensing System.** SAE Paper 912142. Presented at the SAE Aerospace Technology Conference and Exposition, Long Beach, California, September 23–26, 1991, (see N92-11994), 92A39980. (See also 1897.)

A nonintrusive high-angle-of-attack flush airdata sensing system was installed and flight tested in the F-18 High Alpha Research Vehicle. This system consists of a matrix of 25 pressure orifices arranged in concentric circles on the nose of the vehicle to determine angles of attack and sideslip, Mach number, and pressure altitude. During the course of the flight tests, it was determined that satisfactory results could be achieved using a subset of just nine ports.

1891. Duke, E. L.; *Brumbaugh, Randal W.; **Hewett, M. D.; and **Tartt, D. M.: **From an Automated Flight-Test Management System to a Flight-Test Engineer's Workstation.** NASA TM-104242, H-1761, NAS 1.15:104242, AGARD-CP-504, Paper 20. Presented at the 53rd Symposium of the Guidance and Control Panel Air Vehicle Mission Control and Management, Amsterdam, the Netherlands, (ISBN-92-835-0662-6), October 22–26, 1991, October 1991, AD-A253088, 91N32851, #. (See also 1922.)

The capabilities and evolution is described of a flight engineer's workstation (called TEST-PLAN) from an automated flight test management system. The concept and capabilities of the automated flight test management systems are explored and discussed to illustrate the value of advanced system prototyping and evolutionary software development.

*PRC Inc., Edwards, California.
**G and C Systems, Inc., San Juan Capistrano, California.

1892. Lambert, H. H.; Gilyard, G. B.; *Chisholm, J. D.; and **Kerr, L. J.: **Preliminary Flight Evaluation of an Engine Performance Optimization Algorithm.** NASA TM-4328, H-1745, NAS 1.15:4328. Presented at the 27th Joint Propulsion Conference, Sacramento, California, June 24–26, 1991, (see A91-44089), October 1991, 91N32140, #. (See also 1865.)

A performance seeking control (PSC) algorithm has undergone initial flight test evaluation in subsonic operation of a PW 1128 engine F-15. This algorithm is designed to optimize the quasi-steady performance of an engine for three primary modes: (1) minimum fuel consumption; (2) minimum fan turbine inlet temperature (FTIT); and (3) maximum thrust. The flight test results have verified a thrust specific fuel consumption reduction of 1 pct., up to 100 R decreases in FTIT, and increases of as much as 12 pct. in maximum thrust. PSC technology promises to be of value in next generation tactical and transport aircraft.

*McDonnell-Douglas Corporation, St. Louis, Missouri.
**Pratt and Whitney Aircraft, West Palm Beach, Florida.

1893. Glover, Richard D.; and Larson, Richard R.: **A Knowledge Based Application of the Extended Aircraft Interrogation and Display System.** NASA TM-4327, H-1706, NAS 1.15:4327, October 1991, 91N31874, #.

A family of multiple-processor ground support test equipment was used to test digital flight-control systems on high-performance research aircraft. A unit recently built for the F-18 high alpha research vehicle project is the latest model in a series called the extended aircraft interrogation and display system. The primary feature emphasized monitors the aircraft MIL-STD-1553B data buses and provides real-time engineering units displays of flight-control parameters. A customized software package was developed to provide real-time data interpretation based on rules embodied in a highly structured knowledge database. The configuration of this extended aircraft of the rule based package and its application to failure modes and effects testing on the F-18 high alpha research vehicle is discussed.

1894. Noffz, Gregory K.; Curry, Robert E.; Haering, Edward A., Jr.; and *Kolodziej, Paul: **Aerothermal Test Results From the First Flight of the Pegasus Air-Launched Space Booster.** NASA TM-4330, H-1672, NAS 1.15:4330, October 1991, 92N11301, #.

A survey of temperature measurements at speeds through Mach 8.0 on the first flight of the Pegasus air-launched booster system is discussed. In addition, heating rates were derived from the temperature data obtained on the fuselage in the vicinity of the wing shock interaction. Sensors were distributed on the wing surfaces, leading edge, and on the wing-body fairing or fillet. Side-by-side evaluations were obtained for a variety of sensor installations. Details of the trajectory reconstruction through first-stage separation are provided. Given here are indepth descriptions of the sensor installations, temperature measurements, and derived heating rates along with interpretations of the results.

*NASA Ames Research Center, Moffett Field, California.

EC89-0309-3

Pegasus® Rocket Under B-52 Airplane

1895. Anderson, Bianca T.; Meyer, Robert R., Jr.; and Chiles, Harry R.: **Techniques Used in the F-14 Variable-Sweep Transition Flight Experiment.** *Technical Papers*, presented at the AIAA 4th Flight Test Conference, San Diego, California, May 18–20, 1988, pp. 529–548. *Journal of Aircraft*, (ISSN 0021-8669), Vol. 28, October 1991, (see A88-38762), October 1991, pp. 622–629, 91A54368 (See also 1635, 1652.)

1896. Trippensee, Gary: **Update of the X-29 High-Angle-of-Attack Program.** SAE Paper 912006. *Proceedings, 29th International Pacific Air and Space Technology Conference and Aircraft Symposium*, Gifu, Japan, October 7–11, 1991, (see A92-45376 19–01), pp. 375–382, 92A45407.

The X-29A forward-swept wing flight research aircraft flight envelope was expanded to 66 deg angle-of-attack during 1990. Following this flight envelope expansion, a military utility evaluation was performed to investigate the tactical utility of the X-29 configurations at high-angle-of-attack, slow-speed flight conditions. An overall management view and perspective of the expansion process, the technical problems encountered, and the results obtained when compared to the predictions are presented.

1897. Whitmore, Stephen A.: **Development of a Pneumatic High-Angle-of-Attack Flush Airdata Sensing (Hi-FADS) System.** NASA TM-104241, H-1766, NAS 1.15:104241. Presented at the SAE Aerotech 1991 Conference, Long Beach, California, September 23–26, 1991, November 1991, 92N11994, #. (See also 1890.)

A nonintrusive high-angle-of-attack flush airdata sensing system was installed and flight tested in the F-18 High Alpha Research Vehicle. This system consists of a matrix of 25 pressure orifices arranged in concentric circles on the nose of the vehicle to determine angles of attack and sideslip, Mach number, and pressure altitude. During the course of the flight tests, it was determined that satisfactory results could be achieved using a subset of just nine ports.

1898. Richards, W. L.; and *Thompson, Randolph C.: **Titanium Honeycomb Panel Testing.** *Proceedings, Structural Testing Technology at High Temperature Conference*, Dayton, Ohio, November 4–6, 1991, (see A92-51401 21–09), 1991, 92A51411.

The paper describes the procedures of thermal mechanical tests carried out at the NASA Dryden Flight Research Facility on two titanium honeycomb wing panels bonded using liquid interface diffusion (LID) technique, and presents the results of these tests. The 58.4 cm square panels consisted of two 0.152-cm-thick Ti 6-2-4-2 face sheets LID-bonded to a 1.9-cm-thick honeycomb core, with bearing plates fastened to the perimeter of the upper and the lower panel surfaces. The panels were instrumented with sensors for measuring surface temperature, strain, and deflections to 315° C and

482° C. Thermal stress levels representative of those encountered during aerodynamic heating were produced by heating the upper panel surface and restraining all four edges. After more than 100 thermal cycles from room temperature to 315° C and 50 cycles from room temperature to 482° C, no significant structural degradation was detected in the panels.

*PRC Inc., Edwards, California.

1899. *Thompson, Randolph C.; and Richards, W. L.: **Thermal-Structural Panel Buckling Tests.** *Proceedings, Structural Testing Technology at High Temperature Conference*, Dayton, Ohio, November 4–6, 1991, (see A92-51401 21–09), 1991, 92A51409. (See also 1903.)

A titanium-matrix-composite (TMC) hat-stiffened panel of 61 cm sq area and 3.175 cm thick was nondestructively tested to 649 C to examine its buckling characteristics. Compressive loads were applied to the panel in a 978.6 kN uniaxial load frame system. High-temperature testing was performed using quartz lamp heating. A single-strain-age force/stiffness buckling prediction technique was developed to predict panel buckling loads. For the monolithic panel, these test predictions correlated within 10 percent with a finite-element buckling analyses performed elsewhere. Comparisons between force/stiffness predictions and analyses for the TMC panel are in progress.

*PRC Inc., Edwards, California.

1900. DeAngelis, V. M.: **A Historical Overview of High-Temperature Structural Testing at the NASA Dryden Flight Research Facility.** *Proceedings, Structural Testing Technology at High Temperature Conference*, Dayton, Ohio, November 4–6, 1991, (see A92-51401 21–09), 1991, pp. 35–37, 92A51407

Major hot structure test programs conducted at NASA Dryden Flight Research Facility from 1960s to the present are reviewed with emphasis placed on the YF-12A flight load program, which included extensive experimental and analytical tasks. Analytical models of the YF-12A aircraft were generated using NASTRAN and FLEXTAB codes. Experimental data were generated from wind tunnel model tests, laboratory tests performed on the flight vehicle (including Mach-3 thermal simulation that involved heating the entire aircraft's surface after which the aircraft was returned to flight status), and flight tests.

1901. Kehoe, Michael W.; and Snyder, H. T.: **High Temperature Ground Vibration Test Techniques.** *Proceedings, Structural Testing Technology at High Temperature Conference*, Dayton, Ohio, November 4–6, 1991, (see A92-51401 21–09), 1991, pp. 17–26, 92A51404.

This paper describes the experimental modal test techniques and procedures used to conduct uniform, nonuniform, and transient thermoelastic vibration tests. Experimental setup and elevated temperature instrumentation considerations are also discussed. Modal data for a 30.48- by 127-cm aluminum plate heated to a temperature of 371.1 C are presented. These data show the effect of heat on the plate's modal characteristics.

1902. Belcher, Gordon; McIver, Duncan E.; and Szalai, Kenneth J.: **Validation of Flight Critical Control Systems.** AGARD-AR-274, ISBN-92-835-0650-2, AD-A247742, December 1991, 92N20026, #.

The objectives of the research is the following: (1) to provide guidance to those concerned in the Flight Critical Control System (FCCS) validation, namely systems designers and certification authorities; and (2) to identify the areas of research which need to be explored to enable validation of the next generation of FCCS. An attempt was made to review all flight critical control system validation activities which had been completed or were under active consideration, in Europe and the U.S.

1903. *Thompson, Randolph C.; and Richards, W. Lance: **Thermal-Structural Panel Buckling Tests.** NASA TM-104243, H-1778, NAS 1.15:104243. Presented at the *Structural Testing Technology at High Temperature Conference*, Dayton, Ohio, November 4–6, 1991, December 1991, 92N15404, #. (See also 1899.)

The buckling characteristics of a titanium matrix composite hat-stiffened panel were experimentally examined for various combinations of thermal and mechanical loads. Panel failure was prevented by maintaining the applied loads below real-time critical buckling predictions. The test techniques used to apply the loads, minimize boundary were shown to compare well with a finite-element buckling analysis for previous panels. Comparisons between test predictions and analysis for this panel are ongoing.

*PRC Inc., Edwards, California.

1904. *Russell, Philip B.; Lux, David P.; **Reed, R. Dale; *Loewenstein, Max; and *Wegener, Steven: **Science Requirements and Feasibility/Design Studies of a Very-High-Altitude Aircraft for Atmospheric Research.** NASA TM-104983. *NASA Proceedings, 4th Airborne Geoscience Workshop*, (see N91-25445 17–42), 1991, pp. 241–242, 91N25481, #.

The advantages and shortcomings of currently available aircraft for use in stratosphere-troposphere exchange pose the question of whether to develop advanced aircraft for atmospheric research. To answer this question, NASA conducted a workshop to determine science needs and feasibility/design studies to assess whether and how those needs could be met. It was determined that there was a need for an aircraft that could cruise at an altitude of 30 km with a

range of 6,000 miles with vertical profiling down to 10 km and back at remote points and carry a payload of 3,000 lbs.

*NASA Ames Research Center, Moffett Field, California.
**PRC Inc., Edwards, California.

1905. *Yungkurth, C.; *Dawson, F.; **Houck, S.; Corda, S.; and †Trefny, C.: **The F/A-18 External Burning Flight Test.** AIAA Paper 91-5050. Presented at the AIAA 3rd International Aerospace Planes Conference, Orlando, Florida, December 3–5, 1991, 92A44547, #.

A flight test program was undertaken to demonstrate the feasibility of obtaining external burning (EB) data in a flight environment, and to address the question of facility interference in ground test external burning data. Results showed that external burning was effective at reducing transonic base drag in a flight environment having dynamically changing conditions. The flight test program demonstrated that external burning is not just a laboratory phenomenon but is a viable technology for aerospace vehicles.

*Johns Hopkins University, Laurel, Maryland.
**U.S. Navy, Naval Air Test Center, Patuxent River, Maryland.
†NASA Lewis Research Center, Cleveland, Ohio.

1906. Whitmore, Stephen A.; and *Leondes, Cornelius T.: **Pneumatic Distortion Compensation for Aircraft Surface Pressure Sensing Devices.** *Journal of Aircraft*, (ISSN 0021-8669), Vol. 28, December 1991, pp. 828–836, 92A20206.

In this paper a technique of compensating for pneumatic distortion in aircraft surface pressure sensing devices is developed. The compensation allows conventional pressure sensing technology to obtain improved unsteady pressure measurements. Pressure distortion caused by frictional attenuation and pneumatic resonance within the sensing system makes obtaining unsteady pressure measurements by conventional sensors difficult. Typically, most of the distortion occurs within the pneumatic tubing used to transmit pressure impulses from the surface of the aircraft to the measurement transducer. This paper develops a second-order distortion model that accurately describes the behavior of the primary wave harmonic of the pneumatic tubing. The model is expressed in state-variable form and is coupled with standard results from minimum-variance estimation theory to develop an algorithm to compensate for the effects of pneumatic distortion. Both postflight and real-time algorithms are developed and evaluated using simulated and flight data. Covariance selection and filter-tuning examples are presented. Results presented verify that, given appropriate covariance magnitudes, the algorithms accurately reconstruct surface pressure values from remotely sensed pressure measurements.

*University of Washington, Seattle, Washington.

1907. Myers, Lawrence P.; and Walsh, Kevin R.: **Performance Improvements of an F-15 Airplane With an Integrated Engine-Flight Control System.** *Technical Papers*, presented at the AIAA 4th Flight Test Conference, San Diego, California, May 18–20, 1988, pp. 410–418. *Journal of Aircraft*, (ISSN 0021-8669), Vol. 28, (see A88-38747), December 1991, pp. 812–817, 92A20204. (See also 1624, 1625.)

1908. Noffz, Gregory K.; and Curry, Robert E.: **Summary of Aerothermal Test Results From the First Flight of the Pegasus Air-Launched Space Booster.** AIAA Paper 91-5046. Presented at the AIAA 3rd International Aerospace Planes Conference, Orlando, Florida, December 3–5, 1991, 92A17832, #.

Temperature measurements were obtained on the Pegasus booster from launch through Mach 8.0. The majority of sensors were thin-foil temperature gages installed near the surface within the vehicle's ablating thermal protection system. These gages were distributed on the wing surfaces and on the wing-body fairing or fillet. Temperature time histories from these installations are presented. In addition, thermocouples were installed on the surface of nonablating plugs located on the fairing. These sensors were more responsive to changes in flight conditions than the foil gages and allowed a derivation of convective heat flux. A heating rate magnification of 2 was found in the vicinity of the wing shock interaction.

1909. Gupta, K. K.; Petersen, K. L.; and *Lawson, C. L.: **Multidisciplinary Modeling and Simulation of a Generic Hypersonic Vehicle.** AIAA Paper 91-5015. Presented at the AIAA 3rd International Aerospace Planes Conference, Orlando, Florida, December 3–5, 1991, 92A17813, #.

The modeling and simulation of hypersonic vehicles which involve the interaction of a number of major technical disciplines including aerodynamics, structures, heat transfer, propulsion, and control engineering are described. Finite element numerical formulations of individual disciplines including their appropriate integration for multidisciplinary simulation are presented. An efficient unstructured grid generation strategy, evolved by modifying an existing code, is developed.

*Eloret Institute, Claremont, California.

1910. Bjarke, Lisa J.: **Water Tunnels.** *High Reynolds Number Flows Using Liquid and Gaseous Helium*, (see A92-45262 19–34), New York, New York, Springer-Verlag, 1991, pp. 125–130, 92A45266.

Some of the uses of water tunnels are demonstrated through the description of the NASA Ames-Dryden Flow Visualization Facility. It is concluded that water tunnels are capable of providing a quick and inexpensive means of flow visualization and can aid in the understanding of complex fluid mechanics phenomena.

1992 Technical Publications

1911. Fields, Roger A.: **Flight Vehicle Thermal Testing With Infrared Lamps.** NASA TM-4336, H-1779, NAS 1.15:4336. Presented at the Structural Testing Technology at High Temperature Conference, Dayton, Ohio, November 4–6, 1991, January 1992, 92N17226, #.

The verification and certification of new structural material concepts for advanced high speed flight vehicles relies greatly on thermal testing with infrared quartz lamps. The basic quartz heater system characteristics and design considerations are presented. Specific applications are illustrated with tests that were conducted for the X-15, the Space Shuttle, and YF-12 flight programs.

1912. Whitmore, Stephen A.; Moes, Timothy R.; *Leondes, Cornelius T.: **Failure Detection and Fault Management Techniques for Flush Airdata Sensing Systems.** NASA TM-4335, H-1780, NAS 1.15:4335. Presented at the Aerospace Sciences Meeting, Reno, Nevada, January 6–9, 1992, January 1992, 92N17128, #. (See also 1913.)

A high-angle-of-attack flush airdata sensing system was installed and flight tested on the F-18 High Alpha Research Vehicle at NASA-Dryden. This system uses a matrix of pressure orifices arranged in concentric circles on the nose of the vehicle to determine angles of attack, angles of sideslip, dynamic pressure, and static pressure as well as other airdata parameters. Results presented use an arrangement of 11 symmetrically distributed ports on the aircraft nose. Experience with this sensing system data indicates that the primary concern for real-time implementation is the detection and management of overall system and individual pressure sensor failures. The multiple port sensing system is more tolerant to small disturbances in the measured pressure data than conventional probe-based intrusive airdata systems. However, under adverse circumstances, large undetected failures in individual pressure ports can result in algorithm divergence and catastrophic failure of the entire system. How system and individual port failures may be detected using chi sq. analysis is shown. Once identified, the effects of failures are eliminated using weighted least squares.

*University of Washington, Seattle, Washington.

1913. Whitmore, Stephen A.; Moes, Timothy R.; and *Leondes, Cornelius T.: **Failure Detection and Fault Management Techniques for Flush Airdata Sensing Systems.** AIAA Paper 92-0263, Presented at 30th AIAA Aerospace Sciences Meeting and Exhibit, Reno, Nevada, January 6–9, 1992, 92A25719, #. (See also 1912.)

Methods based on chi-squared analysis are presented for detecting system and individual-port failures in the high-angle-of-attack flush airdata sensing system on the

NASA F-18 High Alpha Research Vehicle. The HI-FADS hardware is introduced, and the aerodynamic model describes measured pressure in terms of dynamic pressure, angle of attack, angle of sideslip, and static pressure. Chi-squared analysis is described in the presentation of the concept for failure detection and fault management which includes nominal, iteration, and fault-management modes. A matrix of pressure orifices arranged in concentric circles on the nose of the aircraft indicate the parameters which are applied to the regression algorithms. The sensing techniques are applied to the F-18 flight data, and two examples are given of the computed angle-of-attack time histories. The failure-detection and fault-management techniques permit the matrix to be multiply redundant, and the chi-squared analysis is shown to be useful in the detection of failures.

*University of Washington, Seattle, Washington.

1914. Johnson, Steven A.: **Aircraft Ground Test and Subscale Model Results of Axial Thrust Loss Caused by Thrust Vectoring Using Turning Vanes**. NASA TM-4341, H-1743, NAS 1.15:4341, January 1992, 92N17071, #.

The NASA-Dryden F/A-18 high alpha research vehicle was modified to incorporate three independently controlled turning vanes located aft of the primary nozzle of each engine to vector thrust for pitch and yaw control. Ground measured axial thrust losses were compared with the results from a 14.25 pct. cold jet model for single and dual vanes inserted up to 25 degs into the engine exhaust. Data are presented for nozzle pressure ratios of 2.0 and 3.0 and nozzle exit areas of 253 and 348 sq in. The results indicate that subscale nozzle test results properly predict trends but underpredict the full scale results by approx. 1 to 4.5 pct. in thrust loss.

1915. Murray, James; Moes, Timothy; Norlin, Ken; Bauer, Jeffrey E.; *Geenen, Robert; *Moulton, Bryan; and *Hoang, Stephen: **Piloted Simulation Study of a Balloon-Assisted Deployment of an Aircraft at High Altitude**. NASA TM-104245, H-1785, NAS 1.15:104245. Proposed for presentation at the Sixth Workshop on Civilian and Military Needs for Automated Instrument Platforms in the 1990s and Beyond, Association for Unmanned Vehicle Systems, Menlo Park, California, January 28–30, 1992, January 1992, 92N15986, #.

A piloted simulation was used to study the feasibility of a balloon assisted deployment of a research aircraft at high altitude. In the simulation study, an unmanned, modified sailplane was carried to 110,000 ft with a high altitude balloon and released in a nose down attitude. A remote pilot controlled the aircraft through a pullout and then executed a zoom climb to a trimmed, 1 g flight condition. A small parachute was used to limit the Mach number during the pullout to avoid adverse transonic effects. The use of small rocket motor was studied for increasing the maximum attainable altitude. Aerodynamic modifications to the basic sailplane included applying supercritical airfoil gloves over

the existing wing and tail surfaces. The aerodynamic model of the simulated aircraft was based on low Reynolds number wind tunnel tests and computational techniques, and included large Mach number and Reynolds number effects at high altitude. Parametric variations were performed to study the effects of launch altitude, gross weight, Mach number limit, and parachute size on the maximum attainable stabilized altitude. A test altitude of approx. 95,000 ft was attained, and altitudes in excess of 100,000 ft was attained.

*PRC Inc., Edwards, California.

1916. Ray, Ronald J.; Hicks, John W.; and Wichman, Keith D.: **Real-Time In-Flight Engine Performance and Health Monitoring Techniques for Flight Research Application**. DLR-MITT-92-01. *Proceedings of the 16th Symposium on Aircraft Integrated Monitoring Systems,* January 1992, pp. 311–340, (see N93-15152 04-06), 93N15169, #. (See also 1880.)

Various engine related performance and health monitoring techniques developed in support of flight research are described. Techniques used during flight to enhance safety and to increase flight test productivity are summarized. A description of the NASA range facility is given along with a discussion of the flight data processing. Examples of data processed and the flight data displays are shown. A discussion of current trends and future capabilities is also included.

1917. Ehernberger, L. J.; Haering, Edward A., Jr.; *Lockhart, Mary G.; and *Teets, Edward H.: **Atmospheric Analysis for Airdata Calibration on Research Aircraft**. AIAA 92-0293. Presented at 30th AIAA, Aerospace Sciences Meeting and Exhibit, Reno, Nevada, January 6–9, 1992, 92A25746, #.

In-flight airdata calibrations are used to determine the aerodynamic influence of an airplane on pitot-static pressure measurements of altitude and speed. Conventional flight-test calibration techniques are briefly reviewed and meteorological analysis methods for estimating calibration reference values of atmospheric conditions are described. There are cases where some conventional in-flight techniques are not entirely satisfactory for research aircraft because of added equipment requirements or flight envelope and location limitations. In these cases, atmospheric wind and pressure information can be used to complement conventional techniques. Accuracy of the atmospheric measurements and the variability of upper-air winds and pressure values are discussed. Results from several flight research aircraft show that wind reference calibration is generally less accurate than calibration accuracy standards for civil and research aircraft. Examples of pressure reference altimetry derived from meteorological analyses are also presented for a variety of flight research programs. These flight data show that the reference pressure accuracy provided by meteorological analyses is usually within civil aircraft and flight research airdata calibration accuracy standards. Meteorological analyses altimetry is particularly useful when it is not feasible to restrict the test airplane altitude, location, or maneuver envelope.

*PRC Inc., Edwards, California.

1918. Bosworth, John T.: **Linearized Aerodynamic and Control Law Models of the X-29A Airplane and Comparison With Flight Data.** NASA TM-4356, H-1676, NAS 1.15:4356, February 1992, 92N19174, #.

Flight control system design and analysis for aircraft rely on mathematical models of the vehicle dynamics. In addition to a six degree of freedom nonlinear simulation, the X-29A flight controls group developed a set of programs that calculate linear perturbation models throughout the X-29A flight envelope. The models include the aerodynamics as well as flight control system dynamics and were used for stability, controllability, and handling qualities analysis. These linear models were compared to flight test results to help provide a safe flight envelope expansion. A description is given of the linear models at three flight conditions and two flight control system modes. The models are presented with a level of detail that would allow the reader to reproduce the linear results if desired. Comparison between the response of the linear model and flight measured responses are presented to demonstrate the strengths and weaknesses of the linear models' ability to predict flight dynamics.

1919. Glover, Richard D.: **A Computerized Aircraft Battery Servicing Facility.** NASA CP-3140. Presented at NASA Marshall Space Flight Center, *The 1991 NASA Aerospace Battery Workshop*, February 1992, pp. 37–51, (see N92-22740 13-44), 92N22743, #.

The latest upgrade to the Aerospace Energy Systems Laboratory (AESL) is described. The AESL is a distributed digital system consisting of a central system and battery servicing stations connected by a high-speed serial data bus. The entire system is located in two adjoining rooms; the bus length is approximately 100 ft. Each battery station contains a digital processor, data acquisition, floppy diskette data storage, and operator interfaces. The operator initiates a servicing task and thereafter the battery station monitors the progress of the task and terminates it at the appropriate time. The central system provides data archives, manages the data bus, and provides a timeshare interface for multiple users. The system also hosts software production tools for the battery stations and the central system.

1920. *Shelley, S. J.; Freudinger, L. C.; and *Allemang, R. J.: **Development of an On-Line Parameter Estimation System Using the Discrete Modal Filter.** Presented at 10th International Modal Analysis Conference, San Diego, California, February 3–7, 1992. *Society for Experimental Mechanics, Inc.*, Vol. 1, 1992, pp. 173–183, 94A12488.

Ongoing development of an automated system for monitoring the frequency and damping of time varying structural systems is discussed. A spatial filtering technique called the discrete modal filter is used to uncouple multiple response measurements into modal coordinate responses. Since the modal coordinate responses are the responses of single-degree-of-freedom systems, the frequency and damping may be accurately estimated with short data records. An on-line monitoring system is discussed which may be useful in a variety of applications. The focus in this paper is on the application to aircraft flight flutter testing.

*University of Cincinnati, Ohio.

1921. Ko, William L.; Monaghan, Richard C.; and Jackson, Raymond H.: **Practical Theories for Service Life Prediction of Critical Aerospace Structural Components.** NASA TM-4354, H-1760, NAS 1.15:4354, March 1992, 92N19404, #. (See also 1939.)

A new second-order theory was developed for predicting the service lives of aerospace structural components. The predictions based on this new theory were compared with those based on the Ko first-order theory and the classical theory of service life predictions. The new theory gives very accurate service life predictions. An equivalent constant-amplitude stress cycle method was proposed for representing the random load spectrum for crack growth calculations. This method predicts the most conservative service life. The proposed use of minimum detectable crack size, instead of proof load established crack size as an initial crack size for crack growth calculations, could give a more realistic service life.

1922. Duke, E. L.; Brumbaugh, R. W.; Hewett, M. D.; and *Tartt, D. M.: **From an Automated Flight-Test Management System to a Flight-Test Engineer's Workstation.** AGARD CP-504. *Air Vehicle Mission Control and Management*, March 1992, (see N92-27887 18-01), 92N27907, #. (See also 1891.)

Described here are the capabilities and evolution of a flight-test engineer's workstation (called TEST PLAN) from an automated flight-test management system. The concept and capabilities of the automated flight-test management system are explored and discussed to illustrate the value of advanced system prototyping and evolutionary software development.

*G and C Systems, Inc., San Juan Capistrano, California.

1923. Curry, Robert E.; *Mendenhall, Michael R.; and **Moulton, Bryan: **In-Flight Evaluation of Aerodynamic Predictions of an Air-Launched Space Booster.** NASA TM-104246, H-1803, NAS 1.15:104246. Presented at AGARD Symposium on Theoretical and Experimental Methods in Hypersonic Flows, Torino, Italy, May 4–7, 1992, April 1992, 92N31808, #. (See also 2019.)

Several analytical aerodynamic design tools that were applied to the Pegasus® (registered trademark) air-launched space booster were evaluated using flight measurements. The study was limited to existing codes and was conducted with limited computational resources. The flight instrumentation was constrained to have minimal impact on the primary Pegasus® missions. Where appropriate, the flight measurements were compared with computational data. Aerodynamic performance and trim data from the first two flights were correlated with predictions. Local measurements in the wing and wing-body interference region were correlated with analytical data. This complex flow region includes the effect of aerothermal heating magnification caused by the presence of a corner vortex and interaction of the wing leading edge shock and fuselage boundary layer. The operation of the first two missions indicates that the aerodynamic design approach for Pegasus® was adequate, and data show that acceptable margins were available. Additionally, the correlations provide insight into the capabilities of these analytical tools for more complex vehicles in which the design margins may be more stringent.

*Nielsen Engineering and Research, Inc., Mountain View, California.
**PRC Inc., Edwards, California.

1924. *Smith, John W.; Lock, Wilton P.; and Payne, Gordon A.: **Variable-Camber Systems Integration and Operational Performance of the AFTI/F-111 Mission Adaptive Wing.** NASA TM-4370, H-1748, NAS 1.15:4370, April 1992, 92N22194, #.

The advanced fighter technology integration, the AFTI/F-111 aircraft, is a preproduction F-111A testbed research airplane that was fitted with a smooth variable-camber mission adaptive wing. The camber was positioned and controlled by flexing the upper skins through rotary actuators and linkages driven by power drive units. The wing camber and control system are described. The measured servoactuator frequency responses are presented along with analytical predictions derived from the integrated characteristics of the control elements. A mission adaptive wing system chronology is used to illustrate and assess the reliability and dependability of the servoactuator system during 1524 hours of ground tests and 145 hours of flight testing.

*PRC Inc., Edwards, California.

1925. Myers, Lawrence P.; and Conners, Timothy R.: **Flight Evaluation of an Extended Engine Life Mode on an F-15 Airplane.** NASA TM-104240, H-1764, NAS 1.15:104240, April 1992, 92N29659, #.

An integrated flight and propulsion control system designed to reduce the rate of engine deterioration was developed and evaluated in flight on the NASA Dryden F-15 research aircraft. The extended engine life mode increases engine pressure ratio while reducing engine airflow to lower the turbine temperature at constant thrust. The engine pressure ratio uptrim is modulated in real time based on airplane maneuver requirements, flight conditions, and engine information. The extended engine life mode logic performed well, significantly reducing turbine operating temperature. Reductions in fan turbine inlet temperature of up to 80° F were obtained at intermediate power and up to 170° F at maximum augmented power with no appreciable loss in thrust. A secondary benefit was the considerable reduction in thrust-specific fuel consumption. The success of the extended engine life mode is one example of the advantages gained from integrating aircraft flight and propulsion control systems.

1926. *George, Mike; Bohn-Meyer, Marta; and Anderson, Bianca: **Status of F-16XL SSLFC Numerical Design Validation.** NASA CP-10087. Presented at Langley Research Center, *First Annual High-Speed Research Workshop*, Part 4, April 1992, pp. 1843–1889, (see N94-33517 10-02), 94N33527, #.

The viewgraphs and discussion of the status of the F-16XL SSLFC numerical design validation are provided. The F-16XL Supersonic Laminar Flow Control Program (SSLFC) is a joint effort involving Rockwell's North American Aircraft Division, NASA Ames-Dryden Flight Research Facility, and NASA Langley Research Center. The objectives of the program are to demonstrate that laminar flow can be obtained on a highly swept wing at supersonic speeds, validate the capabilities of a numerical methodology designed to predict boundary layer transition, and validate the capabilities of the methodology in the design of active and passive laminar flow control (LFC) concepts. The F-16XL SSLFC Program consists of the design, fabrication, installation, and flight test of an active laminar flow control glove for the F-16XL. The glove design emphasized the active (suction) control of attachment line and crossflow boundary condition instabilities. The glove design envelop was constrained by the existing geometry, safety of flight considerations, and space requirements for the suction mechanism. The leading edge extension of the glove was limited to 10 inches for consideration of asymmetric flying qualities and the glove height above the existing surface restricted to two inches. The active (suction) portion of the wing extends to nominally 25 percent chord. The glove was constructed of a micro-perforated titanium sheet (hole diameter = 0.025 inches, spacing ratio = 1/8, and sheet thickness = 0.0025 inches). The glove design includes 22 separate chambers to allow suction variation in the chordwise direction. The F-16XL SSLFC program is currently in the flight test phase.

*Rockwell International Corporation, Los Angeles, California.

1927. *Batill, S. M.; *Carey, D. M.; and Kehoe, M. W.: **Digital Time Series Analysis for Flutter Test Data.** AIAA

Paper 92-2103. Presented at AIAA Dynamics Specialists Conference, Dallas, Texas, April 16–17, 1992, pp. 215–223, 92A35674, #.

An application of digital time series analysis to flutter test data processing was conducted. A numerical investigation was used to evaluate the method, as well as its sensitivity to noise and parameter variations. These parameters included those involved with data acquisition, as well as system response characteristics. This digital time series method was then used to predict flutter speed from subcritical response wind tunnel tests. Flutter speeds predicted from forced response, subcritical wind tunnel tests were compared to the experimental flutter speeds.

*University of Notre Dame, Indiana.

1928. Ko, William L.; and Jackson, Raymond H.: **Combined Compressive and Shear Buckling Analysis of Hypersonic Aircraft Sandwich Panels.** AIAA Paper 92-2487. Presented at 33rd AIAA, ASME, ASCE, AHS, and ASC Structures, Structural Dynamics and Materials Conference, Dallas, Texas, April 13–15, 1992, pp. 3198–3225, 92A34603, #. (See also 1859.)

The combined-load (compression and shear) buckling equations were established for orthotropic sandwich panels by using the Rayleigh-Ritz method to minimize the panel total potential energy. The resulting combined-load buckling equations were used to generate buckling interaction curves for super-plastically-formed/diffusion-bonded titanium truss-core sandwich panels and titanium honeycomb-core sandwich panels having the same specific weight. The relative combined-load buckling strengths of these two types of sandwich panels are compared with consideration of their sandwich orientations. For square and nearly square panels of both types, the combined load always induces symmetric buckling. As the panel aspect ratios increase, antisymmetric buckling will show up when the loading is shear-dominated combined loading. The square panel (either type) has the highest combined buckling strength, but the combined load buckling strength drops sharply as the panel aspect ratio increases. For square panels, the truss-core sandwich panel has higher compression-dominated load buckling strength. However, for shear dominated loading, the square honeycomb-core sandwich panel has higher shear-dominated combined load buckling strength.

1929. *Menon, P. K. A.; and Duke, E. L.: **Time-Optimal Aircraft Pursuit Evasion With a Weapon Envelope Constraint.** Presented at 9th American Control Conference, San Diego, California, Vol. 3, pp. 2337–2342, May 23–25, 1990. *Journal of Guidance, Control, and Dynamics*, (ISN 0731-5090), Vol. 15, March–April 1992, pp. 448–456, (A91-30193), 92A 28146. (See also 1782.)

*NASA Ames Research Center, Moffett Field, California and Georgia Institute of Technology, Atlanta, Georgia.

1930. Hicks, John W.: **Development of a Hydrogen External Burning Flight Test Experiment on the NASA Dryden SR-71A Aircraft.** SAE Paper 920997. Presented at SAE Aerospace Atlantic Conference, Dayton, Ohio, April 7–10, 1992, 93A14638.

A captive-carry flight test experiment of the transonic external burning concept using gaseous hydrogen fuel has been proposed for the SR-71A flight research test bed aircraft at the NASA Dryden Flight Research Facility, Edwards, California. This program will be the first large-scale, near-field flight test investigation of this base drag reduction technique at Mach numbers up to 3. Low-speed base drag reduction for supersonic and hypersonic flight vehicles is important in reducing vehicle drag and improving nozzle efficiency. Flight data will be correlated with a concurrent wind tunnel ground test of a similar test apparatus to confirm geometry and component performance scalability predictions and to investigate design parametrics under actual flight conditions. This paper describes the problem of transonic base drag for supersonic and hypersonic aircraft, a planned flight research program to address this problem, the test bed aircraft, and the flight experiment apparatus.

1931. Shideler, John L.; Fields, Roger A.; Reardon, Lawrence F.; and Gong, Leslie: **Thermal and Structural Tests of Rene 41 Honeycomb Integral-Tank Concept for Future Space Transportation Systems.** NASA TP-3145, L-16752, NAS 1.60:3145, May 1992, 92N24205, #.

Two flat 12 by 72 inch Rene 41 honeycomb sandwich panels were tested in a manner to produce combined thermal and mechanical longitudinal stresses that simulated those that would occur in a larger, more complex integral tank and fuselage structure of an earth to orbit vehicle. Elastic strains measured at temperatures below 400 °F are compared with calculated values obtained from a linear elastic finite element analysis to verify the analytical model and to establish confidence in the calculated strains. Elastic strain measurement at higher temperatures (between 600 °F and 1400 °F), where strain measurement is more difficult and less certain, are also compared with calculated strains. Agreement between measured and calculated strains for the lower temperatures is good, but agreement for the higher temperatures is poor because of unreliable strain measurements. Test results indicate that an ascent and entry life cycle of 500 is attainable under high combined thermal and mechanical elastic strains.

1932. Conley, Joseph L.: **User's Manual for AeroFcn: A FORTRAN Program to Compute Aerodynamic Parameters.** NASA TM-104237, H-1675, NAS 1.15:104237, May 1992, 92N32507, #.

The computer program AeroFcn is discussed. AeroFcn is a utility program that computes the following aerodynamic parameters: geopotential altitude, Mach number, true velocity, dynamic pressure, calibrated airspeed, equivalent airspeed, impact pressure, total pressure, total temperature, Reynolds number, speed of sound, static density, static pressure, static temperature, coefficient of dynamic viscosity, kinematic viscosity, geometric altitude, and specific energy for a standard- or a modified standard-day atmosphere using compressible flow and normal shock relations. Any two parameters that define a unique flight condition are selected, and their values are entered interactively. The remaining parameters are computed, and the solutions are stored in an output file. Multiple cases can be run, and the multiple case solutions can be stored in another output file for plotting. Parameter units, the output format, and primary constants in the atmospheric and aerodynamic equations can also be changed.

1933. Zuniga, Fanny A.; Anderson, Bianca T.; and Bertelrud, Arild: **Flight Test Results of Riblets at Supersonic Speeds**. NASA-TM-4387, H-1774, NAS 1.15:4387, <u>June 1992</u>, 94N32880, #.

A flight experiment to test and evaluate the skin friction drag characteristics of a riblet surface in turbulent flow at supersonic speeds was conducted at NASA Dryden. Riblets of groove sizes 0.0030 and 0.0013 in. were mounted on the F-104G flight test fixture. The test surfaces were surveyed with boundary layer rakes and pressure orifices to examine the boundary layer profiles and pressure distributions of the flow. Skin friction reductions caused by the riblet surface were reported based on measured differences of momentum thickness between the smooth and riblet surfaces obtained from the boundary layer data. Flight test results for the 0.0030 in. riblet show skin friction reductions of 4 to 8% for Mach numbers ranging from 1.2 to 1.6 and Reynolds numbers ranging from 2 to 3.4 million per unit foot. The results from the 0.0013 in. riblets show skin friction reductions of 4 to 15% for Mach 1.2 to 1.4 and Reynolds numbers ranging from 3.6 to 6 million per unit foot.

1934. Stewart, James F.; Burcham, Frank W., Jr.; and Gatlin, Donald H.: **Flight-Determined Benefits of Integrated Flight-Propulsion Control Systems**. NASA TM-4393, H-1811, NAS 1.15:4393, Paper 92-2.9.1. Proposed for presentation at the 18th ICAS Congress, Beijing, China, September 20–25 1992, <u>June 1992</u>, 92N27587, #. (See also 1976.)

Over the last two decades, NASA has conducted several experiments in integrated flight-propulsion control. Benefits have included improved maneuverability; increased thrust, range, and survivability; reduced fuel consumption; and reduced maintenance. This paper presents the basic concepts for control integration, examples of implementation, and benefits. The F-111E experiment integrated the engine and inlet control systems. The YF-12C incorporated an integral control system involving the inlet, autopilot, autothrottle, airdata, navigation, and stability augmentation systems. The F-15 research involved integration of the engine, flight, and

inlet control systems. Further extension of the integration included real-time, onboard optimization of engine, inlet, and flight control variables; a self-repairing flight control system; and an engines-only control concept for emergency control. The F-18A aircraft incorporated thrust vectoring integrated with the flight control system to provide enhanced maneuvering at high angles of attack. The flight research programs and the resulting benefits of each program are described.

1935. Stewart, James F.: **Integrated Flight Propulsion Control Research Results Using the NASA F-15 HIDEC Flight Research Facility**. NASA TM-4394, H-1817, NAS 1.15:4394, AIAA Paper 92-4106. Presented at 6th Biannual Flight Test Conference, Hilton Head, South Carolina, August 24–26, 1992, <u>June 1992</u>, 92N27379, #. (See also 1962.)

Over the last two decades, NASA has conducted several flight research experiments in integrated flight propulsion control. Benefits have included increased thrust, range, and survivability; reduced fuel consumption; and reduced maintenance. These flight programs were flown at NASA Dryden Flight Research Facility. This paper presents the basic concepts for control integration, examples of implementation, and benefits of integrated flight propulsion control systems. The F-15 research involved integration of the engine, flight, and inlet control systems. Further extension of the integration included real time, onboard optimization of engine, inlet, and flight control variables; a self repairing flight control system; and an engines only control concept for emergency control. The flight research programs and the resulting benefits are described for the F-15 research.

1936. Gupta, K. K.; *Lawson, C. L.; and *Ahmad, A. R.: **On Development of a Finite Dynamic Element and Solution of Associated Eigenproblem by a Block Lanczos Procedure**. *International Journal for Numerical Methods in Engineering*, (ISSN 0029-5981), Vol. 33, No. 8, <u>June 15, 1992</u>, pp. 1611–1623, 92A41553.

The paper first presents the details of the development of a new six-noded plane triangular finite dynamic element. A block Lanczos algorithm is developed next for the accurate and efficient solution of the quadratic matrix eigenvalue problem associated with the finite dynamic element formulation. The resulting computer program fully exploits matrix sparsity inherent in such a discretization and proves to be most efficient for the extraction of the usually required first few roots and vectors, including repeated ones. Most importantly, the present eigenproblem solution is shown to be comparable to that of the corresponding finite element analysis, thereby rendering the associated dynamic element method rather attractive owing to superior convergence characteristics of such elements, presented herein.

*Eloret Institute, Claremont, California.

1937. Conners, Timothy R.: **Thrust Stand Evaluation of Engine Performance Improvement Algorithms in an F-15 Airplane.** NASA TM-104252, H-1842, NAS 1.15:104252, AIAA Paper 92-3747. Presented at the 28th AIAA, SAE, ASME, and ASEE Joint Propulsion Conference, Nashville, Tennessee, July 6–8, 1992, July 1992, 92N30518, #. (See also 1938.)

An investigation is underway to determine the benefits of a new propulsion system optimization algorithm in an F-15 airplane. The performance seeking control (PSC) algorithm optimizes the quasi-steady-state performance of an F100 derivative turbofan engine for several modes of operation. The PSC algorithm uses an onboard software engine model that calculates thrust, stall margin, and other unmeasured variables for use in the optimization. As part of the PSC test program, the F-15 aircraft was operated on a horizontal thrust stand. Thrust was measured with highly accurate load cells. The measured thrust was compared to onboard model estimates and to results from posttest performance programs. Thrust changes using the various PSC modes were recorded. Those results were compared to benefits using the less complex highly integrated digital electronic control (HIDEC) algorithm. The PSC maximum thrust mode increased intermediate power thrust by 10 percent. The PSC engine model did very well at estimating measured thrust and closely followed the transients during optimization. Quantitative results from the evaluation of the algorithms and performance calculation models are included with emphasis on measured thrust results. The report presents a description of the PSC system and a discussion of factors affecting the accuracy of the thrust stand load measurements.

1938. Conners, Timothy R.: **Thrust Stand Evaluation of Engine Performance Improvement Algorithms in an F-15 Airplane.** AIAA Paper 92-3747. Presented at 28th AIAA, SAE, ASME, and ASEE, Joint Propulsion Conference and Exhibit, Nashville, Tennessee, July 6–8, 1992, 92A49111, #. (See also 1937.)

Results are presented from the evaluation of the performance seeking control (PSC) optimization algorithm developed by Smith et al. (1990) for F-15 aircraft, which optimizes the quasi-steady-state performance of an F100 derivative turbofan engine for several modes of operation. The PSC algorithm uses onboard software engine model that calculates thrust, stall margin, and other unmeasured variables for use in the optimization. Comparisons are presented between the load cell measurements, PSC onboard model thrust calculations, and posttest state variable model computations. Actual performance improvements using the PSC algorithm are presented for its various modes. The results of using PSC algorithm are compared with similar test case results using the HIDEC algorithm.

1939. Ko, William L.; Monaghan, Richard C.; and Jackson, Raymond H.: **Practical Theories for Service Life Prediction of Critical Aerospace Structural Components.**

NASA-TM-4354, H-1760. Presented at the 4th International Conference on Structural Failure, Product Liability and Technical Insurance, Vienna, Austria, July 6–9, 1992. *Structural Failure, Product Liability and Technical Insurance*, H.P. Rossmanith, Editor, Elsevier Science Publishers, Amsterdam, July 1993, March 1992, pp. 495–504, 92N19404, #. (See also 1921.)

A new second-order theory was developed for predicting the service lives of aerospace structural components. The predictions based on this new theory were compared with those based on the Ko first-order theory and the classical theory of service life predictions. The new theory gives very accurate service life predictions. An equivalent constant-amplitude stress cycle method was proposed for representing the random load spectrum for crack growth calculations. This method predicts the most conservative service life. The proposed use of minimum detectable crack size, instead of proof load established crack size as an initial crack size for crack growth calculations, could give a more realistic service life.

1940. *Yuhas, Andrew J.; and Ray, Ronald J.: **Effects of Bleed Air Extraction on Thrust Levels on the F404-GE-400 Turbofan Engine.** NASA TM-104247, H-1806, NAS 1.15:104247, AIAA Paper 92-3092. Presented at the 28th AIAA Joint Propulsion Conference, Nashville, Tennessee, July 6–8, 1992, July 1992, 92N29425, #. (See also 1941.)

A ground test was performed to determine the effects of compressor bleed flow extraction on the performance of F404-GE-400 afterburning turbofan engines. The two engines were installed in the F/A-18 High Alpha Research Vehicle at the NASA Dryden Flight Research Facility. A specialized bleed ducting system was installed onto the aircraft to control and measure engine bleed airflow while the aircraft was tied down to a thrust measuring stand. The test was conducted on each engine and at various power settings. The bleed air extraction levels analyzed included flow rates above the manufacturer's maximum specification limit. The measured relationship between thrust and bleed flow extraction was shown to be essentially linear at all power settings with an increase in bleed flow causing a corresponding decrease in thrust. A comparison with the F404-GE-400 steady-state engine simulation showed the estimation to be within ± 1 percent of measured thrust losses for large increases in bleed flow rate.

*PRC Inc., Edwards, California.

1941. *Yuhas, Andrew J.; and Ray, Ronald J.: **Effects of Bleed Air Extraction of Thrust Levels on the F404-GE-400 Turbofan Engine.** AIAA Paper 92-3092. Presented at the 28th AIAA, SAE, ASME, and ASEE, Joint Propulsion Conference and Exhibit, Nashville, Tennessee, July 6–8, 1992, 92A54009, #. (See also 1940.)

A ground test was performed to determine the effects of compressor bleed flow extraction on the performance of F404-GE-400 afterburning turbofan engines. The two engines were installed in the F/A-18 High Alpha Research Vehicle at the NASA Dryden Flight Research Facility. A specialized bleed ducting system was installed onto the aircraft to control and measure engine bleed airflow while the aircraft was tied down to a thrust measuring stand. The test was conducted on each engine and at various power settings. The bleed air extraction levels analyzed included flow rates above the manufacturer's maximum specification limit. The measured relationship between thrust and bleed flow extraction was shown to be essentially linear at all power settings with an increase in bleed flow causing a corresponding decrease in thrust. A comparison with the F404-GE-400 steady-state engine simulation showed the estimation to be within $\pm$ 1 percent of measured thrust losses for large increases is bleed flow rate.

*PRC Inc., Edwards, California.

1942. Shafer, Mary F.: **In-Flight Simulation Studies at the NASA Dryden Flight Research Facility.** NASA TM-4396, H-1833, NAS 1.15:4396. Presented at the AIAA Simulation Technology Conference, New Orleans, Louisiana, August 12–14, 1991, July 1992, 92N29110, #. (See also 1876, 2075.)

Since the late 1950's, the National Aeronautics and Space Administration's Dryden Flight Research Facility has found in-flight simulation to be an invaluable tool. In-flight simulation has been used to address a wide variety of flying qualities questions, including low-lift-to-drag ratio approach characteristics for vehicles like the X-15, the lifting bodies, and the Space Shuttle; the effects of time delays on controllability of aircraft with digital flight-control systems, the causes and cures of pilot-induced oscillation in a variety of aircraft, and flight-control systems for such diverse aircraft as the X-15 and the X-29. In-flight simulation has also been used to anticipate problems and to avoid them and to solve problems once they appear. Presented here is an account of the in-flight simulation at the Dryden Flight Research Facility and some discussion. An extensive bibliography is included.

1943. *Meyer, Robert R., Jr.; *Curry, Robert E.; and *Budd, Gerald D.: **Aerodynamic Flight Research Using the Pegasus® Air-Launched Space Booster.** AIAA Paper 92-3990. Presented at the 17th AIAA Aerospace Ground Testing Conference, Nashville, Tennessee, July 6–8, 1992, 92A56814, #.

Completed and planned flight research using the Pegasus® as a research vehicle and booster for other hypersonic research vehicles is reviewed. Highlights from flights 1 and 2 are discussed and compared with some analytical results. In particular, attention is given to total vehicle aerodynamics (performance and trim), local aerodynamics (pressure and heat flux distributions), and response of the thermal protection system. Future programs will include a metallic wing test section for laminar flow studies and the use of the Pegasus® to boost a research vehicle to hypersonic speeds. The proposed concepts for a dedicated hypersonic research vehicle project are also discussed.

1944. liff, Kenneth W.; and Shafer, Mary F.: **Space Shuttle Hypersonic Flight Research and the Comparison to Ground Test Results.** AIAA Paper 92-3988. Presented at the 17th AIAA Aerospace Ground Testing Conference Nashville, Tennessee, July 6–8, 1992, 92A56812, #. (See also 2034.)

Aerodynamic and aerothermodynamic comparisons between flight and ground test for the Space Shuttle at hypersonic speeds are discussed. All of the comparisons are taken from papers published by researchers active in the Space Shuttle program. The aerodynamic comparisons include stability and control derivatives, center-of-pressure location, and reaction control jet interaction. Comparisons are also discussed for various forms of heating including catalytic, boundary layer, top centerline, side fuselage, OMS pod, wing leading edge, and shock interaction. The jet interaction and center-of-pressure location flight values exceeded not only the predictions but the uncertainties of the predictions. Predictions were significantly exceeded for the heating caused by the vortex impingement on the OMS pods and for heating caused by the wing leading-edge shock interaction.

1945. Orme, John S.; and Gilyard, Glenn B.: **Subsonic Flight Test Evaluation of a Propulsion System Parameter Estimation Process for the F100 Engine.** AIAA Paper 92-3745. Presented at the 28th AIAA, SAE, ASME, and ASEE, Joint Propulsion Conference and Exhibit, Nashville, Tennessee, July 6–8, 1992, 92A49110, #. (See also 1994.)

An adaptive-performance-seeking control system which optimizes the quasi-steady-state performance of the F-15 propulsion system is discussed. This paper presents flight- and ground-test evaluations of the propulsion system parameter-estimation process used by the performance seeking control system. The estimator consists of a compact propulsion system model and an extended Kalman filter. The extended Kalman filter estimates five engine component deviation parameters from measured inputs. The compact model uses measurements and Kalman-filter estimates as inputs to predict unmeasured propulsion parameters such as net propulsive force and fan stall margin. The ability to track trends and estimate absolute values of propulsion system parameters was demonstrated. For example, thrust stand results show a good correlation especially in trends between the performance seeking control estimated and measured thrust.

1946. Gilyard, Glenn B.; Orme, John S.: **Subsonic Flight Test Evaluation of a Performance Seeking Control**

Algorithm on an F-15 Airplane. AIAA Paper 92-3743. Presented at the 28th AIAA, SAE, ASME, and ASEE, Joint Propulsion Conference and Exhibit, Nashville, Tennessee, July 6–8, 1992, 92A49109, #. (See also 1951.)

The subsonic flight test evaluation phase of the NASA4 F-15 (powered by F100 engines) performance-seeking control program was completed for single-engine operation at part- and military-power settings. The subsonic performance-seeking control algorithm optimizes the quasi-steady-state performance of the propulsion system for three modes of operation: the minimum-fuel-flow mode, the minimum-temperature mode, and the maximum-thrust mode. Decreases in thrust-specific fuel consumption of 1 to 2 percent were measured in the minimum-fuel-flow mode; these fuel savings are significant especially for supersonic cruise aircraft. Decreases of up to approximately 100 R in fan turbine inlet temperature were measured in the minimum-temperature mode. Temperature reductions of this magnitude would more than double turbine life if inlet temperature was the only life factor. Measured thrust increases of up to approximately 15 percent in the maximum-thrust mode cause substantial increases in aircraft acceleration. The subsonic flight phase has validated the performance-seeking control technology which can significantly benefit the next generation of fighter and transport aircraft.

1947. Walsh, Kevin R.: **Summary of the Effects of Engine Throttle Response on Airplane Formation-Flying Qualities.** AIAA Paper 92-3318. Presented at the 28th AIAA, SAE, ASME, and ASEE, Joint Propulsion Conference and Exhibit, Nashville, Tennessee, July 6–8, 1992, 92A48902, #. (See also 2017.)

A flight evaluation as conducted to determine the effect of engine throttle response characteristics on precision formation-flying qualities. A variable electronic throttle control system was developed and flight-tested on a TF-104G airplane with a J79-11B engine at the NASA Dryden Flight Research Facility. Ten research flights were flown to evaluate the effects of throttle gain, time delay, and fuel control rate limiting on engine handling qualities during a demanding precision wing formation task. Handling quality effects of lag filters and lead compensation time delays were also evaluated. Data from pilot ratings and comments indicate that throttle control system time delays and rate limits cause significant degradations in handling qualities. Threshold values for satisfactory (level 1) and adequate (level 2) handling qualities of these key variables are presented.

1948. Binkley, Robert L.; and Mackall, Dale: **System Overview of the NASA Dryden Integrated Test Facility.** NASA TM-104250, H-1831, NAS 1.15:104250. Presented at the 23rd Society of Flight Test Engineers Annual Symposium, Hauppage, New York, August 3–6, 1992, August 1992, 92N32201, #.

The Integrated Test Facility, built at the NASA Dryden Flight Research Facility, provides new real-time test capabilities for emerging research aircraft. An overview of the test facility and the real-time systems developed to operate this unique facility is presented. The facility will reduce flight test risk by minimizing the difference between the flight and ground test environments. This ground test environment is provided by combining real-time flight simulation with the actual aircraft. A brief introduction to the facility is followed by a discussion of the generic capabilities of its real-time systems. The simulation system with flight hardware and the remotely augmented vehicle system is described. An overview of many hardware systems developed for the facility follows. The benefits of applying simulation to hardware-in-the-loop testing on the X-31 Flight Research Program are presented.

1949. DeAngelis, V. Michael; and Anderson, Karl F.: **Thermal-Structural Test Facilities at NASA Dryden.** NASA TM-104249, H-1818, NAS 1.15:104249. Presented at the 23rd Annual Society for Flight Test Engineers Symposium, Hauppauge, New York, August 3–6 1992, August 1992, 92N34202, #.

The National Aero-Space Plane (NASP) has renewed interest in hypersonic flight and hot-structures technology development for both the airframe and engine. The NASA Dryden Thermostructures Research Facility is a unique national facility that was designed to conduct thermal-mechanical tests on aircraft and aircraft components by simulating the flight thermal environment in the laboratory. The layout of the facility is presented, which includes descriptions of the high-bay test area, the instrumentation laboratories, the mechanical loading systems, and the state-of-the-art closed-loop thermal control system. The hot-structures test capability of the facility is emphasized by the Mach-3 thermal simulation conducted on the YF-12 airplane. The Liquid-Hydrogen Structural Test Facility, which is presently in the design phase, will provide the capability of thermally testing structures containing hydrogen.

1950. Burcham, Frank W., Jr.; Maine, Trindel; and Wolf, Thomas: **Flight Testing and Simulation of an F-15 Airplane Using Throttles for Flight Control.** NASA TM-104255, H-1826, NAS 1.15:104255, AIAA Paper 92-4109. Presented at the AIAA Flight Test Conference, Hilton Head, South Carolina, August 24, 1992, August 1992, 92N32864, #. (See also 1961.)

Flight tests and simulation studies using the throttles of an F-15 airplane for emergency flight control have been conducted at the NASA Dryden Flight Research Facility. The airplane and the simulation are capable of extended up-and-away flight, using only throttles for flight path control. Initial simulation results showed that runway landings using manual throttles-only control were difficult, but possible with practice. Manual approaches flown in the airplane were much more difficult, indicating a significant discrepancy between flight and simulation. Analysis of flight data and development of improved simulation models that resolve the discrepancy are discussed. An augmented throttle-only control system that controls bank angle and flight path with appropriate feedback parameters has also been developed, evaluated in simulations, and is planned for flight in the F-15.

1951. Gilyard, Glenn B.; and Orme, John S.: **Subsonic Flight Test Evaluation of a Performance Seeking Control Algorithm on an F-15 Airplane.** NASA TM-4400, H-1808, NAS 1.15:4400. Presented at the 28th AIAA, SAE, ASME, and ASEE Joint Propulsion Conference, Nashville, Tennessee, July 6–8, 1992, August 1992, 92N31275, #. (See also 1946.)

The subsonic flight test evaluation phase of the NASA F-15 (powered by F100 engines) performance seeking control program was completed for single-engine operation at part- and military-power settings. The subsonic performance seeking control algorithm optimizes the quasi-steady-state performance of the propulsion system for three modes of operation. The minimum fuel flow mode minimizes fuel consumption. The minimum thrust mode maximizes thrust at military power. Decreases in thrust-specific fuel consumption of 1 to 2 percent were measured in the minimum fuel flow mode; these fuel savings are significant, especially for supersonic cruise aircraft. Decreases of up to approximately 100 degree R in fan turbine inlet temperature were measured in the minimum temperature mode. Temperature reductions of this magnitude would more than double turbine life if inlet temperature was the only life factor. Measured thrust increases of up to approximately 15 percent in the maximum thrust mode cause substantial increases in aircraft acceleration. The system dynamics of the closed-loop algorithm operation were good. The subsonic flight phase has validated the performance seeking control technology, which can significantly benefit the next generation of fighter and transport aircraft.

1952. Meyer, Robert R., Jr.: **Overview of the NASA Dryden Flight Research Facility Aeronautical Flight Projects.** NASA TM-104254, H-1847, NAS 1.15:104254, AGARD-16. Presented at the AGARD Flight Mechanics Panel, Chania, Crete, Greece, May 11, 1992, August 1992, 92N31261, #. (See also 1981.)

Several principal aerodynamics flight projects of the NASA Dryden Flight Research Facility are discussed. Key vehicle technology areas from a wide range of flight vehicles are highlighted. These areas include flight research data obtained for ground facility and computation correlation, applied research in areas not well suited to ground facilities (wind tunnels), and concept demonstration.

1953. Mackall, Dale; Norlin, Kenneth; Cohen, Dorothea; Kellogg, Gary; Schilling, Lawrence; and *Sheen, John: **Rapid Development of the X-31 Simulation to Support Flight-Testing.** AIAA Paper 92-4176. Presented at the AIAA and AHS, Flight Simulation Technologies

Conference, Hilton Head Island, South Carolina, August 24–26, 1992, 93A13316, #. (See also 1971.)

The X-31 Enhanced Fighter Maneuverability Program has been recognized to form the International Test Organization, with the NASA Dryden Flight Research Facility (NASA-Dryden) as the responsible test organization. The two X-31 research aircraft and engineering support personnel were collocated at NASA-Dryden, with flight test operations beginning in April 1992. Therefore, rapid development of a hardware-in-the-loop simulation was needed to support the flight test operations at NASA-Dryden, and to perform verification and validation of flight control software. The X-31 simulation system requirements, distributed simulation system architecture, simulation components math models to the visual system, and the advanced capabilities the X-31 simulation provides. In addition, unique software tools and the methods used to rapidly develop this simulation system will be highlighted.

*Rockwell International Corporation, Downey, California.

EC93-42152-8

X-31 Airplane

1954. Regenie, Victoria; Gatlin, Donald; *Kempel, Robert; and Matheny, Neil: **The F-18 High Alpha Research Vehicle—A High-Angle-of-Attack Testbed Aircraft.** AIAA Paper 92-4121. Presented at the 6th AIAA Biennial Flight Test Conference, Hilton Head Island, South Carolina, August 24–26, 1992, 93A13273, #. (See also 1970.)

The F-18 High Alpha Research Vehicle is the first thrust-vectoring testbed aircraft used to study the aerodynamics and maneuvering available in the poststall flight regime and to provide the data for validating ground prediction techniques. The aircraft includes a flexible research flight control system and full research instrumentation. The capability to control the vehicle at angles of attack up to 70 degrees is also included. This aircraft was modified by adding a pitch and yaw thrust-vectoring system. No significant problems occurred during the envelope expansion phase of the program.

*PRC Inc., Edwards, California.

1955. Bogue, Rodney K.: **Recent Flight-Test Results of Optical Airdata Techniques.** AIAA Paper 92-4086. Presented at the 6th AIAA, Biennial Flight Test Conference, Hilton Head Island, South Carolina, August 24–26, 1992, 93A13265, #. (See also 2026.)

Optical techniques for measuring airdata parameters have been demonstrated with promising results on high-performance fighter aircraft. These systems can measure the airspeed vector, and some are not as dependent on special in-flight calibration processes as current systems. Optical concepts for measuring free stream static temperature and density are feasible for in-flight as applications. The best feature of these concepts is that the airdata measurements are obtained nonintrusively, and for the most part well into the freestream region of the flowfield about the aircraft. Current requirements for measuring airdata at high angle of attack, and future need to measure the same information at hypersonic flight conditions place strains on existing techniques. Optical technology advances show outstanding potential for application in future programs and promise to make common use of optical concepts a reality. This paper summarizes results from several flight-test programs and identifies the technology advances required to make optical airdata techniques practical.

1956. Knighton, Donna L.: **Design and Utilization of a Flight Test Engineering Database Management System at the NASA Dryden Flight Research Facility.** AIAA Paper 92-4072. Presented at the 6th AIAA, Biennial Flight Test Conference, Hilton Head Island, South Carolina, August 24–26, 1992, 93A13264, #.

A Flight Test Engineering Database Management System (FTE DBMS) was designed and implemented at the NASA Dryden Flight Research Facility. The X-29 Forward Swept Wing Advanced Technology Demonstrator flight research program was chosen for the initial system development and implementation. The FTE DBMS greatly assisted in planning and 'mass production' card preparation for an accelerated X-29 research program. Improved Test Plan tracking and maneuver management for a high flight-rate program were proven, and flight rates of up to three flights per day, two times per week were maintained.

1957. *Bertelrud, Arild; **Kolodziej, Paul; Noffz, Greg K.; and *Godil, Afzal: **Plans for In-Flight Measurement of Hypersonic Crossflow Transition on the Pegasus® Launch Vehicle.** AIAA Paper 92-4104. Presented at the 6th AIAA, Biennial Flight Test Conference, Hilton Head Island, South Carolina, August 24–26, 1992, 93A13260, #.

A flight measurements program is underway to obtain flight data for validating stability theory-based transition estimation techniques for crossflow-induced boundary-layer transition at Mach 6-8. A smooth wing glove, designed to enhance crossflow transition and suppress Tollmien-Schlichting (T-S) instabilities, will be mounted on the delta wing of the first stage of the Pegasus® booster. The instrumentation package will include 'intelligent' software capable of yielding space and time-correlations obtained through extensive use of fast Fourier transforms (FFTs), 'windowing' and multistage compression as well as a variety of techniques for quality assurance. The flight experiment covers a Mach number range (6 to 8) where low background disturbance data cannot currently be obtained in ground facilities. These flight results will support transition estimation code development for application to supersonic laminar flow control (LFC) and National Aero-Space Plane (NASP) class vehicles in areas where crossflow, rather than T-S waves, is the dominant instability mode.

*NASA Langley Research Center, Hampton, Virginia.
**NASA Ames Research Center, Mountain View, California.

1958. *Agarwal, Naval K.; *Miley, Stan J.; *Fischer, Michael C.; Anderson, Bianca T.; and Geenen, Robert J.: **Measurement of Attachment-Line Location in a Wind-Tunnel and in Supersonic Flight.** AIAA Paper 92-4089. *Technical Papers*, presented at the 6th AIAA Biennial Flight Test Conference, Hilton Head Island, South Carolina, August 24–26, 1992, pp. 404–414, 93A11285, #.

For the supersonic laminar flow control research program, tests are being conducted to measure the attachment-line flow characteristics and its location on a highly swept aircraft wing. Subsonic wind tunnel experiments were conducted on 2D models to develop sensors and techniques for the flight application. Representative attachment-line data are discussed and results from the wind tunnel investigation are presented.

*NASA Langley Research Center, Hampton, Virginia.

1959. Bever, Glenn: **The Development of an Airborne Information Management System for Flight Test.** AIAA Paper 92-4113. *Technical Papers*, presented at the 6th AIAA Biennial Flight Test Conference, Hilton Head Island, South Carolina, August 24–26, 1992, pp. 323–332, (A93-11251 01-05), 93A11281, #. (See also 1972.)

An airborne information management system is being developed at the NASA Dryden Flight Research Facility. This system will improve the state of the art in management data acquisition on-board research aircraft. The design centers around highly distributable, high-speed microprocessors that allow data compression, digital filtering, and real-time analysis. This paper describes the areas of applicability, approach to developing the system, potential for trouble areas, and reasons for this development activity. System architecture (including the salient points of what makes it unique), design philosophy, and tradeoff issues are also discussed.

1960. Hamory, Philip J.; and Murray, James E.: **Flight Experience With Lightweight, Low-Power Miniaturized Instrumentation Systems.** AIAA Paper 92-4111. *Technical Papers,* presented at the 6th AIAA Biennial Flight Test Conference, Hilton Head Island, South Carolina, August 24–26, 1992, pp. 309–322, (A93-11251 01-05), 93A11280, #. (See also 2018, 2112.)

Engineers at the NASA Dryden Flight Research Facility (NASA-Dryden) have conducted two flight research programs with lightweight, low-power miniaturized instrumentation systems built around commercial data loggers. One program quantified the performance of a radio-controlled model airplane. The other program was a laminar boundary-layer transition experiment on a manned sailplane. The purpose of this paper is to report NASA-Dryden personnel's flight experience with the miniaturized instrumentation systems used on these two programs. The paper will describe the data loggers, the sensors, and the hardware and software developed to complete the systems. The paper also describes how the systems were used and covers the challenges encountered to make them work. Examples of raw data and derived results will be shown as well. Finally, future plans for these systems will be discussed.

1961. Burcham, Frank W., Jr.; Maine, Trindel; and Wolf, Thomas: **Flight Testing and Simulation of an F-15 Airplane Using Throttles for Flight Control.** AIAA Paper 92-4109. *Technical Papers,* presented at the 6th AIAA Biennial Flight Test Conference, Hilton Head Island, South Carolina, August 24–26, 1992, pp. 282–299, (A93-11251 01-05), 93A11278, #. (See also 1950.)

Flight tests and simulation studies using the throttles of an F-15 airplane for emergency flight control have been conducted at the NASA Dryden Flight Research Facility. The airplane and the simulation are capable of extended up-and-away flight, using only throttles for flight path control. Initial simulation results showed that runway landings using manual throttles-only control were difficult, but possible with practice. Manual approaches flown in the airplane were much more difficult, indicating a significant discrepancy between flight and simulation. Analysis of flight data and development of improved simulation models that resolve the discrepancy are discussed. An augmented throttle-only control system that controls bank angle and flight path with appropriate feedback parameters has also been developed, evaluated in simulations, and is planned for flight in the F-15.

1962. Stewart, James F.: **Integrated Flight Propulsion Control Research Results Using the NASA F-15 HIDEC Flight Research Facility.** AIAA Paper 92-4106. *Technical Papers,* presented at the 6th AIAA Biennial Flight Test Conference, Hilton Head Island, South Carolina, August 24–26, 1992, pp. 247–265, (A93-11251 01-05), 93A11276, #. (See also 1935.)

Over the last two decades, NASA has conducted several flight research experiments in integrated flight propulsion control. Benefits have included increased thrust, range, and survivability; reduced fuel consumption; and reduced maintenance. These flight programs were flown at NASA Dryden Flight Research Facility. This paper presents the basic concepts for control integration, examples of implementation, and benefits of integrated flight propulsion control systems. The F-15 research involved integration of the engine, flight, and inlet control systems. Further extension of the integration included real time, onboard optimization of engine, inlet, and flight control variables; a self repairing flight control system; and an engines only control concept for emergency control. The flight research programs and the resulting benefits are described for the F-15 research.

1963. Powers, Sheryll G.; Webb, Lannie D.; Friend, Edward L.; and Lokos, William A.: **Flight Test Results From a Supercritical Mission Adaptive Wing With Smooth Variable Camber.** AIAA Paper 92-4101. *Technical Papers,* presented at the 6th AIAA Biennial Flight Test Conference, Hilton Head Island, South Carolina, August 24–26, 1992, pp. 201–228, (A93-11251 01-05), 93A11274, #. (See also 1995.)

Results from the wing surface and boundary layer pressures, buffet studies and flight deflection measurement system for the advanced fighter technology integration F-111 mission adaptive wing program are presented. The different aerodynamic technologies studied on the aircraft, and their relationship with each other are described. The wingtip twist measurements provide an insight as to how dynamic pressures for positive normal accelerations affect the wingtip pressure profiles.

1964. Fisher, David F.; *Richwine, David M.; and *Landers, Stephen: **Correlation of Forebody Pressures and Aircraft Yawing Moments on the X-29A Aircraft at High Angles of Attack.** AIAA Paper 92-4105. *Technical Papers,* presented at the 6th AIAA Biennial Flight Test Conference, Hilton Head Island, South Carolina, August 24–26, 1992, pp. 187–200, (A93-11251 01-05), 93A11273, #. (See also 1990.)

In-flight pressure distributions are presented at angles of attack from 15 deg to 66 deg and at Mach numbers from 0.22 to 0.60 at four fuselage stations on the forebody of the X-29A aircraft. Forebody yawing moments are obtained from the integrated pressure distributions and the results are correlated with the overall aircraft yawing moments. Yawing moments created by the forebody were not significant until an angle of attack of 50 deg or above and correlated well with the aircraft left yawing moment.

*PRC Inc., Edwards, California.

1965. Del Frate, John H.: and *Saltzman, John A.: **In-Flight Flow Visualization Results From the X-29A Aircraft at High Angles of Attack.** AIAA Paper 92-4102. *Technical Papers,* presented at the 6th AIAA Biennial Flight Test Conference, Hilton Head Island, South Carolina, <u>August 24–26, 1992</u>, pp. 173–186, (A93-11251 01-05), 93A11272, #. (See also 1993.)

Flow visualization techniques were used on the X-29A aircraft at high angles of attack to study the vortical flow off the forebody and the surface flow on the wing and tail. The forebody vortex system was studied because asymmetries in the vortex system were suspected of inducing uncommanded yawing moments at zero sideslip. Smoke enabled visualization of the vortex system and correlation of its orientation with flight yawing moment data. Good agreement was found between vortex system asymmetries and the occurrence of yawing moments. Surface flow on the forward-swept wing of the X-29A was studied using tufts and flow cones. As angle of attack increased, separated flow initiated at the root and spread outboard encompassing the full wing by 30 deg angle of attack. In general, the progression of the separated flow correlated well with subscale model lift data.

*PRC Inc., Edwards, California.

EC91-491-6

X-29A Airplane With Smoke Generators

1966. *Scardello, Michael A.; *Nesel, Michael C.; and Wheaton, Duane L.: **Real-Time Capture, Archiving, Retrieval, Processing, and Presentation of Large Quantities of Flight Test/Research Information.** AIAA Paper 92-4073. *Technical Papers,* presented at the 6th AIAA Biennial Flight Test Conference, Hilton Head Island, South Carolina, <u>August 24–26, 1992</u>, pp. 44–53, (A93-11251 01-05), 93A11258, #.

An architectural approach that greatly increases the capability to handle the increasingly large quantity of flight test/research data is presented. Attention is given to new and emerging technologies in the mass storage arena, the continuous increases in computational performance, and commercially available analysis and display tools. Consideration is given to the capture, archiving, responsive retrieval, efficient and accurate processing, and presentation of these large quantities of information in a convenient and cost effective manner.

*Perimeter Computer Systems, Inc., Lancaster, California.

1967. Haering, Edward A., Jr.: **Airdata Calibration Techniques for Measuring Atmospheric Wind Profiles.** *Journal of Aircraft,* (ISSN 0021-8669), Vol. 29, No. 4, <u>July–August 1992</u>, pp. 632–639, 92A46792. (See also 1756, 1757.)

The research airdata system of an instrumented F-104 aircraft has been calibrated to measure winds aloft in support of the Space Shuttle wind measurement investigation at the National Aeronautics and Space Administration Ames Research Center Dryden Flight Research Facility. For this investigation, wind measurement accuracies comparable to those obtained from Jimsphere balloons were desired. This required an airdata calibration more accurate than needed for most aircraft research programs. The F-104 aircraft was equipped with a research pilot-static noseboom with integral angle-of-attack and flank angle-of-attack vanes and a ring-laser-gyro inertial reference unit. Tower fly-bys and radar acceleration-decelerations were used to calibrate Mach number and total temperature. Angle of attack and angle of side slip were calibrated with a trajectory reconstruction technique using a multiple-state linear Kalman filter. The F-104 aircraft and instrumentation configuration, flight test maneuvers, data corrections, calibration techniques, and resulting calibrations and data repeatability are presented. Recommendations for future airdata systems on aircraft used to measure winds aloft are also given.

1968. Burken, John J.: **Flight-Determined Stability Analysis of Multiple-Input-Multiple-Output Control Systems.** AIAA Paper 92-4396. *Technical Papers,* Pt. 1, presented at the AIAA Guidance, Navigation and Control Conference, Hilton Head Island, South Carolina, <u>August 10–12, 1992</u>, pp. 439–453, (A92-55151 23-63), 92A55196, #. (See also 1991, 2067.)

Singular value analysis can give conservative stability margin results. Applying structure to the uncertainty can reduce this conservatism. This paper presents flight-determined stability margins for the X-29A lateral-directional, multiloop control system. These margins are compared with the predicted unscaled singular values and scaled structured singular values. The algorithm was further evaluated with flight data by changing the roll-rate-to-aileron-command-feedback gain by +/- 20 percent. Also presented are the minimum eigenvalues of the return difference matrix which bound the singular values. Extracting multiloop singular values from flight data and analyzing the feedback gain variations validates this technique as a measure of robustness. This analysis can be used for near-real-time flight monitoring and safety testing.

1969. *Richwine, David M.; and Fisher, David F.: **In-Flight Leading-Edge Extension Vortex Flow-Field Survey Measurements on a F-18 Aircraft at High Angle of Attack**. NASA TM-4398, H-1783, NAS 1.15:4398. Presented at the AIAA 9th Applied Aerodynamics Conference, Baltimore, Maryland, September 23–25, 1991. September 1992, 92N31276, #. (See also 1888.)

Flow-field measurements on the leading-edge extension (LEX) of the F-18 High Alpha Research Vehicle (HARV) were obtained using a rotating rake with 16 hemispherical-tipped five-hole probes. Detailed pressure, velocity, and flow direction data were obtained through the LEX vortex core. Data were gathered during 1-g quasi-stabilized flight conditions at angles of attack alpha from 10 degrees to 52 degrees and at Reynolds numbers based on mean aerodynamic cord up to 16 x 10 (exp 6). Normalized dynamic pressures and crossflow velocities clearly showed the primary vortex above the LEX and formation of a secondary vortex at higher angles of attack. The vortex was characterized by a ring of high dynamic pressure surrounding a region of low dynamic pressure at the vortex core center. The vortex core, subcore diameter, and vertical location of the core above the LEX increased with angle of attack. Minimum values for static pressure were obtained in the vortex subcore and decreased nearly linearly with increasing angle of attack until vortex breakdown. Rake-measured static pressures were consistent with previously documented surface pressures and showed good agreement with flow visualization flight test results. Comparison of the LEX vortex flight test data to computational solutions at alpha approximately equals 19 degrees and 30 degrees showed fair correlation.

*PRC Inc., Edwards, California.

1970. Regenie, Victoria; Gatlin, Donald; *Kempel, Robert; and Matheny, Neil: **The F-18 High Alpha Research Vehicle: A High-Angle-of-Attack Testbed Aircraft**. NASA TM-104253, H-1846, NAS 1.15:104253, AIAA Paper 92-4121. Presented at the 6th Biennial Flight Test Conference, Hilton Head Island, South Carolina, August 24–26, 1992, September 1992, 92N33404, #. (See also 1954.)

The F-18 High Alpha Research Vehicle is the first thrust-vectoring testbed aircraft used to study the aerodynamics and maneuvering available in the poststall flight regime and to provide the data for validating ground prediction techniques. The aircraft includes a flexible research flight control system and full research instrumentation. The capability to control

the vehicle at angles of attack up to 70 degrees is also included. This aircraft was modified by adding a pitch and yaw thrust-vectoring system. No significant problems occurred during the envelope expansion phase of the program. This aircraft has demonstrated excellent control in the wing rock region and increased rolling performance at high angles of attack. Initial pilot reports indicate that the increased capability is desirable although some difficulty in judging the size and timing of control inputs was observed. The aircraft, preflight ground testing and envelope expansion flight tests are described.

*PRC Inc., Edwards, California.

1971. Mackall, Dale; Norlin, Kenneth; Cohen, Dorothea; Kellogg, Gary; Schilling, Lawrence; and *Sheen, John: **Rapid Development of the X-31 Simulation to Support Flight-Testing**. NASA TM-104256, H-1857, NAS 1.15:104256, AIAA Paper 92-4176. Presented at the AIAA and AHS Flight Simulation Technologies Conference, Hilton Head, South Carolina, August 24–26, 1992, September 1992, 92N33149, #. (See also 1953.)

The X-31 Enhanced Fighter Maneuverability Program has been recognized to form the International Test Organization, with the NASA Dryden Flight Research Facility (NASA-Dryden) as the responsible test organization. The two X-31 research aircraft and engineering support personnel were collocated at NASA-Dryden, with flight test operations beginning in April 1992. Therefore, rapid development of a hardware-in-the-loop simulation was needed to support the flight test operations at NASA-Dryden, and to perform verification and validation of flight control software. The X-31 simulation system requirements, distributed simulation system architecture, simulation components math models to the visual system, and the advanced capabilities the X-31 simulation provides. In addition, unique software tools and the methods used to rapidly develop this simulation system will be highlighted.

*Rockwell International Corp., Downey, California.

1972. Bever, Glenn A.: **The Development of an Airborne Information Management System for Flight Test**. NASA TM-104251, H-1839, NAS 1.15:104251, AIAA Paper 92-4113. Presented at the 6th Biennial Flight Test Conference, Hilton Head, South Carolina, August 24–26, 1992, September 1992, 92N32866, #. (See also 1959.)

An airborne information management system is being developed at the NASA Dryden Flight Research Facility. This system will improve the state of the art in management data acquisition on-board research aircraft. The design centers around highly distributable, high-speed microprocessors that allow data compression, digital filtering, and real-time analysis. This paper describes the areas of applicability, approach to developing the system, potential for trouble areas, and reasons for this development activity. System architecture (including the salient points of what makes it unique), design philosophy, and tradeoff issues are also discussed.

1973. *Hancock, Regis; and Fullerton, Gordon: **X-29 Vortex Flow Control Tests.** *Proceedings, 1992 Report to the Aerospace Profession 36th SETP Symposium*, Beverly Hills, California, September 24–26, 1992, pp. 209–219, 93A38846.

A joint Air Force/NASA X-29 aircraft program to improve yaw control at high angle of attack using vortex flow control (VFC) is described. Directional VFC blowing proved to a be a powerful yaw moment generator and was very effective in overriding natural asymmetries, but was essentially ineffective in suppressing wing rock. Symmetric aft blowing also had little effect on suppressing wing rock.

*USAF Flight Test Center, Edwards AFB, California.

1974. *Finney, M. J.; *Tregay, G. W.; and *Calabrese, P. R.: **Flight Testing of a Fiber Optic Temperature Sensor.** *Proceedings, Specialty Fiber Optic Systems for Mobile Platforms and Plastic Optical Fibers*, Boston, Massachusetts, September 9–11, 1992, pp. 194–203, 93A49476.

A fiber optic temperature sensor (FOTS) system consisting of an optical probe, a flexible fiber optic cable, and an electro-optic signal processor was fabricated to measure the gas temperature in a turbine engine. The optical probe contained an emissive source embedded in a sapphire lightguide coupled to a fiber-optic jumper cable and was retrofitted into an existing thermocouple probe housing. The flexible fiber optic cable was constructed with 200 micron core, polyimide-coated fiber and was ruggedized for an aircraft environment. The electro-optic signal processing unit was used to ratio the intensities of two wavelength intervals and provided an analog output value of the indicated temperature. Subsequently, this optical sensor system was installed on a NASA Dryden F-15 Highly Integrated Digital Electronic Control (HIDEC) Aircraft Engine and several flight tests were conducted. Over the course of flight testing, the FOTS system's response was proportional to the average of the existing thermocouples sensing the changes in turbine engine thermal conditions.

*Conax Buffalo Corporation, Buffalo, New York.

1975. Kehoe, Michael W.; and *Ricketts, Rodney H.: **Getting Up to Speed in Hypersonic Structures.** *Aerospace America*, (ISSN 0740-722X), Vol. 30, No. 9, September 1992, pp. 18–20, 92A55127.

An overview is presented of some of the hypersonic technology that will become the baseline for more advanced commercial aerospace systems and new military transportation systems for carrying astronauts and equipment into space. Attention is given to the X-15 aeronautical research program, the X-20 DYNA-SOAR, and the current X-30 National Aerospace Plane. Consideration is given to FEM analysis methods, modal testing conducted to measure the structure's resonant frequencies, dampings, and mode shapes, and high-temperature, high-speed wind tunnel testing and in-flight measurement of steady and unsteady pressures at Mach 3 and above.

*NASA Langley Research Center, Hampton, Virginia.

1976. Stewart, James F.; Burcham, Frank W., Jr.; and Gatlin, Donald H.: **Flight-Determined Benefits of Integrated Flight-Propulsion Control Systems.** *Proceedings, 18th ICAS Congress*, Beijing, China, Vol. 2, September 20–25, 1992, pp. 1756–1777, 93A14370. (See also 1934.)

The fundamentals of control integration for propulsion are reviewed giving practical illustrations of its use to demonstrate the advantages of integration. Attention is given to the first integration propulsion-control systems (IPCSs) which was developed for the F-111E, and the integrated controller design is described that NASA developed for the YF-12C aircraft. The integrated control systems incorporate a range of aircraft components including the engine, inlet controls, autopilot, autothrottle, airdata, navigation, and/or stability-augmentation systems. Also described are emergency-control systems, onboard engine optimization, and thrust-vectoring control technologies developed for the F-18A and the F-15. Integrated flight-propulsion control systems are shown to enhance the thrust, range, and survivability of the aircraft while reducing fuel consumption and maintenance.

1977. Regenie, Victoria A.; Earls, Michael; Le, Jeanette; and *Thomson, Michael: **Experience With Ada on the F-18 High Alpha Research Vehicle Flight Test Program.** NASA TM-104259, H-1860, NAS 1.15:104259. Presented at the IEEE and AIAA Digital Avionics Systems Conference, Seattle, Washington, October 5–8, 1992, October 1992, 92N34039, #. (See also 2074.)

Considerable experience was acquired with Ada at the NASA Dryden Flight Research Facility during the on-going High Alpha Technology Program. In this program, an F-18 aircraft was highly modified by the addition of thrust-vectoring vanes to the airframe. In addition, substantial alteration was made in the original quadruplex flight control system. The result is the High Alpha Research Vehicle. An additional research flight control computer was incorporated in each of the four channels. Software for the research flight control computer was written in Ada. To date, six releases of this software have been flown. This paper provides a detailed description of the modifications to the research flight control system. Efficient ground-testing of the software was accomplished by using simulations that used the Ada for portions of their software. These simulations are also described. Modifying and transferring the Ada for flight software to the software simulation configuration has allowed evaluation of this language. This paper also discusses such significant issues in using Ada as portability, modifiability, and testability as well as documentation requirements.

*PRC Inc., Edwards, California.

1978. Anderson, Bianca T.; and Bohn-Meyer, Marta: **Overview of Supersonic Laminar Flow Control Research on the F-16XL Ships 1 and 2**. NASA TM-104257, H-1858, NAS 1.15:104257, SAE Paper 92-1994. Presented at the 1992 Aerotech Conference, Anaheim, California, October 5–8, 1992, October 1992, 93N11221, #. (See also 1987.)

NASA is directing research to develop technology for a high-speed civil transport. Supersonic laminar flow control has been identified as a program element, since it offers significant drag-reduction benefits and is one of the more promising technologies for producing an economically viable aircraft design. NASA is using two prototype F-16XL aircraft to research supersonic laminar flow control. The F-16XL planform is similar to design planforms of high-speed civil transports. The planform makes the aircraft ideally suited for developing technology pertinent to high-speed transports. The supersonic laminar flow control research programs for both aircraft are described. Some general results of the ship-1 program demonstrate that significant laminar flow was obtained using laminar flow control on a highly swept wing at supersonic speeds.

1979. Noffz, Gregory K.; Moes, Timothy R.; Haering, Edward A., Jr.; and *Kolodziej, Paul: **Aerothermal Test Results From the Second Flight of the Pegasus® Booster**. NASA TM-4391, H-1827, NAS 1.15:4391, October 1992, 93N10969, #.

A survey of temperature, heat-flux, and pressure measurements was obtained at speeds through Mach 8.0 on the second flight of the Pegasus® air-launched space booster system. All sensors were distributed on the wing-body fairing or fillet. Sensors included thin foil-gauge thermocouples installed near the surface within the thermal protection system. Thermocouples were also installed on the surface of nonablating plugs. The resulting temperature time history allowed derivation of convective heat flux. In addition, commercially available calorimeters were installed on the fillet at selected locations. Calorimeters exhibited a larger change in measured heat flux than collocated nonablating

plugs in response to particular events. Similar proportional variations in heat flux across different regions of the fillet were detected by both the calorimeters and nonablating plugs. Pressure ports were installed on some nonablating plugs to explore the effects of port protrusion and high-frequency noise on pressure requirements. The effect of port protrusion on static-pressure measurements was found to decrease with increasing Mach number. High-frequency noise suppression was found to be desirable but not required on any future flight.

*NASA Ames Research Center, Moffett Field, California.

1980. Anderson, Karl F.: **The Constant Current Loop: A New Paradigm for Resistance Signal Conditioning**. NASA TM-104260, H-1861, NAS 1.15:104260, October 1992, 93N12681, #. (See also 2024, 2025, 2071.)

A practical single constant current loop circuit for the signal conditioning of variable resistance transducers has been synthesized, analyzed, and demonstrated. The strain gage and the resistance temperature device are examples of variable resistance sensors. Lead wires connect variable resistance sensors to remotely located signal conditioning hardware. The presence of lead wires in the conventional Wheatstone bridge signal conditioning circuit introduces undesired effects that reduce the quality of the data from the remote sensors. A practical approach is presented for suppressing essentially all lead wire resistance effects while indicating only the change in resistance value. Theoretical predictions supported by laboratory testing confirm the following features of the approach: (1) dc response; (2) the electrical output is unaffected by extremely large variations in the resistance of any or all lead wires; (3) the electrical output remains zero for no change in gage resistance; (4) the electrical output is inherently linear with respect to gage resistance change; (5) the sensitivity is double that of a Wheatstone bridge circuit; and (6) the same excitation wires can serve multiple independent gages. An adaptation of current loop circuit is presented that simultaneously provides an output signal voltage directly proportional to transducer resistance change and provides temperature information that is unaffected by transducer and lead wire resistance variations. These innovations are the subject of NASA patent applications.

1981. Meyer, Robert R., Jr.: **Overview of the NASA Dryden Flight Research Facility Aeronautical Flight Projects Testing**. AGARD CP-519, *Flight Testing*, October 1992, (see N93-19901 06-05), 93N19916, #. (See also 1952.)

Several principal aeronautics flight projects of the NASA Dryden Flight Research Facility are discussed. Key vehicle technology areas from a wide range of flight vehicles are highlighted. These areas include flight research data obtained for ground facility and computation correlation, applied research in areas not well suited to ground facilities (wind tunnels), and concept demonstration.

1982. Larson, Richard R.; and *Millard, D. Edward: **A Rule-Based System for Real-Time Analysis of Control Systems**. NASA TM-104258, H-1859, NAS 1.15:104258. Presented at the 11th IEEE and AIAA Digital Avionics Systems Conference, Seattle, Washington, October 5–8, 1992, October 1992, 93N11619, #.

An approach to automate the real-time analysis of flight critical health monitoring and system status is being developed and evaluated at the NASA Dryden Flight Research Facility. A software package was developed in-house and installed as part of the extended aircraft interrogation and display system. This design features a knowledge-base structure in the form of rules to formulate interpretation and decision logic of real-time data. This technique has been applied for ground verification and validation testing and flight testing monitoring where quick, real-time, safety-of-flight decisions can be very critical. In many cases post processing and manual analysis of flight system data are not required. The processing is described of real-time data for analysis along with the output format which features a message stack display. The development, construction, and testing of the rule-driven knowledge base, along with an application using the X-31A flight test program, are presented.

*Computer Sciences Corporation, Edwards AFB, California.

1983. McLachlan, B. G.; Bell, J. H.; Espina, J.; Gallery, J.; Gouterman, M.; Demandante, C. G. N.; and Bjarke, L.: **Flight Testing of a Luminescent Surface Pressure Sensor**. NASA TM-103970, A-92175, NAS 1.15:103970, October 1992, 94N35394, #.

NASA ARC has conducted flight tests of a new type of aerodynamic pressure sensor based on a luminescent surface coating. Flights were conducted at the NASA ARC-Dryden Flight Research Facility. The luminescent pressure sensor is based on a surface coating which, when illuminated with ultraviolet light, emits visible light with an intensity dependent on the local air pressure on the surface. This technique makes it possible to obtain pressure data over the entire surface of an aircraft, as opposed to conventional instrumentation, which can only make measurements at pre-selected points. The objective of the flight tests was to evaluate the effectiveness and practicality of a luminescent pressure sensor in the actual flight environment. A luminescent pressure sensor was installed on a fin, the Flight Test Fixture (FTF), that is attached to the underside of an F-104 aircraft. The response of one particular surface coating was evaluated at low supersonic Mach numbers

(M = 1.0–1.6) in order to provide an initial estimate of the sensor's capabilities. This memo describes the test approach, the techniques used, and the pressure sensor's behavior under flight conditions. A direct comparison between data provided by the luminescent pressure sensor and that produced by conventional pressure instrumentation shows that the luminescent sensor can provide quantitative data under flight conditions. However, the test results also show that the sensor has a number of limitations which must be addressed if this technique is to prove useful in the flight environment.

1984. Whitmore, Stephen A.; Moes, Timothy R.; and *Larson, Terry J.: **High Angle-of-Attack Flush Airdata Sensing System**. *Journal of Aircraft*, (ISSN 0021-8669), Vol. 29, No. 5, September–October 1992, pp. 915–919, (see A90-19746), 92A56172. (See also 1758, 1759.)

*PRC Systems, Inc., Edwards, California.

1985. Bjarke, Lisa J.; Del Frate, John H.; and Fisher, David F.: **A Summary of the Forebody High-Angle-of-Attack Aerodynamics Research on the F-18 and the X-29A Aircraft**. SAE Paper 92-1996. SAE Aerotech '92 Conference, Anaheim, California, October 5–8, 1992, 94A12008. (See also 1989.)

High-angle-of-attack aerodynamic studies have been conducted on both the obtained include on- and off-surface flow visualization and static pressure measurements on the forebody. Comparisons of similar results are made between the two aircraft where possible. The forebody shapes of the two aircraft are different and the X-29A forebody flow is affected by the addition of nose strakes and a flight test noseboom. The forebody flow field of the F-18 HARV is fairly symmetric at zero sideslip and has distinct, well-defined vortices. The X-29A forebody vortices are more diffuse and are sometimes asymmetric at zero sideslip. These asymmetries correlate with observed zero-sideslip aircraft yawing moments.

1986. Curry, Robert E.; Meyer, Robert R., Jr.; and Budd, Gerald D.: *Pegasus*® **Hypersonic Flight Research**. SAE Paper 92-1995. SAE Aerotech '92 Conference, Anaheim, California, October 5–8, 1992, 94A12007.

Hypersonic aeronautics research using the Pegasus® air-launched space booster is described. Two areas are discussed in the paper: previously obtained results from Pegasus® flights 1 and 2, and plans for future programs. Proposed future research includes boundary-layer transition studies on the airplane-like first stage and also use of the complete Pegasus® launch system to boost a research vehicle to hypersonic speeds. Pegasus® flight 1 and 2 measurements were used to evaluate the results of several analytical aerodynamic design tools applied during the development of the vehicle as well as to develop hypersonic flight-test techniques. These data indicated that the aerodynamic design approach for Pegasus® was adequate and showed that acceptable margins were available. Additionally, the correlations provide insight into the capabilities of these analytical tools for more complex vehicles in which design margins may be more stringent. Near-term plans to conduct hypersonic boundary-layer transition studies are discussed. These plans involve the use of a smooth metallic glove at about the mid-span of the wing. Longer-term opportunities are proposed which identify advantages of the Pegasus® launch system to boost large-scale research vehicles to the real-gas hypersonic flight regime.

1987. Anderson, Bianca T.; and Bohn-Meyer, Marta: **Overview of Supersonic Laminar Flow Control Research on the F-16XL Ships 1 and 2.** SAE Paper 921994. SAE Aerotech '92 Conference, Anaheim, California, October 5–8, 1992, 94A12006. (See also 1978.)

NASA is directing research to develop technology for a high-speed civil transport. Supersonic laminar flow control has been identified as a program element, since it offers significant drag-reduction benefits and is one of the more promising technologies for producing an economically viable aircraft design. NASA is using two prototype F-16XL aircraft to research supersonic laminar flow control. The F-16XL planform is similar to design planforms of high-speed civil transports. The planform makes the aircraft ideally suited for developing technology pertinent to high-speed transports. The supersonic laminar flow control research programs for both aircraft are described. Some general results of the ship-1 program demonstrate that significant laminar flow was obtained using laminar flow control on a highly swept wing at supersonic speeds.

1988. Del Frate, John H.: **Correlation of Off-Surface Flow Visualization With Yawing Moments for a Forward Swept Wing Aircraft.** *Flow Visualization VI: Proceedings of the 6th International Symposium*, Yokohama, Japan, October 1992, (TA357 I582 1992), Sariger-Verlag, Berlin and Heidelberg, Germany, October 1992, pp. 265–269.

1989. Bjarke, Lisa J.; Del Frate, John H.; and Fisher, David F.: **A Summary of the Forebody High-Angle-of-Attack Aerodynamics Research on the F-18 and the X-29A Aircraft.** NASA TM-104261, H-1862, NAS 1.15:104261, SAE-92-1996. Presented at the SAE Aerotech 1992 Conference, Anaheim, California, October 5–8, 1992, November 1992, 93N12353, #. (See also 1985.)

High-angle-of-attack aerodynamic studies have been conducted on both the F18 High Alpha Research Vehicle (HARV) and the X-29A aircraft. Data obtained include on- and off-surface flow visualization and static pressure measurements on the forebody. Comparisons of similar results are made between the two aircraft where possible. The forebody shapes of the two aircraft are different and the X-29A forebody flow is affected by the addition of nose strakes and a flight test noseboom. The forebody flow field of the F-18 HARV is fairly symmetric at zero sideslip and has distinct, well-defined vortices. The X-29A forebody vortices are more diffuse and are sometimes asymmetric at zero sideslip. These asymmetries correlate with observed zero-sideslip aircraft yawing moments.

1990. Fisher, David F.; *Richwine, David M.; and *Landers, Stephen: **Correlation of Forebody Pressures and Aircraft Yawing Moments on the X-29A Aircraft at High Angles of Attack.** NASA TM-4417, H-1851, NAS 1.15:4417, AIAA Paper 92-4105. Presented at the AIAA Flight Test Conference, Hilton Head, South Carolina, August 24–26, 1992, November 1992, 93N11532, #. (See also 1964.)

In-flight pressure distributions at four fuselage stations on the forebody of the X-29A aircraft have been reported at angles of attack from 15 to 66 deg and at Mach numbers from 0.22 to 0.60. At angles of attack of 20 deg and higher, vortices shed from the nose strake caused suction peaks in the pressure distributions that generally increased in magnitude with angle of attack. Above 30 deg-angle of attack, the forebody pressure distributions became asymmetrical at the most forward station, while they remained nearly symmetrical until 50 to 55 deg-angle of attack for the aft stations. Between 59 to 66 deg-angle of attack, the asymmetry of the pressure distributions changed direction. Yawing moments for the forebody alone were obtained by integrating the forebody pressure distributions. At 45 deg-angle of attack, the aircraft yaws to the right and at 50 deg and higher, the aircraft yaws to the left. The forebody yawing moments correlated well with the aircraft left yawing moment at an angle of attack of 50 deg or higher. At a 45 deg-angle of attack, the forebody yawing moments did not correlate well with the aircraft yawing moment, but it is suggested that this was due to asymmetric pressures on the cockpit region of the fuselage which was not instrumented. The forebody was also shown to provide a positive component of directional stability of the aircraft at angles of attack of 25 deg or higher. A Mach number effect was noted at angles of attack of 30 deg or higher at the station where the nose strake was present. At this station, the suction peaks in the pressure distributions at the highest Mach number were reduced and much more symmetrical as compared to the lower Mach number pressure distributions.

*PRC Inc., Edwards, California.

1991. Burken, John J.: **Flight-Determined Stability Analysis of Multiple-Input-Multiple-Output Control Systems**. NASA TM-4416, H-1837, NAS 1.15:4416, AIAA Paper 92-4396. Presented at the AIAA Guidance, Navigation, and Control Conference, Hilton Head, South Carolina, August 10–12, 1992, November 1992, 93N11178, #. (See also 1968, 2067.)

Singular value analysis can give conservative stability margin results. Applying structure to the uncertainty can reduce this conservatism. This paper presents flight-determined stability margins for the X-29A lateral-directional, multiloop control system. These margins are compared with the predicted unscaled singular values and scaled structured singular values. The algorithm was further evaluated with flight data by changing the roll-rate-to-aileron command-feedback gain by +/- 20 percent. Minimum eigenvalues of the return difference matrix which bound the singular values are also presented. Extracting multiloop singular values from flight data and analyzing the feedback gain variations validates this technique as a measure of robustness. This analysis can be used for near-real-time flight monitoring and safety testing.

1992. *Saltzman, Edwin J.; Del Frate, John H.; Sabsay, Catherine M.; and Yarger, Jill M.: **Pressure Distribution for the Wing of the YAV-8B Airplane; With and Without Pylons**. NASA TM-4429, H-1708, NAS 1.15:4429, November 1992, 93N14451, #.

Pressure distribution data have been obtained in flight at four span stations on the wing panel of the YAV-8B airplane. Data obtained for the supercritical profiled wing, with and without pylons installed, ranged from Mach 0.46 to 0.88. The altitude ranged from approximately 20,000 to 40,000 ft and the resultant Reynolds numbers varied from approximately 7.2 million to 28.7 million based on the mean aerodynamic chord. Pressure distribution data and flow visualization results show that the full-scale flight wing performance is compromised because the lower surface cusp region experiences flow separation for some important transonic flight conditions. This condition is aggravated when local shocks occur on the lower surface of the wing (mostly between 20 and 35 percent chord) when the pylons are installed for Mach 0.8 and above. There is evidence that convex fairings, which cover the pylon attachment flanges, cause these local shocks. Pressure coefficients significantly more negative than those for sonic flow also occur farther aft on the lower surface (near 60 percent chord) whether or not the pylons are installed for Mach numbers greater than or equal to 0.8. These negative pressure coefficient peaks and associated local shocks would be expected to cause increasing wave and separation drag at transonic Mach number increases.

*PRC Inc. Edwards, California.

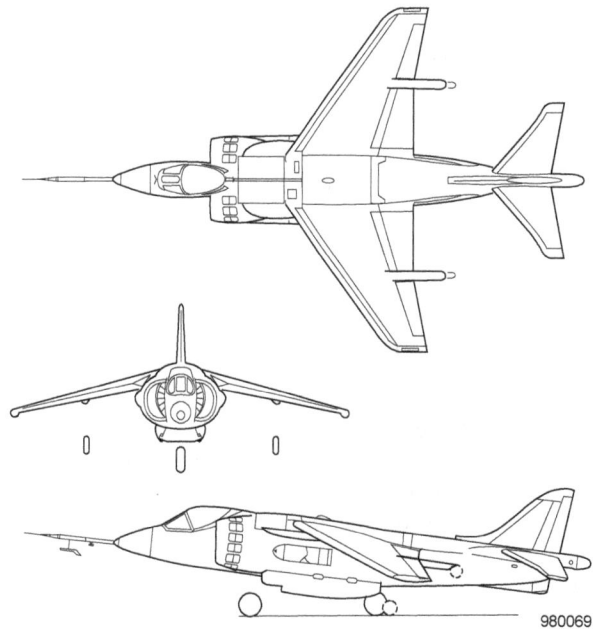

YAV-8B Airplane, Three-View Drawing

1993. Del Frate, John H.; and *Saltzman, John A.: **In-Flight Flow Visualization Results From the X-29A Aircraft at High Angles of Attack**. NASA TM-4430, H-1825, NAS 1.15:4430, AIAA Paper 92-4102. Presented at the 6th Biennial Flight Test Conference, Hilton Head, South Carolina, August 24–26, 1992, November 1992, 93N13322, #. (See also 1965.)

Flow visualization techniques were used on the X-29A aircraft at high angles of attack to study the vortical flow off the forebody and the surface flow on the wing and tail. The forebody vortex system was studied because asymmetries in the vortex system were suspected of inducing uncommanded yawing moments at zero sideslip. Smoke enabled visualization of the vortex system and correlation of its orientation with flight yawing moment data. Good agreement was found between vortex system asymmetries and the occurrence of yawing moments. Surface flow on the forward-swept wing of the X-29A was studied using tufts and flow cones. As angle of attack increased, separated flow initiated at the root and spread outboard encompassing the full wing by 30 deg angle of attack. In general, the progression of the separated flow correlated well with subscale model lift data. Surface flow on the vertical tail was also studied using tufts and flow cones. As angle of attack increased, separated flow initiated at the root and spread upward. The area of separated flow on the vertical tail at angles of attack greater than 20 deg correlated well with the marked decrease in aircraft directional stability.

*PRC Inc. Edwards, California.

374

1994. Orme, John S.; and Gilyard, Glenn B.: **Subsonic Flight Test Evaluation of a Propulsion System Parameter Estimation Process for the F100 Engine**. NASA TM-4426, H-1809, NAS 1.15:4426, AIAA Paper 92-3745. Presented at the 28th AIAA, SAE, ASME, and ASEE Joint Propulsion Conference, Nashville, Tennessee, July 6–8, 1992, November 1992, 93N13155, #. (See also 1945.)

Integrated engine-airframe optimal control technology may significantly improve aircraft performance. This technology requires a reliable and accurate parameter estimator to predict unmeasured variables. To develop this technology base, NASA Dryden Flight Research Facility (Edwards, California), McDonnell Aircraft Company (St. Louis, MO), and Pratt & Whitney (West Palm Beach, FL) have developed and flight-tested an adaptive performance seeking control system which optimizes the quasi-steady-state performance of the F-15 propulsion system. This paper presents flight and ground test evaluations of the propulsion system parameter estimation process used by the performance seeking control system. The estimator consists of a compact propulsion system model and an extended Kalman filter. The extended Kalman filter estimates five engine component deviation parameters from measured inputs. The compact model uses measurements and Kalman-filter estimates as inputs to predict unmeasured propulsion parameters such as net propulsive force and fan stall margin. The ability to track trends and estimate absolute values of propulsion system parameters was demonstrated. For example, thrust stand results show a good correlation, especially in trends, between the performance seeking control estimated and measured thrust.

1995. Powers, Sheryll Goecke; Webb, Lannie D.; Friend, Edward L.; and Lokos, William A.: **Flight Test Results From a Supercritical Mission Adaptive Wing With Smooth Variable Camber**. NASA TM-4415, H-1855, NAS 1.15:4415, AIAA Paper 92-4101. Presented at the AIAA 6th Biennial Flight Test Conference, Hilton Head, South Carolina, August 24–26, 1992, November 1992, 93N11863, #. (See also 1963.)

The mission adaptive wing (MAW) consisted of leading- and trailing-edge variable-camber surfaces that could be deflected in flight to provide a near-ideal wing camber shape for any flight condition. These surfaces featured smooth, flexible upper surfaces and fully enclosed lower surfaces, distinguishing them from conventional flaps that have discontinuous surfaces and exposed or semiexposed mechanisms. Camber shape was controlled by either a manual or automatic flight control system. The wing and aircraft were extensively instrumented to evaluate the local flow characteristics and the total aircraft performance. This paper discusses the interrelationships between the wing pressure, buffet, boundary-layer and flight deflection measurement system analyses and describes the flight maneuvers used to obtain the data. The results are for a wing sweep of 26 deg, a Mach number of 0.85, leading and trailing-edge cambers (delta (sub LE/TE)) of 0/2 and 5/10, and angles of attack from 3.0 deg to 14.0 deg. For the well-behaved flow of the delta (sub LE/TE) = 0/2 camber, a typical cruise camber shape, the local and global data are in good agreement with respect to the flow properties of the wing. For the delta (sub LE/TE) = 5/10 camber, a maneuvering camber shape, the local and global data have similar trends and conclusions, but not the clear-cut agreement observed for cruise camber.

1996. *Erbland, Peter J.; and Bogue, Rodney K.: **Taking the Measure of Aerodynamic Testing**. *Aerospace America*, (ISSN 0740-722X), Vol. 30, No. 11, November 1992, pp. 16–19, 93A13434.

A review is presented of the major challenges for aerodynamic measurement created by advanced aircraft systems that range from turbulence modeling to scramjet engines. Three diverse examples typically challenge current capabilities: modeling of compressible turbulence, validation of complex 3D flow predictions, and thermochemical characterization of chemically active high-enthalpy flows. Various techniques being explored and under development to realize the aerodynamic measurements required are discussed.

*USAF Wright-Patterson AFB, Ohio.

1997. Ehernberger, L. J.: **Stratospheric Turbulence Measurements and Models for Aerospace Plane Design**. NASA TM-104262, H-1865, NAS 1.15:104262. Presented at the AIAA Fourth International Aerospace Planes Conference, Orlando, Florida, December 1–4, 1992, December 1992, 93N13288, #. (See also 1998.)

Progress in computational atmospheric dynamics is exhibiting the ability of numerical simulation to describe instability processes associated with turbulence observed at altitudes between 15 and 25 km in the lower stratosphere. As these numerical simulation tools mature, they can be used to extend estimates of atmospheric perturbations from the present gust database for airplane design at altitudes below 15 km to altitudes between 25 and 50 km where aerospace plane operation would be at hypersonic speeds. The amount of available gust data and number of temperature perturbation observations are limited at altitudes between 15 and 25 km. On the other hand, in-situ gust data at higher altitudes are virtually nonexistent. The uncertain potential for future airbreathing hypersonic flight research vehicles to encounter strong turbulence at higher altitudes could penalize the design of these vehicles by undue cost or limitations on performance. Because the atmospheric structure changes markedly with altitude, direct extrapolation of gust magnitudes and encounter probabilities to the higher flight altitudes is not advisable. This paper presents a brief review of turbulence characteristics observed in the lower stratosphere and highlights the progress of computational atmospheric dynamics that may be used to estimate the severity of atmospheric transients at higher altitudes.

1998. Ehernberger, L. J.: **Stratospheric Turbulence Measurements and Models for Aerospace Plane Design.** AIAA Paper 92-5072. Presented at the 4th AIAA International Aerospace Planes Conference, Orlando, Florida, <u>December 1–4, 1992</u>, (see N93-13288), 93A22342, #. (See also 1997.)

Progress in computational atmospheric dynamics is exhibiting the ability of numerical simulation to describe instability processes associated with turbulence observed at altitudes between 15 and 25 km in the lower stratosphere. As these numerical simulation tools mature, they can be used to extend estimates of atmospheric perturbations from the present gust database for airplane design at altitudes below 15 km to altitudes between 25 and 50 km where aerospace plane operation would be at hypersonic speeds. The amount of available gust data and number of temperature perturbation observations are limited at altitudes between 15 and 25 km. On the other hand, in-situ gust data at higher altitudes are virtually nonexistent. The uncertain potential for future airbreathing hypersonic flight research vehicles to encounter strong turbulence at higher altitudes could penalize the design of these vehicles by undue cost or limitations on performance. Because the atmospheric structure changes markedly with altitude, direct extrapolation of gust magnitudes and encounter probabilities to the higher flight altitudes is not advisable. This paper presents a brief review of turbulence characteristics observed in the lower stratosphere and highlights the progress of computational atmospheric dynamics that may be used to estimate the severity of atmospheric transients at higher altitudes.

1999. Sitz, Joel R.: **The F-18 Systems Research Aircraft Facility.** NASA TM-4433, H-1844, NAS 1.15:4433. Presented at the 1992 Aerotech Conference, Anaheim, California, October 5–8, 1992, <u>December 1992</u>, 93N16753, #.

To help ensure that new aerospace initiatives rapidly transition to competitive U.S. technologies, NASA Dryden Flight Research Facility has dedicated a systems research aircraft facility. The primary goal is to accelerate the transition of new aerospace technologies to commercial, military, and space vehicles. Key technologies include more-electric aircraft concepts, fly-by-light systems, flush airdata systems, and advanced computer architectures. Future aircraft that will benefit are the high-speed civil transport and the National AeroSpace Plane. This paper describes the systems research aircraft flight research vehicle and outlines near-term programs.

EC96-43623-5

F-18 Systems Research Airplane

2000. Hedgley, D. R.: **Silhouette—Hidden Line Computer Code With Generalized Silhouette Solution.** ARC-12721, <u>1992</u>, 94M10039.

Flexibility in choosing how to display computer-generated three-dimensional drawings has become increasingly important in recent years. A major consideration is the enhancement of the realism and aesthetics of the presentation. A polygonal representation of objects, even with hidden lines removed, is not always desirable. A more pleasing pictorial representation often can be achieved by removing some of the remaining visible lines, thus creating silhouettes (or outlines) of selected surfaces of the object. Additionally, it should be noted that this silhouette feature allows warped polygons. This means that any polygon can be decomposed into constituent triangles. Considering these triangles as members of the same family will present a polygon with no interior lines, and thus removes the restriction of flat polygons. SILHOUETTE is a program for calligraphic drawings that can render any subset of polygons as a silhouette with respect to itself. The program is flexible enough to be applicable to every class of object. SILHOUETTE offers all possible combinations of silhouette and nonsilhouette specifications for an arbitrary solid. Thus, it is possible to enhance the clarity of any three-dimensional scene presented in two dimensions. Input to the program can be line segments or polygons. Polygons designated with the same number will be drawn as a silhouette of those polygons. SILHOUETTE is written in FORTRAN 77 and requires a graphics package such as DI-3000. The program has been implemented on a DEC VAX series computer running VMS and used 65K of virtual memory without a graphics package linked in. The source code is intended to be machine independent. This program is available on a 5.25 inch 360K MS-DOS format diskette (standard distribution) and is also available on a 9-track 1600 BPI ASCII CARD IMAGE magnetic tape. SILHOUETTE was developed in 1986 and was last updated in 1992.

376

2001. Gupta, K. K.; Petersen, K. L.; and *Lawson, C. L.: **On Some Recent Advances in Multidisciplinary Analysis of Hypersonic Vehicles.** AIAA Paper 92-5026. Presented at the 4th AIAA International Aerospace Planes Conference, Orlando, Florida, <u>December 1–4, 1992</u>, 93A22302, #.

This paper presents pertinent details of the development and application of an integrated, multidisciplinary finite element analysis tool for the effective modeling and simulation of aerospace vehicles including hypersonic ones. Recent advances in this connection include more efficient CFD solution techniques and also aeroservoelastic stability analysis methods that employ unsteady aerodynamic forces for computation of flutter and divergence speeds. An accelerated Euler solution procedure based on the Aitken acceleration technique has recently been implemented that effects considerable improvement in solution efficiency for the same level of solution accuracy, as evidenced by example problems presented in the paper. A summary of finite element numerical formulations for the various individual disciplines as well as for the unified aeroservoelastic analysis and some relevant numerical examples are also presented in the paper.

*Eloret Institute, Claremont, California.

2002. Bogue, Rodney K.; and *Erbland, Peter: **Perspective on the National Aero-Space Plane Program Instrumentation Development.** AIAA Paper 92-5086. Presented at the 4th AIAA International Aerospace Planes Conference, Orlando, Florida, <u>December 1–4, 1992</u>, 93A22356, #. (See also 2027.)

Development of advanced measurement technology for the NASP program is reviewed. The technical need and the program commitment are discussed which are required to ensure that adequate and timely measurement capabilities are provided for ground and flight testing in the NASP program. Particular attention is given to an assessment of the current development status and a perspective on the features of the NASP program that contributed to the current state of instrumentation technology readiness.

*National Aerospace Plane Joint Program Office, Wright-Patterson AFB, Ohio.

2003. Whitmore, Stephen A.; Moes, Timothy R.; and *Leondes, Cornelius T.: **Development of a Pneumatic High-Angle-of-Attack Flush Airdata Sensing (HI-FADS) System.** *Control and Dynamic Systems*, Vol. 52, pp. 453–511. Integrated Technology Methods and Applications in Aerospace Systems Design Conference, San Diego, California, <u>1992</u>, (see A94-12611 02-01), 94A12622.

The HI-FADS system design is an evolution of the FADS systems (e.g., Larson et al., 1980, 1987), which emphasizes the entire airdata system development. This paper describes the HI-FADS measurement system, with particular consideration given to the basic measurement hardware and the development of the HI-FADS aerodynamic model and the basic nonlinear regression algorithm. Algorithm initialization techniques are developed, and potential algorithm divergence problems are discussed. Data derived from HI-FADS flight tests are used to demonstrate the system accuracies and to illustrate the developed concepts and methods.

*University of California San Diego, La Jolla, California.

2004. *White, David A.; Bowers, Albion; Iliff, Ken; and **Menousek, John: **Flight, Propulsion, and Thermal Control of Advanced Aircraft and Hypersonic Vehicles.** *Handbook of Intelligent Control: Neural, Fuzzy, and Adaptive Approaches*, TJ217.5.H35, <u>1992</u>.

*NeuroDyne Inc., Cambridge, Massachusetts, and MIT Artificial Intelligence Lab., Cambridge, Massachusetts.
**McDonnell Aircraft Co., Hypersonic Thermal Systems, St. Louis, Missouri.

1993 Technical Publications

2005. Budd, Gerald D.; *Gilman, Ronald L.; and *Eichstedt, David: **Operational and Research Aspects of a Radio-Controlled Model Flight Test Program.** NASA TM-104266, H-1881, NAS 1.15:104266, AIAA Paper 93-0625. Presented at the 31st Aerospace Sciences Meeting, Reno, Nevada, January 11–14, 1993, <u>January 1993</u>, 93N18616, #. (See also 2006, 2154.)

The operational and research aspects of a subscale, radio-controlled model flight test program are presented. By using low-cost free-flying models, an approach was developed for obtaining research-quality vehicle performance and aerodynamic information. The advantages and limitations learned by applying this approach to a specific flight test program are described. The research quality of the data acquired shows that model flight testing is practical for obtaining consistent and repeatable flight data.

*PRC Inc., Edwards, California.

2006. Budd, Gerald D.; *Gilman, Ronald L.; and *Eichstedt, David: **Operational and Research Aspects of a Radio-Controlled Model Flight Test Program.** AIAA Paper 93-0625. Presented at the 31st AIAA Aerospace Sciences Meeting and Exhibit, Reno, Nevada, <u>January 11–14, 1993</u>, 93A24742, #. (See also 2005, 2154.)

The operational and research aspects of a subscale, radio-controlled model flight test program are presented. By using low-cost free-flying models, an approach was developed for obtaining research-quality vehicle performance and aerodynamic information. The advantages and limitations learned by applying this approach to a specific flight test program are described. The research quality of the data acquired shows that model flight testing is practical for obtaining consistent repeatable flight data.

*PRC Inc. Edwards, California.

2007. Urnes, James M.; *Hoy, Stephen E.;*Ladage, Robert N.; and Stewart, James: **A Neural Based Intelligent Flight Control System for the NASA F-15 Flight Research Aircraft**. NASA Johnson Space Center, *Proceedings of the Third International Workshop on Neural Networks and Fuzzy Logic*, Vol. 1, (see N93-22351 08-63), January 1993, pp. 109–112, 93N22368, #.

A flight control concept that can identify aircraft stability properties and continually optimize the aircraft flying qualities has been developed by McDonnell Aircraft Company under a contract with the NASA-Dryden Flight Research Facility. This flight concept, termed the Intelligent Flight Control System, utilizes Neural Network technology to identify the host aircraft stability and control properties during flight, and use this information to design on-line the control system feedback gains to provide continuous optimum flight response. This self-repairing capability can provide high performance flight maneuvering response throughout large flight envelopes, such as needed for the National Aerospace Plane. Moreover, achieving this response early in the vehicle's development schedule will save cost.

*McDonnell Aircraft Corporation, St. Louis, Missouri.

2008. *Mendenhall, Michael R.; *Lesieutre, Daniel J.; *Whittaker, C. H.; Curry, Robert E.; and **Moulton, Bryan: **Aerodynamic Analysis of Pegasus®- Computations vs Reality.** AIAA Paper 93-0520. Presented at the 31st AIAA Aerospace Sciences Meeting and Exhibit, Reno, Nevada, January 11–14, 1993, 93A23262, #.

Pegasus,® a three-stage, air-launched, winged space booster was developed to provide fast and efficient commercial launch services for small satellites. The aerodynamic design and analysis of Pegasus® was conducted without benefit of wind tunnel tests using only computational aerodynamic and fluid dynamic methods. Flight test data from the first two operational flights of Pegasus® are now available, and they provide an opportunity to validate the accuracy of the predicted pre-flight aerodynamic characteristics. Comparisons of measured and predicted flight characteristics are presented and discussed. Results show that the computational methods provide reasonable aerodynamic design information with acceptable margins. Post-flight analyses illustrate certain areas in which improvements are desired.

*Nielsen Engineering and Research, Inc., Mountain View, California.
**PRC Inc., Edwards, California.

2009. Iliff, Kenneth W.; and Shafer, Mary F.: **A Comparison of Hypersonic Flight and Prediction Results.** AIAA Paper 93-0311. Presented at the 31st AIAA Aerospace Sciences Meeting and Exhibit, Reno, Nevada, January 11–14, 1993, 93A23006, #. (See also 2168.)

Aerodynamic and aerothermodynamic comparisons between flight and ground test for four hypersonic vehicles are discussed. The four vehicles are the X-15, the Reentry F, the Sandia Energetic Reentry Vehicle Experiment (SWERVE), and the Space Shuttle. The comparisons are taken from papers published by researchers active in the various programs. Aerodynamic comparisons include reaction control jet interaction on the Space Shuttle. Various forms of heating including catalytic, boundary layer, shock interaction and interference, and vortex impingement are compared. Predictions were significantly exceeded for the heating caused by vortex impingement (on the Space Shuttle OMS pods) and for heating caused by shock interaction and interference on the X-15 and the Space Shuttle. Predictions of boundary-layer state were in error on the X-15, the SWERVE, and the Space Shuttle vehicles.

2010. Dana, William H.: **The X-15 Airplane—Lessons Learned.** AIAA Paper 93-0309. Presented at the 31st AIAA Aerospace Sciences Meeting and Exhibit, Reno, Nevada, January 11–14, 1993, 93A23005, #.

The X-15 rocket research airplane flew to an altitude of 354,000 ft and reached Mach 6.70. In almost 200 flights, this airplane was used to gather aerodynamic-heating, structural loads, stability and control, and atmospheric-reentry data. This paper describes the origins, design, and operation of the X-15 airplane. In addition, lessons learned from the X-15 airplane that are applicable to designing and testing the National Aero-Space Plane are discussed.

2011. Whitmore, Stephen A.; Moes, Timothy R.; Czerniejewski, Mark W.; and Nichols, Douglas A.: **Application of a Flush Airdata Sensing System to a Wing Leading Edge (LE-FADS).** AIAA Paper 93-0634. Presented at the 31st AIAA Aerospace Sciences Meeting and Exhibit, Reno, Nevada, January 11–14, 1993, 93A24750, #. (See also 2012.)

This paper investigates the feasibility of locating a flush air-data sensing (FADS) system on a wing leading edge where the operation of the avionics or fire control radar system will not be hindered. The leading-edge FADS system (LE-FADS) was installed on an unswept symmetrical airfoil, and a series of low-speed wind-tunnel tests were conducted to evaluate the performance of the system. As a result of the tests it is concluded that the aerodynamic models formulated for use on aircraft nosetips are directly applicable to wing leading edges and that the calibration process is similar. Furthermore, the agreement between the air-data calculations for angle of attack and total pressure from the LE-FADS and known wind-tunnel values suggest that wing-based flush air-data systems can be calibrated to a high degree of accuracy. Static wind-tunnel tests for angles of attack from −50 to 50 deg and dynamic pressures from 3.6 to 11.4 lb/sq ft were performed.

2012. Whitmore, Stephen A.; Moes, Timothy R.; Czerniejewski, Mark W.; and Nichols, Douglas A.: **Application of a Flush Airdata Sensing System to a Wing Leading Edge (LE-FADS).** NASA TM-104267, H-1886, NAS 1.15:104267, AIAA Paper 93-0634. Presented at the 31st AIAA Aerospace Sciences Meeting and Exhibit, Reno, Nevada, January 11–14, 1993, February 1993, 93N20163, #. (See also 2011.)

The feasibility of locating a flush airdata sensing (FADS) system on a wing leading edge where the operation of the avionics or fire control radar system will not be hindered is investigated. The leading-edge FADS system (LE-FADS) was installed on an unswept symmetrical airfoil and a series of low-speed wind-tunnel tests were conducted to evaluate the performance of the system. As a result of the tests it is concluded that the aerodynamic models formulated for use on aircraft nosetips are directly applicable to wing leading edges and that the calibration process is similar. Furthermore, the agreement between the airdata calculations for angle of attack and total pressure from the LE-FADS and known wind-tunnel values suggest that wing-based flush airdata systems can be calibrated to a high degree of accuracy. Static wind-tunnel tests for angles of attack from −50 deg to 50 deg and dynamic pressures from 3.6 to 11.4 lb/sq ft were performed.

2013. Moes, Timothy R.; Whitmore, Stephen A.; and *Jordan, Frank L., Jr.: **Flight and Wind-Tunnel Calibrations of a Flush Airdata Sensor at High Angles of Attack and Sideslip and at Supersonic Mach Numbers**. NASA TM-104265, H-1875, NAS 1.15:104265, AIAA Paper 93-1017. Presented at the AIAA, AHS, and ASEE Aerospace Design Conference, Irvine, California, February 16–19, 1993, February 1993, 93N19110, #. (See also 2014.)

A nonintrusive airdata-sensing system was calibrated in flight and wind-tunnel experiments to an angle of attack of 70 deg and to angles of sideslip of ±15 deg. Flight-calibration data have also been obtained to Mach 1.2. The sensor, known as the flush airdata sensor, was installed on the nosecap of an F-18 aircraft for flight tests and on a full-scale F-18 forebody for wind-tunnel tests. Flight tests occurred at the NASA Dryden Flight Research Facility, Edwards, California, using the F-18 High Alpha Research Vehicle. Wind-tunnel tests were conducted in the 30- by 60-ft wind tunnel at the NASA LaRC, Hampton, Virginia. The sensor consisted of 23 flush-mounted pressure ports arranged in concentric circles and located within 1.75 in. of the tip of the nosecap. An overdetermined mathematical model was used to relate the pressure measurements to the local airdata quantities. The mathematical model was based on potential flow over a sphere and was empirically adjusted based on flight and wind-tunnel data. For quasi-steady maneuvering, the

mathematical model worked well throughout the subsonic, transonic, and low supersonic flight regimes. The model also worked well throughout the angles-of-attack and -sideslip regions studied.

*NASA Langley Research Center, Hampton, Virginia.

2014. Moes, Timothy R.; Whitmore, Stephen A.; and *Jordan, Frank L., Jr.: **Flight and Wind-Tunnel Calibrations of a Flush Airdata Sensor at High Angles of Attack and Sideslip and at Supersonic Mach Numbers.** AIAA Paper 93-1017. Presented at the AIAA, AHS, and ASEE Aerospace Design Conference, Irvine, California, February 16–19, 1993, (see N93-19110), 93A30931, #. (See also 2013.)

A nonintrusive airdata-sensing system was calibrated in flight and wind-tunnel experiments to an angle of attack of 70 deg and to angles of sideslip of ±15 deg. Flight-calibration data have also been obtained to Mach 1.2. The sensor, known as the flush airdata sensor, was installed on the nosecap of an F-18 aircraft for flight tests and on a full-scale F-18 forebody for wind-tunnel tests. Flight tests occurred at the NASA Dryden Flight Research Facility, Edwards, California, using the F-18 High Alpha Research Vehicle. Wind-tunnel tests were conducted in the 30- by 60-ft wind tunnel at the NASA LaRC, Hampton, Virginia. The sensor consisted of 23 flush-mounted pressure ports arranged in concentric circles and located within 1.75 in. of the tip of the nosecap. An overdetermined mathematical model was used to relate the pressure measurements to the local airdata quantities. The mathematical model was based on potential flow over a sphere and was empirically adjusted based on flight and wind-tunnel data. For quasi-steady maneuvering, the mathematical model worked well throughout the subsonic, transonic, and low supersonic flight regimes. The model also worked well throughout the angle-of-attack and sideslip regions studied.

*NASA Langley Research Center, Hampton, Virginia.

2015. Murray, James E.; Moes, Timothy R.; and Norlin, Ken: **High-Altitude Balloon-Launched Aircraft—A Piloted Simulation Study.** AIAA Paper 93-1019. Presented at the AIAA, AHS, and ASEE Aerospace Design Conference, Irvine, California, February 16–19, 1993, 93A30933, #.

A real-time piloted simulation at the NASA Dryden Flight Research Facility was used to study the feasibility of launching a research aircraft from a high-altitude balloon. In the study, the simulated aircraft was launched in a nosedown attitude at zero airspeed from 110,000 ft. After launch, the pilot flew the aircraft through a near-maximum-lift pullout and then through a zoom climb to a trimmed, 1-g flight condition at the test altitude. The study included parametric variations to measure the effects of launch altitude, gross weight, Mach number limit, and parachute size on the test altitude attained. The aerodynamic model of the simulated aircraft was based on flight test results, low Reynolds number windtunnel tests, and computational models; the model included significant Mach number and Reynolds number effects at high altitude. A small parachute was included in the simulation to limit Mach number during the pullout to avoid adverse transonic effects and their resultant energy losses. A small rocket motor was included in the simulation and was investigated for boosting the aircraft to a higher test altitude. In the study, a test altitude of approximately 95,000 ft was attained without rocket boost, and a test altitude in excess of 100,000 ft was attained using small rocket boost.

2016. Shelley, Stuart J.; Freudinger, Lawrence C.; and Allemang, Randall J.: **Development of an On-Line Modal State Monitor.** Presented at the 11th International Modal Analysis Conference, Kissamee, Florida, February 1–4, 1993.

This paper discusses an ongoing effort to implement vibration health monitoring schemes in an on-line environment. On-line health monitoring or on-line parameter estimation is required to automate the testing procedures currently observed in practice for certain nonstationary or otherwise nonconstant linear systems. Flight flutter testing of aircraft is discussed as a specific and intended beneficiary of this work. Data acquisition hardware is controlled from within a flexible software package for matrix algebra. This development is unique in the sense that a provision is made to perform coordinated transformations such as discrete modal filtering on the data in the acquisition hardware, which can be exploited as a data condensation tool. The results presented in this paper include an overview of the software tools developed to date and experimental results for stationary and nonstationary data.

2017. Walsh, Kevin R.: **Summary of the Effects of Engine Throttle Response on Airplane Formation-Flying Qualities.** NASA TM-4465, H-1888, NAS 1.15:4465, AIAA Paper 92-3318. Presented at the AIAA 28th Joint Propulsion Conference and Exhibit, Nashville, Tennessee, July 6–8, 1992, (see A92-48902), March 1993, 93N23123, #. (See also 1947.)

A flight evaluation was conducted to determine the effect of engine throttle response characteristics on precision formation-flying qualities. A variable electronic throttle control system was developed and flight-tested on a TF-104G airplane with a J79-11B engine at the NASA Dryden Flight Research Facility. This airplane was chosen because of its known, very favorable thrust response characteristics. Ten research flights were flown to evaluate the effects of throttle gain, time delay, and fuel control rate limiting on engine handling qualities during a demanding precision wing formation task. Handling quality effects of lag filters and lead compensation time delays were also evaluated. The Cooper and Harper Pilot Rating Scale was used to assign levels of handling quality. Data from pilot ratings and comments indicate that throttle control system time delays and rate

limits cause significant degradations in handling qualities. Threshold values for satisfactory (level 1) and adequate (level 2) handling qualities of these key variables are presented. These results may provide engine manufacturers with guidelines to assure satisfactory handling qualities in future engine designs.

2018. Hamory, Philip J.; and Murray, James E.: **Flight Experience With Lightweight, Low-Power Miniaturized Instrumentation Systems.** NASA TM-4463, H-1879, NAS 1.15:4463, AIAA Paper 92-4111. Presented at the AIAA 6th Biennial Flight Test Conference, Hilton Head, South Carolina, August 24–26, 1992, (see A93-11280), March 1993, 93N23102, #. (See also 1960, 2112.)

Engineers at the NASA Dryden Flight Research Facility (NASA-Dryden) have conducted two flight research programs with lightweight, low-power miniaturized instrumentation systems built around commercial data loggers. One program quantified the performance of a radio-controlled model airplane. The other program was a laminar boundary-layer transition experiment on a manned sailplane. NASA-Dryden personnel's flight experience with the miniaturized instrumentation systems used on these two programs is reported. The data loggers, the sensors, and the hardware and software developed to complete the systems are described. How the systems were used is described and the challenges encountered to make them work are covered. Examples of raw data and derived results are shown as well. Finally, future plans for these systems are discussed. For some flight research applications where miniaturized instrumentation is a requirement, the authors conclude that commercially available data loggers and sensors are viable alternatives. In fact, the data loggers and sensors make it possible to gather research-quality data in a timely and cost-effective manner.

2019. Curry, Robert E.; *Mendenhall, Michael R.; and **Moulton, Bryan: **In-Flight Evaluation of Aerodynamic Predictions of an Air-Launched Space Booster.** AGARD CP-514. *Theoretical and Experimental Methods in Hypersonic Flows,* presented at Fluid Dynamics Panel Symposium, Torino, Italy, May 4–8, 1992, (see N94-10421 01-02), April 1993, 94N10427, #. (See also 1923.)

Several analytical aerodynamic design tools that were applied to the Pegasus® air-launched space booster were evaluated using flight measurements. The study was limited to existing codes and was conducted with limited computational resources. The flight instrumentation was constrained to have minimal impact on the primary Pegasus® missions. Where appropriate, the flight measurements were compared with computational data. Aerodynamic performance and trim data from the first two flights were correlated with predictions. Local measurements in the wing and wing-body interference region were correlated with analytical data. This complex flow region includes the effect of aerothermal heating magnification caused by the presence of a corner vortex and interaction of the wing leading edge shock and fuselage boundary layer. The operation of the first two missions indicates that the aerodynamic design approach for Pegasus® was adequate, and data show that acceptable margins were available. Additionally, the correlations provide insight into the capabilities of these analytical tools for more complex vehicles in which design margins may be more stringent.

*Nielsen Engineering and Research, Inc., Mountain View, California.
**PRC Inc., Edwards, California.

2020. *Mosier, Marty; *Harris, Gary; and *Whitmeyer, Charlie: **The Pegasus® Air-Launched Space Booster Payload Interfaces and Processing Procedures for Small Optical Payloads**. *Proceedings, Small-Satellite Technology and Applications Meeting*, Orlando, Florida, April 4–5, 1991. Society of Photo-Optical Instrumentation Engineers, Bellingham, Washington, <u>1991</u>, pp. 177–192, (see A93-24151 08-18), 93A24170.

Pegasus® and the PegaStar integrated spacecraft bus are described, and an overview of integration and launch operations is provided. Payload design issues include payload volume and mass capability, payload interfaces, and design loads. Vehicle and payload processing issues include integration and handling methods, facilities, contamination control, and launch operations. It is noted that Pegasus® provides small satellite users with a cost-effective means for delivering payloads into the specific orbits at the optimal time to meet the most demanding mission requirements. PegaStar provides a flexible cost-effective means for providing long-term on-orbit support while minimizing total program risk and cost.

*Orbital Sciences Corp., Fairfax, Virginia.

2021. Brenner, Martin J.: **Actuator and Aerodynamic Modeling for High-Angle-Of-Attack Aeroservoelasticity.** AIAA Paper 93-1419. Presented at the 34th AIAA, ASME, ASCE, AHS, and ASC, Structures, Structural Dynamics and Materials Conference, and the AIAA and ASME, Adaptive Structures Forum, La Jolla, California, <u>April 19–22, 1993</u>, 93A37433, #. (See also 2028.)

Accurate prediction of airframe/actuation coupling is required by the imposing demands of modern flight control systems. In particular, for agility enhancement at high angle of attack and low dynamic pressure, structural integration characteristics such as hinge moments, effective actuator stiffness, and airframe/control surface damping can have a significant effect on stability predictions. Actuator responses are customarily represented with low-order transfer functions matched to actuator test data, and control surface stiffness is often modeled as a linear spring. The inclusion of the physical

properties of actuation and its installation on the airframe is therefore addressed in this paper using detailed actuator models which consider the physical, electrical, and mechanical elements of actuation. The aeroservoelastic analysis procedure is described in which the actuators are modeled as detailed high-order transfer functions and as approximate low-order transfer functions. The impacts of unsteady aerodynamic modeling on aeroservoelastic stability are also investigated in this paper by varying the order of approximation, or number of aerodynamic lag states, in the analysis. Test data from a thrust-vectoring configuration of an F/A-18 aircraft are compared to predictions to determine the effects on accuracy as a function of modeling complexity.

2022. *Pinkelman, J. K.; *Batill, S. M.; Vernon, L. E.; and Kehoe, M. W.: **An Evaluation of Excitation Techniques for Time Domain Based Flutter Data Processing.** AIAA Paper 93-1602. *Technical Papers,* Part 5. Presented at the 34th AIAA, ASME, ASCE, AHS, and ASC, Structures, Structural Dynamics and Materials Conference, and the AIAA and ASME, Adaptive Structures Forum, La Jolla, California, <u>April 19–22, 1993</u>, pp. 2596–2604, 93A34133, #.

Numerically simulated, wind tunnel and flight test experimental data were used to evaluate various types of system excitation sources for subcritical flutter testing. Emphasis was placed upon the determination of modal frequencies and damping from relatively short time series records. Parameter identification based upon digital time series models was used to predict modal characteristics from subcritical test data. Various types of excitation were considered. These were: 1) impulsive loading and the resulting transient free vibration response, 2) random forced response, in which the 'mechanical' forcing function could be directly measured, 3) sine sweep forced response, in which the 'mechanical' forcing function could be directly measured, and 4) forced response from unsteady aerodynamic excitation or turbulence, in which the excitation could only be indirectly inferred from other measurements.

*Notre Dame University, Indiana.

2023. Vernon, Lura: **In-Flight Investigation of a Rotating Cylinder-Based Structural Excitation System for Flutter Testing.** AIAA Paper 93-1537. *Technical Papers,* Part 4. Presented at the 34th AIAA, ASME, ASCE, AHS, and ASC, Structures, Structural Dynamics and Materials Conference, and the AIAA and ASME, Adaptive Structures Forum, La Jolla, California, <u>April 19–22, 1993</u>, pp. 1979–1997, 93A34074, #. (See also 2029.)

A research excitation system was test flown at the NASA Dryden Flight Research Facility on the two-seat F-16XL aircraft. The excitation system is a wingtip-mounted vane with a rotating slotted cylinder at the trailing edge. As the cylinder rotates during flight, the flow is alternately deflected upward and downward through the slot, resulting in a periodic lift force at twice the cylinder's rotational frequency.

Flight testing was conducted to determine the excitation system's effectiveness in the subsonic and transonic flight regimes. Primary research objectives were to determine the system's ability to develop adequate force levels to excite the aircraft's structure and to determine the frequency range over which the system could excite structural modes of the aircraft. The results from the exciter were compared with results from atmospheric turbulence excitation at the same flight conditions. The results from the forced excitation were of higher quality and had less variation than the results from atmospheric turbulence. The forced excitation data also invariably yielded higher structural damping values than those from the atmospheric turbulence data.

2024. Anderson, Karl F.: **The Constant Current Loop: A New Paradigm for Resistance Signal Conditioning**. NASA TM-108744, H-1878, NAS 1.15:108744. Presented at the 39th Instrument Society of America International Instrumentation Symposium, Albuquerque, New Mexico, May 3–6, 1993, <u>1993</u>, 93N25181, #. (See also 1980, 2025, 2071.)

A practical, single, constant-current loop circuit for the signal conditioning of variable-resistance transducers was synthesized, analyzed, and demonstrated. The strain gage and the resistance temperature device are examples of variable-resistance sensors. Lead wires connect variable-resistance sensors to remotely located signal-conditioning hardware. The presence of lead wires in the conventional Wheatstone bridge signal-conditioning circuit introduces undesired effects that reduce the quality of the data from the remote sensors. A practical approach is presented for suppressing essentially all lead wire resistance effects while indicating only the change in resistance value. Theoretical predictions supported by laboratory testing confirm the following features of the approach: (1) the dc response; (2) the electrical output is unaffected by extremely large variations in the resistance of any or all lead wires; (3) the electrical output remains zero for no change in gage resistance; (4) the electrical output is inherently linear with respect to gage resistance change; (5) the sensitivity is double that of a Wheatstone bridge circuit; and (6) the same excitation and sense wires can serve multiple independent gages. An adaptation of the current loop circuit is presented that simultaneously provides an output signal voltage directly proportional to transducer resistance change and provides temperature information that is unaffected by transducer and lead wire resistance variations. These innovations are the subject of NASA patent applications.

2025. Anderson, Karl F.: **The Constant Current Loop - A New Paradigm for Resistance Signal Conditioning.** Presented at the 39th Instrument Society of America International Instrumentation Symposium, Albuquerque, New Mexico, <u>May 3-6, 1993</u>, pp. 465–479, 93A54380. (See also 1980, 2024, 2071.)

A practical single constant current loop circuit for the signal conditioning of variable-resistance transducers has been synthesized, analyzed, and demonstrated. The strain gage and the resistance temperature device are examples of variable-resistance sensors. Lead wires connect variable-resistance sensors to remotely located signal-conditioning hardware. The presence of lead wires in the conventional Wheatstone bridge signal-conditioning circuit introduces undesired effects that reduce the quality of the data from the remote sensors. A practical approach is presented for suppressing essentially all lead wire resistance effects while indicating only the change in resistance value. An adaptation of the current loop circuit is presented that simultaneously provides an output signal voltage directly proportional to transducer resistance change and provides temperature information that is unaffected by transducer and lead wire resistance variations.

2026. Bogue, Rodney K.: **Recent Flight-Test Results of Optical Airdata Techniques.** NASA TM-4504, H-1915, NAS 1.15:4504, SAE-92-1997. Presented at the SAE Aerotech 1992 Conference, Anaheim, California, October 5–8, 1992, <u>May 1993</u>, 94N13791, #. (See also 1955.)

Optical techniques for measuring airdata parameters were demonstrated with promising results on high performance fighter aircraft. These systems can measure the airspeed vector, and some are not as dependent on special in-flight calibration processes as current systems. Optical concepts for measuring freestream static temperature and density are feasible for in-flight applications. The best feature of these concepts is that the air data measurements are obtained nonintrusively, and for the most part well into the freestream region of the flow field about the aircraft. Current requirements for measuring air data at high angle of attack, and future need to measure the same information at hypersonic flight conditions place strains on existing techniques. Optical technology advances show outstanding potential for application in future programs and promise to make common use of optical concepts a reality. Results from several flight-test programs are summarized, and the technology advances required to make optical airdata techniques practical are identified.

2027. Bogue, Rodney K.; and *Erbland, Peter: **Perspective on the National Aero-Space Plane Program Instrumentation Development**. NASA TM-4505, H-1916, NAS 1.15:4505. Presented at the Aero Space Planes Conference, Orlando, Florida, December 1–3, 1992, <u>May 1993</u>, 94N13256, #. (See also 2002.)

A review of the requirement for, and development of, advanced measurement technology for the National Aerospace Plane program is presented. The objective is to discuss the technical need and the program commitment required to ensure that adequate and timely measurement capabilities are provided for ground and flight testing in the NASP program. The scope of the measurement problem is presented, the measurement process is described, how instrumentation technology development has been affected by NASP program evolution is examined, the national effort to define measurement requirements and assess the adequacy of current technology to support the NASP program is discussed, and the measurement requirements are summarized. The unique features of the NASP program that complicate the understanding of requirements and the development of viable solutions are illustrated.

*Air Force Systems Command, Wright-Patterson AFB, Ohio.

2028. Brenner, Martin J.: **Actuator and Aerodynamic Modeling for High-Angle-of-Attack Aeroservoelasticity**. NASA TM-4493, H-1904, NAS 1.15:4493, AIAA Paper 93-1419. Presented at the AIAA, ASME, ASCE, AHS, and ASC Structures, Structural Dynamics and Materials Conference, La Jolla, California, April 19–22, 1993, June 1993, (A93-37433), 94N13255, #. (See also 2021.)

Accurate prediction of airframe/actuation coupling is required by the imposing demands of modern flight control systems. In particular, for agility enhancement at high angle of attack and low dynamic pressure, structural integration characteristics such as hinge moments, effective actuator stiffness, and airframe/control surface damping can have a significant effect on stability predictions. Actuator responses are customarily represented with low-order transfer functions matched to actuator test data, and control surface stiffness is often modeled as a linear spring. The inclusion of the physical properties of actuation and its installation on the airframe is therefore addressed using detailed actuator models which consider the physical, electrical, and mechanical elements of actuation. The aeroservoelastic analysis procedure is described in which the actuators are modeled as detailed high-order transfer functions and as approximate low-order transfer functions. The impacts of unsteady aerodynamic modeling on aeroservoelastic stability are also investigated by varying the order of approximation, or number of aerodynamic lag states, in the analysis. Test data from a thrust-vectoring configuration of an F/A-18 aircraft are compared to predictions to determine the effects on accuracy as a function of modeling complexity.

2029. Vernon, Lura: **In-Flight Investigation of a Rotating Cylinder-Based Structural Excitation System for Flutter Testing**. NASA-TM-4512, H-1883, NAS 1.15:4512, (see A93-34074), June 1993, 94N15783, #. (See also 2023.)

A research excitation system was test flown at the NASA Dryden Flight Research Facility on the two-seat F-16XL aircraft. The excitation system is a wingtip-mounted vane with a rotating slotted cylinder at the trailing edge. As the cylinder rotates during flight, the flow is alternately deflected upward and downward through the slot, resulting in a periodic lift force at twice the cylinder's rotational frequency. Flight testing was conducted to determine the excitation system's effectiveness in the subsonic, transonic, and supersonic flight regimes. Primary research objectives were to determine the system's ability to develop adequate force levels to excite the aircraft's structure and to determine the frequency range over which the system could excite structural modes of the aircraft. In addition, studies were conducted to determine optimal excitation parameters, such as sweep duration, sweep type, and energy levels. The results from the exciter were compared with results from atmospheric turbulence excitation at the same flight conditions. The comparison indicated that the vane with a rotating slotted cylinder provides superior results. The results from the forced excitation were of higher quality and had less variation than the results from atmospheric turbulence. The forced excitation data also invariably yielded higher structural damping values than those from the atmospheric turbulence data.

2030. Burcham, Frank W., Jr.; Maine, Trindel A.; Fullerton, C. Gordon; and *Wells, Edward A.: **Preliminary Flight Results of a Fly-By-Throttle Emergency Flight Control System on an F-15 Airplane**. NASA TM-4503, H-1911, NAS 1.15:4503, AIAA Paper 93-1820. Presented at the 29th AIAA, SAE, and ASME Joint Propulsion Conference, Monterey, California, June 28–30, 1993, June 1993, 94N13254, #. (See also 2031.)

A multi-engine aircraft, with some or all of the flight control system inoperative, may use engine thrust for control. NASA Dryden has conducted a study of the capability and techniques for this emergency flight control method for the F-15 airplane. With an augmented control system, engine thrust, along with appropriate feedback parameters, is used to control flightpath and bank angle. Extensive simulation studies were followed by flight tests. The principles of throttles only control, the F-15 airplane, the augmented system, and the flight results including actual landings with throttles-only control are discussed.

*McDonnell-Douglas Automation Co., St. Louis, Missouri.

2031. Burcham, Frank W., Jr.; Maine, Trindel A.; Fullerton, C. G.; and *Wells, Edward A.: **Preliminary Flight Test Results of a Fly-By-Throttle Emergency Flight Control System on an F-15 Airplane**. AIAA Paper 93-1820. Presented at the 29th AIAA, SAE, and ASME Joint Propulsion Conference, Monterey, California, June 28–30, 1993, 93A49708, #. (See also 2030.)

A multi-engine aircraft, with some or all of the flight control system inoperative, may use engine thrust for control. NASA Dryden has conducted a study of the capability and techniques for this emergency flight control method for the F-15 airplane. With an augmented control system, engine thrust, along with appropriate feedback parameters, is used to control flightpath and bank angle. Extensive simulation studies have been followed by flight tests. This paper discusses the principles of throttles-only control, the F-15 airplane, the augmented system, and the flight results including landing approaches with throttles-only control to within 10 ft of the ground.

*McDonnell Douglas Aerospace, St. Louis, Missouri.

2032. Voracek, David F.: **Ground Vibration and Flight Flutter Tests of the Single-Seat F-16XL Aircraft With a Modified Wing**. NASA TM-104264, H-1906, NAS 1.15:104264, June 1993, 94N11233, #.

The NASA single-seat F-16XL aircraft was modified by the addition of a glove to the left wing. Vibration tests were conducted on the ground to assess the changes to the aircraft caused by the glove. Flight Luther testing was conducted on the aircraft with the glove installed to ensure that the flight envelope was free of aeroelastic or aeroservoelastic instabilities. The ground vibration tests showed that above 20 Hz, several modes that involved the control surfaces were significantly changed. Flight test data showed that modal damping levels and trends were satisfactory where obtainable. The data presented in this report include estimated modal parameters from the ground vibration and flight flutter test.

2033. Orme, John S.; and Gilyard, Glenn B.: **Preliminary Supersonic Flight Test Evaluation of Performance Seeking Control**. NASA TM-4494, H-1909, NAS 1.15:4494, AIAA Paper 93-1821. Presented at the 29th AIAA, SAE, ASME, and ASEE Joint Propulsion Conference, Monterey, California, June 28–30, 1993, June 1993, 94N11205, #.

Digital flight and engine control, powerful onboard computers, and sophisticated controls techniques may improve aircraft performance by maximizing fuel efficiency, maximizing thrust, and extending engine life. An adaptive performance seeking control system for optimizing the quasi-steady state performance of an F-15 aircraft was developed and flight tested. This system has three optimization modes: minimum fuel, maximum thrust, and minimum fan turbine inlet temperature. Tests of the minimum fuel and fan turbine inlet temperature modes were performed at a constant thrust. Supersonic single-engine flight tests of the three modes were conducted using varied after burning power settings. At supersonic conditions, the performance seeking control law optimizes the integrated airframe, inlet, and engine. At subsonic conditions, only the engine is optimized. Supersonic flight tests showed improvements in thrust of 9 percent, increases in fuel savings of 8 percent, and reductions of up to 85 deg R in turbine temperatures for all three modes. The supersonic performance seeking control structure is described and preliminary results of supersonic performance seeking control tests are given. These findings have implications for improving performance of civilian and military aircraft.

2034. Iliff, Kenneth W.; and Shafer, Mary F.: **Space Shuttle Hypersonic Aerodynamic and Aerothermodynamic Flight Research and the Comparison to Ground Test Results**. NASA TM-4499, H-1894, NAS 1.15:4499, AIAA Paper 92-3988. Presented at the 17th Aerospace Ground Testing Conference, Nashville, Tennessee, July 6–8, 1992, (see A92-56812), June 1993, 94N10820, #. (See also 1944.)

Aerodynamic and aerothermodynamic comparisons between flight and ground test for the Space Shuttle at hypersonic speeds are discussed. All of the comparisons are taken from papers published by researchers active in the Space Shuttle program. The aerodynamic comparisons include stability and control derivatives, center-of-pressure location, and reaction control jet interaction. Comparisons are also discussed for various forms of heating, including catalytic, boundary layer, top centerline, side fuselage, OMS pod, wing leading edge, and shock interaction. The jet interaction and center-of-pressure location flight values exceeded not only the predictions but also the uncertainties of the predictions. Predictions were significantly exceeded for the heating caused by the vortex impingement on the OMS pods and for heating caused by the wing leading-edge shock interaction.

2035. Iliff, Kenneth W.; and Shafer, Mary F.: **Extraction of Stability and Control Derivatives from Orbiter Flight Data**. NASA TM-4500, H-1912, NAS 1.15:4500. Presented at the Orbiters Experiments (OEX) Aerothermodynamics Symposium, Williamsburg, Virginia, April 27–30, 1993, June 1993, 94N10707, #.

The Space Shuttle Orbiter has provided unique and important information on aircraft flight dynamics. This information has provided the opportunity to assess the flight-derived stability and control derivatives for maneuvering flight in the hypersonic regime. In the case of the Space Shuttle Orbiter, these derivatives are required to determine if certain configuration placards (limitations on the flight envelope) can be modified. These placards were determined on the basis of preflight predictions and the associated uncertainties. As flight-determined derivatives are obtained, the placards are reassessed, and some of them are removed or modified. Extraction of the stability and control derivatives was justified by operational considerations and not by research considerations. Using flight results to update the predicted database of the orbiter is one of the most completely documented processes for a flight vehicle. This process followed from the requirement for analysis of flight data for control system updates and for expansion of the operational flight envelope. These results show significant changes in many important stability and control derivatives from the preflight database. This paper presents some of the stability and control derivative results obtained from Space Shuttle flights. Some of the limitations of this information are also examined.

EC88-0247-1

Space Shuttle Orbiter

2036. Ennix, Kimberly A.: **Engine Exhaust Characteristics Evaluation in Support of Aircraft Acoustic Testing**. NASA TM-104263, H-1873, NAS 1.15:104263. Presented at the Society of Women Engineers National Conference, Chicago, Illinois, <u>June 1993</u>, 93N32220, #. (See also 2072.)

NASA Dryden Flight Research Facility and NASA Langley Research Center completed a joint acoustic flight test program. Test objectives were (1) to quantify and evaluate subsonic climb-to-cruise noise and (2) to obtain a quality noise database for use in validating the Aircraft Noise Prediction Program. These tests were conducted using aircraft with engines that represent the high nozzle pressure ratio of future transport designs. Test flights were completed at subsonic speeds that exceeded Mach 0.3 using F-18 and F-16XL aircraft. This paper describes the efforts of NASA Dryden Flight Research Facility in this flight test program. Topics discussed include the test aircraft, setup, and matrix. In addition, the engine modeling codes and nozzle exhaust characteristics are described.

2037. Ennix, Kimberly A.; Burcham, Frank W., Jr.; and Webb, Lannie D.: **Flight-Determined Engine Exhaust Characteristics of an F404 Engine in an F-18 Airplane.** AIAA Paper 93-2543. Presented at the 29th AIAA, SAE, ASME, and ASEE Joint Propulsion Conference and Exhibit, Monterey, California, <u>June 28–30, 1993</u>, 93A50267, #. (See also 2059.)

The exhaust characteristics of the F-18 aircraft with an F404 engine are examined with reference to the results of an

acoustic flight testing program. The discussion covers an overview of the flight test planning, instrumentation, test procedures, data analysis, engine modeling codes, and results. In addition, the paper presents the exhaust velocity and Mach number data for the climb-to-cruise, Aircraft Noise Prediction Program validation, and ground tests.

2038. Ko, William L.; and Jackson, Raymond H.: **Compressive and Shear Buckling Analysis of Metal Matrix Composite Sandwich Panels Under Different Thermal Environments**. NASA TM-4492, H-1900, NAS 1.15:4492. Presented at the 7th International Conference on Composite Structures, Paisley, Scotland, United Kingdom, July 1993, <u>June 1993</u>, 93N27263, #. (See also 2039.)

Combined inplane compressive and shear buckling analysis was conducted on flat rectangular sandwich panels using the Raleigh-Ritz minimum energy method with a consideration of transverse shear effect of the sandwich core. The sandwich panels were fabricated with titanium honeycomb core and laminated metal matrix composite face sheets. The results show that slightly slender (along unidirectional compressive loading axis) rectangular sandwich panels have the most desirable stiffness-to-weight ratios for aerospace structural applications; the degradation of buckling strength of sandwich panels with rising temperature is faster in shear than in compression; and the fiber orientation of the face sheets for optimum combined-load buckling strength of sandwich panels is a strong function of both loading condition and panel aspect ratio. Under the same specific weight and panel aspect ratio, a sandwich panel with metal matrix composite face sheets has much higher buckling strength than one having monolithic face sheets.

2039. Ko, William L.; and Jackson, Raymond H.: **Compressive and Shear Buckling Analysis of Metal Matrix Composite Sandwich Panels Under Different Thermal Environments**. *Composite Structures*, (ISSN 0263-8223), Vol. 25, No. 1–4, 1993. Proceedings of the 7th International Conference on Composite Structures, University of Paisley, United Kingdom, <u>July 5–7, 1993</u>, pp. 227–239, (see A93-50376 21-24), 93A50397. (See also 2038.)

Combined inplane compressive and shear buckling analysis was conducted on flat rectangular sandwich panels using the Raleigh-Ritz minimum energy method with a consideration of transverse shear effect of the sandwich core. The sandwich panels were fabricated with titanium honeycomb core and laminated metal matrix composite face sheets. The results show that slightly slender (along unidirectional compressive loading axis) rectangular sandwich panels have the most desirable stiffness-to-weight ratios for aerospace structural applications; the degradation of buckling strength of sandwich panels with rising temperature is faster in shear than in compression; and the fiber orientation of the face sheets for optimum combined-load buckling strength of sandwich panels is a strong function of both loading condition and panel aspect ratio. Under the same specific weight and panel aspect ratio, a sandwich panel with metal matrix composite face sheets has much higher buckling strength than one having monolithic face sheets.

2040. Espana, Martin D.; and Gilyard, Glenn B.: **On the Estimation Algorithm for Adaptive Performance Optimization of Turbofan Engines.** AIAA Paper 93-1823. Presented at the 29th AIAA, SAE, ASME, and ASEE, Joint Propulsion Conference and Exhibit, Monterey, California, June 28–30, 1993, 93A49710, #. (See also 2066.)

The performance seeking control (PSC) algorithm is designed to continuously optimize the performance of propulsion systems. The PSC algorithm uses a nominal propulsion system model and estimates, in flight, the engine deviation parameters (EDPs) characterizing the engine deviations with respect to nominal conditions. In practice, because of measurement biases and/or model uncertainties, the estimated EDPs may not reflect the engine's actual off-nominal condition. This factor has a direct impact on the PSC scheme exacerbated by the open-loop character of the algorithm. In this paper, the effects produced by unknown measurement biases over the estimation algorithm are evaluated. This evaluation allows for identification of the most critical measurements for application of the PSC algorithm to an F100 engine. An equivalence relation between the biases and EDPs stems from the analysis; therefore, it is undecided whether the estimated EDPs represent the actual engine deviation or whether they simply reflect the measurement biases. A new algorithm, based on the engine's (steady-state) optimization model, is proposed and tested with flight data. When compared with previous Kalman filter schemes, based on local engine dynamic models, the new algorithm is easier to design and tune and it reduces the computational burden of the onboard computer.

2041. *Mueller, F. D.; *Nobbs, S. G.; and Stewart, J. F.: **Dual Engine Application of the Performance Seeking Control Algorithm.** AIAA Paper 93-1822. Presented at the 29th AIAA, SAE, ASME, and ASEE, Joint Propulsion Conference and Exhibit, Monterey, California, June 28–30, 1993, 93A49709, #.

The Dual Engine Performance Seeking Control (PSC) flight/ propulsion optimization program has been developed and will be flown during the second quarter of 1993. Previously, only single engine optimization was possible due to the limited capability of the on-board computer. The implementation of Dual Engine PSC has been made possible with the addition of a new state-of-the-art, higher throughput computer. As a result, the single engine PSC performance improvements already flown will be demonstrated on both engines, simultaneously. Dual Engine PSC will make it possible to directly compare aircraft performance with and without the improvements generated by PSC. With the

additional thrust achieved with PSC, significant improvements in acceleration times and time to climb will be possible. PSC is also able to reduce deceleration time from supersonic speeds. This paper traces the history of the PSC program, describes the basic components of PSC, discusses the development and implementation of Dual Engine PSC including additions to the code, and presents predictions of the impact of Dual Engine PSC on aircraft performance.

*McDonnell Douglas Aerospace, St. Louis, Missouri.

2042. Gilyard, Glenn B.; and Orme, John S.: **Performance Seeking Control: Program Overview and Future Directions.** NASA TM-4531, H-1920, NAS 1.15:4531, AIAA Paper 93-3765. Presented at the AIAA Guidance, Navigation, and Control Conference, Monterey, California, August 9–11, 1993, (see A93-51360), August 1993, 94N14855, #. (See also 2043.)

A flight test evaluation of the performance-seeking control (PSC) algorithm on the NASA F-15 highly integrated digital electronic control research aircraft was conducted for single-engine operation at subsonic and supersonic speeds. The model-based PSC system was developed with three optimization modes: minimum fuel flow at constant thrust, minimum turbine temperature at constant thrust, and maximum thrust at maximum dry and full afterburner throttle settings. Subsonic and supersonic flight testing were conducted at the NASA Dryden Flight Research Facility covering the three PSC optimization modes and over the full throttle range. Flight results show substantial benefits. In the maximum thrust mode, thrust increased up to 15 percent at subsonic and 10 percent at supersonic flight conditions. The minimum fan turbine inlet temperature mode reduced temperatures by more than 100 F at high altitudes. The minimum fuel flow mode results decreased fuel consumption up to 2 percent in the subsonic regime and almost 10 percent supersonically. These results demonstrate that PSC technology can benefit the next generation of fighter or transport aircraft. NASA Dryden is developing an adaptive aircraft performance technology system that is measurement based and uses feedback to ensure optimality. This program will address the technical weaknesses identified in the PSC program and will increase performance gains.

2043. Gilyard, Glenn B.; and Orme, John S.: **Performance-Seeking Control—Program Overview and Future Directions.** AIAA Paper 93-3765. *Technical Papers,* Part 2, presented at the AIAA Guidance, Navigation and Control Conference, Monterey, California, August 9–11, 1993, (see A93-51301 22-63), pp. 593–609, 93A51360, #. (See also 2042.)

A flight test evaluation of the performance-seeking control (PSC) algorithm on the NASA F-15 highly integrated digital electronic control research aircraft was conducted for single-engine operation at subsonic and supersonic speeds. The model-based PSC system was developed with three optimization modes: minimum fuel flow at constant thrust, minimum turbine temperature at constant thrust, and maximum thrust at maximum dry and full afterburner throttle settings. Subsonic and supersonic flight testing were conducted at the NASA Dryden Flight Research Facility covering the three PSC optimization modes and over the full throttle range. Flight results show substantial benefits. In the maximum thrust mode, thrust increased up to 15 percent at subsonic and 10 percent at supersonic flight conditions. The minimum fan turbine inlet temperature mode reduced temperatures by more than 100 F at high altitudes. The minimum fuel flow mode results decreased fuel consumption up to 2 percent in the subsonic regime and almost 10 percent supersonically. These results demonstrate that PSC technology can benefit the next generation of fighter or transport aircraft.

2044. Kehoe, Michael W.; and Deaton, Vivian C.: **Correlation of Analytical and Experimental Hot Structure Vibration Results.** NASA TM-104269, H-1943, NAS 1.15:104269. Presented at the SEM Structural Testing Technology at High Temperatures II Conference, Ojai, California, November 8–10, 1993, August 1993, 94N36644, #.

High surface temperatures and temperature gradients can affect the vibratory characteristics and stability of aircraft structures. Aircraft designers are relying more on finite-element model analysis methods to ensure sufficient vehicle structural dynamic stability throughout the desired flight envelope. Analysis codes that predict these thermal effects must be correlated and verified with experimental data. Experimental modal data for aluminum, titanium, and fiberglass plates heated at uniform, nonuniform, and transient heating conditions are presented. The data show the effect of heat on each plate's modal characteristics, a comparison of predicted and measured plate vibration frequencies, the measured modal damping, and the effect of modeling material property changes and thermal stresses on the accuracy of the analytical results at nonuniform and transient heating conditions.

2045. *Ryan, George W., III; and **Downing, David R.: **The Evaluation of Several Agility Metrics for Fighter Aircraft Using Optimal Trajectory Analysis.** AIAA Paper 93-3646. *Technical Papers,* presented at the AIAA Atmospheric Flight Mechanics Conference, Monterey, California, August 9–11, 1993, pp. 293–303, (A93-48301 20-08), 93A48330, #.

Several functional agility metrics, including the combat cycle time metric, dynamic speed turn plots, and relative energy state metric, are used to compare turning performance for generic F-18, X-29, and X-31-type aircraft models. These three-degree-of-freedom models have characteristics similar to the real aircraft. The performance comparisons are made using data from optimal test trajectories to reduce sensitivities to different pilot input techniques and to reduce the effects of control system limiters. The turn performance for all three aircraft is calculated for simulated minimum time 180 deg heading captures from simulation data. Comparisons of the three aircraft give more insight into turn performance than would be available from traditional measures of performance. Using the optimal test technique yields significant performance improvements as measured by the metrics. These performance improvements were found without significant increases in turn radius.

*PRC Inc., Edwards, California.
**Kansas University, Lawrence, Kansas.

2046. *Ogburn, Marilyn E.; *Foster, John V.; Pahle, Joseph W.; Wilson, R. J.; and **Lackey, James B.: **Status of the Validation of High-Angle-of-Attack Nose-Down Pitch Control Margin Design Guidelines.** AIAA Paper 93-3623. *Technical Papers,* presented at the AIAA Atmospheric Flight Mechanics Conference, Monterey, California, August 9–11, 1993, pp. 60–75, (A93-48301 20-08), 93A48308, #.

This paper presents a summary of results obtained to date in an ongoing cooperative research program between NASA and the U.S. Navy to develop design criteria for high-angle-of-attack nose-down pitch control for combat aircraft. A fundamental design consideration for aircraft incorporating relaxed static stability in pitch is the level of stability which achieves a proper balance between high-speed performance considerations and low-speed requirements for maneuvering at high angles of attack. A comprehensive data base of piloted simulation results was generated for parametric variations of critical parameters affecting nose-down control capability. The results showed a strong correlation of pilot rating to the short-term pitch response for nose-down commands applied at high-angle-of-attack conditions. Using these data, candidate design guidelines and flight demonstration requirements were defined. Full-scale flight testing to validate the research methodology and proposed guidelines is in progress, some preliminary results of which are reviewed.

*NASA Langley Research Center, Hampton, Virginia.
**U.S. Navy, Naval Air Warfare Center, Patuxent River, Maryland.

2047. Schilling, Lawrence J.; and Mackall, Dale A.: **Flight Research Simulation Takes Off.** *Aerospace America,* (ISSN 0740-722X), Vol. 31, No. 8, August 1993, pp. 18–21, 93A53769.

The simulation configurations used in research flight test, including nonreal-time, real-time all-software, hardware-in-the-loop, iron bird, and aircraft-in-the-loop, are reviewed. It is concluded that progress in simulation technology will demonstrate new concepts, evaluate designs, enhance the quality of flight test, and minimize flight risks.

2048. Schkolnik, Gerard S.: **Identification of Integrated Airframe-Propulsion Effects on an F-15 Aircraft for Application to Drag Minimization.** AIAA Paper 93-3764. *Technical Papers,* Part 1, presented at the AIAA Guidance, Navigation and Control Conference, Monterey, California, August 9–11, 1993, pp. 569–592, (A93-51301 22-63), 93A51359, #. (See also 2060.)

The application of an adaptive real-time measurement-based performance optimization technique is being explored for a future flight research program. The key technical challenge of the approach is parameter identification, which uses a perturbation-search technique to identify changes in performance caused by forced oscillations of the controls. The controls on the NASA F-15 highly integrated digital electronic control (HIDEC) aircraft were perturbed using inlet cowl rotation steps at various subsonic and supersonic flight conditions to determine the effect on aircraft performance. The feasibility of the perturbation-search technique for identifying integrated airframe-propulsion system performance effects was successfully shown through flight experiments and postflight data analysis. Aircraft response and control data were analyzed postflight to identify gradients and to determine the minimum drag point. Changes in longitudinal acceleration as small as 0.004 g were measured, and absolute resolution was estimated to be 0.002 g or approximately 50 lbf of drag. Two techniques for identifying performance gradients were compared: a least-squares estimation algorithm and a modified maximum likelihood estimator algorithm. A complementary filter algorithm was used with the least squares estimator.

2049. Sim, Alex G.; Murray, James E.; Neufeld, David C.; and *Reed, R. Dale: **The Development and Flight Test of a Deployable Precision Landing System for Spacecraft Recovery.** NASA TM-4525, H-1933, NAS 1.15:4525, September 1993, 94N14853, #. (See also 2110.)

A joint NASA Dryden Flight Research Facility and Johnson Space Center program was conducted to determine the feasibility of the autonomous recovery of a spacecraft using a ram-air parafoil system for the final stages of entry from space that included a precision landing. The feasibility of this system was studied using a flight model of a spacecraft in the generic shape of a flattened biconic which weighed approximately 150 lb and was flown under a commercially available, ram-air parachute. Key elements of the vehicle included the Global Positioning System guidance for navigation, flight control computer, ultrasonic sensing for terminal altitude, electronic compass, and onboard data recording. A flight test program was used to develop and

refine the vehicle. This vehicle completed an autonomous flight from an altitude of 10,000 ft and a lateral offset of 1.7 miles which resulted in a precision flare and landing into the wind at a predetermined location. At times, the autonomous flight was conducted in the presence of winds approximately equal to vehicle airspeed. Several techniques for computing the winds postflight were evaluated. Future program objectives are also presented.

*PRC Inc., Edwards, California.

2050. Thornton, Stephen V.: **Reduction of Structural Loads Using Maneuver Load Control on the Advanced Fighter Technology Integration (AFTI)/F-111 Mission Adaptive Wing.** NASA TM-4526, H-1940, NAS 1.15:4526, September 1993, 94N24295, #.

A transonic fighter-bomber aircraft, having a swept supercritical wing with smooth variable-camber flaps was fitted with a maneuver load control (MLC) system that implements a technique to reduce the inboard bending moments in the wing by shifting the spanwise load distribution inboard as load factor increases. The technique modifies the spanwise camber distribution by automatically commanding flap position as a function of flap position, true airspeed, Mach number, dynamic pressure, normal acceleration, and wing sweep position. Flight test structural loads data were obtained for loads in both the wing box and the wing root. Data from uniformly deflected flaps were compared with data from flaps in the MLC configuration where the outboard segment of three flap segments was deflected downward less than the two inboard segments. The changes in the shear loads in the forward wing spar and at the roots of the stabilators also are presented. The camber control system automatically reconfigures the flaps through varied flight conditions. Configurations having both moderate and full trailing-edge flap deflection were tested. Flight test data were collected at Mach numbers of 0.6, 0.7, 0.8, and 0.9 and dynamic pressures of 300, 450, 600, and 800 lb/sq ft. The Reynolds numbers for these flight conditions ranged from 26 x 10(exp 6) to 54 x 10(exp 6) at the mean aerodynamic chord. Load factor increases of up to 1.0 g achieved with no increase in wing root bending moment with the MLC flap configuration.

2051. Crane, D. Francis; and Hamory, Philip J.: **Reactive System Verification Case Study: Fault-Tolerant Transputer Communication.** NASA TM-108784, A-93103, NAS 1.15:108784, September 1993, 94N15538, #.

A reactive program is one which engages in an ongoing interaction with its environment. A system which is controlled by an embedded reactive program is called a reactive system. Examples of reactive systems are aircraft flight management systems, bank automatic teller machine

(ATM) networks, airline reservation systems, and computer operating systems. Reactive systems are often naturally modeled (for logical design purposes) as a composition of autonomous processes which progress concurrently and which communicate to share information and/or to coordinate activities. Formal (i.e., mathematical) frameworks for system verification are tools used to increase the users' confidence that a system design satisfies its specification. A framework for reactive system verification includes formal languages for system modeling and for behavior specification and decision procedures and/or proof-systems for verifying that the system model satisfies the system specifications. Using the Ostroff framework for reactive system verification, an approach to achieving fault-tolerant communication between transputers was shown to be effective. The key components of the design, the decoupler processes, may be viewed as discrete-event-controllers introduced to constrain system behavior such that system specifications are satisfied. The Ostroff framework was also effective. The expressiveness of the modeling language permitted construction of a faithful model of the transputer network. The relevant specifications were readily expressed in the specification language. The set of decision procedures provided was adequate to verify the specifications of interest. The need for improved support for system behavior visualization is emphasized.

2052. *Groves, Al; **Knox, Fred; Smith, Rogers; and †Wisneski, Jim: **X-31 Flight Test Update.** Presented at the 37th SETP Symposium, Beverly Hills, California, September 1993, (see A95-90866). Society of Experimental Test Pilots, Lancaster, California, September 1993, (ISSN 0742-3705), pp. 100–116, 95A90870.

The goals of the tactical utility flight test are to verify the basic tactical lessons learned in simulation and determine the situational awareness implications of post-stall maneuvering. Tactics and lessons learned from post-stall engagements will supplement current fighter tactics and complement future fighter tactics development. Although the present envelope of the X-31 for carefree post stall (PST) use is limited to 225 KIAS versus 325 KIAS in simulations, the same initial conditions used in 'Pinball II' are being utilized in flight test. Starting conditions up to 325 KIAS are being flown during the build-up phase leading to the full close in air combat (CIC) evaluations. The flight control program has been modified to limit PST entry to below 225 KIAS. Full aft stick application above 225 KIAS cannot command angle of attack (AOA) in excess of 30 deg.

*USN/NAWC, Patuxent River, Maryland.
**Rockwell International Corporation, Los Angeles, California.
†U.S. Air Force/AFFTC, Edwards, California.

EC94-42478-4

X-31 Airplane

2053. Fullerton, C. Gordon: **Propulsion Controlled Aircraft Research.** Presented at the 37th SETP Symposium, Beverly Hills, California, September 1993, (see A95-90866). Society of Experimental Test Pilots, Lancaster, California, September 1993, (ISSN 0742-3705), pp. 78–88, 95A90869.

The NASA Dryden Flight Research Facility has been conducting flight, ground simulator, and analytical studies to investigate the use of thrust modulation on multi-engine aircraft for emergency flight control. Two general methods of engine only control have been studied; manual manipulation of the throttles by the pilot, and augmented control where a computer commands thrust levels in response to pilot attitude inputs and aircraft motion feedbacks. This latter method is referred to as the Propulsion Controlled Aircraft (PCA) System. A wide variety of aircraft have been investigated. Simulation studies have included the B720, F-15, B727, B747 and MD-11. A look at manual control has been done in actual flight on the F15, T-38, B747, Lear 25, T-39, MD-11 and PA-30 Aircraft. The only inflight trial of the augmented (PCA) concept has been on an F15, the results of which will be presented below.

2054. *Kempel, Robert W.; and **Painter, Weneth D.: **Development and Flight Testing of the HL-10 Lifting Body.** Presented at the 37th SETP Symposium, Beverly Hills, California, September 1993, (see A95-90866). Society of Experimental Test Pilots, Lancaster, California, September 1993, (ISSN 0742-3705), pp. 262–286, 95A90872.

The Horizontal Lander 10 (HL-10) lifting body successfully completed 37 flights, achieved the highest Mach number and altitude of this class of vehicle, and contributed to the technology base used to develop the space shuttle and future generations of lifting bodies. Design, development, and flight testing of this low-speed, air-launched, rocket-powered, lifting body was part of an unprecedented effort by NASA and the Northrop Corporation. This paper describes the evolution of the HL-10 lifting body from theoretical design, through development, to selection as one of two low-speed flight vehicles chosen for fabrication and piloted flight testing. Interesting and unusual events which occurred during the program and flight tests, review of significant problems encountered during the first flight, and discussion of how these problems were solved are presented. In addition, impressions of the pilots who flew the HL-10 lifting body are given.

*PRC Inc. Edwards, California.
**National Test Pilot School, Mojave, California.

2055. Espana, Martin D.; and *Praly, Laurent: **On the Global Dynamics of Adaptive Systems—A Study of an Elementary Example.** *SIAM Journal on Control and Optimization*, Vol. 31, No. 5, September 1993, (ISSN 0363-0129), pp. 1143–1166, 93A56355.

The inherent nonlinear character of adaptive systems poses serious theoretical problems for the analysis of their dynamics. On the other hand, the importance of their dynamic behavior is directly related to the practical interest in predicting such undesirable phenomena as nonlinear oscillations, abrupt transients, intermittence or a high sensitivity with respect to initial conditions. A geometrical/qualitative description of the phase portrait of a discrete-time adaptive system with unmodeled disturbances is given. For this, the motions in the phase space are referred to normally hyperbolic (structurally stable) locally invariant sets. The study is complemented with a local stability analysis of the equilibrium point and periodic solutions. The critical character of adaptive systems under rather usual working conditions is discussed. Special emphasis is put on the causes leading to intermittence. A geometric interpretation of the effects of some commonly used palliatives to this problem is given. The 'dead-zone' approach is studied in more detail. The predicted dynamics are compared with simulation results.

*Paris, Ecole Nationale Superieure des Mines, Fontainebleau, France.

2056. Gupta, K. K.; and Petersen, K. L.: **Multidisciplinary Aeroelastic Analysis of a Generic Hypersonic Vehicle.** NASA TM-4544, H-1956, NAS 1.15:4544, AIAA Paper 93-5028. Presented at the AIAA 5th International Aerospace Planes Conference, Munich, Germany, November 30–December 3, 1993, October 1993, 94N27868, #.

This paper presents details of a flutter and stability analysis of aerospace structures such as hypersonic vehicles. Both structural and aerodynamic domains are discretized by the common finite element technique. A vibration analysis is first performed by the STARS code employing a block Lanczos solution scheme. This is followed by the generation of a linear aerodynamic grid for subsequent linear flutter analysis within subsonic and supersonic regimes of the flight envelope; the doublet lattice and constant pressure techniques are employed to generate the unsteady aerodynamic forces. Flutter analysis is then performed for several representative flight points. The nonlinear flutter solution is effected by first implementing a CFD solution of the entire vehicle. Thus, a 3-D unstructured grid for the entire flow domain is generated by a moving front technique. A finite element Euler solution is then implemented employing a quasi-implicit as well as an explicit solution scheme. A novel multidisciplinary analysis is next effected that employs modal and aerodynamic data to yield aerodynamic damping characteristics. Such analyses are performed for a number of flight points to yield a large set of pertinent data that define flight flutter characteristics of the vehicle. This paper outlines the finite-element-based integrated analysis procedures in detail, which is followed by the results of numerical analyses of flight flutter simulation.

2057. Ko, William L.: **Mechanical and Thermal Buckling Analysis of Sandwich Panels Under Different Edge Conditions.** NASA TM-4535, H-1953, NAS 1.15:4535. Presented at the Pacific International Conference on Aerospace Science and Technology PICAST'1, Taiwan, Republic of China, December 6–9, 1993, October 1993, 94N23514, #.

By using the Rayleigh-Ritz method of minimizing the total potential energy of a structural system, combined load (mechanical or thermal load) buckling equations are established for orthotropic rectangular sandwich panels supported under four different edge conditions. Two-dimensional buckling interaction curves and three dimensional buckling interaction surfaces are constructed for high-temperature honeycomb-core sandwich panels supported under four different edge conditions. The interaction surfaces provide easy comparison of the panel buckling strengths and the domains of symmetrical and antisymmetrical buckling associated with the different edge conditions. Thermal buckling curves of the sandwich panels also are presented. The thermal buckling conditions for the cases with and without thermal moments were found to be identical for the small deformation theory. In sandwich panels, the effect of transverse shear is quite large, and by neglecting the transverse shear effect, the buckling loads could be overpredicted considerably. Clamping of the edges could greatly increase buckling strength more in compression than in shear.

2058. Hicks, John W.: **Flight Testing of Airbreathing Hypersonic Vehicles.** NASA TM-4524, Paper-37, H-1934, NAS 1.15:4524. Presented at Space Course 1993, Munich, Germany, October 11–12, 1993, October 1993, 94N15753, #.

Using the scramjet engine as the prime example of a hypersonic airbreathing concept, this paper reviews the history of and addresses the need for hypersonic flight tests. It also describes how such tests can contribute to the development of airbreathing technology. Aspects of captive-carry and free-flight concepts are compared. An incremental flight envelope expansion technique for manned flight vehicles is also described. Such critical issues as required instrumentation technology and proper scaling of experimental devices are addressed. Lastly, examples of international flight test approaches, existing programs, or concepts currently under study, development, or both, are given.

2059. Ennix, Kimberly A.; Burcham, Frank W., Jr.; and Webb, Lannie D.: **Flight-Determined Engine Exhaust Characteristics of an F404 Engine in an F-18 Airplane.** NASA TM-4538, H-1910,NAS 1.15:4538. AIAA Paper 93-2543. Presented at the 29th AIAA, SAE, ASME, and ASEE Joint Propulsion Conference and Exhibit, Monterey, California, June 28–30, 1993, (see A93-50267), October 1993, 94N15141, #. (See also 2037.)

Personnel at the NASA Langley Research Center (NASA-Langley) and the NASA Dryden Flight Research Facility (NASA-Dryden) recently completed a joint acoustic flight test program. Several types of aircraft with high nozzle pressure ratio engines were flown to satisfy a twofold objective. First, assessments were made of subsonic climb-to-cruise noise from flights conducted at varying altitudes in a Mach 0.30 to 0.90 range. Second, using data from flights conducted at constant altitude in a Mach 0.30 to 0.95 range, engineers obtained a high quality noise database. This database was desired to validate the Aircraft Noise Prediction Program and other system noise prediction codes. NASA-Dryden personnel analyzed the engine data from several aircraft that were flown in the test program to determine the exhaust characteristics. The analysis of the exhaust characteristics from the F-18 aircraft are reported. An overview of the flight test planning, instrumentation, test procedures, data analysis, engine modeling codes, and results are presented.

2060. Schkolnik, Gerard S.: **Identification of Integrated Airframe: Propulsion Effects on an F-15 Aircraft for Application to Drag Minimization.** NASA TM-4532, H-1946, NAS 1.15:4532, AIAA Paper 93-3764. Presented at Guidance, Navigation, and Control Conference, Monterey, California, August 9–11, 1993, (see A93-51359), November 1993, 94N24106, #. (See also 2048.)

The application of an adaptive real-time measurement-based performance optimization technique is being explored for a future flight research program. The key technical challenge of the approach is parameter identification, which uses a perturbation-search technique to identify changes in performance caused by forced oscillations of the controls. The controls on the NASA F-15 highly integrated digital electronic control (HIDEC) aircraft were perturbed using inlet cowl rotation steps at various subsonic and supersonic flight conditions to determine the effect on aircraft performance. The feasibility of the perturbation-search technique for identifying integrated airframe-propulsion system performance effects was successfully shown through flight experiments and postflight data analysis. Aircraft response and control data were analyzed postflight to identify gradients and to determine the minimum drag point. Changes in longitudinal acceleration as small as 0.004 g were measured, and absolute resolution was estimated to be 0.002 g or approximately 50 lbf of drag. Two techniques for identifying performance gradients were compared: a least-squares estimation algorithm and a modified maximum likelihood estimator algorithm. A complementary filter algorithm was used with the least squares estimator.

2061. Parker, Allen R., Jr.: **Simultaneous Measurement of Temperature and Strain Using Four Connecting Wires.** NASA TM-104271, H-1945, NAS 1.15:104271. Presented at the SEM Fall Conference and Exhibit on Structural Testing Technology at High Temperature-II, Ojai, California, November 8, 1993, November 1993, 94N15754, #.

This paper describes a new signal-conditioning technique for measuring strain and temperature which uses fewer connecting wires than conventional techniques. Simultaneous measurement of temperature and strain has been achieved by using thermocouple wire to connect strain gages to signal conditioning. This signal conditioning uses a new method for demultiplexing sampled analog signals and the Anderson current loop circuit. Theory is presented along with data to confirm that strain gage resistance change is sensed without appreciable error because of thermoelectric effects. Furthermore, temperature is sensed without appreciable error because of voltage drops caused by strain gage excitation current flowing through the gage resistance.

2062. Gong, Leslie; Richards, W. Lance; Monaghan, Richard C.; and Quinn, Robert D.: **Preliminary Analysis for a Mach 8 Crossflow Transition Experiment on the Pegasus® Space Booster.** NASA TM-104272, H-1954, NAS 1.15:104272. Presented at the Society for Experimental Mechanics, Structural Testing Technology at High Temperature II Conference, Ojai, California, November 8–10, 1993, November 1993, 94N36648, #.

A boundary-layer transition is proposed for a future flight mission of the air-launched Pegasus® space booster. The flight experiment requires attaching a glove assembly to the wing of the first-stage booster. The glove design consists of a spring and hook attachment system which allows for thermal growth of a steel 4130 skin. The results from one- and two-dimensional thermal analyses of the initial design are presented. Results obtained from the thermal analysis using turbulent flow conditions showed a maximum temperature of approximately 305 C and a chordwise temperature gradient of less than 8.9 C/cm for the critical areas in the upper glove skin. The temperatures obtained from these thermal analyses are well within the required temperature limits of the glove.

2063. *Stephens, Craig A.; **Hanna, Gregory J.; and Gong, Leslie. **Thermal-Fluid Analysis of the Fill and Drain Operations of a Cryogenic Fuel Tank**. NASA TM-104273, H-1961, NAS 1.15:104273. Presented at the SEM Structural Testing Technology at High Temperature II Conference, Ojai, California, November 8–10, 1993, December 1993, 94N24495, #.

The Generic Research Cryogenic Tank was designed to establish techniques for testing and analyzing the behavior of reusable fuel tank structures subjected to cryogenic fuels and aerodynamic heating. The Generic Research Cryogenic Tank tests will consist of filling a pressure vessel to a prescribed fill level, waiting for steady-state conditions, then draining the liquid while heating the external surface to simulate the thermal environment associated with hypersonic flight. Initial tests of the Generic Research Cryogenic Tank will use liquid nitrogen with future tests requiring liquid hydrogen. Two-dimensional finite-difference thermal-fluid models were developed for analyzing the behavior of the Generic Research Cryogenic Tank during fill and drain operations. The development and results of the two-dimensional fill and drain models, using liquid nitrogen, are provided, along with results and discussion on extrapolating the model results to the operation of the full-size Generic Research Cryogenic Tank. These numerical models provided a means to predict the behavior of the Generic Research Cryogenic Tank during testing and to define the requirements for the Generic Research Cryogenic Tank support systems such as vent, drain, pressurization, and instrumentation systems. In addition, the fill model provided insight into the unexpected role of circumferential conduction in cooling the Generic Research Cryogenic Tank pressure vessel during fill operations.

*PRC Inc. Edwards, California.
**Hanna Technology Resources, Boulder, Colorado.

2064. Richards, W. Lance: **Strain Gage Measurement Errors in the Transient Heating of Structural Components**. NASA TM-104274, H-1960, NAS 1.15:104274. Presented at the SEM Structural Testing Technology at High Temperature II Conference, Ojai, California, November 8–10, 1993, December 1993, 94N23487, #.

Significant strain-gage errors may exist in measurements acquired in transient thermal environments if conventional correction methods are applied. Conventional correction theory was modified and a new experimental method was developed to correct indicated strain data for errors created in radiant heating environments ranging from 0.6 °C/sec (1 °F/sec) to over 56 °C/sec (100 °F/sec). In some cases the new and conventional methods differed by as much as 30 percent. Experimental and analytical results were compared to demonstrate the new technique. For heating conditions greater than 6 °C/sec (10 °F/sec), the indicated strain data corrected with the developed technique compared much better to analysis than the same data corrected with the conventional technique.

2065. Hedgley, David R., Jr.; and Zuniga, Fanny A.: **A Photogrammetric Solution to a Particular Problem**. NASA TP-3415, H-1888, NAS 1.60:3415, December 1993, 94N22961, #.

A closed-form mathematical solution to the classical photogrammetric problem is presented. Although quite general, the solution is more applicable to problems in which the image-space conjugates are very difficult to match but one of the elements of the pair is not. Additionally, observations are made that should make the solution to the general problem of automatic matching less computationally intensive. This approach was used to analyze flow visualization data for the F-18 High Alpha Research Vehicle. The conditions for this analysis were less than ideal for image-to-object-space transformation.

2066. Espana, Martin D.; and Gilyard, Glenn B.: **On the Estimation Algorithm Used in Adaptive Performance Optimization of Turbofan Engines**. NASA TM-4551, H-1908, NAS 1.15:4551, AIAA Paper 93-1823. Presented at the AIAA Joint Propulsion Conference, Monterey, California, June 28–30, 1993, (see A93-49710), December 1993, 94N21879, #. (See also 2040.)

The performance seeking control algorithm is designed to continuously optimize the performance of propulsion systems. The performance seeking control algorithm uses a nominal model of the propulsion system and estimates, in flight, the engine deviation parameters characterizing the engine deviations with respect to nominal conditions. In practice, because of measurement biases and/or model uncertainties, the estimated engine deviation parameters may not reflect the engine's actual off-nominal condition. This factor has a necessary impact on the overall performance seeking control scheme exacerbated by the open-loop character of the algorithm. The effects produced by unknown measurement biases over the estimation algorithm are evaluated. This evaluation allows for identification of the most critical measurements for application of the performance seeking control algorithm to an F100 engine. An equivalence relation between the biases and engine deviation parameters stems from an observability study; therefore, it is undecided whether the estimated engine deviation parameters represent the actual engine deviation or whether they simply reflect the measurement biases. A new algorithm, based on the engine's (steady-state) optimization model, is proposed and tested with flight data. When compared with previous Kalman filter schemes, based on local engine dynamic models, the new algorithm is easier to design and tune and it reduces the computational burden of the onboard computer.

2067. Burken, John J.: **Flight-Determined Multivariable Stability Analysis and Comparison of a Control System.** *Journal of Guidance, Control, and Dynamics,* (ISSN 0731-5090), Vol. 16, No. 6, pp. 1026–1031, November–December 1993. Presented at the AIAA Guidance, Navigation and Control Conference, Hilton Head Island, South Carolina, August 10–12, 1992, pp. 439–453, (see A92-55196), 94A10805. (See also 1968, 1991.)

2068. Clarke, Robert; Burken, John J.; Bosworth, John T.; and Bauer, Jeffrey E.: **X-29 Flight Control System Lessons Learned.** *Int. J. Control,* Vol. 54, No. 12, 1993, pp. 1–22.

Two X-29A aircraft were flown at the NASA Dryden Flight Research Facility over a period of eight years. The airplanes' unique features are the forward-swept wing, variable incidence close-coupled canard and highly relaxed longitudinal static stability (up to 35-percent negative static margin at subsonic conditions.) This paper describes the primary flight control system and significant modifications made to the system, flight test techniques used during envelope expansion, and results for the low- and high-angle-of-attack programs. Throughout the paper, lessons learned will be discussed to illustrate the problems associated with the implementation of complex flight control systems.

2069. Conners, Timothy R.: **Measurement Effects on the Calculation of In-Flight Thrust for an F404 Turbofan Engine.** *International Journal of Turbo and Jet Engines,* Vol. 10, 1993, pp. 107–125.

A study has been performed that investigates parameter measurement effects on calculated in-flight thrust for the General Electric F404-GE-400 afterburning turbofan engine which powered the X-29A forward-swept wing research aircraft. Net-thrust uncertainty and influence coefficients were calculated and are presented. Six flight conditions were analyzed at five engine power settings each. Results were obtained using the mass flow-temperature and area-pressure thrust calculation methods, both based on the commonly used gas generator technique. Thrust uncertainty was determined using a common procedure based on the use of measurement uncertainty and influence coefficients. The effects of data nonlinearity on the uncertainty calculation procedure were studied and results are presented. The advantages and disadvantages of using this particular uncertainty procedure are discussed. A brief description of the thrust-calculation technique along with the uncertainty calculation procedure is included.

1994 Technical Publications

2070. Banks, Daniel W.; Hall, Robert M.; Erickson, Gary E.; and Fisher, David F.: **Forebody Flow Field Effects on the High Angle-of-Attack Lateral-Directional Aerodynamics of the F/A-18.** AIAA 94-0170. Presented at the 32nd AIAA Aerospace Sciences Meeting & Exhibit, Reno, Nevada, January 10–13, 1994, A94-20550.

A series of wind tunnel and flight investigations have been conducted to characterize the flow field of the forebody region of an F/A-18 configuration at high angles of attack and define its effects on the overall configuration stability at these conditions. The particular experiments included obtaining on- and off-surface flow visualization, surface pressure distributions, and overall aerodynamic characteristics. Early high angle-of-attack high Reynolds number tests indicated strong lateral stability near maximum lift, while low Reynolds number tests and flight tests indicated lateral instability at the same condition. Results from these investigations indicate that these differences are due in part to the dissimilar forebody flow field and its subsequent interaction with the strong leading-edge extension (LEX) and wing flow fields. The forebody flow field is sensitive to cross-flow Reynolds number and protuberances, notably air data probes, near the apex. The high angle-of-attack LEX and wing flow fields show sensitivity to Mach number and leading-edge flap deflection. Variations in this combined flow field were shown to result in distinct changes in lateral stability.

2071. Anderson, Karl F.: **The Constant Current Loop: A New Paradigm for Resistance Signal Conditioning.** *Technology 2003: The Fourth National Technology Transfer Conference and Exposition,* Vol. 2, February 1994, pp. 349–361, (see N94-32420 09-99), 94N32461, #. (See also 1980, 2024, 2025.)

A practical single constant current loop circuit for the signal conditioning of variable-resistance transducers has been synthesized, analyzed, and demonstrated. The strain gage and the resistance temperature detector are examples of variable-resistance sensors. Lead wires connect variable-resistance sensors to remotely located signal-conditioning hardware. The presence of lead wires in the conventional Wheatstone bridge signal-conditioning circuit introduces undesired effects that reduce the quality of the data from the remote sensors. A practical approach is presented for suppressing essentially all lead wire resistance effects while indicating only the change in resistance value. Theoretical predictions supported by laboratory testing confirm the following features of the approach: (1) dc response; (2) the electrical output is unaffected by extremely large variation in the resistance of any or all lead wires; (3) the electrical output remains zero for no change in gage resistance; (4) the electrical output is inherently linear with respect to gage resistance change; (5) the sensitivity is double that of a

Wheatstone bridge circuit; and (6) the same excitation wires can serve multiple independent gages. An adaptation of current loop circuit is presented that simultaneously provides an output signal voltage directly proportional to transducer resistance change and provides temperature information that is unaffected by transducer and lead wire resistance variations. These innovations are the subject of NASA patent applications.

2072. Ennix, Kimberly A.: **Engine Exhaust Characteristics Evaluation in Support of Aircraft Acoustic Testing.** NASA CP-10134. Presented in the 1993 Technical Paper Contest for Women. *Gear Up 2000: Women n Motion,* February 1994, pp. 13–20, (see N94-35961 11-99), 94N35963, #. (See also 2036.)

NASA Dryden Flight Research Facility and NASA Langley Research Center completed a joint acoustic flight test program. Test objectives were (1) to quantify and evaluate subsonic climb-to-cruise noise and (2) to obtain a quality noise database for use in validating the Aircraft Noise Prediction Program. These tests were conducted using aircraft with engines that represent the high nozzle pressure ratio of future transport designs. Test flights were completed at subsonic speeds that exceeded Mach 0.3 using F-18 and F-16XL aircraft. This paper describes the efforts of NASA Dryden Flight Research Facility in this flight test program. Topics discussed include the test aircraft, setup, and matrix. In addition, the engine modeling codes and nozzle exhaust characteristics are described.

2073. Powers, Sheryll Goecke: **A Biased Historical Perspective of Women in the Engineering Field at Dryden from 1946 to November 1992.** NASA CP-10134. Presented in the 1993 Technical Paper Contest for Women. *Gear Up 2000: Women in Motion,* February 1994, pp. 41–61, (see N94-35961 11-99), 94N35967, #.

Being a woman in engineering, and in particular, being the woman with the dubious distinction of having the most years at Dryden, gives the author a long-term perspective on the women who worked in the engineering field and their working environment. The working environment for the women was influenced by two main factors. One factor was the Dryden's growth of 14 persons (2 of them women) at the end of 1946 to the present size. The other factor was the need for programming knowledge when the digital computers came into use. Women have been involved with flight research at Dryden since the days of the first transonic and supersonic airplanes. This paper uses available records, along with memory, to document the number of women in engineering at Dryden, to comment about observed trends, and to make personal observations.

2074. Regenie, Victoria A.; Earls, Michael; Le, Jeanette; and Thomson, Michael: **Experience With Ada on the F-18 High Alpha Research Vehicle Flight Test Program.** NASA CP-10134. Presented in the 1993 Technical Paper

Contest for Women. *Gear Up 2000: Women in Motion,* February 1994, pp. 63–76, (see N94-35961 11-99), 94N35968, #. (See also 1977.)

Considerable experience has been acquired with Ada at the NASA Dryden Flight Research Facility during the on-going High Alpha Technology Program. In this program, an F-18 aircraft has been highly modified by the addition of thrust-vectoring vanes to the airframe. In addition, substantial alteration was made in the original quadruplex flight control system. The result is the High Alpha Research Vehicle. An additional research flight control computer was incorporated in each of the four channels. Software for the research flight control computer was written Ada. To date, six releases of this software have been flown. This paper provides a detailed description of the modifications to the research flight control system. Efficient ground-testing of the software was accomplished by using simulations that used the Ada for portions of their software. These simulations are also described. Modifying and transferring the Ada flight software to the software simulation configuration has allowed evaluation of this language. This paper also discusses such significant issues in using Ada as portability, modifiability, and testability as well as documentation requirements.

2075. Shafer, Mary F.: **In-Flight Simulation Studies at the NASA Dryden Flight Research Facility.** NASA CP-10134. Presented in the 1993 Technical Paper Contest for Women. *Gear Up 2000: Women in Motion,* February 1994, pp. 77–97, (see N94-35961 11-99), 94N35969, #. (See also 1876, 1942.)

Since the late 1950's the National Aeronautics and Space Administration's Dryden Flight Research Facility has found in-flight simulation to be an invaluable tool. In-flight simulation has been used to address a wide variety of flying qualities questions, including low lift-to-drag ratio approach characteristics for vehicles like the X-15, the lifting bodies, and the space shuttle; the effects of time delays on controllability of aircraft with digital flight control systems; the causes and cures of pilot-induced oscillation in a variety of aircraft; and flight control systems for such diverse aircraft as the X-15 and the X-29. In-flight simulation has also been used to anticipate problems, avoid them, and solve problems once they appear. This paper presents an account of the in-flight simulation at the Dryden Flight Research Facility and some discussion. An extensive bibliography is included.

2076. Voracek, David F.; and Clarke, Robert: **Buffet-Induced Structural/Flight-Control System Interaction of the X-29A Aircraft.** *Journal of Aircraft,* (ISSN 0021-8669), Vol. 31, No. 2, March–April 1994, pp. 441–443, 94A60163. (See also 1851, 1852.)

Observed in the lateral-directional axis of the flight-control system is an aeroservoelastic interaction during the high angle-of-attack flight envelope expansion of the X-29A forward-swept wing aircraft. This interaction consists of structural modes that result in commands to the control surface actuators.

2077. Borek, Robert W., Sr.; and *Pool, A.: **Basic Principles of Flight Test Instrumentation Engineering, Volume 1, Issue 2.** AGARD-AG-160-VOL-1-ISSUE-2, Flight Test Instrumentation Series, (ISBN-92-835-0731-2), March 1994, (AD-A282984), 94N33940, #.

Volume 1 of the AG 300 series on 'Flight Test Instrumentation' gives a general introduction to the basic principles of flight test instrumentation. The other volumes in the series provide more detailed treatments of selected topics on flight test instrumentation. Volume 1, first published in 1974, has been used extensively as an introduction for instrumentation courses and symposia, as well as being a reference work on the desk of most flight test and instrumentation engineers. It is hoped that this second edition, fully revised, will be used with as much enthusiasm as the first edition. In this edition a flight test system is considered to include both the data collection and data processing systems. In order to obtain an optimal data flow, the overall design of these two subsystems must be carefully matched; the detail development and the operation may have to be done by separate groups of specialists. The main emphasis is on the large automated instrumentation systems used for the initial flight testing of modern military and civil aircraft. This is done because there, many of the problems, which are discussed here, are more critical. It does not imply, however, that smaller systems with manual data processing are no longer used. In general, the systems should be designed to provide the required results at the lowest possible cost. For many tests which require only a few parameters, relatively simple systems are justified, especially if no complex equipment is available to the user. Although many of the aspects discussed in this volume apply to both small and large systems, aspects of the smaller systems are mentioned only when they are of special interest. The volume has been divided into three main parts. Part 1 defines the main starting points for the design of a flight test instrumentation system, as seen from the points of view of the flight test engineer and the instrumentation engineer. In Part 2 the discussion is concentrated on those aspects which apply to each individual measuring channel, and in Part 3 the main emphasis is on the integration of the individual data channels into one data collection system and on those aspects of the data processing which apply to the complete system.

*National Aerospace Lab., Amsterdam, the Netherlands.

2078. *Kempel, Robert W.; **Painter, Weneth D.; and Thompson, Milton O.: **Developing and Flight Testing the HL-10 Lifting Body: A Precursor to the Space Shuttle.** NASA-RP-1332, H-1942, NAS 1.61:1332, April 1994, 94N34703, #.

The origins of the lifting-body idea are traced back to the mid-1950's, when the concept of a manned satellite reentering the Earth's atmosphere in the form of a wingless lifting body was first proposed. The advantages of low reentry deceleration loads, range capability, and horizontal landing of a lifting reentry vehicle (as compared with the high deceleration loads and parachute landing of a capsule) are presented. The evolution of the hypersonic HL-10 lifting body is reviewed from the theoretical design and development process to its selection as one of two low-speed flight vehicles for fabrication and piloted flight testing. The design, development, and flight testing of the low-speed, air-launched, rocket-powered HL-10 was part of an unprecedented NASA and contractor effort. NASA Langley Research Center conceived and developed the vehicle shape and conducted numerous theoretical, experimental, and wind-tunnel studies. NASA Flight Research Center (now NASA Dryden Flight Research Center) was responsible for final low-speed (Mach numbers less than 2.0) aerodynamic analysis, piloted simulation, control law development, and flight tests. The prime contractor, Northrop Corp., was responsible for hardware design, fabrication, and integration. Interesting and unusual events in the flight testing are presented with a review of significant problems encountered in the first flight and how they were solved. Impressions by the pilots who flew the HL-10 are included. The HL-10 completed a successful 37-flight program, achieved the highest Mach number and altitude of this class vehicle, and contributed to the technology base used to develop the space shuttle and future generations of lifting bodies.

*PRC Inc., Edwards, California.
**National Test Pilot School, Mojave, California.

2079. Ko, William L.: **Mechanical and Thermal Buckling Analysis of Rectangular Sandwich Panels Under Different Edge Conditions.** NASA TM-4585, H-1932, NAS 1.15:4585, April 1994, 94N33704, #.

The combined load (mechanical or thermal load) buckling equations were established for orthotropic rectangular sandwich panels under four different edge conditions by using the Rayleigh-Ritz method of minimizing the total potential energy of a structural system. Two-dimensional buckling interaction curves and three-dimensional buckling interaction surfaces were constructed for high-temperature honeycomb-core sandwich panels supported under four different edge conditions. The interaction surfaces provide overall comparison of the panel buckling strengths and the domains of symmetrical and antisymmetrical buckling associated with the different edge conditions. In addition, thermal buckling curves of these sandwich panels are presented. The thermal buckling conditions for the cases with and without thermal moments were found to be identical for the small deformation theory.

2080. Kehoe, Michael W.; and Freudinger, Lawrence C.: **Aircraft Ground Vibration Testing at the NASA Dryden**

Flight Research Facility, 1993. NASA TM-104275, H-1966, NAS 1.15:104275, NIPS-95-06837. Presented at the 12th International Modal Analysis Conference (IMAC), Honolulu, Hawaii, February 2, 1994, April 1994, 96N16269, #.

The NASA Dryden Flight Research Facility performs ground vibration testing to assess the structural characteristics of new and modified research vehicles. This paper updates the research activities, techniques used, and experiences in applying this technology to aircraft since 1987. Test equipment, data analysis methods, and test procedures used for typical test programs are discussed. The data presented illustrate the use of modal test and analysis in flight research programs for a variety of aircraft. This includes a technique to acquire control surface free-play measurements on the X-31 airplane more efficiently, and to assess the effects of structural modifications on the modal characteristics of an F-18 aircraft. In addition, the status and results from current research activities are presented. These data show the effectiveness of the discrete modal filter as a preprocessor to uncouple response measurements into simple single-degree-of-freedom responses, a database for the comparison of different excitation methods on a JetStar airplane, and the effect of heating on modal frequency and damping.

2081. Freudinger, Lawrence C.; and Field, Richard V., Jr.: **Null Space Pole Estimation Error Bounds.** Presented at the 12th International Modal Analysis Conference (IMAC), Honolulu, Hawaii, February 2, 1994.

Modal parameter estimation algorithms require too much user interaction and are not sufficiently robust to be considered for fully automated test methodologies. This paper presents a preliminary look at a nontraditional approach for identifying the pole values (frequency and damping) derived from one or more free decay time histories. Specifically, multiple independent solutions to the characteristic equation of a typically overdetermined system are found via an eigenvector decomposition of a certain symmetric positive semi-definite matrix. The desired solution vectors span the null space of this matrix. Computational poles are removed using a histogramming approach, and the technique appears to provide robust and unbiased estimates. This report introduces the algorithm and histogramming concepts and shows their use on synthesized and experimental data.

2082. Whitmore, Stephen A.; and Moes, Timothy R.: **Measurement Uncertainty and Feasibility Study of a Flush Airdata System for a Hypersonic Flight Experiment.** NASA TM-4627, H-2010, NAS 1.15:4627, AIAA Paper 94-1930. Presented at the Applied Aerodynamics Conference, Colorado Springs, Colorado, June 20–23, 1994, June 1994, 94N37378, #.

Presented is a feasibility and error analysis for a hypersonic flush airdata system on a hypersonic flight experiment (HYFLITE). HYFLITE heating loads make intrusive airdata measurement impractical. Although this analysis is specifically for the HYFLITE vehicle and trajectory, the problems analyzed are generally applicable to hypersonic vehicles. A layout of the flush-port matrix is shown. Surface pressures are related airdata parameters using a simple aerodynamic model. The model is linearized using small perturbations and inverted using nonlinear least-squares. Effects of various error sources on the overall uncertainty are evaluated using an error simulation. Error sources modeled include boundary layer/viscous interactions, pneumatic lag, thermal transpiration in the sensor pressure tubing, misalignment in the matrix layout, thermal warping of the vehicle nose, sampling resolution, and transducer error. Using simulated pressure data for input to the estimation algorithm, effects caused by various error sources are analyzed by comparing estimator outputs with the original trajectory. To obtain ensemble averages the simulation is run repeatedly and output statistics are compiled. Output errors resulting from the various error sources are presented as a function of Mach number. Final uncertainties with all modeled error sources included are presented as a function of Mach number.

2083. Burcham, F. W., Jr.; Burken, John; and Maine, Trindel A.: **Flight Testing a Propulsion-Controlled Aircraft Emergency Flight Control System on an F-15 Airplane.** NASA TM-4590, H-1988, NAS 1.15:4590, AIAA Paper 94-2123. Presented at the 7th Biennial Flight Test Conference, Colorado Springs, Colorado, June 20–23, 1994, June 1994, 94N35258, #.

Flight tests of a propulsion-controlled aircraft (PCA) system on an F-15 airplane have been conducted at the NASA Dryden Flight Research Center. The airplane was flown with all flight control surfaces locked both in the manual throttles-only mode and in an augmented system mode. In the latter mode, pilot thumbwheel commands and aircraft feedback parameters were used to position the throttles. Flight evaluation results showed that the PCA system can be used to land an airplane that has suffered a major flight control system failure safely. The PCA system was used to recover the F-15 airplane from a severe upset condition, descend, and land. Pilots from NASA, U.S. Air Force, U.S. Navy, and McDonnell Douglas Aerospace evaluated the PCA system and were favorably impressed with its capability. Manual throttles-only approaches were unsuccessful. This paper describes the PCA system operation and testing. It also presents flight test results and pilot comments.

2084. Ray, Ronald J.: **Evaluating the Dynamic Response of In-Flight Thrust Calculation Techniques During Throttle Transients.** NASA-TM-4591, H-1990, NAS 1.15:4591, AIAA Paper 94-2115. Presented at the 7th Biennial Flight Test Conference, Colorado Springs, Colorado, June 20–23, 1994, June 1994, 94N35241, #.

New flight test maneuvers and analysis techniques for evaluating the dynamic response of in-flight thrust models during throttle transients have been developed and validated. The approach is based on the aircraft and engine performance relationship between thrust and drag. Two flight test maneuvers, a throttle step and a throttle frequency sweep, were developed and used in the study. Graphical analysis techniques, including a frequency domain analysis method, were also developed and evaluated. They provide quantitative and qualitative results. Four thrust calculation methods were used to demonstrate and validate the test technique. Flight test applications on two high-performance aircraft confirmed the test methods as valid and accurate. These maneuvers and analysis techniques were easy to implement and use. Flight test results indicate the analysis techniques can identify the combined effects of model error and instrumentation response limitations on the calculated thrust value. The methods developed in this report provide an accurate approach for evaluating, validating, or comparing thrust calculation methods for dynamic flight applications.

2085. Orme, John S.; and Conners, Timothy R.: **Supersonic Flight Test Results of a Performance Seeking Control Algorithm on a NASA F-15 Aircraft.** AIAA 94-3210. Presented at the 30th AIAA, ASME, SAE, and ASEE Joint Propulsion Conference, Indianapolis, Indiana, June 27–29, 1994.

A model-based, adaptive control algorithm called Performance Seeking Control (PSC) has been flight tested on an F-15 aircraft. The algorithm attempts to optimize performance of the integrated propulsion system during steady-state engine operation. The final phase of a 3-year PSC flight test program is described in this paper. Previous studies of use of PSC on the F-15 airplane show improvements in propulsion system performance. Because these studies were conducted using one of two F-15 engines, the full effect on aircraft performance was not measured. During the most recent studies, both engines were optimized to demonstrate the full effect of PSC propulsion system optimization on aircraft performance. Results were gathered over the 1-g supersonic envelope demonstrating benefits of the integrated control approach. Quantitative flight results illustrating the PSC method for deriving benefits from the F-15 integrated propulsion system for Mach numbers up to 2 are also presented.

2086. Clarke, Robert; Burken, John J.; Bosworth, John T.; and Bauer, Jeffrey E.: **X-29 Flight Control System: Lessons Learned.** NASA TM-4598, H-1995, NAS 1.15:4598. Presented at the AGARD Flight Mechanics Panel Symposium, Turin, Italy, May 9–12, 1994, June 1994, 94N34384, #. (See also 2122, 2140, 2215.)

Two X-29A aircraft were flown at the NASA Dryden Flight Research Center over a period of eight years. The airplanes' unique features are the forward-swept wing, variable incidence close-coupled canard and highly relaxed

longitudinal static stability (up to 35-percent negative static margin at subsonic conditions). This paper describes the primary flight control system and significant modifications made to this system, flight test techniques used during envelope expansion, and results for the low- and high-angle-of-attack programs. Through out the paper, lessons learned will be discussed to illustrate the problems associated with the implementation of complex flight control systems.

2087. Anon.: **Fourth High Alpha Conference, Volume 1.** NASA CP-10143-VOL-1, H-2007-VOL-1, NAS 1.55:10143-VOL-1. Preprints for a Conference held at Edwards, California, July 12–14, 1994, 95N14229, #.

2088. Fisher, David F.; and *Lanser, Wendy R.: **Flight and Full-Scale Wind-Tunnel Comparison of Pressure Distributions from an F-18 Aircraft at High Angles of Attack.** NASA CP-10143, Vol. 1. Presented at the NASA Dryden Fourth High Alpha Conference, Edwards, California, July 12–14, 1994, (see N95-14229 03-02), 95N14231, #.

Pressure distributions were obtained at nearly identical fuselage stations and wing chord butt lines in flight on the F-18 HARV at NASA Dryden Flight Research Center and in the NASA Ames Research Center's 80 by 120 ft wind tunnel on a full-scale F/A-18 aircraft. The static pressures were measured at the identical five stations on the forebody, three stations on the left and right leading-edge extensions, and three spanwise stations on the wing. Comparisons of the flight and wind-tunnel pressure distributions were made at alpha = 30 deg, 45 deg, and 60 deg/59 deg. In general, very good agreement was found. Minor differences were noted at the forebody at alpha = 45 deg and 60 deg in the magnitude of the vortex footprints and a Mach number effect was noted at the leading-edge extension at alpha = 30 deg. The inboard leading edge flap data from the wind tunnel at alpha = 59 deg showed a suction peak that did not appear in the flight data. This was the result of a vortex from the corner of the leading edge flap whose path was altered by the lack of an engine simulation in the wind tunnel.

*Ames Research Center, Moffett Field, California

2089. *Cobleigh, Brent R.; **Croom, Mark A.; and †Tamrat, B. F.: **Comparison of X-31 Flight, Wind-Tunnel, and Water-Tunnel Yawing Moment Asymmetries at High Angles of Attack.** NASA CP-10143, Vol. 1. Presented at the NASA Dryden Fourth High Alpha Conference, Edwards, California, July 12–14, 1994, (see N95-14229 03-02), 95N14234, #.

The X-31 aircraft are being used in the enhanced fighter maneuverability (EFM) research program, which is jointly funded by the (U.S.) Advanced Research Projects Agency (ARPA) and Germany's Federal Ministry of Defense (FMOD). The flight test portion of the program, which involves two aircraft, is being conducted by an International Test Organization (ITO) comprising the National

Aeronautics and Space Administration (NASA), the U.S. Navy, the U.S. Air Force, Rockwell International, and Deutsche Aerospace (DASA). The goals of the flight program are to demonstrate EFM technologies, investigate close-in-combat exchange ratios, develop design requirements, build a database for application to future fighter aircraft, and develop and validate low-cost prototype concepts. For longitudinal control the X-31 uses canards, symmetrical movement of the trailing-edge flaps, and pitch deflection of the thrust vectoring system. The trim, inertial coupling, and engine gyroscopic coupling compensation tasks are performed primarily by the trailing-edge flaps. For lateral-directional control the aircraft uses differential deflection of the trailing-edge flaps for roll coordination and a conventional rudder combined with the thrust vectoring system to provide yaw control. The rudder is only effective up to about 40 deg angle of attack (alpha), after which the thrust vectoring becomes the primary yaw control effector. Both the leading-edge flaps and the inlet lip are scheduled with the angle of attack to provide best performance.

*PRC Inc., Edwards, California.
**NASA Langley Research Center, Hampton, Virginia.
†Rockwell International Corporation, Downey, California.

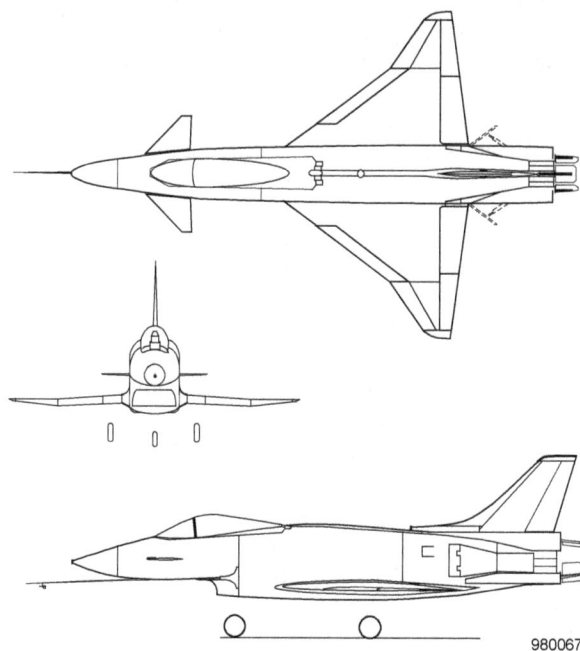

X-31 Airplane, Three-View Drawing

2090. *Hall, R. M.; *Banks, D. W.; Fisher, David F.; *Ghaffari, F.; *Murri, D. G.; **Ross, J. C.; and **Lanser, Wendy R.: **High Alpha Technology Program (HATP) Ground Test to Flight Comparisons.** NASA CP-10143, Vol. 1. Presented at the NASA Dryden Fourth High Alpha Conference, Edwards, California, July 12–14, 1994, (see N95-14229 03-02), 95N14230, #.

This status paper reviews the experimental ground test program of the High Alpha Technology Program (HATP). The reasons for conducting this ground test program had their origins during the 1970's when several difficulties were experienced during the development programs of both the F-18 and F-16. A careful assessment of ground test to flight correlations appeared to be important for reestablishing a high degree of confidence in our ground test methodology. The current paper will then focus on one aspect of the HATP program that is intended to improve the correlation between ground test and flight, high-alpha gritting. The importance of this work arises from the sensitivity of configurations with smooth-sided forebodies to Reynolds number. After giving examples of the effects of Reynolds number, the paper will highlight efforts at forebody gritting. Finally, the paper will conclude by summarizing the charter of the HATP Experimental Aerodynamics Working Group and future experimental testing plans.

*NASA Langley Research Center, Hampton, Virginia.
**NASA Ames Research Center, Mountain View, California.

2091. *Williams, David L., II; *Nelson, Robert C.; and Fisher, David F.: **Free-to-Roll Tests of X-31 and F-18 Subscale Models With Correlation to Flight Test Results.** NASA CP-10143, Vol. 1. Presented at the NASA Dryden Fourth High Alpha Conference, Edwards, California, July 12–14, 1994, (see N95-14229 03-02), 95N14237, #.

This presentation will concentrate on a series of low-speed wind tunnel tests conducted on a 2.5 percent subscale F-18 model and a 2 percent subscale X-31 model. The model's control surfaces were unaugmented; and for the most part, were deflected at a constant angle throughout the tests. The tests consisted mostly of free-to-roll experiments conducted with the use of an air-bearing, surface pressure measurements, off-surface flow visualization, and force-balance tests. Where possible the results of the subscale tests have been compared to flight test data, or to other wind tunnel data taken at higher Reynolds numbers.

*Notre Dame University, Indiana.

2092. Anon.: **Fourth High Alpha Conference, Volume 2.** NASA CP-10143-VOL-2, H-2007, NAS 1.55:10143, Preprints for a conference held at Edwards, California, July 12–14, 1994, 95N14239, #.

2093. *Enns, Dale F.; *Bugajski, Daniel J.; Carter, John; and Antoniewicz, Bob: **Multi-Application Controls: Robust Nonlinear Multivariable Aerospace Controls Applications.** NASA CP-10143, Vol. 2. Presented at the NASA Dryden Fourth High Alpha Conference, Edwards, California, July 12–14, 1994, (see N95-14229 03-02), 95N14249, #.

This viewgraph presentation describes the general methodology used to apply Honywell's Multi-Application Control (MACH) and the specific application to the F-18 High Angle-of-Attack Research Vehicle (HARV) including piloted simulation handling qualities evaluation. The general steps include insertion of modeling data for geometry and mass properties, aerodynamics, propulsion data and assumptions, requirements and specifications, e.g. definition of control variables, handling qualities, stability margins and statements for bandwidth, control power, priorities, position and rate limits. The specific steps include choice of independent variables for least squares fits to aerodynamic and propulsion data, modifications to the management of the controls with regard to integrator windup and actuation limiting and priorities, e.g. pitch priority over roll, and command limiting to prevent departures and/or undesirable inertial coupling or inability to recover to a stable trim condition. The HARV control problem is characterized by significant nonlinearities and multivariable interactions in the low speed, high angle-of-attack, high angular rate flight regime. Systematic approaches to the control of vehicle motions modeled with coupled nonlinear equations of motion have been developed. This paper will discuss the dynamic inversion approach which explicit accounts for nonlinearities in the control design. Multiple control effectors (including aerodynamic control surfaces and thrust vectoring control) and sensors are used to control the motions of the vehicles in several degrees-of-freedom. Several maneuvers will be used to illustrate performance of MACH in the high angle-of-attack flight regime. Analytical methods for assessing the robust performance of the multivariable control system in the presence of math modeling uncertainty, disturbances, and commands have reached a high level of maturity. The structured singular value (mu) frequency response methodology is presented as a method for analyzing robust performance and the mu-synthesis method will be presented as a method for synthesizing a robust control system. The paper concludes with the author's expectations regarding future applications of robust nonlinear multivariable controls.

*Honeywell, Inc., Minneapolis, Minnesota.

2094. *Huber, Peter; and Seamount, Patricia: **X-31 High Angle of Attack Control System Performance**. NASA CP-10143, Vol. 2. Presented at the NASA Dryden Fourth High Alpha Conference, Edwards, California, July 12–14, 1994, (see N95-14229 03-02), 95N14244, #.

The design goals for the X-31 flight control system were: (1) level 1 handling qualities during post-stall maneuvering (30 to 70 degrees angle-of-attack); (2) thrust vectoring to enhance performance across the angle-of-attack. Additional performance goals are discussed. A description of the flight control system is presented, highlighting flight control system features in the pitch and roll axes and X-31 thrust vectoring characteristics. The high angle-of-attack envelope clearance approach will be described, including a brief

explanation of analysis techniques and tools. Also, problems encountered during envelope expansion will be discussed. This presentation emphasizes control system solutions to problems encountered in envelope expansion. An essentially 'care free' envelope was cleared for the close-in-combat demonstrator phase. High angle-of-attack flying qualities maneuvers are currently being flown and evaluated. These results are compared with pilot opinions expressed during the close-in-combat program and with results obtained from the F-18 HARV for identical maneuvers. The status and preliminary results of these tests are discussed.

*Deutsche Aerospace A.G., Munich, Germany.

2095. Yuhas, Andrew J.; Ray, Ronald J.; Burley, Richard R.; Steenken, William G.; Lechtenberg, Leon; and Thornton, Don: **Design and Development of an F/A-18 Inlet Distortion Rake: A Cost and Time Saving Solution**. NASA CP-10143, Vol. 2. Presented at the NASA Dryden Fourth High Alpha Conference, Edwards, California, July 12–14, 1994, (see N95-14229 03-02), 95N14241, #. (See also 2167.)

An innovative inlet total-pressure distortion measurement rake has been designed and developed for the F/A-18 A/D aircraft inlet. The design was conceived by NASA and General Electric Aircraft Engines (Evendale, Ohio). This rake has been flight qualified and flown in the F-18 High Alpha Research Vehicle (HARV) at NASA Dryden Flight Research Center. The rake's eight-legged, one-piece wagon wheel design was developed at a reduced cost and offers reduced installation time compared with traditional designs. The rake features 40 dual measurement ports for both low- and high-frequency pressure measurements with the high-frequency transducer mounted at the port. The high-frequency transducer offers direct absolute pressure measurements from low frequency to the highest frequency of interest, thereby allowing the rake to be used during highly dynamic aircraft maneuvers. Outstanding structural characteristics are inherent to the design through its construction and use of lightweight materials.

2096. Bowers, Albion H.; Regenie, Victoria A.; and Flick, Bradley C.: **F-18 High Alpha Research Vehicle: Lessons Learned**. NASA CP-10143, Vol. 2. Presented at the NASA Dryden Fourth High Alpha Conference, Edwards, California, July 12–14, 1994, (see N95-14229 03-02), 95N14240, #.

The F-18 High Alpha Research Vehicle has proven to be a useful research tool with many unique capabilities. Many of these capabilities are to assist in characterizing flight at high angles of attack, while some provide significant research in their own right. Of these, the thrust vectoring system, the unique ability to rapidly reprogram flight controls, the reprogrammable mission computer, and a reprogrammable onboard excitation system have allowed an increased utility and versatility of the research being conducted. Because of this multifaceted approach to research in the high angle of attack regime, the capabilities of the F-18 High Alpha Research Vehicle were designed to cover as many high alpha technology bases as the program would allow. These areas include aerodynamics, controls, handling qualities, and propulsion.

2097. *Ogburn, Marilyn E.; *Ross, Holly M.; *Foster, John V.; Pahle, Joseph W.; **Sternberg, Charles A.; **Traven, Ricardo; **Lackey, James B.; and †Abbott, Troy D.: **Flight Validation of Ground-Based Assessment for Control Power Requirements at High Angles of Attack.** NASA CP-10143, Vol. 2. Presented at the NASA Dryden Fourth High Alpha Conference, Edwards, California, July 12–14, 1994, (see N95-14229 03-02), 95N14246, #.

Navy study to determine control power requirements at high angles of attack for the next generation high-performance aircraft. This paper focuses on recent flight test activities using the NASA High Alpha Research Vehicle (HARV), which are intended to validate results of previous ground-based simulation studies. The purpose of this study is discussed, and the overall program structure, approach, and objectives are described. Results from two areas of investigation are presented: (1) nose-down control power requirements and (2) lateral-directional control power requirements. Selected results which illustrate issues and challenges that are being addressed in the study are discussed including test methodology, comparisons between simulation and flight, and general lessons learned.

*NASA Langley Research Center, Hampton, Virginia.
**Naval Air Warfare Center, Patuxent River, Maryland.
†Virginia Polytechnic Institute and State University, Blacksburg, Virginia.

2098. Anon.: **Fourth High Alpha Conference, Volume 3**. NASA CP-10143-VOL-3, H-2007, NAS 1.55:10143-VOL-3. Preprints for a conference held at Edwards, California, July 12–14, 1994, 95N14251, #.

2099. Murray, James E.; Sim, Alex G.; Neufeld, David C.; Rennich, Patrick K.; Norris, Stephen R.; and Hughes, Wesley S.: **Further Development and Flight Test of an Autonomous Precision Landing System Using a Parafoil.** NASA TM-4599, H-1987, NAS 1.15:4599, AIAA Paper 94-2141. Presented at the 6th Biennial Flight Test Conference, Colorado Springs, Colorado, June 20–23, 1994, July 1994, 94N33995, #.

NASA Dryden Flight Research Center and NASA Johnson Space Center are jointly conducting a phased program to determine the feasibility of the autonomous recovery of a spacecraft using a ram-air parafoil system for the final stages of entry from space to a precision landing. The feasibility is being studied using a flight model of a spacecraft in the generic shape of a flattened biconic that weighs approximately 120 lb and is flown under a commercially

available ram-air parafoil. Key components of the vehicle include the global positioning system (GPS) guidance for navigation, a flight control computer, an electronic compass, a yaw rate gyro, and an onboard data recorder. A flight test program is being used to develop and refine the vehicle. The primary flight goal is to demonstrate autonomous flight from an altitude of 3,000 m (10,000 ft) with a lateral offset of 1.6 km (1.0 mi) to a precision soft landing. This paper summarizes the progress to date. Much of the navigation system has been tested, including a heading tracker that was developed using parameter estimation techniques and a complementary filter. The autoland portion of the autopilot is still in development. The feasibility of conducting the flare maneuver without servoactuators was investigated as a means of significantly reducing the servoactuator rate and load requirements.

2100. Fisher, David F.; and Cobleigh, Brent R.: **Controlling Forebody Asymmetries in Flight: Experience With Boundary Layer Transition Strips.** NASA TM-4595, H-1992, NAS 1.15:4595, AIAA Paper 94-1826. Presented at the 6th Biennial Flight Test Conference, Colorado Springs, Colorado, June 20–23, 1994, July 1994, 94N36944, #.

The NASA Dryden Flight Research Center has an ongoing program to investigate aircraft flight characteristics at high angles of attack. As part of this investigation, longitudinal boundary layer transition strips were installed on the F-18 HARV forebody, a preproduction F/A-18 radome with a nose-slice tendency, and the X-31 aircraft forebody and noseboom to reduce asymmetric yawing moments at high angles of attack. The transition strips were effective on the F-18 HARV at angles of attack above 60 deg. On the preproduction F/A-18 radome at an angle of attack near 50 deg the strips were not effective. When the transition strips were installed on the X-31 noseboom, a favorable effect was observed on the yawing moment dynamics but the magnitude of the yawing moment was not decreased.

2101. Johnson, Steven; and *Murphy, Kelly: **Pressure-Sensing Performance of Upright Cylinders in a Mach 10 Boundary-Layer**, NASA-TM-4633, H-1977, NAS 1.15:4633, July 1994, 94N37395, #.

An experimental research program to provide basic knowledge of the pressure-sensing performance of upright, flushported cylinders in a hypersonic boundary layer is described. Three upright cylinders of 0.25-, 0.5- and 1.0-in. diameters and a conventional rake were placed in the test section sidewall boundary layer of the 31 Inch Mach 10 Wind Tunnel at NASA Langley Research Center, Hampton, Virginia. Boundary-layer pressures from these cylinders were compared to those measured with a conventional rake. A boundary-layer thickness-to-cylinder-diameter ratio of 8 proved sufficient to accurately measure an overall pressure profile and ascertain the boundary-layer thickness. Effects of Reynolds number, flow angularity, and shock wave impingement on pressure measurement were also investigated. Although Reynolds number effects were negligible at the conditions studied, flow angularity above 10 deg significantly affects the measured pressures. Shock wave impingement was used to investigate orifice-to-orifice pressure crosstalk. No crosstalk was measured. The lower pressure measured above the oblique shock wave impingement showed no influence of the higher pressure generated at the lower port locations.

*NASA Langley Research Center, Hampton, Virginia.

2102. Espana, Martin D.: **Sensor Biases Effect on the Estimation Algorithm for Performance-Seeking Controllers.** *Journal of Propulsion and Power*, (ISSN 0748-4658), Vol. 10, No. 4, July–August 1994, pp. 527–532, 95A68160.

The performance-seeking-control algorithm (PSC) is designed to continuously optimize the performance of propulsion systems. The PSC uses engine deviation parameters (EDPs) characterizing engine deviations with respect to nominal conditions. In practice, the measurement biases (or model uncertainties) may prevent the estimated EDPs from reflecting the engine's actual off-nominal condition. This factor has a direct impact on the PSC scheme exacerbated by the open-loop character of the algorithm. An observability analysis shows that the biases cannot be estimated together with the EDPs. Moreover, biases and EDPs turn out to have equivalent effects on the measurements, leaving it undecided whether the estimated EDPs represent the actual engine deviation or whether they simply reflect the measurement biases. In this article, the effects produced by unknown measurement biases over the estimation algorithm are evaluated. This evaluation allows for identification of the most critical measurements for application of the PSC algorithm to an F100 engine.

2103. Gilyard, Glenn; and Espana, Martin: **On the Use of Controls for Subsonic Transport Performance Improvement: Overview and Future Directions.** NASA TM-4605, H-2002, NAS 1.15:4605, AIAA Paper 94-3515. Presented at the Atmospheric Flight Mechanics Conference, Scottsdale, Arizona, August 1–3, 1994, August 1994, 95N11408, #.

Increasing competition among airline manufacturers and operators has highlighted the issue of aircraft efficiency. Fewer aircraft orders have led to an all-out efficiency improvement effort among the manufacturers to maintain if not increase their share of the shrinking number of aircraft sales. Aircraft efficiency is important in airline profitability and is key if fuel prices increase from their current low. In a continuing effort to improve aircraft efficiency and develop an optimal performance technology base, NASA Dryden Flight Research Center developed and flight tested an adaptive performance seeking control system to optimize the quasi-steady-state performance of the F-15 aircraft. The demonstrated technology is equally applicable to transport aircraft although with less improvement. NASA Dryden, in transitioning this technology to transport aircraft, is specifically exploring the feasibility of applying adaptive optimal control techniques to performance optimization of redundant control effectors. A simulation evaluation of a preliminary control law optimizes wing-aileron camber for minimum net aircraft drag. Two submodes are evaluated: one to minimize fuel and the other to maximize velocity. This paper covers the status of performance optimization of the current fleet of subsonic transports. Available integrated controls technologies are reviewed to define approaches using active controls. A candidate control law for adaptive performance optimization is presented along with examples of algorithm operation.

2104. *Richwine, David M.; and Del Frate, John H.: **Development of a Low-Aspect Ratio Fin for Flight Research Experiments.** NASA TM-4596, H-1993, NAS 1.15:4596, AIAA Paper 94-2133. Presented at the 6th Biennial Flight Test Conference, Colorado Springs, Colorado, June 20–23, 1993, August 1994, 95N16858, #.

A second-generation flight test fixture, developed at NASA Dryden Flight Research Center, offers a generic testbed for aerodynamic and fluid mechanics research. The new fixture, a low-aspect ratio vertical fin shape mounted on the centerline of an F-15B aircraft lower fuselage, is designed for flight research at Mach numbers up to 2.0. The new fixture is a composite structure with a modular configuration and removable components for functional flexibility. This report describes the multidisciplinary design and analysis approach used to develop the fixture. The approach integrates conservative assumptions with simple analysis techniques to minimize the time and cost associated with its development. Presented are the principal disciplines required for this effort, which include aerodynamics, structures, stability, and operational considerations. In addition, preliminary results from the first phase of flight testing are presented. Acceptable directional stability and flow quality are documented and show agreement with predictions. Future envelope expansion activities will minimize current limitations so that the fixture can be used for a wide variety of high-speed aerodynamic and fluid mechanics research experiments.

*PRC Inc., Edwards, California.

2105. Zuniga, Fanny A.; *Drake, Aaron; **Kennelly, Robert A., Jr.; **Koga, Dennis J.; and †Westphal, Russell V.: **Transonic Flight Test of a Laminar Flow Leading Edge With Surface Excrescences.** NASA TM-4597, H-1994, NAS 1.15:4597, AIAA Paper 94-2142. Presented at the 6th Biennial Flight Test Conference, Colorado Springs, Colorado, June 20–23, 1994, August 1994, 95N11158, #.

A flight experiment, conducted at NASA Dryden Flight Research Center, investigated the effects of surface excrescences, specifically gaps and steps, on boundary-layer transition in the vicinity of a leading edge at transonic flight conditions. A natural laminar flow leading-edge model was designed for this experiment with a spanwise slot manufactured into the leading-edge model to simulate gaps and steps like those present at skin joints of small transonic aircraft wings. The leading-edge model was flown with the flight test fixture, a low-aspect ratio fin mounted beneath an F-104G aircraft. Test points were obtained over a unit Reynolds number range of 1.5 to 2.5 million/ft and a Mach number range of 0.5 to 0.8. Results for a smooth surface showed that laminar flow extended to approximately 12 in. behind the leading edge at Mach number 0.7 over a unit Reynolds number range of 1.5 to 2.0 million/ft. The maximum size of the gap-and-step configuration over which laminar flow was maintained consisted of two 0.06-in. gaps with a 0.02-in. step at a unit Reynolds number of 1.5 million/ft.

*Stanford University, Stanford, California.
**Ames Research Center, Moffett Field, California.
†Washington State University at Tri-Cities, Richland, Washington.

2106. *Cotton, Stacey J.; and Bjarke, Lisa J.: **Flow-Visualization Study of the X-29A Aircraft at High Angles of Attack Using a 1/48-Scale Model**. NASA TM-104268, H-1918, NAS 1.15:104268, August 1994, 95N10858, #.

A water-tunnel study on a 1/48-scale model of the X-29A aircraft was performed at the NASA Dryden Flow Visualization Facility. The water-tunnel test enhanced the results of the X-29A flight tests by providing flow-visualization data for comparison and insights into the aerodynamic characteristics of the aircraft. The model was placed in the water tunnel at angles of attack of 20 to 55 deg. and with angles of sideslip from 0 to 5 deg. In general, flow-visualization techniques provided useful information on vortex formation, separation, and breakdown and their role in yaw asymmetries and tail buffeting. Asymmetric forebody vortices were observed at angles of attack greater than 30 deg. with 0 deg. sideslip and greater than 20 deg. with 5 deg. sideslip. While the asymmetric flows observed in the water tunnel did not agree fully with the flight data, they did show some of the same trends. In addition, the flow visualization indicated that the interaction of forebody vortices and the wing wake at angles of attack between 20 and 35 deg. may cause vertical-tail buffeting observed in flight.

*Air Force Flight Test Center, Edwards AFB, California.

2107. Cobleigh, Brent R.; and Del Frate, John: **Water Tunnel Flow Visualization Study of a 4.4 Percent Scale X-31 Forebody**. NASA TM-104276, H-1997, NAS 1.15:104276, September 1994, 95N11898, #.

A water-tunnel test of a 4.4 percent-scale, forebody-only model of the X-31 aircraft with different forebody strakes and

nosebooms has been performed in the Flow Visualization Facility at the NASA Dryden Flight Research Center. The focus of the study was to determine the relative effects of the different configurations on the stability and symmetry of the high-angle-of-attack forebody vortex flow field. The clean, noseboom-off configuration resisted the development of asymmetries in the primary vortices through 70 deg angle of attack. The wake of the X-31 flight test noseboom configuration significantly degraded the steadiness of the primary vortex cores and promoted asymmetries. An alternate L-shaped noseboom mounted underneath the forebody had results similar to those seen with the configuration, enabling stable, symmetrical vortices up to 70 deg angle of attack. The addition of strakes near the radome tip along the waterline increased the primary vortex strength while it simultaneously caused the vortex breakdown location to move forward. Forebody strakes did not appear to significantly reduce the asymmetries in the forebody vortex field in the presence of the flight test noseboom.

2108. *Corda, Stephen; Stephenson, Mark T.; Burcham, Frank W.; and Curry, Robert E.: **Dynamic Ground Effects Flight Test of an F-15 Aircraft**. NASA TM-4604, H-1999, NAS 1.15:4604, September 1994, 95N12191, #.

Flight tests to determine the changes in the aerodynamic characteristics of an F-15 aircraft caused by dynamic ground effects are described. Data were obtained for low and high sink rates between 0.7 and 6.5 ft/sec and at two landing approach speeds and flap settings: 150 kn with the flaps down and 170 kn with the flaps up. Simple correlation curves are given for the change in aerodynamic coefficients because of ground effects as a function of sink rate. Ground effects generally caused an increase in the lift, drag, and nose-down pitching movement coefficients. The change in the lift coefficient increased from approximately 0.05 at the high-sink rate to approximately 0.10 at the low-sink rate. The change in the drag coefficient increased from approximately 0 to 0.03 over this decreasing sink rate range. No significant difference because of the approach configuration was evident for lift and drag; however, a significant difference in pitching movement was observed for the two approach speeds and flap settings. For the 170 kn with the flaps up configuration, the change in the nose-down pitching movement increased from approximately –0.008 to –0.016. For the 150 kn with the flaps down configuration, the change was approximately –0.008 to –0.038.

*PRC Inc., Edwards, California.

2109. Wagner, Charles A.: **Effects of Mass on Aircraft Sidearm Controller Characteristics**. NASA TM-104277, H-2014, NAS 1.15:104277, September 1994, 95N11868, #.

When designing a flight simulator, providing a set of low mass variable-characteristic pilot controls can be very difficult. Thus, a strong incentive exists to identify the highest possible mass that will not degrade the validity of a simulation. The NASA Dryden Flight Research Center has conducted a brief flight program to determine the maximum acceptable mass (system inertia) of an aircraft sidearm controller as a function of force gradient. This information is useful for control system design in aircraft as well as development of suitable flight simulator controls. A modified Learjet with a variable-characteristic sidearm controller was used to obtain data. A boundary was defined between mass considered acceptable and mass considered unacceptable to the pilot. This boundary is defined as a function of force gradient over a range of natural frequencies. This investigation is limited to a study of mass-frequency characteristics only. Results of this investigation are presented in this paper.

2110. Sim, Alex G.; Murray, James E.; Neufeld, David C.; and Reed, R. Dale: **Development and Flight Test of a Deployable Precision Landing System.** *Journal of Aircraft,* (ISSN 0021-8669), Vol. 31, No. 5, September–October 1994, pp. 1101–1108, 95A69243. (See also 2049.)

A joint NASA Dryden Flight Research Facility and Johnson Space Center program was conducted to determine the feasibility of the autonomous recovery of a spacecraft using a ram-air parafoil system for the final stages of entry from space that included a precision landing. The feasibility of this system was studied using a flight model of a spacecraft in the generic shape of a flattened biconic that weighed approximately 150 lb and was flown under a commercially available, ram-air parachute. Key elements of the vehicle included the Global Positioning System guidance for navigation, flight control computer, ultrasonic sensing for terminal altitude, electronic compass, and onboard data recording. A flight test program was used to develop and refine the vehicle. This vehicle completed an autonomous flight from an altitude of 10,000 ft and a lateral offset of 1.7 miles that resulted in a precision flare and landing into the wind at a predetermined location. At times, the autonomous flight was conducted in the presence of winds approximately equal to vehicle airspeed. Several novel techniques for computing the winds postflight were evaluated. Future program objectives are also presented.

2111. Espana, M.; and Gilyard, G.: **Adaptive Wing Camber Optimization: a Periodic Perturbation Approach.** Presented at the 13th IFAC Symposium on Automatic Control in Aerospace, Palo Alto, California, September, 1994.

Available redundancy among aircraft control surfaces allows for effective wing camber modifications. As shown in the past, this fact can be used to improve aircraft performance. To date, however, algorithm developments for in-flight camber optimization have been limited. This paper presents a perturbational approach for cruise optimization through in-flight camber adaptation. The method uses, as a performance index, an indirect measurement of the instantaneous net thrust. As such, the actual performance improvement comes from the integrated effect of airframe and engine. The algorithm, whose design and robustness properties are discussed, is demonstrated on the NASA Dryden B-720 flight simulator.

2112. Hamory, Philip J.; and Murray, James E.: **Flight Experience With Lightweight, Low-Power Miniaturized Instrumentation Systems.** *Journal of Aircraft,* (ISSN 0021-8669), Vol. 31, No. 5, September–October 1994, pp. 1016–1021, 95A69230. (See also 1960, 2018.)

Engineers at the NASA Dryden Flight Research Facility (NASA-Dryden) have conducted two flight research programs with lightweight, low-power miniaturized instrumentation systems built around commercial data loggers. One program quantified the performance of a radio-controlled model airplane. The other program was a laminar boundary-layer transition experiment on a manned sailplane. The purpose of this article is to report NASA-Dryden personnel's flight experience with the miniaturized instrumentation systems used on these two programs. This article will describe the data loggers, the sensors, and the hardware and software developed to complete the systems. It also describes how the systems were used and covers the challenges encountered to make them work. Examples of raw data and derived results will be shown as well. For some flight research applications where miniaturized instrumentation is a requirement, the authors conclude that commercially available data loggers and sensors are viable alternatives. In fact, the data loggers and sensors make it possible to gather research-quality data in a timely and cost-effective manner.

2113. Ehernberger, L. J.; Wurtele, Morton G.; and Sharman, Robert D.: **Simple Atmospheric Perturbation Models for Sonic-Boom-Signature Distortion Studies.** Presented at the NASA Langley Research Center, *High-Speed Research: 1994 Sonic Boom Workshop: Atmospheric Propagation and Acceptability Studies,* October 1994, pp. 157–169, (see N95-14878 03-02), 95N14888, #.

Sonic-boom propagation from flight level to ground is influenced by wind and speed-of-sound variations resulting from temperature changes in both the mean atmospheric structure and small-scale perturbations. Meteorological behavior generally produces complex combinations of atmospheric perturbations in the form of turbulence, wind shears, up- and down-drafts and various wave behaviors. Differences between the speed of sound at the ground and at flight level will influence the threshold flight Mach number for which the sonic boom first reaches the ground as well as the width of the resulting sonic-boom carpet. Mean atmospheric temperature and wind structure as a function of altitude vary with location and time of year. These average properties of the atmosphere are well-documented and have been used in many sonic-boom propagation assessments. In contrast, smaller scale atmospheric perturbations are also known to modulate the shape and amplitude of sonic-boom signatures reaching the ground, but specific perturbation models have not been established for evaluating their effects on sonic-boom propagation. The purpose of this paper is to present simple examples of atmospheric vertical temperature gradients, wind shears, and wave motions that can guide preliminary assessments of nonturbulent atmospheric perturbation effects on sonic-boom propagation to the ground. The use of simple discrete atmospheric perturbation structures can facilitate the interpretation of the resulting sonic-boom propagation anomalies as well as intercomparisons among varied flight conditions and propagation models.

2114. Greer, Donald S.: **Numerical Modeling of a Cryogenic Fluid Within a Fuel Tank**. NASA TM-4651, H-2029, NAS 1.15:4651. Presented at the Second Thermal Structures Conference, Charlottesville, Virginia, October 18–21, 1994, <u>October 1994</u>, 95N13892, #.

The computational method developed to study the cryogenic fluid characteristics inside a fuel tank in a hypersonic aircraft is presented. The model simulates a rapid draining of the tank by modeling the ullage vapor and the cryogenic liquid with a moving interface. A mathematical transformation was developed and applied to the Navier-Stokes equations to account for the moving interface. The formulation of the numerical method is a transient hybrid explicit-implicit technique where the pressure term in the momentum equations is approximated to first order in time by combining the continuity equation with an ideal equation of state.

2115. Ko, William L: **Thermo-Cryogenic Buckling and Stress Analysis of Partially Filled Cryogenic Tank Subjected to Cylinder Strip Heating.** Presented at the JSASS 32nd Aircraft Symposium International Sessions, Kitakyushu, Japan, <u>October 5–7, 1994</u>. (See also 2116.)

Thermocryogenic buckling and stress analysis were conducted on a horizontally oriented cryogenic tank using the finite element method. The tank is a finite length circular cylindrical shell with its two ends capped with hemispherical shells. The tank was subjected to cylindrical strip heating in the region above the liquid-cryogen fill level and to cryogenic cooling below the fill level (i.e., under thermocryogenic loading). The effects of cryogen fill level on the buckling temperatures and thermocryogenic stress field were investigated in detail. Both the buckling temperature and stress magnitudes were relatively insensitive to the cryogen fill level. The buckling temperature, however, was quite sensitive to the radius-to-thickness ratio. The of solutions from different finite element models were compared, and high-stress domains were identified.

2116. Ko, William L.: **Thermocryogenic Buckling and Stress Analyses of a Partially Filled Cryogenic Tank Subjected to Cylindrical Strip Heating**. NASA TM-4579, H-1955, NAS 1.15:4579, <u>November 1994</u>, 95N17417, #. (See also 2115.)

Thermocryogenic buckling and stress analyses were conducted on a horizontally oriented cryogenic tank using the finite element method. The tank is a finite-length circular cylindrical shell with its two ends capped with hemispherical shells. The tank is subjected to cylindrical strip heating in the region above the liquid-cryogen fill level and to cryogenic cooling below the fill level (i.e., under thermocryogenic loading). The effects of cryogen fill level on the buckling temperature and thermocryogenic stress field were investigated in detail. Both the buckling temperature and stress magnitudes were relatively insensitive to the cryogen fill level. The buckling temperature, however, was quite sensitive to the radius-to-thickness ratio. A mechanical stress analysis of the tank also was conducted when the tank was under: (1) cryogen liquid pressure loading; (2) internal pressure loading; and (3) tank-wall inertia loading. Deformed shapes of the cryogenic tanks under different loading conditions were shown, and high-stress domains were mapped on the tank wall for the strain-gage installations. The accuracies of solutions from different finite element models were compared.

2117. Ko, William L.: **Thermocryogenic Buckling and Stress Analyses of a Partially Filled Cryogenic Tank.** Presented at the 2nd Thermal Structures Conference, Charlottesville, Virginia, October 18–20, 1994. *Aerospace Thermal Structures and Materials for a New Era*, Vol. 168, Progress in Astronautics and Aeronautics, <u>1994</u>.

Thermocryogenic buckling and stress analyses were conducted on a horizontally oriented cryogenic tank using the finite element method. The tank is a finite-length circular cylindrical shell with its two ends capped with hemispherical shells. The tank is subjected to cylindrical strip heating in the region above the liquid-cryogen fill level and to cryogenic cooling below the fill level (i.e., under thermocryogenic loading). The effects of cryogen fill level on the buckling temperature and thermocryogenic stress field were investigated in detail. Both the buckling temperature and stress magnitudes were relatively insensitive to the cryogen fill level. The buckling temperature, however, was quite sensitive to the radius-to-thickness ratio. A mechanical stress analysis of the tank also was conducted when the tank was under: (1) cryogen liquid pressure loading; (2) internal pressure loading; and (3) tank-wall inertia loading. Deformed shapes of the cryogenic tanks under different loading conditions were shown, and high-stress domains were mapped on the tank wall for the strain-gage installations. The accuracies of solutions from different finite element models were compared.

2118. Ko, William L.; and Jackson, Raymond H.: **Shear Buckling Analysis of a Hat-Stiffened Panel**. NASA TM-4644, H-2019, NAS 1.15:4644, November 1994, 95N17490, #.

A buckling analysis was performed on a hat-stiffened panel subjected to shear loading. Both local buckling and global buckling were analyzed. The global shear buckling load was found to be several times higher than the local shear buckling load. The classical shear buckling theory for a flat plate was found to be useful in predicting the local shear buckling load of the hat-stiffened panel, and the predicted local shear buckling loads thus obtained compare favorably with the results of finite element analysis.

2119. Espana, Martin D.: **Simple Estimation Algorithm for Performance-Seeking Controllers**. *Journal of Propulsion and Power*, (ISSN 0748-4658), Vol. 10, No. 6, November–December 1994, pp. 914–916, 95A69297.

This study is concerned about the optimization of PSC which is designed to continuously enhance the performance of a propulsion system. The optimization model is a simplified steady-state model of the propulsion system called the compact propulsion system model (CPSM). To characterize the steady-state model, two approaches which include the Kalman filter approach and a simpler Luenberger-type observer are employed. It was observed that simpler Luenberg-type observer is more effective than the Kalman filter approach for such application.

2120. *Saltzman, Edwin J.; and Hicks, John W.: **In-Flight Lift-Drag Characteristics for a Forward-Swept Wing Aircraft and Comparisons With Contemporary Aircraft**. NASA TP-3414, H-1913, NAS 1.60:3414, December 1994, 95N18565, #.

Lift (L) and drag (D) characteristics have been obtained in flight for the X-29A airplane (a forward swept-wing demonstrator) for Mach numbers (M) from 0.4 to 1.3. Most of the data were obtained near an altitude of 30,000 ft. A representative Reynolds number for M = 0.9, and a pressure altitude of 30,000 ft, is $18.6 \times 10(\exp 6)$ based on the mean aerodynamic chord. The X-29A data (forward-swept wing) are compared with three high-performance fighter aircraft: the F-15C, F-16C, and F/A18. The lifting efficiency of the X-29A, as defined by the Oswald lifting efficiency factor, e, is about average for a cantilevered monoplane for M = 0.6 and angles of attack up to those required for maximum L/D. At M = 0.6 the level of L/D and e, as a function of load factor, for the X-29A was about the same as for the contemporary aircraft. The X-29A and its contemporaries have high transonic wave drag and equivalent parasite area compared with aircraft of the 1940's through 1960's.

*PRC Inc., Edwards, California.

2121. Mackall, D.: **HYPERDATA - Basic Hypersonic Data and Equations**. ARC-13185, 1994, 94M10063.

In an effort to place payloads into orbit at the lowest possible costs, the use of air-breathing space-planes, which reduces the need to carry the propulsion system oxidizer, has been examined. As this approach would require the space-plane to fly at hypersonic speeds for periods of time much greater than that required by rockets, many factors must be considered when analyzing its benefits. The Basic Hypersonic Data and Equations spreadsheet provides data gained from three analyses of a space-plane's performance. The equations used to perform the analyses are derived from Newton's second law of physics (i.e. force equals mass times acceleration); the derivation is included. The first analysis is a parametric study of some basic factors affecting the ability of a space-plane to reach orbit. This step calculates the fraction of fuel mass to the total mass of the space-plane at takeoff. The user is able to vary the altitude, the heating value of the fuel, the orbital gravity, and orbital velocity. The second analysis calculates the thickness of a spherical fuel tank, while assuming all of the mass of the vehicle went into the tank's shell. This provides a first order analysis of how much material results from a design where the fuel represents a large portion of the total vehicle mass. In this step, the user is allowed to vary the values for gross weight, material density, and fuel density. The third analysis produces a ratio of gallons of fuel per total mass for various aircraft. It shows that the volume of fuel required by the space-plane relative to the total mass is much larger for a liquid hydrogen space-plane than any other vehicle made. This program is a spreadsheet for use on Macintosh series computers running Microsoft Excel 3.0. The standard distribution medium for this package is a 3.5 inch 800K Macintosh format diskette. Documentation is included in the price of the program. Macintosh is a registered trademark of Apple Computer, Inc. Microsoft is a registered trademark of Microsoft Corporation.

2122. Clarke, Robert; Burken, John J.; Bosworth, John T.; and Bauer, Jeffrey E.: **X-29 Flight Control System Lessons Learned**. *Int'l J. Control*, Vol. 59, No. 1, 1994, pp. 199–219. (See also 2086, 2140, 2215.)

Two X-29A aircraft were flown at the NASA Dryden Flight Research Facility over a period of eight years. The airplanes' unique features are the forward-swept wing, variable incidence close-coupled canard and highly relaxed longitudinal static stability (up to 35-percent negative static margin at subsonic conditions.) This paper describes the primary flight control system and significant modifications made to the system, flight test techniques used during envelope expansion, and results for the low- and high-angle-of-attack programs. Throughout the paper, lessons learned will be discussed to illustrate the problems associated with the implementation of complex flight control systems.

2123. Lokos, William A.; Bahm, Catherine M.; and Heinle, Robert A.: **Determination of Stores Pointing Error Due to Wing Flexibility Under Flight Load**. NASA TM-4646, H-2022, NAS 1.15:4646, AIAA Paper 94-2112. Presented at the 7th Biennial Flight Test Conference, Colorado Springs, Colorado, June 20–23, 1994, January 1995, 95N19044, #.

The in-flight elastic wing twist of a fighter-type aircraft was studied to provide for an improved on-board real-time computed prediction of pointing variations of three wing store stations. This is an important capability to correct sensor pod alignment variation or to establish initial conditions of iron bombs or smart weapons prior to release. The original algorithm was based upon coarse measurements. The electro-optical Flight Deflection Measurement System measured the deformed wing shape in flight under maneuver loads to provide a higher resolution database from which an improved twist prediction algorithm could be developed. The FDMS produced excellent repeatable data. In addition, a NASTRAN finite-element analysis was performed to provide additional elastic deformation data. The FDMS data combined with the NASTRAN analysis indicated that an improved prediction algorithm could be derived by using a different set of aircraft parameters, namely normal acceleration, stores configuration, Mach number, and gross weight.

2124. Anderson, Karl F.: **Current Loop Signal Conditioning: Practical Applications**. NASA TM-4636, H-2026, NAS 1.15:4636. Presented at the 1995 Measurement Science Conference, Anaheim, California, January 26–27, 1995, January 1995, 95N18735, #.

This paper describes a variety of practical application circuits based on the current loop signal conditioning paradigm. Equations defining the circuit response are also provided. The constant current loop is a fundamental signal conditioning circuit concept that can be implemented in a variety of configurations for resistance-based transducers, such as strain gages and resistance temperature detectors. The circuit features signal conditioning outputs which are unaffected by extremely large variations in lead wire resistance, direct current frequency response, and inherent linearity with respect to resistance change. Sensitivity of this circuit is double that of a Wheatstone bridge circuit. Electrical output is zero for resistance change equals zero. The same excitation and output sense wires can serve multiple transducers. More application arrangements are possible with constant current loop signal conditioning than with the Wheatstone bridge.

2125. Powers, Sheryll Goecke: **An Electronic Workshop on the Performance Seeking Control and Propulsion Controlled Aircraft Results of the F-15 Highly Integrated Digital Electronic Control Flight Research Program**. NASA TM-104278, H-2020, NAS 1.15:104278. Presented at a workshop held at Edwards, California, 1993, January 1995, 95N33009, #.

2126. Burcham, Frank W., Jr.; Gatlin, Donald H.; and Stewart, James F.: **An Overview of Integrated Flight-Propulsion Controls Flight Research on the NASA F-15 Research Airplane**. Presented at NASA's *An Electronic Workshop on the Performance Seeking Control and Propulsion Controlled Aircraft Results of the F-15 Highly Integrated Digital Electronic Control Flight Research Program*, January 1995, pp. 1–28, (see N95-33009 12-07), 95N33010, #.

The NASA Dryden Flight Research Center has been conducting integrated flight-propulsion control flight research using the NASA F-15 airplane for the past 12 years. The research began with the digital electronic engine control (DEEC) project, followed by the F100 Engine Model Derivative (EMD). HIDEC (Highly Integrated Digital Electronic Control) became the umbrella name for a series of experiments including: the Advanced Digital Engine Controls System (ADECS), a twin jet acoustics flight experiment, self-repairing flight control system (SRFCS), performance-seeking control (PSC), and propulsion controlled aircraft (PCA). The upcoming F-15 project is ACTIVE (Advanced Control Technology for Integrated Vehicles). This paper provides a brief summary of these activities and provides background for the PCA and PSC papers, and includes a bibliography of all papers and reports from the NASA F-15 project.

2127. Orme, John S.: **Performance Seeking Control Program Overview**. Presented at NASA's *An Electronic Workshop on the Performance Seeking Control and Propulsion Controlled Aircraft Results of the F-15 Highly Integrated Digital Electronic Control Flight Research Program*, January 1995, pp. 31–36, (see N95-33009 12-07), 95N33011, #.

The Performance Seeking Control (PSC) program evolved from a series of integrated propulsion-flight control research programs flown at NASA Dryden Flight Research Center (DFRC) on an F-15. The first of these was the Digital Electronic Engine Control (DEEC) program and provided digital engine controls suitable for integration. The DEEC and digital electronic flight control system of the NASA F-15 were ideally suited for integrated controls research. The Advanced Engine Control System (ADECS) program proved that integrated engine and aircraft control could improve overall system performance. The objective of the PSC program was to advance the technology for a fully integrated propulsion flight control system. Whereas ADECS provided single variable control for an average engine, PSC controlled multiple propulsion system variables while adapting to the measured engine performance. PSC was developed as a model-based, adaptive control algorithm and included four optimization modes: minimum fuel flow at constant thrust, minimum turbine temperature at constant thrust, maximum thrust, and minimum thrust. Subsonic and supersonic flight testing were conducted at NASA Dryden covering the four PSC optimization modes and over the full throttle range. Flight testing of the PSC algorithm, conducted in a series of five flight test phases, has been concluded at NASA Dryden covering all four of the PSC optimization modes. Over a three year period and five flight test phases 72 research flights were conducted. The primary objective of flight testing was to exercise each PSC optimization mode and quantify the resulting performance improvements.

2128. Orme, John S.; and *Nobbs, Steven G.: **Minimum Fuel Mode Evaluation**. Presented at NASA's *An Electronic Workshop on the Performance Seeking Control and Propulsion Controlled Aircraft Results of the F-15 Highly Integrated Digital Electronic Control Flight Research Program*, January 1995, pp. 91–98, (see N95-33009 12-07), 95N33015, #.

The minimum fuel mode of the NASA F-15 research aircraft is designed to minimize fuel flow while maintaining constant net propulsive force (FNP), effectively reducing thrust specific fuel consumption (TSFC), during cruise flight conditions. The test maneuvers were at stabilized flight conditions. The aircraft test engine was allowed to stabilize at the cruise conditions before data collection initiated; data were then recorded with performance seeking control (PSC) not-engaged, then data were recorded with the PSC system engaged. The maneuvers were flown back-to-back to allow for direct comparisons by minimizing the effects of variations in the test day conditions. The minimum fuel mode was evaluated at subsonic and supersonic Mach numbers and focused on three altitudes: 15,000; 30,000; and 45,000 feet. Flight data were collected for part, military, partial, and maximum afterburning power conditions. The TSFC savings at supersonic Mach numbers, ranging from approximately 4% to nearly 10%, are in general much larger than at subsonic Mach numbers because of PSC trims to the afterburner.

*McDonnell-Douglas Corp., St. Louis, Missouri.

2129. Orme, John S.; and *Nobbs, Steven G.: **Minimum Fan Turbine Inlet Temperature Mode Evaluation**. Presented at NASA's *An Electronic Workshop on the Performance Seeking Control and Propulsion Controlled Aircraft Results of the F-15 Highly Integrated Digital Electronic Control Flight Research Program*, January 1995, pp. 99–110, (see N95-33009 12-07), 95N33016, #.

Measured reductions in turbine temperature which resulted from the application of the F-15 performance seeking control (PSC) minimum fan turbine inlet temperature (FTIT) mode during the dual-engine test phase is presented as a function of net propulsive force and flight condition. Data were collected at altitudes of 30,000 and 45,000 feet at military and partial afterburning power settings. The FTIT reductions for the supersonic tests are less than at subsonic Mach numbers

because of the increased modeling and control complexity. In addition, the propulsion system was designed to be optimized at the mid supersonic Mach number range. Subsonically at military power, FTIT reductions were above 70 R for either the left or right engines, and repeatable for the right engine. At partial afterburner and supersonic conditions, the level of FTIT reductions were at least 25 R and as much as 55 R. Considering that the turbine operates at or very near its temperature limit at these high power settings, these seemingly small temperature reductions may significantly lengthen the life of the turbine. In general, the minimum FTIT mode has performed well, demonstrating significant temperature reductions at military and partial afterburner power. Decreases of over 100 R at cruise flight conditions were identified. Temperature reductions of this magnitude could significantly extend turbine life and reduce replacement costs.

*McDonnell-Douglas Corp., St. Louis, Missouri.

2130. Orme, John S.; and *Nobbs, Steven G.: **Maximum Thrust Mode Evaluation**. Presented at NASA's *An Electronic Workshop on the Performance Seeking Control and Propulsion Controlled Aircraft Results of the F-15 Highly Integrated Digital Electronic Control Flight Research Program*, January 1995, pp. 111–120, (see N95-33009 12-07), 95N33017, #.

Measured reductions in acceleration times which resulted from the application of the F-15 performance seeking control (PSC) maximum thrust mode during the dual-engine test phase is presented as a function of power setting and flight condition. Data were collected at altitudes of 30,000 and 45,000 feet at military and maximum afterburning power settings. The time savings for the supersonic acceleration is less than at subsonic Mach numbers because of the increased modeling and control complexity. In addition, the propulsion system was designed to be optimized at the mid supersonic Mach number range. Recall that even though the engine is at maximum afterburner, PSC does not trim the afterburner for the maximum thrust mode. Subsonically at military power, time to accelerate from Mach 0.6 to 0.95 was cut by between 6 and 8 percent with a single engine application of PSC, and over 14 percent when both engines were optimized. At maximum afterburner, the level of thrust increases were similar in magnitude to the military power results, but because of higher thrust levels at maximum afterburner and higher aircraft drag at supersonic Mach numbers the percentage thrust increase and time to accelerate was less than for the supersonic accelerations. Savings in time to accelerate supersonically at maximum afterburner ranged from 4 to 7 percent. In general, the maximum thrust mode has performed well, demonstrating significant thrust increases at military and maximum afterburner power. Increases of up to 15 percent at typical combat-type flight conditions were identified. Thrust increases of this magnitude could be useful in a combat situation.

*McDonnell-Douglas Corp., St. Louis, Missouri.

2131. Conners, Timothy R.; *Nobbs, Steven G.; and Orme, John S.: **Rapid Deceleration Mode Evaluation**. Presented at NASA's *An Electronic Workshop on the Performance Seeking Control and Propulsion Controlled Aircraft Results of the F-15 Highly Integrated Digital Electronic Control Flight Research Program*, January 1995, pp. 121–128, (see N95-33009 12-07), 95N33018, #.

Aircraft with flight capability above 1.4 normally have an RPM lockup or similar feature to prevent inlet buzz that would occur at low engine airflows. This RPM lockup has the effect of holding the engine thrust level at the intermediate power (maximum non-afterburning). For aircraft such as military fighters or supersonic transports, the need exists to be able to rapidly slow from supersonic to subsonic speeds. For example, a supersonic transport that experiences a cabin decompression needs to be able to slow/descend rapidly, and this requirement may size the cabin environmental control system. For a fighter, there may be a desire to slow/descend rapidly, and while doing so to minimize fuel usage and engine exhaust temperature. Both of these needs can be aided by achieving the minimum possible overall net propulsive force. As the intermediate power thrust levels of engines increase, it becomes even more difficult to slow rapidly from supersonic speeds. Therefore, a mode of the performance seeking control (PSC) system to minimize overall propulsion system thrust has been developed and tested. The rapid deceleration mode reduces the engine airflow consistent with avoiding inlet buzz. The engine controls are trimmed to minimize the thrust produced by this reduced airflow, and moves the inlet geometry to degrade the inlet performance. As in the case of the other PSC modes, the best overall performance (in this case the least net propulsive force) requires an integrated optimization of inlet, engine, and nozzle variables. This paper presents the predicted and measured results for the supersonic minimum thrust mode, including the overall effects on aircraft deceleration.

*McDonnell-Douglas Corp., St. Louis, Missouri.

2132. Conners, Timothy R.: **Thrust Stand Test**. Presented at NASA's *An Electronic Workshop on the Performance Seeking Control and Propulsion Controlled Aircraft Results of the F-15 Highly Integrated Digital Electronic Control Flight Research Program*, January 1995, pp. 129–132, (see N95-33009 12-07).

2133. Schkolnik, Gerard S.: **Performance Seeking Control Excitation Mode**. Presented at NASA's *An Electronic Workshop on the Performance Seeking Control and Propulsion Controlled Aircraft Results of the F-15 Highly Integrated Digital Electronic Control Flight Research Program*, January 1995, pp. 133–142, (see N95-33009 12-07), 95N33019, #.

Flight testing of the performance seeking control (PSC) excitation mode was successfully completed at NASA Dryden on the F-15 highly integrated digital electronic control (HIDEC) aircraft. Although the excitation mode was not one of the original objectives of the PSC program, it was rapidly prototyped and implemented into the architecture of the PSC algorithm, allowing valuable and timely research data to be gathered. The primary flight test objective was to investigate the feasibility of a future measurement-based performance optimization algorithm. This future algorithm, called AdAPT, which stands for adaptive aircraft performance technology, generates and applies excitation inputs to selected control effectors. Fourier transformations are used to convert measured response and control effector data into frequency domain models which are mapped into state space models using multiterm frequency matching. Formal optimization principles are applied to produce an integrated, performance optimal effector suite. The key technical challenge of the measurement-based approach is the identification of the gradient of the performance index to the selected control effector. This concern was addressed by the excitation mode flight test. The AdAPT feasibility study utilized the PSC excitation mode to apply separate sinusoidal excitation trims to the controls - one aircraft, inlet first ramp (cowl), and one engine, throat area. Aircraft control and response data were recorded using on-board instrumentation and analyzed post-flight. Sensor noise characteristics, axial acceleration performance gradients, and repeatability were determined. Results were compared to pilot comments to assess the ride quality. Flight test results indicate that performance gradients were identified at all flight conditions, sensor noise levels were acceptable at the frequencies of interest, and excitations were generally not sensed by the pilot.

2134. Orme, John S.: **Performance Seeking Control (PSC) for the F-15 Highly Integrated Digital Electronic Control (HiDEC) Aircraft**. Presented at NASA's *An Electronic Workshop on the Performance Seeking Control and Propulsion Controlled Aircraft Results of the F-15 Highly Integrated Digital Electronic Control Flight Research Program*, January 1995, pp. 146–156, (see N95-33009 12-07), 95N33020, #.

The performance seeking control algorithm optimizes total propulsion system performance. This adaptive, model-based optimization algorithm has been successfully flight demonstrated on two engines with differing levels of degradation. Models of the engine, nozzle, and inlet produce reliable, accurate estimates of engine performance. But, because of an observability problem, component levels of degradation cannot be accurately determined. Depending on engine-specific operating characteristics PSC achieves various levels performance improvement. For example, engines with more deterioration typically operate at higher turbine temperatures than less deteriorated engines. Thus when the PSC maximum thrust mode is applied, for example, there will be less temperature margin available to be traded for increasing thrust.

2135. Burcham, Frank W., Jr.: **Background and Principles of Throttles-Only Flight Control**. Presented at NASA's *An Electronic Workshop on the Performance*

Seeking Control and Propulsion Controlled Aircraft Results of the F-15 Highly Integrated Digital Electronic Control Flight Research Program, <u>January 1995</u>, pp. 159–169, (see N95-33009 12-07), 95N33021, #.

There have been many cases in which the crew of a multi-engine airplane had to use engine thrust for emergency flight control. Such a procedure is very difficult, because the propulsive control forces are small, the engine response is slow, and airplane dynamics such as the phugoid and dutch roll are difficult to damp with thrust. In general, thrust increases are used to climb, thrust decreases to descend, and differential thrust is used to turn. Average speed is not significantly affected by changes in throttle setting. Pitch control is achieved because of pitching moments due to speed changes, from thrust offset, and from the vertical component of thrust. Roll control is achieved by using differential thrust to develop yaw, which, through the normal dihedral effect, causes a roll. Control power in pitch and roll tends to increase as speed decreases. Although speed is not controlled by the throttles, configuration changes are often available (lowering gear, flaps, moving center-of-gravity) to change the speed. The airplane basic stability is also a significant factor. Fuel slosh and gyroscopic moments are small influences on throttles-only control. The background and principles of throttles-only flight control are described.

2136. Burcham, Frank W., Jr.; and Maine, Trindel A.: **Flight Test of a Propulsion Controlled Aircraft System on the NASA F-15 Airplane.** Presented at NASA's *An Electronic Workshop on the Performance Seeking Control and Propulsion Controlled Aircraft Results of the F-15 Highly Integrated Digital Electronic Control Flight Research Program*, <u>January 1995</u>, pp. 193–221, (see N95-33009 12-07), 95N33023, #.

Flight tests of the propulsion controlled aircraft (PCA) system on the NASA F-15 airplane evolved as a result of a long series of simulation and flight tests. Initially, the simulation results were very optimistic. Early flight tests showed that manual throttles-only control was much more difficult than the simulation, and a flight investigation was flown to acquire data to resolve this discrepancy. The PCA system designed and developed by MDA evolved as these discrepancies were found and resolved, requiring redesign of the PCA software and modification of the flight test plan. Small throttle step inputs were flown to provide data for analysis, simulation update, and control logic modification. The PCA flight tests quickly revealed less than desired performance, but the extensive flexibility built into the flight PCA software allowed rapid evaluation of alternate gains, filters, and control logic, and within 2 weeks, the PCA system was functioning well. The initial objective of achieving adequate control for up-and-away flying and approaches was satisfied, and the option to continue to actual landings was achieved. After the PCA landings were accomplished, other

PCA features were added, and additional maneuvers beyond those originally planned were flown. The PCA system was used to recover from extreme upset conditions, descend, and make approaches to landing. A heading mode was added, and a single engine plus rudder PCA mode was also added and flown. The PCA flight envelope was expanded far beyond that originally designed for. Guest pilots from the USAF, USN, NASA, and the contractor also flew the PCA system and were favorably impressed.

2137. Corda, Stephen: **Dynamic Ground Effects Flight Test of the NASA F-15 Aircraft.** Presented at NASA's *An Electronic Workshop on the Performance Seeking Control and Propulsion Controlled Aircraft Results of the F-15 Highly Integrated Digital Electronic Control Flight Research Program*, <u>January 1995</u>, pp. 222–228, (see N95-33009 12-07), 95N33024, #.

Aerodynamic characteristics of an aircraft may significantly differ when flying close to the ground rather than when flying up and away. Recent research has also determined that dynamic effects (i.e., sink rate) influence ground effects (GE). A ground effects flight test program of the F-15 aircraft was conducted to support the propulsion controlled aircraft (PCA) program at the NASA Dryden Flight Research Center. Flight data was collected for 24 landings on seven test flights. Dynamic ground effects data were obtained for low- and high-sink rates, between 0.8 and 6.5 ft/sec, at two approach speed and flap combinations. These combinations consisted of 150 kt with the flaps down (30 deg deflection) and 170 kt with the flaps up (0 deg deflection), both with the inlet ramps in the full-up position. The aerodynamic coefficients caused by ground effects were estimated from the flight data. These ground effects data were correlated with the aircraft speed, flap setting, and sink rate. Results are compared to previous flight test and wind-tunnel ground effects data for various wings and for complete aircraft.

2138. Maine, Trindel A.; Burcham, Frank W., Jr.; *Schaefer, Peter; and Burken, John: **Design Challenges Encountered in the F-15 PCA Flight Test Program.** Presented at NASA's *An Electronic Workshop on the Performance Seeking Control and Propulsion Controlled Aircraft Results of the F-15 Highly Integrated Digital Electronic Control Flight Research Program*, <u>January 1995</u>, pp. 229–244, (see N95-33009 12-07), 95N33025, #.

The NASA Dryden Flight Research Center conducted flight tests of a propulsion-controlled aircraft system on an F-15 airplane. This system was designed to explore the feasibility of providing safe emergency landing capability using only the engines to provide flight control in the event of a catastrophic loss of conventional flight controls. Control laws were designed to control the flight path and bank angle using only commands to the throttles. While the program was highly successful, this paper concentrates on the challenges encountered using engine thrust as the only control effector. Compared to conventional flight control surfaces, the engines are slow, nonlinear, and have limited control effectiveness. This increases the vulnerability of the system to outside disturbances and changes in aerodynamic conditions. As a result, the PCA system had problems with gust rejection. Cross coupling of the longitudinal and lateral axis also occurred, primarily as a result of control saturation. The normally negligible effects of inlet airframe interactions became significant with the engines as the control effector. Flight and simulation data are used to illustrate these difficulties.

*University of Southern California, Los Angeles, California.

2139. Conners, Timothy R.: **PSC Asymmetric Thrust Alleviation Mode.** Presented at NASA's *An Electronic Workshop on the Performance Seeking Control and Propulsion Controlled Aircraft Results of the F-15 Highly Integrated Digital Electronic Control Flight Research Program*, January 1995, pp. 143–145, (see N95-33009 12-07).

2140. Clarke, Robert; Burken, John J.; Bosworth, John T.; and Bauer, Jeffrey E.: **X-29 Flight Control System: Lessons Learned.** AGARD CP-560. Presented at AGARD, *Active Control Technology: Applications and Lessons Learned*, January 1995, (see N95-31989 11-08), 95N32001, #. (See also 2086, 2122, 2215.)

Two X-29A aircraft were flown at the NASA Dryden Flight Research Center over a period of eight years. The airplanes' unique features are the forward-swept wing, variable incidence close-coupled canard and highly relaxed longitudinal static stability (up to 35-percent negative static margin at subsonic conditions). This paper describes the primary flight control system and significant modifications made to this system, flight test techniques used during envelope expansion, and results for the low- and high-angle-of-attack programs. Throughout the paper, lessons learned will be discussed to illustrate the problems associated with the implementation of complex flight control systems.

2141. Gera, J.: **Stability and Control of Wing-In-Ground Effect Vehicles or Wingships.** AIAA 95-0339, Presented at the 33rd AIAA Aerospace Sciences Meeting and Exhibit, Reno, Nevada, January 9–12, 1995.

The static and dynamic stability characteristics of wingships are discussed in the framework of small disturbance stability theory of conventional airplanes. The existence of force and moment derivatives with respect to height for wingship modifies the criteria for longitudinal static stability, and gives rise to a speed subsidence mode. The lateral-directional stability characteristics are influenced only moderately by

ground effect. Consideration of the effect of wind shear and sinusoidal gusts are also given in the paper.

2142. Bauer, Jeffrey E.; Clarke, Robert; and Burken, John J.: **Flight Test of the X-29A at High Angle of Attack: Flight Dynamics and Controls.** NASA TP-3537, H-1984, NAS 1.60:3537, February 1995, 95N22806, #.

The NASA Dryden Flight Research Center has flight tested two X-29A aircraft at low and high angles of attack. The high-angle-of-attack tests evaluate the feasibility of integrated X-29A technologies. More specific objectives focus on evaluating the high-angle-of-attack flying qualities, defining multiaxis controllability limits, and determining the maximum pitch-pointing capability. A pilot-selectable gain system allows examination of tradeoffs in airplane stability and maneuverability. Basic fighter maneuvers provide qualitative evaluation. Bank angle captures permit qualitative data analysis. This paper discusses the design goals and approach for high-angle-of-attack control laws and provides results from the envelope expansion and handling qualities testing at intermediate angles of attack. Comparisons of the flight test results to the predictions are made where appropriate. The pitch rate command structure of the longitudinal control system is shown to be a valid design for high-angle-of-attack control laws. Flight test results show that wing rock amplitude was overpredicted and aileron and rudder effectiveness were underpredicted. Flight tests show the X-29A airplane to be a good aircraft up to 40 deg angle of attack.

2143. *McRuer, Duane T.; and Smith, R. E.: **PIO: A Historical Perspective.** AGARD AR-335. *Advisory Group for Aerospace Research and Development, Flight Vehicle Integration Panel Workshop on Pilot Induced Oscillations*, February 1995, (see N95-31061 11-03), 95N31062, #.

These problems relating to Pilot Induced Oscillations have manifested themselves since the earliest days of manned flight. The earliest recorded examples of PIO date back to the Wright brothers first aircraft. The earliest filmed records date back to just prior to World War 2, with the XB-19 aircraft which suffered a pitch PIO just prior to touchdown. Four classes of PIO have been identified, into which all of the known incidents can be grouped. These are: (1) Essentially Single Axis, Extended Rigid Body Effective Vehicle Dynamics; (2) Essentially Single Axis, Extended Rigid Body with Significant Feel-System Manipulator Mechanical Control Elements; (3) Multiple Axis, Extended Rigid Body Effective Vehicle Dynamics; and (4) PIO's Involving Higher Frequency Modes.

*Systems Technology, Inc., Manhattan Beach, California.

2144. Antal, G.; Brillhart, R.; Hensley, D.; and Freudinger, L.: **Implementation of an Automated**

Approach for Spatial Filtering of Flight Flutter Test Data. Presented at the 13th International Modal Analysis Conference (IMAC), Nashville, Tennessee, <u>February 1995</u>.

An approach to obtaining and evaluating flight flutter data as well as ground test data is presented and evaluated. This approach uses spatial filters to allow many channels of data to be processed such that the primary frequencies of interest can be evaluated on a frequency by frequency basis. In some cases, the filtering is the simple sum and/or difference of signals measured in the test, while in other cases, the filter is created from the mode shapes measured during a ground test or obtained from a finite element analysis. This modal or spatial filtering application allows complex responses of physical degrees of freedom to be refined as single degree of freedom responses corresponding to the modes or shapes of interest. The condensed set of filtered responses provide more meaningful and easily understood information which can be evaluated immediately after data acquisition.

2145. Espana, Martin D.; and Gilyard, Glenn: **Direct Adaptive Performance Optimization of Subsonic Transports: A Periodic Perturbation Technique**. NASA TM-4676, H-2040, NAS 1.15:4676, <u>March 1995</u>, 95N22829, #.

Aircraft performance can be optimized at the flight condition by using available redundancy among actuators. Effective use of this potential allows improved performance beyond limits imposed by design compromises. Optimization based on nominal models does not result in the best performance of the actual aircraft at the actual flight condition. An adaptive algorithm for optimizing performance parameters, such as speed or fuel flow, in flight based exclusively on flight data is proposed. The algorithm is inherently insensitive to model inaccuracies and measurement noise and biases and can optimize several decision variables at the same time. An adaptive constraint controller integrated into the algorithm regulates the optimization constraints, such as altitude or speed, without requiring and prior knowledge of the autopilot design. The algorithm has a modular structure which allows easy incorporation (or removal) of optimization constraints or decision variables to the optimization problem. An important part of the contribution is the development of analytical tools enabling convergence analysis of the algorithm and the establishment of simple design rules. The fuel-flow minimization and velocity maximization modes of the algorithm are demonstrated on the NASA Dryden B-720 nonlinear flight simulator for the single- and multi-effector optimization cases.

2146. *Nelson, Michael L.; *Gottlich, Gretchen L.; *Bianco, David J.; Binkley, Robert L.; Kellogg, Yvonne D.; **Paulson, Sharon S.; †Beaumont, Chris J.; ††Schmunk, Robert B.; ‡Kurtz, Michael J.; and ‡Jaccomazzi, Alberto: **The Widest Practicable Dissemination: The NASA Technical Report Server**. NASA TM-111627,

NAS1.15:111627, AIAA Paper 96-0964, NIPS-96-77253. Presented at Computers in Aerospace, San Antonio, Texas, March 28–30, 1996, <u>March 1995</u>, 96N33940, #. (See also 2147.)

The National Aeronautics and Space Act of 1958 established NASA and charged it to 'provide for the widest practicable and appropriate dissemination of information concerning...its activities and the results thereof.' The search for innovative methods to distribute NASA's information lead a grass-roots team to create the NASA Technical Report Server (NTRS), which uses the World Wide Web and other popular Internet-based information systems as search engines. The NTRS is an inter-center effort which provides uniform access to various distributed publication servers residing on the Internet. Users have immediate desktop access to technical publications from NASA centers and institutes. The NTRS is comprised of several units, some constructed especially for inclusion in NTRS, and others that are existing NASA publication services that NTRS reuses. This paper presents the NTRS architecture, usage metrics, and the lessons learned while implementing and maintaining the services over the initial six-month period. The NTRS is largely constructed with freely available software running on existing hardware. NTRS builds upon existing hardware and software, and the resulting additional exposure for the body of literature contained will allow NASA to ensure that its institutional knowledge base will continue to receive the widest practicable and appropriate dissemination.

*NASA Langley Research Center, Hampton, Virginia.
**Institute for Computer Applications in Science and Engineering, Hampton, Virginia.
†Computer Sciences Corp., Moffett Field, California.
††NASA Goddard Institute for Space Studies, New York, New York.
‡Smithsonian Astrophysical Observatory, Cambridge, Massachusetts.

2147. *Nelson, Michael L.; *Gottlich, Gretchen L.; *Bianco, David J.; Binkley, Robert L.; Kellogg, Yvonne D.; **Paulson, Sharon S.; †Beaumont, Chris J.; ††Schmunk, Robert B.; ‡Kurtz, Michael J.; and ‡Jaccomazzi, Alberto: **The Widest Practicable Dissemination: The NASA Technical Report Server**. AIAA Paper 95-0964. Presented at the AIAA Computing in Aerospace 10, San Antonio, Texas, March 28–30, 1995, A95-90629, <u>1995</u>, pp. 91–103, 95A90641. (See also 2146.)

The search for innovative methods to distribute NASA's information lead a gross-roots team to create the NASA Technical Report Server (NTRS), which uses the World Wide Web and other popular Internet-based information systems as search engines. The NTRS is an inter-center effort which provides uniform access to various distributed publication servers residing on the Internet. Users have immediate desktop access to technical publications from

NASA centers and institutes. This paper presents the NTRS architecture, usage metrics, and the lessons learned while implementing and maintaining the services over the initial 6-month period. The NTRS is largely constructed with freely available software running on existing hardware. NTRS builds upon existing hardware and software, and the resulting additional exposure for the body of literature contained will allow NASA to ensure that its institutional knowledge base will continue to receive the widest practicable and appropriate dissemination.

*NASA Langley Research Center, Hampton, Virginia.
**Institute for Computer Applications in Science and Engineering, Hampton, Virginia.
†Computer Sciences Corp., Moffett Field, California.
††NASA Goddard Institute for Space Studies, New York, New York.
‡Smithsonian Astrophysical Observatory, Cambridge, Massachusetts.

2148. Cox, T.; *Sachs, G.; *Knoll, A.; and *Stich, R.: **A Flying Qualities Study of Longitudinal Long-Term Dynamics of Hypersonic Planes.** AIAA Paper 95-6150, HTN-95-B0383. Presented at the 6th AIAA Aerospace Planes and Hypersonics Technologies Conference, Chattanooga, Tennessee, April 3–7, 1995, 95A90464.

The NASA Dryden Flight Research Center and the Technical University of Munich are cooperating in a research program to assess the impact of unstable long-term dynamics on the flying qualities of planes in hypersonic flight. These flying qualities issues are being investigated with a dedicated flight simulator for hypersonic vehicles located at NASA Dryden. Several NASA research pilots have flown the simulator through well-defined steady-level turns with varying phugoid and height mode instabilities. The data collected include pilot ratings and comments, performance measurements, and pilot workload measurements. The results presented in this paper include design guidelines for height and phugoid mode instabilities, an evaluation of the tapping method used to measure pilot workload, a discussion of techniques developed by the pilots to control large instabilities, and a discussion of how flying qualities of unstable long-term dynamics influence control power design requirements.

*Technical University of Munich, Munich, Germany.

2149. Anderson, Karl F.: **A Conversion of Wheatstone Bridge to Current-Loop Signal Conditioning for Strain Gages.** NASA TM-104309, April 1995.

Current loop circuitry replaced Wheatstone bridge circuitry to signal-condition strain gage transducers in more than 350 data channels for two different test programs at NASA Dryden Flight Research Center. The uncorrected test data from current loop circuitry had a lower noise level than data from comparable Wheatstone bridge circuitry, were linear with respect to gage-resistance change, and were uninfluenced by varying lead-wire resistance. The current loop channels were easier for the technicians to set up, verify, and operate than equivalent Wheatstone bridge channels. Design choices and circuit details are presented in this paper in addition to operational experience.

2150. *Pinkelman, J. K.; *Batill, S. M.; and Kehoe, M. W.: **An Investigation of the Total Least-Squares Criteria in Time Domain Based, Parameter Identification for Flight Flutter Testing.** AIAA-95-1247. Presented at the 36th AIAA, ASME, ASCE, AHS, and ASC Structures, Structural Dynamics and Materials Conference, New Orleans, Louisiana, April 10–13, 1995.

Parameter identification of time series models for linear dynamic structural systems using the least squares and total least squares criteria is investigated. Excitation and response time domain data are used to determine system parameters for autoregressive, moving average (ARMA) models. The method, or criteria, which is used to solve the set of overdetermined simultaneous equations developed from the time domain data affects the solution. A commonly used criteria, least squares, introduces the possibility of significant bias error in the system parameters and leads to bias errors in the modal parameter estimates. An alternative criteria, total least squares, provides an approach which appears to significantly reduce the bias error in the parameter estimates. These methods are applied to a simple, simulated system and then to flight flutter test data with particular emphasis on accurate modal damping estimates.

*Notre Dame University, Notre Dame, Indiana.

2151. Del Frate, John H.: **NASA Dryden Flow Visualization Facility.** NASA TM-4631, H-1972, NAS 1.15:4631, May 1995, 95N27914, #.

This report describes the Flow Visualization Facility at NASA Dryden Flight Research Center, Edwards, California. This water tunnel facility is used primarily for visualizing and analyzing vortical flows on aircraft models and other shapes at high-incidence angles. The tunnel is used extensively as a low-cost, diagnostic tool to help engineers understand complex flows over aircraft and other full-scale vehicles. The facility consists primarily of a closed-circuit water tunnel with a 16- x 24-in. vertical test section. Velocity of the flow through the test section can be varied from 0 to 10 in/sec; however, 3 in/sec provides optimum velocity for the majority of flow visualization applications. This velocity corresponds to a unit Reynolds number of 23,000/ft and a turbulence level over the majority of the test section below 0.5 percent. Flow visualization techniques described here include the dye tracer, laser light sheet, and shadowgraph. Limited correlation to full-scale flight data is shown.

2152. Saltzman, Edwin J.; and Ayers, Theodore G.: **Selected Examples of NACA/NASA Supersonic Flight**

Research. NASA SP-513, H-1836, NAS 1.21:513, NIPS-96-37035, <u>May 1995</u>, 96N22603, #.

The present Dryden Flight Research Center, a part of the National Aeronautics and Space Administration, has a flight research history that extends back to the mid-1940's. The parent organization was a part of the National Advisory Committee for Aeronautics and was formed in 1946 as the Muroc Flight Test Unit. This document describes 13 selected examples of important supersonic flight research conducted from the Mojave Desert location of the Dryden Flight Research Center over a 4 decade period beginning in 1946. The research described herein was either obtained at supersonic speeds or enabled subsequent aircraft to penetrate or traverse the supersonic region. In some instances there accrued from these research efforts benefits which are also applicable at lower or higher speed regions. A major consideration in the selection of the various research topics was the lasting impact they have had, or will have, on subsequent supersonic flight vehicle design, efficiency, safety, and performance or upon improved supersonic research techniques.

2153. Ko, William L.: **Predictions of Thermal Buckling Strengths of Hypersonic Aircraft Sandwich Panels Using Minimum Potential Energy and Finite Element Methods.** NASA TM-4643, H-2009, NAS 1.15:4643, NIPS-95-06451, <u>May 1995</u>, 96N15641, #.

Thermal buckling characteristics of hypersonic aircraft sandwich panels of various aspect ratios were investigated. The panel is fastened at its four edges to the substructures under four different edge conditions and is subjected to uniform temperature loading. Minimum potential energy theory and finite element methods were used to calculate the panel buckling temperatures. The two methods gave fairly close buckling temperatures. However, the finite element method gave slightly lower buckling temperatures than those given by the minimum potential energy theory. The reasons for this slight discrepancy in eigensolutions are discussed in detail. In addition, the effect of eigenshifting on the eigenvalue convergence rate is discussed.

2154. Budd, Gerald D.; *Gilman, Ronald L.; and Eichstedt, David: **Operational and Research Aspects of a Radio-Controlled Model Flight Test Program.** *Journal of Aircraft*, (ISSN 0021-8669), Vol. 32, No. 3, <u>May–June 1995</u>, pp. 583–589, 95A94471. (See also 2005, 2006.)

The operational and research aspects of a subscale, radio-controlled model flight-test program are presented. By using low-cost free-flying models, an approach was developed for obtaining research-quality vehicle performance and aerodynamic information. The advantages and limitations learned by applying this approach to a specific flight-test program are described. The research quality of the data acquired shows that model flight testing is practical for obtaining consistent and repeatable flight data.

*PRC Inc., Edwards, California.

2155. Carter, John F.; and *Nagy, Christopher J.: **The NASA Landing Gear Test Airplane.** NASA TM-4703, H-2045, NAS 1.15:4703, NIPS-96-07731, <u>June 1995</u>, 96N18518, #.

A tire and landing gear test facility has been developed and incorporated into a Convair 990 aircraft. The system can simulate tire vertical load profiles to 250,000 lb, sideslip angles to 15 degrees, and wheel braking on actual runways. Onboard computers control the preprogrammed test profiles through a feedback loop and also record three axis loads, tire slip angle, and tire condition. The aircraft to date has provided tire force and wear data for the Shuttle Orbiter tire on three different runways and at east and west coast landing sites. This report discusses the role of this facility in complementing existing ground tire and landing gear test facilities, and how this facility can simultaneously simulate the vertical load, tire slip, velocity, and surface for an entire aircraft landing. A description is given of the aircraft as well as the test system. An example of a typical test sequence is presented. Data collection and reduction from this facility are discussed, as well as accuracies of calculated parameters. Validation of the facility through ground and flight tests is presented. Tests to date have shown that this facility can operate at remote sites and gather complete data sets of load, slip, and velocity on actual runway surfaces. The ground and flight tests have led to a successful validation of this test facility.

*PRC Inc., Edwards, California.

EC93-41018-6

CV-990 Landing Systems Research Airplane

2156. Burcham, Frank W., Jr., Conners, Timothy R., and *Maxwell, Michael D.: **Flight Research Using F100 Engine P680063 in the NASA F-15 Airplane.** ASME Paper 95-GT-119, H-2037. Presented at ASME Turbo Expo '95, Houston, Texas, <u>June 5, 1995</u>.

The value of flight research in developing and evaluating gas turbine engines is high. NASA Dryden Flight Research Center has been conducting flight research on propulsion systems for many years. The F100 engine has been tested in the NASA F-15 research airplane in the last three decades. One engine in particular, S/N P680063, has been used for the entire program and has been flown in many pioneering propulsion flight research activities. Included are detailed flight-to-ground facility tests; tests of the first production digital engine control system, the first active stall margin control system, the first performance-seeking control system; and the first use of computer-controlled engine thrust for emergency flight control. The flight research has been supplemented with altitude facility tests at key times. This paper presents a review of the test of engine P680063, the F-15 airplanes in which it flew, and the role of the flight test in maturing propulsion technology.

*Pratt and Whitney, West Palm Beach, Florida.

2157. Conners, Timothy R.: **Predicted Performance of a Thrust-Enhanced SR-71 Aircraft With an External Payload.** ASME Paper 95-GT-116, H-2039. Presented at the International Gas Turbine and Aeroengine Congress and Exposition, Houston, Texas, <u>June 5–8, 1995</u>. (See also 2187.)

NASA Dryden Flight Research Center has completed a preliminary performance analysis of the SR-71 aircraft for use as a launch platform for high-speed research vehicles and for carrying captive experimental packages to high altitude and Mach number conditions. Externally mounted research platforms can significantly increase drag, limiting test time and, in extreme cases, prohibiting penetration through the high-drag, transonic flight regime. To provide supplemental SR-71 acceleration, methods have been developed that could increase the thrust of the J58 turbojet engines. These methods include temperature and speed increases and augmentor nitrous oxide injection. The thrust-enhanced engines would allow the SR-71 aircraft to carry higher drag research platforms than it could without enhancement. This paper presents predicted SR-71 performance with and without enhanced engines. A modified climb-dive technique is shown to reduce fuel consumption when flying through the transonic flight regime with a large external payload. Estimates are included of the maximum platform drag profiles with which the aircraft could still complete a high-speed research mission. In this case, enhancement was found to increase the SR-71 payload drag capability by 25 percent. The thrust

enhancement techniques and performance prediction methodology are described.

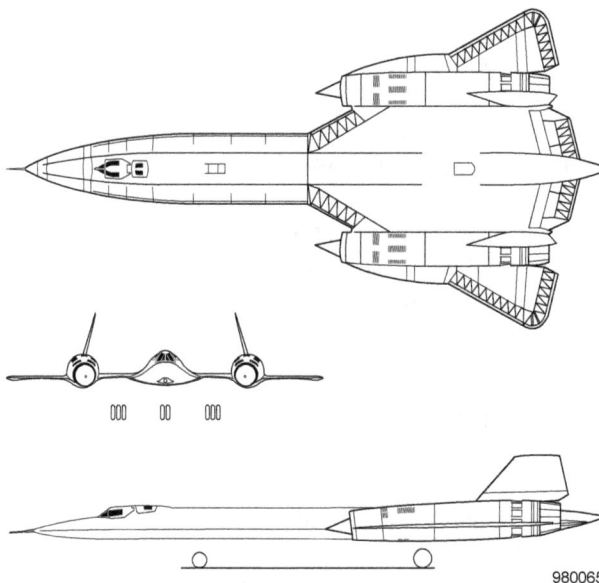

SR-71 Airplane, Three-View Drawing

2158. Schkolnik, Gerard S.; Orme, John S.; and *Hreha, Mark A.: **Flight Test Validation of a Frequency-Based System Identification Method on an F-15 Aircraft.** NASA TM-4704, H-2059, NAS 1.15:4704, AIAA Paper 95-2362. Presented at the 31st AIAA, ASMSA, and ASEE Joint Propulsion Conference and Exhibit, San Diego, California, July 10–12, 1995, <u>July 1995</u>, 95N31846, #.

A frequency-based performance identification approach was evaluated using flight data from the NASA F-15 Highly Integrated Digital Electronic Control aircraft. The approach used frequency separation to identify the effectiveness of multiple controls simultaneously as an alternative to independent control identification methods. Fourier transformations converted measured control and response data into frequency domain representations. Performance gradients were formed using multiterm frequency matching of control and response frequency domain models. An objective function was generated using these performance gradients. This function was formally optimized to produce a coordinated control trim set. This algorithm was applied to longitudinal acceleration and evaluated using two control effectors: nozzle throat area and inlet first ramp. Three criteria were investigated to validate the approach: simultaneous gradient identification, gradient frequency dependency, and repeatability. This report describes the flight test results. These data demonstrate that the approach can accurately identify performance gradients during simultaneous control excitation independent of excitation frequency.

*McDonnell-Douglas Aerospace, St. Louis, Missouri.

2159. Norlin, Ken A.: **Flight Simulation Software at NASA Dryden Flight Research Center**. AIAA 95-3419, H-2052, NAS 1.15:104315. Presented at the AIAA Flight Simulation Technologies Conference, Baltimore, Maryland, August 7–10, 1995, 96N11694, #. (See also 2165.)

2160. Orme, John S.; and Schkolnik, Gerard S.: **Flight Assessment of the Onboard Propulsion System Model for the Performance Seeking Control Algorithm on an F-15 Aircraft**. NASA TM-4705, H-2060, NAS 1.15:4705, AIAA Paper 95-2361. Presented at the 31st AIAA, ASMSA, and ASEE Joint Propulsion Conference, San Diego, California, July 10–12, 1995, July 1995, 95N31425, #.

Performance Seeking Control (PSC), an onboard, adaptive, real-time optimization algorithm, relies upon an onboard propulsion system model. Flight results illustrated propulsion system performance improvements as calculated by the model. These improvements were subject to uncertainty arising from modeling error. Thus to quantify uncertainty in the PSC performance improvements, modeling accuracy must be assessed. A flight test approach to verify PSC-predicted increases in thrust (FNP) and absolute levels of fan stall margin is developed and applied to flight test data. Application of the excess thrust technique shows that increases of FNP agree to within 3 percent of full-scale measurements for most conditions. Accuracy to these levels is significant because uncertainty bands may now be applied to the performance improvements provided by PSC. Assessment of PSC fan stall margin modeling accuracy was completed with analysis of in-flight stall tests. Results indicate that the model overestimates the stall margin by between 5 to 10 percent. Because PSC achieves performance gains by using available stall margin, this overestimation may represent performance improvements to be recovered with increased modeling accuracy. Assessment of thrust and stall margin modeling accuracy provides a critical piece for a comprehensive understanding of PSC's capabilities and limitations.

2161. Haering, Edward A., Jr.; and Whitmore, Stephen A.: **FORTRAN Program for Analyzing Ground-Based Radar Data: Usage and Derivations, Version 6.2**. NASA TP-3430, H-1892, NAS 1.60:3430, August 1995, 95N33193, #.

A postflight FORTRAN program called 'radar' reads and analyzes ground-based radar data. The output includes position, velocity, and acceleration parameters. Air data parameters are also provided if atmospheric characteristics are input. This program can read data from any radar in three formats. Geocentric Cartesian position can also be used as input, which may be from an inertial navigation or Global Positioning System. Options include spike removal, data filtering, and atmospheric refraction corrections. Atmospheric refraction can be corrected using the quick White Sands method or the gradient refraction method, which allows accurate analysis of very low elevation angle and long-range data. Refraction properties are extrapolated from surface conditions, or a measured profile may be input. Velocity is determined by differentiating position. Accelerations are determined by differentiating velocity. This paper describes the algorithms used, gives the operational details, and discusses the limitations and errors of the program. Appendices A through E contain the derivations for these algorithms. These derivations include an improvement in speed to the exact solution for geodetic altitude, an improved algorithm over earlier versions for determining scale height, a truncation algorithm for speeding up the gradient refraction method, and a refinement of the coefficients used in the White Sands method for Edwards AFB, California. Appendix G contains the nomenclature.

2162. Haering, Edward A., Jr.; Ehernberger, L. J.; and Whitmore, Stephen A.: **Preliminary Airborne Measurements for the SR-71 Sonic Boom Propagation Experiment**. NASA TM-104307, H-2068, NAS 1.15:104307. Presented at the NASA High Speed Research Program Sonic Boom Workshop, Hampton, Virginia, September 12–13, 1995, September 1995, 96N12627, #. (See also 2190.)

SR-71 sonic boom signatures were measured to validate sonic boom propagation prediction codes. An SR-71 aircraft generated sonic booms from Mach 1.25 to Mach 1.6, at altitudes of 31,000 to 48,000 ft, and at various gross weights. An F-16XL aircraft measured the SR-71 near-field shock waves from close to the aircraft to more than 8,000 ft below, gathering 105 signatures. A YO-3A aircraft measured the SR-71 sonic booms from 21,000 to 38,000 feet below, recording 17 passes. The sonic booms at ground level and atmospheric data were recorded for each flight. Data analysis is underway. Preliminary results show that shock wave patterns and coalescence vary with SR-71 gross weight, Mach number, and altitude. For example, noncoalesced shock wave signatures were measured by the YO-3A at 21,000 ft below the SR-71 aircraft while at a low gross weight, Mach 1.25, and 31,000-ft altitude. This paper describes the design and execution of the flight research experiment. Instrumentation and flight maneuvers of the

SR-71, F-16XL, and YO-3A aircraft and sample sonic boom signatures are included.

EC95-43024-2

SR-71 and F-16XL Airplanes

2163. Bahm, Catherine M.; and Haering, Edward A., Jr.: **Ground-Recorded Sonic Boom Signatures of F-18 Aircraft Formation Flight.** NASA TM-104312, H-2067, NAS 1.15:104312. Presented at the NASA High Speed Research Program Sonic Boom Workshop, Hampton, Virginia, September 12–13, 1995, <u>September 1995</u>, 96N16433, #. (See also 2188.)

Two F-18 aircraft were flown, one above the other, in two formations, in order for the shock systems of the two aircraft to merge and propagate to the ground. The first formation had the canopy of the lower F-18 in the inlet shock of the upper F-18 (called inlet-canopy). The flight conditions were Mach 1.22 and an altitude of 23,500 ft. An array of five sonic boom recorders was used on the ground to record the sonic boom signatures. This paper describes the flight test technique and the ground level sonic boom signatures. The tail-canopy formation resulted in two, separated, N-wave signatures. Such signatures probably resulted from aircraft positioning error. The inlet-canopy formation yielded a single modified signature; two recorders measured an approximate flattop signature. Loudness calculations indicated that the single inlet-canopy signatures were quieter than the two, separated tail-canopy signatures. Significant loudness occurs after a sonic boom signature. Such loudness probably comes from the aircraft engines.

2164. Norris, Stephen R.; Haering, Edward A., Jr.; and Murray, James E.: **Ground-Based Sensors for the SR-71 Sonic Boom Propagation Experiment.** NASA TM-104310, H-2062, NAS 1.15:104310. Presented at the NASA High

Speed Research Program Sonic Boom Workshop, Hampton, Virginia, September 12–13, 1995, <u>September 1995</u>, 96N16043, #. (See also 2189.)

This paper describes ground-level measurements of sonic boom signatures made as part of the SR-71 sonic boom propagation experiment recently completed at NASA Dryden Flight Research Center, Edwards, California. Ground level measurements were the final stage of this experiment which also included airborne measurements at near and intermediate distances from an SR-71 research aircraft. Three types of sensors were deployed to three station locations near the aircraft ground track. Pressure data were collected for flight conditions from Mach 1.25 to Mach 1.60 at altitudes from 30,000 to 48,000 ft. Ground-level measurement techniques, comparisons of data sets from different ground sensors, and sensor system strengths and weaknesses are discussed. The well-known N-wave structure dominated the sonic boom signatures generated by the SR-71 aircraft at most of these conditions. Variations in boom shape caused by atmospheric turbulence, focusing effects, or both were observed for several flights. Peak pressure and boom event duration showed some dependence on aircraft gross weight. The sonic boom signatures collected in this experiment are being compiled in a data base for distribution in support of the High Speed Research Program.

2165. Norlin, Ken A.: **Flight Simulation Software at NASA Dryden Flight Research Center.** NASA TM-104315, H-2052, NAS 1.15:104315. Presented at the American Institute of Aeronautics and Astronautics Flight Simulation Technologies Conference, Baltimore, Maryland, August 7–10, 1995, <u>October 1995</u>, 96N11694, #. (See also 2159.)

The NASA Dryden Flight Research Center has developed a versatile simulation software package that is applicable to a broad range of fixed-wing aircraft. This package has evolved in support of a variety of flight research programs. The structure is designed to be flexible enough for use in batch-mode, real-time pilot-in-the-loop, and flight hardware-in-the-loop simulation. Current simulations operate on UNIX-based platforms and are coded with a FORTRAN shell and C support routines. This paper discusses the features of the simulation software design and some basic model development techniques. The key capabilities that have been included in the simulation are described. The NASA Dryden simulation software is in use at other NASA centers, within industry, and at several universities. The straightforward but flexible design of this well-validated package makes it especially useful in an engineering environment.

2166. Whitmore, Stephen A.; Davis, Roy J.; and Fife, John Michael: **In-Flight Demonstration of a Real-Time Flush Airdata Sensing (RT-FADS) System.** NASA TM-104314, H-2053, NAS 1.15:104314. Presented at the AIAA Flight Mechanics Conference, Baltimore, Maryland, August 7–10, 1995, <u>October 1995</u>, 96N16908, #.

A prototype real-time flush airdata sensing (RT-FADS) system has been developed and flight tested at the NASA Dryden Flight Research Center. This system uses a matrix of pressure orifices on the vehicle nose to estimate airdata parameters in real time using nonlinear regression. The algorithm is robust to sensor failures and noise in the measured pressures. The RT-FADS system has been calibrated using inertial trajectory measurements that were bootstrapped for atmospheric conditions using meteorological data. Mach numbers as high as 1.6 and angles of attack greater than 45 deg have been tested. The system performance has been evaluated by comparing the RT-FADS to the ship system airdata computer measurements to give a quantitative evaluation relative to an accepted measurement standard. Nominal agreements of approximately 0.003 in Mach number and 0.20 deg in angle of attack and angle of sideslip have been achieved.

2167. *Yuhas, Andrew J.; Ray, Ronald J.; **Burley, Richard R.; †Steenken, William G.; †Lechtenberg, Leon; and Thornton, Don: **Design and Development of an F/A-18 Inlet Distortion Rake: A Cost and Time Saving Solution.** NASA TM-4722, H-2078, NAS 1.15:4722, AIAA Paper 94-2132. Presented at the 7th Biennial AIAA Flight Test Conference, Colorado Springs, Colorado, June 20–23, 1994, October 1995, 96N14003, #. (See also 2095.)

An innovative inlet total pressure distortion measurement rake has been designed and developed for the F/A-18 A/B/C/D aircraft inlet. The design was conceived by NASA and General Electric Aircraft Engines personnel. This rake has been flight qualified and flown in the F/A-18 High Alpha Research Vehicle at NASA Dryden Flight Research Center, Edwards, California. The eight-legged, one-piece, wagon wheel design of the rake was developed at a reduced cost and offered reduced installation time compared to traditional designs. The rake features 40 dual-measurement ports for low- and high-frequency pressure measurements with the high-frequency transducer mounted at the port. This high-frequency transducer offers direct absolute pressure measurements from low to high frequencies of interest, thereby allowing the rake to be used during highly dynamic aircraft maneuvers. Outstanding structural characteristics are inherent to the design through its construction and use of lightweight materials.

*PRC Inc., Edwards, California.
**NASA Lewis Research Center, Cleveland, Ohio.
†General Electric Co., Evendale, Ohio.

2168. Iliff, Kenneth W.; and Shafer, Mary F.: **A Comparison of Hypersonic Vehicle Flight and Prediction Results.** NASA TM-104313, H-2074, NAS 1.15:104313, AIAA Paper 93-0311. Presented at the 31st Aerospace Sciences Meeting and Exhibit, Reno, Nevada, January 11–14, 1993, October 1995, 96N13522, #. (See also 2009.)

Aerodynamic and aerothermodynamic comparisons between flight and ground test for four hypersonic vehicles are discussed. The four vehicles are the X-15, the Reentry F, the Sandia Energetic Reentry Vehicle Experiment (SWERVE), and the Space Shuttle. The comparisons are taken from papers published by researchers active in the various programs. Aerodynamic comparisons include reaction control jet interaction on the Space Shuttle. Various forms of heating including catalytic, boundary layer, shock interaction and interference, and vortex impingement are compared. Predictions were significantly exceeded for the heating caused by vortex impingement (on the Space Shuttle OMS pods) and for heating caused by shock interaction and interference on the X-15 and the Space Shuttle. Predictions of boundary-layer state were in error on the X-15, the SWERVE, and the Space Shuttle vehicles.

2169. Kehoe, Michael W.: **A Historical Overview of Flight Flutter Testing.** NASA TM-4720, H-2077, NAS 1.15:4720. Presented at the AGARD Structures and Materials Panel Meeting, Rotterdam, the Netherlands, May 8–10, 1995, October, 1995, 96N14084, #. (See also 2170.)

This paper reviews the test techniques developed over the last several decades for flight flutter testing of aircraft. Structural excitation systems, instrumentation systems, digital data preprocessing, and parameter identification algorithms (for frequency and damping estimates from the response data) are described. Practical experiences and example test programs illustrate the combined, integrated effectiveness of the various approaches used. Finally, comments regarding the direction of future developments and needs are presented.

2170. Kehoe, Michael W.: **A Historical Overview of Flight Flutter Testing.** AGARD CP-566, H-2041. *Advanced Aeroservoelastic Testing and Data Analysis Conference,* November 1995, (see N96-24337 08-05), 96N24338, #. (See also 2169.)

This paper reviews the test techniques developed over the last several decades for flight flutter testing of aircraft. Structural excitation systems, instrumentation systems, digital data preprocessing, and parameter identification algorithms (for frequency and damping estimates from the response data) are described. Practical experiences and example test programs illustrate the combined, integrated effectiveness of the various approaches used. Finally, comments regarding the direction of future developments and needs are presented.

2171. Powers, S. G.: **Wing.** *McGraw-Hill Yearbook of Science and Technology for 1995,* McGraw-Hill Book Co., New York, New York, Q1.M13 505.8, 1995, pp. 462–465.

Article about the Smooth-Variable-Camber Supercritical Mission Adaptive Wing flown on the Advanced Fighter Technology Integration F-111 Aircraft.

1996 Technical Publications

2172. Gilyard, Glenn: **Development of a Real-Time Transport Performance Optimization Methodology.** NASA TM-4730, H-2085, NAS 1.15:4730, AIAA Paper 96-0093, NIPS-96-09032. Presented at the 34th AIAA Aerospace Sciences Meeting and Exhibit, Reno, Nevada, January 15–18, 1996, January 1996, 96N21251, #.

The practical application of real-time performance optimization is addressed (using a wide-body transport simulation) based on real-time measurements and calculation of incremental drag from forced response maneuvers. Various controller combinations can be envisioned although this study used symmetric outboard aileron and stabilizer. The approach is based on navigation instrumentation and other measurements found on state-of-the-art transports. This information is used to calculate winds and angle of attack. Thrust is estimated from a representative engine model as a function of measured variables. The lift and drag equations are then used to calculate lift and drag coefficients. An expression for drag coefficient, which is a function of parasite drag, induced drag, and aileron drag, is solved from forced excitation response data. Estimates of the parasite drag, curvature of the aileron drag variation, and minimum drag aileron position are produced. Minimum drag is then obtained by repositioning the symmetric aileron. Simulation results are also presented which evaluate the affects of measurement bias and resolution.

2173. Whitmore, Stephen A.; *Petersen, Brian J.; and **Scott, David D.: **A Dynamic Response Model for Pressure Sensors in Continuum and High Knudsen Number Flows With Large Temperature Gradients.** NASA TM-4728, H-2083, NAS 1.15:4728, AIAA Paper 96-0563, NIPS-96-08937. Presented at the 34th AIAA Aerospace Sciences Meeting and Exhibit, Reno, Nevada, January 15–18, 1996, January 1996, 96N19294, #.

This paper develops a dynamic model for pressure sensors in continuum and rarefied flows with longitudinal temperature gradients. The model was developed from the unsteady Navier-Stokes momentum, energy, and continuity equations and was linearized using small perturbations. The energy equation was decoupled from momentum and continuity assuming a polytropic flow process. Rarefied flow conditions were accounted for using a slip flow boundary condition at the tubing wall. The equations were radially averaged and solved assuming gas properties remain constant along a small tubing element. This fundamental solution was used as a building block for arbitrary geometries where fluid properties may also vary longitudinally in the tube. The problem was solved recursively starting at the transducer and working upstream in the tube. Dynamic frequency response tests were performed for continuum flow conditions in the presence of temperature gradients. These tests validated the recursive formulation of the model. Model steady-state behavior was analyzed using the final value theorem. Tests were performed for rarefied flow conditions and compared to the model steady-state response to evaluate the regime of applicability. Model comparisons were excellent for Knudsen numbers up to 0.6. Beyond this point, molecular affects caused model analyses to become inaccurate.

*UCLA, Los Angeles, California.
**Lawrence Livermore National Laboratory, Livermore, California.

2174. *Rudoff, R. C.; *Bachalo, W. D.; Webb, L. D.; Conners, T.; and Ennix, K.: **A Ground Test Application of Laser Doppler Velocimetry to Aircraft Gas Turbine Inlet Flow.** AIAA Paper 96-0112. Presented at the 34th AIAA Aerospace Sciences Meeting and Exhibit, Reno, Nevada, January 15–18, 1996.

Engine inlet velocity flow fields are important for determining inlet flow distortion, optimizing inlet design, and understanding high angle of attack operation. These flow fields are normally measured by expensive, fixed position, and perturbing multi-channel pitot rake sensors. The objective of this study is to show that Laser Doppler Velocimetry (LDV) offers a potential solution to these problems, along with providing high spatial and temporal resolution. Data in the inlet of an F-100 EMD engine was acquired with a state of the art, ruggedized LDV system incorporating a high bandwidth, real-time signal processor. As part of this work, an inlet duct with an optical access and seeding methodology were developed. One-component axial mean and rms velocity profiles were successfully determined under steady state and transient engine run conditions from idle to maximum afterburner. Time-velocity correlations during transient engine maneuvers and an estimate of LDV data rate versus laser power were also obtained. The results show that LDV may be applied to full scale inlets both with and without seeding. Data rates in most cases would be adequate for active feedback control of the engine. The results of this work will be used to guide the development of an in-flight instrument.

*Aerometrics, Inc., Sunnyvale, California.

2175. Hodge, Kenneth E.: **Proceedings of the F–8 Digital Fly-by-Wire and Supercritical Wing First Flight's 20th Anniversary Celebration.** NASA CP-3256-VOL-1, H-1957, NAS 1.26:3256-VOL-1, NIPS-96-76755. Conference, Edwards, California, May 27, 1992, February 1996, 96N32875, #.

A technical symposium, aircraft display dedication, and pilots' panel discussion were held on May 27, 1992 to commemorate the 20th anniversary of the first flights of the F-8 Digital Fly-By-Wire (DFBW) and Supercritical Wing (SCW) research aircraft. The symposium featured technical presentations by former key government and industry participants in the advocacy, design, aircraft modification, and flight research program activities. The DFBW and SCW technical contributions are cited. A dedication ceremony marked permanent display of both program aircraft. The panel discussion participants included eight of the eighteen research and test pilots who flew these experimental aircraft. Pilots' remarks include descriptions of their most memorable flight experiences The report also includes a survey of the Gulf Air War, and an after-dinner presentation by noted aerospace author and historian Dr. Richard Hallion.

2176. Hodge, Kenneth E.: **Proceedings of the F-8 Digital Fly-by-Wire and Supercritical Wing First Flight's 20th Anniversary Celebration.** NASA CP-3256-VOL-2, H-1957, NAS 1.55:3256-VOL-2, NIPS-96-76755. Conference, Edwards, California, May 27, 1992, <u>February 1996</u>, 96N32901, #.

A technical symposium, aircraft display dedication, and pilots' panel discussion were held on May 27, 1992. To commemorate the 20th anniversary of the first flights of the F-8 Digital Fly-By-Wire (DFBW) and Supercritical Wing (SCW) research aircraft. The symposium featured technical presentations by former key government and industry participants in the advocacy, design, aircraft modification, and flight research program activities. The DFBW and SCW technical contributions are cited. A dedication ceremony marked permanent display of both program aircraft. The panel discussion participants included eight of the eighteen research and test pilots who flew these experimental aircraft. Pilots' remarks include descriptions of their most memorable flight experiences. The report also includes a survey of the Gulf Air War, an after-dinner presentation by noted aerospace author and historian Dr. Richard Hallion.

2177. Richards, W. Lance: **A New Correction Technique for Strain-Gage Measurements Acquired in Transient-Temperature Environments.** NASA-TP-3593, H-2043, NAS 1.60:3593, NIPS-96-37020, <u>March 1996</u>, 96N22235, #.

Significant strain-gage errors may exist in measurements acquired in transient-temperature environments if conventional correction methods are applied. As heating or cooling rates increase, temperature gradients between the strain-gage sensor and substrate surface increase proportionally. These temperature gradients introduce strain-measurement errors that are currently neglected in both conventional strain-correction theory and practice. Therefore, the conventional correction theory has been modified to account for these errors. A new experimental method has been developed to correct strain-gage measurements acquired in environments experiencing significant temperature transients. The new correction technique has been demonstrated through a series of tests in which strain measurements were acquired for temperature-rise rates ranging from 1 to greater than 100 degrees F/sec. Strain-gage data from these tests have been corrected with both the new and conventional methods and then compared with an analysis. Results show that, for temperature-rise rates

greater than 10 degrees F/sec, the strain measurements corrected with the conventional technique produced strain errors that deviated from analysis by as much as 45 percent, whereas results corrected with the new technique were in good agreement with analytical results.

2178. Richards, W. Lance; and Monaghan, Richard C.: **Analytical and Experimental Verification of a Flight Article for a Mach-8 Boundary-Layer Experiment.** NASA TM-4733, H-2088,NAS 1.15:4733, NIPS-96-36721. Presented at First International Conference on Computational Methods and Testing for Engineering Integrity, Kuala Lumpur, Malaysia, March 19–21, 1996, <u>March 1996</u>, 96N22128, #.

Preparations for a boundary-layer transition experiment to be conducted on a future flight mission of the air-launched Pegasus® rocket are underway. The experiment requires a flight-test article called a glove to be attached to the wing of the Mach-8 first-stage booster. A three-dimensional, nonlinear finite-element analysis has been performed and significant small-scale laboratory testing has been accomplished to ensure the glove design integrity and quality of the experiment. Reliance on both the analysis and experiment activities has been instrumental in the success of the flight-article design. Results obtained from the structural analysis and laboratory testing show that all glove components are well within the allowable thermal stress and deformation requirements to satisfy the experiment objectives.

2179. Pendleton, Ed; Griffin, Kenneth E.; Kehoe, Michael W.; and Perry, Boyd: **A Flight Research Program for Active Aeroelastic Wing Technology.** AIAA-96-1574. Presented at the AIAA, ASME, ASCE, AHS, and ASC Structures, Structural Dynamics and Materials Conference, Salt Lake City, Utah, April 15–17, 1996, <u>April 1996</u>.

This paper describes a flight research program initiative for the Active Aeroelastic Wing (AAW) concept. AAW technology is also know as active flexible wing technology. This paper introduces key design studies which project significant aircraft weight savings when the concept is applied to new aircraft. The paper also summarizes wind tunnel performance results which provide the basis for the next step in AAW development: a flight research program.

2180. Jenkins, Jerald M.; and Quinn, Robert D.: **A Historical Perspective of the YF-12A Thermal Loads and Structures Program.** NASA TM-104317, H-2079, NAS 1.15:104317, NIPS-96-60615, <u>May 1996</u>, 96N29035, #.

Around 1970, the Y-F-12A loads and structures efforts focused on numerous technological issues that needed defining with regard to aircraft that incorporate hot structures in the design. Laboratory structural heating test technology with infrared systems was largely created during this program. The program demonstrated the ability to duplicate the complex flight temperatures of an advanced supersonic airplane in a ground-based laboratory. The ability to heat and load an advanced operational aircraft in a laboratory at high temperatures and return it to flight status without adverse effects was demonstrated. The technology associated with measuring loads with strain gages on a hot structure was demonstrated with a thermal calibration concept. The results demonstrated that the thermal stresses were significant although the airplane was designed to reduce thermal stresses. Considerable modeling detail was required to predict the heat transfer and the corresponding structural characteristics. The overall YF-12A research effort was particularly productive, and a great deal of flight, laboratory, test and computational data were produced and cross-correlated.

2181. Richards, W. Lance: **Measurement Errors Associated With the Transient Heating of Electrical-Resistance Strain Gages.** *Proceedings of the 42nd International Instrumentation Symposium*, San Diego, California, May 5–9, 1996, May 1996.

Significant strain-gage errors may exist in measurements acquired in transient temperature environments if conventional correction methods are applied. Conventional correction theory was modified and a new experimental method was developed to correct indicated strain gage data errors created in radiant heating environments ranging from 0.6 °C/sec (1°F/sec) to over 56°C/sec (100°F/sec). In some cases the new and conventional methods differed by as much as 30 percent. Experimental and analytical results were compared to demonstrate the new technique. For heating conditions greater than 6° C/sec (10 °F/sec), the indicated strain gage data corrected with the developed technique compared much better to analysis than the same data corrected with the conventional technique.

2182. Szalai, Kenneth J.; *Bonifazi, Carlo; **Joyce, Paul M.; †Schwinghamer, Robert J.; **White, Robert D.; **Bowersox, Kenneth; **Schneider, William C.; ††Stadler, John H.; and **Whittle, David W.: **TSS-1R Mission Failure Investigation Board.** NASA TM-112426, NAS 1.15:112426, May 1996, 97N16648, #.

Reasons for the tether separation during the Tethered Satellite System (TSS-1) Mission are investigated. Lessons learned are presented.

*Italian Space Agency, Rome, Italy.
**NASA Johnson Space Center, Houston, Texas.
†NASA Marshall Space Flight Center, Huntsville, Alabama.
††NASA Langley Research Center, Hampton, Virginia.

2183. Moes, Timothy R.; *Smith, Stephen C.; **Shirakata, Norm; Cobleigh, Brent R.; and Conners,

Timothy R.: **Wind-Tunnel Development of an SR-71 Aerospike Rocket Flight Test Configuration.** NASA TM-4749, H-2108, NAS 1.15:4749, NIPS-96-60616, June 1996, 96N30909, #.

A flight experiment has been proposed to investigate the performance of an aerospike rocket motor installed in a lifting body configuration. An SR-71 airplane would be used to carry the aerospike configuration to the desired flight test conditions. Wind-tunnel tests were completed on a 4-percent scale SR-71 airplane with the aerospike pod mounted in various locations on the upper fuselage. Testing was accomplished using sting and blade mounts from Mach 0.6 to Mach 3.2. Initial test objectives included assessing transonic drag and supersonic lateral-directional stability and control. During these tests, flight simulations were run with wind-tunnel data to assess the acceptability of the configurations. Early testing demonstrated that the initial configuration with the aerospike pod near the SR-71 center of gravity was unsuitable because of large nosedown pitching moments at transonic speeds. The excessive trim drag resulting from accommodating this pitching moment far exceeded the excess thrust capability of the airplane. Wind-tunnel testing continued in an attempt to find a configuration suitable for flight test. Multiple configurations were tested. Results indicate that an aft-mounted model configuration possessed acceptable performance, stability, and control characteristics.

*NASA Ames Research Center, Moffett Field, California.
**Lockheed Martin Corp., Palmdale, California.

2184. Bosworth, John T.; and Stoliker, P. C.: **The X-31A Quasi-Tailless Flight Test Results.** NASA TP-3624, H-2091, NAS 1.60:3624, NIPS-96-60625, June 1996, 96N29644, #.

A quasi-tailless flight investigation was launched using the X-31A enhanced fighter maneuverability airplane. In-flight simulations were used to assess the effect of partial to total vertical tail removal. The rudder control surface was used to cancel the stabilizing effects of the vertical tail, and yaw thrust vector commands were used to restabilize and control the airplane. The quasi-tailless mode was flown supersonically with gentle maneuvering and subsonically in precision approaches and ground attack profiles. Pilot ratings and a full set of flight test measurements were recorded. This report describes the results obtained and emphasizes the lessons learned from the X-31A flight test experiment. Sensor-related issues and their importance to a quasi-tailless simulation and to ultimately controlling a directionally unstable vehicle are assessed. The X-31A quasi-tailless flight test experiment showed that tailless and reduced tail fighter aircraft are definitely feasible. When the capability is designed into the airplane from the beginning, the benefits have the potential to outweigh the added complexity required.

2185. Powers, Bruce G.: **Structural Dynamic Model Obtained From Flight Use With Piloted Simulation and**

Handling Qualities Analysis. NASA TM-4747, H-2075, NAS 1.15:4747, NIPS-96-60624, <u>June 1996</u>, 96N31481, #.

The ability to use flight data to determine an aircraft model with structural dynamic effects suitable for piloted simulation and handling qualities analysis has been developed. This technique was demonstrated using SR-71 flight test data. For the SR-71 aircraft, the most significant structural response is the longitudinal first-bending mode. This mode was modeled as a second-order system, and the other higher order modes were modeled as a time delay. The distribution of the modal response at various fuselage locations was developed using a uniform beam solution, which can be calibrated using flight data. This approach was compared to the mode shape obtained from the ground vibration test, and the general form of the uniform beam solution was found to be a good representation of the mode shape in the areas of interest. To calibrate the solution, pitch-rate and normal-acceleration instrumentation is required for at least two locations. With the resulting structural model incorporated into the simulation, a good representation of the flight characteristics was provided for handling qualities analysis and piloted simulation.

2186.   Pahle, Joseph W.; *Bundick, W. Thomas; *Yeager, Jessie C.; and *Beissner, Fred L., Jr.: **Design of a Mixer for the Thrust-Vectoring System on the High-Alpha Research Vehicle.** NASA TM-110228, NAS 1.15:110228, NIPS-96-64543, <u>June 1996</u>, 96N31389, #.

One of the advanced control concepts being investigated on the High-Alpha Research Vehicle (HARV) is multi-axis thrust vectoring using an experimental thrust-vectoring (TV) system consisting of three hydraulically actuated vanes per engine. A mixer is used to translate the pitch-, roll-, and yaw-TV commands into the appropriate TV-vane commands for distribution to the vane actuators. A computer-aided optimization process was developed to perform the inversion of the thrust-vectoring effectiveness data for use by the mixer in performing this command translation. Using this process a new mixer was designed for the HARV and evaluated in simulation and flight. An important element of the Mixer is the priority logic, which determines priority among the pitch, roll-, and yaw-TV commands.

*Lockheed Engineering and Sciences Co., Hampton, Virginia.

2187.   Conners, Timothy R.: **Predicted Performance of a Thrust-Enhanced SR-71 Aircraft With an External Payload.** NASA TM-104330, H-2179, NAS 1.15:104330. Presented at the PJN: International Gas Turbine and Aeroengine Conference, Houston, Texas, June 5–8, 1996, <u>June 1996</u>, 97N21479, #. (See also 2157.)

NASA Dryden Flight Research Center has completed a preliminary performance analysis of the SR-71 aircraft for use as a launch platform for high-speed research vehicles and for carrying captive experimental packages to high altitude and Mach number conditions. Externally mounted research platforms can significantly increase drag, limiting test time and, in extreme cases, prohibiting penetration through the high-drag, transonic flight regime. To provide supplemental SR-71 acceleration, methods have been developed that could increase the thrust of the J58 turbojet engines. These methods include temperature and speed increases and augmentor nitrous oxide injection. The thrust-enhanced engines would allow the SR-71 aircraft to carry higher drag research platforms than it could without enhancement. This paper presents predicted SR-71 performance with and without enhanced engines. A modified climb-dive technique is shown to reduce fuel consumption when flying through the transonic flight regime with a large external payload. Estimates are included of the maximum platform drag profiles with which the aircraft could still complete a high-speed research mission. In this case, enhancement was found to increase the SR-71 payload drag capability by 25 percent. The thrust enhancement techniques and performance prediction methodology are described.

2188.   Bahm, Catherine M.; and Haering, Edward A., Jr.: **Ground-Recorded Sonic Boom Signatures of F-18 Aircraft in Formation Flight.** *Proceedings of the 1995 NASA High-Speed Research Program Sonic Boom Workshop,* <u>July 1996</u>, pp. 220–243, (see N96-36847 12-01), 96N36858, #. (See also 2163.)

Two F-18 aircraft were flown, one above the other, in two formations, in order for the shock systems of the two aircraft to merge and propagate to the ground. The first formation had the canopy of the lower F-18 in the tail shock of the upper F-18 (called tail-canopy). The second formation had the canopy of the lower F- 18 in the inlet shock of the upper F-18 (called inlet-canopy). The flight conditions were Mach 1.22 and an altitude of 23,500 ft. An array of five sonic boom recorders was used on the ground to record the sonic boom signatures. This paper describes the flight test technique and the ground level sonic boom signatures. The tail-canopy formation resulted in two, separated, N-wave signatures. Such signatures probably resulted from aircraft positioning error. The inlet-canopy formation yielded a single modified signature; two recorders measured an approximate flattop signature. Loudness calculations indicated that the single inlet-canopy signatures were quieter than the two, separated tail-canopy signatures. Significant loudness occurs after a sonic boom signature. Such loudness probably comes from the aircraft engines.

2189.   Norris, Stephen R.; Haering, Edward A., Jr.; and Murray, James E.: **Ground-Based Sensors for the SR-71 Sonic Boom Propagation Experiment.** H-2061. *Proceedings of the 1995 NASA High-Speed Research*

Program Sonic Boom Workshop, July 1996, pp. 199–219, (see N96-36847 12-01), 96N36857, #. (See also 2164.)

This paper describes ground-level measurements of sonic boom signatures made as part of the SR-71 sonic boom propagation experiment recently completed at NASA Dryden Flight Research Center, Edwards, California. Ground-level measurements were the final stage of this experiment which also included airborne measurements at near and intermediate distances from an SR-71 research aircraft. The types of sensors were deployed to three station locations near the aircraft ground track. Pressure data collected for flight conditions from Mach 1.25 to Mach 1.60 at altitudes from 30,000 to 48,000 ft. Ground-level measurement techniques, comparisons of data sets from different ground sensors, and sensor system strengths and weaknesses are discussed. The well-known N-wave structure dominated r sonic boom signatures generated by the SR-71 aircraft at most of these conditions. Variations in boom shape caused by atmospheric turbulence, focusing effects, or both, were observed for several flights. Peak pressure and boom event duration showed some dependence on aircraft gross weight. The sonic boom signatures collected in this experiment are being compiled in a data base for distribution in support of the High Speed Research Program.

2190. Haering, Edward A., Jr.; Ehernberger, L. J.; and Whitmore, Stephen A.: **Preliminary Airborne Measurements for the SR-71 Sonic Boom Propagation Experiment.** *Proceedings of the 1995 NASA High-Speed Research Program Sonic Boom Workshop,* July 1996, pp. 176–198, (see N96-36847 12-01), 96N36856, #. (See also 2162.)

SR-71 sonic boom signatures were measured to validate sonic boom propagation prediction codes. An SR-71 aircraft generated sonic booms from Mach 1.25 to Mach 1.6, at altitudes of 31,000 to 48,000 ft, and at various gross weights. An F-16XL aircraft measured the SR-71 near-field shock waves from close to the aircraft to more than 8,000 ft below, gathering 105 signatures. A YO-3A aircraft measured the SR-71 sonic booms from 21,000 to 38, 000 ft below, recording 17 passes. The sonic booms at ground level and atmospheric data were recorded for each flight. Data analysis is underway. Preliminary results show that shock wave patterns and coalescence vary with SR-71 gross weight, Mach number, and altitude. For example, noncoalesced shock wave signatures were measured by the YO-3A at 21,000 ft below the SR-71 aircraft while at a low gross weight, Mach 1.25, and 31,000-ft altitude. This paper describes the design and execution of the flight research experiment. Instrumentation and flight maneuvers of the SR-71, F-16XL, and YO-3A aircraft and sample sonic boom signatures are included.

2191. Smith, John W.; and Montgomery, Terry: **Biomechanically Induced and Controller Coupled Oscillations Experienced on the F-16XL Aircraft During Rolling Maneuvers.** NASA TM-4752, H-2031, NAS 1.15:4752, NIPS-96-70392, July 1996, 96N33173, #.

During rapid rolling maneuvers, the F-16 XL aircraft exhibits a 2.5 Hz lightly damped roll oscillation, perceived and described as 'roll ratcheting'. This phenomenon is common with fly-by-wire control systems, particularly when primary control is derived through a pedestal-mounted side-arm controller. Analytical studies have been conducted to model the nature of the integrated control characteristics. The analytical results complement the flight observations. A three-degree-of-freedom linearized set of aerodynamic matrices was assembled to simulate the aircraft plant. The lateral-directional control system was modeled as a linear system. A combination of two second-order transfer functions was derived to couple the lateral acceleration feed through effect of the operator's arm and controller to the roll stick force input. From the combined systems, open-loop frequency responses and a time history were derived, describing and predicting an analogous in-flight situation. This report describes the primary control, aircraft angular rate, and position time responses of the F-16 XL-2 aircraft during subsonic and high-dynamic-pressure rolling maneuvers. The analytical description of the pilot's arm and controller can be applied to other aircraft or simulations to assess roll ratcheting susceptibility.

2192. Burcham, Frank W., Jr.; Maine, Trindel A.; Burken, John J.; and Pappas, Drew: **Development and Flight Test of an Augmented Thrust-Only Flight Control System on an MD-11 Transport Airplane.** NASA TM-4745, H-2107, NAS 1.15:4745, NIPS-96-70387, AIAA 96-3742. Presented at the AIAA Guidance, Navigation, and Control Conference, San Diego, California, July 29–31, 1996, July 1996, 96N33120, #.

An emergency flight control system using only engine thrust, called Propulsion-Controlled Aircraft (PCA), has been developed and flight tested on an MD-11 airplane. In this thrust-only control system, pilot flight path and track commands and aircraft feedback parameters are used to control the throttles. The PCA system was installed on the MD-11 airplane using software modifications to existing computers. Flight test results show that the PCA system can be used to fly to an airport and safely land a transport airplane with an inoperative flight control system. In up-and-away operation, the PCA system served as an acceptable autopilot capable of extended flight over a range of speeds and altitudes. The PCA approaches, go-arounds, and three landings without the use of any normal flight controls have been demonstrated, including instrument landing system-coupled hands-off landings. The PCA operation was used to recover from an upset condition. In addition, PCA was tested at altitude with all three hydraulic systems turned off. This paper reviews the principles of throttles-only flight control; describes the MD-11 airplane and systems; and discusses PCA system development, operation, flight testing, and pilot comments.

EC95-43247-4

MD-11 PCA Landing

2193. Ko, William L.: **Thermal and Mechanical Buckling Analysis of Hypersonic Aircraft Hat-Stiffened Panels With Varying Face Sheet Geometry and Fiber Orientation.** NASA TM-4770, H-2097, NAS 1.15:4770. Presented at the 3rd International Conference on Composite Engineering, New Orleans, Louisiana, July 21–26, 1996, December 1996, 97N13249, #.

Mechanical and thermal buckling behavior of monolithic and metal-matrix composite hat-stiffened panels were investigated. The panels have three types of face-sheet geometry: Flat face sheet, microdented face sheet, and microbulged face sheet. The metal-matrix composite panels have three types of face-sheet layups, each of which is combined with various types of hat composite layups. Finite-element method was used in the eigenvalue extractions for both mechanical and thermal buckling. The thermal buckling analysis required both eigenvalue and material property iterations. Graphical methods of the dual iterations are shown. The mechanical and thermal buckling strengths of the hat-stiffened panels with different face-sheet geometry are compared. It was found that by just microdenting or microbulging of the face sheet, the axial, shear, and thermal buckling strengths of both types of hat-stiffened panels could be enhanced considerably. This effect is more conspicuous for the monolithic panels. For the metal-matrix composite panels, the effect of fiber orientations on the panel buckling strengths was investigated in great detail, and various composite layup combinations offering, high panel buckling strengths are presented. The axial buckling strength of the metal-matrix panel was sensitive to the change of hat fiber orientation. However, the lateral, shear, and thermal buckling strengths were insensitive to the change of hat fiber orientation.

2194. Bogue, Rodney K.; Ehernberger, L. J.; *Soreide, David; and **Bagley, Hal: **Coherent Lidar Turbulence Measurement for Gust Load Alleviation.** NASA TM-104318, H-2117, NAS 1.15:104318, NIPS-96-66519, SPIE Paper 2832-05. Presented at the SPIE 1996 International Symposium on Optical Science, Engineering, and Instrumentation, Denver, Colorado, August 4–9, 1996, August 1996, 96N31787, #.

Atmospheric turbulence adversely affects operation of commercial and military aircraft and is a design constraint. The airplane structure must be designed to survive the loads imposed by turbulence. Reducing these loads allows the airplane structure to be lighter, a substantial advantage for a commercial airplane. Gust alleviation systems based on accelerometers mounted in the airplane can reduce the maximum gust loads by a small fraction. These systems still represent an economic advantage. The ability to reduce the gust load increases tremendously if the turbulent gust can be measured before the airplane encounters it. A lidar system can make measurements of turbulent gusts ahead of the airplane, and the NASA Airborne Coherent Lidar for Advanced In-Flight Measurements (ACLAIM) program is developing such a lidar. The ACLAIM program is intended to develop a prototype lidar system for use in feasibility testing of gust load alleviation systems and other airborne lidar applications, to define applications of lidar with the potential for improving airplane performance, and to determine the feasibility and benefits of these applications. This paper gives an overview of the ACLAIM program, describes the lidar architecture for a gust alleviation system, and describes the prototype ACLAIM lidar system.

*Boeing Defense & Space Co., Seattle, Washington.
**Coherent Technologies, Inc., Boulder, Colorado.

2195. Burcham, Frank W.; Jr., Main, Trindel A.; Fullerton, C. Gordon; and Webb, Lannie Dean: **Development and Flight Evaluation of an Emergency Digital Flight Control System Using Only Engine Thrust on an F-15 Airplane.** NASA TP-3627, H-2048, NAS 1.60:3267, September 1996, 97N11179, #.

A propulsion-controlled aircraft (PCA) system for emergency flight control of aircraft with no flight controls was developed and flight tested on an F-15 aircraft at the NASA Dryden Flight Research Center. The airplane has been flown in a throttles-only manual mode and with an augmented system called PCA in which pilot thumbwheel commands and aircraft feedback parameters were used to drive the throttles. Results from a 36-flight evaluation showed that the PCA system can be used to safely land an airplane that has suffered a major flight control system failure. The PCA system was used to recover from a severe upset condition, descend, and land. Guest pilots have also evaluated the PCA system. This paper describes the principles of throttles-only flight control; a history of loss-of-control accidents; a description of the F-15 aircraft; the PCA system operation, simulation, and flight testing; and the pilot comments.

2196. Stoliker, Patrick C.; and Bosworth, John T.: **Evaluation of High-Angle-of-Attack Handling Qualities for the X-31A Using Standard Evaluation Maneuvers.** NASA TM-104322, H-2128, NAS 1.15:104322. Presented at the High-Angle-of-Attack Technology Conference, Hampton, Virginia, September 17–19, 1996, <u>September 1996</u>, 97N12707, #.

The X-31A aircraft gross-acquisition and fine-tracking handling qualities have been evaluated using standard evaluation maneuvers developed by Wright Laboratory, Wright-Patterson Air Force Base. The emphasis of the testing is in the angle-of-attack range between 30 deg and 70 deg. Longitudinal gross-acquisition handling qualities results show borderline Level 1/Level 2 performance. Lateral gross-acquisition testing results in Level 1/Level 2 ratings below 45 deg angle of attack, degrading into Level 3 as angle of attack increases. The fine-tracking performance in both longitudinal and lateral axes also receives Level 1 ratings near 30 deg angle of attack, with the ratings tending towards Level 3 at angles of attack greater than 50 deg. These ratings do not match the expectations from the extensive close-in combat testing where the X-31A aircraft demonstrated fair to good handling qualities maneuvering for high angles of attack. This paper presents the results of the high-angle-of-attack handling qualities flight testing of the X-31A aircraft. Discussion of the preparation for the maneuvers, the pilot ratings, and selected pilot comments are included. Evaluation of the results is made in conjunction with existing Neal-Smith, bandwidth, Smith-Geddes, and military specifications.

2197. Hedgley, David R., Jr.: **A Formal Algorithm for Routing Traces on a Printed Circuit Board.** NASA TP-3639, H-2104, NAS 1.60:3639, NIPS-96-93660, <u>September 1996</u>, 97N11168.

This paper addresses the classical problem of printed circuit board routing: that is, the problem of automatic routing by a computer other than by brute force that causes the execution time to grow exponentially as a function of the complexity. Most of the present solutions are either inexpensive but not efficient and fast, or efficient and fast but very costly. Many solutions are proprietary, so not much is written or known about the actual algorithms upon which these solutions are based. This paper presents a formal algorithm for routing traces on a printed circuit board. The solution presented is very fast and efficient and for the first time speaks to the question eloquently by way of symbolic statements.

2198. Pahle, Joseph W.; Wichman, Keith D.; *Foster, John V.; and *Bundick, W. Thomas: **An Overview of Controls and Flying Qualities Technology on the F/A-18 High Alpha Research Vehicle.** H-2123. Presented at the 5th High-Angle-of-Attack Technology Conference, NASA Langley Research Center, Hampton, Virginia, <u>September 17–19, 1996</u>.

The NASA F/A-18 High Alpha Research Vehicle (HARV) has been the flight test bed of a focused technology effort to significantly increase maneuvering capability at high angles of attack. Development and flight test of control law design methodologies, handling qualities metrics, performance guidelines, and flight evaluation maneuvers are described. The HARV has been modified to include two research control effectors, thrust vectoring, and actuated forebody strakes in order to provide increased control power at high angles of attack. A research flight control system has been used to provide a flexible, easily modified capability for high-angle-of-attack research controls. Different control law design techniques have been implemented and flight-tested, including eigenstructure assignment, variable gain output feedback, pseudo controls, and model-following. Extensive piloted simulation has been used to develop nonlinear performance guidelines and handling qualities criteria for high angles of attack. This paper reviews the development and evaluation of technologies useful for high-angle-of-attack control. Design, development, and flight test of the research flight control system, control laws, flying qualities specifications, and flight test maneuvers are described. Flight test results are used to illustrate some of the lessons learned during flight test and handling qualities evaluations.

*NASA Langley Research Center Hampton, Virginia.

2199. Banks, Daniel W.; Fisher, David F.; *Hall, Robert M.; *Erickson, Gary E.; *Murri, Daniel G.; *Grafton, Sue B.; and *Sewall, William G.: **The F/A-18 High-Angle-of-Attack Ground-to-Flight Correlation: Lessons Learned.** H-2142. Presented at the 5th High-Angle-of-Attack Technology Conference, NASA Langley Research Center, Hampton, Virginia, <u>September 17–19, 1996</u>. (Released as NASA TM-4783, January 1997.)

Detailed wind tunnel and flight investigations were performed on the F/A-18 configuration to explore the causes of many high-angle-of-attack phenomena and resulting disparities between wind tunnel and flight results at these conditions. Obtaining accurate predictions of full-scale flight aerodynamics from wind-tunnel tests is important and becomes a challenge at high-angle-of-attack conditions where large areas of vortical flow interact. The F/A-18 airplane was one of the first high-performance aircraft to have an unrestricted angle-of-attack envelope, and as such the configuration displayed many unanticipated characteristics. Results indicate that fixing forebody crossflow transition on models can result in a more accurate match of flow fields, and thus a more accurate prediction of aerodynamic characteristics of flight at high angles of attack. The wind tunnel results show that small geometry differences, specifically nosebooms and aft-end distortion, can have a pronounced effect at high angles of attack and must be modeled in sub-scale tests in order to obtain accurate correlations with flight.

*NASA Langley Research Center, Hampton, Virginia.

2200. *Steenken, William G.; *Williams, John G.; **Yuhas, Andrew J.; and Walsh, Kevin R.: **An Inlet Distortion Assessment During Aircraft Departures at High Angles of Attack for an F/A-18 Aircraft**. H-2159. Presented at the 5th NASA High-Angle-of-Attack Technology Conference, NASA Langley Research Center, Hampton, Virginia, September 17–19, 1996. (Released as NASA TM-104328, March 1997.)

The F404-GE-400-powered F/A-18A High Alpha Research Vehicle (HARV) was used to examine the quality of inlet airflow during departed flight maneuvers, that is, during flight outside the normal maneuvering envelope where control surfaces have little or no effectiveness. Six nose-left and six nose-right departures were initiated at Mach numbers between 0.3 and 0.4 at an altitude of 35 kft. The entry yaw rates were approximately 40 to 90 deg/sec. Engine surges were encountered during three of the nose-left and one of the nose-right departures. Time-variant inlet-total-pressure distortion levels at the engine face did not significantly exceed those at maximum angle-of-attack and sideslip maneuvers during controlled flight. Surges caused by inlet distortion levels resulted from a combination of high levels of inlet distortion and rapid changes in aircraft position. These rapid changes indicate a combination of engine support and gyroscopic loads being applied to the engine structure that impact the aerodynamic stability of the compressor through changes in the rotor-to-case clearances. This document presents the slides from an oral presentation.

*General Electric Aircraft Engines, Cincinnati, Ohio.
**Analytical Services & Materials, Inc., Edwards, California.

2201. Walsh, Kevin R.; *Yuhas, Andrew J.; **Williams, John G.; and **Steenken, William G.: **Inlet Distortion for an F/A-18A Aircraft During Steady Aerodynamic Conditions Up to 60° Angle of Attack**. H-2124. Presented at the 5th High-Angle-of-Attack Technology Conference, NASA Langley Research Center, Hampton, Virginia, September 17–19, 1996. (Released as NASA TM-104329, April 1997.)

The effects of high-angle-of-attack flight on aircraft inlet aerodynamic characteristics were investigated at NASA Dryden Flight Research Center, Edwards, California, as part of NASA's High Alpha Technology Program. The highly instrumented F/A-18A High Alpha Research Vehicle was used for this research. A newly designed inlet total-pressure

rake was installed in front of the starboard F404-GE-400 engine to measure inlet recovery and distortion characteristics. One objective was to determine inlet total-pressure characteristics at steady high-angle-of-attack conditions. Other objectives include assessing whether significant differences exist in inlet distortion between rapid angle-of-attack maneuvers and corresponding steady aerodynamic conditions, assessing inlet characteristics during aircraft departures, providing data for developing and verifying computational fluid dynamic codes, and calculating engine airflow using five methods. This paper addresses the first objective by summarizing results of 79 flight maneuvers at steady aerodynamic conditions, ranging from –10° to 60° angle of attack and from –8° to 11° angle of sideslip at Mach 0.3 and 0.4. These data and the associated database have been rigorously validated to establish a foundation for understanding inlet characteristics at high angle of attack.

*Analytical Services & Materials, Inc., Hampton, Virginia.
**General Electric Aircraft Engines, Evendale, Ohio.

2202. *Yuhas, Andrew J.; **Steenken, William G.; **Williams, John G.; and Walsh, Kevin R.: **F/A-18 Inlet Flow Characteristics During Maneuvers With Rapidly Changing Angle of Attack**. H-2145. Presented at the 5th High-Angle-of-Attack Conference, NASA Langley Research Center, Hampton, Virginia, September 17–19, 1996. (Released as NASA TM-104327, June 1997.)

The performance and distortion levels of the right inlet of the F/A-18A High Alpha Research Vehicle were assessed during maneuvers with rapidly changing angle-of-attack at the NASA Dryden Flight Research Center, Edwards, California. The distortion levels were compared with those produced by current inlet-engine compatibility evaluation techniques. The objective of these analyses was to determine whether the results obtained for steady aerodynamic conditions were adequate to describe the inlet-generated distortion levels that occur during rapid aircraft maneuvers. The test data were obtained during 46 dynamic maneuvers at Mach numbers of 0.3 and 0.4. Levels of inlet recovery, peak dynamic circumferential distortion, and peak dynamic radial distortion of dynamic maneuvers for a General Electric F404-GE-400 turbofan engine were compared with estimations based on steady aerodynamic conditions. The comparisons were performed at equivalent angle-of-attack, angle-of-sideslip, and Mach number. Results showed no evidence of peak inlet distortion levels being elevated by dynamic maneuver conditions at high angle-of-attack compared with steady aerodynamic estimations. During sweeps into high angle-of-attack, the peak distortion levels of the dynamic maneuvers rarely rose to steady aerodynamic estimations. The dynamic maneuvers were shown to be effective at identifying conditions when discrete changes in inlet behavior occur.

*Analytical Services & Materials, Inc., Edwards, California.
**General Electric Aircraft Engines, Cincinnati, Ohio.

2203. Flick, Bradley C.; Thomson, Michael P.; Regenie, Victoria A.; Wichman, Keith D.; Pahle, Joseph W.; and Earls, Michael R.: **Design and Integration of an Actuated Nose Strake Control System**. NASA TM-104324, H-2134. Presented at the 5th High-Angle-of-Attack Technology Conference, Langley Research Center, Hampton, Virginia, September 17–19, 1996, <u>October 1996</u>.

Aircraft flight characteristics at high angles of attack can be improved by controlling vortices shed from the nose. These characteristics have been investigated with the integration of the actuated nose strakes for enhanced rolling (ANSER) control system into the NASA F-18 High Alpha Research Vehicle. Several hardware and software systems were developed to enable performance of the research goals. A strake interface box was developed to perform actuator control and failure detection outside the flight control computer. A three-mode ANSER control law was developed and installed in the Research Flight Control System. The thrust-vectoring mode does not command the strakes. The strakes and thrust-vectoring mode uses a combination of thrust vectoring and strakes for lateral–directional control, and strake mode uses strakes only for lateral–directional control. The system was integrated and tested in the Dryden Flight Research Center (DFRC) simulation for testing before installation in the aircraft. Performance of the ANSER system was monitored in real time during the 89-flight ANSER flight test program in the DFRC Mission Control Center. One discrepancy resulted in a set of research data not being obtained. The experiment was otherwise considered a success with the majority of the research objectives being met.

2204. Bowers, Albion H.; Pahle, Joseph W.; Wilson, R. Joseph; Flick, Bradley C.; and Rood, Richard L.: **An Overview of the NASA F-18 High Alpha Research Vehicle**. NASA TM-4772, H-2137. Presented at the 5th High-Angle-of-Attack Technology Conference, Langley Research Center, Hampton, Virginia, September 17–19, 1996, <u>October 1996</u>.

This paper gives an overview of the NASA F-18 High Alpha Research Vehicle. The three flight phases of the program are introduced, along with the specific goals and data examples taken during each phase. The aircraft configuration and systems needed to perform the disciplinary and inter-disciplinary research are discussed. The specific disciplines involved with the flight research are introduced, including aerodynamics, controls, propulsion, systems, and structures. Decisions that were made early in the planning of the aircraft project and the results of those decisions are briefly discussed. Each of the three flight phases corresponds to a particular aircraft configuration, and the research dictated the configuration to be flown. The first phase gathered data with the baseline F-18 configuration. The second phase was the thrust-vectoring phase. The third phase used a modified forebody with deployable nose strakes. Aircraft systems supporting these flights included extensive instrumentation systems, integrated research flight controls using flight

control hardware and corresponding software, analog interface boxes to control forebody strakes, a thrust-vectoring system using external postexit vanes around axisymmetric nozzles, a forebody vortex control system with strakes, and backup systems using battery-powered emergency systems and a spin recovery parachute.

2205. Fisher, David F.; *Murri, Daniel G.; and **Lanser, Wendy R.: **Effect of Actuated Forebody Strakes on the Forebody Aerodynamics of the NASA F-18 HARV**. NASA TM-4774, H-2136. Presented at the 5th High-Angle-of-Attack Technology Conference, Langley Research Center, Hampton, Virginia, September 17–19, 1996, <u>October 1996</u>.

Extensive pressure measurements and off-surface flow visualization were obtained on the forebody and strakes of the NASA F-18 High Alpha Research Vehicle (HARV) equipped with actuated forebody strakes. Forebody yawing moments were obtained by integrating the circumferential pressures on the forebody and strakes. Results show that large yawing moments can be generated with forebody strakes. At angles of attack greater than 40°, deflecting one strake at a time resulted in a forebody yawing moment control reversal for small strake deflection angles. At $\alpha = 40°$ and 50°, deflecting the strakes differentially about a 20° symmetric strake deployment eliminated the control reversal and produced a near linear variation of forebody yawing moment with differential strake deflection. At $\alpha = 50°$ and for 0° and 20° symmetric strake deployments, a larger forebody yawing moment was generated by the forward fuselage (between the radome and the apex of the leading-edge extensions), than on the radome where the actuated forebody strakes were located. Cutouts on the flight vehicle strakes that were not on the wind tunnel models are believed to be responsible for deficits in the suction peaks on the flight radome pressure distributions and differences in the forebody yawing moments.

*NASA Langley Research Center, Hampton, Virginia.
**Ames Research Center, Moffet Field, California.

2206. Bowers, Albion H.; and Pahle, Joseph W.: **Thrust Vectoring on the NASA F-18 High Alpha Research Vehicle**. NASA TM-4771, H-2139. Presented at the 5th High-Angle-of-Attack Technology Conference, Langley Research Center, Hampton, Virginia, September 17–19, 1996, <u>November 1996</u>.

Investigations into a multiaxis thrust-vectoring system have been conducted on an F-18 configuration. These investigations include ground-based scale-model tests, ground-based full-scale testing, and flight testing. This thrust-vectoring system has been tested on the NASA F-18 High Alpha Research Vehicle (HARV). The system provides thrust vectoring in pitch and yaw axes. Ground-based subscale test data have been gathered as background to the flight phase of the program. Tests investigated aerodynamic interaction and vane control effectiveness. The ground-based full-scale data were gathered from static engine runs with image analysis to determine relative thrust-vectoring effectiveness. Flight tests have been conducted at the NASA Dryden Flight Research Center. Parameter identification input techniques have been developed. Individual vanes were not directly controlled because of a mixer-predictor function built into the flight control laws. Combined effects of the vanes have been measured in flight and compared to combined effects of the vanes as predicted by the cold-jet test data. Very good agreement has been found in the linearized effectiveness derivatives.

2207. Wichman, Keith D.; Pahle, Joseph W.; Bahm, Catherine; *Davidson, John B.; *Bacon, Barton J.; *Murphy, Patrick C.; *Ostrof, Aaron J.; and **Hoffler, Keith D.: **High-Alpha Handling Qualities Flight Research on the NASA F/A-18 High Alpha Research Vehicle**. NASA TM-4773, H-2138. Presented at the 5th High-Angle-of-Attack Technology Conference, Langley Research Center, Hampton, Virginia, September 17–19, 1996, <u>November 1996</u>.

A flight research study of high-angle-of-attack handling qualities has been conducted at the NASA Dryden Flight Research Center using the F/A-18 High Alpha Research Vehicle (HARV). The objectives were to create a high-angle-of-attack handling qualities flight database, develop appropriate research evaluation maneuvers, and evaluate high-angle-of-attack handling qualities guidelines and criteria. Using linear and nonlinear simulations and flight research data, the predictions from each criterion were compared with the pilot ratings and comments. Proposed high-angle-of-attack nonlinear design guidelines and proposed handling qualities criteria and guidelines developed using piloted simulation were considered. Recently formulated time-domain Neal-Smith guidelines were also considered for application to high-angle-of-attack maneuvering. Conventional envelope criteria were evaluated for possible extension to the high-angle-of-attack regime. Additionally, the maneuvers were studied as potential evaluation techniques, including a limited validation of the proposed standard evaluation maneuver set. This paper gives an overview of these research objectives through examples and summarizes result highlights. The maneuver development is described briefly, the criteria evaluation is emphasized with example results given, and a brief discussion of the database form and content is presented.

*NASA Langley Research Center, Hampton, Virginia.
**ViGYAN, Inc., Hampton, Virginia.

2208. Richards, W. Lance; and *Thompson, Randolph C.: **Titanium Honeycomb Panel Testing**. NASA TM-4768, H-2133, <u>October 1996</u>.

Thermal–mechanical tests were performed on a titanium honeycomb sandwich panel to experimentally validate the hypersonic wing panel concept and compare test data with

analysis. Details of the test article, test fixture development, instrumentation, and test results are presented. After extensive testing to 900 °F, non-destructive evaluation of the panel has not detected any significant structural degradation caused by the applied thermal–mechanical loads.

*PRC Inc., Edwards, California.

2209. Noffz, Gregory K.; and Bowman, Michael P.: **Design and Laboratory Validation of a Capacitive Sensor for Measuring the Recession of a Thin-Layered Ablator**. NASA TM-4777, H-2111, <u>November 1996</u>.

Flight vehicles are typically instrumented with subsurface thermocouples to estimate heat transfer at the surface using inverse analysis procedures. If the vehicle has an ablating heat shield, however, temperature time histories from subsurface thermocouples no longer provide enough information to estimate heat flux at the surface. In this situation, the geometry changes and thermal energy leaves the surface in the form of ablation products. The ablation rate is required to estimate heat transfer to the surface. A new concept for a capacitive sensor has been developed to measure ablator depth using the ablator's dielectric effect on a capacitor's fringe region. Relying on the capacitor's fringe region enables the gage to be flush mounted in the vehicle's permanent structure and not intrude into the ablative heat shield applied over the gage. This sensor's design allows nonintrusive measurement of the thickness of dielectric materials, in particular, the recession rates of low-temperature ablators applied in thin (0.020 to 0.060 in. (0.05 to 0.15 mm)) layers. Twenty capacitive gages with 13 different sensing element geometries were designed, fabricated, and tested. A two-dimensional finite-element analysis was performed on several candidate geometries. Calibration procedures using ablator-simulating shims are described. A one-to-one correspondence between system output and dielectric material thickness was observed out to a thickness of 0.055 in. (1.4 mm) for a material with a permittivity about three times that of air or vacuum. A novel method of monitoring the change in sensor capacitance was developed. This technical memorandum suggests further improvements in gage design and fabrication techniques.

2210. Holzman, Jon K.; Webb, Lannie D.; and Burcham, Frank W., Jr.: **Flight and Static Exhaust Flow Properties of an F110-GE-129 Engine in an F-16XL Airplane During Acoustic Tests**. NASA TM-104326, H-2122, <u>November 1996</u>.

The exhaust flow properties (mass flow, pressure, temperature, velocity, and Mach number) of the F110-GE-129 engine in an F-16XL airplane were determined from a series of flight tests flown at NASA Dryden Flight Research Center, Edwards, California. These tests were performed in conjunction with NASA Langley Research

Center, Hampton, Virginia (LaRC) as part of a study to investigate the acoustic characteristics of jet engines operating at high nozzle pressure conditions. The range of interest for both objectives was from Mach 0.3 to Mach 0.9. NASA Dryden flew the airplane and acquired and analyzed the engine data to determine the exhaust characteristics. NASA Langley collected the flyover acoustic measurements and correlated these results with their current predictive codes. This paper describes the airplane, tests, and methods used to determine the exhaust flow properties and presents the exhaust flow properties. No acoustics results are presented.

2211. *Roudakov, Alexander S.; *Semenov, Vyacheslav L.; *Kopchenov, Valeriy I.; and Hicks, John W.: **Future Flight Test Plans of an Axisymmetric Hydrogen-Fueled Scramjet Engine on the Hypersonic Flying Laboratory.** AIAA 96-4572. Presented at the 7th International Spaceplanes and Hypersonics Systems & Technology Conference, Norfolk, Virginia, November 18–22, 1996,.

Under a contract with NASA, a joint Central Institute of Aviation Motors (CIAM) and NASA team is preparing to conduct the fourth flight test of a dual-mode scramjet aboard the CIAM Hypersonic Flying Laboratory, "Kholod." Ground-launch, rocket boosted by a modified Russian SA-5 missile, the redesigned scramjet is to be accelerated to a new maximum velocity of Mach 6.5. This should allow for the first-time measurement of the fully supersonic combustion mode. The primary program objective is the flight-to-ground correlation of measured data with preflight analysis and wind-tunnel tests in Russia and potentially in the United States. This paper describes the development and objectives of the program as well as the technical details of the scramjet and SA-5 redesign to achieve the Mach 6.5 aim test condition. The purpose and value of a joint Russian-American program to attain overall hypersonic air-breathing technology objectives are discussed. Finally, the current project status and schedules to reach the final flight launch are discussed.

*Central Institute of Aviation Motors, Moscow, Russia.

2212. Richwine, David M.: **F-15B/Flight Test Fixture II: A Test Bed for Flight Research.** NASA TM-4782, H-2113, December 1996.

NASA Dryden Flight Research Center has developed a second-generation flight test fixture for use as a generic test bed for aerodynamic and fluid mechanics research. The Flight Test Fixture II (FTF–II) is a low-aspect-ratio vertical fin-like shape that is mounted on the centerline of the F-15B lower fuselage. The fixture is designed for flight research at Mach numbers to a maximum of 2.0. The FTF–II is a composite structure with a modular configuration and removable components for functional flexibility. This report documents the flow environment of the fixture, such as

surface pressure distributions and boundary-layer profiles, throughout a matrix of conditions within the F-15B/FTF–II flight envelope. Environmental conditions within the fixture are presented to assist in the design and testing of future avionics and instrumentation. The intent of this document is to serve as a user's guide and assist in the development of future flight experiments that use the FTF–II as a test bed. Additional information enclosed in the appendices has been included to assist with more detailed analyses, if required.

2213. Iliff, Kenneth W.; and *Wang, Kon-Sheng Charles: **X-29A Lateral–Directional Stability and Control Derivatives Extracted From High-Angle-of-Attack Flight Data.** NASA TP-3664, H-2118, December 1996.

The lateral–directional stability and control derivatives of the X-29A number 2 are extracted from flight data over an angle-of-attack range of $4°$ to $53°$ using a parameter identification algorithm. The algorithm uses the linearized aircraft equations of motion and a maximum likelihood estimator in the presence of state and measurement noise. State noise is used to model the uncommanded forcing function caused by unsteady aerodynamics over the aircraft at angles of attack above $15°$. The results supported the flight-envelope-expansion phase of the X-29A number 2 by helping to update the aerodynamic mathematical model, to improve the real-time simulator, and to revise flight control system laws. Effects of the aircraft high gain flight control system on maneuver quality and the estimated derivatives are also discussed. The derivatives are plotted as functions of angle of attack and compared with the predicted aerodynamic database. Agreement between predicted and flight values is quite good for some derivatives such as the lateral force due to sideslip, the lateral force due to rudder deflection, and the rolling moment due to roll rate. The results also show significant differences in several important derivatives such as the rolling moment due to sideslip, the yawing moment due to sideslip, the yawing moment due to aileron deflection, and the yawing moment due to rudder deflection.

*SPARTA Inc., Lancaster, California.

2214. Burken, John J.; Burcham, Frank W. Jr.; and *Feather, John: **Flight Test Results of a Propulsion-Only Emergency Control System on the MD-11 Airplane.** H-2144, *AIAA Journal*, December 1996.

A large, civilian, multiengine transport MD-11 airplane control system was recently modified to perform as an emergency backup controller using engine thrust only. The emergency backup system, referred to as the propulsion-controlled aircraft (PCA) system, would be used if a major primary flight control system fails. To allow for longitudinal and lateral–directional control, the PCA system requires at least two engines, and is implemented through software modifications. A flight-test program was conducted to evaluate the PCA system high-altitude flying characteristics and to demonstrate its capacity to perform safe landings. The cruise flight conditions, several low approaches, and four landings without any aerodynamic flight control surface movement were demonstrated. This paper presents results that show satisfactory performance of the PCA system in the longitudinal axis. Test results indicate that the lateral–directional axis of the system performed well at high altitude but was sluggish and prone to thermal upsets during landing approaches. Flight-test experiences and test techniques are also discussed with emphasis on the lateral–directional axis because of the difficulties encountered in flight test.

*McDonnell Douglas Aerospace, Long Beach, California.

2215. Clarke, Robert; Burken, John J.; Bosworth, John T.; and Bauer, Jeffrey E.: **X-29 Flight Control System: Lessons Learned.** *Advances in Aircraft Flight Control,* TL678.A39, 1996, pp. 345–368. (See also 2086, 2122, 2140.)

The X-29A airplanes were evaluated over the full design envelope. The flight control system successfully performed the tasks of stabilizing the short-period mode and providing automatic camber control to minimize trim drag. Compared with other highly augmented, digital fly-by-wire airplanes, the X-29A and its flight control system proved remarkably trouble free. Despite the unusually large negative static margin, the X-29A proved safe to operate within the design envelope.

Appendix A. NASA Contractor Reports

The research described in the following NASA contractor reports was funded by NASA Dryden Flight Research Center.

1964 Contractor Reports

1. *Anon.: **Lunar Landing Research Vehicle: Structural Analysis Handbook**. NASA CR-116780, REPT-7161-954001, April 1964, 72N74854.

There is no abstract available for this record.

*Bell Aerosystems Co., Buffalo, New York.

2. *Anon.: **Lunar Landing Research Vehicle: Weight and Balance Handbook**. NASA CR-127485, REPT-7161-954002, April 1964, 72N74855.

There is no abstract available for this record.

*Bell Aerosystems Co., Buffalo, New York.

3. *Anon.: **Lunar Landing Research Vehicle: Summary of Estimated Performance**. NASA CR-127486, REPT-7161-954003, April 1964, 72N74856.

There is no abstract available for this record.

*Bell Aerosystems Co., Buffalo, New York.

4. *Anon.: **Lunar Landing Research Vehicle: Estimated Handling Qualities**. NASA CR-127487, REPT-7161-954004, April 1964, 72N74857.

There is no abstract available for this record.

*Bell Aerosystems Co., Buffalo, New York.

5. *Kohn, H. T.: **Design Study of an Articulated Binocular Periscope for the F-104B Aircraft**. NASA CR-82002, December 1964, 68N85476.

There is no abstract available for this record.

*Space Systems Lab., Inc., Melbourne, Florida.

1965 Contractor Reports

6. *Conner, F.; *Willey, C.; and *Twomey, W.: **A Flight and Wind Tunnel Investigation of the Effect of Angle-of-Attack Rate on Maximum Lift Coefficient**. NASA CR-321, October 1965, 65N35827.

Wind tunnel tests to determine effect of angle of attack on maximum lift at stall for half-wing models, and single engine, jet propelled aircraft.

*Lockheed-California Company, Burbank, California.

7. *Anon.: **Biodata Processing Study and Program Formulation Final Report**. NASA CR-106213, SR-65-1028/7241, October 1965, 70N77799.

There is no abstract available for this record.

*Spacelabs, Inc., Van Nuys, California.

8. *MacCready, P. B., Jr.; *Williamson, R. E.; *Berman, S.; and *Webster, A.: **Operational Application of a Universal Turbulence Measuring System Final Report**. NASA CR-62025, MRI65-FR-301, November 1965, 66N15232.

Aeronautical turbulence measuring apparatus - gust loading.

*Meteorology Research, Inc., Altadena, California.

1966 Contractor Reports

9. *Anon.: **NASA Water-Cooled Extensometer**. NASA CR-82001, D2-36548-1, January 1966, 69N77051.

There is no abstract available for this record.

*Boeing Co., Seattle, Washington.

10. *Irwin, D. C.: **Landing Dynamics Study for Lunar Landing Research Vehicle**. NASA CR-428, April 1966, 66N23447.

Impact dynamics and effects on lunar landing module performance and landing gear.

*Bendix Corp., South Bend, Indiana.

11. *Anon.: **X-15 Data Display System**. NASA CR-460, May 1966, 66N25560.

Digital data processing techniques for conversion of physiological and environmental response signals from X-15 aircraft pilots.

*Spacelabs, Inc., Van Nuys, California.

12. *Katz, D.; *Emery, J. A.; *Gabriel, R. F.; and *Burrows, A. A.: **Experimental Study of Acoustic Displays of Flight Parameters in a Simulated Aerospace Vehicle**. NASA CR-509, July 1966, 66N32335.

Evaluating acoustic displays of target location in target detection and of flight parameters in simulated aerospace vehicles.

*Douglas Aircraft Co., Inc., Long Beach, California.

13. *Clark, D. C.; and *Kroll, J.: **General Purpose Airborne Simulator - Conceptual Design Report**. NASA CR-544, August 1966, 66N37026.

General purpose airborne simulator with capabilities for model controlled and response feedback types of variable stability operation.

*Cornell Aeronautical Laboratory, Buffalo, New York.

14. *Brigden, W. H.: **Evaluation of a Miniaturized Double-Focusing Mass Spectrometer**. NASA CR-605, November 1966, 67N11341.

Evaluation of miniaturized magnetic double focusing mass spectrometer to measure gas concentrations in flight environment.

*Spacelabs, Inc., Van Nuys, California.

15. *Barrington, A. E.: **Instantaneous Monitoring of Multicomponent Expired Gases**. NASA CR-619, December 1966, 67N11821.

Expired air analyzers with time-of-flight and magnetic deflection mass spectrometers for spacecraft use.

*Geophysics Corp. of America, Bedford, Massachusetts.

16. *Kroll, J.; *Arendt, R. H.; and *Pritchard, F. E.: **Development of a General Purpose Airborne Simulator**. NASA CR-641, November 1966, 67N13179.

Variable stability system development for General Purpose Airborne Simulator (GPAS).

*Cornell Aeronautical Laboratory, Buffalo, New York.

=====

1967 Contractor Reports

17. *Anon.: **Experimentation Program for Development of Phosphor for Cathode Ray Tube**. NASA CR-96002, January 1967, 68N35788.

Phosphor development for cathode ray tubes to extend spectral emission without increasing decay rate.

*Panaura Corp., Chemical Medical Electronics, Pennsauken, New Jersey.

18. *Breeze, R. K.; and *Campbell, G. W.: **The Design, Fabrication and Feasibility Testing of a Prototype Airborne Respiration Analyzer**. NASA CR-741, March 1967, 67N19897.

Design, fabrication, and feasibility testing of prototype airborne respiration analyzer for measuring respiration products and oxygen consumption.

*North American Aviation, Inc., Los Angeles, California.

19. *Meeker, J. I.: **Evaluation of Lateral-Directional Handling Qualities of Piloted Re-Entry Vehicles Utilizing Fixed-Base and In-Flight Evaluations**. NASA CR-778, May 1967, 67N29029, #.

Lateral directional handling qualities of piloted reentry vehicles utilizing fixed base and in flight evaluations.

*Cornell Aeronautical Laboratory, Buffalo, New York.

20. *Anon.: **Study of Fluid Flight Path Control System**. NASA CR-758, REPT-20175-FR1, August 1967, 67N36563.

Flight path stabilization of light aircraft using fluid control system.

*Honeywell, Inc., Minneapolis, Minnesota.

21. *Rodgers, D. L.: **Development and Flight Testing of a Fluidic Control System**. NASA CR-913, REPT-20175-FR2, October 1967, 68N10047.

Three axis fluidic automatic flight control system developed and flight tested.

*Honeywell, Inc., Minneapolis, Minnesota.

22. *Kadlec, P. W.: **Atmospheric Temperature Gradients Related to Clear Air Turbulence in the Upper Troposphere and Lower Stratosphere**. NASA CR-91055, November 1967, 68N26807.

Relationship between atmospheric temperature gradients and clear air turbulence of lower atmosphere.

*Eastern Air Lines, Inc., Miami, Florida.

1968 Contractor Reports

23. *Price, A. B.: **Thermal Protection System X-15A-2 Design Report**. NASA CR-82003, ER-14535, January 1968, 68N25717.

Ablative thermal protection system for X-15 aircraft operating at hypersonic speeds.

*Martin Co., Denver, Colorado.

24. *Price, A. B.: **Full Scale Flight Test Report, X-15A-2 Ablative Thermal Protection System**. NASA CR-82004, MCR-68-15, REV. 1, May 1968, 68N25886.

Flight test and performance analysis of ablative thermal protection system for X-15A-2 aircraft.

*Martin Co., Denver, Colorado.

25. *Price, A. B.; and *Thompson, J. T.: **Application and Refurbishment Procedures X-15A-2 Thermal Protection System**. NASA CR-96000, ER-14539, REV. 1, May 1968, 68N25889.

Operational process manual for ablative thermal protection system of X-15A-2 aircraft.

*Martin Co., Denver, Colorado.

26. *Cockayne, W. G.: **Description of an Energy Management System for the X-15**. NASA CR-96006, June 1968, 69N16923.

Engineering equations of X-15 energy management system and mechanization of equations in SDS 930 and ALERT guidance programs.

*Bell Aerosystems Co., Buffalo, New York.

27. *Burgin, G. H.: **Two New Methods for Obtaining Stability Derivatives From Flight Test Data**. NASA CR-96005-REV, September 1968, 69N33609, #.

New methods for obtaining stability derivatives from flight data.

*Decision Science, Inc., San Diego, California.

28. *Bailey, R. G.: **High Total Temperature Sensing Probe for the X-15 Hypersonic Aircraft**. NASA CR-116772, REPT-12080-FR1, September 1968, 71N23250.

High total temperature sensing probe using fluid oscillator concept for X-15 hypersonic aircraft.

*Honeywell, Inc., Minneapolis, Minnesota.

29. *Smay, J. W.: **Computer-Aided Design of Second and Third-Order Systems With Parameter Variations and Time Response Constraints**. NASA CR-96004, October 1968, 69N14330.

Computerized design of second and third order systems with parameter variations and time response constraints.

*University of Colorado, Dept. of Electrical Engineering, Boulder, Colorado.

30. *Olson, D. E.: **Design Procedures for Dominant Type Systems With Large Parameter Variations**. NASA CR-96003, November 1968.

Fourth order feedback system synthesis with large plant parameter variations.

*University of Colorado, Dept. of Electrical Engineering, Boulder, Colorado.

1969 Contractor Reports

31. *Mc Kay, W.; and *Strane, R.: **Instruction Manual for an Accelerometer Test System**. P/N 231-0000/F/2/-223-008-022-1308/, NASA CR-96010, F-1308, January 1969, 69N36533.

Instruction manual for accelerometer test system.

*Owens-Illinois Glass Co., Pittsburgh, Pennsylvania.

32. *Teper, G. L.: **Aircraft Stability and Control Data**. NASA CR-96008, STI-TR-176-1, April 1969, 69N31783.

Aircraft stability and control data.

*Systems Technology, Inc., Hawthorne, California.

33. *Taylor, F. J.: **Sensitivity Reduction Through Reoptimization**. NASA CR-96009, June 1969, 69N35463.

Optimal system with controlled sensitivity to parameter uncertainty.

*University of Colorado, Dept. of Electrical Engineering, Boulder, Colorado.

34. *Oda, N. T.: **Frequency Response Approach to Design of Adaptive Control Systems Via Model of Specifications**. NASA CR-106209, August 1969, 70N27386.

Frequency response approach to adaptive control systems design by translating from time to frequency domain specifications.

*University of Colorado, Boulder, Colorado.

1970 Contractor Reports

35. *Wykes, J. H.; and *Mori, A. S.: **XB-70 Aerodynamic, Geometric, Mass, and Symmetric Structural Mode Data**. NASA CR-116773, NA-70-158 <u>March 1970</u>, 72N11943, #.

XB-70-1 mass, structural, and aerodynamic data were updated to reflect as closely as possible the characteristics of the airplane at three specific flight conditions which were actually flown; a nominal Mach number of 0.90 at an altitude of 25,000 feet (two cases) and a nominal Mach number of 1.6 at an altitude of 40,000 feet (one case). In-flight response characteristics at a number of points on the vehicle were obtained by exciting a pair of shaker vanes on the nose of the airplane. Data were recorded with the basic stability augmentation system (SAS) operating both alone and together with the identical location of accelerometer and force (ILAF) structural mode control system. Detailed total vehicle weight, mass characteristics, structural frequencies, generalized masses, all aerodynamic data used in the present analyses, and a description of the actual mode shapes are tabulated and presented.

*North American Aviation, Inc., Los Angeles, California.

36. *Veazey, D. R.: **A Literature Survey of Clear Air Turbulence**. NASA CR-106211, <u>March 1970</u>, 70N32002, #.

Literature survey on clear air turbulence.

*Texas A&M University, College Station, Texas.

37. *Lewis, H. Z.: **Computer-Aided Design of Feedback Control Systems With Plant Parameter Variations**. NASA CR-116771, <u>June 1970</u>, 71N13501.

Improving feedback control design by using digital computer techniques.

*University of Colorado, Boulder, Colorado.

38. *Beaulieu, W. D.; and *Martin, A. W.: **XB-70 Flight Test Data Comparisons With Simulation Predictions of Inlet Unstart and Buzz**. NASA CR-1631, <u>June 1970</u>, 70N31577.

XB-70 flight test data comparison with simulated predictions of inlet unstart and buzz.

*North American Rockwell Corp., Los Angeles, California.

39. *Mori, A. S.; *Nardi, L. U.; and *Wykes, J. H.: **XB-70 Structural Mode Control System Design and Performance Analyses**. NASA CR-1557, <u>July 1970</u>, 70N34004.

Damping system for control of structural motion in flexible airframes.

*North American Rockwell Corp., Los Angeles, California.

1971 Contractor Reports

40. *Palsson, T.: **Parameter Uncertainties in Control System Design**. NASA CR-116774, TE-46, <u>May 1971</u>, 71N34414, #.

Design method including effects of parameter uncertainties in design of linear control systems.

*Massachusetts Institute of Technology, Cambridge, Massachusetts.

41. *Warren, M. E.: **Ride Comfort Control in Large Flexible Aircraft; M.S. Thesis**. NASA CR-116775, TE-48, <u>May 1971</u>, 72N13984, #.

The problem of ameliorating the discomfort of passengers on a large air transport subject to flight disturbances is examined. The longitudinal dynamics of the aircraft, including effects of body flexing, are developed in terms of linear, constant coefficient differential equations in state variables. A cost functional, penalizing the rigid body displacements and flexure accelerations over the surface of the aircraft is formulated as a quadratic form. The resulting control problem, to minimize the cost subject to the state equation constraints, is of a class whose solutions are well known. The feedback gains for the optimal controller are calculated digitally, and the resulting autopilot is simulated on an analog computer and its performance evaluated.

*Massachusetts Institute of Technology, Cambridge, Massachusetts.

42. *Incrocci, T. P.; and Scoggins, J. R.: **An Investigation of the Relationships Between Mountain-Wave Conditions and Clear Air Turbulence Encountered by the XB-70 Airplane in the Stratosphere**. NASA CR-1878, H-679, <u>July 1971</u>, 71N31351, #.

XB-70 aircraft for investigating and predicting mountain waves.

*Texas A&M University, College Station, Texas.

43. *Horowitz, I. M.; and *Sidi, M.: **Synthesis of Feedback Systems With Large Plant Ignorance for Prescribed Time Domain Tolerances**. NASA CR-116779, <u>July 1971</u>, 72N27253, #.

There is given a minimum-phase plant transfer function, with prescribed bounds on its parameter values. The plant is imbedded in a two-degree-of freedom feedback system, which is to be designed such that the system time response to a deterministic input lies within specified boundaries. Subject to the above, the design should be such as to minimize the effect of sensor noise at the input to the plant. This report presents a design procedure for this purpose, based on frequency response concepts. The time-domain tolerances are translated into equivalent frequency response tolerances. The latter lead to bounds on the loop transmission function in the form of continuous curves on the Nichols chart. The properties of the loop transmission function which satisfy these bounds with minimum effect of sensor noise, are derived.

*University of Colorado, Boulder, Colorado.

===

1972 Contractor Reports

44. *Miley, S. J.: **A Catalogue of Devices Applicable to the Measurement of Boundary Layers and Wakes on Flight Vehicles**. NASA CR-116776, AASE-71-51, January 1972, 72N18424, #.

A literature search was conducted to assemble a catalog of devices and techniques which have possible application to boundary layer and wake measurements on flight vehicles. The indices used in the search were NACA, NASA STAR, IAA, USGRDR and Applied Science and Technology Index. The period covered was 1950 through 1970. The devices contained in the catalog were restricted to those that provided essentially direct measurement of velocities, pressures and shear stresses. Pertinent material was included in the catalog if it contained either an adequate description of a device and associated performance data or a presentation of applicable information on a particular measurement theory and/or technique. When available, illustrations showing the configuration of the device and test condition data were also included.

*Mississippi State University, Starkville, Mississippi.

45. *Sinha, P. K.: **An Algorithm for Control System Design Via Parameter Optimization; M.S. Thesis**. NASA CR-116778, TE-49, January 1972, 72N26186, #.

An algorithm for design via parameter optimization has been developed for linear-time-invariant control systems based on the model reference adaptive control concept. A cost functional is defined to evaluate the system response relative to nominal, which involves in general the error between the system and nominal response, its derivatives and the control signals. A program for the practical implementation of this algorithm has been developed, with the computational scheme for the evaluation of the performance index based on Lyapunov's theorem for stability of linear invariant systems.

*Massachusetts Institute of Technology, Cambridge, Massachusetts.

46. *Mertaugh, L. J., Jr.: **In-Flight Comparisons of Boundary-Layer and Wake Measurement Probes for Incompressible Flow**. NASA CR-127488, AASE-72-74, March 1972, 72N33270, #.

The results are presented of in-flight comparisons of a number of boundary-layer and wake measurement probes suitable for low-speed flight-test investigations. The tested boundary-layer probes included a traversing total-pressure probe and a hot-film probe mounted on an internally-mounted drive mechanism, a curved and a straight boundary-layer rake, and a traversing hot-film probe with an externally-mounted drive mechanism. The wake measuring devices included a traversing, self-aligning probe, a wake rake, and an integrating wake rate. The boundary-layer data are compared with a common reference velocity profile and comments given regarding the accuracy of the static-pressure and total-pressure measurements. Discussions on the various calibration presentations used with hot-wire and hot-film sensors and various aspects of improving the accuracy of hot-film sensor results are given in the appendix of this report.

*Mississippi State University, Starkville, Mississippi.

47. *McDonald, T. E., Jr.: **Synthesis Procedure for Linear Time-Varying Feedback Systems With Large Parameter Ignorance**. NASA CR-116777, April 1972, 72N27252, #.

The development of synthesis procedures for linear time-varying feedback systems is considered. It is assumed that the plant can be described by linear differential equations with time-varying coefficients; however, ignorance is associated with the plant in that only the range of the time-variations are known instead of exact functional relationships. As a result of this plant ignorance the use of time-varying compensation is ineffective so that only time-invariant compensation is employed. In addition, there is a noise source at the plant output which feeds noise through the feedback elements to the plant input. Because of this noise source the gain of the feedback elements must be as small as possible. No attempt is made to develop a stability criterion for time-varying systems in this work.

*University of Colorado, Boulder, Colorado.

48. *Edinger, L. D.; *Chenk, F. L.; and *Curtis, A. R.: **Study of Load Alleviation and Mode Suppression (LAMS) on the YF-12A Airplane**. NASA CR-2158, December 1972, 73N15033, #.

The potentials and capability for implementing a LAMS (load alleviation and mode suppression) system on the YF-12A for the purpose of flight research were evaluated. The nature of the research is to minimize the design risk in application of LAMS to future aircraft. The results of the study show that the YF-12A would be a suitable test bed for continuing development of LAMS technology. This was demonstrated by defining five candidate LAMS systems and analytically evaluating them with regard to performance and mechanization. Each of the five systems used a different combination of force producers. A small canard vane or a mass-reaction device mounted near the cockpit was considered as a possible LAMS force producer, together with the existing inboard and outboard elevons. It was concluded that a combination of canard vane and outboard elevons would provide the most effective system for the YF-12A.

*Lockheed Aircraft Corp., Burbank, California.

49. *Heffley, R. K.; and *Jewell, W. F.: **Aircraft Handling Qualities Data**. AD-A277031, NASA CR-2144, December 1972, 73N12039, #.

Available information on weight and inertia, aerodynamic derivatives, control characteristics, and stability augmentation systems is documented for 10 representative contemporary airplanes. Data sources are given for each airplane. Flight envelopes are presented and dimensional derivatives, transfer functions for control inputs, and several selected handling qualities parameters have been computed and are tabulated for 10 different flight conditions including the power approach configuration. The airplanes documented are the NT-33A, F-104A, F-4C, X-15, HL-10, JetStar, CV-880M, B-747, C-5A, and XB-70A.

*Systems Technology, Inc., Hawthorne, California.

1973 Contractor Reports

50. *Krishnan, K. R.; and *Horowitz, I. M.: **Synthesis of a Non-Linear Feedback System With Significant Plant-Ignorance for Prescribed Time-Domain Tolerances**. NASA CR-127489, February 1973, 73N19260, #.

The problem considered is the design of a feedback system containing a linear, time invariant, minimum phase plant, whose parameters are known only within given bounds, such that the time response of the system remains within specified limits. A quasi-optimal design, for given design constraints, is one which minimizes the effect of white sensor noise on the input to the plant. An investigation was conducted on the use of the non linear device known as the Clegg integrator in the design of such a system. The describing function of the Clegg integrator has the same magnitude characteristic, apart from a scale factor, as the linear integrator, but has 52 deg less phase-lag, at all frequencies, than the linear integrator; thus, when used in a feedback system, it provides a larger stability margin than the linear integrator. This property allows the nonlinear feedback system to be designed so that the sensor noise is attenuated more than in the linear design.

*University of Colorado, Boulder, Colorado.

51. *Plank, P. P.; and *Penning, F. A.: **Hypersonic Wing Test Structure Design, Analysis, and Fabrication**. NASA CR-127490, August 1973, 73N33883, #.

An investigation to provide the analyses, data, and hardware required to experimentally validate the beaded panel concept and demonstrate its usefulness as a basis for design of a Hypersonic Research Airplane (HRA) wing is reported. Combinations of the beaded panel structure, heat shields, channel caps and corrugated webs for ribs and spars were analyzed for the wing of a specified HRA to operate at Mach 8 with a lifespan of 150 flights. Detailed analyses were conducted in accordance with established design criteria and included aerodynamic heating and load predictions, transient structural thermal calculations, extensive NASTRAN computer modeling, and structural optimization. Optimum beaded panel tests at 922 K (1200 °F) were performed to verify panel performance. Close agreement of predicted and actual critical loads permitted use of design procedures and equations for the beaded panel concept without modification.

*Martin Marietta Corp., Denver, Colorado.

1974 Contractor Reports

52. *Kowalsky, N. B.; *Masters, R. L.; *Stone, R. B.; *Babcock, G. L.; and *Rypka, E. W.: **An Analysis of Pilot Error-Related Aircraft Accidents**. NASA CR-2444, H-827, June 1974, 74N26434.

A multidisciplinary team approach to pilot error-related U.S. air carrier jet aircraft accident investigation records successfully reclaimed hidden human error information not shown in statistical studies. New analytic techniques were developed and applied to the data to discover and identify multiple elements of commonality and shared characteristics within this group of accidents. Three techniques of analysis were used: Critical element analysis, which demonstrated the importance of a subjective qualitative approach to raw accident data and surfaced information heretofore unavailable. Cluster analysis, which was an exploratory research tool that will lead to increased understanding and improved organization of facts, the discovery of new meaning in large data sets, and the generation of explanatory hypotheses. Pattern recognition, by which accidents can be categorized by pattern conformity after critical element identification by cluster analysis.

*Lovelace Foundation for Medical Education and Research, Albuquerque, New Mexico.

53. *Bach, R. E., Jr.: **A User's Manual for Ames (A Parameter Estimation Program)**. NASA CR-163118, June 1974, 82N72452.

There is no abstract available for this record.

*Northeastern University, Boston, Massachusetts.

54. *Johnson, W. A.; and *Teper, G. L.: **Analysis of Vortex Wake Encounter Upsets**. NASA CR-127491, TR-1025-2, <u>August 1974</u>, 74N31500, #.

The problem of an airplane being upset by encountering the vortex wake of a large transport on takeoff or landing is currently receiving considerable attention. This report describes the technique and results of a study to assess the effectiveness of automatic control systems in alleviating vortex wake upsets. A six-degree-of-freedom nonlinear digital simulation was used for this purpose. The analysis included establishing the disturbance input due to penetrating a vortex wake from an arbitrary position and angle. Simulations were computed for both a general aviation airplane and a commercial jet transport. Dynamic responses were obtained for the penetrating aircraft with no augmentation, and with various command augmentation systems, as well as with human pilot control. The results of this preliminary study indicate that attitude command augmentation systems can provide significant alleviation of vortex wake upsets; and can do it better than a human pilot.

*Systems Technology, Inc., Hawthorne, California.

55. *Kadlec, P. W.; and *Buckman, R. C.: **Inflight Data Collection for Ride Quality and Atmospheric Turbulence Research**. NASA CR-127492, <u>December 1974</u>, 75N14745, #.

A flight test program to investigate the effects of atmospheric turbulence on passenger ride quality in large, wide-body commercial aircraft was conducted. Data were collected on a series of flight on a Boeing 747 aircraft. Atmospheric and aircraft performance data were obtained from special sensors, as well as conventional instruments and avionics systems normally available. Visual observations of meteorological conditions encountered were manually recorded during the flights.

*Continental Airlines, Inc., Los Angeles, California.

1975 Contractor Reports

56. *Gupta, N. K.; and *Hall, W. E., Jr.: **Input Design for Identification of Aircraft Stability and Control Derivatives**. NASA CR-2493, H-864, <u>February 1975</u>, 75N17370.

An approach for designing inputs to identify stability and control derivatives from flight test data is presented. This approach is based on finding inputs which provide the maximum possible accuracy of derivative estimates. Two techniques of input specification are implemented for this objective - a time domain technique and a frequency domain technique. The time domain technique gives the control input time history and can be used for any allowable duration of test maneuver, including those where data lengths can only be of

short duration. The frequency domain technique specifies the input frequency spectrum, and is best applied for tests where extended data lengths, much longer than the time constants of the modes of interest, are possible. These techniques are used to design inputs to identify parameters in longitudinal and lateral linear models of conventional aircraft. The constraints of aircraft response limits, such as on structural loads, are realized indirectly through a total energy constraint on the input. Tests with simulated data and theoretical predictions show that the new approaches give input signals which can provide more accurate parameter estimates than can conventional inputs of the same total energy. Results obtained indicate that the approach has been brought to the point where it should be used on flight tests for further evaluation.

*Systems Control, Inc., Palo Alto, California.

57. *McRuer, D. T.; and *Johnston, D. E.: **Flight Control Systems Properties and Problems, Volume 1**. NASA CR-2500, TR-1018-1-VOL-1, <u>February 1975</u>, 75N17371.

This volume contains a delineation of fundamental and mechanization-specific flight control characteristics and problems gleaned from many sources and spanning a period of over two decades. It is organized to present and discuss first some fundamental, generic problems of closed-loop flight control systems involving numerator characteristics (quadratic dipoles, non-minimum phase roots, and intentionally introduced zeros). Next the principal elements of the largely mechanical primary flight control system are reviewed with particular emphasis on the influence of nonlinearities. The characteristics and problems of augmentation (damping, stability, and feel) system mechanizations are then dealt with. The particular idiosyncrasies of automatic control actuation and command augmentation schemes are stressed, because they constitute the major interfaces with the primary flight control system and an often highly variable vehicle response.

*Systems Technology, Inc., Hawthorne, California.

58. *Johnston, D. E.: **Flight Control Systems Properties and Problems. Volume 2: Block Diagram Compendium**. NASA CR-2501, TR-1018-1-VOL-2, <u>February 1975</u>, 75N17372.

A compendium of stability augmentation system and autopilot block diagrams is presented. Descriptive materials for 48 different types of aircraft systems are provided. A broad representation of the many mechanical approaches which have been used for aircraft control is developed.

*Systems Technology, Inc., Hawthorne, California.

59. *Plumer, J. A.; *Fisher, F. A.; and *Walko, L. C.: **Lightning Effects on the NASA F-8 Digital-Fly-By-Wire Airplane**. NASA CR-2524, SRD-26-06, <u>March 1975</u>, 75N22334.

The effects of lightning on a Digital Fly-By-Wire (DFBW) aircraft control system were investigated. The aircraft was a NASA operated F-8 fitted with a modified Apollo guidance computer. Current pulses similar in waveshape to natural lightning, but lower in amplitude, were injected into the aircraft. Measurements were made of the voltages induced on the DFBW circuits, the total current induced on the bundles of wires, the magnetic field intensity inside the aircraft, and the current density on the skin of the aircraft. Voltage measurements were made in both the line-to-ground and line-to-line modes. Voltages measured at the non-destructive test level were then scaled upward to determine how much would be produced by actual lightning. A 200,000 ampere severe lightning flash would produce between 40 and 2000 volts in DFBW circuits. Some system components are expected to be vulnerable to these voltages.

*General Electric Co., Pittsfield, Massachusetts.

60. *Obermayer, R. W.; and *Roe, W. T.: **A Study of Carburetor/Induction Accidents**. NASA CR-143835, March 1975, 75N19208, #.

An assessment of the frequency and severity of carburetor/induction icing in general-aviation accidents was performed. The available literature and accident data from the National Transportation Safety Board were collected. A computer analysis of the accident data was performed. Between 65 and 90 accidents each year involve carburetor/induction system icing as a probable cause/factor. Under conditions conducive to carburetor/induction icing, between 50 and 70 percent of engine malfunction/failure accidents (exclusive of those due to fuel exhaustion) are due to carburetor/induction system icing. Since the evidence of such icing may not remain long after an accident, it is probable that the frequency of occurrence of such accidents is underestimated; therefore, some extrapolation of the data was conducted. The problem of carburetor/induction system icing is particularly acute for pilots with less than 1000 hours of total flying time. The severity of such accidents is about the same as any accident resulting from a forced landing or precautionary landing. About 144 persons, on the average, are exposed to death and injury each year in accidents involving carburetor/induction icing as a probable cause/factor.

*Manned Systems Sciences, Inc., Northridge, California.

61. *Lapins, M.; and *Jacobson, I. D.: **Application of Active Controls Technology to Aircraft Ride Smoothing Systems**. NASA CR-145980, ESS-4039-106-75, May 1975, 76N14138, #.

A critical review of past efforts in the design and testing of ride smoothing and gust alleviation systems is presented. Design trade offs involving sensor types, choice of feedback loops, human comfort, and aircraft handling-qualities criteria are discussed. Synthesis of a system designed to employ direct-lift and side-force producing surfaces is reported. Two

STOL aircraft and an executive transport are considered. Theoretically predicted system performance is compared with hybrid simulation and flight test data. Pilot opinion rating, pilot workload, and passenger comfort rating data for the basic and augmented aircraft are included.

*University of Virginia, Charlottesville, Virginia.

62. *Lange, R. H.; *Cahill, J. F.; *Campion, M. C.; *Bradley, E. S.; *MacWilkinson, D. G.; and *Phillips, J. W.: **Application of Active Controls Technology to the NASA JetStar Airplane**. NASA CR-2561, H-868, June 1975, 75N28049.

The feasibility was studied of modifying a Jet Star airplane into a demonstrator of benefits to be achieved from incorporating active control concepts in the preliminary design of transport type aircraft. Substantial benefits are shown in terms of fuel economy and community noise by virtue of reduction in induced drag through use of a high aspect ratio wing which is made possible by a gust alleviation system. An intermediate configuration was defined which helps to isolate the benefits produced by active controls technology from those due to other configuration variables. Also, an alternate configuration which incorporated composite structures, but not active controls technology, was defined in order to compare the benefits of composite structures with those of active controls technology.

*Lockheed-Georgia Co., Marietta, Georgia.

63. *Hoh, R. H.: **A Pilot Rating Scale for Vortex Hazard Evaluation**. NASA CR-143836, TR-1025-4/1, June 1975, 75N24695, #.

A pilot rating scale is developed for subjective assessment of hazard resulting from wake vortex encounter upsets. The development of the rating scale is based on a survey of 48 pilots regarding the semantic properties of various phrases and a choice of formats for the rating scale. The rating scale can be used to define a hazard/nonhazard boundary as well as to determine a measure of the hazard.

*Systems Technology, Inc., Hawthorne, California.

64. *Koltko, E.; *Katz, A.; *Bell, M. A.; *Smith, W. D.; *Lauridia, R.; *Overstreet, C. T.; *Klapprott, C.; *Orr, T. F.; *Jobe, C. L.; and *Wyatt, F. G.: **F-8 Oblique Wing Structural Feasibility Study**. NASA CR-154841, REPT-2-57000, 5R-3239, November 1975, 77N30107.

The feasibility of fitting a rotating oblique wing on an F-8 aircraft to produce a full scale manned prototype capable of operating in the transonic and supersonic speed range was investigated. The strength, aeroelasticity, and fatigue life of such a prototype are analyzed. Concepts are developed for a new wing, a pivot, a skewing mechanism, control systems that operate through the pivot, and a wing support assembly that attaches in the F-8 wing cavity. The modification of the two-place NTF-8A aircraft to the oblique wing configuration is discussed.

*LTV Aerospace Corp., Dallas, Texas.

65. *Scoggins, J. R.; *Clark, T. L.; and *Possiel, N. C.: **Relationships Between Stratospheric Clear Air Turbulence and Synoptic Meteorological Parameters Over the Western United States Between 12-20 km Altitude**. NASA CR-143837, H-919, <u>December 1975</u>, 76N14711, #.

Procedures for forecasting clear air turbulence in the stratosphere over the western United States from rawinsonde data are described and results presented. Approaches taken to relate meteorological parameters to regions of turbulence and nonturbulence encountered by the XB-70 during 46 flights at altitudes between 12-20 km include: empirical probabilities, discriminant function analysis, and mountainwave theory. Results from these techniques were combined into a procedure to forecast regions of clear air turbulence with an accuracy of 70–80 percent. A computer program was developed to provide an objective forecast directly from the rawinsonde sounding data.

*Texas A&M University, College Station, Texas.

1976 Contractor Reports

66. *Duba, R. J.; *Haramis, A. C.; *Marks, R. F.; *Payne, L.; and *Sessing, R. C.: **YF-12 Lockalloy Ventral Fin Program, Volume 1; Design Analysis, Fabrication, and Manufacturing of Aircraft Structures Using Aluminum and Beryllium Alloys for the Lockheed YF-12 Aircraft**. NASA CR-144971, <u>January 1976</u>, 76N23252.

Results are presented of the YF-12 Lockalloy Ventral Fin Program which was carried out by Lockheed Aircraft Corporation - Advanced Development Projects for the joint NASA/USAF YF-12 Project. The primary purpose of the program was to redesign and fabricate the ventral fin of the YF-12 research airplane (to reduce flutter) using Lockalloy, and alloy of beryllium and aluminum, as a major structural material. A secondary purpose, was to make a material characterization study (thermodynamic properties, corrosion; fatigue tests, mechanical properties) of Lockalloy to validate the design of the ventral fin and expand the existing data base on this material. All significant information pertinent to the design and fabrication of the ventral fin is covered. Emphasis throughout is given to Lockalloy fabrication and machining techniques and attendant personnel safety precautions. Costs are also examined. Photographs of tested alloy specimens are shown along with the test equipment used.

*Lockheed-California Co., Burbank, California.

67. *Duba, R. J.; *Haramis, A. C.; *Marks, R. F.; *Payne, L.; and *Sessing, R. C.: **YF-12 Lockalloy Ventral Fin Program, Volume 2; Design Analysis, Fabrication, and Manufacturing of Aircraft Structures Using Aluminum and Beryllium Alloys for the Lockheed YF-12 Aircraft**. NASA CR-144972, <u>January 1976</u>, 76N23253. (See also 66.)

*Lockheed-California Co., Burbank, California.

68. *Nardi, L. U.; *Kawana, H. Y.; *Borland, C. J.; and *Lefritz, N. M.: **Ride Qualities Criteria Validation/Pilot Performance Study: Flight Simulator Results**. NASA CR-143838, H-936, <u>March 1976</u>, 76N20825, #.

Pilot performance was studied during simulated manual terrain following flight for ride quality criteria validation. An existing B-1 simulation program provided the data for these investigations. The B-1 simulation program included terrain following flights under varying controlled conditions of turbulence, terrain, mission length, and system dynamics. The flight simulator consisted of a moving base cockpit which reproduced motions due to turbulence and control inputs. The B-1 aircraft dynamics were programmed with six-degrees-of-freedom equations of motion with three symmetric and two antisymmetric structural degrees of freedom. The results provided preliminary validation of existing ride quality criteria and identified several ride quality/handling quality parameters which may be of value in future ride quality/criteria development.

*Rockwell International Corp., Los Angeles, California.

69. Steers, L. L.; and Montoya, L. C.: **Study of Aerodynamic Drag Reduction on a Full-Scale Tractor-Trailer**. NASA CR-148806, Department of Transportation, PB-254571/3, DOT-TSC-OST-76-13, <u>April 1976</u>, 76N33142, #.

Aerodynamic drag tests were performed on a tractor trailer combination using the coast-down method on a smooth, nearly level runway. The tests included an investigation of drag reduction obtained with add on devices that are commercially available or under development. The tests covered tractor trailer speeds ranging from approximately 35 to 65 miles per hour and included fuel consumption measurements. The study shows the effects of the various add on devices on the aerodynamic drag, and for some devices on the fuel consumption. Results from a simulation of fuel consumption tests using a computer program are also included.

70. *Muirhead, V. U.: **An Investigation of Drag Reduction on Box-Shaped Ground Vehicles**. NASA CR-148829, KU-FRL-180, <u>July 1976</u>, 76N32127, #.

A wind tunnel investigation was conducted to determine the reduction in drag which could be obtained by making various configuration changes to a box-shaped ground vehicle. Tests were conducted at yaw (relative wind) angles of 0, 5, 10, 20, and 30 degrees and Reynolds numbers of 300,000 to 850,000. The power required to overcome the aerodynamic drag was reduced by a maximum of 73% for a head wind for the best configuration relative to the smooth bottom box-shape, or 75% relative to the rough bottom box-shape. The reduction for a 20 MPH wind at 30 deg to the vehicle path was, respectively, 77% and 79%.

*University of Kansas, Lawrence, Kansas.

71. *Balakrishnan, A. V.; and Maine, R. E.: **Improvements in Aircraft Extraction Programs**. NASA CR-145090, 1976, 77N13043, #.

Flight data from an F-8 Corsair and a Cessna 172 was analyzed to demonstrate specific improvements in the LRC parameter extraction computer program. The Cramer-Rao bounds were shown to provide a satisfactory relative measure of goodness of parameter estimates. It was not used as an absolute measure due to an inherent uncertainty within a multiplicative factor, traced in turn to the uncertainty in the noise bandwidth in the statistical theory of parameter estimation. The measure was also derived on an entirely nonstatistical basis, yielding thereby also an interpretation of the significance of off-diagonal terms in the dispersion matrix. The distinction between coefficients as linear and non-linear was shown to be important in its implication to a recommended order of parameter iteration. Techniques of improving convergence generally, were developed, and tested out on flight data. In particular, an easily implemented modification incorporating a gradient search was shown to improve initial estimates and thus remove a common cause for lack of convergence.

*University of California at Los Angeles, Los Angeles, California.

1977 Contractor Reports

72. *Roberts, P. A.; *Swaim, R. L.; *Schmidt, D. K.; and *Hinsdale, A. J.: **Effects of Control Laws and Relaxed Static Stability on Vertical Ride Quality of Flexible Aircraft**. NASA CR-143843, H-962, April 1977, 77N23127, #.

State variable techniques are utilized to generate the RMS vertical load factors for the B-52H and B-1 bombers at low level, mission critical, cruise conditions. A ride quality index is proposed to provide meaningful comparisons between different controls or conditions. Ride quality is shown to be relatively invariant under various popular control laws. Handling quality variations are shown to be major contributors to ride quality variations on both vehicles. Relaxed static stability is artificially implemented on the study vehicles to investigate its effects on ride quality. The B-52H ride quality is generally degraded when handling

characteristics are automatically restored by a feedback control to the original values from relaxed stability conditions. The B-1 airplane shows little ride quality sensitivity to the same analysis due to the small rigid body contribution to load factors at the flight condition investigated.

*Purdue University, West Lafayette, Indiana.

73. *Jenks, G. E.; *Henry, H. F.; and *Roskam, J.: **Flight Test Results for a Separate Surface Stability Augmented Beech Model 99**. NASA CR-143839, KU-FRL-364, April 1977, 77N21083, #.

A flight evaluation of a Beech model 99 equipped with an attitude command control system incorporating separate surface stability augmentation (SSSA) was conducted to determine whether an attitude command control system could be implemented using separate surface controls, and to determine whether the handling and ride qualities of the aircraft were improved by the SSSA attitude command system. The results of the program revealed that SSSA is a viable approach to implementing attitude command and also that SSSA has the capability of performing less demanding augmentation tasks such as yaw damping, wing leveling, and pitch damping. The program also revealed that attitude command did improve the pilot rating and ride qualities of the airplane while flying an IFR mission in turbulence. Some disadvantages of the system included the necessity of holding aileron force in a banked turn and excessive stiffness in the pitch axis.

*University of Kansas, Lawrence, Kansas.

74. *Whitaker, P. H.: **Development of a Parameter Optimization Technique for the Design of Automatic Control Systems**. NASA CR-143844, H-978, May 1977, 77N27126, #.

Parameter optimization techniques for the design of linear automatic control systems that are applicable to both continuous and digital systems are described. The model performance index is used as the optimization criterion because of the physical insight that can be attached to it. The design emphasis is to start with the simplest system configuration that experience indicates would be practical. Design parameters are specified, and a digital computer program is used to select that set of parameter values which minimizes the performance index. The resulting design is examined, and complexity, through the use of more complex information processing or more feedback paths, is added only if performance fails to meet operational specifications. System performance specifications are assumed to be such that the desired step function time response of the system can be inferred.

*Massachusetts Institute of Technology, Cambridge, Massachusetts.

75. *Gingrich, P. B.; *Child, R. D.; and *Panageas, G. N.: **Aerodynamic Configuration Development of the Highly Maneuverable Aircraft Technology Remotely Piloted Research Vehicle**. NASA CR-143841, NA-76-865, June 1977, 77N26076, #.

The aerodynamic development of the highly maneuverable aircraft technology remotely piloted research vehicle (HiMAT/RPRV) from the conceptual design to the final configuration is presented. The design integrates several advanced concepts to achieve a high degree of transonic maneuverability, and was keyed to sustained maneuverability goals while other fighter typical performance characteristics were maintained. When tests of the baseline configuration indicated deficiencies in the technology integration and design techniques, the vehicle was reconfigured to satisfy the subcritical and supersonic requirements. Drag-due-to-lift levels only 5 percent higher than the optimum were obtained for the wind tunnel model at a lift coefficient of 1 for Mach numbers of up to 0.8. The transonic drag rise was progressively lowered with the application of nonlinear potential flow analyses coupled with experimental data.

*Rockwell International Corp., Los Angeles, California.

76. *Anon.: **Design and Development of a Structural Mode Control System**. NASA CR-143846, NA-77-296, October 1977, 77N33201, #.

A program was conducted to compile and document some of the existing information about the conceptual design, development, and tests of the B-1 structural mode control system (SMCS) and its impact on ride quality. This report covers the following topics: (1) Rationale of selection of SMCS to meet ride quality criteria versus basic aircraft stiffening. (2) Key considerations in designing an SMCS, including vane geometry, rate and deflection requirements, power required, compensation network design, and fail-safe requirements. (3) Summary of key results of SMCS vane wind tunnel tests. (4) SMCS performance. (5) SMCS design details, including materials, bearings, and actuators. (6) Results of qualification testing of SMCS on the "Iron Bird" flight control simulator, and lab qualification testing of the actuators. (7) Impact of SMCS vanes on engine inlet characteristics from wind tunnel tests.

*Rockwell International Corp., Los Angeles, California.

77. *Swaroop, R.: **Analysis of Responses of Cold Pressor Tests on Pilots and Executives**. NASA CR-143847, November 1977, 78N10693, #.

Statistical analyses were performed to study the relationship between cold pressor test responses and certain medical attributes of a group of 81 pilots and a group of 466 executives. The important results of this study were as follows: There was a significant relationship between a subject's cold pressor test response and his profession (that is, pilot or executive). The executives' diastolic cold pressor test responses were significantly related to their medical conditions, and their families' medical conditions. Significant relationships were observed between executives' diastolic and systolic cold pressor test responses and their history of tranquilizer and cardiac drug use.

*System Development Corp., Edwards, California.

78. *Muckler, Fred; *Obermayer, Richard W.; and Nicklas, Douglass R.: **Pilot Performance Measurement Study**. NASA CR-143842, December 1977.

A study was made of aircrew performance in the high-performance YF-12 aircraft in the course of aerodynamic flight testing at the Dryden Flight Research Center. The study objectives were the development of system performance and objective crew performance sets, the investigation of objective, subjective, and physiological crew performance measures, the development of measurements for such applications as crew workload analysis and crew-station control-display evaluation, and the development of practical and feasible automatic and semiautomatic data processing techniques. Five data sources were considered: Physiological recordings, onboard pulse-code-modulation (PCM) and telemetry recordings, audio recordings, crew interviews, and ground-based flight observations and records. A prototype data processing system was developed, and the FORTRAN program listings are included. Complete data reduction was not within the scope of the study, but it was concluded that the measurement sets and data handling methods developed are viable and the this particular aircraft environment is a rich source of human performance data which should prove valuable in modeling human performance in complex, high performance aircraft systems.

*Manned Systems Sciences, Inc. Northridge, California.

1978 Contractor Reports

79. *Johnson, S. H.: **Aircraft Model Prototypes Which Have Specified Handling-Quality Time Histories**. NASA CR-143848, January 1978, 78N14054, #.

Several techniques for obtaining linear constant-coefficient airplane models from specified handling-quality time histories are discussed. The pseudodata method solves the basic problem, yields specified eigenvalues, and accommodates state-variable transfer-function zero suppression. The algebraic equations to be solved are bilinear, at worst. The disadvantages are reduced generality and no assurance that the resulting model will be airplane like in detail. The method is fully illustrated for a fourth-order stability-axis small motion model with three lateral handling quality time histories specified. The FORTRAN program which obtains and verifies the model is included and fully documented.

*Lehigh University, Bethlehem, Pennsylvania.

80. *Porter, R. F.; *Hall, D. W.; *Brown, J. H., Jr.; and *Gregorek, G. M.: **Analytical Study of a Free-Wing/Free-Trimmer Concept; for Gust Alleviation and High Lift**. NASA CR-2946, February 1978, 78N18000.

The free-wing/free-trimmer is a NASA-Conceived extension of the free-wing concept intended to permit the use of high-lift flaps. Wing pitching moments are balanced by a smaller, external surface attached by a boom or equivalent structure. The external trimmer is, itself, a miniature free wing, and pitch control of the wing-trimmer assembly is effected through a trailing-edge control tab on the trimmer surface. The longitudinal behavior of representative small free-wing/free-trimmer aircraft was analyzed. Aft-mounted trimmer surfaces are found to be superior to forward trimmers, although the permissible trimmer moment arm is limited, in both cases, by adverse dynamic effects. Aft-trimmer configurations provide excellent gust alleviation and meet fundamental stick-fixed stability criteria while exceeding the lift capabilities of pure free-wing configurations.

*Battelle Columbus Laboratories, Columbus, Ohio.

81. *Swaroop, R.; and *Ashworth, G. R.: **An Analysis of Flight Data From Aircraft Landings With and Without the Aid of a Painted Diamond on the Same Runway**. NASA CR-143849, February 1978, 78N15692, #.

The usefulness of a painted diamond on a runway as a visual aid to perform safe landings of aircraft was studied. Flight data on glideslope intercepts, flight path elevation angles, and touchdown distances were collected and analyzed. It is concluded that an appropriately painted diamond on a runway has the potential of providing glideslope information for the light weight class of general aviation aircraft. This conclusion holds irrespective of the differences in landing techniques used by the pilots.

*System Development Corp., Edwards, California.

82. *Siegel, W. H.: **Experimental and Finite Element Investigation of the Buckling Characteristics of a Beaded Skin Panel for a Hypersonic Aircraft; Ph.D. Thesis**. NASA CR-144863, April 1978, 78N20534.

As part of NASA's continuing research into hypersonics an 85 square foot hypersonic wing test section of a proposed hypersonic research airplane was laboratory tested. The project reported on in this paper has carried the hypersonic wing test structure project one step further by testing a single beaded panel to failure. The primary interest was focused upon the buckling characteristics of the panel under pure compression with boundary conditions similar to those found in a wing mounted condition. Three primary phases of analysis are included in the report. These phases include: experimental testing of the beaded panel to failure; finite element structural analysis of the beaded panel with the computer program NASTRAN; a summary of the semiclassical buckling equations for the beaded panel under

purely compressive loads. Comparisons between each of the analysis methods are also included.

*University of Kansas, Center for Research, Inc., Lawrence, Kansas.

83. *Anon.: **Description and Theory of Operation of the Computer By-Pass System for the NASA F-8 Digital Fly-By-Wire Control System**. NASA CR-144865, May 1978, 78N22076.

A triplex digital flight control system was installed in a NASA F-8C airplane to provide fail operate, full authority control. The triplex digital computers and interface circuitry process the pilot commands and aircraft motion feedback parameters according to the selected control laws, and they output the surface commands as an analog signal to the servoelectronics for position control of the aircraft's power actuators. The system and theory of operation of the computer by pass and servoelectronics are described and an automated ground test for each axis is included.

*Sperry Flight Systems, Phoenix, Arizona.

84. *Stevens, C. H.; *Spong, E. D.; and *Hammock, M. S.: **F-15 Inlet/Engine Test Techniques and Distortion Methodologies Studies. Volume 1: Technical Discussion**. NASA CR-144866, June 1978, 78N30123, #.

Peak distortion data taken from a subscale inlet model were studied to determine if the data can be used to predict peak distortion levels for a full scale flight test vehicle, and to provide a better understanding of the time variant total pressure distortion and the attendant effects of Reynolds number/scale and frequency content. The data base used to accomplish this goal covered a range from Mach 0.4 to 2.5 and an angle of attack range from -10 degrees to $+12$ degrees. Data are presented which show that: (1) increasing the Reynolds number increases total pressure recovery, decreases peak distortion, and decreases turbulence, (2) increasing the filter cutoff frequency increases both peak distortion and turbulence, and (3) the effect of engine presence on total pressure recovery, peak distortion, and turbulence is small but favorable.

*McDonnell Aircraft Co., St. Louis, Missouri.

85. *Stevens, C. H.; *Spong, E. D.; and *Hammock, M. S.: **F-15 Inlet/Engine Test Techniques and Distortion Methodologies Studies. Volume 2: Time Variant Data Quality Analysis Plots**. NASA CR-144867, June 1978, 78N30124, #.

Time variant data quality analysis plots were used to determine if peak distortion data taken from a subscale inlet model can be used to predict peak distortion levels for a full scale flight test vehicle.

*McDonnell Aircraft Co., St. Louis, Missouri.

86. *Stevens, C. H.; *Spong, E. D.; and *Hammock, M. S.: **F-15 Inlet/Engine Test Techniques and Distortion Methodologies Studies. Volume 3: Power Spectral Density Plots**. NASA CR-144868, <u>June 1978</u>, 78N30125, #.

Power spectral density plots were used to determine if peak distortion data taken from a subscale inlet model can be used to predict peak distortion levels for a full scale flight test vehicle.

*McDonnell Aircraft Co., St. Louis, Missouri.

87. *Stevens, C. H.; *Spong, E. D.; and *Hammock, M. S.: **F-15 Inlet/Engine Test Techniques and Distortion Methodologies Studies. Volume 4: Autocorrelation Functions**. NASA CR-144869, <u>June 1978</u>, 78N30126, #.

Autocorrelation function plots were used to determine if peak distortion data taken from a subscale inlet model can be used to predict peak distortion levels for a full scale flight test vehicle.

*McDonnell Aircraft Co., St. Louis, Missouri.

88. *Stevens, C. H.; *Spong, E. D.; and *Hammock, M. S.: **F-15 Inlet/Engine Test Techniques and Distortion Methodologies Studies. Volume 5: Effect of Filter Cutoff Frequency on Turbulence Plots**. NASA CR-144870, <u>June 1978</u>, 78N30127, #.

The effect of filter cutoff frequency on turbulence plots were used to determine if peak distortion data taken from a subscale inlet model can be used to predict peak distortion levels for a full scale flight test vehicle.

*McDonnell Aircraft Co., St. Louis, Missouri.

89. *Stevens, C. H.; *Spong, E. D.; and *Hammock, M. S.: **F-15 Inlet/Engine Test Techniques and Distortion Methodologies Studies. Volume 6: Distortion Analysis Plots**. NASA CR-144871, <u>June 1978</u>, 78N30128, #.

Distortion analysis plots were used to determine if peak distortion data taken from a subscale inlet model can be used to predict peak distortion levels for a full scale flight test vehicle.

*McDonnell Aircraft Co., St. Louis, Missouri.

90. *Stevens, C. H.; *Spong, E. D.; and *Hammock, M. S.: **F-15 Inlet/Engine Test Techniques and Distortion Methodologies Studies. Volume 7: Cross Correlation Functions**. NASA CR-144872, <u>June 1978</u>, 78N30129, #.

Cross correlation function plots were used to determine if peak distortion data taken from a subscale inlet model can be

used to predict peak distortion levels for a full scale flight test vehicle.

*McDonnell Aircraft Co., St. Louis, Missouri.

91. *Stevens, C. H.; *Spong, E. D.; and *Hammock, M. S.: **F-15 Inlet/Engine Test Techniques and Distortion Methodologies Studies. Volume 8: Cross Spectral Density Plots**. NASA CR-144873, <u>June 1978</u>, 78N30130, #.

Cross spectral density plots were used to determine if peak distortion data taken from a subscale inlet model can be used to predict peak distortion levels for a full scale flight test vehicle.

*McDonnell Aircraft Co., St. Louis, Missouri.

92. *Stevens, C. H.; *Spong, E. D.; and *Hammock, M. S.: **F-15 Inlet/Engine Test Techniques and Distortion Methodologies Studies. Volume 9: Stability Audits**. NASA CR-144874, <u>June 1978</u>, 78N30131, #.

Stability audit plots were used to determine if peak distortion data taken from a subscale inlet model can be used to predict peak distortion levels for a full scale flight test vehicle.

*McDonnell Aircraft Co., St. Louis, Missouri.

93. *Carlin, C. M.; and Hastings, W. J.: **Propulsion/ Flight Control Integration Technology (Profit) Design Analysis Status**. NASA CR-144875, <u>July 1978</u>, 78N29101, #.

The propulsion flight control integration technology (PROFIT) program was designed to develop a flying testbed dedicated to controls research. The preliminary design, analysis, and feasibility studies conducted in support of the PROFIT program are reported. The PROFIT system was built around existing IPCS hardware. In order to achieve the desired system flexibility and capability, additional interfaces between the IPCS hardware and F-15 systems were required. The requirements for additions and modifications to the existing hardware were defined. Those interfaces involving the more significant changes were studied. The DCU memory expansion to 32K with flight qualified hardware was completed on a brassboard basis. The uplink interface breadboard and a brassboard of the central computer interface were also tested. Two preliminary designs and corresponding program plans are presented.

*Boeing Aerospace Co., Seattle, Washington.

94. *Carlin, C. M.; and Hastings, W. J.: **Propulsion/Flight Control Integration Technology (Profit) Software System Definition**. NASA CR-144876, <u>July 1978</u>, 78N29102, #.

The Propulsion Flight Control Integration Technology (PROFIT) program is designed to develop a flying testbed

442

dedicated to controls research. The control software for PROFIT is defined. Maximum flexibility, needed for long term use of the flight facility, is achieved through a modular design. The Host program, processes inputs from the telemetry uplink, aircraft central computer, cockpit computer control and plant sensors to form an input data base for use by the control algorithms. The control algorithms, programmed as application modules, process the input data to generate an output data base. The Host program formats the data for output to the telemetry downlink, the cockpit computer control, and the control effectors. Two applications modules are defined - the bill of materials F-100 engine control and the bill of materials F-15 inlet control.

*Boeing Aerospace Co., Seattle, Washington.

95. *Muirhead, V. U.: **An Investigation of Drag Reduction for Tractor Trailer Vehicles**. NASA CR-144877, KU-FRL-322-1, <u>October 1978</u>, 78N33444, #.

Force and moment data were obtained from a one-twenty-fifth scale wind tunnel model of a cab-over-engine tractor trailer combination. The tests define the aerodynamic characteristics of the baseline (unmodified) vehicle and several modified configurations. The primary modifications consist of: (1) greatly increased forebody corner radii, (2) a smooth fairing over the cab-to-trailer gap, (3) a smoothed underbody, and (4) rear streamlining (boattailing)of the trailer. Tests were conducted for yaw angles from 0 deg to 30 deg. The reduction in drag, relative to the baseline, obtained by combining the modifications are compared for the zero yaw condition with full scale coast down drag results for similar configurations. The drag reductions obtained from the model and full scale tests are in good agreement.

*University of Kansas, Lawrence, Kansas.

96. *Lorincz, D. J.: **A Water Tunnel Flow Visualization Study of the F-15**. NASA CR-144878, NOR-78-176, <u>December 1978</u>, 79N18286.

Water tunnel studies were performed to qualitatively define the flow field of the F-15 aircraft. Two lengthened forebodies, one with a modified cross-sectional shape, were tested in addition to the basic forebody. Particular emphasis was placed on defining vortex flows generated at high angles of attack. The flow visualization tests were conducted in the Northrop diagnostic water tunnel using a 1/48-scale model of the F-15. Flow visualization pictures were obtained over an angle-of-attack range to 55 deg and sideslip angles up to 10 deg. The basic aircraft configuration was investigated in detail to determine the vortex flow field development, vortex path, and vortex breakdown characteristics as a function of angle of attack and sideslip. Additional tests showed that the wing upper surface vortex flow fields were sensitive to variations in inlet mass flow ratio and inlet cowl deflection angle. Asymmetries in the vortex systems generated by each

of the three forebodies were observed in the water tunnel at zero sideslip and high angles of attack.

*Northrop Corporate Labs., Hawthorne, California.

97. *Wolf, J. A.: **Investigation of the Cross-Ship Comparison Monitoring Method of Failure Detection in the HIMAT RPRV; Digital Control Techniques Using Airborne Microprocessors**. NASA CR-144879, <u>December 1978</u>, 79N12064, #.

The Highly maneuverable aircraft technology (HiMAT) remotely piloted research vehicle (RPRV) uses cross-ship comparison monitoring of the actuator RAM positions to detect a failure in the aileron, canard, and elevator control surface servosystems. Some possible sources of nuisance trips for this failure detection technique are analyzed. A FORTRAN model of the simplex servosystems and the failure detection technique were utilized to provide a convenient means of changing parameters and introducing system noise. The sensitivity of the technique to differences between servosystems and operating conditions was determined. The cross-ship comparison monitoring method presently appears to be marginal in its capability to detect an actual failure and to withstand nuisance trips.

*University of Kansas, Center for Research, Inc., Lawrence, Kansas.

1979 Contractor Reports

98. *Grose, D. L.: **The Development of the DAST I Remotely Piloted Research Vehicle for Flight Testing an Active Flutter Suppression Control System**; Ph.D. Thesis. NASA CR-144881, <u>February 1979</u>, 79N17849, #.

The development of the DAST I (drones for aerodynamic and structural testing) remotely piloted research vehicle is described. The DAST I is a highly modified BQM-34E/F Firebee II Supersonic Aerial Target incorporating a swept supercritical wing designed to flutter within the vehicle's flight envelope. The predicted flutter and rigid body characteristics are presented. A description of the analysis and design of an active flutter suppression control system (FSS) designed to increase the flutter boundary of the DAST wing (ARW-1) by a factor of 20% is given. The design and development of the digital remotely augmented primary flight control system and on-board analog backup control system is presented. An evaluation of the near real-time flight flutter testing methods is made by comparing results of five flutter testing techniques on simulated DAST I flutter data. The development of the DAST ARW-1 state variable model used to generate time histories of simulated accelerometer responses is presented. This model uses control surface commands and a Dryden model gust as inputs. The feasibility of the concept of extracting open loop flutter characteristics from closed loop FSS responses was examined. It was shown that open loop characteristics can be determined very well from closed loop subcritical responses.

*University of Kansas, Lawrence, Kansas.

99. *Porter, R. F.; *Hall, D. W.; and *Vergara, R. D.: **Extended Analytical Study of the Free-Wing/Free-Trimmer Concept.** NASA CR-3135, <u>April 1979</u>, 79N22040.

The free wing/free trimmer concept was analytically studied in order to: (1) compare the fore and aft trimmer configurations on the basis of equal lift capability, rather than equal area; (2) assess the influence of tip mounted aft trimmers, both free and fixed, on the lateral directional modes and turbulence responses; (3) examine the feasibility of using differential tip mounted trimmer deflection for lateral control; (4) determine the effects of independent fuselage attitude on the lateral directional behavior; and (5) estimate the influence of wing sweep on dynamic behavior and structural weight. Results indicate that the forward trimmer concept is feasible with the reduced size examined, but it remains inferior to the aft trimmer in every respect except structural weight. Differential motion of the aft trimmer is found to provide powerful lateral control; while the effect of fuselage deck angle is a reduction of the dutch roll damping ratio for nose-down attitudes.

*Battelle Columbus Laboratories, Columbus, Ohio.

100. *Brownlow, J. D.; and *Swaroop, R.: **Beta Distributions: a Computer Program for Probabilities and Fractile Points.** NASA CR-144880, <u>May 1, 1979</u>, 79N21847, #.

A beta distribution is specified by range parameters a b, and two shape parameters alpha and beta 0. The computer program presented calculates any desired probability and/or fractile point for specified values of a, b, alpha, and beta. This program additionally computes gamma function values for integer and noninteger arguments.

*System Development Corp., Edwards, California.

101. *Dobbs, S. K.; and *Hodson, C. H.: **Determination of Subcritical Frequency and Damping From B-1 Flight Flutter Test Data.** NASA CR-3152, <u>June 1979</u>, 79N25426.

The application of the time-lag products correlation/frequency analysis procedure to determine subcritical frequency and damping from structural response measurements made during flight flutter test of the B-1 prototype airplane is described. The analysis procedure, the test airplane, and flight test procedures are discussed. Summary frequency and damping results are presented for six transonic flight conditions. Illustrative results obtained by applying various options and variations of the analysis method are included for one flight condition.

*Rockwell International Corp., Los Angeles, California.

102. *Gowadia, N. S.; *Bard, W. D.; and **Wooten, W. H.: **YF-17/ADEN System Study.** NASA CR-144882, <u>July 1979</u>, 79N27126, #.

The YF-17 aircraft was evaluated as a candidate nonaxisymmetric nozzle flight demonstrator. Configuration design modifications, control system design, flight performance assessment, and program plan and cost we are summarized. Two aircraft configurations were studied. The first was modified as required to install only the augmented deflector exhaust nozzle (ADEN). The second one added a canard installation to take advantage of the full (up to 20 deg) nozzle vectoring capability. Results indicate that: (1) the program is feasible and can be accomplished at reasonable cost and low risk; (2) installation of ADEN increases the aircraft weight by 600 kg (1325 lb); (3) the control system can be modified to accomplish direct lift, pointing capability, variable static margin and deceleration modes of operation; (4) unvectored thrust-minus-drag is similar to the baseline YF-17; and (5) vectoring does not improve maneuvering performance. However, some potential benefits in direct lift, aircraft pointing, handling at low dynamic pressure and takeoff/landing ground roll are available. A 27 month program with 12 months of flight test is envisioned, with the cost estimated to be $15.9 million for the canard equipped aircraft and $13.2 million for the version without canard. The feasiblity of adding a thrust reverser to the YF-17/ADEN was investigated.

*Northrop Corp., Hawthorne, California.
**General Electric Co., Hawthorne, California.

103. *Nardi, L. U.; *Kawana, H. Y.; and *Greek, D. C.: **Ride Qualities Criteria Validation/Pilot Performance Study: Flight Test Results.** NASA CR-144885, <u>September 1979</u>, 79N31193, #.

Pilot performance during a terrain following flight was studied for ride quality criteria validation. Data from manual and automatic terrain following operations conducted during low level penetrations were analyzed to determine the effect of ride qualities on crew performance. The conditions analyzed included varying levels of turbulence, terrain roughness, and mission duration with a ride smoothing system on and off. Limited validation of the B-1 ride quality criteria and some of the first order interactions between ride qualities and pilot/vehicle performance are highlighted. An earlier B-1 flight simulation program correlated well with the flight test results.

*Rockwell International Corp., Los Angeles, California.

104. *Gamon, M. A.: **Testing and Analysis of Dual-Mode Adaptive Landing Gear, Taxi Mode Test System for YF-12A.** NASA CR-144884, LR-28776, <u>September 1979</u>, 79N31192, #.

The effectiveness of a dual mode adaptive landing gear system in reducing the dynamic response of an airplane during ground taxiing was studied. The dynamic taxi tests of the YF-12A research airplane are presented. A digital computer program which simulated the test conditions is discussed. The dual mode system as tested provides dynamic taxi response reductions of 25 percent at the cg and 30 to 45 percent at the cockpit.

*Lockheed-California Co., Burbank, California.

105. *Price, M. A.: **HiMAT Structural Development Design Methodology; Aeroelastic Tailoring of the Canard and Wing Box and Distributed Load Tests**. NASA CR-144886, October 1979, 79N32197, #.

In order to improve aerodynamic performance, a twist criterion was used to design the canard and wing lifting surfaces of two graphite-epoxy research aircraft. To meet that twist criterion, the lifting surfaces were tailored using graphite-epoxy tape. The outer surface of the aircraft is essentially constructed of 95 percent graphite epoxy materials. The analytical tools and methodology used to design those lifting surfaces are described. One aircraft was subjected to an 8g ground test in order to verify structural integrity and to determine how well the desired twist was achieved. Test results are presented and the reductions of both flight and ground strain test gages and their associated stresses are discussed.

*Rockwell International Corp., Los Angeles, California.

106. *Hartmann, G. L.; *Barrett, M. F.; and *Greene, C. S.: **Control Design for an Unstable Vehicle**. NASA CR-170393, December 1979, 83N74196.

There is no abstract available for this record.

*Honeywell, Inc., Minneapolis, Minnesota.

===================================

1980 Contractor Reports

107. *Wykes, J. H.; *Byar, T. R.; *MacMiller, C. J.; and *Greek, D. C.: **Analyses and Tests of the B-1 Aircraft Structural Mode Control System**. NASA CR-144887, H-1109, NA-79-405, January 1980, 80N15073, #.

Analyses and flight tests of the B-1 structural mode control system (SMCS) are presented. Improvements in the total dynamic response of a flexible aircraft and the benefits to ride qualities, handling qualities, crew efficiency, and reduced dynamic loads on the primary structures, were investigated. The effectiveness and the performance of the SMCS, which uses small aerodynamic surfaces at the vehicle nose to provide damping to the structural modes, were evaluated.

*Rockwell International Corp., El Segundo, California.

108. *Lorincz, D. J.: **Flow Visualization Study of the HiMAT RPRV**. NASA CR-163094, NOR-80-128, February 1980, 80N31381.

Water tunnel studies were performed to qualitatively define the flow field of the highly maneuverable aircraft technology remotely piloted research vehicle (HiMAT RPRV). Particular emphasis was placed on defining the vortex flows generated at high angles of attack. The flow visualization tests were conducted in the Northrop water tunnel using a 1/5 scale model of the HiMAT RPRV. Flow visualization photographs were obtained for angles of attack up to 40 deg and sideslip angles up to 5 deg. The HiMAT model was investigated in detail to determine the canard and wing vortex flow field development, vortex paths, and vortex breakdown characteristics as a function of angle of attack and sideslip. The presence of the canard caused the wing vortex to form further outboard and delayed the breakdown of the wing vortex to higher angles of attack. An increase in leading edge camber of the maneuver configuration delayed both the formation and the breakdown of the wing and canard vortices. Additional tests showed that the canard vortex was sensitive to variations in inlet mass flow ratio and canard flap deflection angle.

*Northrop Corp., Hawthorne, California.

109. *Lorincz, D. J.: **Space Shuttle Orbiter Flow Visualization Study; Water Tunnel Study of Vortex Flow During Atmospheric Entry**. NASA CR-163092, NOR-80-82, February 1980, 80N31438.

The vortex flows generated at subsonic speed during the final portion of atmospheric reentry were defined using a 0.01 scale model of the orbiter in a diagnostic water tunnel. Flow visualization photographs were obtained over an angle-of-attack range to 40 deg and sideslip angles up to 10 deg. The vortex flow field development, vortex path, and vortex breakdown characteristics were determined as a function of angle-of-attack at zero sideslip. Vortex flows were found to develop on the highly swept glove, on the wing, and on the upper surface of the fuselage. No significant asymmetries were observed at zero sideslip in the water tunnel tests. The sensitivity of the upper surface vortex flow fields to variations in sideslip angle was also studied. The vortex formed on the glove remained very stable in position above the wing up through the 10 deg of sideslip tested. There was a change in the vortex lifts under sideslip due to effective change in leading-edge sweep angles. Asymmetric flow separation occurred on the upper surface of the fuselage at small sideslip angles. The influence of vortex flow fields in sideslip on the lateral/ directional characteristics of the orbiter is discussed.

*Northrop Corp., Hawthorne, California.

110. *Anon.: **Integrated Research Aircraft Control Technology With Full Authority Digital Electronic**

Control. NASA CR-163100, FR-11792, <u>April 1980</u>, 83N15318.

Baseline definitions for three major areas of the Integrated Research Aircraft Control Technology (INTERACT) program are provided.

*Pratt and Whitney Aircraft Group, Government Products Div., West Palm Beach, Florida.

111. *Radford, R. C.; *Smith, R.; and *Bailey, R.: **Landing Flying Qualities Evaluation Criteria for Augmented Aircraft**. NASA CR-163097, CALSPAN-6339-F-3, <u>June 1980</u>, 81N13969.

The criteria evaluated were: Calspan Neal-Smith; Onstott (Northrop Time Domain); McDonnell-Douglas Equivalent System Approach; R. H. Smith Criterion. Each criterion was applied to the same set of longitudinal approach and landing flying qualities data. A revised version of the Neal-Smith criterion which is applicable to the landing task was developed and tested against other landing flying qualities data. Results indicated that both the revised Neal-Smith criterion and the Equivalent System Approach are good discriminators of pitch landing flying qualities; Neal-Smith has particular merit as a design guide, while the Equivalent System Approach is well suited for development of appropriate military specification requirements applicable to highly augmented aircraft.

*Calspan Advanced Technology Center, Buffalo, New York.

112. *Lorincz, D. J.: **Flow Visualization Study of Spanwise Blowing Applied to the F-4 Fighter Aircraft Configuration; Water Tunnel Test Using a 1/48-Scale Model**. NASA CR-163096, NOR-80-138, <u>August 1980</u>, 81N21009.

Water tunnel studies were performed to define the changes that occur in vortex flow fields above the wing due to spanwise blowing over the inboard and outboard wing panels and over the trailing-edge flaps. Flow visualization photographs were obtained for angles of attack up to 30 deg and sideslip angles up to 10 deg. The sensitivity of the vortex flows to changes in flap deflection angle, nozzle position, and jet momentum coefficient was determined. Deflection of the leading edge flap delayed flow separation and the formation of the wing vortex to higher angles of attack. Spanwise blowing delayed the breakdown of the wing vortex to farther outboard and to higher angles of attack. Spanwise blowing over the trailing edge flap entrained flow downward, producing a lift increase over a wide range of angles of attack. The sweep angle of the windward wing was effectively reduced in sideslip. This decreased the stability of the wing vortex, and it burst farther inboard. Reduced wing sweep required a higher blowing rate to maintain a stable vortex. A vortex could be stabilized on the outboard wing panel when an outboard blowing nozzle was used. Blowing from both an inboard and an outboard nozzle was found to have a favorable interaction.

*Northrop Corp., Hawthorne, California.

113. *Lorincz, D. J.: **Flow Visualization Study of the F-14 Fighter Aircraft Configuration**. NASA CR-163098, NOR-80-150, H-1135, <u>September 1980</u>, 80N33350.

Water tunnel studies were performed to qualitatively define the flow field of the F-14. Particular emphasis was placed on defining the vortex flows generated at high angles of attack. The flow visualization tests were conducted in the Northrop water tunnel using a 1/72 scale model of the F-14 with a wing leading-edge sweep of 20 deg. Flow visualization photographs were obtained for angles of attack up to 55 deg and sideslip angles up to 10 deg. The F-14 model was investigated to determine the vortex flow field development, vortex path, and vortex breakdown characteristics as a function of angle of attack and sideslip. Vortex flows were found to develop on the highly swept glove and on the upper surface of the forebody. At 10 deg of sideslip, the windward glove vortex shifted inboard and broke down farther forward than the leeward glove vortex. This asymmetric breakdown of the vortices in sideslip contributes to a reduction in the lateral stability above 20 deg angle of attack. The initial loss of directional stability is a consequence of the adverse sidewash from the windward vortex and the reduced dynamic pressure at the vertical tails.

*Northrop Corp., Hawthorne, California.

114. *Kalev, I.: **A Computer Program for Cyclic Plasticity and Structural Fatigue Analysis**. NASA CR-163101, H-1139, <u>November 1980</u>, 81N11031, #.

A computerized tool for the analysis of time independent cyclic plasticity structural response, life to crack initiation prediction, and crack growth rate prediction for metallic materials is described. Three analytical items are combined: the finite element method with its associated numerical techniques for idealization of the structural component, cyclic plasticity models for idealization of the material behavior, and damage accumulation criteria for the fatigue failure.

*National Research Council, Washington, D. C.

115. *Anderson, D. L.; *Connolly, G. F.; *Mauro, F. M.; *Reukauf, P. J.; and *Marks, R.: **YF-12 Cooperative Airframe/Propulsion Control System Program, Volume 1**. NASA CR-163099, SP-5317, H-1136, <u>November 1980</u>, 81N13044, #.

Several YF-12C airplane analog control systems were converted to a digital system. Included were the air data computer, autopilot, inlet control system, and autothrottle systems. This conversion was performed to allow assessment of digital technology applications to supersonic cruise aircraft. The digital system was composed of a digital computer and specialized interface unit. A large scale mathematical simulation of the airplane was used for integration testing and software checkout.

*Lockheed-California Co., Burbank, California.

116. *Bergstrom, R. W.; *Doyle, J. R.; *Johnson, C. D.; *Holman, H. Y.; and *Wojcik, M. A.: **Assessment of the Visibility Impairment Caused by the Emissions From the Proposed Power Plant at Boron, California**. NASA CR-163103, SAI-181-EF80-156, H-1143, December 1980, 81N14504, #.

The current atmospheric conditions and visibility were modeled, and the effect of the power plant effluent was then added to determine its influence upon the prevailing visibility; the actual reduction in visibility being a function of meteorological conditions and observer-plume-target geometry. In the cases investigated, the perceptibility of a target was reduced by a minimum of 10 percent and a maximum of 100 percent. This significant visual impact would occur 40 days per year in the Edwards area with meteorological conditions such as to cause some visual impact 80 days per year.

*Systems Applications, Inc., San Rafael, California.

1981 Contractor Reports

117. *Sandlin, D. R.: **Flight Evaluation of the Terminal Guidance System**. NASA CR-163859, January 1981, 81N14991, #.

The terminal guidance system (TGS) is avionic equipment which gives guidance along a curved descending flight path to a landing. A Cessna 182 was used as the test aircraft and the TGS was installed and connected to the altimeter, DME, RMI, and gyro compass. Approaches were flown by three different pilots. When the aircraft arrives at the termination point, it is set up on final approach for a landing. The TGS provides guidance for curved descending approaches with guideslopes of 6 deg which required, for experienced pilots, workloads that are approximately the same as for an ILS. The glideslope is difficult to track within 1/2 n.m. of the VOR/DME station. The system permits, for experienced pilots, satisfactory approaches with a turn radius as low as 1/2 n.m. and a glideslope of 6 deg. Turn angles have little relation to pilot workload for curved approaches. Pilot experience is a factor for curved approaches. Pilots with low instrument time have difficulty flying steep approaches with small turn radius. Turbulence increases the pilot workload for curved approaches. The TGS does not correct to a given flight path over the ground nor does it adequately compensate for wind drift.

*California Polytechnic State University, San Luis Obispo, California.

118. *Muirhead, V. U.: **An Investigation of Drag Reduction for Tractor Trailer Vehicles With Air Deflector and Boattail**. NASA CR-163104, KU-FRL-406-1, January 1981, 81N16955, #.

A wind tunnel investigation was conducted to determine the influence of several physical variables on the aerodynamic drag of a trailer model. The physical variables included: a cab mounted wind deflector, boattail on trailer, flow vanes on trailer front, forced transition on trailer, and decreased gap between tractor and trailer. Tests were conducted at yaw angles (relative wind angles) of 0, 5, 10, 20, and 30 degrees and Reynolds numbers of 3.58×10 to the 5th power 6.12×10 to the 5th power based upon the equivalent diameter of the vehicles. The wind deflector on top of the cab produced a calculated reduction in fuel consumption of about 5 percent of the aerodynamic portion of the fuel budget for a wind speed of 15.3 km/hr (9.5 mph) over a wind angle range of 0 deg to 180 deg and for a vehicle speed of 88.5 km/hr (55 mph). The boattail produced a calculated 7 percent to 8 percent reduction in fuel consumption under the same conditions. The decrease in gap reduced the calculated fuel consumption by about 5 percent of the aerodynamic portion of the fuel budget.

*University of Kansas, Lawrence, Kansas.

119. *Bangert, L. H.; *Feltz, E. P.; *Godby, L. A.; and *Miller, L. D.: **Aerodynamic and Acoustic Behavior of a YF-12 Inlet at Static Conditions**. NASA CR-163106, LR-29623, January 1981, 81N21079.

An aeroacoustic test program to determine the cause of YF-12 inlet noise suppression was performed with a YF-12 aircraft at ground static conditions. Data obtained over a wide range of engine speeds and inlet configurations are reported. Acoustic measurements were made in the far field and aerodynamic and acoustic measurements were made inside the inlet. The J-58 test engine was removed from the aircraft and tested separately with a bellmouth inlet. The far field noise level was significantly lower for the YF-12 inlet than for the bellmouth inlet at engine speeds above 5500 rpm. There was no evidence that noise suppression was caused by flow choking. Multiple pure tones were reduced and the spectral peak near the blade passing frequency disappeared in the region of the spike support struts at engine speeds between 6000 and 6600 rpm.

*Lockheed-California Co., Burbank, California.

120. *Kotsabasis, A.: **The DAST-1 Remotely Piloted Research Vehicle Development and Initial Flight Testing**. NASA CR-163105, February 1981, 81N17038, #.

The development and initial flight testing of the DAST (drones for aerodynamic and structural testing) remotely piloted research vehicle, fitted with the first aeroelastic research wing ARW-I are presented. The ARW-I is a swept supercritical wing, designed to exhibit flutter within the vehicle's flight envelope. An active flutter suppression system (FSS) designed to increase the ARW-I flutter boundary speed by 20 percent is described. The development of the FSS was based on prediction techniques of structural and unsteady aerodynamic characteristics. A description of the supporting ground facilities and aircraft systems involved in the remotely piloted research vehicle (RPRV) flight test technique is given. The design, specification, and testing of the remotely augmented vehicle system are presented. A summary of the preflight and flight test procedures associated with the RPRV operation is given. An evaluation of the blue streak test flight and the first and second ARW-I test flights is presented.

*University of Kansas, Center for Research, Inc., Lawrence, Kansas.

121. *Hartmann, G. L.; and *Stein, G.: **F-8C Adaptive Control Law Refinement and Software Development: June 1976–June 1977**. NASA CR-163093, HONEYWELL-77SRC53, April 1981, 81N22059, #.

An explicit adaptive control algorithm based on maximum likelihood estimation of parameters was designed. To avoid iterative calculations, the algorithm uses parallel channels of Kalman filters operating at fixed locations in parameter space. This algorithm was implemented in NASA/DFRC's Remotely Augmented Vehicle (RAV) facility. Real-time sensor outputs (rate gyro, accelerometer, surface position) are telemetered to a ground computer which sends new gain values to an on-board system. Ground test data and flight records were used to establish design values of noise statistics and to verify the ground-based adaptive software.

*Honeywell, Inc., Minneapolis, Minnesota.

122. *James, R.: **Baseline Mathematics and Geodetics for Tracking Operations**. NASA CR-163102, GMD-802678, April 1981, 81N22453.

Various geodetic and mapping algorithms are analyzed as they apply to radar tracking systems and tested in extended BASIC computer language for real time computer applications. Closed-form approaches to the solution of converting Earth centered coordinates to latitude, longitude, and altitude are compared with classical approximations. A simplified approach to atmospheric refractivity called gradient refraction is compared with conventional ray tracing processes. An extremely detailed set of documentation which provides the theory, derivations, and application of algorithms used in the programs is included. Validation methods are also presented for testing the accuracy of the algorithms.

*GMD Systems, Inc., Lancaster, California.

123. *Muirhead, V. U.: **An Investigation of Drag Reduction for a Standard Truck With Various Modifications**. NASA CR-163107, KU-FRL-406-2, May 1981, 81N23040, #.

A wind tunnel investigation was conducted to determine the influence of several physical variables on the aerodynamic drag of a standard truck model. The physical variables included: a cab mounted air deflector; a boattail on the rear of the cargo compartment; flow-vanes on the front of the cargo compartment; and a forebody fairing over the cab. Tests were conducted at yaw angles (relative wind angle) of 0, 5, 10, 20, and 30 degrees and Reynolds numbers of $3.4 \times 100,000$ to $6.1 \times 100,000$ based upon the equivalent diameter of the vehicles. The forebody fairing and the flow-vane with the closed bottom were very effective in improving the flow over the forward part of the cargo compartment. The forebody fairing provided a calculated fuel saving of 5.6 liters per hour (1.5 gallons per hour) over the baseline configuration for a ground speed of 88.6 km/hr (55 mph) in national average winds.

*University of Kansas, Lawrence, Kansas.

124. *Teper, G. L.; *Dimarco, R. J.; *Ashkenas, I. L.; and *Hoh, R. H.: **Analyses of Shuttle Orbiter Approach and Landing Conditions**. NASA CR-163108, TR-1137-1, July 1981, 81N27113, #.

A study of one shuttle orbiter approach and landing conditions are summarized. Causes of observed PIO like flight deficiencies are identified and potential cures are examined. Closed loop pilot/vehicle analyses are described and path/attitude stability boundaries defined. The latter novel technique proved of great value in delineating and illustrating the basic causes of this multiloop pilot control problem. The analytical results are shown to be consistent with flight test and fixed base simulation. Conclusions are drawn relating to possible improvements of the shuttle orbiter/digital flight control system.

*Systems Technology, Inc., Hawthorne, California.

125. *Schmidt, D. K.; and *Innocenti, M.: **Pilot-Optimal Multivariable Control Synthesis by Output Feedback**. NASA CR-163112, July 1981, 81N28102, #.

A control system design approach for optimal stability augmentation, systems, using limited state feedback theory with the specific inclusion of the human pilot in the loop is presented. The methodology is especially suitable for application to flight vehicles exhibiting nonconventional dynamic characteristics and for which quantitative handling qualities specifications are not available. The design is based on a correlation between pilot ratings and objective function of the optimal control model of the human pilot. Simultaneous optimization for augmentation and pilot gains are required.

*Purdue University, West Lafayette, Indiana.

126. *Muirhead, V. U.: **An Investigation of Drag Reduction for a Box-Shaped Vehicle With Various Modifications.** NASA CR-163111, August 1981, 81N29097, #.

The influence of physical variables on the aerodynamic drag of a box shaped vehicle model was studied. The physical variables included built-in rounded front corners, and two different designs of add on flow vanes for the front of box shaped vehicle with 67 deg and 90 deg of arc. For a diesel powered vehicle, only slightly larger than a family van, the built in rounded front corners provide a calculated fuel saving of about 6.0 liters per hour of driving (1.6 gallons per hour) at 88.6 km per hour (55 mph) in national average winds, as compared to the baseline vehicle having all square corners. The corresponding savings for a baseline vehicle to which front mounted flow vanes were added is competitive. For a gasoline powered vehicle the volumetric fuel savings would be larger by a factor of about 1.7. The fuel savings for a standard size motor home would be greater for the diesel or gasoline powered vehicles by from 30 to 35 percent because of the larger frontal area. Thus projected fuel savings for a standard size motor home powered by gasoline can approach 12.5 to 13.5 liters (3.3 to 3.6 gallons) for each hour driving at highway speeds.

*University of Kansas, Lawrence, Kansas.

127. *Peterson, R. L.: **Drag Reduction Obtained by the Addition of a Boattail to a Box Shaped Vehicle.** NASA CR-163113, August 1981, 81N29094, #.

Coast down tests were performed on a box shaped ground vehicle used to simulate the aerodynamic drag of high volume transports such as delivery vans, motor homes and trucks. The results of these tests define the reduction in aerodynamic drag that can be obtained by the addition of either a boattail or a truncated boattail to an otherwise blunt based vehicle. Test velocities ranged up to 96.6 km/h (60 mph) with Reynolds numbers to 1.3 x 10 the 7th power. The full boattail provided an average 32 percent reduction in

drag at highway speeds whereas the truncated boattail provided an average 31 percent reduction in drag as compared to the configuration having the blunt base. These results are compared with one tenth scale wind tunnel model data.

*California Polytechnic State University, San Luis Obispo, California.

E-38096

Air Flow Testing On Aerodynamics Test Van

128. *Foote, C. H.; and *Jaekel, R. F.: **Flight Evaluation of an Engine Static Pressure Noseprobe in an F-15 Airplane.** NASA CR-163109, NAS 1.26:163109, FR-14915, August 1981, 83N17546.

The flight testing of an inlet static pressure probe and instrumented inlet case produced results consistent with sea-level and altitude stand testing. The F-15 flight test verified the basic relationship of total to static pressure ratio versus corrected airflow and automatic distortion downmatch with the engine pressure ratio control mode. Additionally, the backup control inlet case statics demonstrated sufficient accuracy for backup control fuel flow scheduling, and the station 6 manifolded production probe was in agreement with the flight test station 6 total pressure probes.

*Pratt and Whitney Aircraft Group, West Palm Beach, Florida.

129. *Brock, L. D.; and *Goodman, H. A.: **Reliability Analysis of the F-8 Digital Fly-By-Wire System.** NASA CR-163110, R-1324, October 1981, 82N12079, #.

The F-8 Digital Fly-by-Wire (DFBW) flight test program intended to provide the technology for advanced control systems, giving aircraft enhanced performance and operational capability is addressed. A detailed analysis of the experimental system was performed to estimated the probabilities of two significant safety critical events: (1) loss of primary flight control function, causing reversion to the analog bypass system; and (2) loss of the aircraft due to failure of the electronic flight control system. The analysis covers appraisal of risks due to random equipment failure, generic faults in design of the system or its software, and induced failure due to external events. A unique diagrammatic technique was developed which details the combinatorial reliability equations for the entire system, promotes understanding of system failure characteristics, and identifies the most likely failure modes. The technique provides a systematic method of applying basic probability equations and is augmented by a computer program written in a modular fashion that duplicates the structure of these equations.

*Draper Laboratory, Cambridge, Massachusetts.

130. *Hamer, M. J.; and *Alexander, R. I.: **Optimization of Thrust Algorithm Calibration for Computing System (TCS) for Thrust the NASA Highly Maneuverable Aircraft Technology (HiMAT) Vehicle's Propulsion System**. NASA CR-163121, December 1981, 82N21198, #.

A simplified gross thrust computing technique for the HiMAT J85-GE-21 engine using altitude facility data was evaluated. The results over the full engine envelope for both the standard engine mode and the open nozzle engine mode are presented. Results using afterburner casing static pressure taps are compared to those using liner static pressure taps. It is found that the technique is very accurate for both the standard and open nozzle engine modes. The difference in the algorithm accuracy for a calibration based on data from one test condition was small compared to a calibration based on data from all of the test conditions.

*Computing Devices Co., Ottawa, Ontario, Canada.

131. *Delmundo, A. R.; *McQuilkin, F. T.; and *Rivas, R. R.: **SPF/DB Primary Structure for Supersonic Aircraft (T-38 Horizontal Stabilizer)**. NASA CR-163114, NA-81-649, December 1981, 84N27860.

The structural integrity and potential cost savings of superplastic forming/diffusion bonding (SPF/DB) titanium structure for future Supersonic Cruise Research (SCR) and military aircraft primary structure applications was demonstrated. Using the horizontal stabilizer of the T-38 aircraft as a baseline, the structure was redesigned to the existing criteria and loads, using SPF/DB titanium technology. The general concept of using a full-depth sandwich structure which is attached to a steel spindle, was retained. Trade studies demonstrated that the optimum design should employ double-truss, sinewave core in the deepest section of the surface, making a transition to single-truss core in the thinner areas at the leading and trailing edges and at the tip. At the extreme thin edges of the surface, the single-truss core was changed to dot core to provide for gas passages during the SPF/DB process. The selected SPF/DB

horizontal stabilizer design consisted of a one-piece SPF/DB sinewave truss core panel, a trunnion fitting, and reinforcing straps. The fitting and the straps were mechanically fastened to the SPF/DB panel.

*Rockwell International Corp., Los Angeles, California.

1982 Contractor Reports

132. *Weingarten, N. C.; and *Chalk, C. R.: **In-Flight Investigation of the Effects of Pilot Location and Control System Design on Airplane Flying Qualities for Approach and Landing**. NASA CR-163115, CALSPAN-6645-F-7, January 1982, 82N15074, #.

The handling qualities of large airplanes in the approach and landing flight phase were studied. The primary variables were relative pilot position with respect to center of rotation, command path time delays and phase shifts, augmentation schemes and levels of augmentation. It is indicated that the approach and landing task with large airplanes is a low bandwidth task. Low equivalent short period frequencies and relatively long time delays are tolerated only when the pilot is located at considerable distance forward of the center of rotation. The control problem experienced by the pilots, when seated behind the center of rotation, tended to occur at low altitude when they were using visual cues of rate of sink and altitude. A direct lift controller improved final flight path control of the shuttle like configurations.

*Calspan Advanced Technology Center, Buffalo, New York.

133. *Bailey, R. E.; and *Smith, R. E.: **An In-Flight Investigation of Pilot-Induced Oscillation Suppression Filters During the Fighter Approach and Landing Task**. NASA CR-163116, REPT-6645-F-9, March 1982, 83N13110, #.

An investigation of pilot-induced oscillation suppression (PIOS) filters was performed using the USAF/Flight Dynamics Laboratory variable stability NT-33 aircraft, modified and operated by Calspan. This program examined the effects of PIOS filtering on the longitudinal flying qualities of fighter aircraft during the visual approach and landing task. Forty evaluations were flown to test the effects of different PIOS filters. Although detailed analyses were not undertaken, the results indicate that PIOS filtering can improve the flying qualities of an otherwise unacceptable aircraft configuration (Level 3 flying qualities). However, the ability of the filters to suppress pilot-induced oscillations appears to be dependent upon the aircraft configuration characteristics. Further, the data show that the filters can adversely affect landing flying qualities if improperly designed. The data provide an excellent foundation from which detail analyses can be performed.

*Calspan Corp., Buffalo, New York.

134. *Myers, T. T.; *Johnston, D. E.; and *McRuer, D.: **Space Shuttle Flying Qualities and Flight Control System Assessment Study**. NASA CR-170391, REPT-1174-1, June 1982, 82N28300, #.

The suitability of existing and proposed flying quality and flight control system criteria for application to the space shuttle orbiter during atmospheric flight phases was assessed. An orbiter experiment for flying qualities and flight control system design criteria is discussed. Orbiter longitudinal and lateral-directional flying characteristics, flight control system lag and time delay considerations, and flight control manipulator characteristics are included. Data obtained from conventional aircraft may be inappropriate for application to the shuttle orbiter.

*Systems Technology, Inc., Hawthorne, California.

135. *Mock, W. D.: **A NASTRAN Model of a Large Flexible Swing-Wing Bomber. Volume 1: NASTRAN Model Plane**. NASA CR-170392-VOL-1, NA-76-469-VOL-1, September 1982, 83N14107, #.

A review was conducted of B-1 aircraft no. 2 (A/C-2) internal loads models to determine the minimum model complexity necessary to fulfill all of the airloads research study objectives. Typical model sizings were tabulated at selected vehicle locations, and scale layouts were prepared of the NASTRAN structural analysis model.

*Rockwell International Corp., Los Angeles, California.

136. *Mock, W. D.; *Latham, R. A.; and *Tisher, E. D.: **A NASTRAN Model of a Large Flexible Swing-Wing Bomber. Volume 2: NASTRAN Model Development-Horizontal Stabilzer, Vertical Stabilizer and Nacelle Structures**. NASA CR-170392-VOL-2, NA-76-469-VOL-2, September 1982, 83N14108, #.

The NASTRAN model plans for the horizontal stabilizer, vertical stabilizer, and nacelle structure were expanded in detail to generate the NASTRAN model for each of these substructures. The grid point coordinates were coded for each element. The material properties and sizing data for each element were specified. Each substructure model was thoroughly checked out for continuity, connectivity, and constraints. These substructures were processed for structural influence coefficients (SIC) point loadings and the deflections were compared to those computed for the aircraft detail models. Finally, a demonstration and validation processing of these substructures was accomplished using the NASTRAN finite element program installed at NASA/DFRC facility.

Rockwell International Corp., Los Angeles, California.

137. *Mock, W. D.; and *Latham, R. A.: **A NASTRAN Model of a Large Flexible Swing-Wing Bomber.**

Volume 3: NASTRAN Model Development-Wing Structure. NASA CR-170392-VOL-3, NA-76-469-VOL-3, September 1982, 83N14109, #.

The NASTRAN model plan for the wing structure was expanded in detail to generate the NASTRAN model for this substructure. The grid point coordinates were coded for each element. The material properties and sizing data for each element were specified. The wing substructure model was thoroughly checked out for continuity, connectivity, and constraints. This substructure was processed for structural influence coefficients (SIC) point loadings and the deflections were compared to those computed for the aircraft detail model. Finally, a demonstration and validation processing of this substructure was accomplished using the NASTRAN finite element program. The bulk data deck, stiffness matrices, and SIC output data were delivered.

*Rockwell International Corp., Los Angeles, California.

138. *Mock, W. D.; and *Latham, R. A.: **A NASTRAN Model of a Large Flexible Swing-Wing Bomber. Volume 4: NASTRAN Model Development-Fuselage Structure**. NASA CR-170392-VOL-4, NA-76-469-VOL-4, September 1982, 83N14110, #.

The NASTRAN model plan for the fuselage structure was expanded in detail to generate the NASTRAN model for this substructure. The grid point coordinates were coded for each element. The material properties and sizing data for each element were specified. The fuselage substructure model was thoroughly checked out for continuity, connectivity, and constraints. This substructure was processed for structural influence coefficients (SIC) point loadings and the deflections were compared to those computed for the aircraft detail model. Finally, a demonstration and validation processing of this substructure was accomplished using the NASTRAN finite element program. The bulk data deck, stiffness matrices, and SIC output data were delivered.

*Rockwell International Corp., Los Angeles, California.

139. *Mock, W. D.; and *Latham, R. A.: **A NASTRAN Model of a Large Flexible Swing-Wing Bomber. Volume 5: NASTRAN Model Development-Fairing Structure**. NASA CR-170392-VOL-5, NA-76-469-VOL-5, September 1982, 83N14111, #.

The NASTRAN model plan for the fairing structure was expanded in detail to generate the NASTRAN model of this substructure. The grid point coordinates, element definitions, material properties, and sizing data for each element were specified. The fairing model was thoroughly checked out for continuity, connectivity, and constraints. The substructure was processed for structural influence coefficients (SIC) point loadings to determine the deflection characteristics of the fairing model. Finally, a demonstration and validation

451

processing of this substructure was accomplished using the NASTRAN finite element program. The bulk data deck, stiffness matrices, and SIC output data were delivered.

*Rockwell International Corp., Los Angeles, California.

140. *Hartmann, G. L.; *Wall, J. E., Jr.; *Rang, E. R.; *Lee, H. P.; *Schulte, R. W.; and *Ng, W. K.: **Advanced Flight Control System Study.** NASA CR-163117, HONEYWELL-82SRC5, <u>November 1982</u>, 83N13113, #.

A fly by wire flight control system architecture designed for high reliability includes spare sensor and computer elements to permit safe dispatch with failed elements, thereby reducing unscheduled maintenance. A methodology capable of demonstrating that the architecture does achieve the predicted performance characteristics consists of a hierarchy of activities ranging from analytical calculations of system reliability and formal methods of software verification to iron bird testing followed by flight evaluation. Interfacing this architecture to the Lockheed S-3A aircraft for flight test is discussed. This testbed vehicle can be expanded to support flight experiments in advanced aerodynamics, electromechanical actuators, secondary power systems, flight management, new displays, and air traffic control concepts.

*Lockheed-California Co., Burbank, California.

141. *McGough, J.; *Moses, K.; and **Klafin, J. F.: **Advanced Flight Control System Study.** NASA CR-163120, B-82SRC5, <u>November 1982</u>, 83N15316, #.

The architecture, requirements, and system elements of an ultrareliable, advanced flight control system are described. The basic criteria are functional reliability of 10 to the minus 10 power/hour of flight and only 6 month scheduled maintenance. A distributed system architecture is described, including a multiplexed communication system, reliable bus controller, the use of skewed sensor arrays, and actuator interfaces. Test bed and flight evaluation program are proposed.

*Bendix Corp., Teterboro, New Jersey.
**Grumman Aerospace Corp., Bethpage, New York.

142. *Sandlin, D. R.: **Wind Tunnel Tests of a Free-Wing/Free-Trimmer Model**. NASA CR-170394, <u>December 1982</u>, 83N15263, #.

The riding qualities of an aircraft with low wing loading can be improved by freeing the wing to rotate about its spanwise axis. A trimming surface also free to rotate about its spanwise axis can be added at the wing tips to permit the use of high lift devices. Wind tunnel tests of the free wing/free trimmer model with the trimmer attached to the wing tips aft of the wing chord were conducted to validate a mathematical model developed to predict the dynamic characteristics of a free wing/free trimmer aircraft. A model consisting of a semispan

wing with the trimmer mounted on with the wing on an air bearing and the trimmer on a ball bearing was displaced to various angles of attack and released. The damped oscillations of the wing and trimmer were recorded. Real and imaginary parts of the characteristic equations of motion were determined and compared to values predicted using the mathematical model.

*California Polytechnic State University, San Luis Obispo, California.

1983 Contractor Reports

143. *Holzapfel, W. B.; *Seiler, B.; and *Nicol, M.: **Effect of Pressure on Infrared Spectra of Ice 7.** NASA CR-170300, <u>January 1983</u>, 83N23671, #.

The effect of pressure on the infrared spectra of H2O and D2O ice VII was studied at room temperature and pressures between 2 and 15 GPa with a Fourier transform infrared spectrometer and a diamond anvil high pressure cell. Two librational modes, one bending mode, and various overtone bands are well resolved. The stretching modes, nu sub 1 and nu sub 3 are poorly resolved due to overlap with diamond window absorption. Differences between the spectra of H2O and D2O are discussed.

*University of California, Los Angeles, California.

144. *Anon.: **The YAV-8B Simulation and Modeling. Volume 1: Aircraft Description and Program Summary**. NASA CR-170397-VOL-1, MDC-A7910, <u>January 1983</u>, 83N22193, #.

A FORTRAN batch simulation of the YAV-8B aircraft and supporting documentation are presented. The aircraft is described. Simulation outputs are compared with flight test data.

*McDonnell Aircraft Co., St. Louis, Missouri.

145. *Walker, R.; and *Gupta, N.: **Flight Test Trajectory Control Analysis**. NASA CR-170395, ISI-16, <u>February 1983</u>, 83N18744, #.

Recent extensions to optimal control theory applied to meaningful linear models with sufficiently flexible software tools provide powerful techniques for designing flight test trajectory controllers (FTTCs). This report describes the principal steps for systematic development of flight trajectory controllers, which can be summarized as planning, modeling, designing, and validating a trajectory controller. The techniques have been kept as general as possible and should apply to a wide range of problems where quantities must be computed and displayed to a pilot to improve pilot effectiveness and to reduce workload and fatigue. To illustrate the approach, a detailed trajectory guidance law is developed and demonstrated for the F-15 aircraft flying the zoom-and-pushover maneuver.

*Integrated Systems, Inc., Palo Alto, California.

146. *Anon.: **The YAV-8B Simulation and Modeling. Volume 2: Program Listing.** NASA CR-170397-VOL-2, MDC-A7910, <u>March 1983</u>, 83N22194, #.

Detailed mathematical models of varying complexity representative of the YAV-8B aircraft are defined and documented. These models are used in parameter estimation and in linear analysis computer programs while investigating YAV-8B aircraft handling qualities. Both a six degree of freedom nonlinear model and a linearized three degree of freedom longitudinal and lateral directional model were developed. The nonlinear model is based on the mathematical model used on the MCAIR YAV-8B manned flight simulator. This simulator model has undergone periodic updating based on the results of approximately 360 YAV-8B flights and 8000 hours of wind tunnel testing. Qualified YAV-8B flight test pilots have commented that the handling qualities characteristics of the simulator are quite representative of the real aircraft. These comments are validated herein by comparing data from both static and dynamic flight test maneuvers to the same obtained using the nonlinear program.

*McDonnell Aircraft Co., St. Louis, Missouri.

147. *Johnston, Donald E.; *Myers, Thomas T.; and *Zellner, John W.: **Autonomous RPRV Navigation, Guidance and Control.** NASA CR-179425, NAS 1.26:179425, TR-1180-1, <u>March 1983</u>, 89N14228.

Dryden Flight Research Center has the responsibility for flight testing of advanced remotely piloted research vehicles (RPRV) to explore highly maneuverable aircraft technology, and to test advanced structural concepts, and related aeronautical technologies which can yield important research results with significant cost benefits. The primary purpose is to provide the preliminary design of an upgraded automatic approach and landing control system and flight director display to improve landing performance and reduce pilot workload. A secondary purpose is to determine the feasibility of an onboard autonomous navigation, orbit, and landing capability for safe vehicle recovery in the event of loss of telemetry uplink communication with the vehicles. The current RPRV approach and landing method, the proposed automatic and manual approach and autoland system, and an autonomous navigation, orbit, and landing system concept which is based on existing operational technology are described.

*Systems Technology, Inc., Hawthorne, California.

148. *Hanson, G. D.; and *Jewell, W. F.: **Non-Intrusive Parameter Identification Procedure User's Guide**. NASA CR-170398, TR-1188-1, <u>April 1983</u>, 83N23318, #.

Written in standard FORTRAN, NAS is capable of identifying linear as well as nonlinear relations between input and output parameters; the only restriction is that the input/output relation be linear with respect to the unknown coefficients of the estimation equations. The output of the identification algorithm can be specified to be in either the time domain (i.e., the estimation equation coefficients) or in the frequency domain (i.e., a frequency response of the estimation equation). The frame length ("window") over which the identification procedure is to take place can be specified to be any portion of the input time history, thereby allowing the freedom to start and stop the identification procedure within a time history. There also is an option which allows a sliding window, which gives a moving average over the time history. The NAS software also includes the ability to identify several assumed solutions simultaneously for the same or different input data.

*Systems Technology, Inc., Mountain View, California.

149. *Heffley, R. K.; *Hanson, G. D.; *Jewell, W. F.; and *Clement, W. F.: **Analysis of Pilot Control Strategy**. NASA CR-170399, NAS 1.26:170399, TR-1188-2, <u>April 1983</u>, 83N22212.

Methods for nonintrusive identification of pilot control strategy and task execution dynamics are presented along with examples based on flight data. The specific analysis technique is Nonintrusive Parameter Identification Procedure (NIPIP), which is described in a companion user's guide (NASA CR-170398). Quantification of pilot control strategy and task execution dynamics is discussed in general terms followed by a more detailed description of how NIPIP can be applied. The examples are based on flight data obtained from the NASA F-8 digital fly by wire airplane. These examples involve various piloting tasks and control axes as well as a demonstration of how the dynamics of the aircraft itself are identified using NIPIP. Application of NIPIP to the ATF/F-16 flight test program is discussed. Recommendations are made for flight test applications in general and refinement of NIPIP to include interactive computer graphics.

*Systems Technology, Inc., Mountain View, California.

150. *Deckert, J. C.: **Analytical Redundancy Management Mechanization and Flight Data Analysis for the F-8 Digital Fly-By-Wire Aircraft Flight Control Sensors: July 1978–September 1981.** NASA CR-170396, CSDL-R-1520, <u>April 1983</u>, 85N14844, #.

The details are presented of an onboard digital computer algorithm designed to reliably detect and isolate the first failure in a duplex set of flight control sensors aboard the NASA F-8 digital fly-by-wire aircraft. The algorithm's successful flight test program is summarized, and specific examples are presented of algorithm behavior in response to software-induced signal faults, both with and without aircraft parameter modeling errors.

*Draper Laboratory, Cambridge, Massachusetts.

151. *Weingarten, N. C.; and *Chalk, C. R.: **Application of Calspan Pitch Rate Control System to the Space Shuttle for Approach and Landing.** NASA CR-170402, RECPT-7102 F-1, NAS 1.26:170402, May 1983, 83N24513, #.

A pitch rate control system designed for use in the shuttle during approach and landing was analyzed and compared with a revised control system developed by NASA and the existing OFT control system. The design concept control system uses filtered pitch rate feedback with proportional plus integral paths in the forward loop. Control system parameters were designed as a function of flight configuration. Analysis included time and frequency domain techniques. Results indicate that both the Calspan and NASA systems significantly improve the flying qualities of the shuttle over the OFT. Better attitude and flight path control and less time delay are the primary reasons. The Calspan system is preferred because of reduced time delay and simpler mechanization. Further testing of the improved flight control systems in an in-flight simulator is recommended.

*Calspan Advanced Technology Center, Buffalo, New York.

152. *Muirhead, V. U.: **An Investigation of the Internal and External Aerodynamics of Cattle Trucks.** NASA CR-170400, NAS 1.26.170400, (KU-FRL-541-2), May 1983, 83N26760, #.

Wind tunnel tests were conducted on a one-tenth scale model of a conventional tractor trailer livestock hauler to determine the air flow through the trailer and the drag of the vehicle. These tests were conducted with the trailer empty and with a full load of simulated cattle. Additionally, the drag was determined for six configurations, of which details for three are documented herein. These are: (1) conventional livestock trailer empty, (2) conventional trailer with smooth sides (i.e., without ventilation openings), and (3) a stream line tractor with modified livestock trailer (cab streamlining and gap fairing). The internal flow of the streamlined modification with simulated cattle was determined with two different ducting systems: a ram air inlet over the cab and NACA submerged inlets between the cab and trailer. The air flow within the conventional trailer was random and variable. The streamline vehicle with ram air inlet provided a nearly uniform air flow which could be controlled. The streamline vehicle with NACA submerged inlets provided better flow conditions than the conventional livestock trailer but not as uniform or controllable as the ram inlet configuration.

*University of Kansas, Lawrence, Kansas.

153. *Crouch, K. E.: **Aircraft Lightning-Induced Voltage Test Technique Developments.** NASA CR-170403, LT-82-132, June 1983, 83N26829, #.

High voltage safety, fuels safety, simulation, and response/ measurement techniques are discussed. Travelling wave transit times, return circuit conductor configurations, LC ladder network generators, and repetitive pulse techniques are also discussed. Differential conductive coaxial cable, analog fiber optic link, repetitive pulse sampled data instrumentation system, flash A/D optic link system, and an FM telemetry system are considered.

*Lightning Technologies, Inc., Pittsfield, Massachusetts.

154. *Fisher, R. W.: **Variable Acuity Remote Viewing System Flight Demonstration.** NASA CR-170404, MDC-IRO296, July 1983, 83N29204, #.

The Variable Acuity Remote Viewing System (VARVS), originally developed under contract to the Navy (ONR) as a laboratory brassboard, was modified for flight demonstration. The VARVS system was originally conceived as a technique which could circumvent the acuity/field of view/bandwidth tradeoffs that exists in remote viewing to provide a nearly eye limited display in both field of view (160 deg) and resolution (2 min arc) while utilizing conventional TV sensing, transmission, and display equipment. The modifications for flight demonstration consisted of modifying the sensor so it could be installed and flow in a Piper PA20 aircraft, equipped for remote control and modifying the display equipment so it could be integrated with the NASA Research RPB (RPRV) remote control cockpit.

*McDonnell Aircraft Co., St. Louis, Missouri.

155. *Hoffman, J. A.; and *Sandlin, D. R.: **A Preliminary Investigation of the Drag and Ventilation Characteristics of Livestock Haulers.** NASA CR-170408, NAS 1.26:170408, December 1983, 84N14990, #.

A wind tunnel evaluation of the drag and ventilation characteristics of a conventional (unmodified) and five modified subscale model livestock haulers at 0 deg yaw angle has been made. The unmodified livestock hauler has a relatively high drag coefficient, and a low velocity recirculation region exists in the forward portion of the hauler. The use of a streamlined forebody and enclosed gap reduced the drag coefficient of one model by 42% and improved the rate at which contaminants can be flushed from the cargo compartment by a factor of 2.5. From the limited data obtained, any increase in the fraction of open area of the trailer sides was found to improve the trailer ventilation. The use of a ram air inlet can improve the ventilation within the hauler and remove the low velocity recirculation region at the expense of a modest increase in the truck's drag coefficient. A mathematical model for vehicles with ram air or NACA submerged inlets was developed and appears to adequately predict the ventilation characteristics of livestock haulers.

*California Polytechnic State University, San Luis Obispo, California.

156. *Myers, T. T.; *Johnston, D. E.; and *McRuer, D. T.: **Space Shuttle Flying Qualities and Flight Control System Assessment Study, Phase 2**. NASA CR-170406, REPT-1187-1R, <u>December 1983</u>, 84N14158, #.

A program of flying qualities experiments as part of the Orbiter Experiments Program (OEX) is defined. Phase 1, published as CR-170391, reviewed flying qualities criteria and shuttle data. The review of applicable experimental and shuttle data to further define the OEX plan is continued. An unconventional feature of this approach is the use of pilot strategy model identification to relate flight and simulator results. Instrumentation, software, and data analysis techniques for pilot model measurements are examined. The relationship between shuttle characteristics and superaugmented aircraft is established. STS flights 1 through 4 are reviewed from the point of view of flying qualities. A preliminary plan for a coordinated program of inflight and simulator research is presented.

*Systems Technology, Inc., Hawthorne, California.

157. *Wykes, J. H.; *Kelpl, M. J.; and *Brosnan, M. J.: **Flight Test and Analyses of the B-1 Structural Mode Control System at Supersonic Flight Conditions**. NASA CR-170405, <u>December 1983</u>, 84N13197, #.

A practical structural mode control system (SMCS) that could be turned on at takeoff and be left on for the entire flight was demonstrated. The SMCS appears to be more effective in damping the key fuselage bending modes at supersonic speeds than at the design point of Mach 0.85 (for fixed gains). The SMCS has an adverse effect on high frequency symmetric modes; however, this adverse effect did not make the system unstable and does not appear to affect ride quality performance. The vertical ride quality analyses indicate that the basic configuration without active systems is satisfactory for long term exposure. If clear air turbulence were to be encountered, indications are that the SMCS would be very effective in reducing the adverse accelerations. On the other hand, lateral ride quality analyses indicate that the aircraft with the SMCS on does not quite meet the long term exposure criteria, but would be satisfactory for shot term exposure at altitude. Again, the lateral SMCS was shown to be very effective in reducing peak lateral accelerations.

*NASA Ames Research Center, Moffett Field, California.

1984 Contractor Reports

158. *Schmidt, D. K.; and *Innocenti, M.: **Optimal Cooperative Control Synthesis Applied to a Control-Configured Aircraft**. NASA CR-170411, <u>January 1984</u>, 84N24593, #.

A multivariable control augmentation synthesis method is presented that is intended to enable the designer to directly optimize pilot opinion rating of the augmented system. The approach involves the simultaneous solution for the augmentation and predicted pilot's compensation via optimal control techniques. The methodology is applied to the control law synthesis for a vehicle similar to the AFTI F-16 control-configured aircraft. The resulting dynamics, expressed in terms of eigenstructure and time/frequency responses, are presented with analytical predictions of closed loop tracking performance, pilot compensation, and other predictors of pilot acceptance.

*Purdue University, West Lafayette, Indiana.

159. *Lameris, J.: **Development of a Thermal and Structural Model for a Nastran Finite-Element Analysis of a Hypersonic Wing Test Structure**. NASA CR-170413, H-1219, <u>January 1984</u>, 84N17620, #.

The development of a thermal and structural model for a hypersonic wing test structure using the NASTRAN finite-element method as its primary analytical tool is described. A detailed analysis was defined to obtain the temperature and thermal stress distribution in the whole wing as well as the five upper and lower root panels. During the development of the models, it was found that the thermal application of NASTRAN and the VIEW program, used for the generation of the radiation exchange coefficients, were deficient. Although for most of these deficiencies solutions could be found, the existence of one particular deficiency in the current thermal model prevented the final computation of the temperature distributions. A SPAR analysis of a single bay of the wing, using data converted from the original NASTRAN model, indicates that local temperature-time distributions can be obtained with good agreement with the test data. The conversion of the NASTRAN thermal model into a SPAR model is recommended to meet the immediate goal of obtaining an accurate thermal stress distribution.

*University of Kansas, Center for Research, Inc., Lawrence, Kansas.

160. *Bartlett, M. D.; *Feltz, T. F.; *Olsen, A. D., Jr.; *Smith, D. B.; and *Wildermuth, P. F.: **Airloads Research Study. Volume 2: Airload Coefficients Derived From Wind Tunnel Data**. NASA CR-170410, NA-76-563, <u>January 1984</u>, 84N17174, #.

The development of B-1 aircraft rigid wind tunnel data for use in subsequent tasks of the Airloads Research Study is described. Data from the Rockwell International external structural loads data bank were used to generate coefficients of rigid airload shear, bending moment, and torsion at specific component reference stations or both symmetric and asymmetric loadings. Component stations include the movable wing, horizontal and vertical stabilizers, and forward and aft fuselages. The coefficient data cover a Mach number range from 0.7 to 2.2 for a wing sweep position of 67.5 degree.

*Rockwell International Corp., Los Angeles, California.

161. *Bartlett, M. D.; *Feltz, T. F.; *Olsen, A. D., Jr.; *Smith, D. B.; and *Wildermuth, P. F.: **Airloads Research Study. Volume 1: Flight Test Loads Acquisition**. NASA CR-170409, NA-76-562, January 1984, 84N17173, #.

The acquisition of B-1 aircraft flight loads data for use in subsequent tasks of the Airloads Research Study is described. The basic intent is to utilize data acquired during B-1 aircraft tests, analyze these data beyond the scope of Air Force requirements, and prepare research reports that will add to the technology base for future large flexible aircraft. Flight test data obtained during the airloads survey program included condition-describing parameters, surface pressures, strain gage outputs, and loads derived from pressure and strain gauges. Descriptions of the instrumentation, data processing, and flight load survey program are included. Data from windup-turn and steady yaw maneuvers cover a Mach number range from 0.7 to 2.0 for a wing sweep position of 67.5 deg.

*Rockwell International Corp., Los Angeles, California.

162. *Myers, T. T.; *Johnston, D. E.; and *McRuer, D. T.: **Space Shuttle Flying Qualities Criteria Assessment, Phase 3**. NASA CR-170407, TR-1197-1, February 1984, 84N20565, #.

The crucial flight data measurement and reduction techniques required for the experimental approach are explored. An overview of available flight data is presented, identification of the effective augmented vehicle and pilot models determined, a summary of flight data problems compiled, and further recommendations for the Orbiter Flying Qualities (OFQ) experiment provided.

*Systems Technology, Inc., Hawthorne, California.

163. *Walker, R.; and *Gupta, N.: **Real-Time Flutter Analysis**. NASA CR-170412, NAS 1.26:170412, ISI-24, March 1984, 84N20512.

The important algorithm issues necessary to achieve a real time flutter monitoring system; namely, the guidelines for choosing appropriate model forms, reduction of the parameter convergence transient, handling multiple modes, the effect of over parameterization, and estimate accuracy predictions, both online and for experiment design are addressed. An approach for efficiently computing continuous-time flutter parameter Cramer-Rao estimate error bounds were developed. This enables a convincing comparison of theoretical and simulation results, as well as offline studies in preparation for a flight test. Theoretical predictions, simulation and flight test results from the NASA Drones for Aerodynamic and Structural Test (DAST) Program are compared.

*Integrated Systems, Inc., Palo Alto, California.

164. *Yechout, T. R.; and *Braman, K. B.: **Development and Evaluation of a Performance Modeling Flight Test Approach Based on Quasi Steady-State Maneuvers**. NASA CR-170414, April 1984, 84N27724, #.

The development, implementation and flight test evaluation of a performance modeling technique which required a limited amount of quasisteady state flight test data to predict the overall one g performance characteristics of an aircraft. The concept definition phase of the program include development of: (1) the relationship for defining aerodynamic characteristics from quasi steady state maneuvers; (2) a simplified in flight thrust and airflow prediction technique; (3) a flight test maneuvering sequence which efficiently provided definition of baseline aerodynamic and engine characteristics including power effects on lift and drag; and (4) the algorithms necessary for cruise and flight trajectory predictions. Implementation of the concept include design of the overall flight test data flow, definition of instrumentation system and ground test requirements, development and verification of all applicable software and consolidation of the overall requirements in a flight test plan.

*University of Kansas, Center for Research, Inc., Lawrence, Kansas.

165. *Bacon, B. J.; and *Schmidt, D. K.: **An Optimal Control Approach to Pilot/Vehicle Analysis and Neal-Smith Criteria**. NASA CR-170416, April 1984, 84N21551, #.

The approach of Neal and Smith was merged with the advances in pilot modeling by means of optimal control techniques. While confirming the findings of Neal and Smith, a methodology that explicitly includes the pilot's objective in attitude tracking was developed. More importantly, the method yields the required system bandwidth along with a better pilot model directly applicable to closed-loop analysis of systems in any order.

*Purdue University, West Lafayette, Indiana.

166. *Bowers, A. H.; and *Sandlin, D. R.: **A Comparison of Computer-Generated Lift and Drag Polars for a Wortmann Airfoil to Flight and Wind Tunnel Results.** NASA CR-176963, NAS 1.26:176963, June 1984, 86N28919, #.

Computations of drag polars for a low-speed Wortmann sailplane airfoil are compared to both wind tunnel and flight results. Excellent correlation is shown to exist between computations and flight results except when separated flow regimes were encountered. Wind tunnel transition locations are shown to agree with computed predictions. Smoothness of the input coordinates to the PROFILE airfoil analysis computer program was found to be essential to obtain accurate comparisons of drag polars or transition location to either the flight or wind tunnel results.

*California Polytechnic State University, San Luis Obispo, California.

167. *Myers, T. T.; *McRuer, D. T.; and *Johnston, D. E.: **Flying Qualities and Control System Characteristics for Superaugmented Aircraft.** NASA CR-170419, STI-TR-1202-1, December 1984, 85N13800, #.

Aircraft-alone dynamics and superaugmented control system fundamental regulatory properties including stability and regulatory responses of the basic closed-loop systems; fundamental high and low frequency margins and governing factors; and sensitivity to aircraft and controller parameters are addressed. Alternative FCS mechanizations, and mechanizational side effects are also discussed. An overview of flying qualities considerations encompasses general pilot operations as a controller in unattended, intermittent and trim, and full-attention regulatory or command control; effective vehicle primary and secondary response properties to pilot inputs and disturbances; pilot control architectural possibilities; and comparison of superaugmented and conventional aircraft path responses for different forms of pilot control. Results of a simple experimental investigation into pilot dynamic behavior in attitude control of superaugmented aircraft configurations with high frequency time laps and time delays are presented.

*Systems Technology, Inc., Hawthorne, California.

1985 Contractor Reports

168. *Enns, D. F.: **Model Reduction for Control System Design.** NASA CR-170417, NAS 1.26:170417, March 1985, 85N22398.

An approach and a technique for effectively obtaining reduced order mathematical models of a given large order model for the purposes of synthesis, analysis and implementation of control systems is developed. This approach involves the use of an error criterion which is the H-infinity norm of a frequency weighted error between the full and reduced order models. The weightings are chosen to take into account the purpose for which the reduced order model is intended. A previously unknown error bound in the H-infinity norm for reduced order models obtained from internally balanced realizations was obtained. This motivated further development of the balancing technique to include the frequency dependent weightings. This resulted in the frequency weighted balanced realization and a new model reduction technique. Two approaches to designing reduced order controllers were developed. The first involves reducing the order of a high order controller with an appropriate weighting. The second involves linear quadratic Gaussian synthesis based on a reduced order model obtained with an appropriate weighting.

*Stanford University, Stanford, California.

169. *James, R.; and *Brownlow, J. D.: **Mathematical Analysis Study for Radar Data Processing and Enhancement. Part 1: Radar Data Analysis.** NASA CR-166616-PT-1, H-1287-PT-1, August 1985, 86N13353.

A study is performed under NASA contract to evaluate data from an AN/FPS-16 radar installed for support of flight programs at Dryden Flight Research Facility of NASA Ames Research Center. The purpose of this study is to provide information necessary for improving post-flight data reduction and knowledge of accuracy of derived radar quantities. Tracking data from six flights are analyzed. Noise and bias errors in raw tracking data are determined for each of the flights. A discussion of an altitude bias error during all of the tracking missions is included. This bias error is defined by utilizing pressure altitude measurements made during survey flights. Four separate filtering methods, representative of the most widely used optimal estimation techniques for enhancement of radar tracking data, are analyzed for suitability in processing both real-time and post-mission data. Additional information regarding the radar and its measurements, including typical noise and bias errors in the range and angle measurements, is also presented. This is in two parts. This is part 1, an analysis of radar data.

*GMD Systems, Inc., Lancaster, California.

170. *James, R.; and *Brownlow, J. D.: **Mathematical Analysis Study for Radar Data Processing and Enhancement. Part 2: Modeling of Propagation Path Errors.** NASA CR-166616-PT-2, H-1287-PT-2, August 1985, 86N13354.

A study is performed under NASA contract to evaluate data from an AN/FPS-16 radar installed for support of flight programs at Dryden Flight Research Facility of NASA Ames Research Center. The purpose of this study is to provide information necessary for improving post-flight data reduction and knowledge of accuracy of derived radar quantities. Tracking data from six flights are analyzed. Noise and bias errors in raw tracking data are determined for each of the flights. A discussion of an altitude bias error during all of the tracking missions is included. This bias error is defined by utilizing pressure altitude measurements made during survey flights. Four separate filtering methods, representative of the most widely used optimal estimation techniques for enhancement of radar tracking data, are analyzed for suitability in processing both real-time and post-mission data. Additional information regarding the radar and its measurements, including typical noise and bias errors in the range and angle measurements, is also presented. This report is in two parts. This is part 2, a discussion of the modeling of propagation path errors.

*GMD Systems, Inc., Lancaster, California.

171. *Vaillard, A. H.; *Paduano, J.; and *Downing, D. R.: **Development of a Sensitivity Control Systems**. NASA CR-166619, October 1985, 86N17358, #.

This report presents the development and application of a sensitivity analysis technique for multiloop flight control systems. This analysis yields very useful information on the sensitivity of the relative-stability criteria of the control system, with variations or uncertainties in the system and controller elements. The sensitivity analysis technique developed is based on the computation of the singular values and singular-value gradients of a feedback-control system. The method is applicable to single-input/single-output as well as multiloop continuous-control systems. Application to sampled-data systems is also explored. The sensitivity analysis technique was applied to a continuous yaw/roll damper stability augmentation system of a typical business jet, and the results show that the analysis is very useful in determining the system elements which have the largest effect on the relative stability of the closed-loop system. As a secondary product of the research reported here, the relative stability criteria based on the concept of singular values were explored.

*University of Kansas, Lawrence, Kansas.

172. *Cousineau, R. D.; *Crook, R., Jr.; and *Leeds, D. J.: **Investigation of Seismicity and Related Effects at NASA Ames-Dryden Flight Research Facility, Computer Center, Edwards, California**. NASA CR-170415, November 1985, 86N14706, #.

This report discusses a geological and seismological investigation of the NASA Ames-Dryden Flight Research Facility site at Edwards, California. Results are presented as seismic design criteria, with design values of the pertinent ground motion parameters, probability of recurrence, and recommended analogous time-history accelerograms with their corresponding spectra. The recommendations apply specifically to the Dryden site and should not be extrapolated to other sites with varying foundation and geologic conditions or different seismic environments.

*Soils International, San Gabriel, California.

173. *Schmidt, D. K.; and *Duke, E. L.: **Multi-Input, Multi-Output System Control for Experimental Aircraft**. NASA CR-177017, NAS 1.26:177017, December 1985, 86N28955, #.

Two techniques, direct eigenspace assignment (DEA) and explicit model following (EMF), are used initially to synthesize control laws for the longitudinal dynamics model of a Short Takeoff and Landing (STOL) vehicle in the landing configuration. The vehicle model and the flight control design are presented. The two synthesis techniques are briefly discussed and the handling qualities specifications mapped into the algorithm formulations. The control laws resulting from exercising the algorithms are evaluated in terms of achieved performance and robustness. Since the synthesized control laws involve full state feedback, methodologies were implemented for the control laws using output feedback without adversely affecting performance and robustness. Finally, the salient features o f the two design techniques are summarized and the areas that require further investigation are suggested.

*Purdue University, School of Aeronautics and Astronautics, West Lafayette, Indiana.

1986 Contractor Reports

174. *Myers, T. T.; *Johnston, D. E.; and *McRuer, D. T.: **Space Shuttle Flying Qualities Criteria Assessment. Phase 5: Data Acquisition and Analysis**. NASA CR-166618, NAS 1.26:166618, STI-TR-1206-1, May 1986, 86N24704.

The development of flying qualities experiments (OFQ) as a part of the Orbiter Experiments Program (OEX) was continued. The data base was extended to use the ground based cinetheodolite measurements of orbiter approach and landing. Onboard the cinetheodolite data were analyzed from flights STS 2 through 7 to identify the effective augmented vehicle dynamics, the control strategy employed by the pilot during preflare, shallow glide, and final flare segments of the landing, and the key approach and touchdown performance measures. A plan for an OFQ flying qualities data archive and processing is presented.

*Systems Technology, Inc., Hawthorne, California.

175. *Cruz, R. E.: **An Application of Adaptive Learning to Malfunction Recovery**. NASA CR-166620, H-1325, AD-A158129, AFIT/CI/NR-85-85T, May 1986, 86N25169, #.

A self-organizing controller is developed for a simplified two-dimensional aircraft model. The Controller learns how to pilot the aircraft through a navigational mission without exceeding pre-established position and velocity limits. The controller pilots the aircraft by activating one of eight directional actuators at all times. By continually monitoring the aircraft's position and velocity with respect to the mission, the controller progressively modifies its decision rules to improve the aircraft's performance. When the controller has learned how to pilot the aircraft, two actuators fail permanently. Despite this malfunction, the controller regains proficiency at its original task. The experimental results reported show the controller's capabilities for self-organizing control, learning, and malfunction recovery.

*University of California, Los Angeles, California.

176. *Myers, T. T.; *Dimarco, R.; *Magdaleno, R. E.; and *Aponso, B. L.: **Archive Data Base and Handling System for the Orbiter Flying Qualities Experiment Program**. NASA CR-166622, H-1353, <u>October 1986</u>, 87N14351, #.

The OFQ archives data base and handling system assembled as part of the Orbiter Flying Qualities (OFQ) research of the Orbiter Experiments Program (EOX) are described. The purpose of the OFQ archives is to preserve and document shuttle flight data relevant to vehicle dynamics, flight control, and flying qualities in a form that permits maximum use for qualified users. In their complete form, the OFQ archives contain descriptive text (general information about the flight, signal descriptions and units) as well as numerical time history data. Since the shuttle program is so complex, the official data base contains thousands of signals and very complex entries are required to obtain data. The OFQ archives are intended to provide flight phase oriented data subsets with relevant signals which are easily identified for flying qualities research.

*Systems Technology, Inc., Hawthorne, California.

1987 Contractor Reports

177. *Paduano, James D.; and *Downing, David R.: **Application of a Sensitivity Analysis Technique to High-Order Digital Flight Control Systems**. NASA CR-179429, <u>January 1987</u>, 87N28565, #.

A sensitivity analysis technique for multiloop flight control systems is studied. This technique uses the scaled singular values of the return difference matrix as a measure of the relative stability of a control system. It then uses the gradients of these singular values with respect to system and controller parameters to judge sensitivity. The sensitivity analysis technique is first reviewed; then it is extended to include digital systems, through the derivation of singular-value gradient equations. Gradients with respect to parameters which do not appear explicitly as control-system matrix elements are also derived, so that high-order systems can be studied. A complete review of the integrated technique is given by way of a simple example: the inverted pendulum problem. The technique is then demonstrated on the X-29 control laws. Results show linear models of real systems can be analyzed by this sensitivity technique, if it is applied with

care. A computer program called SVA was written to accomplish the singular-value sensitivity analysis techniques. Thus computational methods and considerations form an integral part of many of the discussions. A user's guide to the program is included. The SVA is a fully public domain program, running on the NASA/Dryden Elxsi computer.

*University of Kansas, Center for Research, Inc., Lawrence, Kansas.

178. *Lan, C. Edward; and *Lee, I. G.: **Investigation of Empennage Buffeting**. NASA CR-179426, H-1393, <u>March 1987</u>, 87N19754, #.

Theoretical methods of predicting aircraft buffeting are reviewed. For the buffeting due to leading-edge vortex breakdown, a method is developed to convert test data of mean square values of fluctuating normal force to buffeting vortex strength through an unsteady lifting-surface theory and unsteady suction analogy. The resulting buffeting vortex from the leading-edge extension of an F-18 configuration is used to generate a fluctuating flow field which produces unsteady pressure distribution on the vertical tails. The root mean square values of root bending moment on the vertical tails are calculated for a rigid configuration. Results from a flow visualization and hot films study in a water tunnel facility using a 1/48 scale model of an F-18 are included in an appendix. The results confirm that the LEX vortex is the dominant forcing function of fin buffet at high angles of attack.

*University of Kansas, Center for Research, Inc., Lawrence, Kansas.

179. *Nelson, Lawrence H.: **Measured and Predicted Structural Behavior of the HiMAT Tailored Composite Wing**. NASA CR-166617, H-1376, <u>March 1987</u>, 89N18530, #.

A series of load tests was conducted on the HiMAT tailored composite wing. Coupon tests were also run on a series of unbalanced laminates, including the ply configuration of the wing, the purpose of which was to compare the measured and predicted behavior of unbalanced laminates, including - in the case of the wing - a comparison between the behavior of the full scale structure and coupon tests. Both linear and nonlinear finite element (NASTRAN) analyses were carried out on the wing. Both linear and nonlinear point-stress analyses were performed on the coupons. All test articles were instrumented with strain gages, and wing deflections measured. The leading and trailing edges were found to have no effect on the response of the wing to applied loads. A decrease in the stiffness of the wing box was evident over the 27-test program. The measured load-strain behavior of the wing was found to be linear, in contrast to coupon tests of the same laminate, which were nonlinear. A linear NASTRAN analysis of the wing generally correlated more favorably with measurements than did a nonlinear analysis. An examination of the predicted deflections in the wing root region revealed an anomalous behavior of the structural model that cannot be explained. Both hysteresis and creep appear to be less significant in the wing tests than in the corresponding laminate coupon tests.

*California Polytechnic State University, San Luis Obispo, California.

180. *Coe, Charles F.: **An Investigation of the Causes of Failure of Flexible Thermal Protection Materials in an Aerodynamic Environment.** NASA CR-166624, H-1389, March 1987, 89N19214, #.

Tests of small panels of advanced flexible reusable surface insulation (AFRSI) were conducted using a small wind tunnel that was designed to simulate Space Shuttle Orbiter entry mean-flow and pulsating aerodynamic loads. The wind tunnel, with a 3 inch wide by 1.75 inch high by 7.5 inch long test section, proved to be capable of continuous flow at dynamic pressures q near 580 psf with fluctuating pressures over 2 psi RMS at an excitation frequency f sub E of 200 Hz. For this investigation, however, the wind tunnel was used to test entry-temperature preconditioned and heat-cleaned AFRSI at q = 280 psf, Prms was nearly equal to 1.2 psi and f sub E = 200 Hz. The objective of these tests was to determine the mechanism of failure of AFRSI at Orbiter entry conditions. Details of the test apparatus and test results are presented.

*Coe Engineering, Inc., Los Altos, California.

181. *Goforth, E. A.; *Murphy, R. C.; *Beranek, J. A.; and *Davis, R. A.: **Flight and Analytical Investigations of a Structural Mode Excitation System on the YF-12A Airplane.** NASA CR-166623, H-1361, April 1987, 87N22685, #.

A structural excitation system, using an oscillating canard vane to generate force, was mounted on the forebody of the YF-12A airplane. The canard vane was used to excite the airframe structural modes during flight in the subsonic, transonic, and supersonic regimes. Structural modal responses generated by the canard vane forces were measured at the flight test conditions by airframe-mounted accelerometers. Correlations of analytical and experimental aeroelastic results were made. Doublet lattice, steady state double lattice with uniform lag, Mach box, and piston theory all produced acceptable analytical aerodynamic results within the restrictions that apply to each. In general, the aerodynamic theory methods, carefully applied, were found to predict the dynamic behavior of the YF-12A aircraft adequately.

*Lockheed-California Co., Burbank, California.

182. *Childs, William I.: **Low Cost Tooling Material and Process for Graphite and Kevlar Composites.** NASA CR-179427, H-1407, June 1987, 90N17834.

An Extruded Sheet Tooling Compound (ESTC) was developed for use in quickly building low cost molds for fabricating composites. The ESTC is a very highly mineral-filled resin system formed into a 6 mm thick sheet. The sheet is laid on the pattern, vacuum (bag) is applied to remove air from the pattern surface, and the assembly is heat cured. The formed ESTC is then backed and/or framed and ready for use. The cured ESTC exhibits low coefficient of thermal expansion and maintains strength at temperatures of 180 to 200 C. Tools were made and used successfully for: Compression molding of high strength epoxy sheet molding compound, stamping of aluminum, resin transfer molding of polyester, and liquid resin molding of polyester. Several variations of ESTC can be made for specific requirements. Higher thermal conductivity can be achieved by using an aluminum particle filler. Room temperature gel is possible to allow use of foam patterns.

*Quantum Composites, Inc., Midland, Michigan.

1988 Contractor Reports

183. *Menon, P. K. A.; and *Walker, R. A.: **Aircraft Flight Test Trajectory Control.** NASA CR-179428, H-1345, AD-A269273, January 1988, 88N16707, #.

Two design techniques for linear flight test trajectory controllers (FTTCs) are described: Eigenstructure assignment and the minimum error excitation technique. The two techniques are used to design FTTCs for an F-15 aircraft model for eight different maneuvers at thirty different flight conditions. An evaluation of the FTTCs is presented.

*Integrated Systems, Inc., Palo Alto, California.

184. *Redner, Alex S.; and *Voloshin, Arkady S.: **Spectral Contents Readout of Birefringent Sensors.** NASA CR-179430, H-1444, April 1988, 88N20673, #.

The objective of the research performed was to establish the feasibility of using spectral contents analysis to measure accurately, strains and retardation in birefringent sensors, and more generally, on transparent materials.

*Strainoptic Technologies, Inc., Norristown, Pennsylvania.

185. *Myers, Thomas T.; *Parseghian, Zareh; and *Hogue, Jeffrey R.: **Orbiter Flying Qualities (OFQ) Workstation User's Guide.** NASA CR-179440, H-1537, June 1988, 89N22612, #.

This project was devoted to the development of a software package, called the Orbiter Flying Qualities (OFQ) Workstation, for working with the OFQ Archives which are specially selected sets of space shuttle entry flight data relevant to flight control and flying qualities. The basic approach to creation of the workstation software was to federate and extend commercial software products to create a low cost package that operates on personal computers.

Provision was made to link the workstation to large computers, but the OFQ Archive files were also converted to personal computer diskettes and can be stored on workstation hard disk drives. The primary element of the workstation developed in the project is the Interactive Data Handler (IDH) which allows the user to select data subsets from the archives and pass them to specialized analysis programs. The IDH was developed as an application in a relational database management system product. The specialized analysis programs linked to the workstation include a spreadsheet program, FREDA for spectral analysis, MFP for frequency domain system identification, and NIPIP for pilot-vehicle system parameter identification. The workstation also includes capability for ensemble analysis over groups of missions.

*Systems Technology, Inc., Hawthorne, California.

186. *Richi, Glen A.: **Debris Prevention Analysis for DFI/OFI/OEI (STS-26 Configuration Only)**. NASA CR-179421, TWR-18091, WBS-4B102-10-08, <u>August 1988</u>, 89N13453, #.

The first 3 shuttle flights to use the Redesigned Solid Rocket Motors (RSRMs) will utilize Development Flight Instrumentation (DFI), as well as Operational Flight Instrumentation (OFI), and Operational Environment Instrumentation (OEI). The OFI consists of high pressure transducers used on both RSRMs to monitor the igniter and motor chamber pressure. DFI consists of assorted strain gages, temperature sensors, accelerometers, girth gages, and low level pressure transducers. The latter are installed on the left hand booster to measure post-separation aerodynamic loading. OEI consists of temperature sensors. After Flight 3, all DFI gages are to be deleted, and only OFI and OEI will be used for subsequent flights. This report deals specifically with debris prevention and hazards concerning the STS-26 flight DFI configuration only. Continued analysis is being done that will adequately address the debris hazards associated with the STS-27 and subsequent flight DFI configurations.

*Morton Thiokol, Brigham City, Utah.

187. *Yeh, Hsien-Yang: **Stress Concentration Around Circular Hole in a Composite Material Specimen Representative of the X-29A Forward-Swept Wing Aircraft**. NASA CR-179435, H-1435, <u>August 1988</u>, 88N26694, #.

The theory of anisotropic elasticity was used to evaluate the anisotropic stress concentration factors of a composite laminated plate containing a small circular hole. This advanced composite material was used to manufacture the X-29A forward swept wing. Observe that the usual isotropic material stress concentration factor is three. However, for composite material, it was found that the anisotropic stress concentration factor is no longer constant, and that the

locations of maximum tangential stress points could shift by changing the fiber orientation with respect to the loading axis. The analysis showed that through the lamination process, the stress concentration factor could be drastically reduced, and therefore the structural performance could be improved. Both the mixture rule approach and the constant strain approach were used to calculate the stress concentration factor. The results predicted by the mixture rule approach were about 20 percent deviate from the experimental data. However, the results predicted by the constant strain approach matched the testing data very well. This showed the importance of the inplane shear effect on the evaluation of stress concentration factor for the X-29A composite plate.

*California State University, Long Beach, California.

188. *Yeh, Hsien-Yang: **Temperature Effect on Stress Concentration Around Circular Hole in a Composite Material Specimen Representative of X-29A Forward-Swept Wing Aircraft**. NASA CR-179439, H-1514, NAS 1.26:179439, <u>August 1988</u>, 89N14456, #.

The theory of anisotropic elasticity was used to evaluate the anisotropic stress concentration factors of a composite laminated plate containing a small circular hole. This advanced composite was used to manufacture the X-29A forward-swept wing. It was found for composite material, that the anisotropic stress concentration is no longer a constant, and that the locations of maximum tangential stress points could shift by changing the fiber orientation with respect to the loading axis. The analysis showed that through the lamination process, the stress concentration factor could be reduced drastically, and therefore the structural performance could be improved. Both the mixture rule approach and the constant strain approach were used to calculate the stress concentration factor of room temperature. The results predicted by the mixture rule approach were about twenty percent deviate from the experimental data. However, the results predicted by the constant strain approach matched the testing data very well. This showed the importance of the inplane shear effect on the evaluation of the stress concentration factor for the X-29A composite plate.

*California State University, Long Beach, California.

189. *Dunipace, K. R.: **Model Reduction Methods for Control Design**. NASA CR-179434, H-1499, <u>August 1988</u>, 88N26144, #.

Several different model reduction methods are developed and detailed implementation information is provided for those methods. Command files to implement the model reduction methods in a proprietary control law analysis and design package are presented. A comparison and discussion of the various reduction techniques is included.

*Indiana University-Purdue University, West Lafayette, Indiana.

190. *Agarwal, A. K.: **Automation Tools for Demonstration of Goal Directed and Self-Repairing Flight Control Systems**. NASA CR-179433, H-1498, August 1988, 88N26121, #.

The coupling of expert systems and control design and analysis techniques are documented to provide a realizable self repairing flight control system. Key features of such a flight control system are identified and a limited set of rules for a simple aircraft model are presented.

*Integrated Systems, Inc., Santa Clara, California.

1989 Contractor Reports

191. *Edwards, S. J.; and *Caglayan, A. K.: **Expert Systems for Real-Time Monitoring and Fault Diagnosis**. NASA CR-179441, H-1540, April 1989, 89N23209, #.

Methods for building real-time onboard expert systems were investigated, and the use of expert systems technology was demonstrated in improving the performance of current real-time onboard monitoring and fault diagnosis applications. The potential applications of the proposed research include an expert system environment allowing the integration of expert systems into conventional time-critical application solutions, a grammar for describing the discrete event behavior of monitoring and fault diagnosis systems, and their applications to new real-time hardware fault diagnosis and monitoring systems for aircraft.

*Charles River Analytics, Inc., Cambridge, Massachusetts.

192. *Menon, P. K. A.; *Badgett, M. E.; and *Walker, R. A.: **Nonlinear Maneuver Autopilot for the F-15 Aircraft**. NASA CR-179442, H-1541, June 1989, 90N11487, #.

A methodology is described for the development of flight test trajectory control laws based on singular perturbation methodology and nonlinear dynamic modeling. The control design methodology is applied to a detailed nonlinear six degree-of-freedom simulation of the F-15 and results for a level accelerations, pushover/pullup maneuver, zoom and pushover maneuver, excess thrust windup turn, constant thrust windup turn, and a constant dynamic pressure/constant load factor trajectory are presented.

*Integrated Systems, Inc., Palo Alto, California.

193. *Rediess, Herman A.: **National Remote Computational Flight Research Facility**. NASA CR-179432, H-1489, September 1989, 91N24210, #.

The extension of the NASA Ames-Dryden remotely augmented vehicle (RAV) facility to accommodate flight testing of a hypersonic aircraft utilizing the continental United States as a test range is investigated. The development and demonstration of an automated flight test management

system (ATMS) that uses expert system technology for flight test planning, scheduling, and execution is documented.

*Sparta, Inc., Laguna Hills, California.

194. *Redner, Alex S.: **Spectral Contents Readout of Birefringent Sensor**. NASA CR-179444, H-1581, REPT-87-955, October 1989, 90N14905, #.

The technical objective of this research program was to develop a birefringent sensor, capable of measuring strain/ stress up to 2000 °F and a readout system based on Spectral Contents analysis. As a result of the research work, a data acquisition system was developed, capable of measuring strain birefringence in a sensor at 2000 °F, with multi-point static and dynamic capabilities. The system uses a dedicated spectral analyzer for evaluation of stress-birefringence and a PC-based readout. Several sensor methods were evaluated. Fused silica was found most satisfactory. In the final evaluation, measurements were performed up to 2000 °F and the system performance exceeded expectations.

*Strainoptic Technologies, Inc., North Wales, Pennsylvania.

195. *Carlson, Leland A.:**Development of Direct-Inverse 3-D Methods for Applied Transonic Aerodynamic Wing Design and Analysis**. NASA CR-186036, NAS 1.26:186036, TAMRF-5373-8903, October 1989, 90N11733, #.

An inverse wing design method was developed around an existing transonic wing analysis code. The original analysis code, TAWFIVE, has as its core the numerical potential flow solver, FLO30, developed by Jameson and Caughey. Features of the analysis code include a finite-volume formulation; wing and fuselage fitted, curvilinear grid mesh; and a viscous boundary layer correction that also accounts for viscous wake thickness and curvature. The development of the inverse methods as an extension of previous methods existing for design in Cartesian coordinates is presented. Results are shown for inviscid wing design cases in super-critical flow regimes. The test cases selected also demonstrate the versatility of the design method in designing an entire wing or discontinuous sections of a wing.

*Texas A&M University, College Station, Texas.

196. *Srivastava, R.; and *Sankar, L. N.: **Numerical Simulation of Unsteady Rotational Flow Over Propfan Configurations: May 1 to November 30, 1989**. NASA CR-186037, November 1989, 90N12500, #.

The objective is to develop efficient numerical techniques for the study of aeroelastic response of a propfan in an unsteady transonic flow. A three dimensional unsteady Euler solver is being modified to address this problem.

*Georgia Institute of Technology, Atlanta, Georgia.

1990 Contractor Reports

197. *Bailey, R. E.; and *Knotts, L. H.: **Interaction of Feel System and Flight Control System Dynamics on Lateral Flying Qualities**. NASA CR-179445, H-1584, CALSPAN-7205-26, December 1990, 91N14353, #.

An experimental investigation of the influence of lateral feel system characteristics on fighter aircraft roll flying qualities was conducted using the variable stability USAF NT-33. Forty-two evaluation flights were flown by three engineering test pilots. The investigation utilized the power approach, visual landing task and up-and-away tasks including formation, gun tracking, and computer-generated compensatory attitude tracking tasks displayed on the Head-Up Display. Experimental variations included the feel system frequency, force-deflection gradient, control system command type (force or position input command), aircraft roll mode time constant, control system prefilter frequency, and control system time delay. The primary data were task performance records and evaluation pilot comments and ratings using the Cooper-Harper scale. The data highlight the unique and powerful effect of the feel system of flying qualities. The data show that the feel system is not 'equivalent' in flying qualities influence to analogous control system elements. A lower limit of allowable feel system frequency appears warranted to ensure good lateral flying qualities. Flying qualities criteria should most properly treat the feel system dynamic influence separately from the control system, since the input and output of this dynamic element is apparent to the pilot and thus, does not produce a 'hidden' effect.

*Calspan-State University of New York Joint Venture, Buffalo, New York.

1991 Contractor Reports

198. *Evans, Alison B.: **The Effects of Compressor Seventh-Stage Bleed Air Extraction on Performance of the F100-PW-220 Afterburning Turbofan Engine**. NASA CR-179447, H-1679, February 1991, 91N20085, #.

A study was conducted to determine the effects of seventh-stage compressor bleed on the performance of the F100 afterburning turbofan engine. The effects of bleed on thrust, specific fuel consumption, fan turbine inlet temperature, bleed total pressure, and bleed total temperature were obtained from the engine manufacturer's status deck computer simulation. These effects were determined for power settings of intermediate, partial afterburning, and maximum afterburning for Mach numbers between 0.6 and 2.2 and for altitudes of 30,000, 40,000, and 50,000 ft. It was found that thrust loss and specific fuel consumption increase were approximately linear functions of bleed flow and, based

on a percent-thrust change basis, were approximately independent of power setting.

*San Jose State University, San Jose, California.

199. *Freudinger, Lawrence C.: **Analysis of Structural Response Data Using Discrete Modal Filters**. NASA CR-179448, H-1693, NAS 1.26:179448, May 1991, 91N22116, #.

The application of reciprocal modal vectors to the analysis of structural response data is described. Reciprocal modal vectors are constructed using an existing experimental modal model and an existing frequency response matrix of a structure, and can be assembled into a matrix that effectively transforms the data from the physical space to a modal space within a particular frequency range. In other words, the weighting matrix necessary for modal vector orthogonality (typically the mass matrix) is contained within the reciprocal model matrix. The underlying goal of this work is mostly directed toward observing the modal state responses in the presence of unknown, possibly closed loop forcing functions, thus having an impact on both operating data analysis techniques and independent modal space control techniques. This study investigates the behavior of reciprocal modal vectors as modal filters with respect to certain calculation parameters and their performance with perturbed system frequency response data.

*University of Cincinnati, Cincinnati, Ohio

200. *Rediess, Herman A.; *Ramnath, Rudrapatna V.; *Vrable, Daniel L.; *Hirvo, David H.; *McMillen, Lowell D.; and *Osofsky, Irving B.: **Hypersonic Research Vehicle (HRV) Real-Time Flight Test Support Feasibility and Requirements Study. Part 1: Real-Time Flight Experiment Support**. NASA CR-179449, H-1677-PT-1, May 1991, 91N24193, #.

The results are presented of a study to identify potential real time remote computational applications to support monitoring HRV flight test experiments along with definitions of preliminary requirements. A major expansion of the support capability available at Ames-Dryden was considered. The focus is on the use of extensive computation and data bases together with real time flight data to generate and present high level information to those monitoring the flight. Six examples were considered: (1) boundary layer transition location; (2) shock wave position estimation; (3) performance estimation; (4) surface temperature estimation; (5) critical structural stress estimation; and (6) stability estimation.

*Sparta, Inc., Laguna Hills, California.

201. *Rediess, Herman A.; and *Hewett, M. D.: **Hypersonic Research Vehicle (HRV) Real-Time Flight Test Support Feasibility and Requirements Study. Part 2:**

463

Remote Computation Support for Flight Systems Functions. NASA CR-179450, H-1700-PT-2, <u>May 1991</u>, 91N24194.

The requirements are assessed for the use of remote computation to support HRV flight testing. First, remote computational requirements were developed to support functions that will eventually be performed onboard operational vehicles of this type. These functions which either cannot be performed onboard in the time frame of initial HRV flight test programs because the technology of airborne computers will not be sufficiently advanced to support the computational loads required, or it is not desirable to perform the functions onboard in the flight test program for other reasons. Second, remote computational support either required or highly desirable to conduct flight testing itself was addressed. The use is proposed of an Automated Flight Management System which is described in conceptual detail. Third, autonomous operations is discussed and finally, unmanned operations.

*Sparta, Inc., Laguna Hills, California.

202. *Hewett, M. D.; *Tartt, D. M.; and **Agarwal, A.: **Automated Flight Test Management System**. NASA CR-186011, H-1699, <u>May 1991</u>, 91N22117, #.

The Phase 1 development of an automated flight test management system (ATMS) as a component of a rapid prototyping flight research facility for artificial intelligence (AI) based flight concepts is discussed. The ATMS provides a flight engineer with a set of tools that assist in flight test planning, monitoring, and simulation. The system is also capable of controlling an aircraft during flight test by performing closed loop guidance functions, range management, and maneuver-quality monitoring. The ATMS is being used as a prototypical system to develop a flight research facility for AI based flight systems concepts at NASA Ames Dryden.

*Sparta, Inc., Laguna Hills, California.
**Integrated Systems, Inc., Santa Clara, California.

203. *Hewett, Marle D.: **Autonomous Aircraft Initiative Study**. NASA CR-186013, H-1609, NAS 1.26:186013, <u>July 1991</u>, 91N26140, #.

The results of a consulting effort to aid NASA Ames-Dryden in defining a new initiative in aircraft automation are described. The initiative described is a multi-year, multi-center technology development and flight demonstration program. The initiative features the further development of technologies in aircraft automation already being pursued at multiple NASA centers and Department of Defense (DOD) research and Development (R and D) facilities. The proposed initiative involves the development of technologies in intelligent systems, guidance, control, software development, airborne computing, navigation, communications, sensors, unmanned vehicles, and air traffic control. It involves the integration and implementation of these technologies to the extent necessary to conduct selected and incremental flight demonstrations.

*G and C Systems, Inc., San Juan Capistrano, California.

204. *Hanna, Gregory J.; and **Stephens, Craig A.: **Predicted Thermal Response of a Cryogenic Fuel Tank Exposed to Simulated Aerodynamic Heating Profiles With Different Cryogens and Fill Levels**. NASA CR-4395, H-1738, NAS 1.26:4395, AIAA PAPER 91-4007. AIAA Session of the ASME/AICHE National Heat Transfer Conference, Minneapolis, Minnesota., July 28–31, 1991, <u>September 1991</u>, 91N31470, #. (See also 1869.)

A two dimensional finite difference thermal model was developed to predict the effects of heating profile, fill level, and cryogen type prior to experimental testing the Generic Research Cryogenic Tank (GRCT). These numerical predictions will assist in defining test scenarios, sensor locations, and venting requirements for the GRCT experimental tests. Boiloff rates, tank-wall and fluid temperatures, and wall heat fluxes were determined for 20 computational test cases. The test cases spanned three discrete fill levels and three heating profiles for hydrogen and nitrogen.

*Hanna Technology Resources, Boulder, Colorado.
**Planning Research Corp., Edwards, California.

205. *Brumbaugh, Randal W.: **An Aircraft Model for the AIAA Controls Design Challenge**. NASA CR-186019, H-1777, NAS 1.26:186019, AIAA PAPER 91-2631. Presented at the AIAA GNC Conference, New Orleans, Louisiana, August 12, 1991, <u>December 1991</u>, 92N13064, #.

A generic, state-of-the-art, high-performance aircraft model, including detailed, full-envelope, nonlinear aerodynamics, and full-envelope thrust and first-order engine response data is described. While this model was primarily developed Controls Design Challenge, the availability of such a model provides a common focus for research in aeronautical control theory and methodology. An implementation of this model using the FORTRAN computer language, associated routines furnished with the aircraft model, and techniques for interfacing these routines to external procedures is also described. Figures showing vehicle geometry, surfaces, and sign conventions are included.

*PRC Systems Services Co., Edwards, California.

1992 Contractor Reports

206. *Kuhn, Gary D.: **Postflight Aerothermodynamic Analysis of Pegasus® Using Computational Fluid Dynamic Techniques.** NASA CR-186017, H-1765, March 1992, 92N21188, #.

The objective was to validate the computational capability of the NASA Ames Navier-Stokes code, F3D, for flows at high Mach numbers using comparison flight test data from the Pegasus™ air launched, winged space booster. Comparisons were made with temperature and heat fluxes estimated from measurements on the wing surfaces and wing-fuselage fairings. Tests were conducted for solution convergence, sensitivity to grid density, and effects of distributing grid points to provide high density near temperature and heat flux sensors. The measured temperatures were from sensors embedded in the ablating thermal protection system. Surface heat fluxes were from plugs fabricated of highly insulative, nonablating material, and mounted level with the surface of the surrounding ablative material. As a preflight design tool, the F3D code produces accurate predictions of heat transfer and other aerodynamic properties, and it can provide detailed data for assessment of boundary layer separation, shock waves, and vortex formation. As a postflight analysis tool, the code provides a way to clarify and interpret the measured results.

*Nielsen Engineering and Research, Inc., Mountain View, California.

207. *Peron, Lee R.; and *Carpenter, Thomas: **Thrust Vectoring for Lateral-Directional Stability.** NASA CR-186016, H-1645, NAS 1.26:186016, March 1992, 92N21357, #.

The advantages and disadvantages of using thrust vectoring for lateral-directional control and the effects of reducing the tail size of a single-engine aircraft were investigated. The aerodynamic characteristics of the F-16 aircraft were generated by using the Aerodynamic Preliminary Analysis System II panel code. The resulting lateral-directional linear perturbation analysis of a modified F-16 aircraft with various tail sizes and yaw vectoring was performed at several speeds and altitudes to determine the stability and control trends for the aircraft compared to these trends for a baseline aircraft. A study of the paddle-type turning vane thrust vectoring control system as used on the National Aeronautics and Space Administration F/A-18 High Alpha Research Vehicle is also presented.

*California Polytechnic State University, San Luis Obispo, California.

208. *Ray, J. K.; *Carlin, C. M.; and *Lambregts, A. A.: **High-Speed Civil Transport Flight- and Propulsion-Control Technological Issues.** NASA CR-186015, H-1794, NAS 1.26:186015, March 1992, 92N21253, #.

Technology advances required in the flight and propulsion control system disciplines to develop a high speed civil transport (HSCT) are identified. The mission and requirements of the transport and major flight and propulsion control technology issues are discussed. Each issue is ranked and, for each issue, a plan for technology readiness is given. Certain features are unique and dominate control system design. These features include the high temperature environment, large flexible aircraft, control-configured empennage, minimizing control margins, and high availability and excellent maintainability. The failure to resolve most high-priority issues can prevent the transport from achieving its goals. The flow-time for hardware may require stimulus, since market forces may be insufficient to ensure timely production. Flight and propulsion control technology will contribute to takeoff gross weight reduction. Similar technology advances are necessary also to ensure flight safety for the transport. The certification basis of the HSCT must be negotiated between airplane manufacturers and government regulators. Efficient, quality design of the transport will require an integrated set of design tools that support the entire engineering design team.

*Boeing Commercial Airplane, Co., Seattle, Washington.

209. *Azzano, Christopher P.: **A Preliminary Look at an Optimal Multivariable Design for Propulsion-Only Flight Control of Jet-Transport Aircraft.** NASA CR-186014, H-1729, NAS 1.26:186014, April 1992, 92N25734, #.

Control of a large jet transport aircraft without the use of conventional control surfaces was studied. Engine commands were used to attempt to recreate the forces and moments typically provided by the elevator, ailerons, and rudder. Necessary conditions for aircraft controllability were developed pertaining to aircraft configuration such as the number of engines and engine placement. An optimal linear quadratic regulator controller was developed for the Boeing 707-720, in particular, for regulation of its natural dynamic modes. The design used a method of assigning relative weights to the natural modes, i.e., phugoid and dutch roll, for a more intuitive selection of the cost function. A prototype pilot command interface was then integrated into the loop based on pseudorate command of both pitch and roll. Closed loop dynamics were evaluated first with a batch linear simulation and then with a real time high fidelity piloted simulation. The NASA research pilots assisted in evaluation of closed loop handling qualities for typical cruise and landing tasks. Recommendations for improvement on this preliminary study of optimal propulsion only flight control are provided.

*San Jose State University, San Jose, California.

210. *McCarty, Craig A.; *Feather, John B.; *Dykman, John R.; *Page, Mark A.; and *Hodgkinson, John: **Design and Analysis Issues of Integrated Control Systems for High-Speed Civil Transports.** NASA CR-186022, H-1787, NAS 1.26:186022, May 1992, 92N31656, #.

A study was conducted to identify, rank, and define development plans for the critical guidance and control design and analysis issues as related to economically viable and environmentally acceptable high-speed civil transport. The issues were identified in a multistep process. First, pertinent literature on supersonic cruise aircraft was reviewed, and experts were consulted to establish the fundamental characteristics and problems inherent to supersonic cruise aircraft. Next, the advanced technologies and strategies being pursued for the high-speed civil transport were considered to determine any additional unique control problems the transport may have. Finally, existing technologies and methods were examined to determine their capabilities for the design and analysis of high-speed civil transport control systems and to identify the shortcomings and issues. Three priority levels - mandatory, highly beneficial, and desirable - were established. Within each of these levels, the issues were further ranked. Technology development plans for each issue were defined. Each plan contains a task breakdown and schedule.

*Douglas Aircraft Co., Inc., Long Beach, California.

211. *Hewett, Marle D.: **High-Speed Civil Transport Issues and Technology Program**. NASA CR-186020, H-1795, NAS 1.26:186020, May 1992, 92N31208, #.

A strawman program plan is presented, consisting of technology developments and demonstrations required to support the construction of a high-speed civil transport. The plan includes a compilation of technology issues related to the development of a transport. The issues represent technical areas in which research and development are required to allow airframe manufacturers to pursue an HSCT development. The vast majority of technical issues presented require flight demonstrated and validated solutions before a transport development will be undertaken by the industry. The author believes that NASA is the agency best suited to address flight demonstration issues in a concentrated effort. The new Integrated Test Facility at NASA Dryden Flight Research Facility is considered ideally suited to the task of supporting ground validations of proof-of-concept and prototype system demonstrations before night demonstrations. An elaborate ground hardware-in-the-loop (iron bird) simulation supported in this facility provides a viable alternative to developing an expensive fill-scale prototype transport technology demonstrator. Dryden's SR-71 assets, modified appropriately, are a suitable test-bed for supporting flight demonstrations and validations of certain transport technology solutions. A subscale, manned or unmanned flight demonstrator is suitable for flight validation of transport technology solutions, if appropriate structural similarity relationships can be established. The author contends that developing a full-scale prototype transport technology demonstrator is the best alternative to ensuring that a positive decision to develop a transport is reached by the United States aerospace industry.

*G and C Systems, Inc., San Juan Capistrano, California.

212. *McRuer, Duane T.; *Myers, Thomas T.; *Hoh, Roger H.; *Ashkenas, Irving L.; and *Johnston, Donald E.: **Assessment of Flying-Quality Criteria for Air-Breathing Aerospacecraft**. NASA CR-4442, H-1758, June 1992.

A study of flying quality requirements for air-breathing aerospacecraft gives special emphasis to the unusual operational requirements and characteristics of these aircraft, including operation at hypersonic speeds. The report considers distinguishing characteristics of these vehicles, including dynamic deficiencies and their implications for control. Particular emphasis is given to the interaction of the airframe and propulsion system, and the requirements for dynamic systems integration. Past operational missions are reviewed to define tasks and maneuvers to be considered for this class of aircraft. Areas of special concern with respect to vehicle dynamics and control are identified. Experience with the space shuttle orbiter is reviewed with respect to flight control system mechanization and flight experience in approach and landing flying qualities for the National Aero-Space Plane (NASP).

*Systems Technology, Inc., Hawthorne, California.

213. *Johnston, Richard P.: **A Preliminary Design and Analysis of an Advanced Heat-Rejection System for an Extreme Altitude Advanced Variable Cycle Diesel Engine Installed in a High-Altitude Advanced Research Platform**. NASA CR-186021, H-1775, NAS 1.26:186021, July 1992, 92N29427.

Satellite surveillance in such areas as the Antarctic indicates that from time to time concentration of ozone grows and shrinks. An effort to obtain useful atmospheric data for determining the causes of ozone depletion would require a flight capable of reaching altitudes of at least 100,000 ft and flying subsonically during the sampling portion of the mission. A study of a heat rejection system for an advanced variable cycle diesel (AVCD) engine was conducted. The engine was installed in an extreme altitude, high altitude advanced research platform. Results indicate that the waste heat from an AVCD engine propulsion system can be rejected at the maximum cruise altitude of 120,000 ft. Fifteen performance points, reflecting the behavior of the engine as the vehicle proceeded through the mission, were used to characterize the heat exchanger operation. That portion of the study is described in a appendix titled, 'A Detailed Study of the Heat Rejection System for an Extreme Altitude Atmospheric Sampling Aircraft,' by a consultant, Mr. James Bourne, Lytron, Incorporated.

*DieselDyne Corp., Morrow, Ohio.

214. *Peron, Lee R.; and *Carpenter, Thomas: **Thrust Vectoring for Lateral-Directional Stability**. NASA CR-186016, H-1645, NAS 1.26:186016, March 1992, 92N21357, #.

The advantages and disadvantages of using thrust vectoring for lateral-directional control and the effects of reducing the tail size of a single-engine aircraft were investigated. The aerodynamic characteristics of the F-16 aircraft were generated by using the Aerodynamic Preliminary Analysis System II panel code. The resulting lateral-directional linear perturbation analysis of a modified F-16 aircraft with various tail sizes and yaw vectoring was performed at several speeds and altitudes to determine the stability and control trends for the aircraft compared to these trends for a baseline aircraft. A study of the paddle-type turning vane thrust vectoring control system as used on the National Aeronautics and Space Administration F/A-18 High Alpha Research Vehicle is also presented.

*California Polytechnic State University, San Luis Obispo, California.

215. Ray, J. K.; Carlin, C. M.; and Lambregts, A. A.: **High-Speed Civil Transport Flight- and Propulsion-Control Technological Issues**. NASA CR-186015, H-1794, NAS 1.26:186015, March 1992, 92N21253, #.

Technology advances required in the flight and propulsion control system disciplines to develop a high speed civil transport (HSCT) are identified. The mission and requirements of the transport and major flight and propulsion control technology issues are discussed. Each issue is ranked and, for each issue, a plan for technology readiness is given. Certain features are unique and dominate control system design. These features include the high temperature environment, large flexible aircraft, control-configured empennage, minimizing control margins, and high availability and excellent maintainability. The failure to resolve most high-priority issues can prevent the transport from achieving its goals. The flow-time for hardware may require stimulus, since market forces may be insufficient to ensure timely production. Flight and propulsion control technology will contribute to takeoff gross weight reduction. Similar technology advances are necessary also to ensure flight safety for the transport. The certification basis of the HSCT must be negotiated between airplane manufacturers and government regulators. Efficient, quality design of the transport will require an integrated set of design tools that support the entire engineering design team.

1993 Contractor Reports

216. *Reilly, Richard J.: **Program for an Improved Hypersonic Temperature-Sensing Probe**. NASA CR-186025, H-1893, June 1993, 93N29066, #.

Under a NASA Dryden-sponsored contract in the mid 1960s, temperatures of up to 2200 C were successfully measured using a fluid oscillator. The current program, although limited in scope, explores the problem areas which must be solved if this technique is to be extended to 10,000 R. The

potential for measuring extremely high temperatures, using fluid oscillator techniques, stems from the fact that the measuring element is the fluid itself. The containing structure of the oscillator need not be brought to equilibrium temperature with the fluid for temperature measurement, provided that a suitable calibration can be arranged. This program concentrated on review of high-temperature material developments since the original program was completed. Other areas of limited study included related pressure instrumentation requirements, dissociation, rarefied gas effects, and analysis of sensor time response.

*Cuyuna Corp., Austin, Texas.

217. *Ward, Donald T.; and *Myatt, James H.: **Preliminary Design of an Intermittent Smoke Flow Visualization System**. NASA CR-186027, H-1917, TEES-AERO-TR-91-1, June 1993, 93N28693, #.

A prototype intermittent flow visualization system that was designed to study vortex flow field dynamics has been constructed and tested through its ground test phase. It produces discrete pulses of dense white smoke consisting of particles of terephthalic acid by the pulsing action of a fast-acting three-way valve. The trajectories of the smoke pulses can be tracked by a video imaging system without intruding in the flow around in flight. Two methods of pulsing the smoke were examined. The simplest and safest approach is to simply divert the smoke between the two outlet ports on the valve; this approach should be particularly effective if it were desired to inject smoke at two locations during the same test event. The second approach involves closing off one of the outlet ports to momentarily block the flow. The second approach requires careful control of valve dwell times to avoid excessive pressure buildup within the cartridge container. This method also increases the velocity of the smoke injected into the flow. The flow of the smoke has been blocked for periods ranging from 30 to 80 milliseconds, depending on the system volume and the length of time the valve is allowed to remain open between valve closings.

*Texas A&M University, College Station, Texas.

218. *Ward, Donald T.; and *Dorsett, Kenneth M.: **Flight Validation of a Pulsed Smoke Flow Visualization System**. NASA CR-186026, H-1914, September 1993, 94N14106, #.

A flow visualization scheme, designed to measure vortex fluid dynamics on research aircraft, was validated in flight. Strake vortex trajectories and axial core velocities were determined using pulsed smoke, high-speed video images, and semiautomated image edge detection hardware and software. Smoke was pulsed by using a fast-acting three-way valve. After being redesigned because of repeatedly jamming in flight, the valve shuttle operated flawlessly during the last two tests. A 25-percent scale, Gothic strake was used to generate vortex over the wing of a GA-7 Cougar and was operated at a local angle of attack of 22 degrees and Reynolds number of approximately 7.8 x 10(exp 5)/ft. Maximum axial velocities measured in the vortex core were between 1.75 and 1.95 times the freestream velocity. Analysis of the pulsed smoke system's affect on forebody vortices indicates that the system may reorient the forebody vortex system; however, blowing momentum coefficients normally used will have no appreciable affect on the leading-edge extension vortex system. It is recommended that a similar pulsed smoke system be installed on the F/A-18 High Angle Research Vehicle and that this approach be used to analyze vortex core dynamics during the remainder of its high-angle-of-attack research flights.

*Texas A&M University, College Station, Texas.

1994 Contractor Reports

219. *Wells, Edward A.; and *Urnes, James M., Sr.: **Design and Flight Test of the Propulsion Controlled Aircraft (PCA) Flight Control System on the NASA F-15 Test Aircraft**. NASA CR-186028, H-1965, NAS 1.26:186028, REPT-94B0005, February 1994, 94N27432, #.

This report describes the design, development and flight testing of the Propulsion Controlled Aircraft (PCA) flight control system performed at McDonnell Douglas Aerospace (MDA), St. Louis, Missouri and at the NASA Dryden Flight Research Facility, Edwards Air Force Base, California. This research and development program was conducted by MDA and directed by NASA through the Dryden Flight Research Facility for the period beginning January 1991 and ending December 1993. A propulsion steering backup to the aircraft conventional flight control system has been developed and flight demonstrated on a NASA F-15 test aircraft. The Propulsion Controlled Aircraft (PCA) flight system utilizes collective and differential thrust changes to steer an aircraft that experiences partial or complete failure of the hydraulically actuated control surfaces. The PCA flight control research has shown that propulsion steering is a viable backup flight control mode and can assist the pilot in safe landing recovery of a fighter aircraft that has damage to or loss of the flight control surfaces. NASA, USAF and Navy evaluation test pilots stated that the F-15 PCA design provided the control necessary to land the aircraft. Moreover, the feasibility study showed that PCA technology can be directly applied to transport aircraft and provide a major improvement in the survivability of passengers and crew of controls damaged aircraft.

*McDonnell-Douglas Aerospace Information Services Co., St. Louis, Missouri.

220. *Deppe, P. R.; *Chalk, C. R.; and Shafer, M.: **Flight Evaluation of an Aircraft With Side and Centerstick Controllers and Rate-Limited Ailerons.** Calspan Final Report No. 8091-2, April 1994. (See also A-235.)

*Calspan Corp., Buffalo, New York.

221. *Cobleigh, Brent R.: **High-Angle-of-Attack Yawing Moment Asymmetry of the X-31 Aircraft From Flight Test**. NASA CR-186030, H-2015, NAS 1.26:186030, AIAA PAPER 94-1803. Presented at the Applied Aerodynamics Conference, Colorado Springs, Colorado, June 20–23, 1994, September 1994, 95N11410, #.

Significant yawing moment asymmetries were encountered during the high-angle-of-attack envelope expansion of the two X-31 aircraft. These asymmetries led to position saturations of the thrust vector vanes and trailing-edge flaps during some of the dynamic stability axis rolling maneuvers at high angles of attack. This slowed the high-angle-of-attack envelope expansion and resulted in maneuver restrictions. Several aerodynamic modifications were made to the X-31 forebody with the goal of minimizing the asymmetry. A method for determining the yawing moment asymmetry from flight data was developed and an analysis of the various configuration changes completed. The baseline aircraft were found to have significant asymmetries above 45 deg angle of attack with the largest asymmetry typically occurring around 60 deg angle of attack. Applying symmetrical boundary layer transition strips along the forebody sides increased the magnitude of the asymmetry and widened the angle-of-attack range over which the largest asymmetry acted. Installing longitudinal forebody strakes and rounding the sharp nose of the aircraft caused the yawing moment asymmetry magnitude to be reduced. The transition strips and strakes made the asymmetry characteristic of the aircraft more repeatable than the clean forebody configuration. Although no geometric differences between the aircraft were known, ship 2 consistently had larger yawing moment asymmetries than ship 1.

*PRC Inc., Edwards, California.

222. *Wang, Kon-Sheng Charles: **In-Flight Imaging of Transverse Gas Jets Injected into Transonic and Supersonic Crossflows: Design and Development**. NASA CR-186031, H-2027, NAS 1.26:186031, November 1994, 95N17418, #.

The design and development of an airborne flight-test experiment to study nonreacting gas jets injected transversely into transonic and supersonic crossflows is presented. Free-stream/crossflow Mach numbers range from 0.8 to 2.0. Planar laser-induced fluorescence (PLIF) of an iodine-seeded nitrogen jet is used to visualize the jet flow. Time-dependent images are obtained with a high-speed intensified video camera synchronized to the laser pulse rate. The entire experimental assembly is configured compactly inside a unique flight-test-fixture (FTF) mounted under the fuselage of the F-104G research aircraft, which serves as a 'flying wind tunnel' at NASA Dryden Flight Research Center. The aircraft is flown at predetermined speeds and altitudes to permit a perfectly expanded (or slightly underexpanded) gas jet to form just outside the FTF at each free-stream Mach number. Recorded gas jet images are then digitized to allow analysis of jet trajectory, spreading, and mixing characteristics.

Comparisons will be made with analytical and numerical predictions. This study shows the viability of applying highly sophisticated groundbased flow diagnostic techniques to flight-test vehicle platforms that can achieve a wide range of thermo/fluid dynamic conditions. Realistic flow environments, high enthalpies, unconstrained flowfields, and moderate operating costs are also realized, in contrast to traditional wind-tunnel testing.

*PRC Inc., Edwards, California.

223. *Suarez, Carlos J.; *Malcolm, Gerald N.; *Kramer, Brian R.; *Smith, Brooke C.; and *Ayers, Bert F.: **Development of a Multicomponent Force and Moment Balance for Water Tunnel Applications, Volume 1.** NASA CR-4642-VOL-1, H-2030-VOL-1, <u>December 1994</u>, 95N18955, #.

The principal objective of this research effort was to develop a multicomponent strain gauge balance to measure forces and moments on models tested in flow visualization water tunnels. An internal balance was designed that allows measuring normal and side forces, and pitching, yawing and rolling moments (no axial force). The five-components to applied loads, low interactions between the sections and no hysteresis. Static experiments (which are discussed in this Volume) were conducted in the Eidetics water tunnel with delta wings and a model of the F/A-18. Experiments with the F/A-18 model included a thorough baseline study and investigations of the effect of control surface deflections and of several Forebody Vortex Control (FVC) techniques. Results were compared to wind tunnel data and, in general, the agreement is very satisfactory. The results of the static tests provide confidence that loads can be measured accurately in the water tunnel with a relatively simple multicomponent internal balance. Dynamic experiments were also performed using the balance, and the results are discussed in detail in Volume 2 of this report.

*Eidetics International, Inc., Torrance, California.

224. *Suarez, Carlos J.; *Malcolm, Gerald N.; *Kramer, Brian R.; *Smith, Brooke C.; and *Ayers, Bert F.: **Development of a Multicomponent Force and Moment Balance for Water Tunnel Applications, Volume 2.** NASA CR-4642-VOL-2, H-2030-VOL-2, <u>December 1994</u>, 95N18956, #.

The principal objective of this research effort was to develop a multicomponent strain gauge balance to measure forces and moments on models tested in flow visualization water tunnels. Static experiments (which are discussed in Volume 1 of this report) were conducted, and the results showed good agreement with wind tunnel data on similar configurations. Dynamic experiments, which are the main topic of this Volume, were also performed using the balance. Delta wing models and two F/A-18 models were utilized in a variety of dynamic tests. This investigation showed that, as expected, the values of the inertial tares are very small due to the low

rotating rates required in a low-speed water tunnel and can, therefore, be ignored. Oscillations in pitch, yaw and roll showed hysteresis loops that compared favorably to data from dynamic wind tunnel experiments. Pitch-up and hold maneuvers revealed the long persistence, or time-lags, of some of the force components in response to the motion. Rotary-balance experiments were also successfully performed. The good results obtained in these dynamic experiments bring a whole new dimension to water tunnel testing and emphasize the importance of having the capability to perform simultaneous flow visualization and force/moment measurements during dynamic situations.

*Eidetics International, Inc., Torrance, California.

===

1995 Contractor Reports

225. *Hallett, John; *Queen, Brian; **Teets, Edward; and *Fahey, James: **Nucleation and Growth of Crystals Under Cirrus and Polar Stratospheric Cloud Conditions.** NASA CR-197991, NAS 1.26:197991, <u>March 1995</u>, 95N24478, #.

Laboratory studies examine phase changes of hygroscopic substances which occur as aerosol in stratosphere and troposphere (sodium chloride, ammonium sulfate, ammonium bisulfate, nitric acid, sulfuric acid), under controlled conditions, in samples volume 1 to 10 (exp –4) ml. Crystallization of salts from supersaturated solutions is examined by slowly evaporating a solution drop on a substrate, under controlled relative humidity, until self nucleation occurs; controlled nucleation of ice in a mm capillary U-tube gives a measured ice crystallization velocity at known supercooling. Two states of crystallization occur for regions where hydrates exist. It is inferred that all of the materials readily exist as supersaturated/supercooled solutions; the degree of metastability appears to be slightly enhanced by inclusion of aircraft produced soot. The crystallization velocity is taken as a measure of viscosity. Results suggest an approach to a glass transition at high molality, supersaturation and/or supercooling within the range of atmospheric interest. It is hypothesized that surface reactions occur more readily on solidified particles - either crystalline or glass, whereas volume reactions are more important on droplets with sufficiently low viscosity and volume diffusivity. Implications are examined for optical properties of such particles in the atmosphere. In a separate experiment, crystal growth was examined in a modified thermal vapor diffusion chamber over the range of cirrus temperature (–30 to –70 C) and under controlled supersaturation and air pressure. The crystals grew at a velocity of 1–2 microns/s, thickness 60-70 micron, in the form of thin column crystals. Design criteria are given for a system to investigate particle growth down to –100 °C, (PSC temperatures) where nitric acid particles can be grown under similar control and in the form of hydrate crystals.

*Prodata, Inc., Burlingame, California.
**PRC Inc., Edwards, California.

226. *McRuer, Duane T.: **Pilot-Induced Oscillations and Human Dynamic Behavior**. NASA CR-186032, H-2042, TR-2494-1, NAS 1.26:4683, March 1995. (Republished as NASA CR-4683, July 1995.)

This is an in-depth survey and study of Pilot-Induced Oscillations (PIOs) as interactions between human pilot and vehicle dynamics; it includes a broad and comprehensive theory of PIOs. A historical perspective provides examples of the diversity of PIOs in terms of control axes and oscillation frequencies. The constituents involved in PIO phenomena, including effective aircraft dynamics, human pilot dynamic behavior patterns, and triggering precursor events, are examined in detail as the structural elements interacting to produce severe pilot-induced oscillations. The great diversity of human pilot response patterns, excessive lags and/or inappropriate gain in effective aircraft dynamics, and transitions in either the human or effective aircraft dynamics are among the key sources implicated as factors in severe PIOs. The great variety of interactions which may result in severe PIOs is illustrated by examples drawn from famous PIOs. These are generalized under a pilot-behavior-theory-based set of categories proposed as a classification scheme pertinent to a theory of PIOs. Finally, a series of interim prescriptions to avoid PIO is provided.

* Systems Technology, Inc., Hawthorne, California.

227. *Ryan, George W., III: **A Genetic Search Technique for Identification of Aircraft Departures**. NASA CR-4688, H-2063, NAS 1.26:4688, AIAA Paper 95-3453, NIPS-96-44492. Presented at the AIAA Atmospheric Flight Mechanics Conference, Baltimore, Maryland, August 7–9, 1995, August 1995, 96N24938, #.

Methods of testing aircraft for departures range from simple, single-parameter criteria to complex, in-flight departure resistance maneuvers. These methods are useful for predicting departure characteristics, but single-parameter methods may be limited in accuracy because of simplifying assumptions made in their derivation. Also, in-flight or simulation testing of departure resistance maneuvers can be limited by the small number of conditions tested. These limitations increase at high angles of attack where the dynamics of the aircraft are more complex. This paper presents a method for using genetic algorithms to augment traditional evaluation criteria. Quasi-random control inputs are generated by a genetic algorithm for a high fidelity X-31 simulation. Each input is evaluated to determine if it causes a departure. The result of the genetic-algorithm-based search is a population, or set, of control input combinations that lead to uncontrolled flight conditions in the simulation. Recognizing possible differences and simplifications between simulation models and the real aircraft, the results show that the method used is effective for finding possible departures caused by inertial coupling and aerodynamic asymmetries. Simulation

data are used to show the results of the genetic algorithm search.

*PRC Inc., Edwards, California.

228. *Gerren, Donna S.: **Design, Analysis, and Control of a Large Transport Aircraft Utilizing Selective Engine Thrust as a Backup System for the Primary Flight Control, Ph.D. Thesis**. NASA CR-186035, NAS 1.26:186035, H-2073, NIPS-95-05901, September 1995, 96N13544, #.

A study has been conducted to determine the capability to control a very large transport airplane with engine thrust. This study consisted of the design of an 800-passenger airplane with a range of 5000 nautical miles design and evaluation of a flight control system, and design and piloted simulation evaluation of a thrust-only backup flight control system. Location of the four wing-mounted engines was varied to optimize the propulsive control capability, and the time constant of the engine response was studied. The goal was to provide level 1 flying qualities. The engine location and engine time constant did not have a large effect on the control capability. The airplane design did meet level 1 flying qualities based on frequencies, damping ratios, and time constants in the longitudinal and lateral-directional modes. Project pilots consistently rated the flying qualities as either level 1 or level 2 based on Cooper-Harper ratings. However, because of the limited control forces and moments, the airplane design fell short of meeting the time required to achieve a 30 deg bank and the time required to respond a control input.

*University of Kansas, Lawrence, Kansas.

229. *Jackson, Michael R.; and *Enns, Dale F.: **A Concept for Adaptive Performance Optimization on Commercial Transport Aircraft**. NASA CR-186034, NAS 1.26:186034, H-2072, NIPS-95-05905, September 1995, 96N14083, #.

An adaptive control method is presented for the minimization of drag during flight for transport aircraft. The minimization of drag is achieved by taking advantage of the redundant control capability available in the pitch axis, with the horizontal tail used as the primary surface and symmetric deflection of the ailerons and cruise flaps used as additional controls. The additional control surfaces are excited with sinusoidal signals, while the altitude and velocity loops are closed with guidance and control laws. A model of the throttle response as a function of the additional control surfaces is formulated and the parameters in the model are estimated from the sensor measurements using a least squares estimation method. The estimated model is used to determine the minimum drag positions of the control surfaces. The method is presented for the optimization of one and two additional control surfaces. The adaptive control method is extended to optimize rate of climb with the throttle fixed. Simulations that include realistic disturbances are presented, as well as the results of a Monte Carlo simulation analysis that shows the effects of changing the disturbance environment and the excitation signal parameters.

*Honeywell Technology Center, Minneapolis, Minnesota.

1996 Contractor Reports

230. Brenner, Marty; *Paduano, James D.; and *Feron, Eric: **Methods for In-Flight Robustness Evaluation**. NASA CR-201886, NAS 1.26:201886, NIPS-96-68177, September 1996, 96N31260, #.

The goal of this program was to combine modern control concepts with new identification techniques to develop a comprehensive package for estimation of 'robust flutter boundaries' based on experimental data. The goal was to use flight data, combined with a fundamental physical understanding of flutter dynamics, to generate a prediction of flutter speed and an estimate of the accuracy of the prediction. This report is organized as follows: the specific contributions of this project will be listed first. Then, the problem under study will be stated and the general approach will be outlined. Third, the specific system under study (F-18 SRA) will be described and a preliminary data analysis will be performed. Then, the various steps of the flutter boundary determination will be outlined and applied to tile F-18 SRA data and others.

Massachusetts Institute of Technology, Cambridge, Massachusetts.

231. *Williams, J. G.; *Steenken, W. G.; and **Yuhas, A. J.: **Estimating Engine Airflow in Gas-Turbine Powered Aircraft With Clean and Distorted Inlet Flows**. NASA CR-198052, NAS 1.26:198052, H-2127, September 1996, 97N26355, #.

The P404-GF-400 Powered F/A-18A High Alpha Research Vehicle (HARV) was used to examine the impact of inlet-generated total-pressure distortion on estimating levels of engine airflow. Five airflow estimation methods were studied. The Reference Method was a fan corrected airflow to fan corrected speed calibration from an uninstalled engine test. In-flight airflow estimation methods utilized the average, or individual, inlet duct static- to total-pressure ratios, and the average fan-discharge static-pressure to average inlet total-pressure ratio. Correlations were established at low distortion conditions for each method relative to the Reference Method. A range of distorted inlet flow conditions were obtained from −10 deg. to +60 deg. angle of attack and −7 deg. to +11 deg. angle of sideslip. The individual inlet duct pressure ratio correlation resulted in a 2.3 percent airflow spread for all distorted flow levels with a bias error of −0.7 percent. The fan discharge pressure ratio correlation gave results with a 0.6 percent airflow spread with essentially no systematic error. Inlet-generated total-pressure distortion and turbulence had no significant impact on the

P404-GE400 engine airflow pumping. Therefore, a speed-flow relationship may provide the best airflow estimate for a specific engine under all flight conditions.

*General Electric Co., Cincinnati, Ohio.
**Analytical Services and Materials, Inc., Edwards AFB, California.

232. *Norby, W. P.; *Ladd, J. A.; and **Yuhas, A. J.: **Dynamic Inlet Distortion Prediction With a Combined Computational Fluid Dynamics and Distortion Synthesis Approach**. NASA CR-198053, NAS 1.26:198053, H-2129, NIPS-96-98519, September 1996, 97N11706, #.

A procedure has been developed for predicting peak dynamic inlet distortion. This procedure combines Computational Fluid Dynamics (CFD) and distortion synthesis analysis to obtain a prediction of peak dynamic distortion intensity and the associated instantaneous total pressure pattern. A prediction of the steady state total pressure pattern at the Aerodynamic Interface Plane is first obtained using an appropriate CFD flow solver. A corresponding inlet turbulence pattern is obtained from the CFD solution via a correlation linking root mean square (RMS) inlet turbulence to a formulation of several CFD parameters representative of flow turbulence intensity. This correlation was derived using flight data obtained from the NASA High Alpha Research Vehicle flight test program and several CFD solutions at conditions matching the flight test data. A distortion synthesis analysis is then performed on the predicted steady state total pressure and RMS turbulence patterns to yield a predicted value of dynamic distortion intensity and the associated instantaneous total pressure pattern.

*McDonnell-Douglas Aerospace, St. Louis, Missouri.
**Analytical Services and Materials, Inc., Edwards AFB, California.

233. *Thomas, Flint O.; *Nelson, Robert C.; and Fisher, David: **Key Topics for High-Lift Research: a Joint Wind Tunnel/Flight Test Approach**. NASA CR-202525, September 1996, 97N11782.

Future high-lift systems must achieve improved aerodynamic performance with simpler designs that involve fewer elements and reduced maintenance costs. To expeditiously achieve this, reliable CFD design tools are required. The development of useful CFD-based design tools for high lift systems requires increased attention to unresolved flow physics issues. The complex flow field over any multi-element airfoil may be broken down into certain generic component flows which are termed high-lift building block flows. In this report a broad spectrum of key flow field physics issues relevant to the design of improved high lift systems are considered. It is demonstrated that in-flight experiments utilizing the NASA Dryden Flight Test Fixture (which is essentially an instrumented ventral fin) carried on an F-15B support aircraft can provide a novel and cost effective method by which both Reynolds and Mach number effects associated with specific high lift building block flows can be investigated. These in-flight high lift building block flow experiments are most effective when performed in conjunction with coordinated ground based wind tunnel experiments in low speed facilities. For illustrative purposes three specific examples of in-flight high lift building block flow experiments capable of yielding a high payoff are described. The report concludes with a description of a joint wind tunnel/flight test approach to high lift aerodynamics research.

*Notre Dame University, Notre Dame, Indiana.

234. *Yeh, Hsien-Yang; and Richards, W. Lance: **Yeh-Stratton Criterion for Stress Concentrations on Fiber-Reinforced Composite Materials**. NASA CR-198054, H-2141, <u>November 1996</u>, 97N12242, #.

This study investigated the Yeh-Stratton Failure Criterion with the stress concentrations on fiber-reinforced composites materials under tensile stresses. The Yeh-Stratton Failure Criterion was developed from the initial yielding of materials based on macromechanics. To investigate this criterion, the influence of the materials anisotropic properties and far field loading on the composite materials with central hole and normal crack were studied. Special emphasis was placed on defining the crack tip stress fields and their applications. The study of Yeh-Stratton criterion for damage zone stress fields on fiber-reinforced composites under tensile loading was compared with several fracture criteria; Tsai-Wu Theory, Hoffman Theory, Fischer Theory, and Cowin Theory. Theoretical predictions from these criteria are examined using experimental results.

*California State University, Long Beach, California.

235. *Deppe, P. R.; *Chalk, C. R.; and Shafer, M. F.: **Flight Evaluation of an Aircraft With Side and Center Stick Controllers and Rate-Limited Ailerons**. NASA CR-198055 (also Calspan Final Report No. 8091-2, April 1994), <u>November 1996</u>, 97N12596, #.

As part of an ongoing government and industry effort to study the flying qualities of aircraft with rate-limited control surface actuators, two studies were previously flown to examine an algorithm developed to reduce the tendency for pilot-induced oscillation when rate limiting occurs. This algorithm, when working properly, greatly improved the performance of the aircraft in the first study. In the second study, however, the algorithm did not initially offer as much improvement. The differences between the two studies caused concern. The study detailed in this paper was performed to determine whether the performance of the algorithm was affected by the characteristics of the cockpit controllers. Time delay and flight control system noise were also briefly evaluated. An in-flight simulator, the Calspan Learjet 25, was programmed with a low roll actuator rate limit, and the algorithm was programmed into the flight control system. Side- and center-stick controllers, force and position command signals, a rate-limited feel system, a low-frequency feel system, and a feel system damper were evaluated. The flight program consisted of four flights and 38 evaluations of test configurations. Performance of the algorithm was determined to be unaffected by using side- or center-stick controllers or force or position command signals. The rate-limited feel system performed as well as the rate-limiting algorithm but was disliked by the pilots. The low-frequency feel system and the feel system damper were ineffective. Time delay and noise were determined to degrade the performance of the algorithm.

*Calspan Advanced Technology Center, Buffalo, New York.

Appendix B. UCLA Flight Systems Research Center Publications

The following papers were published under NASA Dryden Flight Research Center Grant NCC2-374 by the Flight Systems Research Center (FSRC) at the University of California at Los Angeles (UCLA). This program is run under the direction of Dr. Kenneth W. Iliff of NASA Dryden Flight Research Center. The publications listed were written by students or faculty of UCLA unless otherwise noted.

UCLA FSRC 1988 Publications

1.   Catton, Ivan; Issacci, Farrokh; and Heiss, Anton: **Use of Optical Methods for Study of the Dynamic Behavior of Heat Pipes.** *Experimental Heat Transfer, Fluid Mechanics, and Thermodynamics, 1988,* New York, Elsevier Science Publishing Co., Inc., pp. 1656–1661, 91A19821.

Methods for noninvasive study of the dynamic characteristics of the internal behavior of a heat pipe are proposed. The application of twin beam holographic interferometry to simultaneously measure temperature and concentration of a noncondensible is described. Laser Doppler anemometry is recommended for measurement of the local instantaneous velocities in the vapor phase.

2.   Gillis, J. T.: **Multidimensional Point Processes and Random Sampling.** Ph.D. dissertation, UCLA, 1988.

3.   Lincoln, R. A.; and Yao, K.: **Efficient Systolic Kalman Filtering Design by Dependence Graph Mapping.** *VLSI Signal Processing III,* ed. R.W. Brodersen and H.S. Moscovitz, IEEE Press, 1988, Chapter 37, pp. 396–407.

4.   Heister, S. D.; Nguyen, T. T.; and Karagozian, A. R.: **Modeling of Liquid Jets Injected Transversely Into a Supersonic Crossflow.** AIAA Paper 88-0100. Presented at the 26th AIAA Aerospace Sciences Meeting, Reno, Nevada, January 11–14, 1988, 88A22071, #.

Analytical/numerical modeling of the behavior of a single nonreacting liquid jet in compressible (high subsonic and supersonic) crossflows is described here. Inviscid, compressible flow about the elliptical cross-section of the jet is solved numerically, using a procedure modeled after that of Godunov. External boundary layer analysis along the surface of the elliptical cross-section allows determination of an effective drag associated with the jet, which balances centripetal forces resulting from jet deflection. Mass and momentum balances performed along the jet, with and without the inclusion of mass loss due to droplet shedding, are then incorporated so that liquid jet trajectories and bow

shock penetration may be calculated. Comparisons of the predictions are made with experimental results.

5.   Chen, M. J.; and Yao, K.: **Comparison of QR Least-Squares Algorithms for Systolic Array Processing.** *Proceedings, 22nd Conference on Information Sciences and Systems,* March 1988, pp. 683–688.

6.   Lei, S. M.; and Yao, K.: **Proper Scalings in Recursive Lattice Digital Filters for Minimum Round-Off Noises.** *Proceedings, IEEE Conference on ICASSP,* April 1988, pp. 1810–1813.

7.   Chen, M. J.; and Yao, K.: **Linear Systolic Array for Least-Squares Estimation.** *Proceedings, International Conference on Systolic Arrays,* May 1988, pp. 83–92.

8.   Sharman, R. D.; Keller, T. L.; and Wurtele, M. G.: **Incompressible and Anelastic Flow Simulations on Numerically Generated Grids.** *Monthly Weather Review* (ISSN 0027-0644), Vol. 116, May 1988, pp. 1124–1136, 88A45520.

In the numerical simulation of incompressible and anelastic flows, it is necessary to solve an elliptic equation at each time step. When the boundaries of such flows are nonrectangular, it may be advantageous to solve the equations on a new, numerically generated coordinate grid, in which the property of orthogonality has been preserved. Flow equations in general curvilinear coordinates maintaining the conservative form are given for both anelastic models using the momentum equations, and for incompressible models, using the vorticity equation. The general problem of grid-generation in two dimensions is presented, and a quasi-conformal transformation technique is discussed in detail. Some examples of grids generated by this technique are exhibited. Three examples of the flow of a stratified fluid over obstacles are presented, in which the grid-generation permits some new results to be obtained.

9.   Heister, S. D.; and Karagozian, A. R.: **Vortex Modeling of Gaseous Jets in a Compressible Crossflow.** AIAA Paper 88-3270. Presented at the 24th AIAA, ASME, SAE, and ASEE, Joint Propulsion Conference, Boston, Massachusetts, July 11–13, 1988, 88A44815, #.

This paper discusses an analytical/numerical model developed to describe the behavior of gaseous jets injected transversely into a subsonic (but compressible) crossflow. The cross-section of the jet is modeled as an inviscid compressible vortex pair, consistent with experimental observations of the transversejet cross-section. The numerically computed behavior of the vortex pair is used as an input to mass and momentum balances along the jet, forming a model which describes the trajectory, entrainment, and mixing of jets injected into subsonic compressible crossflows.

10. Lincoln, R. A.; and Yao, K.: **Kalman Filtering Systolic Array Design Using Dependence Graph Mapping.**: *Proceedings, 1988 International Conference on Advances in Communication and Control Systems*, <u>October 1988</u>, pp. 654–665.

UCLA FSRC 1989 Publications

11. Cataltepe, Tayfun.: **A Study of Strong Stability of Distributed Systems.** Ph.D. dissertation, UCLA, <u>1989</u>.

12. Marn, Jure: **The Use of Holographic Interferometry for Measurements of Temperature in a Rectangular Heat Pipe.** NASA CR-187424, NAS 1.26:187424, <u>1989</u>, 91N17349, #. Also M.Sc. thesis, UCLA, 1989.

Holographic interferometry is a nonintrusive method and as such possesses considerable advantages such as not disturbing the velocity and temperature field by creating obstacles which would alter the flow field. These optical methods have disadvantages as well. Holography, as one of the interferometry methods, retains the accuracy of older methods, and at the same time eliminates the system error of participating components. The holographic interferometry consists of comparing the objective beam with the reference beam and observing the difference in lengths of optical paths, which can be observed during the propagation of the light through a medium with locally varying refractive index. Thus, change in refractive index can be observed as a family of nonintersecting surfaces in space (wave fronts). The object of the investigation was a rectangular heat pipe. The goal was to measure temperatures in the heat pipe, which yields data for computer code or model assessment. The results were obtained by calculating the temperatures by means of finite fringes.

13. Nguyen, T. T.: **Liquid Transverse Jets in Compressible Crossflows.** Ph.D. dissertation, UCLA, <u>1989</u>.

14. *Chang, Chi-Yung; and Yao, Kung: **Systolic Array Processing of the Viterbi Algorithm.** IEEE Transactions on Information Theory (ISSN 0018-9448), Vol. 35, <u>January 1989</u>, pp. 76–86, 89A39601.

Results on efficient forms of decoding convolutional codes based on the Viterbi algorithm by using systolic arrays are presented. Various properties of convolutional codes are discussed. A technique called strongly connected trellis decoding is introduced to increase the efficient utilization of all the systolic array processors. Issues dealing with the composite branch metric generation, survivor updating, overall system architecture, throughput rate, and computational overhead ratio also investigated. The scheme is applicable to both hard and soft decoding of any rate b/n convolutional code. It is shown that as the length of the code becomes large, the systolic Viterbi decoder maintains a regular and general interconnection structure as well as

moderate throughput rate gain over the sequential Viterbi decoder.

*California Institute of Technology, and Jet Propulsion Laboratory, Pasadena, California.

15. Lei, S. M.; and Yao, K.: **Efficient Systolic Array Implementations of Digital Filtering.** *Proceedings, IEEE International Symposium on Circuits and Systems*, <u>May 1989</u>, pp. 1183–1186.

16. Heister, S. D.; and Karagozian, A. R.: **The Gaseous Jet in Supersonic Crossflow.** AIAA Paper 89-2547. Presented at the 25th AIAA, ASME, SAE, and ASEE, Joint Propulsion Conference, Monterey, California, <u>July 10–13, 1989</u>, 89A46916, #.

An analytical/numerical model for the deflection and mixing of a single gaseous jet in a supersonic crossflow is presented. The jet cross-section is described in terms of the compressible vortex pair resulting from viscous and impulsive forces acting at the jet periphery, and the vortex pair data are combined with data for the mass and momentum balance along the jet axis in order to model the trajectory and mixing of the injected fluid. A numerical technique is employed to solve for the inviscid outer flow and the position of the bow shock which envelopes the jet. The model is shown to be capable of predicting overall jet penetration (for perfectly or slightly underexpanded jets) to within 10 percent of experimental findings, while requiring only a few seconds of computer time.

17. Karagozian, A. R.: **Fuel Injection and Flame Holding in High Speed Combustion Systems.** *Proceedings of the ICASE High Speed Combustion Workshop*, NASA Langley, <u>October 1989</u>. (Also in *Major Topics in Combustion*, ed. Hussaini, M.Y., Kumar, A. and Voigt, R.G. SpringerVerlag, 1992.)

18. Madooglu, K.; and Karagozian, A. R.: **Burning of a Spherical Fuel Droplet in a Uniform Subsonic Flowfield.** Paper No. 89-65. *Proceedings of the Western States Section/The Combustion Institute Fall Meeting*, Livermore, California, <u>October 1989</u>.

19. Heister, S. D.; Nguyen, T. T.; and Karagozian, A. R.: **Modeling of Liquid Jets Injected Transversely Into a Supersonic Crossflow.** AIAA Journal (ISSN 0001-1452), Vol. 27, (see A88-22071), <u>December 1989</u>, pp. 1727–1734, 90A17985, #. (See also B 4.)

UCLA FSRC 1990 Publications

20. Han, Kuoruey: **Randomly Sampled-Data Control Systems.** NASA CR-187425, NAS 1.26:187425, <u>1990</u>, 91N14734, #. Ph.D. thesis, UCLA, 1990.

474

The purpose is to solve the Linear Quadratic Regulator (LQR) problem with random time sampling. Such a sampling scheme may arise from imperfect instrumentation as in the case of sampling jitter. It can also model the stochastic information exchange among decentralized controllers to name just a few. A practical suboptimal controller is proposed with the nice property of mean square stability. The proposed controller is suboptimal in the sense that the control structure is limited to be linear. Because of i. i. d. assumption, this does not seem unreasonable. Once the control structure is fixed, the stochastic discrete optimal control problem is transformed into an equivalent deterministic optimal control problem with dynamics described by the matrix difference equation. The N-horizon control problem is solved using the Lagrange's multiplier method. The infinite horizon control problem is formulated as a classical minimization problem. Assuming existence of solution to the minimization problem, the total system is shown to be mean square stable under certain observability conditions. Computer simulations are performed to illustrate these conditions.

21. Hsieh, S. F.: **On Recursive Least-Squares Filtering Algorithms and Implementations.** Ph.D. dissertation, UCLA, 1990.

22. Jenkins, D. W.; Karagozian, A. R.; and Heister, S. D.: **The Gaseous Fuel Jet in Compressible Crossflow.** Abstract published in *Bulletin of the American Physical Society*, Vol. 35, No. 10, 1990, p. 2298.

23. Kogan, B. Y.; Karplus, W. J.; and Pang, A. T.: **Simulation of Nonlinear Distributed Parameter Systems on the Connection Machine.** *Simulation, Journal of the Society for Computer Simulation*, 1990, pp. 271–281.

24. Li, Hsi-Shang: **Transverse Liquid Fuel Jet Breakup, Burning, and Ignition.** NASA CR-187423, NAS 1.26:187423, 1990, 91N13510, #. Also M.Sc. thesis, UCLA, 1990.

An analytical study of the breakup, burning, and ignition of liquid fuels injected transversely into a hot air stream is conducted. The non-reacting liquid jet breakup location is determined by the local sonic point criterion. Two models, one employing analysis of an elliptical jet cross-section and the other employing a two-dimensional blunt body to represent the transverse jet, were used for sonic point calculations. An auxiliary criterion based on surface tension stability is used as a separate means of determining the breakup location. For the reacting liquid jet problem, a diffusion flame supported by a one-step chemical reaction within the gaseous boundary layer is solved along the ellipse surface in subsonic cross flow. Typical flame structures and concentration profiles were calculated for various locations along the jet cross-section as a function of upstream Mach numbers. The integration reaction rate along the jet cross-section is used to predict ignition position, which is found to be situated near the stagnation point. While a multi-step reaction is needed to represent the ignition process more accurately, the present calculation does yield reasonable predictions concerning ignition along a curved surface.

25. Liu, Kuojuey Ray: **Reliable and Efficient Parallel Processing Algorithms and Architectures for Modern Signal Processing.** NASA CR-191969, NAS 1.26:191969, 1990, 93N16723, #. Also Ph.D. thesis, UCLA, 1990.

Least-squares (LS) estimations and spectral decomposition algorithms constitute the heart of modern signal processing and communication problems. Implementations of recursive LS and spectral decomposition algorithms onto parallel processing architectures such as systolic arrays with efficient fault-tolerant schemes are the major concerns of this dissertation. There are four major results in this dissertation. First, we propose the systolic block Householder transformation with application to the recursive least-squares minimization. It is successfully implemented on a systolic array with a two-level pipelined implementation at the vector level as well as at the word level. Second, a real-time algorithm-based concurrent error detection scheme based on the residual method is proposed for the QRD RLS systolic array. The fault diagnosis, order degraded reconfiguration, and performance analysis are also considered. Third, the dynamic range, stability, error detection capability under finite-precision implementation, order degraded performance, and residual estimation under faulty situations for the QRD RLS systolic array are studied in details. Finally, we propose the use of multi-phase systolic algorithms for spectral decomposition based on the QR algorithm. Two systolic architectures, one based on triangular array and another based on rectangular array, are presented for the multiphase operations with fault-tolerant considerations. Eigenvectors and singular vectors can be easily obtained by using the multi-pase operations. Performance issues are also considered.

26. Zhang, W.: **Nonlinear Damping Model for Flexible Structures.** Ph.D. dissertation, UCLA, 1990.

27. Issacci, F.; Catton, I.; and Ghoniem, N. M.: **Vapor Dynamics of Heat Pipe Startup.** *Proceedings, 7th Symposium on Space Nuclear Power Systems*, Albuquerque, New Mexico, January 1990, pp. 1002–1007.

28. Marn, J.; Issacci, F.; and Catton, I.: **The Use of Single Beam Holographic Interferometry in Temperature Measurements in Rectangular Heat Pipe.** *Proceedings, 7th Symposium on Space Nuclear Power Systems*, Albuquerque, New Mexico, January 1990, pp. 995–1001.

29. Nguyen, T. T.; and Karagozian, A. R.: **Liquid Fuel Jet in Subsonic Crossflow.** AIAA Paper 90-0445. Presented at the 28th AIAA Aerospace Sciences Meeting, Reno, Nevada, January 8–11, 1990, 90A19848, #.

An analytical/numerical model is described which predicts the behavior of nonreacting and reacting liquid jets injected transversely into subsonic cross flow. The compressible flowfield about the elliptical jet cross section is solved at various locations along the jet trajectory by analytical means for free-stream local Mach number perpendicular to jet cross section smaller than 0.3 and by numerical means for free-stream local Mach number perpendicular to jet cross section in the range 0.3-1.0. External and internal boundary layers along the jet cross section are solved by integral and numerical methods, and the mass losses due to boundary layer shedding, evaporation, and combustion are calculated and incorporated into the trajectory calculation. Comparison of predicted trajectories is made with limited experimental observations.

30. Roche, Gregory L.; Issacci, Farrokh; and Catton, Ivan: **Liquid Phase Transient Behavior of a High Temperature Heat Pipe.** Presented at the 7th University of New Mexico, NASA, DOE, and USAF, Symposium on Space Nuclear Power Systems, Albuquerque, New Mexico, January 7–10, 1990, pp. 875–882, 91A19793, #.

The purpose of the study is to develop an analytical model of the transient dynamics of the liquid phase in a including boundary conditions, required to solve the liquid-phases, heat-pipe problem are considered. A simplified solution is formulated by using certain assumptions and integrating the liquid-dynamics equations. A kinetic-theory approach is used to model the phase change. It is pointed out that the model requires a small time step for stability even with the simplifications used in the analysis. At the same time, the study indicates that the transient heat-pipe problem is not amenable to a straightforward simplification such as is used for the vapor phase and requires a full solution of the liquid and vapor phases.

31. Stroes, G.; Fricker, D.; Issacci, F.; and Catton, I.: **Studies of Wick Dryout and Rewet.** *Proceedings, 7th Symposium on Nuclear Space Power Systems*, Albuquerque, New Mexico, January 1990, pp. 1008–1010.

32. Heister, S. D.; and Karagozian, A. R.: **Vortex Modeling of Gaseous Jets in a Compressible Crossflow.** *Journal of Propulsion and Power* (ISSN 0748-4658), Vol. 6, January–February 1990, February 1990, pp. 85–92, 90A21229, #. Translated into Russian as "Vekhrevaya model vzaumodeystvea gazovekh ctooe cbokoviem cnocyshcheem potokom cshemaemoe jedkosti," *Aerokosmecheskaya Technika*, Vol. 8, August 1990, pp. 76–86. (See also B 9.)

33. Balakrishnan, A. V.: **Modeling and Control of Large Space Structures.** Presented at the International Federation for Information Processing, International Conference on Modeling the Innovation, Rome, Italy, March 21–23, 1990, 91A33201, #. Also *Modeling the Innovation: Communications, Automation and Information Systems*, ed.

M. Carnevale, M. Lucertini and S. Nicosia, Elsevier Science Publishers, 1990, pp. 461–469.

Currently NASA, USA, has under active study and development several large structures for deployment in space. These include for instance beam-like trusses to serve as antenna masts and/or basic building blocks for Space Station construction. An important design consideration is that of assuring adequate stability of the structure in the space environment and in addition in the case of antennas, meeting stringent pointing accuracy requirements. This paper addresses some of the basic design considerations involved such as: (1) modeling flexible multibody dynamics, including sensors and actuators, (2) identifying/monitoring model parameters in orbit, and (3) integrated controls-structures optimization with emphasis on novel concepts and techniques.

34. Hsieh, S. F.; Liu, K. J. R.; and Yao, K.: **Applications of Truncated QR Methods to Sinusoidal Frequency Estimation.** *Proceedings, ICASSP 90 - 1990 International Conference on Acoustics, Speech, and Signal Processing*, Albuquerque, New Mexico, April 3–6, 1990, 1990, pp. 2571–2574, 91A19813.

Three truncated QR methods are proposed for sinusoidal frequency estimation: (1) truncated QR without column pivoting (TQR), (2) truncated QR with preordered columns, and (3) truncated QR with column pivoting. It is demonstrated that the benefit of truncated SVD for high frequency resolution is achievable under the truncated QR approach with much lower computational cost. Other attractive features of the proposed methods include the ease of updating, which is difficult for the SVD method, and numerical stability. TQR methods thus offer efficient ways to identify sinusoidals closely clustered in frequencies under stationary and nonstationary conditions.

35. Hadidi, Kh.; Temes, G. C.; and Martin, K.W.: **Error Analysis and Digital Correction Algorithms for Pipelined A/D Converters.** *Proceedings, IEEE International Symposium on Circuits Systems*, May 1990, pp. 1709–1712.

36. Hadidi, Kh.; Tso, V. S.; and Temes, G. C.: **Fact Successive-Approximation A/D Converters.** *Proceedings, IEEE International Symposium on Circuits Systems*, May 1990.

37. Ki, W. H.; and Temes, G. C.: **Offset-Compensated Switched-Capacitor Integrators.** *Proceedings, IEEE International Symposium on Circuits Systems*, May 1990, pp. 2829–2832.

38. Heister, S. D.; and Karagozian, A. R.: **The Gaseous Jet in Supersonic Crossflow.** *AIAA Journal* (ISSN 0001-1452), Vol. 28, (see A89-46916), May 1990, pp. 819–827, 90A32459, #. (See also 2283.)

39. Hadidi, Kh.; Tso, Vincent S.; and Temes, Gabor C.: **An 8-bit 1.3-MHz Successive-Approximation A/D Converter.** *IEEE Journal of Solid-State Circuits* (ISSN 0018-9200), Vol. 25, June 1990, pp. 880–885, 91A19598.

A new successive-approximation A/D converter is described. It combines a string of equal-valued polysilicon resistors and a set of ratioed capacitors in a unique circuit configuration so that a high sampling rate is achieved. The comparator is realized by a chopper-stabilized amplifier to reduce the effect of the offset voltages of MOS amplifiers. The converter performs an 8-b monotonic conversion with a differential nonlinearity less than 1 LSB in 770 nsec. The die area is 3750 sq mil. This new conversion technique can also be utilized in a pipelined A/D converter (Temes, 1985) and enables it to achieve high speed.

40. Issacci, F.; Ghoniem, N. M.; and Catton, I.: **Vapor Flow Patterns During a Start-Up Transient in Heat Pipes.** *Heat Transfer in Space Systems.* Proceedings of the AIAA and ASME Thermophysics and Heat Transfer Conference, Seattle, Washington, June 18–20, 1990, (see A91-38780 16-34), 1990, pp. 41–47, 91A38786.

The vapor flow patterns in heat pipes are examined during the start-up transient phase. The vapor core is modeled as a channel flow using a two dimensional compressible flow model. A nonlinear filtering technique is used as a post process to eliminate the nonphysical oscillations of the flow variables. For high-input heat flux, multiple shock reflections are observed in the evaporation region. The reflections cause a reverse flow in the evaporation and circulations in the adiabatic region. Furthermore, each shock reflection causes a significant increase in the local pressure and a large pressure drop along the heat pipe.

41. Ki, W.-H.; and Temes, G. C.: **Low-Phase-Error Offset-Compensated Switched-Capacitor Integrator.** *Electronics Letters* (ISSN 0013-5194), Vol. 26, June 21, 1990, pp. 957–959, 90A43400.

A modification of the offset-compensated switched-capacitor integrator is described. The resulting circuit has a reduced delay and low gain distortion. It also retains the simplicity and low phase errors of earlier schemes.

42. Marn, J.; Issacci, F.; and Catton, I.: **Measurements of Temperature and Concentration Fields in a Rectangular Heat Pipe.** *Heat Transfer in Space Systems.* Proceedings of the Symposium, AIAA/ASME Thermophysics and Heat Transfer Conference, Seattle, Washington, June 18–20, 1990, (see A91-38780 16-34), 1990, pp. 33–39, 91A38785.

Measurements of the temperature and noncondensible gas fields found in a heat pipe are reported. The heat pipe is rectangular in cross section to facilitate measurements using twin beams interferometry. The heat pipe operating fluid is Freon 113, and air the noncondensible gas constituent. The experimental technique is described, and results are in the form of graphs of temperatures and molar concentration fractions for different regions of the heat pipe. Some interferograms showing the actual flow field under different laser lights are included.

43. Issacci, Farrokh; Catton, Ivan; and Ghoniem, Nasr M.: **Startup Transient Modeling of Vapor Flow in Heat Pipes.** Presented at the 9th ASME, International Heat Transfer Conference, Jerusalem, Israel, August 19–24, 1990, pp. 33–38, 91A19796, #.

The transient behavior of vapor flow during the startup mode of heat pipe operation is analyzed numerically. The vapor core is modeled as a channel flow using a two-dimensional compressible flow model. The centered difference scheme along with a nonlinear filtering technique is employed to overcome non-physical oscillations in flow variables. It is shown that Multiple shockwave reflections are obtained near the evaporation region during the early stage of startup transient. Shock reflections induce time dependent flow reversals which are only transient and disappear as the dynamics approach steady state.

44. Stroes, Gustave; Fricker, Darren; Issacci, Farrokh; and Catton, Ivan: **Heat Flux Induced Dryout and Rewet in Thin Films.** Presented at the 9th ASME International Heat Transfer Conference, Jerusalem, Israel, August 19–24, 1990, 91A19797, #.

Heat flux induced dryout of thin liquid films on an inclined copper plate was studied. Rewet of the dried out area is also considered. The four fluids used to form the thin films exhibited very different dryout and rewet characteristics. The contact angle and hysteresis effects were found to be important, but they must be considered in context with other parameters. No single variable was found to independently determine the pattern of dryout and rewet.

45. *Zhang, W.: **Transition Density of One-Dimensional Diffusion With Discontinuous Drift.** *IEEE Transactions on Automatic Control*, Vol. 35, No. 8, (ISSN 0018-9286), August 1990, pp. 980–985.

The transition density of a one-dimensional diffusion process with a discontinuous drift coefficient is studied. A probabilistic representation of the transition density is given, illustrating the close connections between discontinuities of the drift and Brownian local times. In addition, some explicit results are obtained based upon the trivariate density of Brownian motion, its occupation, and local times.

*University of California, Los Angeles, California.

46. *Lei, Shaw-Min; and Yao, Kung: **A Class of Systolizable IIR Digital Filters and Its Design for Proper Scaling and Minimum Output Roundoff Noise.** *IEEE Transactions on Circuits and Systems* (ISSN 0098-4094), Vol. 37, <u>October 1990</u>, pp. 1217–1230, 91A17916.

A class of infinite impulse response (IIR) digital filters with a systolizable structure is proposed and its synthesis is investigated. The systolizable structure consists of pipelineable regular modules with local connections and is suitable for VLSI implementation. It is capable of achieving high performance as well as high throughput. This class of filter structure provides certain degrees of freedom that can be used to obtain some desirable properties for the filter. Techniques of evaluating the internal signal powers and the output roundoff noise of the proposed filter structure are developed. Based upon these techniques, a well-scaled IIR digital filter with minimum output roundoff noise is designed using a local optimization approach. The internal signals of all the modes of this filter are scaled to unity in the l2-norm sense. Compared to the Rao-Kailath (1984) orthogonal digital filter and the Gray-Markel (1973) normalized-lattice digital filter, this filter has better scaling properties and lower output roundoff noise.

*Bell Communications Research, Inc., Red Bank, New Jersey.

47. Heister, S. D.; McDonough, J. M.; Karagozian, A. R.; and Jenkins, D. W.: **The Compressible Vortex Pair.** *Journal of Fluid Mechanics* (ISSN 0022-1120), Vol. 220, <u>November 1990</u>, pp. 339–354, 91A17658.

A numerical solution for the flow field associated with a compressible pair of counter-rotating vortices is developed. The compressible, two-dimensional potential equation is solved utilizing the numerical method of Osher et al. (1985) for flow regions in which a non-zero density exists. Close to the vortex centers, vacuum 'cores' develop owing to the existence of a maximum achievable flow speed in a compressible flow field. A special treatment is required to represent these vacuum cores. Typical streamline patterns and core boundaries are obtained for upstream Mach numbers as high as 0.3, and the formation of weak shocks, predicted by Moore and Pullin (1987), is observed.

48. Issacci, F.; and Catton, I.: **Transient Flow Patterns and Heat Transfer in Heat Pipes.** NASA CR-200184, NAS 1.26:200184, FED-VOL-102, PVP-VOL-204, NIPS-96-08353. Presented at the Winter Annual Meeting of the American Society of Mechanical Engineers, Dallas, Texas, November 25–30, 1990, <u>1990</u>, 96N70900, #.

The transient behavior of heat pipes during the start-up mode of operation is studied using a 2D transient model to represent the vapor core as well as other regions of the heat pipe. An implicit finite difference scheme is used with different time

scales for the vapor region and the solid regions of the heat pipe to save significant computational time. The transient characteristics of the solid and the liquid phases effect the vapor flow transient behavior. If the working fluid is highly conductive (liquid metals), the compressible waves are generated in the vapor space, which cause flow circulations. The vapor flow transient behavior was found to be two dimensional which cannot simply be modeled as a one-dimensional flow.

49. Landau, D. M.; and Wurtele, M. G.: **Backscattering of Gravity Waves From a Critical Level.** *Proceedings, American Geophysical Union*, San Francisco, <u>December 1990</u>, pp. 1496–1499. (See also B 73.)

50. Zhang, W.: **The Spectral Density of Nonlinear Damping Model: Single Degree of Freedom Case.** *IEEE Transactions on Automatic Control*, Vol. 35, No. 12, <u>December 1990</u>, pp. 1320–1329.

UCLA FSRC 1991 Publications.

51. Balakrishnan, A. V.: **Semigroup Theory and Control Theory.** *Mathematical Theory and Control: An International Conference*, Marcel Dekker, <u>1991</u>.

52. Brashear, L.: **A Study of Estimation of Airdata Parameters.** M.Sc. thesis, UCLA, <u>1991</u>.

53. Cheng, J. W.: **Explicit Models for Proportional Damping in Timoshenko Beams.** Ph.D. dissertation, UCLA, <u>1991</u>.

54. Datta, A.: **Propagation of Gravity, Gravity-Inertia and Lee Waves in Two Dimensions.** M.Sc. project, UCLA, <u>1991</u>.

55. Engquist, B.; and Sjogreen, B.: **Numerical Approximation of Hyperbolic Conservation Laws With Stiff Terms.** *Proceedings of the Third International Conference on Hyperbolic Problems*, ed. B. Engquist and B. Gustafson, Uppsala University, Sweden, <u>1991</u>.

56. Hsieh, S. F.; Liu, K. J. R.; and Yao, K.: **Comparisons of Truncated QR and SVD Methods for AR Spectral Estimations.** *SVD and Signal Processing II: Algorithms, Analysis and Applications*, ed. F. J. Vaccaro, Elsevier Science Publishers, New York, New York, <u>1991</u>, pp. 403–418.

57. Issacci, F.; and Catton, I.: **Use of Spectral Methods for Heat Pipe Analysis.** NASA CR-200185, NAS 1.26:200185, NIPS-96-08351. Presented at the American Institute of Chemical Engineers Symposium, Minneapolis, Minnesota, <u>1991</u>, 96N70899, #. Also ASIChE Symposium Series, Vol. 87, pp. 198–206.

The cost of numerical studies of heat pipe dynamics is prohibitively expensive both in computational time used and in computer resource allocation. The potential of the spectral methods is explored for the heat pipe analysis to significantly reduce the computational efforts. Using data sets from the numerical calculations available from past studies, it is shown that a few first terms of Fourier Series, given the proper trial functions, will satisfactorily represent the data sets.

58. Kogan, B. Y.; Karplus, W. J.; Billett, B. S.; Pang, A. T.; Karagueuzian, H. S.; and Khan, S. S.: **The Simplified FitzHugh-Nagumo Model With Action Potential Duration Restitution: Effects on 2D Wave Propagation.** *Physica D*, Vol. 50, <u>1991</u>, pp. 327–340.

59. Lay, J. H.; and Dhir, V. K.: **Nucleate Boiling on a Macro-Structured Surface Cooled by an Impinging Jet.** *Seventh Proceedings of Nuclear Thermal Hydraulics*, <u>1991</u>.

60. Le, A. T.: **Transverse Gaseous Jet Injection Behind a Rearward-Facing Step Into a Supersonic Crossflow.** M.Sc. thesis, UCLA, <u>1991</u>.

61. Youn, B.: **Flow of Supercritical Hydrogen in Rectangular Ducts.** Ph.D. dissertation, UCLA, <u>1991</u>.

62. *Kalson, Seth Z.; and Yao, Kung: **A Class of Least-Squares Filtering and Identification Algorithms With Systolic Array Architectures.** *IEEE Transactions on Information Theory* (ISSN 0018-9448), Vol. 37, <u>January 1991</u>, pp. 43–52, 91A25021.

A unified approach is presented for deriving a large class of new and previously known time- and order-recursive least-squares algorithms with systolic array architectures, suitable for high-throughput-rate and VLSI implementations of space-time filtering and system identification problems. The geometrical derivation given is unique in that no assumption is made concerning the rank of the sample data correlation matrix. This method utilizes and extends the concept of oblique projections, as used previously in the derivations of the least-squares lattice algorithms. Exponentially weighted least-squares criteria are considered for both sliding and growing memory.

*MIT, Cambridge, Massachusetts.

63. Li, H.-S.; and Karagozian, A. R.: **Breakup of a Liquid Jet in Supersonic Crossflow.** AIAA Paper 91-0689. Presented at the 29th AIAA Aerospace Sciences Meeting, Reno, Nevada, <u>January 7–10, 1991</u>, 91A19415, #. (See also B 104.)

A theoretical study of the breakup of a circular liquid jet injected transversely into a supersonic air stream is conducted. Two different criteria for breakup are explored in the context of a previously developed model for the behavior of liquid jets in compressible crossflow (Heister et al., 1989). The local sonic point criterion first proposed by Schetz, et al. (1980) is explored, in addition to an auxiliary criterion put forth by Clark (1964) based on surface-tension stability. It is found that the local sonic point appears to provide a more reasonable approximation to the actual location of jet breakup, based on comparisons with limited experimental data.

64. Bendiksen, Oddvar O.: **A New Approach to Computational Aeroelasticity.** AIAA Paper 91-0939. Presented at the 32nd AIAA, ASME, ASCE, AHS, and ASC Structures, Structural Dynamics, and Materials Conference, Baltimore, Maryland, April 8–10, 1991, (see A91-31826 12-39), <u>1991</u>, pp. 1712–1727, 91A32007, #.

A novel computational method for aeroelastic stability and structural response calculations is presented in which the entire fluid-structure system is treated as one continuum dynamics problem, by using a mixed Eulerian-Lagrangian formulation and switching from an Eulerian to a Lagrangian description at the fluid-structure boundary. This method effectively eliminates the phase integration errors associated with previous methods, where the fluid and the structure are integrated sequentially by different schemes; it also provides a systematic method for coupling finite element structural codes to finite volume fluid dynamics codes, in a manner that leads to highly vectorizable overall codes. The method is applied to transonic flutter calculations for wings and cascades, using simple finite element models. These results suggest that the method is capable of reproducing the energy exchange between the fluid and the structure with much less error that existing methods.

65. Chang, B.; and Mills, A. F.: **Application of a Low-Reynolds Number Turbulence Model to Flow in a Tube With Repeated Rectangular Rib Roughness.** *Proceedings, 4th International PHOENICS Users Conferences*, Miami, Florida, <u>April 1991</u>, pp. 285–332.

66. Pak, Chan-Gi; Friedmann, Peretz P.; and *Livne, Eli: **Transonic Adaptive Flutter Suppression Using Approximate Unsteady Time Domain Aerodynamics.** AIAA Paper 91-0986. Presented at the 32nd AIAA, ASME, ASCE, AHS, and ASC Structures, Structural Dynamics, and Materials Conference, Baltimore, Maryland, <u>April 8–10, 1991</u>, (see A91-31826 12-39), pp. 1832–1854, 91A32017, #.

A digital adaptive controller is applied to the active flutter suppression problem of a wing under time varying flight conditions in subsonic and transonic flow. Linear quadratic controller gain at each time step is obtained using an iterative Riccati solver. The digital adaptive optimal controller is robust with respect to the unknown external loads. Flutter and divergence instabilities are simultaneously suppressed using a trailing-edge control surface and displacement sensing. A new transonic unsteady aerodynamic approximation methodology is developed which enables one to carry out the rapid calculation required for transonic aeroservoelastic applications. This approximation is based on a combination of unsteady subsonic aerodynamics combined with a transonic correction procedure. Aeroservoelastic transient time response is obtained using Roger's approximation, state transition matrices and an iterative time marching algorithm. The aeroservoelastic system in the time domain is modeled using a deterministic ARMA model together with a parameter estimator. Transonic flutter boundaries of a wing structure are computed, in the time domain, using an estimated aeroelastic system matrix and are in good agreement with experimental data for the low transonic Mach number range.

*University of Washington, Seattle, Washington.

67. Balakrishnan, A. V.: **An Infinite Dimensional Gaussian Markov Process With Non-Nuclear Steady State Covariance.** *Proceedings of the IFIP Working Conference on Stochastic Partial Different Equations,* Charlotte, North Carolina, <u>May 1991</u>.

68. Balakrishnan, A. V.: **Stochastic Partial Differential Equations in Control of Structures.** *Proceedings of the International Conference on SPDEs,* Charlotte, North Carolina, <u>May 1991</u>.

69. Liu, C-T.; Temes, G. C.; and Samueli, H.: **FIT Filter Design Using Quadratic Programming.** *Proceedings, IEEE International Symposium on Circuits Systems,* Singapore, <u>June 1991</u>, pp. 148–151.

70. Zhang, W.: **The Frequency Response of Nonlinearly Damped Flexible Structures.** *International Journal of Control,* Vol. 54, No. 1, <u>July 1991</u>.

71. Kogan, B. Y.; Karplus, W. J.; Karagueuzian, H. S.; and Khan, S. S.: **Simulation of Reentry Processes in a Heart Muscle Using a Massively Parallel Computer.** *Computers in Biomedicine.* Proceedings of the First International Conference, Southhampton, United Kingdom, <u>September 1991</u>, pp. 325–336.

72. Keller, T. L.; Wurtele, M. G.; and Sharman, R. D.: **Implications of the Hydrostatics Assumption on Atmospheric Gravity Waves.** *Proceedings of the 8th Conference on Atmospheric and Oceanic Waves and Stability,* Denver, Colorado, <u>October 1991</u>, pp. 320–323.

73. Landau, D. M.; and Wurtele, M. G.: **Resonant Backscattering of a Gravity Wave From a Critical Level.** *Proceedings of the 8th Conference on Atmospheric and Oceanic Waves and Stability,* Denver, Colorado, <u>October 1991</u>, pp. 244–247. (See also B 49.)

74. Ton, V. T.; Engquist, B. E.; Osher, S. J.; and Karagozian, A. R.: **Numerical Simulation of Inviscid Detonation Waves With Finite Rate Chemistry.** Paper 91-101. *Proceedings of the Western States Section/The Combustion Institute Fall Meeting,* <u>October 1991</u>.

75. Wurtele, M. G.; Datta, A.; and Sharman, R. D.: **Propagation of Resonant Gravity-Inertia Waves.** *Proceedings, 8th Conference on Atmospheric and Oceanic Waves and Stability,* Denver, Colorado, <u>October 1991</u>, pp. 364–367.

76. Issacci, F.; Catton, I.; and Ghoniem, N. M.: **Vapor Dynamics of Heat Pipe Start-Up.** *ASME, Transactions, Journal of Heat Transfer* (ISSN 0022-1481), Vol. 113, <u>November 1991</u>, pp. 985–994, 92A15445.

Vapor dynamics of heat pipes during the start-up phase of operation is analyzed. The vapor flow is modeled by a two-dimensional, compressible viscous flow in an enclosure with inflow and outflow boundary conditions. For high-input heat fluxes, a compression wave is created in the evaporator early in the operation. A nonlinear filtering technique, along with the centered difference scheme, is used to capture the shocklike wave and overcome the cell Reynolds number problem. Multiple wave reflections are observed in the evaporation and adiabatic regions. These wave reflections cause a significant increase in the local pressure and flow circulations, which grow with time. It is shown that the maximum and maximum-averaged pressure drops oscillate periodically because of the wave reflections. Although the pressure drops converge to a constant value at steady state, they are significantly higher than their steady-state value at the initiation of the process. The time for the vapor core to reach a steady-state condition was found to be on the order of seconds.

77. Issacci, F.; Huckaby, D.; and Catton, I.: **Analysis of Heat Pipe Vapor Dynamics Using the Galerkin Method.** NASA CR-203780, NAS 1.26:203780, NIPS-97-18904. *Proceedings of the ASME Winter Annual Meeting,* December 1991, Atlanta, Georgia, <u>1991</u>, 97N70872, #.

The dynamic behavior of the vapor flow is analyzed for the heat pipes with axisymmetric geometry. The results show that the transient process involves multiple symmetric radial wave reflections about the symmetry line, as was observed in the two-dimensional analysis. Each wave reflection causes a significant increase in the local pressure and a large pressure drop along the heat pipe. The cost of numerical studies of heat pipe dynamics is prohibitively expensive both in computational time used and in computer resource allocation. The potential of the Galerkin method is explored for the heat pipe analysis to significantly reduce the computational efforts. Applying a Fourier analysis on the data resulted from the numerical calculations, it is shown that a few first terms of Fourier series, given the proper trial functions, will satisfactorily represent the data sets.

78. Stroes, Gustave; Rohloff, Thomas; and Catton, Ivan: **The Dependence of Capillary Force in Rectangular Channels on Heat Input From Below.** NASA CR-203804, NAS 1.26:203804, NIPS-97-21070. Presented at ASME Annual Meeting, Atlanta, Georgia, <u>December 1–6, 1991</u>, 97N71239, #.

The effect of beat flux on the capillary forces in rectangular grooves has been studied. Tests were simultaneously undertaken on grooves of different depths so that the effect of varying the aspect ratio could be examined. It was found that deeper grooves are generally capable of providing larger capillary forces than shallow grooves when no heat is applied. Upon the introduction of a heat flux, grooves of all depths showed a degradation in the net capillary force that could be provided to pull fluid upwards against gravity. Three stages of meniscus retreat were observed corresponding to three ranges of heat input. Experiments showed that shallow channels tend to be less sensitive to heat loads than deeper channels.

UCLA FSRC 1992 Publications

79. Angell, J. P.: **Parallel Jacobi Algorithms for the Symmetric Eigenvalue Problem and Singular Value Decomposition With High-Dimensional Rotations.** Ph.D. dissertation, UCLA, <u>1992</u>.

80. Balakrishnan, A. V.: **Two Examples of Physically Realizable Processes Whose Spectral Density Is Not Physically Realizable.** *Probability in the Engineering and Informational Sciences*, Vol. 6, <u>1992</u>, pp. 257–259.

81. Chang, B. H.: **Computation of Turbulent Recirculating Flow in Channels, and for Impingement Cooling.** H-2289. Ph.D. dissertation, UCLA, <u>1992</u>.

82. Chen, M. J.; and Yao, K.: **One-Dimensional Least-Squares Systolic Array.** *Advances in VLSI Signal Processing*, ed. M. Bayoumi, Ablex Publications, Norwood, New Jersey, <u>1992</u>.

83. Daneshgaran, F.: **VLSI Architectures for Parallel Implementation of Long Constraint Length Viterbi Decoders.** Ph.D. dissertation, UCLA, <u>1992</u>.

84. Fricker, D.: **A Computational Fluid Dynamics Analysis of the Hypersonic Flights of Pegasus®.** M.Sc. thesis, UCLA, <u>1992</u>.

85. Issacci, F.; Huckaby, D.; and Catton, I.: **Use of the Galerkin Method for Heat Pipe Analysis.** *J. Heat Transfer*, <u>1992</u>.

86. Karagozian, A. R.: **Fuel Injection and Flame Holding in High Speed Combustion Systems.** *Major Research Topics in Combustion*, ed. M.Y. Hussaini, A. Kumar and R.G. Voigt, SpringerVerlag, <u>1992</u>, pp. 237–252.

87. Kogan, B. Y.; Karplus, W. J.; Billett, B. S.; and Stevenson, W. G.: **Excitation Wave Propagation Within Narrow Pathways: Geometric Configurations Facilitating Unidirectional Block and Reentry.** *Physica D*, Vol. 59, <u>1992</u>, pp. 275–296.

88. Landau, Daniel Marc: **Eddy Vortices Produced by Nonlinear Reflection of a Gravity Wave at a Critical Level.** Ph.D. Thesis, UCLA, <u>1992</u>, 93N31155.

The internal gravity waves generated by flow over orography are numerically simulated with a new finite element model. When the vertically propagating wave approaches a critical level (wind flow reversal) the wave interacts with the critical level resulting in wave breaking, reflection of energy from the critical level, and the formation of vortices in the wave field. Without doubt, this problem is of concern to aviators. Although previous studies have addressed reflection and wave breaking, no previous study raised questions examining the validity of its own theories. Here a brash approach is used to expose the weakness and strengths of various theories while comparing them with simulated observations. From the observations we have cataloged several stages during the life cycle of an interacting wave, and have produced an energy budget. Each stage requires a separate theory. Significant amounts of wave reflection occur only during later periods, and we have linked this to the formation of the eddy vortices. While some researchers would be satisfied with the explanation that reflection is merely radiant energy arising from the area of convection and turbulence in the zone of wave breaking near a critical level, they would be very interested to learn that the large amount of energy of the reflected wave may be accounted for not from the release of gravitational potential energy as suggested above but rather from the direct transfer of energy from the mean flow and the energy of the main incident wave. Along this line, a model has been developed which produces results which mimic the observations: a second harmonic reflected wave grows rapidly while interacting with the incident wave.

89. Lay, J. H.; and Dhir, V. K.: **Micro Layer Thickness and Shape of a Vapor Stem During Nucleate Boiling.** *Micromechanical Systems*, ASME DSC–Vol. 40, <u>1992</u>, pp. 259–266.

90. Li, H. S.: **The Instability of a Liquid Jet in a Compressible Airstream.** Ph.D. dissertation, UCLA, <u>1992</u>.

91. Madooglu, K.: **Evaporation and Burning of a Spherical Fuel Droplet in a Uniform Convective Flowfield.** Ph.D. dissertation, UCLA, <u>1992</u>.

92. Mendoza, J.; Fricker, D.; and Catton, I.: **Inverse Heat Conduction in a Planar Slab Composed of Multiple**

Material Layers. *ASME HTD–Vol. 207, Fundamental Problems in Conduction Heat Transfer*, ASME, <u>1992</u>.

93.   Stroes, G. R.: **Dryout on Flat Plates and in Grooved Wicking Structures.** M.Sc. thesis, UCLA, <u>1992</u>.

94.   Stroes, G.; Rohloff, T.; and Catton, I.: **An Experimental Study of the Capillary Forces in Rectangular vs. Triangular Channels.** Presented at the ASME National Heat Transfer Conference, San Diego, California, <u>1992</u>.

95.   Tisdale, E. R.; and Karplus, W. J.: **System Identification With Artificial Neural Networks.** *International Journal of Pattern Recognition and Artificial Intelligence*, Vol. 6, No. 1, <u>1992</u>, pp. 93–111.

96.   Youn, B.; and Mills, A. F.: **Variable Property Flow in Rectangular Ducts With Repeated Rectangular Rib Roughness.** H-2290. *PHOENICS Journal*, Vol. 5, <u>1992</u>, pp. 175–232.

97.   Nguyen, T. T.; and Karagozian, A. R.: **Liquid Fuel Jet in Subsonic Crossflow.** *Journal of Propulsion and Power* (ISSN 0748-4658), Vol. 8, January–February 1992, <u>February 1992</u>, pp. 21–29, 92A21054.

98.   Jenkins, D. W.; and Karagozian, A. R.: **Flame Deformation and Entrainment Associated With an Isothermal Transverse Fuel Jet.** AIAA Paper 92-0236. Presented at the 30th AIAA Aerospace Sciences Meeting and Exhibit, Reno, Nevada, <u>January 6–9, 1992</u>, 92A25699, #.

This paper describes an analytical model of an incompressible, isothermal reacting jet in crossflow. The model represents the flow in the jet cross-section by a counter rotating vortex pair, a flow structure that has been observed to dominate the jet behavior. The reaction surface surrounding the fuel jet is represented as a composite of strained diffusion flames that are stretched and deformed by the vortex pair flow. The results shed new light on the interaction between the vortex pair circulation and flame structure evolution and their relation to the concept of entrainment.

99.   Yao, K.; Lorenzelli, F.; and Kong, J.: **The Equivalence of Total Least-Squares and Correspondence Analysis.** *Proceedings, IEEE Conference on ICASSP*, <u>March 1992</u>, pp. V-305 to V-308.

100.   Bendiksen, Oddvar O.: **Role of Shock Dynamics in Transonic Flutter.** AIAA Paper 92-2121. Presented at the AIAA Dynamics Specialists Conference, Dallas, Texas, <u>April 16–17, 1992</u>, (see A92-35651 14-08), pp. 401–414, 92A35690, #.

A computational study of the influence of shock motion on flutter and divergence in transonic flow is presented. The numerical scheme models the entire fluid-structure system as a single continuum dynamics problem, by using a mixed Eulerian-Lagrangian formulation. No assumptions of small displacements are made, but the effect of viscosity is neglected. The results from this study indicate that the shock dynamics gives rise to limit cycles and highly nonlinear aeroelastic phenomena, such as weak divergence and flutter-divergence interactions. Although the shocks typically are destabilizing at the linear flutter boundary, they often have a strongly stabilizing effect for moderate-amplitude motions. The shocks are thus capable of quenching an emerging bending-torsion flutter motion and turning it into limit cycle flutter. The usefulness of classical flutter and divergence boundary diagrams is severely limited in transonic flow, because much of the global dynamic stability information is lost in such a presentation.

101.   Davis, Gary A.; and Bendiksen, Oddvar O.: **Unsteady Transonic Euler Solutions Using Finite Elements.** AIAA Paper 92-2504. *Technical Papers, Pt. 4.* Presented at the 33rd AIAA, ASME, ASCE, AHS, and ASC Structures, Structural Dynamics and Materials Conference, Dallas, Texas, <u>April 13–15, 1992</u>, (see A92-34451 13-39), pp. 2203–2213, 92A34499, #.

A finite element solution of the unsteady Euler equations is presented and demonstrated for 2D airfoil configurations oscillating in transonic flows. Computations are performed by spatially discretizing the conservation equations using the Galerkin weighted residual method and then employing a multistage Runge-Kutta scheme to march forward in time. A mesh deformation scheme has been developed to efficiently move interior points in a smooth fashion as the airfoil undergoes rigid body pitch and plunge motion. Both steady and unsteady results are presented, and a comparison is made with solutions obtained using finite-volume techniques. The effects of using either a lumped or consistent mass matrix are presented; the finite element method provides an accurate solution for unsteady transonic flows about isolated airfoils.

102.   Pak, Chan-Gi; and Friedmann, Peretz P.: **New Time-Domain Technique for Flutter Boundary Identification.** AIAA Paper 92-2102. *Technical Papers,* presented at the AIAA Dynamics Specialists Conference, Dallas, Texas, <u>April 16–17, 1992</u>, (see A92-35651 14-08), pp. 201–214, 92A35673, #.

A new methodology for flutter boundary identification in the time domain is presented. This technique is based on a single-input single-output deterministic ARMA model and an on-line parameter estimation procedure. It is capable of simultaneous identification of the aeroelastic modal parameters as well as the static offset term which represents the static deformation or state of the aeroelastic system. The capabilities of the method are illustrated by applying it to several examples, such as: damped free oscillations, a two degree of freedom NACA 64A010 airfoil in transonic flight, and a cantilevered rectangular wing in subsonic flow.

Numerical implementations of the new methodology developed in this study demonstrates that it is a cost effective time-domain technique for flutter boundary identification.

103. Wurtele, M. G.; Datta, A.; and Sharman, R. D.: **Gravity-Inertia Wave Propagation in the Presence of Singular Levels.** Presented at the 13th Annual Canadian Conference on Applied Mathematics, University of Alberta, Edmonton, Alberta, Canada, June 1992.

104. Li, H.-S.; and Karagozian, A. R.: **Breakup of a Liquid Jet in Supersonic Crossflow.** *AIAA Journal* (ISSN 0001-1452), Vol. 30, No. 7, July 1992, (see A91-19415), pp. 1919–1921, 92A45860. (See also B 63.)

105. Fricker, Darren; Mendoza, John; and Catton, Ivan: **A Computational Fluid Dynamics Analysis of the Hypersonic Flights of Pegasus.**[®] NASA CR-186023, H-1835, NAS 1.26:186023, August 1992, 92N32560, #.

The performance of a fully viscous, three-dimensional Navier-Stokes solver, PARC3D, was tested. The criteria for judging the performance of the CFD code were based on flight data from the first two flights of the Pegasus. The flight data consisted of heat-transfer rates and sparse pressure coefficients primarily in the fillet region of the vehicle. The code performed remarkably well in all aspects of the tests. As expected, the best heat-transfer results were obtained for the low Mach number simulations. These results are attributed to lack of high ablation rates at the lower Mach numbers since the CFD simulations did not account for ablation at the vehicle surface. As the Mach number increased, the ablative effects became more apparent in the comparisons. This effect was evident at the highest Mach numbers, when PARC3D would be required over the entire fillet region, rather than at a few discrete locations. In this manner, CFD heat-flux profiles could be accurately evaluated. Although the pressure data were sparse, the trends suggest that the code predicts surface pressures with reasonable accuracy. Three of the four locations yield pressures that are consistent, but the CFD results yield pressures below the flight data by a factor of 2 at the fourth location.

106. Fricker, Darren; Mendoza, John; and Catton, Ivan: **A Summary of the Computational Fluid Dynamics Analysis of the Hypersonic Flights of Pegasus.**[®] AIAA Paper 92-4059. Presented at the 28th ASME, AIChE, ANS, and AIAA National Heat Transfer Conference, San Diego, California, August 9–12, 1992, 92A56142, #.

A computational fluid dynamics (CFD) analysis of the hypersonic flights of the NASA's Pegasus launch vehicle was carried out using the PARC code. The flight data included heat transfer rates and sparse pressure coefficients primarily in the fillet region of the vehicle. Since the CFD simulations did not account for ablation at the vehicle surface, the test heat transfer results were obtained for the low Mach number simulations; as the Mach number was increased, the ablative effects at the vehicle surface became more apparent and contributed to the error.

107. Wurtele, M. G.; Datta, A.; and Sharman, R. D.: **Singular Level Dynamics for Gravity- and Gravity-inertial Waves.** *Proceedings, Sixth Conference on Mountain Meteorology*, Portland, Oregon, September 1992, pp. 76–80.

108. Li, H.-S.; and Kelly, R. E.: **The Instability of a Liquid Jet in a Compressible Airstream.** *Physics of Fluids* (ISSN 0899-8213), Vol. 4, No. 10, October 1992, pp. 2162–2168, 92A54964.

The instability of a liquid jet immersed in a coflowing compressible airstream is investigated, for both two-dimensional and circular jets, using a simplified flow model in which the effects associated with the cross-flow component of velocity are ignored. Results of the analysis agreed qualitatively with experimental results in that they suggest a more violent instability when the free-stream Mach number is close to unity. It was also found that a change from convective to absolute instability occurs in this transonic flow regime.

109. Madooglu, K.; and Karagozian, A. R.: **Droplet Burning in a Convective Flowfield With Exact Variation of Gas Properties.** Paper 92-56. *Proceedings of the Western States Section/The Combustion Institute Fall Meeting*, October 1992.

110. Wurtele, M. G.; and Datta, A.: **Lee Waves, Benign and Malignant.** *Measurement and Modeling of Environmental Flows—1992*. Proceedings of the ASME Winter Annual Meeting, Anaheim, California, November 8–13, 1992, Vol. 143, pp. 109–121, 93A50517.

The flow of an incompressible, stratified fluid over an obstacle will produce an oscillation in which buoyancy is the restoring force, called a gravity wave. For disturbances of this scale, the atmosphere may be treated as incompressible; and even the linear approximation will explain many of the phenomena observed in the lee of mountains. However, nonlinearities arise in two ways: (1) through the large (scaled) size of the mountain, and (2) from dynamically singular levels in the fluid field. These produce a complicated array of phenomena that present hazards to aircraft and to lee surface areas. If there is no dynamic barrier, these waves can penetrate vertically into the middle atmosphere (30-100 km attitude), where recent observations show them to be of a length scale that must involve the Coriolis force in any modeling. At these altitudes, the amplitude of the waves is very large, and the waves are studied with a view to their potential impact on the projected National Aerospace Plane. This paper presents the results of analyses and state-of-the-art numerical simulations, validated where possible by observational data.

UCLA FSRC 1993 Publications

111. Huckaby, E. D.: **Heat Pipe Vapor Dynamics Using the Spectral Methods.** M.Sc. thesis, UCLA, 1993.

112. Kim, S.: **A Development of Minimal Time-Change Detection Algorithm (MT-CDA) in System Parameters and Its Applications to Flight Systems.** Ph.D. dissertation, UCLA, 1993.

113. Mendoza, J. C.: **Implementation of the Engquist Filter Into the PARC3D CFD Code for Simulation of the Flights of Pegasus.**® M.Sc. thesis, UCLA, 1993.

114. Ton, V. T.: **A Numerical Method for Mixing/Chemically Reacting Compressible Flow With Finite Rate Chemistry.** Ph.D. dissertation, UCLA, 1993.

115. Youn, B.; and Mills, A. F.: **Flow of Supercritical Hydrogen in a Uniformly Heated Circular Tube.** H-2292. *Numerical Heat Transfer*, Part A, Vol. 24, 1993, pp. 1–24.

116. Garrett, C. J.; Guarro, S. B.; and Apostolakis, G. E.: **Development of a Methodology for Assessing the Safety of Embedded Software Systems.** AIAA Paper 93-1087. Presented at the AIAA, AHS, and ASEE, Aerospace Design Conference, Irvine, California, February 16–19, 1993, 93A30976, #.

A Dynamic Flowgraph Methodology (DFM) based on an integrated approach to modeling and analyzing the behavior of software-driven embedded systems for assessing and verifying reliability and safety is discussed. DFM is based on an extension of the Logic Flowgraph Methodology to incorporate state transition models. System models which express the logic of the system in terms of causal relationships between physical variables and temporal characteristics of software modules are analyzed to determine how a certain state can be reached. This is done by developing timed fault trees which take the form of logical combinations of static trees relating the system parameters at different point in time. The resulting information concerning the hardware and software states can be used to eliminate unsafe execution paths and identify testing criteria for safety critical software functions.

117. Hsieh, S. F.; Liu, K. J. R.; and Yao, K.: **Estimation of Multiple Sinusoidal Frequencies Using Truncated Least-Square Methods.** *IEEE Trans. on Signal Processing*, Vol. 41, No. 2, February 1993, pp. 990–994.

118. Bein, T.; Friedmann, P.; Zhong, X.; and Nydick, I.: **Hypersonic Flutter of a Curved Shallow Panel With Aerodynamic Heating.** AIAA Paper 93-1318. Presented at the 34th AIAA, ASME, ASCE, AHS, and ASC, Structures, Structural Dynamics and Materials Conference, La Jolla, California, April 19–22, 1993, 93A37428, #.

The general equations describing the nonlinear fluttering oscillations of shallow, curved, heated orthotropic panels have been derived. The formulation takes into account the location of the panel on the surface of a generic hypersonic vehicle, when calculating the aerodynamic loads. It is also shown that third order piston theory produces unsteady aerodynamic loading which is in close agreement with that based upon direct solution of the Euler equations. Results, for simply supported panels, are obtained using Galerkin's method combined with direct numerical integration in time to compute stable limit cycle amplitudes. These results illustrate the sensitivity of the aeroelastic behavior to the unsteady aerodynamic assumptions, temperature, orthotropicity and flow orientation.

119. Bendiksen, Oddvar O.: **Nonclassical Aileron Buzz in Transonic Flow.** AIAA Paper 93-1479. Presented at the 34th AIAA, ASME, ASCE, AHS, and ASC, Structures, Structural Dynamics and Materials Conference, La Jolla, California, April 19–22, 1993, 93A37439, #.

A computational study of inviscid, transonic aileron and trailing-edge buzz instabilities is presented. A mixed Eulerian-Lagrangian formulation is used to model the fluid-structure system and to obtain a system of space-discretized equations that is time-marched to simulate the aeroelastic behavior of the wing-aileron system. Results obtained suggest that shock-induced separation may not be an essential driving force behind all buzz phenomena. Several examples are shown where the shock motion interacts with the aileron motion to extract energy from the flow. If the trailing-edge region is sufficiently flexible and the shocks are at the trailing edge, a trailing-edge buzz instability appears possible.

120. Chang, B. H.; and Mills, A. F.: **Turbulent Flow in a Channel With Transverse Rib Heat Transfer Augmentation.** *International Journal of Heat and Mass Transfer* (ISSN 0017-9310), Vol. 36, No. 6, April 1993, pp. 1459–1469, 93A34674.

Turbulent flow in a 2D channel with repeated rectangular rib roughness was numerically simulated using a low Reynolds number form of the k-epsilon turbulence model. Friction factors and average Stanton numbers were calculated for various pitch to rib height ratios and bulk Reynolds numbers. Comparisons with experiment were generally adequate, with the predictions of friction superior to those for heat transfer. The effect of variable properties for channel flow was investigated, and the results showed a greater effect for friction than for heat transfer. Comparison with experiment yielded no clear conclusions. The turbulence model was also validated for a related problem, that of flow downstream of an abrupt pipe expansion.

121. Davis, Gary A.; and Bendiksen, Oddvar O.: **Transonic Panel Flutter.** AIAA Paper 93-1476. Presented at the 34th AIAA, ASME, ASCE, AHS, and ASC, Structures, Structural Dynamics and Materials Conference, La Jolla, California, April 19–22, 1993, 93A37438, #.

FEM is here used to ascertain the stability and aeroelastic response of thin, 2D panels subjected to Mach 0.8-2.5 flows. In the absence of shocks, it is found that the Euler equations used to represent the unsteady flowfield dynamics predict response behaviors resembling those obtained via potential flow methods. Where shocks do play a significant role in the overall motion of the panel, divergence and limit cycle flutter are observed. In the Mach 1.4-1.5 range, flutter involved the higher modes of the panel, tending toward possible chaotic motion.

122. Chang, B. H.; and Mills, A. F.: **Computation of Heat Transfer From Turbulent Impinging Jets.** H-2291. *Proceedings of 6th International Symposium on Transport Phenomena (ISTP-6) in Thermal Engineering*, Seoul, Korea, Vol. IV, May 1993, pp. 245–250.

123. Datta, A.; Wurtele, M. G.; and Sharman, R. D.: **Effect of Singular Levels on Flow of a Stratified Rotating Fluid Over an Isolated Obstacle.** *Proceedings of the Ninth Conference on Atmospheric and Oceanic Waves and Stability*, San Antonio, Texas, May 1993, pp. 199–202.

124. Landau, D. M.; and Wurtele, M. G.: **A Simple Model for the Explosive Growth of Harmonics Reflected From the Incidence of a Gravity Wave on a Critical Level.** *Proceedings of the Ninth Conference on Atmospheric and Oceanic Waves and Stability*, San Antonio, Texas, May 1993, pp. 181–184.

125. Li, Hsi-Shang; and Kelly, Robert E.: **On the Transfer of Energy to an Unstable Liquid Jet in a Coflowing Compressible Airstream.** *Physics of Fluids* (ISSN 0899-8213), Vol. 5, No. 5, May 1993, pp. 1273–1274, 93A39396.

The transfer of energy from a compressible airstream to a coflowing unstable liquid jet via the pressure perturbation at the interface is studied as the Mach number varies continuously from subsonic to supersonic values. The 'lift' component of the pressure perturbation has been demonstrated to predominate up to slightly supersonic free-stream Mach numbers, after which the 'drag' component predominates.

126. Wurtele, M. G.; Datta, A.; and Sharman, R. D.: **Downslope Windstorms Under a Critical Level.** *Proceedings of the Ninth Conference on Atmospheric and Oceanic Waves and Stability*, San Antonio, Texas, May 1993, pp. 189–192.

127. Wurtele, M. G.; Datta, A.; and Sharman, R. D.: **Lee Waves: Benign and Malignant.** NASA CR-186024, H-1890, NAS 1.26:186024, June 1993, 94N10725, #.

The flow of an incompressible fluid over an obstacle will produce an oscillation in which buoyancy is the restoring force, called a gravity wave. For disturbances of this scale, the atmosphere may be treated as dynamically incompressible, even though there exists a mean static upward density gradient. Even in the linear approximation - i.e., for small disturbances - this model explains a great many of the flow phenomena observed in the lee of mountains. However, nonlinearities do arise importantly, in three ways: (1) through amplification due to the decrease of mean density with height; (2) through the large (scaled) size of the obstacle, such as a mountain range; and (3) from dynamically singular levels in the fluid field. These effects produce a complicated array of phenomena - large departure of the streamlines from their equilibrium levels, high winds, generation of small scales, turbulence, etc. - that present hazards to aircraft and to lee surface areas. The nonlinear disturbances also interact with the larger-scale flow in such a manner as to impact global weather forecasts and the climatological momentum balance. If there is no dynamic barrier, these waves can penetrate vertically into the middle atmosphere (30–100 km), where recent observations show them to be of a length scale that must involve the coriolis force in any modeling. At these altitudes, the amplitude of the waves is very large, and the phenomena associated with these wave dynamics are being studied with a view to their potential impact on high performance aircraft, including the projected National Aerospace Plane (NASP). The presentation shows the results of analysis and of state-of-the-art numerical simulations, validated where possible by observational data, and illustrated with photographs from nature.

128. Madooglu, K.; and Karagozian, A. R.: **Burning of a Spherical Fuel Droplet in a Uniform Flowfield With Exact Property Variation.** *Combustion and Flame* (ISSN 0010-2180), Vol. 94, No. 3, August 1993, pp. 321–329, 93A53705.

An analytical/numerical model is developed for single droplet evaporation and burning in a convective flowfield. The model is based on the boundary-layer approach, and chemical reaction kinetics are represented by a one-step, finite-rate reaction mechanism, while variation of gas properties with temperature and gas composition is based on the kinetic theory of gases. Four droplet models differing in the degree of complexity concerning property variation and chemistry are compared. Comparisons are also provided with existing empirical correlations for convective droplet evaporation and burning.

129. Wurtele, M. G.; Datta, A.; and Sharman, R. D.: **Lee Waves: Benign and Malignant.** *Proceedings, Fifth International Conference on Aviation Weather Systems*, Vienna, Virginia, August 2–6, 1993.

130. Kogan, B. Y.; Karplus, W. J.; Billett, B. S.; and Karpoukhin, M. G.: **Excitation Wave Front Transients: A Computer Simulation Study.** *Proceedings of the 15th Annual International Conference of the IEE Engineering in Medicine and Biology Society,* San Diego, California, <u>October 28–31, 1993</u>, pp. 1–2.

131. Garrett, C. J.; Guarro, S. B.; and Apostolakis, G. E.: **Assessing Digital Control System Dependability Using the Dynamic Flowgraph Methodology.** *Proceedings, of the American Nuclear Society, Winter Meeting,* San Francisco, California, <u>November 1993</u>.

UCLA FSRC 1994 Publications

132. Ton, V. T.; Karagozian, A. R.; Marble, F. E.; Osher, S. J.; and Engquist, B. E.: **Numerical Simulations of High-Speed Chemically Reacting Flow.** NASA CR-203703, NAS 1.26:203703, NIPS-97-27703, <u>1994</u>, 97N72166, #. (Also in *Theoretical and Computational Fluid Dynamics,* Vol. 6, 1994, pp. 161–179.)

The essentially nonoscillatory (ENO) shock-capturing scheme for the solution of hyperbolic equations is extended to solve a system of coupled conservation equations governing two-dimensional, time-dependent, compressible chemically reacting flow with full chemistry. The thermodynamic properties of the mixture are modeled accurately, and stiff kinetic terms are separated from the fluid motion by a fractional step algorithm. The methodology is used to study the concept of shock-induced mixing and combustion, a process by which the interaction of a shock wave with a jet of low-density hydrogen fuel enhances mixing through streamwise vorticity generation. Test cases with and without chemical reaction are explored here. Our results indicate that, in the temperature range examined, vorticity generation as well as the distribution of atomic species do not change significantly with the introduction of a chemical reaction and subsequent heat release. The actual diffusion of hydrogen is also relatively unaffected by the reaction process. This suggests that the fluid mechanics of this problem may be successfully decoupled from the combustion processes, and that computation of the mixing problem (without combustion chemistry) can elucidate much of the important physical features of the flow.

133. Ton, V. T.; Karagozian, A. R.; Marble, F. E.; Osher, S. J.; and Engquist, B. E.: **Numerical Simulations of High-Speed Chemically Reacting Flow.** NASA CR-203141, NAS 1.26:203141, NIPS-97-06256, <u>1994</u>, 97N70825, #. (Also Paper No. 93-068. *Proceedings of the Western States Section/The Combustion Institute Fall Meeting,* October 1993.)

The Essentially NonOscillatory (ENO) shock-capturing scheme for the solution of hyperbolic equations is extended

to solve a system of coupled conservation equations governing two-dimensional, time-dependent, compressible chemically reacting flow with full chemistry. The thermodynamic properties of the mixture are modeled accurately, and stiff kinetic terms are separated from the fluid motion by a fractional step algorithm. The methodology is used to study the concept of shock-induced mixing and combustion, a process by which the interaction of a shock wave with a jet of low-density hydrogen fuel enhances mixing through streamwise vorticity generation. Test cases with and without chemical reaction are explored here. Our results indicate that, in the temperature range examined, vorticity generation as well as the distribution of atomic species do not change significantly with the introduction of a chemical reaction and subsequent heat release. The actual diffusion of hydrogen is also relatively unaffected by the reaction process. This suggests that the fluid mechanics of this problem may be successfully decoupled from the combustion processes, and that computation of the mixing problem (without combustion chemistry) can elucidate much of the important physical features of the flow.

134. Balakrishnan, A. V.: **Shape Control of Plates With Piezo Actuators and Collocated Position/Rate Sensors.** NASA CR-204423, NAS 1.26:204423, NIPS-97-27630, Elsevier Science, Inc., New York, New York, <u>1994</u>, 97N72074, #. (Also Paper No. 93-068. *Proceedings of the Western States Section/The Combustion Institute Fall Meeting,* October 1993.)

This paper treats the control problem of shaping the surface deformation of a circular plate using embedded piezo-electric actuators and collocated rate sensors. An explicit Linear Quadratic Gaussian (LQG) optimizer stability augmentation compensator is derived as well as the optimal feed-forward control. Corresponding performance evaluation formulas are also derived.

135. Balakrishnan, A. V.: **Shape Control of Plates With Piezo Actuators and Collocated Position/Rate Sensors.** NASA CR-203142, NAS 1.26:203142, NIPS-97-07898, Elsevier Science, Inc., New York, New York, <u>1994</u>, 97N70844, #.

This paper treats the control problem of shaping the surface deformation of a circular plate using embedded piezo-electric actuator and collocated rate sensors. An explicit Linear Quadratic Gaussian (LQG) optimizer stability augmentation compensator is derived as well as the optimal feed-forward control. Corresponding performance evaluation formulas are also derived.

136. Dillon, C. H.; and Speyer, J. L.: **Parameter Robust Game Theoretical Synthesis for the F-18 HARV.** AIAA 94-3679. *AIAA Guidance, Navigation and Control Conference,* <u>1994,</u> pp. 1242–1249.

137. Kong, Jeffrey: **The Accuracy of Parameter Estimation in System Identification of Noisy Aircraft Load Measurement.** NASA CR-197516, NAS 1.26:197516, <u>1994</u>, 95N19130, #. (Also Ph.D. thesis, UCLA, 1994.)

This thesis focuses on the subject of the accuracy of parameter estimation and system identification techniques. Motivated by a complicated load measurement from NASA Dryden Flight Research Center, advanced system identification techniques are needed. The objective of this problem is to accurately predict the load experienced by the aircraft wing structure during flight determined from a set of calibrated load and gage response relationship. We can then model the problem as a black box input-output system identification from which the system parameter has to be estimated. Traditional LS (Least Square) techniques and the issues of noisy data and model accuracy are addressed. A statistical bound reflecting the change in residual is derived in order to understand the effects of the perturbations on the data. Due to the intrinsic nature of the LS problem, LS solution faces the dilemma of the trade off between model accuracy and noise sensitivity. A method of conflicting performance indices is presented, thus allowing us to improve the noise sensitivity while at the same time configuring the degradation of the model accuracy. SVD techniques for data reduction are studied and the equivalence of the Correspondence Analysis (CA) and Total Least Squares Criteria are proved. We also looked at nonlinear LS problems with NASA F-111 data set as an example. Conventional methods are neither easily applicable nor suitable for the specific load problem since the exact model of the system is unknown. Neural Network (NN) does not require prior information on the model of the system. This robustness motivated us to apply the NN techniques on our load problem. Simulation results for the NN methods used in both the single load and the 'warning signal' problems are both useful and encouraging. The performance of the NN (for single load estimate) is better than the LS approach, whereas no conventional approach was tried for the 'warning signals' problems. The NN design methodology is also presented. The use of SVD, California and Collinearity Index methods are used to reduce the number of neurons in a layer.

138. Lay, J. H.: **Experimental Study in Enhanced Design of Boiling Surface Used in Jet Impingement Cooling and a Complimentary Theoretical Analysis for Fully Developed Nucleate Boiling.** Ph.D. dissertation, UCLA, <u>1994</u>.

139. Li, H. -S.: **Numerical Simulation of the Instability of an Inviscid Liquid Jet in a Coflowing Compressible Airstream.** NASA CR-203155, NAS 1.26:203155, NIPS-97-09946, Elsevier Science, Ltd., United Kingdom, <u>1994</u>, 97N70658, #. (Also *Computers Fluids*, Vol. 23, No. 6, 1994, pp. 853–880.)

The nonlinear interfacial instability of a liquid jet in a coflowing compressible airstream is studied numerically. A high-resolution scheme which has second-order accuracy in space and time is coupled with a Lagrangian marker particle algorithm to visualize the large-scale motion of the interfaces in compressible flow. A numerical algorithm based on an approximate equation of state of a compressible liquid is developed to allow this two-fluid system to be governed by the nonlinear unsteady Euler equations in conservative form. The initial growth of small disturbances given by the simulations agrees well with linear theory. The process of jet disruption in compressible flow is demonstrated to consist of the formation of liquid spikes, interweaving of the gas and liquid and stretching and detachment of the liquid main center core.

140. Madooglu, K.; and Karagozian, A. R.: **Brief Communication: A Simplified Approach to Transient Convective Droplet Evaporation and Burning.** NASA CR-203140, NAS 1.26:203140, NIPS-97-06225, Elsevier Science Publishers, the Netherlands, <u>1994</u>, 97N70835, #. (Also *Combustion and Flame*, Vol. 98, 1994, pp. 170–174.)

Empirical correlations for evaporation rates from single fuel droplets have existed since the 1930s. These correlations, which will be referred to in this article as Froessling/Ranz-Marshall types of correlations, are appropriate to the special cases of steady-state evaporation in the absence of chemical reaction. In a previous article by the authors, the quasi-steady evaporation and burning processes associated with a fuel drop in a convective environment are examined through a droplet model based on the boundary layer approach. For droplet Reynolds numbers of practical interest, this model produces very reasonable steady state as well as quasi-time-dependent droplet simulations, requiring relatively short computational times and yielding good agreement with the above-mentioned empirical correlations. The steady-state case, however, is usually relevant to practical combustor situations only when the drop has reached a nearly uniform temperature since the heating process of the drop cannot be considered to be quasi-steady. In the present study, the transient heating process of the droplet interior during evaporation and/or burning is taken into account, and thus calculations pertaining to the entire life-time of the droplet are carried out. It is of particular interest here to obtain simplified correlations to describe the transient behavior of evaporating and burning droplets; these may be incorporated with greater ease into spray calculations. Accordingly, we have chosen to use stagnation conditions in the present model in a modification of the Froessling/Ranz-Marshall correlations. These modified correlations, incorporating an effective transfer number, produce a fairly accurate representation of droplet evaporation and burning, while requiring only one tenth the computational effort used in a full boundary layer solution.

141. Padgett, M. L.; Karplus, W. J.; Deiss, S.; and Shelton, R.: **Computational Intelligence Standards: Motivations, Current Activities and Progress.** *Computer Standards and Interfaces*, Vol. 16, <u>1994</u>, pp. 185–203.

142. Wang, G. H.: **A Stochastic Adaptive Control Application to Flight Systems.** Ph.D. dissertation, UCLA, 1994.

143. Yao, K.: **SVD-Based Data Reduction and Classification Techniques.** *Advances in Statistical Signal Processing*, JAI Press, Stamford, Connecticut, 1994, pp. 411–431.

144. Youn, B.; Yuen, C.; and Mills, A. F.: **Friction Factor for Flow in Rectangular Ducts With One Side Rib-Roughened.** *Journal of Fluids Engineering*, Vol. 116, 1994, pp. 488–493.

145. Kim, Sungwan: **Minimal Time Change Detection Algorithm for Reconfigurable Control System and Application to Aerospace.** CR-199529, NIPS-95-05569, H-2294, NASA NAS 1.26:199529, 1994, 96N13234, #.

System parameters should be tracked on-line to build a reconfigurable control system even though there exists an abrupt change. For this purpose, a new performance index that we are studying is the speed of adaptation- how quickly does the system determine that a change has occurred? In this paper, a new, robust algorithm that is optimized to minimize the time delay in detecting a change for fixed false alarm probability is proposed. Simulation results for the aircraft lateral motion with a known or unknown change in control gain matrices, in the presence of doublet input, indicate that the algorithm works fairly well. One of its distinguishing properties is that detection delay of this algorithm is superior to that of Whiteness Test.

146. Garrett, C. J.; Yau, M.; Guarro, S. B.; and Apostolakis, G. E.: **Assessing the Dependability of Embedded Software Systems Using the Dynamic Flowgraph Methodology.** *Proceedings of the 4th International Conference on Dependable Computing for Critical Applications*, San Diego, California, January 1994.

147. Garrett, C. J.; Yau, M.; Guarro, S. B.; and Apostolakis, G. E.: **The Dynamic Flowgraph Methodology: A Methodology for Assessing Embedded System Software Safety.** *Proceedings of PSAM-II*, San Diego, California, March 1994.

148. Kogan, B. Y.; Karplus, W. J.; and Karpoukhin, M. G.: **The Effect of Boundary Conditions and Geometry of 2D Excitable Media on Properties of Wave Propagation.** *Fourth NIMC Forum: International Workshop on Dynamism and Regulation in Non-Linear Chemical Systems*, NIMC-AIST, Tsukuba, Japan, March 22–25, 1994, pp. 79–81.

149. Bendiksen, O. O.: **Transonic Flutter Suppression by a Passive Flap.** AIAA Paper 94-l423. *Proceedings, 35th AIAA, ASME, ASCE, AHS, and ASC Structures, Structural Dynamics and Materials Conference*, Hilton Head, South Carolina, April 18–20, 1994.

150. Friedmann, P.; Guillot, and Damien, M.: **A Fundamental Aeroservoelastic Study Combining Unsteady CFD With Adaptive Control.** NASA CR-201434, NAS 1.26:201434, AIAA Paper 94-1721, NIPS-96-61052. Presented at the AIAA Dynamics Specialists Conference, Hilton Head, South Carolina, April 21–22, 1994, 96N72357, #.

This paper describes a two-dimensional aeroservoelastic study in the time domain. The model, which is based on exact inviscid aerodynamics, correctly represents the large amplitude motions and the associated strong shock dynamics in the transonic regime. The aeroservoelastic system consists of a two degree-of-freedom airfoil with a trailing edge control surface. Using first-order actuator dynamics, a digital adaptive controller is applied to provide active flutter suppression. Comparisons between time-responses of the open-loop and closed loop systems show the ability of the trailing edge control surface to suppress non-linear transonic aeroelastic phenomena. A relation between actuator dynamics, sampling time-step and limits on the flap deflection angle to guarantee the effectiveness of the adaptive controller was demonstrated by the results generated.

151. Lorenzelli, F.; and Yao, K.: **On Updating Rate of Jacobi SVD Arrays and Data Nonstationarity.** *Proceedings, SPIE*, Vol. 2296, July 1994, pp. 414–425.

152. Lay, J. H.; and Dhir, V. K.: **A Nearly Theoretical Model for Fully Developed Nucleate Boiling of Saturated Liquids.** *Proceedings of the 10th International Heat Transfer Conference*, Brighton, United Kingdom, August 14–18, 1994.

153. Lorenzelli, F.; Hansen, P. C.; Chan, T. F.; and Yao, K.: **A Systolic Implementation of the Chan/Foster RRQR Algorithm.** *IEEE Trans. on Signal Processing*, Vol. 42, August 1994, pp. 2205–2208.

154. Karplus, W. J.; and Harreld, M. R.: **The Role of Virtual Environments in Clinical Medicine.** *Proceedings of the First Joint Conference of International Simulation Societies (CISS)*, September 1994, pp. 13–17.

155. Balakrishnan, A. V.: **Laser Beam Log Amplitude Temporal Scintillation Spectrum Due to Crosswind. Part 1: Theory.** TR-1-FSRC-1994-PT-1. *Proceedings of the NASA-UCLA Workshop on Laser Propagation in Atmospheric Turbulence*, September 1994, 95N24371, #.

We derive the temporal spectral density of the log-amplitude scintillation of a laser beam due to cross wind. The dependence on the velocity distribution along the propagation axis - magnitude and direction - in relation to the detector position vector in the plane normal to the axis is of main interest in addition to the usual turbulence parameters such as the inner and outer scales. Also studied are the moments of the (normalized) spectral density, which would appear to be less sensitive to these parameters, as providing possible means for monitoring changes in the wind velocity. We begin in Section 2 with a brief review of propagation theory essential for our purposes. The treatment is different from the standard textbook in that we make systematic use of the parabolic approximation of the Helmholtz equation rather than ad hoc arguments for simplification inside the solution integral. The main results, including the spectral density derivation, are in Section 3. Some approximations - which help avoid purely numerical computer evaluation of the integrals and provide some analytical insight - are studied in Section 4.

156. Bendiksen, O. O.: **Eulerian-Lagrangian Simulation of Transonic Flutter Instabilities.** H-2293. Presented at the Symposium on Aeroelasticity and Fluid-Structure Interaction Problems, ASME Winter Annual Meeting, Chicago, Illinois, November 6–11, 1994.

157. Guillot, D.; and Friedmann, P. P.: **Adaptive Control of Aeroelastic Behavior in Transonic Flow.** *Aeroelasticity and Fluid Structure Interaction Problems*, AD-Vol. 44. Symposium Proceedings, ASME Winter Annual Meeting, Chicago, Illinois, November 6–11, 1994, pp. 175–195.

158. Wang, Kon-Sheng Charles: **In-Flight Imaging of Transverse Gas Jets Injected Into Transonic and Supersonic Crossflows: Design and Development.** NASA CR-186031, H-2027, NAS 1.26:186031, November 1994, 95N17418, #. (Also M.S. thesis, UCLA, 1993.)

The design and development of an airborne flight-test experiment to study nonreacting gas jets injected transversely into transonic and supersonic crossflows is presented. Free-stream/crossflow Mach numbers range from 0.8 to 2.0. Planar laser-induced fluorescence (PLIF) of an iodine-seeded nitrogen jet is used to visualize the jet flow. Time-dependent images are obtained with a high-speed intensified video camera synchronized to the laser pulse rate. The entire experimental assembly is configured compactly inside a unique flight-test-fixture (FTF) mounted under the fuselage of the F-104G research aircraft, which serves as a 'flying wind tunnel' at NASA Dryden Flight Research Center. The aircraft is flown at predetermined speeds and altitudes to permit a perfectly expanded (or slightly underexpanded) gas jet to form just outside the FTF at each free-stream Mach number. Recorded gas jet images are then digitized to allow analysis of jet trajectory, spreading, and mixing characteristics. Comparisons will be made with analytical and numerical predictions. This study shows the viability of applying highly sophisticated groundbased flow diagnostic techniques to flight-test vehicle platforms that can achieve a wide range of thermo/fluid dynamic conditions. Realistic flow environments, high enthalpies, unconstrained flowfields, and moderate operating costs are also realized, in contrast to traditional wind-tunnel testing.

UCLA FSRC 1995 Publications

159. Kim, Sungwan: **The Minimal Time Detection Algorithm.** NASA CR-199324, NAS 1.26:199324, 1995, 96N15989, #. (Also IEEE 1994 Aerospace Applications Conference, Vail, Colorado, February 5–12, 1994.)

An aerospace vehicle may operate throughout a wide range of flight environmental conditions that affect its dynamic characteristics. Even when the control design incorporates a degree of robustness, system parameters may drift enough to cause its performance to degrade below an acceptable level. The object of this paper is to develop a change detection algorithm so that we can build a highly adaptive control system applicable to aircraft systems. The idea is to detect system changes with minimal time delay. The algorithm developed is called Minimal Time-Change Detection Algorithm (MT-CDA) which detects the instant of change as quickly as possible with false-alarm probability below a certain specified level. Simulation results for the aircraft lateral motion with a known or unknown change in control gain matrices, in the presence of doublet input, indicate that the algorithm works fairly well as theory indicates though there is a difficulty in deciding the exact amount of change in some situations. One of MT-CDA distinguishing properties is that detection delay of MT-CDA is superior to that of Whiteness Test.

160. Alvarez-Salazar, O. S.; Betros, R. S.; Bronowicki, A. J.; and Manning, R. A.: **Smart Structures Technology for Space Applications.** *Proceedings, 5th International Conference on Advances in Communication and Control,* 1995, pp. 603–613.

161. Braunreiter, D.: **Wind Velocity Estimation From Spectural Density Moment Estimates of Forward Laser Beam Distortion.** Ph. D. thesis, UCLA, 1995.

162. Daneshgaran, F.; and Yao, K.: **The Iterative Collapse Algorithm: A Novel Approach for the Design of Long Constraint Length Viterbi Decoders - Part I.** *IEEE Trans. on Communications*, Vol. 43, 1995, pp. 1409–1418.

163. Daneshgaran, F.; and Yao, K.: **The Iterative Collapse Algorithm: A Novel Approach for the Design of Long Constraint Length Viterbi Decoders - Part II.** *IEEE Trans. on Communications*, Vol. 43, 1995, pp. 1419–1428.

164. Datta, A.: **The Propagation of Gravity Inertia Waves.** Ph.D. dissertation, UCLA, 1995.

165. Karpoukhin, M. G.; Kogan, B. Y.; and Karplus, W. J.: **The Application of a Massively Parallel Computer to the Simulation of Electrical Wave Propagation Phenomena in the Heart Muscle Using Simplified Models.** H-2296. *Proceedings of the Twenty-Eighth Annual Hawaii*

International Conference on System Sciences, ed. L. Hunger and B.D. Shriver, IEEE Computer Society Press, 1995.

166. Kim, S.: **Minimal Time Change Detection Algorithm for Reconfigurable Flight Control Systems.** H-2297. *AIAA Journal of Guidance, Control and Dynamics*, Vol. 18, No. 5, 1995, pp. 1211–1212.

167. Lay, J. H.; and Dhir, V. K.: **Nucleate Boiling Heat Flux Enhancement on Macro-Micro-Structured Surfaces Cooled by an Impinging Jet.** *Journal of Enhanced Heat Transfer*, Vol. 3, No. 3, 1995, pp. 177–188.

168. Lorenzelli, F.; and Yao, K.: **Systolic Array for SVD Downdating.** *SVD and Signal Processing III: Algorithms, Architectures, and Applications*, ed. M. Moonen and B. de Moor, 1995, Elsevier Science Publisher, pp. 243–250.

169. Mortazavian, H.: **Foundations of a Theory of Stochastic Supervisory Control of Discrete Event Systems.** *Proceedings, 5th International Conference on Advances in Communication and Control*, 1995, pp. 800–811.

170. Pak, C.; Friedmann, P. P.; and Livne, E. E.: **Digital Adaptive Flutter Suppression and Simulation Using Approximation Transonic Aerodynamics.** *Journal of Vibration and Control*, Vol. 1, 1995, pp. 363–388.

171. Sharman, R. D.; and Wurtele, M. G.: **Modification of the Richardson Number Field by Lee Waves.** *Proceedings of the 7th Conference on Mountain Meteorology*, Breckenridge, Colorado, 1995.

172. Tan, B.: **Design and Testing of an Automated System Using Thermochromatic Liquid Crystals to Determine Local Heat Transfer Coefficients for an Impinging Jet.** H-2299. M.Sc. thesis, UCLA, 1995.

173. Wang, K. Charles; Smith, Owen I.; and Karagozian, Ann R.: **In-Flight Imaging of Transverse Gas Jets Injected Into Subsonic and Supersonic Crossflows.** *AIAA Journal*, Vol 33, December 1995, pp. 2259–2263.

The development of and results from an airborne flight-test experiment to study nonreacting gas jets injected traversely into subsonic and slightly supersonic crossflows is presented. Freestream/crossflow Mach numbers in the study ranged from 0.6 to 1.2, and planar laser-induced fluorescence imaging of an iodine-seeded nitrogen jet was used to visualize the jet flow. Time dependent images were obtained with a high-speed intensified video camera synchronized to the laser pulse rate. The entire experimental assembly was configured compactly inside a unique flight-test fixture mounted under the fuselage of NASA Dryden's F-104G research aircraft, which served as a flying wind tunnel. Recorded traverse jet images were then digitized to allow analysis of jet trajectory, spreading, and mixing

characteristics. Comparisons of experimental results with model predictions in this transonic crossflow regime show reasonable agreement.

174. Wurtele, M. G.; Datta, A.; and Sharman, R. D.: **Gravity-Inertial Waves and Lee Waves.** *Proceedings of 7th Conference on Mountain Meteorology*, Breckenridge, Colorado, 1995.

175. Wang, K. Charles; Smith, Owen I.; and Karagozian, Ann R.: **In-Flight Imaging of Transverse Gas Jets Injected Into Subsonic and Supersonic Crossflows.** AIAA Paper 95-0516, H-2300. Presented at the 33rd AIAA Aerospace Sciences Meeting and Exhibit, Reno, Nevada, January 9–12, 1995, A95-21364, #.

The development of and results from an airborne flight-test experiment to study nonreacting gas jets injected transversely into subsonic and slightly supersonic crossflows is presented. Freestream/crossflow Mach numbers range from 0.6 to 1.2. Planar laser-induced fluorescence (PLIF) imaging of an iodine-seeded nitrogen jet is used to visualize the jet flow. Time-dependent images are obtained with a high-speed intensified video camera synchronized to the laser pulse rate. The entire experimental assembly is configured compactly inside a unique flight-test-fixture mounted under the fuselage of NASA Dryden's F-104G research aircraft, which serves as a 'flying wind tunnel'. Recorded transverse gas jet images are then digitized to allow analysis of jet trajectory, spreading, and mixing characteristics. Comparisons of experimental results with model predictions show reasonable agreement.

176. Youn, B.; and Mills, A. F.: **Cooling Panel Optimization for the Active Cooling of a Hypersonic Aircraft.** H-2301. *AIAA Journal of Thermophysics and Heat Transfer*, Vol. 9, January–March 1995, pp. 136–143.

177. Holzer, A.; Catton, I.; and Mayinger, F.: **Fluid Dynamics and Performance Limits of Structured Surfaces for Removing Heat.** Diploma Thesis, Munich Technical University, Germany, February 1995.

178. Balakrishnan, A. V.: **On a Generalization of the Kalman-Yakubovic Lemma.** *Journal of Applied Mathematics and Optimization*, Vol. 31, No. 2, March/April 1995, pp. 177–188.

179. Mendoza, J. C.; Huckaby, E. D.; and Catton, I.: **Calculation of Hypersonic Heat Fluxes Using an Artificial Viscosity Model and a Nonlinear Filtering Method.** Presented at the 4th ASME and JSME Thermal Engineering Joint Conference in Maui, Hawaii, March 19–24, 1995.

180. Stroes, G.; and Catton, I.: **An Experimental Study of the Heat Removal Capabilities of Triangular vs. Sinusoidal Capillary Channels.** Presented at the 4th ASME and JSME Thermal Engineering Joint Conference, Maui, Hawaii, March 19–24, 1995.

181. Bendiksen, Oddvar O.; and Davis, Gary A.: **Nonlinear Traveling Wave Flutter of Panels in Transonic Flow.** AIAA Paper 95-1486. Presented at the 36th AIAA, ASME, ASCE, AHS, and ASC, Structures, Structural Dynamics and Materials Conference, New Orleans, Louisiana, <u>April 10–12, 1995</u>, A95-30808, #.

A theoretical and numerical study of traveling wave panel flutter in transonic and low supersonic flows is presented. A mixed Eulerian-Lagrangian formulation is used to model the fluid-structure system and to obtain space-discretized equations that are time-marched to determine panel stability. In the strongly nonlinear transonic range, $M = 0.95$-1.2, the prevailing panel flutter mode is a traveling wave, in the generalized sense, and the panel motions at different chord locations are significantly out of phase. At transonic Mach numbers, the structural and aerodynamic nonlinearities interact to generate traveling wave flutter, even in panels of low chord to width ratios, where previous studies based on linearized aerodynamics predict single-DOF flutter. The presence of traveling wave flutter modes offer another possible explanation for some of the observed discrepancy between earlier calculations based on linear aerodynamic theory and experimental data.

182. Nydick, I.; Friedmann, P. P.; and Zhong, X.: **Hypersonic Panel Flutter Studies on Curved Panels.** AIAA Paper 95-1485, H-2298. *Proceedings, 36th AIAA, ASME, ASCE, AHS, and ASC Structures, Structural Dynamics and Materials Conference*, New Orleans, Louisiana, <u>April 10–12, 1995</u>.

183. Smith, L. L.; Delabroy, O.; Lam, I. T.; Majamaki, A. J.; Karagozian, A. R.; Marble, F. F.; and Smith, O. I.: **PLIF Measurements of Mixing in a Lobed Injector.** Presented at the Central States and Western States Section, The Combustion Institute Spring Meeting, San Antonio, Texas, <u>April 25, 1995</u>.

184. Garrett, Chris J.; Guarro, Sergio B.; and Apostolakis, George E.: **Dynamic Flowgraph Methodology for Assessing the Dependability of Embedded Software Systems.** *IEEE Transactions on Systems, Man and Cybernetics* (ISSN 0018-9472), Vol. 25, No. 5, <u>May 1995</u>, pp. 824–840, 95A86870.

The Dynamic Flowgraph Methodology (DFM) is an integrated methodological approach to modeling and analyzing the behavior of software-driven embedded systems for the purpose of reliability/safety assessment and verification. The methodology has two fundamental goals: (1) to identify how certain postulated events may occur in a system; and (2) to identify an appropriate testing strategy based on an analysis of system functional behavior. To achieve these goals, the methodology employs a modeling framework in which system models are developed in terms of causal relationships between physical variables and temporal characteristics of the execution of software modules. These models are then analyzed to determine how a certain state (desirable or undesirable) can be reached. This is done by developing timed fault trees which take the form of logical combinations of static trees relating system parameters at different points in time. The prime implicants (multi-state analogue of minimal cut sets) of the fault trees can be used to identify and eliminate system faults resulting from unanticipated combinations of software logic errors, hardware failures and adverse environmental conditions, and to direct testing activity to more efficiently eliminate implementation errors by focusing on the neighborhood of potential failure modes arising from these combinations of system conditions.

185. Lay, J. H.; and Dhir, V. K.: **Shape of a Vapor Stem During Nucleate Boiling of Saturated Liquids.** *ASME Journal of Heat Transfer*, Vol. 117, <u>May 1995</u>, pp. 394–401.

186. Stroes, G.; and Catton, I.: **A Simple Analytical Model for the Dryout Location in a Heated Inclined Triangular Channel.** Presented at the IX International Heat Pipe Conference, New Mexico, <u>May 1–5, 1995</u>.

187. Bendiksen, O. O.: **Passive Flutter Suppression Schemes for the Transonic Flow Regime.** Paper No. 65. *Proceedings, International Forum on Aeroelasticity and Structural Dynamics*, Manchester, United Kingdom, <u>June 26–28, 1995</u>.

188. Chung, W. H.; and Speyer, J. L.: **A General Framework for Decentralized Estimation.** *Proceedings, American Controls Conference*, <u>June 1995</u>.

189. Friedmann, P. P.; and Guillot, D.: **Adaptive Control of Aeroelastic Instabilities in Transonic Flow Using CFD Based Loads.** Paper No. 73, H-2295. *Proceedings, International Forum on Aeroelasticity and Structural Dynamics*, Manchester, United Kingdom, <u>June 26–28, 1995</u>.

190. Karplus, W. J.: **The Third-Order Action Potential Model for Computer Simulation of Electrical Wave Propagation in Cardiac Tissue.** *Proceedings of Biomed '95*, Milan, Italy, <u>June 21–27, 1995</u>. Reprinted in *Computer Simulation in Biomedicine*, Southampton, United Kingdom, Computational Mechanics Publications, 1995, pp. 147–154.

191. Lay, J. H.; and Dhir, V. K.: **A Theoretical Study of the Relationship Between Contact Angles and the Shape of a Vapor Stem.** Presented at National Heat Transfer Conference, <u>August 1995</u>.

192. Mendoza, John Cadiz: **A Computational Fluid Dynamics Simulation of the Hypersonic Flight of the Pegasus® Vehicle Using an Artificial Viscosity Model and a Nonlinear Filtering Method.** NASA CR-186033, H-2071, NAS 1.26:186033, <u>September 1995</u>, 96N16635, #. (Also M. Sc. thesis, UCLA, 1995.)

The computational fluid dynamics code, PARC3D, is tested to see if its use of non-physical artificial dissipation affects the accuracy of its results. This is accomplished by simulating a shock-laminar boundary layer interaction and several hypersonic flight conditions of the Pegasus™ launch vehicle using full artificial dissipation, low artificial dissipation, and the Engquist filter. Before the filter is applied to the PARC3D code, it is validated in one-dimensional and two-dimensional form in a MacCormack scheme against the Riemann and convergent duct problem. For this explicit scheme, the filter shows great improvements in accuracy and computational time as opposed to the nonfiltered solutions. However, for the implicit PARC3D code it is found that the best estimate of the Pegasus experimental heat fluxes and surface pressures is the simulation utilizing low artificial dissipation and no filter. The filter does improve accuracy over the artificially dissipative case but at a computational expense greater than that achieved by the low artificial dissipation case which has no computational time penalty and shows better results. For the shock-boundary layer simulation, the filter does well in terms of accuracy for a strong impingement shock but not as well for weaker shock strengths. Furthermore, for the latter problem the filter reduces the required computational time to convergence by 18.7 percent.

193. Balakrishnan, A. V.: **Generalization of the Wittrick-Williams Formula for Counting Modes of Flexible Structures.** *Journal of Guidance, Control, and Dynamics* (ISSN 0731-5090), Vol. 18, No. 6, November 1995, pp. 1410–1415, 96A67841.

A recent (1971) result due to Wittrick-Williams relating the number of modes of a flexible structure to the zeros of a matrix function is generalized and an independent proof given. It is applied to Timoshenko models of a class of interconnected beamlike lattice structures and an interpretation of the zeros given as pinned modes of the structure.

194. Lorenzelli, F.; and Yao, K.: **A Linear Systolic Array for Recursive Least Squares.** *IEEE Transactions on Signal Processing*, Vol. 43, December 1995, pp. 3014–3021.

UCLA FSRC 1996 Publications

195. Balakrishnan, A. V.: **On Superstable Semigroups of Operators.** H-2302. *Dynamic Systems and Applications*, Vol. 5, 1996, pp. 371–384.

196. Balakrishnan, A. V.: **Robust Stabilizing Compensators for Flexible Structures With Collocated Controls.** H-2303. *Journal of Applied Mathematics and Optimization*, Vol. 33, No. 1, 1996, pp. 35–60.

197. Balakrishnan, A. V.; and Butts, R.: **The Proceedings of the NASA-UCLA Workshop on Laser Propagation in Atmospheric Turbulence.** Optimization Software, Inc., 1996.

198. Gerk, T. J.: **Mixing, Ignition, and Burning Processes in Strained Fuel Layers.** M. Sc. thesis, UCLA, 1996.

199. Gerk, T. J.; and Karagozian, A. R.: **Ignition Delay Associated With Strained Fuel Layers.** H-2305. *Twenty-sixth International Symposium on Combustion*, 1996, pp. 1095–1102.

200. Karplus, W. J.; Harreld, M. R.; and Valentino, D. J.: **Simulation and Visualization of the Fluid Flow Field in Aneurysms: A Virtual Environments Methodology.** H-2307. *Proceedings of the Seventh International Symposium on Micro Machine and Human Science*, Nagoya, Japan, IEEE and Nagoya Industrial Research Institute, 1996, pp. 25–31.

201. Kogan, B. Y.; Karplus, W. J.; and Karpoukhin, M. G.: **The Van Capelle and Durrer Model of Cardiac Action Potential Generation and 2DM Propagation: Modifications and Application to Spiral Wave Propagation.** H-2308. *Proceedings of the 1996 Western Multiconference: Simulation in the Medical Sciences*, Society for Computer Simulation, 1996, pp. 106–112.

202. Kogan, B. Y.; Karplus, W. J.; Karpoukhin, M. G.; Roisen, I. M.; Chudin, E.; and Qu, Z.: **Propagation of Electrical Excitation in a Ring of Cardiac Cells: A Computer Simulation Study.** H-2309. *Simulation Modeling in Bioengineering*, Boston, Massachusetts, Computational Mechanics Publications, 1996, pp. 303–313.

203. Kugler, S.; and Dhir, V. K.: **Enhancement of Nucleate Boiling Heat Flux on Macro/Micro-Structured Surfaces Cooled by Multiple Impinging Jets.** H-2311. *Heat Transfer*, Houston, Texas, AIChE Symposium Series, Vol. 92, 1996, pp. 287–293.

204. Lam, I. T.: **Computation of a Scalar Dissipation Rate and Strain Rate in Lobed Injector Flowfields.** M.Sc. thesis, UCLA, 1996.

205. Lorenzelli, F.; and Yao, K.: **Arrays of Randomly Spaced Sensors.** *Advanced Signal Processing Algorithms, Architectures, and Implementations VI. Proceedings of The Society for Optical Engineering (SPIE)*, Vol. 2846, 1996, pp. 122–133.

206. Lorenzelli, F.; and Yao, K.: **An Integral Matrix-Based Technique for Systematic Systolic Design.** *Integration: The VLSI Journal*, Vol. 20, 1996, pp. 269–285.

207. Majamaki, A. J.: **A Mixing Enhancement Study in a Lobed Fuel Injector.** H-2310. M.Sc. thesis, UCLA, 1996.

208. Mitchell, M. G.; Smith, L. L.; Karagozian, A. R.; and Smith, O. I.: **NOx Emissions for a Lobed Fuel Injector/Burner.** H-2312. Presented at Western States Section/The Combustion Institute Fall Meeting, 1996.

209. Rohloff, Thomas J.; and Catton, Ivan: **Development of a Neural Network Flush AirData Sensing System.** *Proceedings of the ASME Fluids Engineering Division*, FED-Vol. 242, 1996.

210. Selerland, T.; and Karagozian, A. R.: **Ignition, Burning, and Extinction of a Strained Fuel Strip.** Paper 96F-100, H-2317. Presented at Western States Section/The Combustion Institute Fall Meeting, 1996.

211. Wurtele, M. G.; Sharman, R. D.; and Datta, A.: **Atmospheric Lee Waves.** H-2318. *Annual Rev. Fluid Mech.*, Vol. 28, 1996, pp. 429–476.

212. Wurtele, M. G.; Datta, A.; and Sharman, R. D.: **The Propagation of Gravity-Inertial Waves and Lee Waves Under a Critical Level.** H-2319. *J. Atmos Sci.*, Vol. 53, 1996, pp. 1505–1523.

213. Harreld, M. R.; Valentino, D. J.; and Karplus, W. J.: **The Virtual Aneurysm: Virtual Reality in Endovascular Therapy.** *Health Care in the Information Age.* Proceedings of Medicine Meets Virtual Reality 4, San Diego, January 1996, ed. H. Sieburg, S. Weghorst and K. Morgan, IOS Press/Ohmsha Publishers, pp. 12–20.

214. Karagozian, A. R.; Wang, K. C.; Le, A-T.; and Smith, O. I.: **Modeling and In-Flight Imaging of Transverse Gas Jets Injected Behind a Rearward-Facing Step.** AIAA Paper No. 96-0914, H-2306. Presented at the 34th AIAA Aerospace Sciences Meeting, January 1996. (Also *Journal of Propulsion and Power*, Vol. 12, 1996, pp. 1129–1136.)

215. Peroomian, O.: **Effect of Density Gradients in Confined Supersonic Shear Layers. I. Two Dimensional Modes.** H-2313. *Phys. Fluids*, Vol. 8, No. 1, January 1996, pp. 225–240.

216. Peroomian, O.: **Effect of Density Gradients in Confined Supersonic Shear Layers. II. Three dimensional Modes.** H-2314. *Phys. Fluids*, Vol. 8, No. 1, January 1996, pp. 241–247.

217. Peroomian, O.; and Chakravarthy, S.: **A Feasibility Study of a Cell-Average-Based Multi-Dimensional ENO Scheme for Use in Supersonic Shear Layers.** AIAA Paper No. 96-0524, H-2315. Presented at the 34th Aerospace Sciences Meeting and Exhibit, Reno, Nevada, January 15–18, 1996.

218. Peroomian, O.; Kelly, R. E.; and Chakravarthy, S.: **Spatial Simulations of a Confined Supersonic Shear Layer at Two Density Ratios.** AIAA Paper No. 96-0783, H-2316. Presented at the 34th Aerospace Sciences Meeting and Exhibit, Reno, Nevada, January 15–18, 1996.

219. Bendiksen, Oddvar O.; and Hwang, Guang-Yaw: **Transonic Flutter Suppression Using Dynamic Twist Control.** AIAA Paper 96-1343. *Technical Papers,* presented at the 37th AIAA, ASME, ASCE, AHS, and ASC Structures, Structural Dynamics and Materials Conference and Exhibit, Salt Lake City, Utah, April 15–17, 1996, (see A96-26801 06-39), pp. 2670–2684, A96-27068, #.

We investigate the feasibility of using dynamic twist control to suppress flutter of wings operating in the transonic flow regime. A simple feedback of the wing twist at a representative span location is used, and the control torque is applied directly to the wing structure. The stabilization mechanism relies on the simple fact that the plunge motion is strongly damped; thus, if the torsional motion can be controlled, the plunge motion can be used to extract energy from the structure. The practical feasibility of implementing such wing twist-control schemes depends on the availability of high-torque actuators and relatively stiff torque tubes. The required control torques are of the order of the torque required to twist a typical wing tip section by 1-3 deg, which is well within the capability of current technology actuators. Because the control systems are simple and robust, involving only the torsional degree of freedom, flutter suppression schemes based on dynamic twist control may find practical applications in fail-safe stability augmentation or in gust-load alleviation.

220. Balakrishnan, A. V.: **Vibrating Systems With Singular Mass-Inertia Matrices.** H-2304. *First International Conference on Nonlinear Problems in Aviation and Aerospace*, Daytona Beach, Florida, May 9–11, 1996, pp. 23–32.

221. Chung, W. H.; and Speyer, J. L.: **A Game Theoretic Filter for Fault Detection and Isolation.** H-2323. Presented at IFAC Meeting, July 1996.

222. Dillon, C. H.; and Speyer, J. L.: **Disturbance Attenuation Approach to Adaptive Control: A Longitudinal Flight Control Example.** AIAA Paper No. 96-3830. *Proceedings of AIAA Guidance Navigation and Control Conference*, San Diego, California, July 29–31, 1996.

Appendix C. Videotapes

1.   Anon.: **The Western Aeronautical Test Range.** NASA TM-104301, NONP-NASA-VT-94-23646, <u>August 1988</u>, 95N10746, Videotape.

An overview of the Western Aeronautical Test Range (WATR) and its connection to NASA Dryden is presented.

2.   Anon.: **HL-10 Dedication Ceremony.** NASA TM-104295, NONP-NASA-VT-94-23640, <u>April 1990</u>, 95N10740, Videotape.

This dedication of NASA's HL-10 lifting body, being put on display at NASA Dryden Flight Research Center, is shown.

3.   Anon.: **NACA/NASA History at Dryden, Part 1 and 2.** NASA TM-104287, NONP-NASA-VT-94-23633, <u>May 1990</u>, 95N10713, Videotape.

Two video tapes of raw material show examples of research activity at the center from the 1950's to the 1980's.

4.   Anon.: **The Crash of Flight 232.** NASA TM-104279, NONP-NASA-VT-94-23627, <u>May 1991</u>, 95N10737, Videotape.

Captain Al Haynes of United Airlines gives a presentation about the DC-10 he captained that crash landed in Sioux City, Iowa in 1989.

5.   Anon.: **NASA and the SR-71: Back to the Future.** NASA TM-104290, NONP-NASA-VT-94-23636, <u>September 1991</u>, 95N10716, Videotape.

A musical video salute to NASA's delivery of three SR-71 aircraft for use in flight research.

6.   Anon.: **Dryden Overview for Schools.** NASA TM-104282, NONP-NASA-VT-94-23630, <u>February 1992</u>, 95N10710, Videotape.

This video provides educators an overview of Dryden for students from late elementary through high school.

7.   Anon.: **Research Excitation System Flight Testing.** NASA TM-104289, NONP-NASA-VT-94-23635, <u>March 1992</u>, 95N10715, Videotape.

Excitation system research at Dryden with an F-16XL aircraft is presented.

8.   Anon.: **Dryden and Transonic Research.** NASA TM-104281, NONP-NASA-VT-94-23629, <u>May 1992</u>, 95N10709, Videotape.

This video on transonic research is given by Dryden engineer Ed Saltzman as part of the 20th Anniversary F-8 Digital Fly-By-Wire (DFBW) and Supercritical Wing (SCW) Symposium.

9.   Anon.: **The Desert Tortoise: A Delicate Balance.** NASA TM-104294, NONP-NASA-VT-94-23639, <u>August 1992</u>, 95N10719, Videotape.

This award winning program looks at the efforts to preserve the desert tortoise in and around the Edwards Air Force Base, California area. It also explains what people should do if they come in contact with a tortoise. This video was produced in cooperation with Edwards Air Force Base.

10.   Anon.: **F-18 High Alpha Research Vehicle Resource Tape.** NASA TM-104299, NONP-NASA-VT-94-23644, <u>August 1992</u>, 95N10744, Videotape.

This video presents raw, unedited material of Dryden's F-18 High Alpha Research Vehicle (HARV) aircraft.

11.   Anon.: **Building the Integrated Test Facility: A Foundation for the Future.** NASA TM-104280, NONP-NASA-VT-94-23628, <u>October 1992</u>, 95N10738, Videotape.

A look at the construction and resources of Dryden's Integrated Test Facility is given.

12.   Anon.: **F-104 Resource Tape.** NASA TM-104296, NONP-NASA-VT-94-23641, <u>October 1992</u>, 95N10741, Videotape.

This video presents raw, unedited material of Dryden's F-104 aircraft.

13.   Anon.: **Dryden Year in Review: 1992.** NASA TM-104285, NONP-NASA-VT-94-23632, <u>January 1993</u>, 95N10712, Videotape.

This video reviews the research work done at Dryden for the year 1992.

14.   Anon.: **F-16XL Resource Tape.** NASA TM-104298, NONP-NASA-VT-94-23643, <u>January 1993</u>, 95N10743, Videotape.

This video presents raw, unedited material of Dryden's F-16XL aircraft.

15.   Anon.: **F-15 835 (HIDEC) Resource Tape.** NASA TM-104297, NONP-NASA-VT-94-23642, <u>February 1993</u>, 95N10742, Videotape.

This video presents raw, unedited material of Dryden's F-15 Highly Integrated Digital Electronic Control (HIDEC) aircraft.

16.   Anon.: **F-18 HARV Presentation for Industry.** NASA TM-104283, NONP-NASA-VT-94-23631, <u>May 1993</u>, 95N10711, Videotape.

This video provides a look at some work done by Dryden's F-18 High Alpha Research Vehicle (HARV) in cooperation with the United States Navy and industry.

17.   Anon.: **F-15 Propulsion Controlled Aircraft (PCA).** NASA TM-104303, NONP-NASA-VT-94-23648, <u>July 1993</u>, 95N10748, Videotape.

This video presentation is a news release highlighting the F-15 Highly Integrated Digital Electronic Controls (HIDEC) Propulsion Controlled Aircraft (PCA) software through June 1993 at Dryden.

18.   Anon.: **X-31 Resource Tape.** NASA TM-104300, NONP-NASA-VT-94-23645, <u>August 1993</u>, 95N10745, Videotape.

This video presents raw, unedited material of Dryden's X-31 aircraft.

19.   Anon.: **Dryden Tour Tape, 1994.** NASA TM-104288, NONP-NASA-VT-94-23634, <u>February 1994</u>, 95N10714, Videotape.

This video provides an overview of NASA's Dryden Flight Research Center. This is the program shown to visitors during the tour at Dryden.

20.   Anon.: **Dryden Overview for Schools.** NASA TM-104302, NONP-NASA-VT-94-23647, <u>February 1994</u>, 95N10747, Videotape.

This video presentation gives a narrated, quick look at the Dryden Flight Research Center and the Center's various projects. The presentation is directed toward a 6th-grade audience and emphasizes staying in school to learn the vital skills needed to succeed today.

21.   Anon.: **NACA/NASA: X-1 Through X-31.** NASA TM-104304, NONP-NASA-VT-94-23649, <u>April 1994</u>, 95N10749, Videotape.

This video presents clips (in-flight, ground crew, pilots, etc.) of almost everything from X-1 through X-31.

22.   Anon.: **Radio Controlled for Research.** NASA TM-104292, NONP-NASA-VT-94-23637, <u>July 1994</u>, 95N10717, Videotape.

This video presents how Dryden engineers use radio-controlled aircraft such as the 1/8-scale model F-18 High Alpha Research Vehicle (HARV) featured to conduct flight research.

23.   Anon.: **LLRV/Apollo 11 25th Anniversary.** NASA TM-104293, NONP-NASA-VT-94-23638, <u>July 1994</u>, 95N10718, Videotape.

This video salutes the 25th anniversary of the Apollo 11's landing on the moon and Dryden's contributions with the Lunar Landing Research Vehicle (LLRV) program.

24.   Anon.: **Dryden Summer 1994 Update.** NASA TM-104305, NONP-NASA-VT-94-23650, <u>July 1994</u>, 95N10750, Videotape.

This video presents a complete, technically detailed report on all Dryden projects, achievements, and employee activities for 1994.

25.   Anon.: **X-31 Tailless Testing.** NASA TM-104306, NONP-NASA-VT-94-23651, <u>September 1994</u>, 95N10751, Videotape.

This video addresses the NASA Dryden and X-31 International Test Organization (ITO) testbed provided for the Pentagon's 'tailless' and quasi-tailless vehicle configuration testing.

Author Index[*]

A

---

[*]Note: The page numbers in bold text are to indicate senior authored paper.

500

503

504

505

506

510

Airplane Index[*]

---

[*]Note: The page numbers in bold text are to indicate photos or drawings.

514

REPORT DOCUMENTATION PAGE

Form Approved
OMB No. 0704-0188

1. AGENCY USE ONLY (Leave blank)	2. REPORT DATE May 1999	3. REPORT TYPE AND DATES COVERED Technical Publication

4. TITLE AND SUBTITLE

Fifty Years of Flight Research: An Annotated Bibliography of Technical Publications of NASA Dryden Flight Research Center, 1946–1996

6. AUTHOR(S)

David F. Fisher

5. FUNDING NUMBERS

WU 953 36 00 000 RR 00 000

7. PERFORMING ORGANIZATION NAME(S) AND ADDRESS(ES)

NASA Dryden Flight Research Center
P.O. Box 273
Edwards, California 93523-0273

8. PERFORMING ORGANIZATION REPORT NUMBER

H-2216

9. SPONSORING/MONITORING AGENCY NAME(S) AND ADDRESS(ES)

National Aeronautics and Space Administration
Washington, DC 20546-0001

10. SPONSORING/MONITORING AGENCY REPORT NUMBER

NASA/TP-1999-206568

11. SUPPLEMENTARY NOTES

Unclassified and unlimited reports from 1946 through 1996.

12a. DISTRIBUTION/AVAILABILITY STATEMENT

Unclassified—Unlimited
Subject Category 99

12b. DISTRIBUTION CODE

13. ABSTRACT (Maximum 200 words)

Titles, authors, report numbers, and abstracts are given for more than 2200 unclassified and unrestricted technical reports and papers published from September 1946 to December 1996 by NASA Dryden Flight Research Center and its predecessor organizations. These technical reports and papers describe and give the results of 50 years of flight research performed by the NACA and NASA, from the X-1 and other early X-airplanes, to the X-15, Space Shuttle, X-29 Forward Swept Wing, and X-31 aircraft. Some of the other research airplanes tested were the D-558, phase 1 and 2; M-2, HL-10 and X-24 lifting bodies; Digital Fly-By-Wire and Supercritical Wing F-8; XB-70; YF-12; AFTI F-111 TACT and MAW; F-15 HiDEC; F-18 High Alpha Research Vehicle, and F-18 Systems Research Aircraft. The citations of reports and papers are listed in chronological order, with author and aircraft indices. In addition, in the appendices, citations of 233 contractor reports, more than 200 UCLA Flight System Research Center reports and 25 video tapes are included.

14. SUBJECT TERMS

Bibliographies, Databases, Flight-tests, High-speed flight aircraft, Research facilities, Research vehicles

15. NUMBER OF PAGES
525

16. PRICE CODE
A22

17. SECURITY CLASSIFICATION OF REPORT	18. SECURITY CLASSIFICATION OF THIS PAGE	19. SECURITY CLASSIFICATION OF ABSTRACT	20. LIMITATION OF ABSTRACT
Unclassified	Unclassified	Unclassified	Unlimited